THE OXFORD COMPANION TO
AUSTRALIAN GARDENS

THE OXFORD COMPANION TO
AUSTRALIAN GARDENS

Edited by

Richard Aitken & Michael Looker

Published in association with the Australian Garden History Society

OXFORD
UNIVERSITY PRESS

OXFORD
UNIVERSITY PRESS

253 Normanby Road, South Melbourne, Victoria 3205, Australia

Oxford University Press is a department of the University of Oxford. It furthers the University's objective of excellence in research, scholarship, and education by publishing worldwide in

Oxford New York

Auckland Bangkok Buenos Aires Cape Town Chennai
Dar es Salaam Delhi Hong Kong Istanbul Karachi Kolkata
Kuala Lumpur Madrid Melbourne Mexico City Mumbai Nairobi
São Paulo Shanghai Taipei Tokyo Toronto

OXFORD is a trade mark of Oxford University Press in the UK and in certain other countries

Copyright © Richard Aitken, Michael Looker 2002
First published 2002

This book is copyright. Apart from any fair dealing for the purposes of private study, research, criticism or review as permitted under the Copyright Act, no part may be reproduced, stored in a retrieval system, or transmitted, in any form or by any means, electronic, mechanical, photocopying, recording or otherwise without prior written permission. Enquiries to be made to Oxford University Press.

Copying for educational purposes
Where copies of part or the whole of the book are made under Part VB of the Copyright Act, the law requires that prescribed procedures be followed. For information, contact the Copyright Agency Limited.

National Library of Australia
Cataloguing-in-Publication data:

The Oxford companion to Australian gardens.

   Bibliography.
   Includes index.
   ISBN 0 19 553644 4.

   1. Gardens—Australia. 2. Gardening—Australia. I. Aitken, Richard.

635.0994

Edited by Trischa Baker
Indexed by Nina Crisp and Richard Aitken
Text designed by Patrick Cannon
Cover designed by Racheal Stines
Typeset by Desktop Concepts Pty Ltd
Printed through the Bookmaker International Ltd .

The Australian Garden History Society is a national membership based organisation that promotes interest in historic gardens and cultural landscapes by examining them in their widest social, historic, literary, artistic and scientific context.
www.gardenhistorysociety.org.au

For JMA

Contents

Foreword	vii
Preface	ix
Acknowledgments	xi
List of Contributors	xv
Note to the Reader	xxviii
A Note Concerning the Illuminated Headpieces	xxix
Entries A–Z	1
Illustration Acknowledgments	663
Index of Gardens	668
Index of Names	678

Foreword

Gardening remains one of the most popular leisure pursuits amongst Australians. It is something of a national pastime. In the tropics or the desert, in a small suburban garden, an inner city courtyard, or a large country garden—or in a tin can on a tiny balcony—nearly all of us manage some form of gardening. Those who do not garden take advantage of others who do, frequenting many of our great public gardens and parks in large numbers. We read books on gardens and gardening by the million. Nurseries are packed with customers on weekends. We have an insatiable appetite for visiting gardens, joining garden organisations, and consuming related magazines and television programs. Much of this is what we call 'popular culture'. That is not to suggest it is meretricious. Who is to say that a clipped box hedge has a higher purpose than a tyre swan? Like most of our population, our gardening traditions and styles are largely imported, and, by nature, diverse. Our varied climates and ability to grow almost anything somewhere on the continent only adds to the melting pot of gardening ideas and opportunities. An indigenous style has yet to emerge. Perhaps it never will. What is certain is that we have had little understanding of the historical context of our gardening endeavours and few, if any, enduring traditions—with the possible exception of the 'back yard'.

With this *Companion* we are able to see, for the first time, our rich gardening heritage and traditions in a broad context. The book covers the territory as comprehensively as possible. We find not only familiar household names and places, but also the quirky, the new, and the unexpected. If there was ever any doubt that Australia has an abundant, and continually developing, cultural tradition associated with gardens and gardening, this volume will dispel it. With its many and diverse entries, of impressive scope, it demonstrates the enormously rich heritage of gardens and gardening in Australia: a heritage developed over more than two centuries since the time of British occupation, and for many centuries before that, as we see from the entries on Aboriginal land management practices for the past 60 000 years. A rich heritage indeed.

The development of this book has stimulated a great deal of research across the country for much of the past decade, and it presents considerable new material drawn from a wide variety of primary sources. This has been gathered together by more than two hundred contributors, from diverse backgrounds. The book also synthesises existing relevant material and places it in context. The illustrations alone—many of which have never before been published—have been chosen with great care, and they add a splendid new dimension to our knowledge.

Foreword

There is no comparable publication on Australian gardens, and indeed few worldwide, that examines in such detail the history of a nation's gardening. The *Companion* will contribute enormously to our current body of knowledge and will become the standard reference text on the subject. I have no doubt its publication will stimulate further interest and research in the field, and will lead to greater efforts to conserve significant historic gardens and designed landscapes in Australia. For this reason the Australian Garden History Society and its members have been generous contributors to the book. Through a substantial financial contribution the Society has enabled many research projects to be undertaken and our members have spent thousands of hours in libraries across the country, indexing and abstracting previously inaccessible magazines and newspapers. All this has yielded new and valuable information. The Society is grateful to its Patron, Margaret Darling, for her generous financial support for this work. A large proportion of the contributors are also Society members, and they have embraced this massive cooperative project with a willing and generous spirit.

The publication of this *Companion* is a major landmark in its field. No other book has attempted such a broad sweep, nor has any other brought together such an impressive array of experts in many disciplines. The *Oxford Companion to Australian Gardens* will sit at the pinnacle of publications on Australian gardens.

Peter Watts
Chairman
Australian Garden History Society

Preface

This *Companion* is long overdue, in terms both of time elapsed since the date of initial commission, and—which is more important—of growth and consolidation in the field of Australian garden history. The lengthy gestation is a product of the relative rawness of garden history as an accepted discipline in Australia, and with that the difficultly in attempting uniform coverage of the subject in such a geographically and historically diverse continent. As a focus for consolidation in a rapidly growing field of endeavour, the *Companion* has provided an unrivalled opportunity for more than two hundred contributors—ranging from garden owners and managers to freelance historians and consultants, and academics in Australia and beyond—to join in a project that will raise the threshold of knowledge about Australian gardens.

The fixed boundaries of our island continent make it possible to isolate and chart the country's garden history, and in the process to offer diverse readings of what has constituted an Australian garden. For many it was a matter of introducing old favourites from 'home'; others saw it as a means to harness the creative opportunities offered by a newly colonised country; to another group it involved the exclusive use of Australian plants; while for some it was the product of an equable climate and the opportunity to grow plants from comparable climates. Each drew on—or ignored—traditions, in response to wider social and cultural forces. As this *Companion* makes clear, there is no single type or style of Australian garden; rather, recurring themes—including memory, acclimatisation, innovation, and adaptation—permeate our garden-making.

Although many disparate threads run through the text, the interconnectedness of the vision offered by the *Companion* is one of its great strengths. By extensive use of cross-referencing (denoted by the use of SMALL CAPITALS), the reader is directed to cognate subjects, places, and personalities. More than 350 entries, many of essay length, present historical aspects and themes in Australian gardens and other designed landscapes. Many longer entries are supported by a range of shorter, specific entries. The different word lengths of the entries also offer some guide to the relative significance of the various subjects, although offsetting factors—such as the need to provide a satisfying amount of detail and to present information in context—also affect the length of particular entries. The individual selection and division of topics has also been tempered by knowledge of other standard works in the field. For example, in the choice of plant genera, there has been no attempt to challenge the encyclopaedic coverage of the *Royal Horticultural Society Encyclopaedia of Gardening*, or Roger Spencer's invaluable *Horticultural Flora of South-eastern Australia*. Rather, the selection highlights

Preface

those plants which have made distinctive contributions in Australia, using yardsticks such as availability and popularity in the nursery trade, the early establishment of specialist societies, and the ubiquity of cultural advice in books and magazines.

More than 350 entries trace the history of significant Australian gardens. The selection of gardens has been made with a view to general significance, rather than to the garden's present condition or standard of maintenance. No attempt has been made to include very recent examples, due in part to the research, writing, and production lead time for a work such as a *Companion*, but also due to the transitory nature of many gardens. Such places are appropriately treated in the glossy compilations that appear with increasing frequency; those achieving significance over a longer time span will be subjects for future editions of this *Companion*. Many places that have not warranted individual entries may, however, be mentioned or discussed in cognate entries, and such places are included in the index at the back of this volume.

The *Companion* includes more than 750 biographical entries summarising the lives of significant figures in the world of Australian garden-making. In undertaking a work such as this, the *Australian Dictionary of Biography* has provided an indispensable starting point and work of reference. Like the thematic entries, the scope of those selected reflects the wide scope of Australian gardens and designed landscapes. It is in this area, perhaps, that most new material is presented, as many of the lives treated have not previously been the subject of any detailed research. This is particularly so for many of those working in regional Australia, and more generally for those working outside the south-eastern capitals.

For some readers this book will answer questions; for others it will pose them. This is as it should be with a work such as the *Companion*. While endeavours have been made to present salient historical facts, the treatment of themes in garden history varies according to the perspective of the contributor and the subject at hand. The contributors have been generous in sharing their expert knowledge, and their individual voices have, as far as possible, been permitted to speak. There is no single answer for some questions, just as there is no linear model for garden history. Events overlap, climates dictate differing responses, approaches vary. Some of the broader questions tackled here will only be fully answered by greater knowledge and analysis: this awaits the products of work now in progress—work on many fronts. The time will come when revised and enlarged editions of the *Companion* can take advantage of this greater understanding, but for the present, assembled here is the most comprehensive compilation of knowledge yet to appear on Australian gardens and their genesis.

Acknowledgments

A project as large as the *Oxford Companion to Australian Gardens* necessarily involves the expertise and cooperation of many people and organisations, and my first debt of gratitude is to my co-editor, Michael Looker. He has been involved in the project almost from its inception and, particularly during its early stages, has contributed to the shape and tone of the finished work. His role in structuring the thematic headwords and checking the veracity of plant names has been particularly valued. More generally, his expertise in the fields of botany, gardening, and horticulture will be readily apparent throughout the text. Michael also administered and contributed to the complex and complementary 'Theoretical Framework for Designed Landscapes in Australia' project, which provided a background for the *Companion's* detailed structure and yielded vital data for many of the entries. Michael's colleagues at Burnley College formed a willing pool of contributors, and the support of Greg Moore and Peter May was instrumental in this cooperative approach.

The involvement of Peter Watts, Margaret Darling, and the Australian Garden History Society has been vital to the completion of the *Companion*. Peter Watts played a key role devising an arrangement whereby research for a database produced under the auspices of the Society could be used exclusively for the *Companion*, and subsequently transformed into an accessible research tool. It is fitting that Peter should be Chairman of the Australian Garden History Society during the year of publication, and I thank him not only for his generous foreword but for his ongoing support and encouragement. Margaret Darling made a very generous donation to match funding from the Australian Garden History Society, without which the *Companion* would surely never have come to fruition. Victor Crittenden has also provided funding for the database project, enabling research to continue well past the publication date of the *Companion*. The vital role of the Australian Garden History Society is justly acknowledged on the title page in its listing as associate publisher with Oxford University Press.

Research for the database has been principally undertaken by Helen Doyle and Helen Botham. Together they have brought much enthusiasm and precision to this task, and have contributed substantially to the thoroughness of the *Companion* entries, particularly those where primary research was required. I also gratefully acknowledge Helen Doyle's friendship and advice throughout the project: her role as a sounding board has greatly assisted my editorial role. Thanks are also due to other researchers employed using Australian Garden

Acknowledgments

History Society funds, including Karen Olsen and Lindl Lawton, and also to the generous voluntary assistance from Society members in Western Australia, headed by Carolyn Middlemis.

A select group of contributors have made contributions that exceed by far what could normally be expected for a project such as this. Richard Clough, David Jones, Colleen Morris, Oline Richards, and Jeannie Sim have each acted as de facto contributing editors, having written many individual entries (ranging from 20 to 75), provided comment on early drafts of headwords, and then made significant input towards supplementing the headword lists and suggesting appropriate contributors. To each I express my heartfelt thanks. Supporting them have been other generous contributors—Anita Angel, Chris Betteridge, James Broadbent, Allan Correy, Ann Cripps, Helen Doyle, Diane Firth, Linden Gillbank, George Jones, Sara Maroske, Carolyn Middlemis, Anne Neale, Lindy Scripps, Jan Seto, Howard Tanner, and John Walter—each of whom provided considerable assistance with writing (typically 10 to 15 entries), made useful comments on draft headwords, and unstintingly gave assistance in matters pertaining to their own state or territory. More generally, I have been overwhelmed by the generosity of all our contributors. Whether providing text, responding to comments, or reviewing other entries, each of those appearing in the List of Contributors has contributed in some way to the final shape of the book, and to its lasting value as a work of reference. To each I express my thanks.

With the unavoidably long gestation for a book such as this, it is a melancholy but fitting task to pay tribute to Margaret Hendry, Joan Law-Smith, Ian McLaren, John Oldham, Richard Ratcliffe, and Barbara van den Broek, who did not live to see their contributions published. Aged 91, John Oldham had been the *Companion*'s oldest contributor, and in the case of Lady Law-Smith, the eloquent entry on spirituality was her final contribution in a distinguished garden-writing career.

Thanks are due to the Australian Heritage Commission for their support of the *Companion* project, especially with funding through the National Estate Grants Programme. This enabled a complementary national project, entitled 'A Theoretical Framework for Designed Landscapes in Australia' to be undertaken, with eight separate reports covering each state and territory, and a national overview report prepared by Richard Aitken, Jan Schapper, Juliet Ramsay, and Michael Looker. The national report, with each of the supporting state and territory reports as appendices, was published in 1997 by Burnley College, University of Melbourne. The designed landscapes project was a major boost to the research effort for the present *Companion* and yielded a considerable amount of new data, especially in those states and territories where little garden history research had previously been undertaken.

In selecting the illustrations I have had great assistance from Anita Angel, Colleen Morris, Oline Richards, Jeannie Sim, Howard Tanner, Lester Tropman, and also many others who assisted with particular images. Thanks are especially due to Howard Tanner for his generosity in funding the inclusion of photographs by Richard Stringer, and to both parties for waiving copyright and permission fees. Many institutions waived or reduced permission fees,

Acknowledgments

and this has made possible the great variety of images selected for publication. Financial assistance from Suzanne Hunt has also assisted in locating and reproducing several illustrations. I note that the illustration captions are my own, lest any infelicities be unwittingly attributed to the contributors of cognate entries.

In adding details of further reading I have been greatly assisted by Georgina Binns, Helen Doyle, Megan Martin, and Colleen Morris. Gil Teague of Florilegium bookshop (Sydney) generously permitted me to browse through his extensive stock to acquaint myself with many relevant books. His detailed catalogues and also those of Anna Buxton (Edinburgh) have also been of great assistance in tracing relevant titles. I am also grateful to Tony Rodd, who at short notice identified all the plants used in the illuminated alphabetical headpieces, and provided their current botanical names.

Many librarians and archivists within Australia's major public collections have assisted with or otherwise facilitated research for the *Companion*, and to all such institutions and their staff I offer my thanks. For privileged access to the collections of specialist libraries, I am particularly grateful to Roanna Ovenden and Megan Martin (Historic Houses Trust of New South Wales), Mark Macnamara (Burnley College), Dr Brent Elliott (Lindley Library, London), Helen Cohn and Jill Thurlow (Royal Botanic Gardens, Melbourne), and Anna Hallett and Miguel Garcia (Royal Botanic Gardens, Sydney).

Much of my research for the *Companion* has been undertaken interstate and overseas, and I am especially grateful to Vivian and June Widgery and Alan Romain (London), Colleen and Richard Morris (Sydney), and Meredith and Dusty Miller (Brisbane) for accommodation over extended periods.

At Oxford University Press, the *Companion* has been favoured by a committed and talented team. The project has spanned the involvement of three publishers: Louise Sweetland, whose idea this was; Peter Rose, whose enthusiasm carried the project through its formative stages; and Heather Fawcett, who patiently guided the project to completion. In the production of this book, I have poked my nose into some dark corners of publishing where authors and editors should not rightly be permitted to stray: I am therefore particularly grateful to Heather Fawcett for her acquiescence in this regard. It has been my great fortune to work with editor Trischa Baker, who has in a thousand unseen ways improved the text, and who has been a great supporter of the book. Geraldine Corridon has sympathetically guided the book through production and offered advice in many areas. The assistance of Paige Amor, Iga Bajer, Natasha Bills, Anna Byrne, Patrick Cannon, Nina Crisp, Cara Gould, Felicity Edge, Ray O'Farrell, Gill Smith, and Georgie Wilkinson is also gratefully acknowledged.

Nigel Lewis has been a great supporter of the project, even during my long absences when our architectural practice owed its existence to his work alone. I am grateful for his tolerance and patience, especially during the editing and production phases of the book over the last five years.

My greatest debt of gratitude is, however, due to Georgina Binns. For the last nine years we have lived in an unhealthy *ménage à trois*: she and I and the *Companion*. Her laptop

Acknowledgments

computer has been appropriated, her living rooms invaded, holidays shared three ways, and her patience sorely tested. I am pleased to record that the *Companion* is now published and will henceforth be banished from our domestic routine.

Richard Aitken

In addition to the acknowledgments above I would like to further mention the following people who have assisted me with this project: Dr Peter May for his comments on the initial list of headwords and for reading and making comments on many horticulturally themed entries; Dr Greg Moore for his comments on the initial list of headwords; and Dr Roger Spencer for his comments on the general structure of the *Companion* and on the thematic and plant-based entries. Finally I owe a great debt of gratitude for the generous support provided to this project by the staff of Burnley College, University of Melbourne. Administrative support and costs were provided over a number of years, in addition to computer technical support, printing and the facilities and catering for the launch of the 'Theoretical Designed Landscapes' project.

Michael Looker

List of Contributors

John Adam is an Auckland-based landscape heritage consultant. He has undertaken extensive research on New Zealand's garden and cultural landscape history, especially local initiatives in scenery preservation.

Richard Aitken is a Melbourne-based architect and historian. He is a member of the Editorial Advisory Board of the British-based journal *Garden History* and has researched and written widely on Australian garden history.

Dr David Aldous is Associate Professor, Burnley College, University of Melbourne. He has long experience in turf management.

Eve Almond is Exhibitions Co-ordinator at Melbourne Museum, and this follows long experience as the inaugural Interpretations Officer at the Royal Botanic Gardens, Melbourne.

Lee Andrews is a Melbourne-based horticulturist in private practice, specialising in the preparation of conservation management plans for gardens and designed landscapes.

Anita Angel is Darwin-based historian who specialises in North Australian history and Australian art history.

Elizabeth Anya-Petrivna is a Melbourne-based museum services consultant caring for house museums. Her research interests include floral decoration, decorative arts, and twentieth-century popular culture.

Dr Helen Armstrong is Professor of Landscape Architecture, and Director, Cultural Landscape Research Unit, Queensland University of Technology. Her research has focused on landscape heritage, design, and more recently on migrant place-making.

Nicholas Bailey is a Senior Lecturer at Burnley College, University of Melbourne, specialising in information technology and its application to horticulture.

Jeannine Baker is a Sydney-based public historian. She has directed and produced documentary films, and researched and curated exhibitions for the Sydney Customs House and the Australian Museum.

Tempe Beaven is a Sydney-based landscape architect whose work has encompassed a range of places from culturally significant gardens to large urban renewal areas.

David Beaver is a practising landscape architect based in the Blue Mountains and specialising in heritage conservation. He edited *Australian Garden History* from 1991 to 1994.

Mandy Bede is a lawyer and former librarian who has maintained her interest in Australian history through the Ephemera Society of Australia.

List of Contributors

Dr Ruth Beilin is a landscape sociologist. She lectures at Burnley College, University of Melbourne, and her research interests include Landcare and catchment management.

Helen Bennett is a researcher in Cultural Heritage, Queensland Environment Protection Agency. She has written on Brisbane's early twentieth-century and interwar urban history.

Dr Ina Bertrand has taught and written about Australian film for many years. She was one of three editors of the *Oxford Companion to Australian Film* (1999).

Chris Betteridge is a heritage practitioner specialising in the analysis, conservation and interpretation of cultural landscapes. His interests include twentieth-century gardens and historic cemeteries.

Margaret Betteridge has pursued a long curatorial career in the field of Australian decorative arts. Her book *Australian Flora in Art* (1979) was a catalyst for revived interest in Australian floral motifs.

Georgina Binns is Music and Multi-media Librarian at Monash University, and has published widely in the field of Australian music history.

Michael Bogle is a curator who has worked with the State Rail Authority (NSW) and with the Historic Houses Trust of New South Wales. His most recent book is *Design in Australia 1880–1970* (1998).

Helen Botham is a freelance researcher and horticulturist specialising in garden history. She has acted as a researcher for the current *Companion*.

Dr David Bowman, Principal Research Fellow, Key Centre for Tropical Wildlife Management, Northern Territory University, is an ecologist who has published widely on ecology and management of Australian landscapes.

Jan Brazier assisted Ken Inglis on his book *Sacred Places: War Memorial in the Australian Landscape* (1998). She is currently archivist at the Australian Museum, Sydney.

Geoffrey Britton is a Sydney-based heritage and design consultant and musician with special professional interests in the assessment and management of culturally significant landscapes.

Dr James Broadbent is a curator and historian whose principal interests are taste and society in colonial New South Wales.

Catherine Brouwer has a landscape architecture practice in Brisbane which includes heritage assessment and conservation planning.

Craig Burton is a Sydney-based architect, landscape architect, and consultant horticulturist and maintains a passionate interest in the history of landscape design in Australia.

Geoff Carr, Melbourne-based horticulturist, is active in the fields of conservation and environmental management, especially as a leading advocate in the fight against environmental weeds.

Angela Cartland has researched childhood and nationalism in early twentieth-century Australia. Her doctoral research at the Australian National University is analysing the social history of the cash register.

Tony Cavanagh has had a long interest in botanical history and the cultivation of Australian plants, especially of the Proteaceae, and in their cultivation overseas.

List of Contributors

Silas Clifford-Smith is an English-born horticulturist who is actively involved with the Australian Garden History Society and the National Trust in New South Wales.

Richard Clough, after a distinguished career in landscape architecture, has devoted his retirement to research and book collecting, especially in the area of Australian colonial horticulture and gardening.

Helen Cohn is a historian and librarian with a particular interest in the history and bibliography of Australian natural sciences. She is Manager of the Library at the Royal Botanic Gardens, Melbourne.

Dr Mimi Colligan was *Australian Dictionary of Biography* researcher in Victoria (1976–87) and contributor of many articles. Her doctoral studies examined nineteenth-century panorama and waxwork entertainments.

Geoff Connellan is a Principal Lecturer, Burnley College, University of Melbourne. He has undertaken extensive research in the modification of plant environments.

Margaret Cook is a Queensland-based historian with a special interest in heritage conservation, especially of places in public ownership or use.

Allan Correy, retired landscape architect and academic, practised in Adelaide and Sydney, and taught at Sydney University. He is currently a visiting lecturer, University of New South Wales.

Jackie Courmadias is Executive Officer of the Australian Garden History Society. Until recently she lived and gardened at Brookdale, a 1920s garden at Mount Macedon.

Ann Cripps is a Hobart-based landscape and garden history consultant. She has had a long involvement with the Australian Garden History Society at a state and national level.

Victor Crittenden is a bibliographer, librarian, and publisher (Mulini Press). His *History and Bibliography of Australian Gardening Books* (1986) remains a standard work.

Rob Cross is Horticultural Research Officer for the Royal Botanic Gardens, Melbourne. He has broad experience in horticulture, including landscape planning, design, and maintenance.

Lorna Crowther is a science graduate and worked as a librarian at Monash Library. For many years she was a volunteer guide at the Royal Botanic Gardens, Melbourne.

Peter Cuffley is an author, historian, and garden designer. His many books have contributed to the Australian revival of cottage gardens, heirloom plants, and period-style gardens generally.

Peter Cuneo is Horticultural Development Officer at Mount Annan Botanic Garden, a branch of the Royal Botanic Gardens, Sydney.

Sallyann Dakis is an Executive Producer for the Australian Broadcasting Corporation's Rural Department in Tasmania and is an active member of the Australian Garden History Society.

Dr John Dargavel, Visiting Fellow, Department of Forestry and Centre for Resource and Environmental Studies, Australian National University, is author of *Fashioning Australia's Forests* (1995).

Dr Kate Darian-Smith is Director of the Australian Centre, University of Melbourne. She is currently writing a cultural history of agricultural shows in Australia.

List of Contributors

Dr Gillian Davies is a volunteer guide at the Royal Botanic Gardens, Sydney, and with Christine Carwardine is researching the career of Charles Fraser.

Catherine de Courcy is a Melbourne-based historian and writer. Her books include *The Zoo Story* (1995), and contributions to *Zoo and Aquarium History* (1999) and *Encyclopaedia of World Zoos* (2001).

John Delpratt lectures at Burnley College, University of Melbourne. His research interests include construction of native plant communities and use of indigenous species for local revegetation.

Judith Deppeler-Hagan is a weaver, gardener, and historian who has lived in Queensland for nearly thirty years.

Trisha Dixon is an author-photographer and keen historian who has published widely on Australian's historic gardens, particularly on the gardens of Edna Walling.

Nicky Downer runs an event management company and has been an active committee member of the Australian Garden History Society in South Australia and nationally.

Helen Doyle is a historian researching landscapes and their meanings, and was an assistant editor for *The Oxford Companion to Australian History* (1998).

Dr Sophie Ducker has had a long career in botany, rewarded by the 1996 Mueller Medal. She has a special interest in botanical history and has published the letters of W.H. Harvey.

Dr Donald Dunbar, recently retired as Senior Lecturer in architecture, University of Canberra. His doctoral dissertation compared flat development in Melbourne and Sydney during the interwar period.

Penny Dunn owned and gardened at the Mount Macedon property Dreamthorpe for over two decades before recently moving to Melbourne.

Dr David Dunstan, lecturer at the National Centre for Australian Studies, Monash University, has written extensively about wine and viticulture, including *Better than Pommard! A History of Wine in Victoria* (1994).

Dr Edward Duyker is the Honorary Consul of Mauritius in Sydney and the author of thirteen books. He is currently writing a biography of J.-J.H. de Labillardière.

Dr Harriet Edquist is Professor of Architectural History and Head of the School of Architecture + Design, RMIT University. Her research focuses on late nineteenth- and twentieth-century Australian architecture and design.

Rodger Elliot has specialised in propagating, growing, cultivating, marketing, and writing about Australian plants. He is a board member of the Royal Botanic Gardens, Melbourne.

Dr Dianne Firth is Head of Landscape Architecture, School of Design, University of Canberra. She has published widely on Canberra's landscape and sits on the ACT Heritage Council.

Kim Fletcher has worked with herbs for over 25 years as a grower, writer, television and radio commentator, and consultant to the commercial herb industry.

Stephen Forbes is Director, Botanic Gardens of Adelaide, and formerly worked at the Royal Botanic Gardens, Melbourne and Sydney. He has a special interest in the South African flora.

List of Contributors

Paul Fox is a Melbourne-based historian who has published widely in the field of cultural history. His book *Clearings* is due for release in 2003.

Jodi Frawley is consultant historian and researcher. Her research interests include the history of recreation and Australia's public parks.

Dr Kevin Frawley is a Canberra-based environmental planner. He has written widely on Australian environmental history especially in relation to forests.

Peter Freeman is a Canberra-based author, illustrator, and conservation architect with an interest in Australian vernacular architecture and regional building typologies.

Dr Robert Freestone is Associate Professor in the School of Planning and Urban Development, University of New South Wales. His research focuses on the history of town planning.

Dr Maurice French, Professor of History and Dean of the Faculty of Arts, University of Southern Queensland, is the author of several books on the Darling Downs.

Dr Don Garden lectures in Australian history and environmental history at the University of Melbourne. He has published mainly institutional and regional histories, including a history of Victoria.

Dr Jennifer Gardner is Curator of the Waite Arboretum, University of Adelaide.

Dr Christine Garnaut is a historian and Research Associate in the School of Architecture and Design at the University of South Australia. Her research interests include town planning and urban design.

T.R. 'Tommy' Garnett is well known as a garden-maker and writer. Upon retirement, his Garden of St Erth at Blackwood (Vic.) became a focus for his observations and writings.

Dr Andrea Gaynor is a lecturer in history at the University of Western Australia and has a special interest in Australian environmental history.

Alex George has written widely on Australian plants and their discovery, best known for his work on banksias. After 33 years in the public service he now works freelance.

Allen Gilbert is a professional horticulturist specialising in organics, budding and grafting, and pruning. He lives on Bruny Island, Tasmania, where he writes and is developing his property using organic principles.

Dr Lionel Gilbert is the author of numerous papers on local and botanical history. His books include a history of the Royal Botanic Gardens, Sydney (1986), and several biographies.

Francine Gilfedder is a freelance historian, horticulturist, and landscape architect who specialises in the conservation and management of cultural and amenity landscapes.

Dr Linden Gillbank, Fellow in the History and Philosophy Department, University of Melbourne, is a historian of Australian botany. Her fascination with plants extends into bush and pasture, far beyond the garden.

Dr Philip Goad is Deputy Dean and Associate Dean (Research), Faculty of Architecture, Building and Planning, University of Melbourne. His research expertise is twentieth-century Australian architecture.

Dr Beth Gott has researched Aboriginal plant use and land management since 1980. She is based at Monash University and has published widely on the subject.

List of Contributors

Dr John Gray, urban forester and landscape architect, was formerly Director, Landscape Architecture, National Capital Development Commission. He has a long-term interest in Canberra, Australia's best known garden city.

Robert Green is a conservation architect employed by Heritage Victoria. He has a long-standing interest in the history of Melbourne's tramways.

Dr Tom Griffiths, Senior Research Fellow in the History Program, Research School of the Social Sciences, Australian National University, has published widely in the field of environmental history.

Dr Derham Groves is a Senior Lecturer at the University of Melbourne. He is interested in cultural rituals and in the quirky side of architecture.

Dr Brigid Hains is currently researching the history of postwar evolutionary biology. Her doctoral studies examined the frontier in Australian environmental history.

Ross Hall is Senior Lecturer in Production Horticulture at Burnley College, University of Melbourne. He is a former president of the International Plant Propagators Society (Australian Region).

Sir Rupert Hamer was Premier of Victoria (1972–81) and his great interest in gardens and the wider landscape has been encapsulated in his promotion of Victoria as the 'Garden State'.

Dr Elery Hamilton-Smith has fifty years experience in the exploration and study of Australian cave areas, and has given special attention to their history.

Richard Heathcote has managed Rippon Lea for the National Trust of Australia (Victoria) for the past decade. His particular interest is in the social history and interpretation of gardens and their gardeners.

Margaret Hendry was a Canberra-based landscape architect. In her retirement she took an active interest in documenting the history of the profession in Australia.

Dr Helen Hewson lectured in botany before involvement with the *Flora of Australia* and the Centre for Plant Biodiversity Research. She is author of *Australia: 300 Years of Botanical Illustration* (1999).

Linda Hipwell is a graduate of Burnley College, University of Melbourne, where her thesis analysed the postwar history of Burnley Gardens.

Dr James Hitchmough, Reader in Landscape, University of Sheffield, was formerly Senior Lecturer in Environmental Horticulture at Burnley College, University of Melbourne.

Dr Katie Holmes teaches history and women's studies at La Trobe University and is currently researching the cultural history of gardens in Australia.

Timothy Hubbard is a heritage architect and planner. He has an interest in historic trees and gardens and is now researching the villa in the landscape.

Joy Hughes is a Sydney-based historian whose research has contributed to the history and conservation of many important nineteenth-century houses and gardens.

Suzanne Hunt is a social historian and is currently developing resources for the study and exhibition of garden history at the State Library of Victoria.

Barney Hutton is a keen gardener. After a long career in teaching he retired to Mount Macedon (Vic.) and with his wife Marion has undertaken considerable research on early nurseries and local history.

List of Contributors

Ian Innes, Horticultural and Landscape Planning Officer, Royal Botanic Gardens, Sydney, trained in landscape architecture and is interested in the history of taste and how this is revealed in garden landscapes.

Pamela Jellie completed a Bachelor of Landscape Architecture at RMIT after an earlier career in teaching. Her special interest is heritage gardens and the cultural landscape.

Dr David Jones is Senior Lecturer in Landscape Architecture at the University of Adelaide. Following doctoral studies into the poetics of Victoria's Western District landscape, he established the University's landscape architecture program and has extensively researched South Australia's cultural landscape and garden history.

George Jones has extensively researched garden history in Geelong and Victoria's Western District, published in *Growing Together* (1984). He was the inaugural honorary life member of the Horticultural Media Association (Vic.).

Ronald Jones trained at Iowa State University and is now a Melbourne-based landscape architect and urban designer in private practice.

Bronwen Keighery, Senior Environmental Officer in the Western Australian Department of Environmental Protection, has extensive experience in community participation in flora surveys.

Greg Keighery, Principal Research Scientist (Biological Survey) in the Western Australian Department of Conservation and Land Management, has published widely on the flora of Western Australia.

Jill Kellow is a lecturer at Burnley College, University of Melbourne, and edits the Burnley Plant Directory (CD-ROM).

Norah Killip has worked as a librarian in Vic. and ACT. She is a keen gardener and amateur historian.

Rohan Lamb has a research interest in engineering heritage and has written on the evolution of the water supply system of Melbourne's Royal Botanic Gardens.

Dr Donald Langmead is Adjunct Professor in the School of Architecture and Design, University of South Australia. He is author of *Accidental Architect* (1994), a biography of George Strickland Kingston.

Anne Latreille is a Melbourne-based writer and editor whose work centres on gardens, landscapes, and the natural environment.

Joan Law-Smith was a botanical artist and writer whose work appeared in many books. Her life was subject of *Kindred Spirits: A Botanical Correspondence* (1999).

Elaine Lawson was formerly Senior Historic Places Curator in the Australian Capital Territory Government managing the conservation of Lanyon, Calthorpes' House, and Mugga-Mugga.

Michael Lehany is a Sydney-based landscape architect with extensive experience in cultural landscape assessment and the conservation of public and private gardens, and cultural landscapes.

Jane Lennon is a Brisbane-based heritage consultant and Australian Heritage Commissioner. For two decades she worked in the Victorian public service, managing numerous significant conservation projects.

List of Contributors

Dr Miles Lewis is Professor in the Faculty of Architecture, Building and Planning, University of Melbourne. His interests include the history of architecture and building technology.

Nigel Lewis is a Melbourne-based architect and heritage consultant with a special interest in the history of designed landscapes.

Dr Barry Long is a consultant physician practising in Adelaide. He has an interest in gardening and garden history, with a particular interest in mazes.

Dr Michael Looker is Director of the Trust for Nature, and previously worked as a Senior Lecturer at Burnley College, and as Horticultural Botanist and then Superintendent of the Royal Botanic Gardens, Melbourne.

Clive Lucas is an architect and writer well known for his involvement with numerous conservation bodies and for his restoration of some of Australia's most important buildings.

Dr David Mabberley is LUF Professor in the University of Leiden, The Netherlands, Honorary Director of the Joseph Banks Archive Project, London, and Honorary Research Associate at the Royal Botanic Gardens, Sydney.

Joy McCann is a historian with a particular interest in rural landscapes. She is currently undertaking doctoral research on rural communities and heritage.

Dr Chris McConville is Senior Lecturer in Australian and Cultural Studies, University of the Sunshine Coast. His most recent publication (co-edited with Lynette Finch) is *Gritty Cities: Images of the Urban* (1999).

Peter MacFie practises as a professional historian. Formerly Historian at Port Arthur Historic Site, he has wide interests in Tasmania's social, penal, landscape, and rural history.

Dr Mary Mackay is a lecturer in the Department of Art History and Theory, University of Sydney. Her doctoral research analysed the Sublime in Australia.

Dr Judith McKay is Curator of Applied Arts at the Queensland Museum. She has written on Ellis Rowan, and recently curated an exhibition *Brilliant Careers* on women naturalists and illustrators.

Dr Ian McLaren was a Victorian parliamentarian, bibliophile, and writer. Much of his exceptional personal library of Australiana is now housed at the University of Melbourne.

Natalie McMaster worked as a teacher librarian and with Jane Edmanson co-edited *Ideas from Private Gardens* (1986). She is a voluntary guide with the Royal Botanic Gardens, Melbourne.

Judy McMaugh was for many years a teacher and most recently a horticultural curriculum specialist for TAFE NSW. She is author of *What Garden Pest or Disease is That?* (1985).

Alan McNeish has a postgraduate degree in History and Philosophy of Science. He assisted Peter Valder in the garden at Nooroo from the late 1950s.

Carmel McPhee, a graduate in History and Applied Science (Horticulture), works as a private landscape consultant and was formerly Manager of National Trust Gardens (Vic.).

Moira Maguire is a freelance writer, editor, and contributor to gardening publications. She is also creating a large garden in country NSW.

Dr Deborah Malor teaches and researches art history and theory in the School of Visual and Performing Arts, University of Tasmania.

List of Contributors

Carol Mansfield is a local historian with a passion for plants and gardens. She also tends a large country garden in the Darling Range (WA).

Dr Julie Marcus is Professor of Social Anthropology, Charles Sturt University. Her research interests include race, gender, and sexuality in Australian society.

Sara Maroske is a historian of Australian science and social history. She is an editor of Ferdinand von Mueller's correspondence and co-biographer of his life.

Dr Susan Martin teaches Australian and English literature at La Trobe University and is currently researching the cultural history of gardens in Australia.

Dr Peter May is Deputy Head of Campus, Burnley College, University of Melbourne. Within the field of environmental horticulture, he has particular interests in urban soils and tree production and establishment.

Patricia Michell gardens in South Australia. Her family has been responsible for many significant gardens and garden design commissions in the state.

Carolyn Middlemis has an active interest in garden history and has co-ordinated historical research undertaken by the Australian Garden History Society (Western Australian Branch).

Simon Molesworth is a Melbourne barrister and long-time Chairman of the National Trust of Australia (Victoria). He has a passionate interest in conservation, including gardens.

Dr Greg Moore, Head of Campus, Burnley College, University of Melbourne University, specialises in horticultural plant science and ecology, with a specific interest in arboriculture.

Dr Brian Morley trained in Europe and the Caribbean and was for two decades Director of the Botanic Gardens of Adelaide and State Herbarium of South Australia.

Colleen Morris is a Sydney-based heritage consultant with a special interest in garden history and the conservation of significant cultural and designed landscapes. She has undertaken conservation plans for many significant properties in NSW.

Ian Morrison is Curator, Australiana, University of Melbourne Library, and is currently compiling a bibliography of Australian almanacs.

Dr Anne Neale is a historian of architecture and gardens. She is a lecturer at the University of Tasmania and her recent doctorate analysed the career of Edward La Trobe Bateman.

Dr Robert Nichol is a professional historian and was recently South Australian State Historian. His publications include important works on Australian cemeteries, including *At the End of the Road* (1994).

Trevor Nottle is manager of the TAFE School of Horticulture in South Australia. His numerous garden books range in subject from old-fashioned roses and cottage gardens to Mediterranean gardening practices.

John Oldham was one of Western Australia's pioneering landscape architects and with his wife Ray co-authored the book *Gardens in Time* (1980).

Dr Karen Olsen is a partner in a Melbourne-based landscape heritage consultancy. Her recent doctoral studies examined historic garden interpretation.

List of Contributors

Frances O'Neill is Senior Historian at Heritage Victoria. Her Master of Arts thesis examined government buildings in Victoria in the nineteenth century.

Jill Orr-Young is the principal of a Melbourne based landscape architecture practice, which focuses on the planning and design of public places.

Helen Page, a graduate in horticulture from Burnley College, works in the regulatory affairs area of agricultural chemicals. She is an active member of the Australian Garden History Society.

Philip Palmer is a landscape architect specialising in heritage landscapes. He has practised in Perth since graduating in 1979 from the University of New South Wales.

Gwen Pascoe is a Melbourne writer. She has recently undertaken postgraduate research on Victoria's horticultural and garden history covering the 1840s to 1860s.

John Patrick is a Melbourne-based horticulturist and landscape architect whose practice has specialised in the study of historic landscapes and gardens.

Dr Pauline Payne, an Adelaide-based historical consultant, teaching part-time at Adelaide University, is co-author (with David Jones) of *Gardens in South Australia 1836–1940* (1998).

Florence Pearce is a Gippsland historian and long-time Boisdale resident where her family farmed for more than eight decades.

Richard Peterson is a Melbourne-based architect. He lectures at the Royal Melbourne Institute of Technology and works as a consultant in the field of heritage conservation.

Jennifer Phipps is Curator of Australian Art (Late Modernism) at the National Gallery of Victoria. She is author of *Artists' Gardens* (1986).

Andrew Picone is an environmental consultant who has recently completed studies in Social Science (Environment) at Royal Melbourne Institute of Technology.

Katrina Place has recently completed postgraduate research at the University of Melbourne on architect Walter Butler and the Arts and Crafts Movement.

Jo Anne Pomfrett is a curator with the Historic Houses Trust of New South Wales. She co-curated an exhibition of Ferdinand Bauer's Australian drawings at Museum of Sydney during 1997–98.

Dr Helen Proudfoot worked as a town planner and historian in Sydney, specialising in heritage studies of buildings, landscapes, and local regions.

Sandra Pullman is currently studying horticulture at Burnley College, University of Melbourne, and has a special interest in the work of early Burnley graduates.

Juliet Ramsay has a background in landscape planning. She has a strong interest in the intangible values of landscapes, and in historic gardens.

Richard Ratcliffe was a Canberra-based landscape architect who specialised in conservation of heritage landscapes.

Bryce Raworth is a practising architectural historian and conservation consultant based in Melbourne. He has a special interest in early twentieth-century design.

Stuart Read is a horticulturist and landscape architect working for the New South Wales Heritage Office.

List of Contributors

Christine Reid is a Melbourne gardening writer who contributes to numerous publications in Australia and overseas. She is a former Victorian co-ordinator of Australia's Open Garden Scheme.

Oline Richards is a retired landscape architect specialising in Western Australian landscape history and heritage conservation. She is author of *War Memorials in Western Australia* (1996) and *Designed Landscapes in Western Australia* (1997).

Dr Libby Robin, Research Fellow, Centre for Resource and Environmental Studies, Australian National University, is author of *Defending the Little Desert* (1998) and co-editor of *Ecology and Empire* (1997).

Tony Rodd, botanical consultant, was formerly Horticultural Botanist at the Royal Botanic Gardens, Sydney. He has recently published a botanical revision of the palm genus *Livistona* in Australia.

Rosemary Rosario is a Perth-based heritage and conservation consultant in private practice.

Dr David Rowe is an architect and heritage consultant. His doctoral thesis analysed the career of architect John Smith Murdoch.

Ken Scarlett is a historian, commentator, and writer on Australian sculpture and public art.

Dr Jan Schapper is a Senior Lecturer in landscape heritage at the University of Melbourne. She is currently a member of the Heritage Council of Victoria.

Lindy Scripps is a consultant historian based in Hobart. She specialises in the research of historic sites in Tasmania, ranging from industrial heritage to historic properties.

Jessie Serle has had long involvement in the conservation of historic properties, including Werribee Park (Vic.). She is the co-author (with Terence Lane) of *Australians at Home* (1990).

Jan Seto trained as an architect and landscape architect. She consults in the field of landscape history and is an active member of the Australian Garden History Society.

Dr Jeannie Sim is a lecturer in landscape architecture at Queensland University of Technology. She specialises in the history of designed landscapes, particularly those in the tropics, and has undertaken conservation plans for several major public gardens.

Phyl Frazer Simons, landscape designer and architect, is the author of *Historic Tasmanian Gardens* (1987) and is the great grand daughter of nursery proprietor Joseph Harris.

Caroline Simpson has an interest in Australian history, including buildings, gardens, and decorative arts. Her collection of early colonial art and furniture is on display at Clyde Bank, Sydney.

Ian Sinnamon, architect and architectural historian, is a former Head of the Architecture Department, University of Queensland, and is now in private practice.

Clive Sorrell is a Lecturer in Arboriculture at Burnley College, University of Melbourne.

Peter Spearritt was until recently Director of the National Centre of Australian Studies at Monash University. His most recent book is *Holiday Business: Tourism in Australia since 1870* (2000).

Dr Roger Spencer is Horticultural Taxonomist at the Royal Botanic Gardens, Melbourne, where he is preparing a horticultural flora for south-eastern Australia and managing a database of plants available in the Australian nursery industry.

List of Contributors

Ian Stephenson is Director, Historic Places ACT, Cultural Facilities Corporation, and was formerly senior curator of the National Trust of Australia (New South Wales).

Elizabeth Stewart is a historian in the Military History Section of the Australian War Memorial. She is author of *Places in the Park* (1991).

Howard Tanner is a Sydney-based architect and writer with a long personal and professional association with landscape design and garden history.

Angela Taylor is a freelance historian with interests in cultural landscapes and forest history. She is the author of *A Forester's Log* (1998).

Dr David Thackray is Head of Archaeology for the English National Trust. He has particular interests in building and landscape conservation and has published widely on cultural resource management.

Paul Thompson started his landscape design company in 1970 and has established a reputation for his innovative use of Australian plants in both public and private landscapes.

Peter Thomson is one of Australia's best known golfers and is now one of the country's foremost golf course designers.

George Tibbits is an architectural historian and Senior Fellow in the Australian Centre at the University of Melbourne.

Lester Tropman, a graduate in architecture from Sydney University, is director of an architectural practice that specialises in heritage conservation.

Dr Peter Valder, retired botanist and author of *Wisterias* (1995), *The Garden Plants of China* (1999), and *Gardens in China* (2002), was responsible for many years for the garden at Nooroo (Mount Wilson, NSW).

Barbara van den Broek was a landscape architect with extensive experience in landscape design and a special interest in the preparation of conservation management plans.

Christopher Vernon is Senior Lecturer in Landscape Architecture, School of Architecture and Fine Arts, the University of Western Australia.

John Viska is a Perth-based lecturer in horticulture and was founding Chairman of the Western Australian Branch of the Australian Garden History Society.

Kevin Walsh is a qualified garden designer, horticulturist, and writer. He has written two books, including the pioneering *Water-saving Gardening in Australia* (1993).

John Walter has a great interest in Australia flora and is a former secretary of the Society for Growing Australian Plants (Victoria). He is currently researching the Society's history.

Darren Watson, an archivist with the National Archives of Australia, completed a Master of Arts degree in 1995 studying the social history of the Royal Botanic Gardens, Melbourne.

Peter Watts has been Director of the Historic Houses Trust of New South Wales since 1981. He has written several books on Australian garden history and was founding secretary of the Australian Garden History Society.

Dr Joan Webb is a former science teacher and university lecturer and has written on natural history subjects, including biographies of George Caley (1995) and Thistle Harris (1998).

Dr Monika Wells is research officer for the Ferdinand von Mueller Correspondence Project. Her doctorate was in the field of medical history.

List of Contributors

Georgina Whitehead is a landscape architect and author of *Civilising the City: A History of Melbourne's Public Gardens* (1997).

Rowan Wilken is a writer who teaches literature and media at Swinburne University of Technology and is a partner in a Melbourne-based landscape heritage consultancy.

James Will is a Senior Lecturer at Burnley College, University of Melbourne, with expertise in plant production and plant breeding.

Glen Wilson has worked as a landscape designer in Melbourne and Canberra. His passionate interest in Australian native plants is reflected in his designs and in his writings.

Gillian Winter is a librarian in the Tasmaniana Library, State Library of Tasmania, and a freelance historian and editor specialising in mid-nineteenth century Tasmanian social history.

Dr Ray Wright is the Parliament of Victoria's Usher of the Black Rod. He has written widely in the fields of pioneer settlement and parliamentary history.

Lauretta Zilles, a former curator at Castlemaine Art Gallery and Historical Museum, has compiled significant research on the history of horticulture in this historic goldfields region.

John Zwar is a Senior Environmental Scientist for Western Mining Corporation at Olympic Dam in South Australia's arid north and is closely involved with the Australian Arid Lands Botanic Garden.

Note to the Reader

This *Companion* comprises a series of entries, shorter or longer depending on the subject, arranged under alphabetical headwords. Each entry is supported by a web of cross-references (denoted by the use of SMALL CAPITALS), drawing attention to other entries where significant related information can be found. There is also an index of names of significant persons, organisations, and places, irrespective of whether these have a separate alphabetical entry. Suggestions for further reading are given at the end of many entries, indicating selected books that are likely to yield significant historical information on their subject. Due to lack of space and the unenviable task of ensuring consistency across such a diverse range of topics, journal articles and unpublished works have been excluded from the further reading suggestions.

For readers who have a particular query or topic in mind, the alphabetical headwords and index will provide the most convenient means of entry into the text. For those with a general interest, the entries on AUSTRALIA, AUSTRALIAN FLORA, GARDEN, HORTICULTURE, PLANTS, and garden STYLES will provide useful points of entry. The general Australian entry is supported by detailed entries on each of the states and territories. Likewise, the major thematic entries are supported by entries on an array of kindred fields, such as AGRICULTURE, ARCHITECTURE, ART, BOTANY, ECOLOGY, FORESTRY, LITERATURE, LANDSCAPE ARCHITECTURE, TOWN PLANNING, and VITICULTURE. In turn, these entries will direct the reader to shorter entries on yet-more-detailed subjects. Thus a general line of enquiry might lead the reader in succession—through the use of cross references—from the general entry on AUSTRALIA to increasingly specific entries on ARCHITECTURE, GARDEN BUILDINGS, GREENHOUSES, and CONSERVATORIES.

A Note Concerning the Illuminated Headpieces

Each alphabetical section of this *Companion* is opened by an illuminated headpiece depicting an Australian plant. These exquisite headpieces were drawn by Edward La Trobe BATEMAN and engraved for the 1861 *Catalogue of the Melbourne Public Library*. They were again used by the Library for its 1865 supplementary catalogue and 1880 catalogue, and their use here represents their first complete republication since 1880. With characteristic attention to detail by the Library and its artist, each chosen plant represented a successive letter of the alphabet. The original catalogues included a list of the botanical names and authorities, and this information is given below. Where this differs from present-day nomenclature, the current name and authority is also given.

Asplenium flabellifolium Cavanilles
Billardiera longiflora Labillardière
Clematis aristata R. Brown
Dichondra repens Forster
Epacris impressa Labillardière
Fabricia laevigata Gaertner—now *Leptospermum laevigatum* (Gaertner) F. Mueller
Gleichenia dicarpa R. Brown
Hardenbergia monophylla Bentham—now *Hardenbergia violacea* (Schneevogt) Stearn
Indigofera silvatica Sieber—now *Indigofera australis* Willdenow
Jasminum lineare R. Brown
Kennedya prostrata R. Brown
Lomaria procera Sprengel—now *Blechnum ambiguum* (C. Presl) Kaulfuss ex C. Christensen
Muehlenbeckia complexa (Meisner)—now *Muehlenbeckia adpressa* (Labillardière) Meissner
Notelaea ligustrina Ventenat—now *Nestegis ligustrina* (Ventenat) L. Johnson
Oxalis microphylla Poiret—now *Oxalis rubens* Haworth
Platylobium obtusangulum Hooker
Quintinia sieberi Alph. De Candolle
Rubus macropodus Seringe—now *Rubus parvifolius* Linnaeus
Stypandra glauca R. Brown
Tetratheca ciliata Lindley
Uncinia tenella R. Brown
Viola hederacea Labillardière
Wittsteinia vacciniacea F. Mueller
Xanthosia dissecta J. Hooker
Youngia thunbergiana Candolle—now *Youngia japonica* (Linnaeus) De Candolle
Zichya latrobeana Meisner—now *Glycine latrobeana* (Meissner) Bentham

ABBOTT, Francis (1834–1903), botanist and gardens administrator, whose long association with the ROYAL SOCIETY of Tasmania Gardens (later ROYAL TASMANIAN BOTANICAL GARDENS), Hobart, ensured their stability and continuity, particularly during the mid-1880s, when the Gardens passed from Society control to that of a board of trustees. Abbott was a member of a scientifically inclined family. His father, Francis Abbott (1799–1883), kept meteorological records for more than thirty-five years, was a member of the Royal Astronomical Society, and was active in the Royal Society. His brothers were among the colony's earliest amateur photographers. Abbott's father and brothers were watchmakers, but young Francis was apprenticed to F.W. NEWMAN, superintendent of the Royal Society's Gardens, in 1850. On the death of his mentor (1859), Abbott was chosen to succeed him. Although already experienced, he was young for such a post, and the Royal Society council sent him to the MELBOURNE BOTANIC GARDENS to confer with its director, Ferdinand MUELLER.

Abbott believed that BOTANIC GARDENS should be scientific, educational, and practical—not merely pleasant places for public recreation. He was keen to foster rare and valuable plants rather than common varieties, and also to establish a complete collection of Tasmanian plants and carry out experiments with grasses and cereals suitable for local conditions. He was also keen that the plants grown should be better provided with informative labels. The Gardens became a centre for exporting plants; many of the exotic trees grown in the colony came from seeds received in exchange by the Gardens. Abbott was awarded a bronze medal for the collection of indigenous seeds and ferns he sent to the Calcutta International Exhibition (1883). Although Abbott wished to discontinue the sale of plants, he willingly supplied them to churches, schools, and government establishments free of charge. He was responsible for Hobart's PUBLIC PARKS and reserves and his influence was particularly evident in the planning and planting of the Queen's DOMAIN.

Zealous and efficient as an administrator, Abbott always worked under financial constraints: the Royal Society had limited funds, and after incorporation (which supplied the Gardens with a secure base as a public institution), the colony faced a long depression. He gave lectures to the Royal Society and was a guide for notable visitors such as botanical artist Marianne NORTH. He was elected a director of the Tasmanian International Exhibition (1894), being responsible for the gardens of the exhibition building. Abbott died at Rossbank, adjacent to the gardens of which he was a still active superintendent. Obituarists recalled 'a genial kindly man, full of practical knowledge' who 'filled his position with credit and ability'.

GILLIAN WINTER

ABORIGINAL ENVIRONMENTAL MANAGEMENT

When Europeans first settled in Australia—this most environmentally unreliable of continents—they described the Aborigines, who had lived off what the land provided for at least 60 000 years, as healthy, well-fed people. The doctrine of *terra nullius* ('land belonging to no one') that had been used to justify European settlement was founded on the idea that Aboriginal people were not cultivating the land—but closer examination has revealed an active system of land management. Over many hundreds of generations they had gained knowledge of the Australian environment and how to treat it so that it continued to provide the necessities of life.

The chief tool of Aboriginal management was FIRE. Edward Curr (1798–1850), a perceptive early settler, said of Aboriginal people that they tilled their land and cultivated their pastures with fire; in recent times this has been described as 'fire-stick farming'. The Australian continent encompasses many different ecological zones and fire was used differently according to the requirements of the people and the nature of the plants. Early accounts describe the open nature of the dry sclerophyll forests in south-eastern Australia, and when Aboriginal burning stopped, the shrub understoreys became thick and impassable. Keeping the forests open permitted the growth of important small tuberous food plants such as lilies, orchids, and the favourite Murnong or Yam-daisy (*Microseris lanceolata*), which do not thrive if they are too shaded. Regular burning also provided fertilising ash and kept the fuel load in the forests to a level at which the fires set by the Aboriginal people were not of a high intensity. The practice was to burn in patches; if the countryside presents a mosaic of areas in different stages of fire recovery and thus with different fuel loads, even lightning-strike fires do not spread widely. Intervals between fires in south-eastern Australia have been estimated at three to five years, at which time biodiversity reaches a maximum level. Some plants that yield fruits, such as Gunyang (*Solanum*

Aboriginal food plants

vescum), one of the Kangaroo Apples, are 'fireweeds'—they appear in profusion after a fire, but after a few years disappear to remain as stored seed in the soil. Thus firing was necessary in order to ensure a regular supply of fruit.

What of areas that were not dry sclerophyll? It seems likely that wet sclerophyll forest was never deliberately fired, but its extent might have been limited by edge burning. These forests did not yield any important food plants, although they did contain medicinal plants and wood for implements such as fire-drills. Grassy plains and stands of certain water-plants that were important for food may have been burnt more often than the forests. Similar carefully controlled burning occurred in southern WA. In arid Central Australia, many of the important food plants providing fruits and seeds behave as fireweeds, so that regular firing ensured maximum production. In tropical areas such as Kakadu (NT), Aboriginal burning maintained the full diversity of plants and animals—a diversity that was adversely affected by the substitution of European burning patterns. Certain areas containing important fire-sensitive food plants were protected from fire, and burning was carefully timed. Many Australian plants have become well adapted to periodic fire as a result of its constant use by Aboriginal people; indeed for some plants, such as the grass-trees, fire is necessary to induce flowering.

In southern Australia, where the staple foods were underground, continual digging-over of the soil by Aboriginal women also had important effects, loosening the soil—and incorporating litter and ash—thereby promoting germination of seeds. They well understood the necessity of leaving some plants to regrow, and to burn after plants had seeded.

The Aboriginal identification with land carried with it a responsibility for maintaining the land's ecological health, which in turn ensured its ability to yield the resources necessary for Aboriginal existence. The invading Europeans encountered people living under a sustainable system; the imposition of European AGRICULTURE has not yet resulted in a similar long-term sustainability.

Comparison of Aboriginal* environmental management with European horticulture and agriculture

European agriculture and horticulture	Koori gathering
Preparation of soil, cultivation	Digging, loosening soil, incorporating litter and ash
Fertilising	Burning at specific times to produce ash
Thinning of perennial plants	Separating clumps of perennials, removing tubers
Sowing and planting	Some tubers left or replanted; burning timed after seeding
Spreading of cultivated plants	Tubers and seeds carried to camps, traded from tribe to tribe

* In this case, the Koori people

David Horton (ed.), *The Encyclopaedia of Aboriginal Australia: Aboriginal and Torres Strait Islander History, Society, and Culture* (Canberra, 1994); Deborah Bird Rose, *Nourishing Terrains: Australian Aboriginal Views of Landscape and Wilderness* (Canberra, 1996); Sylvia Kleinert and Margo Neale (eds), *The Oxford Companion to Aboriginal Art and Culture* (South Melbourne, 2000); Richard Baker, Jocelyn Davies, and Elspeth Young (eds), *Working on Country: Contemporary Indigenous Management of Australia's Lands and Coastal Regions* (South Melbourne, 2001)   BETH GOTT

ABORIGINAL FOOD PLANTS There are about 16 000 NATIVE PLANT species in Australia, and the diet of the Aboriginal people contained a high proportion of plant foods, usually gathered by the women. They used thousands of species—in southern Australia tuberous roots were generally the most used; in the ARID regions, seeds; and in the TROPICS, many more fruits were available.

In the dry sclerophyll forests of southern Australia, which were kept open by regular burning, many small herbaceous PERENNIALS that during the winter, flower in spring and early summer, and die back as water becomes scarce in high summer. They survive this dry period underground as tuberous roots containing stored food; when the autumn rains come they once again put up green leaves. Most of these, including many of the native lilies, were important foods: Chocolate and Vanilla Lilies (*Arthropodium* spp.), Grass Lilies (*Caesia* spp.), Bulbine Lilies (*Bulbine* spp.), Fringe Lilies (*Thysanotus* spp.), and Milkmaids (*Burchardia umbellata*). Aboriginal people also used native orchids, and Murnong or Yam-daisy (*Microseris lanceolata*), formerly very common, was a favoured food.

In the arid regions, seeds of grasses, wattles, and *Portulaca* spp. were a more reliable resource, together with the fruits of Bush Tomato (*Solanum centrale*), which are preserved by drying on the bush. Wattle seeds were eaten green, or ground up when dry. Native Onion (*Cyperus bulbosus*) and Bush Potatoes (*Ipomoea* spp.) provided tubers.

Tropical areas, including RAINFOREST, provided a great variety of foods: lilly-pillies, figs, native grapes, *Pandanus* spp., water-lilies (*Nymphaea* spp.), and Long Yam (*Dioscorea transversa*). Seeds of various cycads and tubers of the Round Yam (*Dioscorea bulbifera*) needed to be processed to remove toxins.

Around rivers and lakes, the water-plants Cumbungi or Bulrush (*Typha* spp.), Water Ribbons (*Triglochin* spp.), and Club-rushes (*Bolboschoenus* spp.) all had tuberous organs that were important foods. Nardoo (*Marsilea* spp.), a small water-fern growing on flooded clay-pans, produces spore capsules that were an emergency food only. Its importance has been exaggerated because it was used by the explorers Burke and Wills in their last days; it destroys vitamin B1 and so is toxic in the long term.

In all areas, tuberous roots could usually be obtained year-round: fruits and seeds were seasonal. FRUITS of some plants such as Muntries (*Kunzea pomifera*) were important because they ripen all at once, while other fruits such as Cherry Ballart (*Exocarpos cupressiformis*) will ripen a few at a time, and so were just 'snack foods'. The Bunya Pine (*Araucaria bidwillii*) is restricted to two small areas of Qld, but when it formed its enormous cones, tribes from long distances around gathered to feast on its plentiful seeds. Aboriginal people used many seasonal 'greens', and knew that the grow-

Aboriginal gardeners

ABORIGINAL GARDENERS have played a vital role in Australian horticultural and agricultural experimentation since European settlement, especially in the TROPICAL north and ARID central zones of the NT, WA, and Qld. This was initially as cheap labour on early settlements, stations, and HOMESTEADS, especially those in remote areas where, as 'live-in help' Aboriginal people provided supervised assistance in the cultivation of subsistence gardens. For instance, from 1906 at Oenpelli (NT), government-appointed Protector of Aborigines, Patrick (Paddy) Cahill (c. 1863–1923), taught local Aboriginal people to grow crops and tropical produce. From the mid-1880s, Aboriginal inmates from Darwin's Fannie Bay Gaol worked in prison-gangs at the DARWIN BOTANIC GARDENS, and in the 1920s Aboriginal gardeners were employed and accommodated on the site. Gardening labour at the Gardens was also provided by young Aboriginal people of mixed racial descent detained at Kahlin Compound, a confinement 'home' established pursuant to the Commonwealth's Aboriginal protectionist policies. Originally located in the vicinity of MYILLY POINT (1913–38) until relocation to Bagot Road, its education program included practical horticultural training on the Compound fruit plantation. As late as the Second World War, Aboriginal workers such as Barramundi Charlie, Topsy, Nellie, and Millie, working on the Katherine River (NT) farming property of Albert Nixon (1906–1990), helped to produce vegetable crops sold to the Army, and were paid 'in kind' for their services. In Alice Springs (NT), the establishment and maintenance of the Olive Pink Flora Reserve in 1956 was in no small part due to assistance provided by Johnny JAMPIJINPA and other Aboriginal workers, and to the indomitable Olive PINK, who strove to attain full wages for her gardening staff. She referred to Jampijinpa as a 'native-born botanist and entomologist'.

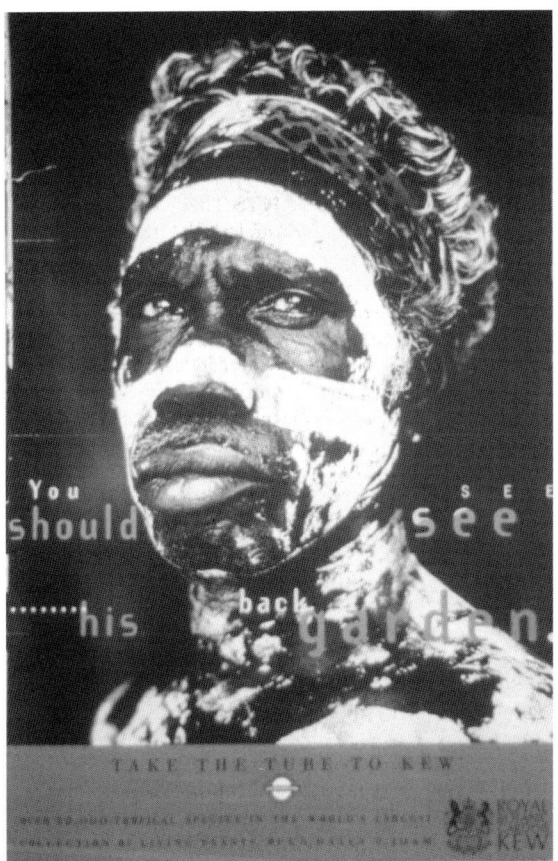

'You should see his back garden': this 1996 London Underground poster advertising the ROYAL BOTANIC GARDENS, KEW, invokes challenging messages about ABORIGINAL ENVIRONMENTAL MANAGEMENT as well as Western notions of PLANT COLLECTING, GARDENS, and HORTICULTURE

Aboriginal people were also trained in European-style gardening activities by missionaries of various denominations from the late nineteenth century, as part of their program of Christian instruction and general education. At many former MISSIONS, especially in northern Australia, traces of tropical and arid-zone agricultural and ornamental gardens exist on many communities; some have been revived as Aboriginal-run MARKET GARDENS and landscaped amenities with the encouragement of the KEEP AUSTRALIA BEAUTIFUL COUNCIL (Northern Territory). Since the 1980s, Aboriginal Land Councils and GREENING AUSTRALIA have worked closely with numerous Aboriginal communities in the Centre and Top End of the NT and the Pilbara, Goldfields, Gulf, and Kimberley regions (WA) to establish LANDCARE education and training programs that incorporate traditional land management with contemporary 'Western' gardening and environmental practices.

European notions of continuous agriculture and property ownership based on defined boundaries were, ironically, crucial in the High Court case *Mabo* (1992), concerning native title, where Koiki (Eddie) Mabo (1936–1992) and others were able to point to clearly identified boundaries on the Murray Islands where their Meriam (Torres Strait Islander) forebears had 'gardened' and cultivated the land for generations. This

ing bases of leaves such as grasses, sedges, and lilies, are soft and palatable; they ate even the bases of grass-tree leaves.

It is possible in many areas of Australia to be taken on bush tucker walks by Aboriginal guides. Many local Aboriginal organisations, universities, schools, municipal councils, and REVEGETATION groups have set up gardens devoted to plants used by Aboriginals. An increasing number of nurseries stock species used by Aboriginal people, and provide information on their cultivation and use. Some species, such as the native lilies, take kindly to cultivation; others, such as the Sweet Quandong (*Santalum acuminatum*), are more difficult. Gathering Aboriginal foods in the wild for the bush tucker market is generally thought impractical, but networks of growers, both amateur and professional, can be found in most states and territories. Herbal medicines and fibres are also important in Aboriginal use of plants.

D. Levitt, *Plants and People* (Canberra, 1981); T. Low, *Wild Food Plants of Australia* (Sydney, 1988); Peter K. Latz, *Bushfires and Bushtucker: Aboriginal Plant Use in Central Australia* (Alice Springs, 1995); J. Robins, *Wild Lime: Cooking from the Bushfood Garden* (Sydney, 1996)   BETH GOTT

Acacia

ABORIGINAL GARDENERS, especially women, were frequently employed in tending MISSION GARDENS; women are shown here preparing land for a VEGETABLE GARDEN during the 1920s at the Church of England's Church Missionary Society Mission at Groote Eylandt in the Gulf of Carpentaria (NT)

contrasted with the far more widespread and geographically diffuse hunter–gatherer traditions of Australia's mainland Aboriginal peoples. ANITA ANGEL

ACACIA, a genus widespread throughout Australia, consisting of more than 600 species, and also represented in Africa, central and southern America, and parts of Asia. Its distribution in Australia, while overlapping the prolific genus EUCALYPTUS, becomes more dominant in the drier areas of the continent. Growth forms vary from prostrate ground-covering shrubs such as *Acacia crispula* to large forest trees such as *Acacia melanoxylon* (Blackwood). Foliage varies from divided fern-like bipinnate leaves to phyllodes (flattened leaf stems) that replace the true leaves.

Many species have been cultivated in gardens for their showy yellow flowers and some are also much valued for their timber. But the faster-growing, medium-sized shrubs and small trees have most often been planted, particularly during the 1960s and 1970s. One drawback is that many acacias are short lived (10-20 years), and their general use in gardens has waned in recent times. However, indigenous acacias have been extensively planted in REVEGETATION schemes, where they not only establish quickly but also provide faunal habitat and are important for soil conservation (as a source of nitrogen). Some species, such as the Blackwood, are long-lived (more than 100 years) and are increasingly being used in urban amenity plantings in south-east Australia. Yet others, such as the popular *Acacia baileyana* (Cootamundra Wattle), have become environmental WEEDS.

Acacia seed has traditionally been a staple ABORIGINAL FOOD: the dried seed is ground between stones to form a flour to make damper. With the gathering interest in bush tucker, additional uses are being found for non-poisonous, seed-bearing species. Wattle seed is now in demand for products such as pastries and breads, and as flavouring, especially in deserts such as ice cream. The acacia is also used as a fodder plant: Mulga, which is widespread in drier regions, has become an important browsing plant.

The Australian common name Wattle may have come from the English reference to the similarity of the twigs of the coastal species observed by early settlers to the stems used in England for interweaving into fences and walls and daubed with mud. Many species carry the common name Wattle—examples are *Acacia mearnsii* (Black Wattle) or *Acacia dealbata* (Silver Wattle)—but others, such as *Acacia harpophylla* (Brigalow) and *Acacia aneura* (Mulga), have retained Aboriginal references. Wattle features strongly as an Australian emblem—the green and gold national sporting colours are thought to be derived from its appearance in flower. The Wattle is also Australia's national FLORAL EMBLEM, and WATTLE DAY has been widely celebrated each year on 1 September.

Maria Hitchcock, *Wattle* (Canberra, 1991) ML

THE ACACIAS (now Loreto College), Marryatville, SA, a suburban MANSION GARDEN laid out in 1874 by Dr J.M. Gunson in conjunction with his new residence, had large park-like grounds and a terraced garden, with an orangery and axially placed fountain. In 1878 (Sir) Edwin Thomas Smith (1830–1919), Mayor of Adelaide (1879–82, 1886–88) and a civic improver of ADELAIDE PARK LANDS and ELDER PARK, acquired the property. He undertook extensive building additions but retained most of the garden structure, including shrubberies along First Creek, terraces, and palm plantings of *Phoenix canariensis* (Canary Island Date Palm) and *Washingtonia filifera* (Cotton Palm). Smith expanded the late Victorian character of the garden—he strengthened the plantings (adding several lathe shade houses and a large zinc-plated conservatory with furnace), developed a winding pathway, edged with terracotta tile, on either side of First Creek, and commissioned Charles ROBINETTE to construct a grotto. The Institute of the Blessed Virgin Mary acquired the property in 1921; although the creek shrubberies and orangery were removed to create playing fields, the general structure of the garden was maintained. DAVID JONES

ACCLIMATISATION might seem only tenuously linked with BOTANICAL and ZOOLOGICAL GARDENS, but in nineteenth-century Australia it connected with and overlapped both. Carrying the meaning 'the process of habituating, or being habituated, to a new climate' the term acclimatisation entered the English language in the 1830s. Several decades later it was applied to the trans-global movement of plants and animals, and acclimatisation societies emerged in a cloud of idealistic rhetoric extolling the importance of introducing ever more examples of Nature's bounty into garden, farm, and forest. Acclimatisation societies would collect, propagate, and distribute useful and ornamental plants and animals. Those that survived and reproduced in the wild or in cultivation in their new homes were deemed to be acclimatised.

After the world's first acclimatisation society was established in France in 1854, two British societies emerged in the early 1860s—in England and in her colonial daughter, Victoria. A driving force in Melbourne was the former editor and co-owner of the Melbourne *Argus* newspaper, Edward Wilson (1813–1878).

When imperial and colonial economies relied so heavily on plants—for timber, cloth, dyes, medicines, and food—potentially useful exotic plants could be test-grown in colonial BOTANIC GARDENS. Before and after the establishment of acclimatisation societies, seeds and plants criss-crossed the oceans en route to botanic gardens for acclimatisation in colonies, whose AGRICULTURE and HORTICULTURE awaited their introduction. The ROYAL BOTANIC GARDENS, KEW, and other British horticultural organisations successfully and sometimes surreptitiously orchestrated the introduction into Britain of plants from all over the world, leaving the English acclimatisation society to focus largely on animals. Through an established and extensive botanical network, plants from Kew reached British colonial botanic gardens long before 'acclimatisation' entered the English lexicon.

In Australian colonies in the mid-nineteenth century, acclimatisation was discussed in philosophical and ROYAL SOCIETIES, and practised in botanic gardens, which were often enlivened zoologically with itinerant waterbirds, symphonious AVIARIES, and mammalian menageries. In Vic., SA, and NSW, acclimatisation societies benefited from botanic gardens and contributed to zoological gardens.

The Acclimatisation Society of Victoria (ASV) was the first Antipodean acclimatisation society. Post-gold-rush Vic. was extremely keen to acquire plants and animals of economic benefit and aesthetic charm. Added to a nostalgia for the sights and activities of 'home', there was an urgent need to provide profit-producing activities for thousands of former gold-seekers. The Director of MELBOURNE BOTANIC GARDENS, Ferdinand MUELLER, was an ardent and active acclimatiser, and was already growing many exotic plants not found elsewhere in the colony. In 1858 the Gardens included bananas, litchi, cherimoir, Paraguayan and Chinese tea, coffee, cork and camphor trees, cotton, cochineal cactus, numerous spice and medicinal plants, and timber trees, including thirty types of oak and forty of pine. A menagerie also graced the grounds, and for several years Mueller's title was Director of the Botanic and Zoological Gardens. Mueller was also secretary of the committee of management for the Gardens' zoological collection. The ASV was established in Melbourne when Wilson joined the zoological management committee (1861). Wilson was ASV president and Mueller vice-president.

The ASV successfully sought membership and government money and land. While Mueller continued to use the Gardens to introduce, propagate, and distribute plants, animal residents were transferred from their paddocks and cages to a site at ROYAL PARK. From 1861 that site was developed as the ASV depot for sea-weary exotic animals awaiting distribution and proliferation. For several years there was enormous enthusiasm for acclimatisation. The ASV was deluged with letters from country towns wishing to set up branch societies, often under the misapprehension that they would thereby gain zoos, and with missionary zeal Wilson spread the word beyond Vic. Wilson visited Sydney in 1861; in 1862 he visited Hobart and wrote a compelling letter to the *South Australian Register*. Patron of the ASV, Sir Henry Barkly, wrote similarly to his fellow governor, Sir George Bowen, in Qld.

Scions of the ASV quickly appeared in Sydney, Adelaide, and Brisbane. In Sydney the Acclimatisation Society of New South Wales was inaugurated late in 1861. The Director of SYDNEY BOTANIC GARDENS, Charles MOORE, was a foundation member, and like Mueller welcomed the Society's growing menagerie in the Gardens. In Adelaide the establishment of the Acclimatisation Society of South Australia in 1862 followed a talk on acclimatisation by the Director of ADELAIDE BOTANIC GARDEN, G.W. FRANCIS, to the Philosophical Society. Francis was the secretary. Following Barkly's letter to Bowen, the Queensland Acclimatisation Society (QAS) was established. A founder and early president was the Clerk of Queensland's Legislative Assembly, L.A. BERNAYS. On acquiring BOWEN PARK, the QAS acclimatised some animals and many plants, including apples, bananas, pineapples, sugar cane, cotton, jute, sorghum, wheat, chicory, coffee, cocoa, and tea. Unlike her sister acclimatisation societies, the QAS did not use BRISBANE BOTANIC GARDENS. Nor did it form a zoo.

The QAS was saved by its strong horticultural emphasis. In the 1870s acclimatisation enthusiasms were waning, although interest in zoological gardens flourished. Acclimatisation societies dwindled and died or added 'zoological' to their name, as occurred in Vic. in 1872, and a decade later in SA. In 1882 the newly reconstituted South Australian Acclimatisation and Zoological Society acquired animals accumulated in the Adelaide Botanic Garden under Francis and SCHOMBURGK, and grounds to house them nearby in Botanic Park. In NSW

Adamson

Acclimatisation societies in Australia

Victoria.
    1861–71 Acclimatisation Society of Victoria
    1872–1910 Zoological and Acclimatisation Society of Victoria

New South Wales.
    1861–c.1882 Acclimatisation Society of New South Wales
    1879–1912 New South Wales Zoological Society

South Australia.
    1862– Acclimatisation Society of South Australia
    1878–81 South Australian Acclimatisation Society
    1882 South Australian Acclimatisation and Zoological Society
    1882–1938 South Australian Zoological and Acclimatisation Society

Queensland.
    1862– Queensland Acclimatisation Society

Tasmania.
    1895– Tasmanian Game Protection and Acclimatisation Society
    1899– North Tasmanian Acclimatisation Society

Western Australia.
    1896– West Australian Acclimatisation Committee

a new society replaced the moribund acclimatisation society. On its establishment in 1879, the aim of the New South Wales Zoological Society was acclimatisation—especially of song birds and game—and in 1883 most of the zoological residents of Sydney Botanic Gardens were transferred to the grounds of the recently formed Zoological Society's grounds at Moore Park. Thus in the 1880s, thanks largely to the efforts of acclimatisation societies, zoological gardens existed in Melbourne, Adelaide, and Sydney.

While the public was keen to marvel at botanical and zoological diversity (especially spectacular examples) on display in botanic and zoological gardens, people and parliaments wanted the economic fruits of plant acclimatisation. Mueller spoke at great length to Victoria's Zoological and Acclimatisation Society on the exotic plants that he considered should be grown in Vic. This grew into his 293-page *Select Plants Readily Eligible for Industrial Culture or Naturalisation* (1876). It rapidly doubled in size, with editions published for NSW as well as Vic., and was printed in several European languages. Meanwhile, Bernays prepared a more tropical volume, *Cultural Industries for Queensland* (1883), on plants he considered suitable for cultivation in Qld.

Useful and beautiful exotic plants continue to be sought for cultivation in Australia without any help from acclimatisation societies. Towards the end of the nineteenth century, newly formed departments of agriculture became involved in this pursuit, as did the CSIRO Division of Plant Industry in the twentieth century.

    Christopher Lever, *They Dined on Eland: Story of the Acclimatisation Societies* (London, 1992)   **LINDEN GILLBANK**

ADAMSON, William (1822–1875), seed merchant and nursery proprietor, was born at White Hills, Banffshire, Scotland. He married in 1851 and migrated to Vic. in the following year. With **Farquharson Smith** (*fl.* 1851–62) Adamson established a business, known later as F.H. BRUNNING Pty Ltd, which has traded continuously from 1852 to the present. Smith is an enigmatic figure. Known mostly as a gardener and seed merchant, he was initially in business, during Melbourne's turbulent post-gold-rush years, with Scottish-born grocer and Melbourne City Councillor George Annand. In 1853 Smith, Adamson and Co. advertised their new grocery establishment as 'Successors to Annand, Smith & Co.'

In 1854 Smith, Adamson and Co. published *The Colonial Gardener, Being a Guide to the Routine of Gardening in Australia; With a Catalogue of Select Kitchen, Garden and Flower Seeds*, heralding the firm's specialisation as seed merchants. This modest thirty-page booklet included a gardening calendar (compiled by 'a thorough gardener'—probably Smith) and a table of sowing times for vegetables, repeated in Adamson's later, renamed *Australian Gardener*. Thus *The Colonial Gardener* was almost certainly the first edition of the book still published as *Brunning's Australian Gardener*. Seeds of superior florists' flowers from England, France, and Germany ('for horticultural competitions') featured, alongside more prosaic agricultural grasses and garden tools, in this earliest known seed catalogue for the colony. Smith produced another small booklet, immodestly titled *The Kitchen Garden: A Complete Treatise on the Kitchen Garden, Containing Practical Information from the Author's Colonial Experience* (1855), and in his review James SINCLAIR sniffily thought this experience should be 'at least from fifteen to twenty years' to justify the claims, when clearly it was far less. *The Colonial Gardener* had advertised 'Gardeners and Land Stewards Recommended', and in publicity accompanying *The Kitchen Garden*, Smith described himself as 'Practical Gardener, Seedsman, &c.', confirming his role as the practical partner and presumably in charge of the nursery at Merri Creek. Smith was a foundation member of the Victorian Gardeners' Mutual Improvement Society (1859).

The partnership Smith, Adamson and Co. was dissolved in 1855. Smith continued alone, and during 1856–57 joined recently arrived horticulturist John RADDENBERRY in business. Debts of this short-lived business were paid by Smith and Adamson, indicating the reunion of the two former partners. By 1856 Adamson had established a nursery at South Yarra, on Punt Road Hill. This was initially under the management of John SMITH (not related to the part proprietor), who after several years left to establish his well-known nursery at Riddells Creek. Between 1857 and 1862 Smith and Adamson supplied many plants to Walter CLARK for Glenara—including 1300 vines, 600 *Maclura pomifera* (Osage Orange) plants for hedges, and a considerable number of specimen trees. In 1858 Smith and Adamson published *The Australian Gardener*—the earliest edition to take this long-lived title—and in 1862 a sixth edition was issued 'to place a knowledge of Cottage Gardening within the reach of every cultivator in this land of our adoption'.

Smith and Adamson dissolved their partnership by mutual consent in 1862, with the business to be carried on by Adamson. According to the *Cyclopaedia of Victoria*, employee Joseph HARRIS then purchased the South Yarra Nursery.

ADAMSON's *Australian Gardener* (1896), first published in the 1850s and still in print as BRUNNING's *Australian Gardener*, appealed to city and country gardeners alike with its popular, practical advice on gardening and horticulture

Adamson continued the wholesale and retail side of the business and by 1862 Alexander STURROCK was working for him; Sturrock revised and corrected the ninth edition of *The Australian Gardener* (1875). Adamson continued to supply customers such as Clark, and he was among the leading seed merchants in the colony. He was an active member of the Victorian Horticultural Improvement Society and had been a subscriber of the Horticultural Society of Victoria since 1857. Adamson (and later his son) was also in business with agricultural merchant Matthew McCaw, dealing principally in grain and dairy produce.

Adamson died in 1875 at his Brighton residence. In the following year Thomas PURVES was appointed manager of the seed business, apparently then at a low ebb after the illness and death of its founder. Adamson's son, William Addison Adamson (1858–1924), also joined the business and ultimately took control of McCaw and Adamson. William ELLIOTT revised *The Australian Gardener* in 1879, greatly broadening its scope. Purves worked hard to rebuild the business and by 1883 was acting as sole city agent for George BRUNNING, who purchased the business in 1887 (when Adamson's widow returned to Scotland). In 1889 Brunning's son, F. Hamilton Brunning, took control of the company—retaining Adamson's name—and worked closely with his father and brothers; Adamson transferred his interests to a stock and station agency, and pursued a career in business and politics. Brunning continued to publish *The Australian Gardener*, with revised editions appearing in 1896 and 1903. On Brunning's death (1905) the Adamson name was finally dropped and the business continued as F.H. Brunning Pty Ltd.   RA

ADCOCK, Thomas (1819–1900), nursery proprietor, from Lincolnshire, England, migrated in 1849 and established Kardinia Nursery in 1851 on about twelve hectares at Highton (Vic.). His brother Henry (1827–1863) arrived in 1854 and established Albion Nursery on an adjacent 2.4 hectares. In 1865 another brother, Edward (1824–1908), joined Thomas at Kardinia Nursery. Their 1857 catalogue—the earliest known to survive—announced 'bulbs and seeds in great variety; also shrubs, ornamental trees and greenhouse plants for sale'; a hothouse built in 1886 enabled propagation of a wider range of plants. Thomas retired in 1891, doyen of Geelong's nursery trade, and Edward continued until the nursery was sold 1896.

George Henry Adcock (1860–1931), son of Edward, was a botanist who learnt from MUELLER (who proposed his fellowship of the LINNEAN SOCIETY in 1895). His 'Census of Plants from the Cape Otway Forest' (1895) and 'Census of Indigenous Plants of the Geelong District' (1897) were published in the *Geelong Naturalist*. He was president of the executive committee for the Geelong Nature Study Exhibition 1905—the first of its kind in Australia—inaugurated by Geelong FIELD NATURALISTS' CLUB, of which Adcock was president in 1897 and 1902. In 1906 he was appointed principal of the government VITICULTURAL college at Rutherglen (Vic.).   GEORGE JONES

ADELAIDE BOTANIC GARDEN SOUTH AUSTRALIA was proclaimed in 1836, and Colonel William LIGHT's 1837 plan of Adelaide showed an area set aside for a BOTANIC GARDEN. It was not until 1854, however, that the Agricultural and Horticultural Society recommended establishment of a forty-seven acre (18.5 ha) botanic garden on the present site. In 1855 George William FRANCIS was appointed superintendent and the garden was opened to the public in 1857. Francis is said to have been influenced by gardens at KEW and Versailles, and the garden still has a northern European landscape style, reflected in its buildings and the FORMALITY of its layout.

Francis resigned in 1865 due to ill health and Dr Richard SCHOMBURGK was appointed his successor—a position he held until his death (1891). Under Schomburgk the Garden continued to flourish. Many of Schomburgk's trees and other plantings, such as the Morton Bay Fig Avenue (1866) and Plane Tree Drive (1874) in adjacent Botanic Park, survive. The eighty-four acre (34 ha) Botanic Park, acquired

Panorama of ADELAIDE BOTANIC GARDEN showing the palm house (1877), one of the chief glories of SCHOMBURGK's directorship; behind it is the circular rose garden formed on the site of Schomburgk's 'class ground' (or SYSTEM GARDEN)

in 1866 after use as a police horse paddock, was dedicated in 1894. In 1868 *Victoria amazonica* (Victoria Waterlily), discovered in northern South America by Schomburgk's brother, flowered in the specially built Victoria House. Since that time cultivation and flowering of this spectacular lily has been associated in Australia with the Adelaide Botanic Garden. Another Schomburgk innovation was the Palm House, specially imported from GERMANY and opened to the public in 1877. One of the finest Victorian GLASSHOUSES in Australia (restored 1993–95), its design (by Gustav Runge) was technically advanced. In 1881, a Museum of Economic Botany was opened to the public. Built in the Greek revival style, it still features a beautiful stencilled ceiling and ECONOMIC BOTANY exhibits are staged in a style suited to the building. It is the only surviving museum of its kind in an Australian garden. During the Schomburgk era, the garden fulfilled recreational and educational functions but also had agronomic importance; new strains of crops (such as wheat, oats, and sorghum), fruit, and vines were tested and distributed to growers and the public.

The next sixty years saw the administrations of three directors: Dr Maurice William HOLTZE (1891–1917), John Frederick BAILEY (1917–32), and Harold GREAVES (1932–47), and were characterised by periods of economic recession and two world wars, resulting in some stagnation of the organisation. The longest-serving director at the Adelaide Botanic Garden was Noel LOTHIAN (1947–80), who re-established the State HERBARIUM in 1955 (headed by Dr Hansjoerg EICHLER), re-established a significant botanical LIBRARY, upgraded staff accommodation facilities, and established seven EXPERIMENTAL plantations of trees and shrubs throughout SA. During Lothian's administration a gardener training scheme began, MOUNT LOFTY BOTANIC GARDEN was created, WITTUNGA Botanic Garden managed, and GOVERNMENT HOUSE grounds made the responsibility of the BOTANIC GARDENS OF ADELAIDE. Dr Brian MORLEY (1980–2000) continued to enhance these initiatives.

Max Lamshed, *The People's Garden: A Centenary History of the Adelaide Botanic Garden, 1855–1955* (Adelaide, 1955)

BRIAN MORLEY

ADELAIDE CHRONICLE: see SOUTH AUSTRALIAN CHRONICLE

ADELAIDE HILLS, a favoured cool-climate area above the Adelaide Plains, forms part of South Australia's Mount Lofty Ranges. A mosaic of valleys and ridges, its high rainfall and generally slightly acidic soils favour apples, cherries, pears, nashi pears, potatoes, winter vegetables (such as cabbages, Brussels sprouts, celery), and soft summer fruits. Originally developed for ORCHARDS, MARKET GARDENING, and timber-getting, it also supported McEWIN's jam operations and early VITICULTURAL attempts. During the 1870s and 1890s many Adelaide families developed HILL-STATION retreats, enabling collection and propagation of favoured species including Japanese maples, dogwoods, azaleas, liquidambars, RHODODENDRONS, CAMELLIAS, FERNS, and CONIFERS. This resulted in colourful spring and autumn displays at BEECHWOOD, Berkeley Vale, Boode House, Bythorne, CARMINOW, Eurilla, FOREST LODGE, Manoah, Mount Lofty House, PANMURE, ST VIGEANS, Thorpe, Tutuila, and WAIROA. Many of

Adelaide Park Lands

The eastern half of this panoramic view of ADELAIDE BOTANIC GARDEN shows other features from Schomburgk's directorship, including the main lake and museum of ECONOMIC BOTANY (1881), between which are the glasshouses comprising the Victoria House, and Schomburgk Range

the original Hills families worked on these new estates, including FAIRHALL, Noble, Searle, SPARROW, and WHIBLEY, together with overseas-trained gardeners such as MENZEL and ROBINSON. Nurseries such as ALDGATE, NEWMAN'S, and LEAWOOD GARDENS were established at this time, and the advice of the GARDEN AND FIELD was respected.

There was a renewed interest in Hills gardens in the 1920s and 1930s, when one could commute by train to Adelaide, and owners pursued garden ideas articulated by ROBINSON, JEKYLL, BAGOT, WALLING, and MELLOR, or followed the fashions expressed by Jack KEMP and SOUTH AUSTRALIAN HOMES AND GARDENS. (BELAIR) NATIONAL PARK, Blackwood Experimental Orchard, and RAYWOOD, BURDETT'S, and ASHBY'S nurseries were established, encouraging native, eclectic, and formal styles found at BROADLEES, The Chestnuts, Mount George, Stangate House, and Yultewirra. Many Hills families—including KEMP, MOSEL, Roberts, and Scott—continued to pursue these horticultural activities, while COTTAGE GARDENING, as at GAMBLE COTTAGE, persisted. In the 1960s LOTHIAN established MOUNT LOFTY BOTANIC GARDEN with CORREY'S designs, and Whibley created the garden image of Stirling Council. The Adelaide Hills have historically been susceptible to bushfires—Ash Wednesday (1983) destroyed many gardens and estates—yet contain a mixture of grand estates, hill-stations, orchards, and cottage gardens, to which has been added in recent years, the production of high quality wines.

TREVOR NOTTLE and DAVID JONES

ADELAIDE OBSERVER (1843–1931), published weekly in SA from 1852 by the proprietors of the *South Australian Register*, included 'Agricultural and Pastoral Interests' among its coverage, with Albert MOLINEUX as agricultural editor. The *Register*, a daily from 1850 to 1930 (originally called *South Australian Gazette and Colonial Register*), was eventually absorbed into the Adelaide *Advertiser*. First published in London in 1836, 'in the capital of the civilised world, with the intention of publishing its second number in a city of the wilderness of which site is yet unknown', under its founding editor George STEVENSON the *Register* exerted a strong influence upon the ideas of colonists. Both the *Register* and the *Observer* provided regular local and international scientific and practical advice on gardening, horticulture, and viticulture; detailed reviews and tours of gardens and orchards, with contributors including Molineux and Henry SEWELL; and reportage of horticultural societies and kindred organisations.

DAVID JONES

ADELAIDE PARK LANDS form an icon of SOUTH AUSTRALIA's capital. Surveyed by Colonel William LIGHT in 1836–37, the plan was directly influenced by the TOWN PLANNING ideas of architect George KINGSTON and the South Australian Colonial Commissioners in London (1835–36). Although the Park Lands were represented on Light's plan, the land was not formally acquired for PUBLIC PARKLAND by Governor Gawler until 1838, and survey and ownership clarification did not prevent extensive clear-felling, quarrying, and over-grazing during the period between 1836 and 1878. Successive City Corporations sought to redress yet financially exploit this situation, permitting the establishment of extensive olive plantations in the 1840s. Under Mayors William Buik and (Sir) Edwin

Smith, Conservator J.E. Brown was commissioned to prepare a *Report on a System of Planting the Adelaide Park Lands* (1880), an amalgam of Picturesque and Gardenesque ideas. Brown commenced executing the plan in 1882–83 but continuing disagreements with City Gardener William Pengilly resulted in Brown's resignation and Pengilly's dismissal. Brown also encouraged the first official Arbor Day planting in Australia in the Park Lands (1889). August Pelzer was subsequently appointed City Gardener (1899) and apparently used the *Report* as a framework to plant and manage the Park Lands.

Town Clerk W.C.D. Veale's overseas study tour (1957) resulted in the development of a golf course, a formal ornamental rose garden, and enhancement of various gardens (including Elder Park). Elsie Cornish was commissioned to design and construct the Pioneer Womens' Garden (1938–39). Various excisions from the Park Lands permitted the establishment of Adelaide Botanic Garden, Botanic Park, Government House, tram sheds, Adelaide Oval, and Adelaide Zoological Gardens. Hassell, consultant planners, prepared a *Park Lands Management Plan* (1999).

J.W. Daly, *Decisions and Disasters: Alienation of the Adelaide Parklands* (Adelaide, 1987) DAVID JONES

ADMIRALTY HOUSE, Kirribilli Point, NSW, has been the official Sydney residence of Australian governors-general since 1914. Originally named Wotonga, the house had several owners between 1845 and 1885; when renamed and enlarged it became the residence of the admiral of the Royal Navy Australian Station. From 1885 to 1985 the garden was maintained by gardeners from Sydney Botanic Gardens. Many fine specimens, including an *Agathis robusta* (Kauri Pine) and several *Ficus macrophylla* (Moreton Bay Fig) and *Araucaria heterophylla* (Norfolk Island Pine) trees, date from the late 1880s: a *Callitris columellaris* (Bribie Island Cypress) on the driveway pre-dates Admiralty ownership. Throughout the garden, paths meander past clipped hedges, mixed borders, rockeries of succulents, and palm beds. On the dramatic harbour frontage, extensive lawns slope away from the house towards rocky cliffs. The lawns are punctuated by several sandstone rocks covered with large clumps of *Dendrobium speciosum* (Rock Orchid). The romantic setting of Admiralty House forms a fine complement to Government House in this outstanding harbourside precinct.

J.S. Kerr, *Admiralty House: A Conservation Plan Prepared for the Department of Housing and Construction* (Sydney, 1987) SILAS CLIFFORD-SMITH

AEOLIA, Randwick, NSW, developed from the 1850s by lawyer and amateur botanist Edwin Daintrey, became a Brigidine Convent early in the twentieth century. Although with substantial additions, the original Edmund Blacket–designed house remains, as does a locally prominent part of the extensive grounds dominated by mature fig trees (including an unusual *Ficus macrophylla* variant); old steps, pillars, and giant clam shells; the carriage drive; and various persistent garden remnants including enormous *Xylomelum pyriforme* (Eastern Woody Pear) trees and *Pereskia aculeata* (Lemon Vine). GEOFFREY BRITTON

AESTHETIC VALUE, ascribed to a place for reasons associated with its beauty, may include formal principles of style and aesthetics but also more subjective concepts such as taste. Taste is often related to aesthetic, especially visual, qualities, but it can also include attributes such as fine craftwork and sound combinations of materials and design, summarised in the old architectural adage 'firmness, commodity, and delight'. At best it can include an informed or knowledgeable appreciation of formal or codified qualities, often expressed in connoisseurship, from the French *connaître* (to know)—with which taste is often confused. At worst it is mere slavish pursuit of fashion.

The Burra Charter guidelines state that 'Aesthetic value includes aspects of sensory perception … such as form, scale, colour, texture, and material of the fabric; the smells and sounds associated with a place and its use'. Aesthetic value is one of the components of cultural significance and is an important component of heritage value. While many landscapes imbued with heritage values also have aesthetic value, places with no appreciable aesthetic value may still be of heritage significance.

Theory relating to aesthetic value has arisen from several areas of thought. The first comes from art, architecture, and related disciplines, and includes ideas of elegance, proportion, and harmony—usually prescribed by a dominant culture. This concept of aesthetic value includes formal aesthetic qualities such as line, form, colour, and texture. More subjective attributes tied to the landscape, such as views and vistas, may also be valued—values derived from Victorian attitudes to landscape and nature. By the last quarter of the eighteenth century, interest in landscape as scenery was heightened by an interest in landscape painting, expressed in the Picturesque. In the early nineteenth century ideas about landscape and scenery were changing, and the concept of taste itself was becoming broader. Formalised rules had been replaced by the idea that individual taste was legitimate. Aesthetic response was no longer dependent solely on the inherent properties of the object perceived, but on the associations registered by the receiver. Aesthetic perception, far from being prescribed, was proving to be changeable and unpredictable, with dramatic consequences for garden styles. JAN SCHAPPER

AFRICA, in particular the Cape of Good Hope, has had a prominent place in Australian garden history since the First Fleet stopped at Cape Town in 1787 to gather supplies and goods for the last leg of its journey to Botany Bay. First Fleeters bought seeds and plants to grow in NSW: Captain Watkin Tench recorded in his diary that Surgeon Arthur Bowes Smyth had in his cabin geraniums and a grapevine from the Cape that 'flourished very much'. Somewhat later Georgiana Molloy spent the considerable sum of £7 17s 6d on seeds in Cape Town on her voyage out in 1829. Without doubt the botanic garden of the Governor of the *Verenigde Oostindische Compagnie* (Dutch East India Company) at Cape Town and the well-stocked orchards and vineyards of the surrounding countryside supplied many of the plants brought to Australia in the early years of colonisation. Mauritius also played an important part in the introduction of plants to Australia: Governor Darling was governor of

Mauritius before coming to NSW, and the botanic gardens there came under his control.

The early horticultural influence of the Cape Province and Mauritius in Australia can still be observed. Many settled areas are populated with naturalised stands of South African plants, particularly BULBS such as *Freesia*, *Sparaxis*, *Crocosmia*, *Watsonia*, *Amaryllis*, and *Babiana*. Various large shrubby aloes are widespread along roadsides and around derelict farmsteads, perhaps first arriving from the Cape as large stem cuttings slung overhead from the cabin roof beams out of the way and safe from the depredations of hungry rats and shipboard livestock.

As the colonies began to explore the possibilities of economic horticulture through ACCLIMATISATION SOCIETIES and fledgling BOTANIC GARDENS, more plants from the Cape were introduced: some native and others, of European origin, possessing commercial value—apple and pear cultivars, wine grapes, olives, and nut trees. Exchanges between plant collectors, botanists, and botanic gardens saw the introduction to Australia of a large variety of ericaceous plants—Proteacae, Euphorbiacae, and Aizoaceae—possibly reaching a peak around the 1930s. The strange SUCCULENT plants of the Cape, such as lithops, haworthias, conophytums, and pleispilos, found high favour with plant collectors, while ROCK GARDEN enthusiasts favoured drought-tolerant crassulas, dwarf aloes, cotyledons, and *Lampranthus* species. Tree-like euphorbias and arborescent aloes were popular additions to vaguely MEDITERRANEAN gardens in warm dry areas.

Since the 1960s, South African plants have begun to be exploited in Australia for the local and export cut-flower trade. Large numbers of leucodendrons, proteas, and allied genera have been established in commercial plantations and supply winter flowers to the country as well as being sent overseas to Japan, Europe, and the USA. TREVOR NOTTLE

AGAVE From ROUSE HILL in the east to WALLCLIFFE HOUSE in the west their spiky silhouettes signal sacred sites, sending the heritage cognoscenti into swoons and striking fear into the hearts of unsuspecting gardeners. In Victorian Britain these graceful monsters were considered 'fine ornaments' on VILLA lawns or urn-bedecked terraces: an infrequent flowering was marked with intense interest and the erection of an elevated viewing platform, but in the fecund colonies, as a member of the Victorian Gardeners' Mutual Improvement Society remarked (1860), it 'thrives and blooms profusely with no care whatever'. Unfettered, agaves multiplied indiscriminately in choice spots along colonial byways and even botanic garden directors were not unmoved by their SUCCULENT beauty. By the mid-twentieth century *Agave americana* was occasionally seen in suburban backyards and was briefly popular—especially in its VARIEGATED form—in pebbled FRONT GARDENS. Recently agaves have again been the subject of admiring glances and eager advances. COLLEEN MORRIS

AGRICULTURAL AND PASTORAL SOCIETIES have played a central role in the development and promotion of new farming techniques in Australia. They were based upon, and maintained ties with, British societies established in the wake of the eighteenth-century agricultural revolution, including the Royal Agricultural Society. In the colonies, where unfamiliar climatic and geographical

Edwardian visitors to the Armytage property COMO, South Yarra (Vic.), disport themselves around a large AGAVE to admire the garden, apparently undaunted by the hostile foliage

Agricultural colleges

features challenged traditional European farming methods, commercial and scientific interest in progressive AGRICULTURE was crucial.

The Van Diemen's Land Agricultural Society (1822) aimed to reward agricultural excellence, and held an annual exhibition of livestock. Similar societies were formed in Sydney (1822), Perth (1829), Adelaide (1839), and Port Phillip (1840). These were restricted associations serving the farming gentry, but agricultural and pastoral societies gradually broadened their membership and activities. As the pastoral industry expanded, agricultural production (particularly wheat) moved further inland, and transport improved, new rural settlements were founded: most boasted their own agricultural society. By Federation, hundreds of societies existed and they continued to form—and close—in accordance with subsequent rural development. These societies fostered agricultural education through publications, model farms, and demonstrations, and worked with related organisations such as breed associations and HORTICULTURAL SOCIETIES. By the late nineteenth century, these efforts were strongly supported by government, which used the societies to promote IRRIGATION, closer settlement, and other schemes. The most influential continue to be the large metropolitan 'Royal' societies, responsible for promoting agriculture statewide and coordinating local and district societies.

The most important activity continues to be an annual show, with competitive judging and prizes for livestock, produce, and technologies. From humble beginnings, shows became substantial exhibitions of colonial resources and wealth. By the 1870s they included extensive displays of agricultural machinery, animals, raw and processed produce, bush skills, sports, equestrian events, domestic arts, flowers, and manufactured goods, with various entertainments and sideshows. These diverse interests are evident in the adoption of the terms 'horticultural' and, especially in Qld, 'industrial' in the official names of societies. Throughout the twentieth century, the metropolitan shows, held over several days on dedicated SHOWGROUNDS, increasingly bridged the gap between urban and rural Australians; in remote areas they assume great social and commercial importance. The grand parade, where the winners in all classes gather in the arena, has become a show tradition. District exhibits—elaborate arrangements of fruit, vegetables, nuts, dairy produce, preserved fruits, jams and pickles, eggs, grains, wool, wine, and other agricultural products—are still a major feature, for example, at Sydney's Royal Easter Show and the 'Ekka' (Exhibition) in Brisbane.

In recent decades, the declining economy of the rural sector, rural depopulation, and other factors affecting farming communities have forced some agricultural societies to close, amalgamate, or reorientate their shows to attract tourists and business interests: about 650 operate today. The rise of small-scale hobby-farming and gourmet food production has given the exhibition and sale of horticultural produce enhanced prominence.   KATE DARIAN-SMITH

AGRICULTURAL COLLEGES have provided EDUCATION and training in agriculture (and horticulture) in Australia since the 1880s, generally based in rural districts, and following British and especially NORTH AMERICAN models. Their origin, examined by Alan Black in the *Australian Journal of Politics and History* (1975), accompanied a call from enlightened agriculturists for 'scientific farming', invoking science as an aid to tradition and empirical knowledge. Farmers (and gardeners), recent migrants, and old colonists ranged from hopeful novices to practical and experienced hands: all needed to acclimatise to the unfamiliar CLIMATES and conditions, and their different needs and expertise were factors in the establishment of AGRICULTURAL AND PASTORAL SOCIETIES, EXPERIMENTAL FARMS, government agricultural departments, and educational colleges. Agitation for these colleges typically began years before their establishment, sometimes with considerable opposition from pastoralists. ROSEWORTHY AGRICULTURAL COLLEGE, SA (1883), was the first in Australia, and other colonies soon followed: Dookie (1886: previously an experimental farm) and Longerenong (1889), both in Vic.; Hawkesbury (1891) and Tocal (1965), both in NSW; Gatton, Qld (1897); WAITE, SA (1924); and Muresk, WA (1926). These residential colleges, principally for boys, promoted systematic and scientific approaches to farming through theoretical and practical lessons with qualified staff (such as G.H. ADCOCK, BRAGATO, J.E. BROWN, GRASBY, LANE-POOLE, MACIVOR, MACKAY, and SHELTON), experimentation programs, and publications. Roseworthy also included VITICULTURE and horticulture in its curriculum; specialised colleges for HORTICULTURE were established at BURNLEY, Vic. (1891) and RYDE, NSW (1946). Many agricultural colleges later affiliated with universities and widened their entry intake to include both male and female students, often with urban campuses linked to traditional rural bases. Agricultural high schools were also established during the early twentieth century in some states.

JEANNIE SIM

AGRICULTURAL GAZETTES AND JOURNALS OF AGRICULTURE, published (generally) monthly by each of the colonial (later state) agriculture departments, contained much of horticultural interest. These were inaugurated in NSW (1890), Tas. (1892), WA (1894), Qld (1897), SA (1897), and Vic. (1902), and were often preceded or supplemented by annual reports, bulletins, and monographs. Prominent horticultural contributors included BOYD, DESPEISSIS, F. TURNER, OSBORNE, and E.E. PESCOTT.   RA

AGRICULTURAL SHOWS: see SHOWGROUNDS

AGRICULTURAL SOCIETIES: see AGRICULTURAL AND PASTORAL SOCIETIES

AGRICULTURE includes the science and practice of cultivating the soil and rearing animals; although the former meaning could equate it with GARDENING, derivation from the Latin *agricultura* (field culture) suggests an obvious difference of scale. While this difference is clear with broadacre cereal crops, the distinction becomes blurred with fruit trees,

Agriculture

AGRICULTURAL COLLEGES, such as Gatton College between Brisbane and the DARLING DOWNS, provided formalised EDUCATION for Australian's farming community, yet their establishment was often opposed in the late nineteenth century by pastoralists with extensive holdings, who were fearful of land selection and closer settlement

grape vines, and vegetables, particularly when they combine to form highly valued CULTURAL LANDSCAPES of ORCHARDS, VINEYARDS, MARKET GARDENS, or similar RURAL LANDSCAPES.

Like the segment of the NURSERY industry devoted to intensive cultivation, agriculture is primarily based on production and market-driven outcomes. The close relationship between agriculture, HORTICULTURE, and gardening is demonstrated where plant cultivars and cultural methods are also used in gardens—rooting stocks in fruit tree production, for example. Such garden usage may have agricultural origins or may utilise specialised non-agricultural techniques: multi-grafting to obtain several cultivars on the same fruit tree, or to have two pollination types necessary for fruit formation are examples of the latter.

Distinctions between agriculture, horticulture, and gardening were less obvious in the eighteenth and nineteenth centuries in Australia. Plant ACCLIMATISATION and experimentation occurred as part of early garden culture, and many EXPERIMENTAL and BOTANIC GARDENS included both ornamental and productive plants. The Royal Horticultural Society of Victoria orchards at BURNLEY, for example, brought these categories together from the 1860s, although by the 1890s the site had been taken over by agricultural interests. Brisbane's BOWEN PARK was another site where experimental (in this case, TROPICAL) horticulture and agriculture coexisted. Many early horticulturists experimented with useful plants and crops rather than ornamental plants in response to economic imperatives. AGRICULTURAL AND PASTORAL SOCIETIES, rather than HORTICULTURAL SOCIETIES, were the norm in Australia (especially rural areas) for similar economic reasons. Scientific agriculture was promoted at a colonial (later state) level by government agricultural departments from the late nineteenth century, which also promoted education through AGRICULTURAL COLLEGES. AGRICULTURAL GAZETTES AND JOURNALS OF AGRICULTURE were a valuable means for governments to disseminate information; the weekly press performed the same role in the private sphere, through papers such as the AUSTRALASIAN. In contemporary agriculture, this function is increasingly being carried out by COMPUTERS, especially through the Internet.

Adverse impacts by agriculture on the ENVIRONMENT—resulting for instance in clearance of large areas of natural vegetation, damage from irresponsible use of CHEMICALS, or soil degradation on a large scale (with effects such as erosion or increased salinity)—have been felt in the garden: gardeners have an increasing awareness of INDIGENOUS VEGETATION and ORGANIC techniques, and a desire to incorporate these in our garden culture. The impact of agriculture is a key concern of environmental politics and history in contemporary Australia, and it has fuelled popular movements such as LANDCARE and GREENING AUSTRALIA.

Samuel Wadham, *Australian Farming, 1788–1965* (Melbourne, 1967); Robin Bromby, *The Farming of Australia* (Sydney, 1986); Geoff Raby, *Making Rural Australia: An Economic History of Technical and Institutional Creativity, 1788–1860* (Melbourne, 1996); Jennifer Cornwall, Gordon Collie, and Paul Ashton, *Sustaining a Nation: Celebrating 100 Years of Agriculture in Australia* (Edgecliff, NSW, 2000) RA and ML

AHLFELD, (Gustav F.) Werner (*fl.*1913–31), nursery proprietor specialising in Australian native plants, operated from Hornsby, in Sydney's north (1926–29). From 1926 he advertised his nursery as 'The House for Native Plants' and conducted 'Our Native Plant Column' for Searl's GARDEN MAGAZINE—one of the earliest regular columns in an Australian GARDEN MAGAZINE on this subject. His pamphlet *The Cultivation of the Native Flowers of Australia* (*c.* 1929), published in Sydney by the Rangers League, was also a pioneering publication on horticultural use of AUSTRALIAN FLORA. RA

AIR RAID SHELTERS With the WARTIME threat of Japanese attack during the 1940s, Australian citizens were encouraged to prepare a 'place in which the whole household can take shelter' should the need arise. The government circulated information on domestic shelters with designs for various garden conditions and household requirements. These ranged from open trenches to partly sunken shelters such as the Anderson shelter, surface (pill-box type) shelters, and fully sunken shelters suited to large PUBLIC GARDENS. The *Australian Garden Lover* (1942) provided gardening tips on camouflaging shelters; nasturtiums topped the plant list for their quick-growing, shallow-rooting habit, and also their cheerful colour 'at a time we need it most'. Surviving shelters are rare: an extant example is found in the BACKYARD of CALTHORPES' HOUSE, Canberra.

ROWAN WILKEN and KAREN OLSEN

ALBERT PARK, Brisbane, gazetted as a park and recreation ground in 1877 and initially controlled by trustees (and later the local council), was planted with shade trees from the BRISBANE BOTANIC GARDENS in 1881. Under the supervision of Philip MACMAHON, the sloping site of Albert Park was developed with flowers, a rose garden, trees, and paths. Recreation facilities included tennis and basketball courts, a cricket pitch, bandstand, and kiosk. During the Second World War air raid shelters were constructed in the park, and some survive. Wartime deterioration prompted a beautification program for the park during the 1950s, involving major replanting and construction of paths and furniture. An amphitheatre was added in 1982. This seven-hectare parkland, complete with a magnificent avenue of *Ficus macrophylla* (Moreton Bay Fig), is a green oasis on the edge of the city. MARGARET COOK

ALBERT PARK, South Melbourne, was established in the mid-1850s. An 1864 plan for its layout is attributed to Clement HODGKINSON. During the 1870s a large lagoon was turned into a LAKE for sailing and rowing; edged with a five-kilometre promenade, this forms the central feature. Like the adjacent Fawkner Park, Albert Park's St Kilda Road frontage was subdivided and sold in 1875. Subsequent excisions reduced its size to 225 hectares. Cricket was played there initially and other sports soon followed, coexisting with cattle grazing that continued well into the twentieth century. Today, indoor and outdoor facilities cater for a wide variety of sports including golf and swimming. The Australian Grand Prix car race has been held there since 1996 despite continuing opposition from some quarters.

J. Barnard and J. Keating, *People's Playground: A History of the Albert Park* (Burwood, Vic., 1996) GEORGINA WHITEHEAD

ALBURY BOTANIC GARDENS, NSW, situated on the Murray River flood plain, occupies four hectares of a

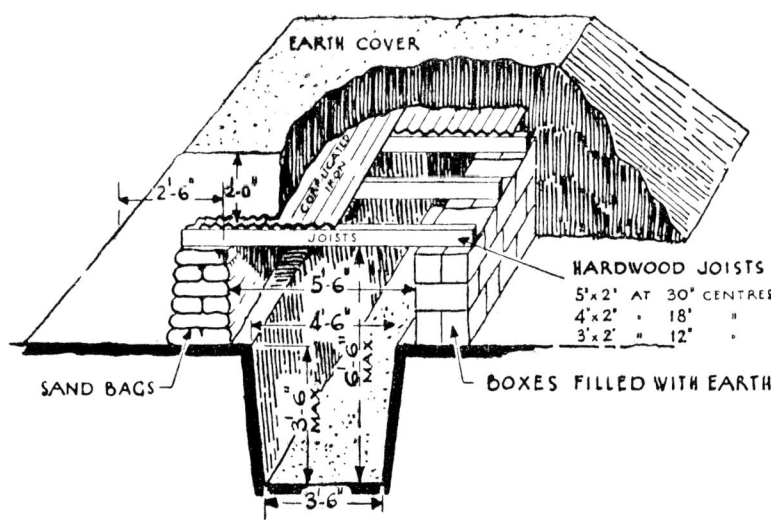

Australian BACKYARDS, as well as PUBLIC PARKS AND GARDENS, were transformed during the Second World War when deteriorating WARTIME conditions dictated the creation of AIR RAID SHELTERS to provide a refuge against the threat of Japanese air strikes

twenty-hectare reserve set aside in 1864. The site, created by diverting Bungambrawartha Creek, was developed after the appointment in 1877 of the first curator, M. Peasley. An avenue of elms was planted along the northern boundary in 1878 but early plantings favoured conifers. The design was modelled on the Union Jack, centred on a shade house and lake. James Edward Richards Fellowes (1859–1939), curator 1901–37, altered this design to create a more picturesque layout—possibly following advice given by William GUILFOYLE in 1886—with a network of meandering paths constructed for internal circulation and the lake converted into three lily ponds. Although now modified, his design and planting established the existing character of the Gardens. Fellowes viewed PUBLIC GARDENS as places 'for recreation and instruction as to what will grow in the different localities' and thought well-kept public gardens were an example to residents, thereby 'making the country a much more desirable place to live in'. The plant collection was maintained by subsequent curators, among them his son, Walter Bennett Fellowes (1896–1944), curator 1937–44. Notable embellishments include a monument to explorer Hamilton Hume (relocated 1884), rotunda (1890), statue of the Greek muse Melpomene (1892), memorial gates (1908), brick curator's cottage (1909), LONE PINE (1936), and rainforest walk (1978).   PAMELA JELLIE

ALDGATE NURSERY is a vernacular name for several significant nurseries established in the Aldgate area of the ADELAIDE HILLS. With Oscar and Bruno MENZEL, Fred Caley SMITH established the Specialist Farm in 1899 on three hectares, which Mrs Caley Smith continued until 1920. It specialised in delphiniums, gladioli, petunias, dahlias, aquilegias, and other bulb species. Henry SEWELL acquired four hectares in 1898 to establish his Cool Climate Nursery; Joseph Beyer and E.R. Beckett served as its managers. In 1929 this nursery was acquired by Herbert KEMP and managed first by Herbert and then by Robert Kemp, whose family still operates the Kemp Nursery. This nursery was prominent in the cultivation and dissemination of acidic-soil-loving plants including ferns, rhododendrons, camellias, azaleas, roses, carnations, hydrangeas, cycads, palms, and perennials, and in supplying and advising upon plants and planting in Adelaide and the Adelaide Hills, particularly between 1920 and 1960. The Claret Ash was first propagated by Tullie WOLLASTON at his RAYWOOD nursery from specimens obtained in this nursery.   DAVID JONES

ALFRED NICHOLAS MEMORIAL GARDENS, Sassafras, Vic.: see BURNHAM BEECHES

ALICE SPRINGS DESERT PARK, NT, developed in 1995–97 and managed by the Parks and Wildlife Commission of the Northern Territory, features AUSTRALIAN FLORA and fauna of three Central Australian ARID ZONE habitats. 'Desert Rivers' features *Eucalyptus camaldulensis* (River Red Gum) along riverine fringes of *Melaleuca glomerata* (Inland Teatree) and *Acacia kempeana* (Witchetty Bush); 'Sand Country' replicates salt lakes and claypans within rolling dunes of red sand, with *Triodia* sp. (Spinifex) as the icon species; while 'Woodland' contains *Hakea subera* (Corkwood), *A. aneura* (Mulga), and *A. estrophiolata* (Ironwood) set among a myriad of grass species. The developed area of fifty hectares sits within a 1500-hectare site, including a section of the West MacDonnell Range, which forms a striking backdrop. INTERPRETATION stresses that there are no exits, only entrances, encouraging visitors and locals alike to respect local environments.   RA

ALLAN, James (1867–1936), rosarian, joined the NATIONAL ROSE SOCIETY of Victoria in 1904 and served as president many times between 1909 and 1936. He was a keen and successful amateur grower, a talented and generous lecturer, and a much-loved figure in the ROSE world. He travelled the world during 1929 and 1930 gaining international experience. He served the National Rose Society with distinction and, with T.A. STEWART and Alister CLARK, formed the backbone of the Victorian group during its first decades.   RA

ALLEN, Charles Ernest Frank (1876–1936), gardens curator and economic botanist, from Rochester, England, completed his training at the ROYAL BOTANIC GARDENS, KEW, in 1904. He spent ten years in Africa, periodically contributing his experiences to the *Journal of the Kew Guild*; a fellow expatriate in St Lucia, Dominica, wrote wistfully of these racy accounts, 'Unlike my old friend C.E.F. Allen, I have no lions, cannibals, or gramophones to write about'. Allen migrated to Qld *c.* 1913 intending to farm on his own account, but soon accepted curatorship of DARWIN BOTANIC GARDENS (following the death of Nicholas HOLTZE) and the position of Inspector of Agriculture. The *Journal* applauded the appointment at a time when Kew-trained graduates were finding difficulty gaining government (or private) appointments in Australia. With the onset of war, Allen joined the Australian Expeditionary Forces, and during this interregnum the Gardens languished. On his return he set about rejuvenating the site as well as providing agricultural advice to Territory farmers.   RA

ALLEN, Joseph (1830–1892), nursery proprietor, native of Northamptonshire, England, migrated to Tas. in 1855 on the *Fortitude*, one of a small group aboard (including William CHANDLER and William SANGWELL) who made careers in horticulture. Indentured as an agricultural labourer under the bounty system to sponsor and Huon district pioneer William Walton, in 1860 he married Catherine Cox (1834–*c.* 1916) at Longford and gradually acquired land on the town outskirts. By the 1870s he had started a nursery to serve the horticulturally rich northern MIDLANDS. After his death his wife ran the business until her own death; it was then managed by family members until the 1940s.

LINDY SCRIPPS

ALLEN, Thomas (1787–1868), landscape gardener, horticulturist, and nursery proprietor, was the first person to advertise and establish a nursery in SA. Born in Edmonton, Middlesex, England, he worked as Garden Steward (1806–20) to the Duke of Clarence (later King William IV) at Bushy Park, and Chief Gardener (1820–31) to King George IV, serving as

'Landscape Gardener & Ground-workman' on the design and planting of London's St James' and Regent's Parks under architect John Nash (1752–1835). Allen married Sarah Weaver (1792–1835), daughter of noted landscape painter Charles Weaver, in 1812.

Migrating to NSW, Allen served as 'Botanist & Cultivator' to the Australian Agricultural Company during the 1830s. Working there as a gardener he also corresponded with J.C. LOUDON. Trading as Thomas Allen & Sons, he advertised in the first number of the *South Australian Gazette and Colonial Register* (1836) offering prospective migrants 'services to Gentlemen Capitalists to select, enclose, layout and plant their gardens in the best manner, both for utility and ornament, on the most reasonable terms, and with the utmost dispatch'. Allen, appointed 'Gardener & Ground-workman' to Governor Hindmarsh, established a nursery on leased land on the banks of the River Torrens (*c*. 1837), offering a 'great variety of Lettuce, Cabbage, and other plants. Also, all kinds of Vegetables on the most reasonable terms.' In 1838 he opened a stall in Adelaide's Gilles Arcade market to sell his vegetables and plants. Lack of success in Adelaide led him to migrate (*c*. 1840) with his family, via Hobart, to Dunedin, New Zealand, where he died. A son, Joseph Weaver Allen (1822–1887), who worked as a gardener in Adelaide, later became a prominent portrait and landscape photographer in New Zealand.   DAVID JONES

ALLITT, William (1828–1893), gardener and nursery proprietor, was born in Co. Kerry, Ireland, and came to London as a youth. From *c*. 1842 he worked in the nursery of E.G. Henderson at St John's Wood, London. Allitt supervised William Bull (1828–1902)—then at the start of a notable career in the British nursery trade—in the hard-wood department at Henderson's. Allitt and his wife Elizabeth arrived in Portland (Vic.) on New Year's Day 1853. After working locally he was engaged in 1858 to lay out PORTLAND BOTANIC GARDENS, and between 1861 and 1866 he was its inaugural curator. Allitt developed the site in the tradition of a systematically arranged BOTANIC GARDEN with squared layout. He botanised extensively, collecting many plants indigenous to the region: the *Portland Guardian* commented in 1859 that 'He aims to cultivate plants of their respective districts so that each [Victorian] Botanic Garden will soon be stocked with the plants of the whole colony'.

Allitt later worked as gardener for pastoralist John Norman McLeod (1816 1886) at Castlemaddie, Tyrendarra (Vic.), and family tradition suggests that he designed gardens for several WESTERN DISTRICT pastoral properties. He also established a small private nursery at Tyrendarra, specialising in begonias (some of his own breeding) and bulbous plants. He corresponded with Ferdinand MUELLER on botanical matters, and in 1883 confessed that the nursery 'at present … does not pay, but I trust that it will do so in time'; Allitt had taken the appointment as postmaster at Tyrendarra in 1879 to supplement his income. He published a long apologia in the *Portland Guardian* (1893) that confirmed his role as a pioneering curator in a regional setting. Allitt was accorded a short obituary in the *Gardeners' Chronicle*, which recorded that 'Styphelia Allitti' was named after this 'estimable man'.   RA

ALLPORT, Joseph (1800–1877), solicitor and horticulturist, with his wife Mary, made a major contribution to horticulture in Tas. Joseph was born in Aldridge, Staffordshire, England, and in 1831 came to Van Diemen's Land with his family, intending to settle on the land. Their foray into farming at Black Brush was unsuccessful and they moved to Hobart, Joseph returning to the law. They established a garden at Faire Knowe, in Upper Liverpool Street, but it was their property in Macquarie Street that later became a drawcard for visitors. Allport acquired Aldridge Lodge, a two-hectare property between Macquarie Street and the Sandy Bay Rivulet in 1841. There they had such a productive fruit and vegetable garden that one of their gardeners briefly ran a greengrocer's shop in town with misappropriated produce. They grew a wide range of fruit including nectarines, peaches, and pears, and nuts such as walnuts and filberts, often successfully exhibited at local horticultural shows. The extensive ornamental garden featured a circular shrubbery enclosed by a clipped box hedge and rarely cultivated plants, some of which Joseph introduced to the colony. The varieties were also built up by seed exchange and by acquisition of seedlings from the Government Gardens, Allport being entitled to receive plants as a member of the ROYAL SOCIETY. Joseph Allport was interested in the ACCLIMATISATION of animals as well as plants and was one of the first to import live fish to Australia. He also experimented with horticultural practices and was widely regarded in the colony as an authority.

Mary Morton Allport (*née* Chapman) (1806–1895), painter and botanical artist, began painting and sketching her surroundings on her arrival in Van Diemen's Land and soon developed a particular affinity for the native flora. In 1832 she advertised in the *Hobart Town Courier* her availability to paint miniatures on commission, including portraits and native flowers on ivory. She painted landscapes, flowers, and natural history subjects and became an accomplished lithographer. Morton Allport (1830–1878) was an important amateur photographer of the 1860s who inherited his parents' love of NATURAL HISTORY and acclimatisation. The Allport Library and Museum of Fine Arts in the State Library of Tasmania forms a memorial to the family.   LINDY SCRIPPS

ALMANACS, annual calendars and compilations of useful information, were originally associated with popular superstitions but swung away from astrology and towards empiricism during the nineteenth century. Australian almanacs typically included government, transport, and postal information, historic dates, and popular medical advice. Their calendric function usually extended to gardening and agriculture, and often included a lunar calendar—early Australian farmers performed much of their work at night. Advice ranged from unsourced hints to detailed instructions for grafting and pruning, essays on soil types, and notes on local and regional climatic conditions. Almanacs often formed an important and inexpensive form of GARDEN BOOK and the gardening calendar format has maintained its popularity, especially when coupled with some form of climatic zoning.

The first Australian almanac was George Howe's *New South Wales Pocket Almanack for 1806*; his almanac continued until the 1830s. In Hobart Town, Andrew Bent and James Ross pro-

Advice on 'Colonial Gardening' from Andrew Bent's *Van Diemen's Land Pocket Almanack* (1824), showing the early primacy of vegetable gardens and the need to remind colonists of seasons in the southern hemisphere

duced rival almanacs during the 1820s and 1830s. By the 1850s, all the major cities boasted several almanac publishers. Long-running titles included *Moore's Almanack* (Sydney, 1852–1939), *Victorian Almanac* (Melbourne, 1858–1927), *Pugh's Queensland Almanac* (Brisbane, 1859–1927), and *Walch's Tasmanian Almanac* (Hobart, 1862–1979), CLARSON, *Shallard & Co.'s* [later *A.H. Massina's*] *Almanac* (Melbourne, 1864–1940), and *Thorne's Queensland Almanac* (Brisbane, 1880–98). Those who contributed horticultural notes to these almanacs included James BACKHOUSE, HILL, PINK, SOUTTER, and WRIGHT.

Ian Morrison and Maureen Perkins, *Australian Almanacs 1806–1930: A Bibliography* (Melbourne, forthcoming, 2003)

IAN MORRISON

ALPINE PLANTS, strictly speaking, are plants that in their natural mountainous habitat are found above the tree line. In horticulture this definition is often broadened to include any small, low-growing alpine-like plant, even though it might come from sea level. Many of these are cultivated in ROCK GARDENS and thus are also referred to as 'rockery plants'. True alpine plants have not been cultivated widely in Australian gardens, although there are specialist growers, collectors, and nurseries, such as Otto Fauser (Dandenong Ranges, Vic.) and Ken GILLANDERS (Tas.), with a wide range of Australian and exotic alpine species.

The alpine flora of Australia is restricted to high country areas of the east coast in NSW, ACT, Vic., and Tas., where the mean summer temperature is below 10°C—insufficient for tree growth. While these areas are comparatively small compared with Australia's land mass, they are important for their hydrology and the high degree of endemism in the floras they contain. Conservation is paramount, especially in the face of an increasing interest in active RECREATION throughout these zones: low temperatures mean vegetation growth is slow, and thus repair of damaged plant communities is difficult. ML

ALSOP, Rodney Howard (1881–1932), Melbourne-born architect and landscape designer, rose to prominence in the first decade of the twentieth century as the designing partner of Klingender and Alsop, with a series of major houses to his credit. His buildings throughout this early period show a clear relationship to the work of English architects such as C.F.A. Voysey and W.R. Lethaby, and a commitment to the principles of the ARTS AND CRAFTS movement, a cornerstone of his work. Alsop's skill in landscape design was shared by Dorothy Hope Lockyer (c. 1894–1968), his wife from 1912, and they collaborated on many garden design projects associated with his architectural practice.

In 1905 Alsop won a Royal Victorian Institute of Architects competition for the design of a suburban domestic garden, and his published scheme incorporated a combination of formal and informal landscape themes, along with elements typical to future work such as terraces adjacent to the house, lawn beds, dividing hedges and low walls, arches over pathways, trellises for climbing plants, a sundial, and a small pond with bridge. In 1910–11 Alsop entered and won a competition for the design for FOOTSCRAY PARK, and although adapted and implemented by others, it featured his characteristic mix of formal and informal landscape themes.

Alsop was concerned from the outset with the landscape design for each of his houses, even in those few cases where a landscape gardener was subsequently involved. Like his contemporaries Walter BUTLER and Walter Burley GRIFFIN, he firmly believed that the design of a building and its setting should be carefully integrated. Domestic gardens associated with Alsop include Edrington, Berwick (1908); Glyn, Malvern (1908); MAWALLOK, Beaufort (1909); WOMBAT PARK, Daylesford (1908–10); Crumpford, Toorak (1916); and the sunken garden at Aberfeldie, Toorak (1925), which reputedly served as a model for the design of the Pioneer Women's Memorial Garden in Melbourne's DOMAIN (1934–35).

Klingender and Alsop dissolved their partnership in 1920 and after a term abroad Alsop returned, specialising in domestic design with clear MEDITERRANEAN influences—as exemplified by his own house, Winster, Toorak (1925). From this time an increased emphasis on formal ITALIANATE garden character can be seen, evident in his winning design (with Conrad Sayce) in the international competition for Winthrop Hall, University of Western Australia (1926).

BRYCE RAWORTH

ALSTON, Harold (1879–1956), horticulturist and journalist, was born in Melbourne, the son of a merchant. He trained as a mine manager at the Ballarat School of Mines but left the mining industry to run his own orchard (1912–19). He then developed a large garden at Diamond Creek (Vic.), where he specialised in roses and daffodils. He became horticultural editor of the *Leader* in 1922 and gardening columnist for its parent, the *Age*, positions he held until 1947; he was also editor of the *Leader* (1941–46). Following retirement Alston revised the 30th to 33rd editions of BRUNNING's *The Australian Gardener* (1949–53), illustrating these with his own photographs. A genial yet retiring man, his public lectures were well attended; they were often illustrated with his own lantern slides. He was well known for his judging at Victorian horticultural shows and was a stalwart member of the Royal Horticultural Society of Victoria and the NATIONAL ROSE SOCIETY. In the year of his death at Braemar, Diamond Creek, aged 77, Alston was still conducting the gardening column of the *Riverlander*.

His son, **Peter Thomas Alston** (1912–2002), followed in his father's footsteps as a horticultural journalist. He joined the *Age* in 1936 and, apart from a stint in the army (1941–46), remained with the paper as a journalist and later senior executive until his retirement in 1977. A long-serving garden editor on the paper, he continued contributing the 'Reader's Questions' column in retirement until the late 1980s.

RA

ALTHOFER, George William (1903–1993) and his brother **Peter Althofer** (1918–1991), seed merchants, nursery proprietors, and promoters of Australian native plants, fuelled the popularity of the Australian BUSH GARDEN movement through their extensive nursery and mail order business. George established his native seed and plant nursery at a time when most gardeners disdained the AUSTRALIAN FLORA and failed to appreciate its horticultural qualities. Although the nursery trade had often carried Australian plants, the exclusive promotion of native plants was then most unusual.

A self-trained botanist, George Althofer began plant collecting in the 1920s and established a small ARBORETUM at Dripstone, on the Central Western Slopes of NSW, which in 1935 became the Nindethana Nursery; on his plant collecting expeditions he was soon accompanied by his brother Peter. The Althofers grew plants from seed collected all over Australia and exchanged specimens from their own area with interested botanists. George Althofer corresponded with the 'orchid man', H.M.R. RUPP, and Victorian botanist W.H. NICHOLLS, among many other colleagues. By 1953 the Nindethana seed catalogue listed some 2000 species, and Althofer exchanged seeds with BOTANIC GARDENS and supplied PUBLIC PARKS AND GARDENS within Australia and overseas. Many authors acknowledged George Althofer's contribution, especially his expertise in growing, and his knowledge of, the genus *Prostanthera* (mintbushes).

George Althofer's ambition for an arboretum or NATIONAL PARK, where the grouping of plants and the way they were to be planted 'intermingling and growing under conditions that would favour natural regeneration', was described in *Wild Life* (1953). Althofer hoped that imported native plants from different parts of Australia would be intermixed with plants indigenous to the area. It was not until 1964, however, that the Soil Conservation Service set aside resumed land on the foreshores of the newly constructed Burrendong Dam near Wellington (NSW) for an ARBORETUM, where Peter Althofer later became superintendent (until 1981). Volunteers planted Burrendong Arboretum with seedlings raised at Nindethana and in the Glen Ora nursery of Peter Althofer and his wife Hazel.

Nindethana nursery was essentially destroyed by a storm in 1964 and closed in 1968. George Althofer's published works included a book about mintbushes, *Cradle of Incense* (1978), and *The Story of Nindethana* (1956). He was honoured by awards from the SOCIETY FOR GROWING AUSTRALIAN PLANTS and the International Dendrology Society. In 1987 Peter and his wife Hazel were jointly awarded the Australian Plant Award by SGAP. For their discovery, the orchid *Diuris althoferi* was named for the brothers.

COLLEEN MORRIS

ALTON, Mount Macedon, Vic., was developed by Sir George Frederic Verdon (1834–1896) following land selection at MOUNT MACEDON by a group of Melbourne gentlemen–scientists who aspired to create HILL-STATIONS as their SUMMER RETREATS. Within a short period (in 1873–74) the land along Alton Road was selected and development begun. Government regulations not only contained residential and fencing clauses, but also stipulated timber tree planting. Verdon engaged TAYLOR AND SANGSTER for supply of plants and possibly landscape design: Sangster wrote a glowing description of the garden in 1885 under the nom de plume 'Hortensis'. Although Verdon was a politician and banker, his sympathies lay with the sciences and arts. His city residence was in the E.S. & A. 'Gothic Bank' in Melbourne's Collins Street, and for Alton he had the eminent English Gothic-revival architect, John Pollard Seddon (1827–1906), design a splendid residence, the basis of the present house.

The 1920s tennis court at ALTON (Vic.) provides a dramatic feature in this late-nineteenth-century HILL-STATION garden, nestled into a steeply sloping site on the side of MOUNT MACEDON

The steep site was terraced with zig-zag paths, and Verdon turned his garden into a dramatically landscaped ARBORETUM of exceptional richness.

Following Verdon's death, several subsequent owners guarded the property until its acquisition in 1927 by pharmacist and philanthropist George Richard Rich Nicholas (1884–1960), whose brother developed BURNHAM BEECHES in the Dandenong Ranges. Nicholas installed a boldly sited tennis court, incorporated much new stonework, redeveloped the kitchen garden, and augmented the planting, particularly with NEW ZEALAND species. Alton survived the 1983 Ash Wednesday fires and was sold by the Nicholas family in 1990. Current owners, the Eshuys family, are engaged in vital regeneration of this outstanding landscaped hill-station and nationally significant tree collection. RA

AMATEUR GARDENER: see LOCKLEY, John Gilmore

AMERICA: see NORTH AMERICA and SOUTH AMERICA

AMERICAN GARDEN, a feature introduced into British gardens from the eighteenth century and popularised by the widespread importation of plants from NORTH AMERICA. By the mid-nineteenth century the term was loosely used, as MCINTOSH recorded (1855), admitting plants 'from most extra-tropical quarters of the globe' especially RHODODENDRONS, azaleas, kalmias, magnolias, and CONIFERS. Requiring damp and peaty soil, these plants were well adapted to many cool elevated parts of Australia, and formed popular subjects in HILL-STATION gardens—albeit rarely invoking the specific American epithet. In the hotter metropolitan capitals, however, unless sufficient shade and moisture could be provided, the American Garden was largely a failure: the north-facing example at Victoria's GOVERNMENT HOUSE (1873) was discontinued after only a year. RA

AMPHITHEATRES, dished oval or circular structures with seats rising in tiers around a central stage, were venues for THEATRE in ancient Greece. They were adopted by many later civilisations, especially those aspiring to reflect a glorious classical past. Thus they were used in landscaping of UNIVERSITIES such as the University of Western Australia and La Trobe University, Bundoora (Vic.), and other educational INSTITUTIONS such as Scienceworks Museum, Spotswood (Vic.). Though mostly found in public situations, their use in private or semi-private landscapes by the GRIFFINS at CASTLECRAG and by WALLING at BICKLEIGH VALE demonstrated an affinity between the arts of landscape gardening, MUSIC, and drama—a vital association in the development of gardens in Renaissance Italy and seventeenth-century France. The pleasing form of natural amphitheatres was also favoured for siting houses and gardens; LOUDON praised this attribute in the setting of ELIZABETH BAY HOUSE. RA

AMUSEMENT PARKS: see PLEASURE GARDENS

ANDERSON (*née* MASON), Ethel Campbell Louise (1883–1958), English-born and Sydney-educated painter, poet, and essayist, married Austin Anderson, a career soldier in the British Army. The couple spent ten years in India, and the war years in England, before returning to Australia in 1924, settling at Ball Green, Turramurra (NSW). Anderson's husband became private secretary to three successive NSW governors. Ethel Anderson was a friend and patron of a group of painters that included Grace Cossington Smith, Roland Wakelin, Roi de Mestre, and Jessie Traill. She contributed prose pieces to various magazines, and her seven publications included a book of essays, *Timeless Garden* (1945), which gathered together experiences of significance to her, especially those linked with gardens. Her descriptions of the GOVERNMENT HOUSE garden and ADMIRALTY HOUSE, with Sydney Harbour as their luminous backdrop; of HILLVIEW at Sutton Forest ('a garden of butterflies'); of YARRALUMLA in Canberra; and several others, are evocative garden pictures. Her daughter, Bethia Foott, wrote *Ethel and the Governors-General* (1992), a book of fond memories.

HELEN PROUDFOOT

ANDERSON, George (*c.* 1841–1905), seed merchant, was born in Edinburgh and migrated to New Zealand *c.* 1865. He spent three years in Vic. before moving to NSW *c.* 1869. In 1873, following the death of William Law, Anderson took over the Sydney branch (established 1863) of LAW, SOMNER AND CO. He took Frederick B. Hall into partnership and the new firm Anderson, Hall and Co. sought to consolidate gains in NSW against established businesses such as those of BAPTIST, FERGUSON, GUILFOYLE, and SHEPHERD. These firms principally dealt in nursery plants, and Anderson's specialty in seeds catered for a rising suburban population of home gardeners. The firm was renamed Anderson and Co. in 1876, and in later catalogues claimed to be 'pioneers of the Packet Seeds business in Australia'. In *Forest Culture and Eucalyptus Trees* (San Francisco, 1876), Ellwood Cooper copied information on species of eucalypts from the Anderson, Hall and Co. catalogue, indicating a contemporary interest in Australian seeds.

George Anderson took sole control of the business in 1877 and immediately published a new edition of Law Somner's *Handbook to the Garden for New South Wales*. Anderson and Co. continued its specialty in seeds and also published further handbooks for the home gardener; its 1895 catalogue lists *The Kitchen Garden and Cottager's Manual*, *The Flower Garden*, and *The Fruit Garden* (in two volumes). Anderson died at his residence, Belmore, Coogee, in 1905. A brief obituary in the *Sydney Morning Herald* noted his prominence in social rather than public circles, and drew attention to his status as an 'old colonist'.

Anderson and Co. continued after the death of its founder; an early achievement of its new management was the publication, in 1907, of three new handbooks, *Anderson's Manual of the Flower Garden and Shrubbery*, *Anderson's Manual of the Vegetable Garden and Orchard*, and *Anderson's Manual of the Farm*, written by Fred TURNER. The firm also reprinted the *War Chest Flower Book* (1917) as *A Book of Garden Gems* in 1923—the same year as it issued a series of booklets on cultivation of popular flowers such as the dahlia and the carnation. Anderson and Co. Ltd (as the company became in 1912) diversified into trees and shrubs, establishing a nursery at Summer Hill; it also offered design and construction services from a landscape department. By the 1960s this department was under the supervision of Harold BLOOM. Impressive catalogues celebrated the 75th and 100th years of operation, but by the mid-1960s the business had folded and one of the longest-established Australian seed merchants closed its doors.   RA

The Sydney premises of ANDERSON, Hall & Co. in Pitt Street, shown in an engraving made for the firm's 1875 catalogue; seed merchants generally maintained a city retail outlet and offices, separate from wholesale stores and nursery grounds

ANDERSON, James (1797–1842) botanic gardens superintendent, was born at Boguham, near Stirling, Scotland. A botanist in West Africa and South America (1821–24), he then served as botanical collector on HMS *Adventure* during Captain Phillip Parker King's hydrographic surveys of the South American coasts (1826–30). Anderson arrived in Sydney in 1832 on the *Brothers*, in which King returned with his family. In 1835, after three years 'wholly engaged in Botanical pursuits', he was appointed Assistant Superintendent of SYDNEY BOTANIC GARDENS. This led to the supervision of a convict gang in trenching and planting HYDE PARK. Having trained his workers, Anderson sought to retain them: they were accordingly 'regularly assigned', and he was to 'pay … every attention instructing them in gardening'.

When Allan CUNNINGHAM resigned as Colonial Botanist and Superintendent in 1837, Anderson applied for the position of Superintendent, in view of his 'long service … Botanical experience … [and] capacity to conduct the Botanical Department'. Impressed by his 'attention and zeal … when … in charge of the Garden during the absence of the Superintendent', the management committee unanimously endorsed the application. Appointed Superintendent (not Colonial Botanist) in 1838, Anderson worked diligently until his death. He was applauded for 'the very many and great improvements' he had effected, the tireless 'pursuit of his favourite science', and his success 'in advancing the interests of horticulturists and floriculturists in this colony'. The genial bachelor's admirers erected a monument in the Devonshire Street Cemetery recording his travels and collection of 'rare botanic specimens'. Relocated to La Perouse in 1901, it was destroyed in 1975. It is comforting to think that Anderson's workers may have brightened their own and others' lives by applying the skills he taught them at a time when such teachers were few.   LIONEL GILBERT

ANDERSON (née SELFE), Maybanke Susannah, (1845–1927), first-wave feminist and educational reformer, born Surrey, England, migrated to Sydney in 1855 with her family. Although known primarily for her key role in the Australian women's suffrage movement, Anderson also maintained a high profile in women's and children's philanthropy in NSW. She was a founding member of the National Council of Women, the Free Kindergarten Union, and the Playground Association. PLAYGROUNDS were seen as a natural extension of kindergarten and educational philosophy—one that encouraged the supervised care of young children otherwise left to their own devices. She agitated for playgrounds to be associated with working communities such as factory or trade-sponsored play areas. Additionally, Anderson lobbied for playgrounds to be incorporated into existing PUBLIC PARKS. The first play area in NSW supervised by the Playground Association was opened at Miller's Point in 1914, followed by playgrounds within Wentworth Park, Glebe (1915), and Moore Park (1917). A volume of her collected work was published in 2001.

Jan Roberts, *Maybanke Anderson: Sex, Suffrage, and Social Reform* (Sydney, 1993) JODI FRAWLEY

ANDERSON, Robert Henry (1899–1969), botanic gardens director, was born at Cooma (NSW). Leaving Sydney's Fort Street High School, he studied agricultural science before joining the AIF, only to be returned from Cape Town when the Armistice was announced. Completing his degree, Anderson joined the SYDNEY BOTANIC GARDENS as a probationary botanical assistant in 1921. He remained there for more than forty-three years, becoming the Gardens' first Australian-born director. Gaining varied experience in the field, the HERBARIUM, and the botanical museum in the last years of J.H. MAIDEN's administration, Anderson also enjoyed systematic work, for example on the family Chenopodiaceae. He wrote papers on weed control and promoted 'a comparatively new subject' when he lectured on 'tree lots for the farm', advocating tree planting to counter erosion, and to provide shelter for stock, useful timber, and habitat for native birds. These views were developed in a bulletin, *Tree Planting on the Farm*, and in *Trees on the Farm* (1932). His wider interest in the forest flora was revealed in *The Trees of New South Wales* (1936), in his FORESTRY lectures at Sydney University from 1925, and in his presidency of the AUSTRALIAN FOREST LEAGUE (NSW) from 1935 to 1937.

Anderson became Botanist and Curator of the Herbarium in 1936 and in 1939 he inaugurated *Contributions from the New South Wales National Herbarium*. At the outbreak of the Pacific War in 1941 he took immediate action to transfer irreplaceable herbarium and library material to the country, far from possible air attack. Wartime fears were eclipsed in the 1950s and 1960s by attacks from local and state authorities resulting in vast upheaval and destruction for a car park and an expressway. The customarily good-humoured Anderson, given to composing light-hearted topical verse and cutting red tape, now had cause for anger, despair, and disillusionment, warning Sydney citizens to be on their guard, for 'there is no saying how far the invader will go'. In the early 1960s Anderson found welcome compensation in negotiating with his friends Alfred and Effie Brunet for the ultimate acquisition by the Gardens of land at MOUNT TOMAH, west of Sydney, where cold-climate plants now flourish around the natural stands of *Eucalyptus fastigata* (Brown Barrel).

LIONEL GILBERT

ANDERSON, William (1828–1909), Scottish-born builder, farmer, and politician, arrived at Belfast (Port Fairy) in 1844 with his parents. After success at the diggings, he purchased land with his father in 1854 at Southern Cross, near Koroit (Vic.), and built a homestead and outbuildings. Anderson became a leading figure in local church and community life, and was elected to the Legislative Council in 1880. A great enthusiast for horticulture and natural history, he helped found the Koroit Acclimatisation Society (*c.* 1862) and developed his property, Rosemount, into a prize-winning farm and famed garden. He was also a long-standing member of the Horticultural Society of Victoria (president 1880–81), and was elected a member of the Royal Geographical Society of Australasia in 1886. Anderson's association with William GUILFOYLE led to a new plan, compiled with the assistance of Robert WHITWORTH, for the KOROIT BOTANIC GARDENS (1880). Anderson's descendants claim Guilfoyle also designed the Rosemount garden, which was acclaimed in the Melbourne *Leader* (1885), although without acknowledgment to Guilfoyle.

Beverley Miller, *From Montrose to Rosemount: The Anderson Family History* (Koroit, Vic., 1996) HELEN DOYLE

ANDREWS, Edward William: see FARM AND GARDEN

ANGAS, George French (1822–1886), painter, lithographer, engraver, and naturalist, was born at Newcastle-upon-Tyne, England. He acquired an interest in natural history and art before travelling to and recording scenes in SA, NSW, South Africa, and New Zealand. His important lithographic and watercolour works were published in *South Australia Illustrated* (1847), *The New Zealanders Illustrated* (1847), and *Savage Life and Scenes in Australia and New Zealand* (1847). Essentially a naturalist with a gift for drawing, in his publications he recorded insects, butterflies, and flowers; Aboriginal and Maori people and their weapons and structures; and the scientific information contained in scenery. Between 1853 and 1860 he was employed at the Australian Museum in Sydney to classify the first public collection of Australian specimens, especially shells.

Angas was the eldest son of merchant, banker, landowner, and philanthropist George Fife Angas (1789–1879), who was chair of the South Australian Co. and promoted the colony for its civil and religious freedoms. He was instrumental in attracting German Lutheran Pastor Kavel and his followers to the colony, providing credit to enable colonisation activities. His estate **Lindsay Park**, near Angaston (SA), was established in 1838 by his manager, Charles Flaxman. The homestead was erected *c.*1850 and Samuel SMITH was engaged as the first head gardener. Great-grandson (Sir) John Keith Angas (1900–1977) inherited Lindsay Park in 1928, and with his wife, Gwynnyth Fay (*née* Good), reorganised the English-style grounds to reflect an American Romantic style, with MEDITERRANEAN traits similar to those advocated by Walter BAGOT. They added a deer park, tennis court, and northern ITALIAN garden features, including statues, pergolas, terraced gardens, and several water features, while retaining old trees, including *Cupressus sempervirens* 'Italica' (Italian Cypress), and a tree-lined driveway. In 1965 racehorse trainer Colin Hayes (1924–1999) acquired the property through a syndicate and established his Lindsay Park Stud.

Sally O'Neill, *George Fife Angas* (Melbourne, 1972); John Tregenza, *George French Angas, Artist, Traveller, and Naturalist, 1822–1886* (Adelaide, 1980) DAVID JONES

ANGOVE, William Thomas (1854–1912), Cornish-born and London-trained doctor and vigneron, migrated to Adelaide in 1883. A keen ornithologist and gardener, he established his practice at Tea Tree Gully (SA), and began planting Shiraz, Riesling, and Black Portugal vines to establish the St Agnes Vineyard specialising in dry red wines of the Burgundy style, which he cultivated for the benefit of his patients and neighbours. In 1910 his eldest son, Thomas Carlyon Angove (1881–1952)—who married the granddaughter of Dr Alexander KELLY—established a brandy and fortified spirits operation at Renmark in the RIVERLAND, one of the first ventures in the region. DAVID JONES

ANLABY, Kapunda, SA, was established by pastoralist Frederick Hugh Dutton (d. *c.* 1849) in 1839. His banker son, Frederick Hansborough Dutton (1812–1890), developed the HOMESTEAD with an extensive terraced garden set in a park of eucalypts and deciduous trees. The grounds featured ornate iron entry gates, a long, tree-lined driveway, house terraces with wide sweeping lawns roamed by peacocks, an ornate balustrade (designed by Walter BAGOT), a mosaic-tiled pathway with a central axis aligned to a circular lily pond and cast iron fountain, picturesque shrubberies, orchid and fern houses, a fern-filled grotto, large rosaries including arches and trellises, a Greek-styled folly water tower, an oval and golf course, orchards, and a deer park. In 1962 the property was inherited by author Geoffrey Dutton (1922–1998) but sold in 1972.
DAVID JONES

ANNEAR, Harold Desbrowe: see DESBROWE-ANNEAR, Harold

ANNUALS are plants that complete their life cycle (seed shoot—flower—seed—death) in one year or growing season. In this way growth through an unfavourable season, such as winter, is avoided. In ARID and semi-arid areas in Australia, ephemeral plants remain as SEED in the ground until moisture initiates germination and then rapid growth to flowering and seed again. Some of these species have been used in Australian native gardens to create annual colour; many of the everlasting daisies are also dried for use in permanent FLORAL ARRANGEMENTS.

Annuals have traditionally been used in Australian gardens to create floral BEDDING schemes, usually planted in highly regimented rows in neat, raised beds to provide temporary COLOUR in PUBLIC PARKS AND GARDENS. Not all plants in these beds are strictly annuals; some may be PERENNIALS (especially herbaceous perennials) grown for a single season's display. Until recently, annuals for these displays were raised in the greenhouses of parks departments; they are now mass-produced by specialist growers, reducing the uniqueness of individual schemes. The cost of maintaining large annual bedding displays is now seen as prohibitive and their use in PUBLIC OPEN SPACE is in decline. Annuals are also raised and maintained in POTS for temporary displays, and are also popular for PATIOS and BALCONY gardens. They are often also grown in hanging BASKETS for the same purpose. Annuals have also been traditionally used in mixed SHRUBBERIES as low border plants and as temporary infills to provide change and annual colour. ML

ANTCLIFF, Allan (1923–1985), VITICULTURAL researcher and vine breeder, completed his studies at the University of Queensland and joined the CSIRO at Merbein (Vic.) in 1947; there he worked on problems of vine physiology and yield. Antcliff initiated the CSIRO program to breed grape vines better adapted to the Australian environment. Necessarily long-term and involving many thousands of crosses, by 1983 more than 40 000 seedlings had been germinated and planted. Improved cloned variants of Sultana resulted. New drying varieties of value included Carina (1975), a small black seedless grape, and Merbein Seedless (1981), a white grape suitable for raisins. Of the wine grapes the red Tarrango (1975) and white Taminga (1985) have attracted the most commercial interest.
DAVID DUNSTAN

ANZAC PARK, Townsville, Qld, reserved in the late nineteenth century as Strand Park, contains several memorials, including a drinking fountain (1908), bandstand (1913), and clock tower (1924). Shady figs and tropical shrubberies edge the city boundary; on the seaward side, tall *Hibiscus tiliaceus* (Cotton Tree), coconut palms, and *Terminalia catappa* (Indian Almond) mask recent waterfront developments. Nearby is the bougainvillea-laden Cliff Gardens waterfall. Extending three kilometres north-west from Anzac Park is The Strand—beachfront parkland that terminates with a rock pool and lookout at Kissing Point. The panorama across Cleveland Bay embraces Magnetic Island, and Castle Hill provides a dramatic inland backdrop. JEANNIE SIM

ANZAC SQUARE, Brisbane, designed by Commonwealth Government Architect John Smith MURDOCH (1916–28), was dedicated as part of the State WAR MEMORIAL on Armistice Day 1930. Classical-revival government office buildings of the inter-war period flank the Square. The classical sandstone Shrine of Remembrance (architects Buchanan and Cowper, Sydney) is located on the upper Ann Street side of the Square with the Queensland Women's Memorial Frieze (sculptor Daphne Mayo, 1932) on the lower level nearby. Around its base and encircling staircases are symmetrical beds of clipped bougainvillea hedges and curved basins of water. The three radiating paths (symbolising the three services) are lined in avenues with an unusual combination of alternating *Butia capitata* (Chilean Wine Palm) and *Brachychiton rupestris* (Queensland Bottle Tree). Lawn covers most of the Square, with small oblong flower beds mirrored on each side of the central path. Along each side of the Square are single rows of *Callitris columellaris*, which provide an evergreen coniferous symbol traditionally associated with MEMORIAL GARDENS. The South African War Memorial, an equestrian statue (1919), was relocated to Anzac Square in 1939. An ill-conceived proposal in the 1970s by Lord Mayor Clem Jones to raise the Square, permitting an underground

This Shrine of Remembrance (1930), part of Queensland's state WAR MEMORIAL in ANZAC SQUARE, Brisbane, seen here in a perspective by George Rae prepared for the Sydney-based winners of the war memorial design competition

car park, was abandoned after community outrage. Anzac Square remains a much-frequented public space and forms a focus for memorial ceremonies.

W.J. Kursey, *History of Anzac Square 1930–1984* (Brisbane, 1985)

JEANNIE SIM

APARTMENTS AND RESIDENTIAL FLATS The trend for external garden space for terraces and other early colonial houses, whether represented by window, VERANDAH, or balcony gardens, remains an essential component of urban lifestyles. Garden spaces take many different forms, from small COURTYARDS, terraces, and PATIOS, to balconies, ROOF GARDENS, gardens-in-pots, and window boxes.

In early urban flats such as Cliveden Mansions, East Melbourne (converted 1911), open space was provided in the form of light wells and service courts. Suburban flats provided opportunities for landscaped gardens: for example, Mayfair, South Yarra, Vic. (1919), included tennis courts, and Ardoch, St Kilda, Vic. (1922), was designed around a 'village green'. Landscaped gardens functioning as entry courts were often formal in design as, for example, at Florida Mansions in Melbourne's St Kilda Road (1915), and The Manar, Potts Point, NSW (1919).

Studley, Toorak, Vic. (1910), designed by Walter BUTLER as his own residence, was converted into flats in 1918. The south-western portion of the original garden survives as the private garden court to these flats. Rather than a formal entry court or a dreary internal light well, the design provided an amenity for tenants and a nostalgic reminder of England, where 'the garden … becomes the outdoor house as the building is the indoor house'. Through a profusion of informal planting, Butler manipulated form and scale to provide romantic illusions—'prized the more for the finding'—that included seats, pond, lion-mask fountain, and paved court with pergola. Importantly, Butler's secluded (rear) garden court provided a pleasing aspect for the rooms and balconies that did not face the street. Although Butler considered it 'most important that no trees of the larger kind be planted in the garden', Studley's garden court provided tenants with a 'common object of strengthening the elevating and ennobling love of idealised nature in a garden', thereby contributing to the incorporation of landscape into the design of flats.

The residential lifestyle in later flats, such as Wyldefel Gardens, Darlinghurst, NSW (1934); Cairo, Fitzroy, Vic. (1936); and Clendon, Toorak (1940) were significantly enhanced by the integration of landscaped garden courts in their design. The anonymity of individual flats with the external form of flat buildings, especially in high-rise blocks, is often relieved by the provision of balconies accommodating gardens-in-pots—for example Stanhill, South Melbourne (1942); The Co-operative Flats, Potts Point (1948–50); and the Domain Park Flats, South Yarra (1959–62). The individual balconies of Harry Seidler's Darlinghouse high-rise apartments (1999) and recreational terraces continue the tradition of external open space as part of the urban aesthetic. Flats resulting from urban consolidation, urban infill, factory conversions, and increased suburban residential density continue to maintain the concept of garden spaces as a necessary component of urban living. Ancher Mortlock Murray and Woolley's Penthouses, Rushcutters Bay, NSW (1967), blur the distinction between flats and townhouses, but their generous landscaped terraces firmly reinforce the value of external living space for urban living.

DONALD DUNBAR

APICULTURE Honey bees from Europe were introduced to NSW in the early nineteenth century, being more able than most indigenous bee species to exploit the honey-producing capacity of EUCALYPTS. Many leading horticulturists contributed to the growing interest in bee-keeping from the mid-century, including SAYCE, DICKINSON, and MACKAY. New Zealand apiarist Isaac Hopkins (1837–1925), author of *Australian Bee Manual* (1886), introduced the portable Langstroth frame-hive in 1877–78, which especially suited Australian conditions: pollen ripening at different times for different trees. The black bee and the more productive Italian bee were introduced in large numbers in the 1880s, the black bee becoming so prolific it was known as the bush bee. Bee-keeping associations were founded in SA, Vic., Qld, and NSW in the 1880s; the *New Zealand and Australian Bee Journal* began publication in the same period.

Production is greatest in NSW, SA, and Vic. Eucalypt forests produce most Australian honey, although bee farmers also rely on prickly pear, lucerne, and clovers. Domestic flower gardens also attract migratory bees during summer. In

Vic., bee-keepers have taken special leases over the tree-tops in a specified radius of crown forest land; other states have more conventional leasing arrangements. The migratory nature of Australian apiculture has not bestowed a rich heritage of bee-farm buildings, but among these is an unusual octagonal bee house at New Norcia (WA).

    Eva Crane, *The Archaeology of Beekeeping* (London, 1983); Peter Barrett, *An Australian Beekeeping Bibliography* (Springwood, NSW, 1996); Eva Crane, *The World History of Beekeeping and Honey Hunting* (New York, 1999)   HELEN DOYLE

ARALUEN, Roleystone, WA, was established in the 1930s as a recreational RESORT dedicated to the service of youth. It was the inspiration of John Joseph ('Boss') Simons (1882–1948), founder and honorary director of the Young Australia League (YAL), a national youth organisation, with headquarters in WA, formed in 1909 to promote the interests of youth and foster pride in Australian identity. Situated on a wooded, fifty-nine hectare valley site in the foothills of the Darling Range, with permanent creek, cascades, granite outcrops, and scenic bushland character, it was an expression of the League's patriotic credo. Araluen became well known not only for its picturesque setting, but also for spring and autumn displays of tulips, flowering shrubs, and deciduous trees, and was a popular destination for camping excursions, outings, and holidays for members and the general public.

Development throughout the 1930s and 1940s was made possible by the philanthropy of individuals and businesses, both in WA and interstate. Rustic bungalows and chalets, named in recognition of prominent donors, were constructed in local stone and timber. YAL members volunteered their time to help with the construction of bridges, walking trails, a swimming pool, pergolas, and extensive terraced gardens planted with Australian and introduced species representing the countries of origin of international visitors or collected on educational tours conducted by the League. The terraced Grove of the Unforgotten, built on the valley hillside, is a distinctive WAR MEMORIAL honouring League members who died in the First World War. Purchased by the WA Government in 1990, the property is now known as Araluen Botanic Park.   OLINE RICHARDS

ARAUCARIA Araucarias make a significant contribution to Australia's CULTURAL LANDSCAPE. They are strong landscape plants with a formal, symmetrical architecture based on distinctive habits, whorled branches with simple branching patterns, and densely and evenly distributed leaves.

    The genus *Araucaria*, which comes mainly from the tropical and warm-temperate forests of OCEANIA, is of GONDWANAN affinity and contains nineteen species—of which a staggering thirteen are endemic to New Caledonia, and two to Australia. Two species occur in South America; the genus name commemorates the *Araucanos*, a Chilean Indian tribe in the region where the *Araucaria araucana* (Monkey Puzzle)—so popular in Victorian England after its introduction in 1795—was obtained. The remarkable *A. bidwillii* (Bunya Pine) from Qld and named for J.C. BIDWILL, is a warm-climate Monkey Puzzle look-alike. It is tantalising to contemplate that the prickly foliage of both these trees probably evolved as a deterrent to browsing dinosaurs when these trees were at a peak in the Jurassic Period some 150–210 million years ago and prior to the breakup of Gondwana. The massive, pineapple-like Bunya cones may weigh more than five kilograms; the seeds, which have the flavour of roasted parsnip, were eaten roasted or boiled by Aboriginals at feasts held every three years.

Although exotic CONIFERS were certainly popular Victorian plants, the native *A. cunninghamii* (Hoop Pine) and Bunya Pine were frequently planted in the mid- to late-nineteenth century, together with the related *Agathis robusta* (Kauri Pine). *Araucaria heterophylla* (Norfolk Island Pine) was another favourite; it is now a signature plant of coastal townships around Australia (and elsewhere in the British and French empires). It has an exceptional ability to maintain its formal shape and straight trunk against strong winds, and has a high tolerance to salt-laden air. To this list can be added *A. columnaris* syn. *A. cookii* (Cook's Pine), an exceptionally slender, columnar tree discovered on the Isle of Pines near New Caledonia by Captain Cook on his second voyage in the Pacific. When mature, it has a dramatic and unaccountable lean to the north.

These araucarias all have a wide climatic tolerance and have been planted since the early days of European settlement in Australia. They now grace many old parks and gardens, standing as prominent silhouettes. Sadly, their use has diminished in recent times through changing fashion and also, particularly in Sydney, due to increased airborne pollutants that strip the wax from leaves, reducing their ability to tolerate salty winds. However, their remarkable forms and landscape potential give us reason for national pride. As recently as 1994 a third living genus of the family Araucariaceae was discovered in a deep, wet, sheltered gorge of the Wollemi National Park some 200 kilometres north of Sydney; it has been named *Wollemia nobilis* (Wollemi Pine). The commercial release of this plant will add another fine subject to horticulture.

    James Woodford, *The Wollemi Pine* (Melbourne, 2000)   ROGER SPENCER

ARBOR DAY, a NORTH AMERICAN concept (begun in Nebraska in 1872 and well known in the USA and Canada by the 1880s), was inaugurated under the auspices of the Australian Natives Association in SA (1889) and NSW (1890). Celebrated in Australia on various dates (usually in autumn), the day was intended to arouse children's interest in planting and preserving trees: it was an effort to turn the tide after a century of forest ringbarking. Increasingly, Arbor Days were directed towards involving schoolchildren, not just visiting dignitaries, as planters. Results varied: one school inspector in Tas. observed (1903) 'Very few teachers failed to do something and of some nothing was expected'. The day persisted in popularity however, and is now commonly celebrated as Arbor Week. The progressive utilitarianism behind Arbor Day was also found in the SCHOOL GARDEN movement, through the work of the AUSTRALIAN FOREST LEAGUE and its allies, and in the role of NATURE STUDY generally.   LIBBY ROBIN

Archaeology

THE PLANTERS

ARBOR DAY was strongly promoted by the various state education departments, especially through their *School Paper* magazines, which generally devoted an annual issue to the importance of tree planting specifically, and NATURE STUDY and conservation generally

ARBORETUM, in Latin signifying 'a place for trees', is mostly used in its dictionary sense as a 'botanical tree garden'. Under this definition, arboreta have been given a specific purpose—usually scientific—complementing ornamental, educational, and amenity aims. Arboreta may form a component of a larger landscape (such as a BOTANIC GARDEN) or stand alone as dedicated PLANTATIONS. A few are privately owned, with restricted access; most form part of PUBLIC OPEN SPACE, and are owned by governments and other public institutions. Collections are often directed towards specific groups; for example, the Mount Dandenong Arboretum (Vic.) has an emphasis on CONIFERS and deciduous TREES, while the PETER FRANCIS POINTS ARBORETUM (Vic.) and BURRENDONG ARBORETUM (NSW) have been solely developed as collections of AUSTRALIAN NATIVE TREES.

The formation of arboreta in Australia paralleled the enthusiasm for the development of botanic gardens and ACCLIMATISATION societies in the nineteenth century. An understanding of growth characteristics of exotic and native tree species in the range of CLIMATIC and SOIL conditions encountered across Australia was the main motivation in their formation. An early and continuing interest has been the investigation of useful species for FORESTRY as well as ornamental use, and for related HORTICULTURAL research. Like their counterparts overseas, education in tree growth characteristics and plant taxonomy for students of the plant sciences, professionals in the field, and the general public has always been a key role of Australian arboreta. Thus many collections have some system of labelling, mapping, and recording to establish at least a base resource for the dissemination of information. Visitor services (including INTERPRETATION) are now considered an important feature of arboreta, as is the importance of PLANT CONSERVATION. Thematic walks highlighting trees of special interest, many of which were planted in the nineteenth century—in the ROYAL BOTANIC GARDENS, MELBOURNE, for example—underline the educational importance and conservation role of the arboretum to a contemporary society.

ML

ARBORICULTURE, a term derived from the Latin *arbor* (tree) in conjunction with 'culture' (care or cultivation), has been in common usage since the 1830s, although the first recorded use of 'arborist' to describe its practitioner dates from 1578. Today the terms arboriculturist and arborist both have currency, with NORTH AMERICAN and Australian usage favouring the shorter term. Arboriculture, while clearly associated with management of TREES, also encompasses large shrubs and palms, and even woody vines. It differs from FORESTRY in its focus on individual plants, and it does not involve the production imperatives usually associated with forestry.

Modern arboriculture deals with all aspects of the care and cultivation of trees. This can involve collection and PROPAGATION of SEED; management practices such as PRUNING and TREE SURGERY, which influence growing and maturing specimens; knowledge of plant pathology related to PESTS AND DISEASES; and removal of aged and senescing specimens that no longer fulfil their intended role. Many of the arborist's techniques prolong the useful life of trees in urban landscapes. Specialist arboricultural skills include the use of ropes and harnesses for climbing, elevated platforms, installation of cables to secure defective canopies, and cavity filling of decayed parts of trees. These techniques have been developed to maximise the safety of arborists and to minimise damage to trees. Arboricultural practices recognise the importance of the whole tree, structurally and functionally, above and below the ground, to ensure that both canopy and root system are appropriately managed.

Richard J. Campana, *Arboriculture: History and Development in North America* (East Lansing, Michigan, 1999)

GREG MOORE

ARBOURS, light, decorative structures—generally with a permeable roof, and often housing simple garden FURNITURE—were popular in French and Italian gardens as summer seats and resting places. They were also popular in British gardens, well adapted to the lightness and elegance of Regency gardens, and also embellished many larger colonial gardens. They were generally of a less permanent nature than SUMMER-HOUSES, perhaps explaining the paucity of extant early examples. Dressed timber (especially lattice or TRELLIS-WORK) or RUSTIC branches were the most common materials, although WIRE-WORK and wrought or cast iron came into use during the mid-nineteenth century. While 'arbour' referred generally to a shady nook, the term 'bower' tended to apply specifically to a leafy one, covered by creepers or CLIMBING PLANTS—well demonstrated by the early example at the ARCHER estate, Brickendon. Larger structures such as PERGOLAS often fulfilled the same function as arbours.

RA

ARCHAEOLOGY is increasingly being used by researchers and managers of HERITAGE PLACES, including historic gardens, to contribute to an understanding of cultural significance and to aid conservation planning. Understanding of the physical changes to a garden's design, layout, and use can often be gained through survey and excavation, coupled with research and analysis. Archaeological results complement the work of the GARDEN HISTORIAN and often illustrate or enhance early written records, maps, and plans. Methods used include the study of aerial photographs, topographical plans, and geophysical surveys to detect or record subtle surface or below-ground features. Excavation, used cautiously, may provide detail of the fabric and construction of features such as paths, beds, and garden buildings, structures, and ornaments. In areas of little disturbance, soil analysis can also provide evidence of vegetation and the history of planting through seed and pollen remains. Above ground, archaeological analysis can aid an understanding of standing structures and works. Archaeological research and analysis has been used effectively at, for example, VAUCLUSE HOUSE, by the Historic Houses Trust of New South Wales, where features of the historic garden were revealed by excavation.

On a wider canvas, archaeology involves studying the landscape and cultural setting of a historic garden, its relationship to a family, building, settlement, or community, and its status and symbolism. The key to archaeology's effectiveness (and relevance) is its thoughtful integration into the conservation process, and close co-operation between archaeologist, garden historian, and all others in the project team.

Naomi F. Miller and Kathryn L. Gleason (eds), *The Archaeology of Garden and Field* (Philadelphia, 1994); Paul Pattison (ed.), *There By Design: Field Archaeology in Parks and Gardens* (Oxford, 1998)   DAVID THACKRAY

ARCHER, Thomas (1790–1850), commissariat officer and pastoralist, was the first of his family to settle in Van Diemen's Land, although he was eventually followed by his father and brothers, all of whom settled on the Norfolk Plains in the north of the colony. From the earliest period of European settlement visitors commented on the area's English or PARK-like appearance. This was due in part to the traditional land management practices of the local Aboriginal people, who had regularly fired the area, and in part to the establishment of pastures based on English grasses and the introduction of hawthorn hedges along boundaries and roadsides.

Thomas Archer arrived in Van Diemen's Land in 1817 to take charge of the Commissariat in Port Dalrymple, and in that year he received the first of his land grants at Norfolk Plains. By further grant and purchase he came to own several properties, including his home estate of **Woolmers**, which comprised nearly 5000 hectares. In 1819 he built a timber house on a knoll overlooking the Lake River, retiring from government service in 1821 to live there permanently. He imported stud sheep, cattle, and horses as well as plant stock, and established a propagating nursery; in 1832 the surplus supplied to other settlers included 100 worked apple trees of different sorts, 100 bearing hawthorns, and fifty gooseberry bushes sent to John Leake of ROSEDALE.

The original ornamental garden may have been a small cottage garden complemented by kitchen and fruit gardens; jasmine grew over the verandah. **William Archer** (1820–1874), third son of Thomas and professionally trained as an ARCHITECT in London, returned to Van Diemen's Land in 1842. He designed an ITALIANATE addition to form a new front to the house, facing away from the river. As part of the extensions, a new garden was created, enclosed within a curved wall and entered through an impressive gateway. The garden was designed around two major axes—one from the house to the Palladian stable at the rear of the garden, the other between the main entrance gate and a gate to the home paddocks. A carriage loop at the front of the house enclosed a circular lawn ornamented with a classical cast-iron fountain; the remainder of the garden was GARDENESQUE in style. Brick-edged paths winding between mixed shrubberies led to a Gothic smoking room (originally set on a barge in the river) and a rustic octagonal summer-house decorated with pine cones. As early as 1856 the gardens were recommended to tourists as particularly fine. Beyond the WALLED GARDEN is the site of extensive kitchen gardens and orchards, and a number of picturesque structures, notably an octagonal pump house (originally horse-powered). The avenue of poplars and the formally clipped cypress hedge are early twentieth-century developments.

William Archer was also a botanist of some note. He spent what time he could from his farming duties to go 'botanising', particularly in the Meander Valley in and around his own estate of Cheshunt. He collected and named many native species and was apparently interested in the cultivation of these plants. His diaries record the dispatch of several native and other plants to friends and relatives. He may also have planted some native species at Cheshunt: in the 1880s a visitor noted that as well as pines, cedars, cypresses, and elms there were several plants not usually found in cultivation, including celery top pines and waratahs. On a trip to England from 1856 to 1859 William Archer contributed botanical drawings to Joseph Hooker's *Flora of Tasmania*, which is dedicated to Archer and Ronald GUNN. Archer was also a member of the ROYAL SOCIETY of Tasmania and presented several papers on horticultural subjects.

Joseph Archer (1795–1853) followed his brother Thomas to Van Diemen's Land in 1821; by 1824 he had acquired the first of his land grants. He eventually owned considerable property in both the Longford and Cressy districts, but his principal residence was **Panshanger**. Both the house and the estate were conceived on a grand scale to reflect the increasing wealth and status of its owner. In the early 1830s Archer added a Grecian revival facade to his existing brick house. The grounds at Panshanger were originally designed to enhance the park-like aspects of the natural setting. Until 1874, part of the grounds were reserved as a DEER PARK. Clumps of English trees, such as oaks and elms, were planted and the eye was drawn to distant VISTAS. Visible from the terrace was a round pigeon tower erected by Archer on his adjoining property, Burlington. Closer to the house was a thatched shed housing a cider mill and a square, castellated water tower that fed the stone fountain in the middle of the lawn as well as the gardens and outbuildings. By the 1870s, many of the trees and shrubs had reached a substantial size, having been planted more than forty years previously: a

The ARCHER property Woolmers (Tas.) retains a fine and early example of a WALLED GARDEN, which is complemented by the axial arrangement of the ITALIANATE front to the house and stable building as well as the main gateways to the drive and home paddocks

stand of acacias—thought to be the largest in Tasmania—reached more than sixty feet high. On the slope below the house were *Pinus pinea* (Stone Pine) and *P. nigra* (Austrian Pine), cypresses, hazel and filbert, poplar, ash, acacia, and laurel. Among the SHRUBBERIES stood an obelisk of Sicilian marble commemorating the first Joseph Archer. Pleasant shady walks wound through the trees and scented flowering shrubs. In parts lily of the valley and violets covered the ground. Weeping willows and osiers were planted along the river. The gardens were described by several commentators as thoroughly English.

In 1824 William Archer (1788–1879), an older brother of Thomas, arrived in Van Diemen's Land. William also acquired several estates either by grant or purchase, settling at **Brickendon**, which was separated from Woolmers by the Macquarie River. A hawthorn hedge lined the approach to Brickendon. The various elements of the grounds as described in 1883 comprised a miniature park, landscaped garden, lawn, and fruit and vegetable gardens. The specimens planted by William Archer were then mature trees, with the pines and hollies thought to be the largest and oldest in Tasmania, and 'gnarled and ancient' hawthorns. Other trees included cedars, cypresses, yews, junipers, araucarias, horse chestnuts, oaks, and elms, while vines and a fig tree were trained up the side of the house. Many of the trees had historical and personal associations—a very typical feature of the period. The garden had many features of the Victorian pleasure garden including shady nooks, winding paths, and a famous nut walk.

LINDY SCRIPPS

ARCHERY GROUNDS Toxophilites—those who pursue the sport of archery—were usually members of clubs, formed in the Australian colonies along the lines of kindred Scottish and English groups. Archery was practised mostly in the upper echelons of colonial society, exemplified by Lady Bowen's occasional archery parties in the 1870s at Victoria's GOVERNMENT HOUSE. Target archery meetings required a field, although the equipment could be set in any park or pleasure garden—Sir Frederick Sargood's RIPPON LEA, for example, where fortnightly bow meetings were held during the 1870s and 1890s. After the shoot, targets and equipment could be stored in a purpose-built structure; the octagonal archery house at Rippon Lea is a rare and unusual extant example. Since the Second World War, target and field archery has grown nationally as an amateur sport through a network of clubs whose members participate in competitions regulated by Archery Australia.

RICHARD HEATHCOTE

ARCHITECTURE has long had a close affinity with garden design by virtue of the relationships between buildings, structures, and landscapes, but especially in Australia by links between house and garden. The profession of architecture was formalised far earlier than LANDSCAPE GARDENING or LANDSCAPE ARCHITECTURE, and the traditional role of architect as designer placed him (or her, from the early to middle years of the twentieth century) at the head of a creative process still rued by many gardeners. Architects often looked to classical sources for their inspiration—either 'ancient' models or Renaissance interpretations—and ITALIANATE influence was a common link between architects and garden design. FORMAL GARDENS—sometimes described as being in the architectural style—were treated by John Arthur Hughes in *Garden Architecture and Landscape Gardening* (1866), among many publications. The term 'garden architect' gained currency during the nineteenth century and was used well into the twentieth.

Francis Greenway (1777–1837), a convicted forger recognised as Australia's earliest professional architect, brought unusual sophistication to both architecture and gardens, advertising in 1835 that he laid out grounds 'in the landscape gardening style'. John Bibb (1810–1862), architectural assistant to Greenway's rival, John Verge (1782–1861), was a keen horticulturist and stalwart member of Sydney's earliest horticultural societies; Verge himself was a designer of Regency-style garden buildings. In Van Diemen's Land, William ARCHER had returned in 1842 from architectural training in London and displayed the vogue for Italianate architecture in his remodelling of Woolmers: his penchant for botany and horticulture was complemented by an interest in landscape design, evidenced by his acquisition in London of plans by Regency architect and garden designer John Buonarotti Papworth (1775–1847), author of *Hints on Ornamental Gardening* (1823) and other pattern books. Melbourne architects PURCHAS and Swyer laid out several gardens mid-century; Purchas also extended his talents to CEMETERY design. This branch of design also suited the formality embraced by the kindred professions of LAND SURVEYING and TOWN PLANNING, whose early practitioners included Colonel William LIGHT and George KINGSTON, best known for their involvement with ADELAIDE PARK LANDS.

As Australian gardens developed, so too did the range of GARDEN BUILDINGS that required architectural input. These ranged from simple KIOSKS and PAVILIONS to elaborate BANDSTANDS, and generally found their most architectonic expression in PUBLIC PARKS AND GARDENS. Architectural links between house and garden formed a transition zone often put to horticultural use—VERANDAHS, CONSERVATORIES, and PATIOS, for example. Architectural decoration drawn from plant forms also enlivened gardens, as is demonstrated by Guilfoyle's use of the Staghorn Fern on his Temple of the Winds at MELBOURNE BOTANIC GARDENS (1901) and Lucien Henri's championing of the waratah for DECORATIVE ARTS. In fact, the ARTS AND CRAFTS influence on Australian gardens convincingly united architecture and garden design, with a leading role being played by architects such as Walter BUTLER and Rodney ALSOP, who stressed the need for unity of design. The GRIFFINS played a key role in drawing the two strands together, successfully clothing the formality of CITY BEAUTIFUL ideas in NATURALISTIC (and nationalistic) garb. The search for an Australian style also saw many architects look to MEDITERRANEAN—particularly Spanish—models for inspiration. These climatically similar buildings and gardens inspired work by Alsop, Walter BAGOT, Harold DESBROWE-ANNEAR, Leslie WILKINSON, and William Hardy WILSON.

MODERNISM also linked architects and garden design, as can be seen in the work of Arthur Baldwinson and Douglas Snelling in the 1940s and 1950s; Robin Boyd (1919–1971) was also a keen observer of garden and landscape design. The use of 'architectural plants'—denoting bold FOLIAGE or strong texture—was a key feature of many schemes, particularly INDOOR GARDENS, of this period. In NSW, Peter Muller (b. 1927) and Bruce RICKARD were both inspired by the designs of North American architect Frank Lloyd Wright (1869–1959), who skilfully integrated landscape and architecture. This theme of responding to the landscape has also recently influenced architects such as Richard Le Plastrier, Glenn Murcutt, Stutchbury & Pape, and Greg Burgess, whereas a sharper urban focus has shaped the work of Denton Corker Marshall, seen convincingly in First Government House Place, forecourt of the Museum of Sydney (1994). RA

ARDAGH, Richard (1850–1922), gardener, rosarian, and nursery proprietor, was born in Melbourne to Irish parents. He returned from a stint on the goldfields in 1870; four years later he started work with florist James SCOTT at Hawthorn. Ardagh began in business on his own account in the late 1870s on a site at Auburn, which he increased over two decades from a quarter-acre lot to two acres (0.8 ha) with nursery and display garden. He was elected a committee member of the Boroondara Horticultural Society in 1882, and remained a stalwart member and honorary secretary for many years. Ardagh was a councillor of Hawthorn Borough (1892–1911) and mayor during 1897–98. He was an advocate for municipal parks and gardens, and initiated street tree planting in the suburb. Ardagh specialised in ROSES and gained high awards at the 1880 Melbourne International Exhibition. At the meeting in 1899 when the NATIONAL ROSE SOCIETY of Victoria was inaugurated, Ardagh occupied the chair. After his death in 1922, tributes acknowledged that for many years he had been one of Australia's leading rosarians. RA

ARD CHOILLE (Gaelic for 'high woods'), Mount Macedon, Vic., was laid out in the early 1890s by William SANGSTER for fellow Scot, industrialist William Peter McGregor (c. 1853–1899), who aimed to establish an estate reminiscent of the

Arid-zone gardens

The unusual and elegant metal SHADE HOUSE (1898) at ARD CHOILLE, Mount Macedon (Vic.) is a reminder of the original owner's business interests in metal mining and testament to the horticultural passions of such HILL-STATION owners

Scottish Highlands. The original residence (destroyed by fire in 1914) sported brick chimneys in a Rob Roy tartan pattern, highland cattle grazed the upper slopes, and a piper tended the vegetable garden. A series of 'lochs' and cascades was constructed down the steeply sloping site and a trout hatchery was established. As the visitor ascended from the residence by terraced paths, a VISTA north to Mount Diogenes (Hanging Rock) opened. Sangster's garden design embodied HILL-STATION characteristics with a fine collection of cool temperate plants, especially CONIFERS. Established trees include *Sequoiadendron giganteum*, *Pseudotsuga menziesii*, *Cedrus atlantica* f. *glauca*, *Cupressus macrocarpa* 'Horizontalis Aurea', *Picea smithiana* and *P. sitchensis*, and *Tsuga heterophylla*. McGregor, for many years chairman of Broken Hill Proprietary Co. Ltd, convincingly demonstrated his company's interests with an elegant metal SHADE HOUSE (1898), now a rare survivor. A large amount of work has been carried out by the present owners, the Cottew family, to revitalise this important MOUNT MACEDON garden and reveal the original Sangster design.   JACKIE COURMADIAS

ARDGARTAN is the earliest remaining garden in Victoria's WESTERN DISTRICT designed by Edna WALLING. Commissioned by Henry John Youngman in 1935, Walling travelled to Grassdale near Hamilton to inspect the site and later returned to complete the planting scheme. The watercolour plan is one of her masterpieces, showing the walled rose garden offsetting the relaxed informality of the park-like grounds. Five generations of Youngmans have lived at Ardgartan since 1888—a continuity reflected in the integrity of the garden.   TRISHA DIXON

ARID-ZONE GARDENS, located in a climatic zone that covers more than two-thirds of the Australian continent, were begun as European settlers moved into the vast arid interior and established pastoral properties, MISSIONS, and communities. Although many areas of inland Australia have the appearance of a huge garden for short periods in favourable SEASONS, with abundant wildflowers and new growth on trees and shrubs, a parched environment is the norm. The harsh CLIMATE, with very hot summers, unpredictable rainfall, scarce and often poor-quality WATER, and often severe frosts in winter, made attempts at gardening difficult. Great distances and limited, slow transport made fresh fruit and vegetables unavailable, giving settlers an incentive to be self-sufficient; gardens provided a balanced diet and reduced the risk of diseases such as scurvy. For example, when water was available, Lutheran missionaries at Killalpaninna (SA) and Hermannsburg (NT) grew vegetables to feed mission staff and local Aboriginal people. Afghan cameleers planted dates at many inland waters as they traversed supply routes between settlements; many of these palms are still thriving.

Some pastoral properties were also noted for their gardens, both ornamental and productive, although fences for shelter and rabbit protection were necessary.

Few local indigenous plants were grown as ornamentals; rather, plants from other areas were brought in to help tame the wilderness. *Schinus molle* (Pepper Tree) from the deserts of Peru and *Nerium oleander* (Oleander) from the Mediterranean and Middle East were widely planted and have naturalised in some places. Unfortunately, some introduced species have become environmental WEEDS; they include *Tamarix aphylla* (Athel Pine) in Central Australia and *Prosopis juliflora* (Mesquite) in arid NSW and Qld. Some local native trees were grown for shade and shelter, and a long process of trial and error largely determined what would survive in different arid zones.

IRRIGATION 'colonies' were established from the late nineteenth century, with the work of the CHAFFEY brothers at Mildura (Vic.) being the best known. The abundant water meant a wide variety of exotic plants could be grown for ornamental and productive purposes, and PALMS became a signature plant in these areas. Most townships in arid zones, however, had limited water supplies and little vegetation due to firewood clearing and the effects of overgrazing by goats (kept for town milk supplies), resulting in severe dust storms. Broken Hill (NSW) was plagued by dust storms and drift sand as a result of vegetation clearance. Through the far-sighted work of Albert MORRIS and others in establishing fenced REVEGETATION areas and SHELTER BELTS (including local native species) around the city from 1936, the problem gradually abated, greatly improving the quality of life for residents. The lessons learnt from such planting schemes have been effectively applied in many other arid-zone communities. Indeed, the mining industry, often accused of environmental damage, was instrumental in the greening of many arid-zone towns before LANDCARE and the ENVIRONMENT became popular causes.

Following the Second World War, new towns to serve mining and other interests were established in Australia's arid zones. In places with minimal tree cover, such as Leigh Creek and Woomera (SA), many arid-zone native species were planted; pleasant, green towns were developed under very harsh conditions. As at Broken Hill, there was considerable trial and error. Kambalda (WA) was noteworthy in that existing trees and shrubs were carefully protected during town construction and incorporated into the new landscape. A similar approach has subsequently been successfully undertaken at other new arid-zone towns including Leigh Creek South and Roxby Downs (SA), and Leinster (WA). More recently, the trend has been to concentrate on local endemic species in public plantings, rather than a mix of species from the arid zones in general.

Examples of gardens in arid zones include Kalgoorlie Arboretum (WA), established in 1954 to test and demonstrate the suitability of native and exotic trees to the semi-arid environment of the goldfields region; the emphasis in this twenty-six hectare garden has been on establishing *Eucalyptus* species and understorey plantings. The OLIVE PINK BOTANIC GARDEN, established in 1956 at Alice Springs (NT) through a variety of desert settings, aims to conserve, display, and promote the study of the Central Australian flora. Endilloe, a private garden established in 1976 near Quorn (SA) by Brian and Fay POWELL, features a wide range of native plants from arid and semi-arid zones. The AUSTRALIAN ARID LANDS BOTANIC GARDEN at Port Augusta (SA), proposed in 1981 and commenced in 1989, was opened in 1996. The garden focuses on the flora of the southern arid zone of Australia, with regional plantings being established; a large Eremophila garden is a major attraction. The AUSTRALIAN INLAND BOTANIC GARDEN, located in a major irrigated horticultural area north of Mildura, is funded by community groups and local government, and supported by an active 'Friends' group. Developed during the 1980s and 1990s, the garden aims to provide education, recreational space, research opportunities, and a venue for conservation. Kalgoorlie–Boulder Native Garden (WA), established in 1995 by the local Landcare group, is a one-hectare arid-zone demonstration garden that aims to encourage garden planting of local native plants, displays the regional flora for visitors, and is an educational resource for school children. The ALICE SPRINGS DESERT PARK, opened in 1997, expands on this concept to embrace both flora and fauna, and interprets traditional ABORIGINAL ENVIRONMENTAL MANAGEMENT and use of arid-zone landscapes. Also in Alice Springs, the power and water authority has a small water-wise demonstration garden at Sadadeen Valley, based on appropriate arid-zone native species, and the Airport Garden is landscaped with regional native plants with interpretive signage—a fitting entry statement to the town.

The use of efficient drip irrigation, automatic irrigation control, utilisation of treated sewer effluent, water harvesting, mulches, and selection of appropriate arid-zone species, along with increasing horticultural knowledge means that gardening in the arid zones is usually successful despite scarce and often poor-quality water supplies, poor soils, and harsh climatic conditions. Indeed, the water-efficient (or XERIC) gardening techniques widely employed in arid Australia could well be utilised elsewhere in the country to make better use of water, our most precious resource.

Norman Hall et al., *The Use of Trees and Shrubs in the Dry Country of Australia* (Canberra, 1972); Horace Webber, *The Greening of the Hill: Revegetation around Broken Hill in the 1930s* (Melbourne, 1992) JOHN ZWAR

ARMATI, Pio Vico (1846–1923), born Marino, Italy, university-educated (Rome and London), arrived in Brisbane in 1872. He commenced business *c.* 1875 as a chemist and

The Eremophilia collection at AUSTRALIAN ARID LANDS BOTANIC GARDENS, Port Augusta (SA), demonstrates ARID-ZONE GARDENING, applicable to large areas across Australia

druggist in Townsville (Qld), then developing as a port for inland goldfields. Armati was a keen gardener, advising on the layout of TOWNSVILLE QUEENS PARK (1878) and later becoming a foundation trustee (1880–88). By 1876 he was advertising seed and plants as agent for Samuel PURCHASE: this exemplified a common connection between the NURSERY trade and kindred businesses, such as pharmacies, in frontier townships.

Peter McLean Armati, *Pio Vico Armati … A Family History* (St Ives, NSW, 1997)   RA

ARMIT, William Edington de Margrat (1848–1901), botanist and public servant, was born at Liège, Belgium, and in 1872 was appointed a sub-inspector in the Queensland Mounted Police. Travelling widely across northern Qld, he collected specimens for MUELLER (who recognised his contributions by naming a plant for him) and published his observations in the *Journal of the Linnaean Society (Botany)*. His 'Notes on Certain Plants of North-Western Queensland Possessing Valuable Medicinal Properties' (1882) substantially drew on local Aboriginal knowledge. During the 1880s and 1890s he travelled and worked in New Guinea, where he died.   RA

ARNIM (née BEAUCHAMP), Mary Annette (Elizabeth) von (1866–1941), novelist, was born in Sydney and spent her childhood there. While in Rome with her father she met her future husband, Graf Henning August von Arnim-Schlagenthin. Married in 1891, Countess von Arnim wrote her first book when living at Nassenheide, a Pomeranian estate close to the Baltic Sea. *Elizabeth and her German Garden* (1898), a major success reprinted many times, recounted an autobiographical tale of garden-making on the sandy plains of Pomerania. Following financial difficulties and the premature death of her husband, she retreated with her children to England, then to Switzerland. Her subsequent twenty-one novels were modestly credited to 'the author of Elizabeth and her German Garden'; *Enchanted April* (1922) was produced as a play (1927) and a film (1935 and 1992).

VICTOR CRITTENDEN

ART The earliest Australian garden images to suggest educated leisure are Joseph LYCETT's PICTURESQUE views of the first private houses on land grants, with specimen pines from Norfolk Island in their gardens. Views by other early colonial artists often show, incidentally, utilitarian gardens with squared and fenced layouts. Most known views of Sydney to 1825 are reproduced by Tim McCormick in *First Views of Australia* (1987), a comprehensive collection containing much of interest to the GARDEN HISTORIAN.

Symbolic gardens were painted early. In an 1824 mourning portrait by Richard Read snr (b. c. 1765), Julia Johnston stands before her family's neo-classical vault in the garden of Annandale, near Sydney. Roses, symbolising love, grow through the picket fence beside what seems to be an oak (hospitality) or perhaps a laurel. An early print (c. 1840) by Phillip Parker King (1791–1856) shows explorer–botanist Allan CUNNINGHAM's memorial situated in an elegant garden of mourning within SYDNEY BOTANIC GARDENS: drooping bamboo and weeping willow flank an obelisk and reflecting pool.

BOTANICAL ILLUSTRATION, which has until recently evoked ambivalence or condescension from art historians, was popular from the early days of European settlement, especially for depictions of native AUSTRALIAN FLORA. This form of art was also made widely available though printmaking and publication in books.

HOMESTEAD and garden portraits by mid- to late nineteenth-century artists such as GLOVER, S.T. GILL, von GUÉRARD, GRITTEN, and TIBBITS carefully delineate ornamental

Fiona Hall's 'Grapefruit (*Citrus paradisi*)', from her series of sardine-tin sculptures *Paradisus Terrestris* (1989–90), draws on John Parkinson's 1629 florilegium, *Paradisus in Sole: Paradisus Terrestris*, using ART to represent the Garden of Eden

as the house. It was only a short visual step—but a huge technological and egalitarian leap—from these depictions to PHOTOGRAPHY, used since the late 1850s, but increasingly, from the late nineteenth century, as a means of recording residences and their attendant gardens.

In the early twentieth century, garden images such as those by Arthur Streeton (1867–1943) and Frederick McCubbin (1855–1917) tended towards informality. William Hardy WILSON redirected this focus with his ordered depictions of early colonial gardens (perhaps acknowledging modernist spareness), notably adding decorative matching tubs of hydrangeas to his measured drawings in *Old Colonial Architecture in New South Wales and Tasmania* (1924). In contrast to Wilson, and more typically of the period, Grace Cossington Smith (1892–1984) painted fragmented flowers and foliage from her Turramurra (NSW) garden with emphasis on form and colour, not on garden views. Others in the modern circle, such as Thea Proctor (1879–1966) and Adrian Feint (1894–1971), also depicted FLOWER ARRANGEMENTS and other domestic aspects of gardening. These reach a hallucinatory apotheosis in the airbrushed depictions of SUBURBAN GARDENS by Howard Arkley (1951–1999).

Recently, SCULPTORS have received garden commissions. *Fern Garden* (1988) by Fiona Hall (b. 1953), of *Dicksonia antarctica* (Soft Tree-fern) planted in spirals, was created for the National Gallery of Australia in Canberra. *The Edge of the Trees* (1994) by Janet Laurence (b. 1949) and Fiona Foley (b. 1964) marks the site of the First GOVERNMENT HOUSE in Sydney. Made from wood, iron, and other materials, it draws on notions of the historic grove and symbolises contact between the Eora people and the first Europeans.

Tim Bonyhady, *Images in Opposition: Australian Landscape Painting 1801–1890* (Melbourne, 1985); Jennifer Phipps, *Artists' Gardens: Flowers and Gardens in Australian Art* (Sydney, 1986); Joan Kerr (ed.), *The Dictionary of Australian Artists: Painters, Sketchers, Photographers, and Engravers to 1870* (Melbourne, 1992); Roy Strong, *The Artist & the Garden* (London, 2000)

JENNIFER PHIPPS

ARTHUR, John (*c.* 1800–1849), founding superintendent gardener of MELBOURNE BOTANIC GARDENS and celebrated bagpipe player, was born in Perthshire, Scotland and worked as a gardener on an estate of the Duke of Argyll before migrating to Australia in 1839. One of a group of selected migrants to arrive in the Port Phillip District, he gained employment at Heidelberg, where he leased land, farming on the fertile river flats and gaining experience working under local conditions, and established a nursery with plants he had brought from Scotland.

Arthur assumed his duties as Superintendent of the Gardens in 1846: his first step was to select five acres (2 ha) of the present Tennyson Lawn for a 'nursery garden'. With two assistants, he set about clearing, grubbing, and trenching the area, which was fenced and laid out in a formal pattern of garden beds and paths forming a parterre as shown in Henry GINN's plan (1856). Arthur planted trees and shrubs from his Heidelberg nursery, including the English elms still stand-

pleasure grounds, and often fruit and vegetable gardens. Glover's own large cottage garden at Patterdale (1837), Van Diemen's Land, is the definitive colonial pastoral image; von Guérard painted homestead commissions within romantic landscapes in which homestead and garden are recorded in encyclopaedic detail. In the naive and obsessively detailed watercolour drawings of Tibbits, garden layout is as important

ing on the Tennyson Lawn. He retained some indigenous vegetation, including *Eucalyptus camaldulensis* (River Red Gum) and *Melaleuca ericifolia* (Swamp Paperbark) fringing the lagoon. From the outset, LA TROBE and his committee supported the hard-working Arthur, who had made excellent progress in establishing a firm foundation for the future development of the Gardens. Visitors could stroll among the healthy young trees and flowering plants, or rest on seats while admiring the views. In 1848, funds were allocated for additional staff including a man for 'Sundays watching'. Arthur's tenure was brief; he died from cholera in the cottage built for him in the Gardens.

LORNA CROWTHER and NATALIE McMASTER

ARTIFICIAL FLOWERS are used as substitutes for fresh flowers in domestic decoration and their history is linked with fashions not only in FLORICULTURE and FLOWER ARRANGEMENT but also of their constituent materials. Floral fads and a general interest in RUSTICITY, introduced to Australia in the nineteenth century, encouraged floral decoration in the home. Handcrafted flowers were a handy alternative in harsh climates and pioneering settlements. Flower studies were deemed a suitable intellectual excursion into the science of BOTANY for women and girls, and a morally edifying encounter with nature. Thus the reconstitution of flowers in materials as diverse as fabric, paper, wool, glass, porcelain, shell, bone, and dried vegetation (such as fruit, especially nuts) was an instructive DECORATIVE ART. Wax was particularly favoured in the nineteenth century for its luminous quality and ease of handling. Conversely, the popularity of synthetic materials in the twentieth century has devalued plastic flowers. First mentioned as items for sale in Australia in the 1820s, artificial flowers were found in fashionable emporiums and at EXHIBITIONS, and a specialised industry—exploitative or artistic, depending on the status of the craftworker—thrived. Artificial flowers provide great versatility, fading neither in draughty halls nor on graves. They eschew the dictates of seasons and climates, bring the exotic within reach of the most modest budget, and can enliven with surreal confections of unnatural hues and tints.

ELIZABETH ANYA-PETRIVNA

ARTS AND CRAFTS The English Arts and Crafts movement centred around the London offices of William Morris (1834–1896), Richard Norman Shaw (1831–1912), and John Dando Sedding (1831–1891). Staff were encouraged to gain a thorough knowledge of every aspect of design, to maintain a respect for local materials and building traditions, and to have an appreciation for Romantic and medieval literature. The movement had a significant impact on garden architecture; the garden was seen as a logical extension of the house design, and that only the architect could create a unity between the two. A battle was declared between formal and landscape gardening, fought by Sir Reginald Blomfield (*The Formal Garden in England*, 1891) and Sedding (*Garden-craft Old and New*, 1892) against William ROBINSON and his followers. In Australia, this battle was fought by Walter BUTLER (Sedding's former assistant) and C. Bogue LUFFMANN in two papers at the Royal Victorian Institute of Architects in 1903.

A formal garden was thought superior to any other for its simplicity. It drew from the design of ITALIANATE gardens as well as the gardens of seventeenth-century designers André Le Nôtre and Isaac de Caux. The garden was treated as a series of external rooms; it was a 'betweenity', creating a threshold between the house and the wildness of nature. The radiating layers included the house, axially planned formal terraces, WILD GARDEN, then, finally, nature. Arts and Crafts gardens drew on a palette of consistent elements—grand front carriageway, terraces, parterre, rose garden, croquet lawn, formal garden beds, tennis court, walls, steps, fernery, wild garden, urns, statues, topiary, arches—arranged according to the dimensions of the site.

Apart from Butler, several Australian architects subscribed to the philosophies of the Arts and Crafts garden, including Robin Dods in Brisbane, and Robert HADDON and Rodney ALSOP in Melbourne. Alsop placed less emphasis on formality and espoused a romantic, rustic ethos for his picturesque Toorak cottages and gardens of the 1910s and 1920s, which anticipated Edna WALLING's Bickleigh Vale. Women played an increasingly important role, and like Gertrude JEKYLL, began to enjoy a direct contact with plants and soil. This was led by the growing emancipation of women, who were venturing into traditional male pursuits, hastened by the after-effects of the First World War. These women often found a voice in journals such as *Australian Home Beautiful* and the *Home*, and in other art forms. Walling was representative of this new generation—she combined her English rural heritage with an appreciation of the natural landscape, and her designs reflected the tension between FORMALITY and NATURALISED garden design.

David Ottewill, *The Edwardian Garden* (London, 1989); Peter Davey, *Arts and Crafts Architecture* (London, 1995); Wendy Hitchmough, *Arts and Crafts Gardens* (London, 1997)

KATRINA PLACE and NIGEL LEWIS

ASHBY, Edwin (1861–1941), plant propagator, nursery proprietor, and naturalist, established in 1902, with his wife Esther (1867–1943), a formal garden and fruit orchard called **Wittunga** at Blackwood in the ADELAIDE HILLS. Born at Capel, Surrey, England, of Quaker parentage, he migrated to Adelaide in 1888 and enthusiastically continued his studies of birds, chitons, and insects, and became passionately interested in the AUSTRALIAN FLORA. Following a bushfire in 1934 that destroyed much of his collections, he concentrated on enlarging his native Australian and South African garden, establishing one of the first specialist native plant nurseries in Australia (1936). An enlightened conservationist, Ashby experimented with alternative methods of propagation and watering systems, developed the 'Ashby deep penetration system', contributed to *Australian Gardening of To-day* (1943) based on weekly articles in the *Express and Journal*, and advocated that 'native shrubs can be grown on the Adelaide Plains at less cost of time and labour than ordinary gardening'. He supported other plant propagators, particularly

ALTHOFER, BURDETT, and MORRIS, often exchanging advice, seeds, and plants. He was honoured in *Banksia ashbyi*.

(Arthur) Keith Ashby (1896–1971), orchardist and grazier, inherited his father's love of both Australian and South African plants, which he enthusiastically promoted by illustrated lectures. In conjunction with his sister Alison he nurtured the Wittunga garden. After retiring from farming he worked full-time in the garden, significantly extending the *Banksia*, *Protea*, *Leucadendron*, *Leucospermum*, and *Erica* collections. Many South African species, particularly ericas, were introduced to Australia through Wittunga. In consultation with his family, Keith donated fourteen hectares to the ADELAIDE BOTANIC GARDEN (1965), publicly opened, in a somewhat modified form, as Wittunga Botanic Garden in 1975.

Alison Marjorie Ashby (1901–1987), noted botanical watercolourist, received some instruction from Rosa FIVEASH and undertook extensive plant collecting journeys in the Australian Alps and Geraldton and Albany areas of WA, depositing thousands of specimens at the Adelaide and Perth Herbaria while adding considerably to the Wittunga collection. She instigated REVEGETATION activities on part of the Wittunga farmland, suggesting that it be 're-clothed in Australian trees and shrubs as part of the green belt around Adelaide', before donating it to the National Trust of South Australia (1957) as Watiparinga Reserve. An Australian Natural History Medallion, the naming of *Acacia ashbyae* and *Solanum ashbyae*, and publication of *Alison Ashby's Wildflowers of Southern Australia* (1981) honour her services to conservation.

Enid Lucy Robertson (b. 1925), systematic botanist, daughter of Keith Ashby, worked at WAITE INSTITUTE (1947–53) and in the Botany Department, University of Adelaide (1953–55, 1967–87). Specialising in conservation and native vegetation management, she revised Part IV of BLACK's *Flora of South Australia* (1957) and wrote *Restoration of Grassy Woodland* (1999). Her achievements have been recognised with an inaugural Australian Heritage Award (1986) and an Australian Plants Award (1991), and in *Posidonia robertsoniae*.

DAVID JONES and BRIAN MORLEY

ASIA is a large and diverse continent, connected to Africa by the Isthmus of Suez and bordering Europe along the Ural Mountains and across the Caspian Sea. Asia is an imprecise construct when considered politically, but useful geographically when considering its collective horticultural impact on Australia. By virtue of its distance from Britain and much of Europe, and its perceived 'exotic' qualities, the Orient—as the area, particularly East Asia, was known until well into the twentieth century—was a fertile influence on gardens and horticulture. ORIENTAL INFLUENCE on garden design was initially transplanted to Australia via Europe, but as a source of plants, Asia has long been both an indirect and direct supplier. This is due to Australia's proximity, especially to South-East Asia, and shipping trade routes to major ports in INDIA, CHINA, and JAPAN.

Most Asian plants were originally brought into Australia through English, Dutch, and German botanic gardens and nurseries. There was a botanic garden in Hong Kong, and John BAPTIST was one who obtained plants directly from it. With the opening up of China (1870s) and Japan (1890s) coincident with burgeoning interest in plant collecting and propagation, many wealthy Australians collected specimens for display in their town or HILL-STATION gardens. Occasionally they undertook grand tours through Japan and China, perhaps en route to Europe, to collect seeds, cuttings, catalogues, and addresses, and to view celebrated local gardens. Following the gold rushes of the 1850s, Chinese gold-seekers established their MARKET GARDENS on the goldfields, although evidence for growth of typical Chinese vegetables is scant until after the Second World War.

The spectrum of Asian plants, especially from cooler regions, as profiled by Peter VALDER in *The Garden Plants of China* (1999), is extensive; it includes many typical species used in Australian gardens. These include apple, apricot, azalea, bamboo, camellia, cherry, chrysanthemum, crab apple, flowering peach, forsythia, giant bamboo, hibiscus, japonica, lily, lotus, magnolia, mulberry, orchid, peonies, plum, rhododendron, rose, tea rose, wisteria, and to a lesser extent *Gingko biloba* (Ginkgo), *Metasequoia glyptostroboides* (Dawn Redwood), and *Cedrus deodara* (Deodar). Many ports were in TROPICAL areas, and indigenous plants and advice were eagerly sought by those in similar climatic regions in Australia, principally Qld and NT. The botanic gardens at Calcutta, Peradeniya, Singapore, Penang, and Buitenzorg—reviewed in McCracken's *Gardens of Empire* (1997)—also provided an alternative network to the more traditional European gardens for curators in tropical and subtropical Australia.

The recent revival of interest in the Vireya Rhododendron, for example, is due to continuing interest in ornamental plant collecting expeditions by both botanic gardens and private collectors (such as Melbourne Vireya expert John Rouse, and Bob CHERRY). In the late twentieth century, South-East Asian countries, principally Vietnam, Thailand, Indonesia, and Malaysia, have greatly enriched Australian horticulture through their MIGRANT gardeners. A wide range of the herbs and vegetables now widely grown, such as *Polygonium odoratum* (Vietnamese Mint) and *Cymbopogon citratus* (Lemon Grass), to name but two, have revolutionised Australian cuisine.

DAVID JONES

ATHELSTONE WILDFLOWER GARDEN AND NURSERY: see PAYNE, Frederick Cyril

ATKINSON, (Caroline) Louisa Waring (1834–1872), botanist, artist, and writer, was the first Australian-born woman to have a novel published in her own land. She was the daughter of Charlotte (*née* Waring) and **James Atkinson** (1795–1834), a farmer from Kent, England, who received Oldbury, Berrima (NSW), as a grant from Governor Macquarie in 1821. He published several papers on agricultural matters between 1826 and 1829—the best known was *An Account of the State of Agriculture and Grazing in New South Wales* (1826), favourably reviewed by LOUDON.

Just eight weeks after Louisa was born, James Atkinson died. Always delicate, she spent her youth writing and collecting, and drawing animals and botanical specimens near

Detail of the tree fern *Todea barbara* from sketchbook of Louisa ATKINSON, demonstrating her lively artistic style—a quality that made her work eminently suited to publication as wood engravings in illustrated newspapers of the mid-nineteenth century

her home—first at Oldbury, and later at Kurrajong in the BLUE MOUNTAINS, and on the South Coast of NSW. A keen horse rider, she would set out on horseback to gain access to deep gullies and high ridges. At 23 she published her first novel, *Gertrude, the Emigrant: A Tale of Colonial Life*, which was to be followed by five more (some were serialised in the *Sydney Mail* 1861–72), and regular columns in the *Illustrated Sydney News* (1853–55), *Sydney Morning Herald*, and *SYDNEY MAIL* (1860–71), where her columns entitled 'A Voice from the Country' were often accompanied by her own sketches.

It was as a botanist, however, that her contributions were most valuable. She corresponded with the leading botanists of the day, including WOOLLS and MUELLER, who named a species of *Nuytsia* (*Atkinsonia ligustrina*) after her. *Xanthosia atkinsoniana*, *Erechtites atkinsoniae* (now *Senecio bipinnatisectus*), and *Epacris calvertiana* also carry her name. In 1869 she married explorer and botanist James Snowden Calvert (1825–1884), who had accompanied Ludwig Leichhardt on his 1844–45 expedition. Always interested in horticulture, he won a medal at the London International Exhibition (1862) for his entry on the possible commercial cultivation of native flax. Suffering ill health, Louisa continued her botanical work, but tragically died just 18 days after giving birth to her only child, a daughter, Louise Snowden Calvert.

Brian H. Fletcher, 'Introduction', in James Atkinson, *An Account of the State of Agriculture and Grazing in New South Wales* (facsimile edition, Sydney, 1975); Patricia Clarke, *Pioneer Writer: The Life of Louisa Atkinson, Novelist, Journalist, Naturalist* (Sydney, 1990); Elizabeth Lawson, *The Natural Art of Louisa Atkinson* (Sydney, 1995) MOIRA MAGUIRE

AUDAS, James Wales Clarendon (1872–1959), botanist, joined the National Herbarium under LUEHMANN as an assistant in 1897; by 1925 he was the senior assistant—a position he gained not with qualifications, but through his experience in the BUSH as well as the HERBARIUM—and held with dedication and enthusiasm until his retirement in 1937. A member and sometime office-bearer of the FIELD NATURALISTS' CLUB of Victoria from 1906, he used its magazine, the *Victorian Naturalist*, to publish the botanical results of numerous official and recreational collecting trips. His botanical reports for three biological surveys of Wilsons Promontory followed its permanent reservation as a NATIONAL PARK in 1908. In 1910 he accompanied A.J. EWART to Victoria's alps, where, astride a bicycle, he collected widely, recording indigenous and weed species. His first visit to the Grampians (1912)—with the Minister of Public Works, investigating its tourist potential—so enchanted him that he revisited the 'wildflower garden of Victoria' many times, noting attractive indigenous plants with apparent horticultural potential. His *Victorian Naturalist* articles formed the basis of his book, *One of Nature's Wonderlands: The Victorian Grampians* (1925).

By the 1930s Audas had gleaned sufficient understanding of Australia's forest flora to produce the first book devoted solely to Australian trees from all states: *Native Trees of Australia* (1934), which was illustrated with many GUILFOYLE photos of trees in the MELBOURNE BOTANIC GARDENS. Prompted by his concern at the continuing destruction of Australian forests and his desire to encourage the planting of Australian trees, Audas wanted it to be 'a popular yet comprehensive' work. He dedicated his last book, *The Australian Bushland* (1950), a pot-pourri of his earlier writings, 'to all Nature-lovers for pride taken in their unique inheritance'. He is the taxonomic author of two Australian plant names and is botanically honoured with the name of a now endangered endemic Victorian orchid, *Caladenia audasii*.

LINDEN GILLBANK

Native Trees of Australia (1934), by James AUDAS, contained many photographs attributed to William GUILFOYLE of specimens in Melbourne Botanic Gardens, including *Archontophoenix cunninghamiana* (Bangalow Palm), an early favourite amongst Australian gardeners

AUSTEN, George Thomas (c. 1847–1921), seed merchant, was born in Sydney and in 1898 established his business in Chinatown near Haymarket. His catalogues indicate an extensive trade with Chinese MARKET GARDENERS; surviving correspondence details the extensive international and interstate network of merchants who supplied the seed. These ranged from large German suppliers (until the First World War) to workers on the Trans-Australian Railway, from whom Austen sought seeds of *Swainsona formosa* (Sturt's Desert Pea). George Thomas Austen jnr (1875–1947) continued the family business.

RA

AUSTRALASIAN (1864–1946), published weekly by proprietors of the Melbourne *Argus*, included an influential horticultural section. Formed by the merger of three weeklies, including the *Yeoman and Australian Acclimatiser* (1861–64), and later incorporating other titles, the paper was among the most prominent of the mainstream weeklies, which in many ways substituted in the colonies for GARDEN MAGAZINES. Essentially a digest of news and entertainment aimed partly at rural readers, the *Australasian* achieved influence outside its colonial borders, was noted for its detailed reporting, and was often quoted by rivals and kindred journals. Horticultural editors included Frederick SEARCH (commenced 1871), Joseph HARRIS (commenced 1885), Emily GIBSON (née Grassick) (1924–46). During the 1880s, William SANGSTER (as 'Hortensis') contributed a series of significant commentaries on leading Victorian gardens, which sat alongside seasonal gardening advice, reviews of the nursery trade, news of horticultural shows and events (often extracted from overseas journals), and trade advertisements. In 1946 the paper became the popular magazine *Australasian Post*, beloved of barbers' shops and schoolboy lockers but devoid of the highly respected horticultural journalism of previous decades.

RA

AUSTRALASIAN ASSOCIATION FOR THE ADVANCEMENT OF SCIENCE: see AUSTRALIAN AND NEW ZEALAND ASSOCIATION FOR THE ADVANCEMENT OF SCIENCE

AUSTRALASIAN NURSERYMAN, SEEDSMAN AND FLORIST: see AUSTRALIAN HORTICULTURE

AUSTRALIA Introduction In 1859, English naturalist Alfred Russel Wallace (1823–1913) drew the famous line that separated the Australian biological realm from the rest of the world, but it took another hundred years before it was understood why Australian stood apart: tectonic forces had contrived a 'second creation'. The gradual breakup of the supercontinent GONDWANA occurred more than 150 million years ago when India, South America, Africa, and Australia left their stationary south-pole mother, Antarctica, and successively drifted northwards. Unlike the other southern continents, Australia remained largely isolated from the rest of the world for most of its northward journey, providing a unique environment where evolution could forge an extraordinary diversity of endemic AUSTRALIAN FLORA and fauna that was later to astonish and perplex Europeans.

During the northward passage, Australia entered an enormously long period of geological quiescence. Vulcanism and associated basaltic flows were the exception rather than the rule. No great mountain chains were built until the leading edge of the continent collided, some 15 million years ago, with South-East Asia to form the fecund archipelago of the Spice Islands and New Guinea. The absence of great mountains starved rivers of great flows, and flat Australia was little affected by glaciers during global ice ages. Without great rivers, glaciers, and volcanoes to rejuvenate landscapes, many Australian SOILS become so deeply weathered that the distinction between rock and soil has become blurred. These deep, old soils trapped an enormous tonnage of salt, deposited in trace quantities by rain over millions of years, to create a time bomb that was detonated by the reckless land clearing and profligate IRRIGATION that followed European settlement.

Australia now straddles the horse latitudes, its CLIMATE dominated by the SUBTROPICAL high-pressure system—a great planetary-sized anticyclone of dry, sinking air. It is thought that the formation of the Antarctic ice sheet about 20 million years ago caused the subtropical high-pressure system to intensify in strength and gradually dry out the continent, from the south to the north, parching the mantle of lush Gondwanan forests and swamps. The high also introduced a new and powerful evolutionary force: landscape FIRE. Scattered throughout modern Australia are relictual habitats, such as RAINFORESTS, that failed to adapt to the recurrent fires that became a characteristic feature of the ENVIRONMENT.

The subtropical high not only gives southern Australia long, blue summer days but also drives terrifying bushfires with fierce, oven-dry north-westerly winds. In the winter months the high provides the steady, dry south-easterly trade winds that desiccate the monsoon-soaked northern Australian savannahs, with resultant annual fires. This climatic system has made Australia the driest and most fire-prone continent on Earth. At least 40 000 years ago—perhaps 60 000—Aboriginal peoples colonised a continent that was already ablaze; the triumph of these colonists was in harnessing landscape fire to make the environment more productive: a process aptly called 'fire-stick' farming.

Australia's environmental history can seem harsh to those raised with Northern Hemisphere environmental sensibilities. At first, many settler-Australians did their best to create gardens and landscapes that denied their ancient continent's apparent stoicism. With time, however, increasing numbers are coming to see beyond the drab 'bush', and to perceive landscapes that house many of Nature's great masterpieces. Increasing pride in the biological heritage of the insular continent they call home is manifest in many NATIONAL PARKS, gardens, and preserved wild lands that so enrich modern Australian landscapes. DAVID BOWMAN

1788–1840 The farm at Farm Cove and the garden at (First) GOVERNMENT HOUSE, Sydney Cove, were established soon after the founding of the colony of NEW SOUTH WALES (1788). This followed the Pacific *Endeavour* voyage of Cook (1768–71), whose exploration aided botanical science through the collaboration of botanists Joseph BANKS and Daniel SOLANDER, and artist Sydney PARKINSON. The later French expedition of d'Entrecasteaux (1791–93) with botanist LABILLLARDIÈRE, and the British *Investigator* expedition of Flinders (1801–03) with botanist Robert BROWN and artist Ferdinand BAUER, consolidated an era of taxonomic classification by the participants, and also botanists such as J.E. SMITH working at 'home'. The antipodean discoveries promoted an enthusiasm for horticultural use of AUSTRALIAN FLORA in the GREENHOUSES and hot houses of Europe, and left a magnificent legacy of BOTANICAL ILLUSTRATION, especially in monographs and periodicals such as CURTIS's *Botanical Magazine*. The influence of Banks also extended to resident plant collectors in the colony (David BURTON, CALEY, GOOD), and his support for the likes of SUTTOR and Allan CUNNINGHAM.

While the rectilinear plots at Farm Cove (now the ROYAL BOTANIC GARDENS, SYDNEY) were for food production, the Government House garden was not entirely utilitarian. In it grew many of the first introductions to Australia of exotic ornamental plants and trees. Its simple, rectilinear plots were roughly symmetrical about a central path that led to the shore of the cove. Hardly to be described as FORMAL, it was the rude antipodean counterpart of thousands of anonymous cottage and farmstead gardens in England: part KITCHEN GARDEN, part ornamental garden, too small and unsophisticated to be touched by the eighteenth-century taste for LANDSCAPE GARDENING. Yet it soon developed a colonial character as its giant bamboo, araucarias, oaks, and *Pinus pinea* (Stone Pine) matured. This symmetrical, rectilinear form and distinctive planting continued throughout the early colonial period: at first for the majority of substantial houses, later for remote HOMESTEADS, and for COTTAGES. The finest surviving example of such a layout is at ROUSE HILL ESTATE (NSW), of the early 1820s.

Increases in population, wealth, and sophistication—not only in NSW, but in Van Diemen's Land (TASMANIA) and the Swan River Colony (WESTERN AUSTRALIA)—brought changes in aesthetic attitudes. The artist and traveller's appreciation of the picturesqueness or SUBLIMITY of native scenery was seldom translated into gardening by the settler, however well informed, who was struggling against the wilderness. J.C. LOUDON realised this when, in the *Suburban Gardener and Villa Companion* (1838), he wrote a section on the 'Geometrical Style' suited to 'wild or unenclosed country':

The suitableness of this style for a country in a wild state must, we think, be obvious to every unprejudiced mind, from the contrast which its clearly defined lines and forms afford

Australia

Australia

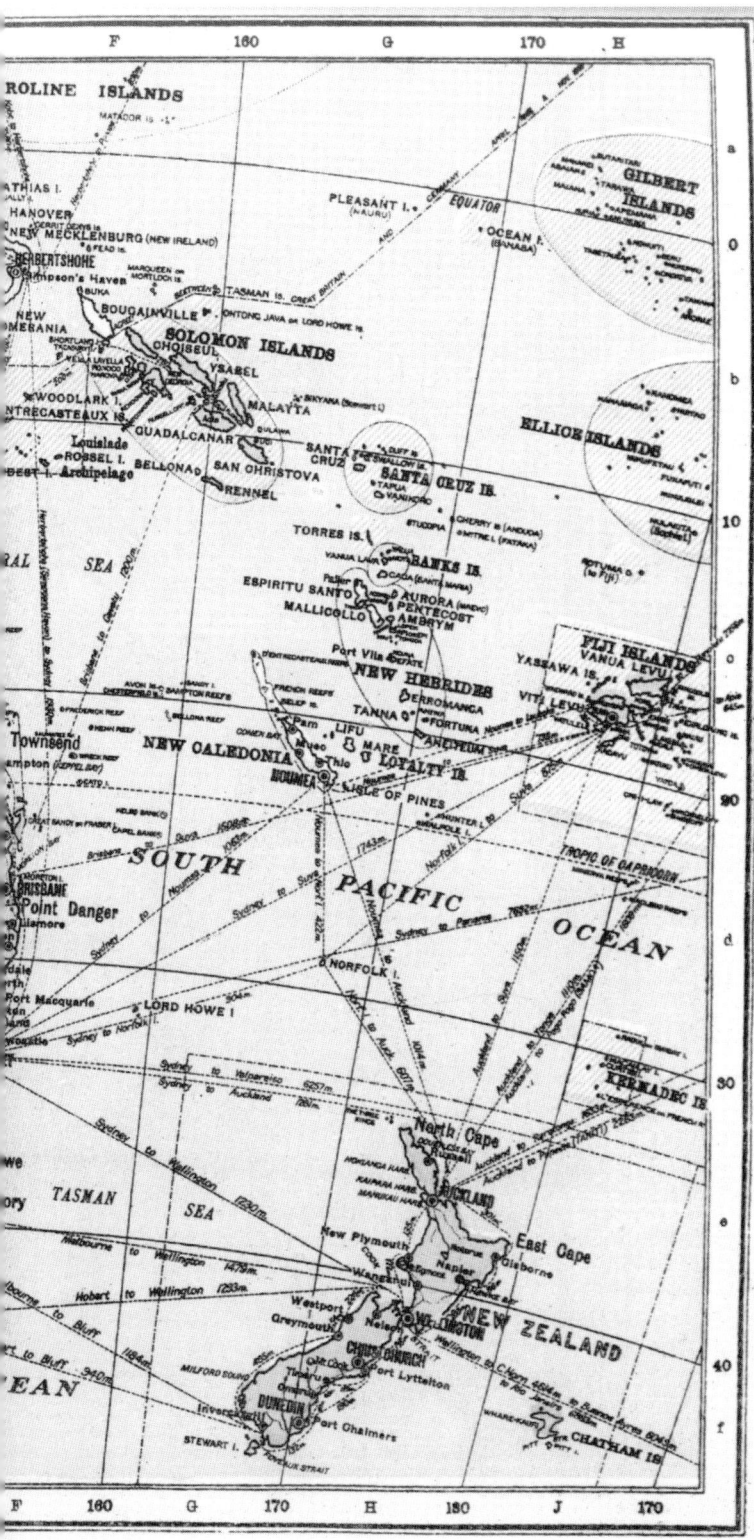

Map of Australia distributed in a handbook to members of the 1914 Australian Meeting of the British Association for the Advancement of Science: when the First World War broke out many delegates were en route aboard ship, and the legend depicting a pink tone for 'British Possessions' and a striped tone for 'Sphere of Influence' assumed heightened significance

Australia

GOVERNMENT HOUSE, NSW (1792), depicted by the Port Jackson Painter: the house overlooked Sydney Cove and for a time its garden, shown here with a walled forecourt and clearly delineated garden beds, was the most sophisticated in Australia

to the irregularity of the surrounding scenery, and from the obvious expression of art and refinement ... [it is therefore calculated] ... to suit newly peopled, and thinly inhabited countries, such as the back settlements of America or Australia.

Thus the rectilinear form persisted in remote areas not only through economic necessity but as a means of subduing the new landscape. Contemporary English fashions in gardening—the PICTURESQUE followed by the GARDENESQUE—were adapted in the towns and their settled districts. In 1810 Elizabeth Macquarie, wife of Governor Macquarie, cleared away what remained of the old garden at Government House, developing it and the Government DOMAIN to accord with her romantic view of Sydney's harbour. Winding walks and drives were constructed around the point and foreshore, and the native landscape's picturesqueness was heightened by the romantic associationism of the Gothick follies she contrived: the government stables, Fort Phillip, and Fort Macquarie. It was a landscape now so domesticated that exotic notes could be added in the form of kangaroos and emus.

Mrs Macquarie's improvements were little emulated. There were still, in the late 1810s and early 1820s, few colonists with the means, taste, and will to do so. Most notably, Captain John Piper built his 'marine villa', Henrietta Villa at Point Piper, with smooth lawns reaching to the bay's edge. Others, such as Alexander Riley of Raby or Sir John JAMISON of Regentville, gave token consideration to fashion by surrounding their carriage sweeps with contoured fences, contrasting with the surrounding roughly or clear-felled paddocks wrested from the BUSH. The ideas of Humphry REPTON were clearly more appropriate to the colonial situation than that of Lancelot 'Capability' BROWN, archetype of the English landscape school promoters (although Brown's name continued to be evoked in reference to landscape gardening of a generally informal or picturesque manner).

The 1820s formed a decade of consolidation. Society was changing from a military to a civil establishment and pastoral wealth was being created. PLANT COLLECTING and plant introductions continued, notably with the Government Botanists Charles FRASER and Allan CUNNINGHAM. Advances were made in VITICULTURE, especially after the arrival of James BUSBY in 1824, but ornamental gardening was of little import until the late 1820s when the increase in immigrant civil servants, and the official granting of 'VILLA allotments' brought a new impetus to the making of gardens.

In the 1830s the colony had a confident, affluent society ready to distinguish itself through its houses and gardens. Foremost, as leaders in society, in taste, and in horticultural science, were Colonial Secretary Alexander McLEAY and leading pastoralist William MACARTHUR. Their gardens at Elizabeth Bay and Brownlow Hill (developed under the superintendence of Robert HENDERSON) and at Camden Park set a standard of design and horticultural expertise that few colonists could hope to achieve, though several tried. More followed in seeking social status through their gardens.

McLeay and Macarthur's botanical and horticultural reputations were wholly grounded in the dominant garden fashion of the 1830s, the Gardenesque—largely formulated in England by their acquaintance and fellow Scot, John

Claudius Loudon. It could have had no better promoters in the colony. Camden Park remains the finest (and largest) garden of the 1830s in NSW. The ARCHER family in Van Diemen's Land set a similar standard in horticulture and garden making. Other colonists of standing, such as the proprietors of the villas on Sydney's Woolloomooloo Hill, or Archibald Windeyer of Kinross, Raymond Terrace (NSW), planned their ideal gardens, with professional advice, but the disastrous financial depression of the early 1840s caused many schemes to be unrealised or curtailed.

Following a system of land grants, introduction of more democratic modes of LAND SURVEY AND SALE by colonial governments expanded the security given by freehold tenure in both rural and urban areas. This security was marked by a period of house and garden making in the earliest colonies. Smaller gardens continued to be simply geometric and symmetrical, but the character of the gardens in the Sydney region was defined by their planting: spires of ARAUCARIAS (Norfolk Island Pine and Hoop Pine, and later, Bunya Pine), the dense masses of native FIGS, and rich combinations of plants from Europe, the Cape, China, and the Americas.

Of the professional gardeners, nursery proprietor Thomas SHEPHERD is the best known because of his published *Lectures on the Horticulture of New South Wales* (1835) and *Lectures on Landscape Gardening in Australia* (1836). Shepherd's Darling Nursery in Sydney was a major source of plants for colonial kitchen and ornamental gardens, but his influence on garden design is less evident. His sensible guidance on the deployment and thinning of native trees in the landscape—his most original contribution—may have been followed, after his death, in landscapes such as FERNHILL, Mulgoa (NSW), of the early 1840s. Gifted individuals such as John THOMPSON and Ronald GUNN assisted in the progress of horticulture, landscape design, and botany in the new colonies. The NURSERY trade remained modest in scale, although dynastic family businesses such as those of the Thomas Shepherd and Hobart's LIPSCOMBE family set a pattern that was repeated in neighbouring colonies by later generations of nursery proprietors and seed merchants.

In the public domain, open space was largely restricted to a handful of urban SQUARES—with the notable exception of Sydney's HYDE PARK—and reservation and development of PUBLIC PARKS AND GARDENS had to wait for government action in succeeding decades.   JAMES BROADBENT

1840–90 This period saw the new colonies of SOUTH AUSTRALIA (1836), VICTORIA (1851), and QUEENSLAND (1859) established in climatically different parts of the continent at a time when newly 'discovered' plants from CHINA, JAPAN, the PACIFIC, and the AMERICAS were increasingly becoming available in commercial nurseries. After the discovery of gold during the 1850s, many new nurseries were established in Australia. These included ANDERSON, FERGUSON, and YATES (NSW); GILES, HACKETT, and McEWIN (SA); HOCKINGS (Qld); CRESWELL, CHANDLER, and DICKINSON (Tas.); ADAMSON, BRUNNING, T.C. COLE, Joseph HARRIS, LANG, LAW, SOMNER AND CO., RULE, John SMITH, and TAYLOR AND SANGSTER (Vic.). These nursery proprietors were not only responsible for introducing the discoveries of PLANT COLLECTORS from English and European nurseries: some, like Michael GUILFOYLE and BAPTIST of Sydney, employed their own collectors in the Pacific.

Wealthy individuals also contributed to the availability of exotic plants. Among these were William MACARTHUR of Camden Park (NSW), and Hugh Glass of Flemington House and Charles Ryan of Derriweit at MOUNT MACEDON (Vic.). People of means also engaged landscape designers such as Michael Guilfoyle, Taylor and Sangster, and Edward La Trobe BATEMAN, whose patrons included the wool barons of Victoria's WESTERN DISTRICT and Melbourne's new professional and mercantile classes. The inspiration for these colonial gardens was J.C. LOUDON's book *The Suburban Gardener and Villa Companion* (1838), and his *Gardenesque*, rather than the British landed estate. An exception was MURNDAL, an Anglo–Irish demesne transported to western Vic. A more utilitarian approach to estate planning was adopted by squatters of Scottish origin, who established linear PLANTATIONS (colloquially known as WINDBREAKS) to protect their livestock.

In the cities the public popularity of gardening was paralleled by the rise of the reading public. In England the writings of Loudon and his wife Jane, Edward KEMP, Charles McINTOSH, and Joseph PAXTON helped popularise horticulture. In Australia, writers such as William CLARSON and James SINCLAIR in Vic., Queensland acclimatiser L.A. BERNAYS, and Louisa MEREDITH and William WOOLLS (who extolled the virtues of indigenous plants and landscapes in the NSW press) catered for middle-class readers who had emigrated from ENGLAND, SCOTLAND, IRELAND, and GERMANY during the gold rushes. Knowledge about colonial horticulture was also disseminated through the lecture programs and exhibitions of HORTICULTURAL SOCIETIES. At the same time, F.M. BAILEY, Joseph MAIDEN, Ferdinand MUELLER, and Richard SCHOMBURGK increased public knowledge of AUSTRALIAN FLORA through their systematic description of the continent's flora, press writings, and evidence given to Royal Commissions. Nevertheless, the celebrated dismissal of Mueller from the Melbourne Gardens might be read as a cautionary tale of how in the colonies the utility of science needed to be artfully dressed. During the 1860s Charles MOORE of the Sydney Botanic Gardens paid attention to this requirement by refashioning the Sydney Gardens in a PICTURESQUE manner, while the BRISBANE BOTANIC GARDENS, under Walter HILL, became noted for trialling plants economically useful to the northern colony. In these circumstances, the colonial botanic garden became an EXPERIMENTAL GARDEN. Through the scientific and imperial networks of BOTANIC GARDENS, local and imported seeds and plants were widely disseminated.

ACCLIMATISATION influenced other aspects of colonial horticulture. Select Committees of colonial parliaments reported on ways that plant introductions from MEDITERRANEAN countries might generate new industries among those who had taken up land under the Selection Acts. As a consequence, mulberries (*Morus nigra*), olives (*Olea europaea*), and cork oaks (*Quercus suber*) attracted the interest of colonial officials. So too did FORESTRY, with the likes of Mueller and William FERGUSON in Vic., and John Ednie BROWN in SA widely distributing timber trees (including North American pines) in order to understand what might be grown where.

In time, the English horticultural styles and fashions of the subtropical, the FERN craze, the PINETUM, and pattern-book picturesque and Gardenesque were adapted to suit colonial climatic conditions. For instance, in Australia the planting of FIGS (*Ficus* spp.), PALMS, aloes, and other SUCCULENTS, advocated by William ROBINSON in *The Subtropical Garden* (1871), created subtropical landscapes unobtainable in northern European winters. Similarly, the Victorian craze for ferns became something grander in the colonies. Here the ideal landscape of the natural fern gully was recreated, not in European glasshouses, but in the open air, or in shade or BUSH-HOUSES derived from European gardening in India. Transformations also occurred in the pinetum, a gardening feature popularised in Britain during the 1830s. A fashion took hold in the southern colonies from the 1850s to the 1880s; in the 1870s and 1880s for instance, John RADDENBERRY planted an extensive pinetum to protect GEELONG BOTANIC GARDENS from sea gales. However, as the use of deciduous trees increased, the pinetum became little more than a line of Pines (*Pinus* spp.) pushed to the perimeter of the garden.

Likewise in the colonies a LAKE, if it continued to exist during drought, not only mimicked European theories of the picturesque but also provided respite from the Australian summer. In such conditions, often only the very wealthy could command a permanent source of water. As a consequence, much colonial gardening practised dry (or XERIC) gardening. These conditions meant other parts of the Empire influenced Australian gardening. For example, the plants of the CAPE PROVINCE suited dry Australian conditions, just as the Indian HILL-STATION inspired Australian counterparts.

Over time, Australian gardening became a fusion of what had been tried and tested in local climatic conditions and the imaginings of many places. These utilitarian, ornamental, and geographic understandings influenced the development of Melbourne Botanic Gardens under William GUILFOYLE. Appointed in 1873, Guilfoyle was simultaneously frontiersman come to the imperial capital, plant hunter on imperial voyaging to the Pacific, and writer whose father was both a garden designer and nursery proprietor. In these Gardens, colonial experience and high-Victorian fashion fused to re-create a gardener's physical and metaphysical navigation of the globe, where the cultivated colonial clearing merged with the elemental forces of nature found on the frontier, and where Australian experience overlapped effortlessly with overseas worlds to create a voluptuous and highly orchestrated gardening ensemble. This bold and sophisticated reading of the colonial contrasted with the trial-and-error experiments of earlier colonial gardening.   PAUL FOX

During the mid-to-late nineteenth century, CONIFERS, particularly ARAUCARIAS such as the Hoop, Bunya and Norfolk Island pines, became dominant specimen trees in AUSTRALIA, their bold silhouette often complemented by rich planting of SHRUBBERIES

1890–1918 This is often described as the Federation period, leading up to and following the union of the colonies into the Commonwealth of Australia (1901). The 1890s was generally a time of economic depression, when a more egalitarian society saw a trend away from the excesses of the land boom of the eastern colonies, although the same period saw an economic boom in WESTERN AUSTRALIA following gold discoveries at Kalgoorlie and Coolgardie.

The 1890s saw late stirrings of the GARDENESQUE, conveyed to new audiences by mainstream Australian GARDEN BOOKS such as *The Australian Gardener* of ADAMSON and BRUNNING, and William ELLIOTT's *Australasian Gardening and Domestic Floriculture* (1897). In the nursery trade, the businesses of the first generation of gold-rush migrants were transferred to the next generation or formed into proprietary limited companies and transferred to business syndicates. Many, such as NOBELIUS (Vic.) and KEMP (SA), moved or established nurseries on the periphery of capital cities, and were expanded to cater for an increase in SUBURBAN GARDENS on quarter-acre blocks. In NSW and Vic. particularly, the depression of the 1890s forced many property owners to subdivide their estates for housing. This, combined with growing population and greatly expanded public transport networks, led to the suburbanisation of Australia's major cities. With an increase in suburban gardens came a corresponding increase in home gardening. The newly egalitarian style of gardening saw a rise in plant specialisation, with DAHLIAS, CHRYSANTHEMUMS, SWEET PEAS, and CARNATIONS coming to the fore, joining the ever-popular ROSE. Specialist nurseries such as those of POCKETT, ROSSI, and BRUNDRETT catered for these enthusiasms, and a great increase in horticultural societies and shows reflected both new specialities and increased suburban activity. New public parks and gardens, especially in capital cities, catered for suburban expansion, but there was consolidation or even stasis in botanic gardens after long and influential directorships by Mueller and Guilfoyle (Melbourne), Moore (Sydney), Schomburgk (Adelaide), Newman and Abbot (Hobart), and MacMahon (Brisbane). Financial cutbacks restricted many botanic gardens, although in NSW the Gardens' Director, J.H. MAIDEN, was particularly influential, especially in his promotion of native FIGS and exotic PALMS to give Sydney a tropical look.

By the end of the Federation period, several technological developments were having a profound effect on garden design. The LAWN MOWER had been refined and was available to a much wider public. The rubber garden HOSE was also much more readily available, and the hose and the mower combined to change the character of our gardens. Buffalo and couch lawns began to occupy more space, and shrubberies and rosaries were increasingly relegated to perimeter beds. Although high cost prevented widespread ownership of cars before the First World War, side driveways had already started to appear, and the motor shed or garage was first featured in garden plans. Popular features of gardens were the LICH-GATE (front) and BUSH-HOUSE (back and sides), while palms and ROCKERIES, both popular in the mid-nineteenth century, gained new favour. The English writings of Gertrude JEKYLL sat alongside female Australian voices such as 'Mrs Rolf BOLDREWOOD' and Mrs Arthur TUCKETT, and standard horticultural works were joined in 1895 by the popular and influential Sydney-based *Yates' Garden Guide*.

The new nationalism encouraged publishers to seek an Australia-wide audience for garden magazines, although long distances, a modest advertising base, and relatively small populations outside the south-east of the continent conspired to thwart such ambitions until the 1920s. The *JOURNAL OF HORTICULTURE* (1906) and *BUILDING* (1907) became prototypes of the new national journal, while the *HOME GARDENER* (1917) prospered and paved the way for successors.

Leading designers including Guilfoyle and Sangster maintained a lingering influence, but stirrings of new voices—such as those of C. Bogue LUFFMANN and Walter BAGOT—began to be heard. A search for appropriate Australian styles in art, architecture, gardening, and literature saw Australia's CLIMATE and the BUSH in a new light. The use of ornamental motifs inspired by AUSTRALIAN FLORA and fauna increased in response to the prevailing sentiments of nationalism, but at the same time a wider international search for comparable climates and design models took place. Much of this was directed towards the MEDITERRANEAN and the new ideas emerging from England and NORTH AMERICA. These ideas affected both horticulture and garden design. In horticulture, the introduction of IRRIGATION settlements in arid zones, a great increase in plant breeding, and advances in entomology and the use of chemicals profoundly changed the reliance on empirical methods handed down from older generations. In garden and landscape design, a renewed emphasis on town planning—especially through the GARDEN CITY and CITY BEAUTIFUL movements and the work of John SULMAN and Charles READE—brought new ideas to public and private spaces. Enlightened planners sought to move away from the crowded row housing of Victorian times and to create developments that separated industrial, commercial, and residential areas and included tree-lined streets and parks. At a more rarefied level, the ARTS AND CRAFTS movement attracted ARCHITECTS, who linked house and garden in a complementary design. This relatively formal style, in which the garden was divided into 'rooms', stood in contrast to the informal or NATURAL style articulated in Luffmann's *Principles of Gardening for Australia* (1903).

The new century brought a new climate of professionalism in horticulture and allied disciplines. The Victorian government established the BURNLEY School of Horticulture in 1891, and with the charismatic Bogue Luffmann as principal (1897–1907) the school soon attracted a wide range of students, including many young women (for whom the Great War had provided new opportunities). Inauguration of the AUSTRALASIAN ASSOCIATION FOR THE ADVANCEMENT OF SCIENCE, the first university chairs of botany at Melbourne (1905) and Sydney (1913), the work of Maiden and R.T. BAKER at the Sydney Technological Museum, and the fruition of research and publication by F.M. BAILEY and others within botanic gardens and herbaria, placed BOTANY on a sound academic footing. The rise of professional

Australia

Detail of a 1911 cartoon from the *Victorian Architectural Students Society Journal* providing a rich parody of the contemporary fascination in AUSTRALIA for the ARTS AND CRAFTS movement in both architecture and garden design

FORESTRY was symbolised by C.E. LANE POOLE, whose approach strongly contrasted with predecessors such as J.E. BROWN. Many government agricultural departments were created late in the nineteenth century, and they built on a scientific approach, represented by appointment of trained entomologists, plant pathologists, and horticultural experts (such as Fred TURNER and E.E. PESCOTT), and the publication of journals bringing agricultural and horticultural advances to those in the field. A strong amateur and commercial tradition was maintained in plant breeding, however—as epitomised by Alister CLARK and by the work of many nursery proprietors.

Although dual patriotic and nationalistic sentiments pervaded the Federation period, nationalism was marked by a rise of interest in the Australian flora, not only for DECORATIVE ARTS, FLORAL EMBLEMS, and horticulture, but for its conservation *in situ*. The annual celebration of WATTLE DAY was one specific manifestation of this interest, but the work of FIELD NATURALISTS' CLUBS and their key supporters, especially in advocacy for NATIONAL PARKS and nature conservation, provided a more general platform for future generations. If the 1890s marked the rise of Federationist sentiment, the selection of Canberra as the site of the new federal capital was its most potent symbol. The AUSTRALIAN CAPITAL TERRITORY, with the GRIFFINS' plan and Charles WESTON's planting, gave great promise as a combination of the threads that had been developing during two decades.

CHRIS BETTERIDGE

1918–45 Urbanisation of Australia's capital cities escalated following the First World War, and TOWN PLANNING became an imperative, now seized by commercial developers and heralding much work by local government. Early voices—for example SULMAN's—were joined by those of others such as J.W. BARRETT (Vic.) and Carl KLEM and William BOLD (WA). Concern for unhealthy living conditions in inner-city areas activated middle-class reformers to establish PUBLIC PARKS and a PLAYGROUNDS movement, promoting fitness and educational programs for the MORAL IMPROVEMENT of the young. By the 1920s these concepts and new building regulations brought an end to the construction of the terrace house. In an atmosphere where improved transport—largely through the electrification of suburban railway networks and increasing car ownership—supported rapid suburban growth, the ideal of 'ample yard space, front and back' became a national aspiration.

Increasing space in GARDEN BOOKS was allocated to the planning of the garden, and the 1916 edition of BRUNNING's *Australian Gardener* claimed to be its first written 'solely for the Home Gardener'. E.E. PESCOTT's *Gardening in Australia* (1926) included schemes for the design of the SUBURBAN GARDEN, and many were given in the pages of GARDEN MAGAZINES. National garden magazines reached a critical mass in circulation, led by AUSTRALIAN HOME BEAUTIFUL (monthly from 1925) and AUSTRALIAN GARDEN LOVER (1925). Smaller journals such as SOUTH AUSTRALIAN HOMES AND GARDENS (1931) and WEST AUSTRALIAN GARDENER

(1932) catered for a local audience, but state-based weekly newspapers—a traditional source of horticultural advice—declined. The predominant image portrayed during the inter-war period was one derived from the late GARDENESQUE style of the Federation period: curved drives led to neat bungalows, flower beds were sharply cut into the smooth green turf, standard roses marched toward the front steps, and trim cypresses and pergolas gave height to the garden. The BUSH-HOUSE enjoyed great popularity, and the plants it contained were often also popular garden subjects—particularly PALMS as feature plants. The back garden was both functional and productive, with Gilbert TOYNE's development of the rotary clothes hoist (patented 1923) paving the way for the Hill's hoist heist of the Australian BACKYARD.

Major new nurseries rose to cater for the suburban demand. Specialists sprang up in all directions and operated from pocket-handkerchief sites, and major new players such as HAZLEWOOD and RIMINGTON gained custom at the expense of older establishments. The NURSERY trade consolidated and developed a unified voice through trade associations and FESTIVALS such as Melbourne's Garden Week. Trees and shrubs increasingly came to dominate gardens, promoted by writers such as Edna WALLING, Harold SARGEANT, and later Ernest LORD, and at the expense of FLORICULTURE, though certainly not causing its demise. Key horticultural specialists and popularisers included Alister CLARK (roses), E.G. WATERHOUSE (camellias), and Russell GRIMWADE (eucalypts). G.K. COWLISHAW and W.A. COMEADOW typified the energetic figureheads who knowledgeably presided over the major HORTICULTURAL SOCIETIES, which experienced record growth in and after the austere years of the Second World War. RADIO broadcasting began in the mid-1920s, and its dissemination of horticultural and gardening information reached great heights of popularity during the 1940s.

The link between CLIMATE and architecture was soon extended to garden and landscape design. Looking to the MEDITERRANEAN, William Hardy WILSON surrounded his neo-Georgian houses with gardens based on his romanticised image of colonial gardens in the Sydney region. The Spanish Mission style of architecture called for simplicity of planting but often maintained existing trees (typically EUCALYPTS), and included paths of crazy paving and rockeries planted with succulents including CACTI—plants that became increasingly popular during the 1930s. Leading garden designer Jocelyn BROWN, writing in Sydney's fashionable *HOME* magazine, and architects such as Leslie WILKINSON and Walter BAGOT, advocated gardens that were a fusion of the formal English garden with the ITALIANATE. The work of Walter BUTLER and Harold DESBROWE-ANNEAR continued the strong input of architects in garden design, just as landscaper Paul SORENSON, based in the Blue Mountains, brought an architectonic quality to gardens, notably at EVERGLADES, his signature work. MODERNISM came slowly to Australian gardens, but Olive MELLOR could comment that both Spanish Mission and the severe lines of the 'modern' required trees of a 'stately character for their enhancement'.

The influence of women designers and horticulturists came to the fore in the period between the wars. Walling (initially through her *Australian Home Beautiful* articles, later through her books, and by word of mouth from admirers), Betty BEGG and Mollie Shannon (through *Australian Garden Lover* articles), Jocelyn Brown, Olive MELLOR, Elsie CORNISH, and Emily GIBSON all made significant contributions to garden design, while Jean GALBRAITH's horticultural advocacy for AUSTRALIAN FLORA was unmatched for its duration or eloquence.

The horticultural use of Australian plants was given a considerable boost in the 1930s by the establishment of specialist nurseries. ALTHOFER, ASHBY, BURDETT, and PARRY all provided plants, while cultural advice from their catalogues was supplemented by the writings of Thistle HARRIS and increasingly frequent articles in garden magazines. This built on the advocacy and legacy of botanic gardens directors, FIELD NATURALISTS, and others such as the GRIFFINS, whose passionate regard for social, aesthetic, and environmental ideals underpinned development (best seen at CASTLECRAG) in which nature and structure interplayed. The Griffins' love of Australian plants mirrored a change in societal attitudes, with artists such as Margaret Preston promoting a national art based on the Australian environment. Whether personal taste ran to native or exotic, *Australian Gardening of To-Day* (1943) encapsulated prevailing horticultural attitudes among gardeners on the cusp of momentous societal change, 'a reminder of the better things of life which even war cannot take from us'.

COLLEEN MORRIS

1945–65 Australia emerged from the anxiety, distress and turmoil of the Second World War faced with overwhelming social change—a major housing shortage, a chronic lack of building materials, and a surge of immigration that would change the size and composition of the population.

Australia's gardening heritage was of mixed lineage. Individuals included established design practitioners (such as WALLING, SORENSEN, Jocelyn BROWN, MELLOR); plant experts (WATERHOUSE, A.S. THOMAS, HARRIS); popular commentators (E.E. LORD, R.G. EDWARDS, HURLEY); and established plant nursery proprietors (NOBELIUS, HAZLEWOOD). These leaders found themselves responding to wide-ranging demand: a plant enthusiast in search of a rare, newly imported CAMELLIA, a young couple looking for a sturdy shrub to suit their new FRONT GARDEN.

These dual forces continue to characterise—and enliven—Australian gardening. But then as now, the largest and most influential component was the general public. Traditionally, most Australians had made and maintained their own gardens, often with help from the long-established mass-market publications from YATES or BRUNNING. The post-war building boom fuelled this do-it-yourself trend. Little information was to be gleaned from PUBLIC PARKS AND GARDENS, which were moving from a horticultural to a recreational emphasis. Looking for guidance and information, gardeners turned to the nearest available expert.

This person could be found in the pages of newspapers, books, and specialist magazines such as *AUSTRALIAN HOME*

Wartime gardening in Australia during the Second World War provided a point of demarcation between the rich horticultural traditions of the inter-war period and the post-war trend towards garden design suited to leisure and recreation

BEAUTIFUL (where Edna Walling's column now promoted AUSTRALIAN PLANTS to home gardeners even as she continued designing large gardens for the wealthy), AUSTRALIAN GARDEN LOVER, or YOUR GARDEN. Lord's *Shrubs and Trees for Australian Gardens* (1948), the classic and enduring reference work of the era, anticipated the change from the comparatively stark gardens of the 1920s and 1930s to gardens of greater horticultural variety. This variety was fostered by individuals such as Peter VALDER at Nooroo, or the CHANDLERS at their nursery at Olinda (Vic.), who brought in interesting plants from around the world.

A further source of expert advice was the local nursery proprietor. After the war many hobbyist plantgrowers, some of them returned servicemen and some with a specialty—azaleas or camellias, for example—set up business around their homes in outer suburbs. They were growers first, retailers second. They provided information and garden advice, even plants free of charge (mostly to impecunious young couples building their first home), and delivered both small and substantial orders. Thousands of seedlings at a time went to designer gardens; a few roses and fruit trees (including a lemon), several shrubs, and a few flower and vegetable seedlings to the owner-built houses in the new suburbs. The housing shortage remained acute and in NSW, more than half the new houses begun in 1952 were owner-built. The result was parallel demand in the nursery industry.

In Eltham (Vic.) the materials shortage spawned the mud-brick movement and the regional, NATURALISTIC style of house and garden exemplified by the work of Alistair KNOX, Ellis STONES, and Gordon FORD. Generally around Australia the twin influences of modernism and local materials made for innovative, trend-setting design. Architect Harry Seidler's uncompromisingly modern house for his parents in Turramurra, Sydney (1948–50), sat in a landscape of low stone walls and sweeping expanses of lawn and gravel (to which his mother added fruit trees, eccentric rockeries, beds of annuals, and vegetables). Peter Muller's Whale Beach house (1954–55) was interpolated into natural bush: a rock outcrop became part of the living room and tree branches were threaded through holes in the roof. Karl LANGER's garden in St Lucia, Qld (1958), was designed with Australian trees and shrubs, and used new techniques such as mulching.

After decades of inactivity, the 1950s saw experimentation and new introductions for native plants. In Vic., Jean GALBRAITH built on the pioneering work of Thistle HARRIS of the late 1930s to produce a guide to local wildflowers (1950) that made information about these plants accessible to gardeners with some expertise; Winifred CURTIS did similar work in Tas. In home gardens, *Grevillea rosmarinifolia* might be seen growing near *Prunus* 'Elvins' (raised in Melbourne in the mid-1950s), a Nellie Kelly passionfruit (also locally raised), and the omnipresent 'Peace' rose—but technical knowledge about native plants was lacking. Melbourne *Age* columnist Peter ALSTON was besieged annually by upset readers who had bought pots of sweet-smelling *Boronia megastigma* and had found out the hard way that this plant needed to be kept damp to survive. In 1957 A.J. SWABY, backed by E.E. Lord, founded the SOCIETY FOR GROWING AUSTRALIAN PLANTS with the theme of preservation by cultivation, attracting thousands of members around the nation. (At the same time the NATIONAL ROSE SOCIETIES and the Australian Camellia Research Society had keen memberships, local HORTICULTURAL SOCIETIES were booming, and in 1953, 30 000 people attended Melbourne's 'Coronation Garden Week'.) Native plants were a major feature at PARRY's Floralands (NSW) and they comprised the whole stock of SCHUBERT in Melbourne and BODDY in Geelong. At the Forests Commission of Victoria's new Wimmera Forest Nursery at Wail, Alf GRAY acquired seed of suitable drought-resistant trees and shrubs from WA. He propagated it, selling the trees (including the spectacular *Eucalyptus torquata* and *E. macrocarpa*) to local farmers for WINDBREAKS—they wouldn't plant the local mallees, which they'd been pulling out for decades. The gorgeously flowering shrubs went to their wives, for their gardens.

After the war most nurseries bundled their plants in newspaper and grew seed and plants in recycled tins. But changes came quickly as Australia's population exploded. The first Victa motor mower appeared in 1953. Dried, pulverised manure came onto the market; seed and fertilisers became available in small bags instead of in bulk from the local grain store; BULBS—an industry developed in the late 1940s by Dutch migrants and led by Cees TESSELAAR—were also bagged. Chain stores began selling plants, but customers who needed advice about cultivation had to be sent round the corner to the nearest nursery. The end of the decade saw the advent of pressure-pack sprays and plastic pots, and of drive-in shopping centres.

The practical horticultural emphasis did not, however, negate inexorable growth in the landscape design profession. John STEVENS opened a design office in Melbourne in 1953 (and wrote a column for gardeners in the *Sun News-Pictorial*); John and Ray OLDHAM were active in Perth and Robin HILL and Alan CORREY in Adelaide—all executing public and city landscapes as well as private gardens. Stevens produced innovative designs informed by a MODERNIST's eye and a plantsman's sensibility ('you must come from that man Stevens', said Melbourne nursery proprietors when gardeners asked for yuccas, agaves, bamboos, *Nandina domestica*, or unusual perennials). With an informal Australian lifestyle similar to that of NORTH AMERICA, COURTYARDS, PATIOS, and BARBECUES proliferated, and in some circles outdoor paving became as important as indoor carpet. The American influence was pervasive, particularly through the writings of Thomas Church (*Gardens are for People*) and James Rose (*Creative Gardens*). Interested landscape professionals had to undertake study overseas; Mervyn DAVIS returned from England and in 1963 initiated moves for an AUSTRALIAN INSTITUTE OF LANDSCAPE ARCHITECTS. BURNLEY College had formalised its certificate course as a diploma of horticulture in 1958; the early 1960s saw tertiary landscape design courses introduced in Adelaide and Melbourne. When Merchant Builders, the fashionable new project home firm, was looking in 1965 for a garden designer to join its highly publicised team, the invitation went to Ellis STONES. He was one of a select group, including Bruce MACKENZIE and Peter GLASS, whose practical landscape achievement gained them AILA associateship.

Generous mentorship characterised Australian garden-making from 1945 to 1965. In Melbourne alone, Edna Walling encouraged Rodger ELLIOT to pursue his love of plants, and gave Ellis Stones and Eric HAMMOND their starts. Hammond's high profile, high standards, and construction expertise remain unsurpassed. His long-established organisation was a proving ground for people such as Glen WILSON and Elliot, as well as for innumerable garden builders who took what they learned onto landscape sites around Australia. Bernhard Schubert allowed Glen Wilson (also trained by Walling) to advertise in his nursery as a designer who used Australian plants. Gordon Ford acquired his plant knowledge from E.E. Lord and was taught landscape design by Ellis Stones. John TURNER and Emily GIBSON encouraged John Stevens in his early days of practice. In WA, Helena KING supported Jean VERSCHUER. As Australia's cities continued to spread, this was a fine foundation on which to build. Houses, freed from the constraints of earlier decades, were becoming larger, smarter, and more complex and allotment sizes were diminishing; but as the baby-boomers reached adulthood the demand for informed expertise in garden-making would continue unabated.

ANNE LATREILLE

1965–2000 This period saw an increase in the number of gardens and designed landscapes, and often a change in location. Freeways and infrastructure projects opened the way

Australia

The BUSH GARDEN movement gained momentum in AUSTRALIA during the 1960s and 70s and, as demonstrated in this Western Australian example, by the late twentieth century had reached a satisfying and complementary fusion of architectural and landscape design

for CARAVAN PARKS, CAR PARKS, RESORTS, and THEME PARKS in the commercial world, many new APARTMENTS AND RESIDENTIAL FLATS and other new forms of mass housing, and a new wave of UNIVERSITY CAMPUSES and other INSTITUTIONAL sites. These constructions posed new challenges that were met by the rise of LANDSCAPE ARCHITECTURE as both a discipline and a profession in Australia. Along with the burgeoning interest in landscape architecture came increased professionalism in ARBORICULTURE, HORTICULTURE, and garden management, reflected in the formation and growth of AUSTRALIAN INSTITUTE OF HORTICULTURE, AUSTRALIAN INSTITUTE OF LANDSCAPE ARCHITECTS, and PARKS AND LEISURE AUSTRALIA. In PUBLIC PARKS especially, there was a shift from old-style park management—under a superintendent with a horticultural focus—to recreation- and leisure-based PUBLIC OPEN SPACES with an increased number of smaller local parks, including linear parks and bicycle tracks. The previous gender imbalance in many of the professions disappeared, or was at least reduced.

Expanded opportunities for formal EDUCATION led to a remarkable rise in standards, from the previously conventional certificates and diplomas to higher degrees, from the early 1980s to the late 1990s. Even within horticulture, doctoral-level studies are now offered in environmental and nursery production horticulture. The widespread introduction of COMPUTERS, with capabilities including word processing, database management, drafting (CAD), and Internet access, revolutionised both education and information exchange. The scope of informal education increased tremendously within public open spaces, especially with the advent of FRIENDS GROUPS, volunteer guides, and special-interest groups associated with botanic gardens and parks. GARDEN BOOKS and MAGAZINES proliferated; they ranged from popular guides (increasingly linked to radio and television shows) to the worthy encyclopaedic volumes of Rodger ELLIOT, Roger SPENCER, Keith WILLIAMS, and John WRIGLEY.

Increased concern about chemicals, herbicides and pesticide use generally, and a heightened recognition of health and safety issues with chemical use in the industry, followed Rachel Carson's *Silent Spring*, which was published in 1962, just prior to the start of the period when DDT use was at its height. However, use of herbicides such as glyphosate, which is classed as a non-residual herbicide, increased to the point that landscape management, including natural area management, became dependent on its application to eradicate a wide range of weeds.

New BOTANIC GARDENS, especially gardens focusing on AUSTRALIAN FLORA, were opened during this period: they included KINGS PARK (1965), AUSTRALIAN NATIONAL BOTANIC GARDEN (1970), and AUSTRALIAN ARID LANDS

Botanic Garden (1996). New satellite botanic gardens were also developed to increase the range of plants displayed or to provide large spaces for new themes—Mount Tomah, Mount Lofty, Mount Annan, Mount Coot-tha, and Cranborne are the major examples. New regional botanic gardens were also developed, often by local governments.

A rising interest in the environment, protests against logging, Green Bans, political interest, and vocal support from a wide spectrum of voices and approaches—such as those of Rupert Hamer, Geoff Mosley, George Seddon, Norman Wettenhall, and David Yencken—saw a new environmental consciousness wedded to an interest in landscape. New organisations such as the Australian Conservation Foundation and the Wilderness Society were formed, and other practical results were achieved in the reservation of new national parks and state parks such as Kakadu and Alice Springs Desert Park (both NT). Rupert Hamer formed the Victorian Convservation Trust (now the Trust for Nature) in Victoria to permanently protect habitat on privately owned land and thus reclaim significant conservation land previously alienated. This was an innovative approach to private land conservation nationally and internationally. However, increasing pressures from tourism and active recreational use placed these fragile places under strain, and major philosophical issues such as commercialisation of public assets remain unresolved. Despite this, new opportunities for engagement with the landscape have paralleled a heightened interest in the horticultural use of Australian plants.

Significant changes in attitude to the Australian flora occurred in this period. Australian plants were used to form bush gardens, and plants were used according to ecological principles and themes—for example, native grasslands. Hostility towards the use of exotics grew, particularly for plants known as environmental weeds. Botanists such as Geoff Carr exposed the large number plants used in Australian gardens that have become weeds in natural bushland. Protection of the little remaining natural vegetation on private land became a critical and urgent issue for biodiversity protection in Australia. Mechanisms such as land purchases, protective conservation covenants on private land owners' titles, and a revolving fund for land purchases to permanently protect rare and threatened habitats were developed by organisations such as the Trust for Nature. Revegetation of previously cleared land was the main concern of organisations such as Landcare, and also of Greening Australia, which focused on indigenous plants obtained from seed sources local to where the plants will eventually be planted.

The nursery industry continued to change during this period, marketing drive-in garden centres from the mid-1960s and organising promotions for particular plants such as the 'plant of the year'. Techniques that allow transportation of large plants, and use of containerised stock and pre-grown turf to form an instant landscape, began to dictate the way new gardens were installed. Instant gardens were given extra impetus by a range of lifestyle TV programs emphasising the speed at which a landscape can be transformed.

Planting fashions in this period included interest in palms and tropical plants, Permaculture, Bonsai, Feng Shui, and a new interest in Asia as a plant source. At the same time the Mediterranean was re-examined as a source of plants and design influences in a similar climate.

The interest of organisations such as the National Trusts, the Australian Garden History Society, and the Historic Houses Trust of New South Wales, and the rise of garden history as a discipline, saw the identification and conservation of heritage places where gardens and designed landscapes were significant. These efforts were assisted in a philosophical sense by the establishment of Australia ICOMOS (which promoted the Burra Charter as a basis for sound conservation practices), and in a practical sense by groups such as the Ornamental Plants Conservation Association. There was a revival of interest in cottage gardens and herb gardens in the 1980s. What started as a general, historically based style later focused on specifically 'heirloom' vegetable varieties (chosen for a variety of aesthetic, culinary, and philosophical reasons) and ornamental plant cultivars. In the field of garden design interest grew markedly in the work of Edna Walling and the Griffins in particular, and also in a broader appreciation of Australia's legacy of designed and cultural landscapes. There was also an increased appreciation of the role of migrants' gardens. Viticulture in Australia was revolutionised by an increasing acceptance of wine drinking, with a correspondingly vast increase in acreages.

There was a strong move, especially towards the close of this period, to hire contract labour to replace the traditional gardener employed on-site. This followed trends observable overseas, particularly in the UK, of large companies tendering for maintenance work. The change contributed to a breakdown in the gardener's traditional custodianship role.

Design for energy efficiency in the landscape was coming into focus and being promoted towards the end of this period. Designs that use less water, as in xeric gardens, can also include planting schemes that reduce heat loads on buildings by using shade during summer, but allow light to penetrate in winter.

Interest in energy efficiency also led to an interest in Mediterranean plants and design influences—in its most popular manifestation causing a veritable Tuscanisation of inner metropolitan suburbs. Interest in art in the garden also increased, with works ranging from public art to more quirky manifestations. Use of the garden as a focus for leisure activities—apart from actual work in the garden—was popularised in the period following the Second World War and continued to expand in later decades. In the public realm, a new interest was shown in urban design, with increasing involvement by those trained in architecture (often with training in another discipline, but also in multidisciplinary teams). New inner-city public parks, plazas, and urban spaces were often developed for sport or entertainment.

Traditional plant breeding and selection programs were radically changed by new techniques in genetic manipulation towards the end of this period. This was controversial, especially in food production. Manipulation for ornamental features, such as flower colour, had only minor impact.

RA and ML

Beatrice Bligh, *Cherish the Earth: The Story of Gardening in Australia* (Sydney, 1973); Howard Tanner and Jane Begg, *The Great Gardens of Australia* (South Melbourne, 1976); Howard Tanner, *Converting the Wilderness: The Art of Gardening in Colonial Australia* (Sydney, 1979); Judith Baskin and Trisha Dixon, *Australia's Timeless Gardens* (Canberra, 1996); Tim Bonyhady, *The Colonial Earth* (Carlton South, Vic., 2000); Paul Fox, *Clearings: Six Colonial Gardeners and their Landscapes* (Carlton South, Vic., forthcoming, 2003)

AUSTRALIAN AGRICULTURIST (1893–1925), 'a monthly journal of progressive agricultural, horticultural and pastoral intelligence', was the sometime official journal of the Horticultural Society of New South Wales. The Society had published its own short-lived journal the *Horticulturist* (1892), and within the pages of the *Australian Agriculturist*, 'The Horticulturist' remained a discrete and substantial section, containing seasonal horticultural hints as well as notes and longer articles. William GUILFOYLE was a notable contributor (1899) in a periodical (later titled *Farm Journal*) whose geographic focus was NSW and Vic. RA

AUSTRALIAN AND NEW ZEALAND ASSOCIATION FOR THE ADVANCEMENT OF SCIENCE (1930–97) began as the Australasian Association for the Advancement of Science (1888–1930); it aimed to encourage scientific effort in all Australasian colonies and, aping its British predecessor, welcomed the public. It linked and sometimes spawned scientific societies. From 1888, a biannual (and later annual) congress, organised in sections, formed its major forum. One enduring consideration was the taxonomy and conservation of the AUSTRALIAN FLORA. No section was dedicated to horticulture, but congresses occasionally included horticultural comment: in 1893 Albert MOLINEUX presented his 'Plea for an Intercolonial State Board of Horticulture' to include economic botany, vegetable pathology, and economic entomology.

Early congresses considered pasture and poisonous plants, and wheat breeding and diseases. J.H. MAIDEN and his colleagues reported on the chemistry, taxonomy, and timber of EUCALYPTS and other potentially useful Australian plants. The inappropriateness of European terms for Australian plants and vegetation was discussed, as was the need for revised colonial Floras, biological surveys, and flora reserves. Regional Floras were presented, and in 1907 Maiden suggested preparation of a new 'Australian Flora'.

Interwar congresses discussed WEEDS, plant PESTS AND DISEASES as well as breeding of better-yielding and disease-resistant crop and pasture plants. A committee recommended certain generic names to the International Botanical Congress. Another committee compiled a 'Bibliography of the Australian Floristic and Ecological Plant-geography' and discussed terms suitable for Australian vegetation. ECOLOGY papers, including T.G.B. OSBORN's saltbush studies of

The landscaping of the Hotel Canberra during the 1920s provided a startling contrast between the rough paddocks of the raw site for the AUSTRALIAN CAPITAL TERRITORY and the confident FORMALITY imposed by Canberra's early civic development

Koonamore vegetation reserve (SA), sharpened public awareness of the need for vegetation conservation.

After the Second World War, ANZAAS continued to emphasise the urgent need to conserve and document Australia's indigenous flora. Following suggestions of plant taxonomists at the 1946 congress, ANZAAS's Systematic Botany Committee was formed to foster the preparation and revision of state Floras, and in 1958 another committee was established to consider preparation of an authoritative and comprehensive national Flora. On receipt of this committee's 1959 report, the Australian Academy of Science recommended a multi-volume Flora of Australia, but the government's response was silence. A meeting at the 1971 congress discussed several Flora proposals. One for a preliminary publication was subsequently accepted by the Australian Academy of Science, and under Nancy BURBIDGE's direction, preparation of the *Australian Plant Name Index* was begun in 1973. In 1979, preparation of the *Flora of Australia* was begun and its first volume (1981, revised 1999) forms an outstanding introduction to the Australian environment and its flora.

LINDEN GILLBANK

AUSTRALIAN ARID LANDS BOTANIC GARDEN, Port Augusta, SA, was established between 1981 and 1984 by the City of Port Augusta with horticulturist John ZWAR. Developed since 1989 with the assistance of Western Mining Corporation and the Electricity Trust of South Australia, and in close collaboration with ADELAIDE BOTANIC GARDEN, this award-winning, 250-hectare project has adopted a regional BOTANIC GARDEN operational model. Stage one (opened 1996) features flora from the southern Australian ARID zone, with much of the horticultural momentum being fostered by Zwar and horticulturist Bernie Haase.

BRIAN MORLEY

AUSTRALIAN CAPITAL TERRITORY came into existence in 1911 as the Federal Capital Territory when NSW ceded 2360 square kilometres to the Commonwealth of Australia. The name was changed to 'Australian' in 1937. The land is owned by the Commonwealth and administered as leasehold, rather than freehold, titles. Part of the foothills of the Australian alps, the area consists of rugged eucalypt-forested ridges, open-wooded hills, and grassland valleys. Relative to other parts of Australia, the climate of the ACT is severe: hot dry summers, freezing winters, strong westerly winds, and low and irregular rainfall. Soils are generally shallow and infertile. Pastoral properties were established from the 1830s and early HOMESTEAD GARDENS include DUNTROON, LANYON, and Yarralumla. Located in sheltered positions, these gardens display a range of exotic and native plants. The two villages of Tharwa and Hall pre-date formation of the territory. The city of Queanbeyan (NSW) sits on the south-east ACT border.

Selected for its picturesque inland setting, bracing climate, adequate water supply, and access to Sydney and Melbourne, much of the territory is used for water catchment and included in Namadji National Park. In the past, Jervis Bay provided the territory's sea port. District-Surveyor Charles Robert Scrivener (1855–1923) chose the city site for 25 000 people in the valley of the Molonglo River because of the site's ability to allow for the simple and easy provision of 'ornamental waters' (now Lake Burley Griffin).. As the site was largely devoid of trees, the government established a nursery at Acton and then at Yarralumla, under the direction of T.C.G. WESTON. Reforestation was a major focus in the early decades and ARBORETA were established to test suitable species (including Westbourne Woods). CONIFERS, hardy exotics, and a range of AUSTRALIAN PLANTS were introduced.

Canberra is the only city of the ACT. As the seat of government, it is the centre for Federal Parliament, for enacting Commonwealth legislation, and for official and social functions of Australia, as well as the official residence of the governor-general (YARRALUMLA House). Diplomatic missions have a notable presence, many with fine gardens. The central part of Canberra has in part been developed to the plan of Chicago landscape architect Walter Burley GRIFFIN, winner of the 1911 international design competition for the Federal Capital of Australia. Griffin's design related the existing landscape and the city in a coherent way: linking the major hilltops of Mount Ainslie and Capital Hill with a land axis, the Molonglo flood plain and Black Mountain with a water axis, and the government ensemble set as a stage facing the formal water basin and auditorium of parklands. Griffin commenced the development of Canberra (1913–20), but due to wartime constraints and bureaucratic difficulties, little was achieved.

Following formal, axial planning principles for the national areas and GARDEN CITY principles for the suburbs, Canberra was developed by subsequent government departments and agencies. John SULMAN, Chairman of the Federal Capital Advisory Committee (1921–25), laid down the pattern of garden suburbs in Reid and Forrest. Under the direction of the Federal Capital Commission (1925–30), Provisional (Old) Parliament House opened in 1927. Garden suburbs to accommodate public servants were developed with hedges instead of front fences, regular street tree planting, local parks (such as Telopea Park), wide verges, and free allocations of plants, which provided a unifying theme to suburban planting. Trees and shrubs of this period favoured seasonal display, with spring-blossom and autumn-leaf colour a feature of street, park, and garden planting. Roses were popular with the National Rose Gardens and Parliamentary Gardens built on formal terraces adjacent to Old Parliament House. The role of parks and gardens agencies has been crucial in maintaining the Garden City character. Weston was followed by Alexander BRUCE, John Hobday, Lindsay PRYOR, David Shoobridge and Ron Murray in directing their programs.

Under the National Capital Development Commission (NCDC) (1958–88), Lake Burley Griffin was built (inaugurated 1964), hilltops were kept free from private development, and public parklands were established around the lake for recreational uses and as a setting for the central city area, including COMMONWEALTH PARK (consultant Sylvia CROWE). With the plan for Canberra to grow to 250 000 people, the NCDC developed a series of satellite towns according to a 'Y-Plan'. Woden/Weston Creek, Belconnen, and Tuggeranong are separated by green space, the National Capital Open Space System, and each town centre has a major park: Glebe Park, Woden Town Park, John Knight Park, and Tuggeranong Town Park. NCDC landscape architects who made a significant contribution were Richard CLOUGH, Harry OAKMAN, Margaret HENDRY, and John Gray. Parliament House on Capital Hill was opened in 1988. It includes a series of internal private garden courtyards and a formal parterre garden, and the larger site is surrounded by informal gardens of Australian plants. With the advent of self-government (1989), responsibility for Canberra's public gardens and green spaces devolved to the National Capital Authority and the ACT Government. In 1993 the population passed 300 000; a new town, Gungahlin, is now being developed by the ACT Government.

In the ACT the focus on gardens and gardening is as much on the public expression of gardens and landscape as on private expression. Canberra is well-treed, spacious, green, and leafy. The AUSTRALIAN NATIONAL BOTANIC GARDENS provide a focus for Australian plants. Private gardens reflect the educated, middle-class nature of the city (such as CALTHORPES' HOUSE and Boxford). The distinctive features of Canberra gardens are primarily influenced by climate, setting, national capital status, the Griffin plan, and government control of development. The climate allows the annual spring festival of Floriade to present a dramatic display of bulbs; the Territory's scenic setting enhances garden vistas such as the Brindabellas from Royal Canberra Golf Course in Westbourne Woods; and the national capital role of the city and its institutions is demonstrated in the garden of the LODGE (prime minister's residence since 1928), the National Sculpture Garden of the National Gallery of Australia, and the courtyard of the Australian War Memorial. The significance of the Griffin plan is demonstrated in Lake Burley Griffin and its parklands, the NATIONAL TRIANGLE, the broad tree-lined avenues and vegetated hilltops, with government control over land and development ensuring well-treed and planned suburbs and managed open space.

Dianne Firth, *A Theoretical Framework for Designed Landscapes in the Australian Capital Territory* (Belconnen, ACT, 1997); John W. Reps, *Canberra 1912: Plans and Planners of the Australian Capital Competition* (Carlton South, Vic., 1997)

DIANNE FIRTH

AUSTRAL(IAN) CULTURIST (1900–04), a monthly journal published in Melbourne and managed and edited by Harry DAVEY, established and boosted its circulation by its affiliation (as official journal) with numerous kindred bodies, including the NATIONAL ROSE SOCIETY of Victoria and various HORTICULTURAL SOCIETIES. Known initially as the *Austral Culturist and Women's Realm*, the magazine devoted itself to 'special industries which are suitable for women': these included APICULTURE, HORTICULTURE, POULTRY, SERICULTURE, and SCENT and other specialised farming. These lofty ambitions soon gave way to commercial realities and editorial space for fruit growing increased. The changes were reflected in many title changes, the journal finally becoming *Fruit World and Journal of Horticulture* (1904). The JOURNAL OF HORTICULTURE OF AUSTRALASIA was formed as a separate magazine by the publisher in 1906 and *Fruit World* continued in publication until 1980. The AUSTRALASIAN NURSERYMAN, SEEDSMAN AND FLORIST (1903) was also established as a separate title by Davey as part of his stable of horticultural titles.

RA

AUSTRALIAN FLORA Introduction The Australian flora has intrigued European visitors since 1697. The observation of First Fleet officer Richard Atkins in 1793 of plants in flower around Sydney as having 'the most vivid and beautiful colours imaginable and many of them most delicately formed' typifies the reaction of many to Australia's plants. Containing more than 25 000 species (ten per cent of the world total) and with eighty-five per cent of these endemic, the flora is renowned for its many and unique 'wildflowers'—from striking kangaroo paws, Sturt's Desert Pea, BANKSIAS, callistemons, and dryandras, through exquisitely delicate verticordias and the startling blues of dampieras and lechenaultias, to the carpets of ephemeral species that clothe deserts of the ARID ZONES after rain.

The richest flora in terms of species density is found on some of the poorest soils—the sandplains and heathlands of WA, where more than 110 species have been recorded in an area of 100 metres square. In contrast, the few remaining tracts of RAINFOREST are often characterised by a multitude of families and genera, with few species within genera. Evolving over 100 million years to cope with drought and nutrient-deficient soils, Australian plants show special features such as deep root systems and symbiotic relationships with soil microbes to gather water and nutrients. FIRE has also shaped the flora, with plants developing protective devices such as thick, insulating bark; SEEDS protected in woody capsules; and the lignotuber—a woody rootstock that allows regeneration after fire. Others are killed by fire but produce large quantities of seed, which accumulates in the soil and germinates in favourable times. Some plants, such as grass trees and many ground orchids, flower best after fire.

Although use of the flora for ABORIGINAL FOOD PLANTS has long traditions, taming the flora for horticulture has been a challenge, as its special requirements have often not been understood; for example, mistakes and misinformation caused a backlash against Australian plants in the 1980s. Most of the basic research in growing Australian plants was done by enthusiastic amateurs from groups such as the SOCIETY FOR GROWING AUSTRALIAN PLANTS. Much of this information is incorporated in the *Encyclopaedia of Australian Plants* by Rodger ELLIOT and David Jones (1980–). After the enthusiasm for BUSH GARDENS of the 1960s and 1970s, the attitude towards Australian plants today is more measured. The varieties of flowers, foliage, and form available are better appreciated, and blending of 'natives' with 'exotics' is well accepted. The use of GRASSES and tufted plants is common, as is the growing of indigenous plants to handle local conditions. Stronger environmental awareness, however, has led to a realisation of the importance of the flora and an understanding of the need to manage rare and endangered species.

Australian flora

Type specimens, from which plants were first described and named, provide raw material for the taxonomy of the AUSTRALIAN FLORA; the recent discovery of *Wollemia nobilis* (Wollemi Pine) continues a long tradition of botanical exploration, categorisation, and naming

Due to continuing land clearing and invasion by exotic environmental WEEDS (more than 3000 species since 1788), as well as PESTS AND DISEASES, the flora is under sustained pressure. Seventy-six plant species are presumed extinct and a further 301 are listed as endangered. The future of the Australian flora will depend on a better understanding of its ECOLOGY and conservation requirements, and on strategies to preserve species, such as reintroduction and habitat restoration through REVEGETATION.   **TONY CAVANAGH**

Botanical exploration, categorisation, and naming
ABORIGINAL peoples were the first to discover and classify Australia's native plants as they learnt how to use them in daily living—as food, medicine, and implements. Their names for plants appear to be confined to those that were useful, and relate to properties of the plant rather than relationships between plants. From a European perspective, recorded discovery began with the second visit of William DAMPIER in 1699 when, for the first time, specimens were collected and taken to England. These were named according to the rather erratic practice of the day, pre-dating the formal starting date of modern botanical nomenclature established by Carl LINNAEUS in 1753. The first Australian plants named under the Linnaean system were two from the west coast: collector unknown, but possibly a member of Willem de Vlamingh's expedition, which discovered the Swan River in 1697 (and if so earlier than Dampier's collection). They were named by the Dutch botanist Nicolaas BURMAN in 1768 (five months before Cook's *Endeavour* voyage left England). At the time they were thought to be from Java, but research later showed them to be Australian. It was the collections of Joseph BANKS and Daniel SOLANDER from the east coast that drew widespread attention to Australia's unique botanical riches.

Banks did not publish his planned grand work on the *Endeavour* voyage, and a number of his specimens were named by botanists who studied them at his home in London's Soho Square—including those first named *Banksia* by the son of Linnaeus. Further early visits that led to publications on the Australian flora were those of Vancouver (1791), d'Entrecasteaux (1792), and Malaspina (1793). The first major work, however, was that of Robert BROWN, botanist on the *Investigator* voyage with Matthew Flinders. With artist Ferdinand BAUER and gardener Peter GOOD, Brown collected several thousand species as they circumnavigated the continent in 1801–02 and during stays at Sydney, Norfolk Island, and Van Diemen's Land. On his return to Britain in 1805, Brown set about preparing a Flora of the continent and in 1810 published the first part, describing some 2000 species (about half the number then known). Although regarded by many as one of the great works in plant systematics, the book sold few copies and Brown did not publish the other part.

Over the next few decades, visitors, and increasingly, settlers, continued to collect plants, but always the specimens were sent to Britain and Europe. There was no resident botanist to study them, nor any place in Australia where they could be stored. Many European botanists named these plants in a wide array of books and journals. It was not until almost 1850 that the first botanist arrived who would stem the one-way flow. Ferdinand MUELLER, a young German who migrated in 1847, began to build up a collection, and became the first official taxonomic botanist when appointed Government Botanist of Vic. in 1853. For more than four decades he worked tirelessly, both in the office and in the field, and through vast correspondence with botanists overseas and with collectors, to establish the National Herbarium of Victoria. Following settlement in various parts of the continent, exploration and botanical discovery moved inland. Besides Mueller himself, significant collectors included CALEY, A. CUNNINGHAM, MITCHELL, Wilhelm Bäuerlen, and Obed D. Evans (NSW); Raymond L. Specht, George McC. Chippendale, and John R. Maconochie (NT); DALLACHY, Karel Domin, DIETRICH, F.M. BAILEY, WHITE, and Stanley T. Blake in Qld; TATE, CLELAND, and BLACK (SA); GUNN, J.D. HOOKER, MILLIGAN, W. ARCHER, and RODWAY (Tas.); WILLIS and A. Clifford Beauglehole (Vic.); and PREISS, DRUMMOND, Ernst G. Pritzel, Ludwig Diels, GARDNER, and William E. Blackall (WA).

Although one of Mueller's ambitions was to write a Flora of Australia, that task fell to a British botanist, George BENTHAM, who had access to the important early collections

Australian flora

housed in European HERBARIA (where most remain to this day). With assistance from Mueller, Bentham published the seven-volume *Flora Australiensis* (1863–78), describing some 8125 species. Thereafter, botanists (amateur and professional) prepared state and local Floras, although even now some areas do not have complete works.

With new plants continuing to be found throughout the land, Bentham's work soon became outdated, but it was not until 1979 that a decision was made to compile a modern Flora. A multi-author work coordinated by the Australian Biological Resources Study, it will comprise forty-seven volumes covering flowering plants, as well as one on FERNS and CYCADS, two on plants of the OCEANIC island territories, and five on lichens and fungi. As companions to the project, lists have been compiled of all names used for Australian plants (published as the four-volume *Australian Plant Name Index*) and of the names accepted as taxonomically correct (*Census of Australian Vascular Plants*).

The major families of flowering plants in Australia are the Leguminosae (wattles, cassia, pea flowers); Myrtaceae (myrtles); Proteaceae (banksias, grevilleas); Asteraceae (daisies); Cyperaceae (sedges); and Poaceae (grasses). The largest genera are the wattles (*Acacia*, more than 600 species), eucalypts (*Eucalyptus*, totalling about 700 species) and *Grevillea* (about 350 species). It is now estimated that there are about 25 000 species of flowering plants in Australia, belonging to some 220 families—the figures vary according to different botanical concepts. With exploration and refinement of classification, new species are continually being recognised.

Flora of Australia, Volume 1: Introduction (Melbourne, 1999)

ALEX GEORGE

Horticultural use outside Australia Australian plants were first grown overseas in 1771 when six species were raised at KEW from seed collected on Cook's first voyage by Joseph BANKS. *Eucalyptus obliqua*, brought back from Cook's second voyage by Captain Furneaux, was the first plant sold (1774) and by 1778, six had flowered in the GLASSHOUSES of Kew. The return of the First Fleet ships enabled seed of over thirty species to reach England in 1789, including five grown in the nursery of LEE AND KENNEDY. Collectors such as David BURTON and Allan CUNNINGHAM from Kew, and William BAXTER for private nurseries, as well as many individuals, provided seeds and plants, so that more than 1200 Australian species were grown in England by 1855. Other London nursery proprietors who specialised in Australian plants included Colville, Henchman, Knight, Loddiges, Mackay, and VEITCH.

The fascination of Victorian gardeners with exotic plants was no less marked in Europe. The Empress Josephine had perhaps a hundred Australian plants in her garden at Malmaison, including boronias, correas, and pea flowers. Carl von HÜGEL grew annuals and climbers, including *Hardenbergia*, outdoors in his garden near Vienna, as well as many species in glasshouses; Anatole Demidoff maintained five huge glasshouses packed with Australian and other exotic plants at San Donato near Florence. Fashions changed from the 1850s, and Australian plants fell from favour as ornamentals. A major cause of decline in their cultivation came with the advent of piped hot-water heating in GREENHOUSES (from remote heat sources), which produced a more humid environment than the drier air produced from internal STOVES, which better suited the growth of Australian plants. (A recent innovation to overcome this problem has been to utilise dehumidifiers.) Australian plants were to go on to meet different needs, however, in afforestation, farming, and in large-scale ornamental plantings.

EUCALYPTUS and *ACACIA* were widely grown overseas during the nineteenth century. Fast-growing eucalypts changed the skyline of California and drained the Pontine marshes near Rome, ridding the area of malaria. In Third World countries, they provided timber, fuel, medicinal oils, and REVEGETATION. In California, more than half a million acacias representing sixty species were planted in Golden Gate Park near San Francisco. Acacias were also used worldwide for sand stabilisation and for tan-bark, and, in the twentieth century, as fast-growing timber trees.

In recent years, the horticultural and economic potential of Australian plants has again been recognised—as pot plants, for cut flowers and foliage, for ornamental planting, and for food. Yet the initiative lies largely overseas. Only ten per cent of the total world supply of Australian cut flowers is produced in Australia. Banksias are grown commercially in Hawaii, Israel, California, and South Africa, while Holland produces nearly one-quarter of the world's 'everlasting' flowers. *Brachyscome*, *Scaevola*, *Bracteantha*, and *Chrysocephalum* are popular in Europe, North America, and Japan where they are mainly grown as 'potted colour'. *Scaerola aemula* (and its many cultivars) is one of the most popular basket plants. The Australian horticultural industry for native plants is still very much in the developmental stage, but extensive current research aims to introduce more varieties to the world horticulture market.

Krystyna Johnson and Margaret Burchett, *Native Australian Plants: Horticulture and Uses* (Sydney, 1996)

TONY CAVANAGH

Horticultural use in Australia Hundreds of generations have made use of ABORIGINAL FOOD PLANTS, and the Australian flora has served many economic purposes as well as providing distinctive markers in CULTURAL LANDSCAPES. Successive generations of European settlers have discovered the horticultural possibilities of the Australian flora and learned in a rather haphazard but cumulative manner from these experiences.

In contrast to use by indigenous Australians of the native flora as a food source, European settlers made an extremely pessimistic assessment of its potential as food. The *Index Plantarum* (1835) by James BACKHOUSE and Ronald GUNN generated much discussion and Backhouse noted in his *Narrative* (1843) that it was 'remarkable … that so few of the indigenous plants of these Colonies yield any fruit suitable for human subsistence. In this respect the Australian regions stand singularly apart, from every other portion of the known world.' It would be a century and a half before 'bush tucker' again attracted as much interest or optimism.

Of far greater importance to the new settlers was the role natural vegetation played in providing shelter from strong

Australian flora

Horticultural use of the AUSTRALIAN FLORA was greatly boosted during the 1920s and 1930s by an alliance between FIELD NATURALISTS and gardeners wanting to replicate decorative aspects of the Australian BUSH in home gardens

winds and sunshine. Although use of Australian plants for ornamental or landscape purposes was not a high priority, landscape features were also formed from BUSH at an early date in both a subtractive manner (to reveal an open area, or to form paths or drives) and in a more positive manner in the retention of the bush (to form a shrubbery, or, following Thomas SHEPHERD's 1836 advice, to selectively retain tree cover). Vistas were also sometimes carved through natural bush for ornamental purposes, and some gardeners also experimented with coppicing local eucalypts. Quick-growing natives (such as the *Acacia* spp.) or retained sections of bush were also used to protect newly planted exotics. The rapid growth, particularly of some eucalypts, made these trees well suited to early street plantings, although they were generally replaced, as the urban fabric of towns and suburbs developed, by sentimental favourites from 'home' such as the elm, oak, and plane.

Transplanting from the bush, especially of small flowers and small shrubs, was an early means of introducing native plants into local gardens. One Victorian garden calendar of 1841 suggested making 'plantations of the indigenous plants and shrubs of the handsomest dwarf growing flowering kinds'. The practice of transplanting from the bush continued for many generations. One source listed a shrubbery containing *Micromyrtus* along with boronias, chorizemas, dwarf grevilleas, hakeas, and pittosporums, mixed with abelias, cistus, coprosmas, escallonias, philadelphus, and proteas.

Links with European traditions were common. Many Australian plants were used as substitutes for European landscape plants—one example is the widespread use of ARAUCARIAS (especially Norfolk Island and Bunya pines) as specimen trees, emulating northern-hemisphere usage of CONIFERS. In their common names, too, European traditions were often recalled—as in the naming of Mountain Ash (*Eucalyptus regnans*) and Silky Oak (*Grevillea robusta*). While Australian plants were favourites in European greenhouses, there was also a market within the Australian nursery industry. Commercial plant collectors of the 1820s and 1830s, such as William BAXTER and James SCOTT, responded to local as well as overseas demand. Australian nurseries began to stock a limited range of Australian plants as early as the 1840s; these included *Telopea speciosissima* (Waratah) and *Crinum flaccidum* (Darling Lily). PLANT BREEDING of Australian species also began at this time: in 1844 William MACARTHUR produced a hybrid of the local *Crinum pedunculatum* and *Crinum scabrum* from Africa.

During the 1850s interest in ACCLIMATISATION grew; it was directed principally at introduction of exotics (both plants and animals) due to a perceived lack of 'Britishness' in the landscape. Empirical trials increasingly included

Australian flora

Australian flora, however, and many Australian species were grown in colonial BOTANIC GARDENS. This interest was fuelled particularly by the interest of government botanists and botanic garden directors such as J.C. BIDWILL, the CUNNINGHAM brothers, and Ferdinand MUELLER. The interest was later shared by many others, including Charles MOORE, William GUILFOYLE, J.H. MAIDEN, and members of the BAILEY family. Australian plants were propagated alongside exotics in botanic garden (and later STATE FOREST) NURSERIES for distribution across the colonies. From the 1850s Australian plants were increasingly offered by commercial nurseries; among the earliest were *Araucaria bidwillii*, *A. cunninghamii*, *Crinum pedunculatum*, *Dendrobium speciosum*, *Doryanthes* spp., *Eremophila maculata*, *Lophostemon confertus*, *Pandorea* spp., *Podocarpus spinulosus*, and *Telopea speciosissima*. In 1860 the Victorian Gardeners' Mutual Improvement Society praised *Eucalyptus globulus* (Blue Gum) and its relatives for park planting. *Acacia baileyana* (Cootamundra Wattle) and *Eucalyptus ficifolia* (Red-flowering Gum) were favourites from the 1870s. In 1894 SEWELL's Payneham Nurseries in Adelaide stocked seeds of more than 125 different species, including twenty-three eucalypts. A great interest in collecting and growing FERNS, many of them Australian, developed during the late nineteenth century.

A general interest in the Australian flora was promoted during the second half of the nineteenth century by writers such as Louisa MEREDITH, Louisa ATKINSON, and William WOOLLS, but it was not until 1892, when H.A. JAMES published his *Handbook of Australian Horticulture*, that a comprehensive treatment of ornamental horticultural use was included in an Australian garden book. A separate chapter on the cultivation of Australian plants listed more than 290 shrubs and trees, sixteen climbers, forty-two ferns, twenty-four orchids, and seventeen cycads and palms. During the last decade of the nineteenth century 'Bulletin School' writers and 'Heidelberg School' landscape painters placed a greater emphasis on Australia's bush heritage, and enlightened voices harnessed this to an emerging nationalism. Both NATURE STUDY and SCHOOL GARDENS helped to promote a study of Australian plants, linked in many instances to the burgeoning FIELD NATURALISTS' CLUBS. R.T. BAKER, noted for his research on economic use of native plants, was a key supporter of the short-lived, Sydney-based Australian Flora Society. Outside botanic gardens, ornamental collections of native plants were uncommon: MARANOA GARDENS, Balwyn (Vic.) was among the earliest examples. In TROPICAL and subtropical areas, RAINFOREST trees (such as *Ficus* spp.) became popular horticultural subjects, especially in PUBLIC PARKS AND GARDENS.

The nationalism surrounding Federation was reflected in horticulture by the inauguration of WATTLE DAY, the search for appropriate FLORAL EMBLEMS, and a spate of nature writing by the likes of Donald MACDONALD and Charles BARRETT, which encouraged the link between bush and garden. Conservation through NATIONAL PARKS and other reserves—especially conservation of flowering plants *in situ*, in response to depletion by over-enthusiastic wildflower show exhibitors and the commercial cut-flower trade—formed a key message of much nature writing. Books such as Guilfoyle's *Australian Plants Suitable for Gardens, Parks and Timber Reserves, Etc.* (1911), E.E. PESCOTT's *The Native Flowers of Victoria* (1914), and Tullie WOLLASTON's *Our Wattles* (1916) assisted in promoting the use of Australian plants, while mainstream gardening books such as Brunning's *Australian Garden* increasingly included appropriate advice on cultivation. Later publications by G.K. COWLISHAW, W. AHLFIELD, James AUDAS, Thistle HARRIS, W.A.W. DE BEUZEVILLE, and Ernest LORD, ranging from pamphlets for enthusiasts to comprehensive works for gardeners and farmers, provided advice that previously had been scarce. Pioneering seed collectors and nursery proprietors, such as John STAER and Andrew MURPHY, were early specialists in a field that grew dramatically during the twentieth century.

The promotion of the Australian flora by Walter and Marion GRIFFIN, through their large-scale town planning and their more modest domestic landscapes, provided a cultural awakening in the professional design world of ARCHITECTURE and LANDSCAPE ARCHITECTURE. Although it was to be several decades before this enthusiasm reached a critical mass, the sculptural beauty of Australian trees in particular appealed to architects, and provided a foil to the stark lines of many MODERNIST designs.

Between the wars, the writings of Jean GALBRAITH and Crosbie MORRISON brought nature writing more directly to a horticulture and garden audience through popular magazines. Influential enthusiasts of this period also included Russell GRIMWADE, William FRANCIS, William BLAKELY, the ASHBY family, Alf GRAY, Albert LINDNER, David GORDON, the PARRY family, and the ALTHOFER brothers. They were joined in the 1940s and 1950s by C.A. GARDNER, Bill CANE, Bernhardt and Dulcie SCHUBERT, and the BODDY family, who catered for the demand for Australian plants and information about their growth. The Western Australian flora was particularly favoured in the temperate southern parts of Australia, while tropical plants were naturally favoured in Qld, the NT, and northern WA. In the late 1940s and 1950s the noted designer Edna WALLING utilised many Australian plants. She appreciated the subtlety of *Westringia*, *Prostanthera*, and *Kunzea ericoides*. Her enlightened book *The Australian Roadside* (1952) championed the importance of natural roadsides and their landscape treatment. Thistle Harris was also prominent, and her books, especially *Australian Plants for the Garden* (1953), strengthened the upsurge in cultivation of Australian plants.

The motto of the Parry nursery Floralands, 'Preservation by Cultivation', also became the motto for the SOCIETY FOR GROWING AUSTRALIAN PLANTS, which has drawn enthusiasts together since 1957. The Society drew in part on the work of earlier organisations such as the Wild Life Preservation Society of Australia (founded by David STEAD), the Sydney-based Rangers League, and various tree preservation societies. This enthusiasm encouraged the development of botanic gardens exclusively devoted to the Australian flora, of which the botanic garden in Perth's KINGS PARK (1965) and the AUSTRALIAN NATIONAL BOTANIC GARDENS in Canberra (1970) were the first examples. Directors and curators of

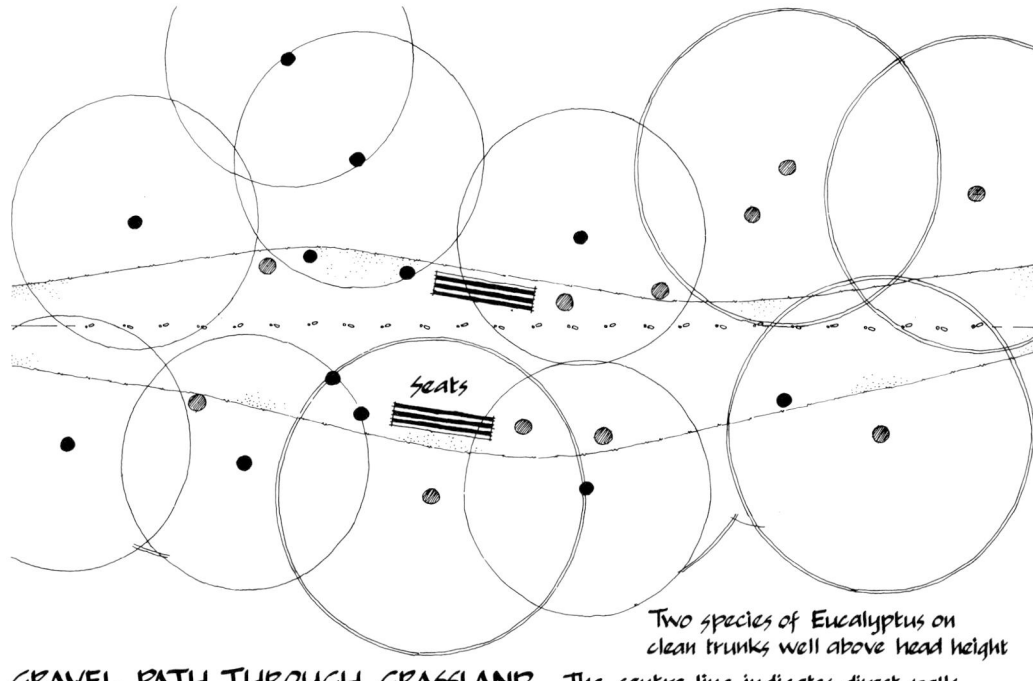

The casual informality to be achieved by landscaping using the AUSTRALIAN FLORA was highlighted in many texts, including Glen Wilson's *Landscaping with Australian Plants* (1975), which provided clear sketch plans for emulation by both home gardeners and professionals

these gardens, especially John BEARD and John WRIGLEY, were key figures in the spread of accurate botanical and horticultural information on Australian plants. More recent examples include MOUNT ANNAN BOTANIC GARDEN (NSW), AUSTRALIAN ARID LANDS BOTANIC GARDEN (SA), ALICE SPRINGS DESERT PARK (NT), and the ROYAL BOTANIC GARDENS, CRANBOURNE (Vic.).

The 1960s and early 1970s saw Australian plants reach a peak in popularity. The BUSH GARDEN of Betty MALONEY in Sydney had its first public opening in 1960 to marvellous acclaim, and the books of Maloney and her sister Jean Walker became best-sellers that succeeded in rousing an awareness of the beauty of Australian plants. Landscape architects and designers including John STEVENS, Grace FRASER, Glen WILSON, Ellis STONES, Bruce MACKENZIE, Marion BLACKWELL, Peter GLASS, and Gordon FORD commonly used Australian plants in their projects. At this time there was an extremely strong desire to cultivate and strengthen the Australian identity, especially in cities and suburbs where much of the local vegetation was under threat because of land clearing and building development. However, many Australian plants were used insensitively, especially eucalypts and melaleucas, and this was often due to a lack of knowledge or understanding of their requirements. The plants sometimes behaved differently in cultivation; wild and ill-informed criticism of Australian plants often came from people inexperienced in their cultivation. In the 1970s and 1980s Bill MOLYNEUX and Sue Forrester were instrumental in introducing a number of Australian plants into cultivation, as Evan Clucas and Leanne Weston did in the 1980s, and continue to do today.

Since the late 1970s the interest in ECOLOGY as well as in local indigenous plants and their cultivation in private and public areas has grown dramatically. In the 1980s worldwide concern for rainforests led to renewed interest in cultivating Australian rainforest plants. The complementary interest in 'bush tucker' began to expand, many rainforest plants having edible portions. The multiplication of indigenous plant nurseries occurred in a relatively short time and purely indigenous plant gardens became more common from the late 1970s. A concurrent interest took place in REVEGETATION, popularised by the work of the BRADLEY sisters. The work of GREENING AUSTRALIA and the various LANDCARE groups have greatly broadened this interest.

By the early 1990s the older-style specialist Australian plant nurseries had diminished in number, but a much wider range of Australian plants was offered by general retail nurseries. Australian semi-herbaceous perennials, such as brachyscomes and scaevolas, are now assembled with non-Australian products, and many people often do not realise they are buying Australian plants. The nursery industry has also increasingly embraced the hybridisation of Australian plants, and Australian orchids such as *Dendrobium* and *Sarcochilus* are now commonly hybridised. The Bush Gems Kangaroo Paw breeding program of Dr Merv Turner resulted in some hybrids becoming entrenched in cultivation, with *Anigo-*

zanthos 'Bush Ranger', *A.* 'Bush Nugget' and *A.* 'Bush Gold' among the favourites. Brachyscomes and bracteanthas have been the focus of breeding programs, and some of the better progeny include *Brachyscome* 'Mauve Delight' and *B.* 'Misty Mauve' while several bracteanthas are now obtainable. Other genera used for successful breeding programs include *Banksia*, *Chamelaucium*, *Correa*, *Eucalyptus*, *Grevillea*, *Hibiscus*, *Lechenaultia*, *Leptospermum*, *Macadamia*, *Microlaena*, *Santalum*, and *Telopea*. One feature of Australian cultivars is the relatively large number selected from wild-sourced material, as the extraordinary variation in some species has led to many cultivars. Increasingly, variants have been recognised and marketed by provenance—nearest town or geographic location, for example. Exploration, evaluation, and harnessing of variation in many Australian species for horticultural use has yet to reach its full potential.

> John Wrigley and Murray Fagg, *Australian Native Plants: A Manual for their Propagation, Cultivation and Use in Landscaping* (Sydney, 1979); W. Rodger Elliot and David L. Jones, *Encyclopaedia of Australian Plants Suitable for Cultivation* (Melbourne, 1980–)
>
> RODGER ELLIOT

AUSTRALIAN FLORAL EMBLEMS: see FLORAL EMBLEMS

AUSTRALIAN FOREST LEAGUE (1912–1950s), 'a band of enthusiasts linked together in the national work of forest preservation' (in the words of Russell GRIMWADE), was established in Vic. (with state branches), as the FORESTRY industry sought broad public support for its advancement. The League's journal, the *Gum Tree* (1917–55), combined with branch publications such as *Jarrah* (Perth, 1918–20), pamphlets, press articles, lectures, and lobbying as the League strove to create 'a Forest Consciousness … in the public mind'. The Victorian branch flourished with Grimwade's support and regarded its most important early achievement as the pressuring of the Victorian Parliament to establish an independent Forests Commission (1919). The League brought its message to CHILDREN through the League of Tree-Lovers and was especially active in NSW, where Thistle HARRIS edited the *Junior Tree Warden* for its Schools Branch. Much of the League's role was taken over from 1944 by the broadly based Save the Forests Campaign (later the NATURAL RESOURCES CONSERVATION LEAGUE OF VICTORIA) and by the increasing professionalism of forestry.　LIBBY ROBIN

AUSTRALIAN GARDENER (1902–10), an Adelaide-based monthly journal, provided detailed advice on planting, and floricultural and horticultural activities, societies, and shows in NSW, Vic., and SA, together with profiles in text and photographs of public and private gardens in those states. The journal shared the market with the long-established GARDEN AND FIELD and the Melbourne-based JOURNAL OF HORTICULTURE, and paved the way for popular national magazines such as AUSTRALIAN HOME BEAUTIFUL and AUSTRALIAN GARDEN LOVER, and the regional SOUTH AUSTRALIAN HOMES AND GARDENS.　DAVID JONES

AUSTRALIAN GARDEN HISTORY SOCIETY (1980–) was formed in the wake of pioneering identification studies of historic gardens, undertaken nationally during 1978–80 under the aegis of the AUSTRALIAN HERITAGE COMMISSION. The Society also harnessed interest generated by the national touring exhibition, *Converting the Wilderness: The Art of Gardening in Colonial Australia* (1979), curated by Howard TANNER. In the accompanying catalogue, Peter WATTS proposed the formation of a society modelled on the (British) Garden History Society, combining scholarly interest with CONSERVATION imperatives.

An inaugural conference in 1980 formally established the Society and set the tone of future annual gatherings with its mix of lectures, discussion, and GARDEN VISITS. Under the patronage of Dame Elisabeth MURDOCH (1980–89), Joan LAW-SMITH (1990–98), and Margaret DARLING (1999–), the Society has successfully brought together a diverse group of people with an interest in the fields of horticulture, landscape design, architecture, and related subjects 'to look at garden making in its wide historic, literary, artistic and scientific context'. Membership increased rapidly during the mid-1980s, especially when the AUSTRALIAN GARDEN JOURNAL was offered to members as the official organ of the Society. A desire to reassert the primacy of GARDEN HISTORY and the independent and authoritative voice of the Society, especially through a journal of its own, led to the publication of *Australian Garden History* (1989–). The structure of a national management committee overseeing (from 1984) state and local branches has combined national responsibilities with local initiatives, accommodating regional differences that often dictate a range of complementary approaches and aspirations.　RA

AUSTRALIAN GARDEN JOURNAL (1983–96), formerly *Garden Cuttings* (1981–83), was edited and published quarterly at Bowral (NSW) by English-trained horticulturist Tim North (b. 1921) and his wife Keva. The journal sought its market among those for whom horticulture and gardening was a passion. Plant-based articles were a major strength; they included series by Brian MORLEY (1986–88) and Stephen RYAN (1990–96). An extensive network of overseas contributors provided an international perspective. GARDEN HISTORY was featured, befitting the journal's role as official journal of the AUSTRALIAN GARDEN HISTORY SOCIETY (1983–89).

> Tim North, *Garden Cuttings: Reflections from an Australian Gardener* (Frenchs Forest, NSW, 1999)　RA

AUSTRALIAN GARDEN LOVER (1925–80), published monthly in Melbourne, achieved a prominent place among Australian GARDEN MAGAZINES due to its longevity, its attempt at national coverage, and the quality of many of its contributors. Known initially as the *Garden Lover* (1925–28), the magazine quickly regained ground previously held by the AUSTRALIAN CULTURIST and JOURNAL OF HORTICULTURE OF AUSTRALASIA, all three published by the Horticultural

Publishing Press of Australasia or its successor from 1923, the Horticultural Press Pty Ltd. The *Australian Garden Lover* aimed at owner–gardeners, especially those on small suburban plots. Competition was provided by the HOME GARDENER, and other smaller, regionally focused magazines; the GARDEN AND HOME MAKER OF AUSTRALIA was incorporated in 1933.

The magazine's heyday came during the 1930s. Ralph BOARDMAN was inaugural editor, followed by Edward Wragg (retired 1951), and then Lindsay Thornton (1951–80); all three had close links to the Victorian nursery industry and also held senior management positions within Horticultural Press. This editorial continuity was matched by the longevity of 'Correa' (Jean GALBRAITH), who started a regular column in 1926, and published her popular *Garden in a Valley* in serial form (1935–39). Betty BEGG and Mollie Shannon also contributed regular garden designs during 1928–32. Alan EDMUNDS was a prolific early contributor. Other contributors were drawn from the ranks of horticultural societies—whose activities received considerable publicity—the nursery industry, and curators of public parks and gardens. A long-running children's page gave encouragement to young readers. Promotion was given to garden festivals, especially Melbourne's Garden Week, demonstrating close links between the editorial team and the organising committees.

Horticulture, especially floriculture and vegetable growing, rather than garden design, was the chief editorial concern of the *Australian Garden Lover*. Lacking the lifestyle approach of its competitors, AUSTRALIAN HOME BEAUTIFUL, and later the HOME, and AUSTRALIAN HOUSE AND GARDEN, the magazine was unable to break much new ground and relied strongly on a rather predictable diet of seasonal gardening advice. Horticultural Press was taken over by Ramsay Ware Stockland Pty Ltd in 1980 and the journal ceased: the professional reader was soon accommodated by that company's new title AUSTRALIAN HORTICULTURE. RA

AUSTRALIAN HERITAGE COMMISSION (1976–) was set up under the *Australian Heritage Commission Act* 1975 following a Commission of Inquiry into the National Estate established by the (Whitlam) Commonwealth Government in 1973 and headed by the Hon. Mr Justice R.M. Hope. The Inquiry was in response to community concern over CONSERVATION of Australia's HERITAGE places—'the things we want to keep', to quote the Hope Report. The Australian Heritage Commission, under its inaugural head David YENCKEN, established a Register of the National Estate, initially drawn from existing NATIONAL TRUST listings, but increasingly incorporating significant cultural and natural heritage places from studies funded from the National Estates Grants Program (NEGP). Although providing no statutory protection for registered places—apart from those controlled by the Commonwealth—the Register gave public recognition to Australia's diverse heritage places. *The Heritage of Australia* (1981) provided an illustrated summary of the Register, which is now available through the Internet. Abstracts of heritage studies and related publications are available on-line through the HERA Database.

Few gardens were included in the Register until the 1980s, when results from pioneering NEGP-funded studies of 1978–80 were assessed for listing. This process was considerably facilitated by Juliet Ramsay's report *Parks, Gardens and Special Trees* (1991), which divided places by type and STYLE. Much data was brought to light in a series of NEGP-funded studies on Australia's DESIGNED LANDSCAPES (1995–98), which formed a significant boost to the research effort for this *Companion*. RA

AUSTRALIAN HOME BEAUTIFUL (1925–), published monthly since October 1925 (and its predecessors *Real Property Annual* (yearly, 1912–22) and *Australian Home Builder* (quarterly, 1922–25)) has been a significant influence on Australian home gardeners. Since its inception, the magazine has devoted itself to 'homemaking in all its various branches', presenting the domestic garden as integral to the broader identity of an Australian 'home beautiful' idyll. Articulating aspirations for a domestic ideal and practical ways of achieving them, its basic role and format (feature

AUSTRALIAN HOME BEAUTIFUL has been one of Australia's most enduring GARDEN MAGAZINES since its first manifestation as *Real Property Annual* (1912); its content gives an unsurpassed overview of popular domestic architectural and garden styles during the twentieth century

Australian Horticulture

articles complemented by monthly columns and advertisements) have changed little throughout its history. Its predominantly Australian coverage has occasionally been complemented by international examples, from the Hollywood mansions of starlets to aristocratic English seats. A 'do-it-yourself' component of the journal formed a crucial connection between stately homes and the realisation of an Australian 'home beautiful', usually in a suburban setting. Advertising, vital for commercial success, was both foil and complement to editorial matter.

Australian Home Beautiful records a vernacular Australian lifestyle and reveals otherwise ephemeral details of home gardening trends within a broader domestic pattern. In charting the SUBURBAN GARDEN's form and function through nine decades, the journal has documented changes or advances in design, structures, technology, plants, and fashion. Design ideas and elements are examined in every conceivable detail, from garden plans and garden buildings to landscape items such as paths, fences, barbecues, and letterboxes. Products of technological development include lawn mowers, irrigation systems, and clothes hoists. Plant selections vary through the decades from bedding plants to mixed shrubberies for the front garden, succulents, alpine plants in rockeries and use of native plants in the garden and for flower arrangements.

The magazine also maps broader social and political changes, albeit unwittingly. Auxiliary publications provided home-making activities to 'Keep your boy fit and happy' during the Depression years, while a much-reduced journal printed on poor quality paper during the Second World War testifies to the pressures of this time.

Through magazines such as the *Australian Home Beautiful*, garden designers and writers such as Edna WALLING and Olive MELLOR recognised the potential demand for 'a magazine not merely for those who contemplate building a house—but for all who have a home of their own in which they take proper pride'. They were able to reach broad audiences with their ideas for lifestyle and design. Despite achieving rather less fame for their efforts, other long-serving editors and staff writers such as W.A.S. (Bill) Shum and C.B. Frond also deserve mention. This tradition continues, and *Australian Home Beautiful* remains a popular vehicle for promotion and consumption of material goods within an Australian suburban culture, if no longer holding such an exclusive grasp of its audience.

Julie Oliver, *The Australian Home Beautiful: From Hills Hoist to High Rise* (McMahon's Point, NSW, 1999) **KAREN OLSEN**

AUSTRALIAN HORTICULTURE (1981–), previously the *Seed and Nursery Trader* (1930s–1981), published monthly to serve the Australian HORTICULTURE and NURSERY industry, can trace its origins to the *Australasian (International) Nurseryman, Seedsman and Florist* (1903–1930s), a trade journal derived from the *AUSTRALIAN CULTURIST*. The transformation in *Australian Horticulture*, and its subsequent rise in journalistic aspirations, was in large measure due to Barry Howard Larkman (1932–1989), managing editor during 1981–83, and Don BURKE, associate editor during the 1980s.

AUSTRALIAN HOUSE AND GARDEN capitalised on the post-war trend towards using gardens as an extension of the living space of the house; many of its articles and ideas looked to the West Coast of the USA for inspiration

Thought-provoking articles by Burke and others challenged and ultimately overturned conservative thinking within the industry, especially in nursery marketing, plant promotions, and media developments. The journal is an important barometer of opinion in horticulture and the nursery industry and is official organ of the AUSTRALIAN INSTITUTE OF HORTICULTURE. **RA**

AUSTRALIAN HOUSE AND GARDEN (1948–) was established in Sydney by publisher K.G. Murray in response to post-war demand for new houses and changed lifestyles. Founding editor Beryl GUERTNER was initially influenced by *American House and Garden* and then, in the 1960s, by California's *Sunset* magazine—especially its advocacy of warm-climate gardening and outdoor living. The early garden illustrations displayed a formal character, showing large gardens established in the 1920s and 1930s, but gradually encompassed more typical suburban images, with timber decks, patios, pergolas, swimming pools, and courtyards providing a focus. An *Annual* (1955–) summarised major trends. Guertner's photographic policy saw every major house shoot contribute to a library of garden images, and this was supplemented by photographer Ed Ramsay. The magazine regularly profiled different plant species and categories (bulbs, annuals, and perennials) and provided a monthly horticultural diary and garden construction articles by Tom Moore and others. An early contributor was Edna WALLING, who illustrated her garden designs at Braemark (Mooroolbark, Vic.) and Lynton Lee (BICKLEIGH VALE), and wrote on 'Good Mulching with Hay'. Long-time gardening correspondents included Reg EDWARDS and Rolfe Bradley. Gardening content was revamped in the 1980s with the introduction of Jennifer Stackhouse's column 'On Home Ground', Tim NORTH's enquiry service, and Michele Shennen's 'Garden Diary'—their articles enhanced by superior photography and colour printing. A long-standing publishing association with *Gregory's Guides* and *Good Gardening* magazine (1971–81) produced numerous allied gardening publications.

HOWARD TANNER

AUSTRALIAN INLAND BOTANIC GARDENS, located in a semi-ARID region on the River Murray in NSW about six kilometres from Mildura (Vic.), was first proposed in 1983. The 150-hectare site was acquired in 1988, with the first planting being undertaken in 1991. The historic relocated Garnpang Homestead serves as a temporary visitor centre, classroom, and social centre for the garden. An IRRIGATION system was installed in 1992 and a salt-tolerant plant section and large rose garden have been established. Development has since commenced on sections featuring American and European plants, followed by plantings of Asian, New Zealand, African, and Australian plants.

JOHN ZWAR

AUSTRALIAN INSTITUTE OF HORTICULTURE (1959–), a professional association embracing horticultural industries including parks and gardens, nursery, landscape design, turf, and floriculture. The Institute was founded in Canberra by James Hamilton Webb (b. 1926), Percy Byron Moore (b. 1924), and Gerald Henry (Tony) Featherston (1915–1980)—during a period that saw rapid development of parks and gardens in the ACT—with the aim of raising the status of HORTICULTURE as a profession akin to that of allied disciplines such as LANDSCAPE ARCHITECTURE and FORESTRY. With approximately 1200 members, it now has branches in all states and territories. The Institute's national council is based in NSW, with its administrative headquarters at Gosford. Reflecting its origins, the Institute continues to have its strongest membership base in NSW, followed by WA, which first established a state council in 1974. Institute news has been published in *AUSTRALIAN HORTICULTURE* since its own journal (1973–81) ceased publication. The Institute promotes professionalism in horticulture, and its aims include improvement of the environment through the science and management of plants; conservation of indigenous flora and habitats; representing qualified horticulturists to government, the industry, and the public; and assisting and promoting horticultural research. It conducts workshops and seminars, and is involved in horticultural education through awards to students and membership of state industry training boards.

JILL KELLOW

AUSTRALIAN INSTITUTE OF LANDSCAPE ARCHITECTS (1967–), now an influential, high-profile organisation with more than a thousand corporate members administered through a National Office in Canberra, was established with Peter SPOONER, Margaret HENDRY, and Richard CLOUGH as first president, secretary, and treasurer respectively. A provisional executive committee to establish an Australian institute of LANDSCAPE ARCHITECTS had been appointed in 1963 to galvanise support and professional status among the burgeoning group of landscape architects in Australia: some then returning from study or work experience in Britain and NORTH AMERICA, or working with a few practising landscape architects from other states during the early 1960s. The Committee established a national council to include one representative from each state and territory, with an additional three to act as an executive. Within two years, this Council, supported by State Groups, introduced conferences, arranged promotional lectures by distinguished landscape architects such as Dame Sylvia CROWE, published a bulletin (the forerunner of *LANDSCAPE AUSTRALIA*), and prepared a constitution to enable incorporation. Initially this took place in Qld, as that state allowed the legal use of the term landscape architect (generally governed by restrictive *Architects Acts*); after the amendment of the ACT *Architects Act* incorporation took place there.

In the 1960s many tertiary institutions offered extension and postgraduate diploma courses in landscape design: as these institutions restructured courses, the Council gave its support in establishing an education policy and accreditation procedure. By the mid-1970s some undergraduate courses operated in the eastern states, resulting in a concentration of landscape architects there. The resulting influx of new graduates soon dominated the profession and AILA membership. By the 20th Congress of the International Federation of Landscape Architects (Canberra, 1982), the majority of members were in private practice, but an increasing number were employed in government service. As membership grew, the Institute authorised Landscape Publications to expand and publish its official journal *LANDSCAPE AUSTRALIA* as a commercial venture. An awards program was introduced to reward professional recognition and excellence; it included the 'Award in Landscape Architecture' (1982) to acknowledge outstanding service by a member of the profession. More recently, some State Groups have introduced similar programs.

As professional services increase and diversify—from landscape assessment, environmental impact statements, master planning, landscape design, expert witness briefs, major national projects, and URBAN DESIGN to the increasing use of electronic technologies—the Institute has introduced a registration procedure to support members as they increase their design skills to meet future challenges.

MARGARET HENDRY

AUSTRALIAN INSTITUTE OF LANDSCAPE DESIGNERS AND MANAGERS (1995–), an organisation 'representing the landscape professional within the industry'. It was formed to serve the needs of qualified landscape designers and landscape managers, who may be ineligible for

AUSTRALIAN INSTITUTE OF LANDSCAPE ARCHITECTS membership, but who, nevertheless, make a major contribution to Australia's DESIGNED LANDSCAPES. ALLAN CORREY

AUSTRALIAN NATIONAL BOTANIC GARDENS, Canberra, is devoted exclusively to the AUSTRALIAN FLORA. While Walter Burley GRIFFIN prepared proposals for the development of botanical reserves and Dr B.T. Dickson of the Council for Scientific and Industrial Research carried out a feasibility study for a conventional BOTANIC GARDEN in 1935, it was Lindsay PRYOR who, on being appointed Superintendent of Parks and Gardens (1944), established the current Gardens. He selected the site on the south-eastern slopes of Black Mountain, where, with two main gullies, an altitude range of 100 metres, and shelter from the west, he saw the possibility of creating a range of microclimates. Influenced by botanic gardens such as those at Santa Barbara (California) devoted to specific floras, he began developing these Gardens using Australian native plants, and gradually formed a policy of devoting them exclusively to study and cultivation of the Australian flora adopted. Dr Erwin Gauba (1891–1964) was employed as botanist in 1950; plants for the garden were collected and propagated at the Yarralumla nursery; and HERBARIUM material was gathered and stored. An ALPINE annexe at Mount Gingera and a coastal one at Jervis Bay were established to allow a greater range of plants to be grown. By the time Pryor left the Department of the Interior (1958), the character of the Gardens had been established.

Pryor's successor, David William Shoobridge (1913–2000), pressed ahead with their development. Dr E. Marie (Betty) Phillips (1917–1977) succeeded Gauba in 1960, greatly extending the areas from which plants were collected, while John WRIGLEY was appointed curator in 1967. With the construction of Lake Burley Griffin the site was redefined and fenced. Herbarium, office, library, depot, and cottages were completed in 1966 and a new herbarium in 1974. The site was first opened to the public in 1964; the official opening following in 1970. The appointment in 1979 of Robert BODEN as inaugural director saw the establishment of the gardens as an independent institution. Following the granting of self-government to ACT (1989) the gardens became a Commonwealth Government responsibility. In 1994 most of the herbarium was moved to the Centre for Plant Biodiversity Research on the CSIRO site.

About 90 000 plants representing more than 5000 species are grown in the forty hectares of the ninety-hectare site that have been developed. These are arranged in both taxonomic and ECOLOGICAL groupings: the granite and Hawkesbury sandstone rock gardens and those based on the swamp, mallee, and temperate rainforest environments are especially notable. RICHARD CLOUGH

AUSTRALIAN NATIVE PLANTS: see AUSTRALIAN FLORA

AUSTRALIAN PARKS (AND RECREATION): see PARKS AND LEISURE AUSTRALIA

AUSTRALIAN PLANTS: see SOCIETY FOR GROWING AUSTRALIAN PLANTS

AUSTRALIAN PLANTS SOCIETY: see SOCIETY FOR GROWING AUSTRALIAN PLANTS

(AUSTRALIAN) TOWN AND COUNTRY JOURNAL (1870–1919), an illustrated weekly newspaper published in Sydney, included considerable horticultural coverage. This was principally directed at economic rather than ornamental horticulture, with agriculturists, pastoralists, and acclimatisers well to the fore. Coverage largely centred on NSW, with occasional excursions into Qld and Vic. T.W. SHEPHERD, its initial 'agricultural and botanical editor', was probably responsible for the extensive series entitled 'Exotic Trees and Plants Suitable for Australia' featured during the first year of publication. Other notable horticultural contributors included Angus MACKAY and Fred TURNER. RA

AUSTRALIAN WATTLE DAY LEAGUE: see WATTLE DAY

AUSTRALIA'S OPEN GARDEN SCHEME (1992–) began in 1987 as Victoria's Gardens Scheme and, following incorporation as a non-profit limited liability company in 1992, has expanded to cover all state and territories. Modelled on well-established British schemes of GARDEN VISITING to (mostly) private gardens, and building on the program organised by John PATRICK in 1984 (for Victoria's sesquicentenary celebrations), the scheme received the initial backing of the Australian Broadcasting Corporation's Victorian Radio Division and Royal Horticultural Society of Victoria. The Victorian scheme introduced the hallmarks of the later national scheme—an informative annual guidebook (giving information on access arrangements and garden notes), well-targeted RADIO publicity, and a modest charge split three ways (between garden owners or their nominated charity, administration, and selected funding of garden projects). As the scheme burgeoned, so too did support from the nursery industry through the Australian Horticultural Corporation. Gardens are chosen by selection panels, using criteria including design strength and quality, significant plantings, historic significance, and standard of maintenance. *The Open Garden* (2000), compiled by Louise Earwaker and Neil ROBERTSON, profiles selected participating gardeners and their gardens. RA

AVENUES, double rows of trees, mark urban and rural landscapes in Australia with formal, scenic, and commemorative elements. They may invite journey or presage arrival, bestow importance to park entrance or GATE, create amenity, frame a VISTA, signify remembrance, or confer power in POLITICAL landscapes. The regularity of their equally spaced trees, usually of the same species, planted on both sides of a road, drive, or path creates their importance. Well grown, their crowns may join to create an archway or 'cathedral' effect in the European manner—as do the elm (*Ulmus* spp.)

Avenues

The planting of tree AVENUES, such as this example through Hobart's Domain, provided a popular nineteenth- and early twentieth-century means of imposing FORMALITY on the Australian landscape

avenues in Melbourne's FITZROY GARDENS and at Bacchus Marsh (Vic.). Most Australian avenues have a lighter, more open appearance due to poorer growth, wide public roadways, or the open crowns of eucalypts.

Avenues in British estates and European town plans were well known when Australia's earliest avenues were planted. The first was probably of *Eucalyptus robusta* (Swamp Mahogany) planted in 1816 along Mrs Macquarie's Drive in Sydney's Government DOMAIN. Jane FRANKLIN's sharp comments led to an avenue of oak, elm, and ash (*Fraxinus* spp.) being planted in 1837 leading to the church at PORT ARTHUR. An early town plan for Rose Hill, Parramatta, (NSW) called for wide, straight, tree-lined avenues, but they did not eventuate. The spread of BOTANIC GARDENS, the creation of PUBLIC PARKS, and TOWN PLANNING for major cities led to further avenues during the 1850s and 1860s. For instance, extensive avenues were planted in Melbourne's Botanic Gardens, Domain, and Government House Reserve under the direction of Ferdinand MUELLER. From being official and special features of the landscape, avenues became common municipal features from the 1890s as street trees were planted: Ballarat (Vic.), for example, established long avenues during the 1870s, and by 1910 had planted every main and cross street. CANBERRA is notable for the thoroughness and beauty of its avenues, initiated by Charles WESTON from 1911. Some have alternating species, while Anzac Parade—leading to the Australian War Memorial—uses several lines of *Eucalyptus globulus* subsp. *bicostata* (Blue Gum) to create a block effect. COMMEMORATIVE avenues of honour form WAR MEMORIALS in many Australian towns.

Private avenues were planted along the driveways to large properties from at least the mid-nineteenth century. The rise of tree consciousness in the 1880s and 1890s, promoted by ARBOR DAY and the provision of free or cheap plants from STATE FOREST NURSERIES, encouraged further plantings. From being features only of large HOMESTEADS, avenues became common in many RURAL LANDSCAPES, where they also served as WINDBREAKS.

Avenues are difficult to maintain against the depredations of traffic engineers, electricity authorities, bush fires, diseases, and accidents. Replacement is particularly difficult and locally contentious, because the trees do not deteriorate or die uniformly. New or replacement avenues in older urban areas are uncommon, although some greenfield housing developments incorporate avenues as features along major access roads.

JOHN DARGAVEL

AVENUES OF HONOUR: see Commemorative and Memorial Gardens

AVIARIES, enclosures—typically decorative, free-standing features in gardens—specifically designed to hold birds in confinement. The earliest recorded example was Marcus Terentius Varro's 'Ornithon' for songbirds at his Roman villa (c. 35 BC). Their renewed popularity world-wide in the eighteenth and early nineteenth centuries was consistent with the creation of new Public Parks and Gardens, zoos, and menageries, coupled with the popular passion for Natural History and field sciences. In Australia, fuelled by an interest in Acclimatisation, aviaries became common features of large private gardens, Botanic Gardens, and Zoological Gardens during the mid- to late nineteenth century, although as the period of the collector and dilettante scientist diminished, other decorative garden elements took their place. An early example remains at Buda (Vic.), where the octagonal structure mimics, in miniature, the distinctive architecture of the house.

FRANCINE GILFEDDER

BABWORTH HOUSE, Darling Point, NSW: see HORDERN family

BACKHOUSE, Benjamin Joseph (1829–1904), self-taught architect, was born at Ipswich, Suffolk, England, and, following a business failure, migrated to Australia, arriving at Geelong (Vic.) in 1853. He worked as a stonemason, and in 1855 started an architectural practice with William Reynolds. Following a return to England in 1860, Backhouse established architectural practices in Qld (1861) and NSW (1868), influential not only for volume of work but as training grounds for apprenticed architects. His involvement with civic improvements included the layout of public spaces and tree planting in Geelong (1850s), street tree planting in Brisbane (1860s), Prince Alfred Park, Sydney (1870), and as a member and long-time chairman of the City of Sydney Improvement Board (1879–1904). A committed socialist and reformer, Backhouse was strongly influenced by his reading of Carlyle, Ruskin, and Morris. His second son, Alfred Paxton Backhouse (b. 1851), was named after Joseph PAXTON, architect of the Crystal Palace.   CRAIG BURTON

BACKHOUSE, James (1794–1869), naturalist, nursery proprietor, and Quaker missionary, was born at Darlington, Durham, England, and educated by a member of the Society of Friends. He trained for two years at a Norwich nursery; his botanical interests allied with deeply held views on prison reform led to his lengthy stay in Van Diemen's Land, Norfolk Island, and NSW from 1832 to 1838. His *Narrative of a Visit to the Australian Colonies* (1843) was warmly reviewed by the *Gardeners' Chronicle*. The *Narrative* contained many prescient observations about colonial society and its ills, but Backhouse also took the opportunity to publish many knowledgable botanical and horticultural observations throughout the text and in an appendix 'Remarks on the Indigenous Vegetable Productions of Tasmania, available as food for man'. This last was an amended republication, with corrections by Ronald GUNN, of his 'Index Plantarum, or an attempt towards a popular description, of some of the most common and remarkable indigenous plants, of Van Diemen's Land', which appeared in *Ross's Hobart Town Almanack for 1835*. Backhouse distributed Australian plants both within Australia and overseas as well as sending exotics to Australia. In addition to many herbarium specimens, Backhouse gave KEW two volumes of his botanical recollections of Australia. He is recognised by the genus *Backhousia*. His brother, Thomas Backhouse (1792–1845), conducted a nursery at York (of which James was a part-proprietor) and E.N. WARD was among those who trained at this celebrated and long-established house.   RA

BACKYARDS The backyard form, a rectangle of open space extending behind the house, was set in industrialising eighteenth-century Europe and modified by nineteenth-century scientific planning. This form was traditionally defined by paling fences—in the nineteenth century left bare, or disguised with plumbago or ivy. By the 1930s, oleander or privet hid palings and created privacy. The 1980s Mediterranean trend saw many palings replaced with rendered walls and bougainvillea.

Backyard content reflected changing ideas of privacy, leisure, work, family, and consumerism. Improvements to plumbing and sewerage, and the coming of the car, affected both form and content. Backyards are traditionally service

For the illustrator of *Australian House and Garden* in 1951, the BACKYARD was little changed in form or purpose from its pre-war manifestation, and the first stirrings of MODERNISM were yet to be felt in this traditional domestic domain

areas, in colonial times containing cart-sheds, stables, tanks, wells and drains, woodpiles, washing lines, fowl-runs, and perhaps a pigsty. Sometimes there was a VEGETABLE GARDEN, or pot plants—rarely grass—sometimes brick paving, mostly hard-packed earth. The form of the yard continues to reflect its service origins. Until well into the 1950s the backyard was accessed through internal service areas—scullery, laundry, or 'trades' porch. A straight path led past the clothes-line to the rear of the block, where toilet, fowl-yard, and sheds for fuel, tools, potting—or pottering—and perhaps a fruit tree, were located, often near a gate to the service lane. In burgeoning suburbia, the backyard form was adapted by a new post-war society. In older suburbs the garage housing the newly acquired family car was accessed from a service lane, but in new areas the car entered from the front, passing the side of the house to the garage clinging to a side fence becoming, de facto, shrubbery. Inside the house, open-plan living areas looked over the backyard, now accessed through sliding doors and a PATIO: laundry and toilet moved indoors. Mown lawns encouraged children's play, and adults entertained with a BARBECUE, signalling a new informality.

The late twentieth-century backyard formed a leisure site, with swimming pools dominating the formal structure. Service areas were disguised behind lattice and clothes-lines made retractable, or replaced by new laundry technologies. The garage became part of the house, the patio was paved, and the lemon tree was potted and topiaried. In rural backyards principles of utility still applied: space was given to tanks and fruit trees; fowl-yard and garages were removed to the house paddock.

Regional variations also occur. In NSW the choko vine departed with the outlawed fowls, but the lemon tree remains. Queenlanders prefer the mango. In Tasmania, sheds for wood and hobbies dominate. Urban consolidation may threaten the suburban backyard, but its culture remains firmly in the national psyche.   DEBORAH MALOR

BAGOT, John (1849–1910), of the influential pioneering pastoral and mining family in SA, spent his early years as part-owner of The Peake, a pastoral lease 1100 kilometres north of Adelaide. He married Lucy Josephine Ayers, daughter of former colonial premier and philanthropist Sir Henry Ayers, in 1878. In 1889 Bagot purchased 9.5 hectares of land at Stirling in the ADELAIDE HILLS: south- and west-sloping land containing a valley between two enclosing spurs. **Forest Lodge**, his Victorian, baronial-style house, built in 1890, of two storeys with a castellated octagonal tower, was designed by architect Ernest Bayer. The layout of the main garden was commenced in the same year, in a late Victorian GARDENESQUE style, by German-trained gardener Ernst MENZEL. Designed with circular patterns traversing the contours as the path layout moved down the valley, often edged with box, rosemary, and juniper, it featured a flower garden near the house and a large rose garden on the western spur. In 1891 Bagot travelled with family and friends to Japan, North America, Scotland, England, and Italy, obtaining ideas and catalogues. Seeds and seedlings were sent back to Menzel with planting and propagation instructions. Bagot also sent back and exchanged seeds and cuttings with other colleagues who were then developing gardens in the Adelaide Hills, including Sir Edward STIRLING and Tom Elder Barr Smith. Bagot's particular interest, and Menzel's expertise, was in CONIFERS. At the lower level of the garden, a cast-iron Victorian fountain and grotto were integrated with an arched Japanese bridge, twin pergolas, and plantings of rhododendrons, bamboo, and wisteria.

Walter Hervey Bagot (1880–1963), John's son, inherited Forest Lodge in 1910. Brought up with his father's fervent interest in shrubs and trees, he was later introduced to and greatly admired northern ITALIAN architecture and landscape design. Bagot obtained an apprenticeship with Adelaide architect E.J. Woods before studying architecture at King's College, London. Returning to Adelaide, he entered into partnership in 1905 with Woods and became a prominent architect influencing public and private architecture and landscape design. His use of light and space, and consciousness of the relationship between the natural and built form, is reflected in his designs. Bagot also served as a governor of the ADELAIDE BOTANIC GARDEN and a commissioner of (BELAIR) NATIONAL PARK. He also influenced the architectural and landscape design of BROADLEES in the Adelaide Hills, and the North Terrace and WAITE campuses of the University of Adelaide, and was a supporter of landscape designer Elsie CORNISH.

Walter Bagot altered and extended the Forest Lodge garden, drawing upon his Italian landscape interests and fashions of the time. He redeveloped the flower garden into a croquet lawn (1911), establishing its clipped euonymus hedges and planting *Cupressus sempervirens* (Italian Cypress) and *Taxus baccata* 'Fastigata' (Irish Yew) to provide accents. In 1917 he started on the lower portion of the garden, establishing the Italian VISTA. On the axis of the Japanese bridge, marble steps descended to a grass sward between two lines of regularly planted Italian Cypress (grown from seeds obtained in Florence). The focal point was an enormous Medici tazza featuring the Judgement of Ajax, set on a classical base, designed as a memorial to his forebears. Flanking the *allée* on both sides were *Pseudotsuga menziesii* (Douglas Fir) and *Sequoia sempervirens* (Californian Redwood). Upon Walter's death, his son, barrister John Hervey Bagot (b. 1910) inherited the property.

In 1929 Walter Bagot had acquired **Nurney House**, North Adelaide, named after the Bagot family home in Ireland, and built in 1847 by his great-grandfather, Captain Charles Hervey Bagot. The house was originally a two-storey residence, enclosed by a four-metre-high limestone wall, with a sweeping drive flanked by geometric garden beds cut into the lawn. In 1930 Bagot designed major alterations to the eastern wing and added a porticoed entrance to the front. An Italianate atrium was added on the southern side, facing the Hills. Enclosed on three sides by vaulted colonnades, steps descended to a recessed parterre garden, edged with clipped rosemary and divided by crossing paths of terracotta tiles. A small, Sienese-tiled circular fountain formed the focal point. In the central arch of the southern wall, a pair of detailed wrought-iron gates provided access to the garden beyond. Sculpture, urns, plaques and fountains complemented the courtyard's simplicity of botanical colour.

TEMPE BEAVEN

BAGOT, Robert Cooper (*c.* 1828–1881), Irish-born surveyor and civil engineer, worked in the Moreton Bay district before moving to Melbourne *c.* 1855. Bagot worked during a period when cricket and other SPORTS facilities were gaining an increasing share of public land, or being incorporated into existing PUBLIC PARKS and recreation reserves. He redesigned the Melbourne Cricket Ground in 1861, transforming the rough paddock into a level, turfed oval surrounded (in YARRA PARK) with trees supplied by MUELLER. Bagot likewise transformed Flemington RACECOURSE during the 1860s, draining the central marsh to form 'the Flat' and persuasively arguing for purchase of 'the Hill'. He brought an egalitarian character to the turf and his changes at Flemington were emulated by racing clubs across Australia.

RA

The vista created by Walter BAGOT at Forest Lodge, Stirling (SA), where an avenue of Italian Cypress leads to an elevated tazza, gives an accomplished ITALIANATE touch that draws on Bagot's architectural training and his extensive travel in Europe

BAILEY, John (1800–1864) and members of his family formed a botanical and gardening dynasty in both SA and Qld for more than a century. Bailey's father was a nursery proprietor and seed merchant in Hackney, London, when John Bailey and his family migrated to Adelaide, arriving in 1839 accompanied by a large shipment of vines and fruit trees. He was an experienced horticulturist and had been invited by Governor Gawler to become the inaugural Colonial Botanist and to oversee the establishment of Adelaide's first BOTANIC GARDEN. Due to the parlous financial state of the settlement, the position lasted only until 1841, so he and his sons established their own business, Bailey's Gardens, also known as Hackney Gardens. Bailey maintained close contact with the English nursery firm Conrad Loddiges and Sons, where he may previously have worked—the firm specialised in Cape Colony (South Africa) bulbs and the flora of New Holland (Australia).

Frederick Manson Bailey (1827–1915), John's second son, was born in Hackney. He did not continue formal schooling after his arrival in Adelaide, and worked in his father's nursery until he tried his luck in the Bendigo (Vic.) goldfields in the early 1850s. He married in 1856 and moved to the Hutt Valley in New Zealand in 1858; by 1861 he had migrated to Brisbane. He opened a seed store in Edward Street, but this venture bankrupted him in 1865. He turned to collecting botanical specimens, which took him to many parts of the colony. In 1874 he was employed as a collector for the Queensland Acclimatisation Society in the Maroochy River area; later in the same year he was appointed Keeper of the HERBARIUM within the Queensland Museum. He wrote *Handbook to the Ferns of Queensland* (1874) and in the following year was also appointed as botanist to the 'Board appointed to Inquire into the Causes of Diseases in Live Stock and Plants'. In 1879 he collaborated with Reverend J.E. Tenison-Woods on a *Census of the Flora of Brisbane* and with Karl Staiger, the Museum's analyst, on *An Illustrated Monograph of the Grasses of Queensland*. The following year, due to staff shortages, he was the temporary Curator of the Museum, and in 1881 he was appointed Colonial Botanist, after Walter HILL retired. Thus, for the first time in Qld, the position of Colonial Botanist was divided from that of the Curator of the BRISBANE BOTANIC GARDENS. Publication of his book *The Fern World of Australia* (1881) coincided with heightened horticultural interest in FERNS.

Bailey and his expanding herbarium remained located within the Museum until 1889, when he moved into the new Department of Agriculture building, the department having been formed two years earlier. He continued his botanical collecting throughout the colony, venturing into the Bellenden Ker range for an important northern collection in 1889. The following decade he collected around the Georgina River in western Qld and on the islands of the Torres Strait, and he accompanied Lord Lamington to New Guinea in 1898. His publications continued: *Catalogue of Plants in the Two Metropolitan Gardens, the Brisbane Botanic Gardens and Bowen Park* (1885), *A Synopsis of the Queensland Flora* (1886), several catalogues to accompany Queensland's exhibits of grasses and woods to various colonial and intercolonial

EXHIBITIONS, *Plants Reputed Poisonous and Injurious to Stock* (1887), *A Companion for the Queensland Student of Plant Life* (1893), and *The Queensland Flora* (1899–1905), as well as many other scientific and popular articles. In 1902, at the age of 75, Bailey refused retirement and continued working without pay for a period. After strong public protest, he was reinstated, but on only half his former pay. In the same year he was awarded the Clarke Medal by the Royal Society of New South Wales. Two years before his death, he produced *The Comprehensive Catalogue of Queensland Plants* (1913).

Over his long career, F.M. Bailey was connected to the wider botanical world through his membership of ROYAL and LINNEAN SOCIETIES in several colonies, as well as election to the Société Royale de Botanique de Belgique. In Qld he was involved in the re-establishment of the Royal Philosophical Society of Queensland (1883), serving in several capacities—president in 1890 and as chair of the Natural History Section during 1886–95. Bailey was also a member of the Biology Section of the AUSTRALASIAN ASSOCIATION FOR THE ADVANCEMENT OF SCIENCE from its inception.

His son, **John Frederick Bailey** (1866–1938), held the position of assistant to the Government Botanist for sixteen years before his appointment as curator of the Brisbane Botanic Gardens in 1905. J.F. Bailey collected widely throughout the state and contributed many articles to the *Queensland Agricultural Journal*. During his eleven-year term, the physical appearance of the gardens changed markedly. A replacement curator's cottage was completed and the retaining wall along the river frontage extended. The gardens were lit by electric power in 1908, greatly enhancing their use as a public venue. Flood mitigation works to straighten the course of the Brisbane River were eventually completed in 1917. This meant that several acres of the gardens were dredged away, many trees planted by Walter Hill were removed, and several buildings moved. Throughout these changes Bailey built a high profile in educational and horticultural affairs. He lectured weekly at Gatton Agricultural College (eighty kilometres west of Brisbane) and travelled widely judging horticultural exhibits. He served on the inaugural Board of Advice on Prickly Pear Destruction (1911) as the Queensland Government attempted to curtail the devastation being wrought throughout southern and central parts of the state. He also re-established close exchange relationships with botanic gardens in Melbourne, Sydney, Ballarat, and Adelaide. At the death of his father, he was appointed Government Botanist and his nephew, F.M. Bailey's grandson, Cyril Tennison WHITE, was appointed as his assistant. Thus the two important horticultural and botanical positions were again combined. Together White and Bailey produced a series of 'Illustrated Notes on the Weeds of Queensland' for the *Queensland Agricultural Journal*. J.F. Bailey was appointed as the Director of the ADELAIDE BOTANIC GARDEN in 1916 where he continued to build the profile of horticultural affairs in the public mind. In 1932 he returned to Brisbane, where he died.

John Rayer Bailey (1914–1956) was appointed Curator of the Brisbane Botanic Gardens in 1946, the position having been vacant for more than six years. He undertook much-needed maintenance of the gardens, and was the first to introduce chemical sprays against weeds and plant diseases. Bailey expanded the succulents collection—established by his predecessor, Ernest BICK—to about 400 species. He also introduced many indigenous species into the collections. The croton collection was expanded, *Callitris* spp. and *Casuarina* spp. were planted by the river, and indigenous species were planted along the length of the old Bunya Drive. By 1951 Bailey had prepared a catalogue of the gardens and produced a pamphlet graphing the flowering periods for about 170 species he thought useful for street planting. His duties also included providing floral and foliage decoration for municipal receptions and official occasions and floats for annual processions and flower shows. His career was cut short by his sudden death.
JUDITH DEPPELER-HAGAN

M.H. BAILLIEU RESIDENCE, Toorak, Vic., designed by Harold DESBROWE-ANNEAR in 1925 and built in 1926, originally had a lofty view north and west to the Yarra River and the city, of which the formal and elaborate garden front took advantage. Desbrowe-Annear's garden was originally conceived as a large terrace intersected by radial paths emerging from a piazza by the house, in the Beaux-Arts manner popular with English and American designers at the time. The completed garden was simplified and comprised two terraces. Much of the significance and success of the Baillieu garden derives from its connection with the architecture of the house, for which Desbrowe-Annear conceived an elaborate garden front in the neo-Georgian style that, with its mellow brickwork and subtle detail, can best be appreciated from the large upper lawn terrace. This terrace is connected with the garden front by a piazza onto which the living rooms open: broad, semi-circular steps in the manner of Gertrude JEKYLL give access to the lawn and an axial path of stone steps set into the lawn lead to a tennis court. The lower terrace along the northern boundary of the property is separated from the upper terrace by a three-metre granite and sandstone wall: stone steps punctuated with classical urns connect the two areas. This terrace has a flagged path lined with herbaceous borders; it originally led, through an arched hedge, to an informal garden of flowering trees and shrubs. Subdivision in 2000 has compromised the rear (west) section of the garden.
HARRIET EDQUIST

BAKER, Euphemia Eleanor (Effie) (1880–1968), was born at Goldsborough (Vic.) and attended Ballarat East Art School, where she developed her interest in PHOTOGRAPHY. She moved to Black Rock (Vic.), setting up an art studio producing toys, drawings, and photographs. She published several booklets of hand-coloured photographs depicting wildflowers (*c*. 1914–17)—early and accomplished examples of this phase of appreciation of the AUSTRALIAN FLORA. Baker converted to the Baha'i faith (1923) and travelled from 1925 to 1936, photographing sacred sites in Palestine and Persia (Iran) and using the results to illustrate *The Dawnbreakers* (1932). She continued her delicate hand-colouring of wildflower photographs until her death in Sydney.
RA

Ballarat Botanic Gardens

eties and technical college students, which illustrated the successful application of Australian floral designs to the DECORATIVE ARTS. These pieces formed the basis of his successful exhibition 'The Australian Flora Applied to Art' at the Museum (1906–44). In *The Australian Flora in Applied Arts—Part 1: The Waratah* (1915) Baker extolled the virtues of the waratah, 'the glory of the Australian bush' as a national symbol and illustrated its successful adaptation to design and decoration.
MARGARET BETTERIDGE

BALCONY GARDENS: see APARTMENTS AND RESIDENTIAL FLATS

BALL, Erica Margery Jane (b. 1930), landscape architect, was born in Sydney and studied horticulture at BURNLEY, gaining her certificate in 1949. Always more interested in large-scale landscapes than in gardens, on the advice of Professor Denis Winston she went to Durham, England, and in 1952–53 studied LANDSCAPE ARCHITECTURE at King's College. Returning in 1953, she became the first Australian landscape architect with an overseas qualification to go into practice. Working from the office of Melbourne architects Leith and Bartlett, she designed landscaping for Housing Commission of Victoria estates developed by the five firms in its panel of architects. She was engaged in 1954 to landscape Melbourne's thirty-hectare Olympic Village at Heidelberg for the 1956 Olympic Games. Edna WALLING and others objected to her use of advanced exotic trees in the village's two small parks, but undaunted, Ball defended her design in the Melbourne *Age*. After her marriage to John Sutherland Edwards in 1957 she ceased her practice and moved to rural NSW.
RICHARD CLOUGH

BALLARA, Point Lonsdale, Vic., is the quintessential seaside SUMMER RETREAT: modest, informal, and low in maintenance. Developed from 1904 for Alfred Deakin (1856–1919), IRRIGATION proponent, influential advocate of Federation, and second Australian prime minister, his family bungalow (1907) sits amidst a clearing in a mix of exotic and retained vegetation. Deakin found solace in clearing undergrowth of the surrounding BUSH while his wife Pattie sketched native ORCHIDS. By their decision to leave Ballara garden primarily indigenous, the Deakins were in the horticultural vanguard.

John Rickard, *A Family Romance: The Deakins at Home* (Carlton South, Vic., 1996)
RA

BALLARAT BOTANIC GARDENS, Vic., developed from 1856 to 1858 on an extensive site overlooking Lake Wendouree, is perhaps the best known BOTANIC GARDEN outside Australia's capital cities. The strong linear form of the original design—the result of a COMPETITION—was laid out by inaugural curator George LONGLEY. Development was focused on the 'botanic department' and nursery ground, buffered by parkland at the north and south. The chief glory was the 'Wellingtonia Walk', a superb avenue of *Sequoiadendron giganteum* (Giant Redwood), whose elephantine trunks and massive tusk-like branches still draw admiring gasps. Other conifers and deciduous exotics were also freely planted

These polished columns installed by R.T. BAKER in the Sydney Technological Museum highlighted the natural grain of timber (*Podocarpus elata* Brown Pine and *Callitris glauca* Cypress Pine), but in their classical inspiration also demonstrated Baker's veneration of the AUSTRALIAN FLORA

BAKER, Richard Thomas (1854–1941), botanist and museum curator, was born at Woolwich, Kent, England, and after education and a teaching position migrated to Sydney (1879). He was appointed assistant curator (to J.H. MAIDEN) at the Sydney Technological Museum in 1888 and curator a decade later. Baker and his colleague, chemist Henry George Smith (1852–1924), collaborated on chemotaxonomic research on EUCALYPTS, which helped to establish the commercial viability of the eucalyptus oil industry. Baker wrote widely on the subject of ECONOMIC BOTANY, including research monographs on Australian eucalypts (1902), pines (1910), hardwoods (1919), and wood fibres (1924). His *Cabinet Timbers of Australia* (1913) followed an earlier work, *Building and Ornamental Building Stones*. Keen to promote the commercial importance of Australian natural resources, Baker organised the Museum's successful contribution of botanical specimens, oils, and polished timber samples to major international EXHIBITIONS overseas, including the Franco–British Exhibition (1908).

Baker's passion for botany and his interest in art were the catalyst for his spirited attempt to establish a national style of decoration. He amassed a collection of more than 200 items, including contemporary craft created by art and craft soci-

This engraving of BALLARAT BOTANIC GARDENS (and its accompanying breathless text) conveyed to astonished English readers of the *Journal of Horticulture and Cottage Gardener* (1874) the reality of development at a place that two decades previously 'had no existence'

during this early stage. In 1877 the first stage of the FERNERY presaged the magnificent structure that formed the undoubted highlight in the late nineteenth and early twentieth centuries. With the donation of twelve Italian statues by local stockbroker and aesthete, Thomas Stoddart, and their housing in an elegant statuary pavilion (1887), the garden was confirmed as a centrepiece of considerable (and justifiable) civic pride of a town whose goldfield riches were transformed into civic and cultural enhancement, funded by both the public and the private purse.

From 1889, tuberous begonias were introduced into displays, beginning a tradition of GLASSHOUSE excellence highlighted by the annual Ballarat Begonia FESTIVAL (1953–). Developments catering for increasing tourism included Lake Lodge (1891) for refreshments, Almeida Pavilion (1907) housing amusement machines, and shelters for picnic parties. 'Fairyland', a wooded grove with bridges and walks on the western shore of Lake Wendouree, became a popular feature, and a ZOOLOGICAL section was established in the north of the reserve. Bequests continued to enhance the gardens in the twentieth century; additions included the avenue of prime ministers' busts (1940–) and a startling conservatory (1995: architect Peter Elliott). The garden retains an exceptional collection of conifers and deciduous trees, and bedding and floral displays continue traditional horticultural techniques. RA

BAMBOO (and its aggregation as a *bambouseraie*) has been a garden feature since early colonial days, especially in Australia's TROPICAL and subtropical regions. It is commonly used as HEDGES and WINDBREAKS, clumped in SHRUBBERIES, beside water, or restrained by pots and tubs (especially for highly invasive temperate running forms whose rhizomes must be contained). There are more than 1000 species of bamboo—of these only three are natives, found in north-east Australia—and many have economic value. Within the grass family, Poaceae, bamboos form a subgroup that can be distinguished by their woody habit and stalked leaves. Habits range from the miniature *Pleioblastus pygmaeus* (Pygmy Bamboo), which grows to thirty centimetres, to the giant bamboos of more than thirty metres. Having a centre of distribution in ASIA, bamboos display a grace and elegance that is strongly associated with ORIENTAL serenity and mysticism. This characteristic is used effectively in JAPANESE gardens and contemplative Zen landscaping.

David Farrelly, *The Book of Bamboo: A Comprehensive Guide to this Remarkable Plant, Its Uses, and Its History* (London, 1996)
ROGER SPENCER

BANCROFT, Joseph (1836–1894), medical practitioner, naturalist, and experimental horticulturist, was a man of wide-ranging botanical and zoological interests. Born in Manchester, England, into a farming family, he migrated to Qld with his wife and children in 1864 to improve his health. They settled in Brisbane where he established a respected practice and created EXPERIMENTAL GARDENS at Kelvin Grove, Wickham Terrace, and Deception Bay. Practical by nature, he investigated the commercial uses of plants, especially their adaptation to Queensland's TROPICAL climate. His private and government researches included experiments with rust-proof wheats, grapes, dates, and rice, and investigations into diseases of sugarcane and bananas. Combining medicine and botany in pharmacology he used native barks and gums to treat bowel infections, found *Duboisia myoporoides* (Solanaceae) to be a source of atropine, and demonstrated that pituri was poisonous to animals. He is most famous for discovering *Filaria bancrofti*, the parasitic worm that causes filariasis.

John Pearn and Lawrie Powell (eds), *The Bancroft Tradition* (Brisbane, 1991) MONIKA WELLS

BANDSTANDS were popular GARDEN BUILDINGS from the mid-nineteenth century, initially in BOTANIC GARDENS, but increasingly in PUBLIC PARKS AND GARDENS. Early use by regimental wind bands—when bandstands were often known as 'orchestras'—was replaced by brass band performances, popularised through competitions, especially among local and work-based groups. Substantial structures were required to hold a band, and architectural elaboration was common, typified by Australia's earliest extant bandstand in FITZROY GARDENS, Melbourne (1864), and also the Hitchcock Memorial Bandstand (1919), centrepiece of JOHNSTONE PARK, Geelong. Prefabricated cast-iron structures were occasionally used, exemplified by the bandstand in ELDER PARK, Adelaide (1881). The great age of bandstand building came in the first two decades of the twentieth century, immediately before the age of RADIO, when embellishment of public gardens and other town reserves for public amusement and recreation was complementing earlier planting imperatives. Sound shells, a North American innovation, replaced traditional octagonal structures following the Second World War.

S. Frederick Starr (ed.), *The Oberlin Book of Bandstands* (Washington, D.C., 1987)   RA

BANGAY, Paul (b. 1963), Melbourne-based garden designer, graduated from BURNLEY College in 1985 and rapidly established a reputation for gardens with FORMAL layouts, strong architectural lines, and simple planting schemes. He cites formal Italian, French, and Spanish gardens and, in Britain, Lawrence Johnston's Hidcote Manor and David Hick's garden in Oxfordshire, as major influences. Bangay has designed more than 600 private gardens in all states of Australia and public projects including the Melbourne Aids Memorial garden. His overseas commissions include gardens in New Zealand, West Indies, Cook Islands, and North America (where he completed the restoration of a large Rusell Page garden in South Hampton, New York). In 1989 he was awarded the Mobil Pegasus award for best individual contribution to the Melbourne FESTIVAL, at which his horticultural exhibition 'Botanica' attracted more than 100 000 visitors. His two books, *The Defined Garden* (1996) and *The Boxed Garden* (1998), demonstrate his stylistic preferences.

SALLYANN DAKIS

BANKS, Joseph (1743–1820), landowner, gentleman-scientist, and explorer, was born in Westminster, London, the only son of William Banks MP (of Revesby Abbey, Lincolnshire), and educated at Harrow and then Eton, where he took up the private study of BOTANY and started a HERBARIUM. At Christ Church, Oxford, he imported a private tutor in botany and, when 23, joined a British ship to study NATURAL HISTORY in Newfoundland, this leading to his being allowed to carry a scientific party, including Daniel SOLANDER (a pupil of LINNAEUS) and the artist Sydney PARKINSON, on Cook's *Endeavour* voyage to the Pacific. He is alleged to have invested some £10 000 in the venture. Based in Tahiti for some three months, the expedition returned to England via New Zealand and the east coast of Australia (where in 1770 Banks named Botany Bay because of its botanical richness), Indonesia, and South Africa, collecting plants as they travelled. From that voyage he introduced the first six AUSTRALIAN PLANTS into cultivation, including *Eucalyptus gummifera* and *Dianella caerulea*.

Banks insinuated himself into royal favour and became effectively a scientific adviser to the unstable George III, taking a deep interest in the running of the royal gardens at KEW. From about 1773 he oversaw their day-to-day running, with William Aiton as superintendent, raising their scientific and horticultural status. Under his management, Kew became the model for the modern BOTANIC GARDEN, evolving into the headquarters for a world-wide network of botanic gardens in the British Empire. Indeed the motive of Banks in pressing for exploration, collecting, and establishing botanic gardens must all be seen in the light of empire-building, particularly Britain's rivalry with Revolutionary France. Banks identified three regions of particular interest to Kew: the Cape, South America, and Australia. He appointed and sometimes supported collectors, particularly Scots with 'the habits of industry, attention and frugality', preferably bachelors. Between them, they introduced some ninety Australian species to Europe, but these were merely a fraction of the 7000 species they brought into cultivation during the reign of George III.

Banks played a key role not only in advocating NSW as a penal colony when a mission for such an enterprise in west Africa in 1785–86 failed, but also in turning Australia into a 'Neo-Europe', through the importing and establishment of European plants and animals, with NSW the model for the other colonies. On the *Endeavour*, he had seen Australia with a landowner's eye, calculating that NSW would support the fruits and vegetables of Europe, particularly the MEDITERRANEAN—telling a Commons Select Committee in 1779 of the cereals, pasture legumes, vegetables, herbs, and soft and stone fruit that could be expected to thrive there. As fruit crops for the First Fleet, Captain Phillip therefore took on lemons, limes, and oranges at Rio de Janeiro and the Cape of Good Hope to add to the peaches and other material loaded at Banks's order in Britain. They were planted on the Government Farm at Farm Cove (later SYDNEY BOTANIC GARDENS), and vegetables were grown on GARDEN ISLAND by the crew of the *Sirius*. Banks hoped the settlement would become self-supporting—and indeed an exporter to Britain—but little of commercial consequence eventuated. With poor results in cultivation in Sydney, he sent out more vegetables, cereals, and fruits for the struggling colonists, the *Gorgon* bringing 200 fruit trees in 1791 and returning with Australian plants packed by Banksian collector David BURTON. Phillip had identified better soils at Parramatta, which became the colony's centre of horticultural and agricultural production; by 1802, there were from the original six peach trees perhaps 160 000 in the Cumberland Plain, producing fruit to be dried, fermented and distilled, or fed to pigs, or eaten fresh.

Banks's resident collector in NSW after Burton was the temperamental George CALEY. His collectors on expeditions included Archibald Menzies on Vancouver's voyage and David NELSON on Cook's third expedition and then on Bligh's breadfruit voyage. Most significant for horticulture was Peter GOOD, the gardener under the supervision of Robert BROWN on Flinders' *Investigator* voyage. He planted seeds of vegetables and fruit crops at points on the continent

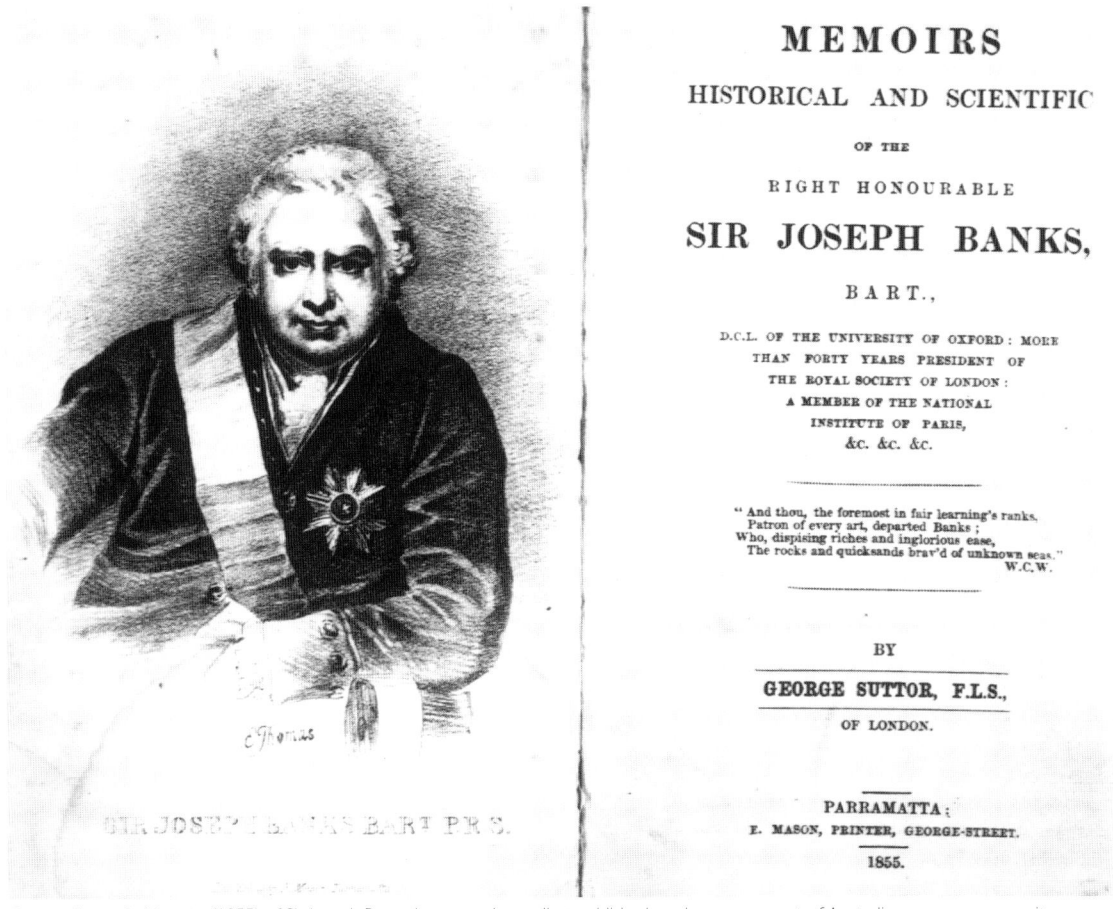

George SUTTOR's *Memoirs* (1855) of Sir Joseph BANKS is among the earliest published works on an aspect of Australian GARDEN HISTORY; it commemorates the role played by Banks as a great patron of Australian botany and horticulture

touched by the voyage, and his seed collections of native plants led to Kew's later pre-eminence in the cultivation of Australian plants—much in vogue in Europe in the early nineteenth century. It was Banks who insisted on a plant cabin on the *Investigator*, as he was to do for the breadfruit on the *Bounty*, and it had been Banks who had supported the market gardener, George SUTTOR, who left England in 1800 with a cargo of plants for NSW. And it was the appointee of Banks, Allan CUNNINGHAM, who became King's Botanist in 1816.

The influence of Banks in appointments in NSW led to the placing of men sympathetic to two-way plant introduction, and he maintained a vast, world-wide correspondence of which they were a part. He was writing to all the governors, from Phillip to Macquarie; Bligh was his nominee, and he supported the candidature of William Paterson; and it was Governor King's son, Philip Parker King, who was to collaborate in pioneering HYBRIDISATION experiments with J.C. BIDWILL and William MACARTHUR.

The influence of Banks on horticulture, as in so many other areas, was as a facilitator rather than an exponent. The nineteenth century in Britain saw a burgeoning of interest in horticulture, notably the development of modern GREENHOUSE cultivation, modern plant pathology and PEST control, experiments in ACCLIMATISATION, and the first systematic programs of plant hybridisation—in all of which Banks was deeply involved. In 1804, he was one of the founders of the (ROYAL) HORTICULTURAL SOCIETY of London, the brainchild of John Wedgwood, Banks contributing to its *Transactions* and being commemorated in the Society's Banksian Medals.

In 1778, Banks was elected president of the Royal Society of London, which post he held until his death. He was one of the 400 richest men in England, and set up at his own expense what has in effect become the Department of Botany in The Natural History Museum, London. He also commissioned BOTANICAL ARTISTS, some of whose work was critical to an understanding of Australian plants—notably the exquisite watercolours of Ferdinand BAUER, who was under the supervision of Robert Brown on Flinders' voyage and later at Banks's house in Soho Square, London. Banks allowed his library to be used by bona fide scientists from all over Europe and beyond and, besides employing Brown as librarian, appointed as assistant there John LINDLEY, who was to become an influential horticulturist and botanist.

Twenty years after the death of Sir Joseph Banks—who had been knighted in 1795—and after the review of Kew by Lindley, that garden became the public garden much as we see it today. His plants had become the core of the botanical collections at what is now the Natural History Museum in 1827. Banks was commemorated in the names of several Australian plants, most notably the genus *Banksia* (Proteaceae), as well as in many place names in Australia—Linnaeus even proposing that the continent itself be called Banksia.

R.E.R. Banks et al (eds), *Sir Joseph Banks: A Global Perspective* (London, 1994); H.B. Carter, *Sir Joseph Banks 1743–1820* (London, 1988); A. Frost, *Sir Joseph Banks and the Transfer of Plants to and from the South Pacific 1786–1798* (Melbourne, 1993)

DAVID MABBERLEY

BANKSIA evolved to its present form about 60 million years ago, just after Australia broke away from the great ancient landmass GONDWANA. At that period the climate was generally TROPICAL, and early banksias probably resembled *Banksia dentata*. As the climate became strongly seasonal the number of species proliferated. Aboriginal peoples found the nectar of the flowers to be a useful food source and gave some names: for example *mangite* for the Bull Banksia of south-western Australia. Often known generically as honeysuckle, modern scientific naming began in 1782, when four species discovered by Joseph BANKS and Daniel SOLANDER in 1770 during the *Endeavour* voyage were described—the generic name honouring Banks. As exploration revealed more of the continent, further species were found, especially in the south-west. Discoveries have continued to the present, the most recent in the 1980s. Seventy-six species are now recognised: sixty in the south-west of WA, fifteen between north-eastern Qld and south-eastern SA (including two in Tas.), and one across the tropical north—this last (*Banksia dentata*) being the only species that grows naturally outside Australia, in New Guinea and the Aru Islands.

Banksias range in form from trees up to thirty metres tall to shrubs growing along the ground. They have tough, usually toothed leaves, flowers in dense spikes, and winged seeds enclosed in woody capsules. Some have flamboyant flowers, others are hidden within the foliage. In many species the fruit will open only when burnt, indicating a long association with natural FIRE in the environment. Many species survive fire and sprout from the old trunk or rootstock, but the others are killed by fire and must regenerate from seed. They are popular garden subjects, and colourful species such as the scarlet *Banksia coccinea* and the orange *B. hookeriana* are prominent in the cut-flower trade. Several species, notably *B. brownii*, *B. goodii*, and *B. cuneata*, are almost extinct in the wild. From their first discovery banksias have attracted artists, with Celia ROSSER being the most notable; two species (*B. attenuata* and *B. serrata*) inspired May Gibbs to create the Bad Banksia Men of her children's story *Snugglepot and Cuddlepie* (1918).

ALEX GEORGE

BANONGILL, Skipton, Vic. William Anderson established this WESTERN DISTRICT pastoral lease in the 1850s, when it was Borrinyallock South before the establishment of Banongill. Horticultural significance came during the Fairbairn family tenure (1895–1975). Along with house extensions in 1904, the spacious north lawn and driveway to the house were landscaped in accordance with the design principles of William GUILFOYLE, a guest of the family. Floral renown came in the 1930s when Charles Osborne Fairbairn (1893–1959) began planting DAFFODILS of the main divisions abundantly, especially on the banks of Mount Emu Creek and beside the driveway. He soon started raising daffodils non-professionally by selective breeding along the lines adopted for sheep and his other interest, racehorses. Of his numerous cultivars, those of greatest merit competed successfully at shows (although he did not register those he named).

GEORGE JONES

BAPTIST, John Thomas (1804–1873), nursery proprietor of Portuguese nationality, probably a native of Madeira, was brought to NSW in 1829. Captain Charles Wilson, appointed Director of Public Works for NSW in 1828, was travelling to Australia in the barque *Swiftsure* when it was damaged during a storm in the Bay of Biscay; during the three months it took to repair the ship in Lisbon, he engaged Baptist. A month after their arrival in Sydney, Baptist's wife and newly born baby died, followed a year later by the death of his two-year-old son. In 1830 he married Emma Phillips, whose convict parents had arrived in NSW ten years previously. Wilson, eighteen months after his arrival, was declared insolvent and dismissed. Without a job and newly married, Baptist opened a butcher's shop in partnership with Ned Shackley, the convict credited with planting the 'Wishing Tree' in the SYDNEY BOTANIC GARDENS. By 1837 they were also selling vegetables grown at the MARKET GARDEN Baptist had established at Surry Hills. In 1832 he was assigned the first of a number of convict workmen, of whom John Moylan (assigned in 1844) was still working for Baptist's son in 1890. The market garden flourished, and from 1839 produce was sold in city markets: daily lists of the vegetables, plants, and floral arrangements survive and show some surprising quantities—for instance the supply of 6 cwt (305 kg) of garlic (1868).

Baptist began collecting ornamental plants, buying from CAMDEN PARK (from 1843), SHEPHERD's Darling Nursery (from 1840), bulbs from England (1842), and choice plants from the Lyndhurst sale (1843), gradually establishing his Surry Hills nursery, named The Garden. Lacking nursery experience, he sought help from Edmund BLAKE on technical issues. The business flourished, and he issued detailed catalogues (1861–75), special leaflets, and regularly advertised in metropolitan and country newspapers throughout Australia and New Zealand (often through his extensive network of agents). He dispatched orders direct to customers and his surviving letters give great detail regarding transport arrangements: for example, orders for northern Vic. first went by ship to SA and then by riverboat up the Murray. He sent employees interstate with consignments of plants for sale: between 1862 and 1869 he sent thirty-seven large consignments of plants to be auctioned in places as far apart as Adelaide, Townsville (Qld), and Dunedin (New Zealand), the auctions often lasting two days. The material he sold was both locally produced and imported, and he regularly received material from England, Germany, France (except during the Franco–Prussian War), and, occasionally, Japan. His employees collected native plants and seeds in the bush—one collector providing 900 *Blandfordia* tubers in 1859. He purchased unusual plants from missionaries and others in the South Pacific area and sent Henry PARCEL to the New Hebrides to collect. Some of these he offered for sale in Europe; he succeeded in selling *Ficus parcelli* (now *F. aspera*) to VEITCH in 1873 for £100. His correspondence with James Veitch had begun in 1856, and their relationship became close after he stayed with him in Exeter in 1863. Baptist made one trip back to Europe, visiting England, Scotland, and Ireland, but not Portugal.

Described as 'a little bustling gentleman', he prospered, gradually acquiring a large property portfolio, and then having sufficient wealth, made several philanthropic gestures. In his first letter to James Veitch he wrote 'I have a young lad about 17 that I intend shall take my place when I depart.' The son, also John Thomas Baptist (1840–1920) was 33 when his father died, and had already spent nine years as a partner in the firm. He continued the business for two years, then for a further ten years ran it as a wholesale nursery. In 1885 he leased it to Shepherd and Co., selling them the remaining stock. They ran the Darling Nursery from this site until it was subdivided and developed for housing after 1900. On Baptist's death the firm's business papers were deposited in the Mitchell Library; they provide a unique and remarkably detailed account of a mid-nineteenth-century NURSERY.

RICHARD CLOUGH

BARBECUES Outdoor cooking was essentially confined to leisure and recreation locations in the first half of the twentieth century. Facilities in PICNIC GROUNDS were usually of a rustic 'parkitecture' style, but they were avoided by seasoned picnickers, who preferred the more informal use of a folding wire grille over an open fire in natural scenic locations. Billy tea and lamb chops were favourite fare. Substantial holiday houses of this period sometimes had specially constructed outdoor fireplaces with grille, associated with a terrace, lawn, or rustic shelter.

Outdoor cooking and entertaining in BACKYARDS began in Australia in the late 1930s, but did not become widespread until the 1950s. Previously, only sophisticated establishments used the rear garden for entertainment, as an extension to living rooms. The change—which introduced the word 'barbecue', derived from the Spanish *barbacoa* and often later abbreviated to BBQ or barbie—was the direct result of NORTH AMERICAN influence. It gave men a new role and steak a new prominence. This cultural revolution transformed the backyard and domestic landscape architecture. Utilitarian activities such as fruit, vegetable, and poultry production, clothes drying, and wood storage, took second place to outdoor living and entertaining. Gully traps gave way to

In its Australian BACKYARD or PATIO setting the BARBECUE has often become a sophisticated form of entertainment, although its unpretentious traditions are never far from the surface, and it embraces the garden setting with casual ease

COURTYARDS and PATIOS, providing space for spindly legged, portable steel barbecues. Masonry structures were often located in dedicated areas further away from the house. More recently, decks attached to houses, combined with a diverse range of barbecue merchandise and exotic menus, have taken the barbecue back to the house, overlooking, rather than being in, the garden.

NIGEL LEWIS

BAROSSA VALLEY, SA, named by Colonel LIGHT because its terrain reminded him of the Barossa Ranges in SPAIN, was first observed to have VITICULTURAL potential by German geologist Johannes Menge (1788–1852), who established an EXPERIMENTAL FARM there in 1839. South Australia Company founder George ANGAS assisted the migration of Lutheran and free-religion settlers to the region; Silesian Lutherans, under Pastor Kavel (1812–1884), settled at Bethany (Bethanien) in 1842, establishing its medieval Prussian *hufendorf* ('farmlet') land pattern. This pattern, also found at Langmeil and Hahndorf, comprised narrow strips of land averaging between 40 and 120 metres wide by about 600 metres or more deep, with barns and *fachwerk* cottages erected at the road end of the allotments, and a central plot for church, school, and manse. Horticultural and agricultural knowledge was brought to the area by scientifically minded GERMAN migrants such as Dr C. Muecke and Richard SCHOMBURGK, who established Büchsfelde near Gawler in 1849.

Johann Gramp (1819–1903) established Jacobs Creek vineyard in 1847 before William Jacob (1815–1902), Henry Evans (1812–1868), Samuel SMITH, William (1804–1871) and Edward Salter (1837–1913), and Joseph Gilbert (1800–1881) established vineyards at Seppeltsfield, Rowland Flat, Evansdale, Lyndoch, Yalumba, Angaston, and PEWSEY VALE in the 1850s and 1860s. Within two decades the Valley was established as a notable wine and agricultural area, and its strict quarantine rules prevented phylloxera infestation in the 1880s. In subsequent years the Basedow, Blass, Burge, Buring, Fiedler, Hentschke, Hoffmann, PENFOLD, Sage, Sobels, and Springbett families have enhanced the viticultural heritage of the region. The Valley is an important Germanic CULTURAL LANDSCAPE and a major 'food bowl' for Adelaide.

Nora Totham, *The Barossa Valley* (South Melbourne, 1978); Annely Aekens et al., *Vineyard of the Empire: Early Barossa Vignerons 1842–1938* (Adelaide, 1988). **DAVID JONES**

BARR, Peter (1826–1909), florist, nursery proprietor, and 'Daffodil King', was, like many gardeners, a Scot. His London nursery specialised in HARDY plants and BULBS, particularly lilies, scillas, hellebores, hostas (funkias), and peonies, at that time somewhat neglected. But DAFFODILS were his great love, and he published *Ye Narcissus or Daffodyl Flower* (1884) and *Chats on Ancient and Modern Daffodils* (1900). Spurred by Parkinson's 1629 statement that there were then nearly 100 types, Barr set out to collect and classify all varieties he could. A possibly apocryphal but *ben trovato* story is that one of his collectors, searching in Portugal for *Narcissus triandrus*, wept, and at his feet was the very plant, hence the popular name, Angel's Tears. One division of narcissus, with a red or yellow cup, was named *barrii*. In the 1890s, George TITHERADGE imported to Australia as complete a collection of named varieties as possible from Barr, some of which later formed the basis of Alister CLARK's breeding program.

Aged 70, Barr handed over the business to his sons and travelled through North America, the Pacific, and many parts of Australia. His accounts in the *Gardeners' Chronicle* (1901) and *Cottage Gardener* (1903–04) provide an overview of Australian gardens and horticulture at the turn of the century—especially the work of William GUILFOYLE at the MELBOURNE BOTANIC GARDENS. Barr was one of the first recipients of the ROYAL HORTICULTURAL SOCIETY Victoria Medal and Honour, and, since his death, the Peter Barr Cup for daffodil-breeding has been awarded annually, the sole Australian recipient being Alister Clark. **T.R. GARNETT**

BARRATT, Enoch Pearson (1812–1895), nursery proprietor, established the Wellington Nursery in 1860, one of the earliest and subsequently largest of the commercial nurseries operating in Perth during the nineteenth century. Barratt, a convict, had arrived in WA in 1852 and was pardoned in 1853. Located initially at his Murray Street residence, the nursery was relocated by 1876 to Wellington (formerly Douro) Street, later with retail premises in Hay Street (1895). Resumption of land for railway purposes in 1892 necessitated relocation of the nursery to a nearby site. His son, James Enoch Barratt, (1845–1906) entered the business in 1880; on his retirement in 1895 it passed to his three sons, Edward James (1871–1937), Albert William (1872–1952), and (Frederick) Walter (1878–1948), who continued the commercial operation until 1904, when the nursery site was sold. The nursery's first advertised plants included *Melia azedarach* (White Cedar); by 1870 stock included grapevines and fruit trees, by 1874, the Western Australian native, *Callitris preissii*, and other ornamental trees, by 1878 seeds, and by 1884 shrubs and roses. As well as exporting its own seeds, the Wellington Nursery was agent for SHEPHERD's Darling Nursery (Sydney) and Suttons Seeds (England). The laying out of gardens and a floral department were other specialities offered. The commercial activities of the nursery had developed from a small business, providing a limited range of productive stock, to one of the colony's largest, catering for the boom experienced after the discovery of gold in WA in the 1890s. **JOHN VISKA**

BARRETT, Charles Leslie (1879–1959), naturalist and writer, worked for many decades as a Melbourne newspaper journalist and wrote more than sixty popular books on NATURAL HISTORY, landscape, and the AUSTRALIAN FLORA. In the 1890s he had been encouraged by Donald MACDONALD to consider writing about nature as a career. Early in the new century Barrett and two other nature-loving friends, calling themselves 'The Woodlanders', established a rural retreat in an old orchard hut on Olinda Creek (Vic.), a pleasant walk from Lilydale railway station, and named it after Thoreau's 'Walden'. Barrett used his Walden observations for his first published articles, in *New Idea*, *Emu*, and the *Victorian Naturalist*, and wove them into his first book, *From Range to Sea: A Bird-Lover's Ways* (1907).

In 1906, thanks to Macdonald's influence, Barrett joined the Melbourne *Herald,* and that paper carried his nature column for thirty-three years, during which he edited the extremely popular series of twelve 'Sun Nature Books', including *Gems of the Bush*, *Australian Birds and Blossoms*, and the *Sun Tree Book*. He also presented a daily series on natural history in the Melbourne *Sun*. His *Victorian Ferns: Descriptions of all the Species Occurring in the State*, co-authored with Richard W. Bond (1934), *An Australian Wild Flower Book* (1942), and chapters in some of his other books focused on plants, but animals and birds generally dominated his writing. His *New Way Gardening* (1933), written with E.E. PESCOTT, was an isolated venture into popular gardening.

Barrett and Crosbie MORRISON were the most prolific nature writers in Australia during the middle of the twentieth century. Barrett had no scientific training but was an active member of many scientific societies. Widely read and widely travelled, his engaging descriptions profoundly influenced popular perceptions of the Australian landscape.

LINDEN GILLBANK

BARSBY, Edward (1821–1878), landscape gardener, florist, seed merchant, and fruiterer, was born at Silby, Leicestershire, England, the son of nurseryman Thomas Barsby. He arrived in Vic. with his wife and children in the early 1850s and subsequently established his business in Portland. Barsby laid out BURSWOOD for Edward Henty, being paid a salary of £100 per annum by Henty at the time the 1856 electoral roll was compiled (at which date Mrs Barsby was advertising lessons in wax flower modelling). By the 1870s Barsby included nursery plants sourced from Thomas LANG among his stock. RA

BARUNAH PLAINS (formerly Long Water Holes), Hesse, Vic., began as a pastoral run in the late 1830s, and in 1851 was acquired by the Russell family. Inauspicious attempts at gardening marked these early years, but following the construction of a homestead *c.* 1866–67 and its extension in 1886 by James Russell (1859–1912), the present extensive grounds with their now-mature trees were landscaped. The site on the Warrambine Creek forms an oasis on the WESTERN DISTRICT plains and contains both parkland and more dressed areas forming the HOMESTEAD pleasure garden. Barunah Plains was retained in Russell family ownership for almost 130 years; it has strong historical links with other family properties such as Golfhill, MAWALLOK, Carngham, and Wurrook, and through early owner John Simson is also linked to TRAWALLA; these links demonstrate the traditional kinship loyalties among immigrant Scottish families and exemplify a major characteristic of the social and cultural history of the Western District. RA

BARWICK, Rodney Lyndon (b. 1952), is among Australia's leading specialist growers of BULBS, and at his Glenbrook Bulb Farm, Claremont (Tas.), he maintains a collection of rare bulbs and liliums from all over the world. Of approximately 150 miniature DAFFODILS world-wide, about one-sixth have been raised by Barwick. With his love of literature, and in response to requests from growers throughout Australia, Britain, and the USA, Rod Barwick produces a detailed biannual catalogue, leavened with idiosyncratic and lyrical touches. ANN CRIPPS

BASKETS, often constructed from rocks and filled with flowering plants, usually annuals, were popular in the decades before and after the Great War, and recommended in many garden books. They were more common in public than in private gardens, and their massive scale brought a touch of Brobdingnag to gardenland. The best surviving examples are at the FLETCHER JONES GARDENS, Warrnambool (*c.* 1948–52). Such baskets are not to be confused with the hanging variety or that affectation of the middle-class cottage gardener, the trug. RA

BATEMAN, Edward La Trobe (1816–1897), ornamental gardener, artist, and designer, was born in Lower Wyke, Yorkshire, England. On his mother's side, the family was well educated and highly cultured: Bateman's uncle was Benjamin Henry Latrobe (1764–1820), the first professional architect in the USA, hydraulic engineer, and author of an unpublished illustrated treatise on the PICTURESQUE; and his first cousin was Charles Joseph LA TROBE, polymath and amateur artist.

Prior to his arrival in Australia in late 1852, Bateman was known primarily as an illuminator, providing the exquisite chromolithography for at least three lavishly illustrated 'gift' books published by architect and designer Owen Jones (1809–1874), two of which had botanical themes. Before working for Jones in London, Bateman had been employed in the Manchester engineering practice of his brother, John Frederic, who was to become the leading hydraulic engineer in Victorian Britain. Bateman's London circle included not only the young Pre-Raphaelite artists such as J.E. Millais, D.G. Rossetti, and Thomas Woolner, but also an older generation including the authors William and Mary HOWITT—who were well acquainted with John and Jane LOUDON—and, through Jones, Henry Noel Humphreys (1810–1879), an influential author, illustrator, and garden journalist.

From his earliest days in Australia, Bateman appreciated the native flora, as well as the rustic simplicity and unconsciously picturesque disposition of many early settlers' houses and gardens. He exhibited illustrations in Melbourne between 1854 and 1869: while popular, their botanical veracity earned the praise of botanist W.H. HARVEY. MUELLER also regarded Bateman's work very highly, commissioning scientific illustrations for Kew. Like his close friend Louisa Anne MEREDITH, Bateman promoted the appreciation of AUSTRALIAN FLORA by his own work in art and design, including a set of decorated initials for the published *Catalogue of Melbourne Public Library* (1861)—employed in the chapter openings in this *Companion*—elegant bindings for Meredith's *Bush Friends* volumes (1860 and 1891), and textile designs exhibited at the 1862 London International Exhibition.

In 1853 La Trobe, then about to return to Europe, asked Bateman to provide a series of views of his beloved cottage and garden at Jolimont, East Melbourne, as a memento, and the Bakewell family of the Plenty Station, north-east of Melbourne, requested a similar set of views of their establishment. So detailed and clear were these highly finished pencil drawings that it has proved possible to identify most of the myriad plants depicted. While his pencil drawings were acclaimed by contemporaries for their Pre-Raphaelite tendencies, Bateman also played a low-key but significant role in the development of Australian landscape painting, with his artist friends Nicholas Chevalier (1828–1902) and Eugene von GUÉRARD both executing famous works while based at Bateman's country establishments at Ferntree Gully and Cape Schanck.

Following an irrevocable breach with William Howitt and the termination of his engagement to William's daughter, the Pre-Raphaelite artist Anna Mary Howitt, Bateman determined to remain in Australia, and, recognising the

Edward La Trobe BATEMAN's 1856–57 design for Fitzroy Square (later FITZROY GARDENS), although almost wholly unexecuted, remains one of the most sophisticated Australian GARDEN PLANS of the mid-nineteenth century

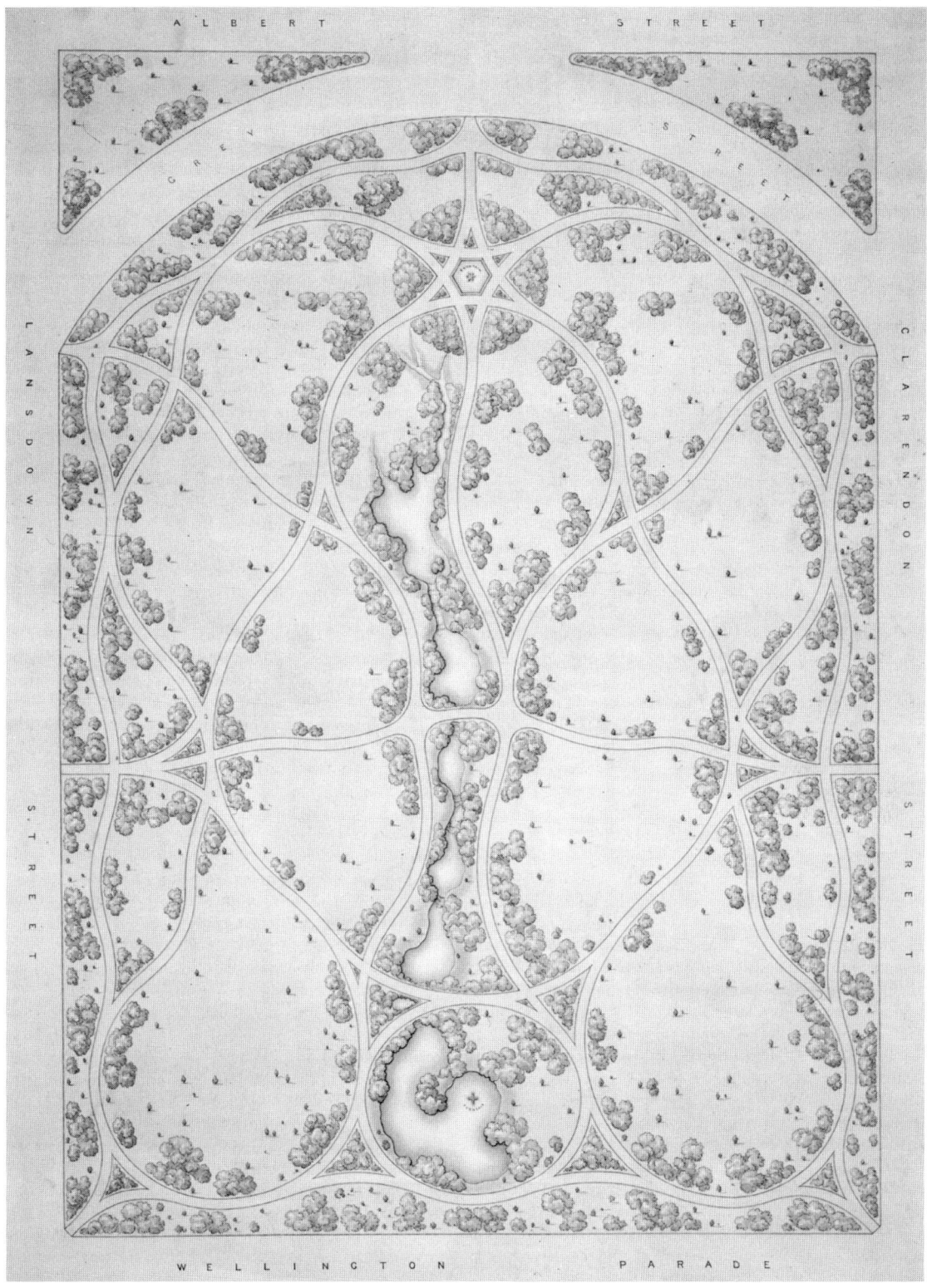

limited scope for earning a living as an artist, turned his hand to garden design, for which his engineering, botanical, and general design experience equipped him well.

Public and institutional gardens designed by Bateman in Vic. include the grounds of the University of Melbourne, including the separate Botanic or SYSTEM GARDEN (1855–64), WILLIAMSTOWN BOTANIC GARDENS (1856), FITZROY Square (now GARDENS) (1856–57), and CARLTON GARDENS (1856–57). A scheme for ST VINCENT GARDENS (1857) is attributable to Bateman, as is a landscaping scheme for the Wesleyan Methodist Church complex, Lonsdale Street, Melbourne (c. 1857). In 1864 he prepared a scheme for the grounds of the proposed new GOVERNMENT HOUSE, Melbourne, in association with Joseph Reed's prize-winning architectural design, but neither was executed. In 1868 Bateman was commissioned to provide designs for the Fawkner, Princes, and Yarra Parks, Melbourne, again largely unimplemented. No evidence has been found to support the oft-repeated claim that Bateman was responsible for designing the MELBOURNE BOTANIC GARDENS.

Bateman's earliest park designs, insofar as they can be established, can be linked with contemporary parks by leading English designers. The parterres, terraces, and *patte d'oie* of vistas at the University of Melbourne can be related to W.E. Nesfield's designs around the Palm House at KEW GARDENS, while the layout at Williamstown, with two straight paths intersecting to quarter the site, and gently serpentine paths weaving around the boundaries, is reminiscent of Loudon's layout for the Derby Arboretum. However, some elements of Bateman's early designs are distinctive, with no obvious contemporary precedent. His concept of centring the formal collegiate Gothic architecture of the university quadrangle on a cool-temperate rainforest grove is remarkable enough, but is quite eclipsed by his apparent derivation of the design of the University's circular botanic garden, including its central moated glasshouse, from the descriptions and illustrations of the mythical Isle of Cythera in the fifteenth-century treatise, the *Hypnerotomachia Poliphili*.

Bateman's subsequent designs for public parks, for which the surviving rendered plan for Fitzroy Square (1856–57) serves as an unmistakable and eloquent exemplar, were quite unlike anything being produced in the English-speaking world at the time. The designs, with their sinuous curves, have a distinctive Continental flavour, of a sort that would not be seen in England until Edouard André's prize-winning design for Sefton Park, Liverpool (1867). The closest parallels among contemporary designers can be found in the work of the German landscape designer Peter Joseph Lenné, himself influenced by the Frenchman, Gabriel Thouin. Bateman had family connections in Germany, so it is not impossible that he had access to reports of Lenné's work.

In Vic., Bateman designed private gardens for Captain and Mrs George Ward Cole, probably St Ninian's, Brighton, but possibly for their town house in William Street, Melbourne (1854); Mrs Mary Cobham at South Yarra (c. 1855); Flemington House for Hugh Glass (1856–65); Barragunda, Cape Schanck, for the Howitt and Anderson families (c. 1865–66); and HERONSWOOD, Dromana, for Professor W.E. Hearn (c. 1864–69). The documented scheme for Wooriwyrite, Kolora, for Thomas Shaw (mid- to late 1860s) demonstrates Bateman's capacity to successfully integrate a house into the wider landscape by means of a carefully designed garden. In 1867 Bateman was on a three-year contract to design and lay out the extensive grounds of CHATSWORTH, Hopkins Hill, near Wickliffe, for John Moffat when he was severely injured in a buggy accident. Although his right arm was paralysed, he recovered sufficiently to see to the laying out of the grounds of Devonshire House, Hawthorn, for Thomas Lambert (1868–69). The original garden layout at RIPPON LEA, Elsternwick, for Frederick Sargood (1868), is also attributable to Bateman.

Bateman returned to Britain in 1869, and settled on the Isle of Bute, Scotland. Despite ill-health he continued to work, designing and laying out at least fifteen gardens, mainly in Scotland, before his death on Bute.

ANNE NEALE

BATH HOUSES Public bath houses, in the style of the *thermae* of the ancient Romans, were revived in England in the mid-nineteenth century as part of a reform movement to promote public health. Private bath houses and Turkish baths had, however, long been popular with the wealthier classes. In Australia, the first substantial bath house was built for Governor Brisbane (1823) on the hill behind GOVERNMENT HOUSE, Parramatta (NSW). Described as being in the form of a Roman *balneum*, it was circular in plan with a domed roof, the tank encircled by a narrow ambulatory divided into rooms. Arches were knocked through the walls (1886) when it was converted into a pavilion (now a prominent landmark of PARRAMATTA PARK). A later bath house (1826) was erected for Sydney's new Government House; a castellated sandstone enclosure on the rocky DOMAIN shoreline, it embraced the PICTURESQUE Gothick style promoted by Elizabeth Macquarie. Alexander MCLEAY planned an ornate bath house for Elizabeth Bay House; while never built, the original plans (1834) show a picturesque octagonal tower built over the harbour and linked to the shore by a balustraded causeway. One of the best late-Victorian examples is found in the garden of WYNSTAY, in the Blue Mountains, NSW (c. 1892). This Turkish bath house, meticulously detailed in polychrome brick and decorative cast iron, included chambers for hot, tepid, and cool water—excess steam was ejected through a vent in the ornate turret. Although converted to a worker's cottage in the 1920s it remains a picturesque element of the garden.   DAVID BEAVER

BAUER, Ferdinand Lucas (1760–1826), botanical illustrator, was born in Austria. His education concentrated on botanical illustration, and in the 1780s he worked on illustrations for John Sibthorp's magnificent *Flora Graeca*. In 1801, at the suggestion of Sir Joseph BANKS, Bauer was appointed by the British Admiralty as natural history painter to Matthew Flinders and the *Investigator* expedition, sent to map the coast of Australia and to document its NATURAL HISTORY. With naturalist Robert BROWN and the expedition's gardener Peter GOOD, Bauer collected thousands of specimens, and made life-size pencil sketches of AUS-

Beach and foreshore reserves

Ferdinand Bauer's watercolour of *Livistona humilis* (Cabbage Palm), painted from specimens collected on islands in the Gulf of Carpentaria in 1802 by Robert BROWN, demonstrates the exquisite delicacy of Bauer's BOTANICAL ILLUSTRATION

TRALIAN FLORA and fauna, annotated with numbers referring to an elaborate, colour-coded chart. After circumnavigating the continent, the expedition ended prematurely when Flinders was arrested and detained on Mauritius while waiting for a replacement ship. Bauer, who had remained in Australia with Brown, eventually returned to England in 1805 and worked for the Admiralty until about 1811, preparing more than 200 finished drawings of plants and animals from his more than 2000 field drawings. Bauer also used his drawings as the basis for his own publication of Australian flora, *Illustrationes florae Novae-Hollandiae* (1813–16). In 1814 he returned to his homeland, where he died. Bauer's ability to combine art and science is widely admired, and his exquisite botanical drawings are distinguished by their extraordinary accuracy. Bauer is remembered in several plant species including *Genoplesium baueri*, *Rhopalostylis baueri*, and *Freycinetia baueriana*, and with his brother Franz Bauer (1758–1840), in the Australian plant genus *Bauera*.

> William T. Stearn, *The Australian Flower Paintings of Ferdinand Bauer* (London, 1976); Marlene J. Norst, *Ferdinand Bauer: The Australian Natural History Drawings* (London, 1989); Peter Watts, Jo Anne Pomfrett, and David Mabberley, *An Exquisite Eye: The Australian Flora & Fauna Drawings 1801–1820 of Ferdinand Bauer* (Glebe, NSW, 1997); David Mabberley, *Ferdinand Bauer: The Nature of Discovery* (London, 1999)

JO ANNE POMFRETT

BAXTER, William (*fl.* 1820s–30s), a Scottish Highlander, was the first privately financed plant collector to be sent to Australia. As gardener to the Comtesse de Vandes (d. 1832), he raised in her garden at Bayswater (London) many of the plants illustrated in early volumes of CURTIS's *Botanical Magazine*. Francis Henchman (*fl.* 1820s) engaged him 'at a very great expense' to collect in Australia. He reached Sydney on the *Royal George* in 1821 when sealing and bay whaling were major industries. Joining their ships, he travelled with them and shared their camps on the south coasts, adjacent islands, and New Zealand, collecting plants and seeds. In 1822 he joined the sealer *Newcastle* on a voyage to Bass Strait and Kangaroo Island. He collected at King George Sound, Cape Arid, and Lucky Bay in western Australia (in the years before its European settlement), the seeds he sent to London being raised in 1824. By 1826 Baxter owned the twenty-ton schooner *Brisbane*; while collecting on the Van Diemen's Land coasts and islands he rescued the shipwrecked crew of the schooner *James*. After the establishment of a garrison at King George Sound he returned there in 1828 'to collect and preserve the most valuable seeds and plants in the neighbourhood' on the understanding that in return for accommodation and assistance everything he collected should in the first instance be sent to the SYDNEY BOTANIC GARDENS, an arrangement that led in 1829 to a dispute with Charles FRASER over the division of the collection.

AUSTRALIAN PLANTS were at the height of their popularity when Baxter's plants became available in Britain. His first shipments were raised by Hugh Low (1793–1863) and John Mackay (*fl.* 1820s–30s), nursery proprietors of Clapton (London), who had an ill-defined arrangement with Henchman. In 1825 two of his introductions were illustrated in Curtis's *Botanical Magazine*, and more than one-third of the illustrations in SWEET's *Flora Australasica* (1827–28) were prepared from his introductions. He returned to England in 1830; in 1831 Joseph Knight (*c.* 1777–1855) of the Exotic Nursery, Chelsea (London), reputedly paid the (improbably) high sum of £1500 for the extensive collection of New Holland plants 'brought from thence by Mr William Baxter'.

RICHARD CLOUGH

BEACH AND FORESHORE RESERVES The beach became the entry point into Terra Australis after the last marine oscillation in the late Pleistocene, by which time Aboriginal occupation of the continent had been established. BANKS and SOLANDER explored along coastlines in 1770 collecting 1600 species unknown to European science, and the aptly named Botany Bay foreshore became a birthplace of Australian plant studies. NATIVE PLANTS along the foreshore—such as tea tree (*Leptospermum laevigatum*), a substitute for 'Chinese tea' (*Camellia sinensis*)—were assessed for commercial and domestic purposes.

As European settlement consolidated on the east coast of Australia, English rights of common lands were superseded by more narrowly defined crown land reserves. Orders preserving access to WATER sources adjacent to Sydney were posted in 1795, while in 1804 all lands within three rods (5 m) of navigable waters were reserved from private ownership, and in 1810 the first RECREATION reserves were set aside. Governor Darling's 1825 instructions on settlement layout resulted in strips of land for public purposes, and survey plans show 'landing places' and 'watering points'. The 1833 Ripon Regulations resulted in the Crown reserving 'to itself all lands within 100 feet of high water mark on the sea coast'. With closer settlement following the 1850s gold rushes, much remaining crown land along the coast was subject to LAND SURVEY AND SALE through both selection and auction. By the 1870s, following public outcry at the potential loss of access to the beach, all remaining coastal frontages were reserved. In Vic. a coastal strip that now includes the Port Campbell National Park was reserved in 1875 'on account of its great natural beauty'.

Beaches and foreshores became valued for recreation and their peculiarly aesthetic attributes were captured by Impressionist painters such as Charles Conder in *Coogee* (1888) and Tom Roberts in *Mentone* (1887) and *Mossman's Bay* (1894). The beach, coastal vegetation, and recreation all figure in these paintings.

Civic improvements in the 1920s saw the formal re-arrangement of many foreshore reserves as PUBLIC GARDENS with distinctive pathways, steps, rockeries, and plantings often featuring ARAUCARIAS. Examples stretch from Rottnest Island in WA to CATANI Gardens at St Kilda (Vic.) and Manly in both Sydney and on Moreton Bay (Qld).

Post-war development, aided by almost universal car ownership, led to beach and foreshore reserves providing CAR PARKS, CARAVAN PARKS, PICNIC GROUNDS, and RESORT developments, with consequent loss of vegetation diversity. Nature has taken revenge with weed invasion, and wind and water erosion. Currently our foreshores are subject to many CONSERVATION initiatives, such as Coastcare projects replanting indigenous species, especially *Banksia* and *Casuarina* spp. The beach as Australia's native front garden has returned as a civic priority.

JANE LENNON

BEALE, Charles (1834–1929), English-born forester, trained in horticulture and botany before migrating to Adelaide in 1857. Appointed district forester for the South East (1876), he established the Leg of Mutton Nursery in the MOUNT GAMBIER LAKES AREA. His son, Albert George Beale (1870–1923), served at Mount Brown and Wanilla before being appointed in charge of BUNDALEER (1914–23). Albert's son, Lance Beale (1906–1987), was the first South Australian graduate of the Australian Forestry School, Canberra, and served at Penola, Myora, before being appointed district forester at Mount Burr (1955–71).

DAVID JONES

BEAMES, Rodney Owen (1947–1994), landscape architect, born in Clare (SA), trained under Allan CORREY and Gavin WALKLEY at the South Australian Institute of Technology. Associated with landscape designs for Walkley's residence, Adelaide Festival Centre, ELDER PARK, RIVER TORRENS LINEAR PARK, Bicentennial Conservatory in ADELAIDE BOTANIC GARDEN, Wollongong Civic Plaza, and several University of Adelaide courtyards, and co-author of *Some Historic Gardens of South Australia* (1981), he was a gregarious advocate of LANDSCAPE ARCHITECTURE and PUBLIC ART.

DAVID JONES

BEAN, William Jackson (1863–1947), botanic gardens curator, born in Yorkshire, England, became a student at KEW in 1883 and rose to become its Curator (1922–29). He developed an intimate knowledge of woody plants and was familiar with the influx of plants introduced at the beginning of the twentieth century, especially from south-west China. He contributed regularly to the *Garden* and *Gardeners' Chronicle*, and wrote numerous books, his most important and enduring work—now in its four-volume eighth edition—being *Trees and Shrubs Hardy in the British Isles* (1914). This contained botanical descriptions on individual taxa as well as invaluable history, based on Bean's personal notes, on introduction and cultivation. This work has been influential in Australia for information on exotic woody plants, many of which were obtained from Britain and thus from the same sources recorded by Bean, and has also been extensively referenced by Australian horticultural literature dealing with exotic woody plants.

ML

BEARD, John Stanley (b. 1916), botanic gardens director, English-born and Oxford-educated, studied and worked in the West Indies (1937–47) and in Natal, South Africa (1947–61). His doctoral thesis was on tropical forestry, and he achieved an international reputation as a botanist and horticulturist for his writings on wattle cultivation and tropical vegetation. He moved to WA in 1961 as foundation director of the state BOTANIC GARDEN (opened 1965) being established at KINGS PARK. During his directorship at Kings Park (1961–70) many of Western Australia's unique NATIVE PLANTS were brought into cultivation for the first time. To promote understanding of their horticultural requirements Beard edited the *Descriptive Catalogue of Western Australian Plants* (1965), published by the SOCIETY FOR GROWING AUSTRALIAN PLANTS: this listed habit, distribution, soil types, and flowering times. Beard established and published the *Vegetation Survey of Western Australia* (1964–81), visiting all parts of the state to map the vegetation—resulting in twenty-six memoirs with large-scale maps. By the time he left to become director of the ROYAL BOTANIC GARDENS, SYDNEY (1970–72), Kings Park was established as a major tourist attraction and a centre for scientific study of Western Australian plants. Returning to Perth upon his retirement, Beard produced popular accounts of his vegetation studies in *Plant Life of Western Australia* (1990), and of his taxonomic and horticultural studies of *Protea* spp. in *Proteas of Tropical Africa* (1993).

BRONWEN and GREG KEIGHERY

BEATON, Donald (1802–1863), Scottish-born gardener and horticultural journalist, commenced his career at Altyre,

The WALLED GARDEN at BEAUFRONT, Ross (Tas.) is among the most impressive surviving examples of this early garden feature in Australia; the use of local sandstone imbues this property with one of the unifying cultural landscape characteristics of the Tasmanian MIDLANDS

Scotland, where he befriended James SINCLAIR. Later positions included a stint at Clapton Nursery (London)—which specialised in orders to and from Australia—before Beaton settled, around 1840, as head gardener at Shrubland Park, Suffolk, England. By mid-century he had become a nationally known figure in Britain. His reputation extended to the colonies through his frequent contributions to the GARDENERS' CHRONICLE and the COTTAGE GARDENER. Beaton was, in the opinion of Brent Elliott (*Victorian Gardens*, 1986), 'doyen of the bedding system and the gardening world's most original stylist'. Although Beaton did not invent massed flower BEDDING, he was a great proselytiser for its merits. Beaton also displayed a great interest in emigration and often published letters from colleagues who had migrated to Australia. He was a friend of both John BAILEY and Edwin SMITH ('and, I might say, he [Smith] left England from my house'); he kept readers in touch with the career of Sinclair; and he reprinted a long letter from Joseph GRAHAM:

> to infuse a little more of the spirit of emigration into the mass of clever young gardeners, who have little chance here to succeed to good situations. For myself, if I [Beaton] were on the right side of forty, I would even throw up a good situation and be off, for the sake of poor relations, if not to rough it out for my own advantage.   RA

BEAUFRONT, Ross, Tas., remains an outstanding example of an English Regency villa set in the Arcadian antipodean landscape. The house (1837) is sited on a gentle rise with an outlook across Elysian pastures to the Macquarie River and mountains beyond, as depicted in an 1840s watercolour in the ALLPORT collection. The von Bibra family (owners since 1914) have kept the simplicity of the bowed west front; an uninterrupted area of mown grass acts as a setting for the house with its broad stone terrace, and gently descends to shrubberies and trees below. Old olive trees abut the house near the front entrance. Extensive original sandstone and brick WALLING, stepped up the sloping hillside behind the house, divides the stable block and the large cutting and vegetable gardens from the pleasure garden. Several early garden ORNAMENTS remain around the homestead, including a classical stone fountain and a sundial (attributed to Daniel Herbert, architect of the nearby Ross bridge).

CHRISTINE REID

BEAUMONT, SA, was the first suburb in Adelaide designed as an urban SQUARE with a central common. The original thirty-eight allotment subdivision, around a central four-hectare common, was designed in 1848 by architect Thomas Price for land owner Samuel DAVENPORT. The Common—an undeveloped grassy expanse with original scattered eucalypts—remained in the care of trustees until transferred to Burnside City Council in 1973.   DAVID JONES

BEBEAH, Mount Wilson, NSW, the house of Edward Cox, was completed by 1880 and its garden laid out. The family, prominent pastoralists, purchased several lots in this BLUE MOUNTAINS township in the 1870s and Bebeah, located on The Avenue (Mount Wilson's main street), contributes strongly to the HILL-STATION character of the village. A clipped azalea hedge lines the main driveway; adjacent to the entry, the contrasting foliage of a *Fagus sylvatica* f. *purpurea* (Copper Beech) and *Acer saccharum* (Sugar Maple) has been used to great effect. A massive *Quercus coccinea* (Red Oak) is one of oldest and most spectacular trees in the garden. The extensive lawns originally included crescent and star-shaped garden beds for specimen trees and GARDENESQUE displays.

DAVID BEAVER

BEDFORD, Mary Josephine (1861–1955), Brisbane-based philanthropist, known as the 'little admiral', was honorary secretary of the Playground Association of Queensland from 1913 to 1954. Her involvement in children's welfare in slum areas of London and Brisbane led her to become a foundation member of Queensland's National Council of Women and the Crèche and Kindergarten Association. Bedford was instrumental in bringing ideas of the social use of open spaces into Australia. In 1911 she travelled to the USA and attended lectures on the PLAYGROUND movement at the Berkeley campus, University of California. This movement was formed on the premise that, with correct guidance and supervision, slum children would grow up to make a more meaningful contribution to society. Bedford was influential in the introduction of important elements in playground design. These included site selection and layout, use of plantings for boundaries and for age and gender delineation, incorporation of field houses and children's libraries, and, most importantly, supervision. Brisbane playgrounds were established in Paddington, Spring Hill, and Fortitude Valley during the 1920s. Whenever the opportunity arose, Bedford was active in circulating information about supervised playgrounds; she actively discouraged the inclusion of unsupervised playgrounds in city PUBLIC PARKS, arguing that without the supervisor directing organised play they fell to improper use and damage. She attended the Second Australian Town Planning Conference and Exhibition (1918), and was a witness at the Royal Commission on Health (1925). After her death, Spring Hill Playground was renamed Bedford Playground in memory of her significant contribution.

JODI FRAWLEY

BEDS AND BEDDING Garden beds in Australia's earliest gardens tended to be formed by the spaces bounded by paths, rather than being expressions of conscious design. In FLOWER beds and SHRUBBERIES—if early paintings can be used as evidence—bare earth between plants was common, and plants were often placed according to GARDENESQUE conventions to best suit their individual attributes. Bare earth continued a tradition, especially in SUBURBAN GARDENS, to prevent perfected nature from being disturbed by WEEDS.

The shape of beds, rather than their planting composition, was perhaps the earliest conscious elevation of beds to a position of pre-eminence in the art of gardening. Circular, polygonal, and other regular shapes lent themselves to FORMALITY, whereas irregular shapes were often a hallmark of PICTURESQUE designs. The relationship between beds was another early design expression, especially in rococo designs, where beds might be grouped to form a PARTERRE. Such beds tended to be separated only by paths; as the nineteenth century progressed, these were increasingly set in LAWN.

By the mid-nineteenth century the planting of beds received increased attention. In Britain and on the Continent massed annual flower bedding had developed apace from the 1840s, but was largely a summer device because of harsh northern winters. The parterre, especially in conjunction with formal gardens, was brought to a state of perfection in England by William Andrews Nesfield (1793–1881); this style was popularised with the advent of PAXTON's Crystal Palace gardens at Sydenham (1854) and the Horticultural Society's garden at South Kensington (1862). Massed flower bedding became common in Australia from the 1860s, and the introduction of its offshoot, ribbon bedding, was variously claimed by Alexander Stephen at YARALLA (NSW) in 1865 and Richard SCHOMBURGK at ADELAIDE BOTANIC GARDEN. Designs were also popularised through illustrated catalogues from Europe. The bedding designs of James PINK—particularly his COLOUR combinations—were widely praised, and were a subject of much theorising and experimentation by gardeners. Massed bedding, often in garish mixed colours, was popularly used in PUBLIC PARKS AND GARDENS; this continues to the present in some areas, especially in FLORAL CLOCKS; both aspects are still well displayed at BALLARAT BOTANIC GARDENS.

The short span of summer flowering (in Britain) and general artifice of massed flower bedding was highlighted by William ROBINSON—although he praised its augmentation (from the 1860s) by the introduction of spring bedding—and he advocated the use of hardy FOLIAGE plants for more durable displays. This subtropical bedding was popularised by Robinson's books and the work of John Gibson (1815–1875) at London's Battersea Park. Robinson's writings also brought advances in foliage beds in FRANCE to an English-speaking audience. The rival merit of foliage bedding was quickly exploited in Australia. With a favourable climate for SUBTROPICAL plants in many parts of coastal Australia, the delights of cannas, cordylines, aralia, and arundo were soon seen in fashionable gardens. MOORE in Sydney and GUILFOYLE in Melbourne both used this form of bedding to great advantage—their compositions often forming shrubberies rather than a changing bedding display. ROCKWORK often formed part of Australian gardens beds, particularly from the 1870s, contributing sculptural and at times voluptuous qualities. Mosaiculture, a three-dimensional form of bedding, often using SUCCULENTS to form vegetal sculptures, was not common in Australia, although an example of the late nineteenth century was created in FITZROY GARDENS, near Sinclair's Cottage—perhaps derivative of SINCLAIR's native Morayshire where the style was, and still is, popular. Carpet bedding—the use of dense, low-clipped foliage—gained only limited popularity in Australia, and was often used in combination with either flower or foliage bedding.

The containment provided by beds has ensured their adaptability to many garden styles, from sophisticated ARTS AND CRAFTS and MODERNIST gardens—where their ARCHITECTURAL possibilities were exploited—to the obsession of the single-plant enthusiast or the artless display of the suburban garden, so conducive to neatness and easy maintenance. The ROSE, in particular, dominated the garden bed. Serious

Beer gardens

View of the floral BEDS in CARLTON GARDENS from the roof of Melbourne's Exhibition Building in the early years of the twentieth century: such high-level views provide an ideal vantage point for extravagant horticultural gestures

challenge was heralded by BUSH GARDENS in the 1960s and 1970s, with their massed plantings and lack of traditional garden bed structure. There has, however, been a revival of interest in bedding, particularly planting composition and colour combinations, as revival styles have come to the fore since the 1980s.   RA

BEECHWOOD (formerly St Wilfreds), Stirling, SA, was established *c.* 1893 by metal broker Frank Snow on the site of an apple orchard in the ADELAIDE HILLS. The garden, laid out by Snow, features conifers, deciduous trees, hydrangeas, lupins, sweeping lawns, an alpine rockery, water gardens, and shade houses for rhododendron and azalea propagation. Snow collected plants extensively in Holland, Germany, and England; he commissioned artist Hans Heysen (1899) to paint a representation of the garden at maturity. The property was acquired by Robert McKirdy in 1950 (and renamed), then by Tom Barr Smith (1969) and the BOTANIC GARDENS OF ADELAIDE (1981). Barr Smith introduced a prefabricated cast-iron and glass conservatory (*c.* 1870), relocated from a family property, Birksgate. Beechwood is entered along a shrub-lined driveway, through a forest, and then controlled vistas of the garden—intended by Snow—are revealed.   DAVID JONES

BEECHWORTH CEMETERY, Vic., demonstrates two distinct periods of development: a squared layout in the first section (surveyed 1854) and a picturesque layout in the 1861 extension. A large Chinese section replete with funerary oven sits within the boundaries, recalling the early history of this mining town. This CEMETERY is distinguished by its collection of mature trees, many with strong associational links—for example the *Cupressus funebris* (Funeral Cypress) which sit amidst indigenous grasses and naturalised bulbs.
   RA

BEEKEEPING: see APICULTURE

BEER GARDENS evolved in 1950s Australia as hybrid descendants of the nineteenth-century hotel PLEASURE GARDEN and its stable yard. By mid-nineteenth century, pub gardens ranged from pleasure gardens and BOWLING GREENS, to the SPORTS GROUNDS, ORCHARDS, and SHOWGROUNDS alongside rural and goldfields hotels, although in the twentieth century the speed of the motor car and the cold eye of the temperance movement hastened their neglect. By the 1950s, however, some hotels—especially those within driving distance of major cities—reopened yards and gardens as drinking and dining space, making use of 'bona fide traveller' regulations. Such beer gardens made a large, cheap, and easily maintained space for weekend drinking crowds.

With extended licensing laws from the 1960s, the beer garden flourished, although, in truth, it shared little with any other Australian garden. At its most basic, it comprised a stretch of lawn on which were scattered crude timber or cheap plastic tables and chairs, with an occasional umbrella. Hoteliers in harbourside Sydney preferred an expanse of concrete with a centrally placed BARBECUE. In more sophisticated establishments, hanging ferns, either plastic or barely living, and a trellis with vines, may have alleviated the impact of the beer garden's concrete, air-conditioning exhaust, or boxes of empty bottles.

The beer garden has won some reprieve as a COURTYARD dining area, pioneered in inner Adelaide during the early 1970s. Now paved and circumscribed by planter boxes or decorative pots, the courtyard serves wine rather than beer. The traditional concrete beer garden has better resisted fashion and common sense in non-metropolitan Australia, especially in the hotter north. CHRIS McCONVILLE

BEGG AND SHANNON Elizabeth Mary (Betty) Begg (1906–1990) and **Mollie Glen Shannon** (1907–1995), landscape gardeners, met when they were students at Ruyton School, Kew (Vic.). They became great friends and, after completing their two-year Certificate of Competency at BURNLEY School of Primary Agriculture and Horticulture in 1926, went into business together. Dissatisfied with pruning and garden maintenance, and frustrated with the lack of landscape training available, they learned surveying. They then spent three months at COOMBE COTTAGE, Melba's house outside Melbourne, working with Edna WALLING. They returned to Kew, where Betty's aunt, Hilda Daniell, was headmistress of Ruyton. She offered to lease them some land at the school and they established the Sylvan Nursery.

The business flourished, and their regular designs for the AUSTRALIAN GARDEN LOVER (1928–32) represented an outstanding achievement for these young women. A 1931 advertisement for 'The Misses Begg and Shannon, Landscape Gardeners and Nurserywomen' in the Garden Lover read: 'Let us plan your property for you and produce a garden of lasting charm and character. We specialise in tubs, and flat-dwellers we arrange to keep supplied with a succession of window-boxes.' This enthusiasm to accommodate those of modest means was reflected in the designs they published, each one accompanied by descriptions of the plants and other features. They exhibited at Garden Week in 1930, where Betty Begg gave a lecture, 'Gardens and Garden Planning from a Woman's Point of View': when it came to garden designing, 'People thought it was fun to have girls!' Mollie Shannon later recalled.

The interest of Begg and Shannon in gardens extended beyond Australia, and one article addressed 'Gardens of Other Countries' (1931). They were saving to go overseas to study design when Mollie married Betty's brother, John, in November 1932; not long after, Betty married Ernie Backhouse, a friend of Mollie's sister. The business wound up, but the pair remained great friends, continuing to create delightful gardens, but only for personal pleasure.

HELEN BOTHAM

(BELAIR) NATIONAL PARK, SA, was proclaimed a NATIONAL PARK in 1891, one of the earliest in Australia and among the first world-wide. Established as a Government Farm (1840), excisions were made for a summer GOVERNMENT HOUSE (1860–80) and STATE FOREST NURSERY (1886–1999) started by John Ednie BROWN. A public campaign led by prominent local citizen Walter Gooch (from 1877) resulted in the reservation of 840 hectares in the ADELAIDE HILLS. Subsequent management decisions permitted recreation developments in the flatter areas and gullies, the planting of native and exotic trees (reflecting contemporary attitudes to conservation) and two MAZES, and construction of sports facilities and picnic grounds (including arbours and pavilions), and lodges for employees. A garden in the an English Italianate style was added to Old Government House in the 1970s. Since 1891, National Park has become a favourite recreation venue, nestled in the cool hills, accessible by rail, and surrounded by eucalypt bush. BARRY LONG

BELEURA, Mornington, Vic., developed from 1863 when the present Renaissance-revival marine VILLA was erected by merchant James Butchart, was owned by a succession of families prominent in the mercantile, political, and pastoral spheres who used the estate as a weekend and SUMMER RETREAT. Following subdivision, Beleura was purchased in 1916 by theatrical entrepreneur (Sir) George Tallis and his wife Amelia: Lady Tallis commissioned Harold DESBROWE-ANNEAR (1920s) to create a formal pool in the carriage loop, thus beginning a long process of formalising the garden. This was continued by her son, Jack Morton (John) Tallis (1911–1996), musician and aesthete, who inherited the property following his father's death (1948). In reshaping and enhancing the pleasure garden he introduced a theatrical flair to Beleura, heightened by his passion for all things ITALIAN and based on long periods spent in Europe. Beleura is now being rejuvenated as a museum and gallery by The Tallis Foundation. RA

BELLA VISTA, Kellyville, NSW, is an important remnant nineteenth-century farm complex established on 1790s land grants. After various early ownerships, including the MACARTHUR family (1801–21), the land was consolidated into a large agricultural enterprise, based on citrus orchards and sheep, by William Thomas Pearce (d. 1865), whose family maintained it until 1950. The surviving core of a dozen farm buildings and homestead is embellished by remnant *Eucalyptus crebra* (Narrow-leaved Red Ironbark) and *E. fibrosa* (Broad-leaved Red Ironbark) and a fine collection of old plantings, the most distinctive of which is the prominent line of *Araucaria bidwillii* (Bunya Pine) and terminating *Pinus pinea* (Stone Pine) marking part of the line of the first entry drive. The Pearce family cemetery remains to the south, off Seven Hills Road. Around the HOMESTEAD is an overlay of formal and kitchen garden plantings (cypress, pomegranate, maybush, camellia) from various estate development phases; the farm courtyard is dominated by early plantings of *Ficus macrophylla* (Moreton Bay Fig). GEOFFREY BRITTON

BELMONT, Raglan, Vic., was settled *c.* 1858 by James Frazer Watkin (*c.* 1828–1896), great-grandfather of the present owner. By 1861 the first stage of the house and lily pond had been built. The garden was progressively developed around the house—with assistance from Watkin's sister-in-law Jane Laura Ninham (*c.* 1841–1894)—which by 1886 had been enlarged three times to its present size. During this time the property operated as a public PLEASURE GARDEN and sports ground, much larger and more elaborate than the surviving garden, with an extensive orchard and a large and fine fernery (demolished 1930s). Vital to the garden was its reliable supply of water, courtesy of dams and races originally cut by Watkin for mining companies.

Belmont is not a 'designed' garden—rather the result of continuous dedicated work by successive generations who gardened for pleasure, just as its exceptional assemblage of farm buildings reflects changing needs. Entered through a LICH-GATE within a cherry laurel hedge, the garden surrounding the house displays a cottage style with close-planted camellias, rhododendrons, magnolias, roses, dahlias, perennials, and self-seeding annuals. Old roses, some dating from the original plantings, add greatly to its charm. Belmont has many fine trees remaining from the early pleasure grounds. The garden sets off an architecturally distinctive timber house, its characteristic sunburst valances repeated in the lich-gate. The lily pond, originally for water storage, was first planted with water-lilies in 1877 and continues so today. Remnant fruit trees stand in surrounding paddocks, and in 1988 a new orchard was planted with trees propagated from old survivors.

HELEN PAGE

BENNETT, (Alexander) Carr (b. 1879), electroculturist, is today remembered for his book *Electroculture: The Application of Electricity to Seeds in Vegetable Growing* (1921). Bennett claimed 'no backyard is too small, no soil too poor' for his system to lessen the family food bill or to give the larger landholder a full living wage from sale of produce. The Bennett system 'consisted in the stimulating of fertile vegetable seeds *before* sowing, by passing weak currents of electricity, and in the use of plentiful waterings to hasten its growth *after* it has been sown'. The idea of stimulating the growth of plants by electricity was not new: Bennett instanced a Finnish professor's experiments with strong currents conducted in wires above growing plants (1885–1905) as well as the use of electrodes, atmospheric electricity, and electrifying chemically coasted cereal seeds. Bennett initially selected land at Dorrigo (NSW) and claimed his ideas gestated after experiencing violent thunderstorms there; he then secured an experimental plot at Armidale and relocated to Lakemba (Sydney) before establishing his St Quentin Electric Experimental Nursery on an acre (0.4 ha) at Boronia Park, Wentworthville. The results are contained in his book—which ends with recipes, including 'Electroculture Soup'—but his was ultimately an isolated crusade.

RA

BENNETT, Charles (*fl.* 1880s–90s), landscape gardener and nursery proprietor, was apparently the son of well-known English rose-breeder Henry Bennett (1823–1890). He arrived in Sydney *c.* 1886 and by 1890 had established the Standard Nursery, Homebush. With CHRYSANTHEMUMS ascendant, Bennett's 1890–91 catalogue was accompanied by his booklet *Practical Treatise on the Culture of the Chrysanthemum* (1890), the earliest Australian monograph on the flower. His *Practical Treatise on the Culture of the Rose* (1891), a modest but early Australian work on ROSES, elicited praise from 'Mrs Rolf Boldrewood' in *The Flower Garden in Australia* (1893).

RA

BENNETT, George (1804–1893), physician–naturalist and author, was born in Plymouth, England, and began travelling at 15. Returning to England in 1821, he studied medicine and obtained his diploma of membership of the Royal

The front garden at BELMONT, Raglan (Vic.), photographed in the early years of the twentieth century, where informal COTTAGE GARDEN plantings complement the intricate, sunburst-filigree timberwork of the gabled verandah roofs

Naturalist George BENNETT demonstrated a keen interest in ACCLIMATISATION and inclusion of an engraving of Richard Hill's Sydney orangery in *Gatherings of a Naturalist* (1860) was part of Bennett's promotion of the orange as a suitable fruit tree for warmer areas of Australia

College of Surgeons (1828) before embarking on further voyages in the Pacific. He first visited Australia in 1829 and on his second visit (1832), ventured inland. His *Wanderings in New South Wales* (1834), the observations of an educated naturalist, also revealed Bennett as a traveller for whom a love of PICTURESQUE scenery elicited 'delightful sensations'.

Awarded a gold medal for his contributions to zoological science once back in England, Bennett returned to Sydney in 1836, establishing a medical practice while maintaining his NATURAL HISTORY pursuits. He became a leading colonist, secretary of Governor Bourke's newly formed 'Committee of Superintendence of the Australian Museum and Botanical Garden' (1836–41), and inaugural president of the Acclimatisation Society of New South Wales (1861). Among other interests he was a member of the Horticultural Society of New South Wales and a friend of artists George French ANGAS and Conrad Martens (1801–1878). Bennett accompanied another friend, Charles MOORE, on expeditions, some recorded in *Gatherings of a Naturalist in Australasia* (1860)—testament to Bennett's continued fascination with Australia and his mature appreciation of it. He also contributed important papers on the orange in Australia for intercolonial and international EXHIBITIONS and contributed to later editions of A.B. Lambert's *Genus Pinus*. George Bennett worked assiduously to improve the appreciation of science, assembling an enormous personal library, and was awarded the Clarke Memorial Medal by the Royal Society of New South Wales (1890). COLLEEN MORRIS

BENSON, Albert Herbert (1861–1930), agriculturalist, British-trained and with POMOLOGICAL experience in California and NSW, arrived in Qld in 1896, instructing at Gatton Agricultural College in fruit culture. He wrote regularly for the *Queensland Agricultural Journal* and published *Fruits in Queensland* (1906), promoting both temperate and tropical fruit growing, especially as a vocation for potential migrants. He became Director of the reorganised Tasmanian Department of Agriculture (1910–15) and Director of Fruit Culture in Qld (1915–27). JEANNIE SIM

BENTHAM, George (1800–1884), English botanist, abandoned the law, and having private means devoted his time to botany. In 1854 Bentham donated his private herbarium to the ROYAL BOTANIC GARDENS, KEW, working there daily from then on. Being in the Kew circle, Bentham was chosen by the Hookers to write *Flora Australiensis* (1863–78), cornerstone of a planned series of colonial Floras. In doing so they appropriated to Kew the favourite project of Ferdinand MUELLER. Bentham in London had access to important early Australian plant collections and comprehensive botanical libraries, and daily contact with fellow botanists. In Australia, Mueller had extensive collections from areas not visited by early collectors and a knowledge of the AUSTRALIAN FLORA in its natural circumstances. Ultimately Mueller ceded authorship to Bentham, thereafter progressively sending his entire HERBARIUM to England for examination, without which the *Flora* would have been less than comprehensive.

B.D. Jackson, *George Bentham* (London, 1906); Marion Filipiuk (ed.), *George Bentham: Autobiography 1800–1834* (Toronto, 1997) HELEN M. COHN

BERNAYS, Lewis Adolphus (1831–1908), public servant and advocate for tropical economic botany, was the youngest son of the Professor of German Language and Literature at King's College, London, where he was educated. Initially he worked in the laboratory of his chemist and botanist brother, Albert James Bernays. After a time in New Zealand, where he farmed and was married, Bernays moved to Sydney, where Charles Nicholson, Speaker of the Legislative Council of New South Wales, employed him for almost seven years. Bernays was appointed as the Clerk of the Legislative Assembly of Queensland on separation from NSW in 1859, employment he retained until his death. Bernays lived in central Brisbane; after 1881, in a residence within the Parliament House grounds.

In 1864 Bernays was appointed secretary to the Brisbane Waterworks Commission; after nearly thirty years, he was raised to membership of the Board itself. He also served forty-four years as a director of the Brisbane Gas Company. He was a trustee of the Queensland Museum during 1878–79 and a member of the ROYAL SOCIETY of Queensland, where he presented several papers on horticultural possibilities for the colony's farmers. He served on the Executive Committee of the Royal Agricultural and Industrial Association of Queensland and was a member of the Brisbane School of Arts. Bernays was a staunch Anglican and held various offices in the lay hierarchy of the church, including the Diocesan Council. From 1868 to 1904 Bernays was a trustee of Brisbane Grammar School, where he directed the arrangement of the drive and tree planting on the site.

Bernays was influential in the establishment and longevity of the Queensland ACCLIMATISATION SOCIETY, serving inaugurally as secretary, later president, and finally becoming vice-patron. In addition, he was trustee of its forty-five acre (18 ha) garden, BOWEN PARK. He developed an active inter-

est in ECONOMIC BOTANY for TROPICAL areas. Among his several publications were *The Olive and its Products* (1872) and *Cultural Industries for Queensland: Papers on the Cultivation of Useful Plants Suited to the Climate of Queensland* (1883). During the 1870s Bernays lobbied for the establishment of a comprehensive HERBARIUM of indigenous species and advocated for the separate appointment of a colonial botanist. His treatise *The Duty of the States in the Teaching of Science and Technology of Plant Life* (1875) comprehensively outlined his plans for support of broad horticultural education within the colony. He was a consistent contributor of plants to the BRISBANE BOTANIC GARDENS, where he was appointed as a Trustee in 1884 after making submissions to government about a reorganisation of the management of public gardens and reserves. His engagement was not so much as a practising amateur gardener; rather he was an advocate and collator of authoritative information regarding horticulture in tropical regions.
JUDITH DEPPELER-HAGAN

BERZINS, Ilmars (1921–1993), the first qualified LANDSCAPE ARCHITECT to practise in Sydney and the first to be employed by any local government authority in Australia, was born in Latvia and studied horticulture at the State Horticultural College and landscape architecture at the University of Technology, Hanover, Germany. Appointed a draftsman in Sydney City Council's newly formed Parks and Gardens Division in 1951, he brought MODERNIST European design styles to a city desperately seeking innovative civic design ideas. Berzins was given many opportunities to create new community spaces and redesign existing parks. He developed a distinctive style that incorporated free-form shapes, sandstone book-leaf walling, naturally sculptured boulders, water-worn pebbles, and strongly contrasting plant forms and textures, all artistically arranged to form pleasing compositions, a marked contrast to the traditional council designs of that time. His most important designs were completed during the 1950s and 1960s, and included the COMMEMORATIVE Sandringham Garden (HYDE PARK), Fitzroy Gardens (Kings Cross), and Arthur McElhone Reserve (Elizabeth Bay), the last remnant of Alexander MCLEAY's famed garden. Berzins was employed by the Sydney City Council for thirty-five years, his final appointment being that of Director of Parks and Recreation.
ALLAN CORREY

BEST, Joseph (1830–1887) and **Henry Best** (1832–1913), vignerons, were sons of David Best (1798–1877), a builder, who arrived in Melbourne in 1839 from Van Diemen's Land. In about 1858 they travelled to Great Western in western Vic., the scene of a gold rush, where they built a slaughterhouse to supply miners with meat. Seeing their business decline and the success of their wine-making neighbours, TROUETTE and Blampied, in 1865 the Bests planted grapes. In 1866 they purchased a property of twenty-eight hectares on the Concongella Creek on the other side of the town and established another vineyard. The Bests lived at Great Western until Henry married in 1872 and moved to a nearby property, Concongella. Both had vineyards of more than sixteen hectares by 1880. A feature of the Great Western winery was its underground cellars tunnelled from the soft rock. They were fortunate also that the railway to Adelaide passed by their Great Western property. It was purchased in 1888, after Joseph's death, by a Ballarat businessman, Hans Irvine, who took three first order of merit awards at Melbourne's Centennial Exhibition (1888–89) with wines made by Joseph. In 1918 Irvine sold to the South Australian wine magnate Benno SEPPELT. After Henry's death his property passed to his son, Charles. He sold to Frederick Thomson in 1918 with the right to market Best's Great Western wines. A feature of the Concongella property is a nursery vineyard containing many rare examples of pre-phylloxera cultivars. It remains in Thomson family hands.
DAVID DUNSTAN

BETCHE, Ernst (1851–1913), botanist, was born at Potsdam, Germany. Delicate from birth—his mother had died in childbirth—Betche was led to embrace an outdoor life, and with his father's indulgence regularly spent his early winters in Italy. After some training and experience in gardening in Germany and Belgium, he went to Wales, where in 1880 he joined a ship for Samoa. Presenting a letter of introduction to the German consul, Betche was enabled to travel to Tonga and the Marshall and Caroline Islands, where he made collections and observations for two papers (published 1881–84). Apart from a fern collection that went to Professor Luerssen of Leipzig, Betche sold his specimens to MUELLER for £12. From Samoa he moved to Townsville (Qld), thence in 1881 to Sydney, where 'within a month' he met J.H. MAIDEN. Thereafter he rarely left NSW.

In 1881, Charles MOORE, director of SYDNEY BOTANIC GARDENS, appointed Betche botanical collector at 12 shillings per day. He joined the LINNEAN SOCIETY OF NEW SOUTH WALES in 1887, and assisted Moore greatly in compiling the *Handbook of the Flora of New South Wales* (1893). Immediately Maiden became director of the Gardens (1896), Betche was appointed botanical assistant at £200 per year, and the two jointly prepared over twenty papers for the Linnean Society, including eighteen in the series 'Notes from the Botanic Gardens, Sydney'. In charge of the HERBARIUM, Betche, despite his deteriorating health, was 'never happy unless at work', averaging, in Maiden's view, twelve hours a day. A quietly courageous, shy man who developed 'a deep knowledge of the flora of Australia', he declined to retire, as late as 1913, when his battle against tuberculosis was almost lost. Betche was fondly remembered as 'a fine character, conscientious, hard-working, unselfish, just'. His chief monument lies in the meticulous work he performed in the herbarium, and in his contributions to Moore's *Handbook* and to Maiden and Betche's *Census of New South Wales Plants* (1916).
LIONEL GILBERT

BEUZEVILLE, James: see DE BEUZEVILLE, Wilfred Alexander Watt

BICHENO, James Ebenezer (1785–1851), author and colonial secretary, was born at Newbury, Berkshire, England. He was called to the bar in 1822 but preferred scientific pursuits: he had been elected a Fellow of the Linnean Society in

1812. He arrived in Van Diemen's Land in 1843 to take up the post of Colonial Secretary. Official duties curtailed his botanical pursuits, but he maintained contact with and sent specimens to colleagues in Britain including Robert BROWN. At different times he was vice-president of the ROYAL SOCIETY and the Mechanics Institute—his lectures there were well attended and covered the variety of the plant kingdom, the beauty of Nature, and horticulture. Northam Cottage, his farm at Moonah, included an established orchard and garden and he was able to observe the success of ACCLIMATISATION of exotic plants under local conditions. On his death his library was bequeathed to the Tasmanian Public Library and his herbarium to the museum of the Swansea Royal Institution, Wales, of which he had been a member. LINDY SCRIPPS

BICK, Ernest Walter (1870–1949), horticulturist and landscape gardener, was born in Somerset, England, and arrived in Brisbane in 1884. He started in 'nursery work' and from 1886 worked for the Queensland Acclimatisation Society at BOWEN PARK, becoming propagator and foreman in 1894, carrying out experimental work. In 1906 he was a gardener at GOVERNMENT HOUSE (Gardens Point), and appointed Head Gardener for Government House after the move to the former FERNBERG, Bardon (1910–12), where he laid out the new garden. He continued with the Department of Agriculture, transferring to head office to be a botanical and entomological collector from 1912, until being appointed Curator of the BRISBANE BOTANIC GARDENS in 1917, where he stayed until retirement in 1940. Bick was a founding member of the Queensland Horticultural Society (1886), and a member of the Royal Society of Queensland (from 1922) and the AUSTRALIAN AND NEW ZEALAND ASSOCIATION FOR THE ADVANCEMENT OF SCIENCE (from 1932).

In 1925 management of the Brisbane Botanic Gardens was handed to Brisbane City Council, much to the disappointment of Bick, who argued strongly for continued connection to the Department of Agriculture and scientific experimental activities. Nevertheless, the Council gained control, and Bick remained as Director. Due to his efforts, experimental activities, exchange, and distribution programs were maintained, and communication continued with the international BOTANIC GARDENS network. During his tenure, Bick supervised several landscape improvements, including realignment of the old Alice Street lagoon, draining of the Fern Island lagoon, and creation of the lower riverside walk and retaining wall; he also encouraged a thriving ZOOLOGICAL collection within the gardens.

Bick was involved in several other landscape design activities, notably at the SHERWOOD ARBORETUM. He was also on the executive committee of the Royal Automobile Club of Queensland, was responsible for the planting of Anzac Memorial Avenue between Petrie and Redcliffe, and supervised mass plantings of *Araucaria cunninghamii* (Hoop Pine) and *Grevillea robusta* (Silky Oak) at Mount Crosby Waterworks (serving Brisbane). Towards the end of his curatorship he engaged in three significant projects: raising plants for the new university grounds at St Lucia, creating gardens in front of the new Women's Hospital at Bowen Hills, and supplying plants for gardens flanking the approaches to Story Bridge at Kangaroo Point.

Bick gave numerous talks; some survive in rough typescript in the Parks History Files of the Brisbane City Council. In 1895 a paper on landscape gardening was published in the *Queensland Horticulturist*, and another on herbaceous perennials appeared in the *Queenslander* (1929). In retirement, Bick resided at La Cima, Coronation Drive, St Lucia. He died while supervising the planting of trees at the new St Lucia campus of the University of Queensland.

JEANNIE SIM

BICKFORD, Nicholas Moysey (1822–1901), gardens curator, retired in 1890 after sixteen years managing Melbourne's city parks and gardens. In this role he had succeeded Clement HODGKINSON, under whom he had worked since joining the public service in 1855 as a member of Hodgkinson's survey party. In 1857, when Hodgkinson assumed responsibility for parkland development, Bickford was appointed senior park ranger. The two men developed a close association: Bickford acted as Hodgkinson's eyes and ears. He was appointed Crown Land Bailiff for Melbourne in 1865, and Inspector of Metropolitan Bailiffs and Overseer of Parklands in 1872. When Bickford took over parkland management in 1874 he did not inherit Hodgkinson's power or authority, but he followed his mentor's precepts faithfully. Hodgkinson would have nodded in approval as Bickford, when laying out Fitzroy's Edinburgh Gardens, dispensed with an 'artistic' plan of 'curved walks and clumps of trees and shrubs … wisely deemed unsuitable', instead substituting straight paths lined with shade trees to connect the surrounding streets across the reserve. In 1882, thirteen reserves previously under colonial government control were given the title of Metropolitan Parks and Gardens. Bickford was appointed their curator, answering to a managing committee representing the Lands Department and Melbourne City Council.

Bickford's son, Ernest John Bickford (b. 1861), moved to Perth in 1894, and became a city councillor active on the Parks and Reserves Committee. There he helped found the Mueller Botanic Society: his interest in ORCHIDS was encouraged by MUELLER, to whom he sent specimens of local species. GEORGINA WHITEHEAD

BICKLEIGH VALE VILLAGE, Mooroolbark, Vic., was developed by landscape designer Edna WALLING from the 1920s. She envisaged a village of simple cottages and gardens complementing the natural bush landscape. She purchased the first parcel of farmland in 1921, shortly after graduating from BURNLEY School of Primary Agriculture and Horticulture. The village was developed around her own home, Sonning, and adjacent nursery, from which she supplied plants to her clients. With the purchase of neighbouring land, Walling set about her work, closely controlling the development by vetting prospective purchasers and designing both home and gardens. She sought to have like-minded people living in harmony with their environment in rustic stone or wooden cottages, reminiscent of the villages of her childhood Dorset.

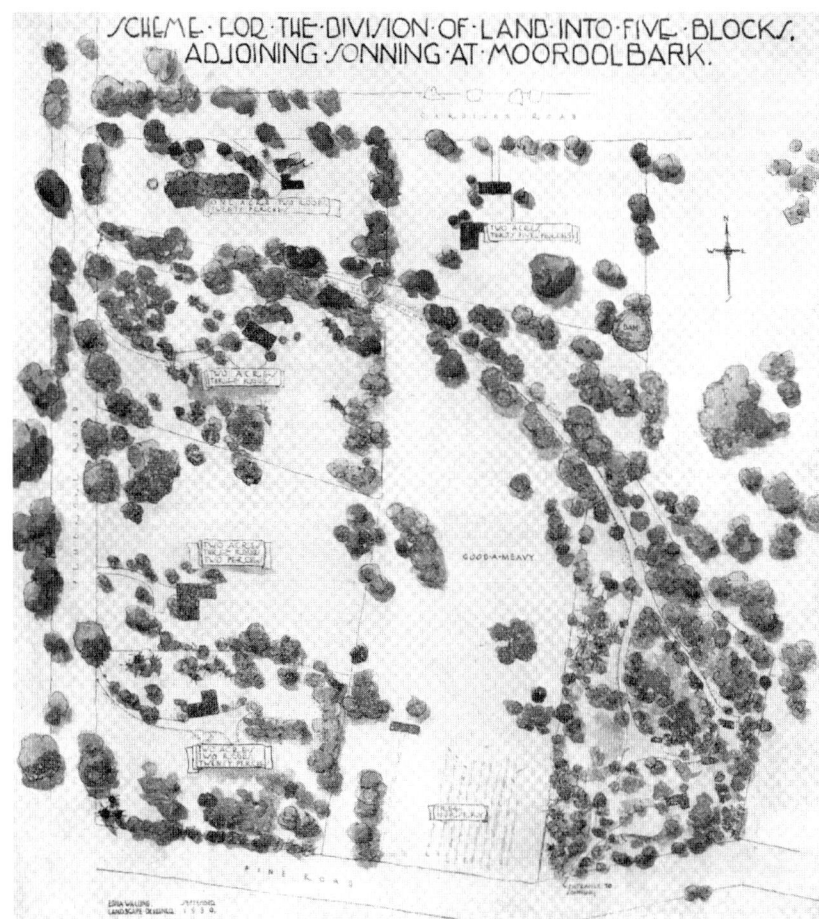

Edna WALLING's estate BICKLEIGH VALE VILLAGE at Mooroolbark (Vic.) was established around her own residence, Sonning, and its plan was depicted in 1930 in *Australian Home Beautiful* when the scheme was still in its formative stage

Bickleigh Vale initially attracted independent single women who were keen to contribute to the strong community spirit. Among the sixteen original cottages were Downderry (where Walling's widowed mother lived), Lynton Lea (home to Walling's close friend Lorna Fielden, a retired teacher, who later moved to Buderim, Qld), Devon Cottage, Glencairn, Mistover, Good-a-Meavy (Walling's home during the 1950s and 1960s, later named The Barn), Wimbourne, Hurst, Cornerways, and Winty. The village was a constant source of inspiration for her writing and photography. The original gardens were quite open, although with the ensuing growth of trees, especially after Walling's embrace of Australian flora, the village is now heavily treed.

Although the original cottages remain, there have been many changes. New residences now sit on subdivided blocks and some of the small cottages, originally designed for single owners, have been massively extended. Walling was able to personally supervise many of the changes to the cottages, which were home to growing families, before moving to Buderim in 1967. Situated at the foot of the Dandenong Ranges, forty kilometres east of Melbourne, the village is now totally surrounded by suburbia, and yet has retained its intrinsic peaceful atmosphere. Roads have remained unsealed, powerlines are underground, and there is still a pervading atmosphere of tranquility and whimsy. However, despite NATIONAL TRUST classification and Register of the National Estate listing, continued subdivision and aggrandisement threaten to undermine the fabric of the village.

TRISHA DIXON

BIDENCOPE, Joseph (c. 1836–1915), amateur horticulturist, was born in Poland and left for England aged 11. Six years later he went to Tas., where he started business as a tailor in Hobart. By dint of great energy and perseverance, he built up a large business and established perhaps the earliest hat manufactory in Australia. His residence, Barton Vale, in West Hobart's picturesquely named Salvator Rosa Glen, possessed a fine garden. Bidencope was an enthusiastic florist and his chrysanthemums, begonias, carnations, and sweet peas were the delight and envy of visitors and fellow exhibitors. He exhibited widely and when interstate, such was his reputation that a display by Bidencope frequently represented the state as a whole. RA

BIDWILL, John Carne (1815–1853), horticulturist and plant explorer, was the eldest son of an Exeter businessman with shipping interests. He showed his adventurous spirit early, going at the age of 17 from England to Canada for more than two years. Soon after his twenty-third birthday he sailed for Sydney on the *Arachne* with his eldest sister, Elizabeth. After his arrival he acted for his family in selecting and applying for 1900 acres (770 ha) of land on the Manning River. While waiting for this to be surveyed he spent five months during early 1839 in New Zealand, a prelude to three further expeditions (1840–48). He sent the plants he collected in 1839—the first from inland areas of New Zealand—to John LINDLEY (apart from an incomplete set that he forwarded to Sir William HOOKER) but much to his annoyance Lindley 'never published one of them'. Bidwill's account of his first visit, *Rambles in New Zealand*, was published in London in 1841. R.T. Pince subscribed for a copy, and James VEITCH subscribed for four: both were Exeter nursery proprietors interested in plant breeding. It seems reasonable to assume that Bidwill gained his knowledge of plant hybridisation from them. Whatever the source of his expertise, he appears to have been the first to introduce PLANT BREEDING to Australia.

While it is not known where he carried out his experiments, he is said to have 'lived out of Sydney'. He worked with both native and exotic plants, the first to be released, in 1843, being a hybrid between two Australian plants—*Hibiscus splendens* and *H. heterophyllus*—which he named 'Hibiscus Sydneyi'. Perhaps it is significant that when he crossed this with 'H. richardsoni' he named the offspring 'H. Pyrmonti', saying 'Pyrmont is out of Sydney'. He crossed the Australian *Crinum pedunculatum* with the South African *C. capense*, while the hybrid belladonna lilies derived from *Amaryllis belladonna* and *Brunsvigia* spp.—now grown all over the world—were first raised by him in 1841. At the time of his first visit to New Zealand he was not known to Allan CUNNINGHAM, but soon after his return he began mixing with a group of influential horticulturists including Phillip Parker King, William MACARTHUR, and James Bowman. He distributed seed to them from the crosses he had made, and carried out crosses in their gardens. This method of working led at times to confusion; *Erythrina bidwillii*, for instance, was named by Macarthur 'E. Camdeni' as he had raised it in his garden there. After being sent to Dean Herbert by Bidwill it was named after him by Herbert, and illustrated in Lindley's *Botanical Register or Ornamental Flower Garden* (1847). This was almost certainly the first illustration to be published of an ornamental garden plant raised in Australia.

Unable or unwilling to pay the price demanded for the land he had selected, he continued his mercantile activities. On a visit to Moreton Bay in 1841 he collected seeds of the Bunya pine, discovered in 1838 by Andrew Petrie (1798–1872), the respected architect and explorer. Two years later he left on the *Arachne* for England, taking collections of both dried and living Australian and New Zealand plants (including the Bunya pine) and plants raised in the colony—among which was a supposed intergeneric hybrid (X *Crinum amaryllis*) which, failing to find a buyer in England, was brought back to Australia. Bidwill had met Joseph Hooker in Sydney in 1841, and King had provided him with an intro-

Araucaria bidwillii (Bunya Pine), named by Sir William HOOKER for J.C. BIDWILL, forms one of the most distinctive CONIFER plantings in early Australian gardens—in common with other members of the ARAUCARIA genus, its bold silhouettes were highly valued

duction to Sir William Hooker, the newly appointed Director of the ROYAL BOTANIC GARDENS, KEW, who named *Araucaria bidwillii* (Bunya Pine) in his honour. Hooker sent him to see the Hon. and Very Rev. William Herbert, the great plant breeder, who encouraged and later corresponded with Bidwill. Returning later in the same year accompanied by his sister Mary, he resumed his work, including the importation and distribution of plants and seeds. He supplied Alexander MCLEAY with one collection of seeds brought back from England and another from Bolivia, having previously presented him with seeds collected in New Zealand and India, as well as peach stones from Kabul. While his introductions were significant, their importance has been exaggerated. He has, for instance, been credited with introducing mangoes and pawpaws for the first time in 1823—when both were already growing in Sydney.

Bidwill spent much of 1845–46 in Tahiti. Macarthur tried to tempt him to return to NSW, offering him the management of Ravensworth, home of Edward Macarthur BOWMAN, at a salary of £200 a year. While rejecting this offer, he accepted enthusiastically his friend's efforts to have him appointed superintendent of the SYDNEY BOTANIC GARDEN—following the death of Nasmith ROBERTSON (1844),

James KIDD had been acting in this position, with indifferent success. In 1847 Governor Fitzroy appointed Bidwill, 'a gentleman of superior qualifications', Government Botanist and Director of the Botanic Gardens at a salary of £300 a year. But his tenure was to be brief. In London the Secretary of State for the Colonies, Earl Grey, on Lindley's advice had already given the same position to Charles MOORE. Bidwill was forced to leave, much to the annoyance of the governor and his advisers: in compensation, he was made Commissioner of Crown Lands at Wide Bay in 1848 at an increased salary, while Moore's was eventually reduced to £200. Bidwill was understandably disappointed and took a dim view of Moore: he bitterly told his brother-in-law William Macdonell to 'soap the snob down, he is donkey enough to swallow any amount of blarney'. Taking up his duties, he established his residence at Tinana, now part of Maryborough (Qld), making two gardens, one near his house and one beside Tinana Creek. In 1851, while marking out a road to Moreton Bay, he was lost in the bush for eight days, suffering from lack of food until rescued by Aboriginals. After this experience his health deteriorated, and in March 1853 he died and was buried 'in his beautiful garden'. In his short life, working, except for five months, in his spare time, Bidwill did more for Australian gardening than most full-time—and more long-lived—horticulturists.

William Edward Bidwill and Airini Elizabeth Woodhouse (eds), *Bidwill of Pihautea: The Life of Charles Robert Bidwill … and a Short History of the Bidwill Family* (Christchurch, 1927).

RICHARD CLOUGH

BISHOP, William James (1893–1967), horticulturist, of Tetratheca, Basket Range (SA), in the ADELAIDE HILLS, gave invaluable service to productive horticulture, especially the fruit and vegetable industry. He chaired the South Australian Fruit Growers' and Market Gardeners' Association (Cherry Section), made regular contributions to the *Grower*, and developed several commercial cherry varieties including Black Douglas. From the 1920s he planted more than 100 different species of CONIFER (mainly obtained from KEMP's nursery) to form an ARBORETUM on his ninety-two hectare property, often visited by dignitaries and plant enthusiasts. *Cupressus bishopii* honours his interest in conifer propagation. The apple and cherry orchards, together with the arboretum, were partly destroyed in the Black Sunday bushfire (1955).

Bishop's eldest son, Douglas Alan Bishop (b. 1923), has also given invaluable service to primary industries, and continues to nurture the Tetratheca orchards and arboretum. He served the apple industry for more than thirty years, locally and nationally—most notably as deputy chairman of the Australian Apple and Pear Corporation and president of the state and national growers' associations. Bishop successfully pioneered sod-culture in Hills' orchards, and established the returnable crate system for the fruit industry. He has had a lifelong commitment to the conservation of the Adelaide Hills environment.

Great-nephew Geoffrey Charles Bishop (b. 1952), historian, of Ferndale, Basket Range, has published several books on the development of horticulture and viticulture in SA, including *Australian Winemaking: The Roseworthy Influence* (1980). He was awarded the *Diplôme d'Honneur* by L'Office International du Vin, Paris (1982).

DAVID JONES and PATRICIA MICHELL

BISSET, Charles Begg (1854–1944), gardener and nursery proprietor, native of Forfar, Scotland, migrated to Sydney in 1883 and worked as head gardener for John Young (1827–1907) at Kentville, Annandale. The leading Sydney building contractor of the time, Young had worked with PAXTON on the Crystal Palace (1851). Young was a pioneering promoter of BOWLS in Australia, and maintained a green at Kentville (used for an early intercolonial match in 1880). The size of the Kentville garden can be appreciated by noting that in 1909 it was subdivided into eighty-seven building allotments. Bisset started his own nursery in Leichhardt, where his son John William Bisset (1884–1967) worked until the 1920s.

Bisset's grandson, **John William (Jack) Bisset** (b. 1909), became the leading commercial ORCHID grower of his generation. Based at Abbotsford (NSW), from the early 1930s he imported, propagated, and hybridised orchids in quantity. In 1938 he mounted an orchid display (mostly Cymbidium hybrids) in the new Sydney store of David Jones—a phenomenal success viewed by almost 20 000 visitors. A year later he staged the first competitive orchid exhibition in Australia; such was his dominance of the orchid world that his regulatory standards stood until this role was assumed by the Orchid Society of New South Wales (of which Bisset was a founder and long-time president) in 1944. Bisset published P.A. Gilbert's *The Charm of Growing Orchids* (1945) and R. Bruce Hogg's *Orchids for Everybody* (1946), and wrote *Cymbidium Culture and Virus Diseases* (1950, co-author H.W. Wilson) and *A Handbook on Orchids* (1951); he also contributed many articles to the horticultural press, and as a great showman was a frequent figure on RADIO and TELEVISION.

RA

BLACK, John McConnell (1855–1951), Scottish-born naturalist and botanist, migrated to Adelaide in 1877. Unsuccessful in farming—but with his interest in ARID-zone flora aroused—he wrote for the *Register* and *Advertiser* among other periodicals, and reported for Hansard in SA until a legacy enabled full-time botanical work (1903). His *The Naturalised Flora of South Australia* (1909) was the first Australian work on the subject. Aged 65 he commenced the *Flora of South Australia* (1922–29, later revised) to replace TATE's *Handbook* (1890). His *Memoirs* were published in 1971.

DAVID JONES

BLACKWELL (*née* PEAKE), Marion Isabel (b. 1928), environmental scientist and landscape designer, grew up on an isolated station in northern NSW. After graduating in science from the University of Sydney, she lectured in mycology at the University of New South Wales before marrying and moving in 1958 to WA. As a student she had undertaken garden and landscape design, and she resumed this work from a home office from the late 1950s while raising a young family, lecturing, and furthering her lifelong hands-on study of ecology. Blackwell and Associates, now directed by her son Tony Blackwell (b. 1956), is one of Australia's longest-established LANDSCAPE ARCHITECTURE practices. Designs include parks, shopping centres, university campuses, domestic gardens, mining towns, and biological survey and rehabilitation work in places as remote and arid as the Kimberley, Pilbara, and Great Victoria Desert. Blackwell continues to promote, collect, and bring into cultivation Western Australian plants: she initiated and guided the important recent publication *The Western Australian Flora: A Descriptive Catalogue* (2000). A mentor and an inspiration to many, her community involvements at all levels, particularly in governance roles, have included the fields of Australian flora, national parks, nature conservation, and the environment. Her influence and her persuasive voice extend beyond her home state. She was inaugural chair of the advisory committee for the AUSTRALIAN NATIONAL BOTANIC GARDENS in Canberra and became an honorary fellow of the AUSTRALIAN INSTITUTE OF LANDSCAPE ARCHITECTS in 1981.

Blackwell's knowledge of the AUSTRALIAN FLORA is encyclopaedic, and her concern and enthusiasm for the natural landscape contagious. A superlative photographer, she sees art and beauty in its every facet. She works closely with indigenous Australians and enjoys nothing more than 'driving the desert' in her own car, plant hunting, and camping out. But while she is passionate about Australia, its plants and landforms, she is not one-eyed. Her innate understanding of ECOLOGY allows her to mix native and exotic plants, choosing the right plant for each location to create urban landscapes—whether in a city or a mining town—of character, beauty, and appropriateness, and to provide comfort for people.

ANNE LATREILLE

BLAKE, Edmund (*c.* 1810–1880), gardener, native of Norfolk, England, worked at Lynn for nursery proprietor Thomas Marshall. In 1833 he destroyed greenhouse and other plants belonging to his employer—valued, according to the *Norfolk Chronicle*, at £400. Sentenced to transportation for seven years, he arrived at Sydney aboard the *Bengal Merchant* in 1835. Described as a 'Gardener Perfect' and aged 24, he was assigned to James and William MACARTHUR. Their property, Camden Park, was then under the direction of (Sir) William Macarthur and a major supplier of newly introduced and locally raised native plants to all parts of Australia and New Zealand. After the departure of Naismith ROBERTSON, divided responsibility for various areas of the ground was established and Blake was given control of the nursery and the raising of newly developed plants. Although there is no evidence that he arrived with any experience of PLANT BREEDING, his contributions led to erythrina, gladiolus, and passiflora cultivars being named after him. The written answers he provided to queries clearly show the breadth of his horticultural knowledge. Blake's wages were £30 a year while Francis FERGUSON, the other leading gardener received £25. Relations between these two were not always cordial, their employers being called on to keep the peace from time to time. In 1840 Blake received a ticket of leave requiring him to remain in the district of Stonequarry, and he remained at Camden Park until his death from apoplexy.

RICHARD CLOUGH

BLAKELY, William Faris (1875–1941), botanist, was born at Wellington Vale, Tenterfield (NSW), and early developed keen interests in the bush and in agricultural and pastoral matters. In 1898 he was appointed gardener at Jenolan Caves, where he further developed his botanical knowledge. In September 1900, during the absence abroad of J.H. MAIDEN, Director of the SYDNEY BOTANIC GARDENS, the acting director, George HARWOOD, had Blakely transferred to the Gardens on probation at seven shillings a day. Permanency soon followed; thereafter, he worked as a grade five gardener until he showed his potential in 1907 by presenting Maiden with 'a highly meritorious list of Economic plants growing in the garden … with suggestions for guides', winning mention in the employees' register.

In 1913 Blakely was transferred to the indoor staff as botanical assistant. Working in the HERBARIUM with Edwin CHEEL and Arthur Andrew Hamilton (1855–1929), he became readily immersed in taxonomic research, becoming especially interested in EUCALYPTS, ACACIAS, and mistletoes, on which he wrote several scientific papers. In mid-1915, Maiden declared Blakely a 'hard-working and naturally gifted diagnostician as regards plants. He is neat in his work and I am very pleased with him.' In 1920 Blakely was promoted to Hamilton's position, and in 1925 was classified Assistant Botanist. In assisting Maiden after 1913 with the *Forest Flora of New South Wales* and *A Critical Revision of the Genus Eucalyptus*, Blakely developed a profound interest in, and knowledge of, trees. Working quietly, he produced at his own expense his celebrated work, *A Key to the Eucalypts: With Descriptions of 500 Species and 138 Varieties and a Companion to J.H. Maiden's Critical Revision of the Genus Eucalyptus* (1934).

LIONEL GILBERT

BLAXLAND (née ANDERSON), Helen Frances (1907–1989), conservationist and author, was a council member of the NATIONAL TRUST OF AUSTRALIA (New South Wales) between 1962 and 1971. Her work led to the establishment of its first historic house, Experiment Farm Cottage, which was opened to the public in 1963 with a collection of early Australian furniture and decorative arts, and colonial garden setting; although now a widely accepted mode of display, at that date these features had not previously been available in Australia for regular public viewing. She was also the founder, in 1961, of the National Trust's major fund-raising group, the Women's Committee, which through its tours 'Looking at Architecture' was influential in promoting the Trust's aims. Her illustrated books on FLOWER ARRANGING, *Flower Pieces* (1946) and *Collected Flower Pieces* (1948), were both practical and popular. The Helen Blaxland Foundation was set up in 1990 to honour her contribution to conservation and for the preservation of Experiment Farm Cottage and Old GOVERNMENT HOUSE, Parramatta, and Lindesay, Darling Point.

CAROLINE SIMPSON

BLEASDALE, Joseph Ignatius (1822–1884), clergyman, analytical chemist, educator, polymath, and wine enthusiast, was a Lancashire-born Catholic who studied for the priesthood at the English College, Lisbon, Portugal, where he also learned about vines and wine. In 1851 Bleasdale arrived in Australia, a country 'that ought to grow good wine'. Appointed to the Geelong and Colac district, he met vignerons there and later became the Victorian authority on wine. In his journalism, analyses of wine samples, and his much-reprinted 1865 presidential address to the Royal Society of Victoria 'On Colonial Wines', he was a knowledgeable and frank critic. He helped organise Melbourne's Intercolonial Exhibition of 1866–67 and chaired the judging of the first real crop of Australian vintages. Bleasdale believed table wine should be enjoyed in the European manner, and was among the first to classify Australian wines according to region. His popularity and wide-ranging intellectual skills did not find him a niche, and his enthusiasm for wine was made fun of. In 1877, in poor health, he resigned from his ecclesiastical appointments and migrated to California, where he died. His name is commemorated by a vineyard (Langhorne Creek, SA) named after him by a friend, Frank Potts.   DAVID DUNSTAN

BLEESER, Florenz August Karl (1871–1942), amateur naturalist and botanist, and postal official, was born in Adelaide and as a child showed an insatiable curiosity for NATURAL HISTORY. Aged 18 he was voluntarily transferred to Palmerston (or Port Darwin, as Darwin was then known) with the Post and Telegraph Department of South Australia. Flo Bleeser travelled extensively throughout the NORTHERN TERRITORY's Top End collecting botanical, marine, and insect specimens, and Aboriginal artefacts. He sent specimens to HERBARIA in Berlin, ROYAL BOTANIC GARDENS, KEW, and MELBOURNE and SYDNEY BOTANIC GARDENS, and became professionally acquainted with many national and international scientists who visited the NT. A number of the species he described now bear his name: *Alectryon bleeseri* (now *Cupaniopsis anacardioides*), *Eucalyptus bleeseri*; *Eragrostis bleeseri* (now *E. cumingii*), *Eriachne bleeseri* (grasses); and *Ptychosperma bleeseri* (rare endemic palm). In 1931 Bleeser erected his house on the present site of Old Admiralty House, The Esplanade, later establishing a BUSH-HOUSE for orchids and ferns, a garden planted with unusual fruit trees (mango, guava, banana, coconut, and cassava), ornamental trees, and palms. Records and duplicate specimens of his botanical collections, as well as Territory artefacts, were displayed in zinc-lined boxes in a cottage 'museum' on the site—the only one of its kind at the time. The Bleeser family was evacuated from Darwin following the Japanese bombing in 1942; the herbarium, bush-house, and collections were destroyed or looted. Only the remains of the bush-house, with its distinctive floor patterning of paving stones from the original Darwin Bakery, have survived. The 'Bleeser Collection' of botanical specimens, housed in the Berlin Museum, was also destroyed by bombing during the Second World War.   JAN SETO and ANITA ANGEL

Arrangement of hydrangeas, water lilies, and cymbidium orchid (with an artfully placed rose—'Golden Dawn'—toning with the yellow centres of the water lilies), photographed by Olive Cotton for Helen BLAXLAND's pioneering Australian work on FLOWER ARRANGING, *Flower Pieces* (1946)

BLIGH (née GORDON), (Rosemary) Beatrice (1916–1973), gardener, writer, lecturer, and historian, inherited her gardening genes from her grandfather, William Forbes Gordon, who established the magnificent garden, MANAR, at Braidwood (NSW). Beatrice (known as Bee) grew up at nearby Wirriwa, Bungendore, and was educated at Frensham, Mittagong. Her early life was that of a typical girl from a well-established country family. A competent horsewoman, she rode successfully as a jockey at local picnic races. She married Francis Leonard Bligh—a direct descendant of Governor Bligh's brother—in 1941, and created the bones of her garden at **Pejar Park** near Goulburn (NSW) while running the property during the Second World War when her husband was overseas. In 1965 Pejar Park won the *Sydney Morning Herald* garden COMPETITION, and three years later Bligh published her first book, *Down to Earth*, describing her battles to create an Australian country garden. Her second book, *Cherish the Earth* (1973), published just after her untimely death, established her as a pioneering GARDEN HISTORIAN, and was the first to explain the background against which Australia's gardening traditions developed. Beatrice Bligh was a Fellow Overseas of the Royal Horticultural Society, London, and a member of the first Garden Committee of the NATIONAL TRUST OF AUSTRALIA (NSW). She lectured widely and left all royalties from her books to the National Trust. Her son Michael (b. 1956) is widely recognised as a leading country garden designer, while his twin brother Hugh is the current custodian of Pejar Park.   MOIRA MAGUIRE

BLOMBERY, Alexander Morris (b. 1913), is one of the most prolific writers and foremost authorities on the propagation, cultivation, and identification of native AUSTRALIAN PLANTS. His *Native Australian Plants: Their Propagation and Cultivation* (1955) appeared at a time when there were few publications on the subject; it was a motivational catalyst for many subsequent authors. *A Guide to Native Australian Plants* (1967) was written especially as a textbook for students of horticulture and landscape architecture. Through his many publications Alec Blombery has educated professional and amateur gardeners in the horticultural value of native plants, and dispelled many myths about the supposed difficulty of cultivating Australian species. *What Wildflower Is That?* (1973) is his most popular book. An early member of the SOCIETY FOR GROWING AUSTRALIAN PLANTS, he has always been among its most enthusiastic supporters. In 1956 he became associated with the newly founded Stony Range Flora Reserve at Dee Why (NSW), and for many years has been its honorary director.

ALLAN CORREY

BLOOM, Harold Maurice (1897–1985), Sydney-born landscape architect, had musical studies in Paris interrupted by the outbreak of the First World War; his arts and law studies were postponed when he was forced to accept responsibility for the family jewellery business. This failed during the Depression, and he obtained a position as garden designer for ANDERSON and Co. Resuming his university studies part-time he graduated with the University Medal for History. In the late 1930s he established his own landscape practice covering housing, open space, and industrial development in Sydney, rural NSW, and overseas. He frequently worked in collaboration with Peter SPOONER in the latter years of a career that extended into his eighties. A founding member of the AUSTRALIAN INSTITUTE OF LANDSCAPE ARCHITECTS, he edited its first *Bulletin* in 1968.

RICHARD CLOUGH

BLUE MOUNTAINS, west of Sydney, a dramatic landscape reaching an altitude of over 1000 metres, comprises windswept heaths, sandstone cliffs, waterfalls, and deep, forested gorges. With the completion of the railway in 1869, the area became fashionable for many of Sydney's prominent citizens to build their SUMMER RETREATS. Sir Henry Parkes built his estate at Faulconbridge in the mid-1870s, and his garden provided a model. Near the house, a series of dry stone walls linked by paths and steps were formed into terraces with lawns, flower gardens, exotic trees, and orchards. More importantly, Parkes extended the garden's perceived boundaries by creating a network of tracks with stone steps and rustic bridges that meandered among the picturesque sandstone outcrops, across a gully of tree ferns, and down to a small waterfall. At Echo Point, Chief Justice Sir Frederick Darley completed his summer residence, Lilianfels, in the early 1880s. A sweeping carriage drive lined with a profusion of flowers led to the house, with its wide verandahs and expansive views over the Jamison Valley. The formal terrace garden at the front served as a HA-HA. A clipped hedge of *Prunus laurocerasus* (Cherry Laurel), with archway openings, separated the developed garden areas from the natural landscape beyond. In similar fashion to Parkes' garden, tracks radiating from Lilianfels led to six cliff-top lookouts.

Remote from the railway and perched on a basalt-capped ridge, Mount Wilson also developed as a HILL-STATION during the 1870s and 1880s. A small and close-knit group of wealthy Sydney families built substantial cottages—such as BEBEAH, DENNARQUE, NOOROO, WYNSTAY, and YENGO—and planned elaborate gardens. Their beloved exotic plants such as oaks, elms, lilacs, and daffodils thrived in the rich volcanic soils and cool climate. Some collected newly introduced plants from NORTH AMERICA and ASIA—cedars,

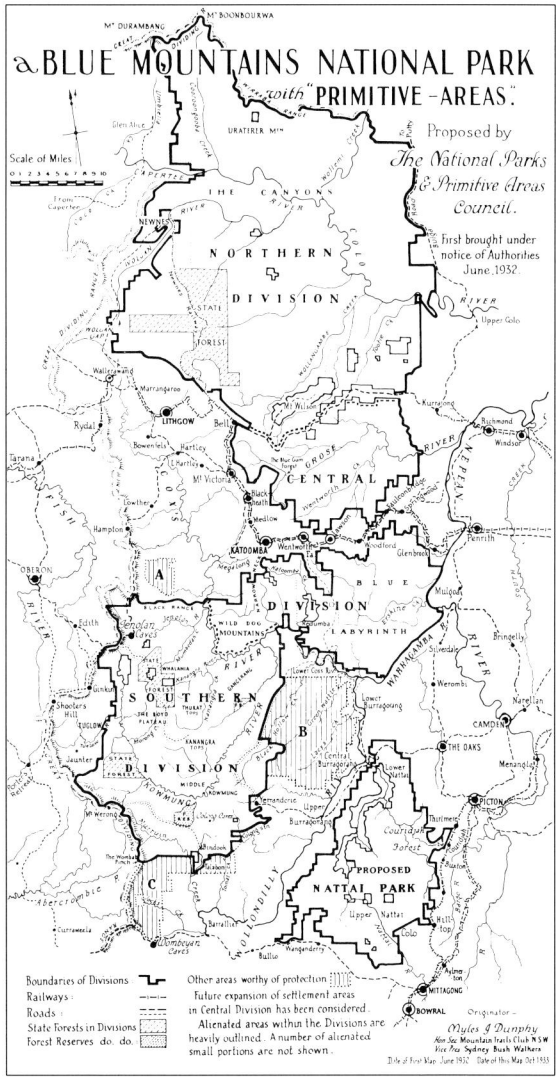

This 1932–33 proposal by Myles DUNPHY for a NATIONAL PARK to encompass the BLUE MOUNTAINS (NSW) built on earlier appreciation of the scenic values of this area and led eventually to widespread recognition of the outstanding natural and cultural assets of this region

maples, rhododendrons, and camellias. The abundant native tree FERNS were generally retained, thus lending a luxuriant, tropical appearance to the otherwise traditional English-style gardens. The gardens were planned to provide seclusion and shade, and few attempted to incorporate mountain views.

The Hydro Majestic at Medlow Bath and the Carrington Hotel, Katoomba, were the grandest of the hotels and guesthouses that flourished on the Mountains during the 1920s. The grounds included a croquet lawn, bowling green, and miniature golf course. Well-made tracks led to nearby CAVES, LOOKOUTS, picturesque rock formations, and a spectacular PICNIC area below cliffs called 'The Colosseum'. The Jenolan Caves were another popular tourist destination.

In 1917 a young Danish gardener, Paul SORENSEN, came to work at the Carrington Hotel for a short time. But he was to have a lasting influence on the area, designing and laying out scores of gardens and supplying a diverse range of cool-climate exotic plants through its nursery. The garden of EVERGLADES, built in the 1930s, is the finest of the gardens in which he worked and demonstrates many characteristics of his work. The Leura Garden Festival originated in the annual public opening of Everglades (instituted in 1936). The annual Blackheath Rhododendron Festival was inaugurated in 1953: the Blue Mountains Rhododendron Society has since developed the Bacchante Gardens to display a wide range of species and cultivars in a native woodland setting. Near Mount Wilson is MOUNT TOMAH BOTANIC GARDEN (opened 1987), the cool-climate garden of the Royal Botanic Gardens, Sydney, which displays mainly southern-hemisphere plants and includes a major ROCK GARDEN. Throughout the region, horticulture is now balanced against conservation imperatives, which have built on the pioneering work of Myles DUNPHY in the 1920s and 1930s in his agitation for a NATIONAL PARK.

C.H. Currey, *Mount Wilson, New South Wales: Its Location, Settlement, and Development* (Sydney, 1968)   DAVID BEAVER

BOARDMAN, Ralph Edwin (1885–1968), horticultural journalist, editor, and publicist, was born at Hitchin, Hertfordshire, England, and as a boy travelled to Melbourne. By 1910 he was assistant manager of the *JOURNAL OF HORTICULTURE OF AUSTRALASIA*, for editor and general manager of the Horticultural Publishing Press of Australasia, Harry H. DAVEY. Boardman became a director of the related company Fruit World Pty Ltd in 1911, and by 1914 he was secretary of the Nurserymen and Seedsmen's Association of Victoria. He was the force behind two horticultural trade exhibitions held in the Melbourne during 1924, the success of which prompted the launch of the long-running Autumn Garden Week FESTIVAL in 1925, with Boardman as secretary and organiser. This launch was paralleled by the establishment of the *AUSTRALIAN GARDEN LOVER*, with Boardman as the inaugural editor; from 1926 he was a director of its publisher, Horticultural Press Ltd. He continued his active involvement in horticulture as director of the Australian Apple and Pear Publicity Campaign (1937–42) and publicity director of the Apple and Pear Marketing Board (1939–49).

RA

BOAS, Harold (1883–1980), architect and town planner, received his architectural training in Adelaide before moving in 1905 to Perth, where he remained professionally active until the age of 90. Boas worked independently until establishing the firm Oldham, Boas, Ednie-Brown and Partners (1920). In 1914, following his election to Perth City Council, he helped to arrange the Perth leg of Charles READE's Australasian Town Planning Tour. After hearing Reade's lectures, Boas was attracted to the fledgling TOWN PLANNING movement and became a foundation member, and first honorary secretary, of the Western Australia Town Planning Association (1916). During service in the First World War, Boas was impressed by the practical application of GARDEN CITY ideas in England. In 1929, as inaugural chair (1928–30) of the Metropolitan Town Planning Commission, he undertook an international study tour to review town planning developments in Britain, Europe, Canada, and North America. This helped shape the Commission's 1930 report—a landmark document that set out a vision and guidelines for the planning of metropolitan Perth. Following its release, Boas persuaded Perth City Council, of which he was still an elected member, to form a Town Planning Committee, advised on and prepared numerous town planning schemes for local government authorities, and established the Perth Town Planning Institute (1931). Among several honours, the HAROLD BOAS GARDENS were opened in West Perth in 1976.

CHRISTINE GARNAUT

BOAS GARDENS, West Perth: see HAROLD BOAS GARDENS

BOATHOUSES Located in private grounds and also on public waterways, these purpose-built structures often used exotic architectural references, forming decorative GARDEN BUILDINGS. An early surviving example of small timber structure for private use sits on the LAKE at RIPPON LEA (*c.* 1890s), while a fine larger building using brick and stone is found at the Thomas Walker Convalescent Hospital on the Parramatta River (1890–93, architect John SULMAN). Rowing clubs and other groups using punts and row boats for LEISURE, RECREATION, or SPORT, gave rise to larger buildings such as the cluster of weatherboard boathouses on Lake Wendouree, Ballarat (Vic.), or examples (now mostly demolished) at TEA GARDENS located overlooking rivers and other bodies of water.   RICHARD HEATHCOTE

BODDY'S EASTERN PARK NURSERY, Geelong, Vic., established in 1951 by (Edward) Morton Murray Boddy (1903–1973), was inspired by Wail STATE FOREST NURSERY, which Boddy had visited when living in Nhill (Vic.). Initially the nursery supplied WINDBREAK trees, grown from seed collected in the Big Desert, to farmers in western Vic. As demand grew, an additional block was purchased and soon Morton, his wife Mollie, and son Ralph (1933–1989) were working full-time in the nursery, producing more than 500 varieties of NATIVE PLANTS by 1956. The mailing list reached 30 000 and production peaked in 1966 with one million plants produced by a staff of twenty. More than 3000

Wistfully captioned 'The Lake Boathouse: Childhood's Pleasure Grounds' in a photographic album of RIPPON LEA assembled in 1903, the year of owner Sir Frederick Sargood's death, this BOATHOUSE continues to bring great pleasure to new generations of National Trust visitors

taxa were advertised in 1960, with some exotics being added in later years to the predominant range of native plants. Morton and Mollie retired from the business in 1966 due to Morton's failing health, and Ralph continued to operate until 1968, when the demands became too great.

GEORGE JONES and JOHN WALTER

BODEN, Robert William (b. 1935), botanist and arborist, has graduate qualifications in forestry and postgraduate qualifications in botany and conservation management. His thesis 'Changing Land Use in the Canberra Region' was accepted by the Australian National University for the degree of Doctor of Philosophy in 1972. After twenty-four years in horticultural and ecological research and environmental management in the ACT and NT, he was appointed foundation Director of the AUSTRALIAN NATIONAL BOTANIC GARDENS in 1979, and over the following ten years guided its development and planned its expansion as an independent cultural institution devoted to the study and conservation of the AUSTRALIAN FLORA. A successful consultant and writer, his *Favourite Canberra Trees* was published in 1993.

RICHARD CLOUGH

BOLD, William Ernest (1873–1953), local government administrator and town planning advocate, was born and educated in England. He migrated to Perth in 1896 where he served as Town Clerk (1901–44). Bold's vision for Perth was underpinned by his belief in municipal socialism, the city plan as 'the keystone of successful municipal effort', the aesthetic goals of the CITY BEAUTIFUL movement, and GARDEN CITY planning principles. He actively promoted the Greater Perth movement, and fair and equitable public access to PUBLIC PARKS, PLAYGROUNDS, and other types of PUBLIC OPEN SPACE. His renowned *Report on World Tour* (1914), a council-sponsored study trip to Britain and North America, set out a visionary and comprehensive program for the future development of Perth. In 1915 Bold drafted legislation that became the basis of Western Australia's *Town Planning and Development Act* (1928). He was a foundation member of the Western Australian Town Planning Association (1916). Bold's influence was not limited to Perth; he is regarded as one of the founders of TOWN PLANNING in Australia.

CHRISTINE GARNAUT

'BOLDREWOOD, MRS ROLF': see BROWNE (*née* RILEY), Margaret Maria

BOLOBEK, Macedon, Vic.: see LAW-SMITH, Joan

BONSAI, a specialised form of plant manipulation and art, miniaturises and shapes woody plants in pots. Originally from JAPAN, bonsai is practised internationally, with many local specialist clubs and enthusiasts throughout Australia, especially after a surge in popularity in the 1960s and 1970s. Plants are restricted in growth by limited soil volumes in pots and by PRUNING. Australia's temperate climate permits outdoor culture of bonsai, compared with their indoor maintenance in cooler areas. Many AUSTRALIAN PLANT species in genera such as *Acacia, Banksia, Ficus, Grevillea, Leptospermum,* and *Melaleuca* are used in addition to traditional Japanese and European subjects such as the maples (*Acer* spp.).

Deborah Koreshoff, *Bonsai: Its Art, Science, History, and Philosophy* (London, 1984)

ML

BONTHARAMBO, near Wangaratta, Vic., a pastoral run from 1838, was developed with a substantial hut and squared garden *c.* 1844—and, more impressively, by a towered Italianate mansion and associated garden from 1857 to 1860, set above a rich river valley dominated by *Eucalyptus camldulensis* (River Red Gum). Developed by Joseph Docker (1793–1865), Bontharambo has seen continuous family management since 1838: a rosemary-hedged family cemetery attests to this long ownership. The garden retains typical features of mid-nineteenth century HOMESTEAD GARDENS, including an elevated site overlooking a watercourse (Ovens River–Reedy Creek), impressive approach drive and avenue, carriage loop, splendid mature specimen trees, groves of fruit trees, a spatial balance between horticultural and leisure pursuits, and contrast between the oasis of the homestead garden and the open farmland. The adoption of ITALIANATE architecture, now reflected in the garden by a formal terrace with square masonry piers—possibly inspired by Docker's visit to Italy in 1853—was among the earliest such garden designs in the colony.

RA

BOOKS: see GARDEN BOOKS

BOORTKOI, Hexham, in Victoria's WESTERN DISTRICT, is arguably Edna WALLING's finest country garden. Commissioned in two stages by the Manifold family in 1937–38, the garden today remains in the sensitive hands of the next generation. Encapsulating Walling's key design elements are low semi-circular stone WALLS, generously proportioned steps, and harmony with the surrounding landscape. Most striking is undoubtedly the massive PERGOLA, situated at the end of a long grassed walk in the WILD GARDEN, totally out of sight of the main garden. The surprise of this structure, once glimpsed, together with the simple planting in the wild garden, with mown paths leading through groups of wild cherry plums, quinces, apples, and hawthorns underplanted by masses of bulbs, is illustrative of Walling's style. This understatement extends to the formal area of garden, exemplified by gnarled apple trees rising out of the mass of perennials at the front of the elegant bluestone homestead.

TRISHA DIXON

BOROONDARA CEMETERY, Kew, Vic., retains significant elements of its original layout and design. The first trustees, representing the principal religious denominations identified in the recently completed census, were appointed in 1858; denominational divisions were apportioned in a similar manner. Frederick Acheson of the Public Lands Office drew up the original plans (1859) and, unusually among Australian CEMETERIES, the design of curved drives made good use of the sloping topography. In 1864 architect Albert PURCHAS was appointed to the Trust and is credited with much of the early landscaping: he was also responsible for the impressive lodge and offices, gates, fences, and seating. Advice on planting was also received from MUELLER and many of his trees survive. Regrettably, extensive planted areas and paths were later sacrificed for burial plots when efforts to extend the cemetery failed. The Springthorpe (1897–1901) and Syme (1908) memorials are outstanding monuments.

ROBERT NICOL

BOSISTO, Joseph (1824–1898), chemist and parliamentarian, born in Leeds, England, arrived in Adelaide in 1848, engaged by manufacturing chemist, F.H. Faulding. After time at Forest Creek diggings (Vic.), where he developed an interest in NATIVE FLORA, especially EUCALYPTS, he settled at Richmond (Vic.). He met Ferdinand MUELLER in Adelaide, and they became lifelong friends. By 1852 Bosisto had opened a pharmacy and was extracting eucalyptus oil. He established distilleries in the Dandenong Ranges and Richmond, manufacturing his famous Parrot brand eucalyptus oil. He was later a partner with chemical firm Felton Grimwade. He was elected to Richmond Council (1860), became Member of the Legislative Assembly for Richmond (1874), and served on many committees including that investigating Grape Phylloxera, then plaguing local VITICULTURE. Bosisto was active in planning for Melbourne's Exhibition Building (opened 1880), and represented Vic. at the Colonial and Indian Exhibition (London, 1886). Having lost most of his money during the 1890s, he was still manufacturing perfume at his Wimmera farm when he died.

MIMI COLLIGAN

BOTANICAL ILLUSTRATION The first published European drawings of AUSTRALIAN PLANTS resulted from the 1699 voyage of William DAMPIER, although it was almost another century before Australian plants were first illustrated for horticulture. The team of Charles L'Héritier (1746–1800), Pierre-Joseph REDOUTÉ, and James SOWERBY combined to produce the *Sertum Anglicum* (1789–92) at much the same time as William CURTIS began his *Botanical Magazine*, and as England established a penal colony at Port Jackson. Redouté drew *Eucalyptus obliqua* for the *Sertum Anglicum*, which was among the first Australian species established for horticulture in England following Cook's Pacific voyages. Redouté became one of the most famed illustrators of horticultural subjects, and Sowerby was among the most prolific horticultural and scientific illustrators. Joseph BANKS played an entrepreneurial role in the botanical exploration of Australia, with significant patronage bestowed on Robert BROWN, Ferdinand BAUER, and Sydney PARKINSON.

Grandly illustrated periodicals proliferated during the first half of the nineteenth century. Among these, *Curtis's Botanical Magazine* continued, illustrated by Sydenham Edwards (1768–1819) until he established his own periodical, the *Botanical Register*, in 1815. Following the death of Banks, William HOOKER began to play a focal role for plant collectors around the world. Although a competent illustrator, he soon employed Joseph Swan (*fl.* 1821–1872) as engraver and Walter Fitch (1817–1892) as artist and lithographer for most of his illustration. Hooker assumed editorship of *Curtis's Botanical Magazine* in 1827 and established his own periodicals, *Exotic Flora* being notable. As Director from 1840 of the ROYAL BOTANIC GARDEN, KEW, he established Kew as the centre of taxonomy and horticultural activity for the world. Hooker's contemporary, John LINDLEY, worked for the ROYAL HORTICULTURAL SOCIETY and similarly facilitated its tradition for horticultural record through art. Lindley became the editor of the *Botanical Register* (1829–47): Sarah Drake (1803–1857) among other artists became a significant illustrator of Australian plants in this and Lindley's other works.

The arrival of Ferdinand MUELLER in Australia in 1847 saw a change of focus away from England. MELBOURNE BOTANIC GARDENS, with Mueller's outstanding HERBARIUM, became the focus for Australian botany, and Kew played a decreasing role, especially after the publication of George BENTHAM's *Flora Australiensis* (1863–78). Mueller pioneered an austerity in the illustration of Australia's plants—Ludwig Becker (1808–1861), Friederich Schoenfeld (*c*. 1810–1868), and Robert Graff (*c*. 1841–1914) playing the major role as illustrators. Australia was in need of identification tools, and colonial Floras were instigated during the latter part of the nineteenth century. The austerity of illustration in the Floras is evident in being sparse or absent.

Several private artists and writers emerged: Ellis ROWAN, Fanny DE MOLE (SA), Fanny CHARSLEY (Vic.), Louisa MEREDITH (Tas.), Rosa FIVEASH (SA), Robert FITZGERALD (NSW), and others contributed to the colour of plant documentation during the last half of the nineteenth century after a period of predominantly black and white (published) illustrations. The end of the century saw the death of Mueller, the rise of Joseph MAIDEN and his illustrator Margaret FLOCKTON at the SYDNEY BOTANIC GARDENS, and of John BLACK, who illustrated his own Floras of SA.

During the first half of the twentieth century PHOTOGRAPHY began to replace illustration in published works. Even so, some illustrated works appeared: Edgar DELL and Emily PELLOE in WA painted for popular publications, William NICHOLLS painted orchids, and Thistle HARRIS arranged for Adam Forster (1850–1928) to illustrate her *Wildflowers of Australia* (1938). All the while, Australian plants continued to be illustrated in overseas journals and magazines including the enduring *Curtis's Botanical Magazine*. Flower painting as an individual art form was championed by Paul JONES.

The last half of the twentieth century saw an emergence from the austerity. A revival was evident by the 1970s, much activity being supported by the Maud Gibson Trust of the Royal Botanic Gardens, Melbourne. Margaret STONES, Celia ROSSER, Ludwick Dutkiewicz (b. 1921), and Betty Conabere (b. 1929) were early players in the revival. Dutkiewicz, in SA, was the first permanently appointed Australian herbarium artist (1953–83). He was later joined by Christine Payne (NSW, 1974), Margaret Saul (Qld, 1975), and Anita Barley (Vic., 1977); Rica ERIKSON drove an emergence in WA. Meanwhile, Stones established herself in England, and Rosser excelled with her *Banksia* paintings. The Australian Biological Resources Study stimulated work for artists through illustration for the *Flora of Australia* (1981–). Much recent work has also been directed at horticultural publications, rather than exclusively botanical ones. There are now teachers and botanical artists' societies in most states and territories. Regular exhibitions are held in most capital cities, and the quality of work is very fine indeed.

Wilfrid Blunt and William T. Stearn, *The Art of Botanical Illustration* (London, 1950; rev. edn, 1994); Janda Gooding, *Wildflowers in Art: Artists' Impressions of Australian Wildflowers 1699–1991* (Perth, 1991); Helen Hewson, *Australia: 300 Years of Botanical Illustration* (Collingwood, Vic., 1999)

HELEN HEWSON

BOTANIC GARDENS The earliest Australian botanic gardens were established in Sydney (1816) and Hobart (1818), which formalised the systematic collection and ACCLIMATISATION of plants in these government gardens. European colonisation of Australia occurred at a time when BOTANY had emerged as a scientific endeavour much expanded from its previous medicinal emphasis. Plants were being collected and described from all parts of the newly discovered world. Botanic gardens evolved as adjuncts to educational institutions, with the earliest such gardens established in Italy at Pisa (1543) and Padua (1545), and England, at Oxford (1621). Under the leadership of Joseph BANKS and later William and Joseph Hooker, the ROYAL BOTANIC GARDENS, KEW (London), became the model for the development of new botanic gardens. Economic as well as scientific imperatives firmed Kew's resolve to become the hub of an imperial network. In Australia, a dialogue with Kew was fundamental in the formation of botanic gardens, whose underlying structure was a living collection of plants with an attached HERBARIUM, consisting of pressed plant specimens, and a botanical LIBRARY, exemplified by the work of Joseph MAIDEN at Sydney.

By the 1850s major botanical gardens had been established in SYDNEY, HOBART, MELBOURNE, ADELAIDE, and BRISBANE. All combined their scientific roles with that of a PLEASURE GARDEN, often a source of conflict for directors, but these gardens were undeniably an integral part of Australia's system of PUBLIC PARKS AND GARDENS. This conflict was nowhere better demonstrated than at Melbourne in the early 1870s, when the scientific zeal of Ferdinand MUELLER was replaced by the landscape brilliance of William GUILFOYLE. The living collection at Kew, as in other major European botanic gardens, was principally laid out according to systematic scientific groupings; different plant types were also separated and grouped to form areas for trees (in an ARBORETUM), SHRUBBERIES, herbaceous plantings and the like. Climatic and geographic themes were also used to group plants, especially in conservatories. Mueller's adherence to these established models was eschewed by Guilfoyle, who combined utility with ornament in his diverse, picturesque groupings. Although the majority of Australian botanic gardens are fenced, with formal hours of opening and strict rules of use, all have free entry, acknowledging their role as important components of open space in the public domain.

Many more botanic gardens had been established throughout the country by the end of the nineteenth century, including significant gardens at DARWIN, ROCKHAMPTON, CAIRNS, and ALBURY. In Vic., many botanic gardens were established in regional towns; although they aspired to horticultural excellence—swelling civic pride—and adhered to some tenets of accepted international standards—such as permanence, plant acclimatisation, accurate nomenclature, and dedicated staff—recreational usage loomed large, and scientific endeavour was minimal. A similar, though smaller, network of 'Queens Parks' was established in Qld during the late nineteenth century. Many of these gardens possessed a range of GARDEN BUILDINGS including PAVILIONS, BANDSTANDS, GREENHOUSES, CONSERVATORIES, SHADE HOUSES, a

C.G.S. Hirst's bird's-eye view (1879) of the BOTANIC GARDENS at Toowoomba (Qld) clearly depicts leisure usage alongside more scientific horticultural pursuits—a complementary pairing that was often strained when recreational and sporting facilities were proposed for such gardens

variety of memorials, and occasionally a small ZOOLOGICAL GARDEN.

In the second half of the twentieth century there was renewed interest in the establishment of botanic gardens; the Botanic Gardens in KINGS PARK (Perth) and the AUSTRALIAN NATIONAL BOTANIC GARDENS (Canberra) were major new additions to the Australian botanic gardens network. Such gardens specialised in the collection and display of AUSTRALIAN FLORA and have subsequently made significant contributions to the understanding, conservation, and cultivation of native plants. The educational program for visitors and school children at the Australian National Botanic Gardens accelerated an important use for botanic gardens which, through much of the twentieth century, had been slow to develop. All the major Australian botanic gardens now have sophisticated visitor services and education programs that provide information and INTERPRETATION at all levels of inquiry into the plant world. At Kings Park and Botanic Gardens, an area managed ecologically to protect and conserve the existing indigenous vegetation provided an important new lead in the horticultural management and research of Australian plants in botanic gardens. This practice has since been adopted in a number of other gardens, most notably at the CRANBOURNE BOTANIC GARDENS, at an annexe to the Royal Botanic Gardens, Melbourne, and at the WOLLONGONG BOTANIC GARDENS.

Another important movement in the second half of the twentieth century was the acquisition, by a number of the major botanic gardens, of satellite sites. In the main, these provided substantial new areas for growing native plants, however, MOUNT LOFTY, an annexe to the Adelaide Botanic Garden, and MOUNT TOMAH, linked to the Royal Botanic Gardens, Sydney, provided a climate for expanding collections more suited to cooler conditions. Coinciding with the establishment of these gardens was the promotion of additional regional gardens located in different climatic zones throughout the country. The North Coast Regional Botanical Garden (Coffs Harbour, NSW), AUSTRALIAN ARID LANDS BOTANIC GARDEN (Port Augusta), AUSTRALIAN INLAND BOTANIC GARDENS (Mildura), and the Monsoon Tropical Botanical Gardens (Mareeba, Qld) are examples of new municipal botanic gardens in the Australian botanic gardens network. These gardens aim to take an active role in local conservation issues through the development of their living collections and educational programs.

There are now large numbers of botanic gardens throughout Australia, ranging from simple, park-like gardens, displaying a limited number of species to the major botanic gardens, with highly developed plant collections and management policies. In addition to traditional systematic and geographic themes, schemes are now employed to display plants. These include horticultural themes, schemes based on plant form and physiology, historic plantings, plants grouped to a particular climatic zone, and plants linked to their conservation status. An increasingly popular method is to develop habitat plantings to display plants in a simulated form of their natural environment—as in the misted rainforest gully at the Australian National Botanic Gardens; the wet and dry sclerophyll, dryland, woodland, bog garden, and rainforest sections of the Wollongong Botanic Gardens; and the range of Western Australian natural ecological association themes displayed at the Kings Park and Botanic Gardens.

The Australian Network for Plant Conservation initiated at the Australian National Botanic Gardens (1991) is developing an important new program for the conservation of Australian species and links with international efforts in plant conservation. Research work, educational programs, and gardens management policies have all been actively engaged in the fulfilment of the needs for plant conservation. The requirement, for example, to collect only wild-source plant material for this program rather than accept gifts or obtain plants from the nursery trade (of unknown wild origin) has substantially changed the collections policies of the major botanic gardens.

Conservation, research, education, and recreation are all active pursuits of modern Australian botanic gardens, aided by 'FRIENDS' GROUPS and guides. In addition, long-established sites also require a strong role in the management of historic landscapes, to reflect early Australian endeavours in the cultivation of plants, systematic botany, and landscape design.

> Edward Hyams and William MacQuitty, *Great Botanical Gardens of the World* (London, 1969); Lucille H. Brockway, *Science and Colonial Expansion: The Role of British Botanic Gardens* (New York, 1979); Carol Henry, *For the People's Pleasure: Australia's Botanic Gardens* (Melbourne, 1988); Donal P. McCracken, *Gardens of Empire: Botanical Institutions of the Victorian British Empire* (London, 1997); Leslie Lockwood, Jan Wilson, and Murray Fagg, *Botanic Gardens of Australia: A Guide to 80 Gardens* (Sydney, 2001) ML

BOTANIC GARDENS OF ADELAIDE: see ADELAIDE BOTANIC GARDEN; BEECHWOOD; MOUNT LOFTY BOTANIC GARDEN; WITTUNGA BOTANIC GARDEN

BOTANY is the study of plants. In the popular imagination the botanist is a kind of glorified gardener—although there are, of course, important connections between botany, HORTICULTURE, AGRICULTURE, and FORESTRY. Perhaps unexpectedly, relatively few academic botanists now work with whole, live plants. The university-based discipline of botany encompasses numerous specialised disciplines—palaeobotany, physiology, anatomy, classification (referred to as systematics or plant biodiversity), genetics, pathology, ecology, biogeography, conservation biology, biochemistry, morphology, and evolution—to name the more important fields. One example of the use of modern techniques is molecular systematics, where plant evolutionary relationships are hypothesised using chemical analysis of the DNA in the plant chromosomes.

The field of plant genetics has produced, by BREEDING and selection, many of our economically important and horticulturally significant garden plants and has, in recent times, taken on a new significance through genetic engineering. This rapidly developing science has major implications for our garden and crop plants. For ornamental plants, the rate of introduction of dramatic NOVELTIES will increase, and for crop plants disease resistance and yields will be a major focus. Substantial gene insertions may pose problems for plant nomenclature, and wider philosophical issues of genetic modification are still to be resolved.

One strong link between botanical science and horticulture is through the BOTANIC(AL) GARDEN—old, established gardens are often, by tradition, termed 'botanic' rather than 'botanical'—where rare and unusual plants are displayed to the public, sometimes as the trophies of PLANT COLLECTING expeditions. SYSTEM GARDENS have also provided this link between horticulture and botany, generally in a more formal, didactic manner than most botanic gardens. In Australia, taxonomic botanists at botanic gardens study not so much the exotic plants in their associated gardens but the native AUSTRALIAN FLORA, although the living collections may be used for research of various kinds. Considerable emphasis is now placed on plant conservation and ECOLOGY.

Another way botanists have an impact on garden plants is through their association with the Latin botanical names, the common currency of communication about the plant world introduced in the eighteenth century by LINNAEUS. This is an uneasy relationship, as botanists introduce unwelcome new names by describing new species, changing names as required by the rules of the *International Code of Botanical Nomenclature*, or researching new classifications and combining or splitting up existing groupings according to their findings.

An attempt to reconcile culture, the environment, and ecology has influenced horticulture, garden design, and horticultural botany in various ways, including the planting of indigenous species for habitat, food, and local landscape character; reduced maintenance and limited or no use of pesticides and fertilisers; increased care with scarce resources such as WATER and energy; a new and more enlightened approach to vegetation and habitat management through studies of FIRE ecology, management of remnants, REVEGETATION, and LANDSCAPE ECOLOGY; WEED research as the natural environment becomes increasingly degraded by human activity and introduced pest plants; and eco-physiology, which examines physiological responses to environmental factors such as drought, waterlogging, and salt resistance, and root physiology as it relates to such matters as interference with pipes and buildings.

Closer to garden plants, horticultural botany concerns itself with their description and documentation. One aspect of this discipline is the formation of accurate lists of plant names using COMPUTER technology. These may range from compilations of plants listed in early NURSERY catalogues to complex, modern-day industrial databases that detail the commercially available plants in Australian nurseries. A recent sophisticated database lists botanical names, including Plant Breeder's Rights and other commercial names, cross-referenced to botanical synonyms, common and other names, and linked in with accounting, barcoding, and stock control at nursery point-of-sales systems. Another important aspect of horticultural botany is the recording of CULTIVARS (cultivated varieties) of garden plants, especially those that have originated in Australia. These must be described

Handbooks such as Florence SULMAN's *Popular Guide to the Wild Flowers of New South Wales* (1913–14), illustrated by Eirene MORT (here depicting *Swainsona formosa*, Sturt's Desert Pea), communicated the results of research in BOTANY to FIELD NATURALISTS and home gardeners

accurately so they may be distinguished from similar cultivars, with their history of origin, breeder and selector and, if possible, a picture or specimen to serve as a permanent record. There is also a great need to record the plants that signal the influences of nursery proprietors and influential growers on our gardens and landscapes.

P.S. Short (ed.), *History of Systematic Botany in Australasia* (Melbourne, 1990); Roger Spencer, *Horticultural Flora of South-eastern Australia* (Sydney, 1995–); *Flora of Australia*, Volume 1: Introduction (Melbourne, 1999)

ROGER SPENCER

BOUGAINVILLEA GARDENS (now Thomas Park), Indooroopilly, Qld, was established by Henry Thomas (1865–1958), who purchased about three hectares of farmland with river frontage in 1898. Throughout the 1920s and 1930s, 'Somerset' or Bougainvillea Gardens was a favourite tourist destination, especially during bougainvillea flowering time. Thomas conducted PLANT BREEDING experiments and developed the vigorous (carmine-pink) *Bougainvillea spectabilis* 'Thomasi'. His gardens featured distinctive Queensland plantings, including palms, shade trees, TROPICAL plants (including fifteen cultivars of bougainvillea), and a twenty-five-metre timber trellis festooned with a single specimen of *B.* 'Thomasi'. Although the garden was purchased by Brisbane City Council for a PUBLIC PARK in 1947, Thomas lived at the site and and tended it until his death. A golf course consumed much of the land and the house was demolished (1962–64), but numerous sturdy bougainvilleas remain.

JEANNIE SIM

BOULEVARDS, broad streets, generally but not necessarily axial and often accentuated by AVENUES of trees, formed a key feature of many Australian towns and cities, especially those where TOWN PLANNING embraced the grid plan or, later, CITY BEAUTIFUL influences. The boulevard—closely related to the ESPLANADE—was originally named for a PROMENADE on demolished fortifications, and came to be symbolised in the nineteenth century by the work of Baron Haussmann in Second Empire Paris. Early Australian examples included North Terrace, Adelaide (1835–37) and the radiating roads of Melbourne (1840s–50s), with many impressive examples in provincial centres: Sturt Street, Ballarat, Vic. (1852), Main Street, Bairnsdale, Vic. (1860), and Deakin Avenue, Mildura, Vic. (1887), for example. CATANI's outstanding Alexandra Avenue, along Melbourne's Yarra River (1896–1901), was later extended to form Yarra Boulevard. Northbourne Avenue, Canberra (1912–18) represents the City Beautiful ideal. The POLITICAL will necessary for intervention of boulevards in pre-existing urban areas has rarely been found in Australia.

RA

BOULTER, Victor John (1890–1975) rhododendron grower, developed an interest in propagating rhododendrons in the 1930s while growing cut flowers at Olinda (Vic.). Reproducing plants he imported from Holland after the Second World War, he was concerned that European varieties were not suitable for hot Australian climates, and he developed cultivars to flower up to two months earlier, during the cooler winter months: many of these, such as 'Denise', 'You Beaut', and 'Jeanette Clarke', are still among the most popular cultivars in Australia. Boulter's sons, Frank John (b. 1924) and Geoffrey Edmund (b. 1926), joined as the business prospered, and Boulters rhododendrons were delivered to retail nurseries across Australia. Although he handed over the nursery to his sons *c.* 1969, Victor continued to hybridise rhododendrons until his death. The traditional business continued as Boulters Olinda Nurseries, run by Frank; in 1985, Geoffrey diversified into growing perennials, fuchsias, and other plants, trading as Boulters Nurseries, Monbulk.

HELEN BOTHAM

BOWEN PARK, Bowen Hills, Qld, was established in 1862 as the garden of the Queensland Acclimatisation Society (QAS), named for the colony's first governor. The forty-five acre (18 ha) creek valley had been cleared and used for brick clay extraction. In 1864 Alexander MACPHERSON was appointed 'park-keeper' (later superintendent) and carried out numerous development works, including a much-praised coral-stone and clam shell fountain. William SOUTTER, overseer 1885–98, brought the park to its peak condition. There

Bowling greens

Retaining many nineteenth-century and early-twentieth-century features, Sturt Street, Ballarat (Vic.) remains one of Australia's finest BOULEVARDS; vigilance is required to protect such DESIGNED LANDSCAPES from the ravages of planners and engineers, which can imperil public open space with inappropriate development

were many decorative features: four statues depicting the seasons, urns, seats, and a huge whale jaw-bone archway. The brick-pits were redeveloped as lagoons, with extensive plantings of waterlilies and bamboo, and bedding displays—especially on and around a quatrefoil-shaped island. A cottage, a bush-house, and a glasshouse supported the experimental plant breeding, growing, and distribution. Some animals were tested (red deer, llamas, and birds), but unusually among Australian ACCLIMATISATION societies, plants were the focus of attention. The Royal National (Agricultural and Industrial) Association (RNA) leased low-lying ground in 1875, and eventually gained most of the original site for its exhibition grounds. The Sandgate railway dissected this former park area (1881) and the new exhibition building (later overlooking the MUSEUM GARDENS) was also erected here (1987).

In 1914, the Brisbane City Council purchased remnant land from the QAS and developed it as the Council's main plant nursery (for a short time) and as a PUBLIC PARK. Bowen Park was officially reopened in 1914 after redevelopment by parks superintendent Henry MOORE to include a bandstand, ornamental gates, and kindred facilities. Between 1915 and 1918 Moore laid out a rose bed with about 1000 plants, and another for 200 massed crotons, replanted the bush-house,

and added numerous seats. In 1938, Moore moved out of NEWSTEAD HOUSE (his official residence) and returned to the cottage in Bowen Park. Between 1932 and 1950 further land was sold to the RNA, leaving the current area of 1.6 hectares. From 1957 to 1959 Harry OAKMAN redesigned the layout of beds, adding curvaceous shrubberies, annual beds, and formal hedging flanking paths and boundaries. Features by Moore and Oakman have survived, but few clues remain to the once-celebrated gardens of the QAS.

Frank Mills, *'The Ekka': The People and Events of Brisbane's Royal National Agricultural and Industrial Association Show* (Brisbane, 1990)

JEANNIE SIM

BOWLING GREENS date from the 1840s in Australia and were first constructed as adjuncts to hotels. Lawn bowls burgeoned as a fashionable and serious recreational SPORT from the 1860s. The sport, derived from the traditional Scottish game, was played on a level 'green' of TURF, usually square (approximately 36-metre sides) and slightly sunken. Few but the largest mansion gardens included a green, but bowling greens on public land, often within existing PUBLIC GARDENS, were gradually developed with seating (often with associated gazebos), plantings (mainly along boundaries), and club facilities housed in a PAVILION. The timber pavilion at St

Kilda (1876) is the oldest surviving bowling pavilion in Vic. Men and women participated, although clubs often had a CROQUET LAWN for the use of associate (female) members, since men's competitions took precedence. Bowling is among Australia's most popular international sports, with over forty-five per cent of the world's bowlers living in Australia.

RICHARD HEATHCOTE

BOWMAN, Edward Macarthur (1826–1872), botanist, was born in Sydney, son of Dr James Bowman, of Lyndhurst, and nephew of William MACARTHUR, of Camden Park, who gave him horticultural training (and financial support). He lived for a time at Ravensworth, a HUNTER VALLEY family property, where he experimented with PLANT BREEDING. During the 1850s he moved to Qld, where he was an enthusiastic plant-raising protégé of J.C. BIDWILL. Throughout central–eastern Qld he collected herbarium specimens for botanists such as MUELLER, and living plants for nursery proprietors. RA

BOYCE, Henry (c. 1852–1910), daffodil specialist and nursery proprietor, established the Deepdene Nursery in Balwyn (Vic.) in 1888 after working as gardener for the Hon. H. Miller in Kew. Modest in scale, his business catered for local needs as well as a growing clientele within the 'daffodil circle'. Boyce was well known and respected among Victorian horticulturists; he served on the committee of the Nurserymen and Seedsmen's Association of Victoria and was a member of the Advisory Board to the BURNLEY School of Horticulture. Following his death, the business was taken over by Fred G. Wood, who had worked for ten years as foreman at the Cremorne Nursery, Richmond, after six years with BRUNNING at the St Kilda Nurseries. E.E. PESCOTT recorded that Boyce was the first in Vic. to grow and deal extensively in DAFFODILS—a legacy recalled by the Royal Horticultural Society of Victoria's Henry Boyce Cup, a perpetual challenge cup for daffodils. RA

BOYCE GARDENS AND RAINFOREST, Toowoomba, Qld, on a six-hectare site watered from a sub-artesian bore, was established by Margaret (1906–1984) and Leslie Boyce (1897–1988) soon after their marriage in 1930. Maintained by them for more than five decades, the garden includes some 700 species of flowering trees, shrubs, and perennials, and is home to eighty bird species. Highlights include a 150-year-old *Ficus superba* var. *henneana* (Cedar Fig), remnant natural RAINFOREST, a *Chorisia speciosa* (Floss Silk Tree) with its giant thorns, and large *Magnolia grandiflora* (Bull Bay). A sunken garden and garden wall incorporating a relocated gargoyle from the Houses of Parliament (London) provide more formal features. In 1969 the site was given to the University of Queensland as an 'educational botanic garden' and in 1974 the University established an External Studies Centre on the estate. The garden provides a key feature in Toowoomba's annual Carnival of Flowers and Green Week FESTIVAL. MAURICE FRENCH

BOYD, (William) Alexander Jenyns (1842–1928), agricultural journalist and school master, was agricultural editor of the QUEENSLANDER from 1874 and founding editor of the respected and widely distributed *Queensland Agriculture Journal*. His publications included *Market Gardening in Queensland* (1910), *Elementary Lessons in Agriculture for the Use of Schools* (1910), and *Flower Gardening for Amateurs* (1911), along with other government publications on cotton, maize, potato, sisal fibre, banana, and pawpaw growing. Boyd's influence on landscape design was felt mostly through the periodical publications with which he was associated and the encouragement he gave to colleagues such as Philip MACMAHON.

The overriding horticultural presence at the *Queenslander* newspaper in the late nineteenth century was Boyd as agricultural editor. He covered a variety of topics from scientific agriculture to creative garden design, and the frequent epithet 'Agricultural Reporter' is thought to refer to Boyd as author; several critical descriptions of major gardens in Qld (GOVERNMENT HOUSE, BRISBANE BOTANIC GARDENS and other PUBLIC PARKS) appeared under this byline.

Boyd's editorship of the Department of Agriculture's *Queensland Agricultural Journal* lasted twenty-four years (1897–1921). Here he gathered the talents of local horticulturists, botanists, and other scientists to advise farmers on the latest experimental findings. Boyd's vision was to unite the farming community by sharing knowledge and experience. The *Journal*'s distribution was intentionally widespread: it was free to any farmer, library, or school within Qld, and to other departments and botanic gardens beyond. Perhaps Boyd's most important contributions to horticulture in Qld were his untiring encouragement of CHILDREN to take up gardening and his emphasis on scientific investigation as the best basis for sound agriculture. JEANNIE SIM

BOYLE, Robert (b. 1949), landscape designer, born at Ivanhoe (Vic.), completed a Diploma of Horticultural Science at BURNLEY College (1969). In his formative years he collaborated with Alistair KNOX, and he works on a diverse range of projects, in both country and city, for all levels of government as well as private clients. His designs often have WATER and ROCKS as prominent components and selected plants are often AUSTRALIAN NATIVES, although exotics are also included. For many years Boyle contributed articles on garden design and ran the national garden planning service for *Australian Home Beautiful*. He lectures at the University of Melbourne, Burnley Campus, on landscape design and construction and in 1991 he was awarded the Victorian College of Agriculture and Horticulture Medal in recognition of his outstanding contribution to landscape design and contracting. RODGER ELLIOT

BRACE, Emmeline Marcia (c. 1872–1922), gardener, was born in Hampshire, England, and proceeded to New Zealand (c. 1907) before settling in Sydney (c. 1909). She was keenly interested in agricultural and horticultural pursuits at a time when their acceptability as a career for women was being promoted, challenging prevailing GENDER divisions. Brace was secretary of the Women's Horticultural and Home Industries Association and an active member of the Feminist

Club and the Girls' Realm Guild. Her obituary in the *Sydney Stock and Station Journal* vividly conveys the then-unconventional lifestyle she and many of her colleagues adopted: 'She dressed like a man in severely cut tweeds, a linen collar, and a felt hat, crushed down upon her short hair, but under this somewhat repellent aspect there was concealed a warm heart and ready hand to help her fellow women.' RA

BRADLEY, Eileen Burton (1911–1976) and **Joan Burton Bradley** (1916–1982), bush regeneration pioneers, both lived in the Sydney harbourside suburb Mosman, and in the 1960s experimented with WEED eradication techniques in nearby Ashton Park. The sisters, both scientists, adopted a systematic approach, and continuously documented results. Their policy was to hand weed, moving from areas least affected to those most affected, mulch with litter collected on site, and foster natural REGENERATION. They eschewed the use of mechanical tools, herbicides, and the planting of seedlings other than those found *in situ*. Their aim was to eradicate all introduced species from remnant bushland and to restore natural ecosystems. Having proved their techniques successful in small areas, they set out using lectures, technical papers, and lobbying to convince land management authorities that large-scale bush regeneration was possible. Joan Bradley described the technique in *Bringing Back the Bush* (1988). Bush regeneration based on the 'Bradley method' is taught at many TAFE colleges, especially in NSW, where trained workers are employed statewide. ALLAN CORREY

BRADLEY, (Henry) Burton (1815–1894), solicitor and horticulturist, was born in London but grew up in Cape Town. He migrated to Sydney in 1832 and in 1839 was admitted as a solicitor. He lived in Paddington, a view of his house, The Terraces, being displayed at the 1867 Paris Exhibition. Bradley was an ardent horticulturist, well known to amateur gardeners of Sydney for his improvement of BULBS. He was an active member of the Australian Horticultural and Agricultural Society and its successor, the Horticultural Society of New South Wales. In 1875 he moved to Llewllyn, Five Dock, devoting himself to philanthropic and public health causes.

A son, **Henry Houghton Burton Bradley** (1845–1918), continued his father's enthusiasm for horticulture. He was a foundation member of the LINNEAN SOCIETY OF NEW SOUTH WALES (1874), wrote for the horticultural press, and gave lectures to local horticultural societies. He was a noted bulb grower and hybridist (especially *Narcissus*), his skill in this field admired by Peter BARR. RA

BRAGATO, Romeo (d. 1914), viticulturist and wine expert who, while studying at Cogneliano, Italy, was inspired to think that Australia would one day rival Italy in wine production. He travelled to Australia and in 1888 met with Rutherglen and Murray district grapegrowers, offering to set up an experimental vineyard and ampelographic collection, analyse soils, and provide scientific lectures and practical assistance. The vignerons wanted Bragato to run a viticultural college. The following year he worked at Great Western, and in 1889 was appointed Victoria's VITICULTURAL expert. For ten years the affable Italian advised local vignerons, boosting their confidence and reporting in the Board of Viticulture's *Journal*. A college was built at Rutherglen in 1897, complete with a model vineyard and winery designed by Bragato. He resigned in 1899 following the collapse of the Victorian wine industry, claiming he had been made a scapegoat for Grape Phylloxera. He went to New Zealand; in 1914 he was found dead in a hotel room in Vancouver, Canada. DAVID DUNSTAN

BRAITHWAITE, John George (1865–1936), gardener, was born in Yorkshire, England, arriving in Melbourne in 1889 to work on private estates. In 1896 he secured the position of City Gardener in Perth, where he supervised the development of parks, reserves, and street tree plantings, as well as a large propagation nursery. The *West Australian* described him as 'the founder and fashioner of … the pleasant places of Perth'. In 1937 he was succeeded by his son Henry Norman Braithwaite (1900–1959), Director of Parks and Gardens until his death, closing a remarkable sixty-three-year span. CAROL MANSFIELD

BREEDING: see PLANT BREEDING

BRICKENDON, near Longford, Tas.: see ARCHER, Thomas

BRIDGES, whether for utilitarian or ornamental purposes, spanning streams, LAKES, and other bodies of water, or gullies, gorges, and declivities, form traditional garden structures included in many Australian gardens. They can link PATHS and circuit walks, and often provide dramatic and otherwise inaccessible views and VISTAS. At a larger scale, bridges have been used in TOWN PLANNING, often as a focus or nexus. Materials range from timber to masonry and metal, using engineering techniques such as suspension, arched, or cantilevered forms. Bridges are often highly valued components of CULTURAL LANDSCAPES, and in the extreme, canalisation of rivers was undertaken to show off bridges to their best advantage and physically to mitigate against flood damage. Like garden buildings, bridges can display a variety of stylistic pretensions, generally complementary to the garden or landscape for which they were designed. Thus at RIPPON LEA the RUSTIC bridges of cast iron imitating timber logs (*c.* 1885) complement the picturesque lake islands they link, while recent structures over Melbourne's Yarra River represent sophisticated, hard-edged URBAN DESIGN. RICHARD HEATHCOTE

BRISBANE BOTANIC GARDENS *City Botanic Gardens*
The Brisbane Botanic Gardens were established in 1855 with Walter HILL the first curator. The site, beside the Brisbane River, was the former Government Garden of the Moreton Bay penal colony, whose boundaries had been laid out by Charles FRASER and Allan CUNNINGHAM in 1828. Hill took the Gardens from an overgrown vegetable plot to an admired pleasure garden with extensive experimental activities, laying the foundations for many important agricultural crops (sugar cane, tropical fruits). His crowning

achievement in design terms was the creation of Fern Island (early 1860s), irregularly planted with exotic and native tropical plants and surrounded by a large collection of giant bamboo (of several species, including *Phyllostachys aurea*). Hill was succeeded by James PINK (1881) and Alexander COWAN (1886), who both continued the horticultural upkeep of the gardens in trying circumstances.

In 1889 Philip MACMAHON was appointed curator, and the second important development phase began. His inventive and organisational abilities had major impacts on the physical form of the gardens. The BUSH-HOUSE, rustic shelters and seats, palms, massed canna displays, and ribbon borders were specialities. After disastrous floods in 1890 and 1893, MacMahon altered pathways and replanted to great effect. The late 1890s saw extensive recreational use, with a kiosk, croquet lawns, and BANDSTAND added. Trees for ARBOR DAY were supplied between 1892 and 1931. When his budget was slashed by half, MacMahon left and was succeeded in 1905 by John Frederick BAILEY, who continued the combined scientific and recreational activities. In 1915–16, Queen's Park (established 1850 along Alice Street) was officially incorporated into the Gardens.

In 1925 E.W. BICK, curator and director (1917–40), protested to no avail when the site was handed to the Brisbane City Council, where it remains. He continued testing plants, particularly those with ornamental potential such as crotons, bougainvillea, and hibiscus, and tended the ZOOLOGICAL collection. During the Second World War, the Gardens and Government DOMAIN became a naval depot. From 1946, new curator John Rayer BAILEY managed the site essentially along park lines, supplying floral tributes for civic functions and continuing Bick's succulents collection. Harold CAULFIELD, director 1956–82, equalled Hill's record twenty-six years of service. The 1974 floods devastated the plant collections and intensified the call for a more secure location. Now titled City Botanic Gardens—and distinct from Brisbane Botanic Gardens, Mount Coot-tha—it remains a peerless historic subtropical garden in the middle of a city centre, and a favourite with visitors. The gardens have been kept as a park with relatively little scientific work since the 1970s, but with increasing educational and INTERPRETATIVE activities. The historic plant collection—especially FIGS, PALMS, and BAMBOOS—has major botanical significance.

Mount Coot-tha This suburban Brisbane site was established following dissatisfaction with the old Brisbane Botanic Gardens site in the centre of the city, which were flood prone and had no potential for expansion. Brisbane City Council began investigating potential sites in 1968, and a fifty-two hectare site on the eastern slopes of Taylor Range, with extensive views of the city skyline, was selected: its potential range of plants is among the widest in Australia. Unusually among Australian metropolitan BOTANIC GARDENS, Mount Coot-tha is under the jurisdiction of local rather than state government. The initial development (1970–73) included a Tropical Display Dome (glasshouse), administrative buildings, and separate pedestrian pathways and vehicular ring road. Planting collections include outstanding Australian and exotic RAINFOREST plants, a fragrant garden, an ARID garden,

BRIDGES offer startling new views of familiar places, and their drama is heightened by the conjunction of WATER and the elevation of the viewer, as in this recent structure over the Yarra River at Melbourne's Southbank

aquatic and bog plants, and tropical herbaceous plants in the glasshouse. Curators have been Barry Dangerfield (1975–80), Harold CAULFIELD (1980–82) and Ross MCKINNON (1983–). In 1998, the Queensland Herbarium (Queensland Department of Environment) relocated here from Indooroopilly, opening the opportunity for sound scientific and educational collaboration.

JEANNIE SIM

BRISBANE GENERAL CEMETERY, Toowong, was intended to replace earlier burial sites that had been haphazardly developed and poorly maintained. Enabling legislation was passed in 1865, trustees appointed in 1870, and the cemetery formally opened in 1875; control was transferred to Brisbane City Council in 1936. In 1875 plans were prepared by the surveyor-general, but the original layout appears to have been the work of engineer George Phillips, who took advantage of the sloping site at the foot of Taylor Range. Improvements were slow, as they relied entirely on profits from fees. A 'dresser' to tend gardens was appointed in 1876, and an annual donation to the Queensland Acclimatisation Society produced a supply of plants and young trees from BOWEN PARK. For many years, the cultivation of flowers within the cemetery grounds was a special feature. These were sold at a moderate cost and, for an additional fee, placed on individual graves for set times or periods. Public resistance due to access problems largely dissipated after provision of a tram service in the early 1900s. Only a portion of the large site was used for burials, and in 1914 excess land was sold to Toowong Town Council for park purposes; proceeds were used to erect cemetery walls, railings, and gates.

ROBERT NICOL

BROADBENT, James (b. 1947), historian and iconoclast, completed his architecture degree at the University of Sydney (1969) with a thesis (jointly with Trevor Allen and Howard TANNER) entitled 'Colonial Garden Design'. Following this pioneering foray into Australian GARDEN HISTORY, he planned reconstructions for lost gardens, including Collingwood (Liverpool, NSW), CLARENDON (Tas.), and ELIZABETH BAY HOUSE (NSW), before his appointment as curator of Elizabeth Bay House (1977), shortly before it was handed over to the newly created Historic Houses Trust of New South Wales (1980). His work, especially with the Trust, has defined the role of the house museum in Australia. Fond of quoting Ruskin's passage from the opening of the 'lamp of memory' (*The Seven Lamps of Architecture*, 1849): 'Do not let us talk then of restoration. The thing is a Lie from beginning to end', his philosophy of minimal intervention has often been at odds with populist voices in the heritage movement. Decisive input into conservation plans, such as that for ROUSE HILL (1990), has seen this philosophy translated into Ruskinian bandaging, challenging for managers and visitors alike. Broadbent's publications and lectures, often complementing exhibitions, have brought a rich new understanding of colonial architecture and society, including its gardens. Key among these is *Gothick Taste in the Colony of New South Wales* (1980, co-author Joan Kerr) and *The Australian Colonial House: Architecture and Society in New South Wales 1788–1842* (1997).

RA

BROADLEES, Crafers, in the ADELAIDE HILLS, was established in 1926 by benefactors Eva and Lily Waite (daughters of Peter WAITE), with Ken MOSEL as head gardener (1925–48). Walter BAGOT designed the residence (1925). Eva Waite developed the garden with assistance from Bagot and Elsie CORNISH, using Gertrude JEKYLL's writings, including *Wall and Water Gardens* (1901) and *Some English Gardens* (1904), inspired by visits to Jekyll-designed English gardens including Brockenhurst. The garden, entered through Bagot-designed cast-iron gates, descends through a CONIFER forest to arrive at a MEDITERRANEAN-influenced residence in a northern ITALIAN garden setting. To the north is the Jekyll-inspired terraced garden with a rose garden, arbour, several water features, small pools and grotto, a middle herbaceous garden, and a lower fruit tree garden, surrounded by extensive planting of rhododendrons, camellias, and hydrangeas.

DAVID JONES

BRONTE HOUSE, NSW, a marine VILLA in the Gothick taste sited overlooking the ocean, was completed in 1845 for Robert and Georgiana Lowe—its picturesque setting sketched by Georgiana. With about one-third of its original curtilage, it was purchased by Waverley Council (1948) then privately leased (1983), although garden reconstruction plans by James BROADBENT and Michael Lehany were only partly implemented. Since 1994 it has been extensively conserved and developed by Leo Schofield (b. 1935), arts impresario and lessee, who gardens in the spirit of the nineteenth century, often using bold subtropical plantings.

COLLEEN MORRIS

BROOME COURTHOUSE GARDEN, WA, was established in 1983 when Broome Botanical Society started a major TROPICAL landscaping project using Community Employment Program funds. Formerly used as Broome Cable Station (1889), the original grounds comprised tennis courts, a well, and vegetable gardens, probably tended by the Indian servants who were associated with the station until its closure in 1914. Used as a courthouse from 1921, the boundary fence and entrance gate (probably 1889) remain.

ROSEMARY ROSARIO

BROWN, George (1929–2002), gardens curator, grew up in Sydney, where he studied at RYDE School of Horticulture. He became a Darwin resident in 1968 after a varied career, commencing as foreman at the DARWIN BOTANIC GARDENS in 1969, rising to become superintendent of Darwin City Council's Parks and Recreation Department. While at the Gardens, he rearranged plants to form botanic groupings and greatly extended the PALM collection, a planting theme that he promoted for wider adoption throughout Darwin after Cyclone Tracy (1974). His career at the Gardens culminated in appointment as curator (1990), before his election—under the slogan 'Go Green with Brown'—as Lord Mayor of Darwin in 1992. A fellow of the ROYAL AUSTRALIAN INSTITUTE OF PARKS AND RECREATION, Brown shared his gardening skills as a RADIO broadcaster for the Australian Broadcasting Corporation. Long lord mayoral tenure gave Brown local prominence, and his wide-ranging opinions, often colourfully expressed and forcefully put, made him a Top End icon.

JAN SETO

BROWN (née GILES), Jocelyn (1898–1971), landscape designer, born near Warwick (Qld), trained as a graphic designer and worked in Sydney. Here she met New Zealand-born **Alfred John Brown** (1893–1976) before he enlisted and left for war service in England and France. Wounded and invalided, he studied at the Royal Institute of British Architects as an Associate member. Jocelyn joined him in England, where they were married in 1920. He was appointed assistant to Louis de Soissons, architect and designer of Welwyn Garden City, a 'new town' at the edge of London of experimental design that embodied GARDEN CITY concepts advocated by reformer Ebenezer Howard. The three years they spent there influenced both Jocelyn and Alfred in their subsequent careers. They returned to Sydney in 1930 after a few years in New Zealand.

Studying the ideas of Gertrude JEKYLL, who was creating gardens in southern England, Jocelyn Brown began to evolve a style drawn from the English Edwardian gardens

plant enthusiast. She delighted in a lavish display of blooms, and enjoyed delineating her favourite flowers. Her best preserved suburban garden is GREENWOOD, St Ives; her two most notable NSW country gardens are ST AUBINS, Scone, and COOLIBAH, Young. Most of her suburban gardens have now disappeared with later subdivisions, and her main legacy today is her gardening articles.

Alfred Brown's TOWN PLANNING ideas were expressed in *Town and Country Planning* (1951, co-author H.M. Sherrard), a standard introductory text that influenced planning students for some decades. It drew attention to the English garden city concept, but at the time the Australian nineteenth-century urban experience had not been seriously studied, and the virtues of the basic colonial grid plans received scant mention.

Helen Proudfoot, *Gardens in Bloom: Jocelyn Brown and her Sydney Gardens of the '30s and '40s* (Kenthurst, NSW, 1989)

HELEN PROUDFOOT

The curved balcony of the residence at BROADLEES, Crafers (SA), designed in 1925 by Walter BAGOT, overlooks an appropriately ITALIAN-influenced garden

where formal built elements were combined with lavish planting to create an ARTS AND CRAFTS design defining outdoor spaces around the house, and making the transition from house to woodland. The house and garden were viewed as a single composition, and the COTTAGE GARDEN, with its old-fashioned favourites, provided the model, rather than the grander landscapes of the eighteenth century or the exotic collections of the nineteenth. She was attracted by the compartmented gardens of southern England and the revival of the earlier Tudor and Jacobean gardens, with their 'outdoor rooms' and controlled VISTAS to terminating points of interest, and walks between lavish planted borders, with intricate planting in selected areas. These elements provided the basis of her designs, more modestly adapted to Australian soil and weather conditions. She used AUSTRALIAN NATIVE PLANTS only at the end of her gardening career, preferring to use the fine forest trees of Ku-ring-gai only as a backdrop to her detailed planting.

Brown's work was stimulated by the planning and planting of her own gardens, first at Woollahra and then, more ambitiously, at Fountains, Lindfield (1938), where Alfred designed the Mediterranean-style house. She became known as a landscape designer when she wrote a monthly column in the *HOME* magazine (1939–42), and opened her own gardens for inspection. Her articles, illustrated by her graceful line drawings, explained her ideas on design, colour, and plant material, based on her practical experience as a

BROWN, John Ednie (1848–1899), silviculturist and forest conservator, was born in Scotland to a distinguished family, strongly associated with FORESTRY and land management. His father, Dr James Brown (1812–1888), Deputy Surveyor-General of Woods and Forests in SCOTLAND, was an authority on silviculture and ARBORICULTURE, and author of *The Forester* (1847). Brown left his Edinburgh school when 15 and spent three years as an apprentice under his father learning the practical management of nurseries, forest estates, and woodlands. He then served as assistant agent and forester on the Invercauld estate, Aberdeenshire. He subsequently moved to England and designed several plantations on estates under his management in Yorkshire and Sussex. In 1871–72 Brown visited North America and wrote his 'Report Upon the Trees Found in California' and 'Forests of the Eastern States of America', awarded the gold medal of the (Royal) Highland and Agricultural Society of Scotland (*c.* 1872). His essay 'The Trees of America' gained a prize from the Scottish Arboricultural Society (*c.* 1872).

Brown was offered the position as South Australia's Conservator of Forests while in Canada. As Conservator (1878–90) he supervised the Forest Board's activities, including the establishment of successful plantations, nurseries, and reserves at Kuitpo (in the ADELAIDE HILLS), WIRRABARA and BUNDALEER (near Jamestown), and at Leg of Mutton, Mount Burr, and Mount McIntyre (all near Mt Gambier). Other plantation sites included Port Road (Adelaide), Kapunda Reservoir, (BELAIR) NATIONAL PARK, and Wooldunga (near Quorn). *Pinus radiata* (Monterey or Radiata Pine), extensively trialled by Brown in these plantations, proved itself to be the most adaptable species for commercial-scale planting.

In 1879 the City of Adelaide engaged Brown to design 'a system of planting suited to the park lands' and to serve as honorary 'Supervisor of the Plantations' (1880-81) to implement the recommendations. His *Report on a System of Planting the ADELAIDE PARK LANDS* (1880) displays an appreciation of contemporary landscape design practice and writings in Britain, Canada, and the USA.

There was considerable tension between Brown and Forests Board chairman, George GOYDER, over Brown's belief that forests exerted a beneficial affect upon climate, and that planting of extensive tracts of trees in arid areas of the colony would increase the amount and reliability of rainfall in those areas. Brown's view, restated in *A Practical Treatise on Tree Planting in South Australia* (1881), accorded with contemporary wisdom, and obtained support from Richard SCHOMBURGK, although many of his practical attempts on the Willochra Plains, and at Mount Brown, HERGOTT SPRINGS, and Oodnadatta, proved unsuccessful. The treatise comprehensively reviewed the silvicultural opportunities of exotic and native trees in the colony, together with the laying-out of rural plantations and STREET TREE plantings. Brown's other publications included *Forest Flora of South Australia* (1882) and *Planting of Olives and Mulberries in the Mallee Lands, Dates in the Far North, and Wattle Cultivation Generally in the Colony* (1885). He successfully introduced ARBOR DAY (1889) into SA before the concept spread to other colonies, and emphasised the need for thorough training for foresters, becoming the first to advocate for a school of forestry in the colonies.

In 1890, NSW Premier Henry Parkes was introduced to Brown and subsequently offered him the position of Director-General of Forests in NSW (1890–93). During his tenure Brown spent much of his time in the field, setting up the forestry regions, supervising the first silvicultural experiments with *Eucalyptus camaldulensis* (River Red Gum), and reviewing options for plantations. Although much foundation work was done, his position, and the department, were abolished in 1893.

In 1895 Brown accepted a consultancy to review forests in WA so that 'the Government would have some reliable information as to the quantity of marketable timber in the colony'. His *Report on the Forests of Western Australia* (1896) provided a comprehensive review of the possibilities and he was subsequently appointed their first Conservator (1895–99). He established softwood plantings, including *Pinus pinaster* (Maritime Pine), sandalwood and wattle plantations, and introduced Arbor Day.

Brown was elected a life fellow in 1890 of the Linnean and Royal Horticultural Societies upon the recommendation of Ferdinand MUELLER. He died unexpectedly at home in Perth following a bout of influenza, aged 51, and was buried in the North Fremantle Cemetery. An under-recognised individual with considerable energy, Brown was the father of economic and scientific forestry in Australia, founding the forestry systems in SA, NSW, and WA, while his apprentice George PERRIN founded those in Vic. and Tas.

DAVID JONES

BROWN, Lancelot ('Capability') (1715–1783), English landscape designer, died half a decade before the First Fleet landed at Sydney Cove, yet his influence loomed over colonial landscaping for a century or more. Brown started learning the rudiments of building and land management in the 1730s and from 1741 worked for Lord Cobham at Stowe, Buckinghamshire, engaged as head gardener and clerk of works in carrying out designs of landscape designer and architect William Kent (1685–1748). Cobham's recommendations brought early commissions, and in the three decades following the mid-century Brown had no serious rival in the country. The success of his landscaping—'place-making' as he termed it—lay with Brown's ability to capitalise on the 'capability' of the place. Dealing with broad acres and substantial budgets, he was able to marshal clumps of planting to control vistas, dam streams, sculpt earth, and route drives—often ruthlessly sweeping away existing impediments such as houses or even whole villages, as recounted in Goldsmith's poem *The Deserted Village*. Such was the taste for landscaped parks in England during the mid-eighteenth century that when reaction came during the PICTURESQUE controversy of the 1790s, Brown was the most prominent target. His work and its context is considered in David Jacques's *Georgian Gardens: The Reign of Nature* (1983), Tom Williamson's *Polite Landscapes* (1995), and a special issue of *Garden History* (2001) which usefully complement Dorothy Stroud's biography.

Few in the colonies possessed the means or inclination to imitate the Brownian landscaped park. It was held up as an ideal by many—architect Francis Greenway invoked 'the celebrated Brown' when describing his scheme for Sydney's DOMAIN—and emulated in some larger NSW and Tas. estates, but more commonly, the appellation 'landscape-garden style' was used interchangeably with 'picturesque' as a kind of opposite to formality. Thomas SHEPHERD, a pupil of Brown's follower Thomas White, included many references to Brown in his lectures, but at this late stage, the English landscape garden had received rich overlays from followers of the Picturesque, and was waking to Loudon's GARDENESQUE, so much so that the Brownian ideal was soon an anachronism to the colonial cognoscenti and its precepts found expression only in the broad rural landscape beyond the HOMESTEAD GARDEN.

Dorothy Stroud, *Capability Brown* (London, 1950, 1975); Roger Turner, *Capability Brown and the Eighteenth-century English Landscape* (London, 1985); Thomas Hinde, *Capability Brown: The Story of a Master Gardener* (London, 1986) RA

BROWN, Robert (1773–1858), botanist, was born at Montrose, Scotland, and educated at the local grammar school and Marischal College, Aberdeen. From 1790 he studied medicine at Edinburgh University. He also took up botany, making excursions in the Highlands, writing Latin descriptions of plants—including Australian species—growing in the botanic garden, and building up a HERBARIUM. Without completing his studies he enlisted in the Fife Fencibles and was appointed surgeon's mate in 1795, when he was posted to Ireland. While on active service, Brown continued his botanical work and trained himself in microscopy. He corresponded with William Withering, who provided him with an introduction to the Portuguese botanist José Francisco Correia de Serra (1751–1823), then working in the herbarium of Sir Joseph BANKS in London, which Brown subsequently visited.

When Brown's school friend Mungo Park declined to go on Matthew Flinders' proposed surveying expedition to

Australia, Correia de Serra put forward Brown's name. Two years later, with a French expedition under Baudin travelling to the Pacific, Banks persuaded the Admiralty to send Flinders on an expedition more ambitious than previously envisaged. Brown was appointed naturalist on the *Investigator*, which left England under Flinders' command in 1801. Brown's team included Peter GOOD, as gardener and collecting assistant, and Ferdinand BAUER, as NATURAL HISTORY illustrator.

PLANT COLLECTING was undertaken on Madeira and at the Cape of Good Hope before reaching western Australia in December: it was to be the most productive of any Australian expedition mounted until then. In just three weeks they collected some 500 plant species in the Albany area alone: almost all were new to science and included the Albany pitcher-plant (*Cephalotus follicularis*). Under Brown's supervision, Good collected live plants for KEW GARDENS. By the end of the expedition, Brown had made more than 6000 plant descriptions—written in Latin, associated with huge numbers of herbarium specimens and cross-referred to Bauer's field sketches—while the live collection at Kew had become the basis for that garden's pre-eminence in the cultivation of AUSTRALIAN PLANTS.

More plants were collected during the *Investigator*'s voyage to Sydney, Brown and his team being the first botanical collectors in what is now Vic. In Sydney the living plants were established in the Governor's garden: the *Investigator* sailed north up the Queensland coast, through Torres Strait and into the Gulf of Carpentaria, virgin territory for the naturalists. With a deteriorating vessel and ailing crew, Flinders returned to Sydney (1803).

Returning to England as a passenger in the *Porpoise*, which carried living plants for Kew and Brown's top set of herbarium specimens for Banks, the vessel struck the Great Barrier Reef and was lost, with only a few seeds saved. Brown, with Bauer and their servants, remained with their collections in Sydney, collecting and drawing. Brown also gathered specimens in the Kent Group and in Van Diemen's Land, where he ascended Mount Wellington and carried out much original exploration, harvesting seeds of plants later successfully raised at Kew. He also used Kingstown (present-day Newcastle) as a base for botanical exploration of the HUNTER VALLEY. In 1805 Brown, with Bauer, left Australia in the hastily refitted *Investigator*, carrying mineral, animal and plant specimens, including seeds, back to England: the living collections were left in the care of Banks's resident collector, George CALEY, and were subsequently lost sight of.

The dried Australian plant specimens were to occupy Brown throughout much of the rest of his long career and they were to be the touchstone for major advances in cytology and palynology as well as systematics and biogeography. Through Banks's influence, Brown (and Bauer) received a salary from the British Admiralty to write up the botanical results of the voyage. This led to the first Flora of Australia, the unfinished *Prodromus Florae Novae Hollandiae et Insulae Van Diemen* (1810), important in re-introducing the 'natural system' of botany to England, as well as monographic works, notably his important paper on Proteaceae (1810). This monograph had been prompted by Brown's work for the

Engraved portrait of Robert BROWN, affixed in homage by Samuel HANNAFORD into his copy of Brown's seminal *Prodromus Florae Novae Hollandia et Insulae Van Diemen* (2nd ed., 1827)

second edition of William Aiton's *Hortus Kewensis* (1810–13), in which many of the species successfully brought into cultivation from the *Investigator* voyage were included. In Aiton's book, Brown also contributed major accounts of Australian Leguminosae and Myrtaceae. As early as 1806, he had drawn up a list of all the Australian plants growing at Kew: some 95 species, including 16 *Banksia* and 10 *Acacia* species.

It had been intended that Brown's *Prodromus* be a forerunner of a magnificent Flora with watercolour illustrations by Bauer, but the project was soon abandoned, though Brown did help Bauer bring out the fifteen plates of his *Illustrationes florae Novae-Hollandiae* (1813–16), another fragment, and, like the *Prodromus*, a financial disaster. With the death of Banks's librarian, Jonas Dryander (1748–1810), Brown was appointed in his place and, at the death of Banks, he was left a life interest in his collections. Banks also intended that Brown be, in effect, botanical consultant at Kew, where Bauer's brother, Franz—with whom Brown was to collaborate in work on fertilisation in orchids—was ensconced for life as resident artist.

In 1827, Brown negotiated with the Trustees of the British Museum, such that Banks's collections passed to the Museum during his lifetime, while he became salaried as Keeper of the Banksian Department, now the Department of Botany in the Natural History Museum, London. In 1830 Brown published a supplement to the *Prodromus*, dealing exclusively with new Australian Proteaceae. In 1837 his unofficial attachment to Kew ended and, in 1840, he had the herbarium collections moved thence to the Museum, before the takeover of Kew by Sir William HOOKER.

Brown was one of the great scientists of the nineteenth century—certainly the greatest British botanist, probably of all time, and certainly the greatest to collect in Australia. He probably named more Australian plant species than any other worker, distinguished by the abbreviation 'R.Br.'. His type specimens are in The Natural History Museum, London, though duplicates have been distributed to collections in Australia, notably ROYAL BOTANIC GARDENS in MELBOURNE and SYDNEY. Brown was commemorated in the names of many geographical features in Australia including Mount Brown (SA), as well as in many Australian plant species: genera named after him are *Brownetera* (now *Phyllocladus*), *Brunonia* (Goodeniaceae), and *Brunoniella* (Acanthaceae).

D.J. Mabberley, *Jupiter Botanicus: Robert Brown of the British Museum* (Braunschweig, 1985); T.G. Vallence, D.T. Moore, and E.W. Groves (eds), *Nature's Investigator: The Diary of Robert Brown in Australia, 1801–1805* (Canberra, 2001).

DAVID MABBERLEY

BROWNE (née RILEY), Margaret Maria ('Mrs Rolf Boldrewood') (c. 1837–1917), author, was orphaned at an early age and brought up by an uncle, Thomas Blomfield, at Denham Court, Ingleburn (NSW), where she tended her own small garden. In 1861 she married Thomas Alexander Browne (1826–1915), celebrated for his books, including *Robbery Under Arms*, written under the pseudonym 'Rolf Boldrewood'. The Brownes moved many times around NSW, with Margaret Maria creating many gardens she was never to see mature. She bore nine children and wrote just one book: *The Flower Garden in Australia* (1893), the first Australian GARDENING BOOK produced by a woman. It was written under the name 'Mrs Rolf Boldrewood' while the Brownes were living in Albury (NSW). Subtitled 'A Book for Ladies and Amateurs', it is as relevant to Australian gardening today as it was at the turn of the century. Written in a calendar-style format, it not only listed what to plant when, but gave detailed descriptions of individual flowers, their history, and growing needs, as well as planting and maintenance tips for shrubs and trees. It was also written from a woman's point of view and the author freely admitted borrowing ideas from other writers to complement her own. The Brownes moved to Melbourne in 1895 but little is known of 'Mrs Boldrewood' after that date. A facsimile edition of *The Flower Garden in Australia* (with an introduction by Victor Crittenden) was published in 1995.

Paul de Serville, *Rolf Boldrewood: A Life* (Carlton South, Vic, 2000).

MOIRA MAGUIRE

BROWNLOW HILL, Cobbitty, NSW: see MCLEAY, Alexander

BRUCE, Alexander Dickson Esson (1884–1967), garden curator and rosarian, is best remembered for his development of Canberra's GARDEN CITY image (1926–38). Scottish-born, after horticultural training in Edinburgh at Heriot-Watt College and the Royal Botanic Gardens, and employment with Cheshire County Council, England, Bruce arrived in WA in 1910 where he became Curator of Parks and Gardens in Fremantle then Subiaco. Following a study tour in 1925 to SA, Vic., and NSW, Bruce was appointed Assistant Superintendent of Parks and Gardens in CANBERRA under T.C.G. WESTON. Following Weston's retirement in 1926, he became Acting Superintendent and Superintendent in 1928. Wholly responsible for the preparation of planting schemes, the selection of trees and shrubs, and planting of the city area, Bruce's influence can be seen in the street tree and park planting of the Federal Capital Commission period. Bruce favoured trees and shrubs for seasonal display, in particular, *Prunus cerasifera* 'Atropurpurea' (Purple Cherry Plum). He introduced large areas of rose plantings, especially along Commonwealth Avenue and around Parliament House, that proved popular tourist features. Extant examples of his work may be seen along Flinders Way, Red Hill (ACT) and at the National Rose Gardens, Parkes (NSW). Bruce was instrumental in forming the Horticultural Society of Canberra and was an energetic president for many years. Bruce terminated his appointment with the Commonwealth Public Service in 1938 and took up work with Sydney City Council, before retiring to Perth. In 1928 he was elected a Fellow of the ROYAL HORTICULTURAL SOCIETY.

DIANNE FIRTH

BRUNDRETT, Samuel (1867–1940), nursery proprietor and rosarian, migrated to Australia c. 1888 from Manchester, England, with family members. After work as a jobbing gardener he started a nursery in Moonee Ponds (Vic.) in 1893, rapidly assuming a position of authority among Victorian rosarians and subsequently becoming one of Australia's leading commercial growers. He was a founding member of the NATIONAL ROSE SOCIETY of Victoria, a successful exhibitor, and a keen promoter of Australian-bred roses, including those of Alister CLARK. Owing to poor water pressure at Moonee Ponds, Brundrett commenced operations in 1926 on the (then) rural acres of Narre Warren, and was soon joined by his son Allen Ambrose Brundrett (1909–1994). Their rose farm was a great success, offering 800 named roses in 1939. The nursery was regularly opened for charity days and, in an era pre-dating widespread car ownership, clients were regularly collected, by appointment, from the local railway station. Allen's son, Bruce Alister Brundrett (b. 1940), joined the business in 1957, and his children continue the family company.

RA

BRUNN, Theodore Herman (1893–1970), landscape gardener and nursery proprietor, was born at Caulfield (Vic.), son of a landscape gardener, and received his early training in gardens at MOUNT MACEDON. Recuperating during 1919 following war service, Brunn toured leading European gardens and nurseries, gaining invaluable experience. On his return, he became manager of Ormond Plant Farm's city business, controlling the landscape department. In 1928 he started business under his own name, and c. 1931 joined with C.E. ISAAC and A. RIMINGTON to form Associated Nurseries Pty Ltd, a joint venture of three well-known Melbourne firms. Brunn lectured on garden planning at the inaugural Garden Week (1925) and was an indispensable member of organising committees for horticultural SHOWS and FESTIVALS. He took great interest in horticultural societies and was a president of the Royal Horticultural Society of Victoria. He was awarded the Veitch Memorial Medal (1968), the highest award by the ROYAL HORTICULTURAL SOCIETY to a person outside Britain. RA

BRUNNING, George (1830–1893), nursery proprietor, was born at Lowestoft, Suffolk, England, where his father, John, was a gardener and seed merchant. George Brunning trained as a gardener at nearby Somerleyton Hall, where formal revivalist W.A. Nesfield had laid out balustraded terraces and a PARTERRE in the late 1840s. Brunning and his brother Charles migrated to Australia, arriving in Melbourne in 1853. George unsuccessfully sought employment in the nursery trade, then in a state of infancy in Vic., and soon accepted a position as a storeman in Melbourne before trying his luck at the Sandhurst (Bendigo) gold diggings. Returning to Melbourne after a few months, Brunning took the management of a small nursery at Richmond, owned by John RULE, which he superintended with success for two years. He returned to England in 1856 to bring out his wife Harriet and young son, George. After his return later that year he began in business on his own account, contracting for the laying out and planting of gardens, while establishing stock for a nursery business. By 1859 he was renting a four-roomed timber cottage in St Kilda.

In 1860 Brunning committed the whole of his time to the nursery business and established the St Kilda Nurseries on Brighton Road, near the corner of Argyle and Inkerman streets, in the heart of a then-fashionable neighbourhood. In 1862 he rented a larger block adjacent to the Grosvenor Hotel further south in Brighton Road, which he occupied until it was sold for housing in 1884. He imported NOVELTIES from England to ensure that he carried the best and most recent plant varieties, especially florists' flowers. He also paid especial care to correct nomenclature in an industry not universally noted for botanical accuracy. By the early 1860s Brunning had been joined by his brother **William Brunning** (c. 1837–1890), who established his own nursery in 1866 on land he selected at Somerville, on the Mornington Peninsula. William specialised in fruit trees and supplied his brother with stock. By 1873 George Brunning was also using Thomas LANG and LAW SOMNER AND CO. as city agents. William's son **John Brunning** (1862–1928) was also a pioneering Somerville orchardist.

In 1883–84, as real estate pressure on his leasehold intensified, George Brunning purchased land and moved his nursery further south down Brighton Road (between Albion and Maryville streets), while also purchasing several subdivided allotments of his old four-acre (1.6 ha) site. At this stage he took his son **George Edward Brunning** (c. 1854–1935) into business, trading as George Brunning and Son, and now directed city business to William ADAMSON as his sole agent. A third son, **Herbert John Brunning** (1864–1949), was also admitted to the family business around this time.

In 1887 George Brunning and William Woodmason purchased the business of William Adamson, retaining the services of long-serving manager Thomas PURVES, and in 1889 **(Frederick) Hamilton Brunning** (1861–1905), Brunning's second son, joined the firm. This strategic purchase gave the family control of a major city outlet and also the publishing rights to *The Australian Gardener*, its predecessor having first been issued by Adamson in 1854. By the time of the 14th edition (1896), the work had been heavily revised by F. Hamilton Brunning.

George Brunning died in July 1893. He had been especially prominent through his overseas and intercolonial exports: he introduced to the colonial trade and popularised many plants, for example the Waltham Cross grape, *Cupressus macrocarpa* (Monterey Cypress), *Schinus molle* (Pepper Tree), and many roses and pelargoniums. When in 1888 celebrated London rosarian William Paul inscribed a presentation copy of his book *The Rose Garden* 'To Mr George Brunning, who has done so much for the advancement of horticulture in

An 1888 lithograph of the St Kilda Nurseries of George BRUNNING & Son recalls an era before real estate pressures forced such inner-suburban NURSERY operations to the city fringes

Buda

Australia' he mirrored a widely shared belief. Encomiums such as 'the largest and finest collection of plants in the Australian Colonies' and 'the most complete establishments of their kind in the Australian colonies' were frequently repeated by contemporary reviewers of the Brunning nurseries and his high business standards were a byword to customers and competitors alike.

Henceforth sons George and Herbert ran the nursery while F. Hamilton Brunning maintained the city depot, which moved from Collins Street to Elizabeth Street in 1900. Special attention during this period to chrysanthemums capitalised on their surge in popularity, while roses had long been a staple of the firm. **Leslie Herbert Ashby Brunning** (1886–1947), son of G.E. Brunning, became a member of staff in 1903; he later revised and edited the 19th (1920) to 28th (1946) editions of *The Australian Gardener*. On the death of F. Hamilton Brunning (1905) the former Adamson business was formed into a proprietary limited company, with Herbert Gill, G.E. Brunning, Purves, and later H.J. Brunning as directors. F.H. Brunning Pty Ltd expanded to encompass a staff of more than sixty, and established a large seed warehouse in South Melbourne. Publication of *The Australian Gardener* continued, with the 1916 edition heavily revised by F.A. Falkner. The Brunning company was reconstituted in 1926, with the parent company retaining farm seed, lawn grasses, bulk vegetable seeds, and export trade, while long-serving staff members GILL AND SEARLE took over the horticultural business, the two companies working co-operatively. The St Kilda Nurseries were also closed in 1926 and the land was subdivided for housing. Brunning Street commemorates the family name. With the relinquishment of the garden trade, L.H. Brunning made the decision to place the publication of *The Australian Gardener* in the hands of Robertson and Mullens Ltd, which (later as Angus and Robertson) has published the work since the 21st edition (1929).

L.H. Brunning wrote several other books, including *Fodder Crops for Australia* (published in 1922 as a souvenir of the 70th year of Adamson's business) and *Australian Home Gardener* (Ideal Home Library, London, 1935)—virtually a reprint of the 23rd edition of *The Australian Gardener* (1934), for which Brunning had added a postscript on cactus culture, then the height of fashion. The London imprint was distinguished by the inclusion of an appendix on garden design with notes and plans by WALLING and MELLOR, and several photographs of gardens, including BURNHAM BEECHES. Harold ALSTON revised the 30th edition (1949) of *The Australian Gardener*, and when Ernest E. LORD revised the 34th edition (1958) the title was changed to *Brunning's Australian Gardener*. The book was (and still is) the flagship for the Brunning name. The business, however, contracted until it sold just lawn seed and a handful of garden requisites—a far cry from its heyday as one of Australian's most important plant nurseries and seed merchants. RA

BUDA, Castlemaine, Vic., is a quintessential product of the Victorian goldrush period and consequent wealth and social change. Developed between 1861 and 1863 by Baptist missionary Rev. James Smith (1816–1898) while convalescing from his enervating Indian circuit, Smith modelled his residence—named Delhi Villa—on the Indian bungalow, with pyramidal roof and encircling slatted verandah. His VILLA garden spilt down the hillside, and it was perhaps this feature that attracted Hungarian silversmith, Ernest Leviny (1818–1905), who purchased the property in 1863. The extent of the early garden is uncertain: Smith was an ardent horticulturist, responsible for acclimatising eucalypts in India, and he may have planted the cypress HEDGE that now forms such a conspicuous feature. Leviny had invested shrewdly in Castlemaine real estate, and he dreamed of one day creating a splendid estate: numerous surviving watercolours of a projected house and garden attest to his aspirations. Unable to start anew, he steadily increased the size of Buda—renamed after his homeland—both by architectural additions and adjoining land purchase. Remodelling continued until the 1890s, and following Leviny's death his wife and daughters lived and gardened at Buda until 1981, when his youngest daughter Hilda died—a remarkable continuity. Subtle changes modified the garden: the nineteenth-century tennis court was remodelled into an ARTS AND CRAFTS–inspired formal garden during the 1920s, and as trees matured, the floral displays contracted through competition, with water-tolerant species faring best in the dry inland climate. Since 1982 Buda has been managed as a museum, with special interpretation of its outstanding historic garden. RA

BUILDING (1907–72), a monthly journal published in Sydney by wife and husband Florence Mary (*née* Parsons) (1879–1969) and George Augustine Taylor (1872–1928), did much to promote architecture, building, and town planning. Florence, among Australia's earliest female architects, edited *Australian* (later *Commonwealth*) *Home* (1925–30), and took on this role for *Building* after the death of her husband. Especially in its first decades, the journal contains much of interest for the garden historian. RA

BULBS, corms, and tubers are usually grouped in HORTICULTURE under the term bulbous plants. While different in makeup, all generally consist of swollen subterranean storage parts—a strategy that allows the plant to deal with dry environments having a short growing season. In Australia bulbs grow in many of these habitats, particularly those from Europe and the MEDITERRANEAN (with genera such as *Narcissus*, *Crocus*, *Hyacinthus*, *Cyclamen*, and *Tulipa*) and from southern AFRICA (with genera such as *Babiana*, *Crocosmia*, *Freesia*, GLADIOLUS, *Ixia*, *Oxalis*, *Sparaxis*, *Tritonia* and *Watsonia*). Bulbs are not prevalent in the AUSTRALIAN FLORA, although *Crinum* and *Calostemma* are examples. More usual are tuberous rooted species, such as *Bulbine bulbosa*, commonly found in grasslands. These species also represent important ABORIGINAL FOOD sources. Although not widely grown in Australian gardens, they have attracted increasing interest, particularly in REVEGETATION schemes.

Bulbous plants figured prominently in early Australian NURSERY catalogues and GARDEN BOOKS, where a separate section was usually devoted to the different species and types. Overseas catalogues in the possession of enthusiasts

The PLEASURE GARDEN at BUDA, Castlemaine (Vic.), enclosed between the house and a massive cypress hedge, provided both a setting for the house and its street frontage, and a sheltered area for the enjoyment of family members and their guests

specialising in early Australian gardens—particularly those from bulb growers in GERMANY and the NETHERLANDS—also provide evidence of a keen interest in the importation and cultivation of bulbous plants. Some of these display images of planting schemes using bulbous plants in formal ribbon BEDDING. A more widespread use of bulbous plants in Australian gardens, however, has been in grouped and informal planting schemes mixed in beds with herbaceous perennials and flowering shrubs. They have also been widely used for their naturalising effect in LAWNS. BREEDING of some species has also been undertaken by Australian enthusiasts, particularly Daffodils (*Narcissus*) which are shown regularly in FLOWER SHOWS and COMPETITIONS.

Australia's climate is well suited to the growth of many bulbous species, especially from southern Africa, although some of these, such as species of *Crocosmia, Gladiolus, Freesia, Sparaxis, Romulea,* and *Watsonia,* have naturalised and become environmental WEEDS.

R.T.M. Pescott, *Bulbs for Australian Gardens* (Melbourne, 1968); A.G.W. Simpson, *Growing Bulbs* (Kenthurst, NSW, 1985); James Hitchmough, *Garden Bulbs for Australia and New Zealand* (South Yarra, Vic., 1989); Jack Hobbs and Terry Hatch, *Bulbs for Gardeners and Collectors* (Balmain, NSW, 1994)   ML

BULCOCK, Robert (1832–1900), was born in England, where he became an overseer in a cotton mill. He arrived in Brisbane in 1855, initially following agricultural pursuits, before setting up in business as a seed and produce merchant in Queen Street. He diversified with nursery plant stock, and by 1861 was also operating as a fruiterer and greengrocer at Ipswich. He took an active interest in political and municipal affairs after retiring as a pioneering member of Queensland's nursery trade.   RA

BUNCE, Daniel (1812–1872), horticulturist, explorer and curator, was born at Chesham, Buckinghamshire, England, and migrated to Van Diemen's Land, arriving at Hobart Town in 1833. His undisputed claim to have trained at KEW is perhaps supported by his plant collecting exploration of Mount Wellington immediately after his arrival. Another early botanising journey took him to Launceston. Bunce was later to publish sets of four albums of about 100 mounted specimens as *Plants from Australia*. By 1835 Bunce was employed at Lightfoot's nursery, fruit, and seed garden on the New Town Road, Hobart Town, which he soon took over and renamed the Denmark Hill Nursery. A list of plants on offer appeared in the *Hobart Town Courier* (15 July 1836), one of the earliest such lists in Australia. Bunce also wrote *The Manual of Practical Gardening*, published from July 1837 in twelve monthly parts. In 1839 Bunce was insolvent and the nursery was sold. He was aboard the *Lord Hobart* when it sailed for Melbourne later that year.

Bunce was soon walking to the Dandenongs and Western Port accompanied by a small party of Aboriginals. It was during this botanising journey that his interest in their language increased, later resulting in his *Language of the Aborigines* (1851). From 1840 Bunce was advertising collections of preserved specimens and seeds—'a present to send home'. In 1841 Bunce proposed the formation of a BOTANIC GARDEN in Melbourne under his supervision, but this was not adopted. Clearly he was not prospering, and that could be the reason for a period of disorderly behaviour including an assault on an acquaintance who had lent him a tent in which to live because of his 'embarrassed circumstances'.

Bunce left in December 1846 as 'naturalist and botanist'—also goatherd as his additional duty—with the second Leichhardt expedition into the interior of Australia. By July 1847 the party returned exhausted, without having achieved its main aims. Many plants, some of them unknown, were recorded, and seed collected. One of the new plants was named *Greevesia cleisocalyx* by MUELLER, but it was later identified as *Pavonia hastata*—a species found in 1767 on the banks of the River Plata in South America. *Panicum buncei*, a grass species discovered at Bokhara Flats (near a creek feeding the Condamine in the DARLING DOWNS), was named for Bunce. His version of the expedition was given in *Travels with Dr Leichhardt in Australia* (1859), which also included his *Australasiatic Reminiscences*. From it the extent of his considerable knowledge of plants can be obtained. A month after the party's return Bunce again accompanied Leichhardt, this time on an expedition to Fitzroy Downs, collecting specimens and seeds before making his way overland back to Melbourne. He presented himself for the ill-fated 1848 expedition, but was rejected. In 1849 Bunce undertook an exploratory tour of the Murray River country, following it course.

In 1850 Bunce was advertising his services as a landscaper with trees for sale—'he may be seen near the hotel St Kilda'. That year his *Australian Manual of Horticulture* was published, followed by his *Hortus Victoriensis* (1851), which was strongly criticised by botanist Ronald GUNN, who showed that it had been taken from a list of plants compiled by James BACKHOUSE in 1834. Bunce's *Hortus Tasmaniensis* (1838) had been suppressed by the publisher. Bunce was in the gold-mining centres of Sandhurst (Bendigo) and Chewton in 1852–53, sending reports to the Melbourne *Argus*. He gained extensive publicity from his books, reports, and letters to newspapers—an editorial in 1851 opened 'According to Bunce and other authorities'.

A 200-acre (81 ha) site east of the town of Geelong was reserved for a botanic garden in 1851 and a cottage for the curator built by 1855. Two years later drives had been laid out and a small collection of plants was in the nursery area, the main need then being an able person to take charge. Bunce was appointed by the trustees, and having at last achieved his ambition he set about his task with enthusiasm, soon deciding that the nursery should form the botanical garden and the remainder parkland with an ARBORETUM. Instead of labels Bunce numbered the plants, and in 1860 published a corresponding 24-page catalogue, priced sixpence.

In 1860 Bunce was a foundation committee member of the Geelong-based Horticultural Improvement Society of the Western District. He wrote two papers for the Society, 'Tree Planting in Towns' (1861) and 'A List of Plants Capable of Resisting Long Drought' (1862). He also contributed notes to the *Victorian Agricultural and Horticultural Gazette*, published in Geelong. In 1863 Bunce was granted a 30-year lease of thirty acres (12 ha) in the Parish of Gnarwarre for use as a medicinal garden and vineyard. By now Bunce had the gratitude of many citizens who appreciated the way the GEELONG BOTANIC GARDENS had been developed. He was locally acclaimed for his success with *Swainsona formosa* (Sturt's Desert Pea), which had become a feature of the Gardens. Praise also came for his generous plant distributions to public and private establishments, principally in Geelong and the WESTERN DISTRICT. Bunce unsuccessfully applied to be superintendent of ADELAIDE BOTANIC GARDENS in 1865. The next year one of his activities was collecting ferns in the Western District, and in 1868 he planned COLAC BOTANIC GARDENS.

Bunce, thrice married (his second wife, Pelonamena, who died in 1859 aged only 25, was pioneer John Batman's youngest daughter), had a chequered adult life but deserves credit for courage as an adventurer, for withstanding adversity, and for his determined pursuit of a botanic gardens curatorial career. He was often erroneously referred to as a Doctor of Botany—a claim he evidently did not deny—but during his time at Geelong he demonstrated he was a capable horticulturist.

Paul Fox, *Clearings: Six Colonial Gardeners and their Landscapes* (Carlton South, Vic., forthcoming, 2003)   GEORGE JONES

BUNDALEER FOREST NURSERY, near Jamestown, SA, was established in 1876 by forester (William) John Jenkins Curnow (1844–1922) as part of the Forest Board initiatives under George GOYDER and John Ednie BROWN. This STATE FOREST NURSERY and its PLANTATIONS became a major trialling base—in conjunction with WIRRABARA Nursery—for economic FORESTRY initiatives in SA. Here the use of *Arundo donax* (Spanish Reed or 'bamboo') for sheathing tubestock was introduced. The nursery provided the majority of seedlings for the ADELAIDE PARK LANDS, and for many parklands and SHELTER BELTS. Species cultivated by Curnow until his retirement in 1914, and thereafter managed by forester Charles BEALE, included EUCALYPTS—particularly *Eucalyptus cladocalyx* (Sugar Gum), *E. camaldulensis* (Red Gum), *E. leucoxylon* (South Australian Blue Gum), *E. globulus* (Blue Gum), *E. marginata* (Jarrah)—pines, sycamores, walnuts, oaks, ash, elms, poplars, willows, and the familiar *Pinus halepensis* and *P. radiata* (Aleppo and Monterey or Radiata Pine), and *Schinus molle* (Pepper Tree).   DAVID JONES

BUNGAREE, a HOMESTEAD estate near Clare, SA, was established in 1841 by grazier George Charles Hawker (1818–1895) and remains in family ownership. The property features a long avenue of deciduous trees, a pair of intricate wrought-iron gates imported from Italy, a Gothic chapel (1864), and outbuildings that have Scottish pattern-book associations. A GARDENESQUE-style garden of lawn expanses with roses, shrubs, and specimen trees, surrounds the two-storey residence (1910).   DAVID JONES

BURBIDGE, Nancy Tyson (1912–1977), English-born botanist and University of Western Australia graduate, undertook ecological and taxonomic work in WA and SA before joining CSIR (later CSIRO) in Canberra (1946–77) where she developed HERBARIUM Australiense (later Australian National Herbarium) into a major centre for AUSTRALIAN PLANT taxonomy. While at ROYAL BOTANIC GARDENS, KEW

Daniel BUNCE outside the picturesque curator's cottage at GEELONG BOTANIC GARDENS (c. 1868) from where he could view the garden he had laid out and tended over two decades

(1938–39 and 1953–54), she investigated Australian plant specimens in British herbaria. Her published papers and *Dictionary of Australian Plant Genera* (1963) manuscript gained her a Doctorate of Science (1961). Other books include *Flora of the Australian Capital Territory* (1970: co-author Max Gray) and *Australian Grasses* (1966–70). With her profound taxonomic knowledge derived from herbaria, taxonomic literature, and the bush, she was seconded from Herbarium Australiense to direct the massive new Flora of Australia project in 1973, orchestrating taxonomic revisions, compiling *Plant Taxonomic Literature in Australian Libraries* (1978), and preparing an Australian Plant Names Index.

LINDEN GILLBANK

BURBURY, Ronald William (1903–*fl*. 1952), CACTI and succulent grower, trained as a musician in Melbourne before turning his horticultural hobby into a profession. He helped found the Cactus and Succulent Society of Australia (*c.* 1924) and in 1935 advertised his garden in Middle Brighton (Vic.) as 'The largest and oldest commercial collection in Australia'. He specialised in ROCKERIES, and his 1936 catalogue was promoted as the first illustrated cactus and succulents catalogue in Australia. 'Although the growing of Cacti and Succulents may seem a long way from music', Burbury observed, the two formed 'an excellent combination, as music is a medium for emotional expression, while those strange little plants are a real expression in themselves, combined with the beauties that music tries to convey'.

STEPHEN FORBES

BURDETT, William (1871–1940), orchardist and horticulturist, and his wife Elsie May (*née* Walker) (1886–1969), established their Australian and South African species WILD-FLOWER garden at Basket Range, in the ADELAIDE HILLS, in the late 1920s. Established after his serious illness and early retirement, the garden matured in the 1930s, becoming a favourite venue for many interstate and overseas visitors. The Burdetts laid out a 'wonderful private garden ... of wilderness and garden art combined', where contoured paths meandered through more than 1000 species, including EUCALYPTS, Erica, and Protea on a seven-hectare rocky spur to arrive at a copse of *Pinus radiata* (Monterey Pine). They obtained seeds from HACKETT's Nursery and from many correspondents in England and South Africa, maintained a competitive friendship with Edwin ASHBY, and sent seeds to Lawrence Johnston of Hidcote in the Cotswolds. Daughter, May Burdett (1911–1985), self-trained naturalist and horticulturist—schooled by the family's numerous Australian collecting trips and propagation successes—maintained the garden following William's death. In 1999 the property, now with 400 species recorded, was acquired by members of the MICHELL family. *Banksia burdettii* and *Eucalyptus burdettiana* honour William Burdett.

DAVID JONES and JOHN WALTER

BURKE, Donald William (b. 1947), horticulturist, journalist, and media personality, followed a childhood interest in gardening by completing certificate courses in horticulture (RYDE) and tree surgery (New South Wales Forestry Commission) before starting work in the NURSERY industry and part-time lecturing. He served in an editorial capacity with *AUSTRALIAN HORTICULTURE* (1981–87), playing a major role in upgrading the journal's professional focus and deploying his persuasive communication skills to great effect with leading articles on the nursery industry. Concurrently, he established his horticultural consultancy (Don Burke and Associates) and horticultural marketing company (Backyard Marketing). Burke's media career began in 1980 with newspaper, RADIO, and then TELEVISION commitments. His signature program, *Burke's Backyard*, began in 1984 on Sydney radio station 2UE and the outstandingly popular television version, filmed each week in his own garden, started on the Nine Network in 1987. Its pioneering 'infotainment' format—now widely emulated—closely linked gardening with wider lifestyle choices. His many books include *The Lazy Gardener* (1983) and numerous spin-off publications such as *Burke's Backyard Magazine* (1998–). A Fellow of the AUSTRALIAN INSTITUTE OF HORTICULTURE, Don Burke maintains a professional interest in horticulture, particularly through a long-established GREVILLEA breeding program. RA

BURMAN, Nicolaas Laurens (1734–1793), Dutch physician and botanist, worked in Amsterdam. His association with Australian BOTANY lies in his description, in 1768, of two plants now known as *Acacia truncata* and *Synaphea spinulosa*. Although then thought to be from Java, they were later recognised as species endemic on the south-west coast of Australia, thus becoming the first AUSTRALIAN PLANTS named under the LINNAEAN binomial system. ALEX GEORGE

BURNHAM BEECHES, Sassafras, Vic., the HILL-STATION developed from 1929 by Alfred Nicholas (1881–1937), displays one of the boldest garden concepts in the state. Alfred and his brother George had amassed considerable wealth from their synthesis of acetylsalicylic acid (or aspirin) when supplies from Germany were cut during the First World War: besides lavishly endowing Melbourne institutions, the two 'Aspro kings' each developed a sumptuous retreat—Alfred in the Dandenong Ranges, and George at ALTON, Mount Macedon. Hugh LINAKER planned the garden at Burnham Beeches and its development was entrusted to English-trained gardener Percy TREVASKIS. The forested approach was accented with *Fagus sylvatica* cultivars (Green and Copper Beech), and selected *Eucalyptus regnans* (Mountain Ash) were retained. On the approach front of the streamlined residence (1930–34: architect Harry Norris), a lawn studded with arboreal rarities (many purchased as advanced specimens) gave but a hint of the splendour that lay beyond. Best seen from the huge picture window, a grand stairway led through terraces of choice ALPINES to a zigzag roadway, its rock retaining walls encrusted with more horticultural treasures. A lake—the culminating feature of the descending layout—was constructed between 1937 and 1939, but Nicholas was denied the pleasure of its completion. Much of the garden, now known as the Alfred Nicholas Memorial Gardens, was donated to the public in 1965, and much-needed rejuvenation has been undertaken since the 1970s. The complement, including the house, was sold in 1981: progressive degradation of original features has marked its subsequent redevelopment. RA

BURNLEY SCHOOL OF HORTICULTURE has, since 1891, under various names and affiliations, been Victoria's principal site—and Australia's first—of formal horticultural EDUCATION. It built on the experimental and educational imperatives of the (Royal) Horticultural Society of Victoria, which developed the site as a horticultural EXPERIMENTAL GARDEN. Later known as Burnley Gardens, its startling formal design by Alfred LYNCH, involving extensive terracing, was initiated in 1861, but was later partly destroyed by floods. Tree plantings commenced in 1861, of which a central *Sequoia sempervirens* (Californian Redwood) and several other exotics survive. A test orchard was established under the direction of William CLARSON (1868–72) and George NEILSON (1872–91): by 1874 it was claimed that the Society had the most comprehensive collection of fruit outside Europe. However, financial difficulties consequent upon the 1890s economic depression saw the Society declare bankruptcy.

In 1891 the Victorian Department of Agriculture took control of the site to develop Australia's first horticultural school. Neilson was retained as curator, offering courses for professional orchardists, and in 1897 C. Bogue LUFFMANN became the first principal of the school. Luffmann laid out ornamental gardens, ponds, orchards, and paddocks on the site, and the gardens became a place of demonstration. The admission of female students for part-time training in 1899 was much criticised at the time, but was soon a popular and lauded feature.

Luffmann resigned in 1908 and was succeeded by John CRONIN (1908–09), E.E. PESCOTT (1909–16), John P. McLennan (1917–21), Frederick RAE (1922–25), and Alexander JESSEP (1926–41). Name changes reflected differing emphases: Burnley School of Horticulture and Small Farming (1915–17), School of Primary Agriculture and Horticulture (1917–58), and Burnley Horticultural College (1958–83). Enrolments increased during the interwar period and half of the certificate course work in the 1920s consisted of practical work in the garden, orchard, and nursery. Graduates from this period included Olive MELLOR (*née* Holttum), Emily GIBSON (*née* Grassick), Edna WALLING, and Betty BEGG and Mollie Shannon. By 1951, 150 ex-service men and women had been given horticultural training under the Commonwealth Reconstruction Training Scheme.

Development of the garden continued. In the early 1960s Ellis STONES designed a rockery for the school; some early features were removed during the 1970s, and in the 1980s an extensive native garden (including a reconstructed native grassland) and water feature were added. New diploma (1958) and degree (1985) courses steadily enhanced educational standards, now complemented by a wide range of part-time vocational and recreational courses. The College became part of the statewide Victorian College of Agriculture and Horticulture (VCAH) in 1983 and its first postgraduate research students were enrolled in 1991, enhancing the role of Burnley College in horticultural research, especially environmental horticulture and nursery production. This was strengthened when VCAH amalgamated with the University of Melbourne, culminating in the formation of the Institute of Land and Food Resources in 1997.

A.P. Winzenried, *Green Grows our Garden: A Centenary History of Horticultural Education at Burnley* (South Yarra, Vic., 1991)
LINDA HIPWELL

Lessons in fruit-tree pruning at BURNLEY SCHOOL OF HORTICULTURE, 1899—this was the first year in which women were admitted for tuition, and this initiative by Principal C. Bogue LUFFMANN proved popular despite being at first controversial

BURRA CHARTER, a 'Charter for Places of Cultural Significance', was adopted by Australia ICOMOS (International Council on Monuments and Sites)—the peak body representing the various conservation professions—in 1979. Named after the mining town in SA where it was officially ratified, the Charter and its associated guidelines separate the assessment of intrinsic importance or 'cultural significance' (embracing aesthetic, historic, scientific, social, and spiritual values), from conservation processes (defined in ascending order of intervention as preservation, restoration, reconstruction, and adaptation). This assessment, or 'conservation analysis', is then widened into a conservation plan that takes these values into account when assessing other aspects (such as financial or legal considerations) and proposing a policy or strategy for works. The applicability of the Charter to gardens has sometimes been questioned by those in the design field, but a recent revision of Charter (1999) specifically included landscapes. The widespread adoption of the Charter at all levels of government and by many private bodies, as well as considerable international interest (especially from Britain), attest to the usefulness of the Charter in setting a framework for sound decision making about culturally significant places such as gardens and designed landscapes.

Australia ICOMOS Incorporated, *The Burra Charter* (Burwood, Vic., 2000)   RA

BURRENDONG ARBORETUM, Wellington, NSW: see ALTHOFER, George and Peter

BURRUNGURROOLONG, Goulburn, NSW, an imposing Italianate HOMESTEAD (1880–81), was erected for Andrew Gibson (1833–1910) on land his family had owned since the 1830s. Approached through open country, the setting is an arboretum of GARDENESQUE design running to the Mulwaree Chain of Ponds. The house has three fronts, each different, with the centre front revealed when, after entering the pleasure garden and passing through the shrubbery, the drive swells into a large circle.   CLIVE LUCAS

BURSWOOD, Portland, Vic., was purchased in 1850 by squatter Edward HENTY, who in 1834 had founded Victoria's first permanent European settlement. Henty and his wife, Anna Maria, built the Regency-style stone house and stables between 1853 and 1855 as a marine VILLA, overlooking Salt Creek, south of PORTLAND BOTANIC GARDENS and the township. Edward BARSBY laid out the three-hectare garden from 1855, probably with help from long-serving gardener William Poland. One of Victoria's earliest surviving domestic gardens, Burswood is a rare early example of GARDENESQUE design, comparable to Maritimo, Portland, and GLENARA, Bulla. A simple carriage loop dominates the house front and to the west is an oval lawn flanked by a SHRUBBERY. Plants of horticultural interest include *Aronia arbutifolia* (Red Chokeberry), *Quercus suber* (Cork Oak), and *Fraxinus excelsior* 'Aurea Pendula' (Golden Weeping Ash). A semi-circular conservatory was removed before 1876.

    FRANCINE GILFEDDER

BURSWOOD PARK, WA, on the Swan River at Perth's eastern entrance, has been progressively created on a former waste disposal area. It is the site of a GOLF club and incorporates Kagoshima Park, a symbol of Perth's JAPANESE sister city relationship. Since the construction of the Perth Casino (1986), Burswood Park has been remodelled in contemporary RESORT style with rolling lawns, lakes, fountains, palm avenues, a wide range of native and introduced trees, and flamboyant displays of perennial and annual flowering plants. Prominence is also given to SCULPTURE and other public art.

PHILIP PALMER

BURTON, David (*c.* 1760s–1792), botanical collector, gardener, Superintendent of Convicts, and the colony's first naturalist, arrived in Port Jackson in September 1791 aboard HMS *Gorgon*. Related through marriage to James Lee, Burton had been retained by Joseph BANKS for £20 a year to supply seeds and botanical specimens exclusively, but it is possible that he also supplied LEE AND KENNEDY. As well as surveying land and reporting on the quality of the soil around the colony, Burton collected enthusiastically, placing on the *Gorgon* in December 1791, sixty tubs containing 221 plants and sown seed. He sent 'all the seeds that I could collect since the Gorgon sailed' on the *Pitt* in April 1792, and further material was dispatched later that year. Much was lost in transport, but Banks at KEW and Lee and Kennedy had his plants in cultivation by 1792. Burton's botanical career was short-lived, as he died in Parramatta in April 1792 from complications following a gunshot wound. Governor Phillip wrote to Banks: 'In this man I lost one whom I cannot replace and whom I could ill spare.' He is commemorated in the Australian plant genus *Burtonia*.

TONY CAVANAGH

BURTON, Pritchard John (*c.* 1825–1905), gardener and herbalist, English-born, arrived in Melbourne with his young family in 1853. He kept a garden on the Yarra River, close to the Richmond Nursery of T.C. COLE. He was reputedly involved in laying out Cremorne Gardens prior to its acquisition by George Coppin. In the late 1850s he took over the orchard and garden at St Heliers, further upstream in Abbotsford. In 1860 Burton was a prize-winner at horticultural and agricultural society shows, and also exhibited models of apples at the Victorian Exhibition (1861). By 1866 he was working as a nurseryman and gardener at Preston, celebrated as a raiser of seedling roses. In the late 1880s he moved to Mount Eagle, establishing his name as a herbalist, connected with 'Mrs Austin's Hospital for Incurables', at nearby Heidelberg. 'He was possessed of special gifts', his Woodrow Nursery regarded by the afflicted as 'a modern Lourdes'.

RA

BUSBY, James (1801–1871), pioneer vine-grower, importer of vine stock, and wine enthusiast, was born into a well-to-do family in Edinburgh. His father worked on the Irish estates of the Marquis of Downshire, where Busby first became interested in agriculture. The family returned to Scotland and decided to emigrate, arriving in Sydney in 1824. Prior to this Busby spent time studying VITICULTURE in Bordeaux, France, with a view to growing vines in NSW. On the voyage out he wrote *A Treatise on the Culture of the Vine and the Art of Making Wine* (1825), a learned work far in advance of the needs of colonists. After securing a land grant he was given charge of the Male Orphan School at Bull's Hill, near Liverpool, where he also taught viticulture and established a vineyard. Busby lost this post in 1826 and became a government official. He retained his enthusiasm for viticulture, in 1830 publishing the simpler *A Manual of Plain Directions for Planting and Cultivating Vineyards, and for Making Wine, in New South Wales*.

Busby returned to England in 1831 to present his case for redress against the school authorities who had dismissed him. He was given the post of British Resident in New Zealand and, after 1833, was thus lost to Australia. Busby first toured the vineyards of SPAIN and FRANCE and collected 678 varieties of vines, sourced from Montpellier Botanic Gardens and Luxembourg Gardens (Paris), among other French and Spanish localities, and Syon House near KEW GARDENS. In a magnanimous gesture he presented these to British authorities to be transported to Sydney to form an EXPERIMENTAL GARDEN to prove their different qualities, and to arrange for their propagation and distribution. Wine and fruit cultivars were included, along with seeds including watermelons, tomatoes, pimentos, cucumbers, lettuce, and endives, and placed on the convict ship *Camden*. The majority survived, and in January 1833 were reported to be in 'the highest state of health and vigour' in the SYDNEY BOTANIC GARDENS. In time they were neglected, and in 1857 rooted out, but not before extensive sections had found their way to properties such as CAMDEN PARK, to the ADELAIDE BOTANIC GARDEN, and to Busby's parents' property, Kirkton, on the Hunter River, where Busby had previously planted 365 varieties, and where his brother-in-law, W.D. Kelman, became an active vigneron and wine maker. Busby published a journal account of his tour in 1833 in Sydney in which he listed and commented on the varieties obtained.

James Busby is rightly regarded as the pioneer of viticulture in Australia. He personally distributed upwards of 20 000 cuttings, and claimed that vineyards in NSW dated from the appearance of his *Manual*. His remarkable collection provided many early Australian vineyards with pre-phylloxera *Vitis vinifera* stocks—restrictions were later imposed on the importation and movement of vines. His collection was also the likely original source of Chardonnay 'discovered' in old vineyards at Mudgee and in the lower HUNTER VALLEY in 1970. Busby was an early prophet of the vine, a disseminator of quality stock, and an advocate of the temperate use of wine as a beverage for the new land.

DAVID DUNSTAN

BUSH Since European settlement the Australian bush has been the subject of myth, national identity, adventure, and pioneering. To most Australians, 'the bush' has two principal meanings: it can mean the 'wild' country of scrub, forest, mountain, and desert, but it can also refer to the rural world, by contrast with the culture of the city. The bush has also been an Aboriginal landscape for many thousands of years. After the arrival of Europeans, however, the bush was interpreted as a counterpoint to a newly arrived civilisation. For most Australian colonists, the bush loomed darkly across the garden fence. Its lack of SEASONAL change and its drab grey-greens evoked criticism or confusion. It was an unruly contrast to pastoral plains and neat, productive gardens. Sometimes Australia's forests, oceans, and rivers seemed SUBLIME, but more often the bush was a dreary wildness, waiting to be transformed. Occasionally the bush was invited into the garden: in formal colonial gardens selected NATIVE TREES and plants were allowed to leap the garden fence, becoming exotic botanical specimens in the process.

In the late nineteenth century some of Australia's HILL-STATION gardens created a wilder landscape, allowing their wooded gardens to unravel gently into the surrounding bush. By then, the bush—the rural world, rather than the wilderness itself—was idolised by writers such as Henry Lawson and Banjo Paterson as the setting for Australian manhood and mateship. The ideal bushman was undomesticated, free to roam in the half-civilised world of the pastoral landscape. The settler on his block, on the other hand, was engaged in a titanic struggle to wrest a living from the bush. The garden became a potent symbol of settling into the country. With fowls and a milking cow, the garden spoke of self-sufficiency, and a woman's touch. The HOMESTEAD GARDEN was an outpost of civilisation, fenced off from marauding stock and the surrounding bush.

By the early twentieth century, white Australians felt more confident of their mastery of the bush, and were able to incorporate it more audaciously in their garden visions. NATURAL HISTORY writers such as Charles BARRETT and Jean GALBRAITH, began to illuminate the bush with their highly differentiated, intimate descriptions of wildflowers, ferns, and scenery. European Australians were gradually persuaded that the bush was not a dreary mass of unchanging foliage. A large popular audience for nature writing in the interwar period ensured that walkers and gardeners alike were alert to the intricate relationships of plants and animals—especially birds—in the bush. Renewed collecting brought more indigenous plants into cultivation, paving the way for a revolution in gardening after the Second World War, when the bush was finally invited to *become* the garden in the simulated natural environments of modern suburbia.

Gregg Borschmann, *The People's Forest: A Living History of the Australian Bush* (Blackheath, NSW, 1999) **BRIGID HAINS**

Charles BARRETT's first book, *From Range to Sea* (1907), with an evocative nocturnal cover image by Ruby Lind, was intended by its author to be 'an enlarged Christmas card' evoking the Australian BUSH and its nature to 'friends in other lands'

BUSHFIRE: see FIRE

BUSH GARDEN became a fashionable term after the publication of *Designing Australian Bush Gardens* (1966) by Betty MALONEY and Jean Walker. They were not the first, however, to advocate a design approach exclusively using NATIVE PLANTS. Certain species—notably PALMS, tree-ferns, and apples (*Angophora* spp.)—attracted early settlers who retained or planted them on their properties. By the mid-nineteenth century newly discovered RAINFOREST species (particularly *Araucaria* spp. and *Ficus* spp.) had also become fashionable. In the 1920s Walter and Marion GRIFFIN encouraged those who moved into their new subdivision at CASTLECRAG (NSW) to plant local species, and Edna WALLING, in her book *The Australian Roadside* (1952), championed the retention of remnant roadside vegetation. Among the first publications to include garden plans featuring only Australian species, was *Australian Plants for the Garden* (1953) by Thistle HARRIS, with plans drawn by Edna Walling and Norman Weekes and planting lists by Harris. Glen WILSON's *Landscaping with Australian Plants* (1975) took the idea further by illustrating gardens designed with a distinctive Australian character. During the 1960s and 1970s Melbourne designers, including Beryl MANN, Gordon FORD, and Ellis STONES, were using mainly native plants, while in Sydney Bruce MACKENZIE, Harry HOWARD, and the NSW Public Works Department designed and redeveloped many parks and institutional grounds (including Taronga ZOO) to reflect their bushland surroundings.

Although bush gardens remain popular, no satisfactory definition has been formulated. Identifying features include exclusive use of native plants, natural materials for construction, absence of manicured LAWNS and BEDS, and informal or NATURAL design and layout that is a reflection, but not a direct copy, of Australian BUSH. Planting palettes range from Australian flora in general, through increasing ECOLOGICAL sophistication to exclusive use of plants indigenous to the locality, as in much recent REVEGETATION. **ALLAN CORREY**

BUSH-HOUSE, a traditional Australian term for a shade house, is a GREENHOUSE structure designed to provide shelter for shade-loving plants (in contradistinction to a GLASSHOUSE

Bush-house

The BUSH-HOUSE was not only a popular feature of Australian gardens, but also widely employed in the NURSERY trade for propagation, storage, and display of plants, as here at the PURCHASE nursery in Parramatta (1878)

or HOTHOUSE). The term 'bush-house' derived from early use of Tea-tree (*Melaleuca*) leaves for roofing; in India and elsewhere such structures were also known as canvas houses, lath houses (timber strips), chick houses (split bamboo), or betel houses (the evergreen creeper *Piper betle*) after their mode of roofing. The term 'bush-house' tended to be applied to smaller, rustic, or rudimentary structures; thus a rough structure shading seedlings in a commercial nursery might be called a bush-house, whereas the more sophisticated joinery of a structure in a large VILLA GARDEN would more commonly receive the epithet shade house or (especially in SA) lath house.

Bush-houses reached a height of popularity from the 1880s to the 1930s; they were used for display purposes (plants in the ground or in pots on shelves), for propagating and resting pot plants (used to decorate VERANDAHS or INDOORS), and as a living space, as in a CONSERVATORY. Advice on the bush-house was a standard feature in horticultural journals and the weekly press from the 1880s. Herbaceous tropical and subtropical plants, such as FERNS, PALMS, ORCHIDS, and Aroids were typically featured. A bush-house given over entirely to ferns was termed a fernery; similarly for orchid-houses. Arguably the most exquisite such structure in Australia is the one at RIPPON LEA, Vic. (*c.* 1884), which is both vaulted in cross-section and curved in plan form. More typically bush-houses were rectilinear in plan, with simple skillion or gable roofs. Originally, thatched roofing provided a shady retreat and turned rain into mist below. Sometimes vines were grown over the structure (especially in Qld), but many experts felt this produced excessive shade. Towards the end of the nineteenth century, sawn timber structures with lattice or TRELLIS work displaced more rudimentary RUSTIC structures. As late as 1950, R.G. EDWARDS considered the bush-house to be the only truly original Australian contribution to gardening. Shade cloth (fine plastic weave) is now generally used in place of timber laths.

The first publication devoted exclusively to the joys of bush-houses was A.E. COLE's *Half-Hours in the Bush-House* (1922). Presenting innovative ideas about battening patterns to vary the amount of sunlight penetration, with dual environments encouraged, Cole considered the bush-house suited to 'the true plant-lover'. He also urged its use for leisure:

> Personally we think no bush-house is complete without a couple of rustic stools and bracket table. When horticultural friends visit us, it is decidedly nice to take a cup of tea among our plants, while for quiet rest and reading our bush-house is the very thing.
> JEANNIE SIM

BUSH TUCKER: see ABORIGINAL FOOD PLANTS

BUTLER, Walter Richmond (1864–1949), architect and garden architect, was born at Pensford, Somerset, England, the son of a farmer. Articled at 15 to architect Alexander Lauder of Barnstaple, Butler moved to London in 1885 and became part of the ARTS AND CRAFTS and domestic revival community led by William Morris and Richard Norman Shaw. In 1888 Butler sailed for Australia, where he quickly established a successful and influential practice with young Melbourne architect Beverley Ussher. Later partners included George C. Inskip, Ernest R. Bradshaw, his nephew Richard Butler, Marcus Martin, and, immediately prior to his retirement (c. 1940), Hugh Pettit.

A designer of great talent and a man of substantial personal charm and faultless presentation, Butler found himself throughout his Australian career in the fortunate position of designing grand houses and HOMESTEADS for Victoria's wealthier citizens, including many prominent in business and the pastoral industry. The large sites upon which he worked provided ample opportunity for the design of gardens, and by the early twentieth century Butler had developed considerable skill as a garden architect, and a definite opinion on the importance of integrating the design of the garden with that of the house. Butler spoke on 'garden design in relation to architecture' to the Royal Victorian Institute of Architects as early as 1903. In his writings he

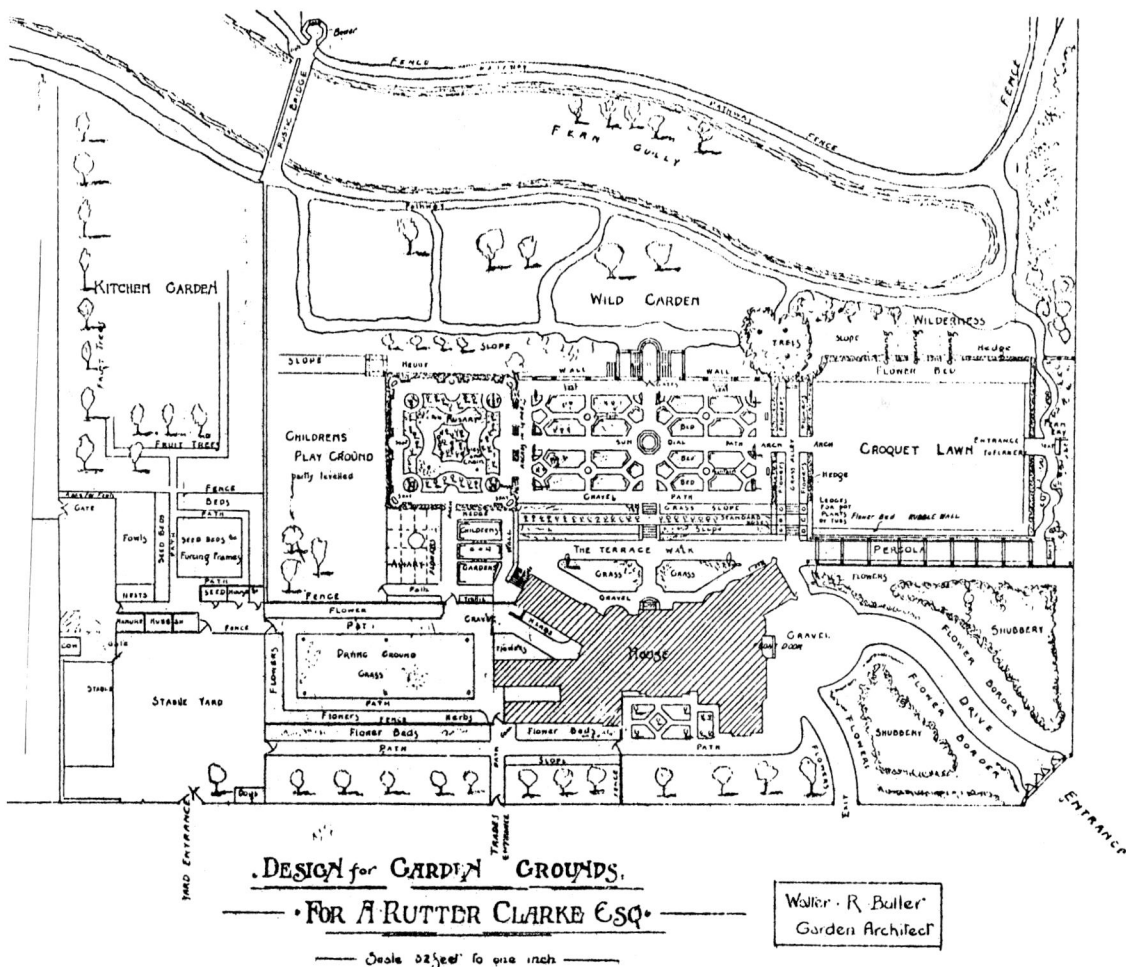

Walter BUTLER's 1906 design for Warrawee, Toorak (Vic.), demonstrated typical ARTS AND CRAFTS planning, with hierarchy of spaces with the most FORMAL elements close to the house

poured scorn on the work of LANDSCAPE GARDENERS, which he believed consisted chiefly of 'wriggling pathways and irregular curves that are utterly devoid of beauty of line', and that 'the chief cause of the errors of proportion and taste seen in this country is that the designing of the house and the planning of the garden are usually done by different men'. While such views were remarkable within the Australian architectural scene, Butler's views on unity of design shared much in common with British and (later) American contemporaries.

Butler's garden designs emphasised regularity of line and FORMALITY of composition, and division of the garden into a series of outdoor 'rooms' of varying character, separated by FENCES, WALLS, or HEDGES. His office produced garden designs for many of his major architectural commissions, including Bishopscourt, East Melbourne (1903), Charlton, Hobart (*c.* 1905), Warrawee, Toorak (1906), Thanes, Kooyong (1907), Kamillaroi, Toorak (1907), Grong Grong, Toorak (*c.* 1908), MARATHON, Mount Eliza (*c.* 1914–24), and Eulinya, Toorak (1925), and is likely to have designed or modified the gardens to many more, including COOMBE COTTAGE. The garden to his own house, Studley, Toorak (1910), was of particular importance as an exemplar of his approach. These commissions indicate an intimate acquaintance with the design principles of Gertrude JEKYLL, William ROBINSON, and J.D. Sedding, and Butler's office library included publications such as Reginald Blomfield's *The Formal Garden in England* (1901 edition), in which he had marked several sentences, including 'Instead of the transition being gradual, there should be no question of where the garden ends'—a sentiment expressed by Butler in both his writing and his garden design.

BRYCE RAWORTH

CACTI and other succulents have at various times been embraced or reviled by Australian gardeners. Cacti, almost entirely confined to the Americas, are members of the cactus family (Cactaceae), while succulents are any plants that store water in fleshy stems or leaves (including cacti).

Opuntia vulgaris (syn. *O. monacantha*) was the first cactus introduced to Australia (1788): Governor Phillip collected plants infested with cochineal scale insect from the vicinity of Rio de Janeiro with hopes of developing a cochineal industry. The history of Prickly Pear (*O. stricta*, syn. *O. inermis*) introduction is less certain: the first known record is of a pot plant in Scone (NSW) in 1839. Various prickly pears, introduced as pot plants and hedges, became environmental WEEDS, infesting 4 million hectares of Qld and northern NSW by 1900, and 24 million hectares by 1926. The introduction of *Cactoblastis cactorum*, a cactus-feeding moth, and other insects, was so successful in eradication that the Commonwealth Prickly Pear Board was disbanded in 1939.

The cultivation of succulents in Europe flourished in the nineteenth century in response to botanical discoveries and advances in GREENHOUSES. In Australia, by 1843 William MACARTHUR had included a number of cacti and succulents in Camden Park's nursery catalogue, and their availability in general nurseries increased rapidly. Cacti and succulents were widely planted in nineteenth-century glasshouses, conservatories, and gardens. In 1880 William GUILFOYLE converted a conservatory at MELBOURNE BOTANIC GARDENS to a house for succulents, and in 1884 Frederick Sargood had a cacti collection at RIPPON LEA. PICTURESQUE garden styles and the ROBINSONIAN subtropical garden appear to have influenced the use of succulents in grotesque ROCKERIES and GROTTOES from the east to the west coast of Australia. The development of specialist societies in Australia began with the Cactus and Succulent Society of Australia in Vic. (*c.* 1924) and coincided with the development of nurseries specialising in cacti and succulents—for example, that of Ron BURBURY. The controversy in the Society that resulted in the *Fuaux Herbarium Bulletin* (1949–53) reflects the earnestness of debate in Australia. Alexis Eric (Lex) Fuaux is the only Australian honoured by specific epithets, in *Mammillaria fuauxiana* and *Mediolobivia fuauxiana*.

Rockeries displaying cacti and succulents retained a steady following in domestic gardens until the 1960s, and, while waning in popularity during the last decades of the

Until its control in the mid-twentieth century, Prickly Pear (*Opuntia* sp.) was a major environmental weed—in this 1898 engraving an officer of the New South Wales Lands Department carries out an inspection of this once-despised member of the CACTUS family

twentieth century, some plants (such as AGAVES) are now finding their way back into respectability. Cactus and succulent collections and displays that are regularly open to the public include Collectors Corner (Keysborough), DAWSON's Cactus Garden (Bendigo), Ralph Field's garden (Tennyson), and Cactus Country (Strathmerton), all in Vic. Collections are also on display at most metropolitan BOTANIC GARDENS, with the Madagascan plants in the palm house at ADELAIDE BOTANIC GARDEN of special interest.

> G.D. Rowley, *A History of Succulent Plants* (Mill Valley, California, 1997); Attila Kapitany and Rudolph Schultz, *Succulents for the Garden* (Teesdale, Vic., 2000) STEPHEN FORBES

CAIRNS BOTANIC GARDENS, Qld, was established in the grounds of Rosebank, Edge Hill, during the 1880s as the private botanic garden of Eugene FITZALAN. Fitzalan was ceded land from the adjoining recreation reserve by the local council so he could develop NURSERIES specialising in native seed stock for distribution throughout Australia. In exchange, Fitzalan opened his gardens to the public, so they could enjoy a day trip from town. The gardens became particularly popular after the opening of the railway to Edge Hill (1885). Early medicinal and economic plantings can be found near the *Samamea saman*, with its thirty-metre canopy and ten-metre-diameter trunk. After Fitzalan's death (1911), the Cairns City Council assumed control of the established gardens. Vince Winkel (curator 1966–84) restored many early features of the gardens, including the rainforest walk on Fitzalan Creek. In 1971 the site was named Flecker Botanic Gardens in memory of local naturalist Dr Hugo Flecker (1884–1957).

JODI FRAWLEY

CALDER (née WRIGHT), Winifred Braithwaite (Winty) (b. 1927), lecturer and consultant in ECOLOGY and ecological planning, was an early member and later (*c.* 1980–87) a distinguished chair of the Landscape Committee of the NATIONAL TRUST OF AUSTRALIA (Victoria). Both here and further afield, she influenced teachers and practitioners, bringing sound landscape planning principles to a wide audience. Her key text, *Beyond the View: Our Changing Landscapes* (1981), explored the complexities of landscape and the need to incorporate an understanding of natural and cultural history into development planning: many of these ideas are now mainstream planning principles. Winty Calder has been a mentor to many young planners and landscape architects, encouraging them to adopt ecological approaches to planning. Her deep love of the countryside has had Victoria's Mornington Peninsula as a focus. JAN SCHAPPER

CALEY, George (1770–1829), botanical collector for Sir Joseph BANKS in NSW (1800–10), was born in Manchester, England, the son of a horse dealer; early in life he was consigned to the drudgery of the stable. His first interest in plants was aroused by a veterinary text with its herbal remedies. He joined the local botanical society and taught himself botany from the textbooks then available, also studying Latin, the universal botanical language. In 1795, seeing a book dedication to Banks, he wrote to Banks asking for assistance in finding a position as a botanist's assistant. Banks arranged for him to work at various gardens in London, including KEW GARDENS, and finally, persuaded by Caley's requests for overseas travel, posted him to NSW in his personal employ. He arrived in 1800.

Caley settled in Parramatta, collecting not only plants, but bird skins, reptiles, mammals, rocks, and wood, sending the bulk of his material back to Banks. But Caley was more than a collector; he gave names to all the plants he collected, wrote descriptions for botanists in London, wrote to Banks on conditions in the convict settlement, and explored well beyond the confines of the colony, looking for new material. In 1804 Caley penetrated further into the BLUE MOUNTAINS than any other European, reaching Mount Banks, which he named for his patron. On his return to England (1810), he again settled in Manchester, but in 1816 became superintendent of St Vincent Botanic Garden in the West Indies. When this closed (1822) Caley returned to England, living in Bayswater until his death.

George Caley is known to history as an eccentric Banksian collector who had frequent disagreements with Governor King and the Rev. Samuel Marsden, but his contribution to the knowledge of AUSTRALIAN FLORA and fauna has been underestimated. He made frequent contacts with the Aboriginal people wherever he travelled, learning their languages and the Aboriginal names for fauna and flora, especially for the EUCALYPTS, in which he was particularly interested. He was the first person to recognise that HYBRIDISATION could occur in eucalypts, his observations being on ironbarks. Caley's contribution to the knowledge of Australian plants lay in his extensive collections, which found their way into the HERBARIA of Europe via wealthy amateur collectors. Here they were accessible to botanists such as Robert BROWN and others who used Caley's material to publish descriptions of the unknown Australian flora. George Caley also contributed to the introduction of Australian native plants in England and Europe by sending seeds to Kew and to commercial merchants such as James Dickson. He is recognised in the orchid genus *Caleana*, and in *Grevillea caleyi*, *Viola caleyana*, *Banksia caleyi*, and *Eucalyptus caleyi*.

> Joan Webb, *George Caley: Nineteenth Century Naturalist* (Chipping Norton, NSW, 1995) JOAN WEBB

CALEY SMITH, Fred: see SMITH, Samuel

CALIFORNIA: see NORTH AMERICA

CALTHORPES' HOUSE, built in 1927 for stock and station agent Harry Calthorpe and his wife Dell, is a remarkably intact 1920s family home in CANBERRA. Original interiors, domestic appliances, and household records reflect sixty years of one family's life. Similarly, the layout and range of plants in the garden is unaltered. The Commonwealth Government's 1984 acquisition of the property for use as a house museum was controversial: the notion of a domestic museum that was architecturally undistinguished, relatively recent, and not associated with a famous person was then unusual. The property is now recognised as a valuable resource, and its SUBURBAN

Panorama (1939) of CALTHORPES' HOUSE, Red Hill (ACT), showing the house and front garden—this image now assists in the CONSERVATION of this SUBURBAN GARDEN as part of a museum property

GARDEN exemplifies 1920s popular fashion. *Cupressus sempervirens* (Italian Cypress) and *C. arizonica* (Rough Bark Arizona Cypress) dominate the front, and the semicircular drive is lined with granite-edged flower beds planted with summer and winter annuals. Hedges of *Ligustrum ovalifolium* (Privet) and *Euonymus* separate the front areas from the informal orchard and vegetable garden at the back, where a cubby house and AIR RAID SHELTER survive.

Anne Bickford, *Calthorpes' House Museum Guide* (Canberra, 1987)   ELAINE LAWSON

CAMDEN PARK, NSW: see MACARTHUR, John

CAMELLIAS, as ornamental garden plants, were introduced to England from China in 1792 and to Australia by 1823–24. A catalogue of plants cultivated in the Sydney Botanic Gardens, prepared in 1828 by Charles FRASER, provides the basis for this date of introduction. The donors of these first plants included the Governor's wife, Lady Brisbane (who forwarded the double red *Camellia rubro plena*), and John Reeves (1774–1856), plant collector of Canton (*C. japonica* 'Alba Simplex'). The Horticultural Society of London forwarded the popular cultivar 'Variegata' in 1824. Alexander MCLEAY, who arrived in the colony in 1826, donated 'Alba Plena' and also grew many other cultivars at Elizabeth Bay House. William MACARTHUR, whose first camellias arrived on board the *Sovereign* in 1831, is recognised as the first major supplier in Australia. Many new cultivars were raised at his Camden Park nursery, including one of the most celebrated Australian cultivars, 'Aspasia'. *Camellia sinensis*, the tea plant, was introduced into NSW as an economic plant through the efforts of Sir Joseph BANKS, and was successfully established by 1796.

Camellias were fashionable in Europe gardens in the middle of the nineteenth century. Interest thus generated led those in the nursery trade to import and propagate many *Camellia* cultivars. Towards the turn of the century the popularity of camellias began to wane, causing a large number of cultivars to be deleted from nursery catalogues. The introduction of the 'The Czar' is considered by many enthusiasts to have revived the popularity of camellias in Melbourne and, to a certain extent, in Sydney. This cultivar was commercially released by R.W. HODGINS, who obtained propagating material from a plant growing at Breslin's Nursery in Camberwell after Breslin's death in 1912. However, it was not until about 1930, when the plants first distributed by Hodgins became established and began to flower well, that the popularity of 'The Czar' increased. Breslin's original stock plant, left *in situ*, was transferred in the early 1950s by Alexander JESSEP to the Melbourne Botanic Gardens, where it still thrives.

The revived popularity of camellias encouraged the introduction of many new cultivars and currently the range is enormous (over 32 000 cultivar names have been received for the international register). This includes not only those formed from the traditionally cultivated *Camellia japonica*, but also those from a number of other species, particularly, *C. reticulata*, *C. sasanqua*, *C. saluenensis*, and hybrids between these species. In 1952 the Australian and New Zealand Camellia Research Society was founded, and it soon produced its first journal. The Society's founding members were Walter HAZELWOOD, Dr C.R. Merrillees (d. 1959), E.G. WATERHOUSE, and Alex Jessep, all of whom researched the history of camellias in Australia and raised many new cultivars. Professor Waterhouse is credited with raising hundreds of new seedlings, including the first reported fully double *C.* X *williamsii* hybrids 'E.G. Waterhouse' and 'Shocking Pink'. The Society has become one of the most active specialist plant societies in Australia, with regular shows and competitions.

The *Camellia* remains one of Australia's most popular garden ornamentals. Enthusiasts and nursery proprietors continue to add new forms to the long list of popular cultivars. In recent years, a broader range of species camellias has gained popularity. The majority of these have smaller flowers by comparison to the traditional cultivar groups, but some, such as *C. oleifera*, have scented flowers, while others have enhanced tolerance to Australian environmental conditions.

ML

CAMFIELD, Julius Henry (1852–1916), gardener and horticulturist, was born at Islington, London, and served his apprenticeship in Kent before working in Regent's Park, London, and then Shooter's Hill, Kent. Arriving in Sydney in 1882, he was immediately appointed by Charles MOORE to the SYDNEY BOTANIC GARDENS and commenced as foreman of the Garden Palace Grounds that year, a demanding position during the redevelopment of the grounds after the Palace burned down in September 1882. Promoted to overseer from 1896, J.H. MAIDEN referred to him as a competent and loyal colleague, and found his fairness in disciplinary matters instructive. Shy and reserved, Camfield had a remarkable personal library and the Sydney Botanic Gardens library owed much to his knowledge of the second-hand book market. A 'sound botanist', he assisted Maiden in the establishment of the New South Wales Herbarium, in addition to keeping his own HERBARIUM for private study, and was the first to collect the rare *Eucalyptus copulans* (1899). As he 'had the greatest objection to appear in print', his detailed knowledge of the flora of the Sydney region was exhibited in a solitary paper, 'Notes on Some Port Jackson Plants' (1898), written with Maiden, whom he also helped to compile the much-quoted 'List of Plants Growing Without Cultivation in the Outer Domain, 1902'. On Camfield's death, Maiden remarked that he usually agreed with Camfield: 'where I did not concur, I always respected his opinion and often doubted my own'. COLLEEN MORRIS

CAMPBELL, Archibald James (1853–1929), civil servant and naturalist, was born at Fitzroy (Vic.), to Scottish parents. He was a leading amateur ornithologist, a keen conservationist, and pursued nature-writing to communicate his love of his chosen field. He was a founder in 1899 of the Victorian Wattle Club—a forerunner of the Australian WATTLE DAY League—and his *Golden Wattle: Our National Floral Emblem* (1921) was a passionate plea for its veneration and cultivation. Ahead of his time in conservation, his biographer recorded 'A pocket full of raisins or oatmeal, a water-flask and an overcoat sufficed him for a day or two walking in the Mallee.' His son, Archibald George Campbell (1880–1954), was an early student of the BURNLEY School of Horticulture (1895–98) and later lectured there; he was also an orchardist at Rutherglen, Pomonal, and Kilsyth (Vic.). RA

CANARY ISLANDS While LINNAEUS catalogued a few distinctive Canary Islands species, including *Dracaena draco* and *Canarina canariensis*, Francis Masson's collecting expeditions from KEW GARDENS and Alexander von Humboldt's descriptions of the Canary Islands flora drew wide attention by the end of the eighteenth century. The comprehensive Flora of Philip Webb and Sabin Berthelot followed (1836–50). The location of the Canary Islands in the Atlantic Ocean—southwest of SPAIN, of which it forms an autonomous region, and en route to Australia for pre-Suez sea voyages—as well as the climatic similarities, facilitated the introduction, cultivation, ACCLIMATISATION, and even naturalisation of Canary Islands flora in Australia. Popular and persistent ornamentals in Australian gardens include *Phoenix canariensis*, *Pinus canariensis*, *Argyranthemum* spp., and *Echium* spp. *Chamaecytisus proliferus* has naturalised as an environmental WEED, yet is still utilised as an ornamental and as a fodder crop. A rewarding flora of SUCCULENTS includes, among many others, *Aeonium* spp., *Ceropegia* spp., and *Euphorbia canariensis*.

STEPHEN FORBES

CANBERRA, ACT: see AUSTRALIAN CAPITAL TERRITORY

CANDOLLE, Augustin Pyramus de (1778–1841), a Swiss botanist, was the first of several family members who became prominent botanists. They amassed a large HERBARIUM, now housed in Geneva, and named many AUSTRALIAN PLANTS from specimens sent to Europe by collectors. Between 1823 and 1873 Augustin, and later his son Alphonse (1806–1893) and grandson Casimir (1836–1918), published *Prodromus Systematis Naturalis Regni Vegetabilis*. Intended as a world Flora, it was never completed, but nonetheless described many hundreds of Australian plants.

ALEX GEORGE

CANE, William Lancashire (1911–1987), nursery proprietor, grower and supplier of previously untried varieties of AUSTRALIAN PLANTS, planted out large numbers of Victorian EUCALYPTS on his property near Maffra in 1940. He established a close friendship with Leo HODGE, breeder of the Poorinda GREVILLEA hybrids, and propagated these hybrids in large numbers for sale. Bill Cane also introduced several grevillea hybrids of his own, named after his nursery, Clearview. A foundation committee member of the SOCIETY FOR GROWING AUSTRALIAN PLANTS, he was renowned for his ability to propagate difficult species and for his eye in spotting interesting variations in bush plants.

JOHN WALTER

CAPE OF GOOD HOPE/CAPE PROVINCE: see AFRICA

CARAVAN PARKS for tourist use emerged in Australia following the inter-war years when the increase in car ownership made it possible for families to build or buy a lightweight plywood vehicle for towing. Caravanning became the affordable holiday for hundreds of thousands of Australian families who wanted a little more luxury and ease of food preparation than tent life provided. By the late 1940s published guides indicated suitable camping grounds, but until the early 1960s most just parked overnight on the roadside, on a BEACH foreshore, or in the local SHOWGROUND or BOTANIC GARDEN (where conflicting uses continue to bedevil managers and users). In the absence of the American fad for mobile homes, caravan parks often remained little more than camping sites until local government health regulations enforced upgrading; even so, elaborate caravan parks, with power and sullage waste facilities, did not become

Suggested CARAVAN PARK entrances from Keith Winser's *Australian Caravan and Touring Manual* (1961), which he felt were important features in 'influencing the caravanner to stop at a park or continue on in search of a more attractive place'

common in Australia until the 1950s. By 1959 the Blue Lagoon Caravan Court, north of Gosford (NSW), offered 'twelve acres of tropical paradise, with the full frontage to the beautiful Blue Lagoon' with bitumen roads, septic sewerage, hot showers, power, bowls, a 'drive-in', and a GOLF COURSE nearby. Most sites were sufficiently large to accommodate a boat; such facilities presaged the RESORT style of park. By 1990 there were 2690 caravan parks in Australia, offering 203 000 powered sites and 71 000 unpowered sites. In and near the major population centres, up to a quarter of residents were 'permanents', out of choice or economic necessity.

Jim Davison and Peter Spearritt, *Holiday Business: Tourism in Australia since 1870* (Carlton South, Vic., 2000)

PETER SPEARRITT

CARLTON GARDENS and the Royal Exhibition Building form a Melbourne icon. The twenty-six hectare site was laid out by Melbourne City Council in the 1850s to Edward La Trobe BATEMAN's elaborate curvilinear plan, later modified by Clement HODGKINSON. Most of this was destroyed for the 1880 International EXHIBITION when the central section was excised as the Exhibition Reserve. Architect Joseph Reed (1822–1890) designed the Exhibition Building and its setting. In front of the building—a compendium of classical architecture with Florentine dome and central entrance as triumphal arch—an imposing FOUNTAIN formed the focus of new paths radiating in a *patte d'oie*. The central *allée* of double paths lined with *Platanus X acerifolia* (Plane Tree) was planted with buffalo grass as a *tapis vert*. William SANGSTER was contracted to build the landscape. He added patterned flower beds, picturesque ponds with subtropical plantings, lawns, and mixed avenues including elms alternating with araucarias. Sculpture, ornate lamps, and an expensive cast-iron perimeter fence were erected. After the 1888 Centennial Exhibition the north garden was reinstated, with oaks, elms, planes, and *Ficus macrophylla* (Moreton Bay Fig) trees lining diagonal paths. A lodge was built (1891) and tennis courts added (1924–27).

The Exhibition Building housed Australia's inaugural Federal Parliament (1901) and then Victoria's Parliament (1901–27), yet the Exhibition Reserve deteriorated during the twentieth century. By the 1950s almost all the open space was used for car parking, most of which has since been displaced by construction of the Melbourne Museum (1996–2000). Although simplified, Carlton Gardens remains the major example of nineteenth-century classicism in an Australian PUBLIC GARDEN.

David Dunstan, *Victorian Icon: The Royal Exhibition Building, Melbourne* (Kew, Vic., 1996)

GEORGINA WHITEHEAD

CARMINOW (formerly The Pinnacles), Mount Lofty, in the ADELAIDE HILLS, was a summer HILL-STATION developed in 1885 by businessman and philanthropist Sir Thomas Elder, and then acquired by newspaper proprietor Sir Langdon Bonython, in 1903. Elder appropriated former wood-cutters' tracks for a path system, planting many deciduous trees and conifers in the 'lower garden'; Bonython developed the extensive 'upper garden' of rhododendrons, azaleas, and camellias within a stringybark forest, much of which was extensively damaged in the Ash Wednesday bushfires (1983).

DAVID JONES

CARNATIONS (*Dianthus* spp.) are native to both Europe and Asia, with many species from the MEDITERRANEAN. Several species, especially *D. caryophyllus*, have long been cultivated in Europe, although the carnation's present form as a florists' flower was the result of extensive hybridisation. Pinks (descendants of *D. plumarius*) and carnations were early favourites in Australian gardens, with T. Horton JAMES recommending them for SA in 1838, only two years after colonisation. Picotees (margined with contrasting colours) and Sweetwilliam (*D. barbatus*) were also favourites, and by 1845 James DICKINSON could list fourteen dianthus in his nursery catalogue. Perpetual-flowering carnations were first raised in France *c*. 1850, and became popular in Australia during the late nineteenth century; they included many fine, locally HYBRIDISED cultivars. Robert HENDERSON was an early populariser, and specialist nurseries flourished from the 1880s, Charles WENTWORTH and Robert POULTER being prominent. Carnation societies (often linked with SWEET PEAS or DAHLIAS) established in Vic. (1901), NSW (*c*. 1901), and SA (1903) were among the earliest specialist HORTICULTURAL SOCIETIES in Australia. Advice was provided in garden magazines and by LOCKLEY's *Carnation Growing Made Easy* (1914) and DENHAM's *Australasian Catechism of Carnation Culture* (1917). Although their cult status was not maintained, carnations formed a popular subject in the COTTAGE GARDEN revival and remain staples of the cut flower trade. For those to whom delicacy is not paramount—for example many in TROPICAL parts of Australia—Queenslander E.W. BICK's 1920 advice is still relevant: 'Don't try to grow carnations ... when gerberas will do so much better.' RA

CAR PARKS first emerged in Sydney and Melbourne in the 1920s, when the growth of car ownership meant that on-street parking spaces in the central business district became hotly contested. Early car parks, often attached to a hotel or garage, only housed a score or so of cars. But in the 1950s and 1960s, with the decline of public transport usage and the increasing role of the car for the journey to work, massive car parks appeared in city centres, and as an integral part of the new car-based shopping centres at Chermside (Brisbane), Chadstone (Melbourne), and Roselands (Sydney). Inner-city car parks, invariably multi-storey, rarely indulge in any landscaping, but many supermarket car parks are single-level, open to the environment, and able to sustain plant life—although narrow garden beds offer a landscape challenge to vegetation rarely attended with success. In the domestic sphere, the motor garage superseded the stable and carriage house during the early twentieth century, and the DRIVE became an important part of even quite modest SUBURBAN GARDENS.

Car parks are now accepted as a central part of urban and RESORT life. Most have time-based charges, which runs counter to the strongly held belief in a right of public access that still applies to our PUBLIC PARKS and BEACHES. Their landscaping is a signature of recent designed landscapes and, with freeway planting, offers bread and butter for landscape architects and contractors. Some parks are still forbidding in appearance, although a few, including the Navy's car park overlooking Sydney's Woolloomooloo Bay, offer parked cars—and their occupants—superb harbour views.

Geoffrey Baker and Bruno Funaro, *Parking* (New York, 1958)
PETER SPEARRITT

CARR, Geoffrey William (b. 1948), environmentalist, ecologist, and horticulturist, developed an interest in plants at an early age and as a teenager joined the Geelong Field Naturalists' Club. Discovering and recording the NATIVE FLORA of Vic., particularly ORCHIDS and other rare plants, became an important interest and formed the basis of his expert knowledge of this flora. It also provided an understanding of the pressures on the ENVIRONMENT by human activities, especially the introduction and subsequent proliferation of WEEDS. Carr fostered the PROPAGATION and cultivation of native plants in the late 1960s through his Geelong nursery, at a time when the BUSH GARDEN movement was burgeoning. In the late 1970s he started Ecological Horticulture, one of Australia's first environmental consultancies. Carr has significantly influenced government policy in the area of environmental weeds, and has been tireless in alerting land managers and the public to their deleterious effects on natural plant communities. ML

CARRICK HILL, Springfield, SA, a large suburban estate, centres on an idiosyncratic house in the Jacobean style built for (Sir) Edward Hayward (1903–1983) and his wife Ursula (*née* Barr Smith) (1907–1970) between 1937 and 1939. The house was designed by architect James Irwin around oak panelling, staircases, and other joinery, brought from Beaudesert, a demolished Tudor and Jacobean country house in Staffordshire, England. The garden was designed by Ursula Hayward and shows her great love of rare trees, flowering shrubs, roses, and bulbs, particularly tuberoses. Taking advantage of sweeping views over Adelaide and the Gulf of St Vincent, it comprises a hedged inner garden, outer park, rill, cutting garden, orchard, nuttery, pleached pear arbour, terraces, and massed roses, all linked by slate paths. The garden evolved during Hayward ownership and was altered when the property passed to public ownership in 1983. In concert with the house and collections, the garden is now being conserved to emulate the Hayward era.

Alan Smith, *Carrick Hill: A Souvenir* (Adelaide, 2000)
TREVOR NOTTLE

CARRON, William (1821–1876) was born at Pulham, Norfolk, England, the son of a gardener, and worked in the botanic garden at Cambridge before moving to Westhall, Suffolk. He and his wife left Cork, Ireland, as bounty migrants; family tradition has it that Carron had charge of plants for ELIZABETH BAY HOUSE when he arrived in Sydney in 1844. After service with the Macleays he moved to T.W. SHEPHERD's Darling Nursery, and in 1847 strongly protested to W.S. Macleay against accusations that he had provided Shepherd with Macleay plants. When Charles MOORE arrived in 1848 as director of SYDNEY BOTANIC GARDENS, he contacted Carron and soon recommended his appointment as botanist to Edmund Kennedy's ill-fated thirteen-man expedition to Cape York. As one of only three survivors, Carron gave evidence at the inquest, and published a moving account of the expedition, recording terrible privations along with botanical observations. After further government service of a clerical nature, and a brief trip to England, Carron was appointed collector for the Sydney Botanic Garden in 1866. He accompanied Moore on excursions to northern NSW and visited Lord Howe Island (1869–71) with Moore and

Aerial view of CARRICK HILL, Springfield (SA), showing the house and its immediate garden compartments in the 1950s enclosed by orchards—such clear documentation has influenced the CONSERVATION and replanting of this important garden

Robert FITZGERALD, returning with a harvest of NOVELTIES, especially FERNS and PALMS. In 1872 Carron reported on twenty forest reserves on the Northern Rivers, and at the end of 1875 left the Gardens to become inspector of forests for the Clarence River district before his early death in Grafton. Moore named the Antarctic Beech, *Fagus carronii* (now *Nothofagus moorei*), and MUELLER commemorated the botanist by the woody climber, *Carronia multisepala* and by a Qld bean tree, *Bauhinia carronii*, but his narrative of one of Australia's most disastrous exploratory expeditions remains Carron's chief memorial.

LIONEL GILBERT

CASCADE TEA GARDEN, South Hobart, was established adjacent to the Cascade Brewery in 1898 when land was leased to Thomas Meredith Lipscombe (son of Frederick LIPSCOMBE). The expansion of tramway lines into the suburbs (1893) gave working-class Hobartians additional recreational choices, and Lipscombe's establishment sat at a tram terminus at the foot of Mount Wellington. The TEA GARDEN featured flowers and fruit trees, with shaded walks and rustic shelters adjacent to the Hobart Rivulet. A small bridge over the stream, huts, and fern dells further enticed the visitor. The attraction was taken over by florist Victor Sayer and his wife, who sold flowers and beverages. The Second World War saw a serious decline until, neglected, the garden was devastated by floods (1960) and bushfires (1967). Hobart City Council has in recent years re-established the Cascade Gardens on the site.

PETER MacFIE

CASLAKE, Charles Robert (*c.* 1891–1961), English-born art metal worker, opened his Melbourne business in 1924. With an uninterrupted family tradition dating back to an eighteenth-century London blacksmith's shop, the business began crafting eagerly sought individualised iron gates and fences for fine Melbourne houses, including CRANLANA and COOMBE COTTAGE. Interstate commissions followed, all produced with justifiable pride in the high-quality materials, design, and craftwork. Sons John, Edward, and Roy all joined the family business, which closed in the late 1980s.

HELEN BOTHAM

CASTELLA, Francois Robert de: see DE CASTELLA, Francois Robert

CASTLECRAG, NSW, a landscaped residential estate located on a peninsula overlooking Middle Harbour on Sydney's North Shore, was developed by Marion Mahony and Walter Burley GRIFFIN; it remains their most enduring community development. The site was purchased by the Greater Sydney Development Association, a company formed in 1919 with Griffin as managing director, and from 1921 shareholders built houses on the dramatic harbourside terrain, with its mix of natural BUSH and denuded land. Restrictive covenants sought to enforce the pervasive aesthetic vision of the Griffins. This included flat-roofed stone and reinforced concrete buildings, 'subordinate to the landscape', which captured sunlight and exploited views to the harbour and reserves through the delicate foliage and sculptural trunks of angophoras and eucalypts. Seemingly a part of the craggy landscape, the houses were austere by contemporary standards; often pergolas for climbing plants melded idealistic architecture with the unpolished environment. Castlecrag's naming was inspired by a prominent rocky outcrop ('Edinburgh Castle') and this Scottish nomenclature was carried through to the roads and the public reserves designed by Griffin for the benefit of the surrounding allotments. Nestled into one of the reserves is the Haven AMPHITHEATRE, where community THEATRE, organised by Marion Mahony, was performed. Estate planning retained sandstone outcrops, islands of bush formed unmanicured reserves, and a continuous foreshore reserve for public use was instituted. The Griffins moved from Melbourne to Castlecrag in 1925 and the estate formed the locus of their idealistic social vision. In 1935–36 the Griffins moved to India, leaving continued implementation to partner Eric Nicholls. Future generations have fought to maintain their vision.

Meredith Walker, Adrienne Kabos, and James Weirick, *Building for Nature: Walter Burley Griffin and Castlecrag* (Castlecrag, NSW, 1994)

COLLEEN MORRIS

CASTLEMAINE BOTANICAL GARDENS, Vic., set aside in 1860, originally comprised approximately seventy acres (28 ha) covering a large, flat area and a reefy hill bisected by Barkers Creek. Reduced to fifty-nine acres (24 ha), the majority of the plantings and features were confined to the area east of the creek, with some in the south-eastern corner of the site. The north-western area was never developed, and still comprises a largely intact indigenous ecosystem retaining some rare species. In 1866 Philip DORAN was appointed the first curator and was responsible for the design. For forty-seven years he oversaw the development of the Gardens and established an impressive collection of native and exotic species, many of which he received from Ferdinand MUELLER. The gardens also featured a summer-house, bridges, nursery, cast-iron fountain, bluestone and iron gates, two lakes with islands, stone weir, tree-fern grove, shelter shed, and band rotunda. Tea rooms were added *c.* 1919 and paths at the southern end were altered. The middle of the twentieth century saw a number of changes, including the unauthorised installation of a caravan park, as well as the removal of the summer-house, band rotunda, second lake, and some of the land. A rose garden was created in the late 1960s. Recent works include the establishment of a *Buddleja* collection and the reconstruction of the band rotunda and summer-house, all aimed at conserving this fine garden, part of the extraordinary network of BOTANIC GARDENS created in Vic. during the mid-nineteenth century.

KEVIN WALSH

CASTENER'S RURAL AUSTRALIAN: see RURAL AUSTRALIAN

CATANI, Carlo Georgio Domenico Enrico (1852–1918), was a civil engineer with a talent for landscape design. After gaining his engineering diploma in Florence, his birthplace, he worked in Italy on railway construction before emigrating in 1876 with friends Pietro Baracchi and Ettore Cecchi. Finding no suitable work in New Zealand they continued on to Melbourne, where the Department of Crown Lands and Survey employed them as draftsmen. Two years later Catani was transferred to the Public Works Department. In 1892 he was appointed Chief Engineer, in charge of such works as draining Koo-wee-rup and Kow Swamps, building roads to Arthur's Seat and Mount Donna Buang, and developing MOUNT BUFFALO (where Eurobin Creek was dammed to form Lake Catani).

His landscaping abilities contributed to the success of perhaps his most important project: the realignment of the Yarra River upstream from Princes Bridge, begun in 1896. Catani's imaginative treatment of reclaimed land along the river's south bank created Alexandra Park, incorporating a sixty-metre wide BOULEVARD with carriage drive, riding tan, bicycle path, and footpath separated by avenues of deciduous trees. The small, ornamental Alexandra Gardens were completed in 1904, and in 1906 he accepted an invitation from Melbourne City Council to join the committee responsible for designing the adjacent Queen Victoria Gardens—all three reserves forming part of Melbourne's DOMAIN.

Catani's last major project was reclamation of St Kilda's foreshore. As a member of the St Kilda Foreshore Trust, formed in 1906, he designed gardens later named after him, taking his inspiration from a beachfront public park in Naples, the Villa Communale. A MEDITERRANEAN influence was particularly apparent in his love of PALMS, which were used extensively along St Kilda foreshore and to a lesser extent in Queen Victoria Gardens and Alexandra Park. ROCKERIES in Alexandra Gardens also included aloes, yuccas, cordylines, agaves, pelagoniums, and other plants adapted to hot, dry conditions. After retiring in 1917 Catani remained on the Foreshore Trust, which continued to implement his plan long after his death. In 1930 a clock tower resembling an ITALIAN campanile was erected to his memory on St Kilda Esplanade.

GEORGINA WHITEHEAD

CATARACT GORGE, Launceston, Tas., a rugged 150-metre deep gorge on the South Esk River, immediately adjacent to the city, is a magnificent example of a naturally SUBLIME landscape, rendered acceptably PICTURESQUE by Romantic appropriation. While the scenery has long been appreciated, it was not until the last decades of the nineteenth century that paths provided ready pedestrian access along the Gorge to the First Basin. Here the Cliff Grounds were developed as a PUBLIC PARK, featuring an extensive and now highly significant collection of conifers around an ORIENTAL-influenced bandstand (1896) and rustic kiosk (*c.* 1900) serving a TEA GARDEN shared with peacocks and local wallabies. The earliest work was privately executed by the Launceston City and Suburbs Improvement Association, including the architect Alexander North (1858–1945), who was responsible for the 'Swiss' gate lodge (1891) hanging off the cliff above King's Bridge. Municipal authorities took control in 1898 and credit for much of what is seen today should go to the parks superintendent, William MCGOWAN. Paths were developed with romantically named focal points: the Giant's Grave, Crusoe's Hut, the Eyrie, and Fairy Dell. In 1904 the Alexandra suspension BRIDGE provided pedestrian access to the southern side of the Gorge, and a walking path to Duck Reach provided an opportunity for a more challenging experience of the natural environment. Early RUSTIC timber shelters were replaced in the 1920s with extraordinary rusticated structures of reinforced concrete.

Cave gardens

The 'Swiss' GATE LODGE (1891) at CATARACT GORGE, Launceston (Tas.) still guards the entrance to one of Australia's most dramatically-sited PUBLIC PARKS, where paths cling to the gorge sides before opening to reveal a tea house set in spacious lawns and shrubberies

The south side of the Basin was further developed from the 1930s, including a swimming pool, kiosk, and extensive lawns. FRANCINE GILFEDDER and ANNE NEALE

CAULFIELD, Harold William (1918–1994), horticulturist and botanic gardens curator, was born and educated in Vic., and gained experience at MELBOURNE and ADELAIDE BOTANIC GARDENS. He was curator of BRISBANE BOTANIC GARDENS (Alice Street) from 1956 to 1982, equalling Walter HILL's twenty-six-year term. His key role in the establishment of the new Brisbane Botanic Gardens at Mount Coot-tha in the early 1970s was one of his finest achievements and followed a Churchill Fellowship (1970) to study BOTANIC GARDENS in the USA, Britain, and Singapore. Caulfield volunteered his time and extensive knowledge in 1984 to assist with tree identification in the old botanic gardens, and this focused attention on the need for conservation work there. His enthusiasm for gardening was also shared with the community through his garden writings for the Brisbane *Courier-Mail* and contributions to local gardening guides.
JEANNIE SIM

CAVANILLES, Antonio José (1745–1804), clergyman and Spain's leading taxonomic botanist of the eighteenth century, spent the period from 1777 to 1781 in Paris, returning to Madrid in 1801 and becoming director of its botanic garden. Remembered by gardeners for his naming of the genus *DAHLIA*, Cavanilles described a number of AUSTRALIAN PLANTS between 1791 and 1799, including the genera *Angophora* and *Bursaria*, from specimens collected around Port Jackson by Fadeo Haenke and Luis Née on the Spanish Malaspina expedition (1793). ALEX GEORGE

CAVE GARDENS In 1834, naturalist George BENNETT commented that, as a result of Thomas MITCHELL's discovery of mammalian fossils at Wellington Caves (NSW), 'caves have become one of the colonial lions'. Certainly, they were among Australia's most popular tourist attractions from the 1870s until 1914—a popularity that continued, albeit shared with many other RESORTS and, increasingly, NATIONAL PARKS. With the discovery and exploitation of cave systems such as Naracoorte (SA), Jenolan (in the BLUE MOUNTAINS), Abercrombie, Wellington, and Yarrangobilly (all NSW), curators often saw the development of gardens—sometimes incorporating picturesque GROTTOS and ROCKERIES—as an extension of the caves themselves. In the 1880s William Reddan, an Irish-trained horticulturist, established a series of gardens at Naracoorte, famed as an attraction in their own right, although now no longer extant. In this, he was assisted by his daughter Agnes, and by photographer William Augustus Francis (son of George FRANCIS). Further south, Paul Krummel and then William ROBINSON developed the MOUNT GAMBIER CAVE GARDEN in the 1870s and 1920s and established its well-known rosary in 1909, while James Umpherston created a nearby fern-edged rowing-pool at Umpherston Cave; both being located in sinkholes. At Jenolan Caves, the premier cave resort for NSW, Joseph MAIDEN designed and planted a series of gardens and rockeries in 1897, a framework that remains intact. At Wombeyan an arboretum of exotic trees was established, and Yarrangobilly has an avenue of *Populus nigra* 'Italica' (Lombardy Poplar) and a thermal swimming pool surrounded by deciduous trees. At the Buchan Caves (Vic.), supervisor Frederick Wilson commenced ornamental planting in 1908. Further planting was designed by Hugh LINAKER during the 1930s and implemented by managers Frank Moon and Albert Sandford. It is associated with a popular caravan park that has won many awards, largely based on the beauty of the site and its trees.

ELERY HAMILTON-SMITH

CEMETERIES The Australian colonies developed in a watershed period in European cultural and social customs in relation to the disposal of human remains. Traditional church graveyards were giving way to large, carefully designed and landscaped cemeteries. The desire for a respectable burial and monument filtered through to all social classes during the nineteenth century. The lead was taken by cemeteries such as Père Lachaise, Paris (1804), Glasgow Necropolis, Scotland (1831), and the ring of private cemeteries developed around London, including Kensal Green (1833), Highgate (1839), Abney Park (1840), Nunhead (1840), Brompton (1840), and Tower Hamlets (1841). These were designed as grand monumented gardens, with appropriate buildings and garden features as well as extensive planting and landscaping. John Claudius LOUDON, the renowned British landscape gardener, horticulturist, and writer, was perhaps the most obvious influence on this process, particularly through his illustrated publication *On the Laying Out, Planting, and Managing of Cemeteries; and on the Improvement of Churchyards* (1843). Large public cemeteries established by public authorities came in the next wave of cemetery development in Britain in the 1850s and 1860s, but these usually lacked the elaborate architectural, design, and landscape input of the private cemeteries.

In the Australian colonies, the public cemetery took the early lead, although in the early years of colonial development there were more pressing priorities than elaborate cemetery planning. The first burials took place in the sandhills around first landfall in all the Australian colonies; early church graveyards and public burial grounds followed utilitarian lines, with limited if any planting. Relatively small areas with basic grid patterns for roads and paths and minimal planting, usually of evergreens, had to suffice. Many of these early burial grounds were soon overtaken by urban development. Aboriginals, and forgotten members of society such as lunatic asylum patients, usually received unmarked plots. A further influence was the growth of the public health movement, which increasingly condemned the siting of burials within towns and populated areas. Under the influence of Edwin Chadwick (1800–1890) in England, sanitary reformers advocated the relocation of cemeteries to the periphery of urban settlement.

Later on, with the increasing availability of suitable plant species, more elaborate cemetery schemes became possible. Among the earliest was an 'impression' of an oval cemetery (later WEST TERRACE CEMETERY) divided by serpentine roads and pathways, included by Colonel William LIGHT in his plan of Adelaide (1837). A more successful implementation was MELBOURNE GENERAL CEMETERY, developed from 1852 under the guidance of Albert PURCHAS. Others of the nineteenth century included BOROONDARA (Melbourne), BRISBANE GENERAL CEMETERY, CORNELIAN BAY (Hobart), GORE HILL and WAVERLEY (Sydney), and KARRAKATTA (Perth). The grandest was Sydney's ROOKWOOD CEMETERY, developed from 1867; Adelaide's PARAFIELD was the most grandiose. Impressive cemeteries were also landscaped in provincial centres and rural townships—examples are SANDGATE, at Newcastle (NSW), and BEECHWORTH (Vic.)

In these larger sites, more complex landscape schemes became possible, though most continued to rely on imposing a geometric layout on a relatively level site. Boroondara, with its hillside location and sweeping drives, was one of the few to take advantage of the existing contours. Most of the larger metropolitan cemeteries incorporated denominational divisions and relatively formal plantings—though this was often heavily influenced by the nature of the local soils, climate, and the availability of water. Evergreens predominated throughout the nineteenth century. Pines (*Pinus* spp.) and cypresses (*Cupressus* spp.) were the most popular, particularly where a formal character was desired. Avenues of trees as well as specimen trees were planted, and there was some use of native Australian plants. Of equal importance was extensive use of shrubs and border plants as well as individual grave plantings, particularly of roses and a wide variety of exotic bulbs. In sites where high levels of maintenance were provided, much use was also made of hedging plants.

Another integral part of large-scale cemetery design was the provision of appropriate buildings and structures, varying from rotundas, waiting shelters, and lich-gates, to chapels, offices, and even mortuary railway stations. Fencing, usually of timber, stone, or iron, also played an important role, both in keeping out wandering animals and delineating individual grave sites. Indeed, some of Australia's finest nineteenth-century ironwork is to be found in cemeteries.

FORMALITY seems to have been the key word for Australia's nineteenth-century cemeteries. There was little influence from the American rural cemetery movement, which largely rejected the grid system of burials and placed graves and associated memorials in an informal pattern often related to the landscape. But the further development of that American concept into schemes that banished the majority of upright memorials and enclosed plots was to have a marked influence on twentieth-century Australian cemetery development.

FAWKNER CEMETERY, established in the northern suburbs of Melbourne under the guidance of Charles HEATH in 1904, was a harbinger of things to come. It retained many traditional Australian features, but Heath became a keen exponent of the garden cemetery movement, closely allied to the GARDEN CITY movement. Other significant influences on cemetery development after the turn of the century were the First World War and the subsequent influenza epidemics. There had been an earlier precedent in the American Civil War, but it was the characteristic Great War military cemetery with its simple, uniform memorials, absence of kerbing, regimented rows, extensive lawn areas, and central Cross of

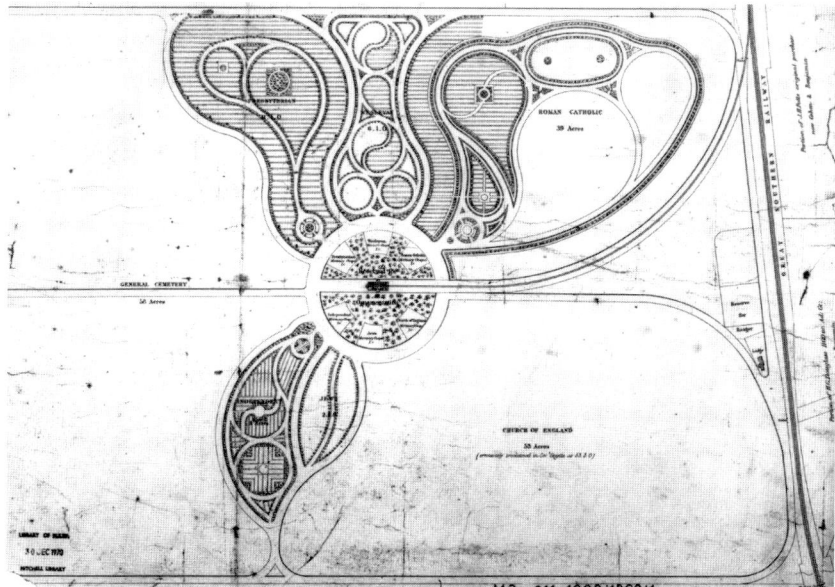

This 1868 plan of the necropolis at Haslem's Creek (later ROOKWOOD CEMETERY), was progressively implemented over succeeding decades; its GARDENESQUE layout and horticultural embellishment accorded with contemporary ideas for garden CEMETERIES

Sacrifice that was to have a profound influence on Australia, where similar cemeteries were developed from 1920. This produced the regimented style of Adelaide's Centennial Park (1936), with an absolute height restriction on monuments to two feet nine inches (84 cm)—though its actual layout and planting owed more to Hubert Eaten's Forest Lawn Cemetery, Los Angeles. A much closer copy of that American model was Adelaide's ENFIELD (1948), Australia's first full lawn cemetery with horizontal plaques set in the extensive lawns. In the twentieth century, Australian cemeteries have also been important repositories for remnant native and exotic vegetation, particularly in areas of sustained urban development, but also in (often neglected) rural sites.

Many nineteenth-century Australian cemeteries succumbed to the popular pioneer park treatment in the second half of the twentieth century, with monuments either discarded or reset in forlorn perimeter displays, earlier plantings ravaged by herbicides, and expanses of lawn introduced. The community's interest in memorialisation continued to decline, particularly as cremation overtook earth burial as the most popular means of disposal. A plethora of niche walls marred many a cemetery landscape, and frequently the ashes might be scattered beyond the boundaries of the cemetery in parks and gardens, and at sea. The memorial trends of the moment include lockets and keepsakes containing ashes, but there has been a return to the standard of earlier centuries, when large numbers of people went unmemorialised.

Celestina Sagazio (ed.), *Cemeteries: Our Heritage* (Melbourne, 1992); Robert Nicol, *At the End of the Road: Government, Society and the Disposal of Human Remains in the Nineteenth and Twentieth Centuries* (St Leonards, NSW, 1994)

ROBERT NICOL

CENTENARY PLACE, a small PUBLIC PARK prominently sited at a major crossroads in Brisbane's Fortitude Valley, on the city's edge, celebrated the centenary of European settlement at Moreton Bay. Designed in 1924 by Henry MOORE, the central PROMENADE, with statues of Robert Burns and politician T.J. Byrnes, addressed a proposed cathedral site adjacent. The original elegant framework of paths, figs and palms remains evident, although garden beds designed by Moore and Harry OAKMAN were slightly modified in 1999 renovations.

CATHERINE BROUWER

CENTENNIAL PARK, lying between Paddington, Woollahra, Bondi Junction, Randwick, and Kensington, NSW, sited on the Lachlan Swamps water supply reserve and originally part of the second Sydney Common (designated by Governor Macquarie in 1811), was developed as a PUBLIC PARK celebrating the centenary of European settlement of Australia (1888). Governor Carrington, whose idea it was for a large regional park for Sydney suited to riding and recreation, recognised the potential of the proposed site and facilitated its realisation. In this he was supported at all levels of government from Premier Henry Parkes to local municipal councils. The 1886 design, attributed to engineer Frederick Augustus Franklin (who had worked under Joseph PAXTON on the Crystal Palace at Sydenham in the 1850s), was laid out by Charles MOORE (appointed in 1887 to supervise its early formation) and his overseer James JONES.

The plan proposed a processional main entry, ornamental gates, plantations, lakes, ornamental water bodies, cascades and fountains, grassed meadows, and areas for sport. Skirting the higher ground were avenues fronted by elegant villas; sale of this land would fund park construction. Erection of a 'State House' on the highest point was envisaged, and although abandoned, parliament voted £50 000 towards park construction, with an emphasis on the Grand Drive. Disagreements arose between the major players over routing of the drive and also over the planting character. Both Franklin and Jones valued the wild character of the indigenous vegetation. This differed from Moore's approach, which advocated the removal of the 'wild vegetation' in favour of a cultivated GARDENESQUE appearance with an emphasis on large grassed areas, although on the exposed site plantings were difficult to establish.

Centennial Park became the venue for events of both national and local significance and has been the focus of recreation in a setting of idealised nature within a context varying from natural wetland to urban development. The initial landscape character established by Moore and Jones was significantly augmented during the first decades of the twentieth century by Joseph MAIDEN, providing the distinctive landscape now associated with this 'People's Park'. Following decades of neglect and vandalism, the establishment of the Centennial Park Trust (1984) once again brought Centennial Park into the public spotlight. The Park's large scale, especially so close to the centre of a major city, is a highly valued attribute.

Paul Ashton and Kate Blackmore, *Centennial Park: A History* (Kensington, NSW, 1988)

CRAIG BURTON

CHAFFEY, George (1848–1932) and his brother **William Benjamin Chaffey** (1856–1926), irrigation pioneers, were born at Brockville, Ontario, Canada, and developed two successful IRRIGATION settlements in California. Alfred Deakin, chairing a Victorian Royal Commission investigating irrigation (1884), visited the Chaffey settlements: George Chaffey, his interest stirred, arrived in Vic. in 1886. He selected a derelict sheep station at Mildura (Vic.), on the banks of the Murray, as the site for his new irrigation settlement, and cabled William to sell their Californian interests and join him. The Victorian Government offered George 250 000 acres (100 000 ha), matched by the South Australian Government, enabling the brothers to select river frontages at Renmark, SA (later part of RIVERLAND). In 1887 agreement was reached with the Victorian Government, and over the next four years George applied his energy and initiative to creating the two settlements, laid out on a handsome scale with broad, tree-lined streets. Many problems beset the endeavour—seepage losses, lack of transport, fruit disease, and the 1893 bank crash—and in 1894 the Chaffeys were declared bankrupt, and government irrigation trusts were established to continue their work. George returned to the USA in 1897 and developed further irrigation projects. William remained in Mildura, establishing a 200 acre (80 ha) ORCHARD and winery. Despite the difficulties, the Chaffey brothers were agricultural pioneers, and they laid the foundations for irrigated horticulture in south-eastern Australia.

J.A. Alexander, *The Life of George Chaffey: A Story of Irrigation Beginnings in California and Australia* (Melbourne, 1928); John P. Fogarty, *George Chaffey* (Melbourne, 1967)

ROHAN LAMB

CHAMBERS, (Thomas) Carrick (b.1930), academic and botanic gardens director, born in Auckland, New Zealand, undertook postgraduate studies at Auckland and Sydney, and also studied at Cambridge University, England (1960–61). He was Professor of Botany at the University of Melbourne (1967–86) and Director of the ROYAL BOTANIC GARDENS, SYDNEY (1986–96). Apart from his research and teaching, Chambers took a close interest in the CONSERVATION and management of culturally significant gardens, including management of RIPPON LEA's garden and research and design of Cook's Cottage garden. While at the University of Melbourne he chaired the committee that oversaw a new master plan (1970–86), resolving problems of campus growth, landscape design, and management, for which he shared an award from the Royal Australian Institute of Architects (1981).

ML

CHANDLER, William (1818–1883), market gardener, was born in London and arrived in Melbourne with his wife and young family in 1853. Giving his occupation as dairyman, Chandler took up market gardening in Glenferrie Road, Malvern (on land purchased between 1856 and 1866), specialising in cauliflowers. His son, **William Chandler** II (1844–1911), nursery proprietor, established his nursery business on land in Malvern adjacent to his father's property. Chandler selected land at The Basin in the Dandenong Ranges 1872–77, which he named Fern Glen, but soon changed to the better known Como. He specialised in cool-climate plants such as rhododendrons, azaleas, and camellias, and was also interested in fruit culture: 'Statesman', one of the seedling apples grown at Malvern, was suited to the export market and was developed in quality at Como. Plants were conveyed to Melbourne for sale (often by auction), and florists, such as RONALDS, were supplied with cut flowers. William had married in 1869, and to cater for their large family, he sold land in 1880 to the Education Department to build a school in this remote area. Many of the Chandler family pursued careers in horticulture, with some achieving prominence in their chosen field.

Alfred Elliot Chandler (1873–1935), son of William II, established the Everson Nursery in 1895 at Boronia, selling his stock of fruit and flowers at the Box Hill Market. 'A.E.' sold the nursery in 1913 and began to farm daffodils and boronia while astutely purchasing and selling land in Melbourne's growing eastern suburbs and pursuing a political career as a shire councillor (from 1901) and in the Legislative Council (from 1919). His son, Gilbert Lawrence Chandler (1903–1974), succeeded him as a shire councillor and was Victorian minister for agriculture (1955–73).

Herbert Theodore Septimus Chandler (1880–1970), son of William II, and his brother (Lawrence) Wreford Chandler (1878–1939), inherited the Como Nurseries on their father's death, but the war prevented Wref from long involvement. Bert continued to run the nursery, orchard, and market garden, and extended the nursery stock by importing rarities from Europe and Japan. He was a keen participant in garden shows and exhibitions, often exhibiting with his cousin David, of Tecoma. His son Thomas Herbert (John) Chandler (b. 1920) inherited Como on his father's death and enhanced the retail business.

David James William Chandler (1887–1955), son of William Chandler's brother, orchardist Thomas David Chandler (1849–1933), established a nursery at Tecoma (Vic.). He specialised in bulbs and supplied plants for Associated Nurseries (run by T.H. BRUNN, C.E. ISAAC, and A. RIMINGTON) and E.E. LORD's short-lived 'Garden Art' business.

Helen Coulson, *The Family of William Chandler, Horticulturist* (Kilsyth, Vic., 1978)　　　　　　　　　　　　　　　　RA

CHANDLER, William Charles (c. 1835–1915), gardener, from Middlesex, England, emigrated to Van Diemen's Land in 1855 and, according to family tradition, gained employment as a gardener at Mona Vale, in the MIDLANDS. He moved to Hobart Town, where he worked as a gardener at GOVERNMENT HOUSE, becoming head gardener following a period gardening on his own account at Granton.

Eldest son **William Charles Chandler** (1863–1944) gained an apprenticeship at the HOBART BOTANIC GARDENS—valuable training for his establishment in 1888 of Chandlers Nursery in Park Street, New Town. Several years later he bought a neglected orchard in Queen Street, Sandy Bay, and moved the nursery to its present site (c. 1892). Between 1899 and 1953 the family maintained a city shop in Liverpool Street, selling plants, seeds, and cut flowers. The nursery continued to expand, and produced extensive catalogues including plants and seeds imported from Holland, Germany, and England. During the 1930s depression, adjoining land was purchased to increase the size of the nursery.

William Chandler had three sons who joined the nursery staff as soon as they left school. William Charles (Bill) (1895–1978) took over the running of the nursery in 1924. Harold Cecil (1900–1991) worked in the business for a short time, but in 1937 was appointed the first superintendent of the Forestry Commission Nursery at Perth (Tas.). Albert Percy (1902–1990) managed the propagation side of Chandlers Nursery. In 1935 the family bought land at Kingston as the soil and growing conditions were ideal for field growing of rhododendrons, boronias, ericas, hydrangeas, and lilies. At Christmas time, blooms of *Lilium regale* were brought to town by the utility load to be sold at the city shop. In 1977, Bill received the Australian Nurseryman's Federal Award of Merit in recognition of his contribution to the nursery industry, and today Chandlers Nursery—one of the longest-established of Australian nurseries still in original family ownership—is run by his son Edward Charles (Ted) (b. 1927) and Ted's son Gregg William (b. 1953).　　　　　　　　　　　　　　ANN CRIPPS

CHARSLEY, Fanny Anne (1828–1915), wildflower artist, one of five artistic daughters of an English coroner, reached Melbourne in 1857. Recognising the beauty of flowers in the BUSH beyond Melbourne gardens, she 'took up the pleasant occupation of collecting and painting the wild flowers around Melbourne … merely as a healthy and interesting pursuit'. In 1867, shortly after her return to England, thirteen of her watercolour drawings were published as hand-coloured lithographs in *The Wildflowers around Melbourne*, which she dedicated to MUELLER for his invaluable botanical help. As the first 'popular' book on Victoria's wildflowers, this exquisitely illustrated volume provided a timely reminder of the grand diversity of antipodean flowering plants awaiting horticultural investigation. While Charsley continued to paint English wildflowers, Mueller remembered her when naming a small daisy, *Helipterum charsleyae*.　　　LINDEN GILLBANK

CHATSWORTH, the celebrated Derbyshire seat of the Dukes of Devonshire, has long been held in awe by Australian gardeners, largely because of the mid-nineteenth-century influence of its head gardener, Joseph PAXTON, but also as a result of the tradition of GARDEN VISITING. Appropriation of its name often coincided with aspirations to emulate its horticultural and landscape design excellence. SHEPHERD and Co., for instance, named their Rooty Hill (NSW) premises Chatsworth Nursery in the early 1860s. The homestead Chatsworth House, Hopkins Hill (Vic.), was erected (1859–60) for John Moffat, and upgraded in 1867 for the visit of Prince Alfred, Duke of Edinburgh, when Edward La Trobe BATEMAN was engaged to lay out the grounds 'on a similar scale of magnificence' to the ducal seat. Chatsworth, Brighton (Vic.), was developed from c. 1864 by merchant William Richard Virgoe (c. 1824–1884). Ably assisted by head gardeners J.F. ROBERTS (c. 1869) and Nathaniel RONALDS (c. 1872–75), Virgoe became a knowledgeable amateur horticulturist; the celebrity of his massive glasshouses amply justified—in the local mind at least—the eponymy of his antipodean homage. A subsequent generation turned private pleasure to commercial gain through Virgoe's Old Chatsworth Nursery.
　　　　　　　　　　　　　　　　　　　　　　　　RA

CHEEL, Edwin (1872–1951), English-born botanist, migrated as a farm labourer to Mackay, Qld (1892), and was employed as a gardener in Sydney's CENTENNIAL PARK (1897). He transferred to SYDNEY BOTANIC GARDENS (1901), where his aptitude for botany—especially lichens—was encouraged by J.H. MAIDEN. In 1908, after botanical study in England, he rose through the ranks at the Sydney Herbarium, taking charge from 1913 to 1936. He was a keen naturalist and advocate for AUSTRALIAN FLORA, involved with many societies, including the WATTLE (DAY) League.
　　　　　　　　　　　　　　　　　　　　　COLLEEN MORRIS

CHEESEMAN, Richard (1855–1916), gardener, florist, and nursery proprietor, was born at Hobart—his family had arrived there in 1854—and came to Melbourne in 1867. He was apprenticed to TAYLOR AND SANGSTER and by 1877 worked as gardener to John Simson at Studley Park; E.E. PESCOTT records that Cheeseman also worked at Toorak House, formerly Victoria's Government House.

Cheeseman purchased an old orchard property on Hawthorn Road, Brighton, and in 1880 established the Union Nurseries. Although he dealt in trees and shrubs, Cheeseman specialised as a FLORIST, capitalising on an upsurge in this branch of the trade. His large nursery provided not only cut flowers but ferns, palms, pot plants, and other desiderata of the parlour and conservatory. He established retail branches in the Eastern Market buildings in 1887, and at St Kilda in 1888; by 1890 he had a florist's shop in Collins Street. Cheeseman was responsible for securing a telephone service for the Brighton district in 1889—doubtless to enhance communication with his city premises. Spring bulbs,

Chemicals

fuchsias, dahlias, carnations, gladioli, azaleas, heaths, bouvardias, camellias, pelargoniums, and roses were all among his early specialities, many of them imported. Cheeseman was well placed to cater for the immense popularity of the chrysanthemum in the 1890s, and exhibited with some success.

Cheeseman increased his nursery in extent from two acres (0.8 ha) in 1885 to fourteen acres (5.7 ha) at the time of his death, becoming one of the leading florists in Melbourne. He was a long-serving committee member of the Brighton Horticultural Society and was secretary from 1884 to 1886. He was a successful exhibitor at horticultural shows, and was later in demand as a judge—adjudicating at the earliest shows of the NATIONAL ROSE SOCIETY of Victoria. He was particularly prominent in the affairs of the Nurserymen and Seedsmen's Association, serving as president of both the state and national bodies. He visited the PACIFIC ISLANDS in 1900–01 with Peter BARR—who thought Cheeseman's nursery 'decidedly the finest' in Melbourne—and his observations were published in pamphlet form. The object of his visit was to establish the Kentia Palm (*Howea forsteriana*) seed traffic on a satisfactory basis. Cheeseman also collected zamias and crotons, and was noted for his interest in HYBRIDISATION: from a chance seedling of weeping cypress obtained from WERRIBEE PARK—sent to Andrew Chirnside by Samuel Wilson of ERCILDOUNE—he raised a much-admired golden form.

Henry Albert (Harry) Cheeseman (1876–1956) and (Colin) Harvey Cheeseman (1884–933), sons of Richard Cheeseman, ultimately took over the family business. Aged just 12, Master Harry Cheeseman had gained an award for 'Six gents' button-hole bouquets' at the special horticultural show held in conjunction with Melbourne's Centennial International Exhibition (1888). The firm of R. Cheeseman and Sons continued in business on its original site until 1983, concentrating on the wholesale trade. RA

CHEMICALS for garden use in Australia to combat PESTS AND DISEASES originally included old remedies such as arsenic, benzole, Bordeaux mixture, Cheshunt compound, common salt, Gishurst compound, lead arsenate, nicotine sulphate, phenyle, soap, sulphur, and tobacco. These were either inorganics or of biological origin, and compared to current chemicals were expensive, ineffective, broad-spectrum, and either non-degradable or too rapidly degradable. Most originated as horticultural and agricultural chemicals which, through trial and error, were found suitable—although not necessarily intended—for garden problems; their use contrary to manufacturers' instructions continues to be a matter of concern.

From the 1930s, chemicals became more sophisticated, leading to the introduction of the broad-spectrum organochlorine insecticides, developed for wartime use, with dichlorodiphenyltrichloroethane (DDT) being the most widely used. DDT was first sold in Australia in 1945. Broad-leaved herbicides were developed for use in cereal crops. Non-specific herbicides were introduced, and found use in gardens for path maintenance. In 1962 the book *Silent Spring*, by American zoologist Rachel Louise Carson (1907–1964), challenged the use of plant protection chemicals. Much anecdotal evidence somewhat diluted the scientifically based environmental concerns raised in the book, and considerable debate ensued. The registration process for new products and uses has increased progressively, and extensive data is now required to support a product's approval. This increase in requirements started in the USA but spread quickly to many countries including Australia. Data on toxicology, metabolism, occupational health and safety, residues, overseas trade issues, environmental chemistry and toxicology, and efficacy must be supplied. It is estimated that such data can cost in the order of US$200 million before a product reaches the market.

Broad-spectrum pesticides kill beneficial insects as well as pests, often upsetting nature's balance; continual use can also lead to resistance. A range of target-specific insecticides, herbicides, and fungicides is now available for use in gardens, and a more sensible approach is now taken to the use of chemicals in gardens, with some level of damage by insects and microorganisms being accepted by most gardeners. Integrated Pest Management (IPM)—successfully integrating biological control, chemical control, and biotechnology—has been developed for specific pest problems. However, some garden problems still require use of chemicals—in conjunction with thoughtful management. Glyphosate products are used widely for total weed control. The use of herbicides such as glyphosate has become so essential in natural area management that restrictions on its use would considerably reduce effective weed control in remnant vegetation and revegetation schemes. Rose growers control black spot and mildew with triforine. Aphid and caterpillars, when in damaging numbers, require treatment by systemic and contact insecticides respectively. Snails cause considerable damage in gardens, and molluscides provide control.

Managers of public gardens have a particular challenge to use chemicals safely. A recent and ongoing problem has been the rapid spread of the Elm Leaf Beetle, which can defoliate a tree and weaken it considerably. Melbourne has one of the finest stands of elm trees in the world, and a safe and effective means of control is still being sought. The challenge is to balance effective control with the use of chemicals acceptable to the urban environment. HELEN PAGE

CHERRY, Robert John (b. 1945), nursery proprietor, plant breeder, and plant explorer, was born in Sydney and spent his formative years on the NSW Central Coast, where he was inspired by the rugged beauty of this Sydney sandstone area. In 1964 he received a certificate in horticulture from the RYDE School of Horticulture. He worked in nurseries for four years before establishing his own retail nursery at Gosford in 1965. In 1972 he purchased his present property of ninety hectares at Kulnara in the Central Coast hinterland, where he established a wholesale nursery, Paradise Plants. An extensive breeding program produced the Paradise range of *Camellia sasanqua*, and in most recent years this has been expanded to include many other CAMELLIA species.

Cherry's ten-hectare private garden merges with the natural bushland. While influenced by European examples, it possesses an individuality of design which, combined with his unequalled collection of plants, makes it outstanding among recently created large-scale Australian gardens. He has collected in New Caledonia and Fiji and has made twenty-five trips to CHINA and South-East ASIA. Since 1989 he has collected and imported many hundreds of plants, growing them in his private quarantine houses before planting them out alongside his camellia and magnolia collections. His collection was acquired with the temperate climate of the Sydney region in mind, and has been grown with the intention of incorporating this new genetic pool through subsequent breeding into plants suited to Australian conditions. RICHARD CLOUGH

CHEYNE, John (c. 1819–1887), gardener, was born in Aberdeen, Scotland, and trained 'under some of the first [i.e. finest] gardeners of their day in England'. He arrived in Qld c. 1865 and started in business as a market gardener (and later fruiterer) at Maryborough. He soon developed the Willow Glen orangery, nursery garden, and pleasure grounds at Tinana, south of Maryborough, then newly accessible via a bridge constructed over the Mary River in the wake of the Gympie gold rush (1867). Omnibuses ran to Cheyne's every Friday and Sunday. He offered cut flowers, fruit, wine, croquet, lawn tennis, and all the accoutrements of a European-style PLEASURE GARDEN, including a summer-house with the letters L O V E embedded in the ceiling, showing 'that the study of art has not banished the presence of the affections'. Cheyne's widow and son Alfred continued the business into the early 1900s. RA

CHILDREN are provided with both accepted and unexpected pleasures in gardens. As formally constructed landscapes, gardens provide an eclectic array of experiences, allowing children a place to understand aesthetic beauty through sensory experiences as well as a venue for NATURE STUDY. Both as a faunal habitat, and as a setting for play with pets, gardens permit and encourage interaction with animals. Through play, and through more structured learning in CHILDREN'S LITERATURE such as textbooks, gardens could 'awaken an interest in botany', often redolent of moral or even religious lessons. Many gardens provide opportunities for play in games such as hide and seek and activities such as tree climbing. Edna WALLING subscribed to the view that 'Where there are children the garden should be planned for their liking, a garden where they can scamper and hide and play ball'. Children have often transformed BACKYARDS, creating their own narratives within these spaces. A fountain could become a wading pool in the heat of the summer, while a hose and sprinkler could become a fountain. Historian Geoffrey Bolton—reflecting a common experience—recalled the suburban footpath, nature strip, and street as venues for neighbourhood contests in 1930s suburban Perth: groups of children would play 'using a tree on the verge as a wicket, a picket as a bat and a tennis ball', improvising a game of cricket; pathways would likewise offer a spot for hopscotch to be chalked out.

Watering eucalypt seedlings in the harsh Northern Territory climate provides CHILDREN at Tennant Creek Preschool Centre (1959) with basic lessons in horticulture and instils the civilising ethos of SCHOOL GARDENS at an early age

In areas where constricted living conditions did not allow for backyards or access to private gardens, municipal governments sought to provide PUBLIC OPEN SPACES for children in the form of PLAYGROUNDS, often complementary to PUBLIC PARKS AND GARDENS. Authorities sought to concentrate on organised play in team games that required adherence to known rules. TENNIS COURTS and other features such as sand pits and wading pools were sometimes added, but the playgrounds consisted mainly of open areas adapted to formal play. While the playgrounds allowed slum children access to fresh air, sunshine, and activity—all contributing to improved physical health—they were also imbued with notions of MORAL IMPROVEMENT. Supervised playgrounds provided places where children could gather safely away from the perceived and genuine dangers of the street. In the more formal setting of the SCHOOL GARDEN, outdoor areas underwent significant changes over time. Paved drill grounds used for assembly and marching activities were increasingly complemented by garden plots. Vegetable and flower gardens were encouraged, the former furnishing a utilitarian lesson for children in providing for themselves. The classroom moved into the garden as an interactive teaching realm for science, botany, drawing, and agriculture. An annual ARBOR DAY, complete with ceremonial tree plantings, encouraged enhancement of school grounds. In the mid-twentieth century, an emerging emphasis on physical education led to larger areas to be set aside for RECREATION and SPORT.

Tigger Wise, *Gardens for Children* (Kenthurst, NSW, 1986)

JODI FRAWLEY

CHILDREN'S LITERATURE Until recently, children's written introduction to the plant world was mostly through their school texts. In *Australian School Science Textbooks 1850–1939: A Bibliography* (1986), Rosemary Polya has argued that specifically Australian environments began to be included in NATURE STUDY in the early 1900s. Geologist and educator Edgeworth David related this to patriotism when he stated (1905) that 'by knowing our land better, we learn to love it better'. MORAL IMPROVEMENT underpinned many texts. The introduction of agriculture and horticulture in schools witnessed the creation of small SCHOOL GARDENS— encouraged by numerous handbooks—in the belief that children's direct experimentation would foster self-realisation, and an ability to work more effectively on the land.

Many of the earliest Australian children's fiction books featured Australian birds and animals in their bush setting, partly in a belief that children had an affinity with nature, but also to inspire its conservation. Stories by Charlotte Barton, Amy MACK, and Louisa Anne MEREDITH were thinly disguised lessons in natural science. In the 1920s and 1930s, the prevailing view that stories were an effective way of imparting knowledge of and respect for the natural environment was illustrated by Kathleen Higgins, *Betty in Bushland* (1937) and Nuri Mass, *Australian Wild-Flower Fairies* (1937). From the 1920s, regular children's columns in gardening magazines, like the one by 'Uncle Dick' in *Australian Garden Lover*, encouraged children to experiment with home gardening.

The garden was often the starting point for fantasy in the stories of Ida Rentoul Outhwaite, Annie Rentoul, and Tarella Quin, although their landscapes were not recognisably Australian. Unlike these English-style fairies, the creations of May Gibbs were based on common bush plants, thereby encouraging children's fondness for their distinctive environment. In the 1950s, both Nan Chauncy and Joan Phipson depicted the harmonious Australian family in an idealised rural setting. The pioneering outback family in Phipson's *Good Luck to the Rider* (1953) rejected city life and created a tranquil, ordered garden out of the wild landscape.

Environmentalism has been the dominant theme of recent picture books that feature gardens. At the forefront has been Jeannie Baker, who explores interconnection, change, and the depletion of wilderness areas in books such as *Window* (1991) and *Where the Forest Meets the Sea* (1987). In *The Hidden Forest* (2000) two children discover the 'mysterious, hidden world' of an underwater kelp forest; the book was inspired by the real-life threat to the kelp of southern Tas. For older children Elizabeth Honey's *Fiddle-back* (1998) and Nadia Wheatley's *The Blooding* (1987) both use conflict to explore a community's attachment to the natural environment. Some recent authors have used the garden theme more metaphorically, to represent children's adaptability to their environment. In Libby Hathorn's *Stephen's Tree* (1979), Stephen's BACKYARD eucalypt flourishes, despite being located in a populous industrial area. TREES have also been used to symbolise strength and renewal, as in Junko Morimoto Kenju's *Forest* (1989), where trees planted by a young boy, much to the ridicule of his village, later become a source of happiness and serenity. In Gary Crew and Shaun Tan's *Memorial* (1999), a Moreton Bay Fig planted after the First World War and now threatened with removal represents the community's living memories.

Rosemary Polya, *Australian School Science Textbooks 1850–1939: A Bibliography* (Bundoora, Vic., 1986); Marcie Muir, *A Bibliography of Australian Children's Books* (2 vols., London and Melbourne, 1970 and 1976); Marcie Muir, *A History of Australian Children's Book Illustration* (Melbourne, 1982)

JEANNINE BAKER

CHINA At present there are few examples of typical Chinese gardens in Australia, the most elaborate and authentic to date being the Garden of Friendship at Sydney's Darling Harbour (1988), designed by the Guangdong Landscape Bureau in Guangzhou. Chinese influences on design and ornamentation have been expressed a little more widely—as, for example, at ERYLDENE (NSW) and in more diffuse examples of general ORIENTAL INFLUENCE.

Although China has had little effect on garden design in Australia, Chinese (and other ASIAN) plants have had a very great impact. Until recently, most of these plants arrived via Europe, having been taken there beginning in the late eighteenth and early nineteenth centuries from Guangzhou, the only port to which, from 1757 on, foreign merchants were allowed access. Following the Opium Wars of 1839–42 and 1856–60, China was obliged to open up most of the country to Westerners, with the result that the richness of the native flora began to be recognised and the great era of plant hunting in China began, with Robert Fortune, E.H. Wilson, George Forrest, and Reginald Farrer being perhaps the best known enthusiasts.

While Chinese plants collected in the wild are grown widely in Australian gardens, the most common are those from Chinese gardens and nurseries—the product of more than 2000 years of Chinese horticultural endeavour. Among the best known are the flowering peaches (*Prunus persica*), tree and herbaceous peonies (*Paeonia suffruticosa* and *P. lactiflora*), flowering quinces (*Chaenomeles speciosa*), wisteria (*Wisteria sinensis*), hibiscuses (*Hibiscus rosa-sinensis*, *H. mutabilis* and *H. syriacus*), and crabapples (*Malus halliana* and *M. spectabilis*). Other Chinese garden plants that have greatly influenced our gardens include CAMELLIAS (*Camellia japonica* and *C. reticulata*), cumquats (*Fortunella japonica*), evergreen azaleas (forms of *Rhododendron X pulchrum* and *R. simii*), CHRYSANTHEMUMS, forsythias (*Forsythia suspensa* and *F. viridissima*), *Rosa banksiae*, *Gardenia augusta*, magnolias (*Magnolia denudata* and *M. liliiflora*), *Murraya paniculata*, daylilies (*Hemerocallis fulva* and *H. lilio-asphodelus*), and *Anemone hupehensis*.

The first Chinese plants known to have been sent to Australia were the oranges, peaches, nectarines, tea plants,

Christmas trees

This advertisement by Sydney seed merchants ANDERSON & Co. in the *Chinese Australian Herald* (1910) was directed at Chinese MARKET GARDENERS, who were among the most enthusiastic customers for vegetable seeds at this time

and ginkgo nuts (*Ginkgo biloba*), which Joseph BANKS had arranged to be taken on board by the First Fleet in 1787. Whether these plants survived the journey and became established is not known, but following this and subsequent importations all these—except perhaps the ginkgo—became established in the early years. Tea and the white mulberry (*Morus alba*), which Banks had sent 'for silkworms', were growing in 1798; peaches and apricots were offered for sale by George SUTTOR in 1804, and other Chinese plants arrived in the early years of the nineteenth century, some directly from China. For instance, John Reeves and Thomas Beale were responsible for sending more than thirty plants from Guangzhou and Macao to Charles FRASER at SYDNEY BOTANIC GARDENS. Included were the ginkgo, tea, two forms of *Camellia japonica*, *Hibiscus rosa-sinensis* and *H. mutabilis*, and a number of useful and ornamental citrus, all of which arrived between 1821 and 1826. *Wisteria sinensis* was probably introduced by Alexander MCLEAY, who had grown it in England and subsequently had it in his Sydney garden, Elizabeth Bay House, along with mandarins, several varieties of lychee, and other plants he had received from China. And by the middle of the nineteenth century Australian nurseries were listing many varieties of Chinese ornamental plants.

Chinese MARKET GARDENING became established in Australia during and after the gold rushes as a result of Chinese migration from the 1850s. It has persisted ever since, expanding in recent times as a result of renewed migration and the rise in popularity of Chinese vegetables generally.

Maggie Keswick, *The Chinese Garden: History, Art, and Architecture* (London, 1978); Peter Valder, *The Garden Plants of China* (Sydney, 1999)

PETER VALDER

CHISHOLM, Nerine Neil (1893–1962), garden designer, studied horticulture at Melbourne's BURNLEY School of Primary Agriculture and Horticulture during 1928–29. She ran a successful garden design business from the 1930s to the 1950s: John STEVENS was a one-time employee. In 1955, the Melbourne *Age* described her joy in designing gardens for 'new Australian' (MIGRANT) gardeners, many of whom had not previously managed a SUBURBAN GARDEN and may have known only European apartment blocks. 'New Australian gardeners take the keenest interest in the native Australian plants', she commented. Chisholm's book *Australian Gardens, Their Planning and Making* (1949) achieved considerable popularity but was overshadowed by the writings of her colleague Edna WALLING. Documented garden schemes of this intense and knowledgeable designer await recognition.

HELEN BOTHAM

CHRIST CHURCH, Longford, Tas., especially the ornamental landscape with its collection of mature trees, is a local landmark, one of few botanically diverse public or INSTITUTIONAL collections outside the state's public parks and botanic garden. The churchyard setting, dating from *c*. 1829, includes a burial ground (containing the ARCHER family vault) and decorative LICH-GATE (1936: architect Louis Williams).

FRANCINE GILFEDDER

CHRISTIE, Hugh Watson (1860–1927), natural history enthusiast, museum collector, and gardener, worked as head lighthouse keeper in the NORTHERN TERRITORY at Point Charles (1893–1917) and Cape Don (1917–25). Despite poor soil, extended dry seasons, the ravages of white ants, and a cyclone (1897), he successfully cultivated tropical fruit and vegetable gardens at Point Charles (pineapples, bananas, pawpaws, limes, melons, coconuts) and experimented with native timbers (kapok) and fibre plants (including cotton), with the assistance of local Aboriginal people. In 1906 and 1908 Christie was awarded gold medals for his collection of NATURAL HISTORY specimens at the Christchurch (New Zealand) and Franco-British Exhibitions.

Kathleen A. Mitchell, *The Christie Families Histories* (Adelaide, 1988)

ANITA ANGEL

CHRISTMAS TREES Much of the uniqueness of an Australian Christmas derives from the bizarre inversion of northern hemisphere rituals transplanted to the southern hemisphere, with its radically different CLIMATE. Fairy lights twinkle on roof-gutters long before the summer sun sets, while true devotees paint hastily fixed or recalcitrant juvenile holly berries with red nail polish for an authentic table centre-piece. To complement the fake snow and roof-top reindeer, a lopped plantation pine (*Pinus radiata*) is purchased from a roadside stall or greengrocer's shop for decoration and display inside a front window of the home. Derived from European, and particularly German, traditions, the decorated Christmas tree was given royal approbation by Queen Victoria and her German-born consort, Prince Albert, at Christmas 1848. A eucalypt bough tied beside a doorway constituted an early Australian form of Christmas decoration, although despite the spectacular landscape contributions made by *Brachychiton acerifolius* (Illawarra Flame Tree), *Eucalyptus ficifolia* (Red-flowering Gum), *Ceratopetalum gummiferum* (Christmas Bush), and *Metrosideros excelsa* (New Zealand Christmas Tree or Pohutukawa)—all of which flower in handsome yuletide shades—the pine is yet to be usurped as the Christmas norm.

KAREN OLSEN and ROWAN WILKEN

CHRONICLE: see SOUTH AUSTRALIAN CHRONICLE

CHRYSANTHEMUMS, herbaceous perennials introduced from their native CHINA and INDIA to Europe from 1794, were present in early Australian colonial gardens, valued for their impressive flowering qualities, ease of cultivation, and suitability to pot culture. Climatically closer to their wild origins in Australia than in Britain, chrysanthemums were particularly valued in FLORICULTURE for their May–July blooms 'while the majority of Flora's embellishments are in a state of nihility'. The writer, Luke WOOFF (1865), also thought them 'one of the gayest and most useful of our garden flowers' but undeservedly neglected; indeed, they were not mentioned in Adamson's *Australian Gardener* (1875 edition). A sharp rise in popularity during the 1890s was perhaps influenced by a reawakened interest in JAPANESE and oriental cultures, but was firmly associated with the expertise and publicity ventures of Melbourne gardener Thomas POCKETT. Increased availability of new varieties brought a new competitive edge to the species, and special sections and even whole shows were devoted to the chrysanthemum. Charles Bennett's *Practical Treatise on the Culture of the Chrysanthemum* (1890) and Pockett's *Essay on the Cultivation of the Chrysanthemum, with a List of Selected Varieties* (1891) were early Australian guides, while garden handbooks of the 1890s, such as H.A. James's *Hand-Book of Australian Horticulture* (1892) and William Elliott's *Australasian Gardening* (1897) gave extensive advice. Although ROSES soon regained ground against their young rival, and CARNATIONS rose in horticultural esteem, chrysanthemums maintained a prominent position, especially in bedding displays in PUBLIC GARDENS, among the HORTICULTURAL SOCIETY fraternity, on the SHOW table, and as cut flowers.

RA

CHURCHILL, David Maughan (b. 1933), botanist and botanic gardens director, born in WA, had an academic career in the Botany Department, Monash University (Vic.), before his appointment as Director of the ROYAL BOTANIC GARDENS, MELBOURNE (1971–85). He maintained a strong interest in vegetation survey work, and under his directorship commenced a COMPUTER-based record and mapping system for the Gardens, which enhanced the scientific evaluation of its living plant collections and assisted with the management and INTERPRETATION of this collection. A key taxonomic interest has been the genus *Borya*, species of which are predominantly found in WA.

ML

CINTRA, Maitland, NSW, retains a large and representative late nineteenth-century VILLA GARDEN (now reduced at the rear) planned to complement the town's grandest ITALIANATE villa (*c.* 1880), designed by local architect William Pender for the Cohen family. The unusual heart-shaped carriage drive, terracotta and cast-iron urns used as garden ornaments, and a squared path layout related to the residence and its central placement on the generous allotment, all add formality to the garden, otherwise softened by shrubberies and typical colonial-era plantings of *Schinus molle* (Pepper Tree) and olives.

COLLEEN MORRIS

CITY BEAUTIFUL MOVEMENT The idea of beautifying buildings, precincts, and cities endures from colonial improvement schemes through to contemporary 'tidy towns' campaigns and URBAN DESIGN projects. The phrase 'city beautiful' as a catchphrase for environmental amelioration entered the professional lexicon with the rise of the modern TOWN PLANNING movement in the early 1900s. This connected with international-cum-imperial impulses toward better civic design and most directly with the heyday of the American City Beautiful Movement, which peaked with Daniel Burnham's Plan of Chicago (1909). Ultimately deemed impractical, partial, and socially regressive, the ethos lingered from the 1920s as one component of comprehensive planning dealing with 'civic art and amenities'.

Urban reformers such as John Fitzgerald in Sydney and W.E. BOLD in Perth saw Australian architecture, planning, and landscape design as inferior by international standards. Cities lacked grand public spaces and VISTAS; riverbanks and waterfronts were being despoiled; street awnings and advertising signs were ugly; monuments were lacking; and 'skyscrapers' were creating havoc with the cohesive skyline inherited from the Victorian era. There was an overall lack of spatial order and aesthetic unity. More attractive cityscapes were linked not just with uplifting people's lives and sense of citizenship but boosting economic and tourism growth. The impulse was more ideological than technical, but a consistent package of public investments was invoked: new city approaches, PUBLIC PARKS and gardens, parkways, improved street furniture, beautification of utilitarian structures, and public buildings in dignified settings, preferably grouped into civic centres.

Many more proposals were mooted than were realised; street parade decorations for nationalistic celebrations continued to hint at more permanent improvements. Walter Burley and Marion Mahony GRIFFIN's 1912 design for CANBERRA assimilated many influences but demonstrably

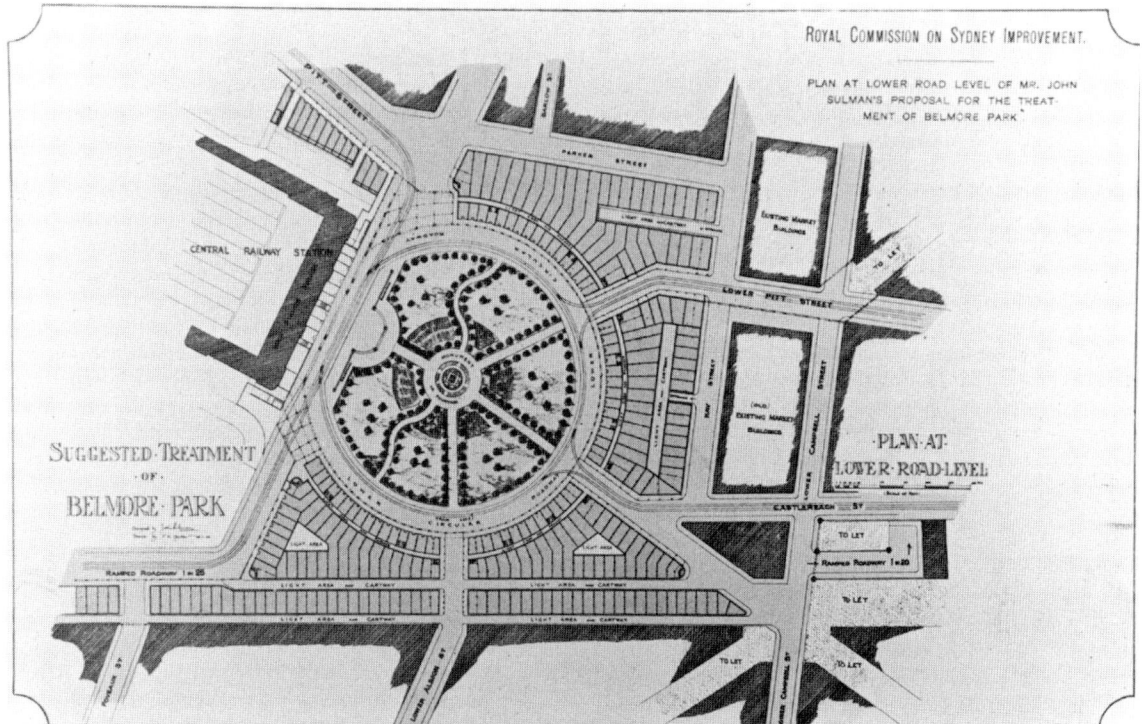

Suggested treatment by John SULMAN for Belmore Park from the report of the Royal Commission on the Improvement of Sydney and its Suburbs (1909), illustrating CITY BEAUTIFUL features such as axial VISTAS, resolution of previously haphazard planning, and a focus on major public buildings

envisaged a monumental city with grand axes and ensembles of public institutions in the city beautiful idiom. Although the Royal Commission on the Improvement of Sydney and its Suburbs (1908–09) codified an overall package of decorative public works, the established capital cities ignored suggestions for expert art commissions and relied on *ad hoc* beautification schemes endorsed by city councils, local authorities, and government boards. POLITICAL and financial obstacles dogged the most ambitious schemes, so tangible achievements were modest. Notable products include Forrest Place (Perth), ANZAC SQUARE (Brisbane), and the Shrine of Remembrance in Melbourne's DOMAIN. The layout and built character of JOHNSTONE PARK (Geelong) and HYDE PARK (Sydney) decisively record the FORMALITY of the city beautiful ideal. Anzac Parade (Sydney) and St Kilda Road (Melbourne) were transformed into attractive city gateway BOULEVARDS. A more diffuse city beautiful aesthetic of symmetry, homogeneity, and neo-classicism can also be read into the inter-war design of commercial offices and public buildings and the master plans for DESIGNED LANDSCAPES such as campuses and model suburbs. ROBERT FREESTONE

CITY PARK, Launceston, Tas., a PUBLIC PARK of outstanding historical interest, has been a focus for horticultural and botanical pursuits, and public recreation, since the first decade of the nineteenth century. Eminent figures associated with the early development of the site include Ronald GUNN and Sir John and Lady FRANKLIN, but City Park owes much to William MCGOWAN, under whom it acquired most of its present form. The eastern half was developed from *c.* 1808 as the site of Government Cottage and the Government Gardens, which utilised a regular squared layout. The western half was occupied from 1841 by the Launceston Horticultural Society and functioned as a BOTANIC GARDEN and semi-private pleasure garden. The dolphin fountain (*c.* 1859), a Crimean War cannon, and possibly a venerable pear tree, survive from this period.

In 1863 the gardens were taken over by the municipal authorities to become a public park. In addition to regular horticultural exhibitions and botanical labelling of trees, permanent ZOOLOGICAL exhibits were incorporated, and provision made for regular musical performances. The park survives as a remarkable example of late Victorian and Edwardian design, with much of its distinctive character derived from surviving structural elements. These include elaborate wrought-iron Coronation Gates (1902–03) and high perimeter fence (1907–15), exquisite 'Queen Anne' gate lodge (1887–89) in the manner of Nesfield's at KEW GARDENS, cast-iron drinking fountain (1887–97), war memorial (1904), and bandstand (1908), as well as the eminently Victorian Albert Hall, a large exhibition building inserted in the north-west corner in 1891. Twentieth-century additions include a Dutch Garden (1921) and a conservatory (1932), modelled after that in Melbourne's FITZROY GARDENS. The Japanese

macaque colony occupies ground used for permanent zoological exhibits since at least 1880. The park layout and planting is broadly GARDENESQUE, with wide paths through sweeping lawns. Mature specimen trees include elms, *Quercus suber* (Cork-oak), *Araucaria* sp., *Cedrus* sp., *Sequoia sempervirens* (Californian Redwood), and *Pinus pinea* (Stone Pine). Some formal flower beds are retained, and the extensive rock-edged shrubbery on the southern boundary with its associated long bench and gravel walk (1908) remains a favoured resort of park visitors.
ANNE NEALE

CIVIC TRUST OF SOUTH AUSTRALIA (1969–), community action group, was formed as a response to community concern in Adelaide over inappropriate building and development on the ADELAIDE HILLS' face in the 1960s. Modelled on the English Civic Trust, it established a system of civic awards and brickbats to applaud or criticise development proposals and projects. In seeking to promote quality design, the Trust became a vehicle for public debate about URBAN DESIGN issues in SA.
DAVID JONES

CLAREMONT, Newtown, Vic., in suburban Geelong, retains a VILLA GARDEN of the Federation period. Originally designed and laid out between 1901 and the 1920s by owner and keen amateur gardener Alexander William Gray (1869–1954), it combined geometric and naturalistic elements in its planting and layout. Claremont has since been meticulously maintained, with few changes, by family members. Annuals and bulbs are still ribbon-planted in extensive front garden beds. The typical complement of garden buildings and structures includes a glasshouse, shade-house, potting shed, cold frames, pergolas, and compost bins.
SUZANNE HUNT

CLAREMONT, Tas.: see LUTANA, Tas.

CLARENDON, Nile, Tas., an estate, granted to James Cox in 1819, originally comprised 2400 hectares. The present house dates from 1838, when the grounds were laid out in the English landscape style favoured by the colonial gentry, featuring an extensive DEER PARK stocked with animals imported by Cox, a lagoon, and an elm avenue. Cox's wife, Eliza, superintended the layout and planting of the gardens surrounding the house: the carriage drive, overlooked by a grand portico, was laid out in lawns and shrubberies, while brick-edged paths criss-crossed the more formal garden at the rear. The original kitchen garden was partly enclosed by outbuildings, and is now planted as a formal flower garden. The house and garden were taken over by the NATIONAL TRUST in 1962, and much of the garden was reconstructed in the 1970s and 1980s after documentation by James BROADBENT.
LINDY SCRIPPS

CLARK, Alister (1864–1949), plant-breeder and versatile sportsman, may be the only person who has received Britain's highest awards for breeding both ROSES (the Dean Hole Memorial Medal, 1936) and DAFFODILS (Peter Barr Memorial Cup, 1948). It was however, his father, **Walter Clark** (1803–1873), who with his wife Annie (*née* Cooper), planted the garden round the great bluestone house **Glenara**, which lies on a shelf of the steep boulder-strewn slopes below Bulla (Vic.). Alister came into possession of the estate by chance since his elder brother, Walter Clark junior, was over-extended financially when the property came up for sale in 1887.

Walter had arrived in Sydney in 1837 with his first wife, Margaret (*née* McKindlay), who died in the quarantine station. He was taken under the wing of the MACLEAY family, and grew rich after becoming manager and part-owner of Macleay properties, including Tubbo, in the Riverina. From these, cattle fed the exploding population of the Victorian goldfields. Walter moved to Melbourne, and before Glenara was built (1857–58), he lived at the fashionable waterfront suburb of St Kilda, where Annie Cooper ran a girls school with her sister. Annie was more than thirty when she married Walter, and it is perhaps not surprising that she never recovered from the birth of her fifth child, Jessie, and died in 1865. The other four children were Aggie (1858), Walter John (1859), Annie (1861), and Alister (1864).

The garden at Glenara was strongly influenced by the siting of the homestead on a benched knoll, dramatically overlooking Deep Creek. Walter kept the invoices (now held by the Royal Botanic Gardens, Melbourne) of all his plant purchases between 1857 and 1872; these show an enormous variety of plants, including thirty-one different roses and fourteen grapes, sourced from leading Melbourne nurseries. His was among the first vineyards planted in Vic. There is evidence that Clark's architects, PURCHAS and Swyer, also assisted in forming garden features around the house, including the fine ITALIANATE balustrading. A TOWER, added in 1872, provided a panoramic view, which had earlier been skilfully portrayed by artist Eugene von GUÉRARD (1867). The garden owed much of its ambience to that of the Macleays' Elizabeth Bay House in Sydney, especially as described by Thomas SHEPHERD in the 1830s.

In 1873, Walter Clark died as result of a buggy accident and the children were left orphans; Walter John was 14, a boy at Scotch College, and his first cousin, John Kerr Clark, was appointed guardian, with the proviso that their father's estate should not be distributed until the youngest of the family, Jessie, turned 21. When that time came (1886), it was found that John Kerr had embezzled much of the money and he was taken back to Scotland, an alcoholic, by Wat Clark, who had married Alister's sister Annie.

Meanwhile, Alister had been to school, first in Hobart, then in England, and at Loretto School in Scotland. From there, he went up to Jesus College, Cambridge, where he became President of the Australian Club and entertained the Australian Test Cricket team. During the voyage back to Australia in 1887, Alister met a wealthy New Zealand family, the Rhodes of Christchurch. Shortly after, he was able to buy 800 acres (325 ha) of Glenara from his father's estate, and he and Jessie went on a walking tour in the South Island of New Zealand, where in 1888 he married Edith (Edie) Rhodes while Jessie married her brother, Heaton, an even more versatile man than his brother-in-law.

Walter CLARK's homestead Glenara, Bulla (Vic.), photographed by Charles Nettleton (c. 1867), showing the splendid ITALIANATE terrace overlooking Deep Creek contrasting with sweeping lawns, conifer-filled shrubberies, and the flanking vineyard and orchard

Putting a manager in Glenara, Alister and Edie Clark went to England, so that Alister could complete his degree in law at Cambridge. During this period, he met well-known gardeners and nursery proprietors, especially those interested in roses and daffodils. It was 1898 before they took up permanent residence at Glenara. In 1897 Clark had joined a syndicate, including Thomas Hanbury (creator of the famous Riviera garden of La Mortola) and Ellen Willmott (of Warley Place), which bought the stock of daffodil BULBS bred by the Rev. G.H. Engleheart. Back in Australia, Clark bought half the stock of a bulb collection made by English Shakespearean actor, George TITHERADGE, who in order to clear up confusion about nomenclature of daffodils, had ordered from Peter BARR bulbs of all named varieties. These bulbs for their BREEDING programs Clark shared with his friend, Leonard Buckland, a solicitor of Camperdown (Vic.), whose exhibits at the important daffodil shows up to the First World War generally beat Clark's. It was he who bred 'Pink 'Un' (illustrated in the *Daffodil Year Book* of 1915), which may well have been the first pink daffodil ever bred. The best known of Clark's daffodils is probably 'Mabel Taylor', still in commerce and used for breeding.

For his roses, Alister Clark aimed to produce varieties suitable for Australian conditions, flowering early and late and needing little water. For his original stock, he commissioned two British nurseries to send him every one of the garden roses that William ROBINSON had named 'great' in his book *The English Flower Garden* (1883), but he drew on many sources, especially the French nursery of Nabonnand, on the Riviera; *Rosa gigantea* was a favourite. Unfortunately, the notebook in which he detailed records of his breeding programs was left in the garden and destroyed. His best known roses include 'Sunny South' (1918), 'Black Boy' (1919), 'Lorraine Lee' (1924), and 'Nancy Hayward' (1937).

Alister Clark was also the founder of the Moonee Valley Race Club, a polo-player, golfer, and Master of the Oaklands Hunt. After his death, racegoers and gardeners from all over Australia financed a MEMORIAL rose garden in ST KILDA BOTANIC GARDENS. In the 1980s, Susan IRVINE resolved to rediscover lost rose varieties—of which he introduced about 200, many (especially those released during the Second World War) now lost—and has found more than fifty. Since 1957 Glenara has been managed by the Rundle family and remains one of Australia's outstanding historic gardens.

T.R. Garnett, *Man of Roses: Alister Clark of Glenara and His Family* (Kenthurst, NSW, 1990)   T.R. GARNETT

CLARKE, Francis Grenville (Frank) (1879–1955), parliamentarian, company director, and horticulturist, was born into the privileged Clarke family of RUPERTSWOOD, Sunbury (Vic.), son of Sir William John Clarke and Janet Marion Clarke (*née* Snodgrass). The young Frank grew up shortly after Rupertswood had been landscaped by William SANGSTER. He inherited a substantial sum on his father's death in 1897, and was prominent in banking and mercantile companies. He was elected to the Legislative Council in 1913, representing various Provinces until his death. Personally—as an ardent horticulturist and nearby resident—and officially—as Minister for Lands and Public Works—he was keenly interested in the MELBOURNE BOTANIC GARDENS, later becoming a member of its Advisory Committee. Clarke published his popular work *In the Botanic Gardens, Melbourne: Their History, Art and Design, with Stories of the Trees* in 1924, with enlarged editions in 1938 and 1944. In it Clarke jokingly proposed a 'League for the Removal of Rotten Round Beds on Lawns' although he was forced to admit that his hero William GUILFOYLE had introduced similar beds. Clarke later channelled his horticultural energies into the Royal Horticultural Society of Victoria (of which he was a long-time president) and his MOUNT MACEDON garden. His garden design ethos was described in an article 'Landscape Gardening' in the *RHSV Year Book* (1943). RA

CLARSON, William (*c.* 1830–1890) horticulturist, printer, and journalist, was born at Tamworth, Warwickshire, England. He arrived in Melbourne in the early 1850s, becoming a member of the Victorian Institute for the Advancement of Science in 1854. He was very active in early printers' union affairs, especially as proprietor and editor of the *Australian Typographical Circular* (1858–60), held to be the earliest labour journal in the colony. In 1859 he joined with Joseph Shallard, Joseph Gibb, and Alfred Massina as a founding partner of the printing firm Clarson, Shallard and Co. (later A.H. Massina and Co.).

As a keen amateur horticulturist, Clarson was elected a member of the Victorian Gardeners' Mutual Improvement Society in 1861. A year later he was elected treasurer of the Melbourne-based Apiarian Society. He was a member of the Horticultural Society of Victoria and in 1868 declined its presidency; Clarson was credited by the *Leader* with the revival of the Society's fortunes following a period of low esteem in the mid-1860s. In 1868 he was appointed to the prestigious position of honorary director of the Society's experimental garden at BURNLEY. Clarson was also interested in the founding of Alfred Hospital, but his eccentric wife, Caroline, began to shower attention upon the hospital's Dr John Blair, whose engagement and subsequent marriage to Mary Hunter changed her devoted friendship to shrewish enmity, manifested in poison pen letters. Blair did not press a libel suit, but Clarson and his wife launched a prosecution of their own. The case opened in 1872, but when there was found to be no case to answer, the misled Clarson, resigning his position at Burnley, abruptly left Melbourne.

Clarson was for many years on the staff of the Sydney *Daily Telegraph*. He was also a contributor, generally anonymous, to journals such as the *Australasian*, *Leader*, and *Illustrated Sydney News*. This material formed the basis of his three horticultural handbooks: *The Fruit Garden* (1878), *The Flower Garden and Shrubbery* (1885), and *The Kitchen Garden and Cottager's Manual* (1886), all of which ran to numerous editions. Clarson went bankrupt in 1888, and early the following year moved from Sydney to take up a position as keeper of the garden and nursery at the newly established Longerenong Agricultural College (Vic.). Later that year he went to Mildura, where he operated as an independent seed merchant and also ran an EXPERIMENTAL GARDEN in conjunction with the newspaper *Mildura Cultivator*, graduating from producing two or three articles a week to acting as editor. He gave lengthy evidence before the Royal Commission on Vegetable Products (*Eighth Progress Report*, 1890), advocating the culture of plants from tropical and semi-tropical regions, especially the pistachio, peanut, carob bean, and *Phoenix dactylifera* (Date Palm).

Clarson, 'distressed by troubles of a private character', committed suicide at Mildura on 30 December 1890; his pathetic note read 'Quite overwhelmed, mind gone, no hope, friendless'—a tragic loss of one of Australia's most versatile horticulturists. RA

CLELAND, George Fullerton (1852–1931), wine merchant, was apprenticed to his uncle, Samuel DAVENPORT, before establishing G.F. Cleland and Co. in 1883. Initially based at BEAUMONT, later expanded at Tanunda, in the BAROSSA VALLEY, the company specialised in wine, spirits, and olive oil. Renowned as an expert on VITICULTURE, Cleland gave long service to industry bodies and to the Royal Agricultural and Horticultural Society of South Australia. His nephew (Sir) **John Burton Cleland** (1878–1971), pathologist and naturalist, made a remarkable contribution to botany, natural science, ornithology, and Aboriginal anthropology in SA. Cleland researched ecological aspects of Aboriginal life and as a 'discriminating plant explorer', he collected and wrote extensively on botany. He served as a commissioner of (BELAIR) NATIONAL PARK (1928–65) among many professional and community interests, and was honoured by naming of the genus *Clelandia* and Cleland Conservation Park in the ADELAIDE HILLS. DAVID JONES

CLIMATE Every PLANT in cultivation has its origins in the wild, even though some have been HYBRIDISED and manipulated in cultivation over long periods. In nature, every plant occupies a particular habitat (the natural range of the species), characterised by properties such as SOIL fertility and climate. Plants develop physiological responses to the climates of their original locations. These responses include such things as varying levels of water stress tolerance or cold tolerance, or requirements for particular temperature regimes for growth and reproduction. The horticulturist takes plants from their area of origin and attempts to grow them in new locations. One of the critical factors for success will be how closely the climate of the new location matches the original location. Early Australian horticulturists were active in ACCLIMATISATION, the evaluation of imported plant material for growth under Australian conditions.

There has always been an element of challenge for some gardeners in attempting to grow plants in areas that are at the limits of their climatic tolerance. A simple example is the use of IRRIGATION to allow plants to survive in ARID areas where natural rainfall does not provide adequate supplies of soil moisture. Other, more complex, strategies include using

GREENHOUSES to modify the temperature regime that a particular location provides, or selecting a sheltered location to reduce the severity of winter cold. By contrast, other gardeners will argue that it is preferable to use plants that are climatically suited to the location of the garden, as that is more likely to give rise to sustainable plantings.

The major climatic variables of concern to the gardener or horticulturist will influence either available moisture or temperature responses. For available moisture, the major factor is rainfall: both total annual falls and seasonal distribution. Higher rainfalls generally allow the gardener to grow plants that are less tolerant of water stress, and a simple classification of climate would use total annual rainfall as a measure of water availability. But the other factor that needs to be considered is the rate at which plants use soil moisture. For example, the WAITE Index, developed at the University of Adelaide during the first half of the twentieth century, rates the available moisture throughout the year by calculating a ratio of rainfall and evaporation.

In the Australian gardening context, the climatic extremes caused by the El Niño Southern Oscillation (ENSO) must also be taken into account. Much of Australia is very dry by world standards, and the variation in rainfall—in particular the severe drought events associated with ENSO—have had an enormous impact on Australia. Some authors, such as Tim Flannery in *The Future Eaters* (1994), argue that the very nature of Australia's flora and fauna was determined by ENSO-induced drought. While ENSO has only been formally described in relatively recent times, the effect of ENSO drought is evident throughout the history of European occupation of Australia. Certainly several ventures to develop marginal farm land for cropping failed as a result of ENSO drought, and the devastating Black Friday (1939), Ash Wednesday (1983), and Sydney (1994) bushfires occurred at the end of ENSO drought periods. In terms of plant selection for Australian gardens, tolerance of periodic severe drought is probably an essential selection criterion.

Low temperatures are of interest for two reasons. In many deciduous species, the breaking of winter dormancy comes as a result of the exposure of the dormant buds to a period of low temperature (called a chilling requirement). Successful cultivation of apples, for instance, requires that the winter be cold enough for the plant to experience a minimum of 1000 hours below 7°C to break bud dormancy. The initiation of flower structures in many spring-flowering BULBS is also dependent on the bulb experiencing adequate chilling after planting.

The other effect of low temperatures on plants is that of low-temperature injury, which is often one of the factors that limits the cultivation of a species in some locations. In TROPICAL species, low-temperature injury can occur at temperatures above freezing, but more usually we are concerned about temperatures at or below freezing point. Freezing of plant tissues causes serious and permanent injury. Depending on the low-temperature tolerance of the species, freezing injury can occur at 0°C or at lower temperatures. Many low-altitude Australian plants are only able to tolerate temperatures a few degrees below zero, while species from higher altitudes have much better freezing tolerance. However, given that Australia is a relatively warm continent, even plants from very high altitudes are not as HARDY as species from colder parts of the world. The successful cultivation of EUCALYPTUS in Europe, for example, is limited to a few species, and to the warmer locations. Plant species from higher latitudes and altitudes are much hardier: some *Betula* species, for instance, are capable of tolerating air temperatures of -40°C or so.

In addition to varying with respect to cold, climates also vary in terms of how warm they are. Each plant species has a temperature range in which its growth will be most successful. This range will obviously be higher in tropical plants than in plants native to ALPINE areas. At temperatures lower than the optimum for a species, plant growth processes will occur more slowly and may be unsatisfactory. Flowering responses in particular are very sensitive to this effect. On the other hand, in temperature ranges higher than the optimum, plant growth will also decrease, primarily because the rate of the photosynthetic reaction is reduced more rapidly at high temperatures than is the respiratory reaction. Plants are rarely exposed to temperatures high enough to kill them outright, but because of the imbalance described above, being grown in a climate that is too warm will result in reduced performance and possibly a slow death by carbohydrate exhaustion.

Because of the importance of matching plant tolerances and garden climate, one goal of horticulture is the production of climate classification schemes that allow the gardener to make sensible plant choices. Some of the schemes that have been developed have been relatively simple, reflecting very significant climatic limitations. Probably the best-known example of this type is the USDA Climate Zones for North America, based on winter minimum temperature—cold-hardiness being such an important element of plant selection in that climate. In the Australian context, some measure of likely water stress is frequently cited as being a more appropriate primary index for comparing climates. Better climate classifications will incorporate a number of elements, as plant performance at a location is usually always influenced by multiple factors. The most recently published scheme for Australia is that devised by T.R. GARNETT in *A Gardener's Guide to the Climate Zones of Australia* (1996), where zones are defined by a combination of total annual rainfall, winter minimum temperature, and summer heat. This system is a useful advance over previous systems, and will undoubtedly be discussed and refined further. To complement this scheme, it will be essential to begin to match plant tolerance against climate zones to allow plant selections to be based on this or similar classifications.

PETER MAY

CLIMBING PLANTS have festooned Australian VERANDAHS, FENCES, ARBOURS, and PERGOLAS since the earliest days of European settlement; exotic climbers such as ROSES, clematis, wisteria, and plumbago are well suited to the CLIMATE. Some favourites, such as *Hedera helix* (Ivy), *Lonicera japonica* (Japanese Honeysuckle), *Macfadenia unguis-cati* (Cat's Claw Vine), *Thunbergia grandiflora* (Blue Thunbergia), and *Dipogon lignosus* (Dolichos) have also become environmental WEEDS. Native AUSTRALIAN PLANTS such as Hardenbergia,

Kennedia, and Hibbertia have been widely planted as climbers. Elizabeth LINTON's book *Some Good Climbing Plants* (1911) was the first exclusively devoted to the subject in Australia, although this LANDSCAPE PLANT TYPE formed a common subject in garden books. In contemporary landscapes, climbers have become useful for providing a mass of vegetation in ROOF GARDENS, where minimal weight for plant and soil is required. They are also increasingly used for growing over structures to reduce heat loads (thus conserving energy) on adjoining buildings and also within URBAN DESIGN projects as *jardins verticaux* (vertical gardens).

RA and ML

CLOUGH, Richard (b. 1921), architect, landscape architect, and educator, was born at Wagga Wagga, NSW, and graduated in architecture at the University of Sydney (1947). He left for London in 1949, encouraged by E.G. WATERHOUSE to study LANDSCAPE ARCHITECTURE, which he did at University College (1950). He worked with Sylvia CROWE on the landscape of Basildon New Town (1954–56), being strongly influenced by her ECOLOGICAL approach to landscape design.

Returning to Australia, he was employed as an architect in Sydney (1956–59) until he took up a position in the National Capital Development Commission, CANBERRA. He was the first landscape architect to be employed by the Commission and remained there until 1981, holding various positions culminating in the directorship of the Landscape and Environment Branch. His landscape planning works included Woden, Weston Creek, and Belconnen, and parts of Tuggeranong and Gungahlin. Major landscape design projects included Anzac Parade, Parkes Place extensions, National Library of Australia, GOVERNMENT HOUSE grounds extensions, Lake Burley Griffin and surrounding parklands, Lake Ginninderra, and Scrivener, Bendora, Corin, and Googong Dams. As a consultant he advised on the landscape design of several school grounds and UNIVERSITY CAMPUSES including The King's School, Parramatta, NSW (with C.E. LANE-POOLE); Macquarie University, Sydney; and the Chancellor's Garden, University of Sydney; and (with Lindsay PRYOR), Flinders University, Adelaide; and La Trobe University, Melbourne. He has also been involved in the design of private gardens—in particular, redevelopment over several decades at NOOROO. He worked with others for the formation of an AUSTRALIAN INSTITUTE OF LANDSCAPE ARCHITECTS and served as its second president (1969–71).

In 1981 Clough was appointed Professor of Landscape Architecture and Head of School of Landscape Architecture, University of New South Wales, a position he held until his retirement in 1986. He has devoted considerable energy to building an outstanding library of Australian gardening books. A modest but genial colleague and mentor to many, his professional achievements have been recognised by numerous fellowships and awards, notably the Australian Award in Landscape Architecture of the Australian Institute of Landscape Architects (1994).

CRAIG BURTON

COFFEE, John Francis (Frank) (*c*. 1852–1929), company director and horticulturist, was born in Warsaw, New York State (USA), and began his career as a journalist, including a stint with the *New York Herald*. He arrived in Sydney in 1881 and started business as a publisher and indentor. McNeil and Coffee published Jonathan Periam's *The Pictorial Home and Farm Manual … with special information in the best and most approved methods of cultivation of all farm and garden products* (1885), an American text 'adapted to the Australasian Colonies' by R.W. Emerson MACIVOR. Coffee travelled extensively, being an early member of the Circumnavigators' Club (New York), and wrote *Forty Years on the Pacific* (1920). He was an enthusiastic horticulturist, and established a nursery garden at Wahroonga that he controlled for fifteen years. He imported many fruit varieties from New York hybridist Luther Burbank—notably the Valencia orange. Coffee provided an atypical American influence at a time when Australia's links with Britain were still largely unchallenged.

RA

COLAC BOTANIC GARDENS, Vic., on a sixteen-hectare site beside Lake Colac, was reserved in 1865. Daniel BUNCE was responsible for the initial planting and design (1868), with a carriage DRIVE later embellished by early curators Josiah Capes Reeve (1874–77), and especially Scottish-trained landscape gardener John McDonald (1877–95). Taking advantage of the lakeside setting, the drive was extended to its present configuration and a pleasure garden established, incorporating a wide range of exotic plants. William GUILFOYLE was commissioned in 1910 to draw up a plan for further improving the gardens. His plan was partly implemented by curators Archibald Campbell (1911–40) and Dugald Leitch (1940–55), maintaining what was, by then, a mature botanical collection. Native plants were added to the gardens by the last resident curator, Donald Greenwood (1955–65). Since then the gardens have been opened up to have a more park-like character, with simplified planting.

PAMELA JELLIE

COLE, A.E. ('Bouquet') (*fl*. 1914–22), Sydney-based gardener and author, came to prominence with the publication of *The Bouquet: Australian Flower Gardening* (*c*. 1914), carelessly credited to 'A.F. Cole' by publisher E.W. COLE. He identified three distinct styles of garden designing: formal ('now happily obsolete'), sub-formal ('still to be seen almost in its purity in many suburban gardens and surrounding the homes of wealthy pastoralists'), and cottage ('delightful … with its rose-covered porches, ivy-clad walls, flowering hedges, mixed flower-beds, and cosy corners'); he recommended 'mixtures of the sub-formal and cottage style are the most suitable and pleasing for Australian homes'. Cole's book was an early Australian title exclusively devoted to the flower garden, its predecessors being works by HOCKINGS, CLARSON, BROWNE, MORTLOCK and TURNER. His next title, *The Australian Floral Almanac* (1916), included the *nom de plume* 'Bouquet', under which Cole contributed to the horticultural press. This was a modest calendrical work 'based upon the conditions prevailing in the warmer parts of New South Wales and Victoria'. It was followed by *Half-hours in the Bush-house* (1922), uniquely devoted to that most

Australian of garden buildings, the BUSH-HOUSE. In this distinctive finale to his publishing career, Cole advocated differential lath spacing to provide multiple environments, specialised houses to suit different horticultural requirements, and specialist notes on pot plants, ferns and palms, foliage plants, orchids, and other ornamental plants. RA

COLE, Edith Marion (1911–1999), Perth-based garden designer, was born in Farnham, Surrey, England. She spent twelve months in Melbourne during 1933–34 working as an assistant to her cousin, Edna WALLING—Cole's mother and Walling's father were siblings. On returning to Perth, Cole established herself as a garden designer, advertising her services in the *West Australian Gardener*. She also contributed several articles on garden design to this magazine in 1934–35, with Walling's influence evident. She described the benefits of well-planned garden layouts and suggested plant combinations, including the native leschenaultia. Cole married in 1941, becoming Edith Cameron.   CAROLYN MIDDLEMIS

COLE, Edward William (1832–1918), bookseller and publisher, migrated from England to the Cape of Good Hope in 1850, where he farmed, and thence to Melbourne in 1852. He started bookselling in 1865 and opened the celebrated Cole's Book Arcade in 1873, gradually enlarging his premises as success endowed the business: in 1896 he incorporated a rustic fernery into the arcade. *Cole's Penny Garden Guide* was abridged from the LAW SOMNER AND CO. *Handbook to the Garden* (1880), a device much used by Cole. His biggest garden success was *Cole's Australasian Gardening and Domestic Floriculture* (1897) by William ELLIOTT. He also published Hamilton McEWIN's *The Fruitgrower's Handbook* and two books by A.E. COLE, and reprinted others, such as John LOCKLEY's *Rose Growing Made Easy*, under his imprint. Cole's *The Happifying Gardening Hobby* (1918), an endearing anthology of words and pictures, embodied his altruistic wish for universal health and happiness.

Cole Turnley, *Cole of the Book Arcade: A Pictorial Biography of E.W. Cole* (Hawthorn, Vic., 1974)   RA

COLE, Thomas Cornelius (1810–1889), horticulturist, nursery proprietor, and pomologist, was born at Sudbury, near Harrow, Middlesex, England, and migrated to the Port Phillip District in September 1841 aboard the *Himalaya*. He landed at Liardet's Beach (now Port Melbourne) with his wife and three children, and resided in Newtown (now Fitzroy), where three more children were born. Cole, in company with a relation, John Cole, afterwards rented a nursery garden at Coburg, on the Merri Creek. T.C. Cole relinquished his share of the business to his partner some time after 1847, and joined his brother George in another garden on the Merri Creek, opposite Northcote. Disastrous floods in 1849 swept the family from their house thrice in thirteen months.

In 1847, T.C. Cole purchased five hectares with Yarra River frontage at the corner of Victoria and Burnley streets, where he established an orchard and nursery. Cole's partnership with his brother George was later dissolved, but Thomas carried on the garden at Merri Creek until the expiry of their lease, when the family took up residence at Richmond. According to E.E. PESCOTT, Cole issued the first catalogue from his Richmond Nursery in 1850, making it one of the earliest produced in the colony. James Kearney's *Plan of Melbourne and Suburbs* (1855) clearly showed the neat, squared beds and orchard of the Richmond Nursery. A year later, James SINCLAIR praised Cole's land 'so snugly sheltered in the bend of the river Yarra, from high and hot winds, where the rich washings, have been accumulating for centuries', and approvingly observed 'the vines ... planted wide apart, and on raised borders, and kept continually mulched with rotten manure [with] the apple and pear-trees ... on raised beds, in a well-dug, rich, and well-sheltered soil, which accounts for their luxuriance'. In 1852 Cole secured, from William MACARTHUR of Camden Park, a collection of CAMELLIAS for propagation—thought to be earliest large-scale introduction of this species into Vic. Cole took a keen interest in the horticultural progress of the colony; he joined with DALLACHY, GINN, and RULE in 1853 to revive the Victorian Horticultural Society, was a prominent member of the Horticultural Society of Victoria, and was a driving force behind the establishment of the Horticultural Society's experimental garden at BURNLEY. Cole was of the old school, and clashed in the pages of the *Yeoman and Australian Acclimatiser* during 1863 with the brash and confident Josiah MITCHELL over the question of exhaustion of soils—the

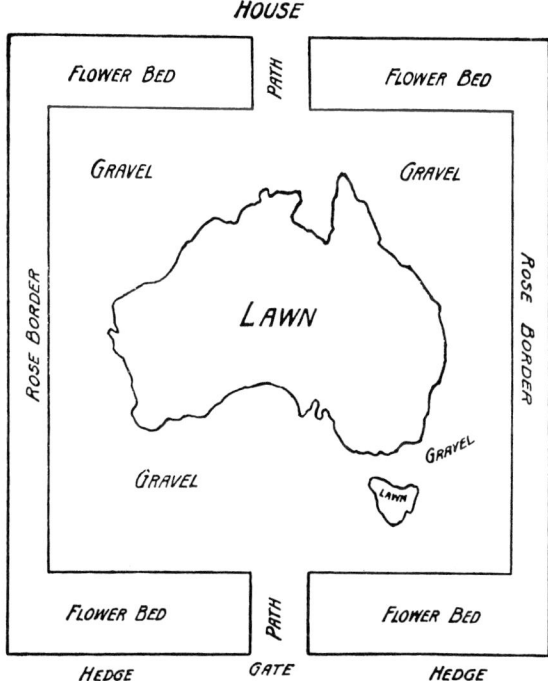

A.E. COLE's design for a front garden (c. 1914), inspired by a bed in Sydney Botanic Gardens—as an alternative to turf, the coast could be delineated in coloured-foliage plants, pot plants half-sunk to represent cities, and different states worked out in carpet-BEDDING plants of contrasting colours

latter scarcely wishing to argue with 'an individual so profoundly ignorant of those recognised principles which, now-a-days, every schoolboy is acquainted with, and which both experience and science combine to affirm'.

In 1853 Cole purchased fifteen hectares of land with a frontage to Tooronga Road, Upper Hawthorn, and by 1860 had established another orchard and nursery, and erected a large brick house on this estate, named Twyford. In 1860 he drew on his long horticultural experience in Victoria, then unparalleled among fellow colonists, to publish *Cole's Gardening in Victoria*, joining the popular handbooks of BUNCE, DICKINSON, ADAMSON, and MCMILLAN, among others in the nursery trade. Besides monthly notes on the kitchen, fruit and flower garden, Cole included authoritative remarks 'On Selecting Fruit Trees', and much of interest regarding garden design. River and creek frontages were to be preferred—or at least an eastern sloping aspect with natural shelter, or 'a plantation of Mimosa [acacia] or other quick-growing trees'. Brick walls or close paling fences of lapped boards responded to local conditions, but Cole generally objected to 'live fences' (hedges) on account of their tendency to impoverish the soil. The gardener's house was to be sited on high ground to facilitate underground irrigation of waste water and liquid manure. Cole recognised the futility of large expanses of LAWN in oppressive Australian summers, and suggested Chamomile rather than turf for bordering flower beds, but he was little concerned with questions of GARDEN STYLE.

In 1862 Cole leased his Richmond Nursery to his son, **John Charles Cole** (1838–1891), who had, a year before, married the eldest daughter of Charles Maplestone (1838–1914), Public Works Department architect, naturalist, and amateur viticulturist. J.C. Cole (and, after his death, his sons) carried on the Richmond Nursery, supplementing the rapidly urbanised site in the mid-1880s with a generous land selection at Fern Tree Gully, which he named Glen Harrow. Cole, who engaged seed merchant David RAILTON as his city agent, specialised in fruit trees and vines, and his many surviving *Descriptive Catalogues* of the 1860s–70s and his paper 'The Apple and its Varieties' in the Department of Agriculture annual report (1874) attest to his excellence in this field. Another son, the Rev. Thomas Cornelius Cole jnr (c. 1836–1879), was also active in Melbourne horticultural circles.

In 1864 T.C. Cole purchased a further 14 hectares adjoining the Twyford estate and leased it to his son **Henry Ungerford Cole** (1843–1904), who established the Shorland orchard and nursery. Like his father and brother, with whom he worked closely, H.U. Cole was noted for his work as a pomological hybridist and judge of fruit at horticultural shows. He was among those in the colonial nursery trade who achieved pre-eminence in raising and distribution of fruit trees. The Shorland Nursery carried on for the early decades of the twentieth century, although by the 1930s Twyford had been demolished and this valuable land subdivided for residential purposes. Charles Frederick Cole, son of H.U. Cole, was born at Shorland and displayed his family's pomological bent, working as Victorian Orchard Supervisor for more than thirty-two years for the Department of Agriculture. C.F. Cole was a prolific writer on horticultural subjects, and also a keen student of his family's history; two useful biographical articles were published using his research (*Wild Life*, 1946, and *Australian Garden Lover*, 1958).

T.C. Cole died at Twyford. A pioneer of Victorian horticulture, his outstanding work in raising seedling fruits and vegetables produced varieties for Australian conditions vastly superior to their predecessors. His obituary in the *Leader* singled out the Edith strawberry and Twyford Bigarreau cherry as particularly ubiquitous among the long list of fruits he hybridised. Many varieties of garden vegetables long perpetuated the name Cole.

George Cole (1822–1868), brother of T.C. Cole, was born in Sudbury, Middlesex, England, and arrived in Melbourne with family members in 1842. With his brother he established a nursery on leased land on the Merri Creek, then started a new nursery of his own on freehold land in Gardener's Creek (later Toorak) Road. Cole's son, George Graham Cole (1855-1946), established the Fernbank Nurseries at Tyabb (Vic.) in 1884, which, along with G.G. Cole & Sons and Coles Nurseries, gave a continuity of family fruit tree nurseries in Tyabb until the close of the twentieth century.   RA

COLEMAN, Edith (1874–1951), naturalist, conservationist, and journalist, was born at Woking, Surrey, England, and arrived in Melbourne in 1887. A versatile naturalist, in 1949 she became the first woman to win the Australian NATURAL HISTORY Medallion. Her original studies of pollination in the ORCHID genus *Cryptostylis* created keen interest among botanists. Combining sound scientific observation with a lyrical appreciation of nature, she wrote many popular articles for the Melbourne press on bush flowers, eucalypts, wattles, native animals, and garden plants. *Come Back in Wattle Time* (1935), her only book, advocated the cultivation of ACACIAS as garden plants. Eclectic in her tastes, Coleman's extensive garden at Walsham, Blackburn, inspired articles on homely old-fashioned plants and medicinal HERBS. During the Second World War she harvested *Angelica* seeds to raise funds for the Red Cross. Walsham's 'tangled wilderness' was also her field for daily observations of nature.   ANGELA TAYLOR

COLONEL LIGHT GARDENS, SA, was designed in 1917 by Charles READE, and established from 1921 as a model garden suburb on a 120-hectare site, six kilometres south of Adelaide. Informed by TOWN PLANNING principles promoted by the British GARDEN CITY Movement, Reade prepared a comprehensive plan without precedent in Australia. Contrary to usual residential subdivisional practice, he considered the site as a whole, devising a scheme that would allow the suburb to be developed along organised lines. Significantly, he anticipated and planned for residents' immediate and projected needs, including separate areas or zones for public buildings, schools, churches, shops, administration offices, and recreation. Reflecting the role of open space in garden city thought, Reade nominated recreation places of different types and sizes including internal reserves behind houses on smaller blocks of land. There were also formal public gardens and tree plantings. Roads varied in line, length, and width. Buildings were set back at varying distances from the street, positioned at corners to create visual interest, or used to terminate long vistas. Sited on ample blocks with space around and between them for gardens, buildings were consistent in form, scale, proportion, and materials. In 1924, three years after the first land sales were announced in Colonel Light Gardens, the state Labor Government initiated Australia's first mass housing project, the Thousand Homes Scheme, on the garden suburb site. As a consequence, additional land was purchased and minor changes were made to Reade's plan in order to accommodate the required number of residential blocks. Colonel LIGHT Gardens remains largely intact today, and is Australia's most complete and intact suburban expression of garden city planning principles.

Christine Garnaut, *Colonel Light Gardens: Model Garden Suburb* (Sydney, 1999) CHRISTINE GARNAUT

COLOUR is principally introduced into gardens through PLANTS—especially through their constituent elements such as FOLIAGE, flowers, fruit, and bark, and their SEASONAL variety—and hard landscape elements such as paving, walls, fences, and other architectural components. Less often and far less predicably—but with rich theatricality—LIGHT and even ephemeral atmospheric effects such as mist or fog are introduced intentionally or by virtue of local geography and CLIMATE.

Considered use of colour in early Australian gardens was primarily achieved through FLORICULTURE, either through flowering annuals, perennials, or shrubs. A promiscuous mix of colour was often sought, but floral BEDDING of carefully delineated colours, either in ribbons or larger beds, was introduced from the 1860s to the 1870s. Advice in Australian garden books or in the horticultural press was infrequent, although bedding schemes in botanic and public gardens—the work of Richard SCHOMBURGK and James PINK for instance—were often described in detail; emulation in private gardens is less well documented. Gertrude JEKYLL's *Colour in the Flower Garden* (1908) described garden design based on the use of flower colour. Her detailed planting plans for specific colour themes were suited to the prevailing ARTS AND CRAFTS style; other influential British voices were Lawrence Johnston (Hidcote Manor), and Harold Nicolson and Vita Sackville-West (SISSINGHURST).

The use of foliage for colour effects, especially ornamental-leaved and VARIEGATED plants, received a boost through local disciples of SUBTROPICAL bedding propagandist William ROBINSON, and William GUILFOYLE was one among many who experimented with its potential. The richness of individual blooms, exemplified by orchids, graced conservatories in cooler areas of Australia during the late nineteenth century, although in tropical areas, especially in Qld, foliage augmented such displays with the widespread (outdoor) use of plants such as crotons.

MODERNISM introduced new boldness to gardens, particularly through architectural elements where colour was often used as a foil to sculptural planting. This theme has been repeated by many post-modernists, and in the example of Dyeworks Park, Prahran, Vic. (1993), boldly coloured striated paving not only recalls the industrial origins of the site but complements the regimented grids and sweeps of planting.

In general, the use of colour as a design principle in Australian gardens has received less attention than other aspects, but recent decades have seen widespread consideration of this key stylistic attribute. Bolobek was one influential garden where careful use of colour was pursued by its creator Joan LAW-SMITH: here white flowers against green foliage provided a consistent and overriding theme.

The use of colour in garden design is based on the colour wheel. The colours of the spectrum can be arranged with the three primary colours—red, yellow, and blue—equally spaced around this circle. All other colours can be made from these primary colours: thus green is a mix of yellow and blue, and the nature of the green depends upon the proportion of each. Similarly, orange derives from yellow and red, and purple from red and blue. Moving around the circle, there is a continuum of gradually changing colour. At the outer edge of the circle these colours are at their boldest and most pure, but in moving to the white centre, each becomes less intense. Thus from scarlet at the edge, reds become less intense and more pink. Moving around the edge, reds give way to purple; in the centre, to less intense mauves. Broken into its many components, the colour circle is an extremely complex intermingling of colour with seamless changes. Further analysis will show that the colour wheel can be divided into two: colours associated with red, orange, and yellow are warm colours, providing a strong visual impact and warmth to a design, though as these colours become softer to the centre of the circle some of their heat is dissipated; by contrast, that part of the colour circle based around greens and blues has a cooler impact. Visually these are recessive colours, and they will tend to recede in any planting scheme.

Garden designers are able to utilise colour to achieve different impacts in a garden. Chosen planting combinations can offer visual excitement or cool and relaxing settings, depending upon the colour balance. Before considering these strategies it is important to recognise the vital roles played by seasonal change, light, and foliage in colour planning. Few plants contribute colour consistently—except perhaps for their foliage—and a planting scheme based on flower colour alone may produce very little display during some seasons. For calculated colour effects to achieve their best, plants need to be in flower consecutively, otherwise effects are lost: this strategy was recognised by Jekyll, Johnston, and Sackville-West, who allotted specific spaces to particular planting schemes. Light plays a significant role in the success of garden planting schemes. Many gardening books emanate from Britain and offer descriptions of colour schemes suited to soft, English light and moist air. Where sunlight is harsher, as it is in most Australian gardens, understated colour schemes of pastel plantings are unable to compete with the intensity of sunlight. Gentle colour schemes appear bleached, especially when viewed from shade; by contrast, stronger flower colours, from the edge of the colour wheel, retain their impact.

JOHN PATRICK

COMEADOW, William Austin (1890–1960), printer and amateur horticulturist, was educated at the Melbourne Technical College. He became a keen horticulturist and long-time office-bearer of the Royal Horticultural Society of Victoria (RHSV). He edited the *RHSV Year Book* (1942–49), prepared the *Australian Horticultural Judges' Handbook for Judges and Exhibitors* (1949), and his company printed the *RHSV Journal* during the late 1940s. When the *Argus*—of which Comeadow was horticultural editor—purchased YOUR GARDEN, the enlarged magazine incorporated the *RHSV Journal*, with Comeadow as editor (1950–54). E.E. LORD illustrated Comeadow's Hawthorn garden in *Shrubs and Trees for Australian Gardens* (1948) and he developed a garden, The Gums, in the hills of Sassafras (Vic.). He was a Melbourne City Councillor for many years, and president of the Moomba Festival Committee (1958). When the enterprising and energetic Comeadow was awarded honorary life membership of the RHSV (1948), president Frank CLARKE said 'what Mr Alister CLARK has meant for the NATIONAL ROSE SOCIETY, Mr Comeadow has meant for the Royal Horticultural Society'. RA

COMMEMORATIVE AND MEMORIAL GARDENS, while similar, can be differentiated: commemoration marks or celebrates a particular event or place, or a person who might still be living; memorials honour and call to memory a deceased individual or group. Particular design characteristics and plant preferences mark each type. For example, in commemorative gardens that INTERPRET the past, the plants may symbolise the event commemorated: ANZAC parks often contain species from particular battlefields where Australians fought, such as pines from Gallipoli and poplars from France. Memorial gardens, designed for individual and personal contemplation, are often more solemn in character, with plants symbolising death and loss—rosemary for remembrance, roses for love and peace, and cypresses, pines, and oaks for both death and life. Most are formal rectangular or circular designs and many are sunken gardens.

Significant historic anniversaries, such as centenaries, are traditionally celebrated by the dedication of great PUBLIC PARKS. Sydney's CENTENNIAL PARK (1888) commemorated the first 100 years of European settlement in Australia, and its sequel, Bicentennial Park (1988), Homebush Bay (NSW), marked 200 years. On an adjacent site a Millennium Park is being constructed. Incorporated into the 1988 redevelopment of Sydney's Circular Quay was First Fleet Park, commemorating the arrival in 1788 of the First Fleet to establish a colony on the shores of Sydney Cove.

Gardens commemorating Australia's early pioneers appear in most states, with examples including Adelaide's Pioneer Women's Garden (1939: designer Elsie CORNISH) and the sunken Pioneer Women's Garden in Melbourne's Domain (1934: designer Hugh LINAKER). Another sunken garden (1938) on the site of the Garden Palace, which stood during 1879–82 in the ROYAL BOTANIC GARDENS, SYDNEY, was dedicated to all Australian pioneers, men and women.

Australia's allegiance to Britain has frequently been commemorated by dedicating parks and gardens to members of the royal family. Examples include various Queens Parks

The PORT ARTHUR Memorial (1999) uses landscape elements such as a reflecting pool and restrained plantings to MEMORIALISE the Broad Arrow Cafe and surrounds

(especially in Qld); Alexandra Park and Gardens (1904) named for Princess Alexandra, and the Queen Victoria Gardens (1905), both in Melbourne's DOMAIN; and the Sandringham Garden (1954)—commemorating both George V and George VI—in Sydney's HYDE PARK North, opened by Queen Elizabeth II. Royal and vice-regal visits are invariably commemorated by tree-planting ceremonies, and all state BOTANIC GARDENS, GOVERNMENT HOUSE grounds, and many PUBLIC PARKS include these special trees; some even retain 'royal oaks' planted for a royal wedding in 1863.

Memorial gardens in the form of ROSE gardens have been particularly favoured to memorialise the deceased, and are often associated with CEMETERIES, crematoria, and WAR MEMORIALS. Living war memorials, in the form of AVENUES of Honour, became popular at the end of the First World War to remember those who had served their country. The first of these was at Ballarat, Vic. (1917–19), planted by the 'Lucas girls' (staff of a local clothing manufacturing firm). The avenue, of 3912 trees, stretched for twenty-two kilometres along the Western Highway, each with a name plaque. Despite the ravages of time, this avenue remains largely intact. Between 1917 and 1921 a staggering 128 such avenues were planted in Vic. alone, with a smaller number in other states. In the eastern states, oaks and elms were the most popular species used, but in WA, planes, sheoaks, and eucalypts were found more satisfactory.

By the end of the Second World War, the planting of memorial avenues had declined in popularity, but one particular project, Remembrance Driveway (1953–), was remarkably successful. Margaret DAVIS suggested the planting of groves of trees along the highways linking Sydney and Canberra to commemorate those who had served. Unlike the formal Avenues of Honour, Remembrance Driveway comprised a series of informal PLANTATIONS located wherever suitable land was available. There are currently more than fifty plantations, with a total of 50 000 trees. Interest in the Driveway was revived during the 'Australia Remembers 1945–1995' celebrations, and, with added government funding, tree planting on a huge scale is being undertaken.

In Cowra (NSW), location of a Japanese prisoner of war camp, an avenue of 2000 Japanese cherries was planted in 1988 to commemorate the strong ties between the town and Japan. The avenue connects the Japanese and Cowra War Cemeteries, the camp site, and the Japanese Garden and Cultural Centre. In Sydney's Bicentennial Park, the Silent Hearts Memorial Garden (1994), established 'In honour of those who have donated their organs and their families who have survived them', reflects values of contemporary society using a garden as its vehicle.   ALLAN CORREY

COMMERCIAL GARDENS, a term embracing gardens and site designs over a wide range of commerce and industry, have at their core private ownership and a profit motive. At their most general, in the field of primary production, they have included ORCHARDS, VINEYARDS, and MARKET GARDENS. Although now often forming CULTURAL LANDSCAPES of considerable interest, unless they were attached to residences or were otherwise on a domestic scale, these examples fell within the utilitarian category of productive horticulture and AGRICULTURE. Wineries were often established within the vineyards, however, and to encourage buyers attractive gardens were developed around the buildings—Seppeltsfield, in the BAROSSA, is a prime example—and recent promotion by the wine industry has placed considerable emphasis on landscape design to attract local and overseas tourists.

Unlikely as it may seem, gardens have long been associated with some types of extractive industry such as gold mining and brickmaking. On mining sites, the manager's residence was often built overlooking the workings, and commonly included an enclosed garden as part of the industrial landscape. At brickworks—often in residential areas—the manager's office was usually surrounded by a well-kept garden to impress visitors and mollify local residents. The same was not true of collieries, where profits came before aesthetics, peoples' health, or the environment. Recently, efforts have been made to establish vegetation on waste heaps and around boundaries to alleviate dust pollution, provide visual screening, reduce noise, and to enhance the general appearance of the workings, particularly on open cut sites. The extensive REVEGETATION programs, begun in the mid-1930s largely through the efforts of Albert MORRIS at Broken Hill (NSW), are some of the most successful of such industrial plantings.

Gardens associated with secondary industry are largely a twentieth-century phenomenon. They initially surrounded residences attached to a factory or works, but, as manufacturing developed, large factory sites were laid out under TOWN PLANNING principles to include extensive gardens for lunchtime use by staff, to provide an attractive setting for buildings, and to ensure the works was in character with its neighbours—often residential areas. Gardens of this type were a feature of Amalgamated Wireless of Australia and Nestlé in Sydney, Southwark Brewery in Adelaide, Cascade Brewery in Hobart, Bryant and May in Melbourne, and H.V. McKAY in Sunshine (Vic.). Perhaps the best known—it became something of an Australian icon—was at the FLETCHER JONES factory, Warrnambool (Vic.). As all these gardens required high maintenance, most have now disappeared or been drastically reduced in size. During the 1920s whole industrial towns, modelled on Ebenezer Howard's GARDEN CITY ideals, were begun at LUTANA (Electrolytic Zinc Company) and Claremont (British confectionery makers, Cadbury Brothers) in Tas., and at the giant open cut coal mine at Yallourn (Vic.) by the State Electricity Commission. One argument used to support these developments was that the health of workers who lived and worked in a 'green' environment would improve, and this would lead to increased production.

After the Second World War development provided opportunities for the creation of innovative industrial landscapes based on ECOLOGICAL design principles. Restoration of surface-mined areas and quarry sites and the surroundings of power stations, and the design of large greenfield sites, have involved the expertise of LANDSCAPE ARCHITECTS, ecologists, and engineers in producing some outstanding industrial landscapes. New business parks—including small business and industrial enterprises located in pre-landscaped

Commonwealth Park

Gondwanaland, a short-lived ZOOLOGICAL GARDEN on Brisbane's south bank, developed in the 1990s on part of the 1988 World Expo site and now demolished, demonstrates the vicissitudes of COMMERCIAL GARDENS

settings such as Tally Ho in Burwood (Vic.), or the decentralised industrial sites in the Albury–Wodonga of the 1980s, where whole corridors for wildlife were revegetated by direct seeding and minimal vegetation clearing was undertaken—represent newer modes of treating commercial and industrial sites.

Urban commercial sites such as shopping plazas represent some of the most difficult situations in which to establish vegetation—often confined to small areas between high-traffic areas such as CAR PARKS and walkways. Altered soil profiles, limited soil root volumes, and the induced climatic aridity of large exposed, hard-paved areas, exacerbate these problems. In many industrial sites soils are not only much altered but can be heavily polluted, requiring significant remedial treatment.

The first gardens to be designed specifically as commercial ventures were the PLEASURE GARDENS developed from the mid-nineteenth century in most capital cities, and, perhaps surprisingly, on Victorian goldfields. Although essentially colonial imitations of the eighteenth-century London pleasure gardens, the Australian versions catered for SPORTING and recreational events such as athletics, dancing, and organised picnics rather than for genteel PROMENADING and masked balls. They were superseded by amusement parks, such as the various Luna Parks popular during the period between the wars, and later THEME PARKS based on the American Disneyland model. Gardens of RESORTS now form the apogee—or nadir—of this mode.

The commercial opportunities in outdoor dining permitted by a generally equable Australian climate has encouraged many hotels and restaurants to exploit new legislation by providing attractive outdoor facilities that often extend onto footpaths and other public areas. However, it is a fine line between permitting certain commercial uses, such as kiosks, to operate in PUBLIC GARDENS, and over-commercialisation in the form of major outdoor entertainment events, which are currently threatening to take over many public parks.

ALLAN CORREY

COMMONWEALTH PARK, Canberra, the National Capital's central PUBLIC PARK, is located within the NATIONAL TRIANGLE, on the foreshore of Lake Burley Griffin and adjacent to 'Civic' (the civic centre). Owned and managed by the Commonwealth Government, its founders intended that it evolve as a place for people, and a show-piece of Australian horticulture. The thirty-four-hectare park is basin-shaped, with an inward focus onto Nerang Pool. It is accessible to pedestrians, cyclists, and vehicles. Regatta Point, where a restaurant and exhibition building is located, commands excellent views across the lake. Development of the originally treeless site proceeded slowly at first. Foundation planting by Charles WESTON in the 1920s was supplemented twenty-five years later by Lindsay PRYOR. The construction of Lake Burley Griffin in the early 1960s led to the creation of Nerang Pool and further informal exotic and indigenous planting. A 1965 master plan by Sylvia CROWE has provided the decisive design input and guided development, which includes a stream valley, marsh garden, amphitheatre, playground, enclosed lawn areas and stage for large crowds, lily pond, rhododendron garden, and restaurant. A conservatory has yet to be built. The park is popular for large annual events, including the Floriade FESTIVAL. Public art and commemorative sites dot the park.

John Gray, *A Park for a Nation: The Story of Commonwealth Park in Australia's National Capital* (Dickson, ACT, 1996)

JOHN GRAY

COMMUNITY FORESTS, a late product of 'progressive conservation' thinking in Australia, had a primary educational purpose of raising consciousness of forests and forest protection, but such projects were also valued as local government 'beautification' projects. Unlike the first ARBOR DAYS (from 1889), when large groups of people stood to attention while dignitaries planted one or two significant trees, everyone got their hands dirty in the creation of a community forest. One early model for massed tree-planting events were the AVENUE of Honour plantations, including the 1919 Ballarat planting by 500 'Lucas girls' (women working in a local factory). Another model was the school plantation, begun in Vic. in the 1920s. The community forest also captured some of the purpose of early ARBORETA—trialling tree varieties, either for FORESTRY or landscape improvement.

Community forests emerged in Vic. as a cooperative venture between the Forests Commission of Victoria and local government following the horrific 1939 bushfires, and also as part of post-war reconstruction. Returning servicemen seeking to build their own homes put so much pressure on depleted timber supplies that the size of new suburban homes was limited to twelve 'squares' (111 square metres). Community forest advocates capitalised on the consciousness of the timber shortage, using the opportunity to educate the public about the need for forest preservation and bushfire prevention. 'Save the Forests Campaign' organiser, Cyril E. ISAAC, conceived the 'community forest' idea, combining his personal experience with the SCHOOL GARDENING movement and local government with the resources of the Forests Commission. Twelve hundred people planted the first community forest in Dandenong (Vic.), in 1944, and 105 000 trees were distributed for public tree plantings during 1945–46.

LIBBY ROBIN

COMMUNITY GARDENS originated in eighteenth-century Britain when plots of land, later called allotments, were set aside by landowners to enable the labouring poor to produce their own vegetables and flowers. A political campaign during the nineteenth century extended the amount of allotment land available, and culminated in the passing of an *Allotments Act* (1887). This law obliged local authorities to provide allotment land, when there was a demand. The amount of allotment land designated has fluctuated, due to events such as the two world wars and the Depression.

Community gardens in Australia have never been the subject of federal legislation, but their purpose when first introduced during the 1940s—to provide people with an opportunity to cultivate edible crops on public land—was similar to that experienced in Britain. An 'Austerity Campaign' invoked by the government during the Second World War actively encouraged citizens to turn their flower beds into productive gardens for the table. Later, when fresh fruit and vegetables became scarce due to a shortage of manpower and the rationing of fertilisers and insecticides in commercial MARKET GARDENS, the campaign was extended to include council land and public institutions. These gardens were referred to as 'Dig For Victory Gardens'.

Escalation of high-density housing in metropolitan areas and a growing awareness of environmental issues increased demand for community gardens in Britain, Canada, the USA, and Australia. The primary focus of these gardens now is to provide a recreational leisure activity and a 'greening' of urban space. The first community-instigated garden in Australia was established in inner suburban Melbourne in 1979, at Collingwood. The Collingwood Community Garden aimed to improve the quality of life and circumstances of people living in nearby public housing estates. Apart from producing food, working in this type of garden offered residents the opportunity to socialise, to take pride in a public space, and to enjoy the therapeutic aspects of gardening. There are currently more than forty such centres operating in Australia; each may control a number of gardens within its jurisdiction, with garden plots available for a nominal fee. Tools, water, and manure are provided free of charge. Some centres have enough funding to support a curator. The gardens vary in size, number and the range of activities undertaken, and are based on active participation at the grassroots level. Community gardens extend from large, highly organised centres with government support (usually local government) to the communal efforts of small groups of people, often culturally linked.

SUZANNE HUNT

COMO, South Yarra, Vic., is a rare surviving example of an early colonial Melbourne estate. With the exception of the 1847 carriage drive from Williams Road, the early garden was replaced by a more grandly inspired landscape, designed and laid out for merchant John Brown (owner 1853–64) by William SANGSTER (1855–66). His ideas, first implemented at Como, recalled the PICTURESQUE tradition of the English gardens. He capitalised on the natural features of the site, including views across the Yarra Valley, and also trialled many recently introduced trees, and established a large orchard. From 1864, under the ownership of Charles and Caroline Armytage, from a wealthy pastoral family with several large holdings in Victoria's WESTERN DISTRICT and Qld, Como became a centre of activity for Melbourne's social elite, the garden often being used for large picnics and other outdoor events. Early elements of the Sangster garden were lost in 1911–21 subdivisions, including a pleasure garden and rosary, flower garden, orchard, orangery, and vegetable and kitchen gardens.

Apart from subdivision, the Armytage family made few changes to the garden during their ninety-five-year ownership, though by 1959, when the property passed to the NATIONAL TRUST, large areas had fallen into disrepair. Of the many early changes made to the garden by the National Trust, the most enduring and significant feature was a water garden designed and built by Ellis STONES (1968). Conservation of the garden in 1996 and 2000 largely reversed other alterations and additions to the Como landscape. Major features that dominate the garden include the

Competition

original carriage drive (1847), an axial vista to the north from Sangster's fountain terrace, a croquet lawn from the Sangster period, the carriage drive west of the house (commenced 1855, truncated 1911), and many mature trees, particularly conifers, from the early to mid-nineteenth century.

Adrea Fox, *The Story of Como* (Melbourne, 1996)

CARMEL McPHEE

COMPETITION has been provided in the realm of gardening and horticulture largely through the activities of HORTICULTURAL SOCIETIES, especially through horticultural and flower SHOWS and garden competitions. Awards at shows, such as the Franklin Trophy (Hobart Town, 1839) initially conferred peer recognition for excellence or outstanding contribution to horticulture, in the manner of the earliest medals awarded by the ROYAL HORTICULTURAL SOCIETY. With burgeoning membership in horticultural societies from the 1850s, show schedules became progressively more complex. Awards, originally confined to flowers, were supplemented by prizes for plants (especially in groups) and soon gardens were included. This was especially true of COTTAGE GARDENS, with the perceived benefits of MORAL IMPROVEMENT never far from the minds of organisers. Garden competitions were generally local, or perhaps regional, in their outlook. Some competitions celebrated local events—memorably demonstrated at Boulder (WA) in 1903–04, to mark the arrival of a long-awaited piped water supply. Newspapers such as the Melbourne *Herald*, *Adelaide Advertiser*, Brisbane *Courier Mail*, *Toowoomba Chronicle*, *Ballarat Courier*, *Geelong Advertiser*, and *Sydney Morning Herald* upheld this tradition with named awards. Such competitions favoured neatness and convention, with matters of taste in regard to garden STYLES often raising their stultifying heads.

Premiums for garden designs (often in the form of a small cash prize and the resulting commission) were sometimes offered as a means of attracting designers, principally for PUBLIC PARKS AND GARDENS. Early examples included Melbourne parklands (1856), PORTLAND BOTANIC GARDENS (1857), BONTHARAMBO (*c*. 1858–60), ST KILDA BOTANIC GARDENS (1860), and, perhaps most controversially, Melbourne's DOMAIN (1872). In recent years, LANDSCAPE ARCHITECTURE competitions have attracted and rewarded innovative schemes for public spaces that might not have found favour within a more traditional mode of commission.

RA

COMPOST is the soil-like end product of decomposed organic materials of plant or animal origin; it may be incorporated into SOIL as a conditioner and organic FERTILISER or spread as mulch. Compost 'recipes' aimed at hastening decomposition while maximising nutrient content owe much to the Indore method, devised in India by Sir Albert Howard early in the twentieth century. Interest in ORGANIC GARDENING saw the formation, after the Second World War, of the Victorian Compost Society, which published *Victorian Compost News* (1947–65). During the 1990s composting became increasingly accepted as a means of reducing waste disposal. Local authorities now compost municipal wastes, and encourage home gardeners to compost kitchen and garden refuse; compost bins and turners for domestic use are readily available. 'Vermicompost' is produced in 'worm farms', notably in Brisbane, where fertiliser is produced on a large scale from sewage and grass clippings. A soil-less growing medium is produced from composting of bark and sawdust.

JILL KELLOW

COMPUTERS The benefits promised by the use of computers to design and manage Australian gardens are now being delivered after many years of expectation. Current systems, which offer high-performance processors, large data storage capacity, and excellent graphic displays, allow for the potential to be delivered in a single desktop unit. Until the late 1970s, computers were only available in large institutions and accessible to a few individuals. The advent of the microcomputer in the form of the Apple II and various CP/M based machines gave computing power to the general public. In the area of horticulture, these machines, largely programmed in the BASIC language, were used primarily for simple plant selection programs. The output from these programs was directed to monochrome screens or low-quality dot matrix printers. In the 1980s, in order to view pictures of plants and overcome display limitations, images were stored on laser disks capable of being viewed using a television. These laser disk players were then linked to computers that allowed for the selection of individual images.

The development of the multimedia computer in the mid-1990s integrated these systems and allowed for the output of images and sound from data stored on CD-ROMS. The display allows for high-quality images to be viewed using millions of colours. These computers have also permitted changes in the way plant keys have been used. Graphics and database attributes, such as those used in the EUCALYPTUS key (EUCLID) produced by the Centre for Plant Biodiversity Research and published by CSIRO (1997), are now used to assist in the identification of plants.

Computers have also been used for producing GARDEN PLANS and as an aid to garden and landscape design. Proprietary Computer Aided Design (CAD) packages, such as Landcadd® (based on Autocad®), have been used mostly in the offices of LANDSCAPE ARCHITECTS due to the high cost of both software and hardware—especially the plotters for outputting designs. They are becoming more popular as a result of increased capabilities for realistic rendering, and for creating 'walk throughs' or VIRTUAL GARDENS that enable clients to gain an impression of how the design will look when constructed and planted.

Municipal authorities and other open space managers are increasingly using computers to monitor and manage their resources. Software includes Geographic Information Systems (GIS), where not only details of plants and other infrastructure are recorded but their position is also stored on an electronic map. The data can be collected using handheld computers linked to satellites.

The Internet is now a large repository of information relating to plants and their culture. Many horticultural institutions are also presenting online information about themselves and their collections. Nurseries are using the Internet for plant

Mr C. Forrest's cottage garden, Boulder (WA), awarded first prize at the local spring show, can be seen as a triumph of COMPETITION but also as a celebration of the Goldfields Water Supply Scheme.

sales. A range of online discussion groups cater for gardeners. The pace of change is both bewildering and exhilarating.

NICHOLAS BAILEY

CONARTY, James (1869–1932), engine driver and amateur vegetable grower, lived and gardened in NSW and Vic. before he settled in Perth c. 1911. He is first recorded winning prizes with his vegetables at the Perth Royal Agricultural Show in 1916, and won the Edwin Rose Trophy in 1922 for a collection of not less than eighteen varieties of vegetables, holding this trophy for four consecutive years. He stopped exhibiting in 1928. Having delivered many lectures throughout Perth on the subject—including those for the Ugly Men's Association, which worked to alleviate the hardships of unemployment—he recorded his knowledge in *Australian Intense Vegetable Culture* (1924). This book was praised for being 'West Australian throughout' and for highlighting methods for growing vegetables in local conditions.

CAROLYN MIDDLEMIS

CONIFER is a loose term, often used indistinguishably in Australia with the term 'pine', although more generally applied to members of the Gymnosperms, particularly those that bear cones. Conifers are commonly taken to encompass eight botanical families that include pines, cypresses, araucarias, podocarps, yews, and others. Together, these families contain some 620 species in about seventy genera. As the common name suggests, they are cone-bearing PLANTS (mostly woody cones but berry-like in the families Cephalotaxaceae and Podocarpaceae); other major distinguishing features include their mainly evergreen needle or scale-like leaves and a distinctive aromatic, sticky resin. Conifers are sometimes also taken to include *Ginkgo biloba* (Maidenhair Tree) and the cone-bearing, palm-like CYCADS. These Gymnosperms stand clearly apart from the flowering plants, or Angiosperms.

The southern hemisphere conifer families Podocarpaceae and Araucariaceae are of GONDWANAN origin and contrast with the familiar northern hemisphere firs (*Abies*), pines (*Pinus*) and spruces (*Picea*) by having many species with broad leaves. The major genera growing naturally in Australia are she-oaks (*Callitris*) in the cypress family (13 species, all states, both coastal and inland), and *Podocarpus* (seven species, mostly from the tropics and subtropics). However, ARAUCARIA (three cultivated Australasian species from TROPICAL and subtropical RAINFORESTS) is perhaps best known in gardens.

The tallest tree in the world, with many extant specimens over 100 metres tall, is *Sequoia sempervirens* (California Redwood); the oldest living tree is probably *Pinus aristata* (Bristle-cone Pine), with one specimen in the American Rockies estimated at about 5000 years old. In Australia *Lagarostrobos franklinii* (Huon Pine)—a tree from Tas. once exploited for its fine-grained, pale timber—exceeds 3000 years life expectancy. X *Cupressocyparis leylandii* (Leyland Cypress) is one of the fastest-growing temperate plants and is widely used as a HEDGE or windbreak.

The nineteenth-century marked a peak of popularity for conifers, as botanical explorers brought back their trophies

Conifer

from western NORTH AMERICA, SOUTH AMERICA, the Himalayas, CHINA, and East ASIA. In Australia, conifers were especially popular in the period 1850–70, when their dark foliage and strong architectural forms added a new and dramatic dimension to the landscape. When these characteristics were later regarded as too formal and sombre, deciduous trees—such as elms, oaks, and planes, and especially those with attractive autumn foliage, so popular in European cities—gained increasing public acclaim.

The relatively recent arrival of conifers in world horticulture has meant that major conifer collections in Australia, especially those in cool-climate gardens, compare favourably in size and maturity with those in notable European and American collections. Many early conifer plantings remain as part of DESIGNED LANDSCAPES, forming the structural framework of BOTANIC GARDENS, PUBLIC PARKS, CEMETERIES (where they were used for their symbolism and folkloric associations inherited from powerful classical and European traditions), SCHOOL and other INSTITUTIONAL GARDENS, and as AVENUES and WINDBREAKS. Pines (especially *P. radiata*) and cypresses (especially *Cupressus macrocarpa* and its cultivars) were particularly suitable as windbreaks, while the araucarias were preferred as dominant specimen trees. The best collections of conifers are in the various botanic gardens and HILL-STATION properties, outstandingly at ALTON, Mount Macedon. The collective use of conifers, especially *Pinus* sp. to form a PINETUM, is still well demonstrated at botanic gardens such as WARRNAMBOOL and WILLIAMSTOWN.

FORESTRY plantations in Australia have been almost exclusively coniferous. Conifers are also often referred to commercially as 'softwoods' in contrast to the 'hardwood' flowering plants, principally EUCALYPTS. *Pinus radiata*, formerly *P. insignis* (Monterey Pine, but known in forestry as Radiata Pine), now rare and endangered in the wild, is the major plantation species in all states with the exception of WA (*P. pinaster*) and Qld (*P. elliottii* and *P. caribaea*). Ferdinand MUELLER suggested as early as 1859—only two years after its introduction—that it had commercial potential. The challenge was first taken up by SA in 1876. Vic. followed in 1880 with the first plantation at MOUNT MACEDON, and in the

The bold masses and silhouettes of CONIFERS have long excited gardeners in Australia, especially those of the cypresses (such as *Cupressus macrocarpa*, Monterey Cypress, shown here) and pines, and the Australian ARAUCARIAS

late 1880s at Creswick and the You Yangs. Canberra plantations were initially established to cover hillsides denuded by clearing and overgrazing and later, in 1925, it was recommended for commercial timber production with the aim of making the ACT self-sufficient in softwood.

In Australian horticulture there are more than 600 conifer CULTIVARS, exhibiting a wide range of habits and foliage colours. They enjoyed a period of great popularity in the 1940s and 1950s, and there has been another resurgence in recent times. Many conifers are prostrate or dwarf, with about 100 of those currently available being selections from Australian PLANT BREEDING. Apart from the strong colours and forms, many are noted for long life expectancy and minimal disease. The Conifer Society of Australia, founded in 1987, caters for enthusiasts of this distinctive group of plant families.

ROGER SPENCER

CONSERVATION of CULTURAL LANDSCAPES and GARDENS is a fine balancing act, seeking to preserve and maintain living spaces that stand on the cusp between the human and natural worlds. In simple terms, any landscape or ENVIRONMENT that has been significantly modified by human impact is a cultural landscape—including a tremendous variety of places such as PARKS, CEMETERIES, BOTANIC GARDENS, suburbs, farming districts, and Aboriginal sacred sites. Our concern here is with underlying values and approaches, rather than techniques.

By its nature, a landscape is a complex whole, not a single artefact. The landscape might include ways of travel (from paths to roadways), boundary lines (from fences to rivers), buildings (from homesteads to hospitals), plants (from remarkable individual specimen trees to ecological communities of grasses and ground covers), or animals (from cattle to wildlife). A landscape might be quite small, but it must have a number of elements that contribute to its general character. For example, a suburban street might form a distinctive mosaic of shady plane trees, inter-war bungalows, low fences, wide nature strips, and mature garden trees. At the smallest scale, a private garden forms a landscape in microcosm, but most landscapes will embody something beyond the private pleasures of the domestic garden. Larger gardens are more easily categorised as landscapes, with their array of features and the diverse experiences of the people who design them, visit them, work and play in them. Even the most important gardens can have their cultural meaning enhanced by a surrounding landscape. The ROYAL BOTANIC GARDENS, MELBOURNE, tell a story not only of picturesque design but of the search for rational recreation and a green oasis in the noisy, polluted city. Each surviving HILL-STATION in MOUNT MACEDON or MOUNT WILSON is valuable, but together they provide an impressive testimony to the lure of cool mountain summers, and the competitive plantsmanship of their Victorian creators. In a landscape, the whole must be greater than the sum of its parts. That is, the landscape must capture some sense of place that transcends its accumulated elements. This character is often the result of social processes and slow evolutionary change, but may be the result of a single designer's eye.

Above all, landscapes are living systems. At a practical level, this has significant consequences for conservation practice. Trees grow old and die, changing the vistas and vertical lines of parks, paddocks, or streets. Other trees grow tall and dominate, changing the patterns of light and shade in a garden. These longer cycles of change must be as successfully managed as the yearly cycles of the seasons, since the vitality of a landscape or garden relies on evolutionary, organic change. However, some changes cannot easily be reconciled with conserving the essential spirit of a place. Most landscapes are the product of particular ways of life, and embody certain social relationships and processes—whether in the form of the deeply cultivated flower beds of great garden estates, or the pleasing green hills of dairying farmland. When these social relationships and processes break down, the landscape may be preserved but be reduced to an empty shell, or museum. In Britain, the NATIONAL TRUST attempts to address this problem by subsidising traditional farmers, such as the sheep-farmers of the Lake District, believing that their lives and livelihoods are a social, community, and ECOLOGICAL good. This neat meshing of natural and cultural conservation is much rarer in the Australian countryside. The colonised landscapes of our continent are not static; they are the outcome of struggles to wrest a living from a new and unforgiving land. Cultural traditions, far from sustaining nature, may be in direct conflict with ecological ideals, as demonstrated in the bitter debates over the rights of cattlemen in the Australian high plains. Many landscapes are historically important because they embody rupture and conflict, not the Arcadian idyll of rural nostalgia. Australia's contemporary countryside was, after all, once Aboriginal land, and the widespread recognition of ABORIGINAL ENVIRONMENTAL MANAGEMENT and cultural landscapes in the past decade is a powerful acknowledgment of this.

Millions of years of evolutionary and GEOLOGICAL processes have formed the raw material of Australia's landscapes, and even the most artificial of our landscapes reflect such elemental foundations as CLIMATE, SOIL, and WATER. Thousands of years of Aboriginal habitation have had a profound impact on vegetation and animal communities, especially in the firing of the land for new grasses, to flush out wildlife, and to clear scrub. In recent decades there has been increased protection of the tangible features of Aboriginal occupation such as middens, rock art, and remnant shelters, which are often fragile and easily damaged by visitors. More subtly, the conservation movement now recognises that physical modification is only one way to give the landscape a vivid cultural life. The Aboriginal cultural landscape is spiritually sustained by a web of meaning and association with places, animals, mountains, caves, rocks, and creeks. These associations, in turn, are the basis for a continuing culture, grounded in place. The recognition that the whole continent carries Aboriginal cultural values has proved an enormous challenge to ideas of wilderness and nature preservation, but has also prompted landmark decisions such as the re-nomination of Uluru–Kata Tjuta to UNESCO's World Heritage List as a cultural landscape in 1994, and the much deeper involvement of local Aboriginal communities in the management of NATIONAL PARKS.

Conservation of plants

Non-Aboriginal cultural landscapes are also an increasing focus of Australian conservation practice. The need to conserve Australia's natural resources has been debated for well over a century now, but the drive to conserve the continent's cultural resources is much more recent. Early attempts at landscape conservation, particularly by the country's NATIONAL TRUSTS in the 1960s and 1970s, tended to analyse the landscape in picturesque terms, rating rural scenery as though it were a three-dimensional painting. The best were orderly, yet organic, full of pleasing sweeping lines, a harmonious continuum of the wild and the cultivated. This approach reached back to the ideal of the PICTURESQUE landscapes of the eighteenth century—an ideal that has indeed shaped some of our most important public and private gardens. Conservation in Australia via the HERITAGE movement has ranged from radical action, symbolised by GREEN BANS, to more measured registers and legislative frameworks, such as those of the AUSTRALIAN HERITAGE COMMISSION.

As in so many aspects of heritage conservation, however, the evaluation of cultural landscapes has become much broader and more eclectic in the past two decades. As architectural historians have turned their interests to the worker's cottage, so landscape historians around the world have turned to the vernacular landscape. To understand the meaning of ordinary landscapes is now seen as key to understanding the social processes, political relationships, and aesthetic ideals they manifest. The cultural landscape can, indeed, represent whole lives, and worlds.

BRIGID HAINS

CONSERVATION OF PLANTS: see PLANT CONSERVATION

CONSERVATORIES, specialised GREENHOUSES having antecedents in seventeenth-century Europe, ranged in Australia from modest plant rooms in domestic buildings—introduced as early as 1826 in the case of ELIZABETH FARM—to major GLASSHOUSES in private, public, and botanic gardens. Domestically, the term was applied to attached and free-standing structures and, depending on the scientific, botanic, or ornamental predilections of its owner, to cool and STOVE houses. Often large plants were grown in soil, or at least in plunged pots, complemented by potted plants on stages. Especially in the public domain, the term often implied architectural ornament or pretension. Fashion was a major influence in their introduction, as it was only in cooler parts of Australia that conservatories were a climatic necessity, and more often a BUSH-HOUSE provided an antipodean equivalent.

Following the repeal of the English glass and window taxes (1845–51), conservatories proliferated in the colonies before falling victim to prohibitive labour costs (mainly for management) in the twentieth century. Some actual buildings and most designs came from overseas sources, including pattern books, prefabricated structures (of wood or cast iron), and the direct experience of European-trained architects. Together with specialised camellia houses, ferneries, vineries, orchid houses, and palm houses, these miniature Crystal Palaces added lustre to domestic establishments. Except for their northern aspect they were virtually indistinguishable from their European counterparts. In Sydney, Thomas SHEPHERD assured Alexander MCLEAY in 1835 that 'particularly a conservatory at a little distance from the house' would transform Elizabeth Bay House into 'one of the most finished residences to be met with in any country'.

Whether it opened off an internal room, formed a link between wings of different dates, occupied the glazed end of a verandah, was a skillion-roofed lean-to or a free-standing structure, the conservatory was an extension of the living space; it provided escape, exercise, occupation, and delectation. It was an ornamental room where the daughter of the house—the latest triumph of the greenhouse—birds, STATUARY, FOUNTAINS, RUSTIC, or WIRE-WORK furniture, and exotic weapons were temporarily displayed at a temperature adapted to humans, which governed the choice of plants. Thus the priorities of the greenhouse or stove house—where plants came first—were reversed.

Major surviving conservatories include those at WERRIBEE PARK, RIPPON LEA, BEECHWOOD, ROSALIND PARK, and at SYDNEY, BRISBANE, and ADELAIDE BOTANIC GARDENS. The concept still appears in the form of glazed atriums in large city buildings, where conservatory-like greenery can link INDOOR GARDENS and outdoor landscapes.

May Woods and Arete Swartz Warren, *Glass Houses: A History of Greenhouses, Orangeries and Conservatories* (London, 1988)

JESSIE SERLE

CONTAINER GARDENING: see POTS AND CONTAINERS

COOCHIN COOCHIN, Boonah, Qld, a pastoral run from 1842, was purchased in 1883 by James Bell (1839–1903) and his wife Gertrude (1855–1946), whose father James Norton

The CONSERVATORY, imported from colder European climates, was generally displaced in Australian home gardens by a SHADE HOUSE, although grand estates such as RIPPON LEA, Elsternwick (Vic.), which could absorb staff and fuel costs, often incorporated this elegant addition to the parlour

(1824–1906), was a keen horticulturist and natural historian, a founding member of the LINNEAN SOCIETY OF NEW SOUTH WALES, and friend of Robert FITZGERALD. The homestead is situated on a sandstone ridge with outlooks over the Boonah–Teviot Brook valley. The gardens, which remain substantially intact, were established and actively maintained by Gertrude Bell. In this she was assisted by ABORIGINAL GARDENERS, including Bunjoey (or Susan as she was also known), who brought local ferns, orchids, and trees from the rainforests and ranges.

Entry to Coochin Coochin is through the south courtyard formed by the kitchen and other outbuildings, marked by an *Araucaria cunninghamii* (Hoop Pine). The north front of the house once addressed formal timber- and brick-edged flower gardens set between gravel paths, with the lawn beyond protected from the west by two *Ficus macrophylla* (Moreton Bay Fig) trees, and a bush-house. Local creek stone now edges garden beds and terraces on the east slope. To the north, a large bougainvillea arbour (1915) and trees enclose the lawn. The grounds beyond, and the walk to the tennis court, have many trees planted by notable visitors, particularly during the 1920s and 1930s, when the Bell family, during their long ownership, entertained freely in these fine gardens.

CATHERINE BROUWER

COOK, Edward Frances George James (*c.* 1894–1975), English-born landscape gardener, was apprenticed from 1909 in several gardens around Ipswich and Grantham (including Harlaxton Manor); following war service, he became head gardener at Bramford Hall (1919–24). He migrated to Australia in 1924 and following a brief period working at MURNDAL he established a landscape gardening business in Melbourne's south-east. Cook became a prominent figure of Melbourne's garden world during the inter-war period, and laid out gardens for many well-known families, notably in Toorak and at MOUNT MACEDON. He contributed to the *Australian Garden Lover*, and in his advertisements he featured work undertaken in conjunction with fashionable Melbourne architects Irwin and Stephenson. His *Vegetable Growing in Australia* (*c.* 1931) was published in WHITCOMBE'S AUSTRALIAN GARDENING HANDBOOKS series. Cook was an Oakleigh councillor, and mayor during 1946–47, taking a keen interest in local parks and gardens. E.F. Cook and Son Pty Ltd ceased business in the late 1950s.

RA

COOK PARK, Orange, NSW, is a fine example of the Victorian-era PUBLIC PARK. Situated adjacent to the town's main street, the park has outstanding mature plantings and many fine features dating from its establishment in 1882. Plantings began in the late 1880s and 1890s under the inaugural gardener, Alfred PATTERSON, a Swedish surveyor and gardener, who had worked for wealthy local merchant and civic leader James Dalton. Cook Park is set out on a radial plan, with a centrally placed octagonal timber bandstand (1908). Unusually, the bandstand retains original gas fittings and music stands. An elegant cast-iron fountain (1891) also stands at the centre, and two sets of notable cast-iron gates (1890 and 1927) mark the imposing entrances from the main street corners. A superb collection of begonias is housed in the Blowes Conservatory (1934), many of the plants sourced from BALLARAT BOTANIC GARDENS. A small lake (1890), ferneries (1938), and sunken gardens complete this well-maintained garden.

RICHARD HEATHCOTE

COOKTOWN BOTANIC GARDENS, Qld, were established in 1878 and reflect the rise of the township as the main port serving far north Qld. BANKS and SOLANDER had collected here more than a century earlier, and Gallop Botanic Reserve (of which the botanic garden now forms a part) retains substantial natural vegetation. The site was revived in the 1980s following neglect from 1917 onwards; it now contains selections of both native and exotic plants, a palmetum, and 'Solander's Gardens', along with nineteenth-century remnant plants, terraces, drains, steps, and other archaeological elements.

JODI FRAWLEY

COOLIBAH, near Young, NSW, a garden planned by Jocelyn BROWN in 1956, was created to complement a country house designed by architect Kenneth McConnel for the Goodall family. This major commission, producing a notable country garden with a distinctive local character, was much looser than her earlier designs. It allowed distant views across the plain; careful planting of native trees outside the garden proper defined and directed the views. An internal vista was to a rocky knoll of granite tors. A gravel drive surrounded the house as a precaution against bushfires, and windbreak belts of trees were established to protect the flower gardens, rose borders, vegetable gardens, and orchard. A mixture of native and imported tree species was used in the planting.

HELEN PROUDFOOT

COOLRINGDON, Cooma, NSW, is a large rambling HOMESTEAD GARDEN at the foothills of the Snowy Mountains. Once centre of pastoralist William Bradley's vast Monaro holdings, Coolringdon was home to Betty Litchfield (formerly Casey, *née* Craig) (1907–1999) throughout the twentieth century. An early avenue of *Pinus radiata* (Monterey Pine) flanks the 1.5 km driveway to the homestead, leading to a late 1840s avenue of *Ulmus procera* (English Elm). The garden encompasses a large area of parkland, formal terracing, creek walks, sunken garden, and courtyard. The formal garden area surrounding the homestead is bounded by a tall stone wall of the 1930s. The homestead and garden are run by the trustees of the estate of Betty Litchfield, and the property is run in perpetuity as a pastoral enterprise with profits allocated to the John and Betty Casey Research Trust run by the University of Sydney.

Trisha Dixon, *Coolringdon Garden* (Canberra, 1998)

TRISHA DIXON

COOMBE COTTAGE, Coldstream, Vic., originally part of Yering station, was bought in 1850 by Paul DE CASTELLA, brother of Hubert. The site was purchased in 1909 by (Dame) Nellie Melba (1861–1931), at that time enthroned as the leading soprano of the age. To increase links with her homeland, Melba developed Coombe Cottage as a retreat from her London residence. An architect's drawing, annotated 'copy to be sent to Mr Guilfoyle' (1911), suggests that William GUILFOYLE may have advised on the earliest section, presumably the sweeping front lawns and beds. The garden was well developed by the early 1920s: its compartmentalised design is redolent of both the ARTS AND CRAFTS movement and Melba's penchant for extending and embellishing the garden. The gate lodge (c. 1925) is attributed to Walter BUTLER, who may have advised on the garden design, including the swimming pool and ROOF GARDEN. Edna WALLING worked at Coombe in 1927, assisted by BURNLEY graduates Betty BEGG, Mollie Shannon, and Joan Anderson, and prepared (unexecuted) plans to convert a tennis court into either a formal lily pond or garden of old-fashioned flowers.

Melba's *Melodies and Memories* (London, 1925)—ghostwritten at Coombe by Beverley Nichols—invokes images of the site to demonstrate Melba's Australianness, yet the garden design has a sophisticated European formality, closeted by a high cypress hedge and eschewing the surrounding countryside. As early as 1971 Walling advocated conservation of the garden—reverentially maintained by family members—as a memorial to Melba, suggesting that its significance would make it the 'Glyndebourne of Australia'. RA

COONAWARRA, SA, is one Australia's great VITICULTURAL regions. It derives its name from an Aboriginal word, believed to mean 'wild honeysuckle'. Its founder was a wealthy district pastoralist, John Riddoch (1827–1901) of Yallum Park, who identified land with good drainage north of Penola. The area is low-lying and flat, with ancient sub-marine origins dating back nearly a million years, when the ocean extended inland as far as the present Naracoorte Range. Only after drainage works (1914–16) was settlement possible off the limestone ridge on which Penola is itself located.

In 1890 Riddoch initiated the 'Penola Fruit Colony' in ten-acre (4 ha) lots, later renamed the Coonawarra Fruit Colony; 400 hectares were laid out, and another 320 later added. Plantings of vines and fruit trees began in 1891 and approximately 120 hectares had been planted by 1899, half with vines. Riddoch supported the settlers and established a nursery and a winery (today Wynn's Coonawarra Estate) and in 1899 sponsored articles in *Garden and Field*, later reprinted in booklet form. An original twenty-six 'colonists' secured holdings ranging from ten to eighty acres (4 to 32 ha). Riddoch's death meant hard times for the Coonawarra 'blockers'. Table wine and apples had been promoted, but Riddoch's trustees turned to brandy production. In 1910 the winery was sold to BAROSSA brandy producer, Chateau Tanunda, who in 1917 sold to another distiller. Transport difficulties and the 1914–18 war inhibited planned export sales of fruit. The vineyards were maintained, though grapes brought low prices when distilled into brandy. In 1936, following a glut, soldier-settlers with fruit blocks were subsidised to move into dairying, and land under vines was reduced from a peak of about 350 hectares to 140.

Brandy was still being made at the old winery in 1946 when the new owner, Austrian-born Tony Nelson of Woodley Wines, changed production to table wine. In 1951 the winery and core vineyards were purchased by David Wynn for the Melbourne-based family wine company S. Wynn and Co. Coonawarra district wine began to achieve a reputation. Other growers, such as the Redman family, sold wine and managed vineyards for Mildara, who purchased land in 1955 and later introduced the 'deep ripping' method of vineyard establishment, breaking the hard cap of limestone to enable better root penetration. Penfold purchased sixteen hectares in 1958 and in 1965 Redman sold the 'Rouge Homme' property to Lindemans, which started a land boom. A distinguishing feature of the region—a ridge-like strip of red soil (*terra rossa*) over limestone, approximately twenty kilometres long and in parts a kilometre wide—has also, more recently, been celebrated. Outlying pockets with the same characteristics have also attracted vineyards. Plantings on both the red and surrounding black soil have seen the region grow into a major viticultural area producing red wines, in particular, of the highest quality. An industry-backed initiative in the 1990s to define the Coonawarra wine region geographically has proved controversial. DAVID DUNSTAN

COPAS, Henry (1838–1918), horticulturist, was born in Slough, Buckinghamshire, England, and trained in Charles Turner's Royal Nurseries (Slough) and James VEITCH and Sons' nursery (Chelsea), undertaking an apprenticeship at the Duke of Sutherland's property, Cliveden. Migrating to Adelaide in 1864, he gained employment in Pitt's Nursery, seeded the new Adelaide Oval lawns (1872), and established his extensive, irrigated market garden and ornamental and fruit tree nursery operations—adjacent to the WIRRABARA FOREST RESERVE, and at Laura—in 1878, before losing the operation through financial difficulties in 1886. In 1905 he established the Findon Nursery at Lockleys, known especially for its roses and fruit trees. His son Henry Walter Copas (1869–1931), grandson Keith Copas (1904–1975), and great-grandson Peter Raymond Copas (1945–1985), continued his horticultural legacy. DAVID JONES

CORNELIAN BAY CEMETERY (originally Hobart Town Public Cemetery), resulted from community pressure to close down unsatisfactory burial sites and to bring concepts of good order and management to CEMETERIES. The winner of a design competition (1871) held by the first trustees (appointed 1866) was surveyor E.J. Burgess, although implementation was undertaken by talented Hobart architect (and former trustee) Henry Hunter (1832–1892). Management ideas and regulations had been adopted from New York's fashionable Greenwood Cemetery, Brooklyn (1838), and the Hobart *Mercury* proudly boasted after the opening (1872) that the new cemetery would become the Père Lachaise of Hobart, a significant tourist attraction. Its waterfront site certainly seemed to offer a romantic setting, but for many years it remained isolated from centres of population and transport routes. The original design, with its nineteen feet (5.8 m) wide grand walks, chapels, and tree borders, was never fully implemented, but mature plantings of conifers—particularly pines and Bhutan cypresses—and old roses combine with the serpentine paths and the elevated promontory site to give an evocative garden cemetery character. ROBERT NICOL

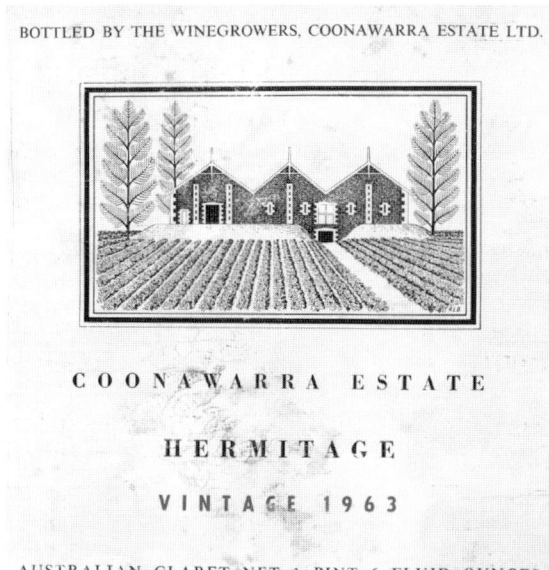

This design by Richard Beck (1912–1985) of the early 1950s, still used by Wynn's COONAWARRA Estate, one of the earliest Australian companies to market wine by region of origin, is a clearly identifiable symbol of this premier South Australian VITICULTURAL region

CORNISH, Elsie Marion (1870–1946), landscape designer, was prominent in Adelaide between 1918 and 1946, and was deemed in her obituary to be 'one of Adelaide's best known landscape gardeners, and … responsible for the design and care of many of the city's most beautiful gardens'. Self-trained, she gained the patronage of many Adelaide establishment families for her domestic projects, and earned the respect of prominent architect Walter BAGOT. Her design work drew reference from the ideas of Gertrude JEKYLL and MEDITERRANEAN design traditions including cottage and northern Italian plants, and she reinterpreted these in the many domestic designs, sunken ROCK GARDENS, entry porches, WALLS and garden features that she personally designed, built, and planted for clients. Her designs display a respect for the local environment, and are reminiscent of the ideas of Jocelyn BROWN and Edna WALLING. Her garden installations often won prizes at the Royal Adelaide Show, competing strongly with KEMP nursery entries, notwithstanding the traditional ideas of chief juror Alfred QUARRELL, expressed in *South Australian Homes and Gardens*. Her most significant projects include the Pioneer Women's Garden (1938–39) in ADELAIDE PARK LANDS, the University of Adelaide embankment (1934–46), and parts of Eringa Hyde Park (1936–37), for the Kidman family. During the 1930s and 1940s her North Adelaide property, later acquired by Gavin WALKLEY, served as a nursery to supply plants to these projects. She also advised the Waite sisters on the layout and planting of their Jekyll-inspired garden at BROADLEES, Crafers.

DAVID JONES

CORREY, Allan Dale (b. 1931), landscape architect, was born in Sydney and educated in horticulture at the ROYAL BOTANIC GARDENS, SYDNEY, and Sydney Technical College; landscape architecture at King's College, University of Durham (UK), and the University of Illinois (USA); and in environmental studies at Macquarie University (NSW). His design philosophy was influenced by the teachings of Brian Hackett and Phil Lewis, and the writings of Garrett Eckbo, Brenda Colvin, Sylvia CROWE, James Rose, and J.B. Jackson. Early designs included the MOUNT LOFTY BOTANIC GARDEN, SA (1961–65), incorporating English picturesque and American romantic ideas, the de Stilj–inspired Art Gallery of South Australia sculpture court (1962), the Burle Marx–influenced western wild garden in the ADELAIDE BOTANIC GARDEN (1963), and numerous domestic and institutional projects in SA. He taught the first landscape design courses offered at the South Australian Institute of Technology and the University of Adelaide (1962–67), often assisting Gavin WALKLEY with initiatives to promote LANDSCAPE ARCHITECTURE and the AUSTRALIAN INSTITUTE OF LANDSCAPE ARCHITECTS. In both teaching and practice he attempted to define a regional Adelaide landscape style and advocated the retention and use of Australian vegetation.

From 1967 to 1970 Correy headed the Landscape Section of the New South Wales Public Works Department, where he was responsible for major state landscape projects, including the redevelopment of Taronga ZOO. He worked as a landscape planner for the State Planning Authority on the Macarthur New Cities development (1970–72) and for Bankstown Municipal Council (1973). From 1978 to 1996 he was Senior Lecturer in Landscape Architecture at the University of Sydney. His career has been shaped by a love of the Australian landscape—initially through bushwalking, but consolidated by rigorous ecological studies—and the imperative to protect its qualities and assert its legitimacy in the broad field of Australian landscape architecture.

DAVID JONES

COSTERMANS, Leon Francis (b. 1933), naturalist and educator, graduated in science (1967), majoring in geology and geomorphology, and botany (1981). He became a secondary school science teacher, then a lecturer in science education and outdoor and environmental education. His two publications, the field guides *Trees of Victoria* (1966), released in 1994 as *Trees of Victoria and Adjoining Areas*, and *Native Trees and Shrubs of South-eastern Australia* (1981), with an introduction describing the major geographic regions and associated vegetation, have been invaluable resources for naturalists and students of horticulture and botany. Costermans has been a strong advocate for many organisations, especially those embracing NATURAL HISTORY, NATIONAL PARKS, CONSERVATION, and REVEGETATION, including GREENING AUSTRALIA and the Victorian National Parks Association.

JILL KELLOW

COTTAGE GARDENER (1848–60), later the ***Journal of Horticulture and Cottage Gardener*** (1861–1915), was, after the *GARDENERS' CHRONICLE*, the most influential British horticultural journal circulating in the colonies during the mid-nineteenth century. It was held by many Australian public LIBRARIES and HORTICULTURAL SOCIETIES, and was doubtless in the collections of many private subscribers. The journal title should not confuse; it was, as one commentator aptly put it, 'for the occupiers of a cottage to which a double coach-house was attached'. Founding editor, George William Johnson (1802–1886), was also well known for his *Cottage Gardeners' Dictionary* (1852)—a work that went into many editions and was popular in Australia until at least the 1940s. His pioneering *History of English Gardening* (1828) was a prelude to the many historical articles published in the *Cottage Gardener*. Principal among the early contributors was Donald BEATON, who through his regular column was strongly supportive of the emigration of GARDENERS to Australia. The journal also demonstrated a general interest in antipodean gardening—for instance, in its very positive review of *Principles of Gardening for Australia* by Charles Bogue LUFFMANN (1903). RA

COTTAGE GARDENS European settlement in Australia began at a time when increasing attention was being given to smaller houses and their attendant gardens. In Britain, enlightened reformers saw the need for improved living conditions for ordinary workers, including space to grow VEGETABLES, FRUIT, HERBS, and FLOWERS. Following LAND SURVEY AND SALE and given the availability of land in and around the towns and villages of the Australian colonies, a great emphasis was placed on detached cottages with room for a garden. From this evolved the dream of a family home on its own 'quarter-acre block'. Pioneering conditions ensured that most of the earliest gardens in both town and country were of a similar character to the traditional cottage garden in England. Within the protection of a fence of palings, pickets, or sticks, as many vegetables were grown as conditions would allow; fruit trees were established, and livestock kept. A few flowers, grown for sentiment, were a first step towards the creation of antipodean gardens, often as floriferous as any at 'home'.

Hot summers—and in many places, low or unreliable rainfall—meant that some of the tender plants favoured in English cottage gardens were restricted to cool, well-watered areas. Other cottage flowers adapted readily, and some thrived. We know from diaries, letters, and contemporary publications, that gardeners were very resourceful. Exchanging seeds, cuttings, bulbs, corms, tubers, and rooted plants was a notable activity. With improving prospects including more leisure time, people took to gardening in ever-greater numbers. Newspapers, magazines, and popular garden books contributed to this trend. Cottage gardening became a regular subject in publications both in Britain and Australia. Two early Victorian examples were RULE's *Economical Gardening for Cottagers* (1859), and *The Cottage Gardener* (1862), a guide and catalogue published by Ballarat nursery proprietor George SMITH.

By the end of the nineteenth century, English cottage gardens and their 'old fashioned' plants were becoming an important influence in the making of fashionable gardens on every scale. Australian cottage gardens could be divided into three categories. First, there was a continuation of the old unsophisticated approach: a free-growing garden, both functional and decorative, in association with a cottage or modest house. Secondly, there were cottage gardens that included, to a greater or lesser degree, aspects of FORMAL traditions. Even the humblest of Australian dwellings could be given gardens with axial plans, geometric BEDS, and in some examples, complicated PARTERRES. Borders were carefully laid out with plants such as *Dianthus plumarius* (Cottage Pink) or *Buxus sempervirens* 'Suffruticosa' (Dwarf Edging Box), reliable in a range of temperatures and during periods of low rainfall. Finally, there were schemes influenced by writers, artists, and garden designers who were in turn inspired by the most attractive of the old cottage gardens. In England, Gertrude JEKYLL travelled country lanes in search of herbaceous plants and old roses. Her turn-of-the-century garden designs combined informal plantings, especially of HERBACEOUS BORDERS, with a formal framework of paths, steps, terraces, walls, and pergolas.

Books and magazines with plans and illustrations helped spread the romantic cottage style in Australia in the early decades of the twentieth century. From the 1920s, writer and designer Edna WALLING was a powerful force in maintaining and extending the cottage garden ideal. Her book *Cottage and Garden in Australia* (1947) challenged the stark spaces and hard lines of MODERNISM with a combination of woodland effects and cottage plantings. Her use of the word 'cottage' in the 1940s carried over from earlier times—by then the modest family dwelling was more prosaically called a 'home'. The term 'bungalow' as a fashionable description had peaked in the 1920s, during the boom in the Californian bungalow style.

Typically, Australian cottage gardens have included plants from regions with a MEDITERRANEAN climate, including BULBS from South Africa, SUCCULENTS from Mexico, wildflowers from California, shrub daisies from the CANARY ISLANDS, the moss rose and common lilac from Iran, and sages from Central and South America. Cottage garden favourites from the Mediterranean itself include *Digitalis* (foxgloves), *Consolida* (larkspurs), *Lavandula* (lavenders), *Lathyrus* (sweet peas), *Iberis* (candytufts), hypericums, and *Rosmarinus officinalis* (Common Rosemary).

A straight path running from the gate to the front door was almost universal in Australian cottage gardens in the nineteenth century. If there was a formal layout of beds, they were usually balanced on this central axis. Even the smallest FRONT GARDENS were given edged beds in squares, rectangles, diamonds, circles, and ovals. Shrubs were used for hedging, as a background to beds, or as central features. The use of ornamental trees depended on available space and current fashions. Fruit trees were sometimes planted in the front garden, or as a group to one side in a small ORCHARD. More typically, they were a part of the utilitarian character of the BACKYARD. When shrubs and climbers were also used, a softening of the plain geometry of sheds, outhouses, and fences was achieved. VERANDAHS became an integral part of Australian domestic architecture, providing shelter for plants in POTS and support for all manner of CLIMBING PLANTS. Honeysuckle and other fragrant species were helpful in disguising the odours of unsewered toilets. Artemisia hedges planted alongside poultry runs were believed to deter lice. Raspberries, strawberries, and gooseberries were all popular;

Courtyards

This COTTAGE GARDEN on the goldfields at Hill End (NSW), photographed c. 1870–75, displays a remarkable FORMALITY in the layout of its garden beds, startling to modern eyes when juxtaposed with the rudimentary slab and bark hut

passionfruit flourished in most regions, as did pumpkins and melons. The all-important vegetable garden varied in scale and was generally set out in a simple grid pattern of rectangular beds edged with bricks, stones, tiles or timber.

Prosperity and expanding suburbia in the decades following the Second World War produced a diversity of gardening fashions. The use of AUSTRALIAN PLANTS reached a high level of acceptance followed in turn by a new wave of interest in traditional gardens. New books both reflected and encouraged a gathering momentum. Nurseries answered a burgeoning demand for 'cottage' or 'heritage' plants; ancillary industries offered picket fences, rose arches, rustic garden furniture, bird baths, and ornaments. As long as there are cottages, their gardens will evolve in response to changing fashions. The cottage style has become an enduring tradition that suits a variety of garden settings.

Victor Crittenden, *The Front Garden: The Story of the Cottage Garden in Australia* (Canberra, 1979); Anne Scott-James, *The Cottage Garden* (London, 1981); Peter Cuffley, *Cottage Gardens in Australia* (Canterbury, Vic., 1983); Trevor Nottle, *The Cottage Garden Revived* (Kenthurst, NSW, 1984)

PETER CUFFLEY

COTTESLOE WAR MEMORIAL TOWN HALL AND CIVIC CENTRE (formerly Overton Lodge), WA, was built c. 1898 by barrister Richard William Pennefather. Mining promoter Claude Albo de Bernales (1876–1963) purchased the property in 1911 and remodelled the existing house and garden during the mid-1930s. To create large lawn areas, rich soil was brought in from the Darling Ranges. Features of these terraced gardens include extensive limestone walls with Italianate balustrades, a tennis court and pavilion overlooking the Indian Ocean, and sunken gardens with water-lily ponds. It was these qualities that saw the site used as a location (evoking Majorca) in the film *Let's Get Skase* (2001). Cottesloe Municipal Council purchased the property in 1949 and altered aspects of the garden to suit public use.

CAROLYN MIDDLEMIS

COURTYARDS Early British settlers coming to terms with Australia's hot CLIMATE quickly adopted the VERANDAH and the informal, well-planted courtyard as important adjuncts to outdoor living. Sometimes for practical reasons, courtyards were hard-paved and WALLED to screen activities from view—as at ELIZABETH FARM, Parramatta, NSW (1833). The most typical courtyard was formed by the back of the house and two secondary wings, and was open on the fourth side. This pattern is clearly seen at Burrundulla, Mudgee, NSW (1864), where river cobbles flag the space, which is overhung by an old grapevine supported by a hardwood trellis. In the first half of the twentieth century this pattern was embellished with MEDITERRANEAN detail, the fourth side becoming a classical colonnade at ERYLDENE, Gordon, NSW (1913), a massive PERGOLA at Hazeldean, near Cooma, NSW (1937), or a simple arcade at designer Marion Hall Best's house at Woollahra, NSW (1934). The Woollahra house became, with the addition of a colourful Marimekko fabric tent roof and lush SUBTROPICAL planting, one of the most memorable images of the 1960s, its arcades framing views to a JAPANESE-inspired garden.

Spacious, architecturally enclosed domestic courtyards are rare in Australia. A fine Edwardian example was Kilmory, Point Piper, NSW (1915), with a central octagonal FOUNTAIN, stone flagging, and an encircling verandah at upper level. The cortile of the Renaissance, with its vaulted arcades and grilled windows, provided the basis of the remarkable extension to Nurney House, North Adelaide (1930), created by architect Walter BAGOT. Here HEDGES of clipped rosemary edged the central pathways, which met at a shallow dish fountain. A more 'Hollywood Spanish' version was Boomerang, Elizabeth Bay, NSW (1926), where open colonnades framed views to tiled ponds and lush planting. A Roman-inspired courtyard was proposed by architect John D. Moore in his book *Home Again* (1944). His vision of 'a pisé house with a central courtyard for the hot dry country', with a central fountain surrounded by low shrubs, and the summer sun shielded by retractable canvas blinds was inspired, but probably unrealised.

Large INSTITUTIONS, especially the older UNIVERSITIES and some HOSPITALS and schools, often featured large architectural courtyards or quadrangles, typically a simple arrangement of paths and lawns with the occasional accent tree. The Thomas Walker Hospital, Concord, NSW (1891–93), retains paired formal courtyards with exquisite Queen Anne colonnades about lawns set with central terracotta fountains. A similar formal arrangement is found at Old Parliament House, Canberra (1927), whose two courtyards are dominated by poplars and temple-like pergolas (now altered) within a framework of white classical forms. At the University of Sydney, Professor E.G. WATERHOUSE introduced jacarandas, cypress pines (*Callitris* sp.), azaleas, and camellias around the main buildings. These are used to memorable effect in the Vice Chancellor's Quadrangle (1925), which is traversed by sandstone paths and accented by a pair of French statues cast in bronze. Several modern courtyards are found in Canberra, ranging from University House (1949–54), the Trade Offices (1972–74), and Parliament House (1981–88), using highly structured patterns of paving, planting, ponds, and abstract sculpture within a formal plan. In the domestic sphere, the PATIO accompanied a vogue for outdoor living after the Second World War, and today tight urban courtyard gardens extend what are effectively rooms into the landscape.

HOWARD TANNER

COWAN, Alexander Menzies (*fl.* 1880s–90s), horticulturist and nursery proprietor, was trained at the ROYAL BOTANIC GARDENS, KEW, and left in 1880 for Brisbane. He worked in the nursery trade and, highly recommended by Sir Joseph Hooker, succeeded James PINK as Head Gardener at the Brisbane Botanic Garden (1886). Like Pink, he resigned from this position (in 1889) after conflict with the Board of Trustees. Cowan contributed 'Flower Gardening' and 'Orange Cultivation in Queensland' in Alfred Midgley's *The Queensland Illustrated Guide; for the Use of Farmers, Fruit-Growers, Vignerons, and Others* (1888) and joined Pink in a commercial nursery in the early 1890s. Cowan subsequently moved to WA, his whereabouts being reported in the *Journal of the Kew Guild*. He served as Superintendent of Rottnest Park from *c.* 1895, and died several years prior to 1922 (when Kew botanist E.H. Wilson sought his whereabouts).

JEANNIE SIM

COWLEY, Ebenezer (*c.* 1849–1899), horticulturist and nursery manager, was born at Fairford, Gloucestershire, England, and was raised and married in South Africa. He was a sugar cane planter at Coorparoo (outer Brisbane) during the 1880s. In 1889, he was appointed overseer at Kamerunga STATE NURSERY, west of Cairns on the Atherton Tableland. Located beside the Barron River, amid lush rainforest, Cowley's work included experimenting with various tropical ECONOMIC plants, distributing such plants to the public, recording weather information, and preparing displays for the Cairns Agricultural Show. Cowley visited New Guinea in 1893 to collect indigenous varieties of sugar cane. His garden writing contributions included a list of indigenous TROPICAL shade trees published in SHELTON's *Tree-planting for Shade and Ornament* (1892), annual reports to the Department of Agriculture, and, from March 1898, a regular column, 'Field and Garden Notes for Tropical Queensland', in the *Queensland Agricultural Journal*. His horticultural advice ranged from recommending some of the gardening practices of local Chinese MARKET GARDENERS to recognising the need in the tropics to concentrate heavy work during the cooler months.

JEANNIE SIM

COWLISHAW, (George) Keith (1901–1983), lawyer, horticulturist, journalist, and collector, was born at Mosman (NSW), son of stock and station agent George Owen Cowlishaw. He lived for much of his life at a family home, Telopea, Mosman, which was featured in *Our Beautiful Homes* (*c.* 1910). Its handsome garden was host to Cowlishaw's horticultural expertise and experimentation—such were his standards that in 1928 he retained only five out of 5000 hybridised watsonia seedlings—and its walls were lined with his burgeoning collection of books and paintings. He was a stalwart council member of the Royal Horticultural Society of New South Wales and for a time edited its official journal, *Garden and Home Maker of Australia* (1925–33). Cowlishaw was a frequent contributor to other journals, touching especially on the flower garden and PLANT BREEDING. He displayed a special interest in BULBS, including those from the Cape, and was a member of the South African National

COURTYARDS, periodically fashionable with architects and designers, have once again become a focus for garden designers working within the tight space constraints of many urban sites

Botanical Society. His book *All About Palms: Australia's Native and Cultivated Species* (1929) was the first Australian work on its subject, and his pamphlet *The Cultivation of Australian Native Plants* (*c.* 1932), published in Sydney by the Rangers' League, was also a pioneering work: one of the first to give practical instructions in cultivation rather than mere admiration of wildflower blooms or select incorporation of Australian trees into otherwise exotic planting schemes. His advice that 'The well-planned and properly planted Australian garden leaves one the impression that the house was built into the garden, and not the garden built about the house' was at odds with most suburban development of the inter-war period. Cowlishaw inherited sufficient wealth to pursue his collecting and gardening full-time, rising to be among the first rank of Australian horticulturists. His horticultural LIBRARY was reputedly the best in Sydney, and after his death his collection was auctioned by Sotheby's (1984). The National Library of Australia now holds the 'Cowlishaw Gardening Book Collection'.

RA

CRAIGOW, Richmond, Tas., was granted to physician and farmer James Murdoch (1785–1848), who also possessed a farm with medicinal garden at nearby Risdon Creek. By 1829 he produced herbal 'waters' from lavender, peppermint, and rosemary, as well as medicinal opium and grapes for wine. Perched on a rise, the Gothic-styled Craigow homestead (*c.* 1880) and fernery overlooks a box-hedged circular driveway bounded by a picket fence. It is approached by three formal avenues, which are rare survivors in this relatively dry climate: the oldest, winding from the Richmond Road, is dominated by araucarias, oaks and conifers, and the second and current, a steep drive, uses elms under-planted with bulbs and drained by cobblestone gutters. A third avenue of she-oaks leads to the farm yard.

PETER MacFIE

CRANBOURNE BOTANIC GARDENS, Vic.: see ROYAL BOTANIC GARDENS, CRANBOURNE

CRANBROOK, Bellevue Hill, NSW, is centred on the Italianate house (1859) built for brewer Robert Tooth (1821–1893) and sold to merchant Robert Towns (1794–1873) in 1864. Its elaborate grounds were described in the *Horticultural Magazine* (1866). The house, with views to Sydney Harbour, sat on a grassy plateau with a thirty-metre long conservatory to one side, and below it three terraces descended to a shrubbery and a miniature lake. As the state's GOVERNMENT HOUSE (1901–17), a massive sandstone terrace was added to complement the new ballroom. As Cranbrook School (1918–), the grounds have been increasingly built over, although the original landscaped driveway still links gates, gatehouse, and residence. Major specimen trees—*Agathis robusta* (Kauri Pine), *Araucaria cunninghamii* (Hoop Pine) and *A. hetrophylla* (Norfolk Island Pine), *Ficus virens* (White Fig), and *Butia capitata* (Chilean Wine Palm)—remain from the historic garden, as does architect J. Horbury Hunt's recreational PAVILION (*c.* 1875).

HOWARD TANNER

CRANLANA, Toorak, Vic., was designed in 1932 by Harold DESBROWE-ANNEAR. Originally commissioned in 1928 by retailer Sidney Myer (1878–1934) to design a new house, the architect proposed for it an extensive formal garden similar to the original scheme for the nearby M.H. BAILLIEU garden (1925). With the onset of the Depression, the project for a new house was abandoned, but Myer and his wife Merlyn (née Baillieu) (1900–1982) enlarged their property by acquiring land to the north and commissioned the architect to design a modified version of the garden, together with the front wall and gates (wrought by CASLAKE).

A straight gravel drive in front of the house divided the garden into two areas, both of which Desbrowe-Annear envisaged as extensions of the house set within a highly formalised plan of a circle (articulated by planting) within a square (boundary walls). Within this frame (of which only the northern section was completed to his plans) a grid of paths divided the garden into sections. An upper, walled terrace on axis with the front entry of the house lead to a lower, larger sunken WALLED GARDEN, in the midst of which is a shaped lily pond of the kind illustrated in JEKYLL and Weaver's *Gardens for Small Country Houses* (1912), and two axially placed fountains. Beyond, a long, informal, flagged walk terminated at either end by nineteenth-century Italian statues extended the length of the northern boundary. While the terrace can be compared with North American landscape designer Beatrix Farrand's fountain terrace at Dumbarton Oaks (1921–47), it can equally be seen as a development of earlier themes in Desbrowe-Annear's work, enhanced by an expanded use of freestone walls and ornaments in the Jekyll manner. Both architect and client owned editions of Jekyll and Hussey's *Garden Ornament*, and it is probable that this provided a discussion point. Myer might also have known Sir Edwin Lutyens (1869–1944), with whom Jekyll collaborated on many gardens, and who was commissioned to design the Myer memorial tomb in Box Hill cemetery.

HARRIET EDQUIST

CRESSBROOK, Qld, established in 1841 by David Cannon McConnel (1818–1885), was the first property taken up in the Brisbane River valley when the Moreton Bay region was opened to pastoral settlement. Cressbrook is the oldest HOMESTEAD GARDEN in Qld, and remains in the McConnel family. Extensive gardens, including stone-edged terraces with gravel paths, croquet lawn (and later a tennis court), nursery, vegetable gardens, and orchard were established primarily to the north and west of the house. A gravel path and steps led down the slope and through grape vine–covered trellises to the river. An *Araucaria bidwillii* (Bunya Pine) planted in 1842 by David McConnel remains. The impressive siting, along the edge of a curving, north-facing river terrace with an outlook to the paddocks, the Brisbane River, and the D'Aguilar Range, permits panoramic views. Unusually for Qld, the garden includes *Quercus robur* (English Oak) and *Ulmus parvifolia* (Chinese Elm), in addition to *Araucaria bidwillii*, *Jacaranda mimosifolia*, and *Celtis sinensis*.

CATHERINE BROUWER

CRESWELL, Charles Frederick (*c*. 1826–1895), nursery proprietor, seed merchant, and florist, was born in Gloucester, England, and arrived with his parents in Van Diemen's Land in 1843. In 1849 he left for a stint at the Californian diggings and travelled before returning to Australia. He married Sarah, daughter of nursery proprietor Frederick LIPSCOMBE, in 1853, and in 1856 took over the business in Murray Street, Hobart Town, that Lipscombe had established in 1840. The business grew, and by the 1860s it included the Tasmanian Seed Stores in Murray Street, a branch in Liverpool Street supplying fresh fruit and vegetables, and a nursery in Macquarie Street. It imported high grades of garden, agricultural, and pastoral seeds from Europe and America, grew various seeds under contract for the seed trade, and collected indigenous seeds for export. Creswell was involved in a wide variety of agricultural and horticultural interests and was a long-serving committee member of the Gardeners' and Amateurs' Horticultural Society. A founder of the Southern Tasmanian Agricultural, Pastoral and Horticultural Society (1874), his great practical and theoretical knowledge was credited for much of the success of their early shows and exhibitions. Creswell was also highly regarded in his later position as chairman of the Hobart Fruit Board.

In 1872 his son **Charles Frederick Creswell** (1858–1916) joined the branch business in Melbourne, and in 1880 undertook the management of the company's Sydney seed house in George Street. On the death of his father he returned to Hobart to run the business. The Melbourne business was taken over in 1883 by William James Taylor, son of William Taylor of TAYLOR AND SANGSTER. C.F. Creswell jnr. was a Fellow of the Royal Horticultural Society and wrote on horticulture for various journals. Creswell's son Harvey Creswell (1884–1945) was also involved in the family seed business, as was his son Harvey Strathmore Creswell (1905–1965). H.S. Creswell expanded the seed-packaging business, including the area of specialist turf seeds. The growing conditions for seed production were ideal in Tas., and Ch. Creswell & Co., with their reputation for quality and service, became involved in packaging and seed distribution under licence for other companies throughout Australia. Although sold by the family in 1970, the Creswell seed business continues to operate.

ANN CRIPPS

CRIBB, Joan Winifred and **Alan Bridson Cribb**: see HERBERT, Desmond Albert

CRIBB, John George (1830–1905), born near Bristol, England, arrived in Brisbane with family members in 1849. Although trained as a lithographic artist in London and a banker in Brisbane, horticulture was his passion: his large garden on the River-road (now Coronation Drive) was 'a private ACCLIMATISATION ground on a small scale'. He introduced many useful fruit varieties from North America, and was a frequent and knowledgeable contributor to the local horticultural press.

RA

CRICHTON, David Alexander (*c*. 1824–1906), gardener, horticulturist, and journalist, undertook his professional training in Britain. He fought with the Dragoon Guards in the Crimean War, taking part in the Battle of Alma. Crichton migrated to Australia, becoming gardener to Robert Towns at CRANBROOK, Rose Bay (NSW). He gave papers to the

Harold DESBROWE-ANNEAR's garden scheme for the Myer property, CRANLANA, Toorak (Vic.), photographed during its early development for *Australian Home Beautiful* (1934), displayed the designer's fondness for geometric planning

Horticultural Society of Sydney on 'The Orange' and 'The Apple' (1864) and occasionally chaired the Society's meetings. By 1877 he was agricultural and horticultural editor of the *WEEKLY TIMES* (Melbourne); at various times he also undertook these duties for the *Federal Australian* (Melbourne) and *Tribune* (Sydney). In January 1877 he published the first monthly issue of his *Horticultural Magazine and Garden Guide*: twenty-four issues appeared (bound annually and sold in book form as the *Australian Horticultural Magazine and Garden Guide*), each devoted to popular flowers, fruits, and vegetables. During the early 1890s Crichton acted as fruit expert to the Victorian Department of Agriculture, lecturing and reporting across the colony. With IRRIGATION then providing an impetus to citrus culture in Vic., Crichton published *The History, Uses, and Culture of the Orange, and Other Species of the Citrus Family*. His major work, *The Australasian Fruit Culturist* (1893), was the most comprehensive Australian book on its subject, and drew on his extensive European and Australian experience. Here he advertised himself as 'Horticultural Agent, Land & Agricultural Agent, and Valuator', willing to advise 'upon the capabilities of land & the best means of utilising it [and] … the formation of orchards, vineyards, parks, and gardens', the septuagenarian Crichton being among the most experienced of Victoria's horticulturists. RA

CRONIN, John (1865–1923), horticulturist and botanic gardens director, was born at Clunes (Vic.), and spent his early working life in the mining industry there. Subsequently moving to Melbourne, he followed the lead of younger brother, Maurice, in obtaining employment at MELBOURNE BOTANIC GARDENS as a labourer in early 1886. Two years later he was promoted to gardener, and was apparently entrusted with various specialist duties by the director, William GUILFOYLE. With promotion in the Gardens painfully slow, Cronin opted to leave for a position as an orchard inspector with the Department of Agriculture (1896). While in this capacity, working in the Murrumbeena area, Cronin acquired a reputation among fruit growers for his knowledge and innovation, most notably in relation to PRUNING techniques. Through applying these to the Jonathan apple tree he made a considerable contribution to the industry. In 1908 Cronin was appointed principal of the BURNLEY School of Horticulture, but held this position for only twenty months before the recommendation of retiring William Guilfoyle facilitated his nomination as Curator (and from 1920–21, Director) of Melbourne Botanic Gardens. He retained this post for the next fourteen years.

Cronin was very active in horticultural circles, serving as secretary and president of the Victorian Horticultural Society, and freely giving his time to lecture and judge at horticultural gatherings. In his favoured field, HYBRIDISATION, he achieved world-class results with watsonias and dahlias. Within the Gardens, Cronin introduced lectures and examinations to enhance staff qualifications, and carried out improvements in the Australian section and adjacent DOMAIN. In the main, however, he limited himself to the maintenance of Guilfoyle's completed plan—no mean task, given the labour shortages imposed by the First World War and post-war government economising. By 1922 there were fifteen unfilled staff positions, and strident criticism in the press and parliament concerning the general condition of the Gardens. To his credit, Cronin's abilities were never questioned, but there was no doubt that serious illness in 1922–23 limited his power to properly fulfil his duties. In 1926, through the combined efforts of the NATIONAL ROSE SOCIETY, the Nurserymen and Seedsmen's Association of Victoria and others, the Cronin Memorial Horticultural Scholarship was founded to honour John Cronin's contribution to Australian horticulture.   DARREN WATSON

CROQUET GROUNDS were often found in the gardens or grounds of large nineteenth-century residences where sufficient level LAWN space enabled this popular Victorian garden game to be played. Although court size and configuration of wickets could be varied according to available space, club (competition) matches required a court 35 x 28 yards (32 x 25.6m). Croquet clubs, established as early as 1800–10 in colonial Australia, usually sported several full- and half-sized courts, although the game later became an adjunct to lawn BOWLS. As equipment was demountable and therefore easily transported (usually in wooden chests), no structures for storage were required, although small timber shelters often provided seating and protection against sun and rain. Croquet was a mixed-sex sport that enjoyed its peak in popularity during the first half of the nineteenth century, after which it was surpassed by the newly fashionable game of lawn TENNIS.   RICHARD HEATHCOTE

CROWE, Sylvia (1901–1997), English landscape architect, produced landscape master plans for new towns, reservoirs, power stations, hospitals, and other places during redevelopment after the Second World War, as well as forestry landscape guidelines. From the 1950s to the 1990s she published significant textbooks on LANDSCAPE ARCHITECTURE, including *Garden Design* (1958), and was a leader of her profession. She significantly influenced Australian landscape architecture during the 1960s and 1970s when concerns about environmental deterioration were emerging. Her books were read widely, and she was respected personally by many Australians. During visits in 1964 (twice) and 1977 she spoke about landscape issues to politicians, government agencies, professionals, and the public. As International Federation of Landscape Architects vice-president she assisted in the formation of the AUSTRALIAN INSTITUTE OF LANDSCAPE ARCHITECTS. She advised the National Capital Development Commission on CANBERRA's development and COMMONWEALTH PARK planning. AILA awarded her an honorary fellowship (1979) and the Award in Landscape Architecture (1990).

> Geoffrey Collens and Wendy Powell (eds), *Sylvia Crowe* (Reigate, Surrey, 1999)   JOHN GRAY

CRUDEN FARM, Langwarrin, Vic.: see MURDOCH (née GREENE), Elisabeth Joy

CUFFLEY, Peter Leonard (b. 1944), social historian and garden designer, owes his love of gardens to family traditions and a childhood in the Dandenong Ranges (Vic.). He was inaugural curator of history at Sovereign Hill, Ballarat, Vic. (1972–75). His books, including *Cottage Gardens in Australia* (1983) and *Creating Your Own Period Garden* (1984; revised in 1991 as *Traditional Gardens in Australia*), tapped into a burgeoning historical consciousness. Intuitive and tinged with nostalgia, his garden writings and paintings evoke style as well as substance.   RA

CULTIVAR, a term formed from the conjoining of the words 'cultivated variety', is used to distinguish variants in plants that have usually been bred or selected for some ornamental feature (such as colour or shape of flowers or leaves, or habit). Although often raised in gardens, cultivars can be selected from the wild, often as single-plant variants, and maintained in cultivation. The term was incorporated into the *International Code of Nomenclature for Cultivated Plants* (1953), where article one states: 'Cultivated plants are essential to civilization. It is important, therefore, that a precise, stable, and internationally accepted system should be available for their naming.' The code specifies that cultivars be given a non-Latinised, 'fancy' or vernacular name of no more than three words in length, placed in single quotation marks, generally after the botanic name—for example, *Camellia japonica* 'Great Eastern'—or directly after the generic name if the species name is not established—for example, *Prunus* 'Elvins'. Cultivar nomenclature is not only used for ornamental plants but in forestry and agriculture for the naming of economically important plants. The cultivar name in this case is often placed after the common name for the crop—for example, Strawberry 'Red Gauntlet'.   ML

CULTURAL LANDSCAPES are 'natural' landscapes that have been physically modified by human activity over time, or have acquired particular cultural significance for a community. The term 'landscape' originated in Old English to denote a tract of land. By the eighteenth century, it was associated with landscape painting and became synonymous with 'natural' scenery possessing distinguishing characteristics and features. Cultural landscapes were first described as such in the early twentieth century by human geographers such as Carl Sauer to explain the importance of cultural influences in shaping the distinctive physical character of different landscapes over time. By the 1970s, the landscape was studied as a tangible 'document' of human history. Seminal work by cultural geographers such as David Lowenthal, Yi-Fu Tuan, and Donald Meinig encouraged a wider interpretation of cultural landscapes, and people's attachment to them, by seeking to understand the intangible values, perceptions, and ideologies implicit in particular landscapes. The concept has gained currency among social scientists, planners, and land managers, and is widely used in the field of heritage conservation. Gardens are DESIGNED LANDSCAPES, where 'natural' elements have been intentionally selected and arranged to fulfil a particular purpose. Much of the scholarship on cultural landscapes in Australia is contained in articles and study reports, including work by Jane Lennon, Ken Taylor, and Jim Russell, and the AUSTRALIAN HERITAGE COMMISSION.

Australia's cultural landscapes embrace more than 60 000 years of human history. The Tasman Peninsula, for example, is a rich cultural landscape associated with Aboriginal occupation, a British convict penal colony, and successive eras of farming, forestry, and mining. Together, they form an evocative record of cultural forces that have shaped Australia. Where a landscape is an actual or symbolic manifestation of something valued by a group of people, they may experience profound grief when their bonds with that landscape are broken. The Uluru–Kata Tjuta National Park, for example, is recognised on the World Heritage List both for its scenic grandeur and for its powerful religious and social associations with the Anangu Aboriginal people. The Anangu believe that their ancestral heroes created Uluru and Kata Tjuta in the Dreamtime. The Anangu's cultural history and identity are inextricably linked with that landscape.

Significant cultural landscapes are often identified during local environmental planning processes. CONSERVING them may involve retaining significant features or associations within a dynamic physical and social setting, and balancing competing land uses to ensure that the landscape and its history continue to enrich or inform the lives of present and future communities.

W.G. Hoskins, *The Making of the English Landscape* (London, 1955); D.W. Meinig (ed.), *The Interpretation of Ordinary Landscapes: Geographical Essays* (New York, 1979); D.N. Jeans and P. Spearritt, *The Open Air Museum: The Cultural Landscape of New South Wales* (Sydney, 1980); Deborah Bird Rose, *Nourishing Terrains: Australian Aboriginal Views of Landscape and Wilderness* (Canberra, 1996); George Seddon, *Landprints: Reflections on Place and Landscape* (Cambridge, 1997)

JOY McCANN

CUNDALL, Peter (b. 1927), horticulturist, broadcaster, and writer, grew up in Manchester, England, and emigrated in 1950. Professionally involved with garden design and horticulture, Cundall received a Churchill Fellowship (1974) to study gardening television programs internationally. He has been a regular broadcaster since 1969 with ABC RADIO in Tas. and nationally. He was an inaugural presenter for *Gardening Australia* on ABC TELEVISION (1989), and since 1990 he has been its avuncular anchor, broadcasting—and writing in the *Gardening Australia* magazine—with knowledgeable enthusiasm. ORGANIC GARDENING is a passion.

RA

CUNNINGHAM, Allan (1791–1839) and **Richard Cunningham** (1793–1835), botanic gardens superintendents and explorers, were born at Wimbledon, England, sons of a Scottish gardener and his English wife. Having served briefly in a law office, Allan found more congenial work at the ROYAL BOTANIC GARDENS, KEW, where the curator William Townsend Aiton (1766–1839) was then revising his father's plant catalogue, *Hortus Kewensis*. In preparing this for publication between 1810 and 1813, and the more convenient *Epitome* in 1814, Aiton had some help from Allan and much from Richard, who in 1808, aged 15, had also joined him. Association with Kew's living plants and with Acton's publications gave him valuable experience of the unique AUSTRALIAN FLORA.

In 1814, Allan applied to Sir Joseph BANKS, then *de facto* director of Kew, to be a collector, declaring 'it is a love of plants, and to search for them in their wild state, and a wish to make myself useful in the Capacity of a Collector, that now urges me to address you'. He hoped to ensure 'that the Royal Collection at Kew may exceed all other Collections in the Riches of new, beautiful and desirable plants'. Despite this exuberance, Banks coolly advised that Allan's ambition might be realised if, as Aiton believed, he possessed the qualities 'of honesty, sobriety, diligence, activity, Humility & Civility'. Such 'Essential Qualifications' assured 'a traveller Respect among Strangers & assistance from those in high office'. A yearly salary of £180 was offered, with a request to

The view from Tower Hill towards Illowa, in Victoria's WESTERN DISTRICT, illustrates a CULTURAL LANDSCAPE shaped by a century and a half of farming, bringing with it fences, hedges, windbreaks, and modest farm cottages

be frugal. Allan Cunningham and fellow-collector James BOWIE sailed in October 1814 for two years' collecting in Brazil, before respectively proceeding to NSW and South Africa. Richard remained at Kew for another eighteen years as Aiton's amanuensis and cataloguer of the rich harvest received from Banks's collectors.

Arriving in Sydney on the convict transport *Surry* in December 1816, Allan reported to Governor Macquarie, who recommended he join surveyor John Oxley's forthcoming expedition to the rivers beyond the BLUE MOUNTAINS. Once established at Parramatta, the botanist eagerly gained field experience to prepare for this and future journeys. During the 1817 expedition, Oxley was accompanied by both Charles Fraser, the Governor's botanist, and Allan Cunningham, the King's botanist. They worked harmoniously to the benefit of the Governor's garden in Sydney and the King's garden in Kew.

Between 1817 and 1822 Allan sailed with Lieutenant Phillip Parker King on four extensive coastal surveys. He then spent most of the period 1822–29 exploring widely in NSW, particularly in such botanically rich areas as the Blue Mountains, Illawarra, Hunter Valley, Liverpool Plains, Hastings River, and Moreton Bay. He discovered Pandora's Pass through the Liverpool Range, named the DARLING DOWNS, and found the gap now bearing his name on the road between the Downs and Brisbane. In 1826 he visited NEW ZEALAND, and in 1830 Norfolk Island, before returning to England to work on the masses of specimens and notes he had accumulated and to write for learned journals.

In 1832, following the death of his erstwhile companion, Charles FRASER, Allan was offered the post of Colonial Botanist and Superintendent of the SYDNEY BOTANIC GARDENS. He declined in favour of his brother, and although 'exceedingly unwell', actively interceded for Richard, writing commendations and contacting referees. He also wrote an important 'Memorandum relative to the Colonial garden at Sydney', suggesting how it might become more truly scientific—and, indeed, how Richard might effect this. With support from Aiton, Robert BROWN, and Sir William Hooker, Richard was appointed at £200 per year. He arrived on the convict transport *Mary* in January 1833 to begin a career destined to be short and tragic. Dr George BENNETT voiced concern when he expressed the hope that now Sydney would 'soon have a "*Botanic Garden*", in lieu of a repository for turnips and carrots'. Richard promptly compiled a report on the Gardens, with a plan showing 'Kitchen', 'Fruit', 'Experimental', and 'Botanic' sections, and suggested improvements. He dutifully attended to routine matters, distributed thousands of fruit and ornamental trees, shrubs, and vines 'to the several Government establishments and private Individuals', and made collecting trips to Emu Plains, the Blue Mountains, Illawarra, New Zealand, Norfolk Island, and Van Diemen's Land. In March 1835 Richard joined Major Thomas MITCHELL's expedition into the interior, and was shortly reported missing. In searching for plants he frequently ranged the country on either side of the line of route, and on one such diversion became lost. He fell in with some Aboriginals, but apparently alarmed them by wandering in their camp at night, and so was killed, on about 20 April.

Again offered the Sydney post, Allan accepted, returning on the *Norfolk* in February 1837 to find that Governor Bourke had appointed 'A Committee of Superintendence of the Australian Museum and Botanical Garden'. Instead of feeling free to exercise the professional freedom he had sought for his brother, Allan believed that his scientific aspirations would be bureaucratically thwarted. Now ailing with advanced tuberculosis, he felt professionally and physically 'in great measure unfitted for the future management' of the Gardens, and submitted his resignation in November 1837. It was accepted as from 1 January 1838, although Governor Gipps, who arrived in February, unsuccessfully sought a rapprochement. The press declared 'Mr Cunningham would no longer consent to remain a mere cultivator of official cabbages and turnips' and so had resigned 'in disgust', thereby over-simplifying the causes of contention. Sadly debilitated, Cunningham returned from New Zealand in October 1838 and died in a Gardens cottage on 27 June 1839. P.P. King lamented: 'Alas, poor Allan! he was a rare specimen—a genus of himself; an enthusiast in Australian geography; devoted to his own science, Botany; a warm friend, and an honest man'.

The Cunninghams' contribution to horticulture lay chiefly in making improvements in Sydney's Botanic Gardens, distributing plants for ornamental and economic purposes, and in making Australasian plants more widely known both locally and in England. The Cunningham name is commemorated in the specific epithets of many Australian plants and Allan forms the subject of a biography. Richard's grave lies beneath eucalypt trees blazed by Lieutenant Henry Zouch on the Bogan River near Tottenham (NSW); Allan's remains have rested since 1901 within a memorial obelisk erected in the Sydney Botanic Gardens in 1844; memorial plaques to both brothers grace St Andrew's Church, Rose Bay.

W.G. McMinn, *Allan Cunningham: Botanist and Explorer* (Melbourne, 1970)   LIONEL GILBERT

CURTILAGE Over the past five decades, TOWN PLANNERS—later, HERITAGE advocates—have become increasingly concerned with the notion of curtilage: the primary landscape or garden setting of a house (or other building or place) and the extent to which it might be compromised by development. Most Australian MANSIONS and even grand VILLAS originally possessed ample gardens. Some, such as RIPPON LEA and RAHEEN (Vic.), retain their gardens and landscape settings, although even these have lost paddocks and former productive areas. Others, including ELIZABETH BAY HOUSE in Sydney and Labassa in Melbourne, have been subjected to severe residential subdivision pressure, obliterating most of their original grounds. The curtilage of INSTITUTIONAL sites, especially HOSPITALS and UNIVERSITIES, has long been compromised, mostly by internal rather than external developments.

Many planning cases hinge on heritage and curtilage issues, particularly in Sydney, where high real estate values create intensive pressures on land use, and NSW has been at the forefront of debate over definition and protection of curtilages. The planning debacle of the late 1990s that allowed a new high-rise block of units (dubbed 'the toaster') to overlook the Sydney Opera House created renewed

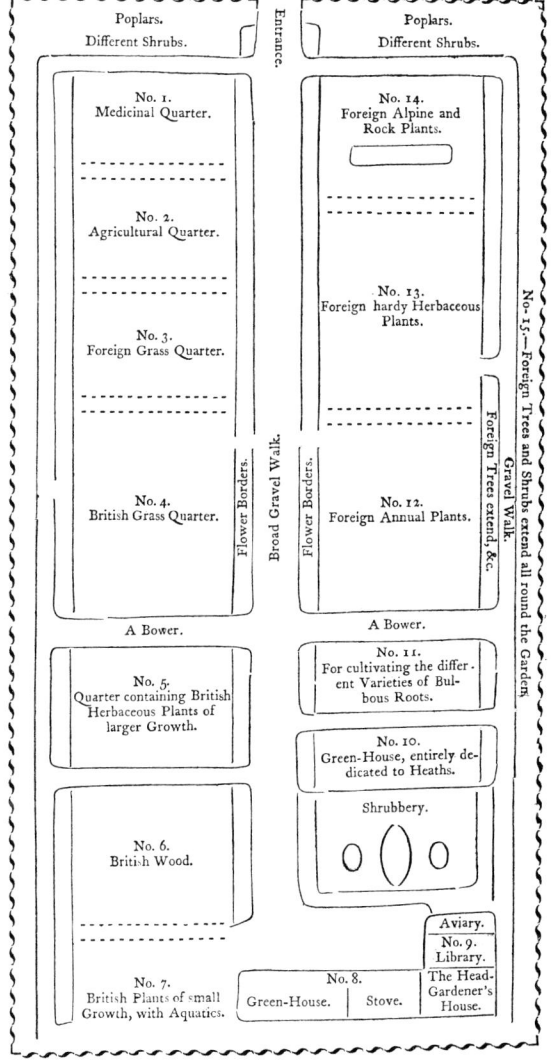

Plan of the BOTANIC GARDEN established in the 1790s by William CURTIS in the inner London suburb of Brompton—although privately owned and open only to subscribers, the formal planning provided a precedent for colonial botanic gardens established in succeeding decades

interest in issues of curtilage—particularly because of the way that building blocked VISTAS, rather than from more traditional concerns about land encroachment.

Heritage Office and Department of Urban Affairs and Planning (NSW), *Heritage Curtilages* (Sydney, 1996)

PETER SPEARRITT

CURTIS, William (1746–1799), horticulturist, author, and founder of the *Botanical Magazine*, was born in Alton, Hampshire, England. Although trained as an apothecary, Curtis had shown a keen interest in NATURAL HISTORY since childhood. The sale of his practice enabled him to devote himself fully to this pursuit at the age of 25. In his 'Botanic Gardens' at Lambeth and Brompton, he cultivated ornamental and economically important plants. A man of 'energy and ideas but undisciplined purpose', Curtis wrote and lectured on such diverse topics as insects, plants of medical interest, agricultural use of grasses, Linnaeus's system of botany, and the cultivation of sea-kale. However, he is best known for *Flora Londinensis* (1775–98), one of the finest illustrated English Floras, featuring coloured plates and text of plants indigenous to London. Poor sales and high costs led Curtis to try to recoup his losses with the *Botanical Magazine* (1787–) to fill a need for information on exotic plants then being introduced to Europe. Each issue had high-quality, hand-coloured plates—a feature retained, astonishingly, until 1948—of foreign plants cultivated in Great Britain, with scientific descriptions by eminent botanists, and cultivation notes. No periodical has so well chronicled the change in garden fashions and tastes over two centuries. The illustrated plants came from all continents (more than 450 were from Australia up to 1864) and were chosen for their horticultural merit or botanical distinction. The *Botanical Magazine* today survives as part of the *Kew Magazine*, with which it was incorporated in 1984.

Ray Desmond, *A Celebration of Flowers: Two Hundred Years of Curtis's Botanical Magazine* (London, 1987)

TONY CAVANAGH

CURTIS, Winifred Mary (b. 1905), botanist, has, through her extensive work on Tasmania's flora, contributed to the introduction of many plants into horticulture. Arriving from England in 1939, she began teaching at the University of Tasmania. Her revision of RODWAY's *Tasmanian Flora* (1903) expanded into the authoritative *Student's Flora of Tasmania* (1956–94). She also prepared the botanical and ecological text for *The Endemic Flora of Tasmania* (1967–78), authenticating the specimens sent to Margaret STONES for illustration. She received a doctorate of philosophy (1950) and of science (1968) from the University of London and as University of Tasmania Honorary Research Fellow continued her taxonomic work long after retirement (1966). In naming endemic plants, she honoured Herbert KING and Lord TALBOT and gave the specific epithet *tasmanica* to an attractive *Epacris* and a beautiful, but extremely rare, non-fruiting *Lomatia*. Tasmanian plants named in her honour include the genus *Winifredia* and various species and subspecies *curtisiae*.

M.R. Banks et al. (eds), *Aspects of Tasmanian Botany: A Tribute to Winifred Curtis* (Hobart, 1991)

LINDEN GILLBANK

CUSHING, John (d. c. 1820), Irish-born gardener, came to prominence as the author of *The Exotic Gardener; in which the Management of the Hot-House, Green-House and Conservatory, is fully and clearly delineated according to modern practice* (Dublin, 1811). Cushing was a departmental foreman with LEE AND KENNEDY, the celebrated London nursery proprietors who specialised in 'New Holland plants', then fashionable in the northern hemisphere. The first London edition appeared in 1812, dedicated to Sir Joseph BANKS, with later editions in 1814 and 1822. LOUDON (1822) declared it 'by far the best work which has appeared on the culture of ornamental exotics', and MCINTOSH in his *Practical Gardener* (1829) cited 'the late Cushing' as an authority.

Exotic plants, including the many Australian genera listed by Cushing, would not thrive in the northern latitudes, he wrote, 'unless art steps forward to their assistance' in the form of a HOTHOUSE, GREENHOUSE, or CONSERVATORY. He dealt at length with propagation and management, placing great stress on use of soil suited to the endemic location of each plant. The fashion in England for AUSTRALIAN FLORA soon waned as floral riches from other countries outshone their Austral cousins, but Cushing's book remained one of the earliest devoted to their culture. A short memoir of this neglected figure appeared in the GARDENERS' CHRONICLE (1963). RA

CYCADS, primitive, seed-producing plants with a PALM-like appearance and known from the fossil record to have flourished over much of the earth at the same time as the dinosaurs during the Mesozoic period, are now represented by a limited number of genera and species. Several endemic genera—*Bowenia*, *Macrozamia*, and *Lepidozamia*—are found in Australia, in addition to *Cycas*, which is more widely distributed throughout India, China, Japan, Madagascar, and East Africa. In cultivation, the cycads are slow in growth but produce strong, ornamental evergreen FOLIAGE. Collections are held in major Australian BOTANIC GARDENS and some private gardens, notably in Qld and NT. Several are grown in the nursery trade, especially *Cycas revoluta* (Sago Palm—although not a true palm), which is popular for pot culture and indoor use. Cycad seeds were used as ABORIGINAL FOOD PLANTS, repeatedly soaked in water to remove toxins then pounded into flour, a process not comprehended by early explorers, who became extremely ill after inadequate preparation prior to consumption. ML

DAFFODILS: see *Narcissus*

DAHLIA, a genus indigenous to Central and South America, has a long history of cultivation, with the elongated stems of *Dahlia imperialis* (Tree Dahlia) used by the Aztecs to convey water from springs and streams. Named in 1791 by Antonio Cavanilles for Swedish botanist Andreas Dahl (1751–1789), this perennial herbaceous plant with tuberous roots reached England in 1798. Dahlias—also known as Georginas for a time—were much hybridised from the 1830s, leading to the development of modern show varieties. James Dickinson listed the scarlet *Dahlia frustranea* (*D. coccinea*) in 1845, and by 1858 Francis Henty could inform F.W. Newman that Portland Botanic Gardens had 'some magnificent Dahlias ... I think above a hundred varieties were introduced last year'. Their extraordinary popularity in floriculture from the 1830s to the 1850s—regarded as second only to the rose—was dulled by the fashion for floral bedding of the mid-century, although this led to the development of dwarf dahlia varieties to suit the new style. In Australia, 'the majestic mien of the plant, the size and symmetry of the flowers, the brilliant and infinite variety of its splendid colours, combined with easy management, growing and flowering in every soil and in every climate ... finds a hearty welcome', wrote Luke Wooff in 1864. The many new varieties became a favourite of the show table, and in 1901 a Carnation and Dahlia Society was founded in Vic. The first Australian monographs, John G. Lockley, *Dahlia Growing Made Easy* (1908) and E.E. Pescott, *The Dahlia in Australia* (1920), coincided with attention from Australian hybridists such as George Kerslake, John Cronin, Mrs Fred Caley Smith, and Edward Gray. From the 1920s to the 1950s dahlias continued their ascendancy, especially in the suburban garden and rural gardens, and the nursery industry—including large firms such as Hodgins and small specialist growers—catered for this burgeoning market. A periodic dip in fashion between the 1960s and 1980s—notwithstanding the activities from 1972 of Eaglehawk Dahlia and Arts Festival (Vic.)—has lately been halted, and the merits of dahlias in both subtle and strident forms are again being assessed.   RA

Unconcerned by the dictates of fashion, a DAHLIA enthusiast at Ballarat (Vic.) uses umbrellas to cover prized blooms in the garden

DALLACHY, John (*c.* 1803–1871), botanic gardens superintendent, was born in Scotland. His gardening apprenticeship included experience at Haddo House (1824–25), seat of the Earl of Aberdeen, and at the Horticultural Society's garden at Chiswick, London (1826); by the early 1840s he had risen to become head gardener at Haddo. In 1847 he went to Ceylon to manage a coffee plantation. He arrived in Melbourne in 1848, where he was employed as gardener by stockbroker J.B. Were of Brighton. On the death of John Arthur in 1849, Dallachy was appointed Overseer of the Melbourne Botanic Gardens. He maintained Arthur's parterre and continued to implement Henry Ginn's plan, including new walks forming a promenade. After severe flooding in 1849, the lagoon was excavated, its edges straightened, and the silt used to make large flower beds to complement the ornamental style of the parterre.

From 1850 the Gardens became a popular venue for horticultural shows and Dallachy was a great supporter of Victoria's nascent horticultural societies. By 1851 the Gardens contained approximately 5000 exotic and 1000 native plants, and a catalogue of plants (1852) listed more than 1200 cultivated trees, shrubs, and flowers. Visitor numbers increased during the early 1850s, although there were severe maintenance problems with a hot, dry summer in 1851. After the departure of garden staff for the diggings, no new work was carried out during 1852. In 1853, when a musical concert attracted hundreds, the *Argus* praised the well-kept Gardens and its floral displays.

Dallachy made three trips east and north of Melbourne in 1849–50. He accompanied Ferdinand MUELLER on his first expedition in 1853 to MOUNT BUFFALO, returning with plants and seeds for the Gardens, and 1000 packets of seeds were distributed to BOTANIC GARDENS within Australia and overseas. Local supporters also received plants and cuttings. Dallachy was promoted to Superintendent in 1853 with an increase in salary, although a period of financial stringency followed, with funds and staffing reduced, and only maintenance work being carried out until 1856. Nevertheless, the cultivated area was increased by three acres (1.2 ha) during the period 1853–57. After Mueller was appointed Director in 1857, Dallachy became Curator, with reduced powers and responsibilities. At Mueller's direction he collected in Vic. and NSW until 1861, when he was retired. He continued as a collector for the Gardens in Qld until his death. Dallachy was highly regarded as a plant collector and his name is commemorated in the scientific names of a number of plant species, including *Acacia dallachiana* and *Eucalyptus dallachiana*. During difficult times, he used his considerable horticultural skills to develop a picturesque botanic garden enjoyed by its many visitors.

LORNA CROWTHER and NATALIE McMASTER

DALVUI, Noorat, in Victoria's WESTERN DISTRICT, once formed part of the Black family property MOUNT NOORAT. Niel Walter Black (1864–1908) commissioned William GUILFOYLE to prepare a garden design, and Guilfoyle forwarded his plan, plant list, and instructions in 1898. The survival of these instructions is a major source for Guilfoyle's design philosophy:

> red, yellow and variegated leafage should be among the greenery ... [There] will be harmony of foliage for the backgrounds, and there will be variety and contrast enough, in their foregrounds ... With some of the hardy pines and deciduous trees, it would be wise to place as many as eight or nine in a mass, next to a mass of a different kind or tint of foliage ... Superfluous stones can be made use of for grand rockeries ... [with] a little taste on the part of your Gardener in hollowing out some stones, and placing them on top of others or leaving crevices between them for such showy things as Echeverias and Mesembryanthemums.

By 1900 tree planting and construction of the lake had commenced, and during 1907–08, the residence (architects, Ussher and Kemp) was erected in the established garden setting.

Black was lost at sea when the *Waratah* disappeared without trace between Durban and Cape Town. The Dalvui estate was reduced by subdivision in 1911, and the homestead was purchased by the Palmer family, who had previously commissioned Guilfoyle to landscape their property, The Bend, Terang. It remained in their ownership until 1974. Photographs of *c.* 1908–10 show that Guilfoyle's intentions were largely implemented, and Dalvui remains one of his finest surviving private gardens.

RA

DAMPIER, William (1651–1715), English privateer, adventurer, and NATURAL HISTORIAN, made the first authenticated collection of AUSTRALIAN PLANTS in 1699 when he landed at Dirk Hartog Island, East Lewis Island, and Lagrange Bay on the north-west coast. Twenty-three HERBARIUM specimens of flowering plants and a seaweed survive, now housed at Oxford University, including a species of *Dampiera* (a genus named after him), and the Sturt Pea, recently placed in its own genus *Willdampia*.

A.S. George, *William Dampier in New Holland: Australia's First Natural Historian* (Melbourne, 1999) ALEX GEORGE

DANGAR, Henry (1796–1861), surveyor and pastoralist, employed first by the government and then the Australian Agricultural Company, established Neotsfield, near Singleton (NSW), where a house was built 1827–33 under the supervision of his brother William Dangar (1800–1868). The Dangar

The first published BOTANICAL ILLUSTRATIONS of the AUSTRALIAN FLORA, included in William DAMPIER's book *A Voyage to New Holland, &c. In the Year 1699* (1703), depict plants collected along the western coastline of Australia

brothers established pastoral properties throughout NSW, and their descendants, especially Albert Augustus Dangar (1840–1913) at Baroona, near Singleton, and Gostwyk, Uralla, designed the landscapes of their properties with formal gardens—at Neotsfield these included statuary and white marble urns—avenue plantings, shelter belts, planting clumps in paddocks, and other appurtenances of large HOMESTEAD estates such as deer paddocks, glasshouses, croquet lawns, and tennis courts. A.A. Dangar planted the significant features of Gostwyk, including elm avenues well-established by 1890s, and of Palmerston, Armidale, defined and largely enclosed by 1880s hawthorn hedges. Other properties associated with the family include Grantham, Potts Point (now demolished) and Rotherwood, Sutton Forest.

Elisabeth Mary Dangar, *The Dangars from St Neot, Cornwall: Genealogical Table with History & Biographies* (Sydney, 1964)

COLLEEN MORRIS

DARDEL, James Henry (*c.* 1810–1901), vine grower, orchardist, and former soldier, migrated from Switzerland to Port Philip in 1840, probably inspired by the appointment of Charles Joseph LA TROBE as Superintendent—La Trobe's wife Sophie was from Neuchâtel, the same Swiss Canton as Dardel. He established the first of his Paradise VINEYARDS at Batesford (Vic.), on the Moorabool River, on leasehold land and became one of the most successful of the Geelong district vignerons; he was also instrumental in establishing and working vineyards for many others in this early period. As late as 1866 he was credited with having personally planted fifty-five hectares of Victorian vineyards. Among those who made use of his services were the Ryrie brothers at Yering in the early 1840s, who claimed 'he also put us in the way of making wine'.

DAVID DUNSTAN

DARLING (née ANDERSON), Margaret (b. 1923), garden enthusiast, was born in Melbourne and devoted her privileged social position to voluntary work for conservation organisations and in indulging her passion for gardening. In both she was tireless, practical, and hardworking. From the early 1960s she worked for the Women's Committee of the NATIONAL TRUST OF AUSTRALIA (Victoria), establishing its shops, which raised millions of dollars for the Trust: vital to its important CONSERVATION role. She took a particular interest in the Trust's gardens and served on the COMO and RIPPON LEA garden committees. She was a Trust councillor (1966–90), serving as president or vice-president (1980–90). She then chaired the AUSTRALIAN GARDEN HISTORY SOCIETY (1990–99), a position she served with distinction, and is its current Patron. An amateur but wily publisher, Margaret Darling was responsible for the publication of the five books written by or associated with her great friend Joan LAW-SMITH, and also for a biography of Edna WALLING by Peter WATTS. The proceeds from these ventures assisted either the National Trust and the Australian Garden History Society. She gardens actively at Woomargama, her property in southern NSW (acquired 1965), where she has developed a large and wonderful country garden.

PETER WATTS

DARLING DOWNS, Qld, forms a band of open rolling plains country to the west of the Great Dividing Range, bounded by Toowoomba, Warwick, and Dalby, and the Condamine River. Volcanic eruptions laid down the deep black clay soils of the southern and western Downs and the red soils around Toowoomba; subsequent erosion provided the distinct granite spurs and basalt cones separating the long, fertile valleys where native grasses grew 'as high as a horse's belly'. Mean temperatures range from 3°C in July to 28°C in January; moist easterly winds prevail in summer, with severe frosts and drying westerlies in winter. For 30 000 years, the region was home to the Wakka Wakka linguistic group for whom the intricate ecosystems of the Bunya Mountains in the north provided a cultural focus.

Situated at the northern end of Australia's fertile crescent, the Downs became the 'jewel in the diadem of squatterdom' from the 1840s. Squatters dominated the region until colonial governments resumed their estates in the 1890s. By 1914, the selectors—stereotyped by Steele Rudd's *Dad and Dave* stories—had triumphed: family farms and tractors, cereal crops and silos, dairy farms and cheese factories, piggeries and bacon factories came to dominate the landscape. From the coming of the railway in 1867, Toowoomba developed not only as the transport and administrative hub, but as the gateway to the vast south-west Qld and north-western NSW; it came to dominate the region.

The wealthier squatters had erected large homes and established formal HOMESTEAD GARDENS: the most distinctive of these were Goomburra, TALGAI EAST, Yandilla, JIMBOUR, JONDARYAN, and Harrow. It was Toowoomba, however, that developed as 'The Garden City', establishing the first two AGRICULTURAL and HORTICULTURAL SOCIETIES in Qld. From the 1870s, German settlers established MARKET GARDENS, ORCHARDS, and VINEYARDS in the city's environs: the most famous was that of Henry Roessler (1847–1934), which was open to the public on Sundays. At the same time, the city officials drained the swamps, widened the streets, planted willows and camphor laurels as shade trees, established a BOTANIC GARDEN and started the clearing of TOOWOOMBA QUEENS PARK. Above all, private citizens proudly developed their own gardens—so much so that one (1928) writer claimed Toowoombaites, after work, rushed home to their gardens rather than loitering in the pubs or promenading in the streets: an outstanding local property is the BOYCE GARDEN AND RAINFOREST on the range escarpment. Although the first garden competition was probably held in September 1918, it was not until September 1950 that the city launched its annual Carnival of Flowers FESTIVAL to celebrate the city's garden image. During the 1980s, Toowoomba created Australia's largest Japanese garden, thus emphasising the importance of gardens to local tourism and economic diversification on the Darling Downs.

D.B. Waterson, *Squatter, Selector and Storekeeper: A History of the Darling Downs, 1859–93* (Sydney 1968); Maurice French, *A Bibliography for the History of the Darling Downs and Adjacent Regions* (Toowoomba, Qld, 1979); Maurice French, *A Pastoral Romance: The Tribulation and Triumph of Squatterdom* (Toowoomba, Qld, 1990); Maurice French (ed.), *Travellers in a Landscape: Visitors' Impressions of the Darling Downs 1827–1954* (Toowoomba, Qld, 1994)

MAURICE FRENCH

DARWIN, Charles Robert (1809–1882), naturalist and evolutionary theorist, spent a comfortable but unremarkable childhood in Shrewsbury, England, before attending Edinburgh and Cambridge universities. A keen naturalist in his youth, he was fascinated by plants and animals, and assiduous in collecting fossils and insects. In 1831, aged 22 and with unfinished medical training behind him, Darwin embarked on HMS *Beagle* as naturalist on what proved to be one of the most influential voyages of scientific exploration undertaken in the nineteenth century. For nearly six years *Beagle* explored South America, Australia, and a host of islands in the Pacific and Atlantic oceans, giving Darwin ample opportunity to observe botanical, zoological, and geological phenomena, and the indigenous peoples of the countries visited. Darwin assembled so much in the way of specimens, observations and information that he was provided with enough raw materials to keep himself fruitfully occupied for the next forty-six years.

In January 1836 Darwin had his first close look at Australia when *Beagle* anchored in Port Jackson (NSW). From there *Beagle* sailed to Van Diemen's Land and King George Sound. Darwin commented on the thriving state of Sydney, in particular comparing the SYDNEY BOTANIC GARDENS more than favourably with those in South America. Expeditions to the Blue Mountains and the hinterland of Hobart Town and King George Sound gave Darwin first-hand exposure to the extraordinarily different flora and fauna of the continent. Australia also provided him with a wealth of examples of the consequences to native biota of human activities and the introduction of exotic species. After three months in Australian waters, *Beagle* headed home, reaching London in October 1836.

Darwin was extraordinary for the breadth of his interests, encompassing as they did all branches of the natural sciences. In his work he was most influenced by Alexander von Humboldt (1769–1859), German explorer of South America, the geological theories of Charles Lyell (1797–1875), and John Henslow (1796–1861) and Adam Sedgwick (1785–1873), professors respectively of botany and geology at Cambridge University. Joseph HOOKER, himself a scientific visitor to Van Diemen's Land and pioneering student of phytogeography, became a close friend and one of Darwin's most constant supporters. Darwin is best known for his book *On the Origin of Species* (1859), a revolutionary theory of evolution that has underpinned, informed, and provoked debate on the origin and development of all forms of life ever since. He also published seminal works on barnacles, the formation of coral atolls, variation in domesticated species, and volcanoes. His botanical researches embraced insectivorous plants, movement in plants, fertilisation of plants (particularly orchids), flower morphology, and plant adaptation, all the subjects of substantial publications. Darwin died a highly respected scientist and a towering figure of nineteenth-century biological research.

A.J. Marshall, *Darwin and Huxley in Australia* (Sydney, 1970); M. Allan, *Darwin and his Flowers* (London, 1977); F.W. and J.M. Nicholas, *Charles Darwin in Australia* (Cambridge, 1989); A. Desmond and J. Moore, *Darwin* (London, 1991)

HELEN M. COHN

DARWIN BOTANIC GARDENS is the successor of the Government Garden planted by William HAYES in 1869 for the first permanent settlement (Palmerston) at Port Darwin in the NORTHERN TERRITORY (of SA). Following the death of Hayes, Maurice HOLTZE was appointed Government Gardener (1878–91), and he supervised the Gardens' transfer (with the assistance of Chinese labour) to a site in Fannie Bay (1879). Here, despite the poor soil, he successfully continued experimentation with economic crops.

In 1886 the Gardens were relocated to their present site, not far from Fannie Bay Gaol, which provided prison labour, mostly by Aboriginal inmates—an economy measure Holtze found unsatisfactory. Despite this, and inadequate government funding, his experimental work testified to the Territory's 'agricultural capabilities', which he ardently, and optimistically, believed could be realised on a commercial scale. His son, Nicholas Holtze, succeeded him in the newly created position of Curator (1891–1913) and applied himself primarily to the cultivation of rice and fibres. He introduced an ornamental aspect to the Gardens, implementing his father's plan for an impressive avenue of coconut palms, all but destroyed by Cyclone Tracy (1974). He continued the practice of distributing cuttings, plants, and shrubs to local residents, thereby contributing to the 'greening' of the city. Following Holtze's death, the Gardens entered a period of neglect.

From 1911 to 1957, the Darwin Botanic Gardens were curated by a succession of Commonwealth Government appointees, but attempts to reorganise and stabilise the site—as a scientific and educational institution and a public amenity—were impeded by the frequent absences of Holtze's successor, C.E.F. ALLEN, two world wars, and a cyclone (1937). Army occupation of the site during the Second World War contributed to the Gardens' neglect. Civil administration returned to the city in 1945, and despite lack of funds, Italian-born Isadore (Jack) Agostini (*c.* 1893–1956) was appointed Foreman Gardener, responsible for 'the unenviable task' of rehabilitating the Gardens. Some degree of experimentation with economic plants was also undertaken.

In 1957, the Gardens came under the control of the newly constituted Darwin Municipal Council. Following curatorships of A.J. Mackenzie (1958–64) and Brian Edwards (1964–71), George BROWN was appointed Superintendent of Parks and Recreation. Cyclone Tracy destroyed or damaged more than three-quarters of the trees and other early features, but under Brown's supervision the Gardens made a rapid recovery, with the addition of a PALM garden, RAINFOREST gully, ORCHID shadehouse, and recreational facilities. In 1990, administration of the Gardens reverted to the Northern Territory Government. Histories by June Bauer (1980) and Helen Wilson (1994) document the geographical shifts, natural disasters, and administrative changes that have defined major phases of development.

ANITA ANGEL and JAN SETO

DAVENPORT, Samuel (1818–1906), pastoralist, politician, and advocate for economic horticulture, played a major role in advancing and diversifying colonial SOUTH AUSTRALIA's agricultural and horticultural activities. Born in Sherbourne,

Entrance to the Government Garden at Port Darwin depicting the gardener's cottage and collection of economic plants, photographed in 1874 prior to the establishment of DARWIN BOTANIC GARDENS on its present site

Oxfordshire, England, to a banking family, he migrated to Adelaide in 1843, establishing a mixed farming operation at Macclesfield before successfully venturing into large-stock pastoralism. He served as a member of the Legislative Council (1847–66), was president of the South Australian Chamber of Manufactures, Royal Agricultural and Horticultural Society of South Australia, and Royal Geographical Society of Australasia (South Australian Branch), and represented SA at EXHIBITIONS in London (1851 and 1886), Philadelphia (1876), resulting in the introduction of North American agricultural machinery into SA, Sydney (1879), and Melbourne (1880 and 1888). Davenport was responsible for the design of Macclesfield and BEAUMONT, with their distinctive village commons. He was also an ardent experimenter and advocate of almond, olive, and vine cultivation, directly participating in these pursuits at Macclesfield and Beaumont, and in writing about their potential in *Some New Industries for South Australia* (1864), *The Cultivation of the Olive* (1870), *The Extraction of Scents from Plants* (1864), and *Notes on the Olive and its Values to Country suitable for its Growth* (1904), among other pamphlets and lectures. In his pamphlet he implored the cultivation and production of olive oil, silk, flower-farming, and tobacco culture. Davenport, knighted in 1884 and appointed KCMG in 1886, died a patrician figure at his Beaumont residence.

DAVID JONES

DAVEY, Harry Hubert (1869–1941), horticulturist, editor, and publisher, was a pioneer of Australian horticultural publishing, especially in the field of MAGAZINES. Born at South Yarra (Vic.), his first publishing venture was to establish the *AUSTRAL(IAN) CULTURIST*, which served as a springboard for his company, the Horticultural Publishing Press of Australasia. Davey established separate periodicals for the fruit and nursery trades and also for home gardeners, the *JOURNAL OF HORTICULTURE OF AUSTRALASIA*. In these endeavours, he was ably supported by R.E. BOARDMAN. He worked with great energy to promote horticulture in Australia, and in 1912 he upgraded the *Journal*, renaming it *Home and Garden Beautiful*. His impressions of America following his visit to the Panama–Pacific International Exposition (1915) introduced readers to NORTH AMERICAN influences, with observations of GARDEN CITIES and Californian bungalows. Davey was a co-convenor of the meeting at which the NATIONAL ROSE SOCIETY of Victoria was founded, a council member of the Inventors Society of Victoria, a vice-president of the Carnation and Dahlia Society of Victoria, and a key player in both the nursery and fruit trades.

RA

DAVIDSON, William (1805–1837), botanist, nursery proprietor, and garden superintendent, was born in Northumberland, England, and prior to migrating to Van Diemen's Land in

1827, was head gardener on the Benwell estate (Northumberland) of Robert Walker. Described as a man of education, refinement and of some means, Davidson arrived in the colony with 800 trees, 200 grape vines, seeds, cuttings, a complete supply of garden utensils and implements, and £500. In 1828 Lieutenant-Governor Arthur appointed Davidson as the first Superintendent of the Hobart Town Government Gardens—precursor to the ROYAL TASMANIAN BOTANICAL GARDENS—and it was under Davidson's leadership that the rare surviving internally heated 'Arthur Wall' was constructed for the growing of exotic fruits and flowers, as well as a glasshouse attached to the wall, in which he produced arguably Australia's first pineapples. Davidson was also instrumental in the collection and exchange of endemic plants to Ireland and England, and grew more than 130 natives gathered from the slopes and summit of Mount Wellington. In a colourful account of what it dubbed 'the cabbage bag affair', the *Colonial Times* described the dismissal of Davidson by Colonel Arthur in 1834 for the disposal of four cabbages, four turnips, and four cauliflowers from the government gardens without Arthur's authorisation. In 1831 Davidson was granted an allotment bounded by Davey Street, Elboden Street, and Garden Crescent, on which he created a substantial private garden. He died aged just 33, and his headstone is in ST DAVIDS PARK, Hobart.　　　SALLYANN DAKIS

DAVIS (née REARDON), Margaret (1908–2000), gardener, writer, broadcaster, and pilot, married fellow flying student Arthur Davis in 1925 and became the second woman to hold a pilot's licence in Australia. In 1944 Davis organised the first of several annual flower shows in the Sydney Domain in aid of the Red Cross. When these were discontinued in 1949 she called a meeting to form a GARDEN CLUB, and the inaugural meeting of the Garden Club of New South Wales (now known as Garden Clubs of Australia) was held in November 1950 with Davis as founding president. One of its earliest achievements was to create a living memory to the members of the Australian armed forces, in the Remembrance Driveway, a series of COMMEMORATIVE tree plantations between Sydney and Canberra. Club affiliation expanded throughout Australia, now comprising over 500 clubs with more than 30 000 members. Sydney-based, Davis lectured and travelled widely, and wrote several books on gardening, including *A Garden in Pots* (1969), *Living Flower Arrangements* (1971), *The Small Garden* (1977), *Balcony Gardens* (1981), and, aged 89, *Retire to Your Garden* (1997). She was a regular guest broadcaster for the ABC and a early advocate of conservation. For health reasons Davis retired to Honolulu and then Santa Barbara, California, honoured by the naming of several flowers, including the award-winning camellia, 'Margaret Davis'.
　　　MOIRA MAGUIRE

DAVIS, Mervyn Twynam (1917–1985), landscape architect, studied horticulture at BURNLEY (dux in 1946) following service with the Women's Auxiliary Australian Air Force as a transport driver. She worked as a jobbing gardener before employment at ADELAIDE BOTANIC GARDEN as a technical

Founding president of the Garden Clubs of Australia, Margaret DAVIS, planting the first tree of Remembrance Driveway in 1954, at Goulburn (NSW)

assistant from 1949. In 1951 she moved to MELBOURNE BOTANIC GARDENS, where she worked as a herbarium assistant until 1956, when she went to England and studied LANDSCAPE ARCHITECTURE at King's College, Durham. The following year she spent three months on a fellowship at the International Agricultural Study Centre, Wageningen University, Netherlands.

Becoming an individual member of the International Federation of Landscape Architects for Australia on her return, she set out to establish a local institute. Largely as a result of her initiatives, this was achieved when the AUSTRALIAN INSTITUTE OF LANDSCAPE ARCHITECTS was formed in 1967. From her return in 1959 until 1963 she worked for architects and engineers and as a consultant, designing the landscaping for the Sports Complex, Monash University (Vic.), and for the Perth Airport (1962). The success of these works led to her appointment the following year as technical officer in landscape architecture, Commonwealth Department of Works, the first person to occupy this position, where she became responsible for projects in Australia and New Guinea. Large-scale works included the Hobart, Launceston, Tullamarine, and Canberra airports, the Naval

Depot at Cockburn Sound, Dockyards at Williamstown, East Sale RAAF Base, and Broadmeadows Army Establishment, in addition to many smaller ones. The varied nature of these projects and their large scale marked a significant change in the role of women in the profession—a change she pioneered. Her achievements were acknowledged in 1970 when she became one of the first fellows of the AILA.

RICHARD CLOUGH

DAWSON, George Russell (1870–1959) and **Edward James Harrison** (1864–1949), nursery proprietors, were partners in Dawson, Harrison and Co., established in WA in 1901. Dawson had come to Perth in the 1890s from Vic. after working there at the Hinton and Dawson nursery in Caulfield. Harrison, a trained horticulturist, worked at Hampton Court gardens, England, before going to Egypt, helping to lay out the Mena Hotel Gardens and becoming a gardener at Lord Kitchener's residence. By 1903 the partners had four acres (1.6 ha) at Belmont and subsequently 100 acres (40 ha) at Forrestfield. Their first retail outlet was located in Central Arcade opposite the Perth Railway Station, later relocated to various sites in Barrack Street.

The partnership was dissolved *c.* 1921, with Harrison continuing to trade at Belmont as E.J. Harrison and Son, and George Dawson establishing a new nursery at Forrestfield, trading as Dawson Harrison. Harrison's business continued until 1972, producing potted stock and glasshouse lines while Dawson grew roses, ornamentals, and fruit trees at Forrestfield. Dawson's business was continued by his sons (Russell) William (1905–1999) and George Dawson (1910–1989). After making enquires to its American headquarters in Detroit, Bill Dawson was awarded the first Interflora membership for Australia (*c.* 1930). He broadcast a regular fifteen-minute RADIO gardening program from the 1930s to the 1970s, and during the Second World War produced a booklet, *My Victory Garden*, which aimed to inform Western Australians how they could utilise their quarter-acre blocks to become self-sufficient. At Forrestfield in the mid-1960s the Dawsons set up Perth's first garden centre, and the business is now run by a third generation.

JOHN VISKA

DAWSON, Thomas Henry (1902–1986) and **Justin Moray Gill** (1903–1996), ran Dawson's Cactus Garden and nursery in White Hills, Bendigo (Vic.), from 1933 to the 1980s. The DISPLAY GARDEN still retains an impressive stand of *Pachycereus pringleii*, and a range of mature CACTI and succulents. Proclaiming 'We grow the rare ones', an early Dawson and Gill catalogue included more than 2000 species. Prior to 1952 Dawson imported wild-collected plants from Mexico, and as required, these plants were quarantined in a registered quarantine house within the garden.

STEPHEN FORBES

DEANS, William C. (*fl.* 1909–49), was first listed in Brisbane directories in 1909 with a store in Stanley Street, and was included in the trade listing of seed merchants and nursery proprietors in 1913, the year he published his *Queensland Fruit Culture*. In 1928 he compiled his major work, *The Australian Flower Garden*, drawing on sources from GLENNY onwards. Describing himself as a LANDSCAPE ARCHITECT—an early Australian use of the term—his book covered design and planting of the flower garden, including directions for the bush-house, rockeries, tennis courts, and bowling greens. It was one of few garden books published in Qld to that date, and joined those by HOCKINGS, WRIGHT, and TRELOAR. Deans resided at Hawthorne and 'Deans Nurseries', Nudgee Road, Hendra, was still operating as late as 1949.

RA

DE BEUZEVILLE, Wilfred Alexander Watt (1884–1954), forest ecologist and botanist, was born at Bombala (NSW), the son of a pastoral station manager. His grandfather, **James Beuzeville** (1809–1887), was descended from French refugees who in the early eighteenth century had established a silk-weaving firm in London. James spent eight years in Europe, mainly Spain, as a sericulturist before migrating to Australia in 1848. On his arrival in Sydney he advocated experiments in SERICULTURE, and with the backing of a group including T.S. MORT, superintended a short-lived experimental silk institution. Although bankrupted, he continued his crusade through letters and an illustrated booklet, *Practical Instructions for the Management of Silk Worms*. Many of his descendants reverted to the earlier form of 'de Beuzeville', among them his grandson.

Wilfred joined the NSW Department of Forestry in 1912 and was soon surveying the resources of the Pilliga scrub under E.H.F. SWAIN. A bearded and somewhat eccentric figure, according to colleagues, 'Boozy' thought nothing of camping in the forest by crawling up a hollow log for the night. He rose within the Department (after 1916, Forestry Commission) and showed great interest in the NATIVE FLORA, particularly EUCALYPTS. He corresponded with J.H. MAIDEN and contributed to his *A Critical Revision of the Genus Eucalyptus* (1903–33). He wrote *Australian Trees for Australian Planting* (1947) at a time when interest in CONSERVATION of natural resources was burgeoning, and was instrumental in promoting the planting of native plants, especially through the work of STATE FOREST NURSERIES.

RA

DE CASTELLA, Francois Robert (1867–1953), viticulturist, was the son of Swiss-born Hubert de Castella (1825–1907), vigneron and author, of St Hubert's vineyard in Victoria's YARRA VALLEY. In 1883 Francois left Australia to study natural science at Lausanne, Switzerland, and vine growing and wine making in France. On his return (1886) he managed St Hubert's, but his father sold his share in the vineyard in 1890 and Francois joined the Victorian Department of Agriculture. He wrote the influential *Handbook on Viticulture for Victoria* (1891) but was retrenched in 1892. He became manager of Chateau Dookie for the Bank of Victoria. Following the outbreak of Grape Phylloxera at Bendigo (1894), de Castella condemned the Victorian Government's eradication of affected vineyards. Instead, he supported regional quarantine and the introduction of phylloxera-resistant American rootstocks, as was the trend in Europe. But his advice was ignored. In 1907, with the Victorian wine industry on the verge of collapse, he was again appointed VITICULTURAL expert with the Department of Agriculture. Sent to Europe to gain information, his work over the ensuing decades provided a scientific and practical basis for the reconstitution of phylloxera-affected vineyards in central and northern Vic. His tour also led to the introduction of cultures of flor yeasts for making delicate, dry sherries of the fino type, encouraging a popular beverage and increased planting of sherry varieties. Following his retirement in 1936 the Phylloxera Board of South Australia commissioned him to report on the grape varieties of SA. His achievements, especially in ampelography, were widely recognised and he was appointed to the French *Ordre du Mérite Agricole* in 1937. His recollections of early Victorian wine growing were published in the *Victorian Historical Magazine* (1942–44).

DAVID DUNSTAN

DECORATIVE ARTS using motifs from AUSTRALIAN FLORA defined the visual imagery for a national style of decoration that emerged in the final quarter of the nineteenth century, responding to a growing sense of national identity as Australia embraced the idea of Federation. Lucien Henry (1850–1896), a French-born artist and communard, arrived in Sydney from political exile in 1879: he sensed the stirrings of nationalistic fervour and in an essay in *Australian Art* (1888) promoted a style of 'National Art' based on the unique characteristics of the indigenous flora and fauna. Henry argued that 'the waratah, the stenocarpus and the banksia … could replace the lotus flower and palmette designs that express the qualities of the Classical World'. Then, to prove that a new Australian order could be created, he produced a folio of extraordinary and sometimes fanciful designs inspired by local flora. Henry transmitted his enthusiasm to students at Sydney Technical College, and as they accepted teaching appointments interstate, his influence infiltrated design schools and technical colleges across the continent.

Henry left Australia in 1891, but his legacy flourished. Stylistic forms of Australian flora readily adapted to the prevailing influence of Art Nouveau and the ARTS AND CRAFTS movements, illustrated best in the work of Melbourne cabinet-maker, Robert Prenzel. Waratahs, flannel flowers, and stenocarpus appeared as ornament on Federation-style architecture, while overseas manufacturers, such as English potteries, discovered lucrative domestic markets for locally inspired wares. The success of this movement was captured by Richard Thomas BAKER, whose collection at the Sydney Technological Museum formed the basis for his book *Australian Flora in Applied Art. Part 1: The Waratah* (1915) and the enduring interest in this art form. In NSW, Eirene MORT proposed a national school of design with the idea of producing articles based on Australian motifs. Her work, and that of her contemporaries in the New South Wales Arts and Crafts Society, demonstrate a serious commitment to that philosophy. At the Hobart Technical College, Henry's former student Lucien Dechaineux attempted to establish a regional style of decoration, while members of the Tasmanian Arts and Crafts society including Mildred Lovett, Maude Poynter, and Ellen Payne successfully worked Australian floral designs to create a local Arts and Crafts style. A similar movement developed through the Perth Technical School under the tutelage of James Linton and at the School of Art in Adelaide where the Principal, Laurence Howie, encouraged his students to create uniquely Australian crafts. In Qld, however, it was the outbreak of war that produced a patriotic style, championed by cabinet-maker, L. J. Harvey. Although Henry's national style of decoration failed to eventuate, the work of many Australian contemporary decorative artists, including Jenny Kee and Linda Jackson (fabric), Puzzle (silver and jewellery), and Tony Bishop and Michael Retter (marquetry), has brought international recognition to the unique forms of the Australian flora.

Margaret Betteridge, *Australian Flora in Art from the Museum of Applied Arts and Sciences, Sydney* (South Melbourne, 1979)

MARGARET BETTERIDGE

DEER PARKS were created in the Australian colonies in the early nineteenth century, imitating the medieval English tradition of keeping deer for the royal hunt. In Australia, such parks were occasionally formed in the DOMAINS and gardens adjoining GOVERNMENT HOUSES, and in larger PUBLIC PARKS, principally for aesthetic rather than sporting purposes. Grazing deer were considered an ornamental addition, assisting colonists to emulate PARK-like English landscapes. Private deer parks also provided game for the colonial gentry, who rode to hounds and considered venison a delicacy: they appear to have been most prolific in Tas., where deer were first introduced in 1829. Deer were also released into the bush, first at St Marys, NSW (1808), and in the 1860s in parts of Vic. and Qld for sporting and ACCLIMATISATION purposes. In parts of western Vic., in the hills east of Melbourne, and at ROYAL NATIONAL PARK, SYDNEY, deer continue to thrive. The western Melbourne suburb, Deer Park, recalls the former site of the Melbourne Hunt Club.

HELEN DOYLE

DELAHAYE, Félix (1767–1829), one of the earliest European gardeners to work in Australia, was born in Caumont, Eure, France. Aged 17, he gained employment in the botanical garden of the Académie des Sciences in Rouen and in 1788 was employed at the Jardin du Roi in Paris under André Thouin. In 1791 Delahaye joined d'Entrecasteaux's expedition, as a gardener, and worked diligently under the direction of LABILLARDIÈRE. During their first sojourn at Recherche Bay in Van Diemen's Land (1792), he planted chicory, cabbages, sorrel, radishes, cress, and potatoes. Unattended, the garden did not prosper. Delahaye, detained by the Dutch in Java until 1797, nevertheless continued to care for breadfruit plants he had collected in Tonga, which were eventually introduced to Mauritius and the French Antilles. In 1798 Delahaye became chief gardener at Trianon and then, in 1805, at the Empress Josephine's estate at Malmaison. He died in Versailles.

Edward Duyker and Maryse Duyker, *Bruny d'Entrecasteaux: Voyage to Australia and the Pacific* (Carlton South, Vic., 2001)

EDWARD DUYKER

DELATITE, Mansfield, Vic., retains the outline of an 1830s bark outstation and 1849 cottage 300 metres north-east of the present homestead, the site marked by three cedars

A modern DEER PARK at Quorn Hall (Tas.), echoes the mid-nineteenth-century interest in ACCLIMATISATION, which embraced both fauna and flora

planted in 1937 as a memorial to Antoinette Ritchie. The simple 1860s house of Alfred and George Chenery, who named it Delatite, remains alongside the present house (1890); the Chenerys also laid out a small garden and an orchard. *Rosa* 'Fortune's Yellow' planted in 1890 along the homestead verandah still blooms profusely and the drive of *Pinus macrocarpa* (Monterey Pine) was planted in 1898. The design of today's fine garden, begun in 1903, is attributed to Antoinette Ritchie (1870–1936), wife of Geoffrey Ritchie (1862–1923), who managed the property from 1902 then purchased (as part of a syndicate) in 1904. Set against a background of trees and shrubs, the garden contains curving flower beds, extensive lawns, and three magnificent pear trees from Chenery's orchard. From 1936, daughter-in-law Sylvia Noel Ritchie (1903–2000), together with a relative and Burnley trainee Miss May Fisher, modified and maintained the garden, planting the box-hedged rose garden and many more shrubs and trees. Sylvia Ritchie is credited with the introduction to Australia of *Rosa* 'Albertine' (1952).

HELEN PAGE

DELL, Edgar (b. 1901), London-born botanical artist, son of a nurseryman and garden contractor, arrived in Perth in 1924, having studied art in London. By the 1930s his meticulous watercolours of NATIVE PLANTS attracted the attention of the government botanist, C.A. GARDNER, and Dell's work illustrated Gardner's *Flowers of Western Australia* (1933–35) and *Poison Plants of South-western Australia* (1937). The whereabouts of the original artwork remains unknown.

CAROL MANSFIELD

DE MOLE, Fanny Elizabeth (1835–1866) and her sister **Harriet Jane De Mole** (1837–1891), botanical artists, were born in London and privately educated. In 1856 the sisters arrived with family members in SA. Fanny, of delicate health and 'confined to a wheelchair and couch', drew and painted the NATIVE FLORA, with twenty hand-coloured lithographs published in *Wild Flowers of South Australia* (London, 1861)—the first book of its kind for SA. A superb folio, fewer than 100 copies were produced. Family involvement in its production seems likely, and Harriet (like her sister) was a regular prize-winner for her watercolours of landscapes and flowers at South Australian Society of Arts exhibitions. Margaret De Mole (1844–1918), a daughter of horticultural advocate George STEVENSON and niece to Fanny and Harriet, inherited LEAWOOD GARDENS from Margaret Gorton (1807–1874) and it remained in her family until 1926.

DAVID JONES

DENBIGH, Bringelly, NSW, began in 1812 as a 1100 acre (445 ha) grant to merchant Charles Hook (*c*. 1762–1826), whose house was commenced *c*. 1817. Denbigh was next purchased by parson Thomas Hassall (1794–1868), who extended the homestead with a two-storey annexe and service buildings and built Heber Chapel (1828) nearby. Charles McIntosh purchased Denbigh in 1868 after leasing the property in 1866; during continuous family ownership, it has been used for breeding Clydesdale horses, dairying, and as an Ayrshire cattle stud. Denbigh is rare as one of few very early colonial properties to retain its original grant boundaries. It retains a large complex of outbuildings, and has fine views and a charming garden with early plantings of eucalypts (attributed to Hassall), *Araucaria bidwillii* (Bunya Pine), *Ceratonia siliqua* (Carob Tree), *Schinus molle* (Pepper Tree), cypresses, olives, agaves, and *Brachychiton populneus* (Kurrajong). Similar plantings survive at Heber Chapel and adjacent St Paul's Cemetery, Cobbitty (1842).

GEOFFREY BRITTON and COLLEEN MORRIS

DENHAM, Ilma (Elma) (1891–1971), carnation specialist and nursery proprietor, managed the Lanville Carnation Nursery, Thornbury (Vic.), an early female foray into the nursery trade. She hybridised numerous carnation varieties in the years around the First World War and in 1917 (as Elma Denham) wrote the *Australasian Catechism of Carnation Culture*, later extensively revised for a new edition (1921).

The book, arranged in the form of questions and answers, acknowledged her indebtedness to fellow specialists R. POULTER and Son and ERREY Bros. and gave instruction on cultivation and propagation. She included a history of the carnation and observed that 'Australian hybridists are quietly working and producing varieties which are, I am tempted to say, better than a lot of the boomed imported novelties.' Denham included remarks on 'The symbolism and expression of carnation colors', advising ladies 'to amuse themselves and unfold all their lovers' or husbands' secrets according to the carnation they wear'. Among Australian gardening books, her *Catechism* was one of the earliest by a female author, and one of the earliest specifically devoted to the CARNATION.   RA

DENISON, William Thomas (1804–1871), engineer, colonial governor, and horticultural enthusiast, was born in London, and had a distinguished career as an engineer in the Royal Engineers and the Admiralty before being knighted in 1846 and appointed Lieutenant-Governor of Van Diemen's Land (1847–55). His extensive library reflected a broad interest in the natural sciences. He was interested in the practical uses of Tasmanian timbers and in the improvement of agricultural production: as an active patron of the ROYAL SOCIETY, he presented several papers on topics including manures suited to turnip crops and potato planting. In his later posting as New South Wales Governor (1855–61), where he oversaw the inauguration of responsible government (1856), Denison proved an energetic leader. He supported agricultural pursuits and presided over the Australian Horticultural and Agricultural Society. His skilful handling of the inquiry into Charles MOORE's management of SYDNEY BOTANIC GARDENS (1855) saw Moore retained but Denison required, and supported, improvements. From his vice-regal positions he facilitated plant exchanges for colonial BOTANIC GARDENS, distributed seeds of economic value, and 'gave an impetus not only to gardening, but to every other industrial and scientific pursuit, encouraging them by practice, and lending a willing hand in furthering projects likely to benefit the community at large'. Denison returned to England in 1868 after a period as Governor of Madras.   LINDY SCRIPPS and COLLEEN MORRIS

DENNARQUE, Mount Wilson, in the BLUE MOUNTAINS, NSW, was designed in 1878 as a SUMMER RETREAT for Edward Merewether (1820–1893), a former general superintendent of the Australian Agricultural Company. The garden was laid out in the 1890s and incorporated many mature native tree ferns retained on the lot. Indeed, Dennarque is reputedly an Aboriginal name for Tree Fern. The main drive is lined with rhododendrons and lilacs, while the extensive lawns are dotted with specimen trees. The facade of the house is flanked by majestic specimens of *Cedrus deodara* (Himalayan Cedar).   DAVID BEAVER

DESBROWE-ANNEAR, Harold (1865–1933), architect and garden designer, born at Happy Valley, Bendigo (Vic.), moved with his family to Melbourne in 1870 where he was articled to the architect William Salway in 1883. He hyphenated his name in 1889 and adopted a monogram based on the initials DA, an ARTS AND CRAFTS–inspired homage to German artist Albrecht Dürer (1471–1528). Best known for his innovative and early functionalist houses during the first fifteen years of the twentieth century, Desbrowe-Annear's interests after the war turned towards Beaux-Arts design and TOWN PLANNING, manifest in a series of published but unexecuted plans for Melbourne. At this time he became well known locally for a number of large neo-Georgian houses in the wealthy inner suburbs of South Yarra and Toorak, and it is in connection with these works that his reputation as a garden designer is based.

Desbrowe-Annear's interest in garden design was probably sparked when he collaborated in 1910 with the artist Blamire Young (1862–1935) on the design for the garden of the MacGeorge House at Fairy Hills, Alphington—a formal design based on the geometry of the circle. Contemporary debate and local examples by architects such as Walter BUTLER were important precedents, and English and American theory and practice undoubtedly informed his gardens, particularly the work of Gertrude JEKYLL and architect Edwin Lutyens (1869–1944), the more formal designs of Reginald Blomfield (1856–1942) in England, and in the USA the work of landscape architect Beatrix Farrand (1856–1959) as well as the architect Charles Platt (1861–1933). None of the few surviving plans of Desbrowe-Annear's gardens contain planting keys, and his designs show none of the impressionistic use of plants found in the work of Jekyll, Farrand, or Edna WALLING. Compared with these three, Desbrowe-Annear's gardens are somewhat austere, in the formalist manner of Blomfield.

The Fairbairn (1919) and Kiddell (1926) gardens, in adjacent South Yarra streets, were ITALIANATE gardens designed to accompany refurbishments of Victorian houses in the fashionable neo-Georgian manner. Both were defined by one long walk of large flagstones set in lawn between garden beds, and a cross axis embellished by a colonnade. In both, lily ponds bordered by iris and emphasised by sculpture intersected the main walk, and formed a focal point. Planting was exotic—in the Kiddle garden it included poplars and birches, clipped box hedges, standard roses, and hydrangeas.

The most ambitious of Desbrowe-Annear's gardens were designed for Toorak residences of M.H. BAILLIEU (1925) and Sidney Myer at CRANLANA (1932). These were both originally conceived as large terraces intersected by radial paths emerging from a semi-circular piazza by the house, and their plans bear a close relationship to the Beaux-Arts plan for Melbourne that Desbrowe-Anear published in 1922. They were also part of larger schemes that included tennis courts, kitchen gardens, and service areas. In both cases, however, these plans were modified when the gardens were built. Three other gardens for houses designed by Desbrowe-Annear— Mulberry Hill, Baxter (1926), Westerfield, Frankston (1924), and Fairview, Kew (1924)—may also have had his input. In Desbrowe-Annear's last garden, Katanga, Malvern (1932), a narrow boundary path connected the three elements of the site plan: the centrally placed house, its formal garden on the west, and informal kitchen garden to the east. This compact and well-balanced plan can be compared with Jekyll and Weaver's 'Scheme for a narrow plot'.

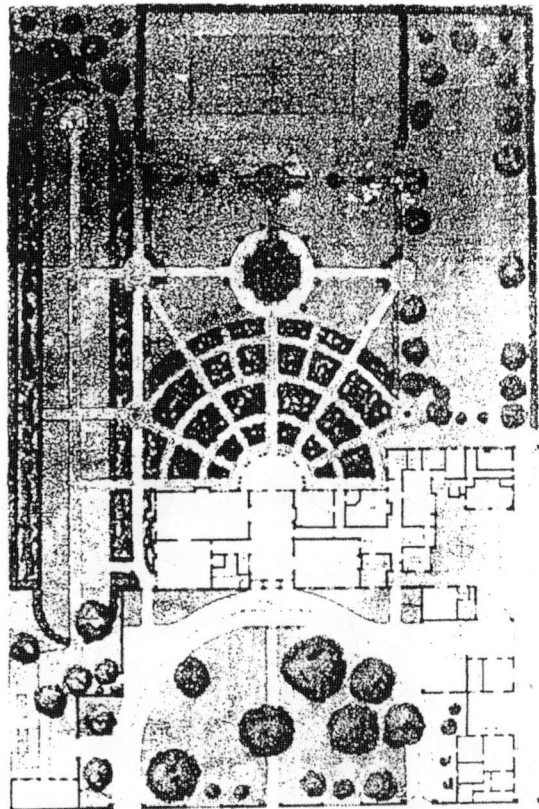

An unexecuted plan (1929) for CRANLANA, Toorak (Vic.), by Harold DESBROWE-ANNEAR, incorporating the geometric planning that characterised his final years—the radial and concentric path layout of the garden front was a device he had earlier used for the M.H. BAILLIEU residence

Desbrowe-Annear's garden designs were always conceived in relationship to the architecture of the house, and employed simple geometries of connection: axes, semi-circles, and grids. He was not particularly innovative, but his gardens were nonetheless significant in continuing the traditions of English garden design established at the end of the nineteenth century that emphasised the unity of design between the house and its site.   HARRIET EDQUIST

DESCHAMPS, Joseph Clement (1813–1878), vine grower, of Neuchâtel Canton, Switzerland, was a twelfth-generation French Burgundian vigneron who in 1853 migrated to Vic. Deschamps knew Lieutenant-Governor Charles Joseph LA TROBE, staying with him before establishing in the Kyneton district. Beaten by frost and bushfire, in 1859 he accepted the contract to establish a large commercial VINEYARD at Yering with his sons, Auguste, Louis, and Clement. Deschamps then purchased land at Lilydale, planted vineyards for his sons and 'retired' to Canterbury, near Melbourne, and a modest vineyard. Lilydale's description as 'the wine village' owed much to the picturesque vines of the Deschamps family: Auguste's Lilydale Vineyard to the east of the town, the Olinda Vineyard of Louis about a mile on the western side, and Clement's Market-Street vineyards adjoining it on a rise to the west. Their enterprise faded with the nineteenth century. A third generation, sons of Auguste, started the Yeringa vineyard but sold in 1904.
                            DAVID DUNSTAN

DESIGNED LANDSCAPES are a form of CULTURAL LANDSCAPE that have been intentionally created or designed. Gardens are one of the most easily recognisable forms, but the term includes a far wider range of places, such as specialised plantings in ARBORETA, ORCHARDS, and PARKLANDS; manifestations of TOWN PLANNING and URBAN DESIGN, including AVENUES, BOULEVARDS, DOMAINS, ESPLANADES, GREEN BELTS, and STREET TREE planting; INSTITUTIONAL sites such as CEMETERIES, HOSPITAL GARDENS, RAILWAY GARDENS, SCHOOL GARDENS and UNIVERSITY CAMPUSES, SHOWGROUNDS, and ZOOLOGICAL GARDENS; some grounds associated with SPORT, such as GOLF COURSES and RACECOURSES; and some COMMERCIAL sites, the outer margins of which may include CARAVAN PARKS, CAR PARKS, and THEME PARKS.

One VINEYARD or orchard in isolation might constitute a designed landscape, but in aggregation, as in the COONAWARRA region or BAROSSA VALLEY, they are usually considered to form a cultural landscape. Likewise, just as an individual HOMESTEAD GARDEN with its constituent parts may form a designed landscape, a wider grouping of farm buildings and other features of the RURAL LANDSCAPE, such as FENCES, HEDGES, and WINDBREAKS, more typically form a cultural landscape. Designed landscapes may reveal important clues about economic and social circumstances, aesthetic preferences, and historical events that have shaped them, such as LAND SURVEY AND SALE. By understanding their history and learning to read their physical character, a keen observer may gain insights into the cultural attitudes and values of those who have designed and used them.   JOY McCANN

DESPEISSIS, Adrian Jean Marie (1860–1927), agriculturist, viticulturist, and horticulturist, was born on the estate of his French sugar-planter family at Mapou, Mauritius. He was studying medicine at Port-Louis when he was sent to India by the government to investigate cane-sugar importing. He was appointed the Mauritian executive commissioner at the Colonial and Indian Exhibition, London (1886) and stayed to study at the Royal Agricultural College, Cirencester. In 1890, after further agricultural study in Paris and practical viticultural experience in the Médoc wine region and at Montpellier, he was appointed as consulting viticulturist and inspector of agriculture for the NSW government (his father at this time was an adviser to the Colonial Sugar Refining Co. in Sydney). In 1894 Despeissis went to WA, where he helped to establish the Bureau of Agriculture, becoming its viticultural and horticultural expert and inspector. His *Handbook of Horticulture and Viticulture of Western Australia* (1895) ran to three editions by 1921 and he wrote many journal articles. He visited Algeria, Spain, and Portugal in 1906 to study VITICULTURE, and on his return rose within the Agriculture Department. He investigated tropical agriculture in Qld, Malaya, Singapore, and Java in 1910, and retired in 1912 after two years as commissioner for tropical agriculture for the north-west of WA. He subsequently established a vineyard at Guildford (WA), and served a term as director of agriculture in Fiji (1923). RA

DICKINSON, James (1806–1888), nursery proprietor and horticulturist, was born in the English Lake District, where he soon mixed in the company of botanists and imbibed the wild romantic scenery beloved of poet William Wordsworth and celebrated in numerous picturesque guidebooks, notably those by Thomas West (1778) and William GILPIN (1786). James, now a Lancastrian merchant, his wife Fanny and their five children were living in Liverpool when he was charged in 1837 with receiving stolen wool. He was transported on the *Minerva* to Van Diemen's Land in 1838 to begin his fourteen-year sentence. His behaviour was reported as 'exemplary' by the ship's surgeon and he received his ticket of leave in 1842. His wife and their four living children emigrated in 1843, and the family settled in Hobart. As a Quaker, he attended the Friends' Meeting House in Murray Street. The Society let him the vacant ground next door, where by 1845 he had established a florist's business. He was made overseer of the Royal Society's botanic garden, a position he accepted on the understanding that he be permitted two afternoons a week to attend to his own business. His *Catalogue of Annual and Herbaceous Plants, Flowering Bulbs and Tubers, Ornamental Shrubs, Forest Trees, Fruit Trees, and Culinary Plants and Seed* (1845) is one of the earliest Australian nursery catalogues known to survive. In it, Dickinson apologised for its paucity 'accounted for by the statement that it is only the second season, with very limited capital, since the Collection was attempted'. Dickinson collected indigenous seeds and explored the hinterlands; in a letter under the nom de plume 'Tyro' to the *Hobart Town Courier* (1845) he wrote of the Wellington Falls: 'This piece of scenery [is] magnificent as any country could boast of—a scene where the wild, the grand and the sublime are merged in the romantic, the stupendous and the terrible'.

In 1845 Dickinson exchanged plants with the Royal Society, but within four years he was complaining that the Society's liberal policy on plant exchanges was threatening his livelihood in the nursery business. He was secretary of the Gardeners' and Amateurs' Horticultural Society of Hobart Town when it issued its booklet on *Properties of Florists' Flowers*, after the definitions of George GLENNY. In 1855 his major work, *The Wreath: Gardener's Manual, Arranged for the Climate of Tasmania* (edited by John Morgan) was published, the first Tasmanian guide since BUNCE's *Manual of Practical Gardening* (1838). Dickinson acknowledged the assistance of Joseph ALLPORT and quoted many standard English works in his mainly practical remarks.

By 1856 Dickinson, denied a land grant in Tas., had settled in Vic., at Morang then Portarlington. During the early 1860s he was a frequent contributor to the *Yeoman and Australian Acclimatiser*, discussing topics as diverse as medicinal plants, grasses, bees, and silkworms. He advertised his services as a botanical collector and during 1870 exchanged plants with MUELLER. Dickinson died at Hepburn, a pioneer of the Australian NURSERY TRADE and one of the few convicts who made a lasting contribution to Australian horticulture. RA

DIETRICH (née NELLE), (Konkordia) Amalie (1821–1891), naturalist and collector, spent a decade in Qld (1863–72). Her collecting was not the gentle recreational pursuit deemed so acceptable for nineteenth-century European women. It was vocational and arduous. Until her marriage in 1846 to the pharmacist Wilhelm Dietrich, Amalie lived in Saxony and learned from her mother about plants and their medicinal uses. Her husband, who (falsely) claimed kinship with the famous botanical Dietrichs, taught her NATURAL HISTORY, and the couple made an irregular and unreliable living by collecting, preparing, and identifying plants, insects, and minerals.

Dietrich's Australian work was prompted by a combination of unrelated factors: her marital situation, German economic and scientific interests, and Queensland immigration policy. After Wilhelm's affair with a younger woman, Amalie sought work as a collector to support herself and her young daughter. Godeffroy and Sohn, a German shipping and trading firm that later went bankrupt (1879), was expanding into the Pacific, and wanted natural history and ethnographic items for sale and display in the Museum Godeffroy in Hamburg. Dietrich gained a ten-year contract. Godeffroy's only female collector, she arrived at Moreton Bay on a Godeffroy ship carrying German migrants attracted by gold and land grants. After collecting around Brisbane she sailed north and collected near Gladstone, Rockhampton, Mackay, Lake Elphinstone, and Bowen. On remote agricultural settlements she sometimes stayed with German migrants.

Dietrich lived above the Godeffroy Museum and worked on her unique collections, whose size and significance make her one of the most important naturalists to collect in Australia. Taxonomists working on her collections described many new species and named some in her honour—insects, algae, mosses, ferns, and flowering plants with specific epithets *amaliae*, *dietrichiae*, and *dietrichiana*.

Charitas Bischoff (née Dietrich) wrote an immensely successful book, which presented a partly fictitious portrait of her adventurous and determined plant-loving mother.

LINDEN GILLBANK

DISPLAY GARDENS have largely been used to exhibit plants, horticultural products, and GARDEN BUILDINGS and ORNAMENTS for COMMERCIAL advantage, often in conjunction with a NURSERY, a garden SHOW, or FESTIVAL. An early (and partly extant) example was attached to the TAYLOR AND SANGSTER nursery at MOUNT MACEDON, where the 1874 valuation separately listed stock in pots and that planted out in garden borders. The advent of Garden Week in Melbourne (1925) formalised a mode of commercial exhibit, utilising temporary display gardens, previously seen at AGRICULTURAL SHOWS. The term has also denoted a stylistic mode in domestic gardens invoking attributes such as neatness, order, and public appreciation, usually in the FLOWER GARDEN. RA

DIXON, Kingsley Wayne (b.1954), research botanist and horticulturist, is Director (Science Directorate) of KINGS PARK AND BOTANIC GARDEN, Perth. Following a PhD in botany from the University of Western Australia (1981) he joined the botanical staff at Kings Park. As head of research (1984) he focused on the biology, conservation, and horticultural development of the AUSTRALIAN FLORA. His most significant research achievement was the discovery that smoke from burning plants was a hidden trigger in the germination of many of Australia's beautiful yet difficult-to-PROPAGATE species. His personal interest in Australian ORCHIDS combined with collaborative research in tissue culture and cryogenics to harness these technologies for the first time to overcome a crisis in conservation of some of Australia's rarest species. Dixon has been an invited speaker and lecturer on Australian plants to a wide audience, including national and international forums.   ML

DIXON (née **BURKITT**), **Patricia Annesley** (b. 1953), garden writer and photographer, was born in Goulburn (NSW), and her career has been greatly influenced by her rural background. Researching Edna WALLING's gardens propelled her GARDEN HISTORY writings, including *Gardens in Time* (1988) and *The Vision of Edna Walling* (1998), both written with Jennie Churchill. Trisha Dixon edited *Australian Garden History* (1995–2000) and her photography has featured in many books and magazines, including her *Garden Design and Style* (1991) and *Gordon Ford: The Natural Australian Garden* (1999).   RA

DOMAINS, particularly as describing grounds attached to the early GOVERNMENT HOUSES, appear to be distinctly Australasian in concept. The term's general English usage was wider, applying to royal domains and also to individual property or a personal environment generally. In Australia its meaning evolved into a specialised form of public land, and also became directly linked with the early BOTANIC GARDENS.

The term was interchangeable for a time with the legal (Old French) spelling 'demesne', which was used in at least one Sydney plan, by C. Cartwright (1816). This showed the area now called the Domain in Sydney, a gently sloping area encircling the present ROYAL BOTANIC GARDENS, SYDNEY (then called the Outer Domain). It is still intensively used for public occasions, meetings, rallies, public oratory, sport, and concerts, and is regarded as a significant place in Sydney's public life. This domain was attached to the First Government House (1788) at Sydney Cove. Failed attempts to grow wheat and corn were made there, plunging NSW into an uncertain and hungry period before supply ships reached it from England in 1791. At Parramatta, a domain surrounded (Old) Government House, and it was here that the first successful crops were grown under the watchful eye of Henry Dodd. Extensive at first, stretching to Toongabbee, Governor Macquarie forbade casual trespassers on the town side. By 1857, however, the domain lost its close link with the governor, and the parkland was reduced to 63 hectares and renamed PARRAMATTA PARK.

In Hobart, the Government Domain was located on the rocky knoll on Macquarie Point, by Governor Macquarie in 1811. The location was confirmed by Governor Arthur (1826), who had plans to relocate Government House to this scenic and 'judiciously' chosen spot, but the present building was not completed until the 1850s. The domain was then stated to be 'set apart for the use and recreation of the citizens of Hobart Town', for which purpose it is still used. It adjoins the ROYAL TASMANIAN BOTANICAL GARDENS and now encompasses 152 hectares of an original 240. Remnants of native vegetation survived early nineteenth-century grazing and deliberate policy from the late nineteenth century to create a park-like environment, now represented by a PINETUM and exotic tree plantings. At Launceston, land once adjoining the government cottage now forms part of CITY PARK.

In Brisbane, Charles FRASER and Allan CUNNINGHAM selected an area of 17 hectares for a public garden in 1827. When the district was thrown open for free settlement (1839), a new town plan was put in place, but the Government Garden was confirmed. After separation from NSW (1859), Governor Bowen moved into a newly built Government House at the northern border of BRISBANE BOTANIC GARDENS. When the governor moved to Fernberg the vice-regal link was lost. Since then the area has been built over, skirted by the Riverside freeway, used as a car park, and a small remnant made over as the Domain parkland.

In Melbourne, Lieutenant-Governor LA TROBE created another permutation of this pattern when he chose Government House grounds overlooking the Yarra River in 1845 and a nearby valley for the nucleus of a garden, now the ROYAL BOTANIC GARDENS, MELBOURNE, 'for rearing and cultivating plants'. In conjunction with the construction of Government House (1872–76) a competition was held and the scheme of Joseph SAYCE was selected and partially implemented. Ferdinand MUELLER had previously densely planted the area, and William GUILFOYLE subsequently modified the landscape design. The King's Domain—now managed by the Melbourne City Council—is one of a number of separate but conjoined reserves that still maintain Government House as a focus.

In Adelaide, Government House was sited in the expansive ADELAIDE PARK LANDS. The term 'domain' was supplanted in SA by 'park lands', and George GOYDER required the provision of park lands for every new town surveyed in SA and NT, in part to enable both tree planting and recreation.

The town plan of Perth, laid out in 1829, incorporated a generous government domain extending from Barrack Street to the Causeway. However, most of this prime riverfront land was soon sold for private residential development, leaving a small domain of 4.5 hectares where the first permanent Government House was erected in 1834–35. Stirling Square, an undeveloped reserve adjoining the Government House, was declared a public park in 1845 and is today Perth's oldest public park. The lower section of Pier Street along the western boundary of the Government House site was closed in 1858 and included in the Government Domain when the present Government House was under construction. The Government Domain, which originally had a river frontage, and the adjoining Stirling Gardens—sometimes referred to collectively in the past as the Government Domain—remain

Cartwright's plan of the 'Governor's Demesne' (1816) is amongst the earliest Australian garden plans, and provides crucial evidence of the early history of Sydney's DOMAIN, GOVERNMENT HOUSE, and the ROYAL BOTANIC GARDENS, SYDNEY (located at the head of Farm Cove)

a dominant element in the St Georges Terrace/Barrack Street historic precinct. Of all the capital city domains only Perth lacked a contiguous botanic garden.

Generally, the domains, together with the botanic gardens, have performed an important role in the evolution of the form of Australian capital cities, providing valuable PUBLIC OPEN SPACE in the metropolitan cores and mediating the basic grid to provide a distinctly Australian mixture of land uses.

HELEN PROUDFOOT

DORAN, Philip (1830–1913), horticulturist and botanic garden curator, was born in Hull, England, the son of a gardener. He served his apprenticeship under Joseph PAXTON at CHATSWORTH, and assisted in laying out the Crystal Palace grounds at Sydenham. He arrived in Australia in 1855, and in Castlemaine (Vic.) in 1857 he advertised: 'Parterres, Gardens, Pleasure Gardens, &c., laid out, stocked and kept in order at modest charges … Designs for horticultural buildings, arbors, rustic seats, &c done to order.' In 1866 he became inaugural curator of CASTLEMAINE BOTANIC GARDENS, a position he held for forty-seven years until his death. He was responsible for the design of the garden, including its ornamental lake and some of the structures, including the summer-house. During his curatorship he oversaw the transformation of the land from a mined-out creek flat to an ornamental garden featuring gravel paths, lakes with islands, fernery, garden buildings, formal entrance gates, and garden ornament such as a fountain. Throughout this period he managed the gardens as BOTANIC GARDENS, labelling plants and receiving unusual and experimental species from Daniel BUNCE, William GUILFOYLE, Charles MOORE, and, most often, Ferdinand MUELLER. Doran's duties also included other parks and reserves in the municipality, and his STREET TREE planting was particularly noteworthy. In 1874 his contribution to the Castlemaine Botanical Gardens was acknowledged by Mueller, who named the small Central Australian shrub *Dicrastylis doranii* for him.

KEVIN WALSH

DOWNING, Andrew Jackson (1815–1852), landscape gardener and horticultural writer, started his career in the family nursery business at Newburgh, New York. Strategically located in the Hudson River Valley, home to North America's finest collection of landscaped estates, the young Downing soon produced his first book, *A Treatise on the Theory and Practice of Landscape Gardening Adapted to North America* (1841), its subtitle *With a View to the Improvement of Country Residences* clearly delineating its intended audience of wealthy rural improvers. Downing was a protégé of LOUDON, especially in his literary pursuits and his boundless energy, and like his mentor, wrote authoritatively on both architecture and landscape. His *Fruits and Fruit-trees of North America* (1845) was widely consulted by Australian POMOLOGISTS, and his two architectural works directly or indirectly influenced many designers working in Australia in the mid-nineteenth century. His English-born architectural partner, Calvert Vaux (1824–1895), later collaborated with Frederick Law OLMSTED. Downing edited the *Horticulturist* (1846–52), best known in Australia through the republication of its editorials as *Rural Essays* (1853). Later editions of the *Treatise* embraced an appreciation of native (American) trees, thereby lessening his philosophical dependence on Loudon's GARDENESQUE style, but the lofty tone was a fixture. Downing spun a dream of the ideal country residence only to realise that it was unattainable for all but the most wealthy. In the *Horticulturist* he increasingly catered for more modest establishments and his untimely death in a steamboat accident perhaps prevented these more liberal ideas from reaching a wider post–gold rush audience in Australia.

George Tatum and Elisabeth Blair MacDougall (eds), *Prophet with Honor* (Washington, D.C.,1989); David Schuyler, *Apostle of Taste* Baltimore, 1996); Judith K. Major, *To Live in the New World: A.J. Downing and American Landscape Gardening* (Cambridge, Mass., 1997)

RA

DOWSE, Frank Robert (1902–1983), landscape gardener and garden superintendent, born at Bury St Edmunds, Suffolk, England, the son of a head gardener, worked at Biddulph Grange (Staffordshire) and Hever Castle (Kent), before migrating to Vic. in the early 1920s to work at BALLARAT BOTANIC GARDENS. After two years there, and seven years with the Melbourne City Council, working on the Alexandra and FITZROY GARDENS, Dowse spent much of the Depression as curator of the St Kilda Cemetery. He then lived and worked in Springvale, where he established a nursery.

Dowse was superintendent of parks and reserves in Launceston from 1946 to 1967, succeeding William McGOWAN. He was largely responsible for the design of Launceston's suburban parks, including the Trevallyn Reserve, Punchbowl Reserve, Newstead Reserve, Victoria Square (Windmill Hill), Ockerby Gardens, and the Elizabeth Gardens at Invermay. In these and in his modifications to other PUBLIC PARKS, his inclination was towards simpler and slightly more tailored schemes than those of his predecessors, characteristically replacing the distinctive rough rock-work of McGowan with more tailored walls of cement-jointed cut basalt. In addition to his professional expertise, Dowse had a colourful turn of phrase and an overwhelming enthusiasm for gardening, all of which contributed to the success and enduring popularity of his weekly gardening show on RADIO (1950–66). He was held in such esteem that on his retirement there was a public campaign to rename CITY PARK after him: this eventually resulted in a new F.R. Dowse gateway.

ANNE NEALE

DRAINAGE of a garden is just as important as IRRIGATION in providing a balanced level of moisture in the soil. Consideration of how to remove excess WATER, either from rain or salt-laden groundwater, is essential in achieving ideal ground conditions for plants to thrive and also to extend the range of plants able to be grown. Drainage falls into two broad categories based on the quality of the water gathered: fresh water (such as surface run-off following rain) and groundwater (such as swampy soil).

Effective drainage was identified as a major source of improved health for an increasingly urbanised population during the nineteenth century, removing excess water as well as sewage; the rapid segregation of these two functions into stormwater and sewerage systems formalised their separate roles. Stormwater drainage, usually effected by pipe (enclosed) or channel (open), has included systems of timber, stone, brick, earthenware, terracotta, concrete, and plastic products. When fresh, as is the case of surface run-off following rain, water is often reused for irrigation. This has generally been achieved by surface drains lining the sides of paths with stone, brick, or earthenware half-pipes that typically drained into a larger underground network of wood-stave, terracotta, or brick pipes. In larger gardens, this water was often stored in an ornamental LAKE. One of the most sophisticated drainage (and irrigation) systems taking full advantage of natural features is RIPPON LEA, where the elaborate nineteenth-century system still provides a working and largely subterranean museum display. ROOKWOOD CEMETERY exhibits a much bolder aesthetic use of drains, with deep, brick-lined channels presenting a distinct landscape feature. At an early date, the MELBOURNE BOTANIC GARDENS was largely self-sufficient in its water needs, quarrying its own stone for drains, collecting rainwater via surface drains and from building roofs, and storing this in lakes and tanks within the gardens. For urban gardens, reticulated water supplies such as Launceston (1857), Melbourne's Yan Yean supply (1857), Hobart's Mountain Water Supply (1861), and the goldfields scheme of Coolgardie and Kalgoorlie, WA (1903), reduced reliance on self-sufficiency in water supply.

Subsoil drainage has been less developed in Australia in small gardens, and is generally confined to larger schemes. The use in Britain of patent draining tiles for boggy or swampy soil was little imitated here, although localised drainage via agricultural pipes has been a popular (if frequently misunderstood) remedy. Large-scale drainage accompanied major irrigation projects as part of managing the water table. Where extra water was added to dry land—for example, in the closer settlement schemes of the Murray–Darling basin—the leached, subsurface salt-laden water was carried away in open channels. Alternatively, low-lying, waterlogged land—such as the Koo-wee-rup swamps (Vic.)—that was otherwise unsuitable for cultivation had the water level lowered by drainage, thus allowing its development. The traditional view of swamps as unhealthy and requiring a heavy engineering approach to manage and control them is fast being replaced by a valuing of wetlands as important conservation and revegetation zones. Changed attitudes are also encouraging onsite drainage management, especially in housing and large institutional and commercial developments through the use of swales, wetland plantings, and plant selection that deals sensitively with wet and dry edaphic conditions. At La Trobe University, Bundoora, Vic., a lake system includes filtering ponds for urban run-off and planting that collects injurious compounds and oxygenates the water. Water that has passed through soil is often polluted by salts, and can be detrimental to soil quality and plant growth, necessitating drainage. Run-off water carrying excess nutrients (often from FERTILISERS) is now causing considerable concern, as it has great potential to damage ecological systems; slow-release chemicals and increased monitoring are two avenues for its control, if not its abatement.

ROHAN LAMB

DRINKING FOUNTAINS The movement to provide drinking WATER in public places developed in the middle of the nineteenth century and was quickly supported by the temperance lobby. By the turn of the century, substantial drinking fountains were essential utilitarian and decorative elements of PUBLIC GARDENS and reserves. Most of the more elaborate fountains also served as MEMORIALS commemorating individuals and events; some were gifts from benefactors and community groups. Early examples were often of decorative cast iron, but soon stone was universally adopted for durability. Designs were based on cemetery monuments, and many featured small temple-like structures housing the water outlets. Horse troughs and drinking bowls for dogs were incorporated into a few designs, and some fountains were capped with elaborate gas lamps. More modest fountains have been incorporated in URBAN DESIGNS since the 1940s, using a variety of modern materials.

ROBERT GREEN

DRIVES, roads or carriageways used for vehicular transport between the private residence and public roadway. In early colonial settlement, drives were associated primarily with MANSION and HOMESTEAD estates, enabling access principally for a carriage of the property owners and their guests. Connected to the public road at a GATE or LODGE, the drive formed a significant design element; it oriented and directed the visitor, revealed the beauty and extent of the property, and announced the residence at its terminus. Driveway plantings, such as AVENUES or mixed SHRUBBERIES accentuated these functions, often by developing a sense of enclosure or by framing VISTAS. A serpentine form was particularly popular for landscapes designed in a PICTURESQUE mode. The drive usually terminated in a turning circle or bay, while a subsidiary drive continued to the outbuildings, such as stables and buggy-house. These functional and aesthetic characteristics—which also applied to many INSTITUTIONAL sites and occasionally carriage drives through large PUBLIC PARKS—continue to characterise driveway design for large properties.

As city populations grew during the nineteenth century, the drive was adapted to VILLA residences on smaller SUBURBAN blocks, yet still reflected the luxury of private transport commensurate with high social status. Constricted sites resulted in tighter circular or horseshoe layouts, with stables being accessed from a separate public road or lane. The suburban driveway circle provided an ideal bed for a specimen tree or floral BEDDING. The First World War saw vast changes to living patterns in all aspects of Australian life. Domestically, the burgeoning GARDEN SUBURB, modest costs for domestic construction, and increasing home ownership testified to a rising middle class. Technological changes included the introduction of a revolutionary means of conveyance—the automobile.

While car ownership was beyond the reach of most new small home buyers, by the 1920s suburban home builders provided for a driveway—even if they never intended to own an automobile themselves. Again, space constraints of subdivision relegated the drive to its most economical form: a direct path running from the street frontage along the side of the house to the BACKYARD. Simple two-strip concrete drives, with an auxiliary pedestrian path to the house, became an inexpensive norm. This pattern soon became integral to suburban planning, and still dominates. Automobiles also provided for an important new GARDEN BUILDING, the garage, and a new public facility, the CAR PARK.

Since the 1960s, the 'two-car family' has required additional space for drive and garage facilities. The pressure on garden space today is evident when front lawns are overrun with family vehicles, suggesting a complete evolution from front garden to car park. Despite earning vilification as a garden intrusion, the drive has also facilitated a new garden zone

The DRIVE at CRUDEN FARM, Langwarrin (Vic.), lined by an avenue of *Eucalyptus citriodora* (Lemon-scented Gum), provides an understated yet elegant approach to this fine country estate

for multiple use; adaptations range from a green for lawn bowls of the 1920s to a popular BARBECUE area, a cricket pitch, or apron for a basketball hoop. **KAREN OLSEN**

DRUMMOND, James (*c.* 1784–1863), botanist, plant collector, and horticulturist, born at Hawthornden, Scotland, spent his early working life in southern Ireland where he was curator of Cork Botanic Garden (1808–28). He became an associate of the Linnean Society in 1810 and published papers on the Irish flora. His younger brother, Thomas, was well known as a plant collector in North America. James Drummond arrived in Australia on the *Parmelia* with the official party at the founding of the Swan River Colony (1829). He was appointed government naturalist, a position without salary, but with the prospect of becoming superintendent of the government garden should one be established. Although disappointed in his aspirations for permanent government office, as one of the few experienced horticulturists in the colony he contributed to its earliest horticultural history, most notably over the period 1829–34, and achieved widespread recognition as Western Australia's pre-eminent nineteenth-century botanist and a plant collector *extraordinaire*.

Drummond established three ACCLIMATISATION gardens in WA during the first years of settlement, all short-lived. The first, on Garden Island off the coast near Fremantle, was hastily planted, soon after arrival, with nine cases of plant stock donated by the Horticultural Society in London and Drummond's own private stock of plants and seeds, only to be left behind when the official party moved to permanent quarters on the mainland two months later. A second garden at Guildford was soon abandoned, and the third, established in 1831 on the river foreshore at Perth, was described in LOUDON's *Encyclopaedia of Gardening* (1834). This first PUBLIC GARDEN in Perth—not to be confused with the present STIRLING GARDENS, established in 1845—was incorporated in the grounds of Government House in 1834. Its demise was a personal blow for Drummond, and thereafter the botany of WA became the focus of his life's work.

Drying grounds

He made extensive botanical collections for subscribers in England, the result of numerous expeditions on foot and horseback over vast areas of south-west WA. Drummond's biographer, Rica ERICKSON, has identified the provenance and extent of his so-called six collections, numbering several thousand species. He was a long-standing correspondent with Sir William Hooker at KEW GARDENS and his papers, articles, and correspondence were published in newspapers and scientific journals in WA and England. A series of ten such articles on the Western Australian flora was published in the local *Inquirer* newspaper (1842). His services to botanical science were officially recognised in 1846 when he received an honorarium of £200. Specimens collected by Drummond are held in twenty-five herbaria in Britain, Europe, the USA, and Australia. Some seventy plants are named after him (originally 119 before taxonomic revision), and a memorial seat in KINGS PARK AND BOTANIC GARDEN (1968) commemorates his life and work.

Rica Erickson, *The Drummonds of Hawthornden* (Osborne Park, WA, 1969)   OLINE RICHARDS

DRYING GROUNDS, or drying greens, were introduced into colonial NSW from Europe. Drying grounds were areas of scythed grass, edged with other sweet-smelling shrubs such as lavender. Spread across grass and bushes, laundered linens dried in the sun, acquiring a gentle perfume in the process. Drying grounds usually existed on larger estates with the luxury of land that could be spared from food production. The area was sometimes fenced and separate from the garden proper, or adjacent to the laundry and servants' quarters behind the house. Where drying was restricted to smaller BACKYARDS, lines and props lifted washing off the ground. By 1924 Gilbert TOYNE had developed the rotary clothes hoist, forerunner of the Hills Hoist, although garden plans published as late as the 1940s show lines in designated 'drying areas', separated by hedges from the rear garden—a legacy of the drying ground.   DEBORAH MALOR

DUNCAN, Walter Hughes (b. 1939), rosarian and nursery proprietor, is descended from the Duncan family of HUGHES PARK, SA. On completing his secondary schooling he joined his family's pastoral company, and remains a director. Aged 19 he joined the NATIONAL ROSE SOCIETY of South Australia and quickly rose to prominence as a successful grower and exhibitor of modern and old-fashioned ROSES. He was active in all aspects of the society's business, elected to the committee (1962), vice-president (1964), president (1972–74), and honorary life member (1978). He maintained strong

TOYNE's Rotary Clothes Hoist, advertised in *Australian Home Beautiful* as early as 1924, revolutionised Australian DRYING GROUNDS, and later became a suburban icon

family connections to the Royal Agricultural and Horticultural Society of South Australia, especially as a committee member of its Horticultural and Floricultural Committee (elected 1976) and as a member of the Board of Management. During 1963–72 he won two Banksian Medals of the ROYAL HORTICULTURAL SOCIETY (UK) and nine Bronze Medals awarded at the Royal Adelaide Show.

Duncan developed a keen interest in growing and exhibiting plants in containers for use in imaginative garden-like floor displays and allied also to his interest in growing roses he became a professional rose grower at Hughes Park. He rejuvenated the extensive gardens of the homestead, including a large hedged vegetable garden, adding a new rose DISPLAY GARDEN. His business annually produces approximately 150 000 plants of old and new roses under contract to major retail outlets and for direct sale. Duncan is widely respected for his judging and lecturing; he is a horticultural raconteur who shows a deep appreciation of the ways of gardeners.

TREVOR NOTTLE

DUNEIRA, Mount Macedon, Vic., was developed from the 1870s by pastoralist Suetonius Henry Officer (1830–1883) and saw long occupation and further development (1890–1940) by the family of James Smith Reid (d. 1922). Duneira is unusual among MOUNT MACEDON gardens for its gently undulating ground and consequent open parkland design, in contrast to more typical terraced HILL-STATIONS. The six-hectare garden, which complements an impressive SUMMER RESIDENCE (1875–76), gatehouse, and outbuildings, enjoys deep soils and a damp climate particularly favourable to a diverse range of trees. Of particular note is the half-kilometre formal DRIVE lined with elms—one of the best private AVENUES in Vic.; this is underplanted with spring-flowering crocus species and bluebells. The garden contains excellent examples of popular nineteenth-century plantings, including holly hedges, avenues of oak and Spanish Chestnut, and extensive rhododendron plantings. A 'secret garden' hidden by dense *Prunus lusitanica* (Portugese Laurel) hedges is divided into 'rooms', one of which contains a magnificent *Prunus* 'Shirotae' while another conceals a small glasshouse.

PENNY DUNN

DUNPHY, Myles Joseph (1891–1985), draftsman and conservationist, developed a passion for bushwalking during his teenage years and soon became aware that the natural areas he loved so much were threatened by population growth and economic development. His own specially designed maps of the BLUE MOUNTAINS and other walking areas provided the basis for walks by many thousands of others. In 1932 he was a founder of, and the driving force behind, the National Parks and Primitive Areas Council. Using the Council as advisers and a sounding board, Dunphy developed plans for many NATIONAL PARKS and reserves throughout eastern NSW. Although a number of these proposals were progressively agreed by government, and parks established during the 1930s, the recognition of others has been slower. But today, most areas Dunphy recommended for protection are national parks or protected areas, some of them being gazetted only in recent years. Thus, Dunphy is arguably the greatest visionary of the Australian parks movement. His son, Milo Kanangra Dunphy (1929–1996), director of the Sydney Total Environment Centre, followed in his footsteps.

Patrick Thompson (ed.), *Selected Writings: Myles Dunphy* (Sydney, 1986)

ELERY HAMILTON-SMITH

DUNTROON, Canberra, ACT, was taken up as a pastoral run in 1825 by prominent Sydney merchant Robert Campbell (1769–1846), granted 4000 acres (1620 ha) of land on the Limestone Plains as compensation for the loss of his ship on government service. Robert's fourth son, George (1818–1881), moved to Duntroon—part of an inheritance from his father—with his wife Marianne (1827–1903), creating one of Australia's finest country estates. Marianne, a plant collector, botanist, gardener, and watercolourist (specialising in flower painting) laid out the garden in 1854; it included a MAZE (*c.* 1871) based on the Hampton Court maze and a conservatory (1875). The two-storey Scottish baronial extension (*c.* 1861) to the 1832 homestead was also designed by Marianne. Duntroon, within the new federal capital, was leased to the Army after Marianne's death and Duntroon College (the first military college in Australia) was opened in 1911. The garden has been restored in recent years and is a rare example of a Victorian-era garden in Canberra, enhanced by its many mature trees, particularly a pair of *Phoenix canariensis* (Canary Island Date Palm).

Joan Kerr and Hugh Falkus, *From Sydney Cove to Duntroon: A Family Album of Early Life in Australia* (London, 1982)

TRISHA DIXON

DURHAM HALL, Jembaicambene (near Braidwood), NSW, retains a homestead from 1841 and an earlier slab hut. The surviving garden dates from the early 1840s and a *Wisteria sinensis* planted at the original front door survives from this era. The front garden is arranged about an axial circular box hedge that edged the original carriageway, now grown into a maze-like labyrinth. A towering old *Cedrus atlantica* (Atlas Cedar) dominates the garden and provides a canopy over the carriage loop. There are many old roses, some of which remain unidentified, and a rare shrub, *Desmodium amethyustinum*. Since 1855, the Royds family have been custodians of this significant early HOMESTEAD GARDEN.

Astrida Upitis (ed.), *Durham Hall Garden* (Canberra, 1992)

TRISHA DIXON

DURROL, Mount Macedon, Vic., was developed during 1900–01 by Clara Josephine Woods and her husband, William Foster Woods, chairman of the Melbourne Stock Exchange; their timber residence, with its picturesque assemblage of bays and complex roof forms, remains exceptionally intact. Durrol was sold to Stanley Anketell Allen, father of the present owner, Karin McKinnon, during a period when his young family had decamped to MOUNT MACEDON to escape the flu epidemic in Melbourne. In 1928, Allen's wife (Edith) Mervyn commissioned Edna

Dutch influence

WALLING to design an addition (only partly implemented) to the original garden. It was ITALIANATE in concept, with the awkward slope of the site deftly handled by creating a strong axis to join the garden compartments. Bushfires in 1983 altered the southern part of the garden, with the loss of big conifers and other trees and shrubs. Spared were a rare *Ilex aquifolium* 'Pendula' (Weeping Holly), *Ilex aquifolium* 'Ferrox' (Porcupine Holly), and two *Tilia* x *europaea* (Linden). Durrol forms part of an outstanding precinct of HILL-STATIONS and offers a fine balance between intensively maintained garden, bushland, and service areas.

JACKIE COURMADIAS

DUTCH INFLUENCE: see THE NETHERLANDS

DWIGHT, (Horace) John de Fraine (b. 1908), landscape gardener and horticulturist, London-born, trained in horticulture in Buckinghamshire, migrated to Sydney in 1928 and established a landscape gardening practice before moving to Adelaide in 1946. Dwight served as Foreman at ADELAIDE BOTANIC GARDEN (1950–54) before being appointed Parks and Gardens Officer for the South Australian Housing Trust (1954–73). He wrote the Trust's *Gardening Handbook* (1957) and supervised the Trust's gardening activities. Established in 1936, the Trust provided public housing throughout SA, including the satellite new town Elizabeth (1949–55), designed by Henry Percy Smith (b. 1913) leading a multi-disciplinary team, under the chairmanship of Alexander Maurice Ramsay (1914–1978). Dwight's *Handbook*—given to each tenant—included garden designs, planting calendars, and plant lists appropriate for the Adelaide Plains. His *Gardening Handbook: Port–Pirie, Port Augusta, Home Gardens* (1970) covered ARID-ZONE GARDENS.

DAVID JONES

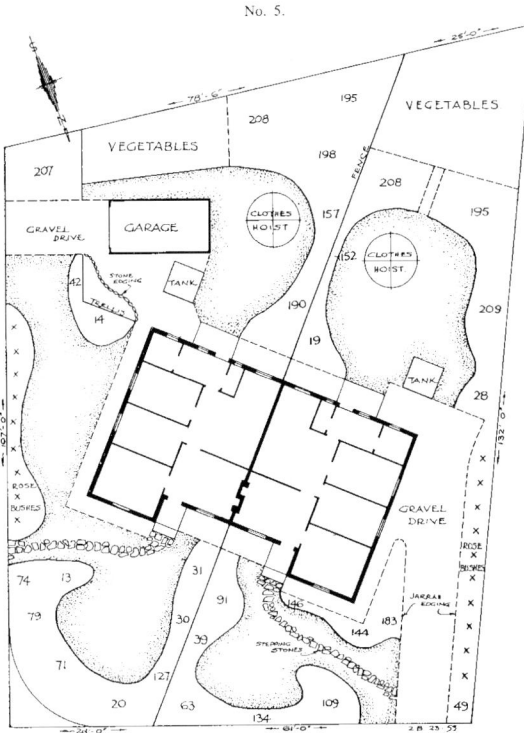

Plans by John DWIGHT from his *Gardening Handbook* (1957), prepared for the South Australian Housing Trust, were intended to guide home gardeners at the Trust's new estates, including the satellite town of Elizabeth

EARTH GARDEN (1972–), a quarterly magazine published in Balmain (NSW), by Keith Vincent Smith (b. 1939) and Irene Smith (b. 1942), emphasising practical ECOLOGY and ORGANIC production of basic necessities. Such environmental sensitivity was proposed as 'an alternative to the nine-to-five drag'. The Smiths sold the magazine in 1989 and it has continued to find new and loyal audiences, through its emphasis on a self-sufficiency, which, rather than standing against conventional suburbanism, can be theoretically and practically incorporated into an urban professional lifestyle.
CHRIS McCONVILLE

EASTERN BEACH, Geelong, Vic., designed by architect Harry Hare (1924–25) as the result of a COMPETITION, comprises a 1.6 hectare CITY BEAUTIFUL–inspired landscape of sloping lawns and exotic trees, formal paths negotiating the steep site overlooking Corio Bay (frequently likened to the Bay of Naples in the nineteenth century), kiosk, pavilion, rotundas, and a monumental staircase with lamp standards and fountain. In 1937–38 City Surveyor Ian McDonald designed the semi-circular bath with a timber promenade and curved sea wall, and a circular concrete children's pool (known locally as the '50/50 pool' after a well-known brand of orange and lemon cordial but also for the reputed composition of the water). The landscaped ensemble ranks among Australia's finest inter-war BEACH resorts.
DAVID ROWE

EASTERN PARK, Geelong, Vic.: see GEELONG BOTANIC GARDENS.

EAST POINT RESERVE, Fannie Bay, a peninsula recreation area enclosed by coastal headlands at the mouth of Port Darwin, has since the late nineteenth century been the site for LEISURE activities in the tropical Top End of the NT. PICNIC outings to the 'jungle' areas of mangrove and monsoon vine forests were popular with early Darwin residents, with swimming restricted to the 'dry season'. The first civilian Government Resident (1870–73), Captain Bloomfield Douglas (1822–1906), organised target shooting sessions at East Point for his daughters. The site became part of a circuit—including Fannie Bay Gaol, DARWIN BOTANIC GARDENS, and Palmerston (Port Darwin) Museum—for escorted visits of official guests and dignitaries. Darwin Club hotelier, Fannie Eliza Bell, treated hotel guests to picnics at East Point between 1910 and 1915, accompanying them to picturesque spots in her stylish sulky—a practice continued in the early 1930s by hoteliers in Parap, who accommodated aviators and airline passengers after their arrival at the original airstrip (now Ross Smith Avenue). During the Second World War, the land was occupied by the Army as a strategic defence and command post that included a six-inch gun emplacement, now part of the East Point Military Museum complex. From the 1960s, East Point was protected and developed as a special reserve, today featuring walking and cycling tracks, foreshore landscaped picnic areas, a lake, interpretative walks, sporting facilities, and a wallaby reserve. It remains one of the city's scenic LOOKOUT sites for viewing sunsets, particularly during the 'build-up', and electrical storms during the 'wet season'.
ANITA ANGEL

EAST TALGAI, near Allora, Qld, a sheep station on the DARLING DOWNS, was acquired in 1865 by pastoralist George John Edwin Clark (1834–1907). From the encircling verandahs of the homestead (1868), designed by architect Richard Suter (1827–1894), the views included the garden, Dalrymple Creek, pastures, and mountains beyond. Suter and his wife Mary became close friends of George and Ellen Clark, with many visits resulting in fifty-nine watercolours painted by Mary (1868–85). Combined with surviving gardening ledgers (1868–1937), these provide an unequalled record of a HOMESTEAD GARDEN in Qld. Daniel Lawson, head gardener 1872–1900, regularly judged fruit and vegetables at the Warwick show. Apart from productive kitchen gardens and an ORANGERY, there were lawns for tennis and croquet, standard roses edging the drive, a herbaceous border-edged Long Walk, and coniferous specimen plantings in the wide lawns surrounding the homestead.

Barbara Lord, *East Talgai and its Environs: A Series of Watercolours by Mary Handfield Suter* (Toowoomba, Qld, 1995)
JEANNIE SIM

EAVES, Samuel Hinder (1842–1927), horticulturist, nursery proprietor, seed merchant, and florist, was born in Bridport, Bedfordshire, England. He arrived in Brisbane in the 1860s and was employed by Queensland's first governor, Sir George Bowen, as gardener. In 1864 Eaves set up his Breakfast Creek Nursery at Albion, with a retail shop in

Brisbane's Queen Street—a combination that continued into the twentieth century. In his 1897 catalogue, Eaves claimed to have been trained at the largest horticultural establishments in Britain and offered his services thus: 'being thoroughly conversant with the principles and practice of landscape gardening, I am prepared to furnish plans, and to contract for laying out and planting parks, orchards and gardens in the very best styles, and at most moderate rates'. As yet, examples of his design work have not been located, but he was possibly part of the team, with Walter HILL, that laid out the gardens and grounds of GOVERNMENT HOUSE (1861–62). The plants on offer for the 1897–98 season included conifers, palms, cycads, crotons; carpet bedding and ribbon border plants; dracaenas, cannas, hedge, and edging plants; greenhouse and hothouse plants; a huge listing of roses; herbaceous plants and succulents—an eclectic mixture of temperate, tropical, exotic, and native species. Eaves vied with HOCKINGS and SUMMERLIN as the leading nursery proprietor in Qld in the late nineteenth century. His son Alfred Eaves (b. 1870) joined the business in the 1890s, which family members continued into the 1940s.   JEANNIE SIM

ECKERSLEY, Richard Hugo (b. 1949), Melbourne-based garden designer and a graduate of BURNLEY College, started Eco Landscape Design in 1976, under which banner he continues to design and construct gardens. His designs, which have been widely displayed in lifestyle magazines such as *Vogue Living*, *Belle*, and *Australian House and Garden*, challenge traditional safe suburban garden styles by their manipulation of space and colour. He has also expanded the range of designer products available for use in the landscape with the introduction and promotion of materials such as Eco Pebbles and Pavers. With business partner and co-designer Lisa Stafford (b. 1961), Rick Eckersley published the book *Living in the Garden: Australian Style* (1993). He has also co-hosted a gardening programme on Melbourne radio 3AW (1989–).   ML

ECOLOGY There is growing recognition of the ecological role played by gardens. While often small individually, domestic gardens frequently constitute the largest collective area of 'greenspace' in towns and cities and are potentially of high ecological significance. As an example of this, much of the tree canopy of urban Australia is provided by trees growing in private gardens. Gardens are also potentially valuable catalysts in changing attitudes to unsustainable lifestyles, by encouraging recycling and wise resource use.

What is an ecological garden? Querying supporters of different gardening traditions elicits a range of responses. The most frequent vision is of a garden based upon plant species native to the region or country in which it is located. It is generally assumed—and in Australia there is some research to substantiate this—that by containing NATIVE PLANTS a garden will also provide a valuable faunal habitat or food source.

The strong FIELD NATURALIST movement in Australia fostered an interest in ecology from the turn of the century, as did formal educational initiatives ranging from elementary botany and NATURE STUDY texts such as those by Agnes Brewster and Constance LE PLASTRIER to university teaching by T.G.B. OSBORN and A.A. LAWSON from the 1920s. Outside the gardens of the wealthy, gardening in Australia had strong utilitarian origins, and while some native species were cultivated in nineteenth-century gardens, in the main ecological content was little considered. The garden as a place with significant native plant content did not begin to manifest itself in the mainstream until the development of BUSH GARDENS in the 1960s. While loosely responding to local conditions and themes, the bush landscape style typically involved a rather eclectic landscape of native shrubs and trees and to a lesser degree herbs, arranged around a rustic ground plan of meandering gravel paths, small ponds, rocks and logs. Individual specimen planting usually lacked the repetition evident in natural vegetation.

In the late 1980s a new version of the native bush landscape with much clearer ecological goals emerged. This was based on refinement of the concept of 'nativeness' from Australian plants in general to those indigenous to a specific region or place. Initially this movement was largely driven from outside the garden tradition by those involved in the developing urban ecology movement. The STYLE was underpinned by a desire to develop and maintain local landscape character (as represented by vegetation) and conserve local populations (genetic assemblages) of indigenous plants. Unlike the taxonomic eclecticism of the traditional bush garden, these landscapes used only local species, with much stronger emphasis on GRASSES and other herbaceous understorey species. It seems reasonable to assume that gardens composed of indigenous species will provide superior habitat for invertebrates and other species that have evolved specific relationships with particular plant species. Initially, design was conspicuously absent from the indigenous garden style, but gradually the visual opportunities offered by the exciting textures and colours of tussock grasses contrasted with the trunks of native trees has been recognised by garden designers and combined with contemporary cultural references in the form of timber decking, sophisticated paving, and contemporary design materials such as steel. The development does not improve the ecological merits of this landscape type, but it does provide the opportunity for these landscapes to be seen as a garden genre that attempts reconciliation between culture and ecology. It is also important to recognise that valuable foraging and in some cases breeding habitat can also be provided in gardens by non-native species. This is appreciated by urban conservation agencies in Europe, but has had relatively little impact as an idea in Australian gardens.

Another vision of the ecological garden involves gardens designed to minimise negative impacts on the surrounding or regional environment. Sustainable gardens are a broad church—from the utilitarian puritanism of the PERMACULTURE movement through to more relaxed gardens that try to avoid plants that are likely to escape and become WEEDS displacing local native species, are not dependent on the regular use of PESTICIDES and FERTILISERS for maintenance, and do not require significant inputs of scarce resources such as

The museum of ECONOMIC BOTANY (1879) in ADELAIDE BOTANIC GARDEN was one of Director Richard SCHOMBURGK's showpieces; it displayed exhibits in an elegant Greek revival building, and was easily the most impressive museum of any of the Australian botanic gardens

WATER and energy. The indigenous garden is an example of this garden style, but this mode can also be based on carefully selected exotic species, either alone or in combination with native species. An increasingly important version of the latter is the low-water-use garden, derived to a significant degree from the XERIC GARDEN of western NORTH AMERICA.

All of the garden styles discussed thus far possess 'real' ecological content. Ecological ambience, if not substance, may also be conferred by plantings designed to demonstrate the rhythms, patterns, and layers found in naturally occurring vegetation. Repetition of a single species across a site and planting species in matrix-like as opposed to block arrangements is important in capturing a sense of nature. This style of ecological planting can be achieved with exotic as well as native species. It is widely used (with herbaceous planting) in central Europe and Germany in particular.

From an ecologist's perspective, however, the litmus test of truly ecological gardens is whether they demonstrate the recruitment of new desirable native species (that is, they are self-sustaining). These types of gardens are becoming more common in northern Europe and North America, but are difficult to implement in Australia's urban areas and urban fringes due to the tendency of new plants establishing in plantings to be aggressive weeds rather than desirable natives or cultivated species. The process of plant recruitment is most satisfactorily managed in gardens on very infertile soils, subsoils, or sands, which restrict the vigour of at least some exotic weeds. Gravel paths are a familiar location in which this process currently (unintentionally) occurs. General understanding of this type of gardening is restricted, but may well represent the ecological garden of the future.

Eric Rolls, *They All Ran Wild: The Story of Pests on the Land in Australia* (Sydney, 1969); William Lines, *Taming the Great South Land: A History of the Conquest of Nature in Australia* (Sydney, 1991); Tim Flannery, *The Future Eaters: An Ecological History of the Australasian Lands and Peoples* (Sydney, 1994); Ann Hamblin (ed.), *Visions of Future Landscapes: Proceedings of the Australian Academy of Science, 1999* (Kingston, ACT, 2000); Martin Mulligan and Stuart Hill, *Ecological Pioneers: A Social History of Australian Ecological Thought and Action* (Cambridge, 2001)

JAMES HITCHMOUGH

ECONOMIC BOTANY, the study of useful plants, is in one sense as old as humanity. At a more formal level, it was part of the commercial and scientific exploration of the eighteenth and nineteenth centuries when botanists attempted to classify 'newly discovered' plants in a scientific way, and also to scrutinise them for their possible value as sources of food, fibre, medicine, timber, dye, or garden decoration. As BOTANIC GARDENS were established or enlarged to receive, nurture, classify, and transfer such plants, their staff took over the work of exploring and collecting, and gradually acquired the technical ability to improve and adapt plants for commercial production.

KEW GARDENS was central to this process, for one of its functions was to distribute plants of economic and horticultural value to any of the colonies where suitable conditions for their cultivation existed. Joseph BANKS, appointed inaugural director in 1773, was excited by the 'untapped plant resources of distant lands', and sent out such collectors as William Bligh, whose 1787 voyage in HMS *Bounty* was primarily an expedition to collect Breadfruit (*Artocarpus altilis*) from Tahiti for cultivation in the West Indies. George CALEY was Kew's first official Australian collector.

Subsequent directors William and Joseph Hooker influenced many discoveries concerning the potential exploitation and introduction of indigenous and exotic flora in overseas territories, especially through botanic gardens. The best known of these introductions were rubber and cinchona (for quinine), from Central America to southern Asia. In 1848, William Hooker established a Museum of Economic Botany to display the collection he had used in lectures at Glasgow University, and expanded it to display the 'vegetable products of the Empire'; it became, in effect, a permanent international EXHIBITION. Economic botany is still high among Kew's priorities; for example, the seedbank contains seeds of potential crops for deserts and semi-arid lands. The Sir Joseph Banks Centre for Economic Botany was opened in 1990.

In Australia, economic botany was part of a two-way process—primarily through Kew—that involved importation, ACCLIMATISATION, and distribution of exotic plants and evaluation and exploitation of native vegetation. Ferdinand MUELLER, Victoria's first Government Botanist, reported in 1853 that perhaps the most important part of his research was to 'reflect upon the practical usefulness of our vegetable creation, either with regard to medicine, manufactures, or in a domestic point of view'. This way of looking at plants may still be explored at the Museum of Economic Botany in ADELAIDE BOTANIC GARDEN (opened in 1881), where displays include essential oils, gums and resins, fibres, dyes, foods and beverages, timber, and a permanent carpological collection. Likewise, Sydney's Powerhouse Museum holds the nucleus of the outstanding collection on which the research of R.T. BAKER was based.

> Lucille H. Brockway, *Science and Colonial Expansion, the Role of the British Royal Botanic Gardens* (New York, 1979); A. Frost, *Sir Joseph Banks and the Transfer of Plants to and from the South Pacific 1786–1798* (Melbourne, 1993); Donal P. McCracken, *Gardens of Empire: Botanical Institutions of the Victorian British Empire* (London, 1997)   GWEN PASCOE

EDDY (née JAMIESON), Nancy Gilmour (b. 1916), tropical gardening enthusiast and amateur botanist and historian, arrived in the NORTHERN TERRITORY in 1935; her Darwin garden was, by the mid-1950s, 'an oasis amid the fast-growing townscape', with an immaculate lawn of native grass and more than 100 native trees and plants. Eddy studied botany (teaching herself Latin) and attracted the attention of professional botanists in Australia and abroad. For more than a year she worked at the DARWIN BOTANIC GARDENS, identifying and labelling 1000 botanical specimens. For many years she was on call at Royal Darwin Hospital, where her botanical expertise assisted in poisoning cases, particularly for children who had ingested poisonous plants. She gave numerous illustrated talks to local schools, women's organisations, church and gardening clubs, as well as to interstate audiences. She wrote many articles for the *North Australian Monthly* (1955–65), chiefly concerning gardening, and between 1954–83 she was a horticultural judge at the Darwin Show. In 1963, Eddy was awarded a Fellowship of the Royal Society of South Australia and was presented life membership of Darwin Garden Club in 1978.   ANITA ANGEL

EDGAR, James Scott (1842–1902), botanic gardens curator and tropical horticulturist, was born in Inverness, Scotland; family sources indicate that he worked at the ROYAL BOTANIC GARDENS, KEW. He migrated to Sydney in the mid-1860s, and following work with the railways department, was appointed inaugural curator of ROCKHAMPTON BOTANIC GARDENS (1873–1901). He undertook considerable ACCLIMATISATION work with plants suited to the TROPICS, including introductions from MUELLER. The agricultural reporter of the *Queenslander* (1883) considered that due largely to his efforts, the district was no longer considered in a 'dry belt' and impossible to cultivate. Edgar was a great advocate of shade trees, planting many in Rockhampton streets, and also in the Gardens. He was especially fond of FIGS, including the native *Ficus macrophylla* (Moreton Bay Fig), and devised an ingenious planting method consisting of upright hollow logs 'a foot or more in diameter and about 5 feet high' filled with soil, simulating the adventitious habit of seedling figs in rainforest tree clefts.   JEANNIE SIM

EDMUNDS, (Walter) Alan (1894–1969), horticulturist, humorist, self-described poetaster, and horticultural journalist, was born in Launceston (Tas.). After serving at Gallipoli, he married in London and on his return to Australia (1922) took up a block at Red Cliffs (Vic.) under the Soldier Settlement Scheme. He worked as a journalist for the *AUSTRALIAN GARDEN LOVER* from 1925, contributing under the *noms de plume* 'A.E.' and 'Hortus'; his jocular style may also indicate authorship of other features, such as the humorous column 'Through Mr Periwinkle's Spectacles'. Edmunds worked from the early 1930s in the advertising department and later as horticultural expert for the Vacuum Oil Company in an age when oil companies had a direct interest in horticultural CHEMICALS and a vested interest in promoting long-distance motor travel to view wildflowers. His principal works, *An Introduction to the Ancient Art of Growing the Espalier Beautiful* (1940) and *Espalier Fruit Trees: Their History and Culture* (c. 1946), promoted the traditional French technique of ornamental PRUNING and training; these were the first dedicated English-language books on the subject (save for a translation of Lorette's French classic). Addressed 'to that most charming of Australian fauna—the Esthetic Backgardener', Edmunds combined historical touches with practical guidance based on specimens in the remarkable circular fruit garden at his Deepdene home in Melbourne's east. He wrote with an engaging humour, hoping for the day when the Australian garage wall, clad in espaliers, would 'look like something by Corot'. His writings were also sprinkled with verse of dubious literary merit:

> Ants tickle/The fickle/Cor-nicle/Of aphids on whom they intrude/(As they sit on the node in the nude!)/They do it just laughing/And joking while quaffing/The sweet/They entreat/The aphid to excrete!/I'm no prude, but it does seem rude!

During the Second World War, Edmunds became a committed socialist and this interest suffused his later writings. His children's book, *A Jackaroo's Jingles about Australian Birds and Animals* (1940), was published by the Horticultural Press and revised editions of his books appeared during the 1950s and 1960s.   RA

Education

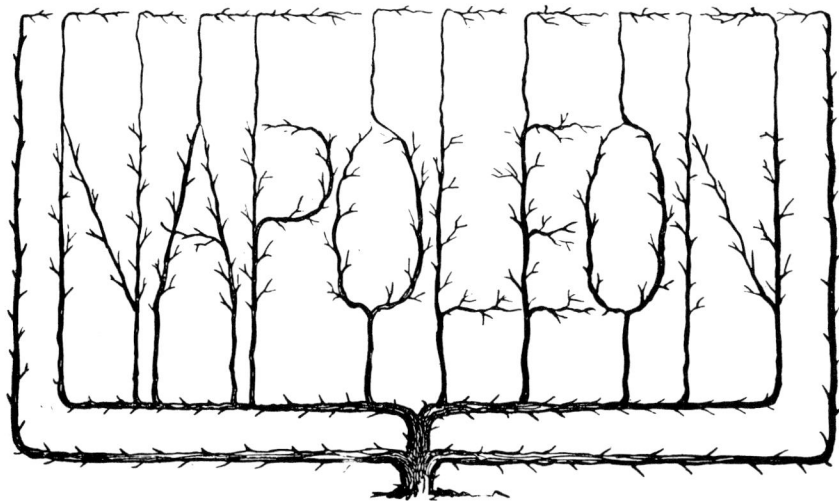

Alan EDMUNDS reproduced this ESPALIERED 'Napoleon', taken from an 1850s French gardening magazine, in his *Espalier Fruit Trees* (c. 1946) and urged his 'leftish readers to emulate his horticultural example by doing an equally handsome STALIN on the back fence in Plum blossom!'

EDNIE-BROWN, John: see BROWN, John Ednie

EDUCATION for HORTICULTURE and GARDEN design has evolved considerably to meet changing needs and expectations. In Australia's first years of European settlement, horticulture and agriculture were, of necessity, directed almost entirely to food production. As wealthy free settlers arrived, more gardens for beauty and pleasure were developed alongside KITCHEN GARDENS, and professional GARDENERS found employment. Most had been trained under a traditional apprenticeship system in Britain or Europe, usually starting in their early teens, and they in turn trained others in the colonies.

From the 1830s to the 1840s mechanics' institutes opened in larger cities and towns. They developed LIBRARIES, and the largest offered evening lectures in scientific subjects including BOTANY and GEOLOGY. Their educational role was complemented for gardening and horticulture by the establishment of BOTANIC GARDENS, often with attached HERBARIA or museums, HORTICULTURAL SOCIETIES that conducted lectures and HORTICULTURAL SHOWS, a vigorous weekly horticultural press, importation and local publication of GARDENING BOOKS and MAGAZINES, and a tradition of lecturers speaking on gardening at diverse gatherings. From the late nineteenth century, primary school teachers were directed to develop SCHOOL GARDENS so pupils could learn to grow flowers and vegetables.

By 1886 the organisation that began as the Sydney Mechanics School of Arts and later developed into Sydney Technical College had a permanent agriculture lecturer who also taught gardening and flower culture. At around this time AGRICULTURAL COLLEGES were established, including Roseworthy, SA (1883), Burnley, Vic. (1891), Hawkesbury, NSW (1891), and Gatton, Qld (1897). ROSEWORTHY was the first Australian college to offer tuition in VITICULTURE, and BURNLEY the first with horticulture as a major focus, followed in NSW by the Sydney Technical College (1938). The RYDE SCHOOL OF HORTICULTURE was established in 1948.

In the early years horticultural courses were of a general nature and provided trained staff for all aspects of work in nurseries, parks, and gardens. As the horticulture industry developed, the need for more specialised training and education was reflected in courses. In the ACT, horticultural courses began in 1946 when, as in other states, the Commonwealth Reconstruction Training Scheme arranged training for soldiers returning after the Second World War. Certificates and diplomas with turf, gardening, and nursery specialisations were first available in WA in the 1960s through the Technical and Further Education (TAFE) system and in Tas., urban horticulture at certificate level was first offered in Hobart by TAFE in 1977. By the mid-1980s there were TAFE courses throughout Australia providing training for all levels and types of horticultural work, from skilled assistants to tradespeople, supervisors, and managers.

By the mid-1990s changes introduced by the Commonwealth Government were taking effect in horticultural training. Competency standards describing what horticulturists should be able to achieve at work were developed, and began to be used as a basis for training and as a measure of achievement at certificate levels. The system aimed to encourage on-job training and assessment.

In universities, horticulture was for many years offered only as part of an agriculture qualification. The first horticulture courses concentrated on fruit and vegetables, but later, degrees in the production and use of ornamental species were introduced. Burnley College was the first with a degree in amenity (now environmental) horticulture, in the early 1980s. Now, in addition to undergraduate degrees, some universities offer masters degrees, doctorates, and graduate diplomas. There is increasing emphasis on the environmental effects of horticultural activity. Specialist degrees have been developed in this and other technical areas; for example, Curtin University of Technology (WA) offers a Bachelor of Agribusiness (Horticulture) and Griffith University (Qld) offers a Bachelor of Park Management. Other university study focuses on the science of horticulture and equips graduates for research.

Education in LANDSCAPE ARCHITECTURE began in 1965, with part-time landscape design graduate diplomas available through the University of New South Wales, and the Royal Melbourne Institute of Technology in conjunction with Burnley College. Undergraduate degrees were first offered at the University of New South Wales and the Canberra College of Advanced Education in 1974. Now, landscape architecture is offered in all states and territories except Tas. and the NT.

Pathways from TAFE diplomas to university are becoming better planned, and access to horticultural training and education is also becoming easier. Distance education is available through a number of institutions including Charles Sturt University, the University of New England, and the Open Training and Education Network of TAFE NSW. The full effects on standards of increased emphasis on competency-based training will not be apparent for a number of years.

JUDY McMAUGH

EDWARDS, Reginald George ('Taffy') (d. 1966), horticultural journalist, spent his boyhood near Aylesbury, Buckinghamshire, England. Following several years in Canada, he came to Australia (c. 1913) and soon learned to love the 'springtime livery' of its bush. By 1930 Reg Edwards was gardening editor of the Sydney *Daily Telegraph*. He later acted in this capacity for other titles in the Consolidated Press stable, the *Australian Woman's Weekly*, *Sunday Telegraph*, and *Home Budget*. He lectured in agriculture at Sydney Technical College, was an early gardening broadcaster on stations 2GB, 2UE, and 2UW, and later, as 'Taffy', he contributed a column to YOUR GARDEN.

The Australian Garden Book (1950) was his major work, and its thoughtful comments on Australian gardens were the result of keen observation. It filled a niche between works by Nerine CHISHOLM and Ernest LORD, was more substantial than the guides of BRUNNING, HUNT, HURLEY, and YATES, and was one of the first large-format gardening books published by the major publishing houses (in this case Angus and Robertson). Edwards bemoaned the lack of 'a purely local gardening sense or system of design', decrying the 'overcrowded English herbaceous border, the formal Continental bed … or the hideous Italian garden'. Greater ingenuity and originality had been shown in our ROCK GARDENS (which suited a 'rugged country like Australia') than in general garden planning, and Edwards praised the BUSH-HOUSE as 'the only original touch that I can see we Australians have introduced to our gardens'. A revised edition of *The Australian Garden Book* appeared in 1958. Through his writings Edwards was a generous contributor to Australian horticulture. RA

EICHLER, Hansjoerg (1916–1992), German-born botanist and taxonomist, was inaugural keeper of the HERBARIUM at ADELAIDE BOTANIC GARDEN (1955–73). With Noel LOTHIAN's support, he drew together the Richard SCHOMBURGK, Ralph TATE, and John McConnell BLACK collections and permanent loans to the University of Adelaide, and completed the *Supplement to J.M. Black's Flora of South Australia 1943–57* (1965). Appointed curator at Herbarium Australiense (National Herbarium) in Canberra (1973–81), he supported the *Flora of Australia* project and received the Willdenow Medal (1979) from Berlin-Dahlem Herbarium.

DAVID JONES

ELDER PARK, originally set aside as part of (ADELAIDE) PARK LANDS in LIGHT and KINGSTON's plan, was transformed into a civic green in the early 1880s under Mayor Edwin Smith, in conjunction with the development of Torrens Lake and John Ednie BROWN's Park Lands plan. The octagonal BANDSTAND (1881–82) donated by philanthropist Sir Thomas Elder (1818–1897) remains the dominant feature of the Park; its cast-iron components with domed cupola were fabricated by Macfarlane's Saracen Foundry in Glasgow, Scotland. It has become a focal point for cultural and musical festivals (joined in 1973 by the adjacent Festival Centre, with its striking steel-framed forms and paved forecourt). Elder Park was incorporated into the Riverbank Precinct master plan (1999).

DAVID JONES

ELIZABETH BAY HOUSE, NSW: see McLEAY, Alexander

ELIZABETH FARM, Parramatta, NSW: see MACARTHUR, John

ELLIOT, (Winston) Rodger (b. 1941), nursery proprietor and horticultural writer, established the Austraflora nursery, at Croydon (Vic.), in 1959, later moving to Bayswater (1963) then Montrose (1968). He worked (part time) for Edna WALLING (1960–61) and for Eric HAMMOND (1961–66). In 1972 he began his long association with *Your Garden*, writing on AUSTRALIAN PLANTS. Among his many books and articles, the comprehensive *Encyclopaedia of Australian Plants* (1980–), written with David Lloyd Jones (b. 1944) and now almost completed in nine volumes, is a major contribution to Australian horticulture. Austraflora was leased in 1973 and sold in 1982 to enable him to concentrate on horticultural consulting and a wholesale propagating nursery, Australian Tube Plants.

In much of his professional work Elliot has been ably partnered by his wife Gwendoline Margaret (*née* Parry) (b. 1940), especially as an author, tour leader, nursery proprietor, and garden maker—the garden created by Rodger and Gwen Elliot at Montrose (1982–92) set a standard for its use of Australian plants. Elliot continues to promote Australian plants through his writing, lecturing, and involvement with Outback Plants, a firm that markets Australian plants through licensed propagators and growers in the USA, Europe, Britain, and Japan. Elliot is internationally recognised for the development and promotion of Australian plants and has received many awards and honours, capped by the Australian Natural History Medallion (1995) and the ROYAL HORTICULTURAL SOCIETY's Veitch Gold Memorial Medal (1999).

ML

ELLIOTT, Alexander (1824–1901), horticulturist and university gardener, born in Peebleshire, Scotland, was educated

The BANDSTAND (1881–82) in Adelaide's ELDER PARK, prefabricated by Macfarlane's Saracen Foundry in Glasgow, Scotland, with its elegant detailing, exotic architectural references, and its fine acoustic properties, remains the archetype of Victorian bandstands

in Edinburgh, where he also trained as a landscape gardener, following his father's vocation. He arrived in Melbourne in December 1856, and was employed at the MELBOURNE BOTANIC GARDENS under DALLACHY and then MUELLER. In 1857, he designed and laid out the PORTLAND BOTANIC GARDENS following his success in a design COMPETITION. In January 1860 he was appointed Head Gardener at the University of Melbourne, a position he held until his death. His duties included landscape gardening, supervision, propagation, maintenance, and new work; he dealt with the complications of overflowing cesspits, investigated which professor was using excessive water, and argued for more adequate finances. He claimed that the UNIVERSITY GROUNDS were almost covered by 'a tangled mess of wattle-trees and gums' in 1860, and, although this was an exaggeration, as head gardener for more than forty years, he presided over a transformation.

Elliott was a figure of authority in Victorian horticultural circles. He helped inaugurate the Grand United Order of FREE GARDENERS of Australasia in Melbourne (1864). He was sought as a judge for horticultural shows and his claim to have studied botany is reinforced by his participation in an expedition to the Dividing Range near the head of the Yarra to collect 'seeds or plants of new or rare native shrubs' for TAYLOR AND SANGSTER, and in his preparation of WARDIAN CASES of plants in exchanges with the museum in Wellington, New Zealand.

GWEN PASCOE

ELLIOTT, Robert George (1874–1962), rosarian and author of *The Australasian Rose Book* (1920), typified those who saw MORAL IMPROVEMENT in horticulture in general and floriculture in particular. Elliott lived in modest surroundings in Brunswick, an inner Melbourne suburb with proud working-class traditions. A stalwart of the local horticultural society, he spoke directly to workers and gardeners through lectures, articles in the *Home Gardener*, and a lengthy series on 'Beautification' in the *Victorian Railways Magazine* (1926–27)—seeking to 'stimulate the interest of railwaymen in brighter stations as well as better home gardens'—which was reprinted in the *Teachers' Gazette*. His book was an early Australian monograph on roses, following works by those such as Thomas JOHNSON (1866), Charles BENNETT (1891), and J.G. LOCKLEY (1907), and pre-dating the important contributions made by the *Australian Rose Annual* (1928–) and ROSSI's *Modern Roses in Australasia* (1930).

RA

ELLIOTT, William (1813–1897), horticulturist, nursery proprietor, and editor, was born in Northumberland, England, the son of a gardener, and migrated to Vic. in 1853. He was a founding committee member of the Ballarat Horticultural Society (1859) and in 1860 Ballarat nursery proprietor Thomas LANG was joined by Elliott ('of the Creswick Nursery') as a partner. In that year Elliott was also elected as a corresponding member (for 'gardeners and amateurs of acknowledged ability, who may be elected without an annual subscription') of the recently formed Victorian Gardeners' Mutual Improvement Society, doubtless aided by his links with Lang, and his strong duo of proposers—Josiah MITCHELL and William HYNDMAN. Elliott was elected a member of the rival Horticultural Society of Victoria in 1871, but played little part in the activities of either society.

At about this date, Elliott was appointed horticultural editor of the *LEADER* newspaper, where his discretion, knowledge, and practical experience were valued. With a wide circulation in south-eastern Australia, especially in country districts, the *Leader* provided regular horticultural news and comment in a period with few specialised horticultural journals. Elliott censured William GUILFOYLE in 1882 about private commissions, and in 1890 described the MELBOURNE BOTANIC GARDENS fern gully as the 'meanest and most despicable', but his editorial policy was mostly one of free interchange of news and opinions.

Elliott edited the tenth edition (1879) of ADAMSON's *Australian Gardener*, the first edition to include extensive remarks on the flower garden; his significant revision of the text was very little changed in the 1884 edition, and much of his flavour can be detected in subsequent nineteenth- and early twentieth-century editions. Elliott's eminence in the horticultural world was confirmed by his authorship of an essay on 'Horticulture' in *Victoria and its Resources* (1893), which provided an authoritative summary of horticulture in the colony, including remarks on public parks and gardens, botanic gardens, horticultural societies, and private gardens (where he observed that 'Flower gardening is chiefly of the old-fashioned style, massing or any other form of bedding being rarely attempted').

Elliott's major published work was *Cole's Australasian Gardening and Domestic Floriculture*, dated 1896 on the title page by E.W. COLE, but in fact published posthumously in 1897. In it Elliott drew on his considerable experience in both Britain and Australia, enunciating 'principles laid down by the best landscape gardeners', especially English landscape gardener Edward KEMP, whose book *How to Lay Out a Garden* he extensively copied in both style and substance. *Australasian Gardening* was exceedingly popular, attested by many reissues and abridgments. Elliott remained active in his chosen field until the last, and his death ended almost half a century of unobtrusive service to colonial horticulture. RA

ELMS (*Ulmus* species and cultivars) are large deciduous trees of Europe, Asia, and North America. First imported in 1803, they have been planted widely in cool temperate areas of eastern Australia, with a few in WA and southern Qld; Vic. has the largest number. Although Australian trees were used in streets and parks in Vic. in the colony's early years, by the 1880s they had been supplanted by exotic trees such as elms. To the homesick early settlers, elms in particular evoked the rural English landscape. They were planted in streets, parks, large gardens, and avenues, and often chosen for avenues of honour after the First World War. Fine AVENUE plantings such as Melbourne's Royal Parade and those of numerous country towns remain.

The most widely planted trees in the early years were the tall and stately *Ulmus procera* (English Elm) and *U.* X *hollandica* (Dutch Elm), although early nursery catalogues reveal that a wide range of species and CULTIVARS was available from the 1860s. In recent decades, smaller-growing, non-suckering cultivars such as *U. glabra* 'Camperdownii' (Weeping Wych Elm), *U. glabra* 'Lutescens' (Golden Elm), and the semi-evergreen *U. parvifolia* (Chinese Elm), have replaced the larger trees in popularity, although *U. minor* (Field Elm), especially in its VARIEGATED form, is still used in Vic. for public plantings. Rarer species and cultivars may be found in collections such as that of MOUNT LOFTY BOTANIC GARDEN and WAITE Arboretum (SA), and in various regional BOTANIC GARDENS, notably that of BALLARAT (Vic.).

Australia is fortunate in having a significant number of mature elms, since most northern hemisphere trees were killed during the 1970s by a virulent form of Dutch Elm Disease (*Ophiostoma ulmii*), a fungal wilt disease. Elm Bark Beetles, which spread the disease, have been found in Australia, and the fungus may arrive also despite stringent quarantine controls. Meanwhile the Elm Leaf Beetle (*Pyrrhalta luteola*) is a serious problem. In 1991 this major pest was only known from the Mornington Peninsula (Vic.). At that time, it was hoped that a parasitic wasp introduced from North America would provide control, but elms defoliated by the beetle are now a common sight in Melbourne. The Friends of the Elms group was formed by concerned Melburnians, with the aim of funding research into the pests and diseases threatening these trees, which are such a significant component of the city's landscape.

Roger Spencer, John Hawker, and Peter Lumley, *Elms in Australia* (South Yarra, Vic., 1991) JILL KELLOW

EMERALD COUNTRY CLUB, Vic.: see NOBELIUS, Carl Axel

ENDILLOE ARID-LAND GARDEN, near Quorn, SA: see POWELL, Brian Martin

ENFIELD CEMETERY, SA, opened in 1947, was Australia's first full lawn CEMETERY, with horizontal memorial plaques set in extensive LAWNS. The design by Rex Lloyd and Andrew Benko, winners of a 1945 competition, was based on concentric circles, radiating paths and roads, and provision for chapels, fountains, a crematorium, and a grand entrance; Benko—who supervised implementation—also provided community areas with central memorials. Hungarian-born Benko (*c*. 1903–1997) had trained as an architect in Italy, receiving his doctorate from the University of Milan in 1930. After working in Milan, he migrated to SA shortly before the outbreak of war, sponsored by Kenneth Milne, arguably Adelaide's most influential architect of the period. In association with Rex Lloyd, Benko developed and maintained a keen interest in TOWN PLANNING. His work at Enfield was praised in 1949 by Harry Sheppard, visiting Professor of Landscape Architecture at the University of California, who asserted that Benko's design and layout were equal to anything in the world.

Slow development and financial stringencies led the controlling trust in the 1960s to enter into a 'pre-need marketing scheme' with a private company and to rename the cemetery Evergreen Memorial Park, but the concept collapsed amid public controversy, threatening the viability of the cemetery. A long period of recovery, consolidation, and renewal in the 1980s and 1990s finally saw the original lawn cemetery concept achieved. ROBERT NICOL

ENGLAND, by virtue of its dominant part in the British imperial schema, has provided the major external influence on Australian gardens and horticulture. At the time of British colonisation of 'New Holland' (1788), England had only achieved political union with WALES (1536) and SCOTLAND (1707); IRELAND soon following uneasily (1801–1922). The arrival of the First Fleet and the planting of the British flag at Sydney Cove followed a period of intensive exploration worldwide by major political powers, which also included

England

Portuguese, Spanish, Dutch, and French expeditions. The AUSTRALIAN FLORA exercised a fascination for English botanists and horticulturists, which resulted in comprehensive taxonomic efforts as well as cultivation at 'home' in heated GREENHOUSES.

The botanical effort centred in England on the ROYAL BOTANIC GARDENS, KEW, especially through the agency of Joseph BANKS and William and Joseph Hooker, culminating during the nineteenth century with BENTHAM's *Flora Australiensis*. Illustrated periodicals, epitomised by the *Botanical Magazine* of William CURTIS, assisted in the transfer of this botanical knowledge to the horticultural world. Banks played a particularly crucial role in his appointment of plant collectors, and in his encouragement of early settlers such as George SUTTOR. Kew was also an important training ground for emigrant gardeners—although rivalled by many of the larger private gardens and nurseries—and heavily promoted its own importance (and rued the period from the late nineteenth century when its influence waned).

The horticultural importance of Australian plants in England had waned far earlier than this, when plant houses changed from heated flues to steam and water pipes—with a consequent loss of dryness in atmosphere so crucial to successful cultivation of many Australian plants. The nurseries and proprietors that had been closely involved in the introduction of Australian plants, such as VEITCH, LEE AND KENNEDY, James BACKHOUSE, and Low, were also important training grounds for gardeners, and English nurseries provided the major influence (with Scotland) on an industry that increased dramatically in Australia from the 1850s and 1860s. The garden of the (ROYAL) HORTICULTURAL SOCIETY at Chiswick and that of the Royal Botanic Society at Regent's Park in London also complemented Kew as training grounds. These horticultural society and BOTANIC GARDENS, along with the large private gardens (such as CHATSWORTH, Derbyshire, and Trentham, Staffordshire), also provided stylistic precedents for Australian gardens.

At the time of the first European settlement in Australia, the English landscape garden was the prevalent style of the landed classes. This was translated directly to Australia by Thomas SHEPHERD, who worked for Thomas White (a pupil of 'Capability' BROWN), but by the time of Shepherd's celebrated lectures in the mid-1830s, the PICTURESQUE, SUBLIME, and GARDENESQUE had provided more appropriate antipodean models for LANDSCAPE GARDENING. The influence of practitioners and theorists such as William GILPIN (and his nephew W.S. Gilpin), Uvedale PRICE, Humphry REPTON, and John Claudius LOUDON coincided with a period of extensive rural and urban development. Loudon, in particular, took a keen interest in Australia, with correspondents

The welcome given in Melbourne to 'A Primrose from England', where the central Marian figure lovingly contemplates the infant plant, was given suitably romantic treatment in a painting by Edward Hopley, subsequently reproduced for a mass audience by lithographic and engraved (1858) editions

such as Alexander MCLEAY and John THOMPSON communicating advances in horticulture and garden design to English audiences, and assisting in the spread of Loudon's ideas in the colonies. English garden magazines—especially the GARDENERS' CHRONICLE and COTTAGE GARDENER and the books and journalism of Donald BEATON, George GLENNY, Shirley HIBBERD, Edward KEMP, John and Jane Loudon, Robert MARNOCK, Joseph PAXTON, and William ROBINSON—played a major part in the transfer of knowledge from England to Australia.

Of the generation attracted by the gold rushes of the 1850s, those who made the greatest impact on Australian gardening and horticulture were predominantly British (among whom the English formed a majority). Whether transporting plants in WARDIAN CASES, filling positions as head gardeners or botanic gardens directors, importing seeds, writing GARDEN BOOKS, or leading debate in GARDEN MAGAZINES and the weekly horticultural press, the English voice was looked on as one of authority. These voices included the likes of Lewis BERNAYS, George BRUNNING, William CLARSON, William ELLIOTT, Joseph HARRIS, Josiah MITCHELL, and Henry SEWELL.

In the late nineteenth and early twentieth centuries, horticultural and garden design trends initiated or popularised in England were transported to Australia through published books, newspapers and journals, and through personal experience. Thus the influence of significant figures such as William Robinson, Gertrude JEKYLL, Reginald Blomfield, H. Inigo TRIGGS, and Thomas MAWSON, and new styles such as the ARTS AND CRAFTS, were absorbed by Australian gardeners and designers. In the horticultural world, visits from key figures such as Peter BARR, publications from a new generation at Kew that included William BEAN, and the results of plant collecting by Reginald Farrar (and the consequent resurgence of interest in the rock garden and alpine plants), had a lasting impact on planting preferences in temperate parts of Australia. England was an important source of MODERNISM, exemplified by the writings of Christopher Tunnard (*Gardens in a Modern Landscape*, 1938) and also transferred later through the LANDSCAPE ARCHITECTURE profession and its leading figures such as Sylvia CROWE.

English horticultural traditions continued through the twentieth century, with the English love of plants providing a strong influence on Australian garden design. English nurseries, such as Hillier with its vast catalogues of plants, continued to provided the source of new exotic arrivals in the Australian nursery trade. Gardens, such as SISSINGHURST in Kent, were a source of inspiration to exotic plant arrangements in the Australian domestic garden. Influential English garden writers such as John Brookes, Beth Chatto, Penelope Hobhouse, Christopher Lloyd, and Rosemary Verey remain the source of much garden doctrine espoused by an influential sector of the contemporary domestic garden movement, especially garden makers in cooler-climate gardens such as those in the BLUE MOUNTAINS (NSW) and MOUNT MACEDON (Vic.), but also in many SUBURBAN GARDENS. The contemporary fashion for GRASSES in English gardens has also been embraced in Australia. However, there has also been a reaction to an excessive dependency on English references, with many Australian gardeners now looking to more comparable climates and to native Australian landscapes for inspiration.

Tension between garden makers and the environmental movement is common to both Australia and England; in Australia this is highlighted by attitudes to exotic plants (and hence the potential for environmental WEEDS) and the use of horticultural CHEMICALS, while in England there are serious concerns about excessive mining of natural resources such as peat, and collection of pebbles from beaches for garden use. There is also a shared focus on garden making that reduces water consumption.

While direct reference to actual English gardens has waned, an inherited passion for garden making remains a strong influence in the Australian landscape. This is highlighted by the recent spate of TELEVISION lifestyle programs providing garden advice and featuring garden makeovers, derived from their highly popular English counterparts.

George W. Johnson, *A History of English Gardening* (London, 1829); Alicia Amherst, *A History of Gardening in England* (London, 1895); Miles Hadfield, *Gardening in Britain* (London, 1960); Blanche Henrey, *British Botanical and Horticultural Literature before 1800: Comprising a History and Bibliography of Botanical and Horticultural Books Printed in England, Scotland, and Ireland from the Earliest Times until 1800* (London, 1975); David C. Stuart, *Georgian Gardens* (London, 1979); David Jacques, *Georgian Gardens: The Reign of Nature* (London, 1983); Brent Elliot, *Victorian Gardens* (London, 1986); David Stuart, *The Garden Triumphant: A Victorian Legacy* (London, 1988); Jane Brown, *The Art and Architecture of English Gardens* (London, 1989); Martin Hoyles, *The Story of Gardening* (London, 1991); Christopher Thacker, *The Genius of Gardening: The History of Gardens in Britain and Ireland* (London, 1994); Ray Desmond, *Biographical Dictionary of British and Irish Botanists and Horticulturists including Plant Collectors, Flower Painters, and Garden Designers* (London, 1994); Martin Hoyles, *Bread and Roses: Gardening Books from 1560 to 1960* (2 vols., London, 1994 and 1995); Mavis Batey, *Regency Gardens* (Princes Risborough, Buckinghamshire, 1995); Tom Williamson, *Polite Landscapes: Gardens and Society in Eighteenth-Century England* (Stroud, Gloucestershire, 1995); Ray Desmond, *Bibliography of British and Irish Gardens* (Winchester, Hampstead, 1996); Donal P. McCracken, *Gardens of Empire: Botanical Institutions of the Victorian British Empire* (London, 1997); Jane Brown, *The English Garden Through the Twentieth Century* (Woodbridge, Suffolk, 1999); Todd Longstaffe-Gowan, *The London Town Garden 1700–1840* (New Haven and London, 2001)

RA and ML

ENVIRONMENT in Australia has been altered as a result of human settlement, initially by the 'fire-stick farming' of the Aboriginal peoples, and later by the more radical strategies of Europeans. Whether myopic opportunists or careful planners for long-term wealth and progress, European settlers saw the environment as an exploitable commodity. They cleared and felled compulsively, dramatically reducing the forest and vegetation cover (especially RAINFOREST), then introduced IRRIGATION methods to counter the unprofitable dry CLIMATE. Pastoral and farming practices upset the fine balance that ABORIGINAL ENVIRONMENTAL MANAGEMENT had long maintained on the grasslands, and in the long term this led to erosion and salinity. The pursuit of mineral wealth wreaked havoc on the countryside while assisting industrial development of the cities. The growing population led to rapid urbanisation in the major coastal settlements.

Settlers generally perceived the Australian BUSH as essentially foreign and hostile, and built homes and planted gardens in an effort to civilise it. Through ACCLIMATISATION societies, they introduced the familiar plants, birds, and other animals of 'home' to ornament the strange new country. At the same time, however, some cultivated the AUSTRALIAN FLORA, replanting bush flowers in domestic gardens.

By the 1890s and early 1900s, the civilised bush was a place enjoyed for RECREATION. Interest in scenery preservation and the healthy outdoors coincided with an extended railway network, the reservation of NATIONAL PARKS, and the growth of local tourist RESORTS. Driving and rambling through the bush, as well as PICNICKING and camping, became characteristic of the Australian lifestyle. This new appreciation of the natural environment was part of growing patriotic sentiment. Australian plants, especially the gum (*EUCALYPTUS*) and the wattle (*ACACIA*), were promoted as symbols of the new nation, and by the 1920s and 1930s many other species had won approval in domestic gardens. ECOLOGY emerged as a separate discipline as botany progressed beyond the confines of plant taxonomy. Negative perceptions of the environment persisted, however—especially in images of ravaging bushfires, lost children, and in the simple battle for survival on the land—but alongside this was an increasingly sentimental and nostalgic landscape of gum trees.

Greater appreciation of the natural environment developed alongside, and in response to, ongoing degradation caused by farming and mining. Increased politicisation of environmental issues from the 1960s, and louder calls for CONSERVATION, had one effect in the BUSH GARDEN phenomenon of the 1960s and 1970s. In the outback, political lobbying for environmental protection operated in tandem with Aboriginal land rights, as at Kakadu (NT).

At the beginning of the new century, the natural environment has become increasingly elusive. Environmentalists see the bush as infested with an increasing number of WEED species. Identifying an indigenous historic environment has become problematic, if not near-impossible, as rich cultural overlays coexist with natural values. REVEGETATION has become an imperative, although the protection of remnant vegetation and ecosystems is an even higher priority for biodiversity. At the same time, many new SUBURBAN GARDENS in the major cities seem more intent on reproducing commercial variants of stylised European gardens than in looking to Australian species and styles.

J.M. Powell, *Environmental Management in Australia 1788–1914: Guardians, Improvers, and Profit* (Melbourne, 1976); Eric Rolls, *A Million Wild Acres* (Sydney, 1981); Geoffrey Bolton, *Spoils and Spoilers: Australians Make Their Environment 1788–1980* (Sydney, 1982); Eric Rolls, *From Forest to Sea: Australia's Changing Environment* (St Lucia, Qld., 1993); George Seddon, *Landprints: Reflections on Place and Landscape* (Cambridge, 1997); Graeme Aplin, *Australians and their Environment: An Introduction to Environmental Studies* (South Melbourne, 1998); Ian R. Tyrrell, *True Garden of the Gods: Californian–Australian Environmental Reform 1860–1930* (Berkeley, California, 1999); Tim Bonyhady, *The Colonial Earth* (Carlton South, Vic., 2000)

HELEN DOYLE

ENVIRONMENTAL WEEDS: see WEEDS

ERCILDOUNE, Burrumbeet, Vic., was established as a pastoral station by Scottish brothers Thomas (1818–1903) and Somerville (1819–1878) Learmonth, in 1838. Trees were planted from this date, reputedly from seedlings shipped from SCOTLAND. A network of paths, beds, hedges, creepers, fruit trees, willows, a rosary, and an ornamental lake were also added. The garden was developed considerably after 1859 when the house was extended in Scotch baronial style. Samuel Wilson (1832–1895), a keen ACCLIMATISER and a founder of the Acclimatisation Society of Victoria, purchased the property in 1873 and further developed the garden. He maintained extensive shrubberies and ornamental grounds, and added a walled garden and glasshouse. Through the surrounding parkland of eucalypts and *Acacia implexa* (Lightwood), he planted a carriage drive with alternating *Pinus radiata* and *Cedrus deodora*. Wilson also established a DEER PARK and fish hatchery, kept numerous exotic birds, and added the extra 'E' to the property's name. Nellie Melba occupied Ercildoune briefly in 1907. Alan Currie, son of J.L. Currie of TITANGA, owned the property from 1920 to 1964. Although subsequently altered, Ercildoune remains a significant Australian HOMESTEAD GARDEN, retaining the walled enclosure, remnant box-hedged PARTERRES, a low stone wall, and several lakes.

HELEN DOYLE

ERICKSON (née SANDILANDS), Frederica Lucy (Rica) (b. 1908), historian, naturalist, botanical illustrator, and school teacher, was born and brought up in south-west WA where she grew to love the bush. She taught herself botany and NATURAL HISTORY, and painted wildflowers in the field, while corresponding with eminent botanists and naturalists across Australia. Erickson's books include *Orchids of the West* (1951), *Triggerplants* (1958), and *Plants of Prey* (1968), each based on original research and supported by her accurate and detailed watercolour illustrations. The first of her many engaging histories was *The Drummonds of Hawthornden* (1969), a biography of Western Australia's first resident botanist, James DRUMMOND. She also edited seven (of thirteen) volumes of *The Dictionary of Western Australians* (1979–94). Her botanical illustrations have been exhibited at the Art Gallery of Western Australia and Perth's Alexander Library. Several awards recognise Rica Erickson's outstanding contributions to natural history and the arts, including an honorary doctorate of letters from the University of Western Australia (1980).

Bronwen Keighery, *Sharing a Wonderful Dream: An Exhibition* (Perth, 1991)

CAROL MANSFIELD

ERREY, William Henry (1838–1912), nursery proprietor and plant breeder, came from Heathfield, Sussex, England, and with family members including his father Thomas, brother Thomas Peter Errey (1847–1934), and cousin David Errey (1834–1916), migrated to Vic. in 1857. W.H. Errey settled in Camperdown (Vic.), establishing a nursery in the early 1860s. His eldest son, Gilbert Gurnett Errey (1880–1961), worked with him from 1892. Gilbert realised the advantages of specialising and began hybridising CARNATIONS with success. His brothers (Thomas) Henry Errey (1884–1928) and Edwin Errey (1890–1918) also joined the firm. Another brother, Sidney Arnold Errey (1887–1964), joined when W.H. Errey was contemplating expanding into GLADIOLUS (c. 1907)—Sid securing land for that purpose. In 1912, after the death of W.H. Errey, the firm was registered as Errey Bros.; Gilbert was business manager, Sid farm manager, and Edwin assisted at the two nurseries but was killed in action in the battle of the Somme. Sales soared after the war and Sid had mass-production well organised. Gilbert's son, Reginald Gilbert Errey (1909–1974), joined after leaving school, succeeding with breeding gladioli that found favour domestically and overseas. Carnations were discontinued in 1932, attention turning to Reg's special interest, the iris. The nursery closed in 1966.

T.P. Errey had 'the family love of flowers and dabbled in the nursery business', moving to Cobrico c. 1875. He was a butcher in Cobram, but by 1881 was growing and selling fruit, vegetables, and plants at Cobrico. He was involved with W.H. Errey in the establishment of Camperdown Horticultural Society (1880). He 'knew hard times' and in 1892 left Cobrico, finally settling at Hazeldene in 1896, establishing a nursery and orchard. In 1908 he moved to Lilydale, but it is evident that he lacked the business acumen of his successful brother. His youngest son William Gilbert Errey (1887–1969) continued at Hazeldene. From 1905 he imported liliums from Japan and developed a nursery of rare bulbs and perennials, adopting the trade name Gilrey. In 1919 he moved to Warburton, and later Lilydale. He was federal president, Australian Iris Society, and foundation president, Australian Lilium Society.

The Errey family members were remarkable for the breadth of their horticultural expertise and for their success in the fickle world of the carnation, iris, gladiolus, and lilium.

GEORGE JONES

ERYLDENE, Gordon, NSW: see WATERHOUSE, Eben Gowrie

ESPALIER, a French term derived from the Italian *spalle* (to shoulder), refers to the training and manipulation (especially by PRUNING) of TREES against a WALL. It was traditionally used in Europe for FRUIT trees, to take advantage of the protection a wall offered. While now mainly used for fruit trees, other woody ornamental plants such as CAMELLIAS may be used. Plants may also be trained to stand alone. Many patterns and branching systems are employed and illustrated in the horticultural literature, some with descriptive names such as 'Candelabra', 'Belgian fence', 'Fan' shape, 'U' shape, and 'Serpentine'. In Australia, where most climates do not require the extra warmth provided by a wall for optimum plant growth, the method has been used rather to enable the growing of fruit trees in small urban spaces and to achieve ornamental patterns in garden design. Alan EDMUNDS was a vocal proponent for the technique from the 1930s to the 1950s.

ML

ESPLANADE, a level piece of ground, especially one used for public PROMENADE, is derived from the space separating a citadel (or fortress) from its town, especially in France or Spain (*esplanada*). Esplanades shares similarities with BOULEVARDS, but the latter are often graded, and generally built on two sides, rather than fronting or separating two major or dissimilar elements. With level ground as its key attribute, the esplanade is especially suited to bodies of water, especially along BEACH fronts or on the margins of rivers or lakes, where it is often known as the Strand. Well-known Australian esplanades include Sydney's Circular Quay, THE STRAND (Townsville, Qld), and the beach fronts of Bondi and Manly (NSW). Many less-celebrated esplanades provided in town plans by early land surveyors form valuable PUBLIC OPEN SPACES, as in Tas., where almost all towns and suburbs with water frontage, no matter how feeble the ebb or flow, have this feature.

RA

EUCALYPTUS While ACACIA is Australia's FLORAL EMBLEM and its green and gold colours are incorporated into the nation's sporting image, the genus *Eucalyptus* is overwhelmingly the symbol of Australia's natural vegetation. Both genera, however, are widespread and prominent in Australia's woody biota; *Acacia* being generally more dominant in drier areas while *Eucalyptus* dominates less harsh zones, although *Acacia* is often present in the understorey in these regions.

The name Eucalyptus was coined in 1788 by French botanist Charles-Louis L'Héritier de Brutelle (1746–1800), based on a specimen of *Eucalyptus obliqua* collected in 1777 on Bruny Island off the coast of Tas. Etymologically the name Eucalyptus was formed from the Greek *eu* (well) and *kalypto* (to cover), referring to the flower bud, which has a cap (operculum) protecting the flower until being shed at maturation.

The genus *Eucalyptus*, embracing some 700 species, includes a wide range of forms from small shrubs, such as *Eucalyptus vernicosa* (Varnished Gum) from south-west Tas. to some of the tallest hardwood trees in the world, and *E. regnans* (Mountain Ash) native to Tas. and Vic. It also consists of broad-crowned woodland trees and the so called 'mallee' forms, which are multi-trunked and grow in drier localities. While a large number of eucalypt species form a specialised organ called a lignotuber, which in the adult tree consists of a woody mass of dormant buds at the base of the main stem, in mallee forms it is well developed and is the main method of regeneration after canopy destruction by drought or fire—its typical multi-stemmed form. These lignotubers or 'mallee roots' have been much valued as a fuel.

In addition to a wide range of height and growth forms, the eucalypts also possess different bark types, which have been used to characterise various groups. In general, these

Eucalyptus

Eucalyptus globulus (Blue Gum), engraved after the drawing by REDOUTÉ and published by Labillardière (1800) was among the earliest published BOTANICAL ILLUSTRATIONS of the genus EUCALYPTUS

can be divided into the 'gum barked' species (where the bark is shed leaving a more or less smooth finish) and the 'rough barked' species (where the bark persists in various formations such as the tessellated appearance of the 'boxes' or the furrowed bark of the 'stringybarks' and 'ironbarks'; in the former the bark is fibrous while in the latter it is hard). Many of the 'gum barked' species, such as *Eucalyptus mannifera* (native to the Canberra region and a feature of the National Gallery of Australia Sculpture Garden) and *E. scoparia* possess smooth white powdery trunks of strong ornamental value.

Another feature of the eucalypts is their production of different leaf types in size, shape and colour (known as heterophylly) at different growth phases. Four stages are generally recognised: seedling, juvenile, intermediate and adult. The juvenile foliage in some species such as *Eucalyptus globulus* (Blue Gum) is markedly different from the adult foliage. In this species the juvenile leaves are bluish in colour and rounded while the adult leaves are green and long, and narrow in shape. The juvenile foliage is considered desirable for the cut FLOWER trade and in Britain seedlings are used in annual bedding schemes as dot plants to add FOLIAGE texture and interest. To maintain the juvenile form in many of these species over time it is necessary to periodically coppice plants by cutting them back to the ground.

First impressions of the eucalypts for timber use were not complimentary. In his *Journal* (1790), John WHITE expressed a common perception that 'the timber of this country is very unfit for the purpose of building. Nor do I know any one purpose for which it will answer except for firewood; and for that it is excellent: but in other respects it is the worst wood that any country or climate ever produced.' The eucalypts now represent an enormous timber resource, supplying hardwood with a range of durability and strength characteristics for building, cabinet-making, fencing, fuel, and paper pulp. The essential oils that provide the eucalypts with their characteristic aromatic smell and produce the blue haze over the Australian landscape as they volatise into the atmosphere in summer have long been recognised for their medicinal value. The early European settlers described them as being particularly useful for the treatment of dysentery. The peppermint tree (*Eucalyptus piperita*) was so named because of the similarity of its essential oil to the peppermint (*Mentha piperita*) traditionally used in Europe. This term has now been applied to a group of eucalypt species which have a similar peppermint oil odour.

Many Australian gardening books suggested that the numerous forms and features of the eucalypts lend themselves to a wide range of conditions and uses in the landscape. However, as a tree for cultivation in gardens the eucalypt has had a mixed reception. Although acknowledged for its ornamental value and representativeness as part of a uniquely Australian landscape style, its evergreen canopy, which precludes light in small domestic spaces during winter in south-eastern states, its constant leaf shedding, and its propensity to exclude the growth of other vegetation beneath its canopy (due partly to the toxic affect of its leaves) have tempered enthusiasm for its use. In addition, its natural tendency to shed limbs without notice has dampened enthusiasm of PUBLIC OPEN SPACE managers, increasingly conscious of litigation. This, in conjunction with its lack of a formal habit, has restricted its use in highly urban areas, where formality often constrains architectural designs and thinking. Eucalypts are largely SEED raised rather than cloned, and often display considerable variation in growth form within a given species. Recent research, undertaken by Dr David Beardsall at Victoria's Knoxfield Research Station, has attempted to improve this situation by developing seed orchards of elite Australian trees, especially those already found desirable for urban planting such as *Eucalyptus leucoxylon* (Yellow Gum). This program was commenced as a direct response to the huge public outcry in 1992 and divided public opinion over the planting of *Platanus* X *acerifolia* (Plane Tree) rather than native eucalypt specimens as STREET TREES in central Melbourne.

Various fashions for different *Eucalyptus* species have changed over time, often in tandem with other AUSTRALIAN PLANTS. Ferdinand MUELLER, experimented widely with a range of Australian trees and especially promoted *Eucalyptus globulus* (Blue Gum), for widespread and avenue planting, earning him the sobriquet 'Blue Gum Mueller'. While this early interest in this tree subsided it was briefly revived during the 1970s when a wide range of eucalypt species were being tried alongside other Australian plants. Its fast growth rate, eventual large size, and potential root damage to buildings, especially when planted in small inner suburban gardens, soon caused its widespread removal. This period, however, was important for the introduction of a wide range of eucalypt species into cultivation, particularly smaller growing species such as *Eucalyptus caesia* (Gungurru). New interest in ECOLOGICAL plantings and REVEGETATION has kindled interest in the use of indigenous species obtained from local seed sources.

ML

EVERGLADES, Leura, NSW, a three-hectare garden on steeply sloping land overlooking the Gordon Falls valley, was laid out by Paul SORENSEN between 1932 and 1947 for industrialist Henri Van de Velde (1879–1947). Composed of 'outdoor rooms'—in this case separated by level change rather than hedges or walls—it is a pioneering MODERNIST design. The garden comprises terraces stepping down the slope, supported by drystone retaining WALLS—the most dominant feature of the design—constructed from ironstone collected on site. The terraces, each with its own character, were originally furnished with sculptures, most of which have since been lost. The Studio Terrace has a studio–gymnasium at the northern end and a view over the valley to the south. It also contains the Garden Theatre, formed with the recycled façade of a Sydney bank building as its backdrop. The Cherry Terrace leads to the art deco residence (1935). In this upper section of the garden all planting is exotic, with a strong use of deciduous and coniferous trees. A grove of flowering cherries is underplanted with bluebells, and there are mass plantings of rhododendrons, azaleas, and maples. The view over the valley is deliberately hidden from most of the garden, with its dramatic impact revealed fully only from the house and from a LOOKOUT on the path to the lower gardens, where mostly native plants are used. This path leads eventually to a stream garden and grotto pool. Everglades was acquired by the NATIONAL TRUST in 1962.

RICHARD RATCLIFFE

EVERIST, Selwyn Lawrence (1913–1981), botanist, toxicologist, and naturalist, was director of the Queensland HERBARIUM (1954–76). Beginning as a clerk in 1931, Everist was encouraged to matriculate and study science by his employer, C.T. WHITE; he eventually concentrated on ECONOMIC BOTANY, and, after the war, poisonous plants and WEEDS. As director, he modernised and expanded the Herbarium, especially in the 1970s, after relocating to new quarters at Indooroopilly (1968). His 'History of the Queensland Herbarium and Botanic Library 1855–1976' in *Austrobaileya* (1982) provides insight into many aspects of Australian botanical history.

JEANNIE SIM

EWART, Alfred James (1872–1937), botanist, born and educated in Liverpool, England, gained doctoral degrees from Leipzig, London, and Oxford, after plant physiological research. In Melbourne from 1906, as Victoria's Government Botanist and foundation professor of botany and plant physiology at the University of Melbourne, Ewart quickly directed his attention to Victoria's indigenous and introduced plants. To facilitate the recognition of WEEDS—which, under Victorian law, required destruction—he prepared illustrated descriptive articles that grew into *The Weeds, Poison Plants, and Naturalized Aliens of Victoria* (1909), written with his National Herbarium assistant, James Richard Tovey (1873–1922). Some of the weeds were reputedly garden escapees, and the long list of naturalised aliens indicated the extent of the invasive changes to Victoria's flora.

To clarify the taxonomy of indigenous and introduced plants, Ewart published new records and corrected old ones in local journals. Chairing the Field Naturalists' Club of Victoria's Plant Names Committee, Ewart was surprised that so little importance was given 'to many native plants of pronounced decorative value for garden purposes'. Some INDIGENOUS PLANTS in the Committee's list, published in *A Census of the Plants of Victoria* (1923), were recorded as 'decorative', 'ornamental', or 'worthy of garden cultivation', including alpine species of the genus recently named in his honour—*Ewartia*.

Ewart reported on agricultural and forestry issues and on the flora of Victoria's alps, Wilsons Promontory, and the NT. His *Handbook of Forest Trees for Victorian Foresters* (1925) described Victorian trees and shrubs, and exotic pines. During the 1920s Ewart was a full-time professor and no longer Government Botanist, but he prepared a new *Flora of Victoria* (1930), the first since MUELLER's *Key to the System of Victorian Plants* (1888).

LINDEN GILLBANK

EXHIBITIONS, like HORTICULTURAL SHOWS and garden FESTIVALS, have exerted a considerable although often indirect influence on Australian gardens and horticulture. Major international exhibitions in London (1851, 1862, 1873–74, 1886, 1899), Paris (1855, 1867, 1878, 1889, 1900), Dublin (1865), Vienna (1873), Philadelphia (1876), and Chicago (1893) provided models for the intercolonial and international exhibitions held in Australia. These were periodically supplemented by major horticultural congresses and exhibitions in the European capitals. The landscaped setting of the buildings of the exhibitions were highly influential: PAXTON's Crystal Palace, London (1851, re-erected Sydenham 1854); the Paris exhibition (1867) by Jean Charles Adolphe Alphand and Jean-Pierre Barillet-Deschamps (especially as reported by William ROBINSON) and Alphand's work at the 1889 exhibition; and the influence on the CITY BEAUTIFUL MOVEMENT of the World's Columbian Exposition (Chicago, 1893) being key examples reported extensively to Australian readers in the *Gardeners' Chronicle*, the *Cottage Gardener*, and the *Illustrated London News*, among others. While attendance at international conferences seems commonplace in the jet age, in the nineteenth century, travel to exhibitions overseas was a time-consuming undertaking.

Notable Australian exhibitions, often held as preludes to international exhibitions, were held at Melbourne (1854, 1861, 1866–67, 1875, 1880–81, 1888–89), Sydney (1870,

1873, 1879–80), Adelaide (1887–88), Brisbane (1876, 1877, 1897), Launceston (1891–92), and Hobart (1894–95). In recent times, Brisbane hosted the 1988 World Expo. Other influential exhibitions, including the First Australian Exhibition of Women's Work (Melbourne, 1907) touched on gardens. Economic rather than ornamental concerns were foremost in these exhibitions—promoting commerce and encouraging immigration—although special horticultural shows were often held simultaneously, and a leisured appreciation of the FERNERIES and other garden displays (such as BEDDING in adjacent PUBLIC GARDENS) was immensely popular. Botanic garden directors and government botanists such as Mueller and F.M. Bailey joined leading names from the nursery trade as key exhibitors, with items ranging from eucalyptus oil to wax fruit models.

J.E. Findling and K.D. Pelle (eds), *Historical Dictionary of World's Fairs and Expositions* (New York, 1990); David Dunstan, *Victorian Icon: The Royal Exhibition Building, Melbourne* (Kew, Vic., 1996); Judith McKay, *'A Good Show': Colonial Queensland at International Exhibitions* (special issue of Memoirs of the Queensland Museum: Cultural Heritage Series, Brisbane, 1998); Peter Proudfoot, Roslyn Maguire, and Robert Freestone (eds), *Colonial City, Global City: Sydney's International Exhibition 1879* (Darlinghurst, NSW, 2000)   RA

EXPERIMENTAL GARDENS AND FARMS, employing various degrees of empirical and scientific investigation of HORTICULTURE and AGRICULTURE, flourished in the nineteenth century in Australia. In one sense, all early gardens and farms involved the necessity of experimentation in unfamiliar climates for their emigrant owners and managers. The earliest colonial government or BOTANIC GARDENS were viewed from afar—especially at KEW—as experimental stations, and ACCLIMATISATION certainly became a key horticultural agenda in the mid-nineteenth century as directors such as MUELLER and HILL used country sites (as well as their own metropolitan sites) for experimentation. In Qld—perhaps more than any other colony—the local acclimatisation society was skewed towards flora rather than fauna, and was able to conduct horticultural trials at BOWEN PARK. Agricultural and HORTICULTURAL SOCIETIES frequently wrote or spoke of the need for experimental farms and gardens, but few progressed beyond worthy ideas. Those that did—such as the model farm at Royal Park, Vic. (1858)—were often dismal failures, derided by 'practical men' who felt such ventures were best left to the free market. In the area of POMOLOGY, the (Royal) Horticultural Society of Victoria started its BURNLEY Gardens on a handsome government reserve, having high hopes for trialling and fixing nomenclature of 'the most approved' fruit

The outdoor display by Sydney hardware and horticultural providers, F. Lassetter & Co., at an EXHIBITION held at Prince Alfred Park during the 1870s, featured fountains, plant stands, and lawn mowers

Experimental gardens and farms

varieties, but the venture foundered after a few decades as diligent nursery proprietors demonstrated that it was possible to undertake in the commercial sphere what had idealistically been hoped for in the public. In other horticultural spheres, this commercial and private experimentation—especially with plant breeding—contributed immeasurably to the range of plants available to Australian gardeners: the names of CLARK of Glenara (ROSES) and WATERHOUSE of Eryldene (CAMELLIAS) being two of the best known.

Large-scale private initiatives such as the Arundel Model Farm (1853) near Bulla (Vic.), were rare, but many landowners trialled crops and plants in the quest for better yields. As the agriculture departments of each colony were established, so too were government-owned experimental farms specialising in local crops (such as sugar, wheat, fodder grass, and fruits) or trialling a range of plants and livestock suited to local climates. The newly established AGRICULTURAL COLLEGES, some being former experimental farms, were part of this network. STATE FOREST NURSERIES also fulfilled many experimental roles in their specified field. In recent times, the growing of genetically modified plants has caused a great deal of controversy, especially for their potential to pollute the genetic make-up of neighbouring unmodified crops.

JEANNIE SIM

FAIRALL, Arthur Robert (1921–1970), horticulturist, was born in, and trained in, South Africa. In 1962 he moved to Perth as inaugural superintendent of the BOTANIC GARDEN at KINGS PARK. He laid out the Botanic Garden and maintained records, with Russell Blake (b. 1919), the Garden foreman, of plants with horticultural potential. Compiled into *Western Australian Native Plants in Cultivation* (1970), published shortly after Fairall's death, it was the first complete book on its subject. GREG and BRONWEN KEIGHERY

FAIRHALL, Alfred Ernest (1871–1945), landscape gardener and amateur geologist, was born in Greymouth, New Zealand; in 1889 he moved to Melbourne, where he completed a five-year apprenticeship with TAYLOR AND SANGSTER before establishing his own business. In 1894 he moved to Adelaide, becoming head gardener to pastoralist and politician John Duncan at his residence Strathspey at Mitcham, and at his HUGHES PARK homestead at Watervale for three years. Fairhall then worked at HACKETT's Nursery at Kent Town, at Alexander George Downer's residence at Belair, and at Gurrawarra, Crafers, for Alexander Thomas Magarey, before being engaged in 1897 by (Sir) Edward and Lady Stirling at ST VIGEANS, where he worked on their renowned RHODODENDRON collection in the ADELAIDE HILLS for almost a quarter of a century. DAVID JONES

FARM AND GARDEN (1858–63), a monthly journal published in Adelaide, provided detailed advice and information on agriculture, horticulture, and gardening in SA drawn from colonial contributors and 'kindred British and Colonial publications'. Edited by newspaper proprietor **Edward William Andrews** (1812–1877), the journal was instigated in 1857 under the auspices of the South Australian Agricultural and Horticultural Society, on the recommendation of horticulturist Daniel Ferguson (1837–1905), 'to advance the productive interests of the colony'. The journal succeeded the failed monthly SOUTH AUSTRALIAN HORTICULTURIST (1856). Andrews, born in Walworth, Surrey, England, arrived in Adelaide in 1839 and became engaged in mercantile pursuits before becoming editor and proprietor of the *South Australian Register* and the ADELAIDE OBSERVER. Known for his energetic interest in community affairs, with *Farm and Garden* Andrews established a strong 'agronomical' publication based on practical and scientific horticultural and agricultural information and advice. Andrews stopped publication due to unprofitability, but maintained a 'Farm and Garden' column in the *Observer* until the Society sponsored the publication of GARDEN AND FIELD under the editorship of Albert MOLINEUX in 1875. DAVID JONES

FAWKNER, John Pascoe (1792–1869), Victorian pioneer, was born at Cripplegate, London. After his father was sentenced to fourteen years' transportation for possessing stolen goods, the family sailed with David Collins and his party on the *Calcutta* to establish a settlement in the Port Phillip District (1803). The settlement, near present-day Sorrento, was abandoned after a few months, and the party moved to Hobart Town. Fawkner had many occupations: shepherd, convict, sawyer, newspaper editor, printer, bookseller, stationer, publican, lending library and carriage proprietor, merchant, commission agent, 'bush lawyer', member of parliament, and nursery proprietor. In 1829 he established a nine-acre (3.6 ha) garden and nursery near Windmill Hill, Launceston, Van Diemen's Land. This produced the first fruit trees for the HENTYS of Portland, as well as the seeds, plants, and 2500 fruit trees that Fawkner sent to Port Phillip on the *Enterprise*. His employees began a farm and garden near Batman's Hill in Melbourne, but were induced to move to the south side of the Yarra. In 1839 Fawkner began to develop Belle Vue Park, a 780-acre (315 ha) farm at 'Pascoeville' (now Oak Park in Melbourne's north), of which several acres became a nursery. His invoices (1839–46) list imported plants, seeds, and garden equipment from Britain, Van Diemen's Land, and NSW. In 1848 Fawkner called the public meeting that resulted in the establishment of the Victorian Horticultural Society. Fawkner's copy of LOUDON's *Observation on Laying out Farms in the Scotch Style* (held in the State Library of Victoria) is a reminder of his farming interests.

C.P. Billot, *The Life and Times of John Pascoe Fawkner* (Melbourne, 1985) GEORGE JONES and GWEN PASCOE

FAWKNER CEMETERY, Vic. (originally New Melbourne General Cemetery) was, along with the Springvale Necropolis (1901), a product of a long, drawn-out campaign to have MELBOURNE GENERAL CEMETERY superseded. Intended to serve the needs of the northern metropolitan area, it was finally established in 1904. Its new trust purchased 284 acres (115 ha) at Fawkner, and the original fan-shaped layout was designed by

Richard Daintree's 1858 photograph of Clunes (Vic.), during the early phase of gold mining, clearly indicates the importance of FENCES to the settlement process—the boundary fence of the pastoralist's pre-emptive right cuts diagonally across the scene while the modest fenced plots of miners define smaller and more egalitarian allotments

architect Charles HEATH after extensive investigation of contemporary overseas ideas on cemetery development. The final plan (1911) included both formal and informal planting, denominational divisions, chapel sites, waiting rooms, a formal entrance from Sydney Road, and a railway platform. Heath took a lifelong interest in the project, becoming secretary and manager. His work at Fawkner was carried on by his son Frank, an ardent supporter of American concepts of cemetery design and of the professionalism of cemetery development and management.

ROBERT NICOL

FEAKES, Daniel (1863–1936), Government Gardener, was born in Suffolk, England, arriving in Perth in 1887. Apparently trained at KEW GARDENS, he quickly found employment at the Government Gardens (now STIRLING GARDENS), subsequently (1896–1919) holding the positions of superintendent, director, and Government Gardener. This 'true gentleman' was responsible for PUBLIC PARKS and reserves under colonial (then state) government control, including advising on work in KINGS PARK, and gardens at both GOVERNMENT HOUSE and Parliament House.

CAROL MANSFIELD

FEDERATION GARDENS: see AUSTRALIA 1890–1918

FENCES The network of fences that forms a pattern across the Australian landscape is so ubiquitous as to be invisible to the initial gaze. Yet fences are pervasive, making barriers of boundaries so that public access by footpaths over private properties is rare in Australia. Colonial artists depicted domestic gardens fenced primarily to stave off the threatening wilderness—mentally as much as physically. Fences have defined boundaries against the bush, contained stock, barred intruders, separated land uses, defined ownership, and secured possession. Fences imposed order and reorganised space, in marked contrast to the symbiotic relationship of the Australian Aboriginal people with the land. Scholarly study of fences in Australia is recent and partial, but is already perceived as a rich source of evidence for landscape interpretation and settlement history.

Only after 1847, when the Secretary of State for the Colonies offered security of tenure during leasehold to squatters and compensation for improvements such as building dams and fences, did enclosure proliferate in Australia. Split post-and-rail fences had been confined to home paddocks of perhaps thirty hectares, and domestic gardens enclosed with split picket or paling fences. As freehold tenure increased, fences followed the surveyors to define purchased property boundaries. But only after the 1850s gold rushes, when wages doubled, was it cheaper to build fences and replace shepherds. As early as the 1840s, wire fencing was said to be cheaper than post-and-rail, and sheep were said to be improved if left undisturbed behind fences. A medium-sized sheep property could consume 30 000 trees to produce fence posts—fences not only defined, but denuded the land. Although iron posts and droppers were available from the 1870s, the 'star' picket was not patented until 1926—but was then almost universally adopted. Hedgerows were planted in Tas. and parts of Vic., and extensive drystone walls survive in Victoria's WESTERN DISTRICT, often from the 1850s. Only leased land remained unfenced.

Split timber picket or paling fences enclosed urban and rural domestic gardens from an early date, and portable IRON FENCES (or hurdles) were imported from the 1850s and locally manufactured soon after. Sawn pickets—with decorative heads and simple profiles until the 1870s—became more stylised. From 1890 until 1920, pickets were taller, in diverse organic profiles often varying in height, with turned posts. The Australian rights to manufacture the American Cyclone brand were secured in 1898, and their woven, crimped, and later chain-link fences, on a tubular steel frame, sometimes with decorative timber posts, became popular. Cast- and wrought-iron palisades set into dressed basalt plinths (or dwarf walls in SA) and capped with cast spearheads, were favoured for architecturally pretentious urban fences until 1900, and many fine examples survive.

All of these fences were transparent. Except for suburban paling fences, whether split or sawn, or corrugated iron boundary fences, visibility of the garden beyond the fence was invariably desirable. William ELLIOTT, in *Cole's Australasian Gardening* (1897), recommended that otherwise fences should be 'kept out of sight as much as possible … hidden by vegetation … climbing plants, shrubs or hedges'. Solid fences and WALLS, presumably for security, are an innovation of the last twenty years in Australia, with relatively few exceptions (including HEDGES). Open gardens without fences were fashionable for a short time—from the 1950s to the 1970s.

Richard Peterson, *Fences and Gates c. 1840–1925: A Guide to Identification, Conservation and Restoration of Historic Fences and Gates* (Melbourne, 1988). **RICHARD PETERSON**

FENG-SHUI ('wind–water') is the ancient Chinese system of placing buildings and objects in the landscape with the view of obtaining personal good fortune. It is still practised in Asia, and, only in the last few years, has also become highly popular in the West, including Australia. Feng-shui is based on the belief that powerful forces inhabit the landscape. *Qi* ('the breath of nature') is the positive, life-giving force that flows in invisible 'streams' through the earth, and *sha qi* ('the noxious vapour') is the negative, destructive force produced by anything that is straight—such as pathways, roads and walls. The aim is to find or attract *qi*, which brings good luck, and to avoid or repel *sha qi*, which brings bad luck. By observing for centuries the environmental conditions that appeared to foster both *qi* and *sha qi*, feng-shui experts developed a complex set of rules for finding the best, or the luckiest, sites for buildings and towns (dwellings for the living), and graves and cemeteries (dwellings for the dead). In general, such a site has a high mountain to the north (symbolised by a black tortoise), a slightly lower mountain to the east (symbolised by an azure dragon), an even lower mountain to the west (symbolised by a white tiger), and a meandering river to the south (symbolised by a red finch). **DERHAM GROVES**

FENTON, John (b. 1935) and his wife **Cicely Fenton** (b. 1938), farm foresters and pastoralists, challenged assumptions behind WESTERN DISTRICT pastoral traditions that tree removal aided profitability when, in 1956, they began a broad-scale tree planting and wetlands establishment program at Lanark, Branxholme (Vic.). Recipients of a National Tree Farmer Award (1993), their property is an innovative model for sustainable landscapes. John received an honorary doctorate from the Royal Melbourne Institute of Technology (1997) for his achievements. **DAVID JONES**

FERGUSON, Francis (1824–1892), gardener and nursery proprietor, migrated to Sydney in 1849 possessing considerable English horticultural experience. J.G. VEITCH recorded that Ferguson 'learned his business at CHATSWORTH and other large English gardens', while in correspondence with Robert MARNOCK—who reprinted two letters in his *Gardeners' and Farmers' Journal*—Ferguson asked to be remembered to John Spencer, head gardener at the celebrated seat of Bowood, Wiltshire, probably indicating experience there. He also thanked 'Messrs Mackay and McLelland' whose 'urgent request' caused Ferguson to come to Australia: Mackay may have been John Bain Mackay (1795–1888), nursery proprietor of Chelsea and Hackney in London.

After arrival, Ferguson was soon engaged as superintendent to Sir Thomas MITCHELL at his country estate—a situation he found 'in every respect an uncomfortable one'. After three months he moved to become one of William MACARTHUR's tenants at Camden Park, and was subsequently a propagator, plant collector, and gardener until *c.* 1857. By the time Ferguson was at Camden Park, Macarthur had converted part of his garden into a nursery, and as early as 1850 Ferguson was earning £25 per annum (and other entitlements) plus '10 per cent on all that is sold', which considerably increased his remuneration. He praised Macarthur to Marnock as 'a good practical botanist, and quite a votary of Flora [possessing] … one of the most extensive plant collections in this country'. Ferguson's friendship with Marnock saw him donate a case containing thirty-three plants to the Royal Botanic Society's gardens at Regent's Park, London. At Camden, Ferguson, the enterprising newcomer, clashed with gardener Edmund BLAKE, and the pair maintained a jealous rivalry.

Ferguson's Australian Nursery was established at Camden in 1858, with the support of Macarthur, who supplied Ferguson with imported NOVELTIES. The Australian Nursery was an agent for James Veitch and Sons, and by 1868 Ferguson himself had agents in Auckland, Wellington, Wanganui, and Dunedin (New Zealand). The business expanded, by 1880, to become Francis Ferguson and Sons, Australian Nurseries, Camden, Sydney, and Double Bay, with a central depot in George Street. One garden known to have been designed by Ferguson is Ellensville (*c.* 1890) at Mount Hunter near Camden. After Ferguson's death the business passed to one of his younger sons, and was run with the assistance of a relative, Alf Little. The business moved from its original site but continued to operate from Camden, and by 1904 had opened at Hurstville. During the twentieth century the nursery was operated by family members in various localities until the sale of the Mittagong Nursery in 1970. The name Ferguson's has been retained by the present owners, the Pike family. Stately *Jubaea chilensis* (Chilean Wine Palm) and araucarias, reminders of Francis Ferguson's connection with Camden Park, grace the original Australian Nursery site—one of the oldest nursery sites in Australia. **CRAIG BURTON and COLLEEN MORRIS**

FERGUSON, William (*c.* 1827–1887), gardener and forester, presumably British-born, is thought to have arrived in Melbourne in 1856. In the late 1850s and 1860s he worked as a gardener in Melbourne—for J.H.Brooke at Mount Eagle, Heidelberg, and Hugh Glass at Flemington House—and was active in horticultural circles, in particular the Victorian Gardeners' Mutual Improvement Society. In 1869 Ferguson was appointed Overseer of Forests and a Crown Land Bailiff in the Department of Crown Lands and Survey. It was a difficult assignment, complicated by the fact that Ferguson's departmental superior, the formidable Clement HODGKINSON, questioned the utility of his appointment: Hodgkinson held the firm opinion that locally based crown land bailiffs were better placed to protect the forests than a single overseer. Competing demands on Ferguson's time were also problematic. In December 1869 Ferguson was dispatched to the MELBOURNE BOTANIC GARDENS with instructions to improve the austere landscaping and planting of director Ferdinand MUELLER. The two clashed repeatedly, and Ferguson found himself embroiled in the very pubic debate over Mueller's position. In 1870, as part of a WESTERN DISTRICT forests inspection, Ferguson visited Hamilton, where he laid out the HAMILTON BOTANIC GARDENS. He also arranged for shrubs and trees to be sent to Hamilton from the Melbourne Botanic Gardens. Although Ferguson's plan was superseded by William GUILFOYLE's 1881 design, a number of surviving conifers are reminders of Ferguson's contribution.

In 1872 Ferguson was removed from the Gardens and ordered to MOUNT MACEDON with instructions to establish a STATE FOREST NURSERY. His position had now been absorbed into the fledgling Department of Agriculture. He started work in December 1872, and took to the task with great energy, concentrating initially on clearing the site and installing drainage. Gradually the site was transformed. From September 1873 all plants distributed to the many reserves managed by the Lands Department came from Mount Macedon. It also became a centre for the training of foresters, and for the education of reformatory boys. In 1882 Ferguson joined the Melbourne Public Parks and Gardens Committee, and in 1886 he appeared as an expert witness before the Royal Commission on Vegetable Products. Following the sudden death of Ferguson at the State Nursery, George PERRIN was appointed Conservator of Forests. Ferguson's work at Mount Macedon confirms Hodgkinson's assessment that he was 'a scientific and practical arboriculturalist'.

Paul Fox, *Clearings: Six Colonial Gardeners and their Landscapes* (Carlton South, Vic., forthcoming, 2003) RAY WRIGHT

FERN, James (1834–1918), gardener and trade unionist, arrived in Australia from Scotland in the 1860s, and for many years worked at the SYDNEY BOTANIC GARDENS. He was one of the founders of the NSW Gardeners' Union, and represented that body on the Trades and Labor Council in 1890, an early advocate for the disparate body of GARDENERS found throughout the workforce. RA

FERNBERG, Bardon, Qld: see GOVERNMENT HOUSE, Queensland

FERNHILL, Mulgoa, NSW, exemplifies sophisticated colonial landscape planning. In the 1840s, landowner Edward Cox (1805–1868) thinned the natural woodland to resemble English parkland and retained apple gums (*Angophora floribunda* and *A. subvelutina*) to provide an informal avenue to the drive that winds through the property, across stone bridges and gullies, affording vistas of the Greek Revival homestead on its hilltop, St Thomas's church in the valley, and Sydney on the horizon. Late twentieth-century owners have made Fernhill an elaborate country estate, but the important colonial framework is still discernible.

HOWARD TANNER

FERNS AND FERNERIES Ferns are distinctive plants with a fascinating evolutionary history that has long intrigued naturalists and horticulturists. While reaching their most abundant levels of diversity in the world's wet tropics, ferns are also encountered in much cooler, and sometimes drier, habitats. They exist in many forms, from tiny filmy ferns only one cell thick, to towering, twenty-metre-high tree ferns. Today's ferns belong to an ancient group of plants that date back approximately 200 million years. Pre-dating flowering plants, ferns reproduce through the production of spores rather than seeds. Although continually evolving and adapting to modern environmental conditions, many ferns are living reminders of Australia's GONDWANAN heritage. Australia is home to approximately 430 species of the estimated 9000 found world-wide. RAINFORESTS, from the wet tropics of north Qld to the cool temperate regions of western Tas., provide some of the most important habitat for the majority of Australian ferns. Many ferns prefer soil (terrestrial) while others favour the trunks and branches of trees (epiphytic) and some are quite happy on rocks (lithophytic). Generally ferns are most abundant along creeks and waterways, where moisture is assured and humidity is maintained. Some ferns—*Cheilanthes* spp. for example—have adapted to semi-ARID environments of inland Australia, possessing the ability to rejuvenate their seemingly dead foliage after rain.

In 1808 the first ferns from Australia arrived in Britain, including *Platycerium bifurcatum* (Elkhorn), still widely cultivated. Ferns became increasingly popular in Britain from the 1840s, and remained fashionable at least until the early 1900s. Through a chance discovery, Nathaniel Ward invented the WARDIAN CASE in the 1830s. This sealed glass container—much like a miniature conservatory—enabled fern enthusiasts to cultivate the more delicate ferns that required high humidity and stable atmospheres. Wardian cases were particularly useful for the cultivation of the exceptionally delicate filmy ferns (*Hymenophyllum* spp.) popular around the 1880s. Australian interest in ferns was partly due to Britain's influence on popular culture, but also due to the plentiful supply found in the wild.

Fern collecting—or 'fern hunting' as it was more melodramatically known—was a favoured pastime of both the middle class and the wealthy. The popularity of ferns led to a great demand, and many nurseries employed people who regularly collected large quantities from the wild. Fern gullies gradually became degraded from over-collecting, and in time the rarer species became locally extinct, forcing expeditions to go further abroad to find the more common species.

The massive lathed timber FERNERY at BALLARAT BOTANIC GARDENS, erected in stages during the 1870s–80s, was among the grandest of the vegetal cathedrals that graced Australia's botanic gardens during the late nineteenth and early twentieth centuries

The popularity of *Dicksonia antarctica* (Australian Soft Treefern) was due in large measure to its ease of transplantation and cultivation, requiring only to be cut off at the base, even for mature specimens (now illegal without a permit). Many trees were also felled in the rainforests of NSW and Qld simply to collect the highly prized epiphytes. The axe came down hard on vast areas of Australia's rainforests, much to the dismay of botanists and naturalists alike. However, not all fern collecting was carried out in such an unscrupulous fashion. At times, expeditions were simply rescue missions by those who could not bear to see such wonders of nature cleared, heaped, and burnt. Today the majority of ferns are grown from spores, as collection from the wild is illegal.

A graceful habit and basic cultural requirements have led to the widespread use of ferns in gardens and as INDOOR PLANTS world-wide. In Victorian times, fern collecting was a serious business, and to grow a wide variety of ferns, elaborate shade houses (or GLASSHOUSES in cooler climates) were constructed to replicate the natural environments. These specialised structures enabled collections of ferns to be displayed and propagated under suitable conditions. The earliest examples in Australia were simple BUSH-HOUSES or shade houses, providing protection from dry, hot, cutting winds while allowing adequate ventilation and necessary shading. Shaded open-air ferneries, especially in conjunction with GROTTOS or ROCKERIES, were also common in the late nineteenth century. By the 1870s many private and public gardens maintained ferneries as features, and at GEELONG and BALLARAT BOTANIC GARDENS, very large timber ferneries formed veritable cathedrals of ferns. A sophisticated example can still be seen at RIPPON LEA, where a metal-framed and timber-lathed structure of double-cusped configuration and considerable elegance contains an environment nearly forty metres in length, with naturalistic landscaping of paths, a creek, waterfalls and rockwork beds displaying more than three hundred types of ferns.

David Allen, *The Victorian Fern Craze, A History of Pteridomania* (London, 1969); Rod Ritchie, *Seeing the Rainforests in Nineteenth Century Australia* (Paddington, NSW, 1989)

ANDREW PICONE and RICHARD HEATHCOTE

FERTILISER One of the functions of SOIL is to supply PLANTS with nutrients, the chemical elements essential for plant growth. Often, the ability of a soil to supply a nutrient or nutrients is less than the plant's requirements and plant growth or performance is limited as a result. For centuries, humans have added nutrients to soils to supplement nutrient supplies. The materials used to do this are fertilisers. Originally, naturally occurring materials or plant or animal by-products (ashes, manures, blood, ground rock, COMPOSTS) were used. During the nineteenth century, as a better scientific understanding of soil and plant chemistry developed, purer sources of plant nutrients were used to supplement soil nutrient supplies (for instance, naturally occurring minerals such as potassium nitrate or rock phosphate). The agricultural and garden CHEMICAL industry then began to manufacture fertilisers. Examples are salts such as ammonium nitrate or ammonium phosphate or organic molecules such as urea. Since the 1950s, fertiliser manufacturers have developed slow-release fertilisers that can supply nutrients for extended periods of time, reducing the risks of toxicity or of leaching losses of nutrients. During the twentieth century, concerns about human impact on soil health led to the development of various alternative approaches to maintaining soil fertility. At first confined to the ORGANIC movement, many other gardeners have now adopted these practices. Irrespective of the approach taken to fertiliser use, informed decisions are needed. Ideally, fertiliser requirements are established by plant and soil analysis, but domestic and ornamental plantings are commonly fertilised on the basis of rule of thumb and prior experience.

PETER MAY

FESTIVALS with garden themes have a tradition dating from Roman times, where the fruits of the vine were celebrated. The modern sense of the word as a series of performances or events dates from the Baroque period, and it is from this tradition that Australian garden festivals indirectly descend. HORTICULTURAL SHOWS provided a forerunner to garden festivals, and although wide-ranging in their scope, these were usually of very limited duration—rarely longer than a single day. ARBOR DAY and WATTLE DAY provided other, more closely focused, precedents, while EXHIBITIONS represented an extended festival form.

The earliest and longest running Australian garden festival is Garden Week, held annually in Melbourne since 1925. During 1924 two horticultural trade exhibitions had been held in autumn and spring, and their success led to the inauguration of an annual event. Conducted under the auspices of the Nurserymen and Seedsmen's Association of Victoria, the festival had close links with the NURSERY trade, and was viewed by participants as a showcase for their products and talents. Commercial and professional organisation, rather than the honorary efforts of horticultural societies, was a key difference between garden festivals and horticultural shows, and the two continue to run parallel courses.

Local government—a third player with substantial resources and an eye to tourist promotion—instigated the second major festival, the Grafton Jacaranda Festival, NSW (1935–). Its format of a floral pageant with the crowning of a Jacaranda Princess was repeated by the Toowoomba Carnival of Flowers, Qld (1950–) and Ballarat Begonia Festival, Vic. (1953–). At Toowoomba a garden COMPETITION was held concurrently; the Ballarat festival, based at BALLARAT BOTANIC GARDENS, drew on the special expertise developed by gardens staff for tuberous begonias. In each case, local traditions developed: the floodlighting of trees at Grafton, a carnival at Toowoomba, and the annual creation of a floral carpet at Ballarat. Huon Valley Apple Festival, Cygnet, Tas. (inaugurated 1952), Mersey Valley Apple Festival, Spreyton, Tas. (inaugurated 1956), and Eaglehawk Dahlia and Arts Festival, Vic. (1972–) also capitalised on local horticultural specialties. The horticultural society tradition provided a basis for the long-running Chelsea Flower Show, Brisbane (inaugurated 1947), named after the illustrious English show and commenced in the wake of the war as a fund-raiser for Red Cross. A Floral Festival in Sydney had also commenced about the time of the Second World War.

Floriade (1987–), Canberra's month-long spring festival, features mass plantings of perennials and bulbs, and art work in

FESTIVALS with floral themes are fine mirrors of popular culture, and the float at Ballarat's 1966 Begonia Festival conveying the Queen of Begonias and quest finalists could scarcely be surpassed for its aesthetic and social significance

a picturesque lake-side setting. The Melbourne International Flower and Garden Show (1996–) is a showcase for both horticulture and landscape design, and builds on the experience—and Australian participation—of international festivals world-wide.

RA

FIELD, Barron (1786–1846), London-born judge and natural historian, was called to the bar in 1814 and was soon appointed judge of the Supreme Court of New South Wales. He and his wife arrived in Sydney in 1817, prelude to a stormy judicial career. Known to Charles Lamb, Leigh Hunt, and William Wordsworth, Field had developed a passion for poetry. Combining this with his interest in NATURAL HISTORY, he published *First Fruits of Australian Poetry* (1819). The poems 'Botany Bay Flowers' and 'The Kangaroo' extravagantly described such plants as the native heath (*Epacris longifolia*) and fringed violets (*Thysanotus* spp.), and such animals as the kangaroo, platypus, and 'sooty swan', provoking the cruel criticism: 'Thy poems, Barron Field, I've read/And thus adjudge their mead:/Such a crop proclaims thy head/A barren field indeed.' Undaunted, Field published a second edition (1823), again anonymously. He served as president of the Agricultural Society of New South Wales (1822) and was active in the short-lived Philosophical Society of Australia, precursor of the Royal Society of New South Wales, taking special interest (with poetic effusion) in the Society's project of erecting a memorial at Kurnell in 1822 to 'James Cook and Joseph BANKS, the Columbus and Maecenas of their time'. Field returned to England in 1824 where, after further judical appointments in Ceylon and Gibraltar, he retired.

Field's signal contribution to natural history was to compile *Geographical Memoirs of New South Wales* (1825) 'by various hands', including his own. Included were geographical, geological, meteorological, astronomical, anthropological, and botanical papers, and Field's accounts of his own journeys, revealing a conscious attempt to understand, though 'neither botanist nor poet truly', why the dominant trees of the bush were 'all as unpicturesque as the shrubs and flowers are beautiful'. He loved the Illawarra RAINFORESTS, but considered 'Australia is a land of contrarieties, where the laws of nature seem reversed'. Of more scientific significance were two papers by Allan CUNNINGHAM, a journal, and 'A Specimen of the Indigenous Botany …' with illustrations and descriptions of new species, including *Fieldia australis*. Some of Field's plant specimens are preserved at Oxford.

LIONEL GILBERT

FIELD NATURALISTS' CLUBS AND SOCIETIES

When Europeans began to establish gardens in Australia they knew and liked very little about its indigenous plants, and maintained a strong desire to keep them beyond the fence line. As gardens proliferated, the AUSTRALIAN FLORA was fitted into taxonomic categories, and sometimes the garden. While ROYAL SOCIETIES considered flora and fauna in a wider context, other groups—then very popular in Britain—arose to focus solely on NATURAL HISTORY. From 1880, Australian naturalists' and field naturalists' clubs, societies, and royal society sections provided meetings and field excursions to present and discuss natural history specimens and observations. Generations of members interested in plants on both sides of the garden fence have learned about Australian plants through field naturalist activities and publications.

Although some groups metamorphosed or died, the earliest still survives—the Field Naturalists' Club of Victoria (FNCV, established 1880), publisher of the *Victorian Naturalist* (1884–). Established by a group of friends who enjoyed bush rambles and informal meetings where they discussed their catch of specimens, its fifty-four original members—whose wide range of occupations included pharmacy and medicine, publishing and photography, religion and science—enjoyed monthly meetings and excursions, including 'field days' at Brighton, Oakleigh, and other rail-accessible, subsequently suburbanised areas round Melbourne, and 'camp-outs' as far afield as King Island and east Gippsland. MUELLER helped identify plant specimens collected. Early kindred Victorian societies included Ballarat Field Club and Science Society (1882) at Ballarat's School of Mines, and Geelong Field Naturalists' Club (1880), briefly associated with Gordon (Technical) College, which published the *Geelong Naturalist* (1891–1931).

A short-lived Sydney society echoed FNCV rules. In 1881 the Field Naturalists' Club (called sometimes Naturalists' Field Club) held field days and monthly meetings at Sydney's Mechanics' School of Arts. Later, the Natural History Association (1887), formed in association with that School, became the Field Naturalists' Society of New South Wales (1890). Encouraging 'the study of nature and the collection, preservation, and systematic classification of specimens' it organised excursions by tram, train, and steamer to accessible districts, including Manly, the Botany Swamps, Shark Island, and Parramatta, but, like other naturalists' groups, did not survive the 1890s depression.

In the 1890s natural history societies existed in Perth (re-emerging as the Mueller Botanic Society), Adelaide (Boys' Field Club), Rockhampton (Qld), and Brisbane, while in SA and Qld royal societies had field naturalists' sections. Professor Ralph TATE successfully led moves to establish the Field Naturalists' Section of the Royal Society of South Australia (1883) which, decades before its conversion to the Field Naturalists' Society of South Australia (FNSSA, 1959), began producing the *South Australian Naturalist* (1919–). Colonial Botanist F.M. BAILEY inspired and led the shorter-lived Field Naturalists' Section of Queensland's Royal Society (1886), whose excursions were predominantly botanical. Members collected specimens of many hundreds of species around Brisbane, and in the early 1890s construction of the Brisbane–Gympie railway line made rich RAINFORESTS accessible, facilitating extensive plant collections from which Bailey documented many new species.

Early in the twentieth century state clubs were established in NSW (1900), Tas. (1904), and Qld (1906), and began publishing their *Australian Naturalist* (1906–64), *Tasmanian Naturalist* (1907–), and *Queensland Naturalist* (1922–). Government Botanists RODWAY and WHITE were leading members of the Tasmanian and Queensland clubs. The New South Wales Naturalists' Club amalgamated with the Flora Society in 1912 and became the Naturalists' Society of New South Wales, which the Wildlife Preservation Society incorporated in 1964.

Western Australia's Mueller Botanic Society published a plant list in its *Journal* (1899–1903) and was renamed West Australian Natural History Society (1903), and then Natural History and Science Society of Western Australia (1909), which held meetings and field excursions until its 1914 conversion to the Royal Society of Western Australia. A decade later Dominic Louis Serventy (b. 1904) set up the Western Australian Naturalists' Club, which attracted many Royal Society members and later published the *Western Australian Naturalist* (1947–). Club 'recorders' were responsible for naming and discussing members' specimens: Walter Mervyn Carne (1885–1952) identified fungi, WEEDS, and economic plants, and C.A. GARDNER native plants. A group of ORCHID enthusiasts developed around Emily PELLOE and contributed to the orchid display she organised annually at the Royal Show. More recently, the Northern Territory Field Naturalists' Club

(1977) in Darwin published the *Northern Territory Naturalist* (1978–).

Before the Second World War, several regional clubs were established, including Barrier Field Naturalists' Club (1918) by Albert MORRIS at Broken Hill (NSW), and North Queensland Naturalists' Club (1932) by Hugo Flecker (1884–1957) in Cairns. In the optimistic post-war years regional clubs proliferated, including the Launceston Field Naturalists' Club (1949), whose members collected extensively for the Endemic Flora of Tasmania project financed by their patron Lord TALBOT DE MALAHIDE. A huge meeting organised by Morwell Horticultural Society established Victoria's Latrobe Valley Field Naturalists' Club (1960). During the 1960s, fourteen western Victorian clubs federated, more than twenty Victorian clubs affiliated with the FNCV, and six clubs affiliated with the FNSSA.

HERBARIUM and BOTANIC GARDEN staff were often club members. So too were NATURE STUDY teachers in city and country schools, and some clubs had junior groups for students. Many clubs had specialist groups, often including BOTANY and nature PHOTOGRAPHY. The FNCV also had standing committees on MARANOA GARDENS and NATIONAL PARKS, and groups on wildflower gardens and native plant preservation. Pleased that Victoria's Country Roads Board had 'made a garden of considerable interest' by fencing a patch of blue orchids by the Hume Highway, Winifred WADDELL established the FNCV's Wildflower (later Native Plants) Preservation Group (1949), which became the Native Plants Preservation Society of Victoria (1952).

An increasing awareness of environmental threats to species and their habitats ensured that by the mid-twentieth century, naturalists' groups aimed to conserve, as well as observe, the indigenous flora. Australian flora and wildlife reserves, sanctuaries, and national parks bear eloquent witness to clubs' successful conservation efforts, without which Australia's botanical heritage would be the poorer.

Field naturalists' clubs continue to shape our understanding of the indigenous flora in several important ways. Specimens collected by members have enriched club, regional, and state herbaria. Club journals carry indigenous botanical records in excursion reports, botanical surveys, and sometimes descriptions of new taxa. Mueller published descriptions of more than 100 new species of Australian plants in the *Victorian Naturalist*, where WILLIS and others have since described hundreds more. As well as carrying Flecker's census of north Queensland plants, the *North Queensland Naturalist* (1932–92) included descriptions of orchids and other new species. In 1971, when Flecker's name was given to CAIRNS BOTANIC GARDEN, the North Queensland Club's huge herbarium, including twenty-four type specimens, was incorporated into CSIRO's new tropical herbarium in Atherton.

Reliable information about the distribution and rarity of indigenous plants is crucial for conservation-compatible land use decisions so that species are not pushed to extinction. After publication of the FNCV Plant Names Committee's *A Census of the Plants of Victoria with their Regional Distribution and Vernacular Names* (1923), the *Victorian Naturalist* carried further taxonomic and distribution information, and in the 1980s the Western Victorian Field Naturalists' Clubs Association facilitated a breath-taking project—the survey of Victoria's flora, region by region, by long-standing member of the Portland Field Naturalists' Club, (Alexander) Clifford Beauglehole (b. 1920). He was helped by regional field naturalists' clubs, and published hundreds of name changes and new records for Victoria's flora in the *Victorian Naturalist*. Clubs have also stimulated public interest in native plants and their conservation through spectacular wildflower exhibitions, informative public and classroom discussions, and popular plant books.

LINDEN GILLBANK

FIGS consist of species of the large, mostly tropical genus *Ficus*, mostly trees or, less commonly, shrubs or climbers. The ficus of the ancients was the edible fig of the MEDITERRANEAN, its name formalised by Linnaeus as *Ficus carica*. At least one CULTIVAR of edible fig was brought to Australia by the First Fleet; they proved hardy under local conditions and at least sixteen cultivars were available by the mid-nineteenth century. Australia has forty-two native *Ficus* species, thirty-three confined to the tropics and only one (*F. coronata*) extending south as far as Vic. Best known is *F. macrophylla* (Moreton Bay Fig), named in 1807 from a plant cultivated in Paris, its source probably the Illawarra or Hunter region of NSW (native there as well as at Moreton Bay). Described by MUELLER as 'Perhaps the grandest of Australian avenue-trees', it was planted in warm-temperate regions around the world, and by the mid-twentieth century some huge specimens were recorded. The closely allied *F. rubiginosa* (Port Jackson or Rusty Fig) is a common tree of the Sydney region, where it also makes fine park specimens; it is noteworthy for its habit of self-seeding above the ground, commonly on brick walls, rock cuttings, and palm crowns. Planting of figs in PUBLIC PARKS and large gardens reached its height in the late nineteenth and early twentieth centuries: J.H. MAIDEN wrote an enthusiastic article in 1908 on suitable species in the *Agricultural Gazette* (NSW). From the 1920s to the 1950s another native fig, *F. microcarpa* var. *hillii* (Hill's Fig), was in vogue, at least in Sydney and Brisbane (where it had been found in a city park and first named *F. hillii* by F.M. BAILEY in 1891). In city parks of TROPICAL Australia are found some fine specimens of *F. benghalensis* (Banyan) with its spectacular multiple trunks.

TONY RODD

FILM has been associated with gardens from the end of the nineteenth century, when PLEASURE GARDENS were in vogue. In these, patrons could wander along the paths among the garden beds, pausing for conversation and refreshments at food stalls or at stages to watch vaudeville performances. They catered for huge crowds: at Perth's Ye Olde Englishe Fayre more than 6000 were in attendance on the night of 8 February 1897, to enjoy films of the 1896 Melbourne Cup. Their successors were the 'picture gardens', which were popular in all states by the First World War. In small communities this was sometimes the only venue; but larger settlements (both suburban and rural) could afford gardens as well as a building, usually working in tandem: the gardens open in fine weather, the hall in cold or wet weather. Some of these were

Isabelle Huppert and Robert Menzies star in the FILM *Cactus* (1986), directed by Paul Cox, in which untouchable beauty is the central theme of a love affair involving a blind CACTUS fancier

gardens only in name: they were simply a corrugated iron fence surrounding rows of deckchairs on bare ground facing a large screen. But some were true gardens, the seats placed on well-kept lawns, the screen surrounded by garden beds and the fences covered with flowering creepers. These survived in some areas longer than in others, notably in WA (such as the SUN PICTURE GARDENS, Broome), NT, and Qld, where the weather was more reliable. Some continued long enough to benefit from the 1990s revival in seasonal open air entertainments. Thus Mosman Park Picture Gardens (WA) was one of those to reopen after many years, and the ROYAL BOTANIC GARDENS, MELBOURNE, was one of several public venues to offer film presentations in summer.

Meanwhile, gardens themselves were being recorded on film, the subject of early documentaries, amateur footage, and professional newsreels—sources rarely consulted by GARDEN HISTORIANS. The MCKAY MEMORIAL GARDENS (Vic.), for example, appeared on film during the 1930s, with halating dahlias dazzling the local audience. Amateur film-making increased following the Second World War, and 16mm colour film (introduced into Australia by Kodak in 1935) was a popular medium for early films of Australian flora, where the rich palette of, say, WA wildflowers, could be brought to a horticultural society audience previously content with hand-coloured lantern slides. With the advent of Super 8 film in the 1960s and 1970s, and video from the 1980s, gardens again became popular locations and themes for home movies.

Gardens also appeared incidentally, but significantly, in feature films. From the silent days, private gardens were often class markers. Perhaps the most obvious example is the contrast between the dusty vacant lot that forms the playground for the Woolloomooloo children in *The Kid Stakes* (1927), and the magnificent garden of the Potts Point mansion, where the children's goat wreaks such havoc among the carefully tended roses, and where they dress quickly among the bushes after an illicit dip in the private swimming pool while the gardener fumes. Similarly, the terraced garden of the mansion in *The Woman Suffers* (1918) reminds viewers that wealth did not necessarily bring happiness. There are telling glimpses of public gardens in feature films, too. In the 1919 version of *The Sentimental Bloke*, the Bloke rests on a park bench in SYDNEY BOTANIC GARDENS, watching promenading girls, and in the 1932 version, Melbourne's FITZROY GARDENS is the location for some comic–dramatic business. After the feature film revival of the early 1970s, gardens were used to evoke a particular historic period in a costume drama: thus exteriors were filmed in the grounds of MARTINDALE HALL (SA) for *Picnic at Hanging Rock* (1975), and in *The Getting of Wisdom* (1977) Laura Tweedle Rambotham (Susannah Fowle) runs from her oppressive schooling into a freer future in the gardens outside.

In more recent Australian films, gardens have occasionally played a more substantial role in theme and content. The theme of the TREE in Jane Campion's *Sweetie* (1989) or the tragic desolation of the BACKYARD in *Muriel's Wedding* (1994) are powerful examples. Director Paul Cox has made telling use of plants and gardens in his films, often as a means of evoking larger themes such as decay and renewal. His *Man of Flowers* (1983) strongly draws on botanical and horticultural references, while *Cactus* (1986) contains both gentle parody of the CACTUS and Succulent Society and far more subtle and powerful images of blindness and tactility. Kathryn Millard's *Parklands* (1996) draws on this more subtle thematic use of gardens to evoke the character of Adelaide in the 1960s. Finally, the professional gardener has appeared as a major figure in two films of the 1990s. No matter how irritated viewers may be at Lenny's (Mark Little's) incompetence, all gardeners will sympathise with his plight as the greens at the bowling club turn yellow-brown despite his best endeavours in *Greenkeeping* (1993). The final sequence of *The Sum of Us* (1994) not only shows us Greg (John Polson) at work planting, but draws back into a crane shot over the gardens, with the Sydney Opera House in the distance, and a sense of Jeff's (Russell Crowe's) hope and joy encapsulated in the image of nature's beauty and abundance.

Brian McFarlane, Geoff Mayer, and Ina Bertrand (eds), *The Oxford Companion to Australian Film* (Melbourne, 1999)

INA BERTRAND

FINEDON, Frank (*c.* 1864–1935), proprietor of the Victoria Nursery, West Maitland (NSW), arrived from Britain as an assisted immigrant in 1886. His lasting achievement was *The Australian Kitchen Garden* (1897), a substantial guide to VEGETABLE GARDENING with illustrations provided by William ADAMSON and a tabular monthly calendar of operations from Thomas LANG and Co. The *Australasian* praised the publication, citing its 'plain practical manner', while the author's preface drew attention to his especial treatment of salad plants. RA

FIRE is a significant ecological factor that has shaped the evolution of plant species and affected the development of whole plant communities in Australia. The advent of ABORIGINAL ENVIRONMENTAL MANAGEMENT heralded a marked increase in the frequency of fire, and within a far shorter time span, the introduction of European land management practices has also seen fire as a significant environmental issue.

The role of fire is a factor that can affect vegetation just as much as soil type, rainfall, and temperature. The frequency of fire and the intensity of its heat are two primary determinants that influence the impact of fire on vegetation. Vegetation may be scorched—where the plants are affected by a blast of hot air and are not really burnt—or they may be singed, causing superficial burning of plant tissues such as foliage, fruits, or bark. While these processes are often not lethal, burning causes irreversible changes to the composition of plant tissues due to the high temperatures. Although fire is often described as destructive by the popular press and other media—and urbanisation of many bushfire-prone areas has led to many tragic deaths and property losses—this is rarely the case when a natural fire burns through an AUSTRALIAN PLANT community. While some species and certain individual specimens may be damaged or even killed by the fire, Australian plants and plant communities have evolved to cope with fire, and their recovery is usually both rapid and complete. Indeed some communities can only exist because of the periodic occurrence of fire of an appropriate intensity.

In relation to gardens and other designed landscapes, it must be recognised that fire will periodically occur and affect both native and exotic vegetation. It is imperative that the role of fire is properly understood, and that vegetation be managed—both with predictive strategies before fire occurs, and management strategies after fires establish. Some plants, such as many ACACIA species and the gum-barked EUCALYPTS, are very sensitive to fire, as are many of the exotic CONIFERS. However, other eucalypts, many deciduous species, and even some of the conifers (such as redwoods and the deciduous conifers) are quite capable of recovering from serious fires. South-eastern Australia and parts of WA are among the most fire-prone places on the planet. Major bushfires have affected gardens in the ADELAIDE HILLS, MOUNT MACEDON, and Victoria's Dandenong Ranges, as well as in the outskirts of Sydney and Brisbane. Many of the gardens in these areas can be described as HILL-STATION gardens, and the fact that they are hilly and forested makes them likely candidates for regular major fires.

'When the fire took the fencing, Joe asked dad if he didn't think it a splendid sight': an ironic view of FIRE depicted by illustrator A.H. Fullwood in *On Our Selection* (1899) by Arthur H. Davis ('Steele Rudd')

Fire can be a significant regenerative influence on native plant communities, and the thoughtful gardener needs to consider the role of fire and the adaptations that so many species—both native and exotic—possess, in the proper management of parks, gardens, and designed landscapes both before and after fire. Such an approach, especially in areas of high risk, would be reflected in both the selection of species and the garden design. Fire will always be part of the ecology in many Australian regions, and this knowledge should inform land use and management decisions.

Stephen J. Pyne, *Burning Bush: A Fire History of Australia* (New York, 1991) GREG MOORE

FISCHER, (Detlef) Ludwig Theodor (1809–1902), gardener and botanist, was born in Treetz, Holstein, Denmark. Apprenticed at the Hamburg Botanic Garden, he worked in gardens in the Netherlands, Nymphenburg Garden near Munich, and Schönbrunn, Vienna, before being appointed head gardener at the University of Kiel's BOTANIC GARDEN in 1832. Migrating to SA in 1848, he settled at Bugle Ranges adjacent to properties owned by Ferdinand MUELLER and

Friedrich KRICHAUFF. He started collecting specimens for Mueller and was the first to propose the genus *Duttonia*, named by Mueller. Fischer established fruit tree nurseries at Macclesfield, Strathalbyn, and Mount Barker, in particular raising Gravenstein and Calville Blanche apples. Old age and total blindness forced him to reside with his son-in-law Krichauff in Norwood for several years before his death.

DAVID JONES

FITZALAN, Eugene Fitzherbert Albini (1830–1911), botanical collector, horticulturist, and nursery proprietor, was born at Londonderry, Ireland. He was trained in the gardens of the Earl of Enniskillen and at the VEITCH nursery, Chelsea (London). Motivated by his interest in botany, he joined others going to Mexico to search for new species in Latin America. On returning to England, he decided to go to Australia, arriving in Vic. in 1849 with plants he had been commissioned to bring. He settled in Geelong, working in vineyards and laying out several gardens there and in Melbourne. During a botanical trip he met MUELLER, establishing a lifelong friendship. Fitzalan's next enterprise came in 1855, when he took up tenancy of a thirty-acre (12 ha) portion of land on the Barwon River, Geelong, which he named Elvaston Gardens (presumably after William Barron's celebrated garden at Derbyshire, England). Here he established a PLEASURE GARDEN with seats and bowers, and where tea and refreshments were supplied. It doubled as a nursery stocked with fruit trees, flowers, bulbs, and herbs, but before the year closed Fitzalan was insolvent and the entire stock was sold.

Fitzalan left for Qld. in 1859 and opened a seed and plant shop in Brisbane. In 1860 he joined the schooner *Spitfire*, commanded by Lieutenant J.W. Smith, as botanical collector, going as far north as Port Denison before returning to Brisbane. Specimens collected during the expedition were sent to Mueller, who prepared an essay, saying 'by the zealous exertions of Mr Fitzalan, botanical collections were formed of so considerable interest, that I deemed the material sufficient for the issue of a special document on its elucidation'. When the Queensland Government formed a settlement at Port Denison (renamed Bowen in 1861), Fitzalan, his wife, and three children were among the first party of settlers. Fitzalan purchased land at Bowen, cultivated his plants, and made plant-hunting journeys up the northern coast, his particular interest being ORCHIDS. In 1887 he left his large nursery garden and moved to Cairns, where he established another nursery garden and from where, during a ten-year residency, he exported large numbers of orchids, palms and palm seeds, ferns, and other plants. Fitzalan then retired to South Brisbane, where he lived until his death. That Fitzalan's collections were so highly regarded by Mueller attests to the validity of this tribute by J.H. MAIDEN: 'He was one of those botanical pioneers to whom Australian, and particularly Queensland botany owes much'. *Randia fitzalanii* (syn. *Gardenia fitzalanii*), *Psychotria fitzalanii* (syn. *Uragoga fitzalanii*), *Eulophia fitzalanii* (syn. *Graphorkis fitzalanii*), and the orchid *Eria fitzalanii* were named for him.

Gertrude Kelly, *Eugene Fitzalan: Botanist, Pioneer & Poet 1830–1911* (Bowen, Qld, n.d.)

GEORGE JONES

FITZGERALD, Robert David (1830–1892), surveyor, orchidologist, and botanical artist, was born in Tralee, Ireland, and, in 1856, after studying civil engineering at Queens College, Cork, migrated to Sydney. He soon obtained a position as draftsman in the Surveyor-General's section of the NSW Lands Department and, advancing through promotions, was given charge of the roads branch (1868) and became Deputy Surveyor-General (1873), a position he held until the office was abolished in 1887.

In Ireland, Fitzgerald had been a keen ornithologist, and upon his arrival in Australia he took an interest in her NATURAL HISTORY, developing his talent as a delineator of living plants, not only depicting their parts but representing plants in their natural habitats. For the HORTICULTURAL MAGAZINE he contributed lithographs (1866–68) that formed the earliest illustrations in an Australian GARDEN MAGAZINE. In 1864 he accompanied survey draftsman Walter Scott Campbell (1844–1935) to Wallis Lake, north of Newcastle (NSW), and in 1869 he visited Lord Howe Island with Charles MOORE and William CARRON, collecting FERNS and PALMS, among

An engraved view of Lord Howe Island, after a sketch by Robert FITZGERALD (1869), depicting Kentia palms, figs, and the native pandanus collected on a PACIFIC ISLAND expedition undertaken in the company of Charles MOORE and William CARRON

other specimens. Fitzgerald returned to the island in 1871 and again in 1876, making botanical collections. He discovered *Sarcochilus fitzgeraldi* near the head of the Bellinger River in northern NSW, and as he devoted more time to the study of ORCHIDS, he travelled to every Australian colony. From *c*. 1872 Robert Fitzgerald and his family lived at Hunters Hill (NSW), in a prefabricated timber house that had originally been erected in the grounds of the Paris Industrial EXHIBITION (1854). This house was set in about two acres (0.8 ha) of a naturalistic garden he developed, and Fitzgerald excavated a 'remarkable fernery' in the sandstone rock. Roofed with glass and watered from a large tank that trickled water down the walls among his handwork of artificial rock, Fitzgerald grew hundreds of species of ferns, mosses, orchids, and other plants.

Dedicated to Charles DARWIN, the first volume of Fitzgerald's monumental *Australian Orchids* was issued in seven parts between 1875 and 1882, and four parts of the second volume were issued prior to his death; a fifth part was published posthumously by his friend Henry Deane (1847–1924). These gave detailed descriptions and illustrations of 183 species and subspecies. Fitzgerald drew the first lithographs on stone, and hand-coloured the prints himself, though later lithographs were the work of Arthur Stopps (1833–1931) and were hand-coloured by artists from Fitzgerald's instructions and sample sheets. This work drew praise from both George BENTHAM and J.D. HOOKER; Hooker considering it 'a work which would be an honour to any country and any botanist'.

COLLEEN MORRIS

FITZHARDINGE (née MacMASTER), Olive Rose (1881–1956), rose hybridist of Warrawee (NSW), bred and introduced several Hybrid Tea roses—under her husband's name, Mrs Hardinge Fitzhardinge—with the aim of 'hoping to raise Roses stronger and more suited to our land of sunshine'. She worked from her small suburban garden, and the roses were introduced commercially by the HAZLEWOOD Nursery, Epping (NSW), and some by Conrad Pyle at his West Grove nursery, Pennsylvania (USA). Registered varieties included 'Warrawee' (1935); 'Lady Gowrie', 'Lubra', 'Mrs C.E. Prell', 'Prudence' (1938); and 'Captain Bligh', 'Governor Philip', 'Lady Edgeworth David', 'Sirius' (1939). 'Warrawee' and 'Lubra' are her only roses still commercially available in Australia.

TREVOR NOTTLE

FITZPATRICK (née JOHNSON), (Alice) May (1910–1985), tropical gardening enthusiast, newspaper columnist, and foundation president of Darwin Garden Club (1958), was born in Leongatha (Vic.) and arrived in the NT in 1943. She settled in Darwin in 1949, and lived there for thirty-one years. Like Nancy EDDY, she educated herself, mainly by reading South African gardening texts and by experimentation in her home garden. Through her work for the Darwin Garden Club, which met monthly in members' gardens 'to exchange ideas, slips and seeds' and awarded various gardening prizes, May Fitzpatrick contributed significantly towards the greening of a city that had suffered extensive environmental damage during the Second World War. Darwin was then dominated by public servants on short-term transfers and, recognising that gardening in the TROPICS was a challenge to newcomers, she shared her local knowledge through articles (under the name Alice-May) in the *Northern Territory News* (1957–72), later compiled as *Gardening in Darwin* (1985). She was also the driving force behind production of a cookbook, *Darwin Gardeners Gourmet Guide* (1978), detailing the cultivation and culinary preparation of fruit and vegetables particularly suited to local requirements.

JAN SETO AND ANITA ANGEL

FITZROY GARDENS, Hobart, was developed into a PUBLIC PARK only after plans by the colonial government early in the nineteenth century to create a BOTANIC GARDEN on the site failed (the adjoining Garden Crescent was named in anticipation). In 1834 Lieutenant-Governor Arthur deferred a request to develop the garden, and in 1840 the reserve was leased for grazing. Further initiatives by local residents to develop part of the reserve as a PROMENADE and pleasure ground—although approved in 1851—also never eventuated, and by 1854 the land was offered to the ROYAL SOCIETY of Van Diemen's Land for a museum with botanic and ZOOLOGICAL GARDENS. Two years later, the Society decided the site was not sufficiently central; the area then became a rubbish dump, and eventually the land was handed over to the City of Hobart (1886). In 1901 the mayor suggested plans be prepared for the laying out of the reserve so the area could be made 'attractive and ornamental'—the landscape genesis of this genteel, English-style park, fronting an elegant Georgian crescent, with sweeping views across Sandy Bay, Battery Point, and the River Derwent.

SALLYANN DAKIS

FITZROY GARDENS, near Melbourne's Parliament House, occupies land set aside by 1848 for public RECREATION. Clement HODGKINSON began laying gardens out in 1859, discarding Edward La Trobe BATEMAN's plan prepared when the twenty-six-hectare reserve was briefly under Melbourne City Council control. Fences kept out stray livestock and the paths, which connected surrounding streets, were also fenced to control behaviour and keep visitors out of extensive uncultivated areas. It was a garden of trees with few flowers. Remnant indigenous eucalypts were retained, and while most new planting was evergreen (especially conifers), elms lined many paths. An eroded creek bed carrying street run-off was converted to a fern gully. Numerous cement copies of antique statues were positioned along the paths, and a classical bandstand, rotunda, and fountains stocked with goldfish contributed to the ornamentation. Two staff lodges were also built, one (now demolished) occupied by gardener James SINCLAIR.

By the time John GUILFOYLE succeeded Nicholas BICKFORD as curator (1891), the trees were overcrowded, with many in poor condition. Guilfoyle introduced a different character, mainly around the principal walks, featuring massed flowers, ribbon borders, dramatic foliage plants in the SUBTROPICAL style, and lawns. He enlarged and relocated the nursery, and excavated its old site to form a pond and mound

The ITALIANATE character of Melbourne's FITZROY GARDENS, evident in the 1870s through the use of statuary, a classical ROTUNDA, and conifer plantings, faded in the early twentieth century as sweeping lawns replaced crumbling antique figures and senescent pines

planted with rhododendrons. A kiosk incorporating another bandstand was built in 1908—a period when public toilets were built and fences dismantled. Yet two-thirds of Fitzroy Gardens were still relatively uncultivated when Melbourne City Council acquired complete control of most inner city reserves in 1917. The changes Guilfoyle initiated were completed during J.T. SMITH's curatorship; garden beds and lawn replaced thousands of trees. Moreton Bay figs were removed—smaller, tidier species being preferred—and Hodgkinson's statues disappeared, although not without controversy. A propagator's lodge was built in 1928, the conservatory in 1930, and 'Captain Cook's Cottage' was re-erected nearby in 1934.

In 1929 the Council assumed control of the adjacent six-hectare **Treasury Gardens**. Laid out in 1867 by Hodgkinson and similar in concept to its larger neighbour—but without statues or fountains—it was subsequently managed by the director of MELBOURNE BOTANIC GARDENS. William GUILFOYLE built a JAPANESE Garden around the pond in 1902, but little else had changed when Council employed some of the growing numbers of jobless men to clear the 'beautiful bit of unspoilt nature' and bring it to a similar level of cultivation as Fitzroy Gardens. After the Second World War, the Japanese Garden was bulldozed; Fitzroy Gardens was simplified, with some paths and garden beds being grassed, and herbaceous perennials being replaced with shrubs. Of all Melbourne's PUBLIC PARKS AND GARDENS, these two have long been seen as representative of its garden city image, inspiring affection and a place in the public imagination.

GEORGINA WHITEHEAD

FIVEASH, Rosa Catherine (1854–1938), botanical artist, trained at the Adelaide School of Art and Design and taught privately. Fiveash was invited to illustrate J.E. BROWN's *The Forest Flora of South Australia* (1882–90), and her services were increasingly sought by scientists, including E.C. STIRLING, J.M. BLACK, botanist Edgar Ravenswood Waite (1866–1928), and orchidologist Richard Sanders Rogers (1861–1942). Lord Tennyson and Robert Barr Smith donated a collection of her works to the South Australian Art Gallery (1900), and she presented a portfolio to the state (1937) including illustrations republished as *Australian Orchids* (1974).

DAVID JONES

FLAGSTAFF GARDENS, one of Melbourne's oldest PUBLIC GARDENS, became a popular resort when a flagstaff was raised on the hilltop in 1840 to signal between harbour and town, and hence the scene of celebrations upon news of Victoria's separation from NSW. The settlement's first burial ground was also located on the site—now marked by a memorial erected in 1871. After its use as a magnetic observatory, local residents petitioned the government in 1862 to develop the derelict seven-hectare reserve as gardens. Although not as elaborate as FITZROY GARDENS and with different topography, Clement HODGKINSON prepared and implemented a plan using similar features. West Melbourne Bowling Club was permitted to occupy 0.5 ha in 1867. Substantial changes to the Gardens' character occurred under John GUILFOYLE and J.T. SMITH, and after the Second World War. City buildings now hide the panoramic views once enjoyed from the hilltop.

GEORGINA WHITEHEAD

FLEMING, James (*c.* 1758–*c.* 1803), convict gardener, transported from London for seven years for stealing clover seeds, arrived in Sydney in 1800. Employed by Governor King as a gardener at Parramatta, he was botanist on the Colonial

Schooner *Cumberland* (1802–03), under surveyor Charles Grimes (1772–1858), mapping vegetation and writing the report of the journey to the Kent and King Islands and Port Phillip Bay. Fleming made the first description of the northern parts of that bay, and at the Yarra Falls, Studley Park, sowed seeds of European 'greens'. In Sydney he made detailed lists of ornamental and useful European plants found at the time in the colony (recorded in the Brabourne collection of Banks papers, Mitchell Library). He also prepared live plants for Sir Joseph BANKS. Pardoned on the way home tending these plants on the *Glatton*, he was much recommended 'as a good Gardener and Botanist' by Rev. Samuel Marsden (1764–1838).

SOPHIE C. DUCKER

FLETCHER JONES GARDENS, Warrnambool, Vic., were developed from 1948 by clothing manufacturer (David) Fletcher Jones (1895–1977) around his Pleasant Hill works. The unpromising site was filled and levelled to accommodate neatly mown lawns, rockeries, low-shrub planting, a sunken lily pond, and pergola. Sculptures such as the Sputnik (a tall, triangular metal fountain), Sphere & Trilon (copied from the 1938 Chicago World Fair), and a large tripodal water tank (1967) complemented the sculptural qualities of the factory buildings. A quintessential FJ man—in bas-relief near the lily pond—subtly brought the image of permanent press trousers and crisply pressed shirts into the open: garden and product reinforced each other. Rose beds featured, and the lawn was dotted with floral BASKETS, spaced like sunbathers on a crowded beach trying hard, but never quite succeeding, to maintain the least possible contact with their neighbours. Neatness ruled, and the garden became a model for the post-war generation of SUBURBAN GARDENERS of a style later christened by George SEDDON 'Fletcherian' or 'Blackpool municipal'.

RA

FLOCKTON, Margaret Lilian (1861–1953), botanical artist and illustrator, born in England, the daughter of an artist, studied art (including lithography) at the South Kensington Art School. In 1881 she accompanied her sister to Sydney, where she worked for seven years as a commercial artist for printing and publishing firms. She then opened a studio, where her students included J.H. MAIDEN's daughter. In the 1890s her paintings, including WILDFLOWER studies, appeared in the annual exhibitions of the Art Society of New South Wales.

She worked at SYDNEY BOTANIC GARDENS (1901–27) preparing lithographs for Maiden's two 8-volume series, *Forest Flora of New South Wales* (77 parts, 1902–25) and *A Critical Revision of the Genus Eucalyptus* (75 parts, 1903–31), in which he acknowledged her as 'practically a joint author'. Plate 69 of the *Critical Revision* included her meticulous representations of foliage, flowers, and fruit of a new Western Australian variety that Maiden had named in honour of 'the accomplished artist' of his two masterworks. In 1915 he raised her taxonomic reward to specific rank and established the new species—*Eucalyptus flocktoniae*—which Thistle HARRIS included among the 'lovely smooth-barked' eucalypts in her *Australian Plants for the Garden* (1953). With a high reputation as a lithographer, Flockton continued its long tradition of use by botanical illustrators into a period when it was not a common art form. She published a small book, *Australian Wild Flowers* (1908), containing twelve plates printed by colour lithography, which were reproduced as large lithographs and as an 'Art Series' of postcards.

LINDEN GILLBANK

FLORA: see AUSTRALIAN FLORA and HERBARIUM

FLORAL CLOCKS, though relatively few in number, have been a popular novelty in Australian PUBLIC PARKS AND

The FLETCHER JONES GARDENS, Warrnambool (Vic.), developed from 1948 to beautify a clothing factory, remain a popular feature: the vision of subdued and ordered nature they present is a recurring theme in Australian SUBURBAN GARDENS

GARDENS throughout most of the twentieth century. Horologically functional and usually several metres in diameter, they were incorporated into landscaped banks with the dial decorated seasonally with thousands of small plants in the carpet BEDDING manner. The idea of making a floral clock dates from the late nineteenth century. Important early examples were found at Water Works Park, Detroit, USA (1893, built by Elbridge Scribner) and the extant clock at West Princess Street Gardens, Edinburgh (1903, built by John McHattie). The earliest floral clocks in Australia date from the late 1920s and include the extant example at Sydney's Taronga Zoo (1928) and the now-removed example at Melbourne's Royal Agricultural Showground (1930). Floral clocks also feature in Melbourne's DOMAIN, BALLARAT BOTANIC GARDENS, ROYAL TASMANIAN BOTANICAL GARDENS, and Perth's KINGS PARK.   SILAS CLIFFORD-SMITH

FLORAL EMBLEMS Heraldic designs have traditionally assumed an arrangement of visual devices unique to a person or place to express identity. One of the most successful devices in establishing national identity throughout history has been the botanical motif—be it the English rose, the French fleur-de-lis, the Indian lotus, the Welsh leek, or the Canadian maple leaf. AUSTRALIAN FLORA has likewise resulted in rich experimentation and tradition in ART, the DECORATIVE ARTS, and LITERATURE.

Australia's first coat-of-arms, proclaimed in 1908, was devoid of floral ornament. It was replaced in 1912 by a second version, incorporating the badges of the six states against a background of wattle. The choice of wattle was the result of spirited public debate between the members of the WATTLE DAY League, established in Melbourne, and R.T. BAKER and his NSW supporters, who considered the waratah a more fitting national symbol. Official recognition for Golden Wattle (*Acacia pycnantha*) as Australia's national flower was not formally granted until the bicentenary of European settlement (1988).

The first state to proclaim a floral emblem was Vic. Although the Scarlet Bottlebrush (*Callistemon macropunctatus*) had been proposed in 1931, the Common Heath (*Epacris impressa*) was officially recognised in 1958. Qld marked its statehood centenary (1959) with the formal adoption of the Cooktown Orchid (*Dendrobium bigibbum*). Other floral emblems formally adopted were the MANGLES Kangaroo Paw (*Anigozanthos manglesii*), WA (1960); Sturt's Desert Rose (*Gossypium sturtianum*), NT (1961); Sturt's Desert Pea (*Swainsona formosa*), SA (1961); Waratah (*Telopea speciosissima*), NSW (1962); Blue Gum (*Eucalyptus globulus*), Tas. (1962); and Royal Bluebell (*Wahlenbergia gloriosa*), ACT (1982). As part of the commemorations and celebrations in 2001, all states and territories have adopted a Centenary of Federation floral emblem.

Anne Boden, *Floral Emblems of Australia* (Canberra, 1985)
MARGARET BETTERIDGE

FLORICULTURE, the cultivation of flowers as a dedicated pursuit, whether massed in the FLOWER GARDEN or as isolated specimens for the SHOW table, came to prominence in the early nineteenth century. *A Concise and Practical Treatise on the Growth and Cultivation of the Carnation, Pink, Auricula, Polyanthus, Ranunculus, Tulip, Hyacinth, Rose and other Flowers* (1812) by English florist Thomas Hogg (1771–1841) reflected a taste for growing and exhibiting individual flowers that had commenced as a recreational pastime for self-employed artisans and working men in late eighteenth-century England. In describing himself as a 'florist' rather than a 'nurseryman', Hogg assumed that the difference was clearly understood; a florist grew a restricted range of flowering plants and often showed them in COMPETITION; nurseries stocked a far wider range of flowering plants, including trees, shrubs, and frost-tender greenhouse plants. 'Florists' flowers' were HARDY outdoor plants that with skilled cosseting produced flowers of perfect symmetry according to strict rules developed as 'ideals of perfection' for each kind of plant. At shows or 'florists' feasts', often held in inns, groups of devotees to a particular plant, such as the Auricula, would meet, show their best flowers, and afterwards feast—often with much alcohol consumed in boasts and toasts. It was a pastime that found adherents in Australia too, once the early years of economic hardship and the struggle to establish had passed. Daniel BUNCE, writing for the month of April in his *Manual of Practical Gardening* (1838), acknowledged Hogg as his mentor and passed on tips for growing Auriculas successfully in Van Diemen's Land. Local experience and changing plant fashions saw some florists' flowers fall from favour, while others rose to prominence.

The Auricula was mentioned as a rather demanding plant for Australian florists in David CRICHTON's ambitious *Australian Horticultural Magazine and Garden Guide* (1877–78), but by this time other, more easily grown, flowers were favoured by competitive exhibitors seeking perfection and prize money. CAMELLIAS, CHRYSANTHEMUMS, cyclamen, GLADIOLUS, NARCISSUS, and pansies emerged as new, hybridised NOVELTIES and caught the attention of flower gardeners; but hyacinths, ROSES, and tulips kept their place as established favourites on the exhibition bench. Tulips, auriculas, and polyanthus (Primroses), being difficult to bring to perfection, slowly waned in popularity while others, such as the Ranunculus and Pink, were regarded as old-fashioned, and relegated to the COTTAGE GARDEN rather than the show hall.

A shift away from cut flowers to potted specimen plants around 1880 also changed the kinds of plants preferred by florists for exhibition. While auriculas were always shown as entire plants, other florists' flowers had been shown as 'cuts'. The plants were collected, but only the flowers were important. The change in focus from flowers alone to entire plants in bloom changed thinking about which plants were desirable for the show bench. Variety in FOLIAGE and plant form became just as important as flower form. In particular FERNS, CACTI, succulents, ORCHIDS, and geraniums were elevated in importance.

The Australian CLIMATE also had an impact on the development of floriculture. Being generally much warmer than the English climate, the Australian climate allowed more frost-tender plants to be grown without the protection of glass and heat. This meant that plants regarded as the preserve

Flower arrangement

of those wealthy enough to afford costly heated STOVES and CONSERVATORIES could be grown outdoors in Australia. Slowly, new flower and plant fashions took hold; orchids, begonias, bromeliads, ferns, geraniums, and FUCHSIAS were grown in BUSH-HOUSES, while cacti and other succulents were grown on rockeries and as potted specimens. DAHLIAS became highly popular, as did PELARGONIUMS, calceolarias, and SWEET PEAS. Roses emerged triumphant as the best loved, most admired, and widely popular flower for home gardeners and competitive exhibitors; a position which, arguably, they have maintained to the present. Each kind of plant had its devotees; HORTICULTURAL SOCIETIES dedicated to the major plant groups were formed from the early twentieth century to popularise the plants (or their cut flowers) through shows and educational programs. A heightened interest in plant BREEDING accompanied this passion for individual flowers, and some Australian breeders, notably Alister CLARK, achieved international fame.

From the work of amateur florists acting as plant breeders gradually developed the modern commercial flower culture and floristry. The nursery trade had traditionally embraced floriculture, and many businesses maintained separate florists' outlets (usually in city centres). Others, such as RONALDS (Vic.) and SEARL (NSW) were primarily florists, but also dealt in general nursery stock. While hybridising was once the province of dedicated amateurs, this role was gradually taken over by commercial breeders. Increasing specialisation also saw the separate development of breeding, propagation, and cut-flower industries and the growth of import and export markets for cut flowers, especially flowering AUSTRALIAN NATIVE PLANTS. Amateur growers and exhibitors have declined in numbers in the late twentieth century, replaced by other leisure and recreation activities or a more general interest in gardening. FLOWER ARRANGING, a traditional female domestic role, has broadened its scope, and new cult figures—such as Melbourne's Kevin O'Neill (1941–1997)—have brought new boldness to floristry and taken full advantage of the benefits offered by air freight in their popularisation of TROPICAL flowers.

Brent Elliott, *Flora: An Illustrated History of the Garden Flower* (London, 2001)   **TREVOR NOTTLE**

FLOWER ARRANGEMENT 1788–1915 Flower arranging as a part of interior decoration satisfies a common need for artistic self-expression (and sometimes self-congratulation) and has a long history, closely linked to successive waves of PLANT COLLECTING and ACCLIMATISATION. Settlers arrived in Australia with European plants and with plants from the Cape of Good Hope; Elizabeth Macquarie is the earliest-recorded colonial flower arranger. Using mostly Old World rather than native flowers, predominantly middle-class women enjoyed the aesthetic and supposed MORAL benefits of reproducing styles of arrangement familiar to them and using a choice of blooms based on established fashions and the meanings of flowers: for Alexander McLEAY's eightieth birthday China roses and hollyhocks vied with blandfordias and impomeas. Flowers popular during the nineteenth century included anenomes, bignonias, candytuft, chrysanthemums (despite connotations of death), convolvulus, fuchsias, larkspurs, honeysuckle, lilies, lily-of-the-valley, mignonette, pansies, passionflowers, pelargoniums, primroses, roses, stocks, sweet peas, tulips, violets, virginian stocks, wallflowers, and wisteria. Containers—whether glass, ceramic, metal, antique, or makeshift—changed along with taste, and some lent themselves to certain flowers. Matched pairs of both trumpet and spill vases, specimen vases, tiered glass stands (some etched), épergnes, and metal vases—echoing current revival styles in household silver—dominated for much of the century. From the 1850s onwards, colonists found some rational use for the eclectic ceramics now pouring out of Europe and appearing at EXHIBITIONS.

Flower arrangements are as subject to taste and fashion as tassels and fringes, and can give a sharp impression of the date of illustrations, although some fashions survived with only subtle changes. Despite continuities, the profile, scale, and character of arrangements responded to overseas and local publications, FERN-mania, revolutionary changes in interior decoration, artificial lighting, and changing garden STYLES. Nosegays, mixed bunches in baskets, and stumpy, drooping-edged bouquets gradually succumbed to larger, more assertive effects such as a branch of magnolias under a glass dome. The CLIMATE encouraged the wanton use of flowers and greenery, and the overscaled arrangements seen during Australia's first royal visit (1867) were precursors of the floral elephantiasis that later overwhelmed tables and mantelpieces.

From the 1880s, artistic and Aesthetic notions saw asymmetry and off-beat flowers oust paired vases from mantelpieces. Seeds, weeds, feathery grasses, bamboo, pampas, and date-palm fronds appeared in tandem with INDOOR PLANTS, animal products, and native weapons. Instead of the single vase of flowers recommended by Mrs Beeton, dining tables now sported floral copses, the effect magnified by plateaux of mirrored glass or carried up into the gasolier. The rich, and their professional flower arrangers, excelled themselves: a simulated fern gully filled the entire stage at Melbourne's Cliveden for the Flower Ball of 1890. At the turn of the century, *Art Nouveau* favoured cooler colours; interest in JAPAN popularised chrysanthemums and prunus; nationalism boosted flannel flowers and gum tips. Roses, now flatly massed or in Edwardian trumpet vases, enjoyed a revival, and clivias and hydrangeas raised their heads. 'Novelty' justified white china swans, gilt wheelbarrows, and discarded sailors' hats (varnished) as containers. When the First World War broke out, the clean-up and first stirrings of MODERNISM still had a way to go.

JESSIE SERLE

1915–2000 Flower arrangement in the early decades of the last century commonly featured single varieties of flowers in individual vases—perhaps reflecting an increasing specialisation in the suburban garden, and a consequent focus on single species such as ROSES, CARNATIONS, SWEET PEAS, and ORCHIDS—or a perceived vulgarity regarding multiple blooms. A middle-class household might contain several vases in one room, dotted about and creating a medley of blooms. White flowers had a mixed reception: some used lilies in wedding bouquets while others linked them with death and mourn-

Flower arrangement

Norman SPARNON's 'Ten Shredded Aspidistra Leaves', from his book *The Poetry of Leaves* (1970), presents a Japanese-influenced FLOWER ARRANGEMENT that, after three decades, still strains the boundaries of conventional taste

ing. Sweet-scented flowers were prized, and vases were often placed at head-height on fretted timberwork, sideboards, and pot stands. Potted plants were mixed in rooms with freshly cut blooms. The heightened interest in Australian native flowers and foliage for decoration continued through to the 1930s, especially sprays of gum leaves and wattle blossom.

The 1930s saw the heyday of the flower show, whether staged by a horticultural society or a local church auxiliary, with individual blooms as well as floral table arrangements with a suite of matched bowls or vases (often Moorcroft and Royal Doulton); the 'mixed bowl' arrangement was among the most coveted of awards. These local flower shows fostered the growing interest in 'floral art'. Popular flowers included asters, aquilegias, clarkias, daffodils, delphiniums, grape hyacinths, heuchera, lily of the valley, nasturtiums, pansies, Russell lupins, snapdragons, and zinnias, backed where appropriate by foliage such as asparagus fern. Roses, and now DAHLIAS and GLADIOLUS, were great favourites, the latter in large, often highly coloured bunches.

During the 1930s artist Adrian Feint (1894–1971) adopted the flower vase as his leitmotif, and used imaginative combinations of grasses, leaves, and fruit, as well as flowers, in his designs. Thea Proctor (1879–1966), a trend-setter, advocated a study of Japanese flower arrangement and simpler arrangements. The influence of these local artists was considerable: Margaret Preston (1875–1963) in particular assembled a dazzling array of flower pieces over the decades 1920–50. They were given prominence in art magazines, and she featured native flowers, using them as formal subjects or massed groups.

A move was made towards Modernism with the introduction of dried flowers for arrangements and a greater emphasis on INDOOR PLANTS, especially as architectural features.

Notwithstanding these trends, when Helen BLAXLAND published her *Collected Flower Pieces* in the 1940s, the grouping of similar species in the same vase was still fashionable in Australia, and bunched clumps of roses and hydrangeas were also used. There were also, however, combinations of different species in the same vase to form a balanced composition, with the vase itself forming part of a design. Constance Spry, as London's most fashionable flower arranger, dismissed the prejudice against white flowers and the use of mixed flowers in vases, and started a vogue for them. She visited Australia during the mid-1950s as the guest of David Jones department store, disseminating her floral style through demonstrations and books.

By the mid-1950s Ikebana arrangements were fashionable, portrayed skilfully in the books of Norman SPARNON, whose carefully chosen blooms were arranged in simplified, austere, balanced combinations. There had always been ARTIFICIAL FLOWERS of various media, but dried native flower arrangements, popular from the 1970s to the 1990s, suited increasingly busy lifestyles. FOLIAGE, which became available commercially after the 1950s, began to dominate many arrangements, and with widespread air transport and use of refrigeration, tropical flowers began to appear in temperate latitudes. The introduction of 'oasis' foam in the 1960s also had a profound effect on the shape of arrangements and the ease of arranging flowers. Ubiquitous white Gypsophila and green foliage as filler became a florist's trade mark as a finishing touch, and there was always a constant search for 'new' varieties to add to their stock. Many varieties had bigger, stronger blooms, but had lost their old perfume. Elaborate set piece pieces featuring Australian and South African flowers were still in local vogue at the end of the twentieth century.

Florists' shops have had a major influence on the style and content of flower arrangements, especially in their production of posies, wreaths, and floral gifts. The rise of professional florists—and even celebrity florists, such as Kevin O'Neill—encouraged a new boldness, especially in colour and size. At the start of the twenty-first century two opposing trends dominate. On one hand, there is a complicated array of different floral species to select for arrangements for interior decoration, and several schools of thought about the design. On the other, there is a tendency to dispense with 'arrangement' entirely, with a bunch of single-species florists' flowers left as they come, and just placed in a vase.

HELEN PROUDFOOT

Julia S. Berrall, *A History of Flower Arrangement* (London, 1953; New York, 1968); Beverley Nichols, *The Art of Flower Arrangement* (London, 1967); Mary Rose Blacker, *Flora Domestica: A History of Flower Arranging 1500–1930* (London, 2000)

FLOWER GARDENS Settlers travelling to Australia in the First Fleet brought with them from Cape Town flowering plants as well as those intended for agriculture. Arthur Bowes SMYTH had in his cabin flowering geraniums as well as grape vines ready for his eventual garden at Sydney Cove. Early views of Sydney clearly show two kinds of decorative gardening: grand landscape gardens such as that of Captain Piper's marine villa, fronting an expansive lawn—with its separate flower and vegetable gardens hidden from view behind the house—and more casual, small-scale COTTAGE GARDENS.

Plants that grew during the rainy months were favoured, as WATER for IRRIGATION was scarce and needed for productive crops and household use. Many South African BULBS and PERENNIALS, such as watsonias and Agapanthus, were valued for their beauty and toughness. Succulent plants such as aloes and AGAVES were also planted widely. Apart from water, flower gardening was limited by the availability of plants and skilled horticulturists. The palette of flowering plants gradually expanded as the NURSERY TRADE developed, giving flower gardeners greater variety and choice. Garden and plant fashions were well understood from the flow of British books, and experiments in ACCLIMATISATION on a domestic scale gradually produced more appropriate local advice. S.T. GILL's charming watercolour views of Prospect House show that even on the dry Adelaide Plains, keen and fashion-conscious gardeners followed the rage for collections of exotics displayed in the GARDENESQUE manner. At the same time, cottage gardening continued to satisfy those confined to the quarter-acre plot, and there was a gradual shift away from production to ornament.

By the end of the nineteenth century a growing population, improved economic circumstances, and the spread of reticulated water supplies enabled the full treasure trove of exotic importations to be more widely planted. Various garden STYLES made references to Japan, Renaissance Italy, North America, and England, and most relied to some extent on flowering plants grouped in compartments, be they masonry-walled beds of the ARTS AND CRAFTS style or BEDS cut into lawn in more Gardenesque arrangements. Brief encounters with Spanish Mission architecture accompanied by gardens of CACTI and succulents, the advent of MODERNISM, and BUSH GARDENS made little impact on devotees of the flower garden, and the designs of Edna WALLING and the English flower garden maintained its position as the preferred style for gardens large and small. After the Second World War the spread of suburbs based on GARDEN SUBURB ideals shifted the focus of gardeners away from growing plants for recreation to using them to create a setting for a lifestyle that was based on car use and recreation away from home. Flowers became less important, and lawns with a background of shrubs and trees, chosen for minimum maintenance, took over as the dominant feature of gardens.

The late twentieth-century fashions for romantic English gardens based on the ideas of Vita SACKVILLE-WEST and Rosemary Verey—who in turn had found inspiration in the writing of Gertrude JEKYLL and the idealised watercolour pictures of Alfred Parsons and the Surrey School—could be seen as a reaction to the simpler uniformity of the American style. Now Australian gardeners are struggling with the naturalised garden as exemplified by James van Sweden (USA) and Piet Oudolf (Netherlands). The emphasis is on massing perennials, GRASSES, SHRUBS, and BULBS selected for their ability to maintain themselves in the local climate with minimum care. The challenge will be to avoid the temptation to adopt the palette described by the authors of the ideas, and instead to develop a fresh palette according to what will grow 'naturally' in Australian conditions and respect local ECOLOGIES.

Trevor Nottle, *Old-fashioned Gardens* (Kenthurst, NSW, 1992)

TREVOR NOTTLE

FLOWER SHOWS: see HORTICULTURAL SHOWS

FOLIAGE is a vital part of planting composition in garden design. It provides texture and COLOUR and strongly develops form and structure in planting themes. Deciduous plants herald the change in SEASONS and can importantly alter light availability to the immediate surrounding environment by providing shade in summer but allowing light in during winter. On the other hand, evergreen plants produce stability and consistency in the planted form throughout the year. The vast majority of Australian plants are evergreen, although a few—such as *Brachychiton acerifolius* (Illawarra Flame Tree)—are summer deciduous. Many, such as the EUCALYPTS, are sclerophyllous, having leaves hard in texture and stiffened and strengthened by structural fibres. While these attributes are now generally admired and provide a unique and local identity to Australian gardens, they contributed to an early undesirable perception of a harsh landscape. The nineteenth-century fashion for cultivating Australian RAINFOREST plants reinforced the admiration of lush foliage over smaller and harder-textured plants.

Foliage as a character in plant selection was a strong fashion in nineteenth-century Australian plantings—one that distinguished what MUELLER termed 'scenic plants'. Many nursery catalogues listed numbers of plants primarily on their foliage attributes even though their flowers were also a strong ornamental feature. One BRUNNING's catalogue, for example, listed *Wigandia caracasana*, a large-leaved South American shrub with strongly ornamental purple flowers, listed in William ROBINSON's book *The Subtropical Garden* (1871) as a highly desirable garden plant and as a 'bold and handsome foliaged plant'. This plant was also used in the landscapes of William GUILFOYLE along with other coloured foliage and succulents to develop his planting styles. TROPICAL and subtropical bedding—with picturesque effect being more important than pattern—had been introduced by Jean-Pierre Barillet-Deschamps (1824–1875) in his work in Paris in the 1860s, in London by John Gibson (1815–1875), and generally through the writings of Robinson, and locally in the work of Guilfoyle and Charles MOORE. While some Australian plants, *Grevillea robusta* (Silky Oak) for instance, were—and to a limited extent still are—used as foliage bedding plants, most of the ornamental-leaved plants introduced by Australians came from OCEANIA. Foliage has also played an important part in FLOWER ARRANGING and selection of INDOOR PLANTS.

As nursery technology developed in the second half of the twentieth century to produce the majority of plants for sale in plastic pots, the importance of foliage became secondary to flowers: a 'successful' plant came to be seen as one able to come into flower while still in its nursery container. With a stronger interest developing in Australian plants, building on the BUSH GARDEN movement of the 1960s and 1970s, there was a much wider acceptance of the subtle differences between plants with reduced and less lush-looking foliage. Recently there has been a resurgence of interest in plants that display ornamental foliage characteristics, especially with the increased use of GRASSES, including Australian native species.

ML

FOOD PLANTS: see ABORIGINAL FOOD PLANTS

FOOTSCRAY PARK, Vic., permanently reserved in 1911, was saved from suburban development in 1908 by a spirited newspaper campaign and the generosity of the Victorian Racing Club (which had acquired the land to control a prime vantage point overlooking Flemington and to prevent noxious trades establishing on the river opposite this premier RACECOURSE). A design competition judged by William GUILFOYLE was won by Rodney ALSOP, and the park was laid out by long-serving curator David MATTHEWS. It is probable

Whether in the confines of the GLASSHOUSE or SHADE HOUSE, or in open garden BEDS, in the late nineteenth century the use of FOLIAGE challenged the supremacy of flowers in the realm of ornamental horticulture

that the general layout, the architectural use of stone retaining walls, and the varying small structures are the most direct remnants of Alsop's proposal. Road widening severed a strip of parkland during the 1960s, but Footscray Park still remains one of Melbourne's most intact parks from the Edwardian and inter-war period, with characteristic features including rustic stonework, pergolas, ornamental ponds, and an extensive palm collection. The unusual linear plan and terraced layout are both a direct response to the awkward site, and the main axial pathway skilfully exploits the sloping site and gives formality to the design.   RA

FORD, Gordon Craig (1918–1999), landscape designer and pioneer of the BUSH GARDEN, spent a formative childhood as the son of a Presbyterian minister in small country towns in central NSW: 'my playgrounds were callitris and casuarina forests,' he later wrote. Settling in Eltham (Vic.), he worked with Ellis STONES in 1952–54. Ford then established his own landscape company, specialising in designs to blend unobtrusively with the mud-brick houses of the area, a direct heritage from Stones and Edna WALLING.

His work included domestic, public (for example, work at Melbourne's ROYAL PARK and Monash University), and commercial landscapes (such as the Décor Corporation factory at Scoresby, Vic.). They reflected two concepts central to his design philosophy: to arrange the garden as an asymmetrical juxtaposition of mass and void—an idea he adapted from English landscape architect Brenda Colvin (1897–1981)—and to design the garden landscape to disguise the boundary. Texture and shape of foliage, rather than flower colour, were integral to his landscapes. While he favoured using AUSTRALIAN PLANTS, particularly eucalypts such as *Eucalyptus maculata* (Spotted Gum) and melaleucas, he was not averse to exotic plants. His own garden, Fülling at Eltham, and the adjacent garden, also designed by him, remain superb examples of his skill in arranging rocks and water in a way that suggests the natural landscape. In *Gordon Ford: The Natural Australian Garden* (1999), Ford and his wife and collaborator, Gwen, reflected on fifty years of designing and constructing NATURAL GARDENS.   CHRISTINE REID

FOREST LODGE, Stirling, SA: see BAGOT, John

FORESTRY as the organised protection and management of forests was slowly established in the various Australian colonies, states, and territories between 1870 and 1920 in the face of opposition from agriculturists and lands departments. It adopted the British imperial model of reserving areas of crown land as state forests and establishing state forest services, staffed by a cadre of trained foresters, to protect and manage them. Its main purpose was to ensure the supply of timber but it also protected water catchments. It largely ignored forests on private land and Australia's extensive woodlands.

Several early foresters, such as John Ednie BROWN, had British training and practical experience in estate management, plantation development (or ARBORICULTURE), and the management of stands of trees (or silviculture). The New South Wales Forest Service established an internal training

The NATURALISTIC garden created by Gordon FORD at his property Fülling, Eltham (Vic.), draws strongly on the use of thick understorey plantings to contrast with the sprinkling of slender emerging eucalypt trunks

scheme that produced notable foresters such as E.H.F. SWAIN. The Victorian School of Forestry, established in 1910, provided formal class-work and practical experience in its STATE FOREST NURSERY, plantations, and native forest silviculture.

After the First World War, the Commonwealth established the Forestry and Timber Bureau and the Australian Forestry School to train graduate foresters. Both were headed by C.E. LANE-POOLE. A national target of 10 million hectares of state forests agreed upon in 1920 was not reached until 1966. Research enabled eucalypt wood to be used for paper pulp. Forestry flourished after the Second World War with the assistance of enhanced access roads, improved fire protection, and research into silviculture, but the high demand for timber seriously overcut and inadequately regenerated the native forests; those near pulp mills were clear-felled. Plantations had to be expanded. There were more than 1.2 million hectares of plantations by 1997, providing half of the sawlogs being produced. The 0.9 million hectares of conifer plantations are mostly *Pinus radiata* (Monterey or Radiata Pine) in southern Australia; *P. eliottii* (Slash Pine), *P. caribaea* (Cuban Pine), and *Araucaria cunninghamii* (Hoop Pine) in Qld and some *P. pinaster* (Maritime Pine) in WA. The 0.3 million hectares of hardwood plantations are mostly *Eucalyptus globulus* (Blue Gum), *E. nitens* (Shining Gum), *E. regnans* (Mountain Ash), and *E. grandis* (Flooded Gum). Investment in eucalypt plantations was expanding this area rapidly at the end of the 1990s. Some of the plantations were established by industrial companies and by an enthusiastic farm forestry movement encouraged by government schemes. Tree planting and the protection of remnant vegetation is encouraged by LANDCARE groups around the country.

Intractable conflicts throughout the 1970s and 1980s over the clearing of native forests for pine plantations, clear-felling of native forests for woodchip exports, and felling of rainforests and old-growth forests, led to the 1992 *National Forest Policy Statement*. Detailed regional assessments form the basis for creating a comprehensive system of conservation reserves and assuring wood supplies for industry from the remaining state forests, which are to be managed in an ecologically sustainable way.

L.T. Carron, *A History of Forestry in Australia* (Canberra, 1985); Athol Meyer, *The Foresters* (Hobart, 1985); John Dargavel, *Fashioning Australia's Forests* (Melbourne, 1995)

JOHN DARGAVEL

FORMALITY in Australian gardens has not been confined to any one garden STYLE, but has been a recurring theme as succeeding generations have wrestled with the balance between art and nature. The squared garden layouts of early VEGETABLE GARDENS, with bed and path layouts based on dimensions best suited to those tending the plots and the nature of the crops therein, had little to do with art and much in common with contemporary farm layouts; these vernacular utilitarian origins have persisted in the vegetable patch and the quincuncial grid of the ORCHARD. Even if an axis on the cottage front door transcended utility by introducing an ornamental note, 'geometric' seems rather too grand to describe these pragmatic rectilinear plots.

The recognition of art in the garden—whether produced by the levels and regular slopes of the 'ancient' or geometric style or by the polished curvature of the 'modern' or informal style—was under debate in the early nineteenth century. In this context, 'ancient' style included the Renaissance and baroque and did not necessarily imply any parallel with classical antiquity. The revival of formal gardens in Britain embraced the necessity of restoring formal gardens and avenues that had survived the BROWNIAN onslaught, as an accompaniment to revivalist architectural styles—especially as a means of anchoring an old residence to the landscape by use of terraces—and the introduction of CONSERVATORIES into the garden as an ARCHITECTURAL accompaniment.

J.C. LOUDON recommended the geometric style for countries 'in a wild state', citing contrast and an 'obvious expression of art and refinement', and unstated, as a means of imposing order on the newly acquired and unfamiliar landscape. This was clearly demonstrated in the LAND SURVEYS (especially geodetic surveys) and grid town plans of Australia, schemata scrutinised by Paul Carter in *The Road to Botany Bay* (1987). Loudon also recommended the geometric style for public parks and gardens (calculated to display PROMENADING visitors to advantage), and this formality is seen in many early examples Sydney's HYDE PARK, Melbourne's urban SQUARES, and BOTANIC GARDENS at BALLARAT, GEELONG, and PORTLAND—albeit often now richly overlaid. This style was also well adapted to SYSTEM GARDENS, where geometric disposition perfectly complemented botanical categorisation, and in CEMETERIES, where regularity was conducive to economy—again recommended by Loudon's 1843 treatise on the subject. The geometric style was also adopted for FLOWER GARDENS, especially those fronting the constricted sites of early COTTAGES, VILLAS, and terrace houses, where they formed a miniaturised, egalitarian form of the PARTERRE. The formality and neatness implied by geometry well suited the MORAL dimension of FRONT GARDENS, still echoed in Australia's SUBURBAN GARDENS.

Even the GARDENESQUE style could admit formality, especially in gardens that displayed Loudon's 'axis of symmetry' (1840). Such axes did not need to reflect perfectly geometric arrangements, but in 'cultivated and refined examples' could include unequal sides requiring 'the eye of a philosophical artist to detect the axis'. The most fluid Australian examples of these symmetrical garden designs were by Edward La Trobe BATEMAN in the late 1850s, and recall the Owen Jones *Grammar of Ornament* school of illuminated design.

Charles McINTOSH postulated four styles of gardening in his *Flower Garden* (1838): the Italian (characterised by terraces); the French (by parterres); the Dutch (by regular formality and the 'clumsy artifice' of 'clipt evergreens'); and the English (an artful imitation of nature). The first three were manifestly formal, and the Italian style, whose chief British exponent was Charles Barry (1795–1860), arrived in Australia during the mid-century. The terraces at GLENARA (1857–58) and BONTHARAMBO (1857–60) typify its early manifestation, and countless villa gardens in suburbs and towns, tile-edged, balustraded, and urn-bedecked—echoing the prescriptions of *Garden Architecture and Landscape Gardening* (1866) by J.A. Hughes—represent a more common expression. Alfred LYNCH's plan for the Horticultural Society of Victoria gardens at BURNLEY (1861) was an unusually sophisticated public example and Victoria's GOVERNMENT HOUSE (1872) a prominent later exemplar.

Much TOWN PLANNING of the early twentieth century, especially that falling within the ambit of the CITY BEAUTIFUL MOVEMENT, relied on formality through spatial order, symmetry, and axial planning. Allied to ARCHITECTURE and craftwork, the influence of the ARTS AND CRAFTS Movement brought renewed interest in formal modes of garden design, albeit softened by planting. MEDITERRANEAN INFLUENCES, especially via NORTH AMERICA, built on acceptance of Arts and Crafts designs at a time when Australian architects and designers were assessing climatically similar models in the quest for a distinctive Australian style. The early work of Edna WALLING, culminating in her design for MAWARRA (1929–32), and the late work of Harold DESBROWE-ANNEAR exemplify this influence. To later generations, MODERNISM brought elements of formality to architecture, but associated landscapes were often planned to soften and complement rather than accentuate. In much recent LANDSCAPE ARCHITECTURE, particularly in the public domain, formal elements have accentuated architecture over landscape. At a domestic level, revived interest during the 1980s in hedges and Italian elements has producing static, low-maintenance gardens that suit new and chaotic urban lifestyles.

Reginald Blomfield, *The Formal Garden in England* (London, 1892); Mark Laird, *The Formal Garden: Traditions of Art and Nature* (London, 1992)

RA

FORREST, John (1847–1918), explorer, surveyor-general, and politician, was born in Bunbury (WA), and rose to become the most influential figure in the West, fortuitously at his peak during the 1890s gold boom. During 1869 to 1883 he led three successful, gruelling expeditions through uncharted inland Australia, where he collected significant numbers of botanical specimens for Ferdinand MUELLER. In recognition of services to botanical science Forrest was elected Fellow of the LINNEAN SOCIETY (1882). During the 1890s he was inaugural president of the Natural History and Science Society, later the Mueller Botanic Society. Knighted in 1891, Forrest, far-sighted and confident, was the colony's first premier (1890–1901), overseeing the passing of the *Parks and Reserves Act* and becoming first president of KINGS PARK Board (1895–1918). Forrest's wife, Margaret Elvire (née Hamersley) (1844–1929), was an accomplished BOTANICAL ARTIST who accurately portrayed Western Australian wildflowers for Mueller. Her collection of seventy-three watercolours is held by the Art Gallery of Western Australia.

CAROL MANSFIELD

(JOHN) FORREST NATIONAL PARK: see JOHN FORREST NATIONAL PARK

FORTUNA, Bendigo, Vic., retains remnants of the lavish garden laid out *c*. 1858 around the Second Empire–style villa built for mining magnates Christopher and Theodore Ballerstedt. Significant extensions and alterations to the house and garden were carried out between 1871 and 1934 for mining entrepreneur George Lansell (1823–1906) and his family. This hilltop garden once contained extensive lakes, garden buildings, and statuary: the distinctive fountain (1879) is a replica of one seen by Lansell at Pompeii.

FRANCINE GILFEDDER

FOSTER, John Harvey (1944–1994), historian, grew up in Melbourne and maintained a lifelong interest in gardens and gardening, perhaps passed down from his grandfather Charles Bowmont Taylor, a gardener at MOUNT MACEDON and (according to Foster) grandson of William Sangster's partner, William TAYLOR. Foster's academic interests related to German-Jewish history—especially through a lectureship at the University of Melbourne from 1971—but a personal passion was GARDEN HISTORY. He was a perceptive researcher, skilful writer, and engaging lecturer, covering sources and themes then rarely tapped. His output in this field was modest though memorable: several articles and one book, *Victorian Picturesque: The Colonial Gardens of William Sangster* (1989). His unpublished garden essays are being edited for publication. Foster's last book, *Take Me to Paris, Johnny* (1993), an elegant and moving tribute to his partner Juan, reveals his rich humanity.

RA

FOUNTAINS play an important part in bringing WATER into garden and landscape designs, often in connection with features such as LAKES and pools, yet few early colonial examples are known. Jets, cascades, and fountains had been popular in formal European gardens from the Renaissance and Baroque periods, although they had fallen from favour in Britain during the eighteen-century landscape gardening movement: it was not until the rise of formal gardens in the early to mid-nineteenth century that they again flourished.

A basic requirement was a reliable water source, and in Australia this was often lacking. The earliest examples were gravity-fed from an elevated source—as at MCLEAY's Elizabeth Bay House (1835–40) and VAUCLUSE HOUSE (1861–62), both in Sydney. A burst of fountain building came with the provision of reticulated water supplies to Australia's capital cities in the 1850s and 1860s—somewhat later in major provincial towns. Accompanied by swellings of municipal pride, these fountains (and DRINKING FOUNTAINS) were commonly constructed in urban SQUARES (for example in PRINCE's SQUARE, Launceston, Tas.: 1859); BOTANIC GARDENS and PUBLIC PARKS (for example the River God Fountain, FITZROY GARDENS, Melbourne: 1862); and BOULEVARDS (for example Sturt Street, Ballarat, Vic.: 1860s). Some were locally crafted, others imported. Imported fountains were most often of composition stone (from manufacturers such as Austin and Seeley) and cast iron (typically from Coalbrookdale). Portland cement—moulded in panels or blocks, or cast over a reinforcing frame, or a combination of these—was also a popular material for local and imported examples alike. Stone was also used, commonly marble or granite, although the Stanford Fountain,

The FOUNTAIN at FORTUNA, Bendigo (Vic.), modelled on an original viewed by owner George Lansell at Pompeii, lent a touch of classical grandeur to this expansive garden, wholly in keeping with the aspirations of its gold-rich owner

Gordon Reserve, Melbourne (1867) is of basalt. Late nineteenth-century examples also employed terra cotta, often with a faience finish, as at Memorial Gardens, Narrandera, NSW (1922).

Fountain design in Australia tended towards formality—a mode favoured for VILLA GARDENS—often with tiered circular basins and sculpture associated with classical allegorical images, such as the Archibald Fountain, HYDE PARK, SYDNEY (1932). Some were constructed for EXHIBITIONS, and the Exhibition Fountain (1880) in Melbourne's CARLTON GARDENS is perhaps the supreme example. Informal structures employing cascades and rustic-work occasionally found favour (for example, at ROSALIND PARK, Bendigo, Vic.: 1880) and in the domestic setting these were often associated with ROCKERIES. Jets as a device were first employed at MELBOURNE BOTANIC GARDENS in 1864, and more recently at Lake Burley Griffin, Canberra (1970). Commemorative imperatives generated many fine examples: Robert WOODWARD's El Alamein Fountain, Kings Cross, Sydney (1961), is an icon of Australian MODERNISM. Many other fine fountains and water sculptures have been erected in recent decades, including those at the Adelaide Festival Centre, in KINGS PARK and beside Parliament House (WA), and the water wall and moat at the National Gallery of Victoria.

COLLEEN MORRIS

FOWLER, William (1822–1897), gardener, was born at Glasgow, Scotland. After apprenticeship under William Hooker at Glasgow Botanic Gardens he worked at KEW GARDENS. From 1848 he 'wandered about the world'; in Tas. he assisted Ronald GUNN to collect for the Kew herbarium. From Australia he moved to North America to Baltimore, Maryland, and for forty years was gardener at Clifton Park, the celebrated estate of John Hopkins, where he took a special interest in acacias, eucalypts, and other AUSTRALIAN PLANTS. RA

FOWL HOUSE Poultry has been an important adjunct to residential gardens, especially in the period to the mid-twentieth century. Horticultural training usually included poultry management, while the amateur could learn from books such as H.R. Harris, *The Poultry Book for Australasia* (c. 1906), or the journal *The Australian Hen* (1900–22). The fowl house, universally located in the BACKYARD, was generally a utilitarian structure with a fenced run. Occasionally, more sophisticated structures were provided; the fowl house (1854) at Tasmania's GOVERNMENT HOUSE, for instance, was a medieval fantasy, all gablets and half-timbering. A macabre adjunct involving poultry was the cock-fighting pit, very occasionally found in domestic backyards. RA

FOX, Paul Francis (b. 1953), is a Melbourne writer and historian whose wide interests include the social and cultural history of gardens, designed landscapes, and natural history. As Thomas Ramsay Science and Humanities Scholar at the Museum of Victoria (1989–91) he curated the exhibition 'Drawing on Nature'. In 1999 he was part of the winning team for the contemporary design of the Federation Garden in Sydney's CENTENNIAL PARK. His writings have been published in numerous journal articles, catalogue essays, and a forthcoming book, *Clearings* (2003). Ideas are his principal concern and his writing is illuminated by humanist understandings and incident. RA

FRANCE Although her formal gardens had their origins in Italy, 'the French brought nature to heel', and grand designed landscapes, especially the use of long (often PLEACHED) AVENUES became synonymous with the French garden: the quintessential French garden at the close of the eighteenth century was also intimately related to a political show of power. Despite Louis Napoleon's romance with the *jardin anglais*, the major town planning changes to Paris (1853–70) under the direction of politician Baron (Georges) Eugène Haussmann (1809–1891) and landscape designer Jean Charles Adolphe Alphand (1817–1891) reinforced the formal SQUARE and grand BOULEVARD as precedents for international practice in urban design. (The GRIFFIN plan for Canberra and later planting of the new capital, the Shrine vista in Melbourne, and the 1927 plan for HYDE PARK, Sydney, brought this theme to an Australian audience.)

An integral adjunct of French (and British) political power was colonisation, prompting a race for prospective settlement sites in the South Pacific. Early French expeditions visiting New Holland were led by Bougainville (1766–69) and La Pérouse (1785–88). Greater botanical interest came from D'Entrecasteaux (1791–93)—accompanied by botanist LABILLARDIÈRE and gardener DELAHAYE—and Baudin (1800–03), who had three botanists, including Jean-Baptiste Leschenault (1773–1826), after whom *Lechenaultia* was named. In 1818 Louis de Freycinet's expedition visited WA, where plant collector Gaudichand (1789–1854) discovered several new species. These expeditions resulted in a flow of plants—both live, and dried as HERBARIUM specimens—from New Holland (Australia) to France, though botanically overshadowed by the British due to a lack of French publication.

Seeds from Baudin's expedition were shared by the Empress Josephine with André Thouin of the Jardin des Plantes, Paris, and also propagated at Malmaison. In 1827–28 Charles FRASER credited Thouin with introducing approximately 100 plants to the SYDNEY BOTANIC GARDENS, an amount, according to Jardin des Plantes policy, 'in proportion to similar favours received, or returns expected'. As the other colonial capitals and larger provincial cities established BOTANIC GARDENS, interchange of plants with French counterparts—such as Montpellier, Rouen, and Brest—increased. Australian VITICULTURE owed much to France, drawing on French expertise and plant stock; some, like BUSBY, had studied there, while others such as TROUETTE and DESPEISSIS were of French origin. Australian olive production and SERICULTURE likewise drew on French expertise. French cultivars of ROSES and other ornamental plants featured in the colonial nursery trade from the mid-nineteenth century, with an increasing number imported directly from France.

The Paris EXHIBITIONS (especially 1855, 1867, 1878, and 1889) captured the public imagination in Australia, in much the same way as those in London. The 1855 exhibition focused the attention of the horticultural press on advances in Parisian parks and gardens, as did the 1867 *Exposition Universelle*. Chief Gardener to the City of Paris, Jean-Pierre Barillet-Deschamps (1824–1875), was then experimenting in Parisian parks with South Seas plants—his work was publicised in Alphand's lavish *Les Promenades de Paris* (1867–73), copies of which were scarce, but not unknown, in Australia. Charles MOORE attended the 1867 exhibition with William ROBINSON, correspondent for the *Times* of London. Robinson's books *Gleanings from French Gardens* (1868), *Parks, Promenades and Gardens of Paris* (1869), and *The Subtropical Garden* (1871) reported the fashion for subtropical foliage and transformed aspects of the craze into stylistic manifestos for emulation by British (and Australian) gardeners. These featured bold-foliaged plants such as *Wigandia caracasana*, *Montanoa bipinnatifida*, and palms, all readily grown in Australia's temperate regions. In Sydney, this influence was further strengthened by Moore's 1884 appointment of French-trained gardener James JONES. In Melbourne, William GUILFOYLE adopted the subtropical style, adding to it plants gained from his experience of the AUSTRALIAN FLORA on the Tweed River and that of the Pacific Islands.

Despite the impact on architecture and interior design of *l'Art Nouveau*, the 1925 Paris Exposition (expressed in the art deco style), and the leading part played by France in MODERNISM, French influence on gardens in Australia was slight in the twentieth century. More recently, however, as international trends have been promoted through LANDSCAPE ARCHITECTURE, designers of urban parks have increasingly looked to French examples such as Parc de la Villette for inspiration.

William Howard Adams, *The French Garden 1500–1800* (New York, 1979); Kenneth Woodbridge, *Princely Gardens: The Origins and Development of the French Formal Style* (New York, 1986); Dorothee Imbert, *The Modernist Garden in France* (Newhaven and London, 1993); Barbara Abbs, *French Gardens, A Region by Region Guide* (London, 1995)

COLLEEN MORRIS

FRANCIS, George William (1800–1865), botanist, horticulturist, and botanic gardens director, was born and grew up in east London, and later wrote that he could read French and Latin and had studied botany as a child. In his twenties he travelled to Italy, France, and Spain. Between 1825 and 1844 he lectured on botany and chemistry and worked as a writer and journalist. Wide-ranging publications included *An Analysis of British Ferns and their Allies* (1837) and a monthly publication, the *Magazine of Science and School of Arts* (1839). After unsuccessfully applying for the chair of botany at King's College, London, in 1840, he taught in Boulogne, France (1844–46). He married twice, and in 1849 the Francis family migrated to Adelaide. Within three months of arrival he was encouraging the government to fund a BOTANIC GARDEN, following previously unsuccessful attempts using both public funds and private subscriptions. Francis, granted a lease of one of these sites, pressed for a properly funded botanic garden while working as a local government surveyor and valuator, and recommending plantings for Adelaide's city squares and gardens including Victoria Square.

In 1855 the government agreed to establish the publicly funded ADELAIDE BOTANIC GARDEN on a new sixteen-hectare site with Francis as inaugural superintendent and secretary. With six labourers, Francis began fencing this site. He planted hedging plants, and planned a north-south entrance walk and circular beds and shrubberies. He may have been influenced by the design of gardens established in Regent's Park, London. A stream running across the Garden facilitated the construction of lakes and ponds. Exchanges were initiated with Australian and overseas colleagues. GLASSHOUSES, EXPERIMENTAL GARDENS, and a ZOOLOGICAL section were established, and a *Catalogue of Plants* (1858) produced. Francis enhanced the scientific and educational role of the Gardens by establishing a LIBRARY, HERBARIUM, and a botanical museum, while beautifying the grounds with fountains and flower beds. Over a decade, this 'founding father' of Adelaide Botanic Garden laid excellent foundations.

Francis gave advice on civic plantings and provided newspaper articles on horticultural and practical household matters. He was a fellow of both the Linnean Society and the Horticultural Society of London. In SA he actively supported the Library and Mechanics' Institute, the Acclimatisation Society, the Philosophical Society, and the Agricultural and Horticultural Society. After his death, a parsimonious government refused his widow a pension.

Barbara J. Best, *George William Francis, First Director of the Adelaide Botanic Garden: A Biography* (Adelaide, 1986)

PAULINE PAYNE

FRANCIS, Peter: see PETER FRANCIS POINTS ARBORETUM, near Coleraine, Vic.

FRANCIS, William Douglas (1889–1959), farmer and self-taught botanist, assisted in the clearing of virgin rainforest at Kin Kin, near Gympie (Qld), for a family farm. As EVERIST observed: 'While engaged in cutting down the rainforest, Francis became interested in the identity of the trees he was helping to destroy. He was also in an excellent position to collect good herbarium material from the fallen trees.' In 1919 he was appointed Assistant Government Botanist, working as deputy to C.T. WHITE at Queensland Herbarium for thirty-one years; he later served as Government Botanist (1950–54) for Qld. A painstaking photographer and observer, he had two main interests: the classification, identification, distribution, and ecology of RAINFOREST trees, and the structure and chemical composition of protoplasm. He spent a year during 1930–31 on exchange at KEW. His monument is *Australian Rain-Forest Trees* (1929; 4th edn, 1981), which Everist considered 'the authoritative work on the subject and a milestone in the extension of botanical knowledge to the community at large'.

RA

FRANKLIN (née GRIFFIN), Jane (1792–1847), promoter of science and second wife (m. 1828) of Sir John Franklin (1786–1847), Arctic explorer and lieutenant-governor of Van Diemen's Land (1837–43), was born in London, the daughter of a wealthy silk merchant. Although she had little formal education she read extensively and was credited by

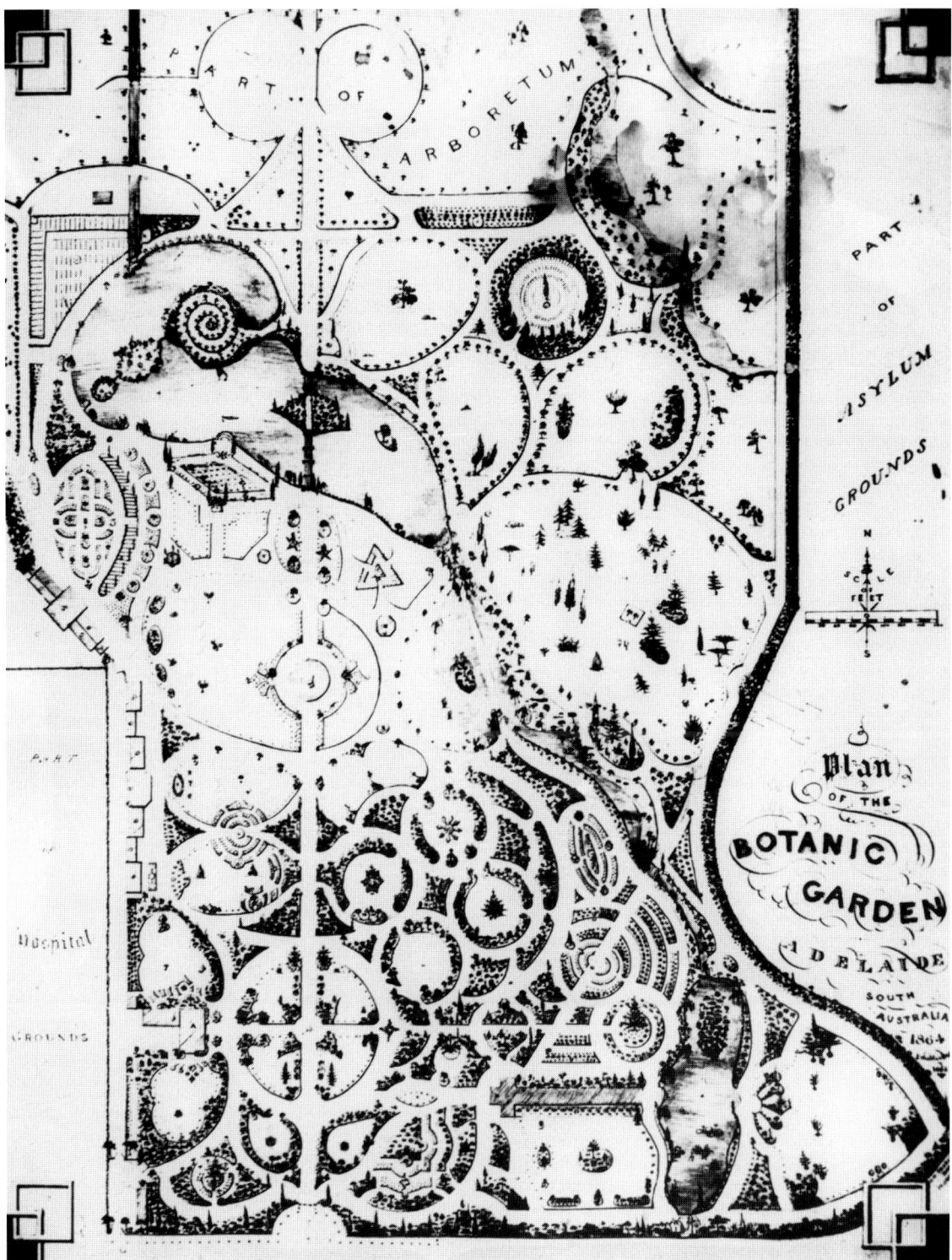

This plan of ADELAIDE BOTANIC GARDEN (1864), prepared by inaugural Superintendant George FRANCIS, depicts a grand European-influenced vision for the Garden—features such as the axial entry and walk, and the main and top lakes, as well as some of the path layout still survive

historian John West (1852) with 'a masculine intellect and adventurous spirit'. Under her influence Sir John Franklin founded the Tasmanian Natural History Society (1839), which later became the ROYAL SOCIETY of Tasmania. As a result of the Franklins' activities, the colony became the intellectual centre of Australia during this period. In 1842 the Franklins journeyed overland to Macquarie Harbour, Lady Franklin being the first European woman to do so. During this expedition the shrub later named *Acradenia frankliniae* (Whitey Wood) in her honour was discovered. In 1839 Lady Franklin purchased 130 acres (53 ha) at Kangaroo Bottom (now the suburb of Lenah Valley) with the intention of establishing a BOTANIC GARDEN with an initial emphasis on rare INDIGENOUS PLANTS. On the property, named Ancanthe, she had a museum of natural history built. The building, in the style of a Greek temple, housed a LIBRARY and NATURAL HISTORY specimens that had been collected by or presented to Lady Franklin. The Franklins left the colony in 1843, and in 1853 the museum was closed and the collection dispersed. Lady Franklin also encouraged the gardeners of Hobart through the presentation of prizes at horticultural shows.

LINDY SCRIPPS

FRANKLIN SQUARE, Hobart, a semi-formal urban SQUARE and PUBLIC PARK, was constructed between 1864 and 1866 on the site of a former GOVERNMENT HOUSE and grounds. It is bounded on three sides by streets, and on the fourth side by the Treasury offices. Symmetrical garden beds and oak trees, now mature, were planted around a fountain and pool surmounted by a statue of Sir John FRANKLIN. Although the basic structure of the park is still evident, a number of original features, including the rock garden at the base of the statue's plinth, have been replaced, and the park has not been fenced since 1944. Franklin Square has traditionally been used as a meeting place and more recently as a location for protest rallies.

LINDY SCRIPPS

FRANKLYN VALE, Grandchester, Qld, a pastoral run on Laidley's Plains (named by Allan CUNNINGHAM in 1829), was first taken up in the early 1840s. In 1849 the Laidley Run was sold to Thomas Sutcliffe MORT, who divided the run into two, the portion named Franklyn Vale being managed by his brother Henry (who had previously managed CRESSBROOK Station); after the marriage of his daughter Kate to Edward Crace (1871), the present homestead was erected and the couple installed as managers. The early layout, including a carriage loop and courtyard set within a distinctive framework of *Araucaria bidwillii* (Bunya Pine) plantings, had been established by Henry Mort. After a succession of managers (1877–84), Arthur and Constance Mort took up residence in 1894 and Constance was responsible for considerable new planting. The property, still in Mort family ownership, includes a tennis pavilion by architect Robin Dods and shrub beds set within the early layout.

RA

FRASER (FRAZER or FRAZIER), Charles (1791–1831), botanist and botanic gardens superintendent, was born at Blair in Perthshire, Scotland. He became a gardener, probably for the extensive estates of the landlord, the Duke of Atholl, and subsequently had connections with the botanic gardens of Edinburgh and Glasgow. He enlisted as a private in a Foot Regiment in 1815 and arrived in Sydney in 1816 to stay, joining the 46th Regiment later that year. Governor Macquarie quickly found this 'botanical soldier' and appointed him Colonial Botanist (collector)—in contradistinction to the King's botanist, Allan CUNNINGHAM. He was ordered to accompany surveyor John Oxley on his 1817–19 expeditions exploring the Lachlan, Macquarie, and Hastings river systems. Many hundreds of new species were collected, dried, and dispatched to collectors and curators, principally to Earl Bathurst, Secretary of State for the Colonies, and the botanic gardens of Glasgow and Edinburgh.

Charles Fraser took over care of the 'Exotics' in the Government Gardens in 1818 but did not have general supervision until 1820, with official appointment in January 1821 as inaugural Superintendent. Over a decade he organised the development of SYDNEY BOTANIC GARDENS from the governors' kitchen garden to a world-renowned BOTANIC GARDEN, receiving and sending plants and seeds to all the major horticultural centres as well as to penal settlements and major gardens in NSW. Initially food plants were grown—fruit trees, olives, and grapes being particularly successful—and liberally distributed among the settlers. As more economic and ornamental plants were given to him, he trialled, propagated, and grew these under difficult conditions: with poor soil, inadequate water, and no GLASSHOUSES. Being a skilled horticulturist, he succeeded where others had failed, and became respected by governors, botanists, and explorers alike.

Fraser participated in two further major expeditions, to make collections, one in 1827 with Captain James Stirling in western Australia to determine a site for settlement. The second, under Captain Patrick Logan in 1828, was to the Moreton Bay area, where they ascended the ranges and he laid out the 'New Garden', which became the BRISBANE BOTANIC GARDENS. Some of the plants collected on this journey were planted out in Sydney Botanic Gardens, notably *Araucaria cunninghamii* (Hoop Pine) and *Waterhousea floribunda* (Weeping Lilly Pilly), now huge canopy trees at the southern end of the present palm grove. Apart from collecting in NSW, and on the major expeditions, Fraser made many collecting trips to Van Diemen's Land, especially for cryptogamous plants, which were prized by his principal recipient, W.J. HOOKER, then Professor of Botany at Glasgow. He also collected from Norfolk Island.

Fraser died from a stroke returning from an arduous collecting expedition to a favoured area around Bathurst (NSW), and was buried at St John's Church, Parramatta. His specimens are now principally in the herbaria at KEW; Natural History (formerly British) Museum, London; Oxford; and some have returned to Sydney. George BENTHAM's *Flora Australiensis*, when finally completed in 1878, gave Fraser numerous attributions and Joseph MAIDEN in 1908 listed twenty-nine species named for him (although some have later been renamed).

GILLIAN DAVIES

The simple arrangement of low-slung homestead complete with verandah, carriage drive, and boundary plantings of *Araucaria bidwillii* (Bunya Pine) combine to make FRANYLYN VALE a quintessential Queensland HOMESTEAD complex

FRASER, Grace Ella (b. 1921), landscape designer and conservationist, was born in Melbourne and initially trained as an accountant assistant. She completed the certificate course (including garden design) at BURNLEY (1943–44), where wartime productive horticulture offered prospects for worthwhile outdoor work with plants. At Burnley she later supervised retraining of ex-servicemen and taught from 1948 to 1950. She developed a keen interest in plant pathology, which she pursued with CSIRO in Canberra (1945–48), and at Edinburgh and Cambridge (1950–52). On her return to Melbourne, Emily GIBSON facilitated her appointment to Tintern Church of England Girls Grammar School as grounds development manager for its new twenty-hectare East Ringwood site (1953–58). Fraser worked with John STEVENS (1959–64) on landscape projects, including Monash University, ICI House, Royal Children's Hospital, and Western Suburbs Memorial Park. Following Stevens' appointment to Australian National University, Canberra, she completed work in hand and commenced private practice (1964–86). Projects included the Australian plant garden, ROYAL PARK; Alexander Park, Sandringham; Camberwell Girls Grammar School; BP administration building, Western Port; Lake Ginninderra, Canberra (with Beryl MANN); and Frankston Golf Course. Since the 1960s, conservation and planning issues on the Mornington Peninsula have been a major interest. PAMELA JELLIE

FREE GARDENERS' SOCIETY The Grand United Order of Free Gardeners of Australasia was established in Melbourne in 1864, and in the following year a charter to set up branches or Lodges in Vic. was granted by the Grand Lodge of SCOTLAND. By 1906 Lodges existed in all Australian states, with many members, such as founder Alexander ELLIOTT, both Scotsmen and professional GARDENERS. As a friendly society, the Order raised funds through voluntary subscriptions from members, providing them with medicines and medical attendance, and relief to widowed mothers. Monthly meetings enabled members to socialise and conduct rituals based on the symbolism of the Garden of Eden and Christian teaching. Free Gardenery applied the art of cultivating the ground and its symbols to the development of the mind in intelligence and virtue. At the Society's zenith, more than twenty-five Lodges existed in Melbourne, where the Order continues. A short history was compiled by Bro. W.G. Mitchell (1958). RICHARD HEATHCOTE

FRENCH, Charles (1842–1933), gardener, naturalist, orchidologist, and entomologist, was born in Lewisham, Kent, England, and arrived in Vic. aged about ten. He was later (c. 1858) apprenticed to James SCOTT, from whose nursery he reputedly wheeled young trees, including now famous elms in the FITZROY GARDENS and a Californian Redwood that today towers over the BURNLEY gardens. He worked at the nurseries of Alex Bogie and Joseph HARRIS, and from 1865 at MELBOURNE BOTANIC GARDENS, where, on replacing Ferdinand MUELLER in 1873, William GUILFOYLE put him in charge of plant propagation and the fernery.

French enjoyed bush rambles with friends, who often met at his house in the Botanic Gardens to discuss their excursions and collections. His idea of a NATURAL HISTORY club led to the establishment, in 1880, of the FIELD NATURALISTS' CLUB of Victoria (FNCV), at whose first meeting he presented a talk on Victorian ferns. In the 1880s French was Mueller's senior HERBARIUM assistant in the Botanic Museum, and travelled widely in Vic. with FERNS and ORCHIDS his main interests. He shared his enthusiastic expertise in cultivating native ones, and his descriptions of all known Victorian orchids were published in the *Victorian Naturalist* (1884–87). He was a fellow of the Linnean and Royal Horticultural Societies in England, and the *Naturwissenschaftliche Gesellschaft Isis* (Isis Natural History Association) in Germany.

French also had entomological interests. In the Botanic Gardens he pursued his British boyhood love of netting butterflies, and prepared a report on timber-boring insects for the Department of Agriculture in 1874. Following insect damage to crops and orchards, French was appointed Victoria's first government entomologist (1889). French supervised a growing staff of plant disease inspectors and developed a standardised spraying and fumigation program for fruit trees. He retired in the year the fifth and final volume of his *Destructive Insects of Victoria* (1891–1911) was published.

Charles Hamilton French (1868–1950) as a child accompanied his father on collecting trips and to FNCV meetings, and acquired his interests, including a wide knowledge of Victoria's flora. In 1883 he joined his father in the Botanic Museum as a junior herbarium assistant and helped prepare Mueller's *Key to the System of Victorian Plants* (1885–88). He travelled throughout Vic. collecting plant specimens for Mueller and insects for his father. Appointed assistant entomologist (1895), he again joined his father, and in 1913 succeeded him as government entomologist. In 1929 he was promoted to government biologist. On his retirement in 1933 he devoted much time to FNCV activities and MARANOA GARDENS, becoming curator in 1944. In the bush, inconspicuous orchids and insects rarely escaped his searching eyes. E.E. PESCOTT dedicated his *Orchids of Victoria* (1928) to 'Charles French, Senior and Junior, Father and Son, pioneers in research work in Victorian Orchidology'. LINDEN GILLBANK

'FRIENDS GROUPS' of botanic gardens, national parks, and zoological gardens have, especially since the 1970s and 1980s, played an important—and extremely informed—voluntary role in areas such as fund raising, lobbying, publicity, and interpretation. This movement sprang from the North American docent system of volunteers (especially in museums and art galleries) and even earlier European precedents involving privileged access for members of privately managed gardens and kindred institutions. Originally operating independently, many Australian 'friends groups' are now linked by state councils, and a peak national body, the Australian Federation of Friends of Museums. Perhaps more diverse in membership than comparable groups in galleries, garden 'friends' form an influential group, with their high profile indicative of the vital role of their achievements and aspirations. EVE ALMOND

FRONT GARDENS The vernacular front garden, especially forming a key feature of Australian SUBURBAN GARDENS, presents a desired self-image of its keeper, usually neat and tidy, declaring communal responsibility; but it can also reveal non-conformist tendencies. Whether the garden is the traditional combination of LAWN, SHRUBS, ANNUALS; a riot of painted STATUARY and ROCKWORK; or a tangle of native GRASSES and eucalypts; it also makes a statement about the personality of the owner. In a highly urbanised country, LAND SURVEY AND SALE has until relatively recently favoured single dwellings, or at its tightest, terrace housing, rather than multi-storey housing, with consequent space for front gardens and BACKYARDS.

Stylistically, the vernacular front garden has rocked between nostalgic anachronism and fashion victim. The tiny colonial COTTAGE GARDEN, behind protective palings, included tough species such as PELARGONIUMS and olives, as HEDGES or in POTS. In the 1850s, scythed grass and citrus trees of VILLAS framed small PARTERRE entrances, and SHRUBBERIES evolved. Gardens have since become larger, the house moved back on the block, as by mid-century there was less need for the utilitarian aspects of the backyard. Front gardens also became more complex. With Federation, selected elements of the GARDEN SUBURB—curving paths, shrubberies, decorative island BEDS of GARDENESQUE plantings, and lattice structures—were taken up to complement the bungalow, viewed from the complementary NATURE STRIP through an open wire or iron fence.

Two technological advances had major influences on the front garden: the early twentieth-century 'domestication' of concrete and the move from hand mower to the powered LAWN MOWER after the Second World War. Do-it-yourself concrete defined the PATH and twin-strip DRIVEWAY, and outlined beds in toothpaste-like ribbons. The front garden was protected by other concrete products—GNOMES, 'classical' figures, swans, flamingos, SHELLS, and Aboriginal figures (with spears) have been favoured at various times—and by myth (plastic bottles of water spread on the lawn to deter dogs). With the lawn mower, the garden owner could attain that pinnacle of neatness, the all-lawn front garden, with perhaps a single ROSE bush, or decorative LETTERBOX to break the sward, and garden beds driven to the boundary fences. FENCES protected in many areas, although they are not as ubiquitous as in earlier days. Functionalist modernity introduced car driveway strips as permanent fixtures, paralleled by straight paths, spaces filled with lawn, edged with rose beds or mixed annuals, a masonry fence or privet hedge, and with foundation plantings near the house. These last elements have largely remained as the foundation of suburban front gardens: only plant stock indicates a response to fashion—carpet roses, Mondo grass, English box, PALMS, and golden diosma being indicators of late twentieth-century trends. The BUSH GARDEN of the 1960s and COURTYARD gardens of the 1990s have perhaps offered the greatest challenge to the front gardening mores.

Popular garden practice evolved through advice in early ALMANACS, NURSERY catalogues, popular GARDEN BOOKS and guides by ADAMSON and BRUNNING (Vic.), HEYNE (SA), HOCKINGS (Qld), Walch (Tas.), and YATES (NSW), GARDEN MAGAZINES, and broadcasts on RADIO and TELEVISION. All have been interpreted on a vernacular, personal level in the front garden and imposed over a plan well established by the 1930s. The intrigue of the personal meeting the public in the front garden has attracted many commentators ranging from Peter CUFFLEY to George SEDDON. DEBORAH MALOR

In its book *Liquid Gold: Australia* (1959) the Australian Publicity Council sought to attract migrants to the IRRIGATION districts of Vic. and NSW, and to the Snowy Mountains Hydro-Electric and Irrigation Scheme, by depicting the nation's comfortable and prosperous outlook, ranging from FRONT GARDENS to factories

FRUIT, defined botanically as the matured ovary of a seed plant, can also include other parts of the flower. There is a great array of fruit types, and they can be divided into fleshy fruits such as apple (pome), tomato (berry), plum (drupe), and rose (hep), and dry fruits such as hazel (nut), eucalyptus (capsule), pea (pea), and elm (samara). These groups can be further divided, in the case of fleshy fruits, into those formed from single flowers (including all those mentioned) and multiple flowers formed from more than one flower (an inflorescence) such as the pineapple, mulberry, and fig. For dry fruits a further division is made between those that split to release seed (dehiscent), such as the pea, and those that do not split (indehiscent), such as nuts.

Fruit growing forms an important part of Australia's DESIGNED LANDSCAPES. On the broad scale of vineyards, VITICULTURE—often in IRRIGATED areas conducive to growing a wide range of fruit, including citrus—has formed a specialised but significant component of fruit growing. TROPICAL fruits also form a specialised branch of fruit growing, one of great significance in tropical areas of Qld and NT. In gardens, plants that produce edible fruit have been widely grown; sometimes in larger SUBURBAN GARDENS and rural HOMESTEAD GARDENS areas for growing fruit trees have been formalised into designated ORCHARDS. POMOLOGY formed a cornerstone of nineteenth- and early twentieth-century horticulture. In small urban and COURTYARD gardens, trees manipulated to grow against a wall as an ESPALIER have also been used. Fruit have also been widely used in gardens for their ornamental value, ranging from traditional *Malus* spp. (Crab Apple) to Australian native plants such as the pink-purple fruit of *Acmena smithii* (Lilly Pilly) to the rich purple fruit of *Dianella* spp. Early Australian nursery plant catalogues also promoted the use of trees that were both ornamental and useful, such as the *Eriobotrya japonica* (Loquat), which has large bold FOLIAGE and produces yellow fruit at once ornamental and edible.

Paul Baxter, *Growing Fruit in Australia* (Melbourne, 1981); L. Glowinski, *The Complete Book of Fruit Growing in Australia* (South Melbourne, 1991); H. Frederick Janson, *Pomona's Harvest: An Illustrated Chronicle of Antiquarian Fruit Literature* (Oregon, 1996)

ML

FRUIT TREES: see ORCHARDS

FUCHSIA, a genus named in honour of German herbalist and botanical illustrator Leonhart Fuchs (1501–1566), was introduced into cultivation in Europe from South America and the first plants offered in England by James LEE in 1753. While the majority of species arrived from Central and South America, other species, such as the small flowering

Furniture

ground cover, *Fuchsia procumbens*, were introduced from New Zealand and Tahiti. The circumstances surrounding the introduction of fuchsias into Australia are uncertain, but a range of CULTIVARS was available in nurseries by the mid-nineteenth century. The majority were imported from Europe, and consisted of the popular lines produced as a result of hybridisation and selection by NURSERIES and individual PLANT BREEDERS. As with other cultivar groups, the First World War disrupted breeding programs, and the popularity of fuchsias waned. After the Second World War there was a renewed upsurge in interest, particularly for cultivars raised in the USA. The American Fuchsia Society (established 1928) was central to this revival, and is now the world registration authority for new cultivars. Many new forms have since been raised in Australia, and a large number of fuchsia societies have been established—most importantly the Australian Fuchsia Society, founded in Adelaide in 1970. In addition to the large number of cultivars now formed from traditionally grown species, such as *Fuchsia magellanica*, *F. coccinea*, and *F. fulgens*, and cultivated in shrub beds, as ornamentals, in hanging baskets, and as POT PLANTS for INDOOR display, a wide range of other species such as *F. arborescens*, *F. boliviana*, *F. corymbiflora*, and *F. splendens* has been also been planted in Australian gardens.

ML

FURNITURE in Australian gardens cannot be separated from furniture made, used, or stored on VERANDAHS. In that traditional and vernacular Australian middle-ground between house and garden, mingled furniture was made for use both inside and out. Frequently a piece of furniture progressed—or rather was relegated—from inside to verandah to garden as fashion and the condition of the piece changed. This appears to be so for one of the earliest documented garden seats recorded at Sydney's ELIZABETH BAY HOUSE by 1841: an early nineteenth-century sofa frame, depleted of its upholstery and given a rudimentary ornamentation of lattice-work. By the mid-nineteenth century, purpose-made wooden garden or verandah benches or settles were common, often with solid seats, railed backs, and curved or shaped arms. They are well documented in early photographs of SYDNEY BOTANIC

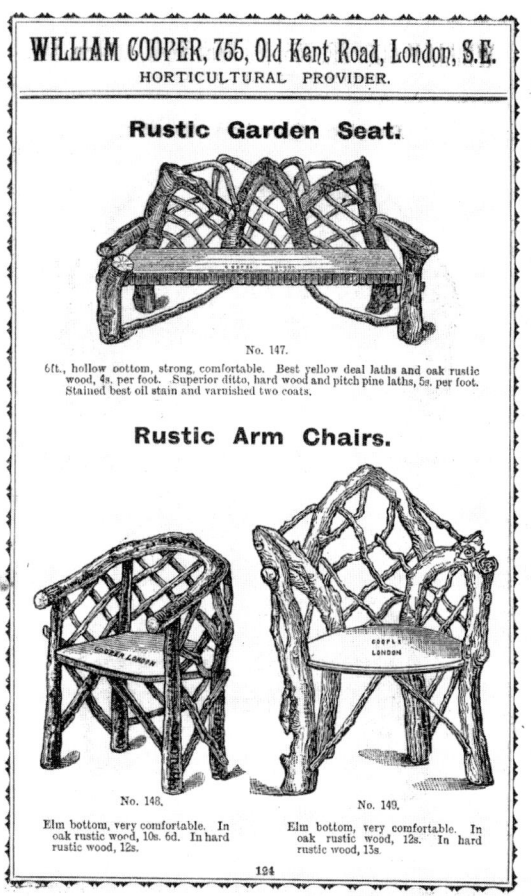
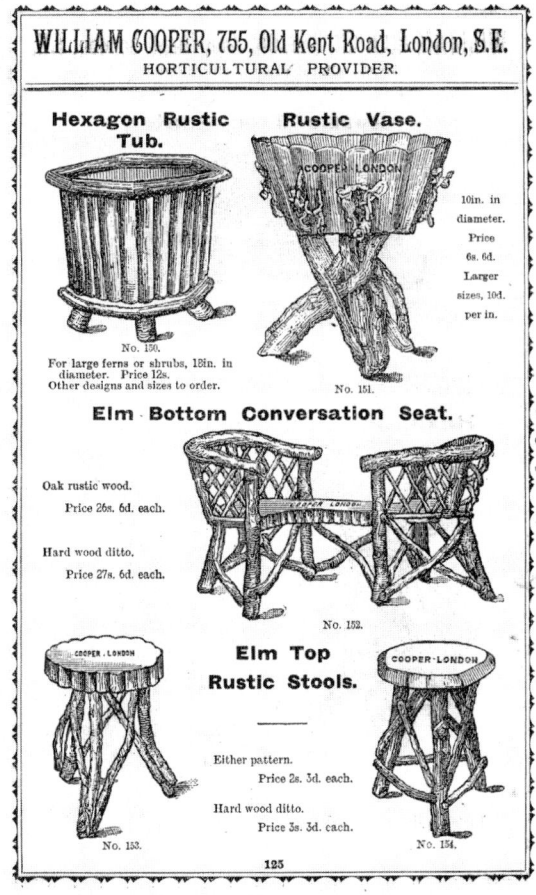

Numerous local manufacturers and importers supplied garden FURNITURE through mail-order catalogues and emporiums in the nineteenth century, with tastes running from the chaste to the overtly RUSTIC

Furniture

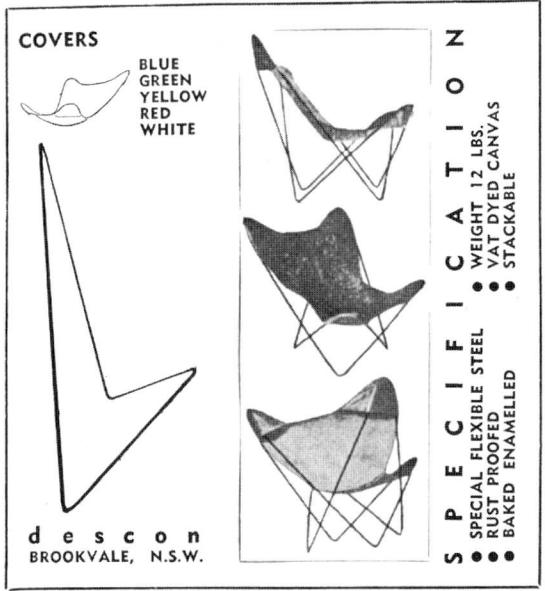

MODERNISM swept through the Australian FURNITURE market as post-war PATIOS and COURTYARDS demanded furniture suited to a new aesthetic of leisure

GARDENS, and fine examples (*c.* 1860), painted dark green, remain in the front verandah for which they were made at ROUSE HILL (NSW). The type continued throughout the nineteenth century and until recently was still found on railway platforms and waiting rooms. Such wooden settles lost popularity during the second half of the century when cast iron became increasingly available.

By the late 1860s cast iron furniture of English, American, and Australian production was used extensively in entrance halls, verandahs, and gardens. At Elizabeth Bay House, full cast-iron seats (probably Coalbrookdale) stood on either side of its front door in the late 1850s, but more commonly used in public and private gardens well into the twentieth century were benches with cast-iron ends joined by wooden slats. The designs of these benches and ends showed the range of mid- and late nineteenth-century styles: Gothick, Louis revival, RUSTIC and naturalistic, Renaissance revival, and Aesthetic movement. These styles persisted long after their fashion had passed for interior design. They were available in several painted colours, bronze-green, Aesthetic green, and deep Brunswick green being common.

A lighter, although not quite so durable or strong alternative to cast-iron furniture, and available from the mid-nineteenth century until well after the First World War, was furniture of woven WIRE, imported, locally made, or home-made. Chairs, settees, and tables were available in addition to plant stands and other garden ornaments. An early twentieth-century variant of metal garden furniture, popular in Qld, was the bench of galvanised pipe frame with woven-wire seat and back. Wooden furniture, of natural, twisted branches in the rustic taste was also popular—and a cheap alternative to cast iron—at the end of the nineteenth century. There were also easily moved pieces such as deck chairs—light, wooden frames hung with canvas, or caned—or more substantial pieces such as swing seats, complete with canvas UMBRELLAS.

Woven furniture of cane, willow, rattan, and similar pliable, natural materials was first imported from China and India and used both inside and on verandahs. By the late nineteenth century, the woven basket chair was ubiquitous, not yielding to seagrass and rattan furniture until the 1920s. Cheap imports as well as locally made cane and rattan furniture have continued to be sold, although its popularity was first challenged by such innovations as Lloyd-loom furniture and, in the 1960s, light, aluminium-framed furniture with weather-resistant plastic or nylon webbing, exemplified by the vastly popular folding 'banana lounge'.

At the beginning of the twentieth century, fashion, influenced largely by English ARTS AND CRAFTS, Queen Anne and Georgian Revival designers, turned again to wooden benches of simpler, vaguely classical, form; although dark green continued as a practical, neutral colour, white and cream gained favour. Cast-iron and wood benches were also replaced—particularly in public gardens—by benches of bent strap iron with thinner wooden laths—a functional type that has continued to be made. Traditionally wrought (blacksmith) iron was rarely used for furniture, although the term was used popularly after the Second World War, and the general availability of welding machines brought forth furniture of curved, welded strap steel, commercially produced but frequently home-made.

Of other materials, benches of carved and moulded stone were used infrequently in the late nineteenth and early twentieth centuries, and only in grander gardens. However, in the Sydney area in the second half of the twentieth century, garden seats and 'settings' (tables and benches) of highly figured Gosford sandstone made by sandwiching together many rusticated-edged layers, were popular in suburban gardens. Cast concrete benches and tables, generally of debased Italianate or classical form and often coloured and finished to resemble sandstone, gained popularity between the wars. This taste has continued to the present, with more sophisticated casts, often influenced by such English firms as Haddonstone. Rarer for garden furniture, but popular for garden ornament, was naturalistically modelled concrete fondue rustic-work. Ceramic or earthenware furniture appeared in Australian gardens in the early nineteenth century with the importing of Chinese barrel-shaped stools. At the end of the century a few earthenware rustic garden chairs were made by Australian potteries, but these were rare. At BABWORTH HOUSE (NSW) in the early twentieth century wooden slatted benches with ceramic ends manufactured by Royal Doulton were used. Stone and ceramics were, however, much used for garden ORNAMENTS.

Garden furniture other than chairs, benches, and tables was rare. Benches often contained storage boxes for equipment for outdoor games; old boxes and cupboards were often placed on the verandah for similar uses. Plant stands and plant stages, however, ranged from improvised structures of planks

239

Furniture

and logs to elaborately designed pieces of furniture. Like seat furniture, the earliest documented plant stands were of simple wooden construction, with receding tiers of shelves—or, like the surviving stands at Bedervale, Braidwood (NSW), of table-like form, perhaps fitted with tin drip trays. Cast iron appears to have been less popular than woven wire for stands in the late nineteenth and early twentieth centuries. The popularity of purpose-designed plant stands seems to have declined between the wars, although improvised examples abound: they were adapted from old tables, perforated metal industrial scrap, water pipe, or steel reinforcing mesh. Stands for individual pots and jardinières included, throughout the nineteenth century, Chinese ceramics and, in the twentieth century, rustic wood, wrought iron, and cast and rustically modelled cement in imitation of logs.

The wheel of fashion returned to a taste for decorative neo-Victorian metal benches, generally flimsy and of light cast aluminium, in the last quarter of the twentieth century. At the same time there was a revival of Edwardian wooden benches in the manner of Lutyens, usually made of imported teak, unpainted and left to weather.

Terence Lane and Jessie Serle, *Australians at Home: A Documentary History of Australian Domestic Interiors from 1788 to 1914* (Melbourne, 1990) **JAMES BROADBENT**

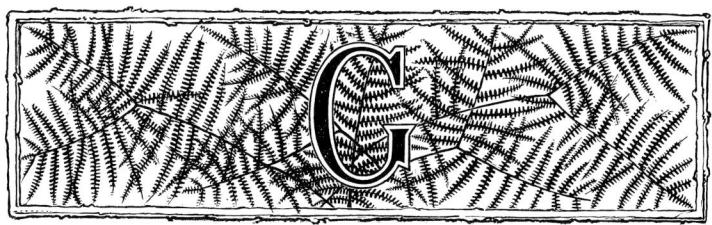

GALBRAITH, Jean ('Correa') (1906–1999), botanist, naturalist, writer, and gardener, lived at Tyers in Gippsland (Vic.). At her family home, Dunedin, she worked with her father and mother to make and maintain a garden whose beauty she shared with fellow gardeners throughout Australia over seven decades of writing—in periodicals, newspapers, and books. A love of plants was fundamental to her being; learning about plants was of immense, continuing interest. Through her long life she encouraged this in others.

The Galbraiths, devout members of the Christadelphian faith who saw God's hand in every facet of Nature, led a simple life at Dunedin based around a farm and garden so productive that they were virtually self-sufficient. Often ill as a child and thus a voracious reader, Jean was encouraged by her parents to take an interest in the garden, the birds that visited it, and the surrounding bushland. She left school at 14. Then, aged 16, she met the botanist H.B. WILLIAMSON at a FIELD NATURALISTS' CLUB wildflower show in Melbourne. Seeing her thirst for knowledge, he suggested she send him plants for identification. Their eight-year correspondence and friendship built the foundations of botany for her.

Galbraith once said she could not live without writing. In 1925 her letters and observations began appearing in the monthly magazine, the (AUSTRALIAN) GARDEN LOVER, under the pen-name 'Correa', which she chose for the sheets of this Australian plant that cloaked the hillsides around Dunedin. From 1931 to 1975 she wrote a regular column in this magazine, 'From Day to Day in the Garden'. An inspirational and constant voice in gardening journalism can have a profound effect on generations of gardeners (as witness Vita Sackville-West's writings in the *Observer*). Galbraith's readers were legion, and the news that she was to leave the *Australian Garden Lover* after fifty years brought a cry of despair from one: 'You mean you're going to say goodbye? I can't bear that you should stop writing! Dear Correa, it has been so wonderful, all these years, the way you have been able to share the things that surround you.' When, through age and failing eyesight, Galbraith had to discontinue the articles she contributed to the *Age* newspaper (1985–92), there were similar dismayed letters.

Jean Galbraith's major publications contributed immeasurably to the body of knowledge about indigenous plants. These are *Wildflowers of Victoria* (1950, republished 1956 and 1967), and Collins' *Field Guide to the Wildflowers of South-East Australia* (1977). The first, written at the instigation of Winifred WADDELL, was the first comprehensive such publication since Ferdinand MUELLER's *Key to the System of Victorian Plants* (1886–88). The second took five years of research and writing, and involved travelling thousands of kilometres, often in remote areas—a tall order for anyone, much less a tiny, frail woman in her sixties. The strength of

Jean GALBRAITH's garden at Dunedin, Tyers (Vic.) was depicted on the cover of her autobiographical *Garden in a Valley* (1939)—writings that introduced countless readers to the seasonal joys of life in rural Australia

each book is the bridge built between botany as a science, and amateurs who want to find out more about AUSTRALIAN PLANTS. Many such people take these books to the bush for identification purposes, many grow in their own gardens the plants Jean helped them to appreciate. Her other important books—*Garden in a Valley* (1939, republished 1985), *A Gardener's Year* (1987), and *A Garden Lover's Journal* (1989)—encourage a wider appreciation of gardening, and promote her belief in gardens as sources of solace, delight, and spiritual renewal. But she also found pleasure in garden chores, and in growing things. At Dunedin, the garden that evolved with her and which she left in 1993, she loved to experiment with new or interesting plants, particularly ALPINES, and the front verandah held a clutch of pots containing the rare, the more common, and the sickly. She called it 'intensive care'.

Galbraith is remembered in skirt, thick stockings, and sensible shoes on bushwalks and camping expeditions, carefully selecting tiny specimens of plants, with an eagle eye that picked out the minutest variations (and that led to the discovery, and naming, of *Dampiera galbraithiana*, 1989, and *Boronia galbraithiae*, 1993). She received the Australian Natural History Medallion in 1970. Dedicated conservationist and generous teacher (from radio broadcasts for schoolchildren to botany lessons by correspondence for the artist, Joan LAW-SMITH, published in 1999 in *Kindred Spirits*), close friend to many 'names' in Australian gardening (including the botanist J.H. WILLIS, and the designer Edna WALLING, with whom she collaborated on several proposed books), Jean Galbraith remains an inspiration to many. This would have surprised her, because for her the plant world was simply a way of life, while writing books about gardens was 'like sending ships into strange seas and finding in every port, not strangers, but friends.' ANNE LATREILLE

GAMBLE COTTAGE, Blackwood, SA, retains a small COTTAGE GARDEN developed *c.* 1900–10 by Harriet Victoria Gamble (1866–1940) and her daughters Clara and Edith. As the daughters grew elderly, the property was transferred to the Mitcham City Council, which in turn sought assistance and advice from a group of interested local citizens, constituted as a FRIENDS GROUP. The sisters' recollections have assisted in rejuvenation of the garden, which is maintained with a display of hardy annuals, bulbs, herbaceous perennials, roses, flowering shrubs, climbers, and small trees to represent a decorative SUBURBAN GARDEN of *c.* 1900.

TREVOR NOTTLE

GARDEN The artificial construct that *Homo sapiens* calls (in English) a 'garden' is as much a contemporary product of evolution as the nest of a weaver-bird, the web of a spider, the mound of a termite colony, the den of a polar bear, or a tract of rainforest. Almost all of us are now aware of the 'web of life' into which gardens fit, though we constantly tear holes in it. Religion has been described as attempts to climb the same mountain by different routes and from different starting points; and indeed, religion and gardening have much in common—including the most fervently espoused cults. It is in this context that Australian gardens and gardening should be viewed.

In their book *Gardens in Time* (1980), John and Ray OLDHAM juxtapose two striking images: one of an Egyptian pyramid, and the other of a pyramid hill in a wild area of north-western Australia. In some cultures, notable shapes, whether natural or made by conscious human manipulation, are components of what we call gardens—witness the upright rocks of Chinese gardens, the sand gardens of Japan, or the geological formations that are sacred sites for Aboriginal Australians.

Fruit pigeons (and other animals) make their own gardens; the seeds from the fruits they have eaten germinate elsewhere to create new groves; hippopotamuses fertilise with their droppings their own grazing grounds. Hunter–gatherer becomes agriculturist, who becomes HORTICULTURIST. Monks, as scientists, test plants for medicinal purposes; as evangelists they ascribe symbolic meaning to plants such as rose and lily; the beginning of things is set in a (well-watered) garden. As communities become more settled (and even when they do not) aesthetics merge with utility. Other motives enter. The paradise gardens of Asia were hunting parks. The pursuit of pleasure, the display of wealth, and of the power of humans over nature (still potent factors in garden-making) acquire greater emphasis. The scientists of BOTANY step in—describing, classifying, analysing, experimenting.

Turn now to AUSTRALIA. The Aboriginal inhabitants, over time and presumably by trial and error, acquired a comprehensive knowledge of the PLANT products of their areas, how to get rid of poisons in some of them and when were the most prolific SEASONS for fruit and tubers. ABORIGINAL ENVIRONMENTAL MANAGEMENT, through the practice of 'fire-stick farming', constantly altered the floristic component of the surroundings (though perhaps not by as much as the vagaries of climate). One assumes that they could not have helped being aesthetically moved by the displays of blossom and their scent; but I know of no evidence that suggests that Aboriginal Australians consciously manipulated these elements into what Europeans call gardens.

Some of those Europeans, when they first arrived, were so moved by the wealth of plant life that they named their landfall Botany Bay. But their first efforts at cultivation were utilitarian, and because they did not understand the soil or the climate, they nearly starved. Later, in their ignorance—which continues still—they grievously misused that SOIL, not least by the introduction of cloven-footed animals, foreign grasses, and escaped garden plants and the translocation of some native plants so that they too became WEEDS.

As they became more secure (but still felt isolated), they sought to recall, in architecture and in gardens, what they had known at 'home'. Experience in India played a big part; there, in the hot season—and they found Australia hot—the governing classes migrated to the hills. MOUNTS WILSON and MACEDON, and the ADELAIDE HILLS filled the role of Simla and Darjeeling. Gradually, very gradually—after all, what is 200 years' experience compared with that acquired over thousands of years around the MEDITERRANEAN and in CHINA?—the new settlers adjusted; but the styles of gardening and the varieties of plants grown have generally followed—and still follow—those of other countries.

There was, after their first discovery, a burst of interest in Europe in growing plants indigenous to Australia; but it died down as newly collected plants flooded in from other parts of the world. In Australia itself, the interest in the NATIVE FLORA flickered, and at one point in the twentieth century became intertwined with nationalism. Until recently, little attention has been paid to the effects of GEOLOGY, geography, symbiosis and, above all, differences in CLIMATE on gardening (in which respect south-east Tas. most closely resembles Europe). For many Australian plants, occasional FIRES are necessary for their persistence and health, which makes them unsuitable for suburban gardens. Since most Australians live in cities, or on the outskirts of cities, comparatively few understand the dangers and advantages of fire to the ENVIRONMENT.

The main factors affecting gardening have remained what they always were—climate, especially rainfall and sunlight, and geology, and since European settlement, money. Wealthy individuals have made large gardens, often with imported plants; but quarter-acre blocks have deterred experimentation. Subsistence gardening or the growth of grouped 'allotments' for gardens has been rare. MIGRATION from cultures other than the British has resulted in changes of content (for example, a Polish lady fills her garden with beetroot for borscht); but the basic skills and TOOLS remain little changed, except for some mechanisation. Capital cities and provincial centres created BOTANIC GARDENS, especially after gold had generated wealth; but the struggle between the scientific and municipal aims for them has never been resolved. Although Alister CLARK deliberately tried to breed roses to suit Australian conditions, there has been comparatively little deliberate HYBRIDISING with that aim in mind.

In the years following the Second World War, there was a hiatus in gardening knowledge. Most GARDENING BOOKS were imported. AUSTRALIA'S OPEN GARDEN SCHEME and the publication of books based on Australian experience, especially with native plants, have done much to foster enthusiasm and to give gardeners confidence to try plants and methods more suitable for where they live. The evolution of Australian gardens will continue. Microscopy and genetic manipulation, and a more detailed understanding of evolution, have made even the concept of 'species' debatable, and replaced folk wisdom with scientific analysis. But interest in gardening is great, and helps to provide the flow of money needed to continue its evolution.

J.C. Loudon, *An Encyclopaedia of Gardening* ... (London, 1822 and later editions); Marie Luise Gothein, *A History of Garden Art* (London, 1928); D. Clifford, *A History of Garden Design* (London, 1962); Miles Hadfield, *Gardens* (London, 1962); Julia S. Berrall, *The Garden: An Illustrated History from Egypt to the Present Day* (London, 1966); Norman T. Newton, *Design on the Land: The Development of Landscape Architecture* (Cambridge, Mass., 1971); G.B. Tobey, *A History of Landscape Architecture: The Relationship of People to Environment* (New York, 1973); Geoffrey and Susan Jellicoe, *The Landscape of Man: Shaping the Environment from Prehistory to the Present Day* (London, 1975); Anthony Huxley, *An Illustrated History of Gardening* (London, 1978); Christopher Thacker, *The History of Gardens* (London, 1979); Geoffrey and Susan Jellicoe, Patrick Goode, and Michael Lancaster, *The Oxford Companion to Gardens* (Oxford, 1986); William Howard Adams, *Nature Perfected: Gardens Through History* (New York, 1991); Martin Hoyles, *The Story of Gardening* (London, 1991); Monique Mosser and Georges Teyssot (eds), *The History of Garden Design: The Western Tradition from the Renaissance to the Present Day* (London, 1991); Charles W. Moore, William J. Mitchell, and William Turnbull jnr, *The Poetics of Gardens* (Cambridge, Mass., 1988); Jane Brown, *The Pursuit of Paradise: A Social History of Gardens and Gardening* (London, 1999); John Dixon Hunt, *Greater Perfections: The Practice of Garden Theory* (Philadelphia, 2000)   T.R. GARNETT

GARDEN AND FIELD (1875–1940), a prominent monthly journal based in Adelaide, provided detailed advice and information on advances in agriculture, horticulture, gardening, and forestry throughout SA, and occasionally neighbouring colonies (later states). Established by Albert MOLINEUX, with the support of E.W. ANDREWS, and published under the auspices of the Royal Agricultural and Horticultural Society of South Australia, it became the most consistent and significant publication of its type in Australia up to the Second World War. Molineux's editorial policy was simple: 'First of all (as no country ever has, or can prosper when agriculture is neglected) we wish to see the very best system of farming initiated and sustained'. By the early 1880s, the journal's motto was 'Science and Experience to guide, Intelligence to comprehend, and Industry to execute'. Members of the Chamber of Manufactures, Royal Agricultural and Horticultural Society, Field Naturalists' Club, and local scientists, botanists, aboriculturists, agronomists, and horticulturists provided regular contributions, together with extracts—often translated— from European and North American scientific publications. Molineux served as editor until 1891, when educator and natural science enthusiast W. Catton Grasby (1859–1930) purchased the journal and continued its strong editorial direction, enabling Molineux to concentrate on his work with the Agricultural Bureau. The journal absorbed the *Dairy Farmer* (1905–08) and the *Fruit Growers' and Gardeners' Bulletin*, and had minor title changes, including *Australian Garden and Field* (1907–20).   DAVID JONES

GARDEN AND THE HOME (1923–24), published monthly in Sydney, was the official organ of the Horticultural Society of New South Wales, the National Rose Society of New South Wales, and other horticultural societies. Under editor and publisher R.A. Williams, the magazine included coverage from the eastern mainland states. It contained Edna WALLING's contributions 'From the Victorian notebook'—among her earliest published articles and plans—and other content focusing on FLORICULTURE. The *Garden and the Home* was superseded by GARDEN AND HOME MAKER OF AUSTRALIA.   RA

GARDEN AND HOME MAKER OF AUSTRALIA (1925–33), published monthly in Sydney, divided its horticultural coverage between the SUBURBAN GARDENER and the plant enthusiast. AUSTRALIAN FLORA also took its place alongside exotic favourites under the capable hand of editor

Garden books

G.K. COWLISHAW. The journal became the official organ of the Royal Horticultural Society of New South Wales, but struggled to achieve national coverage in editorial content and advertising, and was absorbed by the AUSTRALIAN GARDEN LOVER. RA

GARDEN BOOKS for Australian conditions commenced in the 1830s with works issued by NURSERY proprietors, although prior to this ALMANACS had provided essential horticultural guidance to the new settlers. British gardening and agricultural works had been imported by settlers dating from the First Fleet, but they were not always immediately useful due to SEASONAL and CLIMATIC differences between the northern and southern hemispheres. Works by SHEPHERD (NSW), BUNCE (Tas.), and MCEWIN (SA) all drew on the nursery backgrounds of their authors, although Shepherd's *Lectures on Landscape Gardening in Australia* (1836) stood alone for many years as a locally published work on design. McEwin also included guidance on VITICULTURE, a field that produced other early horticultural texts, notably by BUSBY (NSW) and NASH (WA), in the 1820s–40s. Most of the early works, such as those by JAMES (SA), Bunce and DICKINSON (Tas.), ADAMSON, COLE, and SINCLAIR (Vic.), and HOCKINGS (Qld), adopted a seasonal arrangement, generally broken into monthly sections. These works of the 1830s to the 1850s were simple instruction books, concentrating primarily on FRUIT and VEGETABLE growing, and secondly on FLORICULTURE. Only occasionally was there mention of more advanced ideas on layout and design.

Gardens and ORCHARDS were encouraged primarily as a source of food, even for the small householder, although most of these early books were directed at the professional GARDENERS employed by the more affluent members of colonial society. By the 1850s and 1860s, Australian garden books—many were really pamphlets—were increasingly directed at the 'amateur', the small householder, and often the housewife. Gardening was promoted as a source of MORAL IMPROVEMENT and a means of keeping the family happy and healthy. These early works were rarely illustrated and were intended for use in the bush-house or garden shed rather than the sitting room.

By the latter part of the nineteenth century books had become more sophisticated, with the FLOWER GARDEN taking up more of the space; but it was not until the twentieth century that SHRUBS began to have a separate section of their own. Again, nursery proprietors and seed merchants such as HEYNE (SA), BRUNNING, LAW SOMNER, MCMILLAN, and STURROCK (Vic.), and TRESEDER (NSW), were all authors of popular works, many revised through several editions. Horticultural journalists such as MACKAY and WRIGHT (Qld), CLARSON and ELLIOTT (Vic.), and MOLINEUX (SA), also drew on their considerable experience to produce books during the 1870s–90s. During this period GARDEN MAGAZINES were also published locally, although few achieved a lifespan of more than a decade, due in part to the vigorous weekly horticultural press of the major newspaper proprietors. During the nineteenth century—and indeed well into the twentieth—garden books were essentially directed at local audiences, and few made the intercolonial transition. In part this was historical, due to major political factors, but climatic factors also saw localised information and distribution, especially for tropical Qld and cool temperate Tas. Another trend that consolidated from the late nineteenth century was the publication of English books with an Australian imprint, especially by Cassell & Co. and Ward Lock & Co., although this had commenced with colonial imprints of Loudon's *Encyclopaedia of Cottage, Farm and Villa Architecture* (McGarvie, Sydney, and Howe, Hobart Town, 1833) and Abercrombie and Mawe's *Every Man His Own Gardener* (Tegg, Sydney, 1836).

Three books stand apart for their publishing longevity: those by Adamson and Brunning (Vic.), Walch (Tas.), and YATES (NSW). Smith and Adamson's *The Colonial Gardener* (1854) was the precursor to *Brunning's Australian Gardener*, still in print after a century and a half, an unsurpassed publishing span. The *Handbook of Garden and Greenhouse Culture in Tasmania* (1870), anonymously written and published by J. Walch and Sons, ran through many editions to the 1940s, with successive revisions by WADE, WALKER, KAY, and Alan Cruickshank. *Yates' Garden Guide* (1895) remains in print after more than a century.

The *Handbook of Australian Horticulture* (1892) by H.A. JAMES was Australia's first horticultural blockbuster. Issued in twelve monthly parts during 1891–92, its 522 pages were interleaved with twelve chromolithographed plates (by Signor Guglielmo Auteriello)—the first colour illustrations in an Australian gardening book—and also contained numerous engraved illustrations. It followed the formula of earlier handbooks, but in its physical size and comprehensiveness looked forward to post–Second World War books by E.E. LORD, Thistle HARRIS, Noel LOTHIAN, and Reg EDWARDS. Another innovation was the introduction of books in uniform format issued as part of a series, commenced in a tentative manner with handbooks by William Clarson (1878–86) and John LOCKLEY (1907–14) and firmly established by the Australian Practical Handbooks (1920–21) and WHITCOMBE'S AUSTRALIAN GARDENING HANDBOOKS (1926–31) of publisher Whitcombe & Tombs.

Apart from Shepherd's *Lectures*, garden design was subordinated to horticulture until seminal works of the new century such as C. Bogue LUFFMANN's *Principles of Gardening for Australia* (1903) and Edna WALLING's *Gardens in Australia: Their Design and Care* (1943). This is not to deny the influence of books such as William Elliott's *Australasian Gardening and Domestic Floriculture* (1897) or E.E. PESCOTT's *Gardening in Australia* (1926); but what set Luffmann and Walling apart was their freshness of thought and focus on design philosophy. Another key field that saw its major works first appear in the twentieth century was the horticultural use of the AUSTRALIAN FLORA. Australian native flowers and shrubs were often mentioned in early books and discussion of the difficulty in growing the flowers was emphasised. Native shrubs were more easily accommodated in these gardens, but no mainstream garden book suggested planting and growing a completely native garden until the appearance of *Australian Plants for the Garden* (1953) by Thistle Harris, which was followed during the 1950s and 1960s by the books written by proponents of the BUSH GARDEN such as Alec BLOMBERY, Betty MALONEY and Jean Walker, and Glen WILSON.

Photography overtook earlier printing techniques such as wood engraving for illustrations in the early years of the twentieth century, and dust jackets first appeared *c.* 1915, at first with text, but soon assuming their current decorative illustrated format. Gardening books since the 1960s have become more specialised and more decorative. Sumptuous coloured photographs of magnificent blooms meet the eye at every turn of the page. Books continue to appear on specialised LANDSCAPE PLANT TYPES, although taxonomic revisions delight the botanist but bedevil the publisher. GARDEN HISTORY has seen a large increase of books published since the mid-1970s, and biographies of major figures appear at a steady rate. Some books are still written by nursery proprietors but now more often it is the garden journalist or 'TV' gardener who is able to link horticultural literature and commerce. In the colonial period garden books were primarily written by men. Since the first in Australia by women ('Mrs Rolf BOLDREWOOD', 1893; Mrs Arthur TUCKETT, 1905; E.H. LINTON, 1911; and Elma DENHAM, 1917), they outnumbered men as writers, and one suspects that women have always been the major practitioners of the gardening art and most receptive audience for LITERATURE, be it practical or of more lofty ambit.

John A. Ferguson, *A Bibliography of Australia* (Sydney, 1943–69); Victor Crittenden, *A History and Bibliography of Australian Gardening Books* (Belconnen, ACT, 1986).

VICTOR CRITTENDEN

GARDEN BUILDINGS, sometimes called garden ARCHITECTURE, encompass buildings for both plants and people, with many combining the two functions. The word 'building' is derived from the Old English *byldan* (dwelling) suggesting a structure capable of enclosure to permit habitation, and the presence of a roof forms a useful point of demarcation between garden buildings and other garden structures.

The most obviously habitable garden buildings are those for human occupation, such as GATE LODGES and cottages for caretakers, gardeners, and curators. While hermits or other recluses abound in the mythology of the Australian BUSH, hermitages are rare, and the term is generally used in an ironic manner to denote remoteness, although TREE HOUSES— particularly in the hollow trunks of giant *Eucalyptus regnans* (Mountain Ash)—perhaps form an antipodean manifestation. Shelter sheds, those worldly shrines of SCHOOL GARDENS, and transport shelters (embracing cabs, trams, and buses) form conspicuous examples of habitable garden buildings in the public landscape. Allied to such buildings are utilitarian adjuncts such as sheds (for tools, storage, or indoor activities such as potting), AIR RAID SHELTERS, BATH HOUSES, FOWL HOUSES, FRUIT houses and cool stores, privies and toilets, pump houses, and even tank-stands, all common elements of gardens, especially those linked to RURAL LANDSCAPES. In common with less utilitarian buildings, these examples often possessed ornamental qualities.

Garden buildings used for ornament include ARBOURS, AVIARIES and dovecotes, GROTTOES, KIOSKS, LICH-GATES, ROTUNDAS, and TEMPLES. Such buildings, although of diverse lineage, generally fall within the eighteenth-century French concept of *fabrique*, derived from the lexicon of painting and meaning constructions erected in a garden for an ornamental or PICTURESQUE end and generally imbued with meanings beyond their immediate function. Buildings intentionally constructed as garden follies are, however, rare in Australia.

Buildings for LEISURE, RECREATION, and SPORT encompass many buildings found in PUBLIC PARKS AND GARDENS, as well as private gardens. Those for leisure include BANDSTANDS, belvederes, gazebos and LOOKOUT TOWERS, BOAT HOUSES, and SUMMER-HOUSES. Those for recreation and sport include grandstands, PAVILIONS, and kiosks—in this sense

This timber PAVILION (1993) at HEIDE, Bulleen (Vic.), has a lightness of touch and appropriateness to its situation (in this case in a SCULPTURE GARDEN) often sought but rarely achieved in the design of Australian GARDEN BUILDINGS

Garden City Movement

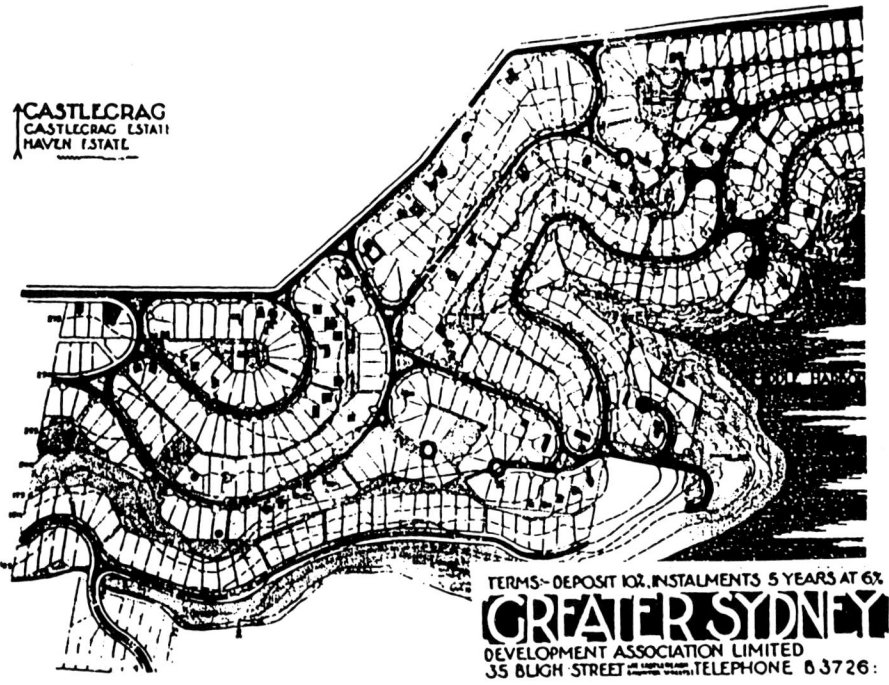

The GRIFFIN plan of CASTLECRAG (NSW) embodies many GARDEN CITY attributes, especially in its retention of natural features, incorporation of public parkland reserves, and the enlightened social vision of its promoters

often focusing as much on the provision of refreshments as on viewing. Specialised buildings, such as an ARCHERY house, were sometimes erected in gardens as an adjunct to outdoor activities. Cubby-houses and tree houses provided PLAY opportunities for CHILDREN. Many garden buildings, such as TENTS and pavilions for FESTIVALS, EXHIBITIONS, SHOWS, and other forms of entertainment, were temporary or demountable. On a smaller scale, UMBRELLAS provide temporary (and demountable) shelter and protection.

HORTICULTURE has spawned diverse buildings, some generic and others highly specialised. Those for aiding the growth of plants, especially through CLIMATIC modification (including temperature, wind, rain, and frost) can usefully be considered collectively under the term GREENHOUSES. Depending primarily on the nature of materials and internal environment, this term embraces generic structures such as GLASSHOUSES, CONSERVATORIES, HOTHOUSES, and STOVES and specialised houses for ORCHIDS, PALMS, vines, and the Victoria Lily. These all employ glass or other transparent or translucent materials and have design precedents in Britain and Europe. More typical in Australia are BUSH-HOUSES or shadehouses, with specialised variants used for ferns and other decorative INDOOR PLANTS, and for PROPAGATION.

The siting of buildings can form focal points in gardens, especially in gardens employing elements of FORMALITY; but equally, in more naturalistic settings, they can be recessive or hidden, waiting to surprise and delight. Likewise, their design expression can complement a surrounding garden or landscape, especially where bold architectural treatment has been employed, or they may be so RUSTIC as to be mistaken for 'nature's hand'.

RA

GARDEN CITY MOVEMENT *Garden Cities of To-Morrow* (1902) was the manifesto of Ebenezer Howard (1850–1928) for clusters of new town–country magnets to chart a 'better and brighter civilisation' than industrial metropolitanism. The realisation of these ideals at Letchworth (1903) near London generated wide interest in environmental reform. Howard's ideas were adapted at two scales: cellular town growth and the layout of communities 'on garden city lines'. Promoted internationally by the rising TOWN PLANNING movement, these ideas proved most adaptable to suburban extension.

In Australia, the Garden City Movement crystallised as a post–CITY BEAUTIFUL environmental ideal to rid urban development of its 'happy-go-lucky' character. Leading advocates and technicians included John SULMAN, Charles READE, Carl KLEM, and Saxil Tuxen (1885–1975). The desired package of garden city principles evolved through trial and error. Dominant values revolved around family house and garden precincts, tree-lined streets, open space hierarchies, community facilities, and classification of roads. Above all, the garden community would be a complete social and physical entity.

The development of garden suburbs, industrial villages, and new towns was stimulated by varied circumstances: as public housing experiments, as demonstration estates, to reward returned soldiers, to tame factory workers, and to make money. The government showpieces were Daceyville (1912) in Sydney, COLONEL LIGHT GARDENS (1921) in Adelaide, and Melbourne's Garden City (1926). Walter Burley GRIFFIN, who had designed several Melbourne subdivisions, masterminded the unique social and conservation experiment of CASTLECRAG (1921) in Sydney. Less nobly but more ubiquitously, the garden suburb became a speculative device resulting in geometric mazes of prematurely subdivided land. Claremont and LUTANA in Hobart were industrial estates planned on garden city lines. The South Australian *Town Planning and Development Act* 1920 provided a positive framework for enlightened new town design, but the most notable achievements were suburban CANBERRA (1920s), A.R. LA GERCHE's Yallourn, Vic. (1921), and irrigation towns such as Theodore (1924) in Qld.

The Depression killed the classic garden suburb, but site planning innovations continued to evolve and mature after the Second World War, particularly in public housing estates. Planning and local government legislation codified ideas into regulations. As this process of institutionalisation proceeded, the term 'garden suburb' reclaimed its populist meaning as a precinct of trees and gardens. At the same time, the professional standing of the low-density suburb as the desired residential environment was challenged by shifts towards higher density estates in response to changed demographic, cultural, and public finance conditions.

What became more prominent from the 1930s were the metropolitan aspects of the idea: the urban containment formula of satellite towns and GREEN BELTS. This template was adopted in Sydney's first metropolitan master plan (1948), although the green belt was unable to withstand pressure of urban growth. More successful was Canberra, whose metropolitan form was textbook garden city from the late 1960s, with Howard-like towns separated by green belts and composed of neighbourhood-scale planned suburbs.

Robert Freestone, *Model Communities: The Garden City Movement in Australia* (Melbourne, 1989)

ROBERT FREESTONE

GARDEN CLUBS: see HORTICULTURAL SOCIETIES

GARDENERS Shackles were an adjunct to shovel and hoe for Australia's first working gardeners when clearing and planting of ground for the government farm and Government House garden by convicts at Sydney Cove commenced, only weeks after the First Fleet's 1788 landing. Convict gardeners continued to be utilised on government gardening projects, including BOTANIC GARDENS in Sydney, Hobart, and Brisbane, for the next fifty years. Though they were rarely experienced horticulturists, exceptions such as John RICHARDSON and James KIDD found relatively responsible government positions open to them within the limitations of their penal servitude. Social development, however, soon fostered a demand for gardening skills among settlers also, and in 1837 Governor Bourke initiated a scheme for training young convicts in gardening at SYDNEY BOTANIC GARDENS, so that they might find redeeming employment as 'ticket of leave' servants with the wealthier settlers.

Incentives for the qualified, non-convict gardener to emigrate to remote Australia were limited prior to the 1850s. Fare for passage was relatively expensive, and few garden establishments, public or private, could offer positions promising professional advancement after arrival. Those who undertook the voyage generally favoured commercial ventures in ORCHARDING, the NURSERY TRADE, or MARKET GARDENING, especially in NSW, SA, and Tas. However, successive gold discoveries from 1851 onwards precipitated a tremendous influx of nationalities and occupations, with its fair share of professional gardeners. Of these, the majority were ENGLISH, but with SCOTS, IRISH, and GERMANS also well represented. Many were influenced by glowing reports in European horticultural journals of high wages and high prices for vegetable products. This, however, inevitably proved only half the reality and, while horticulturists established prior to the rush reaped rich rewards for their produce, the 'new chum' found his high wages partially nullified by the inflated prices of the gold-rush period. More often than not the caches of seeds that were carried with an eye to future wealth were sold or given away.

Ideally the migrant gardener was able to secure a live-in position, with board or rations in addition to wages (around £2 6s a week in Melbourne in 1853). Yet, while the best positions could entail overseeing two to three garden labourers—employed for the menial work of hoeing, trenching and weeding—most often they were single-handed. Consequently, outside botanic and PUBLIC GARDENS there was little room for the formal trade-learning structure of apprentice, journeyman, master gardener, and head gardener. When added to a falling off in the number of migrating British gardeners (the most highly regarded) the result was a perceived shortage of skilled men by the 1870s. Additional reasons pointed out by contemporary horticultural writers included the new style in larger gardens of systematic bedding out with a narrow range of flower and succulent varieties, and the preference of young colonial gardeners for football and cricket over evenings of study. As one respected Victorian professional propounded in 1874, 'I can see no coming race of gardeners; the garden lads of this colony take no interest in their work'. More pragmatic commentators called for the introduction of EDUCATIONAL facilities for the training of young gardeners. It was, however, not until 1891 that Australia's first school of horticulture was opened at BURNLEY in Melbourne, offering a two year Certificate of Horticulture course.

For those at the lower end of the trade the question of intensive horticultural training was largely irrelevant to their work; which frequently also encompassed the care of livestock as well as chopping wood and cleaning boots. Hours of work for gardeners generally were particularly long in the hot summer months, when one might be required to be hand watering until 11 p.m., and to work on Sundays without additional pay. In many plant nurseries ten-hour working days remained a reality into the early twentieth century. Continuing high wages compensated during the 1870s–80s, but economic downturn in the 1890s brought increasing instances of exploitation, or 'sweating', by employers. Labour organisations for gardeners were well established by this time. Their precursors, like the United Gardeners' Benefit Association founded in Victoria in 1875 or the FREE GARDENERS' SOCIETY, had tended to be in the nature of friendly societies, offering assistance in cases of distress and loans for travelling to distant situations. From the 1890s, however, the Gardeners' Union in NSW and the Victorian Gardeners' Association were actively engaged in lobbying for improved standard conditions. In Vic. this resulted in the formation of a Wage Board for gardeners, its first determination in 1912 setting minimum wages. The attendant debates highlighted two factors that would continue to hinder professional development: that the trade lacked a clear hierarchy, and the perception of gardening as an idyllic pastime. 'What better occupation could a man have than looking after a beautiful garden?' enquired one glib parliamentarian.

It was, however, the lack of any alternative occupation that forced many men to seek casual gardening work during the Depression years of the 1930s. Ironically, the result was a backlash against the fixed wage levels gained by professional jobbing gardeners in the earlier settlements, since many householders baulked at employing men out of considerations of charity if it meant having to pay award rates. The male gardening professional had also found competition from a different quarter. By the 1920s some women, mainly graduates of the Burnley Horticultural College, were beginning to make inroads on a professional level. Inspired by Gertrude JEKYLL in England, and on the heels of local forerunners such as Ina HIGGINS, came Edna WALLING, Olive MELLOR, and others who took on garden maintenance and landscaping work.

The introduction of horticultural courses redefined landscape management over the twentieth century, providing a stronger scientific base. Professional gardening was increasingly developed into a trade, achieved through an apprenticeship system and applied almost entirely to the landscapes of PUBLIC OPEN SPACE. The disciplines that embrace gardening have struggled for professional recognition against the overwhelming tradition of amateur gardening, which continues to flourish and maintain the vast number of domestic gardens.

Joan Morgan and Alison Richards, *A Paradise Out of a Common Field: The Pleasures and Plenty of the Victorian Garden* (London, 1990) **DARREN WATSON**

GARDENERS' CHRONICLE (1841–), published weekly in London, was the most widely read horticultural journal in Australia during the nineteenth and early twentieth centuries. Self-proclaimed as 'The Times of Horticulture', it was generally held by colonial botanic gardens, horticultural societies, major subscription and public libraries, as well as numerous private subscribers. The *Gardeners' Chronicle and Agricultural Gazette* (as it was constituted during the period 1844–73) was initially edited by Joseph PAXTON and John LINDLEY. Until this date, LOUDON's *Gardener's Magazine* (1826–44) had been the only major foray into horticultural journalism, apart from expensive colour plate works such as the *Botanical Magazine* (1787–1984) of William CURTIS or Maund's *Botanic Garden* (1825–51). Initially taking four to six months to reach Austral shores by sea, this time-lag less-ened to several weeks by the turn of the century. Measured in tone, the *Chronicle* authoritatively reported on advances in horticulture and landscape design; in this way colonial readers could read influential reports from France by William ROBINSON or follow Kingdon Ward's botanical explorations. The *Chronicle* took a close interest in development of colonial gardens and horticulture, particularly BOTANIC GARDENS, often reprinting or abstracting annual reports or significant papers (such as MUELLER's 'The Use of Botanic Gardens' in 1872). It recommended, among others things, Buffalo Grass as suitable for Australian conditions (1871), gave detailed observations of Australian horticulture by J.G. VEITCH (1866), and, as illustrations became more freely used from the late 1880s, illustrated several Australian gardens. Following mergers with kindred publication in 1969 and 1976, the *Chronicle* continued as *Horticulture Week*. RA

GARDENER'S MAGAZINE AND JOURNAL OF RURAL ECONOMY: see SINCLAIR, James

GARDENESQUE, a term first used by John Claudius LOUDON in his *Gardener's Magazine* (1832), described a STYLE of garden design that could be instantly recognised as a work of art. This responded to the neo-Platonic arguments of French academician A.C. Quatremère de Quincy (1755–1849) that gardens laid out in a PICTURESQUE style were not distinguishable from wild nature and so could not be considered as works of fine art. Central to the Gardenesque, which many argue is a planting (as opposed to design) style, was for single plants to be allowed to grow so that none touched another object and each displayed its character to the optimum: 'if touched by the hand of the gardener, only to be improved in their regularity and symmetry'. The *Scottish Gardener* (1856) argued that the Gardenesque method of planting existed long before Loudon's time but he 'was the first to discriminate and define' it. By then Loudon's advice had been 'ignored altogether' or 'confounded with its abuse'. This referred to the transformation of the Gardenesque by a new generation of authors, one of the first being Edward KEMP in *How to Lay out a Small Garden* (1850): 'There are three principal kinds of style recognised in landscape gardening:—the old formal or geometrical style; the mixed, middle, or irregular style, which Mr Loudon called the gardenesque; and the picturesque.' Kemp saw the objects of the 'mixed style' as 'beauty of lines, and general variety. Roundness, smoothness, freedom from angularity, and grace rather than dignity or grandeur, are its numerous indications.'

In Australia, Loudon's recommendations and the Gardenesque in its transmuted form were both manifest. As early as 1838, in his *Manual of Practical Gardening*, Daniel BUNCE recommended: 'When any of the shrubs have made long rambling shoots, so as to interfere with each other, you should go over them with a knife and reduce such plants to regular order, so that each may be seen distinctly without crowding up on one another.' At SYDNEY BOTANIC GARDENS, Charles MOORE thinned planting to allow 'more regular and natural development' (1857) and expended enormous effort over the years, through blasting and filling, to transform the rocky

Gardenesque

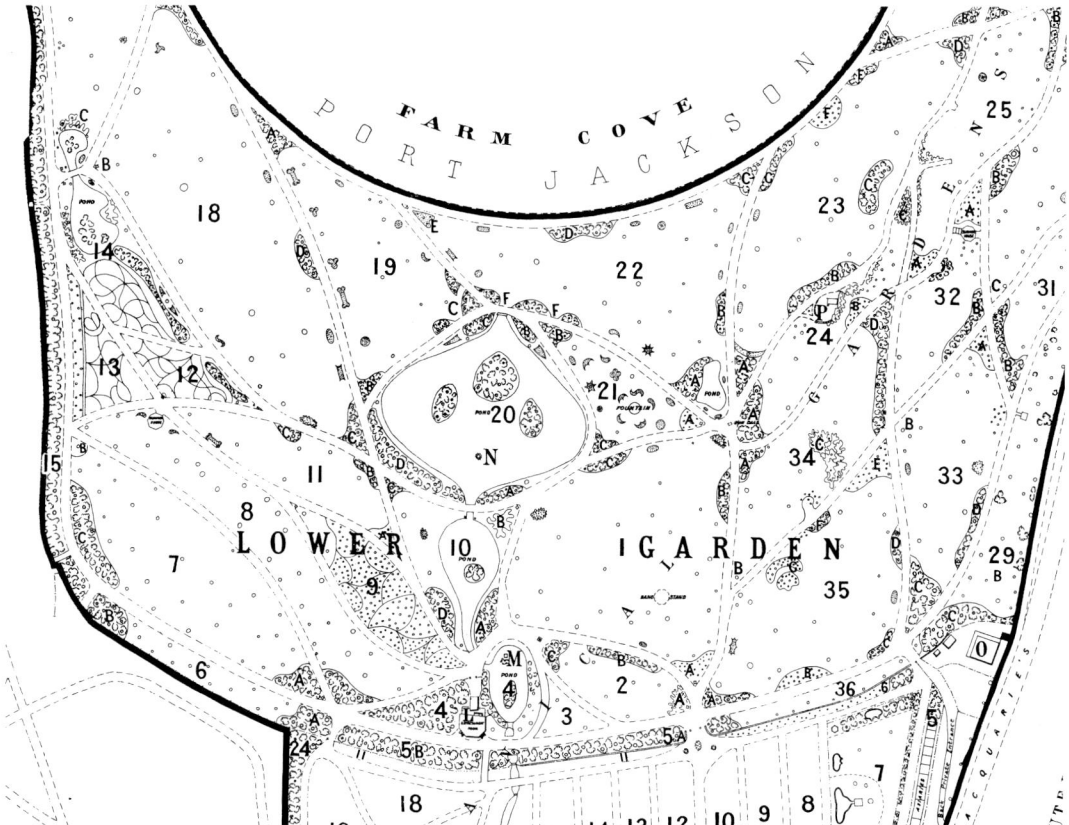

This 1897 plan of SYDNEY BOTANIC GARDENS recorded Director Charles MOORE's achievements over four decades, including this detail of his GARDENESQUE design for land progressively reclaimed from Farm Cove from the late 1840s to the 1870s

Sydney Harbour site to a landscape that was smooth and free from irregularity—a practice confirming gardenesque values, and one also implemented in the development of CENTENNIAL PARK.

In 1860 prominent Victorian gardener William FERGUSON proposed the principle of separately grouping evergreen and deciduous trees, adopted by the Victorian Gardeners' Mutual Improvement Society and recommended for 'general practice by all planters in this Colony as far as circumstances will permit'. Ferguson exhibited a thorough understanding of the concept of Gardenesque as espoused by Loudon: while the first object in planting was to form a decorative feature, the second was to show the individuality of trees or shrubs in such a way as both the whole and the parts could be appreciated. Ferguson recommended (1863) that 'in general I would adopt the gardenesque manner of planting trees and shrubs, especially in the pleasure ground and near the house … the gardenesque manner of planting and managing includes the application of pruning and thinning, at all future periods of growth of the trees and shrubs, so as to keep each plant perfectly distinct from those around it'. The idea of growing individual species of exotic trees was very popular, to the 1870s at least, but they were rarely thinned as Loudon had intended.

The 'art of the gardener' meaning implied by Kemp coincided with wealth from gold discoveries in Vic. and NSW and a consolidation of early pastoral wealth (with freehold tenure), and this neatly dovetailed with embellishment, grandiosity, display, and the necessary wealth for many gardeners. By 1865, the Horticultural Magazine could speak of a neat entrance with a highly ornamental gate as being Gardenesque, with Fiona, the Darling Point estate of Edward Knox—replete with aviary, elaborate conservatory, Gothic cottage, and flower beds edged with glass tiles—displaying the 'merits' of the style. The interpretation of the Gardenesque popularised in Australian GARDENING BOOKS was that of Kemp rather than Loudon. Although William ELLIOTT, in *Australasian Gardening and Domestic Floriculture* (1897), followed Loudon's recommendation that if indigenous trees were to be planted then they should be planted singly and 'recognised as coming under the dominion of art', both Elliott and TRESEDER in *The Garden* (1880)—and others—published Kemp's words verbatim, bringing the Gardenesque to a new generation of gardeners.

Significant exceptions to this transformation and popularisation of the style included the depth of understanding of Loudon's Gardenesque concepts exhibited by J.E. BROWN in his report on the ADELAIDE PARK LANDS (1880); Brown planned for a picturesque effect while fulfilling Gardenesque ideals—although gardening staff failed to comprehend and implement his planting plan; and by William SANGSTER at WOMBAT HILL BOTANIC GARDENS, where he proposed redesigned walks, thinned plantings, avenues, lawns, and a rosary (1885), to transform 'chaos' to an 'orderly and gardenesque appearance'.

The majority of nineteenth-century domestic Gardenesque examples have disappeared, but for the purposes of education and the display of individual plants, the style was eminently suited to BOTANIC GARDENS. The best surviving examples are thus at the SYDNEY and ADELAIDE BOTANIC GARDENS, and also in many PUBLIC PARKS, INSTITUTIONAL GARDENS, and CEMETERIES. ROOKWOOD CEMETERY, designed at the zenith of the Gardenesque popularity, although regrettably now devoid of its requisite high-Victorian ornamentation, is arguably the largest Gardenesque landscape in Australia. Despite enduring criticism for spottiness, the Gardenesque (or grotesque, some would say), was the predominant landscape aesthetic during the nineteenth century—the period when the culture of gardening was established in Australia—and it has endured, in spirit if not name, in many SUBURBAN GARDENS.

COLLEEN MORRIS

GARDEN FESTIVAL: see FESTIVAL

GARDEN FURNITURE: see FURNITURE

GARDEN GAZETTE (1902–03), published monthly in Melbourne, had an importance belied by its mere fourteen-issue lifespan. Covering traditional ground of popular garden flowers, ferns, and orchids, the *Gazette* also featured generous coverage of private gardens and 'the somewhat neglected beauties of our public gardens and parks'. RIPPON LEA and the MELBOURNE BOTANIC GARDENS were thus favoured with detailed illustrated articles; in fact William GUILFOYLE used the journal as a veritable mouthpiece for the latter, and published notable articles on palms and rockwork. RA

GARDEN HISTORY as a scholarly pursuit has made its greatest strides in Australia since 1980, and in the formation of the AUSTRALIAN GARDEN HISTORY SOCIETY. The Society united a disparate group whose interests ranged across traditional history disciplines, but especially those with an interest in architecture, art, botany, gardening, horticulture, literature, landscape architecture, and town planning. The work of the Society, especially through its journal, annual conferences, and garden visits, drew strongly on research and assessment being undertaken for the AUSTRALIAN HERITAGE COMMISSION, the exhibition and catalogue of the same title (*Converting the Wilderness: The Art of Gardening in Colonial Australia*), conservation initiatives of the NATIONAL TRUST OF AUSTRALIA, and existing research interests of members. Garden history had, of course, been an active interest of many prior to this time.

In much garden making of the mid- to late-nineteenth century, historically based garden STYLES required a sound knowledge of history, and several popular writers such as J.C. LOUDON provided considerable guidance on stylistic antecedents. In the field of horticulture, the allied discipline of botany has played a strong part in reinforcing the need for accurate records. The Australian and New Zealand Camellia Research Society, for instance, drew on this tradition—and on the informed interest of key members such as E.G. WATERHOUSE and Tom SAVIGE—in their plant breeding cultivar registration activities, which depend so strongly on historical knowledge and accuracy.

Gardeners have not traditionally been to the fore in recording history, whereas their more methodical colleagues in the world of botany, by dint of scientific training, have left more coherent records and have maintained, for example, a tradition of comprehensive obituaries for deceased colleagues in established scientific journals. By contrast, biographical notes and descriptive histories of gardens and gardeners have relied on a much more haphazard system of reporting in newspapers and GARDEN MAGAZINES. It is those who combined botanical and horticultural skills, such as Joseph MAIDEN, Director of Sydney Botanic Gardens (1896–1924), who pioneered the recording of garden history. Aided by an enquiring mind and a relentless (perhaps even obsessive) zeal to record history, Maiden published scores of papers giving invaluable historical notes on GARDENERS and botanists, HORTICULTURAL and SCIENTIFIC SOCIETIES, PLANT COLLECTING, and SYDNEY BOTANIC GARDENS to name the most pertinent. Maiden published some of the pioneering Australian biographical writings in his fields, and followed isolated early examples such as George SUTTOR's biography of Joseph BANKS (1855). Maiden wrote thoughtful appreciations or obituaries of his staff—even lavatory attendants were accorded a sentence or two in annual reports on their retirement or death—and generally laid the foundation for modern historical research into Australian botany and horticulture. At Melbourne Botanic Gardens, Ambrose NEATE fulfilled a similar although much lesser role. The centenaries of various botanic gardens were marked by historical publications (for example Sydney 1916, Melbourne 1946, Adelaide 1955), but such commemoration was rare in private gardens. The history of the nursery trade was championed in Vic. by E.E. PESCOTT and in NSW by Roy RUMSEY and Walter HAZLEWOOD.

In recent decades, the close links between garden designers and the nursery industry have been supplemented by the professionalisation of landscape architecture as a discipline, bringing with it a tradition of publication and promotion that will serve as an invaluable historical record to future generations. The largely craft-based gardening and nursery trades have left almost no major collections of manuscript papers or business records in public collections, relatively few GARDEN PLANS (apart from notables such as GUILFOYLE and WALLING), and even scant coherent photographic evidence in public collections.

Those prominent in the field of Australian garden history during recent decades—such as Rica ERICKSON, Beatrice BLIGH, Lionel GILBERT, James BROADBENT, Howard TANNER, Peter WATTS, John FOSTER, Anne LATREILLE, Paul FOX, Trevor NOTTLE, and Trisha DIXON—have now published a sizeable body of work, but comprehensive treatment of many subjects is still required.

Richard Aitken et al. (eds), *A Theoretical Framework for Designed Landscapes in Australia* (Burnley, Vic, 1998); Michael Conan (ed.) *Perspectives on Garden Histories* (Washington, D.C., 1999)

RA

GARDEN ISLAND, a small island in Sydney Harbour, was named by Governor Phillip in 1788 when a party from HMS *Sirius*, finding reasonable soil and water, established a garden there for the ship's company. Their initials carved in rock and dated 1788 survive. In 1883 Garden Island became the Australian headquarters of the Royal Navy, and has played a major role in Australia's defences. Amid institutional development, a mature garden is maintained at the island's north end.

CAROLINE SIMPSON

GARDEN MAGAZINE (1923–27) was published monthly by Sydney florists SEARL's Limited in a similar, although more commercial style, to the *Gardening Bulletin* of Adelaide nursery proprietors E. & W. HACKETT (1917–50). A regular 'Native Plant Column' (from 1926) by W. AHLFELD was an innovative feature in a magazine primarily aimed at the suburban home gardener. The *Garden Magazine* continued as *Garden* (1927–28).

RA

GARDEN MAGAZINES as a form of populist literature hold an integral place in the development of gardening as an important part of domestic culture. With a thirst for knowledge and increasing capacity to indulge in LEISURE activities during the nineteenth century, the middle classes looked for reliable information to guide their endeavours. In response, editors and publishers initiated journals that continued the tradition of introducing new exotics to the buying public and provided practical advice for the home gardener. The 1830s and 1840s in Britain saw a burgeoning of horticultural periodicals; the public appetite for horticulture coincided with technological advances that made printing faster and paper-making much cheaper. Most of these new journals lasted for only a few years, falling victim to low editorial standards, poor production quality, and a glutted market. Even fewer were generally available in Australia.

The works of J.C. LOUDON, John LINDLEY, and William ROBINSON were among the most influential to have found their way into Australian homes and LIBRARIES. Loudon's *Gardener's Magazine and Register of Rural and Domestic Improvement* (1826–44) covered, as its title suggests, 'subjects as inexhaustible as the vegetable kingdom and among the most interesting that concern domestic life'. The conjunction of HORTICULTURE with AGRICULTURE was also apparent in the *GARDENERS' CHRONICLE*, where rural economy and general news took their place beside the horticulture for which Lindley was editor. The *Gardeners' Chronicle* is still being published, now titled *Horticulture Week*; each of its many name changes reflecting a greater shift away from domestic gardening towards the nursery and landscape industries. In contrast, the *Garden*, founded in 1876 by Robinson, whose writings so influenced the work of landscape designers such

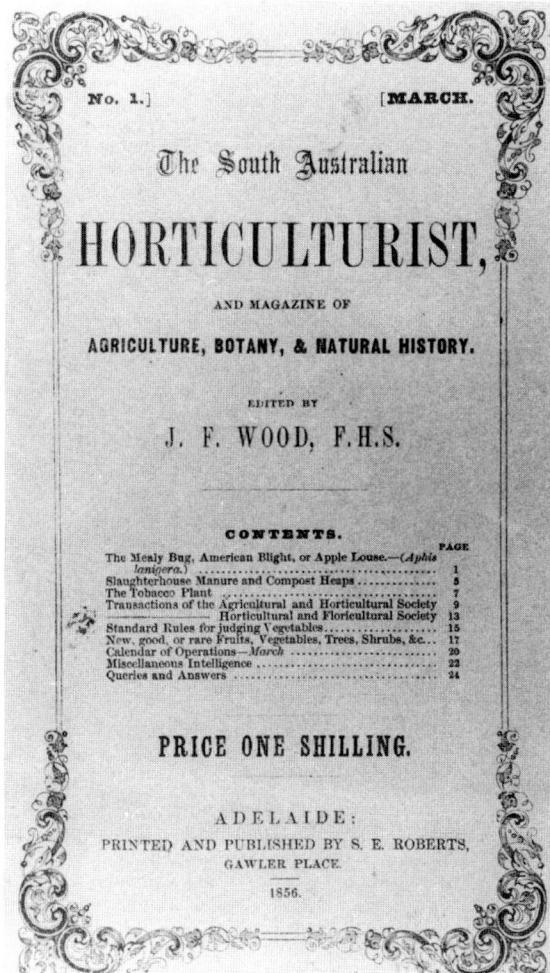

Although many Australian GARDEN MAGAZINES, such as the *SOUTH AUSTRALIAN HORTICULTURIST* (1856), only managed short publication spans, their educative contribution and influence on debate about gardening and horticulture was immense

as William GUILFOYLE, maintained a strong focus on gardening as domestic culture.

In Australia, horticulture first took its place in the general periodical literature. The earliest vehicles for horticultural journalism in Australia were not the specialised gardening magazines such as were being produced in Britain. Rather they were periodicals such as the SYDNEY MAGAZINE OF SCIENCE AND ART, the official publication of the Australian Horticultural and Agricultural Society and the Philosophical Society of New South Wales. Early attempts at establishing specialised horticultural magazines met indifferent success, the Victorian *RURAL MAGAZINE* and *SOUTH AUSTRALIAN HORTICULTURIST* each surviving less than a year. Later magazines fared hardly better. The pious hopes expressed in the *GARDEN GAZETTE* that it would be seen as the long-awaited 'first-class organ' to promote the interests of Victoria's many

Garden ornament

horticultural and gardening groups proved unfounded when it folded in 1903 after barely a year.

The combination of horticulture with agriculture was a feature of colonial journals such as the VICTORIAN AGRICULTURAL AND HORTICULTURAL GAZETTE, GARDEN AND FIELD, the AUSTRALIAN AGRICULTURIST and, following the establishment of Departments of Agriculture in the several colonies, their various AGRICULTURAL GAZETTES AND JOURNALS OF AGRICULTURE. Gradually in the twentieth century, however, gardening established an independent if slightly precarious presence in the periodical market, not least because it became more firmly aligned with the domestic garden. This is perhaps epitomised by the AUSTRALIAN GARDENER, which professed its principal aim to be 'encouraging in every possible way the beautifying of home surroundings'. FLORICULTURE, and not the farm, vineyard, or orchard, was to be its principal topic, and its popularity may be gauged by its circulation of 12 000 copies monthly. One of the most successful of the popular gardening magazines was the AUSTRALIAN GARDEN LOVER, the title of which was intended to convey the uplifting qualities of horticulture. For more than five decades this magazine informed and encouraged the gardening public across Australia. Unfortunately, falling advertising revenue and decreasing circulation forced its closure in 1980. Of similar longevity is YOUR GARDEN, founded in 1947 in response to the post-war boom in house-building and still going strong.

While these magazines had as their primary focus the outdoor part of the domestic environment, gardening had a necessary place in magazines that had a greater emphasis on the indoor environment. The HOME with its high production values and striking design gave increasingly more space to gardening as it guided the tastes and activities of middle Australia in the inter-war period. AUSTRALIAN HOME BEAUTIFUL and later AUSTRALIAN HOUSE AND GARDEN have been perhaps more important popular magazines that combine horticultural journalism with the practicalities of creating and maintaining the Australian oasis that is home and garden. With its emphasis on the practical, *Australian Home Beautiful* has had a central role in shaping public expectations of what constitutes good domestic horticulture. The equally popular *Better Homes and Gardens* has more recently extended the reach of horticultural journalism by developing into a successful TELEVISION program. By the association of garden with home, horticulture is defined as an essential part of domestic culture. More specialised magazines highlight horticultural trends, particularly those that deal with individual plant groups. *Australian Plants*, published by the SOCIETY FOR GROWING AUSTRALIAN PLANTS, is devoted solely to the propagation, cultivation, and identification of the AUSTRALIAN FLORA. Those interested in ORCHIDS are particularly well served, with *Australian Orchid Review*, the *Orchadian*, and *Orchids Australia*. So too are ROSARIANS, with *Australian Rose Annual* and the various state-based publications. The history of gardening in Australia in all its aspects is the subject *of Australian Garden History*.

Newspapers have consistently provided an important popular avenue for the publication of information aimed at the home gardener. Some of Australia's earliest leading newspapers—dailies and, especially, weeklies—carried horticultural columns, notably the SYDNEY MAIL and (AUSTRALIAN) TOWN AND COUNTRY JOURNAL (NSW); ADELAIDE OBSERVER and SOUTH AUSTRALIAN CHRONICLE; QUEENSLANDER; TASMANIAN MAIL; AUSTRALASIAN, LEADER, and WEEKLY TIMES (Vic.); and WESTERN MAIL (WA). As the principal means of disseminating information, the newspaper—relatively inexpensive and readily accessible—was an ideal medium for circulating horticultural information. Gardening columns carried considerable authority, having been written by leading horticultural figures such as William SANGSTER and T. W. SHEPHERD. These columns provide a mirror of changing horticultural practices and trends in domestic gardening. The garden section remains an indispensable part of most newspapers even if the popularity of home gardening is not always matched by the number of column centimetres.

Professionals are also well served by periodicals, some of which continue longstanding scientific practice, primarily through the inclusion of refereed articles and their mode of exchange among botanic gardens and other professional libraries. International journals, including many from Britain and other parts of Europe, North America, and Asia, form an indispensable complement to those locally published. Extensive citation through databases and abstracts increases the usefulness of such journals, and a growing number are being made available electronically by use of COMPUTERS and the World Wide Web. Many of Australia's botanic gardens and professional bodies produce well-respected journals, with LANDSCAPE AUSTRALIA and AUSTRALIAN HORTICULTURE among the most relevant to those in the garden world.

Helen M. Cohn, *Australian Plants, the Garden, and Botany in the Nineteenth Century Periodical* (Clayton, Vic., 1995)

HELEN M. COHN

GARDEN ORNAMENT: see ORNAMENT

GARDEN PLANS, as physical objects, are two-dimensional representations of three-dimensional landscape spaces. Produced or printed on a variety of surface materials (linen, tracing paper, card, and synthetic materials such as architectural film), plans can be rendered in media ranging from graphite, pen and ink, to watercolour, spirit-based pens, and adhesive overlays. Plans for gardens are traditionally represented in plan view or as elevations, and sometimes as sectional or detail drawings. Axonometric views and perspectives ('bird's eye' or, in Edward Lutyens' words, 'worm's eye' views) are less common. Although once rare, three-dimensional modeling is increasing through the use of COMPUTER rendering technology and the creation of VIRTUAL GARDENS. Increasingly, garden plans are created and stored digitally.

Plans are vital to the art of garden design (including its associated ARCHITECTURE), and are used in various ways throughout the design process: as documentation of existing conditions, as working or developmental sketches, as concept or presentation drawings (often for public display or publication), and as working or technical drawings during construction (or reconstruction). They may also become legal documents when linked to TOWN PLANNING processes.

Garden therapy

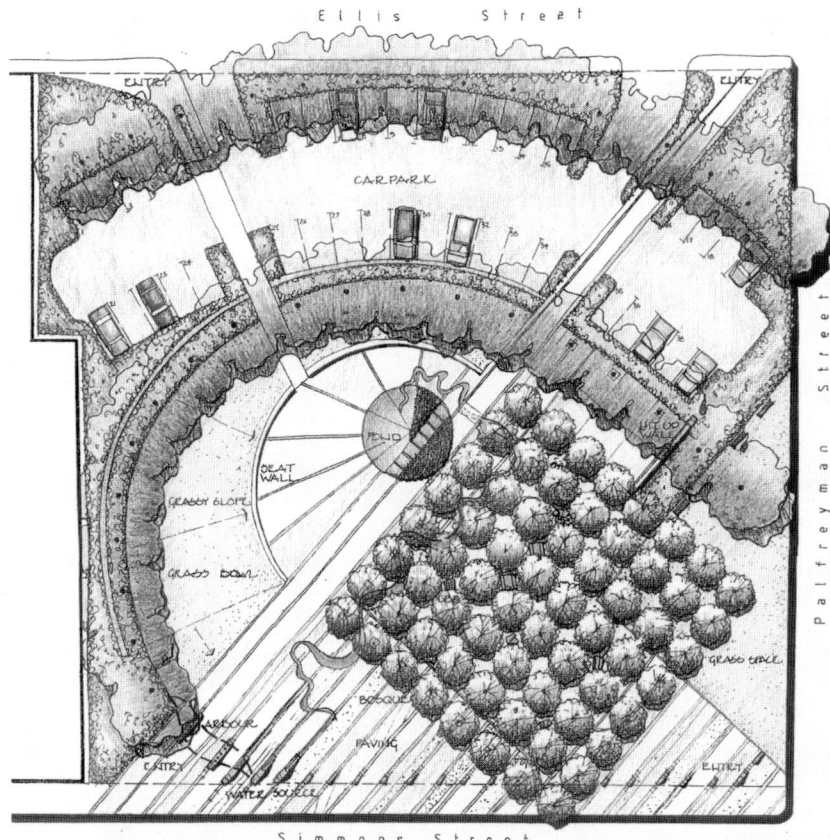

GARDEN PLANS such as this 1994 rendering of Dyeworks Park, Prahran (Vic.) remain a vital and traditional means of communication for LANDSCAPE ARCHITECTS and garden designers

Over time, plans become an important record of a place or a designer's *oeuvre*, and an invaluable archival resource for GARDEN HISTORIANS and gardeners. Plans assist in the assessment of a garden's development and significance, aid in rejuvenation or reconstruction of compromised or derelict gardens in CONSERVATION projects, especially of HERITAGE PLACES. As historical documents, plans also reveal tastes and STYLES in design and plant use, and important breaks from standard cultivation or practice. Moreover, they can reveal the extent or limit of a designer's horticultural knowledge —understanding of plant selection, positioning, and nomenclature, are often all exposed on plans. In addition to these technical features, garden plans are increasingly being appreciated for their aesthetic qualities as art objects for collection, publication, and display. Australian garden designers noted for the production of outstanding plans include William GUILFOYLE, Marion Mahony and Walter Burley GRIFFIN, Edna WALLING, Jocelyn BROWN, Emily GIBSON, and Betty MALONEY and Jean Walker.

Their range of potential roles suggests that garden plans are more than a basic site description. A plan is both a laboratory for testing the designer's vision for a place, and a tool that marries this vision with the fulfilment of a client's brief. Plans thus become an intermediary space between private thought and design, and public scrutiny and veto.

ROWAN WILKEN and KAREN OLSEN

GARDEN STYLES: see STYLES

GARDEN SUBURB: see GARDEN CITY MOVEMENT

GARDEN THERAPY is used for the treatment of physical and mental ailments, and also as a means of general well-being: in Australia almost forty per cent of the population uses gardening as a form of RECREATION. Two principal advantages of garden therapy are physical exercise and mental relaxation. This is not a new concept; gardening was used in earnest in Australia for its therapeutic effects after the First World War. Veterans' HOSPITALS such as Bodington at Wentworth Falls (NSW) actively used gardening for both physical and mental therapy.

SENSORY GARDENS are an important tool used in garden therapy. Sensory gardens use the gratification of the sense of sight through the use of COLOUR and its combinations; the sense of smell in perfumes and odours; and in some cases the sense of touch through the use of textures. The Fragrant

Garden visiting

Garden in Erina (NSW) is one such sensory garden. The senses of smell and touch are especially important when designing gardens for blind people.

Formal horticultural therapy is now used in a number of institutions such as prisons, rehabilitation centres, and nursing homes. In institutions such as these, gardening is used as physical therapy to increase physical strength, endurance, and flexibility, as a small amount of time working in the garden can return physical strength to people recovering from an accident or operation, or provide exercise for the aged who are unable to participate in more strenuous activities. Garden beds are often raised to allow ease of access and use for the aged or people in wheelchairs. Many types of gardens can provide therapy including vegetable gardens, gardens with native Australian plants, and ornamental flower gardens.

As important as the physical benefit of gardening is the mental relaxation and satisfaction that can be achieved through association with a garden. It is known that the ancient Egyptians recommended to their mentally disturbed patients that they walk in the gardens to sooth their troubled minds. Physical work in a garden is not necessary to gain a benefit from it. Simply sitting in a garden and enjoying the atmosphere can be an important part of the healing process, for both physically and mentally injured people. A number of gardeners claim that they feel a form of SPIRITUAL renewal when working in their gardens or by simply being in them. Being in a garden can allow a person to feel the therapeutic effects of being in touch with Nature and feeling the passing of the SEASONS.

Martha Tyson, *The Healing Landscape: Therapeutic Outdoor Environments* (New York, 1998)   LESTER TROPMAN

GARDEN VISITING has played a significant role in both LEISURE and EDUCATION for Australian gardeners. PUBLIC PARKS AND GARDENS, BOTANIC GARDENS, and DOMAINS established during the nineteenth century in populous centres, formed popular places of resort, especially in an era when public admission to private gardens was rare. Leisure activities, including PROMENADING, attendance at HORTICULTURAL SHOWS (which were often held in botanic gardens), PICNICKING, and the pure SENSORY pleasure available from appreciation of a garden, are coupled with more vigorous RECREATIONAL pursuits, as major activities in the public realm. INTERPRETATION of gardens as a means of offering the garden visitor a richness of experience has greatly increased in recent decades, although this has, through museums of ECONOMIC BOTANY and other special displays, traditionally formed part of the role of major botanic gardens.

Regular opening of private gardens, now such an established part of the garden scene in Australia through AUSTRALIA'S OPEN GARDEN SCHEME, has greatly increased garden visiting for both leisure and recreation. Private parks and gardens in Britain from the eighteenth century had generally opened their gates—upon proof of respectability—to interested visitors. By the mid-nineteenth century, gardeners especially were encouraged by reforming writers such as J.C. LOUDON to visit gardens as part of their education. DOWNING (1859) cited a 'liberal proprietor' in Philadelphia who freely opened his garden and claimed this had 'greatly increased the popular taste' of local gardeners who had availed themselves of this opportunity. Such visiting in Australia in the nineteenth century was much more likely to be a special occasion, coinciding with a horticultural show, garden party, or charity fete. The RIPPON LEA garden was opened for visiting for long periods during the First World War on payment of a small donation to aid Red Cross. Regular garden openings, in the now-familiar manner, were held sporadically during the middle years of the twentieth century and with encouragement by groups such as the NATIONAL TRUST (both to its own properties and to private gardens as fund raisers) accelerated from the 1980s. Today, the limits of curiosity and appreciation are being constantly tested, as an increasing range of gardens are opened for visiting and emulation.   RA

GARDNER, Charles Austin (1896–1970), botanist, was born in Lancaster, England, and arrived in WA in 1909. Appointed a botanical collector in the Forests Department in 1920, he transferred to the Department of Agriculture in 1924 and was appointed Government Botanist and Curator of the Western Australian Herbarium in 1929, a post he held until retirement in 1960. He travelled and collected widely in WA, describing eight new genera and more than 200 species of plants. A very accomplished artist, especially in ink, he illustrated most of his own scientific and popular publications. Gardner also lectured in botany at the University of Western Australia (1924–62). He was an early force in conservation, instrumental in the establishment of major NATIONAL PARKS (Kalbarri, Fitzgerald River, and Cape Arid) in southern WA. Gardner's books included *A Systematic Census of Plants Occurring in Western Australia* (1930), *The Toxic Plants of Western Australia* (with H. Bennetts, 1956), and *Grasses of Western Australia* (1952), and a long series of articles on trees of WA, reprinted as *Eucalypts of Western Australia* (1970). Perhaps his major contribution to popular appreciation of AUSTRALIAN FLORA was the series *Flowers of Western Australia* (1933–35), illustrated by watercolours of Edgar DELL and first produced as a weekly series in the WESTERN MAIL. Published in book form as *Wild Flowers of Western Australia* (1935), it remains in print, fourteen editions later.

GREG and BRONWEN KEIGHERY

GARNET, (John) Roslyn (1906–1998), chemist, naturalist, and parks advocate, was born and educated in South Gippsland (Vic.). In a life devoted to NATURAL HISTORY and its conservation, J. Ros Garnet served variously as president, secretary, and councillor (1946–69) of the FIELD NATURALISTS' CLUB of Victoria (FNCV), and tirelessly pursued his interest in NATURAL HISTORY, particularly the native ORCHIDS, writing and publishing a multitude of papers and several books. As secretary of the FNCV Standing Committee on National Parks and National Monuments (1946–52) he played a leading role in drafting the bill that resulted in the (first) *Victorian National Parks Act* 1946, but probably his greatest influence lay in constant public advocacy for the parks movement. He served on the committee of management of

Gates and gate lodges

The GATE lodge (1887–89) at CITY PARK, Launceston (Tas.) provides a picturesque element at the entrance, and complements the fine surviving collection of garden buildings and structures of this important PUBLIC PARK

Wyperfeld National Park (1956–75), and was a founder and long-standing secretary of the Victorian National Parks Association (1952–74). Garnet was awarded the prestigious Australian Natural History Medallion in 1996. He was both mentor and inspiration to thousands who shared his love and concern for the Australian BUSH.   ELERY HAMILTON-SMITH

GARNETT, Thomas Ronald (b. 1915), teacher, ornithologist, garden-maker, scholar, and writer, spent the first half of his life in England, where he studied classics at Cambridge, played cricket for Somerset, and was mentioned in dispatches as an RAF squadron leader. He had already made many gardens when he came to Geelong Grammar School in Australia (1961) to round off forty years as a schoolmaster, twenty-one of them as headmaster. In 1973 he retired to an expanse of scrubby bushland around a stone cottage at Blackwood in Victoria's central highlands. Here T.R. Garnett, with his wife Penelope and other family members, created the much-visited Garden of St Erth, one of Australia's first private gardens opened to the public in the modern era, in which grew plants from all corners of the globe. Articles from 1980–95 for the *Age* newspaper (where he was gardening editor 1979–85) developed his reputation as a creative, respected, often controversial authority on gardening matters. His books include *Stumbling on Melons* (1984) and *A Gardener's Potpourri* (1986), a biography of Alister CLARK: *Man of Roses* (1990), *The Evolution of a Gardener* (1993), and *From the Country: An Anthology* (2001). In 1984 he helped with the government sesquicentenary project to rejuvenate Victoria's country BOTANIC GARDENS; in the early 1990s he (successfully) advocated the establishment of an independent board for the ROYAL BOTANIC GARDENS, MELBOURNE. He defined a series of CLIMATIC zones for Australian gardeners, part of his many widely recognised achievements.

ANNE LATREILLE

GATES AND GATE LODGES If Australians are naturally defensive, if our home is our castle even more than the Englishman's, if property has a value beyond dollars, then access is barred or gained at the gate, where DRIVE or PATH meets FENCE. More than preventing invasion of property, the gate is a potent image of possession and of control. It stands to protect the home, the expression of our individual identity, the shrine of our place-making. It secures against a threatening world, as it did earlier from a threatening wilderness.

The gate may also present as an emblem, a succinct announcement of the identity of the occupants of the house beyond. It may seek to impress, to aggrandise, as it did in many gate lodges built in Australia. The gate lodge was a statement of pretension and status, beyond practical function. Frequently it was picturesquely Gothic in manner, whatever the architectural style of the house beyond. Some may have been influenced by designs from pattern books, such as MOUNT NOORAT (1873–76) or Invergowrie, St James Park, Hawthorn, Vic. (c. 1850). Others were classically derived, as at STONNINGTON (1890) and RUPERTSWOOD (1871–72). Yet others were set before public buildings or other INSTITUTIONAL sites, such as the former Royal Mint, Melbourne (1871–72), which functioned as a guardhouse.

Other than a cattle-grid—that most minimal of entrances—the simplest and generally earliest gates were mere continuations of the fence, and barely visible. Sliprails of sapling poles, perhaps fixed through horseshoes to form simple rural gates, are now rare, but timber parallel bar and braced gates survive, secured with a looped chain or timber sliding-piece. Iron gates could be fabricated by a blacksmith, and bolted or welded together. Patent cast- and wrought-IRON rural gates, such as those manufactured by H.V. McKAY at Sunshine, are still common. They were succeeded in the early twentieth century by Cyclone's gates of tubular steel, clad with wire mesh in vehicular or pedestrian widths.

The company's suburban gates were much more decorative, with curlicue metal ribbon flourishes and woven, crimped, or chain-linked wire mesh panels. The low brick fences from the 1930s to the 1950s had mild steel geometric gates by Cyclone and others. More stylish gates came from works such as CASLAKE, in Melbourne.

Timber-latticed, high side gates screened the activities of the BACKYARD. At least from the 1880s, timber merchants such as James Moore in South Melbourne offered ranges of elaborate timber gates, with decorative fretwork, turned spindle palisades, and decorative panels. Gateposts were usually more impressive, and often higher, than fence posts. Earlier, massive red gum posts were decoratively axed with notches, like lesser totem poles. Later, more finely finished posts were decorated with applied, mitred-timber mouldings, drilled decoration, cast-iron finials, chamfered angles, and cast-lead rosettes. Foundry catalogues depict posts assembled from cast-iron panels, bolted together. Iron gates had wrought palisades of spearheads, sometimes over a decorative frieze. Occasionally, the entire gate was a decorative, cast panel. The grandest iron gates were imported from British foundries, or designed by architects of the house, as at Rupertswood. Mild steel replaced wrought iron in the twentieth century.

Only from the 1960s to the 1980s did we generally trust leaving domestic driveways unimpeded by gates. But a failure of nerve has more recently heralded their return to the suburbs.

Tim Mowl and Brian Earnshaw, *Trumpet at a Distant Gate: The Lodge as Prelude to the Country House* (London, 1985)

RICHARD PETERSON

GATTER, George Prowlin (*c*. 1828–1886), rhubarb specialist and the son of an English nurseryman, arrived in Vic. in 1855. E.E. PESCOTT records that Gatter shared a tent on the Bendigo goldfields with Joseph HARRIS and then became head foreman for the PERRY brothers. In 1861 he established his own nursery at Box Hill. A year later his father, William, sent out a consignment of named rhubarb varieties, apparently the colony's first. Gatter moved to Burwood, where he was joined by his son (James) George Gatter (1864–1942); later generations continued in market gardening at Hallam.

RA

GEELONG BOTANIC GARDENS, Vic. Following local calls for public gardens in 1848, supported by Superintendent LA TROBE, the Town Council appointed a committee of horticulturists to advise on establishing a BOTANIC GARDEN (1850). Their unanimous choice was a 200-acre (81 ha) piece of undulating treeless land at Limeburner's Point. La Trobe reserved the garden in 1851—the first in the colony outside Melbourne—and appointed trustees to form a committee of management. Control passed to the Council in 1874. The initial plan for the whole area to be gardens with walks and drives was later found too ambitious. The five-acre (2 ha) nursery near the centre became the botanic garden, the remainder a botanical parkland, **Eastern Park**.

Planting began in earnest when Daniel BUNCE was appointed curator (1857). He and his successor John RADDENBERRY set the framework for an extensive plant collection. Today the most significant tree is a *Ginkgo biloba* (Maidenhair Tree) that came as a seed in 1859 and developed aerial roots at an early age (the only such specimen known outside China and Japan to exhibit this feature). A *Fagus sylvatica* var. *purpurea* (Copper Beech), *Quillaja saponaria* (Soap Bark Tree), *Eucalyptus maculata* (Spotted Gum), and *Juniperus thurifera* (Spanish Juniper) are also exceptional. A *Jubaea chilensis* (Chilean Wine Palm) planted *c*. 1867 is splendidly symmetrical, protected during its formative years inside Raddenberry's huge FERNERY (1885–87). For sixty years its ferns, palms, and other plants were a great attraction. The garden was enlarged in 1959, a FRIENDS group formed in 1985, and a master plan for further development completed in 1995.

George Jones, *Growing Together: A Gardening History of Geelong—Extending to Colac and Camperdown* (Belmont, Vic., 1984)

GEORGE JONES

GELDING, John (*c*. 1828–1900) and brother **William Gelding** (*c*. 1839–1897), nursery proprietors, seed merchants, and florists, established their business in 1861, trading from Sydney's George Street Markets with a nursery at Double Bay; by 1869 they transferred to Petersham, where the business was known as the Victoria Nursery. John Gelding had previously worked as gardener for Sir Charles Cowper at Camden, Sir William MACLEAY, and for six years as overseer of Sir Daniel Cooper's estate at Rose Bay after his arrival in Sydney in 1853. John Gelding achieved lasting recognition as editor of the HORTICULTURAL MAGAZINE; he was presented with a testimonial by fellow members of the Horticultural Society of New South Wales in 1869 in gratitude for his services as secretary of the Society (which ultimately spanned *c*. 1862–77) and as honorary editor. As the more prominent brother, John was also Government Judge of Orchards throughout the colony, and founding president of the Horticultural Association of New South Wales (*c*. 1893); after his death the Association commissioned a portrait of him to hang in its rooms.

COLLEEN MORRIS and SILAS CLIFFORD-SMITH

GENDER permeates many facets of gardens and gardening—its influence attributed to many of the differences found in the designs, choice of plants, and gardening practices of men and women. Woman has been seen as at home in the garden, whether it be garden of Eden, the medieval flower garden, a nineteenth-century cottage garden, or a small twentieth-century subdivision of our cities. She is invariably depicted among the flowers, her femininity aligned with the delicate style and perfume of the species she cultivates. Occasionally she can be found mowing the lawn or digging a trench, but more often she bends gently to catch the scent of a flower, or stands elegantly, hose in hand, watering her blooming patch. Man in the garden adopts a very different pose. He is shown at work, and is more often found pushing the wheelbarrow or in the vegetable garden, than cultivating beauty among the flowers—unless they be roses. The implications of such stereotypes include a general dismissal of the

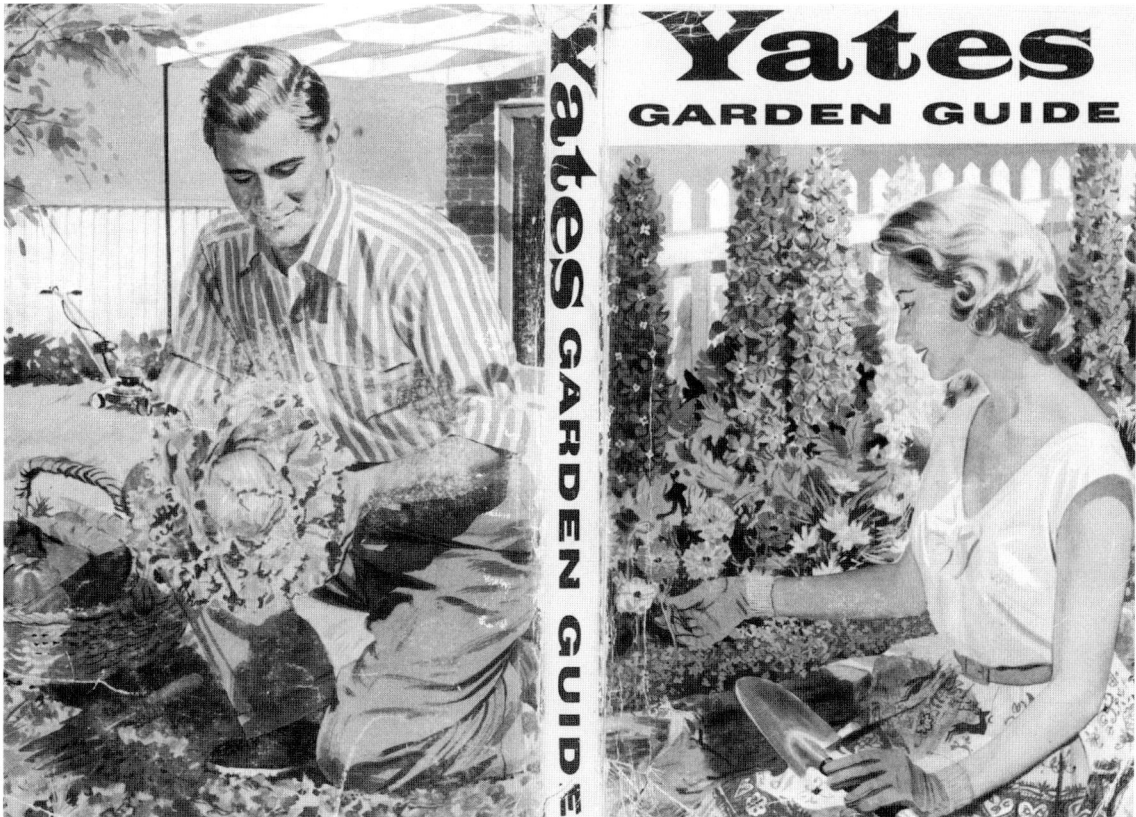

Nowhere were GENDER differences more apparent in the realm of gardening than in depictions of work in the home garden as portrayed in popular GARDEN BOOKS

importance of women's work in the garden and a reinforcing of cultural attitudes about men and women: women garden for pleasure, men are involved with the more serious business of work and productivity.

Gender differences are both cultivated in the garden and reflected there. Women's involvement with flowers, herbs, and medicinal plants may have had practical derivations in the earliest of gardens, and the tradition of women caring for gardens can be found in the Adonis gardens of classical Greece; but by the nineteenth century, the association between the delicate bloom and scent of flowers became intimately connected with understandings of femininity. Within the confines of the garden, young, middle-class girls would be transformed into blooming maidens and eventually into good wives and mothers. The 'femininity' of the flower garden was further reinforced by its physical and functional location to the house. Boys learnt other, more practical lessons. 'Serious' gardening, however—designing, digging, propagating, and producing, for both profession and pleasure—was done by men.

The first book addressed to women gardeners, William Lawson's *The Country House-Wifes Garden*, appeared in 1617 and while men were out creating the 'landscape garden' in the eighteenth century, there is ample evidence of women's involvement in smaller scale flower and herb gardens. By the nineteenth century, women began to feature more regularly in English gardening books, both as authors and as readers. The best known of these were Jane LOUDON and, later, Gertrude JEKYLL. In Australia, the first gardening books by women were by 'Mrs Rolf BOLDREWOOD' (1893) and Mrs Arthur TUCKETT (1905). Many of these early gardening books by women in Britain, North America, and Australia repeat a theme that women are capable of the hard physical work involved in the garden, and that it could serve as a place of creativity and empowerment in a society that otherwise sought to marginalise and denigrate their contributions. There is also a shared belief that attractive gardens and a settled home life went together; that men attached to homes with gardens would be less inclined to go in search of other pleasures: gardens settled the souls of restless Australian men. For Australian women on rural properties, the garden could be a crucial means of transforming an alien landscape into an area of fertility and domesticity, sometimes with the assistance of Aboriginal servants. Gardens, and women's work in them, was a crucial means of 'settling' Australia.

By the late nineteenth century women were being encouraged to take up horticulture as a profession. In England, special colleges such as Swanley and Waterperry were established to train women in horticulture, but in Australia women joined men as pupils at Victoria's BURNLEY School of Horticulture in 1899. Women's magazines exhorted women to pursue horticulture, believing them specially equipped in the 'art that doth mend nature'. The loss of a generation of men in the First World War opened up new opportunities for women. The earliest and best-known women graduates from Burnley—including Ina HIGGINS, Olive MELLOR (née Holttum), Millie GIBSON (née Grassick), and Edna WALLING—formed a cohort of women who were to become successful landscape gardeners in the inter-war years. Their entry into horticulture was not uncontested; as with other professions women sort to enter, the likelihood of their marrying and bearing children was used as an argument against professional training.

While women were gradually establishing themselves in gardening as a profession, men still dominated both professional and amateur HORTICULTURAL SOCIETIES. The Amateur Horticultural Society of Hobart, formed in 1900, allowed ladies at four meetings a year, and permitted their participation in competitions, but only men could be full members. By contrast, the scientifically oriented LINNEAN SOCIETY OF NEW SOUTH WALES permitted women as members. But horticultural societies increasingly provided opportunities for both men and women to exhibit flowers and vegetables in urban and rural competitions throughout Australia.

Distinctions in the types of gardens that men and women make and design have provoked repeated comment throughout the twentieth century. Discussion was not limited to whether women prefer flowers and men vegetables—a representation common in *Yates Garden Guides*—but also whether men were more attracted to a regimental style of planting—straight rows and squares—and more concerned with design than plants. Walling, writing in *Australian Home Beautiful* (1926), observed that men were more inclined to gravel footpaths, prize blooms, and impressing passers-by, women to secluded, seductive gardens. Walling did not believe that gardens should be a place for flaunting one's horticultural abilities. Other writers commented on the likelihood of marital conflict arising in the garden over differing visions of its design and the treatment of plants therein. The title of an article in the journal *Garden and Home Maker of Australia* (1931) put it this way: 'The Husband in the Garden: a warning as to the perils involved in having both'. The belief that men and women do garden differently is firmly held, if not empirically sustainable. Perhaps the shared nature of space in the garden makes its use more contested—unlike the home, which is usually seen as a woman's domain. Despite resistance to women's entry into horticulture, they have made significant inroads into the professions and are now widely employed as landscape architects, horticulturists, and even head gardeners. Many other women find the garden a place of creativity and relaxation, especially once the demands of career or children lessen. Their visions of a garden may differ from men's, and the garden will continue to serve as a space where differences in gender are both manifest and constructed. Gardens may convey images of tranquillity, domesticity, and harmony, but a little digging can uncover many other ideas, conflicts, and accommodations.

Deborah Kellaway (ed.), *The Virago Book of Women Gardeners* (London, 1995); Sue Bennett, *Five Centuries of Women and Gardens* (London, 2000)   KATIE HOLMES

GEOLOGY Landforms are often controlled by rock type and structure, so geology is regularly reflected in widespread changes to vegetation even where other major influences such as CLIMATE and aspect remain the same. Australia—with Africa, India, New Zealand, South America, and Antarctica—split from the greater landmass of GONDWANA and drifted away over millions of years. Thus modern plants and animals in each country may share common ancestors. The geological history of Australia extends well back in time, with rock formations known to date from at least 3.5 billion years ago. Some landforms may have changed little in many millions of years. This is in contrast with the northern hemisphere, where extensive glacial erosion and uplifting occurred during the late-Tertiary and Quaternary eras. In Australia, landscapes similar to that of Europe can only be found in Tas. and in elevated parts of the south-east of the continent. These locations have developed strong gardening cultures, such as HILL-STATIONS tradition, based on European influences; they remain important areas for the NURSERY industry. Not only do they have a cooler climate but often deeper, richer soils have formed—soils in which a wide range of plants common in European gardens, such as rhododendrons, magnolias, and maples, flourish.

The generally low-lying and stable landscapes of much of Australia have produced deep weathering profiles (or regolith) capped by old and often deeply leached SOILS, and with extensive salt accumulations at depth. These deposits can rise to the surface when landscapes are altered and vegetation is removed. Salinity has rapidly become one of the most environmentally damaging effects of European land management practices in Australia. Horticultural techniques, enhanced knowledge, and research—including appropriate selection of plants—are being applied by professionals and amateurs alike, through a wide range of government and non-government organisations such as LANDCARE groups and GREENING AUSTRALIA, in an attempt to redress land degradtion.   ML

GEORGE, Alexander Segger (b. 1939), botanist, natural historian, and editor, was born and educated in Perth, completing a Bachelor of Arts degree that embraced the study of botany. Following employment in the Western Australian Herbarium (1959–81), he was appointed inaugural executive editor (1981–93) for the multi-volume *Flora of Australia*. While his knowledge and experience are broad, he has specialised in Orchidaceae, Myrtaceae, and Proteaceae, with BANKSIA being the genus for which he is best known. He has published widely, and his *The Banksias* (1981–2000), with artist Celia ROSSER, records all *Banksia* species and ranks among the great Australian botany books. Alex George's botanical career is inextricably linked with his interest in horticulture. He has collected new species that have entered horticulture, and has inspired many amateurs in the study of native plants, for example, through his association with the

Western Australian Wildflower Society and the Australian Plant Society's Grevillea, Banksia, Dryandra, and Verticordia study groups. He has written, contributed to, and illustrated with excellent photographs many popular science books featuring native plants, such as *Flowers and Plants of Western Australia* (1973).   HELEN HEWSON

GERANIUMS: see PELARGONIUMS AND GERANIUMS

GERMANY and its garden traditions have had a significant influence on Australian gardens. In particular this was through the influence of those who migrated to Australia from the Germanic states, especially to SA, Vic., and Qld, in the nineteenth century; they formed one-tenth of South Australia's population by 1900. The Germanic states from which they came—which gradually unified during these years under a dominant Prussia—produced gardeners who were held in high regard in nineteenth-century Europe. The apprenticeship system under which they trained covered botany, plant propagation and care, simple chemistry, and garden design; the system encouraged young men to travel around northern Europe gaining experience. John Claudius LOUDON, who praised the Germans as a 'scientific … and a reading people', wrote in 1833 that 'all the best gardens in Poland, Russia and Italy are in the care of Germans'. Loudon thought the harsh climate in Germany encouraged a careful approach to gardening; and that knowledge of horticulture was more widespread in Germany than in France. In Prussia, practical horticulture, including grafting, was taught in primary schools.

Nineteenth-century German BOTANIC GARDENS with significant collections of plants included Leipzig, Giessen, Stuttgart, Altdorf, Rintel, Ratisbon, Ulm, Jena Königsberg, Dresden, Munich, and Berlin, as well as the two famous gardens of Nymphenburg (Bavaria) and Schönbrunn (Austria), which both included AUSTRALIAN PLANTS in their collections. German gardeners were exposed to a variety of landscape design styles, from the Baroque to the English styles, through examples in important private and public gardens such as the Hortus Palatinus (Heidelberg), Veitshöchheim (Würzburg), Grosser Garten (Dresden), Favourite (Mainz), and Herrenhausen (Hanover); others of note were Schloss Augustusburg (Brühl), Schlossgarten (Schwetzingen), Wörlitz (Dessau), Wilhelmshöhe (Kassel), and Sanssouci (Potsdam). These gardens provided examples of the use of PARTERRES, FOUNTAINS, STATUES, LAKES, GROTTOES, and fine AVENUES of trees. To Loudon, the gardens in Munich and Magdeburg showed a good understanding of the principles of LANDSCAPE GARDENING. Throughout the Germanic states there was an appreciation of silviculture—a significant percentage of the landscape was wooded, as it still is today—as forestry practice went back for centuries. German migrants to Australia were familiar with the practice of tree planting along roads and the use of FORMAL avenues in landscape design. The German tradition of PLEASURE GARDENS, with elements of public garden, beer garden, and amusement park, was another strand of influence in garden design.

Coming to Australia in the nineteenth century, German-born scientists and horticulturists of note—including

The plan of a 'Gentleman's Garden' included in Ernst HEYNE's *The Amateur Gardener* (1881) transferred stylistic ideas directly from GERMANY to Australia, combining productive areas of the kitchen garden and orchard within an ornamental layout

MUELLER, SCHOMBURGK, HOLTZE, HEYNE, and Johannes Menge (1788–1852)—set an example in careful horticultural practices and enthusiastic experimentation with a wide range of plants from around the world. The correspondence of Schomburgk and Mueller refers to sources in northern Europe, South-East Asia, North America, and South America, with one important example being phylloxera-free rootstock sent from California in the 1880s. Both Schomburgk and Mueller used formal plantings of trees in their designs, and both made good use of conifers. They were energetic supporters of tree planting for civic parks and cemeteries, and wrote extensively about introduced and native varieties suitable for both landscaping and commercial use. Schomburgk also made some use of hedges and garden 'rooms' (popular in sections of German garden design) and limited use of parterre planting (then fashionable in nineteenth-century Europe). Schomburgk's German imports included statuary and the important prefabricated palm house at ADELAIDE BOTANIC GARDEN. Along with other scientific men and 'thinking' people, both men participated in learned societies and supported research and education in the applied plant sciences of horticulture, viticulture, forestry, and agriculture. With support from German-born parliamentarians F.E.H.W. KRICHAUFF and M.P.F. Basedow, SA established Australia's first agricultural college at ROSEWORTHY (1883) and its first forestry department (1876).

Nineteenth-century German emigrants who had no special training in horticulture were more likely to concentrate on utilitarian plants rather than garden flowers, growing herbs, vegetables, vines, and fruit trees (such as apple, pear, and mulberry). Through their practical survival skills they made their own contribution to settler society. Their twentieth-century counterparts, especially in the post-war years, have tended to be quiet achievers whose gardening traditions have not been dramatically different from those of mainstream Australia. There has of late, however, been an upsurge of interest in the contribution of the German scientific and horticultural fraternity and the German lifestyle in colonial times. Recent German influence has included the experience of banning herbicide use in urban greenspace, and ecological approaches to planting design, especially the use of herbaceous perennials mixed within a grassy matrix.

Patrick Bowe, *Gardens in Central Europe* (Woodbridge, Suffolk, 1991); Rod Home, *Science as a German Export to Nineteenth Century Australia* (London, 1995); Charles Quest-Ritson, *Gardens of Germany* (London, 1998).   PAULINE PAYNE

GIBSON (née GRASSICK), Emily Matilda ('Millie') (1887–1974), horticultural journalist, lecturer, and landscape designer, of Scottish parentage, migrated to Australia in 1911 and later settled in Melbourne. She studied part-time at BURNLEY School of Horticulture (1914–16), and on graduation worked in the Melbourne office of Walter Burley GRIFFIN, receiving tutelage from Max Meldrum in painting and Bertha Merfield in design. In 1918 she returned to Burnley as an instructor, filling a position vacated by Olive MELLOR. She toured Europe (1922–24), and during this time spent a brief stint working in the office of the notable London landscape firm Milner Son and White. In 1924 she became a horticultural journalist with the *Australasian* and the *Argus*, writing for the latter under the nom de plume 'Culturist'. During her twenty-two years as a writer for these publications, she is reported to have averaged more than 2000 letters annually in response to incoming correspondence. It was also at this time that she met and married (1934) *Argus* agricultural writer John Gibson.

From 1947 to 1953 Gibson returned once more to Burnley, retraining ex-service personnel for the post-war horticultural workforce. During the same period she consulted for the major commercial and industrial architecture firms of Stephenson and Turner, and Buchan Laird and Buchan, collaborating on occasion with fellow designers Grace FRASER and John STEVENS. Known for encouraging women to pursue professional landscape design and for fostering links with King's College at Durham University (England), Gibson was also involved with the Lyceum Club's 'garden circle'. Knowledge of Gibson's design style is relatively scant, although she is well regarded for using native and exotic species to develop hospitable garden settings from exposed and barren sites. For this reason, she has come to be seen as a pioneer of INDUSTRIAL landscape design. Incomplete physical remnants are in most cases the only evidence of her design work, and many of her GARDEN PLANS for industrial clients were never implemented. She is reputed to have destroyed all of her drawings and plans on retirement, but a small collection is held by the State Library of Victoria.

ROWAN WILKEN

GILBERT, Lionel Arthur (b. 1924), teacher and historian, was born and educated in Sydney and taught at primary, secondary and tertiary level in NSW until his retirement in 1984. His doctoral thesis, 'Botanical Investigation of New South Wales, 1811–1880' (Armidale, 1971), eclipsed the most detailed previous treatments of the subject by J.H. Maiden. Gilbert has many publications, chief among which is *The Royal Botanic Gardens, Sydney: A History 1816–1985* (1986), and biographies of William WOOLLS (1985), H.M.R. RUPP (1992), and J.H. MAIDEN (2001).   RA

GILES, Charles (c. 1807–1887), nursery proprietor, born at Fowey, Cornwall, England, arrived at Adelaide in 1839 with eleven years' training and apprenticeship in a Devon nursery and some experience in the hotel business. With his wife Hannah (née Long, c. 1807–1879) he took up farming on South Road at a property he called Bold Venture. By 1846 he had established himself sufficiently to purchase at auction approximately 160 hectares of land in the foothills of the ADELAIDE HILLS near Magill (later known as Norton Summit)—but not before he had thoroughly sampled the soils. Walking from Bold Venture every Monday morning, he worked for a week at a time at this property, and soon had two hectares of cherries under cultivation. Naming this property **Grove Hill**, he planted extensive stone fruit orchards and set up a production nursery, as well as clearing land for farming. Giles was the first South Australian orchardist to export cherries—packed in cork dust—to Covent Garden, where they achieved high prices for fruits out of season. An expert orchardist, he also grew many varieties of apples and pears with great skill, and perry and cider were commercially produced using 300 French oak barrels to mature the pressed juices. Slate fermenting vats still remain set up in the grounds of Grove Hill.

In 1857, with his son Charles (c. 1846–1932), Giles established the Exotic Nursery, a retail outlet at Kent Town. Here he traded a wide range of forest and fruit trees, ornamental plants, flowers, and shade-house plants. A keen and successful exhibitor at horticultural shows, Giles travelled by horseback from Norton Summit to Adelaide and Mount Barker with baskets of camellias and fruit so expertly packed that delicate flowers were unblemished and the bloom on the fruits was unmarked. Giles was a significant importer of plants from England, NSW, and elsewhere: there are still to be found at Grove Hill, WARDIAN CASES stamped 'VEITCH and Co.' and painted with 'Charles Giles, Grove Hill', as the consignee. Undeterred by the high loss rates, Giles tenaciously continued importing plants to meet the competition of his rivals. He made several return trips to England to buy plants—stopping at Ceylon on the voyage over, to see new CHINESE and JAPANESE plant NOVELTIES before travelling on to English nurseries and KEW. Son Charles and his son-in-law, horticulturist John Francis Pascoe (c. 1837–1912), took charge of the Exotic Nursery from 1861 to 1875 while Giles retained the facilities and gardens at Grove Hill as a private pleasure ground. A visit by Ferdinand MUELLER, accompanied by his correspondent Otto TEPPER, was the occasion for the plant-

S.T. GILL's 1850 watercolour of Prospect House, the Adelaide residence of J.B. Graham, who had made his fortune in copper mining at Burra Burra (SA), reveals a fantastic GARDENESQUE setting in which the flat site is richly compensated by an intricate pattern of garden BEDS

ing of a presentation tree, a *Cupressus cashmeriana* (Cashmere Cypress), which still stands as a fine mature specimen.

A determined and successful business man, Charles Giles owned city properties as well as farms and hotels in the further corners of SA and in the NT, including the Grove Hill gold mine. The diversity of his enterprise extended to a jam factory in Kent Town where stone fruits from Grove Hill were made into conserves. Family tradition relates that he was proud of his achievements, fair and honest, especially on matters of quality and accuracy of nomenclature. Draft letters written in a fine cross-hatched copperplate show that he was forthright in complaining about poor standards and the quality of plants and seedlings received; stern letters to Dutch bulb dealers complained of named double hyacinths turning out to be mixed single sorts. Closer to home, he felt his requests to the superintendent of the infant ADELAIDE BOTANIC GARDEN had been dealt with unjustly, even though he had been generous with his gifts of plants.

Following the death of Giles the Exotic Nursery ceased to operate at Kent Town, and Grove Hill passed to his grandson, Charles William Wycliffe Giles (1869–1942). The property is still owned by the Giles family (fifth and sixth generations) and is now the site of a cool-climate vineyard and wine cellar. Remarkably, the buildings at Grove Hill are substantially unaltered since they were first built. Several ranges of heated GLASSHOUSES, a boiler house, and bothy were built into a steep hillside; a large packing shed and several barns as well as a large residence were constructed with fine book-leaf slate masonry. The extensive grounds were serviced by a system of underground drains, and dry-stone retaining walls hold terraces where tree peonies, camellias, and flowering plants were grown. Of particular interest is a grove of more than one hundred camellia 'trees', known to have been imported in the 1850s from MACARTHUR's Camden Park nursery and from European nurseries. Many of these plants retain their original enamelled identity numbers: camellia authority Tom SAVIGE, adjudged this the best historic CAMELLIA collection in the southern hemisphere.

TREVOR NOTTLE

GILL, Samuel Thomas (1819–1880), English-born artist, arrived in SA with his parents and siblings in 1839. Already proficient as a draughtsman, he established a studio in Adelaide, specialising in 'correct likenesses' of people, animals, residences, and local scenery. He travelled widely, and relocated in 1852 to Vic., quickly exploiting the visual wealth of the diggings, before a short stay (1856–62) in Sydney. A skilled lithographer, he published several series of prints, but it is his watercolours that attract the GARDEN HISTORIAN for their minute observation of detail, outstandingly demonstrated in his views of Prospect House, North Adelaide (1850) and his series on the months and SEASONS (*c*. 1847).

Keith Macrae Bowden, *Samuel Thomas Gill, Artist* (Maryborough, Vic., 1971); Geoffrey Dutton, *S.T. Gill's Australia* (Sydney, 1981); Ron Appleyard, Barbara Fargher, and Ron Radford, *S.T. Gill, The South Australian Years 1839–1852* (Adelaide, 1986)

RA

GILL, Walter (1851–1929), forest conservator, botanist, and photographer, supervised the maturation of South Australia's forestry industry as conservator of forests (1890–1923). Born in Welford, Northamptonshire, England, he trained in the family's Dorset nursery, F. Gill and Co., before migrating to

Adelaide in 1876. Gill was appointed sub-inspector of crown lands (1884) and then placed in charge of the WIRRABARA forest plantations and nursery (1886), before succeeding J.E. BROWN as conservator. He used his enthusiasm and skill in photography to portray and illustrate the activities and achievements of the Woods and Forests Department, including the successful mass cultivation of *Pinus radiata* (Monterey Pine) in South Australia's south-east. He also supervised (unsuccessful) attempts at date PALM cultivation, and continued the free distribution of seedlings throughout the state.

DAVID JONES

GILLANDERS, Kenneth David (b. 1930), nursery proprietor and plant collector, was born in Melbourne and from 1955 to 1975 worked for CHANDLER's Como Nurseries, specialising in rare plants. In 1975 he moved to Tas. and established Woodbank Nursery at Longley in the foothills of Mount Wellington—an ideal site for growing alpines. He began collecting rare Tasmanian endemic plants, which he supplied to overseas collectors, notably to KEW and Munich Botanic Gardens. Many of the rare plants grown in the nursery have been propagated from variants in the native Tasmanian flora collected by Gillanders, such *Eucryphia lucida* 'Pink Cloud' (Pink Leatherwood). In 1987 he began PLANT COLLECTING trips to Chile, Bolivia, Ecuador, China, and South Africa, concentrating on rare plants that would be tolerant of conditions in Tas., and hence in cooler areas of Australia. Gillanders has written and lectured widely on ALPINE PLANTS and Tasmanian mountain flora, and wrote, as co-author, *Know Your Rock Garden Plants and Dwarf Bulbs* (1973).

ANN CRIPPS

GILL AND SEARLE PTY LTD, seed merchants and nursery proprietors, was established in 1926 when F.H. BRUNNING Pty Ltd was reconstructed—a move precipitated by the sale of their leasehold premises in central Melbourne. With links to the parent company, three former employees took over the retail horticultural portion of the business (covering garden seeds, seedlings, trees, shrubs, and garden requisites). Herbert Fitzmaurice Gill (1871–1957), a cousin of Walter GILL, joined Brunning in 1886 and became a director in 1906. His brother, (Ernest) Reginald Notton Gill (1878–1957), commenced with Brunning in 1892 and in 1909, preferring an outdoor life, switched to the growing of flower and vegetable seedlings for the company. Alexander Waldemar Searle (*olim* Schultz) (1887–1963) commenced with the company in 1904 and from 1922 was manager of the city shop. Premises for Gill and Searle were secured at 73 Elizabeth Street, opposite the former Brunning shop, and visitors were welcomed at their Grendon Nursery in North Brighton. The nursery passed from family control in 1961 after almost four decades as a byword for floricultural excellence in Vic. and, retaining the name Gill, has continued to trade at several new locations.

RA

GILPIN, William (1724–1804), English clergyman and champion of the PICTURESQUE, travelled extensively through Britain (1769–76). His tour journals, illustrated with pen and wash drawings, formed the basis of his published *Observations*, including popular works on the Wye River (1782), the Lake District (1786), and the Highlands of Scotland (1789), which almost single-handedly invented and defined picturesque beauty. As Malcolm Andrews has observed in *The Search for the Picturesque* (1989), Gilpin also helped to promote, if not inaugurate, the fashion for Picturesque touring. Many of the elite who travelled to the colonies in the early nineteenth century certainly demonstrated Picturesque tastes based on Gilpin's influence, and reading the early writings of George BENNETT, direct influence can be detected. Gilpin translated his observations into a practical landscape manifesto through *Remarks on Forest Scenery* (1791), which analysed the contributions of individual trees, and then their collective value of as clumps, copses, and forests.

Nephew and pupil **William Sawrey Gilpin** (1762–1843) assisted his uncle with illustrations and later commenced a successful career as a landscape gardener. His style drew on the Picturesque, brought to the public (including Australia) through his *Practical Hints upon Landscape Gardening* (1832). His designs found particular favour in Scotland, and among emigrant Scottish gardeners, William SANGSTER was one who looked to Gilpin, transcribing parts of the *Practical Hints* as a reference. Gilpin's career is assessed by Piebenga (*Garden History*, 1994).

William D. Templeman, *The Life and Work of William Gilpin (1724–1804), Master of the Picturesque and Vicar of Boldre* (Urbana, Illinois, 1939); Carl Paul Barbier, *William Gilpin: His Drawings, Teaching, and Theory of the Picturesque* (Oxford, 1963)

RA

GINN (GHINN), Henry (1817–1892), architect and horticulturist, was born in Box Hill, Sussex, England, and after being articled to London architect William Cubbitt, arrived in Sydney in 1835. He designed the Garrison Church (1840), Millers Point, and worked in the Colonial Architect's Office. Ginn arrived in Melbourne in 1846 as Clerk of Works to the Port Phillip District and then became Victoria's Colonial Architect (1851–53). He was actively involved, in his professional and personal capacities, in the creation of the MELBOURNE BOTANIC GARDENS; he presumably provided the first plan (1846), designed the under-gardener's cottage (1850), served as honorary secretary and as a member of the committee of management, and prepared the first two annual reports (1851–52). A meeting in his office (1853) revived the Victorian Horticultural Society (established 1849), of which he was honorary secretary. Ginn continued as secretary of the revived Society but returned to England during 1854–69, denying the colony his experience during a period of immense horticultural development.

GEORGE TIBBITS

GLADIOLUS, from the Latin *gladius* (sword, giving rise to the common name Sword Lily), is the name given to a large group of related species mostly from South Africa, although cultivated varieties are the result of extensive and complex hybridisation from the 1820s onwards. Gladioli (plural) are corms (see BULBS) and in Australia have been valued since the mid-nineteenth century for their great beauty and size, and ease of culture (according to E.E. Pescott, *Bulb Growing in Australia*, 1926, one of the earliest Australian books on bulbs). In 1874 Thomas LANG offered seventy-seven varieties of European origin, and thirty-six raised by his son-in-law William Harvie. From the early 1900s they were exceeding popular, especially on the SHOW table. Specialist growers such as ERREY Bros offered more than 100 varieties during the 1920s, admirably adapted for FLOWER ARRANGING. Their cosiness in the SUBURBAN GARDEN led satirist Barry Humphries (in the guise of Edna Everage) to parody 'glad-dies' in the show *Excuse I* (Sydney, 1965), since when Everage has been their most vocal apologist. RA

GLASS, Peter (1917–1997), artist, conservationist, and landscape architect, was born in Camberwell (Vic.). He studied painting with Max Meldrum and joined the artists' colony at Eltham, purchasing land there in 1936 and later building his own mud brick house and studio. In the 1950s he worked for influential environmental designer Alistair KNOX. From the 1960s he practised independently and in partnership with Gordon FORD as a landscape designer creating small and large-scale gardens in the NATURAL STYLE in both city and country, Belodun Point, Gippsland (Vic.), being a notable example. A foundation member of the AUSTRALIAN INSTITUTE OF LANDSCAPE ARCHITECTS, he was noted for his use of AUSTRALIAN PLANTS and with his wife, Cecile, established a native plant nursery in the 1960s.

RICHARD CLOUGH

GLASSHOUSES, glazed GREENHOUSES—the two terms often used interchangeably—were popular GARDEN BUILDINGS in private and public gardens from the mid-nineteenth century. Like their heated variants, HOTHOUSES, glasshouses of some architectural pretensions were often known as CONSERVATORIES. Conversely, utilitarian structures used for protecting or forcing vegetables were commonly known as pits or frames. The best examples of glasshouses are now found in BOTANIC GARDENS and larger PUBLIC PARKS, with fine examples at ROSALIND PARK, Bendigo, Vic. (1897), and botanic gardens in SYDNEY (1970–71), BRISBANE, Mount Coot-tha (1970–73), ADELAIDE (1987–89), and BALLARAT, Vic. (1995). Specialised environments are demonstrated by fine early structures for PALMS (1877) and the Victoria Lily (1868) at Adelaide Botanic Garden.

John Hix, *The Glass House* (London, 1974; rev. edn 1996); Georg Kohlmaier and Barna von Sartory, *Houses of Glass: A Nineteenth-century Building Type* (Cambridge, Mass,, 1986); Sylvia Saudan-Skira and Michel Saudan, *Orangeries: Palaces of Glass, Their History and Development* (Cologne, 1998) RA

GLEDSWOOD, in a park-like setting at Catherine Field, NSW, was built *c.* 1829 for James and Elizabeth Chisholm.

This striking GLASSHOUSE at BALLARAT BOTANIC GARDENS (1995), widely recognised for its innovative design drawing on historical precedents, has added a rich new centrepiece to a BOTANIC GARDEN of undoubted cultural significance

Glenalta

The garden, expanded by James Kinghorne Chisholm, was described in the *Horticultural Magazine* (1870). Romanticised by W. Hardy WILSON in 1920—'In a wide circle camellias grow, ring within ring, their dark glossy leaves almost hidden under scarlet, white and striped flowers, blooming when morning frosts sparkle on the meadow beyond. The grape twines over its pergola and woodbine overhangs the paths that wind about this luxuriant garden'—it inspired the planting of Wilson's own garden at Purulia. Although the garden has been altered, Gledswood's signature plantings of ARAUCARIAS are a landmark from the former Cow Pasture Road between Liverpool and Camden. COLLEEN MORRIS

GLENALTA, Stirling, SA, an elegant nineteenth-century garden in the ADELAIDE HILLS, was established by South Australian statesman (Sir) John William Downer (1843–1915) from 1880. Son James Frederick Downer and his wife Florence extended and developed the garden from the 1920s to the 1940s. Since 1987 Geoffrey and Robyn Steward have restored and enhanced the terraced garden, and new plantings of unusual trees, including *Sapium sebiferum* (Chinese Tallowwood), *Nyssa sylvatica* (Tupelo), and *Taxodium distichum* (Swamp Cypress), sit well with the existing mature woodland. Excavations revealed a typical Edwardian water garden and a stone dell now planted with miniature conifers. Notable features are the lawn terraces, a row of giant poplars, and a recently planted herbaceous border. The Adelaide Hills' seasonal variation is demonstrated by the woodland's late winter bluebells and camellias, through to summer-flowering perennials and the outstanding autumn foliage of the trees. NICKY DOWNER

GLENARA, Bulla, Vic.: see CLARK, Alister

GLEN HARROW, Belgrave, Vic.: see COLE, T.C.

GLENHOLME, Ballarat, Vic, erected in 1869 by government surveyor Henry Morres and owned during 1874–89 by merchant J.J. Goller, retains an extraordinarily intact VILLA GARDEN of the mid-nineteenth century. Located close to Lake Wendouree, Glenholme was sited in a rich mining precinct and the sunken oval front lawn today recalls its origin as a mining dam. The property was purchased by the Cuthbert family in 1901 and their descendants have since exercised sensitive custody. Mature exotic trees, clipped box hedges bordering crushed quartz paths, a gnarled wisteria shading the verandah, shrubberies, and a large service garden and vegetable garden recall its early layout and planting. In an age when re-created Victorian-era gardens are now popular, Glenholme assumes outstanding significance for its authenticity. RA

GLENNY, George (*c*. 1793–1874), English horticultural journalist and author, is best remembered for his influence in the mid-Victorian period on FLORICULTURE. Born in London, he started growing tulips when only a boy, and his outspoken views were soon heard through journals and at meetings. In 1832 he founded the Metropolitan Society of Florists and Amateurs and commenced the *Horticultural Journal* (1832–39), in which he published his papers on the 'Properties of Flowers'—widely regarded as his most important contribution to floriculture. His fixed standards for florists' flowers governed horticultural SHOWS from the mid-century onwards. His standards, widely adopted in Australia, were separately published in 1850 by the Gardeners' and Amateurs' Horticultural Society of Hobart Town, and included in books by DICKINSON (1855) and HOCKINGS (1875).

Glenny edited numerous journals, including the *Gardener's Gazette* (1837–47), the first horticultural periodical in a newspaper format; and the *Horticultural Magazine* (1845–50), which included special issues on the Vegetation of New Holland, the Banksia, the New Holland Pitcher Plant, and Gardening and Farming for Colonists and Emigrants; and contributed notes on florists' flowers to the *Cottage Gardener* from 1851. He published numerous horticultural handbooks in the early 1850s, all freely available in the colonies, including *Flower Garden & Greenhouse*, *Practical Gardening … including Landscape Gardening*, and *Fruit & Vegetable Garden*, as well as numerous other titles. An obituary spoke of Glenny as 'immoderately egoistic, exacting, and quarrelsome', but the influence of his publications, his tireless advocacy for horticulture, and his role in the promotion of horticultural societies were widely recognised. RA

GLOVER, John (1767–1849), English-born landscape painter, arrived in Van Diemen's Land in 1831, possessing a sound technique in the Claudean manner. He brought English shrubs and song birds, and established his estate Patterdale (named for the English Lake District township where he had once lived) at Mills Plains on the northern slope of Ben Lomond. His pastoral scenes portraying the Australian landscape echo the English *beau ideal* of a gentleman's park. Despite this backward glance, art historian John McPhee has observed that 'his paintings are the first to realise and portray the eucalypt in its bushland setting as a peculiarly national symbol'. His house paintings provide superb depictions of gardens, albeit occasionally taking the form of a capriccio, juxtaposing different seasons. Glover's works are held by many Australian galleries, and several of his books—left to the Evandale Subscription Library and still held by the Queen Victoria Museum (Launceston)—attest to his keen interest in gardening.

John McPhee, *The Art of John Glover* (Melbourne, 1980)
 RA

GNOMES, small, human-like, coloured statues used as garden ORNAMENTS, became a common feature in Australian gardens during the twentieth century. With origins in European folklore, such figures were mass-produced in German and Austrian potteries during the nineteenth century. From the 1860s these were exported to Britain, where they became known as gnomes, after the German *gnomenfiguren* (miniature figures). Imported to Australia from the early twentieth century, they were sold as 'continental garden figures'. Their popularity peaked in Australia with the 1937 release of the film *Snow White and the Seven Dwarfs*. Gnomes

and animal figures have been popular in the vernacular SUBURBAN GARDEN, particularly in poorer socioeconomic areas, as well as their sometimes jocular use in the more mannered confines of the QUIRKY GARDEN. They slipped—but did not completely disappear—from fashion during the 1970s (along with other figures of derision such as concrete Aboriginals) and early examples, particularly with original colouring, are rare.
SILAS CLIFFORD-SMITH

GOLF COURSES Golf came to Australia with the early settlers, dragging and dropping its familiar seaside links features on a dry and often hostile landscape. The results, a century or more later, are mixed and varied. Few Australian golf courses reached the lofty ambitions of their founders, but those that did, such as the Royal Melbourne courses, have achieved world-wide fame, and are listed among the great championship venues. Other more modest facilities are little more than dirt fairways amid sparse and spare struggling eucalypts. In ARID ZONES, the 'sand scrape' (a 'green' of oiled sand) is a characteristic Australian feature where WATER and TURF are scarce. Each course is considered, by its members, a social centre of community importance.

All courses and clubs made some attempt at beautification, in some cases replicating familiar European landscapes. Pines, elms, willows, and the like are common around the nation, but generally, for good reasons of economy and maintenance, native AUSTRALIAN PLANTS have increasingly been used, sometimes out of their own environment, since Australia is a large continent of diverse climate, and what thrives in north Qld is naturally a stranger in Vic. It is common enough, however, for beautification to include tall trees only to separate one hole from another. Inclusion of small indigenous plants and groundcovers has largely been overlooked. In southern climes, the ubiquitous *Leptospermum laevigatum* (Tea-tree) has been too often planted and propagated, leading to the demise of more sensitive species that are unable to compete. Happily this practice is now being reversed. Many courses have allowed a natural temptation for planting to override the golf aspect, although after all a course is a SPORTING arena, and tube stock can become a mighty problem twenty years on, as seedlings take on an unintended canopy.

Generally speaking, Australian golf courses are happy environments that allow golfers to commune closely with Nature, even if with the frustration of a lost ball or difficult lie. There are as yet no Australian courses that are so highly manicured as to appear artificial—a recent US development that either offends or delights, depending on the eye of the beholder. Golf courses generally are accepted as valuable pieces of real estate, providing breathing space in crowded suburban districts and offering haven to native birds and other fauna. As city densities increase, courses become increasingly important to the general environment, playing the role of 'parks and gardens' by increasing urban green-space and forming a vital part of good urban planning. And with 1500 courses Australia-wide (as at 1996), covering 48 000 hectares, employing 6500 maintenance staff, golf has considerable horticultural potential.
PETER THOMSON

GONDWANA The concepts of plate tectonics and continental drift were first espoused by German meteorologist and geologist, Alfred Lothar Wegener (1880–1930), in 1912. His theory proposed that the earth's continents were parts of massive geological plates that moved around the surface of the planet due to the movements of its molten core. Prior to the Jurassic period (210–145 million years ago) all the earth's current continents were massed to form one super land mass called Pangaea. During the Jurassic period, Pangaea began to split into two massive super continents—Laurasia in the north and Gondwana in the south. Gondwana consisted of the land masses that now constitute Africa, South America, Australia, Antarctica, and India, as well as smaller components such as Madagascar and New Zealand. The splitting process has continued for millions of years, and the continents are still moving; it has been estimated that the Australian land mass continues to move northward at approximately six centimetres per year.

Many significant groups of PLANTS evolved before the fragmentation of Pangaea, and the subsequent splitting of Gondwana has led to some interesting patterns of distribution of southern plant genera. Many northern-hemisphere CONIFERS are not represented on southern landmasses, and the so-called southern conifers are a clearly distinct group. The genus *Nothofagus* is shared among Australia, South America, and New Zealand while the Proteaceae are well represented in Africa and Australia. A similar pattern emerges in the distribution of the genus *ACACIA*. The southern landmasses that once made up Gondwana also share the fossil heritage of the glossopterid flora, which is now seen as the likely predecessor of the modern angiosperm group.
GREG MOORE

GOOD, Peter (d. 1803), foreman at the royal gardens at KEW, had successfully conveyed a selection of living plants there from the East India Company's garden in Calcutta when chosen as the gardener aboard the *Investigator* (under Matthew Flinders), which sailed for Australia in July 1801. Good collected live plants and seed, sent to both Sir Joseph BANKS and Kew Gardens. He died in Sydney in June 1803; Flinders wrote of Good as a 'botanical gardener, a zealous worthy man [whose death] … was regretted by all.' He is commemorated in the Australian genus *Goodia*.

Phyllis I. Edwards (ed.), *The Journal of Peter Good: Gardener on Matthew Flinders' Voyage to Terra Australis 1801–03* (London, 1981)
JOAN WEBB

GOODMAN, Richard (1833-1917), orchardist, was born in Essex, England, the son of a horticulturist. Arriving in Melbourne in 1857, he went to work in the Geelong nursery of Thomas ADCOCK. He moved to Gippsland in 1858, where he was pastoralist Archibald McLeod's head gardener at Bairnsdale for six years. In 1861 he selected 100 acres (40 ha) on the Mitchell River flats at Picnic Point (Vic.) where he grew fruit and vegetables: ORCHARDING and MARKET GARDENING were major nineteenth-century industries in the Bairnsdale district. Son Charles John Goodman (1863–1910) trained at Cremorne Nursery, Richmond (Vic.), returning to Bairnsdale to establish a fruit tree nursery in 1888. By 1901, when the first catalogue was distributed Australia-wide, the nursery comprised 70 acres (28 ha) with over one million trees including 150 varieties of apples. Later sales went to New Zealand and South Africa. His son William Goodman (1867–1951) established the Goodman Seeds company in Bairnsdale in 1894. Goodman descendants still retain an interest in the family businesses.

FLORENCE PEARCE

GORDON, David Morrice (1899–2001), grazier and horticulturist, born in Talbot (Vic.), developed his garden Myall Park at Glenmorgan in south-west Qld from 1941. Devoted exclusively to AUSTRALIAN FLORA, this ninety-hectare garden and HERBARIUM of 7000 specimens specialises in plants from ARID, semi-arid, and dry SUBTROPICAL regions. Three grevilleas named after the daughters of David and his wife Dorothy Curtis (née Gemmell) (1930–1985), botanical artist, originated here: *Grevillea* 'Robyn Gordon' and *G.* 'Sandra Gordon' are still garden favourites. Gordon was awarded the Australian Plants Award of the SOCIETY FOR GROWING AUSTRALIAN PLANTS in 1994. Myall Park Botanic Garden Ltd (formed 1991) continues the Gordons' vision.

Betty McKenzie, *One Man's Dream: David Gordon and Myall Park Botanic Garden* (Glenmorgan, Qld, c. 1995) RA

GORE HILL CEMETERY, NSW, served the burial needs of Sydney's north shore. The site was chosen by local parliamentarian and land owner William Tunks in association with surveyor John Armstrong, who in 1867 planned the fourteen-acre (5.6 ha) cemetery with denominational and general use sections and for future extension. The site was heavily wooded, and Tunks advocated retention of some of the natural vegetation for shade and ornamentation. The first burial took place in 1877. Early management was divided, with denominations taking individual responsibility and Tunks chairing the trust responsible for the general section. Each section acquired a distinctive character: the Catholic one, for example, was extensively planted with palms to define the main paths, while early plans for the Presbyterian and Congregational sections provided for landscaping with curved paths leading to open circles. A combined committee was formed in 1884 and attempted a more uniform landscaping scheme, but pressure for burial space has destroyed much of the early layout and some early planting. Despite this, Gore Hill remains an evocative nineteenth-century site in name and character. ROBERT NICOL

GOVERNMENT HOUSES in Australia housed—and continue to house—representatives of British royalty; this vice-regal inheritance became a powerful symbol of imperial authority in the colonies. These residences and their extensive gardens were generally contiguous with a BOTANIC GARDEN and DOMAIN, and often had a riverside or harbourside location. The government houses were planned on a generous scale and formed self-sufficient estates, although many of these working estates have now been truncated through the loss of horse paddocks and altered through the conversion of service areas: Tas. is the outstanding exception. The design of vice-regal gardens (and houses) was tempered by the need to provide for both private and public usage. Many featured FORMAL gardens, designed for large functions, and these are now among the best surviving examples from the nineteenth century. While the ebb and flow of successive governors and their families could precipitate changes to the gardens, often these were transitory, with continuity provided by head gardeners (many of whom were long-serving) or managers (typically associated with an adjacent botanic garden). A SUMMER RETREAT was often provided for the governor, especially a HILL-STATION (such as HILL VIEW, NSW). With Federation, the office of governor-general was formalised—the NSW governor had previously rejoiced in this title—and Vic. and NSW vied to provide his residence. Although the state governor of NSW moved to CRANBROOK, to its great chagrin the 'mother colony' became a seldom-visited outpost and Victoria's larger government house, conveniently located near the seat of parliament, was used until the move to CANBERRA in 1927.

Vice-regal patronage of horticulture through horticultural shows, horticultural societies, and in the importation of plants, provided an important stimulus: FRANKLIN and DENISON (in the nineteenth century) and GOWRIE (in the twentieth) typified this role. More generally, the circle centred on Government House provided an aspirational model for polite society and invitation into this world was keenly sought. Large garden parties for charities often provided a foil against exclusivity, and republican sentiment continues to challenge traditional modes of use. COLLEEN MORRIS

Australian Capital Territory Yarralumla, a nineteenth-century pastoral property, with owners including Terence Aubrey Murray and Frederick Campbell, was resumed by the Commonwealth in 1913. Yarralumla House became a hostel for politicians and was the venue of the first cabinet meeting in the Federal Capital Territory (1924). With Parliament's move from Melbourne to CANBERRA in 1927, **Yarralumla** became the official residence of the governor-general. The picturesque fifty-three hectare setting, with northerly views across Lake Burley Griffin to Black Mountain and southerly vistas to the Brindabella Ranges, comprises indigenous and exotic tree and shrub plantings, a vegetable garden, wild garden, small lake, and resident population of kangaroos. T.C.G. WESTON and Lindsay PRYOR made additions to the gardens during the residency of Lord Gowrie; Edna WALLING, E.G. WATERHOUSE, Paul SORENSEN, and Richard CLOUGH also advised on the garden design and details during various incumbencies. With the formation of Lake Burley Griffin in 1963, the National Capital Development Commission established a water-gate and foreshore plantings.

C.D. Coulthard-Clark (ed.), *Gables, Ghosts, and Governors-General: The Historic House at Yarralumla, Canberra* (Sydney, 1988) DIANNE FIRTH

New South Wales Some of the earliest illustrations of European-influenced gardens in Australia depict (First) Government House, Sydney Cove (from 1788). Pressure for viable agricultural land saw the establishment of an alternative seat

Government houses

This garden party (1912) at the Government Residence, Darwin, demonstrates a pragmatic design requirement for GOVERNMENT HOUSE gardens and grounds: ample open space, close to the residence, in which to conduct public functions

of government at Parramatta, with the consequent erection of (Old) Government House (1790s) and the establishment of a DOMAIN (later subdivided to form PARRAMATTA PARK and several major government institutions). This house initially overlooked a squared garden, and was sited on the brow of Rose Hill terminating an axial roadway, one of Australia's earliest conscious TOWN PLANNING schemes.

Extensive improvements to the Governor's Domain on Sydney and Farm Coves were undertaken by Governor Lachlan Macquarie and his cultured wife Elizabeth, including an enclosing wall (1811–12) and avenue plantings, Mrs Macquarie's Road (1813–16) encircling the promontories, and stables (1817–19, architect Francis Greenway). These PICTURESQUE embellishments provided a sophisticated landscaped park for (First) Government House as well as an ideal setting for the new government house (1838–45) with long VISTAS over the harbour. Here, English architect Edward Blore provided plans for a castellated pile that complemented the stables and consolidated a stylistic trend for harbourside mansions. The urn-bedecked western terrace (1845)—a rare antipodean example of a raised SHRUBBERY—was balanced to the east by a formal terrace (1861–64), characterised by balustraded walks enlivened by a central fountain and parterre beds.

The current curtilage of the garden was formalised in 1917 and this preserved the nucleus of the early pleasure garden. Tall vertical elements, provided by araucarias—especially *A. columnaris* (Captain Cook's Pine)—and subtropical plantings including a massive *Ficus macrophylla* (Moreton Bay Fig), define the character of the garden: 'I do not know any garden where dark is darker, or bright more bright' rhapsodised Ethel ANDERSON in 1945. **COLLEEN MORRIS**

Northern Territory Known as the Government Residence (or Residency) until 1912, this house has been the official home of successive South Australian Government–appointed Residents followed by Commonwealth Government–appointed Administrators since 1870. Favourably sited on a natural plateau above Darwin Harbour, the house was substantially redesigned in 1878–79 by future Government Resident (1890–92) and Melbourne architect John George KNIGHT, together with surveyor Gilbert Rotherdale McMinn (1844–1884). Despite extensive cyclone damage (1897, 1937, and 1974) and Second World War bombing and subsequent reconstruction, the house's early aesthetic and physical characteristics remain intact, and the property continues to set a standard for refinement in TROPICAL living and outdoor formal receptions. Landscaping effectively began with Knight's extensive fencing, terracing, and path layout in the mid-1870s, the remnants of which exist in the commemorative 'Knight's Walk'. 'Abbott's Walk' acknowledges the horticultural beautification instigated by Administrator C.L.A. Abbott's wife, Hilda, during his term of office (1937–46). Extensively relandscaped in the 1980s, the 1.3 hectare garden features a wide variety of lush exotic and native plantings, ornamentals, trimmed shrubbery, a shadehouse, orchid and cycad features, and a herb garden, located beyond and around the sweeping carriage loop entry drive, and central island Flagpole Lawn.

Paul Rosenweig, *The House of Seven Gables: A History of Government House* (Darwin, 1996) **ANITA ANGEL**

Queensland Old Government House (1861–62) originally sat in a thirty-acre (12 ha) DOMAIN at Gardens Point (Miajin to the original Aboriginal inhabitants), bounded south by the Brisbane River, east by the BRISBANE BOTANIC GARDENS, and north-west by Parliament House. Designed by architect Charles Tiffin, government house was sited prominently at the end of the George Street ridge. Thus, vessels arriving up the river saw the house in an appropriately grand setting of open grassland with picturesque clumps of trees, and visitors from the town side could marvel at the adjacent botanic wonders and the dignified parliament house. With major contributions by Lady Diamantina Bowen, wife of the first governor, the government house domain was laid out by Walter HILL. In 1910, the governor moved to Fernberg (Bardon), and Old Government House was used by the newly established University of Queensland. Since then, development for Queensland University of Technology and its precursors have progressively taken up almost all of the former domain, except for the low-lying riverside areas. Since 1973 the house has formed headquarters and a museum for the NATIONAL TRUST of Queensland. A small reserve for the house includes a remnant rainforest garden and shell fountain.

Queensland's current Government House—formerly **Fernberg** ('distant mountain')—now in suburban Brisbane, was developed by Johann Christian Heussler between 1860 and 1865. In 1882, the property was sold to pastoralist and businessman John Stevenson, MLA, who extended the house in an Italianate style (1889–90). Fernberg was selected as a temporary home for the Queensland governor in 1910, but soon became the permanent residence with E.W. BICK as head gardener (1910–12). The house sits on a ridge amid four hectares of ornamental formal gardens and twelve hectares of remnant bushland of spurs and gullies, partly cleared for picturesque, park-like effect. The garden primarily provides spaces for vice-regal events, making great use of floral bedding displays, massed azaleas, roses, and tropical plantations. Productive activities (cut-flowers and bush-house plants) and private recreation (tennis, swimming pool) are carried out behind the scenes. Formal hedging is found everywhere using bougainvillea, *Murraya paniculata* (Orange Jessamine), and variegated *Duranta erecta* (Pigeon Berry). *Cedrela odorata* (Cigar Box Cedar) and jacarandas vie with the old gum trees as shade trees. Sweet peas covering columns of chicken-wire were a favourite springtime feature when Sir John and Lady Goodwin created woodland walks amid the back bushland in 1928, adding foot bridges over gullies, and about 1000 flowering trees, such as jacarandas, wattles, and poinsettias. Recent road-widening has reduced the size of the grounds but the character of the place remains intact and its elevated verdant location makes it a local landmark.

JEANNIE SIM

South Australia The main vice-regal residence in Adelaide (1837) was constructed for Governor Hindmarsh, although successive governors remodelled and extended the house, including new gates and guard house (1874), resulting in its amalgam of Regency and Italianate styles. ADELAIDE BOTANIC GARDEN director George FRANCIS laid out the garden (1855–65) and Garden staff were thereafter responsible for its management. It was home from 1928 to 1934 to Lady Hore-Ruthven (later Lady GOWRIE) and she recrafted the garden, with assistance from J.F. BAILEY and H. GREAVES, into the more pronounced GARDENESQUE mode that characterises the garden today. During 1971–76 Governor Sir Mark Oliphant sought to 'open up' the garden; he erected a fountain and arbour amid its neatly maintained lawns and specimen trees, with the drive forming the main structural element of the garden. Summer government houses were constructed at BELAIR (1860–80) and Marble Hill (1879) in the ADELAIDE HILLS; Marble Hill was destroyed in the 1955 bushfires.

DAVID JONES

Tasmania Government House, Hobart, replaced an earlier structure (that site later developed as FRANKLIN SQUARE), and was occupied in 1858 following a protracted building campaign. The site fronted the Derwent estuary and abutted the Government DOMAIN and Government Garden (later ROYAL TASMANIAN BOTANICAL GARDENS). Plans of 1856 (possibly by the architect of Government House, William Porden Kay) showed a design that formed the basis of the existing garden, laid out by landscape gardener William THOMAS overseeing a party of convicts. A key feature was the clear demarcation between surrounding paddocks and the PLEASURE GROUNDS. On the east, a shrubbery and arboretum provided screening, while on the south, from an elegant balustraded terrace, long vistas to the Derwent were obtained: an oak avenue, believed to date from the 1840s, was the only feature to cut through the paddocks until the advent of the railway (1870s) and much later the roadway. A quarry within the grounds was converted into a lake in the mid-1870s.

The garden at Government House was an almost complete transplantation of British landscaping ideals to the antipodes, and closely followed the prescriptions of LOUDON. Today this is evident in the formal terraces, careful planning of the approach drive, use of discrete garden compartments, mature evergreen trees that complement the picturesque outlines of the residence, and the carefully controlled vistas. This garden, which also retains early outbuildings and KITCHEN GARDEN, is one of the most intact and evocative mid-nineteenth-century gardens in Australia.

RA

Victoria Government House, in Melbourne's DOMAIN, was erected between 1871 and 1876. It was designed and documented by the Public Works Department, and replaced Toorak House. The site had been planted with trees by MUELLER, but a competition for the layout of the newly reserved Government House grounds (1872) produced no suitable design and the scheme of Joseph SAYCE was approved in 1873. The subsequent story of Sayce's dismissal and William GUILFOYLE's coincidental appointment at the adjacent MELBOURNE BOTANIC GARDENS (with responsibility for the landscaping of Government House grounds and the Domain) has been recounted by several authors. The bones of Sayce's scheme were retained by Guilfoyle, and he oversaw the dramatic reshaping of the ground to permit a vista to and from the city, conceived the hierarchy between the inner and outer lawns, created a fern gully, implemented clumped planting on the lawns, enhanced the curvature of the drive, and undertook considerable tree planting: many of these features were illustrated in Guilfoyle's *Report* (August 1873) and their early development was documented in panoramic photographs by Holtermann. Balustraded terraces and a princely expanse of gravel separated the residence from the grounds, permitting a flower garden, and tennis and croquet courts. An extensive kitchen garden and stables complex formed a buffer between the residence and botanic gardens.

Australia's governors-general resided here from 1900 to 1930, with the governor relocated to STONNINGTON in

The garden of Western Australia's GOVERNMENT HOUSE in central Perth, although reduced from its original size, provides a spacious setting for the residence, and also incorporates many significant garden elements that recall the rich history of the site

suburban Malvern. Hugh LINAKER truncated the grounds during 1933 as part of the Domain landscaping, although the essential features of the inner pleasure grounds were retained, and the grounds are now among the grandest surviving nineteenth-century gardens in Australia.   RA

Western Australia Recognised as one of Perth's most significant heritage places, the site has been occupied as the principal vice-regal residence since the founding of the colony, when temporary timber buildings were erected there. The present picturesque Victorian Tudor-style building was first occupied in 1864 and replaced a more modest residence built in 1835. The below-ground remains of this Reveley-designed building are now an important archaeological site within the grounds.

A government ACCLIMATISATION garden was established in 1831 by colonial botanist James DRUMMOND. This garden, originally adjoining the government house site and later incorporated within the governor's domain, was located near the present garden party lawn (not in Stirling Gardens, as some have previously claimed). It became, in turn, the nucleus of the vice-regal kitchen garden, vineyard, and orchard, which was transformed in the late 1880s and 1890s, into the pleasure grounds that exist today, under the guidance of Jeremiah SHEATH and Daniel FEAKES. Now covering a modest four hectares, the grounds originally included stables, paddocks, and an early 1900s experimental septic system in the area now occupied by the Perth Concert Hall. The ornamental pond in the lower grounds is a vestige of the original river shoreline that once extended to the boundary of the site. The front walling and main driveway date from the convict period (1850–68), while approximately one-third of the mixed collection of trees, which includes local eucalypts, Western Australian peppermints, oaks, olives, oleanders, and palms, are significant nineteenth-century plantings.

OLINE RICHARDS

GOWRIE (née POLLOK), Zara Eileen (1879–1965), Irish-born garden and kindergarten proponent, was wife of Sir Alexander Hore-Ruthven, later Baron Gowrie (1872–1955), who served as Governor of SA (1928–34) and NSW (1935–36), and Governor-General (1936–1945). Lady Gowrie thus resided in three GOVERNMENT HOUSES and ADMIRALTY HOUSE, from where she promoted Red Cross activities, horticultural societies and shows, and horticulturists and garden designers (including CORNISH and BURDETT). She also contributed to Olive MELLOR's *The Garden Lovers' Log* (1940), diplomatically praising gardens Australia-wide.

DAVID JONES

GOYDER, George Woodroofe (1826–1898), surveyor-general, was born in England and studied surveying and railway design before migrating to Sydney in 1848. In 1851 he joined the South Australian civil service as a draftsman, rising to become surveyor-general (1861–94), establishing the colonial land survey patterns throughout SA, and responsible for innovations in agriculture, forestry, irrigation, and land reclamation. Goyder was instrumental in establishing the northern surveys, reinventing the ADELAIDE PARK

LANDS town model, and surveying parts of the NORTHERN TERRITORY including recommending the site of Palmerston (Darwin) as its capital. The Goyder Line (1866), which delineated the limits of drought (and therefore pastoral survival), became infamous following a disastrous drought in 1880, when ill-advised government land selection policies (sanctioning development beyond the line) were exposed. In 1873 he recommended the preservation of forest trees, foreshadowing the establishment of a Forest Board (1875) and the appointment of J.E. BROWN as conservator. Goyder was also interested in water conservation and scientific land management, advocating and studying the latest engineering advances in the use of artesian bores for inland areas, irrigation works along the River Murray, and drainage works in the South East. Known as 'Little Energy', his diminutive stature disguised his reputation as the most able, efficient, and honest public service administrator in the colony, overseeing the largest development phase in the colony while managing surveying, mine inspection, valuation, forestry, crown lands, and subdivision design portfolios within the one department.

Michael Williams, *George Woodroofe Goyder: A Practical Geographer* (Adelaide, c. 1982)   DAVID JONES

GRACEMERE, near Rockhampton, Qld, was settled in the early 1850s by pastoralists William (1818–1896) and Charles (1813–1861) Archer, Norwegian migrants of Scottish ancestry. The original slab homestead survives and the property is still in Archer family ownership. The homestead and associated outbuildings were located on the centre of a low peninsula extending to the curve of a large lagoon or mere. The garden was established in a grand Victorian manner, with the sensitive incorporation of the surrounding landscape of sweeping lagoon and low hills beyond, and plantings of accents such as *Araucaria bidwillii* (Bunya Pine) and other araucarias, a clump of bamboo at the mere, and palms. Nearer the house, the GARDENESQUE style was used for the extensive flower gardens, which included annuals. *Petrea volubilis* now extends along the long verandah, in front of which the oval lawn, once used for croquet, is raised from the gravel walkway by local stone edging. The Archers were associated with the Queensland Acclimatisation Society and grew many fruit and other trees unusual in the TROPICS. The orchard, on the gentle slope to the mere, was incorporated as part of the pleasure garden with an orange tree-lined walk. A trellis supporting grape vines covered the walk to the mere, where papyrus was planted near the bathing pavilion. A notable addition from early in the twentieth century is the profusion of bougainvillea. Long droughts in the 1990s and reduced maintenance have hastened the loss of several major trees and much of the finer plantings in this highly significant garden.

CATHERINE BROUWER

GRAHAM, Joseph (1828–1894), nursery proprietor and seed merchant, was born in Perthshire, Scotland. He migrated to NSW in 1853 following training as a gardener. To boost his finances he initially worked as a sawyer in Brisbane; through the agency of Donald BEATON his early colonial experiences and observations were recounted in the *Cottage Gardener* (1854). Graham commenced a nursery and seed business in 1857, occupying premises in Sydney's George Street Markets. He prospered and in 1868 made his home, Lilydale, at Marrickville, establishing extensive nursery gardens there and also later at Auburn. He served twenty-one years of 'aldermanic usefulness' with Marrickville council (1869–90), being mayor for eight of those years. Eschewing a career in parliament, he instead gave service as a member of many public bodies, notably as treasurer and an inaugural trustee (1879) of the (ROYAL) NATIONAL PARK, during a period of much tree planting and beautification of this large reserve. His life was one of 'constant usefulness and benevolence'—an industrious Scot who grasped the opportunities emigration provided.   RA

GRANT, Alexander (1848–1906), Scottish-born gardener, worked under James McNab at Edinburgh Botanic Gardens, demonstrating skill as a microscopist, before migrating to Sydney in 1878. His first position was as gardener for Thomas Walker at YARALLA, then at Rosemont, Woollahra, before planning and laying out SWIFTS, Darling Point. He entered employment at SYDNEY BOTANIC GARDENS in 1882 and was officially designated as Propagator in 1896. A specialist in fungi, Grant improved the collection of the herbarium, initiated an exchange program with other botanical institutions, and is thought to have supplied the specimens Dr Tassi of Siena, Italy, described in *Fungi Novi Australiani* (1900). He also undertook mycological work for the Department of Agriculture in an honorary capacity. The importance of Grant's career was outlined by the president of the LINNEAN SOCIETY OF NEW SOUTH WALES in his 1907 address.   COLLEEN MORRIS

GRASBY, (William) Catton: see WESTERN MAIL

GRASSES (Gramineae and Poaceae) include around 650 genera and 10 000 species underpinning cultures as pasture and cereals, of which 150 genera and 950 species are native to Australia. Grasses are botanically distinguished from other grass-like plants by various morphological characters including the disposition of the individual florets (flowers) into spikelets and of the spikelets into an inflorescence (flowerhead), the distinction of the leaf into a sheath and blade and, typically, hollow cylindrical stems. In most situations grasses are readily distinguished from sedges (Cyperaceae), rushes (Juncaceae), and rope-rushes (Restionaceae).

The interest of European settlers in Australian native grasslands was principally in exploiting their value as pasture. As a result, native grasslands have been highly modified or even obliterated through trampling by introduced hoofed animals, overgrazing, pasture 'improvement', and changes in fire regimes. Significant native grassland species include *Themeda triandra* (Kangaroo Grass) and *Danthonia* spp. (Wallaby Grass) in temperate Australia, *Poa* spp. (Tussock Poa) in ALPINE areas, and *Astrebla* spp. (Mitchell Grass) and *Sorghum* spp. in TROPICAL Australia. Hummock-forming *Plectrachne* (including *Triodia*) spp. (Spinifex) are widespread and often dominant in ARID Australia.

Low-slung and festooned in vegetation, GRACEMERE, near Rockhampton (Qld), typifies the early Queensland pastoral HOMESTEAD—important remnants of the garden also survive despite losses due to drought and a maintenance regime much reduced from its nineteenth-century heyday

Although some efforts to improve *Danthonia* spp. for pasture were made during the early twentieth century, the selection of Australian native grasses for horticultural use has only recently been revisited. The use of native tussock grasses, such as *Poa labillardieri* (Tussock Poa) for landscape plantings, and of *Microlaena stipoides* (Weeping Grass) for lawns and the re-creation of native grasslands reflects current interest in NATURALISTIC styles, and increasing emphasis on habitat conservation and sustainable horticulture. The extensive and innovative use of grasses and grass-like plants by American landscape architects, especially as displayed in Wolfgang Oehme and James van Sweden's *New American Garden* (1990), has also influenced Australian LANDSCAPE ARCHITECTS. Outstanding exotic ornamentals such as *Miscanthus sinensis* are enjoying a revival of interest.

Historically, grasses in their various manifestations have been important to gardens. Grasses are utilised functionally or aesthetically as sports turf, amenity lawns, grasslands, wildflower meadows, and as ornamentals. The early development of LAWNS in early Australian gardens is of interest, but as yet little studied. The eighth edition of Miller's *Gardener's Dictionary* (1768) observed that English lawns should extend for 'never less than thirty or forty acres' (12–16 ha), which was generally achieved by enclosing existing pasture or by planting hayseed from nearby pasture. In Australia, the development of extensive lawns was limited, and probably followed the exploitation of native pastures and the establishment of improved pastures. Interestingly, officer Watkin Tench observed small tussock grasses to be abundant in Sydney in the 1790s. Although BAMBOOS are illustrated in early Australian gardens, few other ornamental grasses are apparent.

The WEED potential of pasture, amenity, and ornamental grasses is significant. For example, *Cortaderia selloana* (Pampas Grass) and *Pennisetum villosum* (Feathertop) were introduced to Australia as ornamentals in the nineteenth century, and are both now widely recognised as noxious weeds in south-eastern Australia.

STEPHEN FORBES

GRASS ROOTS (1973–), an Australian craft and lifestyle magazine emphasising domestic economics, garden culture, and, more distinctively, communitarian lifestyles. The editors David (b. 1946) and Meg Miller (b. 1947) have also produced a series of books and compendia under the *Grass Roots* imprint. Originating in the post-hippie 1970s, the *Grass Roots* style, reminiscent of the American back-to-nature optimism of that era, has now been meshed with concern for family values and concern for the global ENVIRONMENT, to reach a mass audience at the turn of the century.

CHRIS McCONVILLE

GRAY, Edward Waters (c. 1869–1937), garden curator, was born at Salisbury, Wiltshire, England, and arrived in Vic. with his family c. 1877. They settled at Kyneton and after a stint with the *Kyneton Guardian*, Gray was appointed c. 1887 as under-curator at Kyneton Botanic Gardens. In 1903 he accepted the curatorship of Port Fairy Botanic Gardens, then enjoying high popular esteem, and after a short transfer to Footscray (1904) he returned to take charge at Kyneton on the death of curator Orames (1905). Keenly interested in ARBORICULTURE, Gray became a valued member of the VICTORIAN TREE PLANTERS' ASSOCIATION. He was an accomplished 'DAHLIA man' and a prolific contributor to the horticultural press, notably the *Home Gardener*. A son, Harold Charles Gray (1899–1950), was curator of SUNSHINE GARDENS c. 1939–50.

Another son, **Alfred John Gray** (1896–1981) forester, nursery manager, and seed collector, was assistant forester at Macedon STATE FOREST NURSERY (1920–45) and pioneered arid-lands REVEGETATION through provenance seed harvesting and supply of plants at the Wail Forest Commission Nursery, near Dimboola, Vic. (1946–55). The nursery was transformed from a small producer of *Eucalyptus cladocalyx* (Sugar Gum) to an operation supplying a variety of local flora and a range of western Australian mallee EUCALYPTS that produced 10 000 plants in its first year. A system of veneered board forestry tubes was developed, and Wail nursery soon became an inspiration to enthusiasts of native AUSTRALIAN PLANTS. Alf Gray left Wail in 1955 and was employed by David GORDON for three years as a collector. During one three-month trip to WA he collected seed and detailed growing conditions for more than 1000 species.

Two of Alf Gray's sons, Kenneth Alfred (1924–1951) and Roy Gordon Gray (b. 1927) worked at Wail. Kenneth later managed an arid lands nursery at Port Augusta (SA) for Woomera (1953–65), managed Belair Woods and Forests Nursery (1968–73), and advised Colonial Sugar Refinery Ltd on mine site restoration (1973–83). During 1978 he acted as consultant to UNESCO on revegetation projects in Mexico City. With his son John Gray (b. 1948) he established Tetratheca Nursery (1975) and founded Blackwood Seeds (1982–92), harvesting native seeds for revegetation projects.

JOHN WALTER and DAVID JONES

GREAVES, Harold (1882–1959), horticulturist and botanic gardens director, had a lifelong association with ADELAIDE BOTANIC GARDEN. Born in North Adelaide, he was employed at the Garden in 1894, rising to directorship (1932–48). During his tenure he negotiated extensions to the Garden, including the sunken garden development. Notwithstanding a depressed economy, he was active in assisting planting programs along Anzac Highway (SA), at Mildura (Vic.), and STRATHALBYN SOLDIERS' MEMORIAL GARDENS. Greaves planned floral arrangements for the state's centenary celebrations (1936), served as a Commissioner to (BELAIR) NATIONAL PARK, and implemented a policy that encouraged greater public access to and understanding of the Garden and its collections.

DAVID JONES

GREEN BANS In 1971 the impeccably middle-class group 'The battlers for Kelly's Bush', reluctantly and having exhausted all other options, approached the Builders Labourers' Federation, led by John Bernard (Jack) Mundey (b. 1929), an outspoken communist, to prevent A.V. Jennings from redeveloping a small strip of harbourside open space in Sydney's Hunters Hill. Mundey, a consummate wordsmith, coined the phrase 'green ban'—so much more acceptable to the media than 'black ban' with its overtones of oppressive union power—to describe the resultant action. Subsequent green bans were pronounced, gaining widespread support from working-class residents of the Rocks threatened by the Liberal state government with losing their rented terrace houses to high-rise office and apartment blocks. Other bans followed on Victoria Street, Kings Cross, and on prominent inner-city freeway routes. Since then some freeways have gone ahead, and the southern portion of the Rocks has been given over to office and residential blocks. In retrospect, the green bans represented a high point in union power and union interest in environmental politics, which these days tends to focus more on uranium mining than on preserving urban space. That battle is now left to local councils, which in most states are frequently overridden by planning ministers of various political persuasions, subject as they are to the vagaries of influence and self-interest.

> Richard Roddewig, *Green Bans: The Birth of Australian Environmental Politics* (Sydney, 1978); Jack Mundey, *Green Bans and Beyond* (Sydney, 1981); Meredith Burgmann and Verity Burgmann, *Green Bans, Red Union* (Sydney, 1998)

PETER SPEARRITT

GREEN BELTS emerged as a desirable element in modern Australian planning during the post-Federation movement for TOWN PLANNING. The encircling ADELAIDE PARK LANDS, a legacy of its colonial plan (1837), provided an early model. GARDEN CITY ideology shaped local thinking by promoting the green belt as a means of redressing the absence of metropolitan open space arising from uncontrolled nineteenth-century expansion, and as a tool for structuring and organising metropolitan space. A range of schemes was prepared. The function of the green belt—sometimes called a 'lung', 'girdle', or 'ring'—was variously perceived to contain expansion, frame and separate new from existing development, reserve natural bushland, and provide contact with nature, PUBLIC OPEN SPACE for RECREATION, and land for agriculture. The most comprehensive of the early twentieth-century proposals, the HOPE–Klem Perth Endowment Lands Scheme (1925), was realised west of Perth. The green belt was a favoured planning tool in city master plans and New Town schemes of the 1940s–50s before the rise of the regional city.

Stephen Hamnett and Robert Freestone (eds), *The Australian Metropolis: A Planning History* (Allen & Unwin, Sydney, 2000)

CHRISTINE GARNAUT

GREENHOUSES The enhancement of growing conditions for PLANTS through some form of covering or enclosure has been practised by gardeners since Roman times. Many terms have been used to describe plant-growing enclosures, and in some cases differentiation between them is unclear. European nomenclature has also been used in Australia with little discrimination, and can cause considerable confusion in the interpretation of GARDEN BOOKS and other literature from Europe. The first use of the word greenhouse is attributed to English gardener John Evelyn (1620–1705). His definition—'an enclosure for growing greens'—is still relevant as an omnibus term to cover a range of enclosed or partially enclosed GARDEN BUILDINGS or spaces that involve the key principles of temperature modification, protection from frost, and the promotion of plant growth. The role of the greenhouse in the horticultural development of Australia has been mainly associated with functional performance rather than for architectural effect. Australian greenhouses have been widely used to propagate plants, produce out-of-season vegetables, provide environments for exotic plants, and display valued and interesting plant specimens. They have also been extensively used for providing controlled environmental conditions in plant research.

Throughout their history, greenhouses and their variants have formed key elements of gardens. Strategies to provide favourable conditions for temperature-sensitive plants ranged from removal to a protected space, such as an ORANGERY, for temporary storage, to dedicated plant buildings, with light-transmitting roofs and some heating, known as the STOVE or HOTHOUSE. Many greenhouses did not have supplementary heating, and the term coldhouse has been used in USA and Europe (although not commonly in Australia) to describe unheated greenhouses. GLASSHOUSES, in which the enclosing material was predominantly of glass, formed a particularly important element in the pleasure grounds, as well as in the more utilitarian confines of the nursery.

Australia's CLIMATE did not demand extensive use of greenhouse-type structures to provide favourable conditions for plant display or growth. In most areas Australian gardeners early recognised the need for protection from high levels of solar radiation, particularly for many introduced plants, and built BUSH-HOUSES, ranging from simple structures or enclosures using branches and other vegetation forms to more elaborate shadehouses of timber slats, or knitted or woven shadecloth, designed to reduce the level of sunlight and still allow appropriate air movement.

Apart from the bush-house, the type of greenhouse structure utilised in Australia until the mid-twentieth century was predominantly based on European precedents. Significant design features of the modern greenhouse—large expanses of covered areas and climate-controlled environments—can be traced to the innovative work of J.C. LOUDON and Joseph PAXTON, particularly Loudon's metal glazing bars, which allowed curvilinear surfaces, and Paxton's experiments at CHATSWORTH, which demonstrated the ridge and furrow roof design, mechanised timber preparation systems for glazing, and hot water pipe heating.

The modification of the greenhouse temperature has been the main focus of greenhouse engineers over the last two centuries. Heating systems have evolved from crude open fires to precision-controlled heating pipes. Some early furnaces were harmful both to gardeners and to plants as a result of the production of toxic fumes. The early nineteenth century was a period of major development in greenhouse heating systems in Europe. Initially steam was employed, and

GREENHOUSES embrace a wide spectrum of GARDEN BUILDINGS for the growth of plants, ranging from decorative CONSERVATORIES and GLASSHOUSES (such as this palm house at MELBOURNE BOTANIC GARDENS, photographed in 1861), to more humble and utilitarian BUSH-HOUSES

then the application of the thermosiphon principle to hot water in metal pipes resulted in the availability of many different types of hot water systems in the early 1830s. A circuit of pipes was connected to a boiler and the hot fluid would automatically move around the circuit as a result of the cooling of water in the pipe (thermosiphon effect). Until this time there had been a strong reliance on inefficient and often ineffective furnace-type heating systems.

Supplementary heating has not been a major issue for many parts of Australia. Greenhouses in colder regions, such as southern Vic. and Tas. were often fitted with heating systems. Piped systems, both plain and finned, supplied by boilers (fired using gas, liquid, or solid fuel) are now widely used in Australian greenhouses. The most common type of heating in use today is convection heating supplied by furnaces, which has the advantage of low initial cost and simple distribution of heat. However, many greenhouse operators prefer pipe-based heating as it provides a more gentle application of heat to the plant. Solar greenhouses have some or all of their night-time heating supplied by stored heat derived from solar energy absorbed during the day. This energy may be absorbed within the greenhouse space, by separate solar collectors, or both. This principle of solar energy entrapment is applicable on a global scale, giving rise to the term 'greenhouse effect' to describe an increase in the temperature of the atmosphere close to the earth's surface.

Glass (or timber for bush-houses) was the main enclosing surface for greenhouses until other materials, such as plastic sheets and film, were introduced. All permitted varying amounts of natural light to be transmitted to enable plant growth. The availability of low-cost polyethylene film in the 1960s had a major impact on greenhouse development in Australia. The production of plants and crops under cover was readily accessible to horticultural producers and home owners. The early designs were based around pipe frames formed into a hemisphere or tunnel; overheating was a significant disadvantage of these designs. The greenhouse climate was improved through the raising of the tunnel frame on to a wall, typically one to two metres high. Over the past decade there have been further design refinements through the incorporation of more effective natural ventilation systems. The need for rapid air exchange under hot conditions is recognised by greenhouse managers as being essential for healthy plant growth. Technologies are now available that also allow light levels, greenhouse air and plant root temperatures, relative humidity, and carbon dioxide to be automatically controlled so that optimum conditions for specific plant groups can be maintained.

John Hix, *The Glass House* (London, 1974; rev. edn 1996); Keith Garzoli (ed.), *Greenhouses* (Canberra, 1988)

GEOFF CONNELLAN

GREENING AUSTRALIA (1982–) is a national federation of non-government not-for-profit organisations in each state and territory. It works with rural and city groups, including farmers, schools, and businesses, to assist in the protection and restoration of Australia's landscapes, especially through work in REVEGETATION and in support of LANDCARE. Born out of an urgent need to protect and enhance Australia's biodiversity, its mission is 'to engage the community in vegetation management to protect and restore the health, diversity and productivity of our unique Australian landscapes'. A national network of field officers is supported by technical and training specialists.

ML

GREENMOUNT, Mackay, Qld, was established in 1862 by pastoral explorer John Mackay (1839–1914). In that year, John Cook selected nearby Balnagowan, and his son Albert Cook (with his wife Vida) established the present Greenmount homestead and gardens in 1914 on a portion of Mackay's estate. Greenmount's formal gardens complemented the hill-top homestead siting and enjoyed a panoramic outlook over cattle and cane lands, and the Pleystowe mill, in which the family had an interest. A gravel drive passed the front verandah and a large, horseshoe-shaped mixed shrubbery, centred on the entry, enclosed a segmented circular flower bed. The garden's basic structure has been maintained and is planted with TROPICAL favourites such as crotons, acalyphas, and ixoras. Trees around the homestead include figs (*Ficus* sp.), araucarias, nauclea, flame trees, and *Cinnamomum camphora*. Avenues of mangoes line the driveway and route to the mill.

CATHERINE BROUWER

GREENOAKS, Darling Point, NSW: see MORT, Thomas Sutcliffe

GREENWOOD, St Ives, NSW, designed by Jocelyn BROWN between 1941 and 1945, when she and her husband lived there, was one of her most accomplished designs. It had a seventy-metre frontage to Mona Vale Road, then a country road from Gordon along the ridge, sloping down gently to the tall timbers of the Dalrymple–Hay Reserve. She planned a structure of wide, level grassy walks between long HERBACEOUS BORDERS, descending down the slope, with the built element of a sunken garden and pool creating a major cross axis on one of the walks. The terracing and planting of Greenwood complemented the site, and the great trees of the Reserve provided a superb backdrop to the garden.

HELEN PROUDFOOT

GREVILLEA, a large genus of AUSTRALIAN PLANTS (comparable numerically to *ACACIA* and *EUCALYPTUS*) with a majority of species endemic, was named for Charles F. Greville (1749–1809), a founder of the (ROYAL) HORTICULTURAL SOCIETY. Falling within the family Proteaceae, most are low-to-medium shrubs with prickly leaves, often found among rocks and in heathlands, although there are a few trees. These include *Grevillea barklyana* and *G. robusta* (Silky Oak), native to northern NSW and Qld and widely used since the nineteenth century as a specimen tree in large parks and as a street tree, with its timber valued for furniture and turnery. Many hybrids and CULTIVARS have been recognised in the genus, particularly the 'Poorinda' group selected by LEO HODGE. Most of these are shrubs selected from hybrids, although *Grevillea* 'Poorinda Royal Mantle' is a vigorous-growing ground cover. There are many new subtropical 'fern leaf' hybrids using the flamboyant northern species *Grevillea banksii*, *G. pteridifolia*, and *G. whiteana* as parents. Showy cultivars such as *Grevillea* 'Robyn Gordon', and *G.* 'Superb'—involving *G. banksii* from south-eastern Qld and *G. bipinnatifida* from WA—have been strongly promoted in the nursery trade in recent times. Flowers, which can be grouped into several different and distinct arrangements including the Spider flowers, Toothbrush grevilleas, and Plume grevilleas, are well known as bird attractants and have been popular in Australian native plantings and BUSH GARDENS. Grevilleas are, however, intolerant of high soil phosphorous levels and therefore often excluded from much altered and highly fertilised garden soils. An additional concern for conservation within the species is the ease with which introduced garden forms are able to hybridise with indigenous species corrupting local gene pools.

Botanically there are two major groups or sub-genera within the genus. One group has symmetrical, individual, usually white, flowers. This group includes *Grevillea manglesii* and *G. paniculate*. The other group has asymmetrical individual flowers. It includes *Grevillea robusta* and *G. banksii*.

Peter Olde and Neil Marriott, *The Grevillea Book* (Kenthurst, NSW, 1994–95)   ML

GREVILLEA PARK, Bulli, NSW, was established on a sixteen-hectare site in 1987, although the first planting did not occur until 1993. The park was laid out to a design by Ray Brown (b. 1947), who acts as volunteer curator, with almost one-fifth of the site now developed. Specialising in the Proteaceae family, the park contains one of Australia's largest collections of GREVILLEA and many species of *Persoonia*. As well, the park includes a large collection of *Prostanthera* and 0.4 ha is developed as RAINFOREST. All plants are wild-sourced to ensure species and not garden hybrids are grown. Essentially a private garden with limited but regular openings run by volunteers, the Grevillea Park has been described by Bill Payne, editor of AUSTRALIAN PLANTS, as the best NATIVE GARDEN in NSW.   JOHN WALTER

GRIFFIN, Walter Burley (1876–1937) and **Marion Lucy Mahony** (1871–1961), landscape architects and architects, married in 1911. In their native USA, Walter and Marion Griffin until only recently were remembered as but protégés of that nation's most celebrated architect, Frank Lloyd Wright (1867–1959). In Australia, Walter Griffin has received much greater attention stemming from his design (1911) for the federal capital, CANBERRA. Walter's enduring association with the capital, however, has obscured not only recognition of his larger *oeuvre*, but also Marion's contribution. Common to both nations is the perception of the Griffins as architects. This perception is far too restrictive and diverges significantly from fact: the Griffins practised LANDSCAPE ARCHITECTURE, which complemented and ran parallel to architecture.

The Griffins' Australian landscape work is better understood by first examining the American context that shaped Walter's, and subsequently Marion's, approach to landscape architecture. Educated in both architecture and 'landscape gardening' at the University of Illinois (1895–99), Griffin early worked with Wright, joining his staff—then including Mahony—in 1901. Among other roles, Griffin served as Wright's landscape architect. Upon receipt of a commission, Wright conceived the general site organisation and Griffin prepared detailed landscape designs: this collaboration eventuated in a mutual design approach. Seeking to unite house and garden, Wright typically organised grounds by extending the dwelling's plan geometry outwards into its surrounds, engaging the entire block. This geometric order then was expressed in the planting and in the design of pergolas, courtyards, terraces, and pools. Naturalistic plantings predominated at the block perimeter, providing a frame to contain and effectively foil the geometric matrix of house and garden. Leaving Wright's employ in 1906, Griffin further evolved his design approach. Enlarging Wright's architecturally derived geometry, Griffin drew upon the 'architecture of plants' as another source of geometry, even adapting botanical forms as garden plans. Griffin's resultant designs fused this almost Platonic geometry with PICTURESQUE naturalism and reflected his search for communion with nature. For him, this ideal was not to be realised through the simulation of a romanticised wild nature, but through nature's more rational use and cultivation. By 1912, Griffin's practice entailed garden, university campus, and suburban estate design. Also in 1912, his now legendary Canberra design was selected by international competition. Most of the 137 competitors responded to the rugged inland site as if it were a *tabula rasa*, distorting it into conformity with varied aesthetic formulae. Alternatively and central to his success (together with Marion's exquisite renderings of the design), Walter organised his plan in accordance with the existing topography, appropriating the site itself as the new nation's primal monument.

At Commonwealth invitation, Walter travelled to Australia in 1913 to explain his design. In response to the landscape previously only imagined, he assessed that the 'gum tree, instead of being one continual monotony, strongly appealed' to him. Apart from their aesthetic appeal, the gums, for Griffin, were central to the character of the larger landscape. Appointed 'Federal Capital Director of Design and Construction' during the visit, Walter and Marion moved to Australia in 1914. Concurrent with Walter's Commonwealth duties, the Griffins began private practice in Sydney and Melbourne. Quickly seizing every opportunity to study the AUSTRALIAN FLORA, they soon applied their new knowledge in a design for Melbourne's Newman College (1915–17). Featuring native flora, the campus garden—Marion recalled—was organised by Walter's 'method of planting together according to colour'. Although developed in the USA, this method was executed there with native and exotic plants. Here, however, he sought to realise it almost exclusively with native flora. Collaboratively designed with Marion and Emily GIBSON (their first apprentice landscape architect), this Australian flora garden is one of the first by landscape architects. Of equal significance is that the project marked Marion's formal entrée into the practice of landscape architecture: coincident with this project, she published her views—under the title 'landscape architect'—and publicly lectured on that profession. Marion advocated, for instance,

Marion Mahony GRIFFIN's drawing of the native *Angophora costata* (Apple Gum) at CASTLECRAG (*c.* 1925) captures a highly refined and complementary vision of architecture and landscape

trees'. These eucalypts not only layered a patina of antiquity over the new community, but they also acknowledged the Griffins' conviction that such flora was central to Australia's place distinctiveness.

Unfortunately, Walter's efforts at Canberra were eventually undermined by calculated political antagonisms, culminating in abolition of his position in 1920. Although demoralised, the Griffins nonetheless elected to remain in Australia and continue private practice. Seeking to resolve a perceived dialectic between nature and culture, they saw the holistic parallel design of landscape and architecture as offering a habitable 'second' nature—one referential to its increasingly remote, primeval counterpart. This was best realised in their masterwork community design, CASTLECRAG (1920–35), near Sydney. There the Griffins rehabilitated and conserved a bushland site, folding roadways and dwellings into the contours of the Castlecrag promontory: architecture receded in deference to nature and landscape was given primacy. Castlecrag residents themselves, the Griffins at last and if only fleetingly, realised ideals rejected at Canberra. By the mid-1930s, their practice was extensive and included built works in ACT, NSW, Qld, SA, and Vic., and unrealised projects in WA. Enlarging this achievement, Walter travelled to India in 1935 to take up new commissions; Marion followed the next year to assist. Although anticipating only a temporary absence, Walter never returned: he died of peritonitis in Lucknow in 1937. After completing projects at hand, Marion returned to Sydney and organised for their partner Eric Milton Nicholls (1902–1965) to continue the practice. She returned alone to her native Chicago in 1938. Today, scholarship on their work is burgeoning, and admiration of the Griffins exceeds anything they knew in their lifetimes.

Donald Leslie Johnson, *Canberra and Walter Burley Griffin: A Bibliography of 1876 to 1976 and a Guide to Published Sources* (Melbourne, 1980); Peter Harrison, *Walter Burley Griffin: Landscape Architect* (Canberra, 1995); Jeff Turnbull and Peter Navaretti, *The Griffins in Australia and India* (Carlton South, Vic., 1998); Anne Watson (ed.), *Beyond Architecture: Marion Mahony and Walter Burley Griffin: America, Australia, India* (Sydney, 1998) **CHRISTOPHER VERNON**

that flower beds were 'tolerable' only in 'circumscribed recesses', so as not to 'interfere with the integrity of a quiet stretch of green' or 'conflict with the simplicity of the whole scheme'. Curiously, Marion was not known as a landscape architect in the USA, nor did she inscribe drawings with the title. Once in Australia, perhaps it was her enchantment with the landscape and climate that became catalysts for new direction. The Griffins also were avid naturalists and conservationists. These concerns were early displayed in Walter's community design for Eaglemont (*c.* 1915), near Melbourne. Here he co-joined development with conservation, including reserves situated so as 'to conserve ancient Red gum

GRIMWADE, (Wilfrid) Russell (1879–1955), businessman, philanthropist, and horticulturist, was born in his family's Caulfield mansion, Harleston, which he and his brothers later gave to Melbourne Grammar. In 1903, as a young chemist, he became director of the new research laboratory of his father's pharmaceutical business, Felton, Grimwade and Company, and in 1907 he became a partner. He later became a director of the subsidiary company, J. BOSISTO and Company. On his father's death (1910) he inherited substantial interests in various family companies, including what became Drug Houses of Australia Limited in 1929. He served on the boards of family companies and the advisory bodies of scientific institutions. Diverse business interests allowed him to integrate his philanthropic and horticultural interests.

As a centenary gift to Victorians in 1934, Grimwade donated Cook's Cottage, which was rebuilt in the FITZROY

GARDENS. Until his resignation in 1935, he served for more than a decade on the MELBOURNE BOTANIC GARDENS Advisory Committee, and from 1945 on the Maud Gibson Trust, which he hoped would foster the culture of AUSTRALIAN PLANTS for suburban gardens. Many hundreds of specimens collected by Jim WILLIS and others during the 1947 'Grimwade Expedition' to south-west Australia enriched Victoria's National Herbarium.

Gardens at **Miegunyah**, his Toorak residence, and Westerfield, his country farm near Frankston, were important sources of satisfaction and pleasure, and reflected his diverse interests and passions. On purchasing Miegunyah in 1910 he kept exotic and Australian specimen trees in the large open lawn edged by a dense, curvilinear shrubbery. On adjacent land purchased in 1911 he developed a formal garden and two unusual features—an informal woodland and an ARBORETUM of Australian trees. The formal rose garden of axial design was surrounded by an English Box hedge inside a perennial border. Ellis STONES placed a sculpture in its pool in 1938 and later converted a disused tennis court into a woodland glade, with informal plantings of silver birches, naturalised bulbs, and stone steps.

Miegunyah's EUCALYPT-rich arboretum was emblematic of Grimwade's interest in Australian FORESTRY and the cultivation and use of Australian trees. He claimed that no genus could compare with *Eucalyptus* for hardwoods and cabinet timbers; he photographed eucalypt leaves, buds, flowers, and fruit, and made an intricate cabinet from native timbers for his extensive collection of eucalypt fruit capsules. His photographs illustrated his *An Anthography of the Eucalypts* (1920), which was 'to assist in the identification of species, to stimulate research, and to promote cultivation of the Eucalypts'. He thanked CRONIN for specimens and ST JOHN for tutelage. The enlarged 1930 edition received professional forestry approval in LANE POOLE's review. Grimwade campaigned tirelessly for forest conservation. A member and sometime president of the AUSTRALIAN FOREST LEAGUE's Victorian Branch, he contributed money and articles (as 'Operculum') to its journal during the campaign to establish the Forests Commission of Victoria in 1919. Later he was a leading SAVE THE FORESTS CAMPAIGN spokesman. His philanthropy included forestry education and research.

In 1920 Grimwade purchased Westerfield and, even before house-building, began planting eucalypts and acres of lavender and geranium. Now he could grow medical and perfume plants, whose sometimes unsuccessful plantations by J. Bosisto and Company he had prompted. He planted hundreds of eucalypts of more than fifty species, many varieties of wattle, an orchard and olive grove, and lavender, geranium, peppermint, and boronia, installing a still for their oil distillation. During the Second World War staff were switched from commercial flower production to drug plants, and a drying-shed was erected for extraction purposes.

Miegunyah's garden provided solace during his illness and the place for his funeral. In his will Sir Russell Grimwade—knighted in 1950—asked that 'the trees in the grounds shall be cherished and, when any of them die, or suffer damage, they shall be replaced with discretion', and provided a bequest that financed a new imprint of Melbourne University Press—Miegunyah Press. On the death of his wife Mabel Louise (*née* Kelly) in 1973, Miegunyah was left to his alma mata, the University of Melbourne, whose School of Biochemistry bears his name in recognition of his largest lifetime gift. By 1987, when the university sold Miegunyah, the significance of its garden had been widely recognised: the house survives, but the garden has now been largely subdivided for housing. LINDEN GILLBANK

GRITTEN, Henry (1818–1873), English-born 'landscape and architectural painter', trained and exhibited in London before travelling to NORTH AMERICA, where his commissions included views of Springside at Poughkeepsie, New York (1852), now celebrated as the only extant garden of A.J. DOWNING. He arrived in Vic. in 1853 and spent time in Melbourne, Sydney, Hobart, and Launceston. His topographic paintings of houses and gardens, including Quorn Hall, Tas. (1861), The Lodge, New Town Park, Hobart (*c*. 1850s–60s), and Melbourne from the Botanic Gardens (*c*. 1867) exhibit a keen appreciation of garden detail. RA

GROTTO, from the Italian *grotta*, the Latin *crypta* (a crypt or subterranean passage or chamber), and in turn the Greek *krypte* (vault), may be a natural CAVE or cavern, usually damp and dripping with mosses and FERNS. The garden grotto is usually an artificially created structure or cave-like recess, built as an ornamental feature. With its origins in biblical times as a symbolic place for reflection and communion with nature, the grotto is often cited in classical sources (such as Plato's allegory in his *Republic* comparing the passage of life to a sojourn in a cave). The grotto was revived during the Renaissance and reached dizzy heights of baroque ornamentation and theatricality in the highly artificial gardens of sixteenth-century France and Italy and, later, Wagnerian Germany. The grotto found a sympathetic response in the English landscape garden, where, as a 'natural' feature amid more artificial elements, it was designed to stimulate the imagination, either as an accompaniment to a muse or as a place of contemplation.

In Australia during the late nineteenth and early twentieth centuries, grottoes were developed in some grander gardens to recreate nature in miniature and to provide suitable habitat niches for a range of TROPICAL and bold-foliaged plants including PALMS, AGAVES, bromeliads, and ORCHIDS. Examples survive at YARALLA and BABWORTH HOUSE (NSW), WERRIBEE PARK (Vic.), and WAIROA (SA), and in the works of Charles ROBINETTE. Many Australian Catholic Church properties including convents, monasteries, and schools feature grottoes dedicated to the Virgin Mary or saints. A number of QUIRKY or eccentric gardens also feature grottoes, often decorated with SHELLS and other found objects.

Naomi Miller, *Heavenly Caves: Reflections on the Garden Grotto* (New York, 1982) CHRIS BETTERIDGE

GROUND COVER is a general term used in gardening to describe plants covering the ground, although in natural area management it may be used to describe a rich mix of

Grove Hill

The GROTTO at YARALLA, Concord (NSW), developed c. 1910, provides a suitably dramatic setting for palms and other bold-foliaged plants

understorey plants, while in PUBLIC OPEN SPACE management it usually refers to a massed monoculture of low-growing plants: plants for that use are often woody and spreading, although a successful ground cover planting may be made of non-spreading plants placed sufficiently close to form a knitted canopy. The use of these planting schemes became fashionable in the latter part of the twentieth century as a way of providing greater function in planting design. Properly formed, ground cover planting may suppress weed growth and minimise management input. This increase in landscape design use has been reinforced by its use in creating ground patterns, popularised by the Brazilian landscape architect, Roberto Burle Marx—especially patterns that can be viewed from elevated positions, such as high-rise buildings. Their popularity has become such that Peter Thoday, an influential horticultural consultant in Europe, stated in relation to the use of ground covers in design 'that bare soil has become tantamount to indecent exposure'. Added impetus to the use of ground covers has also occurred in modern landscapes in an attempt to create planting schemes for greater safety in public spaces. By taking the middle shrub layer out but having ground covers and trees, visual contact between separate areas can be maintained. Contemporary landscape designers and horticultural managers are experimenting with a more naturalistic, less monocultural approach to ground covers by using flowering herbaceous plants (or flowering forbes) in a native GRASSY matrix. ML

GROVE HILL, Norton Summit, SA: see GILES, Charles

GUÉRARD, (Johann Joseph) Eugen(e) von (1811–1901), artist, played a significant role in documenting Australian colonial landscapes and its pastoral expansion as well as botanical, geological, and zoological features. Born in Vienna, he was apprenticed and studied art in Vienna, Naples, and Dusseldorf, under his artist father, and Johann Wilhelm Schirmer, adopting the style of the Austrian Biedermeier school of art. In 1852 he arrived in Geelong (Vic.) and began his extensive travels and artistic output. The tinted lithographs in his book *Australian Landscapes* (1866) were a remarkable study of the landscape, as were his oil paintings of Tower Hill (1855), Ferntree Gully (1857), Stoney Rises (1857), Mount William (c. 1856), and Mount Kosciuszko (1870). While these record the first inklings of European encroachment, his views of Basin Banks (1857), Purrumbete (1858), MENINGOORT (1861), Yalla-y-Poora (1864), and Koort-koort-nong (1860) display fully the symbols of pastoral advancement through his other main subject, the HOMESTEAD.

From 1870, appointed the first master of painting at the Melbourne National School of Art and curator of the National Gallery of Victoria, von Guérard instructed many of the later Heidelberg School of Australian artists, asserting the importance of landscape painting. Active in the Royal Society of Victoria, in 1882 he returned to London, where he died. Eugene von Guérard was Australia's most important romantic landscape painter during the third quarter of the nineteenth century, and his works remain widely admired. In the 1970s, his view of Tower Hill was used as evidence for the REVEGETATION of Tower Hill Reserve in Victoria's WESTERN DISTRICT.

Marjorie Tipping, *Eugene von Guérard's Australian Landscapes* (Melbourne, 1975); Candice Bruce, *Eugen von Guérard* (Canberra, 1980); Candice Bruce, Edward Comstock, and Frank

McDonald, *Eugene von Guérard, 1811–1901: A German Romantic in the Antipodes* (Martinborough, New Zealand, 1982); Alison Carroll and John Tregenza, *Eugene von Guérard's South Australia: Drawings, Paintings and Lithographs from Journeys in South Australia in 1855 and 1857* (Adelaide, 1986)

DAVID JONES

GUERTNER, Beryl Greta (1917–1981), founding editor of the popular magazines *Australian House and Garden* and *Good Gardening*, and the author of numerous gardening guides, was born at Katoomba and raised in Wagga Wagga (NSW). From an early age she was interested in exotic flowers and plants. She came to Sydney in 1938 and worked in the publicity department of Paramount Pictures and as a journalist on the *Daily Telegraph*. From 1949 to 1970 at Warrimoo in the BLUE MOUNTAINS, Guertner and her friend Kate Warmoll (b. 1921) created a sophisticated country retreat. The imaginative garden was filled with unusual plants, with fieldstone walls easing the transition towards the natural landscape of sandstone shelves, angophoras and waratahs.

From 1948 until her death she was a senior editor with the K.G. Murray Publishing Company, which later included Gregory's Guides & Maps Pty Ltd. For twenty-five years she edited AUSTRALIAN HOUSE AND GARDEN, steadily developing its gardening component. She also initiated *Good Gardening* (1971–81), a practical illustrated magazine for mainstream gardeners in Australia and New Zealand. Her first gardening handbook, *Gregory's Guide to Better Gardens* (1963), ran to many editions; in the same year she brought out the *Australian Book of Flower Arrangements*. She compiled and edited many books between the 1960s and the 1980s (many undated), including *Gregory's Australian Guide to Better Outdoor Living* (c. 1964) and *Landscape Planning for Small Gardens* (1968). Retiring from a city career in 1973, she created a subtropical garden alongside the lagoon at Macmasters Beach. Here her extensive reading, research, and the development of the garden assisted her role as a prolific author and editor. Recalled as a strong and engaging personality, Guertner's work recognised the mass-market tastes of the period, while offering insights into contemporary design and horticultural practice, and adventurous planting choices.

HOWARD TANNER

GUILFOYLE, John Austin (1852–1909), horticulturist, is best known as curator of Melbourne's city parks and gardens. The son of Sydney nursery proprietor Michael GUILFOYLE, he ran off to sea in his teens, but soon returned to help work his family's plantation on the Tweed River (NSW). For twenty years he engaged in agricultural pursuits in Qld and SA, including a stint in the Department of Woods and Forests under John Ednie BROWN, and expeditions to New Guinea and Solomon Islands collecting ORCHIDS. In 1890 Nicholas BICKFORD employed him in renovating the CARLTON GARDENS after Melbourne's Centennial Exhibition. Following Bickford's retirement, Guilfoyle was appointed Curator, Metropolitan Parks and Gardens, in 1891.

Unlike his older brother William GUILFOYLE, John appears not to have had any particular gift for landscape design. Rather, he applied his skills as manager and horticulturist to admirable effect during a career coinciding with the 1890s depression and characterised by meagre budgets. Guilfoyle was the first professional horticulturist to manage the city's gardens, then dominated by trees; under his guidance they slowly changed to include greater areas of lawn, shrub beds, and flowers. A major achievement was his creation of the precursor to the Melbourne City Council Parks and Gardens Department, providing horticultural training and raising most of the plants required. His interest in acquiring less-common species led to exchanges with BOTANIC GARDENS locally and abroad. Guilfoyle never married, dying prematurely from heart disease in Carlton Gardens lodge, where his sister had kept house.

GEORGINA WHITEHEAD

GUILFOYLE, Michael (c. 1809–1884), nursery proprietor and landscape gardener, received his early training in London and rose to the position of foreman at the Royal Exotic Nursery, King's Road, Chelsea. This nursery, established in 1808 by Joseph Knight (and later owned by VEITCH), specialised in GREENHOUSE and STOVE plants, including newly introduced AUSTRALIAN NATIVE PLANTS. Guilfoyle was a member of the West London Gardeners' Association and at their meetings contributed to discussions on the cultivation of these plants. His eldest son, William GUILFOYLE, told J.H. MAIDEN that Knight had such a belief

Beryl GUERTNER, forceful and direct in her views, was the influential founding editor (1948–73) of AUSTRALIA HOUSE AND GARDEN and author or editor of numerous garden and home-making guides produced by the Sydney-based K.G. Murray Publishing Company

in his father's abilities that 'he sent him to many parts of the Kingdom to lay out or remodel parks and gardens frequently without even inspecting his work'.

In 1845 Knight took the first steps towards retirement, and in 1849 Guilfoyle and his family, wife Charlotte (née Delafosse) and son William, migrated to Sydney aboard the *Steadfast*. He established a nursery in Kellick Street, Redfern, which soon failed. He was then fortunate in obtaining the patronage of T.S. MORT, the wealthy industrialist and active horticulturist. In 1846 Mort had purchased Percyville, a cottage standing in more than seven acres (2.8 ha) of ground at Darling Point, and immediately began transforming the house (renaming it Greenoaks) and the grounds, which became 'the leading and model private garden of New South Wales', described at length in the *Horticultural Magazine* (1865). Mort was president of the Horticultural Society of New South Wales, the publisher of the magazine, and Guilfoyle was listed in it as one of the 'good and first-rate gardeners' formerly employed at Greenoaks. Mort owned land at Double Bay, down the hill from Greenoaks, where he had his vegetable garden, orchard, and offices, and Guilfoyle occupied a cottage there (at the corner of South and Ocean streets). By 1851 he had established a nursery on three and a half acres (1.4 ha) of land belonging to Mort. This site, lying between South and Cross streets, was sandy and low-lying, with a watercourse draining the nearby swamp into the bay, flowing through its centre. This stream provided a reliable water supply for the nursery. When the swamp was reclaimed, the watercourse was filled—becoming Swamp Street (now renamed Guilfoyle Avenue).

In 1851 Guilfoyle issued the first catalogue of his Exotic Nursery, whose name recalled his place of employment in England. It listed almost 1500 plants and shows that he was already competing with SHEPHERD, BAPTIST, and HENDERSON, the leading Sydney nursery proprietors of the previous decade. As the business grew so also did his family of thirteen children (two of whom died as infants). Three boys—William, Michael, and John GUILFOYLE—worked in the nursery, William becoming a partner in 1862. By 1860 the nursery consisted of a 'home, shop, store, greenhouse and gardens', and in 1864 Mort leased these to Guilfoyle for twenty-one years at an annual rent of £150. This was the year when John Gould VEITCH, after visiting the major nurseries of NSW, wrote that 'if not the largest [it was] … one of the best nurseries in the colony. The stock consists almost entirely of flowering and evergreen trees and shrubs and Coniferae. The collection of the latter is probably one of the most complete in the colony.' The increase in stock was indicated in the catalogue prepared for Guilfoyle by John MACGILLIVRAY in 1862, where 2500 different plants were listed. He overcame the difficulty of propagating jacarandas in 1868, enabling the widespread use of this spectacular flowering tree for the first time. He also raised new varieties of popular plants such as verbena, camellia, and azalea, and attempted to popularise both in Australia and Britain the plants introduced from the PACIFIC ISLANDS by Charles MOORE in 1850 and by his son William, who accompanied HMS *Challenger* on its voyage in 1868.

The interest of father and son in both ornamental and economic TROPICAL plants led Guilfoyle to consider taking up land in the Tweed River district of NSW. He visited the area in 1869, and his sons William, John, and James selected land forming part of the Cudgen scrub. The properties appear to have been managed as a unit, with William responsible for the nursery and the tropical garden surrounding the house at Cudgen and John for the broad acres planted with sugar and tobacco. William had effectively left the Double Bay nursery in 1868 and in 1875 Guilfoyle relinquished the lease, moving his nursery to a smaller site in Elswick Street, Leichhardt. This was closed two years later when he retired. He died at his home, Athelstone, Windsor Street, Paddington.

In his first catalogue Guilfoyle advertised 'Gardens laid out and planted with Plants suited to their soils'. William stated that his father 'laid out scores of gardens around Sydney and in the country', and R.T.M. PESCOTT that the 'Government of New South Wales sought Michael Guilfoyle's assistance on the development of the Domain and Botanic Gardens in Sydney' and that 'he took a prominent part in designing those gardens as they exist to-day'. Support for this latter statement has not been forthcoming. It is known however, that he supplied the plants and carried out the landscaping of Prince Alfred Park and Argyle Place in Sydney.

Unlike other prominent nursery proprietors of the time, once in Australia, Guilfoyle played little part in the horticultural societies and seldom contributed to their shows. He did, however join with T.W. SHEPHERD in 1854 in attacking Charles MOORE's management of SYDNEY BOTANIC GARDENS, especially his practice of exchanging plants, accusing him of publishing reports with the 'intention to mislead'; in the following year he appeared before the Select Committee set up to investigate the allegations. This did not prevent him seeking two cases of *Araucaria hetrophylla* (Norfolk Island Pine) from Moore a year later.

Michael's son William—who referred to his father as 'generalissimo'—claimed he was 'an exceedingly strict man, treating his sons with Spartan severity'. Nevertheless, it is the achievements of his sons William and John that make him such a significant figure. While both informed J.H. Maiden that he never gave either of them a single lesson in LANDSCAPE GARDENING, he provided the opportunities for both to acquire the knowledge and skills that formed the foundations for their careers.

RICHARD CLOUGH

GUILFOYLE, William Robert (1840–1912), landscape designer and botanic garden director, was born at Chelsea, London, son of Michael GUILFOYLE. The family arrived in Sydney in 1849, and Michael Guilfoyle established a nursery and landscape business in Double Bay. William was the eldest of eleven surviving children and, along with his brothers Michael and John GUILFOYLE, was involved in the family business from its beginning. After leaving school he undertook a number of field trips to northern NSW and southern Qld, collecting and sketching plants. By the time he was 22, he was an experienced horticulturist and had become a partner with his father in the family nursery.

In 1868 William accompanied the British warship, HMS *Challenger*, on a five-month tour of the South Pacific, calling at Samoa, Tonga, Fiji, New Hebrides, and New Caledonia. Guilfoyle collected extensively for the SYDNEY BOTANIC GARDENS and for the family nursery. He recorded the voyage with a series of watercolour sketches and a detailed account in the *SYDNEY MAIL*, which so impressed Ferdinand MUELLER at MELBOURNE BOTANIC GARDENS, that the Victorian Government Botanist forwarded it to London for publication. Mueller was already familiar with the work and reputation of Guilfoyle, writing regularly to encourage and advise the younger man and had proposed him for LINNEAN SOCIETY fellowship in 1867.

Soon after William's return, the Guilfoyle family selected approximately 250 hectares of land at Cudgen (NSW), on the Tweed River, for a sugar plantation and experimental nursery, and the congenial correspondence between Mueller and the Guilfoyles continued. Subsequently Robb and Company established a flourishing sugar mill at Cudgen; one of the directors was James Joseph Casey (1831–1913), then Victoria's Commissioner of Crown Lands. Casey met the Guilfoyles during his visits to Cudgen and was obviously extremely impressed by William. In 1873 Casey appointed William Guilfoyle 'Curator of Botanic and Domain Gardens', Melbourne, as a replacement for the unpopular Mueller.

Outraged and embittered, Mueller wrote to colleagues seeking their support for his reinstatement. In his correspondence he variously refers to Guilfoyle as 'a young cousin of the Minister of the Department, an inexperienced Nurseryman of Sydney, devoid of all scientific knowledge' and 'the cousin of the Minister's wife, a completely unscientific gardener'. Such charges of nepotism were also reported in the contemporary press, but have not been proven.

Guilfoyle set about extensively remodelling Melbourne Botanic Gardens, beginning near the director's house where choice plants, including camellias and azaleas imported from the family nursery, could be safely held. Over the summer of 1874–75 he successfully transplanted hundreds of semi-mature CONIFERS from Mueller's PINETUM to provide a PICTURESQUE landscape framework throughout the Gardens. Guilfoyle replaced his predecessor's system of narrow paths and dense avenue plantings with wide, serpentine paths curving around expansive LAWNS. The careful positioning of SHRUBBERIES as well as individual beds and specimen trees, in relationship to the ornamental lakes, created scenic panoramas and VISTAS. Guilfoyle's changes were well received, and he was appointed director in 1875. Progressively, other areas of the Gardens—including the Fern Gully, Australian Border, and Eastern and Tennyson Lawns—were developed, culminating in the realignment of the Yarra River during 1897–1901.

The Princes Lawn at MELBOURNE BOTANIC GARDENS, landscaped by William GUILFOYLE during the mid-1870s and demonstrating his stylistic and planting preferences, was the first public example of his work, and its popular reception laid the foundation for his outstanding success as a garden designer

William GUILFOYLE, pictured in 1902 under a specimen of *Phoenix canariensis* (Canary Island Date Palm) in MELBOURNE BOTANIC GARDENS, is the epitome of an accomplished garden designer and plant enthusiast whose many garden projects—both public and private—were rapidly maturing

Guilfoyle's landscape skills lay in his ability to combine the public's demand for a picturesque 'pleasure garden' with the scientific requirements of a well laid-out, labelled BOTANIC GARDEN where individual plants could be seen to advantage, as in the GARDENESQUE style. Drawing upon his earlier experiences, he also embraced the current gardening fashion for TROPICAL and subtropical plants, using coloured and VARIEGATED foliage plants to great advantage, both outdoors and in his CONSERVATORIES. Thatched-roofed SUMMER-HOUSES, again suggestive of the South Pacific islands, were added, along with other Gardenesque elements such as RUSTIC bridges and seats, grotesque ROCKERIES, and ornamental urns. Compared with Mueller's situation Guilfoyle was certainly helped by a vastly increased budget and superior IRRIGATION system, but he also employed his horticultural knowledge, practical experience, and ability to visualise landscape designs wisely.

In addition to his duties in the Botanic Gardens, Guilfoyle was also responsible for implementing Joseph SAYCE's landscape plan for Victoria's GOVERNMENT HOUSE and the surrounding DOMAIN, and for the design of various metropolitan and provincial public and institutional gardens. These included Trinity College grounds, Parkville (1876), WARRNAMBOOL BOTANIC GARDENS (1877), KOROIT BOTANIC GARDENS (1880), Horsham Botanic Gardens (1880), HAMILTON BOTANIC GARDENS (1881), Princes Park, Maryborough (1883), Camperdown Botanic Gardens (1885), Parliament House, Melbourne (1888), Melbourne Teachers Training College, Carlton (1892), and Japanese Garden, TREASURY GARDENS, Melbourne (by 1904). He also advised on botanic gardens at Sale, Vic. (1881) and Albury, NSW (1886), and drew up a plan to remodel the COLAC BOTANIC GARDENS (1910), although only a small proportion of his suggestions there were executed. In addition, Guilfoyle designed a number of private country gardens. Those with unequivocal evidence of his involvement include Derriweit Heights, Mount Macedon (prior to 1896, destroyed by bush fires in 1983), DALVUI, Terang (1898), MOOLERIC, Birregurra (1903–10), TURKEITH, Birregurra (1905–06), Banool, Yarra Glen (c. 1905), and MAWALLOK, Beaufort (1909). Presumably he also laid out the garden for his own country property, Mount Yule, at Healesville. A number of city gardens have also been attributed to him, but all require further verification.

In his early career at the Gardens, Guilfoyle concentrated on courting his political masters with timely and detailed reports of his progress. As his reputation increased, he became more in demand around the colony as a brilliant, original, but practical landscape designer. However, he was not without his critics. An 1882 article in the LEADER accused him of neglecting the Melbourne Botanic Gardens to design private gardens for wealthy country patrons. This criticism may have had some foundation, for Guilfoyle had already been censored by his superiors in the Lands Department for being away from Melbourne too often. Consequently the plans for Koroit and Horsham Botanic Gardens were completed by R.P. WHITWORTH under Guilfoyle's direction. Whitworth had earlier collaborated with Guilfoyle on the production of the *Official Guide to Victoria* for the 1880 Melbourne International Exhibition. Its keyed plan for the Botanic Gardens entry bears some resemblance to those in Guilfoyle's own comprehensive *Catalogue of Plants under Cultivation in the Melbourne Botanic Gardens, Alphabetically Arranged* (1883).

Always interested in potentially useful plants, Guilfoyle prepared extensive displays of plant products, such as timbers and fibres, for various international and intercolonial EXHIBITIONS. He also established an extensive medicinal garden in the 1880s at the Melbourne Botanic Gardens, and opened a Museum of Economic Botany and Plant Products in 1892. His writings again became more prolific in his later years and included extensive articles in the *Bankers' Magazine of Australasia* concerning his 1890 trip to Europe, regular contributions on native species to the *Victorian Naturalist*, and two guide books (1902, 1908) to the Melbourne Botanic Gardens.

Contemporary photographs and descriptions show William Guilfoyle to have been rather short and stout, with a flowing moustache tobacco-stained from cigar chain-smoking. Always strict with staff, he became even more irascible in later years as gout and arthritis forced him to use a wheelchair. However, his private letters to his wife Alice (née Darling), whom he had married in 1889, and to family friends such as the Ramsays at Mooleric, reveal an affectionate, kindly, and hospitable person. Despite his poor health, Guilfoyle's term in office was extended to 1909, four years past the normal retirement age of 65—a sign of the enormous public respect and confidence in him.

Guilfoyle's love of all AUSTRALIAN PLANTS, not just the then fashionable tropical and subtropical species, pervaded all his designs. His final work, *Australian Plants Suitable for Gardens, Parks, Timber Reserves, Etc.* (1911), drew on his considerable horticulture experience and helped promote the use of native plants in the private and public domains. Indeed, Guilfoyle's outstanding ability to design—and to implement and manage—gardens within the picturesque tradition using both native and exotic plants, coupled with his strong commitment to public education and his lifelong interest in horticultural research and economic botany, put him head and shoulders above his nineteenth-century contemporaries in Vic. and perhaps Australia.

R.T.M. Pescott, *W.R. Guilfoyle 1840–1912: The Master of Landscaping* (Melbourne, 1974); Paul Fox, *Clearings: Six Colonial Gardeners and their Landscapes* (Carlton South, Vic., forthcoming, 2003)　　　　　　　　　　　　EVE ALMOND

GULLIVER, Thomas Allen (*c.* 1809–1873), gardener, was born in Dorset, England, and arrived in Melbourne *c.* 1857 with his wife and two sons, **Thomas Allen Gulliver** (1848–1931) and **Benjamin Thomas Gulliver** (1851–1938), both born at Helston, Cornwall. Thomas Gulliver worked at MELBOURNE BOTANIC GARDENS from *c.*1860 and did Thomas jnr (*c.* 1863– 70). Gulliver's sons sailed as botanical collectors aboard the HMS *Eagle* under Francis Cadell's captaincy during an 1867 exploration of South Australia's NORTHERN TERRITORY. The pair sent plants from the Gulf of Carpentaria and Arnhem Land to MUELLER and several were named in their honour. During the early 1870s the Gulliver brothers botanised in Tas. Seeking botanical work in Qld without success, Thomas jnr joined the Post and Telegraph Department and in the 1870s supervised construction of the Cape York (Qld) telegraph line. Thereafter he was postmaster at Townsville and as a keen horticulturist presided over beautification of the town. By the late 1870s Benjamin was listed as a 'nurseryman and seedsman' in Townsville, where he established the Acacia Vale Nursery (*c.* 1881). The venture prospered and its PLEASURE GARDEN was a favoured RESORT 'where wines, mineral waters, tea, and fruits were dispensed, and bouquets of roses provided … with the exception of music and dancing we imagined ourselves once more on the Continent'.　　　　　　　RA

GUNN, Ronald Campbell (1808–1881), botanist and public servant, whose assiduous collecting and annotating of specimens did most to document and disseminate information about Tasmania's flora, was born at the Cape of Good Hope, the son of an army officer. Gunn was educated in Scotland for a military career but the success of his brother in Van Diemen's Land brought him to the colony in 1830. Appointed superintendent of convicts in the north of the colony, he formed a friendship with the landholder Robert William Lawrence who, with Thomas Scott, a merchant, collected plants for the eminent English botanist W. J. HOOKER. Lawrence enlisted Gunn's help and the loss Gunn felt at Lawrence's death in 1833 only sharpened his desire to continue their work. Posted to Circular Head as a police magistrate in 1834, he continued to collect botanical specimens, animals, birds, and shells, corresponding with a fellow collector in the area, Dr Joseph MILLIGAN. A grateful Hooker sent Gunn books, journals, and plants. The following year Gunn, together with the Quaker missionary James BACKHOUSE, published in the *Hobart Town Almanack* a list of INDIGENOUS PLANTS and animals.

Sir John FRANKLIN's appointment as the lieutenant-governor of Van Diemen's Land ushered in a period of active support for Gunn's botanical endeavours. Returning to Hobart he became the secretary of the Horticultural Society (1839) and the Tasmanian Society (1840). As Franklin's private secretary he met scientific visitors to the colony, including J.D. Hooker, the son of W. J. Hooker. He accompanied the Franklins on exploration trips and assisted Lady Franklin to lay out the botanic garden at her Ancanthe estate near Hobart. In 1841, he returned to Launceston to manage the Lawrence estates and became a substantial landholder, a politician (1855–60), and influential in many organisations, including the Northern Agricultural Society and the Launceston Horticultural Society. Gunn kept the Tasmanian Society active until 1848 when it was amalgamated with the ROYAL SOCIETY of Van Diemen's Land, established by Lieutenant-Governor Eardley-Wilmot in 1843. Gunn was a contributor to, and editor of, the prestigious *Tasmanian Journal of Natural Science* (1842–49).

He was elected Fellow of the Linnaen Society (1850) and Fellow of the Royal Society (FRS) (1854), the first Tasmanian to achieve FRS status. J.D. Hooker dedicated his *Flora Tasmaniae* to Gunn, in acknowledgment of his extensive specimen collecting and accompanying notes 'that display a remarkable power of observation'. A volume of W.H. HARVEY's *Phycologia Australia* (1863) was also dedicated to Gunn. His HERBARIUM was presented to the Royal Society of Tasmania (1878) but was transferred to the National Herbarium of New South Wales in 1904. His splendid LIBRARY was dispersed in 1924, when his Launceston estate, Newstead, was sold. Subdivision of the property destroyed the botanic garden he had established there in 1833. Gunn's Plains, Lake Gunn, and streets in Devonport and Launceston commemorate him. Some twenty-five species of plants bear his name, as do a bandicoot and four shellfish species.

A.M. Buchanan, *The Tasmanian Collecting Localities of Ronald Gunn and Joseph Milligan* (Hobart, 1985); Frank Ellis (ed.), *Van Diemen's Land Correspondents by T.E. Burns and J.R. Skemp: Letters from R.C. Gunn, R.W. Lawrence, Jorgen Jorgenson, Sir John Franklin and others to Sir William J. Hooker, 1827–1849* (Launceston, 1961)

GILLIAN WINTER

HACKETT, Elisha W. (c. 1826–1914), seed merchant and nursery proprietor, arrived in SA in 1850 and established his business as a corn and seed merchant in Rundle Street, Adelaide, in 1852. He was joined in his enterprise shortly afterward by his younger brothers Walter and George, and between them they built up a flourishing trade. **Walter Hackett** (1827–1914), born in Chichester, Sussex, England, arrived in SA c. 1852—at the request of his brother—having previously migrated to Melbourne to try his hand at the diggings. He was a committee member of the Royal Agricultural and Horticultural Society of South Australia, and a commissioner for several intercolonial and international EXHIBITIONS. **George Hackett** (d. 1895) arrived in SA c. 1851. The business continued to grow after Elisha made a trip to England in 1860, during which he built up contacts among seed merchants there. Carrying a wide range of stock, originally bought in from other nurseries, but soon grown at their own premises at Marryatville, they were a leading South Australian nursery of the era. Indeed, photographs show Walter Hackett as a proper 'toff', wearing a cut-away coat and grey topper as he strode down Rundle Street, looking every inch the successful entrepreneur.

By the 1870s, the business was trading as E. & W. Hackett, and other family members joined. **George Alfred Hackett** (1851–1940), son of George Hackett, was born in Adelaide and trained at the SHEPHERD nursery, Sydney, for five years and spent many years (1874–1916) with the family firm. **(Walter) Champion Hackett** (1864–1938), son of Walter, joined the firm in 1880 as a director, and had a fine record of service to South Australian horticulture and the nursery trade. Father and son between them served almost seven decades as secretary of the South Australian Horticultural and Floricultural Society (c. 1879–1946). Champion also served as national president of the Australian Nurserymen and Seedsmens' Association, on the executive and as a judge for the Royal Agricultural and Horticultural Society of South Australia, and chaired the FIELD NATURALISTS' section of the Royal Society of South Australia.

The business continued into the new century with flourishing wholesale and retail divisions selling agricultural seeds, general garden plants, orchard stocks, flower and vegetable seeds, horticultural and agricultural sundries, glasshouse plants, ferns and orchids, fertilisers, florists requirements, and bee-keepers' requisites. NOVELTIES and new introductions from European and American seed houses included a wide range of introductions from VEITCH, Burpee, Carter, Sutton, Vilmorin, and other suppliers. The diverse offerings—Okra, Japanese Cape Gooseberry (*Physallis alkekengi*), Chinese Artichoke (*Stachys affinis*), Capsicum 'Golden Queen', Salsify, Curly Kale, and Tree Tomato—suggest that epicurism is not a recent phenomenon. Decorative plants were also a keenly contested area of sales for the bigger nurseries, and extensive lists of ROSES were a feature of Hackett's trade, along with a surprising range of stovehouse plants, fuchsias, pelargoniums and geraniums, ferns and lycopods, chrysanthemums, palms, cycads, cacti, and aquatic plants. The firm also published a monthly magazine, the *Gardening Bulletin* (1917–c. 1950); it was one of few Australian nurseries to undertake this role, especially in such a sustained manner. Hackett's business enterprises continued into the early 1950s when they were finally wound up and sold off.   TREVOR NOTTLE

HACKETT, John Winthrop (c. 1848–1916), Irish-born editor, newspaper proprietor and politician, migrated to Australia in 1875. In 1883 he joined Charles Harper as partner in the *West Australian* newspaper, publisher of the WESTERN MAIL. As confidant of Premier FORREST, a Legislative Councillor (1890–1916), and editor of Perth's leading newspaper, Hackett was a highly influential public figure closely associated with numerous cultural and educational endeavours in WA during the 1890s and early 1900s. These included establishment of the University of Western Australia, ZOOLOGICAL GARDENS (South Perth), KINGS PARK, KARRAKATTA CEMETERY, ACCLIMATISATION Committee, and tourist development of the scenic CAVES in the south-west. He was knighted in 1911.

Deborah Vernon Hackett (*née* Drake-Brockman) (1887–1965), who married Hackett in 1905, forged a remarkable career as a community worker and mining entrepreneur. She edited the *Australian Household Guide* (Perth, 1916), which included a chapter advising how to garden on Perth's sandy soils, seeking to create 'a series of plant pictures … [having] order and method without their being noticeable … the ideal garden is an orderly disorder'.   OLINE RICHARDS

HADDON, Robert Joseph (1866–1929), architect, trained in London before his arrival in Melbourne in 1889. He worked in Vic., Tas., and WA before setting up in practice in

Melbourne (1901). He strove for originality in design, responding to local materials and climate. Although he undertook few documented garden designs, his ARTS AND CRAFTS sympathies and artistic inclination—he was a skilled delineator and colourist—ensured that he viewed house and garden as an ensemble, ideas expressed in the chapter 'Gardening' in his *Australian Architecture* (1908). RA

HA-HA (or sunk fence/wall), of seventeenth-century French origin and popularised by the eighteenth-century English landscape movement, consisted of a ditch and FENCING or walling to provide separation or protection (especially from animals) without loss of VISTAS. The angular mode employed a wall on one side of the ditch (with or without associated fencing or walling) while the trapezoid model employed a light fence in the centre of the ditch. The former was most common in Australia, almost exclusively employed in HOMESTEAD GARDENS, with fine examples at WERRIBEE PARK, SALISBURY COURT, and MAWALLOK. The ha-ha was also used in nineteenth-century lunatic asylums, where HOSPITAL patients could be confined without the need for excessively high walls. The derivation of the term is obscure, but the use of exclamation marks in eighteenth-century LANDSCAPE GARDENING texts suggests the surprise and jocularity to human viewer and stock alike of the 'ha! ha!'. RA

HAMEL NURSERY, WA, was established in 1896 by the Commissioner of Crown Lands as a STATE FOREST NURSERY for the propagation of native trees (as shade and SHELTER BELT trees for farmers) and pine seedlings (for forest department PLANTATIONS). The initial site at Guildford was abandoned in favour of a more suitable one on the De Hamel Estate at Drakesbrook, south of Waroona, in 1897. Alfred McFarlane (1852–1916) was the first officer-in-charge and early plant lists show that about seventy species of natives and exotics were grown, with the native species later increasing to 120. GREENING AUSTRALIA took over the running of the site from the Forests Department in 1988. An ARBORETUM of mature native and exotic specimens survives, including *Quercus suber* (Cork Oak), old *Camellia* cultivars, plus one of the few stands of *Telopea speciosissima* (Waratah) in the state. JOHN VISKA

HAMER, Rupert James (Dick) (b. 1916), Premier of Victoria (1972–81), came to office following the Little Desert furore, and a consequent policy shift, with new legislation giving increased attention to environmental affairs. He played a major role in ensuring the effective implementation of that legislation and providing considerable personal leadership in environmental policies. The first ministry of conservation in Australia was established under his government. Other bodies established within the ministry included the Land Conservation Council, Environment Protection Authority, Victoria Conservation Trust (now Trust for Nature), and a completely reshaped National Parks Service. The Melbourne and Metropolitan Board of Works was also empowered to purchase large land areas within the metropolitan area as the basis of a new regional parks system. His government ensured the professionalism of land resource management, and provided a massive increase in the number and size of protected areas in Vic. He revived 'The Garden State' title and used it to energetically promote the state's image. Sir Rupert Hamer was knighted (KCMG) in 1982.

ELERY HAMILTON-SMITH

HAMILTON, Richard (1792–1852), vigneron, migrated from Long Island, New York, to Adelaide in 1837. He acquired thirty-two hectares at Warradale in Adelaide, naming the property Ewell after his home village in Surrey, England. With vines acquired from Cape Town en route, he established a vineyard (mainly Shiraz, Grenache, Pedro Ximenes, Muscatel, and Doradillo) that eventually covered sixty-three hectares. His son Henry Hamilton (1826–1907) continued the Ewell vineyard operation and established further vines at Oaklands Park. Henry's son Frank Hamilton (1859–1913) inherited the wineries, which continued as a limited company. Many of the original vineyards were subsumed in Adelaide's suburban expansion, but the company progressively acquired land at Happy Valley, Springton (1938), Eden Valley (1967) in the BAROSSA VALLEY, Wood Wood on the Murray River, and Sandy Hollow vineyards in the HUNTER VALLEY. DAVID JONES

HAMILTON BOTANIC GARDENS, Vic., set aside in 1853 on a four-hectare site near the town centre, was formally gazetted in 1870 and developed from that date. William FERGUSON set out the gardens with three perimeter rows of trees, including cypresses, pines, and sequoias. But it was the contribution of William GUILFOYLE in 1881 that largely established their design and present character. His extant plan included the encircling path shrubberies of irregular shape, large sweeping lawns dotted with specimen trees, and a lake in the low-lying ground. He also recommended suitable planting groups. A curator's cottage was erected in 1882 and the lake and island were created in 1883. The Edwardian period is now seen in the planting of palms *Butia capitata* (Chilean Wine Palm) and *Washingtonia robusta* (Thread Palm) among mainly oaks, elms, and conifers. COMMEMORATIVE and other features added to the gardens include ornamental gates at Thompson Street (1893) and French Street (1908–09), Australian Natives Association fountain (1908), Thomson memorial fountain (1918–21), Country Womens' Association glasshouse (1934), and King George V bust (1937). The garden still retains a menagerie with kangaroos and emus, and an aviary, ZOOLOGICAL features fashionable in nineteenth-century public gardens. A splendid Edwardian BANDSTAND was relocated to the gardens in 1988 from nearby Melville Oval. These features, along with the maintenance of the collection of mature trees and shrubs, and annual floral displays, reflect civic pride in the gardens, making them one of the most intact examples of Australia's nineteenth-century provincial BOTANIC GARDENS and among the best-preserved examples of Guilfoyle's work. PAMELA JELLIE

HAMMET, Ivo (1896–1975) naturalist, book collector, and grower of Australian plants, was born in Geelong (Vic.).

While officer-in-charge of publications in the Customs Department in Melbourne, Hammet built up a notable library of Australiana, including many works of NATURAL HISTORY. His interest in AUSTRALIAN PLANTS was stimulated by accounts of the flora by early explorers and he determined to introduce bush plants into cultivation, expressing the objectives of a 1940s native garden movement as 'Preservation through Cultivation'. He was president of the FIELD NATURALISTS' Club of Victoria (1944–45), foundation president of the SOCIETY FOR GROWING AUSTRALIAN PLANTS in 1958, and was actively involved with MARANOA GARDENS. He contributed the chapter on 'Natives and Wildflowers' in Keith Winser's *Complete Australian Garden Manual* (1953) and gave many lectures emphasising the importance of the indigenous flora. Hammet was extremely knowledgeable on the cultivation requirements of Australian plants in an era when they were little grown, and his fine garden in Ivanhoe was lavishly praised by Thistle HARRIS in *Australian Plants for the Garden* (1953).   TONY CAVANAGH

HAMMOND, Eric Herbert (1898–1992), landscape constructor, brought his trade to an art form in more than sixty years of practice. He was known for his meticulous attention to detail and for his technical expertise. In its heyday the E.H. Hammond organisation, employing fifty people, was said to be the largest such firm in Australia. Its regular advertisement on the back cover of YOUR GARDEN offered construction services in 'tennis courts, swimming pools, bowling greens, sports grounds, rock gardens, lawns & fish ponds, paved terraces, rustic furniture, fencing & pergolas' using thirteen different kinds of soil, rocks, flagging, and gravel.

After active service in the First World War, Hammond, who had trained in nursery work as a teenager, became an orchardist at Kilsyth (Vic.), driving a horse and cart to Prahran Market. In 1922 he set up as a landscape contractor. He travelled on a bicycle equipped with special carriers for tools and materials, and put in long hours at the local library—the only available source of information on garden design—to supplement his practical experience.

In 1924 he began building gardens for Edna WALLING. Their long association was marked by mutual regard, and it is said they never had an argument. He called her Edna—a liberty accorded to no other employee—while she referred to him as Mr Hammond. His work for her included grand gardens such as MAWARRA in the Dandenong Ranges, with a stone-edged octagonal pool and an extraordinary double flight of stone steps, and Churston, Toorak, with two tennis courts, a swimming pool, pergolas, stone steps, and walls with iron balustrading. Hammond worked for many other designers, and also carried out his own designs. Important construction projects included the forecourt of the ICI Building (Melbourne's first modern office tower) for John STEVENS, the surface of the Melbourne Cricket Ground for the 1956 Olympic Games, and the Eastern Freeway landscape in the early 1970s. But four-fifths of his work was in home gardens, and no job was too small. In 1940, with Olive MELLOR and Ellis STONES, he had been one of the first landscapers in Melbourne to advertise his services in the classified telephone directory. The only category available to them was 'gardeners'.

Dressed in collar and tie, with highly polished shoes, his appetite for hard work was prodigious and he made no secret of the fact that he wanted to be the best in his field. He would insist that his men redo work that did not meet his exacting standards. Even after his sons took over the business he remained active until well into his eighties, still liking to 'give the boys a hand with a rake'. A concession to advancing age was to adjust his morning alarm clock from 4.30 a.m. to 5.30 a.m.

Hammond was one of the first affiliate members of the AUSTRALIAN INSTITUTE OF LANDSCAPE ARCHITECTS, becoming an honorary fellow in 1974. In 1987 he received the Victorian Landscape Contractors Association's inaugural

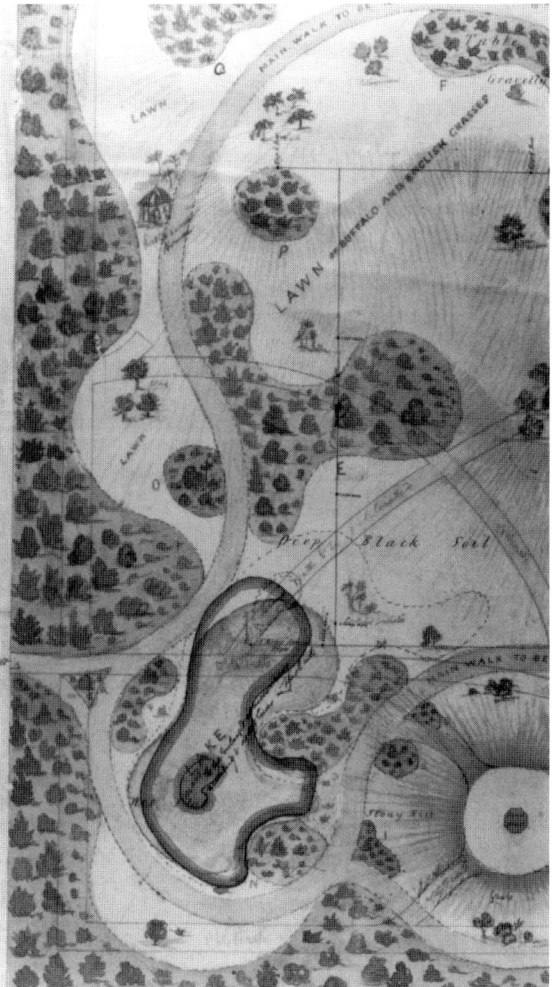

This detail of William GUILFOYLE's plan for HAMILTON BOTANIC GARDENS (1881) reveals his mode of sketching over a base plan provided by the client—here the rigid design of the 1870s is overlaid with the suggested picturesque layout of sinuous paths, shrubberies, and lake

award for a distinguished contribution to the landscape industry. There are many Melbourne garden owners who—probably without knowing it—enjoy the benefits of beautifully prepared lawns, perfectly drained paved terraces, and sturdy rock walls originally constructed by the Hammond organisation.

ANNE LATREILLE

HANDASYDE, McMILLAN & CO. (c. 1861–66), seed merchants, nursery proprietors, and florists, traded from Elizabeth Street, Melbourne, and by 1863 their Yarra Nurseries in South Yarra added extensive nursery stock to the business. **Gilbert Handasyde** (c. 1824–1869) grew up on his family's Pinkie Hill Farm at Inveresk, near Edinburgh, and as nursery proprietors and seed merchants the Handasyde name was well known in Scotland. Handasyde emigrated c. 1845, initially proceeding to Jamaica. He arrived in Melbourne in 1853 and by 1857 he was trading there as a merchant.

The life of **Thomas McMillan** (fl. 1854–71) is much more of a mystery. He apparently worked in the British nurseries of Dicksons and Co. and Drummond and Sons before emigrating. The first definite record of McMillan trading in Melbourne is an extended article in the RURAL MAGAZINE in 1855, where he was noted as a 'seedsman and nurseryman'. His 1860 catalogue, comprising a *Select List of Flower Seeds sold by McMillan & Co.* included close to 200 species and cultivars not previously listed by Victorian nurseries. NORTH AMERICAN plants, particularly from the western United States and Mexico, made up a quarter of the new introductions. In 1859, two booklets written by McMillan were published. One was *Plain and Practical Hints on the Cultivation and Management of the Melon, Cucumber, Gourd, and Vegetable Marrow*. The other, *Rule's Economical Gardening for Cottagers; Being Concise Directions for Cultivating Useful Culinary Vegetables*, was written for John RULE who in 1850 had established the Victoria Nursery in Richmond.

Handasyde, McMillan & Co. was responsible for introducing a range of plants to Victorian horticulture. The 1864 and 1865 catalogues included many species not previously listed by Victorian nurseries. Species from the Americas, especially from North America, featured strongly. The company also demonstrated a keen interest in AUSTRALIAN FLORA, listing almost sixty species indigenous to many parts of Australia. The short-lived partnership ended in 1866. Handasyde continued trading as a seed merchant and florist, while McMillan formed a new partnership in 1867 with John Grant, trading as Grant and McMillan. This too was short-lived, with Grant forming another partnership by 1869 with a Mr Cameron at Flemington. McMillan was not listed in the nursery trade again. Frederick William Handasyde (1862–1930) continued his father's interest in horticulture, although not professionally. He was the secretary of the NATIONAL ROSE SOCIETY of Victoria (1905–10).

ROB CROSS

HANDRECK, Kevin Arthur (b. 1938), soil scientist in the CSIRO Division of Soils in Adelaide, has made significant contributions to Australian HORTICULTURE. Through many growing trials and publications, he has been able to identify the physical, nutritional, and irrigation requirements for ornamental plants grown under Australian conditions, thus changing the Australian NURSERY industry. He has published widely, in both the professional and amateur fields. His gardening guide, *Gardening Down Under* (1993), identifies the conditions for best garden growth in southern Australia. *Growing Media for Ornamental Plants and Turf* (1984), co-authored with N.D. Black, is the standard horticultural text for professional understanding of plant growth requirements, especially SOILS. Kevin Handreck is a member of many professional organisations, and is a contributor to the International Plant Propagators' Society. He has a lasting interest in the genus *Begonia*, and is active in Australian begonia societies.

JAMES WILL

HANNAFORD, George (1852–1927), apiarist and orchardist, was born in Hartley Vale (SA), and became overseer of the Government Experimental Farm at Mannahill. In 1880 he moved to Dingo Flat at Cudlee Creek, in the ADELAIDE HILLS, where he established an orchard, engaged in forestry, wattle and hop growing, and developed his Gipsy Apiary with several hundred hives housing imported Italian queen bees. Hannaford was the first South Australian to successfully export apples to England and Germany (1896). A son, Ernest Hayler Hannaford (1879–1955), continued the APICULTURE venture, maintaining 360 colonies of bees, yielding ten tons of honey annually.

DAVID JONES

HANNAFORD, Samuel (1827–1874), bank clerk and botanist, was born in Devonshire, England, where he botanised and published a Flora of his home town, Totnes: *Flora Tottenensis* (1851). Because he suffered ill health, the bank helped with his emigration and employment at the Bank of Australasia in Warrnambool and Geelong (Vic.). He arrived in Australia in 1852. Apparently well educated and versed in English botanical literature and a correspondent of Sir William HOOKER, he brought a library including BROWN's *Prodromus florae Novae Hollandiae* (1810) and SWEET's *Flora australasica* (1827–28). He remained active in botany and wrote *Jottings in Australia* (1856), *Sea and River-side Rambles in Victoria* (1860) and *The Wild Flowers of Tasmania* (1866) 'with a complete list of indigenous ferns and instructions for their cultivation'. He collected plants for Ferdinand MUELLER and seaweeds for the visiting Professor W.H. HARVEY, so that genera and species were named for him. By 1865, married and with several children, he was unable to manage his affairs; he 'borrowed' funds and lost his job as bank teller, but later established himself as a newspaper editor and librarian at the Tasmanian Public Library in Hobart.

Interested in horticulture, Hannaford was editor of the VICTORIAN AGRICULTURAL AND HORTICULTURAL GAZETTE (1857–61) until it ceased due to the lack of funds. Not to be defeated, in 1861 the Horticultural Improvement Association was formed in Geelong with Hannaford as secretary, again editor of the *Transactions of the Horticultural Improvement Association of the Western District* and giving the inaugural address. After two years, due again to lack of funds, the journal also folded, but Hannaford continued to write for the *Illustrated Journal of*

Australasia and Monthly Magazine with unsigned articles. These are frequently duplicated paragraphs taken from his books, or vice versa. Hannaford voiced the sentiment of many early settlers in Australia that they were at a total loss as to the unknown AUSTRALIAN FLORA and the lack of pertinent publications. Acknowledging the great help in his early work, particularly of Mueller and the arrival of the newly published *Flora Tasmaniae* (1855–60) of J.D. Hooker and W.H. Harvey's *Phycologia australica* (1858–63), Hannaford tried to popularise these for the general public in his writings. He was certainly a moving force in bringing gardeners and naturalists of his period together, not only by writing for diverse societies and soliciting others to do so but also by his correspondence to such figures as Daniel BUNCE, Mueller, Ronald GUNN, and Harvey.

SOPHIE C. DUCKER

HARDY, a term used in Britain to signify plants that are able to grow outdoors throughout the year, thus has specific reference to cold tolerance. In Australian horticulture, the term has taken on a more general meaning; it could refer to any or all of a range of CLIMATIC tolerances—such as cold, heat, drought—and is thus non-specific. In this context, the term can be misleading and is less useful in matching plants to a particular site than by making direct reference to individual specific tolerances—for example, being drought tolerant or drought hardy.

ML

HARDY, Thomas (1830–1912), vigneron, was born at Gittisham, Devon, England, and migrated to Adelaide in 1850. First gaining employment under John REYNELL, in 1853 he commenced his VITICULTURE pursuits establishing a Shiraz and Grenache vineyard, together with an orchard, at Bankside, near Adelaide. Hardy produced his first wine in 1857, commenced shipments to England in 1859, and by 1863 his fourteen-hectare vineyard had plantings of Shiraz, Roussillon, Muscat, Mataro, Grenache, and Zante currant. The Zante was a show-piece and Hardy trained the vine to grow some 400 metres over the verandahs and trellises of Bankside. In 1876 Hardy acquired the Tintara Winery in the MCLAREN VALE, originally established by A.C. KELLY, and expanded the vineyard into some 220 hectares of vines that excelled in their production of burgundies and clarets. In 1887 Thomas Hardy & Sons Pty Ltd was formed, an award-winning company with a London distribution agent. By 1895 Hardy's was the largest wine producer in the colony, producing more than 1.5 million litres of wine. An advocate of wine growing, Hardy toured and lectured extensively in Europe, America, and South Africa, became acquainted with the latest vine disease research in Britain and at Montpellier Viticultural College, and published widely, including *Notes on Vineyards in America and Europe* (1885) and *A Vigneron Abroad: Trip to South Africa* (1899).

James J. Hardy (1856–1904) continued his father's work, supervising the family company and promoting wine cultivation. The Bankside winery was destroyed by fire in 1904. The company also acquired additional vineyards at Dorrien (BAROSSA VALLEY), Waikerie (RIVERLAND), and Keppoch (COONAWARRA), and acquired the major Western Australian wine exporter, Emu Wine Holdings, in 1976 before merging to form BRL Hardy Ltd.

Hardy & Sons Ltd, *The Hardy Tradition* (Adelaide, 1953)

DAVID JONES

HAROLD BOAS GARDENS, West Perth, commemorates pioneering architect and town planner, and Perth city councillor, Harold BOAS. The design, by landscape architects BLACKWELL and Cala (1973), remodelled one of Perth's early PUBLIC GARDENS, Delhi Square (1900). Flowing spaces and undulating landforms integrate old and new plantings, creating a richly varied and enclosed environment. An artificial watercourse flows through a valley formed in the centre of the site, providing a focus. The sight and sound of running WATER are rare attractions in the Perth climate and help to create a tranquil respite from the surrounding urban environment.

PHILIP PALMER

HARRIS, Joseph (1833–1925), horticulturist, nursery proprietor, and politician, was born in Henbury, near Bristol, England, from an eighteenth-century family of nursery proprietors in Taunton and Bristol. His father had a three-acre (1.2 ha) nursery—still called Nursery Gardens—and a Bristol seed shop. REPTON's Blaise Castle landscape, adjoining his school, Henbury Grammar, was an early influence on him.

Coming to Melbourne in 1854, he pushed his luggage ashore in his wheelbarrow, journeyed to Korong, found no gold, and returned to work at Smith and ADAMSON's Melbourne seed shop. About 1862 be bought their Floral Nursery, backing onto Caroline Street from Punt Road, South Yarra. His tinted photo-card shows this early Victorian house and glasshouse with one of the city horse cabs that passed every ten minutes. Profiting from land prices, he sold out in 1870, buying HANDASYDE AND MCMILLAN's nursery in Yarra Street, and Lee Villa, Avoca Street. In 1873 he became a St Kilda councillor, then twice mayor. He was extricated from bankruptcy in the 1880s by his son-in-law, the Belgium Consul, but nevertheless retired in 1885, a man of means, to his Marina Cove estate at Mornington. From 1880 for twenty-nine years he was in turn a member of the Legislative Assembly for St Kilda then South Yarra; was for twenty-five years horticultural editor of the *AUSTRALASIAN*; served for twenty years on the Metropolitan Parks and Gardens Committee; and acted as chairman of the Board of Vegetative Disease Control and government nominee on the Horticultural Board of Advice.

Widely travelled in northern Australia, the Pacific Islands, and Europe, his 1865 catalogue contained plants from New Caledonia and the Chatham Islands. It offered transport of plants indigenous to Australia in WARDIAN CASES to Europe, China, and South America, and claimed that he raised the largest pot-grown plants in Victoria, unlike 'half-starved' stock from Sydney. On his land at Mount Martha summit, earlier intended for a governor's marine residence, he planted *Pinus canariensis* (Canary Island Pine) *c.* 1867, and later gave 200 trees to Mount Martha Park. He brought cork oak from Tuscany and tea from Ceylon; with Ferdinand MUELLER, whom he helped keep in office, he experimented in plants for

MELBOURNE BOTANIC GARDENS. His listed plantings of now-immense araucarias, *Waterhousea floribunda* (Weeping Lilly Pilly), rare *Afrocarpus falcatus*, and *Cassine crocea*, are in the eighty-six acres (35 ha) left to the Scouts as Joseph Harris Park.

Harris, with William GUILFOYLE and Mueller, gave public lectures at Burnley Horticultural College, and in 1891, in 'Undeveloped Sources of Wealth', he espoused horticultural education for women and other far-sighted ideas. His home, Marina, with blackamoors at the entrance, 'relics and records', and a famous cypress hedge, was burnt in 1915; only the Japanese tea-house escaped. With BRUNNING, CHEESEMAN, and former employees RIMINGTON and NOBELIUS, Harris helped build Victoria's impressive early nursery trade.

PHYL FRAZER SIMONS

HARRIS, Thistle Yolette (1902–1990), educator, botanist, author, and conservationist, was born in Sydney and became a passionate advocate of AUSTRALIAN FLORA and fauna. She was educated at Redlands School, Cremorne, and at the University of Sydney, and after several years as a science teacher in secondary schools became a lecturer in science education at Sydney Teachers' College (1938–61). She was awarded a Master of Education degree (1945) and studied for a Diploma in Landscape Design (1968–69) at the University of New South Wales; at the age of 83 she was awarded an honorary doctorate by the University of Wollongong.

Thistle Harris, as a girl of sixteen, met the naturalist David STEAD when taken to a meeting of the New South Wales Naturalists' Society by a teacher. Thus began a long relationship, working together in the Wild Life Preservation Society of Australia and for other causes. She became his third wife in 1951 following the death of his second wife, but had been living with Stead at his home in Watson's Bay since 1939.

As an author of books on the Australian flora, Harris was an early advocate for the growing of Australian native plants in the garden. Her first book, *Wildflowers of Australia* (1938), with coloured plates by Prussian-born pharmacist, Adam Forster (*olim* Karl Ludwig August Wiarda) (1848–1928), was ahead of its time, and *Australian Plants for the Garden* (1953) met a growing need for people interested in growing native plants, even though the text had shortcomings. A passion for the high country took Harris to Kosciuszko every summer for many years, and after visits to the high country in Tas. she produced *Alpine Plants of Australia* (1970). Three volumes of *Gardening with Australian Plants* (1977–80) followed.

Following David Stead's death (1957), Harris was anxious to establish a fitting memorial for this early conservationist, so she established a wildlife sanctuary called Wirrimbirra at Bargo, south of Sydney, in 1963, and the David G. Stead Memorial Wildlife Research Foundation of Australia undertook its management. In 1965, anxious to preserve the sanctuary for the future, she donated the property to the NATIONAL TRUST OF AUSTRALIA (New South Wales) with the Foundation as manager. School children were encouraged to visit the sanctuary for educational purposes, and volunteers acted as educational officers. In 1971, with financial assistance from the Gould League of New South Wales, a building was erected to act as a Field Studies Centre, and in 1973 a teacher from the Education Department was appointed to be a full-time education officer. Thus her dream of a sanctuary that was also an educational facility was realised, and from the time of her retirement (1961) until her death Harris worked tirelessly on behalf of Wirrimbirra.

Joan Webb, *Thistle Y. Harris (A Biography of Thistle Yolette Stead)* (Chipping Norton, NSW, 1998)

JOAN WEBB

HARRISON, Edward: see DAWSON, George Russell

HARTMANN, Carl Heinrich (d. 1891), nursery proprietor, arrived in Qld *c*. 1865 and worked as a gardener at Middle Range, Toowoomba, part of a large German community on the DARLING DOWNS. By the late 1870s Hartmann had opened the Range Nursery, specialising in fruit trees (particularly oranges). He was a frequent contributor to the horticultural press and was active in local horticultural circles, being an office bearer of the Darling Downs Horticultural Association in its formative years. His *Travels & Adventures in the Gulf Country and New Guinea: with an account of the New Guinea Mission* (1887) paints him as an intrepid botanist and plant hunter. His splendid collection of crotons, ferns, and palms, collected in part with Louis BERNAYS and botanist Wilhelm Bäuerlen, was destroyed on the return voyage:

> I watched the grand but disastrous phenomenon of wave after wave dashing over the ship … My feelings at this time are easier imagined than described, when I saw the sea-water trickling over my splendid collection of plants … I went below and stripped off my wet clothes and donned pajamas only, in case of accident to be ready for the swim. Mr Douglas and I now went to have some tea and biscuits.

RA

HARVEY, William Henry (1811–1866) botanist, was born in Summerville, Limerick, Ireland. He had an early botanical association with Sir William HOOKER and as colonial treasurer in South AFRICA published *Genera of South African Plants* (1838), forerunner of *Flora Capensis*, the important publication with Otto Wilhelm Sonder (1812–1881); their three volumes appeared during 1859–65. He named among others the garden plant *Mackaya bella* and was a skilled lithographer, thus illustrating his numerous books. Appointed to Trinity College, Dublin—first as keeper of the HERBARIUM and later professor of botany—he specialised in and published on seaweeds. In 1854–56 he travelled in Australia's southern states and the Pacific Islands collecting a herbarium to finance his travels, describing in his letters people and plants in the bush and in private gardens. He was a contributor to all the volumes of Joseph Hooker's *Botany of the Antarctic Voyage* (1844–60). Harvey's Australian letters are published in *The Contented Botanist* (1988).

SOPHIE C. DUCKER

HARWOOD, George (1842–1915), gardener, was born at Taunton, Somerset, England, and trained at the nurseries of Keems, Williams and Co. He arrived in Sydney in 1862 and was employed by H.B. BRADLEY at Paddington. Director

Charles MOORE appointed Harwood to the staff of the SYDNEY BOTANIC GARDENS in 1873 to work in the hothouses; he was promoted to overseer (1884) superintendent (1891), and during Joseph MAIDEN's absence overseas in 1900–01, acting director. Shy but competent, he retired in 1914: the exacting Maiden felt that with the exception of Moore, Harwood had 'been more concerned in development of the Botanic Gardens than any other man ... I shuddered lest he be taken away from me in the early years of my Directorship'. The cultivar *Hibiscus rosa-sinensis* 'George Harwood' was named in his honour, and its image embellished a lavish illuminated address presented to him by his colleagues on his retirement.

COLLEEN MORRIS

HASCOMBE, Mount Macedon, Vic., was established as a SUMMER RETREAT during the period 1874–76 by Robert Lewis John Ellery (1827–1908), government astronomer and leading member of Victoria's scientific community. The property passed through several hands, including solicitor Robert Selman Whiting (who owned neighbouring ALTON during 1924–27), before long ownership and development by Sir Thomas and Lady Ramsay (1940s–80s)). The highest garden on MOUNT MACEDON, Hascombe epitomises the terraced HILL-STATION style of the Victorian era and is notable for its collections of mature rhododendrons, conifers, copper beeches, Japanese maples, and species such as *Pseudopanax crassifolius* introduced from NEW ZEALAND at the start of the twentieth century. The property, encompassing ten hectares, five and a half of which are gardened, retains many fine trees, including *Abies pindrow* (West Himalayan Fir), *Ulmus glabra* 'Horizontalis', *Agathis australis* (New Zealand Kauri), and a pair of *Taxus baccata* 'Fastigiata' (Irish Yew). Fortunately Hascombe survived the 1983 bushfires with little damage and, now owned by Lindsay and Paula Fox, the steep hillside woodland areas have been naturalised with plantings of rare, cool-climate bulbs, such as *Cardiocrinum*, *Erythronium*, anemone, *Galanthus*, and *Fritillaria* species; herbaceous borders have been extended and innovative plantings flower for an extensive period throughout summer. The nineteenth-century working areas of the property are remarkably intact and include gardener's cottage, stables, and vegetable and picking gardens.

PENNY DUNN

HATELEY, Garnet Alexander Stanley (1883–1960), was a pioneer grower of AUSTRALIAN PLANTS. He grew mostly EUCALYPTS in the plantation he established in the 1940s on his property near Stawell (Vic.). Believed to contain approximately 200 species of eucalypt, the plantation was very well known during his lifetime, but has now largely disappeared. 'Garney' Hateley was not a field collector of species, but compiled his collection by corresponding with other pioneer enthusiasts such as George ALTHOFER and David GORDON.

JOHN WALTER

HAWKINS, William Richard (*c.* 1860–1948), nursery proprietor, was born at Weymouth, Dorset, England, and came to Victoria in his youth. He worked with many Melbourne nursery proprietors, including Thomas LANG and W.R. VIRGOE. He leased John Holt's Sand Hill nursery at Kew for some years and then worked at Bendigo with G.W. KNIGHT.

The upper LAKE at HASCOMBE, Mount Macedon (Vic.) provides a serene vantage point at the highest point of this terraced HILL-STATION garden

He later took over his father's business at Brighton, transferring to Box Hill, where he specialised in tomato plant growing. Hawkins wrote for the *Journal of Horticulture of Australasia*, became a key figure in Melbourne's Garden Week FESTIVAL, acted as secretary of the Brighton Horticultural Society and vice-president of the Royal Horticultural Society of Victoria for more than thirty years, and was a long-time member of the Nurserymen and Seedsmens' Association of Victoria. On his death, the *Age* described Hawkins as 'one of the state's best known horticulturalists', while E.E. PESCOTT acknowledged his valuable help in compiling 'Pioneers of Horticulture in Victoria' (1940). RA

HAWTER, Jacob (1863–1926), horticulturist and nursery proprietor, was born in Switzerland, and worked as a foreman horticulturist at Crystal Palace, London, in 1882, before making his way to WA in 1887. Hawter, along with fellow countryman and nurseryman Charles Lauffer (d. 1903), established Helena River Nurseries later that year. Contemporary accounts relate the arduous labour by these men as they cleared land, constructed buildings, and established nursery stock. In 1893 the nursery was syndicated, later to become the Helena Vineyards Co. Ltd. In the early 1890s Hawter left to establish the Darling Range Nurseries nearby in Glen Forrest, said to be 'one of the most extensive nurseries of fruit trees and vines in Western Australia'. Advertised in 1901 as 'The "Darling" Nurseries', branches were located at Sawyer's Valley, Harvey, and Mullalyup, the latter known as Blackwood Nursery. CAROLYN MIDDLEMIS

HAYES, William Brelsford (*c.* 1839–1878), amateur horticulturist and the NORTHERN TERRITORY's first government gardener (appointed 1871), was born in Galway, Ireland, and migrated to SA *c.* 1864. As a member of GOYDER's 1868–69 survey party, he planted the Territory's first official garden (on the foreshore of Francis Bay between old Fort Hill and Stokes Hill), within a week of his arrival at the new settlement of Palmerston (now Darwin), using a variety of vegetable seeds brought by German-born Frederick Hermann Heinrich Schultze (*c.* 1804–1902), the expedition's official naturalist. Two further 'subsistence gardens' were planted near Doctor's Gully (1870) and, with the assistance of CHINESE labour, the first EXPERIMENTAL GARDENS (1871) was established about a mile from the Telegraph Station. By the mid-1870s, the Government Gardens provided fresh produce and plants to a growing number of private residents, as well as to 'government officials and the sick'. Despite lack of funding from the South Australian administration, Hayes pioneered experimentation with tropical AGRICULTURE, especially crops of economic value (such as fibres and sugar cane), developed further by his successors, Maurice and Nicholas HOLTZE, at DARWIN BOTANIC GARDENS. He also established the practice of distributing cuttings and plants to prospective agriculturists in the region. Hayes submitted samples of sugar cane, yams and sweet potatoes, and specimens of tree fungi to the EXHIBITIONS in Melbourne (1875) and Philadelphia (1876), and a selection of timbers to Paris (1878). At his death, the nine-acre (3.5 ha) experimental gardens included tropical fruit trees, exotic timbers, and ornamentals, a propagating house, and a gardener's cottage. ANITA ANGEL

HAZLEWOOD, Harry H. (1882–1959) nursery proprietor and rose expert, left school in 1898 and worked at Arthur YATES' seed store in Sussex Street, Sydney, until 1905. He gained experience in the Melbourne nurseries of BRUNNING, CHEESEMAN, and HODGINS, and at the Cremorne Nursery. On returning to Sydney he worked for ROSÉN and as a propagator for VOLLMER and Vessey. Well trained, he established his own nursery in 1908 on a portion of the family orchard at East Carlingford (NSW). Takings for his first trading year (1909) totalled £37. In 1910 Hazlewood entered into an agreement to supply plants to ANDERSON and Co. (previously supplied by SEARL and Sons) and in that year his brother **Walter Gordon Hazlewood** (1884–1980), nursery proprietor and camellia expert, bought a partnership in the nursery for £200. The first catalogue of Hazlewood Bros Nursery was issued in 1911, when their stock of trees, shrubs, and roses totalled 50 000. In 1921 the nursery was expanded, incorporating additional land for rose stock, which amounted to 100 000 plants in 1922. Difficulties created by the 1930s depression were exacerbated by termination of the agreement with Anderson and Co. (1932), but the brothers recovered to become one of Australia's leading retail nurseries, introducing many new plants to Australia and reintroducing others that had not been available for many years. The nursery was moved twice more, to Carlingford and then Dural. The retail business was closed in 1965 and the last catalogue was issued in 1973.

While the brothers co-operated in running the nursery, each had his own area of specialisation. Harry Hazlewood concentrated on ROSES, each year reviewing new roses for the *Australian Rose Annual* (1928–59). He was the second recipient of the T.A. STEWART Memorial Plaque awarded by the NATIONAL ROSE SOCIETIES of Australia and New Zealand. Walter Hazlewood's interest lay in trees and shrubs. CAMELLIAS were his specialty, and he developed the practice of raising them from cuttings; he introduced many CULTIVARS. In 1930 he took cuttings of all the 107 camellias growing at CAMDEN PARK, and after flowering them was able to name sixty-four varieties—the others being seedlings without merit, or duplicates. The results of his investigations were published in various American journals until the Australian and New Zealand Camellia Research Society produced its first annual (1954). He was a founding member of the society and a frequent contributor to its publications. His *Handbook on Trees, Shrubs and Roses* (1960) gave the results of over fifty years' experience.

David (Rex) Hazlewood (1886–1968), landscape designer and teacher, who had been a photographer before joining his brothers (*c.* 1926), was a keen naturalist. He became the firm's landscape designer, providing advice to city and country clients. After leaving the firm (1935) he became a consultant to suburban councils, architects, and private clients. He gave advice to the Remembrance Driveway Committee and designed the planting of the North Parramatta Cemetery and the Warwick

Farm Racecourse. He contributed the chapter 'Garden Design' to *Planning the Australian Homestead* (1947) by Kenneth McConnel, an architect with whom he collaborated. In the early 1950s he lectured on landscape design in relation to planning to students studying for the postgraduate diploma in Town and Country Planning at the University of Sydney. A challenging teacher, he gained the respect of all students, who found the use of NATIVE PLANTS—illustrated by examples of his own work—particularly revealing. Unfortunately, bouts of ill-health curtailed what was for its time an innovative practice.

RICHARD CLOUGH

HEATH, Charles (1867–1948), architect, surveyor, and cemetery planner, was born in Melbourne and after architectural training in the 1890s he took his young family to WA, where he worked at Fremantle Harbour and Geraldton (designing the ESPLANADE there). He returned to Melbourne in 1904 and took up the position of secretary/manager from 1905 of the new FAWKNER CEMETERY. Heath designed the layout based on his extensive investigation of cemeteries overseas, supervised the landscaping, and lived on site (to oversee implementation of his scheme).

Heath's interest in the cemetery was carried on by his son **Frank Heath** (1907–1980), who also developed an influential position as architect, TOWN PLANNER, and CEMETERY reformer in Melbourne. An architect trained at the University of Melbourne, he became secretary of the Cremation Society of Victoria, a member of the American Landscape Association, council member of the Victorian Town Planning Association, an associate of the Royal Institute of British Architects, and correspondent for the International Federation of Housing and Town Planning (based in Brussels). His professional credits included many garden designs for large residences, the Brisbane Crematorium and Gardens of Remembrance, additions to the Melbourne Crematorium, and landscape work at Fawkner and MELBOURNE GENERAL CEMETERY. His publications included *The Trend in Modern Cemetery Development* and, jointly with F.O. Barnett and W.O. Burt, *We Must Go On: A Study in Planned Development and Housing* (1944), as well as a chapter, 'Trees and Modern Town Planning', for E.E. LORD (1948).

ROBERT NICOL

HEDGES The art of TOPIARY, or clipping plants into various shapes, has a long history and was much used in Roman times. Clipping to form a continuous hedge has been the greatest use of this method of plant manipulation, especially to provide a formal framework in the landscape. Extensive use of hedging was made in Renaissance gardens to provide structure and an architectonic quality to gardens, and the various revivals of FORMALITY in gardens, from ITALIANATE to ARTS AND CRAFTS, have drawn strongly on this element. The hedging of plants provides a perfect medium in the landscape to create formal spaces, axes, symmetry, and containment. This latter use has also been extensively used in Australian landscapes to create visual and functional screens, particularly for protection from the wind—and in wider RURAL LANDSCAPES as WINDBREAKS—and as an alternative to FENCING. (Fences were originally prohibited from front boundaries in the ACT, while hedging was permissible; although contributing to the GARDEN CITY concept, many of the species planted were weedy rosaceous subjects, such as *Cotoneaster* spp. and *Pyracantha* spp., which were dispersed by birds into the surrounding native bush.) In addition to structuring the landscape, hedging plants can also add texture and colour. Tapestry plantings, such as the one that lines the entrance driveway at WOMBAT PARK (Vic.), incorporate more than one species in a single hedge to form a mixture of foliage textures and colours.

A wide range of species has been used for hedging, including exotic species such as *Maclura pomifera* (Osage Orange), *Buxus sempervirens* (Box), *Ligustrum ovalifolium* (Privet), *Photinia glabra* (Photinia), and *Cotoneaster* and *Pyracantha* spp, and

The massive cypress HEDGE at BUDA, Castlemaine (Vic.), planted in the 1860s, had by the turn of the century outgrown its intended size, presenting a MAINTENANCE headache for successive generations of gardeners

native AUSTRALIAN PLANT selections such as *Leptospermum* spp. (Tea-tree), *Callistemon* spp. (Bottle Brush), *Pittosporum undulatum* (Sweet Pittosporum)—widely used in the nineteenth century although now an environmental WEED—and *Grevillea*, *Melaleuca*, and *Westringia* spp. The CONIFERS have been widely used for their neat trimmed appearance and dense foliage, especially *Cupressus macrocarpa* (Monterey Cypress), which is fast-growing and forms a hedge of imposing proportions at maturity. CLIMBING PLANTS have also been used for hedging; when a fence is used for support the resultant clipped climber and structure is known as a 'fedge', with many fine examples executed in *Muehlenbeckia complexa* (Wire Vine or Maidenhead Creeper).   ML

HEDGES, (William) Henry (1821–1893), gardener, 'of wide British experience', arrived in Vic. in 1857 and served as head gardener to leading Belfast (Port Fairy) landowner William Rutledge (1806–1876). In 1859 Hedges designed the twenty-four-acre (10 ha) Belfast BOTANIC GARDENS; his plan, since lost and only partially implemented, included serpentine paths and a central oval, around which a carriage drive was later flanked with she-oaks. In 1865 the gardens were described as 'the best out of Melbourne'. Hedges joined the New Zealand gold rush in 1861, and on returning, replaced William ALLITT in 1866 as curator of PORTLAND BOTANIC GARDENS. His removal in 1884 was apparently linked to inappropriate behaviour, which included displaying a 'scarcely decent' statue.   HELEN DOYLE

HEIDE, Bulleen, Vic., was developed from 1934 when art patrons, Sunday (*née* Baillieu) (1904–1981) and John Reed (1901–1981), purchased a weatherboard farmhouse on 15 acres (6 ha) overlooking the Yarra River. The garden they created was central to their lifestyle, and artists they supported (including Sidney Nolan and Joy Hester) were expected to assist with its maintenance and planting. Neil Douglas created a wild garden, and with the help of Sam Atyeo and John Reed an orchard was planted. A friend, Barrett Reid (d. 1995), sympathetically maintained the garden from 1982. The Heide I garden contains mature specimen trees, a walled 'heart' garden, an avenue of Osage Orange (*Maclura pomifera*), and a fine rose collection. In 1967 the Reeds moved to Heide II, where Sunday created a new kitchen garden. Since the Reeds' death, Heide II has operated as a museum for modern art with its grounds embellished by SCULPTURE. A master plan competition design (1998–99), won by O'Connor & Houle (architects) in association with Paterson + Pettus (landscape architects), will link existing and proposed elements and incorporate adjoining Banksia Park.   LINDA HIPWELL

THE HEIGHTS, Newtown, Vic., is a rare surviving example of a mid-nineteenth-century provincial suburban estate. Designed in the GARDENESQUE style, the garden surrounds an elegant prefabricated German timber dwelling constructed between 1854 and 1856 for Charles Ibbotson (*c.* 1813–1883), plant enthusiast and trustee of GEELONG BOTANIC GARDENS (1857–74), and his wife Mary-Anne. On 1.3 hectares overlooking the Barwon River valley and Barrabool Hills, the garden is dominated by conifers and evergreen oaks, including several notable *Quercus ilex* (Holm Oak) and *Pinus halepensis* (Aleppo Pine). The mature tree canopy provides both structure and shade to dense shrubberies that follow narrow, curving gravel paths and create a strong sense of seclusion from the street. The original curving gravel drive lined with mature box hedging retains its separate entrance and exit points.

During 1938–39, the Whyte family redesigned the house, and garden areas in its immediate vicinity. New features, which reflected popular garden trends, included a paved terrace, stone courtyard, circular feature lawn with specimen trees and associated herbaceous perennial and bulb borders, formal pond and fountain, rose arbour walk, and wrought-iron entrance gates. A collection of rare and unusual shrubs and picking garden were regrettably lost through subdivision (1975). Outbuildings from both major ownerships include

The suburban estate of THE HEIGHTS, Newtown (Vic.), photographed during the 1860s and showing the garden after a decade's growth, encapsulated the mid-Victorian love of shrubberies, dark-hued conifers, and carefully placed ornamentation

stables, grooms' cottage, and water tower, and 1930s timber dovecote and elegant garden shed. The property has been owned and managed by the NATIONAL TRUST OF AUSTRALIA (Victoria) since 1975.   CARMEL McPHEE

HEINZE, Kevin Carl (b. 1928), gardener, broadcaster, and author, is dedicated to helping others through gardening. After a career in nurseries, council gardens, and the Melbourne Botanic Gardens from c. 1940—leading to the position of Horticultural Supervisor, Melbourne City Council—he became well known in Vic. for his RADIO and TELEVISION broadcasts. His trademark greeting 'Hello there' and farewell 'Cheerio' as host of *Sow What* on ABV2 (1967–88) set the scene for his gently encouraging, practical guidance for home gardeners. Appointed Gardening Consultant for the Education Department of Victoria in 1975, he was able to pursue his mission to develop CHILDREN's feelings of self-worth through gardening—a role he still cherishes through his interest in SCHOOL GARDEN awards. Inspired by him, the Kevin Heinze Garden Centre, Doncaster, Vic. (1979–) provides, through the efforts of dedicated volunteers, GARDEN THERAPY for disabled and disadvantaged people. Heinze has written several popular gardening books and continues his weekly gardening advice on ABC Radio.

Kevin Heinze with John McArthur, *Cheerio for Now: My Life and Thoughts* (Melbourne, 2000)   HELEN BOTHAM

HENDERSON, Robert (c. 1797–1865), gardener and nursery proprietor, was born in Scotland and arrived as a free settler in NSW in 1826, having been recruited by Alexander McLEAY, the colonial secretary, at the Cape of Good Hope. Later that year the garden of McLeay's official residence in Bridge Street was 'reckoned & with justice, the neatest in Sydney'. McLeay was granted land at Elizabeth Bay in October 1826 and Henderson commenced supervising the development of the grounds for the planned house. A gardener's cottage was erected on this fifty-six-acre (23 ha) estate in 1827, which he occupied while in charge of the workforce—said, at times, to have numbered twenty men. He was also in charge of the development of the grounds at Brownlow Hill near Cobbitty.

In 1831 Henderson married Elizabeth Joslyn Shepherd, eldest daughter of Thomas SHEPHERD, of the Darling Nursery. Shepherd died in 1835, and in accordance with his will Henderson became a trustee of his estate. He left Elizabeth Bay before the house there was completed, and with Shepherd's widow Jane (née Henderson) ran this important nursery until his wife's half-brothers were old enough to take control (the eldest being eleven at the time of his father's death). While doing this, Henderson established the Camellia Grove Nursery in Erskinville Lane, Newtown, and by 1841 was living there with his family. This nursery became renowned for its FLORISTS' flowers and fruit trees. The account given in the *Horticultural Magazine* (1864) recounts the decline of the nursery after the discovery of gold and its subsequent revival after the return of Henderson's son, Robert Theophilus, from the diggings. By this time Henderson was ill, and in 1853 he had relinquished his trusteeship of the Shepherd estate. In an obituary, John GELDING called him 'one of the first and best gardeners of New South Wales … we never came in contact with him without feeling a degree of pleasure at his frankness and cheerfulness'. Thirty-one years earlier Baron von HÜGEL had noted after visiting the ground of Elizabeth Bay House that he was 'an energetic man who lives only for his job'.

While his estate, valued at £2000, was left to be divided equally among his children, Robert Theophilus Henderson (1837–1909), the eldest surviving son, continued the nursery business. He was a very active member of the Horticultural Society of New South Wales and renowned for his ROSES, his collection in the 1860s being the largest in the colony. He raised many new plants, especially DAHLIA varieties, prompting John LOCKLEY to dedicate *Dahlia Growing Made Easy* (1908) to Henderson.   RICHARD CLOUGH

HENDRY, Margaret Janet (1930–2001), landscape architect, trained at BURNLEY in Vic. and Manchester University, and worked under Sylvia CROWE in England. She was active in the formation of the AUSTRALIAN INSTITUTE OF LANDSCAPE ARCHITECTS and worked in CANBERRA for the National Capital Development Commission (1963–73). Foundation senior lecturer in landscape architecture at the Canberra College of Advanced Education (University of Canberra) 1974–87, she has played an active role in promoting, archiving, and researching LANDSCAPE ARCHITECTURE in Australia.   DIANNE FIRTH

HENRY, Kathleen Vivian (Kitty) (1904–1966), garden designer and florist, who became a gardener when it was considered a daring occupation for a woman, landscaped many of Hobart's substantial gardens and established a national reputation as one of the country's leading florists. Growing up in the remote orcharding district of Birch's Bay in southern Tas., her family moved to a rambling old house, Ellington, in the prestigious Hobart suburb of Sandy Bay when she was 16. At 24 she was designing and managing a number of Sandy Bay gardens; she went on to landscape gardens on the established farming properties of Tas., her style a mixture of WALLING and JEKYLL. Her own garden has been described as a multi-layered 'wilderness', crammed with exotic plants and bulbs. Her floral arrangements were much sought after; Queen Elizabeth II on her 1954 visit was so impressed by the bouquets presented to her that she asked to meet the florist, and Henry was presented to the young Queen. Henry was a foundation member of the NATIONAL ROSE SOCIETY in Tas., a floral art lecturer for the Adult Education Board, and a member of the Australian Women's Land Army during the Second World War. After her death, the National Rose Society placed a memorial plaque on a carved sandstone fountain in their rose garden on Hobart Glebe as a tribute to Kitty Henry.   SALLYANN DAKIS

HENTY (née TATTERSFIELD), Carol (1936–1991), garden writer, born in New Zealand, helped awakened public awareness of major Australian and European gardens and landscapes through a series of photo essays for *Belle*

magazine (1974–) undertaken from 1979. Her evocative stories and photographs capture the essence of gardens as diverse as those in the Vatican, Italy; in England; and in Australia at Ballarat, Mount Macedon, Bowral, and Cowra (the Japanese garden). Her interest in GARDEN HISTORY culminated in her book *For the People's Pleasure: Australia's Botanic Gardens* (1988), a pioneering survey of this important resource.
HOWARD TANNER

HENTY, William (1808–1881) horticulturist, solicitor, and politician, was born in West Tarring, Sussex, England. In 1837 he followed his father and five of his brothers to the Australian colonies, settling in Van Diemen's Land at Launceston. He entered into partnership as a solicitor with John Ward Gleadow in 1837. Henty became prominent in horticultural circles in the north of the colony. He was a driving force, with Ronald GUNN, in the Launceston Horticultural Society (founded 1838). Henty was its president 1841–56 (during Gunn's absence in Hobart), and was responsible for negotiating the establishment of the Society's gardens (now CITY PARK). Henty continually lobbied successive colonial governors for funds to support the gardens, with some success. His booklet *On Improvements in Cottage Husbandry* (1849), provided guidance for smallholders in the colonies. In 1856, following the granting of self-government in Tas., he was elected to parliament and served as colonial secretary for six years. He maintained an interest in horticultural activities, and through the Gardeners' and Amateurs' Horticultural Society of Hobart offered prizes for grapes grown in the open air. He resigned his post in 1862 and returned to England, where he died.

Edward Henty (1810–1878), pioneer pastoralist and horticulturist, brother of William, was the first squatter in Vic. He arrived at Portland Bay in 1834 accompanied by a small party and bringing with him a large number of fruit trees, and seeds of vegetables and other plants, which he subsequently planted. He was soon joined by his brother, **Francis Henty** (1815–1889), who brought the first merino sheep to the district. The brothers were chiefly responsible for the establishment of PORTLAND BOTANIC GARDENS; its objectives were to collect native plants of the area and to introduce plants from the other colonies and overseas. Edward, whose town garden BURSWOOD overlooked the Gardens, was said to spend hundreds of pounds each year on obtaining plants from all over the world for his own purposes, giving any surplus to the Gardens in return for other plants to add to his collection. Francis corresponded with many BOTANIC GARDENS, including those in Melbourne, Sydney, and Hobart, in order to promote plant exchanges.

Lynnette Peel (ed.), *The Henty Journals: A Record of Farming, Whaling and Shipping at Portland Bay, 1834–1839* (Carlton, Vic., 1996)
LINDY SCRIPPS

HERBACEOUS BORDERS are regarded worldwide as a key feature of an English FLOWER GARDEN. Comprised of PERENNIAL plants set against a background of dark green HEDGING or a high masonry WALL, carefully arranged to create subtle harmonies and skilfully managed to be in peak bloom over the months of high summer, this display demands high levels of horticultural skill, rich soils, regular water supplies, mild weather conditions, good timing, and a huge palette of plants from which a gardener may compose the planting scheme. Even in England that is quite a task. Advocates with the artistry to design herbaceous borders—such as Gertrude JEKYLL, who remains unsurpassed as a creator of such garden features—assumed the ready availability of high levels of skilled labour and the vast numbers of plants needed to fulfil her schemes. As a practitioner and theoretician Jekyll defined an ideal that has proven difficult to maintain in modern times, and frustrating to implement in many CLIMATES outside the cool-temperate zones of the world. Recent developments of the idea, such as the kidney-shaped island beds advocated by plantsman Alan Bloom in the mid-twentieth century, are no more amenable to transplanting to alien climes than the traditional paired borders, twenty metres long and four metres deep, with a central grassed path edged in stone paving.

More readily adapted to Australian conditions is the idea of a mixed border containing flowering SHRUBS, GRASSES, small CLIMBING PLANTS, FOLIAGE plants, shrub ROSES, small TREES, BULBS, and ANNUALS (often found in COTTAGE GARDENS). Developed after the Second World War in England in response to shortages of skilled labour and plants, the idea has as its strongest and most creative designer Christopher Lloyd (b. 1921). His vigorous approach to mixing all manner of plants and experimenting with hot colours and TROPICAL foliage effects has energised gardeners everywhere to move on from the traditional herbaceous border. More recent European developments include the use of mixed herbaceous perennials within a grassy matrix to provide a rich tapestry of colour to mimic and enhance natural grassland scenes, especially those of the American prairies and European meadows, and simultaneously reduce MAINTENANCE, which constrains the wide use of the traditional herbaceous border in contemporary landscapes.

In Australia, David Glenn (b. 1943) of Lambley Perennials Nursery, Ascot (Vic.) has been a significant importer of plants selected for their ability to perform well under Australian conditions, and a leading proponent of the mixed border. He has introduced many hybrids of his own raising, especially *Agapanthus* 'Jehan', *Geranium* 'Criss Canning', *Kniphofia* 'James Nottle', and foliage plants such as *Marrubium* 'Scallop Shell'. Among his most adaptable imports have been many grasses, sedums, and yuccas. Graham Roger Cooke (b. 1942) of Romantic Cottage Gardens, Frankston (Vic.), has sought to introduce a range of perennials that will perform well in summer heat and drought without heavy, frequent irrigation. Jeremy Mark Francis (b. 1951) has developed a pair of mixed borders based on the traditional model at his Cloudehill garden in Olinda (Vic.), incorporating contemporary garden art; his evolving design consciously strives to redefine the ideal with plants generally tolerant of Australian conditions. Many herbaceous perennials suited to Australian conditions have become environmental weeds, however, and their introduction into the garden thus requires careful screening.
TREVOR NOTTLE

HERBARIUM This is essentially a plant museum, where specimens of all kinds of PLANTS (including flowering plants, ferns, fungi, mosses, liverworts, lichens, and marine and freshwater algae) are stored for scientific study. Most are preserved as dried, pressed specimens, either entire plants when small, or representative parts when large (for example, shrubs and trees). They are identified and stored, usually mounted on large sheets of stiff paper, all specimens of each species, together, in folders or packets in pigeon-holes. For some samples, liquid preservation is preferable, commonly in alcohol-based fluid. Each collection bears a label with the scientific name of the plant, locality, and habitat where it was found, the name of the collector and date, and data on the plant not evident from the specimen (such as size, flower colour, scent). The ultimate goal is an accurately named collection that represents the complete range of variation and geographical occurrence of every species (including naturalised plants) in a region such as a state or country. Stored under suitable conditions, plant specimens last for hundreds of years.

In Australia, all major herbaria are public institutions in government departments or under statutory authorities, most being associated with BOTANIC GARDENS. Many universities have smaller collections. There is also a tendency towards small regional herbaria managed by local volunteers. Many fine private collections have also been assembled.

Herbaria are staffed by taxonomists or systematic BOTANISTS (whose role is to study the classification and relationships of plants), by specialists with tasks such as molecular analysis, and by curators and technicians. Staff may also include ecologists (who study plants in relation to their environment) and artists. The results of research are published as scientific papers and books. These range from descriptions of new species to reviews of particular groups of plants (such as a genus or family), or all the plants of a defined geographic area or vegetation type (for example, the Sydney region, or mangroves). The published synthesis of the taxonomic information on the plants of a region is known as a Flora. Herbaria maintain comprehensive LIBRARIES of botanical books and journals, in which the names, classification, and other aspects of botanical research have been published.

Many herbaria provide a service for business and the public, identifying plant specimens and supplying information on every species discovered in their region. Because large areas of Australia have not been thoroughly explored botanically, and because there are relatively few botanists, it will be many decades before herbaria approach their goal of complete coverage. For lesser-known groups such as fungi and algae, only a small proportion is known of the species believed to occur.

The first public herbarium in Australia was established in Melbourne in 1853. Until then, all specimens (such as those collected on Cook's and Flinders' voyages) had been taken or sent to European herbaria, where most remain to this day. There are now major herbaria in all state and territory capitals, as well as smaller ones in other towns and university botany departments. In general, each concentrates on the plants of its particular region. ALEX GEORGE

HERBERT, Desmond Albert (1898–1976), Melbourne-born botanist and educator, was appointed government botanist in WA in 1918. He lectured in agricultural botany at the University of Western Australia before accepting a professorship in plant physiology and plant pathology at the University of the Philippines (1921). He moved to the University of Queensland in 1924 as lecturer, and then foundation Professor of Botany (1948–65). His influence on agricultural and botanical students and the development of AGRICULTURE in Qld was significant. His interest in the influence of CLIMATE on geographical plant distribution was first expressed in his doctoral thesis and recurred in several publications. He was a vital and well-liked member of local scientific and horticultural groups. As part of the war effort, Herbert was co-author (with C.T. WHITE and R.E.P. Dwyer) of *Friendly Fruits and Vegetables* (1943), an early 'bush food' manual for the Royal Australian Air Force. His genial nature and skill at communicating were in great demand: he lectured on horticulture for the Australian Broadcasting Commission and wrote garden advice for the *Sunday Mail*. His book, *Gardening in Warm Climates* (1952),

Desmond HERBERT's book *Gardening in Warm Climates* (1952), its cover featuring a typical TROPICAL garden, was a major contribution to Australian gardening and horticultural literature by this Brisbane-based botanist

illustrated with photographs by J.R. BAILEY, was targeted at gardeners in the subtropical 'Brisbane Zone', stretching on the coastal strip from Rockhampton (Qld), south to Grafton (NSW)—'the zone in which the jacaranda grows to perfection'—and filled a void among Australian GARDENING BOOKS.

Herbert's daughter, **Joan Winifred** (b. 1930), and her husband **Alan Bridson Cribb** (b. 1925), both botanists, have worked closely in the sphere of NATURAL HISTORY. Together they have published a definitive series of books on NATIVE PLANTS and their properties: *Wild Food in Australia* (1975), *Useful Wild Plants in Australia* (1981), and *Wild Medicine in Australia* (1981).

JEANNIE SIM

HERB GARDENS The first herb garden in Australia was established in 1788 at Sydney Cove to provide medicinal plants for the first colonial HOSPITAL to supplement medical supplies brought with the First Fleet. This garden failed to thrive. Subsequent arrivals brought sufficient supplies to reduce the need for locally grown herbs. Most colonists grew familiar herbs such as sweet bay, marshmallow, garlic, plantain, horehound, calendula, fennel, yarrow, briar roses, and mint to treat illness and to provide flavourings and fragrances for the home. Many of these escaped to become WEEDS. Some doctors grew herbs such as opium poppy, peppermint, hemlock, rue, lavender, and deadly nightshade, but for much of the nineteenth and twentieth centuries doctors, herbalists, and colonists relied extensively on imported botanicals, extracts, isolates, synthetic drugs, and proprietary medicines. People in country areas grew medicinal herbs, but treatment relied as much on substances found in the pantry as in the garden.

The focus was not on herb gardens as such; herbs were simply included wherever possible in ornamental or KITCHEN GARDENS. Lavender, rosemary, thyme, calendula, pinks, geraniums, wormwood, and other fragrant herbs featured prominently in FLOWER GARDENS, while garlic, parsley, thyme, sage, marjoram, and mint were grown among vegetables. Box and thyme were favoured for HEDGES.

The need to supplement scarce drugs during two world wars revived interest in the wider use of herbs. Writing in the first edition of *Your Garden* magazine in 1947, herbalist Edith COLEMAN reflected on the history and usefulness of herbs and encouraged readers to develop gardens specifically for them.

By the mid-1950s, several small herb nurseries were supplying a limited range of common herbs. In 1955 Felix Mermet of Glenelwyn Herbal Farm, Gundarene via Coramba (NSW), self-published *Culinary, Scented and Medicinal Herbs: Description, Cultivation and Uses*—a booklet said to be the first on herbs published in Australia. In that year Rosemary (b. 1922) and John Hemphill (b. 1918) established Somerset Cottage, Dural (NSW), which became well-known as a specialist herb nursery with neatly laid-out display gardens. In 1959 Rosemary Hemphill's book *Fragrance and Flavour* was published to international acclaim. This, and her subsequent books, stimulated widespread interest in herbs in the 1960s and 1970s.

The 1970s and 1980s saw the popularisation of herbal medicine, the publication of numerous books and articles on herbs, and the formation of a number of herb societies. Herb gardens became popular in private as well as public gardens and parks. Design ranged from informal to formal with gardens often reflecting a theme, such as medicinal or culinary. While most herbs were of European origin, the 1980s and 1990s saw the introduction of many species from ASIA and the Americas. Herbs as ornamental and useful plants are at the height of their popularity today.

Kim Fletcher, *Herbs in Australian Gardens* (Fitzroy, Vic., 1988)

KIM FLETCHER

HERGOTT SPRINGS and **Lake Harry** were the sites of major *Phoenix dactylifera* (Date Palm) PLANTATION experiments in SA. Initially advocated by J.E. BROWN in *Plantings of … Dates in the Far North* (1885), the plantation at Hergott Springs (now Marree) was commenced in 1887 by Brown. He was assisted with donations from William GUILFOYLE and the French government, later with Algerian Sahara and Tunis provenance species, which proved successful in growth and harvests under conservator Walter GILL, but were reliant upon bore water that varied in salinity levels. Labour shortages, water problems, and the First World War combined with a severe drought and dust storms to devastate the 300 palms in 1914. The Lake Harry plantation, established in 1891 on nearby Muloorina Station, consisting of some 2700 trees, suffered the same fate as Hergott Springs.

DAVID JONES

HERITAGE PLACES in the Australian context are those places considered to have cultural significance, defined by the BURRA CHARTER as 'aesthetic, historic, scientific, social or spiritual value for past, present or future generations'. They are places that we judge worthy of retention and CONSERVATION as evidence of our heritage. Many landscapes and gardens constitute heritage places but have, in general, received less attention than other types such as buildings.

An important consideration when establishing cultural significance is to determine to whom the place may have significance. It may be significant to an individual, to a minority group or local community, to the state or nation, or it may have international significance as exemplified by World Heritage sites. 'Place' is this sense is defined as meaning 'site, area, land, landscape, building or other work, group of buildings or other works and may include components, contents, spaces and views'. Increasingly, intangible values—such as social or spiritual value to a community—have became important markers of heritage, and gardens and landscapes such as Thoreau's Walden Pond or The Cross at MOUNT MACEDON demonstrate this symbolic value.

Heritage landscapes are diverse in scale and attributes, but often present shared dilemmas. Wilderness areas and natural landscapes are arguably the best identified, and are primarily defended using scientific information. They may also have great AESTHETIC VALUE and a wonderful sense of space and isolation, but these values are harder to defend. Landscapes of Aboriginal significance are often viewed with Eurocentric eyes as natural landscapes, but may be rich in cultural meaning as cultural sites. Agricultural and pastoral landscapes demonstrate post-European settlement changes to the broader landscape. Even mining and FORESTRY landscapes may have heritage value. Parks and gardens are probably the largest and best-known category of heritage landscape places.

An understanding of heritage landscapes implies an understanding of natural processes overlain by cultural features. Much of our difficulty in dealing with landscape heritage stems from the fact that landscapes embody a confusing mix of so-called natural and cultural features. On one hand we have natural landscapes predominantly set aside for values relating to ecology and biodiversity. On the other, landscapes such as CULTURAL LANDSCAPES are considered to be of value in demonstrating human habitation over time.

Theory relating to heritage places in the landscape has arisen from both architectural conservation and nature conservation. These two strands embody very different points of view, and provide a wide range of theory and practice with which to understand and conserve heritage places.

Graeme Davison and Chris McConville, *A Heritage Handbook* (North Sydney, 1991); Michael Pearson and Sharon Sullivan, *Looking after Heritage Places: The Basics of Heritage Planning for Managers and Administrators* (Carlton, Vic., 1995); C. Michael Hall and Simon McArthur (eds), *Heritage Management in Australia and New Zealand: The Human Dimension* (Melbourne, 1996)   JAN SCHAPPER

THE HERMITAGE, Narbethong, Vic., the HILL-STATION developed from 1894 by German-born ethnographic and landscape PHOTOGRAPHER John William Lindt (1845–1926), was a key tourist destination that did much to popularise the forests and FERN gullies of the Black Spur and Healesville area. Lindt selectively retained existing trees and ferns, interplanting with exotics in terraced beds, around a lily pond, and on open banks. The garden was approached through a rustic LICH-GATE and, drawing on memories of his New Guinea and OCEANIAN photographic excursions (1885–92), Lindt created a network of elevated walkways over gullies linking TREE HOUSES in the towering *Eucalyptus regnans* (Mountain Ash). The garden retains massive specimens of *Cryptomeria japonica* 'Elegans' and *Eucalyptus cypellocarpa* (Mountain Grey Gum) and fine examples of *Tilia X europaea* (Linden) and *Abies nordmanniana* (Caucasian Fir). Following Lindt's death, The Hermitage was used as a guest house, for a time owned by BURNLEY graduate Joan Anderson, who, with later sympathetic owners (including John and Valerie Stafford), venerated and conserved this outstanding estate.

Shar Jones, *J.W. Lindt: Master Photographer* (Melbourne, 1985)
                                  RA

HERONSWOOD, Dromana, Vic., enjoys a spectacular site, north-facing to the sea, yet protected from prevailing southerly winds by Arthurs Seat. The Gothic-revival house of the 1860s, built for Professor William Edward Hearn (1826–1888), was designed by Edward La Trobe BATEMAN, who is also credited with its landscaping. Many of the fine, large trees including a *Ficus macrophylla* (Moreton Bay Fig), cypresses, and araucarias, significantly the *Araucaria columnaris* (Cook Island Pine), date from this period. In the valley below, Hearn established an orchard, from which mulberry, apple, and pear trees survive. Heronswood was also the home, from 1903 to 1929 of Henry Bournes Higgins (1851–1929), judge and brother of Ina HIGGINS, who added a tennis court below the driveway. Palms and Himalayan cedars, still prominent in front of the house, were planted in the 1930s.

Photographer J.W. Lindt, famed for his ethnographic photographs in New Guinea, recreated a hilltop 'village' in the 1890s, complete with TREE HOUSES and aerial walkways, at THE HERMITAGE, Narbethong (Vic.)

In 1983 Clive Blazey (b. 1944)—son of Alan Blazey (1911–1983), founder in 1935 of Hortico—and his wife Penny (b. 1946) purchased Heronswood as a home and base for their mail order garden club and seed business, Diggers Club (1978–). They have developed the garden from a seaside holiday landscape to a DISPLAY GARDEN of eight different rooms, featuring cottage annuals, vegetables, and perennials for a dry climate. Seed is imported from sources worldwide with a particular emphasis on heirloom vegetable varieties. In 1996 the Blazeys purchased the Garden of St Erth, Blackwood (Vic.), from Tommy GARNETT, and have rejuvenated this goldfields garden, incorporating autumn borders as well as spring bulb displays.   CHRISTINE REID

HEYNE, Ernst Bernhard (1825–1881), botanist and horticulturist, was born in Meissen, Saxony, the son of doctor. He graduated from the University of Leipzig with a diploma in botany and was said to be an accomplished mathematician and linguist. He gained practical experience in the plant sciences working at the Royal Botanic Gardens, Dresden, and was to have led a botanical expedition to Spain but this was cancelled due to the political upheaval of 1848. Heyne's brother, Carl, fled to the USA in 1848 after killing an officer in a duel. While not implicated himself, Heyne decided he also would emigrate. He left Hamburg for Melbourne, where he arrived in 1849, after serving a family as tutor on the voyage. His letters describing the voyage, the Australian landscape, and society, together with advice for migrants, were published in German as *Australia Felix* (Dresden, 1850). His widowed mother, who ran a school in Dresden, and his sister Agnes, both followed in 1851. In Melbourne his mother continued her career as a teacher while Heyne, after working as a gold escort officer, was appointed chief plantsman at MELBOURNE BOTANIC GARDENS in 1854.

After Ferdinand MUELLER became director of these Gardens in 1857, Heyne worked as his secretary and assistant, accompanying him on collecting trips in southern Australia. He is commemorated by *Aster heynei* (now *Olearia xerophila*), and *Cyperus heynei* (now *Cyperus ornatus*). Heyne is credited with finding a specimen of the tree fern *Dicksonia antarctica* (now extinct in SA) in 1870 on the southern slopes of the Mount Lofty Ranges. His collection of South Australian seaweeds, considered important, is now lost, and his large HERBARIUM was destroyed after his death.

Moving to Adelaide in 1869, Heyne purchased a property at Norwood for a nursery and opened a city shop in Rundle Street for seed and plant sales. Trade was assisted by the prosperity of the 1870s, boom years for the South Australian economy, and an expanding housing market that witnessed increased spending on domestic gardens. Heyne not only provided plants and seeds suitable for local conditions but helped to educate people about gardening techniques. His *Fruit, Flower and Vegetable Garden* (1871) was enlarged into the *Amateur Gardener for South Australia* (1877), which ran into four editions. Heyne set out some general rules for gardening; they allowed for varying conditions in different parts of the colony, and provided guidance for its MEDITERRANEAN climate. He proposed suitable plants for the kitchen garden and home orchard, recommended the way to prepare the ground, and advised when different varieties could be planted. For the flower garden and for general design he instructed his readers to consider the habits of plants, whether they were tall, compact, or slow-growing. He discussed different varieties of edging, lawn, and hedging plants, plants for verandahs and trellises, the use of native species, how paths should be made, and ribbon borders designed. He listed hardy plants suitable for outdoor planting and others suitable for shade houses and glasshouses, finishing with a monthly calendar, sections of which were often printed in the local newspapers. This was a significant publication of its time in Australia, more so for its sound regional advice. It was informed by the educational policies of Prussia, where practical horticulture was taught in primary schools and where dependence on good soil care was recognised by successive generations.

Heyne became secretary to the Vignerons' Club; the grateful club presented him with a gold watch in 1876. He contributed regular articles for the *South Australian Register*, the *Observer* and specialist publications, paying especial attention to forage plants, pasture grasses, and forest trees, and to the best methods of treating plant diseases. He published *Vines and their Synonyms* (1869) and, putting his linguistic skills to good use, he translated German, Spanish, and French articles and pamphlets on VITICULTURE. He also contributed to discussions sponsored by the Chamber of Manufactures on trees and crop plants that were suitable for trials in SA, among them sultanas and other vines, tobacco, sunflower, and mulberries (for SERICULTURE), supporting the pleas of his fellow colonists Samuel DAVENPORT and Richard SCHOMBURGK for crop experimentation. Their willingness to experiment and to use knowledge and skills from Europe, North America, and the Cape put SA in the forefront of applied research.

Heyne was one of many migrants from the GERMANIC states who settled in SA and made a significant contribution to botany and the applied sciences of horticulture, viticulture, and agriculture. Among these were Schomburgk,

This bamboo house, a distinctively South Australian version of the BUSH-HOUSE, illustrated by E.B. HEYNE in his book *The Amateur Gardener* (1881), used closely spaced bamboo stalks rather than timber laths to create a shady GREENHOUSE

Friedrich KRICHAUFF, M.P.F. Basedow, and C.W.L. Muecke, together with Heyne's fellow nursery proprietors, C.F. Neumann (NEWMAN), Ludwig Wertheimer, and Friedrich Seesle. Suffering from the effects of asthma and nearly blind, Heyne sold the Rundle Street business to Wertheimer and Seesle shortly before his death. Part of the business was carried on at the Norwood premises by his wife Maria Wilhemine Laura (née Hanckel) (1842–1934).

Ernst Heyne was survived at the time of his death by three daughters and a son, Carl Franz (1876–1948), who was then a student at the newly established ROSEWORTHY AGRICULTURAL COLLEGE. Carl bought into the Rundle Street business in association with Anderson Potter. His son Franz Waldemar (Wally) Heyne (b. 1913) and grandsons followed him in the nursery business. The Rundle Street shop closed, but under Roger Heyne (b. 1944), son of Wally, Heyne's Nursery (now located in Beulah Park) is still thriving, arguably the longest-running family nursery business in Australia.

PAULINE PAYNE

HIBBERD, (James) Shirley (1825–1890), horticulturist, florist, journalist, and author, was born in Stepney, London. Before the age of 25 he was editing a weekly newspaper and had written *Brambles and Bay Leaves*, essays on rural life. Having married and taken up residence in Pentonville, he soon turned his attention to urban horticulture, the results of which appeared as *The Town Garden: A Manual for the Management of City and Suburban Gardens* (1855). He moved to Stoke Newington in London's then comparatively undeveloped west, where he established an experimental garden and indulged his passion for NATURAL HISTORY. His *Rustic Adornments for Homes of Taste, and Recreations for Town Folk, in the Study and Imitation of Nature* (1856 and later editions) was perhaps his most influential book on the colonial consciousness; its objects were not merely wishful thinking for many in the post-goldrush period, but goals within easy reach. His delight in the apiary, AVIARY, ROCKERY, FERNERY, WARDIAN CASE, and, to a lesser extent, the aquarium, was well suited to Australia's rapidly growing population of urban dwellers. His design advice treated the GARDENESQUE as a mixed style in the manner of KEMP and McINTOSH, and many manifestations of RUSTIC-WORK can be traced to his general influence. He edited *Floral World* (1858–75) and the *Gardeners' Magazine* (1861–90), which both circulated in the colonies, as did his later books, including *The Fern Garden* (1869) and a series of handbooks for amateur gardeners. Hibbard's career is analysed by Wilkinson in 'The Preternatural Gardener' (*Garden History*, 1998).

RA

HIGGINS, Frances Georgina Watts (Ina) (1858–1948), professional horticulturist, landscape gardener, and feminist, was born in Ireland and migrated to Vic. with her parents and six siblings (the eldest being Henry Bournes Higgins, future justice of the High Court and owner of HERONSWOOD) in 1870. She was among the first intake of female students at the BURNLEY School of Horticulture, and obtained her diploma *c.* 1900. She subsequently toured Europe, studying gardens and horticulture in Britain, France, and Italy. By 1907 Higgins had returned to Melbourne, and was heavily engaged in her role as the honorary secretary to the Victorian committee hosting the first Australian Exhibition of Women's Work. Over the next few years she gained recognition as an accomplished landscape gardener, with several gardens to her credit. Acknowledged at the time as one of the first women to take up gardening and horticulture professionally in Australia, she strongly advocated it as a potential career for women generally—citing its healthy nature and the inherent advantages of the female gardener through deftness and attention to detail. Speaking in 1913, she referred to the aptitude of women for all forms of nursery work and garden design, and the possibilities for their specialising in these fields. Indeed, the main danger that Higgins perceived for the woman gardener or horticulturist was in undervaluing her own skills, and settling for less than equal pay with men. GENDER equality, she argued, should be the basis for a successful co-operative approach to professional horticulture.

DARREN WATSON

HIGGINS, Walter Herbert (1869–1934), Geelong estate agent and bulb merchant, gained his widest fame from DAFFODILS at a time when they were being rapidly developed. He was not a breeder but imported new varieties for growing into marketable stocks. As secretary of Geelong Horticultural Association from 1899 he was instrumental in organising its first bulb show that year. He displayed 100 varieties, and 121 the following year. At his North Shore Bulb Farm he was also growing tulips, hyacinths, anemones, ranunculus, irises, and freesias. In 1908, while mayor of Geelong, he supplied tulips for planting at Government House (STONNINGTON). Catalogues from 1907–25 (held by Royal Botanic Gardens, Melbourne) demonstrate his strong contribution to Australian horticulture.

GEORGE JONES

HIGHFIELD, near Circular Head, Stanley, Tas., built 1832–35 as the residence for Van Diemen's Land Company's first manager, Edward Curr, is an important site in Australian garden history, although little remains of the original garden today. Circular Head was described in 1828 as a place where 'Nature has done everything in variegating this place with hill and dale and making it the most picturesque and best adapted soil for habitation on the North Coast of this island', and by 1833 Highfield possessed 'a pretty flower garden and an extensive and well-stocked kitchen garden'. Henry Hellyer's view of *The Lawn Front* (1832) shows the recently extended property 'handsome ... with a verandah, large French windows and very comfortable-sized rooms'. Watercolours of the 1840s depict the Regency villa and its garden in great detail, with irregular paths and planting, and nearby, in a glade in the surrounding forest, a classical funerary monument, erected after Curr's young daughter died tragically. In 1856 the company's agent described the house as 'standing in a lawn of three acres, surrounded by shrubberies and connected with a garden and orchard, comprising an area of upwards of two acres. A park of 30 acres, and an enclosure adjoining of 43 acres, are considered as the grounds attached to the house'. Subsequent owners from 1856 made only minor alterations to the house,

HIGHFIELD, near Circular Head (Tas.), was depicted in this 1840 watercolour as an elegant Regency villa, its decorative GARDENESQUE front garden complementing the ornamental architectural touches of the bow window and trellised verandah

which remains remarkably intact. The historic site is now administered by the Tasmanian Government, and garden reconstruction, using the 1840s watercolours as a guide, is being undertaken. CHRISTINE REID

HILL, Robin Sinclair (b. 1931), landscape designer, born in Adelaide, trained at KEMP's Nursery and Stanley Street Art School, North Adelaide, and during 1952 travelled through eastern Europe and Italy. Strongly influenced by European landscape design and the compositional principles of American landscape architect Thomas Church (1902–1978), Hill established Massey & Hill in 1956, the first landscape design practice in Adelaide. Hill's work was prominent during the 1950s–70s and his most significant projects were the MICHELL garden (1964) and the IPEC building grounds (1964), both undertaken with architect Peter Muller (b. 1927), his Le Corbusier–influenced residence at Horsnells Gully (1964–65), and the O'Halloran Hill REVEGETATION scheme (1975–80). Design characteristics including creative manipulation of ground planes, use of vegetation for textures and forms, and use of crazy paving and dry-stone walling formed the core of his design ideas and teachings. DAVID JONES

HILL, Walter (1820–1904), botanic gardens superintendent and colonial botanist, was born in Scotsdyke, Dumfries, Scotland, and trained as a gardener at the Royal Botanic Gardens, Edinburgh, for two years before appointment to the ROYAL BOTANIC GARDENS, KEW (1843–51). He carried a letter of introduction to gentleman and botanist, William Sharp MACLEAY, when he migrated to Sydney in 1852, but initially Hill sought his fortune in the Victorian goldfields. He returned to join Frederick Strange and four others on an exploratory party to Percy Island off Mackay (Qld), which ended in a fatal altercation with local Aboriginals. Soon after, Hill was employed to re-establish the government gardens in Brisbane, neglected since the closure of Moreton Bay penal settlement (1842).

Hill was appointed superintendent of the BRISBANE BOTANIC GARDEN in 1855 and, on separation from NSW (1859), Queensland's Colonial Botanist. The original garden reserve of about six acres (2.5 ha) was soon expanded to twenty-eight acres (11.5 ha), and endowed with a grant of £600. Hill made his first annual report to parliament in 1861; he listed forty-eight recently introduced species of plants and twenty-seven varieties of vines, twelve of pineapples, eight of bananas, and ten types of oranges. Three years later he reported successful results of the experiments made with tea, coffee, sugar, cinnamon, allspice, ginger, indigo, and tobacco. Hill established an oak plantation between the original lagoon and the Brisbane River in which eighteen species of European, Asian, and American oaks were planted to investigate for tanning purposes. He had also managed to obtain one specimen of *Cinchona calisaya* (Peruvian Fever Tree) for the Brisbane Gardens, and hoped for more from his contacts with Sir William Hooker at Kew and the Governor of Madras, India. There had been a concerted effort to establish this valuable medicinal tree (which yields quinine) throughout tropical areas of the British Empire, and Hill responded enthusiastically. Though the plants acclimatised adequately the project was not a success, as he was unable to interest farmers in plantation forestry of the tree.

Hill was influential in the establishment of the sugar industry in Qld. In 1862 a sugar planter from Barbados, John Buhot (1831–1881), arrived in Brisbane. With considerable help from Hill and his experimental cane stands, Buhot succeeded in granulating about five pounds (2.3 kg) of crystal sugar from seven gallons (26.5 L) of liquor. In 1870, Hill distributed more than 50 000 sugar cane cuttings of thirty-six varieties from the Brisbane gardens to coastal Qld; by 1876 more than 75 000 cuttings of fifty varieties were dispersed.

Hill is also credited with the introduction and acclimatisation of several other economic plants. He sought grasses and fibre crops, dye plants, mulberries, grapevines, and pineapples and all manner of tropical fruits—including the important horticultural species of mangoes, paw paw, and ginger—from around the world to acclimatise and distribute throughout the colony. He was also interested in indigenous flora with horticultural potential—he introduced *Macadamia integrifolia* into the gardens from Queensland's bush. Aware of the denudation from the forest of valuable species, Hill established a *Toona australis* (Australian Red Cedar) nursery at Oxley Point near Brisbane. He was also responsible for colonial forest reserves and for several years was the government's Agriculture Selector. He supplied trees and shrubs to many government institutions for beautification of their grounds and for shade purposes. With his overt support, branch BOTANIC GARDENS—often known as Queen's Parks—were gazetted in ROCKHAMPTON, TOOWOOMBA, MARYBOROUGH, and IPSWICH, during the 1870s. Hill desired experimentation with plants in various climatic zones of the colony; though over time, these regional gardens reverted mainly to recreational PUBLIC PARKS.

Hill was fully aware of the Brisbane gardens as a prime public recreational space in the city. He landscaped and had paths made through much of the area under his control. The first jacaranda in Qld was planted there in 1864 (and survived until 1980). Bedding flower gardens were established, lagoons dug for waterlilies, and fern islands constructed. Bamboo groves were planted and a Bunya pine avenue was established in memory of fellow botanist, John Carne BIDWILL. In the same year, Hill had a fine stone drinking fountain erected—the first source of pure drinking water in the gardens. Like most curators of colonial botanic gardens, Hill had a problem retaining skilled labour in the gardens for both experimentation and beautification.

Hill was interested in educating the public about the new plants they encountered. On several occasions he labelled major plantings, with only temporary success. From his several collecting expeditions and donations and exchanges with similar institutions, Hill established a HERBARIUM. He made large collections for local AGRICULTURAL SHOWS and intercolonial and international EXHIBITIONS, and in 1875 completed a catalogue of the plants in the gardens. During 1865–84 he contributed the gardeners' calendar to *Pugh's Almanac*. In 1862 he established a LIBRARY of botanical titles, open to his gardeners from 8 o'clock in the morning; the public waited until 9 o'clock for entry. Unfortunately the building in which the books were housed deteriorated and by 1875 Hill was forced to package the books until renovations were complete. His own residence in the gardens suffered a similar lack of maintenance, as did the greenhouse.

Walter Hill was retired from service on his sixtieth birthday and withstood an unpleasant departmental inquiry into his stewardship of the gardens. By then he had already moved to Canobie Lea at Eight Mile Plains, south of Brisbane, where he remained.   JUDITH DEPPELER-HAGAN

HILLARY, Cyril Hamilton Corby ('Hovea') (1889–1968), horticulturist, rosarian, and public servant, was born in Adelaide, moved to WA in 1895, and worked in London

The fern island at BRISBANE BOTANIC GARDENS, photographed in 1878, was one of the major developments of inaugural Superintendent Walter HILL, and reflected the contemporary enthusiasm for FERNS as well as Hill's skilful use of ferns in bold-foliaged groupings

between 1937 and 1948. Hillary was an instigator and foundation secretary of the NATIONAL ROSE SOCIETY of Western Australia, and later its president for fourteen years. Highly respected as gardening writer ('Hovea') for the *West Australian* (1933–68)—a role later taken by his daughter Joan (b. 1926)—he also contributed to the *Farmers Weekly* and broadcast garden talks on RADIO and TELEVISION.

CAROL MANSFIELD

HILL RIVER STATION, near Clare, SA, was established *c.* 1840 as a pastoral property by William Robinson (1814–1889). Charles Brown Fisher (1818–1908), grazier, acquired the property in 1855 and commenced an extensive tree planting and development program, continued by John Howard ANGAS (1823–1904) when he purchased the property in 1876. Dudley Angas and his American wife, Mary Christina (*née* Abbott), reshaped the HOMESTEAD GARDEN in an American romantic style in the 1920s, including a swimming pool, while maintaining the integrity of the shelter belts and tree-lined driveway.

DAVID JONES

HILLS HOIST: see TOYNE, Gilbert

HILL-STATIONS might be considered paradises where the exigencies of the Australian CLIMATE (apart from BUSHFIRES) appear to have been softened. Here, assisted by abundant WATER, gardening was practised without the stoicism of HOMESTEAD GARDENING on the unrelenting plains. Amid mountain cool, the horticultural rarity could be raised by nursery proprietors and gardened by wealthy residents so that the botanical discoveries of the age of imperialism luxuriated on terraced slopes against the backdrop of remnant indigenous forest.

In an age when Anglo-INDIAN concepts of space and place influenced colonial mindsets globally, MOUNTS MACEDON and WILSON, and the ADELAIDE HILLS were likened to Simla and Darjeeling. In due course the governor, like his raj counterparts, followed his colonial subjects to these upland retreats, giving these sanatoria added social cachet. While Australian hill-stations may be perceived as pleasure domes for wealthy elites escaping the rigour of city life, business, and the cares of office, not as easily characterised are the attitudes of their residents to the natural landscape. (Frederick) Eccleston Du Faur (1832–1915), who founded Mount Wilson in 1870, was instrumental in leading an 'expedition' into the Grose River valley of the BLUE MOUNTAINS in 1875, and later successfully lobbied to have Ku-ring-gai Chase (NSW), made a NATIONAL PARK in 1894. The establishment of (BELAIR) NATIONAL PARK in the Adelaide Hills in 1891 also suggests those who gardened the hill-station clearing found beauty in nature, although in this instance the flatter areas and gullies were planted with exotics as well as indigenous trees. At Macedon, one of the conditions imposed by the government on the colonial cognoscenti and scientific gentlemen who took up the original land selections of the early 1870s was to plant exotic trees at a stipulated rate—a response to the timber-getter denuding much of the Mount. In these circumstances it is not surprising to find experimental STATE FOREST NURSERIES and forests of exotics and indigenous timbers being established on hill-stations by colonial governments.

In the inter-war period of the twentieth century, the role of hill-stations as sites of European fantasy and longing intensified as city magnates (whose fortunes were made in retailing and industry) cultivated an up-to-the-minute aesthetic of woodland gardening popular in England at the time, especially with plants brought back from the ORIENT, during the second half of the nineteenth century.

And what of the present? Changes induced by natural disasters, especially bushfires, coupled with lack of understanding about Australian ECOLOGY and inevitable subdivision pressures, pose the question of how these past landscapes sit within a changing culture. Answers depend in part on how we perceive—and garden—the future of this continent.

Pat Barr and Ray Desmond, *Simla: A Hill Station in British India* (London, 1978)

PAUL FOX

HILLVIEW, Sutton Forest, NSW, in the SOUTHERN HIGHLANDS, was the vice-regal summer residence from 1882 to 1958. Sixteen governors of NSW resided there, each adding their touch to the garden. Although first granted in 1822, the garden was not developed until the house was erected (1872–75). Situated on a hill overlooking open grazing land towards Moss Vale, the grounds were already 'beautifully laid out' (1882) when Charles MOORE superintended additional planting in keeping with their new vice-regal status. After 1958 the size of the garden doubled under the enthusiastic guidance of owner Edward Klein (1901–1989), an eccentric, self-taught scholar and philosopher who visualised 'a place for contemplation and the getting of wisdom'. Klein tilled the entire three-hectare garden by himself, often working through the night by lamplight. The existing stonework and embellishments emanate from this era, which ended when Klein gifted Hillview back to the state government (1985), although the property is once again in private ownership.

TRISHA DIXON

HIRSCHI, Friedrich (1813–1870) and **Carl Lenné** (1827–1910), horticulturists and viticulturists, ran a nursery business together in Castlemaine (Vic.), in the wake of the gold rushes. Hirschi was born in Switzerland where in Berne he studied agriculture and gardening. He arrived in Australia during the early 1850s and in 1854 set about acquiring land in Castlemaine for a public BOTANIC GARDEN. Thwarted in his ambitions, in 1856 he purchased six acres (2.5 ha) on Barkers Creek, and planted numerous grape vines, fruit trees, shrubs, flowers, and tobacco. In that year he went into business with Lenné, born in Cologne, Prussia, who had a practical horticultural education: family tradition suggests he may have been a nephew of celebrated German landscape designer, Peter Joseph Lenné (1789–1866). Arriving in Adelaide in 1854 Lenné soon came to Castlemaine and also purchased land on Barkers Creek. In 1857 they opened a shop in Castlemaine selling their plants and produce, and the following year the Mount Alexander Nursery and Tea Garden advertised for sale 20 000 fruit trees (ninety-six varieties), 16 000 trees and shrubs, 24 000 vines, as well as numerous berries, pot plants, and items of pottery. In 1862 they claimed to have the largest stock in Victoria.

Around this time the partnership ceased. Lenné briefly went into business with E. Nicolai before moving to Bendigo, then Echuca, with his family where he commenced a successful nursery business that continued until his death. Family members were subsequently involved with LAW SOMNER and Hortico. At the time of Hirschi's death in 1870, he owned 10 acres (4 ha) of gardens and a licensed hotel. He was actively involved with the Castlemaine Horticultural Society and the Castlemaine and District Vinegrowers Association, as well as serving on council. He is recognised as a local pioneer of VITICULTURE.   LAURETTA ZILLES

HITCHMOUGH, James Donald (b. 1956), academic, came to Australia to take up a lecturing position at BURNLEY Horticultural College, Vic. (1983) after completing a PhD at the University of Bath, England. Appointed Senior Lecturer in Environmental Horticulture (1988), he was primarily responsible for the change in title and emphasis at Burnley from 'amenity horticulture' to 'environmental horticulture' for this discipline. His main concern during a decade in Australia was to educate horticultural students and professionals alike in the scientific management of vegetation in PUBLIC OPEN SPACE. His numerous professional papers and four books continue to strongly influence and guide Australian professional horticulture training and practice, particularly *Urban Landscape Management* (1994), now a standard reference for environmental horticulture. Engaged in a wide range of landscape issues, his current focus is the development of nature-like landscapes, particularly re-created GRASSLANDS using a rich diversity of flowering herbaceous plants, which he has continued to apply on his return to the UK.   ML

HOBART BOTANIC GARDENS, see ROYAL TASMANIAN BOTANICAL GARDENS

HOBBS, Jonah (1836–1913), orchardist and nursery proprietor, was born in Hillcott, Wiltshire, England, and migrated to Adelaide in 1847. After a gardening apprenticeship, he established the successful Glen Nursery at East Marden (SA), specialising in vegetables, fruit trees, and orchard tree cultivation. Upon acquisition of the neighbouring Lochend and Lochiel Park pastoral properties in Campbelltown (now adjacent to RIVER TORRENS LINEAR PARK), he established an extensive nursery that the *Cyclopaedia of South Australia* (1909) described as the 'foremost of fruit orchards of the State'.   DAVID JONES

HOCKINGS, Albert John (1826–1890), merchant and nursery proprietor, was born in London, arrived in NSW in 1840, and moved to Brisbane in 1847. He began as general-store owner in 1848, taking over Daniel Peterson's Stockton Store (established in 1842). In 1858 at South Brisbane he established one of the earliest commercial nurseries in Qld; this business continued until the close of the century. Hockings published the first Queensland gardening monograph, *Queensland Garden Manual* in 1865, which reached a third edition by 1888. His next book, *The Flower Garden in Queensland: Containing Concise and Practical Instructions on the Cultivation of the Flower Garden, and the Management of Pot Plants, in Australia*, was published in 1875. These gardening guides dominated the local scene during the 1860s–80s due to the simple descriptions of what could and could not be done in the unfamiliar CLIMATES and localities of Qld and because they offered a cheaper source of information than the standard British works by J.C. LOUDON and others (from which he freely quoted, such as GLENNY on florists' flowers). He also made gardening contributions to local publications (such as *Pugh's Almanac*) and his numerous nursery catalogues provided information, although only one (1865) is known to survive.

As a seed and plant merchant he supplied both wholesale and retail, and served farmers and gardeners all over Qld by post or railway. At its height, Hockings' business included the main nursery at Montague Road (near his residence, The Oaks), South Brisbane, a store in Queen Street, North

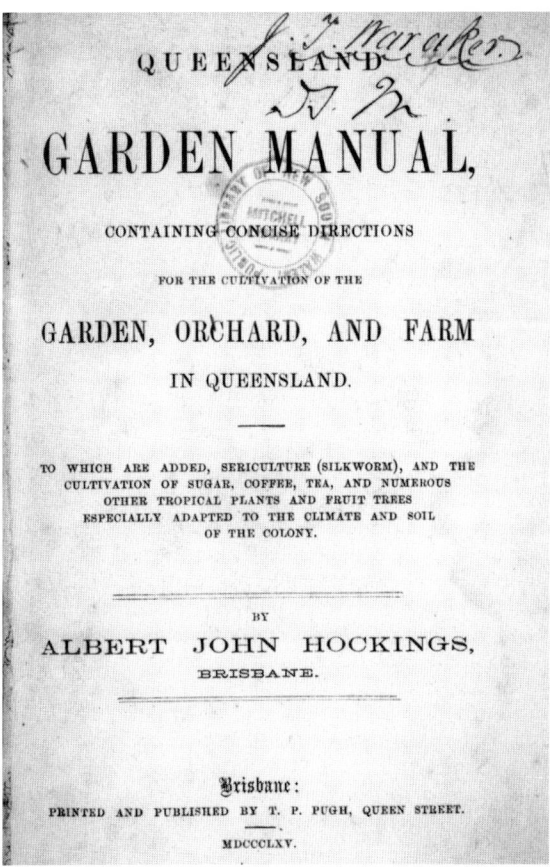

The *Queensland Garden Manual* (1865) of A.J. HOCKINGS was the earliest Australian GARDEN BOOK specifically addressing TROPICAL and subtropical climates; it also incorporated a catalogue of kitchen garden, flower, and agricultural seeds and fruit trees, and is the earliest surviving catalogue for Qld

Brisbane, and another nursery at Eagle Junction. In 1877, his son **Albert Thomas Hockings** (*c.* 1856–1928) became a partner in the firm, renamed Hockings and Son.

A.J. Hockings was a leading citizen in the colony: he was a founding member of the Queensland Acclimatisation Society, a trustee for the Mechanics' Institute and for Musgrave Park (South Brisbane), a Brisbane City Council alderman and mayor twice (1865, 1867), and Member of the Legislative Assembly for Wickham (1877–78). His important contributions to horticulture in Qld included ACCLIMATISING and HYBRIDISING plants for sale (especially fruit trees), supplying all sorts of ornamental and useful plants, seeds, agricultural, and garden equipment, and especially for his firm's helpful garden manuals.

JEANNIE SIM

HOCKINGS, (Francis) David (b. 1928), horticulturist and founding member of the SOCIETY FOR GROWING AUSTRALIAN PLANTS in Qld, has been an avid promoter of NATIVE PLANTS, especially through his books *Propagation of Australian Plants* (1969), *Friends and Foes of Australian Gardens* (1980), *Australian Gardener's Guide to Flowering Trees* (1982), and his numerous contributions to SGAP publications. Hockings worked as an ornamental plant specialist and horticulturist with the Queensland Department of Primary Industries. He was awarded the AUSTRALIAN INSTITUTE OF HORTICULTURE's Award of Excellence in 1986.

JEANNIE SIM

HODGE, Leomin (1904–1994), HYBRIDISER of GREVILLEAS and grower of AUSTRALIAN PLANTS, was born at Meredith (Vic.) and moved to East Gippsland with his family in 1905. He farmed his property, Poorinda, at W Tree and here during the 1940s grew native plants to lawn specimen standard. Arthur SWABY described the garden in 1958 as 'one of the best private native gardens in Australia'. Using hand pollination techniques, Leo Hodge developed forty-five grevillea hybrids and named selected CULTIVARS after Poorinda.

JOHN WALTER

HODGINS, Robert Wyburn (*c.* 1865–1947), nursery proprietor, established his business *c.* 1893, initially at Northcote (Vic.). Specialising in roses, he soon relocated to a larger site at Essendon, and his son **Basil Robert Hodgins** (1895–1947) joined the company. Hodgins Nurseries diversified into shrubs and trees, their detailed yearly catalogues forming a fine record of plant fashions during the inter-war period. As a schoolchild, Basil began collecting exotic ORCHIDS, soon becoming an authority. By 1930 he had specialised in cymbidiums, which did not require artificial heat in Australian CLIMATES, and therefore appealed to those unable to afford a specialised orchid house. HYBRIDISING was another talent, and in collaboration with T.W. POCKETT he bred stiff-stemmed DAHLIAS of rich and varied colourings. Family members continued the nursery until the early 1970s. RA

HODGKINSON, Clement (1819–1893), surveyor, scientist, land manager, and bureaucrat, was born in Southampton, England. In 1839, after qualifying as a surveyor and railway engineer, he migrated to NSW where he became a pastoralist and, from 1842, a contract surveyor. In 1843, economic hardship and the death of his wife persuaded him to return to England. Hodgkinson published an account of his experiences—*Australia, from Port Macquarie to Moreton Bay* (1845)—and between 1844 and 1851 worked as a railway engineer in England and on the Continent, and as a lecturer at the Putney College of Geodetic Engineering.

In 1851 Hodgkinson sailed for Melbourne where, in early 1852, he joined the Survey Office as a draftsman. He was successively appointed assistant-surveyor, surveyor in charge of the Melbourne Survey District, Acting Surveyor-General and, in 1858, Deputy Surveyor-General of the Department of Crown Lands and Survey. In 1861 he became Assistant Commissioner, or administrative head, of Crown Lands and Survey. Hodgkinson was the colony's most influential land manager—he was the father of 'selection before survey' and Victorian state FORESTRY, was a member of numerous boards and royal commissions, and was head of the most powerful government agency in the colony. Hodgkinson shaped the CULTURAL LANDSCAPE of Victoria.

Within this much wider management context, Hodgkinson personally controlled the identification, management, modification, or revocation of Victoria's crown land reserves including PUBLIC PARKS, GARDENS, and recreation sites. He supervised the landscaping of the Treasury, FITZROY, and FLAGSTAFF GARDENS where his rule was total: he drafted the plans, selected the trees, shrubs, statues, and fountains, chose the workmen, sold the clippings, and maintained a secret fund to finance garden developments. In pioneer Melbourne, the Fitzroy Gardens won wide praise. Yet Hodgkinson's gardening reach extended well beyond the city, for he travelled the colony dispensing advice and censure, and maintained a voluminous official correspondence concerned with park and garden management.

In May 1873 Hodgkinson, overworked and beset by acute administrative problems, reluctantly accepted the additional position of Inspector General of Metropolitan Parks, Gardens and Reserves. Ironically, at a time when his influence was at its greatest, his Department was sinking into a bureaucratic quagmire. A series of official inquiries into Lands Department maladministration charged that his supervision was partly to blame—for Hodgkinson, despite his many gifts, was a poor administrator incapable of delegation and absorbed by minutiae. In May 1874, ill and humiliated, he resigned.

During his retirement Hodgkinson landscaped the MELBOURNE GENERAL CEMETERY, served on many boards and, in March 1882, joined the Melbourne Public Parks and Gardens Committee. Hodgkinson's reputation as a LANDSCAPE GARDENER is equivocal, his work now judged pedestrian. His standing as Victoria's greatest land manager attracts no such qualification.

Ray Wright, *The Bureaucrats' Domain: Space and the Public Interest in Victoria 1836–84* (Melbourne, 1989)   RAY WRIGHT

HOLLAND: see THE NETHERLANDS

HOLLIDAY, (Harold) Ray (b. 1924), horticulturist and landscape designer, and his brother **Ivan Holliday** (b. 1926), horticulturist and town planner, have made a contribution to horticulture in advocating the use of plants species suited to SA, particularly indigenous and AUSTRALIAN NATIVES. Ray established Athelstone Wildflower Garden and Nursery at Black Hill (formerly F.C. PAYNE's nursery) and served as landscape manager for the new suburb of West Lakes before establishing a landscape design practice responsible for many projects, including the design and planting of The PADDOCKS (1971–72) and Monarto City Centre (1975). Ivan wrote *Growing Australian Plants* (1964) with Noel LOTHIAN (the first Australian planting and design guide for SA), *Australian Plants for Adelaide Gardens* (1990), and several field guides on Australian trees and shrubs.   DAVID JONES

HOLLINSDALE, Charles (*c.* 1819–1882), English-born seed merchant, arrived in Hobart Town by 1850. He traded as a 'fruiterer and colonial produce salesman' in Liverpool Street, with gardens in Proctor Road. Hollinsdale worked assiduously on behalf of gardeners and others along Sandy Bay Rivulet for the improvement of the main road, which he described as an 'impassable puddle'. He gained prizes for cut flowers, and, with John LATHAM, was one of the principal Hobart seed merchants of the mid-Victorian period.   RA

HOLTZE (HOLZ), Maurice (Waldemar) William (1840–1923), botanist, horticulturist, and botanic garden director, was born in Hanover, Germany. He studied and graduated in botany and horticulture at the Imperial Gardens in St Petersburg, Russia (now known as the Komorov Institute), and served four years as assistant in the Gardens at Hildesheim, followed by three years in a Hanover nursery. He then served as First Class Assistant at the Herrenhausen Royal Gardens, near Hanover, while studying botany under Professor Johannes Leunis. He married Evlampia Mesinzoff, daughter of a Russian captain, in 1867 before returning to Germany.

In 1872 the family migrated to Australia, landing in Melbourne, and travelled to the new settlement at Palmerston (now Darwin) in the NORTHERN TERRITORY of SA. After initially working as a gaol warder, Holtze was appointed Government Gardener (1878–91) of what became DARWIN BOTANIC GARDENS, originally a ten-acre (4 ha) portion of the 'park lands' in Fannie Bay. Holtze designed this garden, drawing on his European training and experience, as 'an umbrageous paradise' but few of his plantings have survived cyclones of 1897, 1937, and 1974. Holtze, and his son Nicholas, consolidated and extended economic agricultural experimentation pioneered in NT by William HAYES. Crops tested included sesame seed, tapioca, arrowroot, bananas, cotton, jute, rice, and opium poppy, many samples of which were submitted successfully in intercolonial and international EXHIBITIONS. In 1887 Holtze visited Canton, Hong Kong, Macao, Saigon, Singapore, and Batavia to study tropical agriculture, and his report recommended Indian over Chinese labour for northern plantations. In 1888 he was appointed Forester for the NT. Father and son also collected and listed local seeds and plants, sending many specimens to MUELLER. Holtze was a good linguist with warm social qualities; the family home in the Gardens served as a centre of culture and hospitality.

Appointed Director of ADELAIDE BOTANIC GARDEN (1891–1917) after Richard SCHOMBURGK's death, Holtze developed a fine collection of aquatic plants, redesigned flower-beds and garden features to suit prevailing tastes, replanted older trees, and provided roses for civic plantings. His 'type orchard' established at Mylor in the Mount Lofty Ranges in 1899 provided over 2000 varieties of apples and pears. While Holtze was not able to get the financial support

The elderly Maurice HOLTZE, pictured, towards the end of his directorship of ADELAIDE BOTANIC GARDEN, using a tricycle on his inspection rounds—a quaint image of paternal stewardship

given to his predecessor Schomburgk, resulting in some diminution of the scientific role of the Gardens, the recreational aspect of the Gardens was maintained and Holtze improved staff working conditions. A Fellow of the Linnaean Society and the Royal Society of South Australia, Holtze was awarded the Imperial Service Order (1913) for his services to botany. Several plants found in NT, including *Polyalthia holtzeana* and *Eugenia holtzeana*, have been named in his honour.

Aged just 23, **Nicolas (Nicholas) Holtze** (*c.* 1868–1913), amateur horticulturist, botanist, and public servant, succeeded his father as first official Curator of the Darwin Botanic Gardens, although severe financial constraints made the appointment part-time. Hoping the gardens might become self-supporting through the growing of crops, he experimented with sisal plants, cotton, and rice, believing, as his father had, in the agricultural potential of the Territory. He was actively involved in local horticultural societies and exhibitions, and curated a local museum that showcased Territory produce. A talented, capable, and successful—but overworked—public servant, he rose to be Acting Government Resident. His early death, following a 'brief botanising expedition' to Katherine, was attributed to an acute attack of dyspepsia, but may have been in part attributable to the stress he was said to be suffering regarding 'operations in the Gardens', following the handover of the administration of the Territory from SA to the Commonwealth.

Wynnis J. Ruediger, *The Holtze Saga* (Adelaide, 1988)

PAULINE PAYNE

THE HOME (1920–42) was published by (Sydney George) Ure Smith (1887–1949) as a stable-mate to his prestigious *Art in Australia* (established 1916). The *Home* design was refined from contemporary overseas women's magazines, and it became, in style and content, a unique document of inter-war Australian middle-class life, depicting its smart social set, aspirations, likes and dislikes, fashions, and yearning for MODERNITY. Gardens and gardening were included and gradually gained more space and illustrations. There was emphasis on 'good taste' and gardens were seen as essential complements to the house.

Ure Smith, with a fine flair for visual design, introduced stylish cover designs by graphic artists such as Thea Proctor, Hera Roberts, Margaret Preston, and Percy Leason. He employed photographers such as Max Dupain and Harold Cazneaux, and published their innovative black and white photographs. There was a selection of Australian short stories, as well as articles about interior design, architecture, and fashion. He assembled a group of talented artists and writers in the 1920s, and the magazine went from being a quarterly to a monthly. Based in Sydney, it nevertheless had a strong Melbourne and Victorian component. By the mid-1920s there was a special section on domestic architecture and gardens, mainly by John Berry or Hardy WILSON, and illustrated pieces on aspects of horticulture—such as one in July 1928 on cactus growing, a current craze. There was admiration for FLORAL ART and decoration, thus drawing it into the modern fashionable circle. Into the 1930s, gardens and flowers were to command more attention, and popular garden writer S.H. HUNT wrote regular practical articles on horticulture.

Ure Smith sold the *Home* to John Fairfax and Sons in 1934, when circulation figures were at 7000. They saw it as a competitor to *Vogue*. He stayed on as editor until 1939, when he resigned, leaving Leon Gellert in charge, and the magazine began to lose some of its vigour and style and shrink in size. The tone of fashionable sophistication was maintained, however, and the gardening articles were lent a special sparkle when Jocelyn BROWN began regular contributions (1939–42). These were carefully considered articles embellished with her graceful line drawings, which discussed landscape design as well as growing flowers.

Nancy D. Underhill, *Making Australian Art 1916–49: Sydney Ure Smith, Patron and Publisher* (South Melbourne, 1991)

HELEN PROUDFOOT

HOME AND GARDEN BEAUTIFUL, see JOURNAL OF HORTICULTURE OF AUSTRALASIA

HOME GARDENER (1917–54), published monthly in Melbourne, was a practical and inexpensive aid to the amateur gardener. Thomas A. Browne, editor for three decades, and publishers Mitchell and Casey, made a timely entry into the market as Melbourne's ring of orchards and paddocks was being transformed into suburbs of quarter-acre blocks. The Great War had also given a stimulus to gardening, not only in the practical need for produce but also the desire to excel in floriculture—both aspects fully covered by the *Home Gardener*. Contributors were frequently prominent in the local nursery trade and horticultural societies. Little space was given to garden design, but new horticultural trends were given timely attention. Thus G.K. COWLISHAW commenced a CACTUS column in 1934 and new varieties of sweet peas, lilies, and gladioli were prominently featured. Interstate coverage increased during the journal's heyday in the 1920s–30s, but during the post-war period the magazine was outclassed in production and content by new rivals.

RA

HOMESTEAD GARDENS The presence of the homestead (or station) garden from earliest European settlement of Australia guarantees it a seminal position in Australian cultural history. Interpreted by historians as a symbol of cultivation and the characterisation of the European *vis-à-vis* the wilderness, the homestead garden charts shifts in European taste, cultivation, perception, and colonisation of the Australian landscape.

Early homestead gardens may also be interpreted as a frontier space where women created a space beyond the sheep run and animal husbandry of their menfolk. Women perceived the frontier as garden, painting it from either the homestead or the verandah; the professional male landscape painter—such as Tasmanian settler and artist John GLOVER, in *A View of the Artist's House with Garden* (*c.* 1834)—viewed homestead and garden from the wider landscape. Not all gardens created by women were confined by the garden fence. Women such as Georgiana MOLLOY in WA and Louisa ATKINSON in NSW, with their interest in botany and botanical rambles, integrated the natural world with the cultivated in a highly sophisticated way.

The garden as the feminine space of the frontier also allowed other spaces to be created: spaces that varied from male frontier experience. For example, in Port Phillip District Susannah Cotton and her husband, the ornithologist squatter John, gave employment to Aboriginal women weeding the garden around their homestead, Doogallook, in a rare European acknowledgment of Aboriginal women's skill with the digging stick.

Despite this, the homestead garden existed within a contested landscape for much of its first hundred years. Not only was there contestation between Aboriginal people and Europeans; after the gold rushes of the 1850s, squatter (later known by the respectable euphemism 'pastoralist') and selector (would-be small farmers) both claimed the same landscape by using house and garden as symbols to assert economic power and dominance.

Scientific ideas, especially about ACCLIMATISATION, also impinged upon the homestead garden. By the 1860s, squatters influenced by their memories of the landscape of first sight perceived the detrimental changes their flocks wrought on the indigenous landscape. Some came to be haunted by this vanished landscape, and people such as William Henry Bacchus (1820–1887), of Peerewur station (Vic.), took to growing indigenous GRASSES in his garden to re-establish them as native pastureland. For others, the ghosts of memory were laid to rest by reading the natural world ravaged by colonisation as evidence of Darwinian survival of the fittest, whereby the successful adaptation of the acclimatised plant was seen as evidence of the superiority of the European importation over the indigenous Australian. In these circumstances, the homestead garden came to be conceived of as an ideal world standing apart from the surrounding landscape; a place of refuge from the elemental forces of nature that periodically crippled the productive landscape.

Not all settlers perceived the homestead garden in this way. Some gardens jumped the fence literally—by means of the HA-HA—others were sited with views of naturally occurring LAKES or lagoons, or of distant mountains, so that the PICTURESQUE reading of the Aboriginal-fired landscape of grasslands and trees as a gentlemen's PARK was replaced by metaphors drawn from Scottish estate management of the plantation, where taste and utility were satisfied equally. In Victoria's WESTERN DISTRICT, with its high percentage of Scottish settlers, sparse tree cover and windy plains, plantations in particular marked out homestead and wider landscape. By the end of the century, a number of gardeners, working as landscape FORESTERS in other parts of the country, were successfully creating plantation landscapes on homestead properties.

Throughout this period, wealthy pastoralists continued to strive to create ideal landscapes against the odds of rabbits and drought; the homestead gardens of William GUILFOYLE, created at the beginning of the twentieth century, may be considered the final flowering of the high-Victorian country garden. There were other cultural movements at work at this time that would create a different aesthetic by revisiting the colonial past. Hardy WILSON's *Cow Pasture Road* (1920) and *Old Colonial Architecture in New South Wales and Tasmania* (1924), drawing on a decade of investigation, idyllicised the Georgian colonial past. In a movement that saw Professor E.G. WATERHOUSE and others like him seek out the MACARTHUR camellias of Camden Park (NSW), the early homestead became an inspiration for an elite that, in the aftermath of the First World War, imagined itself a county gentry inhabiting an English Georgian world. Englishness now became a sought-after state of mind, and in the world of gardening, Edna

In Frederick Kruger's photograph (c.1880) of Windemere, near Lara (Vic.), the property of George Fairbairn, the FENCE of the HOMESTEAD GARDEN is echoed in the middle distance by PLANTATIONS of eucalypts, planted in counterpoise to the denuded hills of the nearby You Yangs

WALLING created gardens that satisfied this longing. The re-creation of MICALAGO homestead and gardens on the Monaro (NSW) by Professor Leslie WILKINSON in 1945 and owner Mrs Ryrie (with advice from Walling), may be seen as an expression of the continuing influence of the colonial Georgian ideal in post-war Australia.

The homestead garden in its rise and decline reflects contemporary economic history. After the wool boom of the early 1950s created by the Korean War, rising costs saw the homestead garden beholden to the cost of labour and accordingly simplified—a change not reversed until the 1980s, when the historic homestead garden came to be seen as culturally important and worthy of conservation. However, this discovery of the past, unlike that of the interwar period, has failed to be a springboard for innovative design. Tradition, not modernity, is the sine qua non of contemporary homestead garden design.

A new perspective on an old theme of homestead gardening has arisen since the 1980s. Movements such as Land for Wild Life and LANDCARE, with their planting of trees in the wider landscape, evoke the desire to re-create the vanishing landscape first articulated in the 1860s as well as to protect and enhance biodiversity values. In cash-strapped rural communities concerned with environmental degradation, government funding for wildlife corridors and the protection of remaining natural habitats has seen the wider landscape, rather than the homestead garden, become the focus of attention of many who farm the land.

> Howard Tanner, *Converting the Wilderness: The Art of Gardening in Colonial Australia* (Sydney, 1979); Peter Freeman, *The Homestead: A Riverina Anthology* (Melbourne, 1982); Peter Watts and Margaret Barrett (eds), *Historic Gardens of Victoria: A Reconnaissance* (Melbourne, 1983); James Broadbent, *The Australian Colonial House: Architecture and Society in New South Wales 1788–1842* (Sydney, 1997) PAUL FOX

HOOKER, William Joseph and **Joseph Dalton Hooker**: see ROYAL BOTANIC GARDENS, KEW

HOPE, Percy G.S. (1885–1979) and **Carl H. Klem** (1883–1952), surveyors and brothers-in-law, were partners in the Perth-based firm Hope and Klem (established 1911). Klem was active in the state's Town Planning Association from 1917, and became a member of the Western Australian Town Planning Commission in 1928. Hope and Klem were key Australian practitioners of GARDEN CITY planning principles, applying them to designs for new suburbs such as Dalkeith (1911), Mount Lawley Estate No. 3 (1923), Ascot Garden Suburb (1927), and Wembley Downs (1928). Their most notable achievement was a visionary scheme adopted by Perth City Council for the Endowment Lands (1925), a large tract of unimproved land west of the capital. Influenced by garden city planning thought and by guidelines proposed in 1917 by William BOLD, the Hope–Klem plan incorporated towns on the coast (City Beach) and inland (Floreat Park) as satellites of the capital city. City Beach was 'Perth's first example of a contour controlled layout'. The two towns were separated from the metropolis and from each other by a reserved GREEN BELT that included parklands, pine forest, and golf course. Hope and Klem are remembered for their advocacy and practical implementation of TOWN PLANNING 'on garden city lines'. CHRISTINE GARNAUT

HORDERN family, descendants of Anthony (1788–1869) and Ann Hordern—who established a Sydney retailing dynasty exemplified by Anthony Hordern and Sons' Palace Emporium—created many celebrated gardens around their residences.

Anthony Hordern II (1819–1876) built Retford Hall in 1865 at Darling Point, an ITALIANATE villa with terraced gardens (destroyed) descending to the shores of Sydney Harbour; his son Anthony ('Tertius') Hordern III (1842–1886) built Shubra Hall in 1869, a high-Victorian villa on a landscaped hilltop (now Presbyterian Ladies College) at Croydon. Another son, Samuel (1849–1909), acquired a large rural holding east of Bowral, in the 1880s: his country 'seat', **Retford Park**, was approached along a long, tree-lined drive leading to the *porte-cochère* of the towered, iron-verandah'd house, surrounded by a park setting of imported trees and laurel hedges.

Samuel's eldest son, (Sir) Samuel Hordern (1876–1956), acquired Mount Adelaide on the Darling Point ridge and created a vast new residence and landscaped setting in an ARTS AND CRAFTS style (*c.* 1912): formal stairways descended from the porte cochère to sunken gardens and GROTTOES distinguished by an important botanic collection. Known as **Babworth House**, this great estate was designed by architects Morrow and De Putron, who also designed nearby Hopewood House (1914) for his brother Lebbeus Hordern (1891–1928): only its inventive gateways, domed gatehouse, and several key trees survive. Sir Samuel also resided at Retford Park: Lady Hordern took a keen interest in both gardens; another brother, Anthony (Tony) Hordern (1889–1970), also used Morrow and De Putron to create at **Milton Park**, Bowral, an expansive hilltop bungalow (1910) adjacent to Retford Park. The site was graded to form a series of garden platforms and enclosures descending to a rose garden, herbaceous border, and oak glade underplanted with bluebells. Tony's second wife, Mary, rearranged the garden at Milton Park to achieve striking colour combinations that survive today.

Sir Samuel Hordern's son, also Samuel (1909–1960), commissioned Professor Leslie WILKINSON to design a generous MEDITERRANEAN-inspired villa (1936) on Bellevue Hill, whose arcaded forecourt recalled Renaissance *cortile*, though filled with lush subtropical plants; the main garden has a formal terrace, accented by large plane trees and banks of hydrangeas framing an outlook over Sydney Harbour to Manly.

Two cousins maintained an interest in gardening. Edward Carr Hordern (1853–1940) purchased Chislehurst, Chatswood, in 1905: it had very elaborate Edwardian gardens in spacious grounds (destroyed). His brother Alfred (1859–1932) had architect J. Horbury Hunt design a shingle-style house, Highlands (1892), at Wahroonga; its thirty-four acres (14 ha) were known as 'Hordern's bush'. His zealous wife Caroline (Carrie) at times employed up to fourteen gardeners in the production of a showpiece garden; after Alfred's death she transformed his weekender, Kalua (*c.* 1922), at Palm Beach to provide a spectacular subtropical setting, including transplanted ten-metre-high palms.

HOWARD TANNER and GEOFFREY BRITTON

HORSLEY, Horsley Park, NSW, is the remnant core of a farm established from a 2000-acre (810 ha) grant to Major (later Colonel) George Johnston (1764–1823). The grant passed to his daughter Blanche and *c.* 1832, after marrying Captain George Weston and a subsequent stay in India, the celebrated Indian Bungalow–inspired house was built. Much admired by later architects, Horsley became a model for houses such as W. Hardy WILSON's Eryldene. The hilltop HOMESTEAD and its distinctive 'street' of outbuildings are signposted by a magnificent old avenue of *Araucaria bidwillii* (Bunya Pine) along the original entry drive and groups of mature trees around the garden. Though the vineyard, orchard, and deer enclosure have gone there are many surviving features—front drive loop garden with an uncommon Delhi Plum, *Tecomaria capensis* (Cape Honeysuckle) maze, *Ficus macrophylla* (Moreton Bay Fig) trees flanking the top of the drive, and brick spoon drains.

GEOFFREY BRITTON and COLLEEN MORRIS

HORTICULTURAL BOOKS: see GARDEN BOOKS

HORTICULTURAL MAGAZINE AND GARDENERS' AND AMATEURS' CALENDAR OF NEW SOUTH WALES (1864–71) was published under the auspices of the Horticultural Society of Sydney (from 1865, of New South Wales) 'for the purpose of giving a full report of the Society's monthly proceedings, noticing and fully reporting on all new rare Plants, Fruits, and Vegetables'. The monthly issues included an introduction by honorary editor John GELDING, a summary of the transactions, exhibits, and papers presented to the Horticultural Society, and, from 1865, meteorological observations taken at YARALLA by its gardener Alexander Stephen. These were interspersed with reports of horticultural shows, 'Notes' on various genera, regular columns such as the 'Flower Department' and 'Ornamental and Landscape Gardening', original articles, and descriptions of prominent gardens. Regular contributors included William WOOLLS and Luke WOOFE. Issues in the period 1866–68 contained lithographed botanical illustrations—'truthful renditions' of his subjects—by Robert FITZGERALD; they were the earliest illustrations in an Australian GARDEN MAGAZINE. By 1869 subscriptions to the *Horticultural Magazine* were dropping, and after the magazine was discontinued in 1871, the *Sydney Mail* printed the Horticultural Society's transactions under 'Horticultural Notes'. The seven yearly volumes of the *Horticultural Magazine*—an outstanding achievement in a publishing field not noted for longevity in the nineteenth century— form a unique record of the state of gardening and horticulture in NSW during the 1860s, provide valuable insights into nineteenth-century horticultural tastes, and contain invaluable descriptions of prominent Sydney estates.

COLLEEN MORRIS

HORTICULTURAL MAGAZINE AND GARDEN GUIDE: see CRICHTON, David

HORTICULTURAL MAGAZINES: see GARDEN MAGAZINES

HORTICULTURAL SHOWS have been a feature of Australian gardening and horticulture since the formation of the earliest HORTICULTURAL SOCIETIES in the 1830s. Indeed, the voluntary efforts of horticultural society members have distinguished horticultural shows from other, more commercially oriented garden FESTIVALS. The earliest horticultural shows, in Sydney (1838), Launceston (1838), Hobart Town (1839), Melbourne (1850), and Moreton Bay (*c.* 1853), were commonly held in the town's government or BOTANIC GARDEN, or other suitable public venue. TENTS or demountable buildings were often used to house exhibits, which were usually set on timber stages grouped according to category. Schedules were issued in advance outlining categories and to provide adequate notice both for participants and for visitors. These early shows were often titled 'horticultural exhibitions', indicating a mix of COMPETITIVE and non-competitive exhibits. The *Gardeners' Chronicle*, reporting in 1842 on a show conducted by the Australian Floral and Horticultural Society, felt that its readers 'may be anxious to know how such matters are managed in New Holland, and what are the prominent subjects of cultivation there'. It professed surprise 'to learn that there is very little difference between a garden exhibition of Sydney and one in an English country town', but commented 'We find no instance of New Holland plants being produced, with the solitary exception of two flowering specimens of the Doryanthes excelsa, each of which was 15 feet long. European plants and vegetables were evidently the great source of interest.'

Flowers—especially those termed florists' flowers—and vegetables were the most common forms of exhibit at these early shows, although potted plants and even groups of plants became increasingly common as the nineteenth century progressed. FOLIAGE plants such as ferns and crotons were commonly included in shows from the 1860s and 1870s, and special sections began to be devoted to distinct plant groups. At the start of the twentieth century, special shows dedicated to popular flowers such as ROSES and CHRYSANTHEMUMS became common, and accompanied the rise of specialist societies. Horticultural shows, usually of only one or two days' duration, acted as a showcase for the host society. Many catered for amateur and professional gardeners alike, although definitions of 'amateur' filled many column-inches in the horticultural press.

Apart from shared knowledge and good-natured competition, LEISURE was a key motive of shows. MUSIC was often featured, and vice-regal patronage, if it could be obtained, was a great boost. In short, horticultural shows became a keenly anticipated social occasion, where an office-bearer might have the privilege of shaking a gubernatorial hand, or indicating a particular point of merit on the show table to the assembled party. Venues increasingly tended towards large halls, and even, in the case of Melbourne's Horticultural Hall (1874), a purpose-built structure. The early use of natural light, filtered through canvas, was thus augmented in the mid-nineteenth century by gaslight (and towards the turn of the century by electricity), enabling night viewing.

Horticultural societies

The format of shows has changed little over a century and a half, although with increasing competition in the leisure market, their survival cannot be assured. Specialist trade gatherings, garden FESTIVALS, and the transformation of commercial NURSERIES into garden centres (with displays, talks, and special events) have also eroded and transformed public support. Perhaps the tradition will be left to AGRICULTURAL AND PASTORAL SOCIETIES, which often still include horticultural sections in their shows, as they have done since their inception in the early nineteenth century.   RA

HORTICULTURAL SOCIETIES were established in Australia from the 1820s and 1830s, but it was the period from the 1850s onwards that witnessed their greatest growth. Many of these societies were glorified AGRICULTURAL AND PASTORAL SOCIETIES, with the addition of the word 'Horticultural' often justified by a few extra prizes for plants at the annual agricultural show. Initially there were few true horticultural societies outside capital cities, with the possible exceptions of Geelong (which acted as an entrepôt for Victoria's WESTERN DISTRICT) and Launceston (Tas.). As agricultural, pastoral, and mining activities brought wealth to colonial townships—especially in Vic. and NSW after the gold rushes of the 1850s—additional societies were established. Two basic divisions emerged among members and their respective societies, derived from British precedents. The first, for gentlemen 'amateurs' of wealth and standing, and for those at the pinnacle of the horticultural professions, was modelled on the (ROYAL) HORTICULTURAL SOCIETY of London, founded in 1804. The second, for working gardeners, was based on gardeners' mutual improvement societies of the 1830s. Of the two major Melbourne-based societies, the (Royal) Horticultural Society of Victoria typified the former, while the Victorian Gardeners' Mutual Improvement Society was modelled on the latter. In the more socially exclusive societies, money could often purchase fellowships and life memberships. Women, if they were mentioned at all in rules, were generally excluded from membership until the 1890s, and in some cases until well into the twentieth century. SCIENTIFIC SOCIETIES, such as the LINNEAN SOCIETY OF NEW SOUTH WALES, provided essential links between botanists as well as those with a wider interest in NATURAL HISTORY. Most horticultural societies had a relatively small membership base and fluctuations in support were the norm. Strong

The HORTICULTURAL SHOW of the Horticultural Society of Western Australia, held in Perth's Queen's Hall (1907), demonstrates both traditional show tables and also naturalistic groupings of bold-foliaged plants, popular from the 1870s

antipathy also existed between rival societies, and there was generally an unwillingness to merge; this was founded on an explosive mix of social, financial, and personal factors, and rarely on horticultural ideology. Ideology was often discussed, however—as in 1860 when the Victorian Gardeners' Mutual Improvement Society considered a motion that proposed the GARDENESQUE as the preferred mode of grouping trees—but rarely caused lasting rancour.

EDUCATIONAL imperatives formed a strong impetus for many societies. This ranged from informal discourse at regular meetings, to lectures and even occasional excursions. LIBRARIES were often discussed but less often formed. Great difficulty existed in sustaining magazines or regular publications, and early periodicals, such as the SYDNEY MAGAZINE OF SCIENCE AND ART, FARM AND GARDEN, and HORTICULTURAL MAGAZINE, were generally published under the auspices of a society but by a commercial publisher. Some later magazines, such as the WEST AUSTRALIAN GARDENER, were longer lived, but always faced strong competition from commercial publications. EXPERIMENTAL GARDENS or trial grounds to test plant cultivars, especially those of fruit and popular flowers, were occasionally established, but rarely did these supplant testing undertaken by the commercial NURSERY trade.

Competitive aspects such as SHOWS and garden COMPETITIONS were a major activity and consumed much committee time, in both organising and staging. Venues were required, schedules distributed, certificates printed, doors attended, exhibits staged, judging undertaken, and prizes awarded. To this list, for the elite societies, could be added vice-regal patronage and musical entertainment. Monetary prizes or certificates were the norm and rarely were commendations for improved plant cultivars (in the manner of the Royal Horticultural Society) issued or even mooted.

Venues for meetings, shows and buildings were a recurring problem for most societies. TENTS for shows and rented premises for meetings were the norm in the nineteenth century, but the larger shows were increasingly housed in town halls or other large public buildings. Melbourne's Horticultural Hall (1874) was an isolated example of a dedicated venue combining offices, library, meeting rooms, and hall.

The early decades of the twentieth century were marked by the formation of specialist societies, including those focused on a single species (for example, the ROSE, SWEET PEA, DAHLIA, and CARNATION), special interests (such as NATURAL HISTORY, especially through the various FIELD NATURALISTS' CLUBS AND SOCIETIES), and discrete suburban locations (often a splitting of previous wider groupings, such as the various 'South Suburban' or 'Northern Suburbs' horticultural societies). These groups achieved their peak membership and influence in the years around the Second World War. Among the major metropolitan societies directed at professional gardeners there was a move away from a nineteenth-century self-help and an ehos of mutual benefit towards a more militant stand on issues of wages and conditions, leading some decades later to unionisation of the various branches of the trade. Among those involved in construction and design, this progression led to the formation of professional institutions.

The formation in 1950 of the Garden Club of New South Wales by Margaret DAVIS commenced a movement that placed gardens rather than horticulture firmly centre stage. The social role of gardens and gardening, rather than the more competitive world of horticulture, resulted in a predominantly female membership among the affiliated garden clubs. The post-war period also saw an explosion in the number of special interest groups, with the Australian CAMELLIA Research Society and SOCIETY FOR GROWING AUSTRALIAN PLANTS among the most influential. Post-war suburban growth and the consequent need for garden advice also fostered the establishment of many smaller societies, often at a suburban level.

Since the 1960s many societies in kindred fields, and devoted to wider landscape conservation issues including environmental degradation, revegetation, and conservation (as private initiatives and by formal reservation through the national parks system)—such as the Wilderness Society, LANDCARE and GREENING AUSTRALIA groups, the Australian Conservation Foundation, and various other conservation councils—have captured the public and political imagination.

RA

Australian Capital Territory Established to coincide with the first wave of residents to the new federal capital, the Horticultural Society of Canberra played an important role in marshalling public support to implement CANBERRA'S GARDEN CITY concept. After initial difficulties, the society was constituted in 1929 with Alexander BRUCE, Superintendent of Parks and Gardens, as president. With viceregal patronage and encouragement, especially from Sir Isaac Issacs (1931–36) and Lady GOWRIE (1936–45), the society engaged a large proportion of the Canberra population through annual, seasonal, and monthly exhibitions, pruning demonstrations, and garden competitions. It was instrumental in developing the National Rose Gardens (1933), a co-operative venture between the Society, the Department of the Interior, and nation-wide donations of roses. Since 1948 the Society has published the *Canberra Gardener*, with a focus on gardening for local conditions. As well as the long-standing SOCIETY FOR GROWING AUSTRALIAN PLANTS (Canberra Region), the ACT supports a diverse range of gardening clubs and horticultural groups with special interests.

DIANNE FIRTH

New South Wales The first attempt to form an AGRICULTURAL SOCIETY in NSW (1818) was dropped when Governor Macquarie declined to be patron of a society where emancipists were not freely admitted. The Agricultural Society of New South Wales (1822–26) was formed under the patronage of Governor Brisbane, and continued as the Agricultural and Horticultural Society (1826–36)—the quiet demise of which was 'enshrouded in mystery'. Horticultural interest was upheld by the Australian Floral and Horticultural Society (1836–48) and members of the fledgling wine industry formed the Hunter River Vineyard Association (*fl*. 1847–54). The Australasian Botanic and Horticultural Society (1848–56), catering for the elite (and with Governor Fitzroy as first president), amalgamated with the Horticultural Improvement Society of New South Wales (1855–56) to form the Australian Horticultural and Agricultural Society (1856–*c*. 1860). Although

Horticultural societies

The opening of the Launceston Horticultural Fete (1847) in the garden of the local HORTICULTURAL SOCIETY (now CITY PARK)—an early and unusual example of a subscription garden in the Australian context

short-lived, this was effectively the precursor of both the Horticultural Society of New South Wales and the Agricultural Society of New South Wales. The Horticultural Society of New South Wales (1862–) enjoyed a meteoric rise in popularity in its first years, when the HORTICULTURAL MAGAZINE was instigated, but appears to have terminated c. 1879 due to disagreement among members. It was revived in 1886, and has continued as the Royal Horticultural Society of New South Wales since 1931. The LINNEAN SOCIETY OF NEW SOUTH WALES (1874–) attracted a more scientifically minded membership.

In areas where agricultural and horticultural pursuits were concentrated, regional societies were formed. In northern NSW, colonists formed societies at Moreton Bay (1853), Clarence (1866), and the Hunter River region (by 1867). Parramatta, site of the first successful agricultural pursuits by British colonists in Australia, was the base for several early agricultural societies before establishment of the Horticultural Society of Parramatta (1877). Other suburban horticultural societies included Eastern Suburbs and Western Suburbs, both formed by 1877 when support for the Horticultural Society of New South Wales was in a lull, and Ashfield Horticultural Club (by 1890).

The Horticultural Association of New South Wales (1893) was formed by professional gardeners; around the turn of the century specialist societies included a carnation society and the short-lived Australian Flora Society (fl. 1906). The rise of the garden suburb during the 1910s and 1920s spawned a new generation of local societies just as post-war suburbanisation saw a new wave of societies. A notable development was the establishment by Margaret DAVIS of the Garden Club of New South Wales (1950), progenitor of many affiliated clubs. Several professional bodies are based in, or have numerically strong branches in, NSW—including a large proportion of AUSTRALIAN INSTITUTE OF HORTICULTURE members.

COLLEEN MORRIS

Northern Territory The Agricultural, Horticultural, and Industrial Society of North Australia (c. 1902–09), the first locally driven society of its kind in Darwin, aimed to promote economic investment in the NT. It mounted at least eight exhibitions and exhibited in colonial and international EXHIBITIONS. The Society established a permanent museum collection (1903), curated by Nicholas HOLTZE, and encouraged agriculture and horticulture through lectures, prize-giving, and promotional tours to its museum and to DARWIN BOTANIC GARDENS for visiting dignitaries and steamship passengers in transit.

Since the 1950s many specialist societies have been established, supporting a wide range of horticultural interests and activities, both recreational and commercial. In the monsoonal north these include the Royal Agricultural Society of the Northern Territory (1951–), Darwin Garden Club (1958–98), Nightcliff Garden Club (c. 1964–84), Darwin Bonsai Club (1969–), Orchid Society of the Northern Territory (1974–), Rural Garden Club (1977–), Rare Fruit Council of Australia (1981–2001), Northern Territory Palm and Cycad Society

(1983–), Top End Native Plant Society (1984–), Top End Herb Group (1987–), Northern Territory Horticultural Association (an umbrella group formed in 1993 with affiliated bodies covering the nursery industry, and mango, citrus, banana, rambutan, and flower growers), and orchid groups in Nightcliff, Litchfield, and Katherine. Groups addressing horticultural and wider landscape conservation issues across the NT include GREENING AUSTRALIA and the NATIONAL TRUST OF AUSTRALIA (Northern Territory). The KEEP AUSTRALIA BEAUTIFUL COUNCIL also acts as an advisory and referral body in horticultural matters.

JAN SETO and ANITA ANGEL

Queensland The colony's earliest horticultural society—the Moreton Bay Horticultural Society (1853–56)—conducted exhibitions and, importantly, petitioned for the establishment of the BRISBANE BOTANIC GARDENS. Its role was soon taken over by the Queensland Acclimatisation Society (1862); like its predecessor and uniquely among Australian ACCLIMATISATION societies, it focused on plants, particularly those of economic value. The first wave of AGRICULTURAL SOCIETIES began on the DARLING DOWNS, Ipswich, Beenleigh, and Rockhampton during the 1860s and 1870s, culminating in the establishment of the Queensland-wide (Royal) National (Agricultural and Industrial) Association, which began the 'The Ekka' (Exhibition) in Brisbane (1875). The second wave of general societies (1870s–80s)—focusing on agriculture or pastoralism, sometimes combining with industrial or mining interests, but with only a passing interest in horticulture (such as market gardens, orchards, and vineyards)—continued the spread into northern and western districts, with consolidation into smaller districts with the next wave (1890s–1920s).

The establishment of the Darling Downs Horticultural Society (c. 1884) and the Queensland Horticultural Society (1886)—later the Royal Horticultural Society of Queensland (RHSQ, 1955)—were important developments, marking the 1890s as a peak time for horticulture in Qld. The publication of the *Queensland Horticulturist* by the RHSQ marked an auspicious early achievement for its members. Country and suburban societies were not generally established until the twentieth century. Specialisation of the horticultural groups began with a section of the Royal Horticultural Society devoted to orchids (1904), then widened to include the Queensland Dahlia Society (1928), the NATIONAL ROSE SOCIETY of Queensland (1930), and the Queensland Orchid Society (1934). These proliferated after the Second World War, with groups including Brisbane (1957) and Queensland (1959); sections of the SOCIETY FOR GROWING AUSTRALIAN PLANTS; the Australian Hibiscus Society (1967), based in Brisbane; and the Bromeliad Society of Queensland (1967)—reflecting the state's special tropical and subtropical horticultural needs.

JEANNIE SIM

South Australia The South Australian Agricultural Society (established 1839) merged with the South Australian Horticultural Society in 1844 to form the Royal Agricultural and Horticultural Society of South Australia, whose history is recorded in *Royal Show* (1983) and *Teamwork* (1995). The *SOUTH AUSTRALIAN HORTICULTURIST*, *FARM AND GARDEN*, and *GARDEN AND FIELD* were published under its auspices. VITICULTURE was promoted through this predominantly AGRICULTURAL SOCIETY following establishment of an earlier 'Association for the Introduction of Vines' (1840).

Floricultural societies included the South Australian Horticultural and Floricultural Society (1856–1923) and the Carnation and Sweet Pea Society of South Australia (*fl.* 1903–18), the latter strongly associated with Alfred QUARRELL. The South Australian Gardeners' Mutual Improvement Association (1872) was formed (with George STEVENSON as its first president) to promote the interests of professional and amateur gardeners. Incorporated as the South Australian Gardeners' Society (1880–1909), its monthly meetings provided advice and display of plants and attracted the involvement of leading figures in gardening and horticulture, with proceedings often being recorded in the *REGISTER*. A prominent member, Ernst MENZEL, was also secretary of the Mount Lofty Gardeners Society (*fl.* 1890–1900) in the ADELAIDE HILLS.

The South Australian Association of Nurserymen and Seedsmen (1908–), formed to promote the interests of the industry, became the South Australian Association of Nurserymen in the 1940s before being incorporated as the South Australian Horticultural Association in 1985 and merging with the United Farmers' and Stockowners' of South Australia in 1989. The *Grower* (1946–89) was its main publication. Its early history is recorded in SWINBOURNE's *Years of Endeavour* (1982).

Horticultural societies in rural centres and in suburban Adelaide were established during the twentieth century. Some changed their focus from horticulture to gardening—as for example the Thebarton Floriculture and Horticultural Society (1923), which became the Thebarton Garden Club in 1964. Many, particularly in rural areas, remained allied to agricultural societies. Groups interested in the wider landscape and its conservation have also been formed in recent decades, mirroring national trends.

DAVID JONES

Tasmania Ronald GUNN was instrumental in forming horticultural societies in both Launceston (1838) and Hobart (1839). Launceston Horticultural Society held its first show in December 1838 in the Government Cottage, offering prizes (sponsored by the FRANKLINS) for the best COTTAGE GARDEN and to the individual who best furthered the interests of horticulture, whether by importation or otherwise. In 1841 Gunn and William HENTY negotiated the grant of the present CITY PARK for the establishment of the Society's garden, embracing both botanic and ornamental objectives. By 1850, amateur gardeners dissatisfied with the Society and feeling unable to compete with the landed gentry who employed professional gardeners, broke away and formed the Launceston Gardeners' and Amateur Horticultural Society. With declining membership, the Launceston Horticultural Society amalgamated with its rival in 1868 to form the Northern Horticultural Society.

Gunn convened a meeting to establish a horticultural society in Hobart Town although, unlike Launceston, the society

Horticultural societies

did not establish a garden. This role was undertaken, between 1844 and 1886, by the ROYAL SOCIETY of Van Diemen's Land for Horticulture, Botany, and the Advancement of Science, when it was handed control of the former Government Gardens (now the ROYAL TASMANIAN BOTANICAL GARDENS). In 1845 the professional gardeners formed a Gardeners' Society, which amalgamated with the Hobart Horticultural Society in 1851 to form the Gardeners' and Amateurs' Horticultural Society of Hobart Town. By the early 1870s membership was declining, and the Society could not afford to hold its shows or offer worthwhile prizes. Abandonment and failure of its shows in 1874 led to cessation of activities; disaffected members dispersed and formed new groups, including the Tasmanian Agricultural, Pastoral, and Horticultural Society, and the West Hobart Amateur Horticultural and Cottage Gardeners' Society, which also transmuted several times. The Amateur Horticultural Society was formed in 1900 for 'gentlemen amateurs', and soon absorbed Hobart's earlier horticultural society.

Every township had its AGRICULTURAL AND PASTORAL SOCIETY whose shows offered an opportunity to exhibit flowers and produce. Some towns, such as Kempton and Queenstown, also had a horticultural society or garden club, but in smaller centres these were generally short-lived. Specialist societies were unusual until recent decades, perhaps because of small membership numbers and also because the Hobart Horticultural Society, for example, had separate sections for camellias and rhododendrons, roses, and daffodils, responsible for specialist shows.   LINDY SCRIPPS

Victoria The Victorian Horticultural Society (1848–c. 1853), Melbourne Floral and Horticultural Society (fl. 1855), and Victorian Vineyard and Fruit Garden Association (fl. 1855) formed precursors for the two principal colonial horticultural societies, the Horticultural Society of Victoria (1856; Royal prefix granted 1885) and Victorian Horticultural Improvement Society (1859; until 1862 Victorian Gardeners' Mutual Improvement Society and later Victorian Horticultural Society). The Horticultural Society catered for wealthy amateur gardeners, elite professional gardeners and nursery trade representatives; it conducted HORTICULTURAL SHOWS and an EXPERIMENTAL GARDEN at BURNLEY, while the Horticultural Improvement Society followed the British model and concentrated on lectures and shows.

Another outlet for horticulture was provided by agricultural and pastoral societies, which often included horticultural sections in its shows. Such societies were established at Geelong (1855), Beechworth (c. 1862), Bendigo (c. 1863), and South Bourke, based at Box Hill (c. 1872). Where sufficient population existed, horticultural societies were established in country towns, reflecting the development of pastoralism, gold, agriculture, closer settlement, and irrigation. Major societies were those at Ballarat (1859); Geelong: Horticultural Improvement Association of the Western District (1860–66), and Geelong Horticultural Improvement Society (1888–95) and its successors; Castlemaine (by 1861); Benalla (by 1882); and Mildura (by 1890). Suburban and metropolitan societies were established at Richmond (c. 1853), Brighton (1862), Williamstown (by 1865), and Brunswick (by 1886), while the South Suburban Horticultural Society (by 1865) catered for those of the bayside suburbs who did not aspire to the pretensions of their Brighton brethren. These societies combined monthly meetings comprising lectures and competitive exhibits, with annual or seasonal shows. Some had modest libraries, and many published annual reports, but only the Geelong society published transactions.

Specialist societies reflecting the popularity of certain plants developed from the turn of the century. The NATIONAL ROSE SOCIETY of Victoria (1899) and Carnation and Dahlia Society of Victoria (1901), which later embraced sweet peas, typified this national trend; the Cactus and Succulent Society (1930s) began in Vic. and later achieved national coverage. The new ring of suburbs, which encouraged plant specialists, also spawned new horticultural societies, such as those at Ivanhoe (1906), Essendon (by 1906), Malvern (by 1907), and Canterbury (by 1913). Popular movements represented by the WATTLE DAY League (c. 1915) and AUSTRALIAN FOREST LEAGUE (1912) also flourished. Moral and educational virtues were represented by the Victorian State Schools Horticultural Society (c. 1911) and War Relief Gardeners' League (1916).

Professional horticultural bodies followed the rise of unionised labour (Victorian Gardeners' Association: 1902), education at BURNLEY (Women Horticulturists' Association of Victoria: 1918), and influence of local government (Town Planning and Parks Association of Victoria: 1914 and VICTORIAN TREE PLANTERS ASSOCIATION: 1926); later professional societies were often state chapters of national organisations.

Interest in CONSERVATION of the ENVIRONMENT, both natural and cultural, saw many groups formed in the post-war period: Compost Society of Victoria (1945), NATURAL RESOURCES CONSERVATION LEAGUE OF VICTORIA (1951), NATIONAL TRUST OF AUSTRALIA (1956), SOCIETY FOR GROWING AUSTRALIAN PLANTS (1957), AUSTRALIAN GARDEN HISTORY SOCIETY (1980), and ORNAMENTAL PLANT COLLECTIONS ASSOCIATION (1988), and many LANDCARE groups.   RA

Western Australia The Agricultural and Horticultural Society of Western Australia was established soon after the first colonists arrived in 1829. The Society published a *Journal* for 1842, 'conducted through the press' by editor R. W. NASH, and intended 'to be a source of information abroad, and guide and stimulant to exertion at home'. This Society eventually became the Royal Agricultural Society, and remains active. The role of the Horticultural Society of Western Australia (c. 1885–1957) was being questioned in 1886 after only a few exhibitors had participated in the show: 'Every grower must regard the attendance at the shows of this society as one of the many public duties we owe to the requirement of a well-organised community'. The Albany Horticultural Society can trace its beginnings to 1889, making it the oldest continuing country horticultural society in WA. The Mueller Botanic Society (1897) was proposed by E. J. BICKFORD and established upon lines similar to the LINNEAN Society (UK). Ferdinand MUELLER, after whom the Society was named, had shown a 'deep concern in the flora of this colony' and the need to investigate and classify INDIGENOUS PLANTS. After several name changes this Society became the Royal Society of Western Australia (1913), currently associated with the Museum of Western Australia. A need to regulate horticultural activities within the state saw the formation of the Western Australian Horticultural Council (1932). Still in existence, this body of affiliated societies reflects the aims and needs of the horticultural community. This Council published the WEST AUSTRALIAN GARDENER. More than 120 horticultural societies current operate in WA.

CAROLYN MIDDLEMIS

HORTICULTURAL TECHNIQUES increasingly rely on mechanisation and a greater scientific understanding of plant growth and environmental conditions in their development. Traditional hand TOOLS and manual methods have steadily been replaced by a wide range of specifically designed small machinery, or are no longer practised, as a result of a deeper scientific understanding of cultivation requirements, especially in MAINTENANCE and within the NURSERY industry. Economic imperatives, along with much-altered and often degraded environments—in which it has become increasingly difficult to establish vegetation—have emphasised the need for a more scientific approach. COMPUTER technology has revolutionised horticultural machinery, environmental monitoring, and measuring equipment as well as information and communications systems used by landscape practitioners. Continuing research into plant growth and environmental conditions has overturned many previously followed practices, especially many outlined in nineteenth-century horticultural literature. In ARBORICULTURE, for example, a better understanding of branch attachment and structure has led to improved methods of canopy management, enabling trees to live longer, particularly in PUBLIC OPEN SPACES, where safety is of prime importance. In Australia, research into techniques that promote water efficiency (such as XERIC GARDENS), WEED control, and eradication of PESTS AND DISEASES (using integrated approaches with an emphasis on biological control to avoid a total reliance on CHEMICALS) has become an important focus to deliver more sustainable DESIGNED LANDSCAPES. Similarly, techniques developed to support more NATURALISTIC designs—with an emphasis on ECOLOGICAL associations—have become an important part of contemporary horticultural practice.

ML

HORTICULTURAL THERAPY: see GARDEN THERAPY

HORTICULTURE, derived from the Latin *hortus* (garden) and culture, is often confused with gardening. While clearly interrelated, horticulture is differentiated by its emphasis on developing a scientific approach to the cultivation of PLANTS and landscape management. Gardening, on the other hand, is practised as a craft, largely informed by the scientific understanding and technological advances made in the discipline of horticulture. Both are undertaken as professions, although horticulture has demanded increased EDUCATION at the tertiary level to develop and improve its research base and to fulfil its requirement for the training of people who design and manage a diverse range of landscapes. Over the past decades, educational institutions such as BURNLEY COLLEGE have started degree programs—from undergraduate to doctorate level—within the discipline. The demand for research and for courses at tertiary level has been driven by the greater technical degree of competence required in landscape management, especially in NURSERY production and within urban locations, as well as to remedy environmentally degraded RURAL LANDSCAPES. Training at this level is almost entirely directed at PUBLIC OPEN SPACE management rather than domestic gardens, still largely the domain of the amateur GARDENER, albeit often with well-qualified assistance. Significant differences between amateur gardening and professional horticulture are also related to scale, usage, and maintenance, although the empirical knowledge of gardeners has traditionally been a significant influence on horticulture.

The term 'horticulture' has been used widely: in addition to its reference to gardens it has been especially used in AGRICULTURE to refer to intensive cropping (as in fruit and vegetable growing in MARKET GARDENS or VITICULTURE) to distinguish these production systems from broad-acre cropping (for crops such as wheat). Agriculture and FORESTRY are the main applied land-management systems followed in Australia; they have been formalised since the late nineteenth century through government departments, educational institutions, and research programs. Although these two disciplines are still dominant, horticulture has gained increasing importance throughout the twentieth century and is recognised through professional bodies such as the AUSTRALIAN INSTITUTE OF HORTICULTURE.

Several terms have been used in the application of horticulture to gardens and public open space. Historically this came under 'amenity horticulture'—a term still widely used in Britain for production activities unrelated to agriculture or forestry, and especially for management of parks and gardens. The other term widely used, especially in the USA, is 'ornamental horticulture'. Both terms, however, have only limited application to the current concerns within the discipline. Amenity horticulture has developed a strong RECREATIONAL emphasis, and although recreation is an important component, it does not cover the discipline as a whole. Ornamental horticulture implies an aesthetic treatment that ignores the strong functional role. Since the 1990s the term 'environmental horticulture' has been used, especially in Australia and the USA. This term recognises a greater understanding of natural biological processes, especially using the scientific discipline of ECOLOGY as its basis. In fact it is closely related to applied ecology and the burgeoning field of LANDSCAPE ECOLOGY.

The prominent European horticulturist Peter Thoday suggests that three main components act on the vegetation in any landscape site, whether FORMAL or NATURALISTIC in STYLE: the genome (or genetic make-up of vegetation), the influence of the environment on vegetation, and human manipulation of vegetation. Contemporary approaches attempt to reduce, as much as possible, human manipulation to create more sustainability in the landscapes managed. Functionally, vegetation is increasingly being used for its ability to ameliorate harsh

Horticulturist

urban environments, to create greater energy efficiency (by reducing heat loads), to lower water usage, and to better control urban runoff, rather than being seen merely as design ornamentation. In rural landscapes, environmental horticultural technology and management systems are being used to assist in the restoration and re-creation of ecosystems in an attempt to redeem degraded land.

Several specialisations beyond general landscape management are recognised within environmental horticulture: ARBORICULTURE (the management of TREES), nursery production horticulture (PROPAGATION and production of plants), and landscape construction (implementation of landscape design plans).
ML

HORTICULTURIST: see AUSTRALIAN AGRICULTURIST

HOSES AND SPRINKLERS specifically designed to improve the efficiency of applying WATER to gardens and lawns were developed in France and England during the 1860s; their use became common in Australia following development of reticulated water supplies during the mid- to late nineteenth century. Improved water efficiency encouraged the development of domestic gardens and the popular use of hoses and sprinklers. Not all gardeners were convinced about the efficacy of using sprinklers, however, considering them to be injurious to the health of plants, and preferred to continue to water by hand-held hose.

An early system involved transferring water stored in elevated tanks or reservoirs via a series of underground pipes (terracotta or lead) to encompass the walls of a dwelling. Water cocks or taps were installed in the pipe at intervals, and leather hoses of varying lengths—fitted with a brass cock and a rose head, pierced with holes of different sizes—were attached by using a screw fitting. Another ingenious method, for watering large areas, used a series of metal pipes joined together by flexible leather hose and fitted with small sprinkler heads across the top; wheels made the heavy metal hose easier to move. Canvas or India rubber hoses covered with cotton were in vogue during the latter part of the nineteenth century, but proved to be unsuitable because of their tendency to burst due to kinking or rotting. In 1898 a more pliable rubber product helped to eliminate these problems by coating both the exterior and interior cotton lining of the hose. In 1908 the Dunlop Rubber Company was the first to manufacture this type in Australia.

The technology for attaching hoses to tap heads and hose ends for sprinkler fittings has ranged from metal attachments of various kinds—wire or string ties, metal screw fittings, wire clips—to plastic click-on fittings. The period from 1910 to the 1930s saw innovation in both design and marketing, with advertisements for the 'Butterfly', 'Rain King', 'The Fairy', 'Perfection', 'Skattra', 'Pixie', and 'The Frog'; the progress of Melbourne's Gay Sprinkler Company was closely monitored by the horticultural press, and illustrations of fashionably dressed ladies demonstrated the ease of watering the garden using the new products.

The first moulded plastic hoses in Australia were developed in 1945 by John Derham, proprietor of Nylex. The hoses were red in colour to match the shade of 'ripe red tomatoes'. Further developments in watering technology included the introduction of 'soaker' hoses during the 1950s and 'do it yourself' plastic irrigation systems in the 1970s. Recent innovations have included protective layers on hoses to mitigate the effects of the sun's ultraviolet radiation. More important however, with an increasing acknowledgment of the suitability of XERIC GARDENING practices to many parts of Australia, is a new focus on targeted IRRIGATION. This can serve individual plants or garden beds and control time, duration, and intensity of water application.

SUZANNE HUNT

HOSPITAL GARDENS first appeared in medieval hospitals attached to monasteries and commonly included an ORCHARD, VEGETABLE GARDEN, large medicinal garden (perhaps with narcotic plants), vines, and fish ponds. Often used by members of holy orders, these were places of SPIRITUAL rejuvenation. Surgeon John WHITE, after landing at Sydney Cove (1788), complained that 'not a comfort or convenience could be got' for his patients, prompting Governor Phillip to set aside land for a vegetable garden—the first hospital gar-

In the generally dry CLIMATES found across much of Australia, inexpensive rubber (and later plastic) HOSES proved a great boon for home gardeners, although in recent decades there has been a general reassessment of plant selection to reduce WATER consumption

den in Australia, and one of the earliest European attempts at gardening in the new colony.

Institutions designed exclusively for the treatment of the mentally ill were largely a product of the nineteenth century, those in Australia being modelled on prototypes, or influenced by writings, from Britain and North America. An important aspect of Quaker Samuel Tuke's description of The Retreat (1813), York, England, was the therapeutic role the landscape played in treatment. James BACKHOUSE provided Governor Brisbane with a copy of Tuke's book in 1835 prior to the construction of Tarban Creek, the first purpose-built asylum in NSW. The siting of the hospital above the Parramatta River obeyed PICTURESQUE principles of landscape design—a pretension for the benefit of bureaucrats, however, rather than patients.

J.C. LOUDON also commented on the importance of gardens for people's psychological well-being (1832) but it was not until the 1860s that this was related to a patient's environment. The 'moral therapy' philosophies of doctors such as Thomas Kirkbride in the USA and John Connolly in England paralleled the reverence for nature by American poet Ralph Waldo Emerson (1803–1882) and landscape artists Thomas Cole (1801–1848) and Frederic Church (1826–1900). Kirkbride's ideas were influential in the design, under the direction of Frederic Norton Manning (1839–1903), of Callan Park Mental Asylum, Rozelle (NSW)—the first hospital in Australia to be designed and landscaped using these principles (1876–84). Trees were seen as imperative in the treatment of melancholy; the use of a sunk wall to allow distant VISTAS for patients was recommended; airing courts were to have gardens; SUMMER-HOUSES provided quiet airy spots for rest; and productive farms, with patient involvement in maintenance, were considered essential.

Similar principles governed general hospital design: fresh air and sunlight were considered essential for convalescent patients and for the dissipation of miasmas or infectious gases. The landscape was an important spatial element in much hospital planning, and gardens were an integral design component. Gardens were considered therapeutic; they were valued for their role as places of exercise during convalescence, and admired for their aesthetics by staff, patients, and visitors.

Hospital expansion, economic constraints, and changes in patient treatment have had a major impact on hospitals, especially as INSTITUTIONAL GARDENS, and in many places these are now reduced to token planting around the entrance. Some new hospitals incorporate gardens in their design (for example, the Children's Hospital, Westmead, NSW), especially for GARDEN THERAPY. Many large asylums are significant as grand DESIGNED LANDSCAPES, often containing notable plant collections. Some redundant sites have been severely compromised by privatised development, others have been sympathetically adapted for alternative institutional use. The sensitive management of the remainder provides a challenge for the whole community.   COLLEEN MORRIS

HOTHOUSE, a GREENHOUSE where some form of heating supplements direct absorption of solar radiation during the day. Early hothouses, often called STOVES, used dry heat, but by the early nineteenth century this was provided by steam; later, hot water was conveyed in pipes through the interior of the house (usually from a dedicated boiler located close to the building). Electric heating, using radiant and convection systems linked to internal and external sensors, has been another significant design change. Hothouse plants were rarely sunk into earth; instead, timber stages usually held potted plants ranging from those being PROPAGATED to tender exotics (especially ORCHIDS) on display. When attached to a residence or of unusual size or architectural distinction, the hothouse was commonly known as a CONSERVATORY. Specialised hothouses, such as vineries, housed plants requiring specific environmental conditions and large-scale production requirements. The term 'hothouse' was also applied generically in the columns of the overseas gardening press to classify a wide collection of TROPICAL or tender plants, but in Australia the shade of a BUSH-HOUSE was more often required for such plants.   RA

HOWARD, Amos William (1848–1930), English-born nursery proprietor and pasture improvement pioneer, migrated to Adelaide in 1876 and established a plant nursery at Blakiston, in the ADELAIDE HILLS. In 1889, while inspecting land nearby for purchase, he noted a kind of clover (later identified as subterranean clover, *Trifolium subterraneum*), that improved pastures and upgraded soil fertility. He sold this in commercial quantities from 1907 and within half a century some eight million hectares in southern Australia had been sown with the clover.   DAVID JONES

HOWARD, Harry Stanton (1930–2000), architect, landscape architect, and planner, was born and educated in Sydney. He graduated in architecture from the University of Sydney and completed a diploma in town and regional planning. Howard was a committed modernist and, following work with architect Sydney Ancher, and in the office of Edwards Madigan Torzillo, he established an independent practice, sharing a design office in North Sydney with colleagues including Bruce RICKARD and Bruce MACKENZIE. Strongly influenced from childhood by the bush gullies of the North Shore, Howard became a leading advocate for AUSTRALIAN FLORA through his landscape designs, and was among those who contributed to a distinctive 'Sydney School', which responded strongly to the local landscape. He worked on site planning and landscape design of many schools during the 1960s, and created fine institutional expressions of the BUSH GARDEN ethos. He was consultant landscape architect to Lane Cove Council for two decades, guiding the creation of a municipal landscape in harmony with the ecological and aesthetic values of the indigenous bush. Howard lectured part-time at the University of New South Wales from the early 1960s, and was a generous educator and mentor.

In 1978, Harry Howard received a commission—the design of the landscape setting of the High Court and National Gallery in Canberra—that was to become his most highly acclaimed work. The design of its Sculpture Garden, located within the NATIONAL TRIANGLE, was developed with his associate Barbara Buchanan and architect Roger Vidler; it turned the erstwhile building site into a brilliant microcosm of the Australian bush, studded with SCULPTURE and redolent of SENSORY experiences found in our unique landscape. Completed in 1982, the Sculpture Garden is an outstanding and mature expression of Australian LANDSCAPE ARCHITECTURE. Howard received the Australian Award in Landscape Architecture from the AUSTRALIAN INSTITUTE OF LANDSCAPE ARCHITECTS in 1996—the highest award of that group, of which he had been a foundation member. RA

HOWITT, William (1792–1879), author and traveller, and his brothers Richard (1799–1870), poet, and Godfrey (1800–1873), physician and natural scientist, were born in Derbyshire, England. William and his wife, Mary (née Botham) (1799–1888), are credited with 180 published works. In Australia, the best known of these is *Land, Labour, and Gold; or Two Years in Victoria* (1855), written as the result of William's experiences during the years 1852–54. This book shows his concern for social issues, but also reveals his interest in NATIVE PLANTS and in colonial gardens. The Howitts moved in cultured colonial circles, and were well acquainted with Edward La Trobe BATEMAN and Lieutenant-Governor C.J. LA TROBE. William and Mary settled in Rome in 1870, and may have been responsible for planting EUCALYPTS that drained malarial swamps. A son, Alfred William Howitt (1830–1908), was a noted artist and scientist.

Richard arrived in Port Phillip in 1840 with his younger brother and farmed near Heidelberg until 1844. His *Impressions of Australia Felix during Four Years Residence in that Colony* (1845) was regarded as 'the most reliable description of Australian life at that date'. Godfrey, a graduate of the University of Edinburgh, arrived in Port Phillip in 1840 with members of his wife's family (Bakewell). He erected a prefabricated cottage on land which, by 1845, extended from Collins Street to Flinders Lane with a frontage to Spring Street, where he had a 'notable garden'. He maintained pastoral interests near Yea and Cape Schanck and a farm at Caulfield. He was involved with many medical and scientific associations and societies, including the Royal Society of Victoria, and enjoyed a wide reputation as a botanist and entomologist. GWEN PASCOE

HOWLETT, Frederick (1832–1913), horticulturist, was born at Ampton, Suffolk, England, and arrived in Melbourne in 1856. While a clerk at the University of Melbourne he took a keen interest in the development of HORTICULTURE and ACCLIMATISATION. He joined the Victorian Horticultural Improvement Society in 1875 (vice-president 1877, president 1884) and was a regular winner of the cottage garden and amateur classes at Society shows. His papers on floriculture were popular and informative, though moralistic in style. In 1887 he took up 275 acres (110 ha) outside Morwell (Vic.), and his farm, Spring Grove, became his nursery where he developed an experimental ORCHARD. He was the energetic founding secretary of the Dairymen's and Fruitgrowers' Association. As a local councillor he strenuously promoted the planting of productive trees in his district. In 1910 he retired to Sandringham, where he continued his experiments with varieties of fruits and vegetables suitable for local conditions. NORAH L. KILLIP

HÜGEL, Carl (Charles) Alexander Anselm von (1795–1870), Austrian diplomat, army officer, courtier, and naturalist, travelled to the Swan River Colony, Van Diemen's Land, Norfolk Island, and NSW in 1833–34, recording his observations on vegetation, people, and gardens, and collecting seeds and HERBARIUM specimens. On his return to Europe he became famous for his gardens, where he cultivated fashionable 'New Holland plants'—some 350 new species of which were described from his specimens (for example, *Melaleuca huegelii* and *Hardenbergia*, named after his sister, Countess von Hardenberg). From Europe he corresponded with William MACARTHUR and William HOOKER, and his descriptions of the AUSTRALIAN FLORA stimulated the interest of Ferdinand MUELLER. In addition to his botanical legacy, the 1994 English translation of Hugel's *New Holland Journal* (1833–34) has brought his views of the state of colonial horticulture and society to a wider audience.

COLLEEN MORRIS

HUGHAN, Robert (1833–1898), gardener and viticulturist, was born at Sorbie, Wigtownshire, Scotland, and was a gardener to the Earl of Galloway. He migrated to Geelong (Vic.) in 1854 with the intention of starting a vineyard, although on arrival he initially undertook six months' gardening employment with Charles Ibbotson. Hughan then established a vineyard at Highton—a success until the phylloxera outbreak brought about its destruction c. 1880. He had twelve children, of whom some of the sons and their descendants took up gardening occupations. A grandson, Randolph Hughan (1865–1956), settled in Mildura in 1895 as a supervisor of irrigation, then in 1901 took up the curatorship of HAMILTON BOTANIC GARDENS, a post he held for forty-four years. GEORGE JONES

HUGHES, (Edwin) Albert ('Elfin') (1876–1958), horticulturist, journalist, broadcaster, and commercial traveller, was born in New Zealand and lived in Adelaide before moving to Perth c. 1917. The warm acknowledgment he received on his arrival to WA hints at his prior achievements. In May 1925 Hughes began the first weekly gardening column in the *West Australian*, and he contributed regularly for eight years. He brought together this information in *Every Amateur's Gardening Guide* (c. 1931)—with the cover title *The Westrala Gardener*—'a simple treatise for amateurs in town, suburban, and country gardens'. His knowledge, enthusiasm, and energetic attitude made him an ideal pioneering garden broadcaster on RADIO station 6WF (1926–27). Hughes was honorary secretary of the Floricultural and Horticultural Society in 1917 and responsible for arranging its annual flower shows. SWEET PEAS were his passion: 'he only had to be in your house for ten minutes before he was in the garden with a spade in his hands'. CAROLYN MIDDLEMIS

HUGHES PARK, Watervale, SA, an extensive pastoral holding in the Clare Valley, was the home of Sir Walter Watson Hughes (1803–1887), a Scottish-born pastoralist, mine-owner, and public benefactor. He established Hughes Park in 1862, drawing upon his Wallaroo mine profits. Here he

The *Westrala Gardener* (c. 1931) by E.A. HUGHES, was intended by its author to spread 'more widely and minutely a knowledge of flower growing'—sentiments well conveyed by its evocative cover

planted the first Riesling vines in the locality and established a twenty-nine-hectare park of Scottish conifers and deciduous trees. A gift of £20 000 in 1871 by Hughes helped establish the University of Adelaide and formed the Chair of Classics and Philosophy.

Hughes Park was inherited by his nephew, Sir John James Duncan (1845–1913), pastoralist and politician, who in 1891 extended the residence. He established the walled garden (with clipped olive hedge), unusual triangular citrus grove, and a tapered netting cage covering vines and espaliered fruit trees. His eldest son, John Grant Duncan (1882–1962), inherited the property in 1913 (and became known as John Grant Duncan-Hughes in compliance with the will of his great-uncle Walter Watson Hughes). After the death of Duncan-Hughes, the property was managed by his nephew, John James Duncan (1913–1997), who assumed full ownership in 1990. Hughes Park now operates as a family trust managed by his sons Walter Hughes DUNCAN (b. 1939) and John Gordon Duncan (b. 1943).

Walter Duncan, who now lives at Hughes Park, started restoration of the house and gardens in 1973. He planted the tree-lined drive and established the homestead garden, retaining many existing trees and blending exotic plants into the original setting. He also developed an extensive ROSE garden (with more than 700 varieties of heritage roses) as a DISPLAY GARDEN for his specialist nursery business.

TREVOR NOTTLE and DAVID JONES

HUNT, Sidney Herbert (c. 1883–1962), horticultural journalist, broadcaster, and nursery proprietor, was born at Moonta (SA) the son of a miner, but spent the early part of his career in Bendigo (Vic.). He moved to Sydney c. 1927 and described himself in the early 1930s as an 'Adviser in Garden Craft' to the *Australian Garden Lover, Home, Garden Gossip, Women's Budget, Fashion and Society, Australian Traveller,* 'and other leading metropolitan and provincial journals'. Hunt was a contributor to the Sydney *Sun,* and it was from these articles that he self-published his *Gardening Simplified* (1934). Likening the garden to the 'best room in the home', Hunt provided easily understood advice on horticulture and 'Landscape Art' for amateur gardeners. He believed that 'curves are lines of beauty, and, when properly used in conjunction with others that are straight and direct, for contrast sake, they add greatly to the measure of success attained'; he urged gardener designers to avoid incongruity and recommended that gardens should have 'due regard to the architecture and size of the dwelling, and the extent and shape of the ground surrounding it'. The cover of *Gardening Simplified* featured a portrait of Hunt at the microphone of Sydney commercial radio station 2UW, where he was a pioneering horticultural broadcaster; as the medium developed he spread his talents to other stations in Sydney, Katoomba, and Orange (NSW). He was also a proprietor of Sydney-based Hunt & East Pty Ltd with Cecil Arthur Wentworth East (1909–2001), seed and plant merchants, and took full advantage of his media profile in the firm's advertising; specialising in rare seeds, plants, and bulbs, Hunt & East traded under the banner 'The Friendly Garden Store'. *Gardening Simplified* ran to seven largely unchanged editions by 1952, and for several decades rivalled the guides of YATES and BRUNNING in popularity. RA

HUNTER VALLEY, NSW, a favoured horticultural region 200 kilometres north of Sydney, comprises a series of broad valleys enclosed by mountain ranges, rising in the north to 1556 metres (Barrington Tops) with snow gums and stands of rare *Nothofagus moorei* (Antarctic Beech). The valleys drain via the Hunter River to the sea at Newcastle.

Grape growing and wine making were introduced into the Hunter Valley by James BUSBY and James King in the 1830s and consolidated by Dr H.J. Lindeman at Cawarra from 1843 onwards. Along the Hunter River are picturesque nineteenth-century towns, including Morpeth, Maitland, Singleton, and Muswellbrook, often dominated by a spired or towered church on a rise and set within parkland or cemetery. On the slopes overlooking the river are historic buildings with columned verandahs and overgrown gardens with cast-iron seats and urns, overhung by huge, lichen-draped fig trees, all contributing to a general air of nostalgia.

The early colonial homesteads of the lower Hunter such as Dalwood, Aberglasslyn, and Tomago have had chequered careers, and only traces of their original gardens survive. In the Singleton area pastoral prosperity gave rise to houses such as Baroona (1869–93) and Minimbah (1875–77)—vast, towered piles encircled by verandahs, often dominating a hilltop and set within a sweep of tall trees and garden. The big houses and churches speak of confidence and continuity: in the grounds of All Saints Church, Singleton, is a substantial stone temple, the mausoleum of the DANGARS of Baroona.

VITICULTURE dominates the landscapes around Pokolbin and Broke. Further up the Hunter Valley are major horse studs with their characteristic high-fenced paddocks and manicured settings: Coolmore (Jerrys Plains) and Arrowfield (Scone) are examples. The Scone district has notable gardens such as the homestead garden at Turanville, and several splendid landscaped estates including ST AUBINS (designed by Jocelyn BROWN), the historic White family property Belltrees, and the Packer family grazing property and polo grounds at Ellerston, which has a modern lake and gardens designed by Andrew PFEIFFER.

Philip Cox, Howard Tanner, and Meredith Walker, *The Hunter Valley* (South Melbourne, 1978)   HOWARD TANNER

HURLEY, Percy Joseph (Peter) ('Waratah') (*c.* 1893–1983), horticultural journalist, attributed his interest in gardening to his wife; from their marriage in 1924 they maintained a quarter-acre garden at their home in East Lindfield on Sydney's North Shore. Hurley joined the *Sun* in 1930 and first began writing for the *Sydney Morning Herald* in 1937; from 1953 he also wrote for the *Sun-Herald*. He contributed to many garden journals and was for many years a council member of the Royal Horticultural Society of New South Wales. His first garden book, *Grow Your Own Vegetables* (1943), appeared in the same year as the first edition of his popular travel book, *In Search of Australia*. His major work was *An Encyclopaedia for Australian Gardeners* (1946), the first Australian GARDEN BOOK to adopt an encyclopaedic presentation and, on Hurley's admission, based on *Johnson's Gardeners' Dictionary*, first published more than a century earlier and then still in print. Hurley confined himself to plants and design features commonly used in Australian gardens; the popularity of his *Encyclopaedia* was confirmed by its revision for nine editions over fifteen years. Later gardening books included *Australian Rose Growing for Amateurs* (1947), which included advice for different climatic regions and five plans of formal rose gardens, and *This Week in Your Garden* (1951); he also edited Stan Kelly's *40 Australian Eucalypts in Colour* (1949). Hurley, writing as 'Waratah', retired from the *Sydney Morning Herald* in 1969,

Cressfield, near Scone (NSW), built by Archibald Little in the 1830s and painted by Conrad Martens in 1862, is typical of HOMESTEAD GARDENS in drier areas of Australia with its broad expanses of gravel and hardy plants

widely acknowledged as an authority of his generation and proclaiming that gardening was 'good for you psychologically and morally … you're not just sitting and watching something grow, you're taking part in it'.   RA

HYBRIDISATION: see PLANT BREEDING

HYDE PARK, Perth, was originally *Boodjamooling*, a wetland with abundant wildlife and useful plants that was a popular meeting place for Aboriginal people. From the mid-nineteenth century the Third Swamp Reserve (as it was then known) was a fringe-dwellers' camp and watering point for stock. Although earmarked for residential development, attempts to drain the wetland interfered with domestic water supplies, and in 1897 the area was instead declared a recreation reserve. It was fenced and landscaped during 1897–99, and renamed Hyde Park. The *Jacaranda mimosifolia* (Jacaranda) avenue in the south-eastern portion was established in 1921, a colourful addition to planting dominated by *Platanus* X *acerifolia* (Plane Tree), *Ficus macrophylla* (Moreton Bay Fig), *Phoenix canariensis* (Canary Island Date Palm), *Araucaria* spp., and *Cinnamomum camphora* (Camphor Laurel) trees. Barbecue and playground facilities were added during a major renewal in 1965. Today the park is a popular venue for picnics, photography, and quiet relaxation.   ANDREA GAYNOR

HYDE PARK, Sydney, occupies land within the area marked out by Governor Phillip in 1792 as township land for the city. By Governor Macquarie's time, on 11 February 1810, it was formally reserved as open space, the first PUBLIC PARK set aside in Australia. It was delineated only as a space at the end of Macquarie Street, where the military held parades, and townspeople cut firewood and carted off soil. It became a favourite place for cricket, a PLAYGROUND for local schoolboys, a RACECOURSE, and—with its slightly elevated position—a PROMENADE. In 1854 the *Public Parks Act* was passed and a Hyde Park Improvement Committee formed. The central walkway, aligned with Macquarie Street, was established as its major axis, with a FIG avenue, and it began to attract some civic monuments. Control was vested in the Sydney Municipal Council in 1904.

Hyde Park is now a defined space of sixteen hectares at the edge of the city centre, ringed by roads, and used daily by many Sydneysiders. It was refashioned in the late 1920s after construction of the underground railway, which necessitated massive excavations and vast disturbance over five years (1924–29). A design COMPETITION (1926) for a restored and refurbished Hyde Park (along 'up-to-date lines') was won by engineer Norman Weekes (1888–1972), with a finely delineated design drawn by young architect Raymond McGrath (1903–1977). This design evolved with the active criticism of the assessors, John SULMAN, architect Alfred Hook, and Town Clerk W.G. Layton, who wrote a masterly report assessing the design, pointing out its shortcomings, and enunciating the design philosophy favoured. There was a move to include NATIVE PLANTS, and E.H. WARD, curator of SYDNEY BOTANIC GARDENS, became the chief adviser—he was responsible for the planting of the great, dense AVENUE of *Ficus microcarpa* var. *hillii* (Hill's Fig).

Desirable attributes were listed: the need for shade, restriction of plant species, open grassed areas rather than shrubberies. Specimen trees were considered 'out of place'; flower beds were tolerated in restraint. The desired quality was 'quietude'—the park would be a haven from the bustle and noise of the city. Trams and buses, routed through the park by Weekes, were eliminated. Civic monuments were thought appropriate, and two of the most successful of the period were attracted—the Archibald Fountain (1932) by French sculptor François Sicard, at the northern end, and the Anzac Memorial (1929–34) by architect C. Bruce Dellit (1900–1942) at the southern end: an inspired Art Deco monument of blocky, buttressed forms. With fine sculptures under Raynor Hoff's direction, its symbolism departed from neo-classical forms used in many WAR MEMORIALS, and incorporated symbols special to Australia—such as the rising sun and figures of brooding servicemen—which gave monumental strength to the large granite structure.

HELEN PROUDFOOT

HYDROPONICS is a form of plant culture that does not use soil. In the most common hydroponic systems, nutrients are supplied in solution and the plant is supported in an inert medium such as sand, gravel, plastic chips, perlite, expanded clay, rockwool, or similar. The nutrients are then trickled through the medium. Some commercial crops are grown in a film of water flowing in a shallow trough or gutter (nutrient film technique). Plants have been grown in water for centuries but the origins of hydroponics as we understand it lie in the eighteenth century, when scientists grew plants in water with some soil added to try to gain a better understanding of plant nutrition. By the nineteenth century scientists had found that dissolved salts could be used to provide essential nutrients in solution. The term hydroponics was coined in the early 1930s, when workers were developing commercial systems for greenhouse culture of plants using nutrient solutions. The technique was first used in Australia in the late 1930s. Hydroponic production was recognised as being useful where existing soil conditions were poor, and the United States Army used the technique to grow fresh vegetables for troops serving in the Pacific during and after the Second World War. Hydroponic culture has long been of interest to hobbyist growers who enjoy the challenge it presents, but it has also proved useful in some commercial applications including vegetables such as tomatoes, lettuce, and herbs, and cut flowers such as roses, carnations, and gerberas. World-wide, commercial hydroponic vegetable growing is estimated to cover approximately 30 000 hectares.   PETER MAY

HYNDMAN, William (1822–1883), gardener, was born in Argyllshire, Scotland and worked as a gardener in both Scotland and Ireland before employment at Trinity College, Dublin, collecting specimens for practical classes and preservation in a HERBARIUM. Hyndman arrived in Melbourne in

Hyndman

1855 and by March 1856, he was working at the MELBOURNE BOTANIC GARDEN. He then took a position as 'botanical porter' at the University of Melbourne, where, for more than a year, he assisted in laying out the SYSTEM GARDEN, but resigned after friction with the Professor of Natural Science, Frederick McCoy. By early 1859 he was working with Edward La Trobe BATEMAN, who had been commissioned by the city council to design the CARLTON and FITZROY GARDENS. As the Melbourne City Corporation gardener, Hyndman's responsibilities included Carlton Gardens, Murchison, Lincoln, Macarthur, and Argyle SQUARES, West Melbourne Reserve, and Victoria Parade. In 1869, with three men, he was looking after eight miles (13 km) of walks and more than 18 000 trees. Problems included damage done by goats, dogs, and vandalism, and robberies. There were complaints about weeds, mismanagement, and access. Redmond Barry and Ferdinand MUELLER appreciated his talents as an 'experienced practical gardener', with 'great experience in forming public plantations', but despite this recognition, Hyndman was suspended in April 1870 for ring-barking several Blue Gums, without authority, and left the council's service to establish a nursery in North Fitzroy.

GWEN PASCOE

INDIA was progressively administered by Britain until 1947 following the granting of a charter to the East India Company (1600). When New Holland was claimed by the British in 1770, India was among the nearest imperial outposts; indeed, between 1814 and 1835, the Church of England in Australia was part of the see of Calcutta. India's rich traditions of landscaping were overlaid with British-influenced gardens. From India and Ceylon (as well as Burma, Malaya, and Java) came the tradition of HILL-STATIONS, derived from the elevated SUMMER RETREATS of the British officials established at Ootacamund, Darjeeling, and Simla (India) and Nuwara Eliya (Ceylon)—the latter much visited by Anglo–Australian travellers after the opening of the Suez Canal (1869). GARDENERS with firsthand experience in India included John DALLACHY, who, during 1847–48, had managed the Earl of Aberdeen's Ceylonese estates; Baptist minister John Smith, who established Delhi Villa (later BUDA) in 1861–63 while convalescing at Castlemaine; and Christopher MUDD, who travelled there as botanist for the Prince of Wales during 1875–76. Some officers of the East India Company, such as Charles Weston of HORSLEY and Arthur Pooley Onslow, came to NSW, and several administrators in NSW had served in India or the East Indies, bringing with them rich cultural influences. Many British army officers retired from India to Tas. during the early nineteenth century, perhaps seeking the freedom of a colonial lifestyle in a more familiar climate. Qld also had close links with India during the nineteenth century, and Walter HILL and his successors acquired Indian books and journals for the library of the BRISBANE BOTANIC GARDENS. German scientists were prominent in India (as they were in Australia); in India they developed the imperial model of FORESTRY, which was gradually extended to other territories: Indian forest service conservator F.D'A. Vincent visited Vic. and recommended the model in 1887, and Inspector-General of Forests in India, B. Ribbentrop did the same when he visited in 1895. From India also came the tradition of agri-horticultural societies, adopted in Australia in a society that shared a need for experiments with a need for plant acclimatisation (especially of economic plants) and also had a sparse population without the momentum to successfully maintain horticultural societies away from the main metropolitan centres.

From India came many fruits and vegetables, RHODODENDRONS and also *Ficus benjamina* (Weeping Fig). Exchanges between BOTANIC GARDENS in India—especially Calcutta, particularly during the directorship of Nathaniel Wallich—and Australia also enriched horticulture. Thomas Augustus Firminger (1812–1884), in his book *Gardening in Upper India and Bengal* (1863), spoke to a local audience—but that audience was widely mirrored in Australia in the need for shade rather than glass, and cooling rather than heat. Surveyor John THOMPSON wrote from Sydney to LOUDON (*Gardener's Magazine*, 1840): 'The droughts to which we are so continually subject render abortive all attempts at maintaining a garden in the English style; and point out to me, that stonework, and terraces, and large shady trees, the characteristics of Hindostanee gardens, are more suited to our climate than English lawns and flower-beds'—an observation only partially embraced by colonists.

Sylvia Crowe and Sheila Haywood, *The Gardens of Mughul India* (London, 1972); C.A. Bayley (ed.) *The Raj: India and the British 1600–1947* (London, 1990); Ray Desmond, *The European Discovery of the Indian Flora* (Oxford, 1992); James L. Westcoat and Joachim Wolschke-Bulmahn (eds), *Mughal Gardens: Sources, Places, Representations, and Prospects* (Washington, D.C., 1992)

RA

INDIGENOUS PLANTS: see AUSTRALIAN FLORA

INDOOR PLANTS Nineteenth century are absent from the visual record of Australia's earliest colonial years, possibly due to the initial dearth of flower POTS and sheltering VERANDAHS. There were plant rooms at ELIZABETH FARM by 1826, and the section on 'the management of Plants in Rooms' in Daniel BUNCE's *Manual* (1838) suggests an established habit in the south at least—as do references to CONSERVATORIES in Van Diemen's Land soon after. Plant stands of WIRE-WORK, iron, and timber, a bouquet stand, and ornamental china flower pots appear in house sales of Sydney bankrupts in the 1840s. Stands were fitted with zinc (later galvanised iron) trays and sometimes nets to support cut flowers immersed in wet sand to prolong their life. Purpose-made cast-iron trays and ceramic saucers protected surfaces. As with containers for FLOWER ARRANGEMENTS, ornamental pots and urns changed style as one revival succeeded another, and multiplied as mass production increased the options. New decorative theories dominated the final quarter of the nineteenth century, with metal and ceramic containers from the Middle and Far East being popular. Easels and ceramic pedestals and jardinières set off pot plants, and plain terracotta pots were often casually swathed in drapery.

The advent of house plants was closely related to the arrival of GREENHOUSES, PALM and ORCHID houses, and FERNERIES. Ideally, plants came into the house at their peak. Whether seen in the attached conservatory or the house proper, the great divide was between greenery and coloureds, which lit up interiors. Although mentioned in Australian horticultural literature, window boxes and WARDIAN CASES were less common than in colder countries. Indoor plants (listed roughly in order of chronological popularity during the nineteenth century) included lilies, geraniums, begonias, coleus, fuchsias, ferns, cinerarias, calceolarias, primulas, cordylines, orchids, tradescantias, succulents, aspidistras, and palms of all sorts.

From at least the 1870s the dolefulness of the summer fireplace was relieved either with greenery or an admixture—coral or seashells set among rocks and ferns to imitate nature; cut flowers tucked promiscuously into a moss-drenched mantelshelf protected by a glass plateau; or creepers such as ivy or tradescantia descending curtain-like or climbing almost to the ceiling. Verandahs and COURTYARDS were transitional spaces where tiered wooden stands were acceptable, where TRELLIS might support passionflowers, and where staghorns and other semi-tender plants created an illusion of coolth, sometimes shielded by blinds. Special occasions and the rooms of parade received special attention: at GOVERNMENT HOUSE, Hobart, a tree fern, arching over a cornucopia of summer flowers, substituted for the traditional CHRISTMAS TREE in the 1840s and later *Araucaria hetrophylla* (Norfolk Island Pine) did duty on a mantelpiece for a Hobart wedding. A wedding at WERRIBEE PARK in 1894 saw the hall lined with pots in plant stands, 'with huge palms and greenery carrying the decoration to the ceiling on either side of the staircase'. Late in the century, plants became virtual items of furniture or semi-architectural elements as cosy corners and bower-like spaces were created using plants, flowers, and peacock feathers.   JESSIE SERLE

Twentieth century In the twentieth century, the palm (especially *Kentia* sp.), aspidistra, *Monstera deliciosa*, Maidenhair Fern, terrarium, hanging basket of fuchsias, and cactus became successive clichés. Some of these had previously been used indoors—particularly palms, ferns, and fuchsias—and their use (especially in older houses) until the mid-century continued a mode of display little changed from the nineteenth century. Timber pot stands and metal jardinières continued as favourite accessories, with wire-work stands generally still confined to the verandah. Changes in architectural style, especially on the advent of MODERNISM, brought a changed approach, however. Plants assisted in defining or subdividing rooms, provided links between indoor and outdoor spaces, and, through bold foliage, complemented geometric architectural patterns and textures. Enthusiasm for tropical plants, especially those with bold, brightly coloured, and variegated foliage, came into fashion during the 1960s, well demonstrated in the catalogues of *Decorative Plants* issued by Jack KREMPIN; they were incomplete without white-painted WIRE-WORK or wrought-iron stands. BONSAI provided an oriental touch in interiors during this period, alongside Ikebana floral arrangements. By the final decades of the twentieth century, indoor plants had become a widespread domestic feature, and the popularity of spaces that shared both indoor and outdoor attributes—such as courtyards, PATIOS, sunrooms, and APARTMENT balconies—augmented the verandah's traditional dominance as the site for the most impressive displays.

In the latter part of the twentieth century the atrium and other wide, lofty, spaces became regular features of large commercial buildings such as hotels, office complexes, and shopping malls. Widespread creation of planned interior landscapes responded in part to German research that revealed the benefits of using living plants to humanise otherwise sterile spaces. In the movement known as *Burolandschaft*, plants unified and complemented architecture and interior design, divided and screened, created sightlines, directed pedestrians, and formed impressive entrance displays. Widespread utilisation of plants indoors was further facilitated by advances in electrical lighting technology, and by the development of mechanical control of temperature and humidity within buildings. Electrical lamps specifically designed to produce horticulturally appropriate spectral energy increasingly provided the range of light necessary for photosynthesis in plants. Plant species commonly used for interior displays in Australia include *Anthurium, Aralia, Aspidistra, Caladium, Chamaedorea, Chlorophytum, Cissus, Croton, Dracaena, Ficus, Hedera, Howea, Monstera, Nephrolepis, Philodendron, Phoenix, Rhapis, Sansevieria, Schefflera,* and *Spathiphyllum*— generally plants with dramatic foliage that tolerate low levels of light. Today, in Australia, the production, installation, and management of plants for indoor use in domestic and commercial buildings is a multimillion-dollar industry. However, interior plants are often placed as an afterthought, and many installations fail because basic horticultural requirements of irrigation, drainage, light, or maintenance have been overlooked in the design process.   CLIVE SORRELL

Tovah Martin, *Once Upon a Windowsill: A History of Indoor Plants* (Portland, Oregon, 1988); Terence Lane and Jessie Serle, *Australians at Home: A Documentary History of Australian Domestic Interiors from 1788 to 1914* (Melbourne, 1990)

INDUSTRIAL LANDSCAPES: see COMMERCIAL GARDENS

INSTITUTIONAL GARDENS include those associated with long-established public institutions—such as BOTANIC and ZOOLOGICAL GARDENS, HOSPITALS, gaols, CEMETERIES, churches, SCHOOLS, UNIVERSITIES, art galleries, parliament and GOVERNMENT HOUSES, and RAILWAYS—and, more recently, occur in the form of private business parks for industrial and COMMERCIAL sites.

Many existing public institutions were established during the mid-nineteenth century—a period of considerable prosperity resulting from mineral wealth as well as agricultural and pastoral productivity—and many exhibited identifiable characteristics. The buildings, for example, were of solid construction in masonry or brick, ornately designed in the Victorian manner, and built to last. Surrounded by extensive

Institutional gardens

Railway gardens were once the most numerous of institutional gardens, and due to an extensive system of competitions, among the most keenly maintained; this prize-winning station garden, photographed in 1959, is at Glenbrook (NSW)

grounds often laid out in the fashionable Gardenesque style, with curving gravel driveways and paths, dense evergreen shrubberies, large specimen trees, ornate fountains and ornamental pools, they were generally enclosed by high masonry walls or iron palisade fences with elaborate cast-iron entrance gates. These grounds, designed to impress arriving visitors, provided an attractive setting for the buildings, isolating them from the surrounding community. Reticulated irrigation systems increasingly facilitated year-round watering, and this encouraged the development of expanses of manicured lawns and colourful displays of bedding plants. Grounds such as these required constant maintenance by a staff of skilled gardeners, but since wages were low and gardeners plentiful, this was rarely seen as a problem. A house provided at a moderate rent within the grounds for the head gardener meant this was once a highly sought-after position.

Originally the various institutions used their grounds in different ways. Ornament was a high priority, but this was perhaps just the most obvious impression to visitors, staff, and inmates. Other more complex factors were also involved. Railway gardens, for instance, encouraged pride in the workplace. The therapeutic value of plants and green spaces was well known, and hospitals and lunatic asylums encouraged patients and their visitors to walk and sit in the well-kept gardens. In some cases, in asylums and gaols, for instance, trusted inmates assisted in some of the day-to-day maintenance where it was considered beneficial or appropriate. Several of these larger institutions incorporated vegetable gardens or plant nurseries, with the produce and plants being used across a network of kindred institutions.

Changes within society in attitudes and values, as well as technological and electronic developments, have frequently had an impact on institutional gardens, usually to the detriment of their original or early character. For example, accommodating social changes has not been easy for established cemeteries and churchyards. Many of these landscapes have heritage value: significant buildings and monuments, intricate patterns of driveways, pathways, and open drainage channels, and a valuable diversity of plant species. Attempts to incorporate modern vaults and mausolea, lawn graves, and parking areas have rarely been successful. Grounds maintenance has been particularly difficult, as the original layouts, designed for manual labour, have not been amenable to mechanised forms of maintenance. Raising money for continuing restoration, conservation, and day-to-day maintenance is difficult, and the use of volunteer labour has limitations.

The impact of such changes is always most keenly felt at established sites. By comparison, their modern counterparts have fared better, since space for extension can be incorporated at the initial planning stage and many fine new institutional gardens have been created. Enhanced access to some previously restricted spaces is an encouraging development in recent institutional garden design—Australia's new Parliament House being a prominent example.

Recent political pressure to reduce costs and maximise usage has also brought many changes. Construction of additional buildings and expansion of parking areas has meant the loss of many trees and green spaces, and high-maintenance horticultural displays have been replaced by minimum-maintenance alternatives. In some cases, whole institutions have been relocated, resulting in entirely new uses; this has often

Interpretation

required a total redesign, in which heritage items are conserved and new activities incorporated, with varying degrees of success. Some institutions, such as botanic gardens and zoos, are increasingly being forced, in order to raise funds, to include facilities for popular entertainment—often at odds with the primary purpose of the institution or, less obviously but perhaps more insidiously, diverting valuable staff resources from core activities. Commercial sponsorship is at its most effective when respective interests are well matched, and managers of institutional gardens are increasingly forced to confront such arrangements as public funding is reduced.

The corporate business park can be considered a modern form of institutional garden. While emphasis is on aesthetics to promote a strong corporate image, the needs and comfort of visitors and staff are also carefully considered. Adequate parking, outdoor eating, entertainment, sporting, and childcare facilities all form an important part of the overall design. In stark contrast to their government counterparts, these corporate grounds are meticulously maintained, as this is seen by shareholders as a legitimate expense.

ALLAN CORREY

INTERPRETATION, in environmental and cultural heritage conservation practice, is the way visitors learn about and value a place. It includes the philosophy, methods, and media that present gardens to a visiting public. The term was initially defined in 1957 (and subsequently popularised) by US National Park Service officer Freeman Tilden (1883–1980) as 'an educational activity which aims to reveal meaning and relationships through the use of original objects, by first hand experience, and by illustrative media, rather than simply to communicate factual information'. Tilden's principles for interpretation, and their ensuing guidelines, have formed a foundation for further development by Australian interpreters in HERITAGE PLACES and landscapes such as NATIONAL PARKS, historic landmarks, and private and public gardens.

Interpretation takes many forms, and is utilised in all gardens open to the public, from BOTANIC GARDENS and PUBLIC PARKS to private properties opened through AUSTRALIA'S OPEN GARDEN SCHEME. Visitors might be given a map, brochure, or guide book, or learn about the site through a guided tour. Other media include on-site signs along preferred routes—or audiovisual presentations, and theatrical 'activation' in the garden, although those techniques are not so commonly employed.

While recognised as a fundamental element in key Australian garden CONSERVATION guidelines such as the Australia ICOMOS BURRA CHARTER, interpretation is often seen as being of secondary importance to other conservation activities, such as restoration or reconstruction. Conversely, some practitioners argue that all conservation practice is simply a form of interpretation. Critics judge interpretation as merely a mechanism for marketing sites in a cultural tourism industry. However, despite these varied and sometimes vexed theoretical issues, visitors still derive pleasure and new knowledge about gardens from informal learning through interpretive practices.

Very broadly, interpretation can apply to any way a garden is 'read' for its meaning. We might describe Australian gardening as an interpretation of 'place-making' since colonial settlement, and a garden design utilising native plants might be interpreted as a microcosm of Australian bushland. Many garden writers world-wide propose that all gardens and garden making are interpretations of a lost Garden of Paradise or Eden.

KAREN OLSEN

INVERGOWRIE, Exeter, NSW, has a substantial garden established from 1937 by steel manufacturer Cecil Hoskins (1889–1971), laid out by Paul SORENSEN, and restored c. 1980 by the Fieldhouse family. Its older trees date from a YATES nursery, established here c. 1890. Dogwoods and oaks accent the curving entry drive. The wisteria-draped, Tudor-style house overlooks wide lawns set with specimen trees. To the east, banks of rhododendrons and other intensively planted areas conclude in the Dell, a secluded valley with flowering cherries, azaleas, and tree ferns in a wooded setting.

HOWARD TANNER

IPSWICH QUEENS PARK is one of a few parks in Qld designated prior to colonial separation from NSW (1859). A site of 207 acres (84 ha) was set aside in 1858 at the request of the local community, which sought a recreation reserve that suitably reflected the affluence of the town. Ipswich notables, including Dr Henry Challinor and George Thorn snr, formed the board of trustees. The two spine ridges of silicified magnesian limestone provided stone for landscape detailing including gateways, wall terraces, and kerbing, lending a distinctive regional character. Although gazetted as BOTANIC GARDENS in 1862, the emphasis of this PUBLIC PARK has always focused on community RECREATION.

JODI FRAWLEY

IRELAND Like their counterparts from ENGLAND and SCOTLAND, the Irish figured among the botanists, collectors, gardeners, and those in the seed and nursery trade of colonial Australia. Nineteenth-century Irish immigration to Australia, which peaked in the 1850s and 1860s, generally reflected the demographic at home; settlers were predominantly Catholic and mostly small farmers or rural labourers. The highest proportion of Irish settled in Vic., where, by the 1870s, roughly a quarter of the population had Irish origins. However, it was the Protestant Irish, especially the Anglo-Irish, who were the most prominent of Irish-born colonial garden owners and horticulturists. In Ireland, prestigious and privileged institutions such as botanic gardens and universities, patronised by the Irish Ascendancy and closely associated with equivalent institutions in England and Scotland, were for a long time barred to Catholics; as a result, they worked in less prestigious horticultural fields as gardeners and in the nursery and seed trade. This pattern was perpetuated in the colonies, where the leading Irish horticulturists brought training and connections from Trinity College, Dublin; Glasnevin Botanic Gardens (where Charles MOORE's brother was director); Cork Botanic Gardens (where

Scotsman James DRUMMOND had been curator); and doubtless from Belfast Botanic Gardens. Others had worked in the gardens and demesnes of the Anglo-Irish aristocracy—a group critical in establishing the political and educational institutions of colonial Vic. Australian horticulturalists and botanists with Irish connections included William ALLITT, Richard ARDAGH, Eugene FITZALAN, Robert FITZGERALD, James JONES, William HAYES, William HYNDMAN, Phillip MACMAHON, John and Patrick O'SHANESY, and Thomas REEDY. William HARVEY was a notable visitor, and Baron TALBOT de Malahide a discerning patron.

It is difficult to discern particular Irish influences on Australian gardening, and to determine Irish origins of exotics cultivated in Australia. The dual indigeneity of many plants to both Ireland and England, compounded by the effects of a long British presence in Ireland, meant that although many of the same plants were brought to Australia by the Irish and the English, they came to be popularly regarded as distinctively English. The Irish Strawberry Tree (*Arbutus unedo*) is perhaps one exception. The particular Irish characteristics of the HOMESTEAD GARDENS of the colonial Anglo-Irish, comparable with those of the English gentry, are, as a result, hazy. The grand oak avenue planted by the Winter Cooke family at MURNDAL in Victoria's WESTERN DISTRICT perhaps came from Irish-sourced plant stock, or at least expressed Anglo-Irish, rather than English, sentiments. The large number of Irish religious who came to Australia perpetuated a clearer Irish landscape tradition in the orderly gardens of their churches, convents, and monasteries.

The colonial gardens of Irish rural labourers and small farmers were smaller, plainer, and necessarily more practical. Vegetables were grown for home and market, and ornamentation was less of an imperative. There was, nevertheless, a particular fondness for the flowers of home (particularly popular were roses, rhododendrons, fuchsias, and daffodils), and clippings of shamrock from home were kept by MIGRANTS for sentimentality and good luck. In areas of concentrated Irish settlement, such as the rich agricultural district around Belfast (Port Fairy), Koroit, and Killarney in south-west Vic., aspects of an Irish landscape are discernible. Here, Irish tenant farmers planted a patchwork of potato and onion fields, and grew Hawthorn hedgerows. Some measure of Irish ingenuity was also evident, such as a bed-edging treatment using glass bottles (of unambiguous origin). Significantly, the local botanic gardens at KOROIT and Port Fairy were curated by Irish brothers, James and Edward Prior.

Edward Hyams, *Irish Gardens* (London, 1967); E.C. Nelson and A. Brady (eds), *Irish Gardening and Horticulture* (Dublin, 1979); Edward Malins and Patrick Bowe, *Irish Gardens and Demesnes from 1830* (London, 1980); Keith Lamb and Patrick Bowe, *A History of Gardening in Ireland* (Dublin, 1995)

HELEN DOYLE

IRON FENCES Until after the Great War virtually all iron in Australia was imported. Cheaper labour costs in Europe and more effective mass production encouraged the importation of iron FENCES of all sorts, especially from Britain. The earliest indication of wire fencing is in an advertisement by J.H. Porter of London in 1839, directed to settlers in SA, but until the introduction of galvanising by Porter and others about four years later, wire fencing would have had few advantages.

By the 1850s (though rarely individually dated) one finds a range of metal fences. There was the hairpin type, in which wrought-iron bars in an elongated U-shape overlapped each other or alternated with plain rods, and were usually supported by wrought-iron straps as cross rails. There were various forms of self-contained panel or hurdle, usually spiked into the ground, as well as individual standards and strainer posts, in either wrought or cast iron, designed to carry fencing wire. The whole range can be seen in British catalogues, especially those of C.D. Young & Co. of Edinburgh and Glasgow.

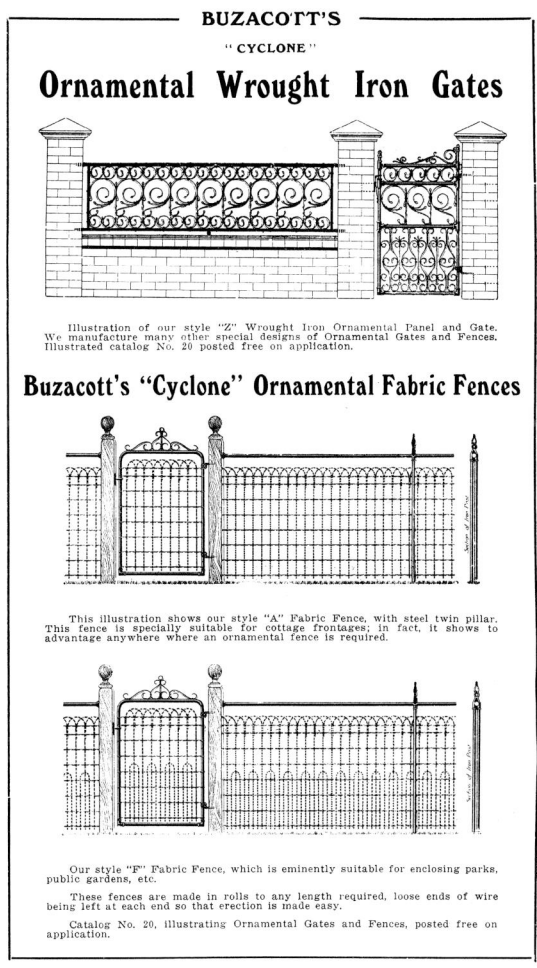

Cyclone IRON FENCING, introduced to Australia from the USA at the beginning of the twentieth century, was produced locally under license and distributed by numerous manufacturers, such as Brisbane- and Sydney-based Buzacott & Co.

Formal urban fences were at first made of cast-iron palisade bars, each with an ornamental spear at the top, the base set into a stone plinth and run with red lead in the manner that remained standard through the rest of the century. Much more elaborate cast-iron gates and fences were imported later in the century, especially from Walter Macfarlane's Saracen Foundry, Glasgow, but their use was confined to the grandest properties.

In 1859 the Carron Rolling Mills in Melbourne began rolling scrap wrought iron to produce small square and round sections. Henceforward, the standard palisade bar was a plain wrought-iron rod onto which the ornamental cast-iron spearhead was placed while hot, shrinking and locking itself into position as it cooled. By then only the larger and more opulent fences used cast bars, usually distinguished by their more elaborate fluted or other forms. Towards 1880 this fashion was reversed, and wrought iron came to be seen as superior, provided that it was individually crafted (though the results are less apparent in fencing than in roof ridging and finials).

By the 1870s one of the most assiduous British exporters was Francis Morton, of Liverpool and London, who had developed a form of standard that was used for everything from the smallest fence post to the largest telegraph pole. It was hollow and slightly tapered, and formed in two halves, each with flanges that were bolted or riveted together. He also made more conventional iron gates with criss-cross bracing. The Sydney agent, George Royce, advertised that he could supply and erect Morton's buildings anywhere within a hundred miles (160 km) of a rail head at a fixed cost—a particular inducement in Qld, where a series of independent spur lines ran inland from the coast. It is probably for these reasons that Morton fences and gates are now to be found at Ravenswood and Charters Towers.

Corrugated-iron fencing has been an important fencing material since the 1850s, when it first appeared. Initially most commonly in the five-inch (130 mm) pitch, during the 1860s the modern three-inch (80 mm) size became more common. Substantial examples would be capped in timber, whereas functional party and back fences were not, though the top might be cut into zig-zag spikes to deter intruders. In the period 1880–1920 forms of ornamentally perforated corrugated-iron fencing were marketed, though very few examples survive today. In the Edwardian period it was not uncommon for some of the grander timber fences to contain panels of corrugated ripple iron—of one-inch (32.5 mm) pitch.

The Adelaide plumbers Walter and Ernest Hume (later to develop an international spun concrete pipe business) developed rolled-steel ribbon fencing, which was exhibited at the Sydney Agricultural Show in 1907, and became popular as street-frontage fencing in country towns, though less so in the cities. Soon afterwards, Cyclone wire fencing was introduced from the USA and manufactured locally under licence. It was sometimes combined with steel ribbon in the same fence or gate, though more commonly used separately.

In the cities, more pretentious fencing in the twentieth century was generally not of iron, but ornamental wrought-iron panels set between pillars and above dwarf walls were common until well after the Second World War. More specifically, rural forms of fencing, such as star posts with barbed wire or wire netting, were also found in suburban gardens, especially in the functional areas. MILES LEWIS

IRRIGATION in Australia has been at the forefront of the thoughts of agriculturists and horticulturists alike since the beginning of European settlement, as each attempts to manage their WATER resources for maximum benefit. Achieving a balance in the application of water requires an understanding of irrigation as well as DRAINAGE principles. Only with these in balance will their objectives be met. This applies not only to gardens but also to whole CULTURAL LANDSCAPES, with the degree of intervention required being largely determined by the CLIMATE. Most settlement was initially based around naturally occurring fresh water sources such as rivers. The first successful private attempts to increase farm production using irrigation took place in Tas. during 1830, when the marshland of the Derwent Estuary was reclaimed and tidal fluctuations were harnessed via a series of sluices. Other early schemes, such as at MOUNT ELRINGTON, Braidwood (NSW), were restricted to gravity-fed dams on streams some distance away and hand-dug channels carrying water to the garden. The use of groundwater from bores in SA, NT, and Qld was developed during the twentieth century.

The viability of closer settlement schemes in the drier parts of Australia, particularly northern Vic., the RIVERLAND (SA), and the Murrumbidgee Irrigation Area (NSW), was successful only after the provision of a continuous, reliable water supply. Many of these regions were flat, and gravity alone could not be used. It was not until the introduction of steam-powered pumps during the 1860s that settlement was possible. Initially, most irrigation was by individual landowners. Late nineteenth-century developments had their origins in state-sponsored initiatives to open up the interior. The Victorian Government was influential on many practices, with legislation establishing local trusts to manage water resources, sometimes combined with private development. The largest and most innovative of these were CHAFFEY brothers' settlements at Mildura (Vic.) and Renmark (SA). These towns were based on NORTH AMERICAN settlements with well laid out streets and generous STREET TREE plantings. These developments in previously unoccupied areas allowed for the planning of towns and cities using the latest TOWN PLANNING principles, well demonstrated by the designs of Walter Burley GRIFFIN for Leeton and Griffith in the Murrumbidgee Irrigation Area.

Plant selection is considerably limited or extended by the available water. Domestic and public gardens, generally confined in size, are unlikely to have an independent water supply. Early gardeners without a constant water supply were restricted in their choice of planting and relied on rainwater only, with gardens going dry over summer. Larger homestead gardens generally fared better, drawing from springs or wells on the property, or from nearby watercourses (often the main determinant for initial siting). In cities, the advent of larger suburban blocks coincided with introduction of reticulated water, resulting in more ambitious gardens and LAWNS with greatly increased water usage.

The basic designed landscape elements of early IRRIGATION areas included the water channel lined with PALMS, and the hedged house on its 'block', with ORCHARD and VINEYARD filling the available land

When many public and botanic gardens were established in the mid-nineteenth century, reticulated water systems did not exist in most cities. In the case of MELBOURNE BOTANIC GARDENS, sited on the banks of the Yarra River, the various methods of irrigation were representative of the way many early gardens evolved. Water was initially hand-carted from the Yarra by bucket and water carts, and rainwater from roofs was stored in tanks. Ornamental windmills were used with limited success, although when reticulated water reached Melbourne in 1857 the Gardens were not connected and a separate system evolved using a succession of steam-powered pumps to draw water from the Yarra. Water was stored in a reservoir at the highest point in the gardens, and galvanised iron pipes and open channels distributed the water around the gardens. The Gardens also relied on water stored in the ornamental LAKE; reticulated supply was finally connected in 1931, when the dams supplying Melbourne reached excess storage capacity. At RIPPON LEA, Elsternwick (Vic.), an exceptional scheme drew water from several springs in the surrounding neighbourhood and piped the water to an ornamental lake. The water, pumped over a waterfall (which aerated the water as well as providing aesthetic pleasures), was then pumped though pipes to sprinklers throughout the garden.

Perhaps one of the potent forces determining the design and management of contemporary Australian landscapes is the need for water conservation. A range of initiatives—from better water delivery to individual plants via drippers and computer-driven watering systems to selecting plants that will survive with little supplemental water—is being used. The concept of the 'brown park', where water is not applied during summer, is increasingly being implemented, especially in peripheral landscapes such as roadsides. The use of 'grey water' recycled from washing machines and baths and the use of rainwater collected on site using tanks are also helping to conserve water resources. Manipulating the landscape using swales (mounds of earth) to direct storm water around the landscape for use on site rather than taken away via storm water drainage is also used. Planting undertaken on these sites is matched to the water supply at different points around the landscape. The concept of XERIC GARDENS (or the proprietary Xeriscape method) has been used to promote water conservation.

Margaret Mason-Cox, *Lifeblood of a Colony: A History of Irrigation in Tasmania* (Hobart, 1994)   ROHAN LAMB

IRVINE (*née* BERGER), Susan (b. 1928), teacher and rose enthusiast, was born at Dalby (Qld), grand-daughter of

Tasmanian architect Henry Hunter. After teaching in NSW, Tas., and Vic., she was appointed, as Mrs St Leon, headmistress of Lauriston School for girls in Melbourne. On retirement after ten years, she bought Bleak House outside Malmsbury (1982). There, after extensive renovations described in *Garden of a Thousand Roses* (1992), she started a nursery and bookshop. In 1983, she began to collect named varieties bred by Alister CLARK and, in 1985, married Bill Irvine, inaugural chairman of the independent board of the ROYAL BOTANIC GARDENS, MELBOURNE. In 1985 they moved to Gisborne, where Susan Irvine made another garden crammed with roses and presided over by a horse's head to commemorate the first rose issued by Alister Clark, 'Lady Medallist'. In 1996 they moved to Deloraine (Tas.), where she continues to garden, lecture, and write.

T.R. GARNETT

ISAAC, Cyril Everett (1884–1965), educator, horticulturist, parliamentarian, and conservationist, was born in Brunswick (Vic.), and trained initially as a teacher, working in the Victorian Education Department from 1900 to 1922. His ideas about education were entwined with his love of horticulture. He was an enthusiastic entrant in the Australian Natives Association SCHOOL GARDEN competitions, founder of the Victorian State Schools' Horticultural Society (1910), and supervisor of school gardening (1913–22). His eldest son, **Cyril Hampden Isaac** (1910–1971), inherited a love of gardens, and like his father made a distinguished career as a nursery proprietor in Melbourne's south-eastern suburbs. In 1922 C.E. Isaac left the Education Department and started Flowervale Nursery at Noble Park. C.H. Isaac established his own business in nearby Carnegie in 1931, and took over Flowervale when his father entered the Victorian Parliament (1940). Throughout the 1930s the Isaacs worked together on floral BEDDING displays for Melbourne's Royal Agricultural Show, including a Persian carpet and FLORAL CLOCK (reputedly the world's first with a moving second hand). C.H. Isaac was a great admirer and supporter of his father's work but avoided the spotlight of public life, expressing himself through horticultural design. C.E. Isaac was a very focused parliamentarian, concentrating on education, forestry, and national parks. He launched the 'Save the Forests Campaign' (later the NATURAL RESOURCES CONSERVATION LEAGUE) in 1944 to 'build a forest conscience in all Victorians' after the tragic 1939 bushfires. The campaign established a nursery to support COMMUNITY FORESTS and Isaac promoted tree-planting and forest protection through his popular radio broadcasts.

LIBBY ROBIN

ISLAMIC GARDENS: see MIDDLE EASTERN INFLUENCES

ITALIANATE INFLUENCES The influence of Italy on Australian gardens dates from the earliest colonial times. Both practical and aesthetic, it has long been evident in the MEDITERRANEAN plants chosen for gardens and in domestic architecture, and argued for because of the similarity in climates. In the nineteenth century the Italianate style dominated the architectural 'Battle of the Styles', which was also reflected in garden design. In the twentieth century the influence of Italy melded with the Colonial and the so-called Spanish Mission revival into a general Mediterranean idiom. Italian influences have also been linked with domestic architecture, especially through the emergence of the villa form, seen in MANSION GARDENS, suburban VILLA GARDENS, and HOMESTEAD GARDENS. To a limited extent, there has also been a scientific influence through continuing associations with BOTANIC GARDENS. Finally, because of the work of certain individuals, Italian influences can be traced in some PUBLIC GARDENS.

Italian details used in the nineteenth century included terraces and PARTERRES; parapet walls and steps; axes linking a garden with the broader landscape; FOUNTAINS and pools; and assorted classical ORNAMENTS such as urns, vases, pedestals, columns, and STATUES. Typical Mediterranean plantings included pines, cypresses, PALMS, citrus, CACTI and other succulents, and evergreen HEDGES. These were combined to maximise topography, contrast, and silhouette. More sophisticated gardens in Australia also contained inherent Italian values: the dominance of structure over planting, the superiority of art over nature, and a demonstration of prestige by the owner. The fact that some details have become a pastiche today should not detract from the enduring influence of Italy in Australia.

Italy had long influenced gardens through painting and literature, especially the ideal landscapes of artist Claude Lorraine (1600–1682). In this cultural climate, the Italianate style of architecture was 'invented' by the British architects John Nash (1752–1835) and Sir Charles Barry (1795–1860). Essentially a souvenir style—and not without a political dimension—it was promoted in architectural pattern books, some of which included advice on gardening. Osborne House (1845–61), Queen Victoria's villa on the Isle of Wight, gave the style imperial approval. In Australia, that approval was sealed by Victoria's GOVERNMENT HOUSE (1871–76)—a mansion designed as a villa and set in a broad landscape in a garden planned by Joseph SAYCE, borrowing both aspect and prospect from the adjacent MELBOURNE BOTANIC GARDENS.

The colonial version of the Italianate villa seems first to have emerged in Van Diemen's Land. Examples include the remodelling of the ARCHER property, Woolmers (*c*. 1842), and of ROSEDALE (1846). William Archer's design for MONA VALE (1865) at Ross is perhaps the grandest private example of an Italianate villa and its garden in Australia. The artist John GLOVER, a keen domestic gardener at Hobart and Patterdale, has been called the 'English Claude'. In NSW, where the Gothic revival dominated, the influence of Italy is less clear. Not all the villas and their gardens built on the Woolloomooloo hill from the late 1820s were classical in origin, but Conrad Martens' painting *View from Rose Bank* (1840) captures the dreamy Arcadian ideal that lay behind the Italianate style. YARALLA (from 1860) at Concord and Belmont Park (1892) at Richmond were perhaps the most ambitious Italianate examples in NSW, with all the essential ingredients of the style. Early houses and their gardens in Victoria include: Bishopscourt, East Melbourne (*c*. 1849); Toorak House (*c*. 1850); GLENARA

Italianate influences

The atrium at Nurney House, Adelaide, designed by its owner Walter BAGOT in 1930, reflected his passion for ITALIAN architecture and gardens, and was an unusually sophisticated Australian response to Mediterranean sources

(1857); and Pine Grove, Richmond (after 1866), developed by George Coppin, who was famous for his PLEASURE GARDEN, the Cremorne Gardens.

The influence of Italy has been both direct and indirect. Many upper middle-class Australians included Italy in their version of the Grand Tour. The Manifolds of Purrumbete in Victoria's WESTERN DISTRICT went abroad during the construction of their new Italianate homestead, completed in 1886. William GUILFOYLE visited them in 1887, and three years later made a study tour that started in Italy. His successor and biographer, R.T.M. PESCOTT, wrote: 'The fame of the beautifully landscaped gardens of Italy, particularly in the north, had always appealed to Guilfoyle, and he was anticipating that they would provide him with many new ideas to incorporate in his developing garden in Melbourne. He was greatly disappointed with what he saw, however.' Walter BAGOT, Rodney ALSOP, Emily GIBSON, and Jocelyn and Alfred BROWN all travelled in Italy in the 1920s, but equally, other designers in the Italianate mode relied largely on published sources.

The influence of Italy has come indirectly through publications such as those by J.C. LOUDON and A.J. DOWNING. Importantly, they stressed the link between house and garden and promoted the notion of a suburban villa lifestyle. Then the books of the Americans, Charles Platt (1861–1933) and Edith Wharton (1862–1937), advanced the aesthetics of Italian gardens. Wharton, who had lived in Italy as a child, wrote *Italian Villas and their Gardens* (1904), which was influential on Edna WALLING. Julia Cartwright's *Italian Gardens of the Renaissance and Other Studies* was published in London in 1914. Walling owned *Italian Gardens of the Renaissance* (1925) by Shepherd and Jellicoe, and it influenced her design philosophy and presentation. Georgina Masson's *Italian Gardens* (1961) was a post-war influence.

Many public pleasure gardens and parks incorporated Italian ingredients. The Italian engineer Carlo CATANI, as a

Italianate influences

member of the St Kilda Foreshore Trust from 1906 to 1918, designed improvements typical of the Mediterranean tourist Meccas. The Mediterranean imagery in Hollywood films was almost irresistible. Popular magazines such as AUSTRALIAN HOME BEAUTIFUL promoted Mediterranean—and specifically Italian—design, for example in Walling's article 'The Italian Influence in our Australian Gardens' (1933).

While many older Italianate gardens survive in Australia, two recent design strands have emerged. The first is the gardens of post-war MIGRANTS, who have brought a love of vegetable and fruit growing to unexpected new urban pockets, and also a long viticultural tradition. The second is seen in urban gardens, where the formality of Italianate designs neatly links architectural (and generally low-maintenance) elements such a hedges, paving, and garden ornaments, with travel aspirations and a cosmopolitan outlook.

David Coffin (ed.), *The Italian Garden* (Washington, D.C., 1972); John Dixon Hunt, *Garden and Grove: The Italian Renaissance Garden in the English Imagination, 1600–1750* (London, 1986); Elisabeth Blair MacDougall, *Fountains, Statues, and Flowers: Studies in Italian Gardens of the Sixteenth and Seventeenth Centuries* (Washington, D.C., 1994); John Dixon Hunt (ed.), *The Italian Garden: Art, Design, and Culture* (Cambridge, 1996)

TIMOTHY HUBBARD

JAMES, Henry Alfred (c. 1850–1936), amateur horticulturist and writer, lived in the Sydney suburb of Summer Hill. He worked in the public service as an examiner in the Mines Department, and on his retirement in 1915 had charge of the records branch. A talented amateur horticulturist specialising in ferns, James was a driving force behind the Ashfield Horticultural Club, sometime president of the Western Suburbs Horticultural Society, gold medallist of the Horticultural Society of New South Wales, and a Fellow of the Royal Horticultural Society. He contributed horticultural notes to the SYDNEY MAIL, and was not averse to referring favourably in the third person to his own horticultural talents. In 1890 he published *Practical Horticulture for Australian Readers*, reprinting a series of articles he wrote for the *Sydney Morning Herald*. His magnum opus, the *Handbook of Australian Horticulture*, appeared in twelve monthly parts during 1891–92. The *Handbook*, published in Sydney by Turner & Henderson and illustrated by Signor Guglielmo Autoriello (as well as many stock engravings from A. Blanc of Philadelphia, not otherwise acknowledged), was a massive folio volume of more than 500 pages with colour illustrations—the earliest in an Australian GARDENING BOOK. In addition to comprehensive horticultural advice, James included notes on garden design, happily noting the passing from favour of formal flower beds and praising 'a natural system of gardening [endeavouring] … to introduce, as much as possible, a careless gracefulness'. He also included a long section on AUSTRALIAN PLANTS, placing himself in the vanguard of popular gardening authors. In his later years James lived in the Blue Mountains at Glenalva, Hazlebrook; his obituary in the *Sydney Morning Herald* attributes to him the laying out of the public gardens at Lawson and Hazlebrook. RA

JAMES, (Thomas) Horton ('Rubio') (c. 1792–1867), colonial chronicler, included the earliest published garden guide for SA in his *Six Months in South Australia … with Advice to Emigrants; to which is added a Monthly Calendar of Gardening and Agriculture. Adapted to the Climate and Seasons* (London, 1838). He had previously written a pamphlet on the *Sandwich and Bonin Islands … together with hints on the probability … of introducing British manufactures into … Japan* (1832) and as 'Rubio' later published *Rambles in the United States and Canada during the year 1845, with a short account of Oregon* (1846). James, whose book was written after a stay of three and a half months from January to May 1838, and received mixed reviews, inscribed this 'little manual of gardening' to the 'Land Owners of South Australia'. It remained the only published garden guide for SA, apart from ALMANACS, until George McEwin's manual (1843). RA

JAMISON, John (1776–1844), physician, 'landed proprietor', and horse-racing patron, was a founder (1822) and long-time president of the AGRICULTURAL SOCIETY of New South Wales. He began cultivating grapes in 1817 and engaged Frederick Meyer c. 1830 to construct seven acres (3

This FLOWER ARRANGEMENT, 'Native Flowers', illustrated by H.A. JAMES in his *Handbook of Australian Horticulture* (1892), was an unusual depiction of the AUSTRALIAN FLORA amongst contemporary GARDEN BOOKS—for many decades only a few enlightened advocates of the native flora saw its beauty

ha) of terraced VINEYARD, surrounded by china rose and lemon HEDGES, at Regentville, his celebrated estate near Penrith (NSW). Jamison presided over a boom period for AGRICULTURE and lived lavishly, but fell victim to the 1840s depression, and died relatively poor. COLLEEN MORRIS

JAMPIJINPA (YANARILYI), John (c. 1923–1973), Warlpiri entomologist, botanist, and gardener, was raised west of Coniston Station (NT), and later took the surname Yanarilyi by deed poll so that his descendants would always know that their land was the hill and waterhole of this name. During the Second World War he worked for the Australian Army. Afterwards he was pleased to take on the role of gardener (1961–72) on the newly gazetted flora reserve in Alice Springs (now the Olive Pink Botanic Gardens). Olive PINK ensured that he received a full wage rather than the allowance usually paid to ABORIGINAL GARDENERS and employees. He had a knowledge of local flora and fauna, invaluable in choosing a successful environment for their plantings. Pink always said that his work really 'made' the garden. He died in his middle years. Never a Christian convert, at his daughter's request, he was buried by a Catholic priest. JULIE MARCUS

JAPAN After the fall of the Tokugawa Shogunate (1868) and the opening up of Japan, Japanese gardens became fashionable in the West. In Australia, however, the major impact of this change came from the sudden availability of Japanese garden plants. The establishment in 1890 of the Yokohama Nursery Co. and others such as K. Wada of Numazu enabled nursery proprietors and others in Australia to obtain plants direct from Japan. In addition to general catalogues in English, they issued illustrated catalogues of azaleas, camellias, cherries, hydrangeas, lilies, magnolias, maples, peonies, and others whose long popularity with the Japanese had led to the development of many beautiful cultivars previously unavailable to Australian gardeners.

The first informed knowledge of Japanese gardens came with the appointment in 1922 of Arthur Lindsay Sadler (1882–1970) to the chair of Oriental Studies at the University of Sydney. In 1932 his article 'The Way of Tea' appeared in the *Home* magazine and the tea ceremony garden he had built at his home at Warrawee was also described and illustrated that year. In 1933 the first of many editions of his book *Cha-no-yu, the Japanese Tea Ceremony* was published in Japan and England. It was the earliest work dealing with this subject to be published in English. It contained a scholarly account of Roji, gardens attached to tea houses. In the same year his *Art of Flower Arrangement in Japan* was published in England. This was at that time the only authoritative work, other than Condor's *Theory of Japanese Flower Arrangements* (1889), to have been written in English.

With the resurgence of the Japanese economy after the Second World War cultural ties with Australia were fostered, with several sister-city relationships being formed. These led in many instances to the sponsoring of the construction of Japanese gardens. One such is at the Campbelltown City Bicentennial Art Gallery, NSW (1988), designed by Australian landscape architect Alan Cheung working in collaboration with Tatsuya Togashi, Chief of Design and Construction, Koshigaya, Campbelltown's sister city. The construction was also a collaborative effort with a team of workers coming from Koshigaya to erect the buildings. This garden being small, enclosed, and creating a landscape seen from inside the gallery, is much closer to a traditional Japanese garden than those that form incidents in larger parks or gardens.

A much larger and more elaborate example, based on Edo period stroll gardens, is the Japanese Garden at Cowra (NSW). During the Second World War, Cowra was the site of the prisoner-of-war camp from which, in 1944, the Japanese prisoners staged a breakout that led to the deaths of 231 Japanese and four Australians. In 1964 the Japanese government built a war cemetery, designed by Shigeru Yura, for Japanese nationals who had died in Australia during the war. Some years later, citizens of Cowra suggested the building of a garden as a symbol of friendship and goodwill. With support from the Australian and Japanese governments, Ken Nakajima (1914–2000) of Tokyo was engaged as designer. Stage one was completed in 1978 and stage two started eight years later with Mr Nakajima's son supervising construction. The garden is situated on the outskirts of this inland town, on a five-hectare site with typical rock outcrops and indigenous trees in both garden and surrounding setting. Nakajima has succeeded in creating a unique garden blending successfully Japanese and Australian landscape elements.

Lorraine Kuck, *The World of the Japanese Garden from Chinese Origins to Modern Landscape Art* (New York and Tokyo, 1968)
RICHARD CLOUGH

JEAVONS, Mary (b. 1955), landscape architect, specialises in the design of CHILDREN's environments of all kinds, including early childhood centres, primary and secondary school grounds, and play environments for children with disabilities. This interest developed when she worked as Executive Officer for the Playgrounds and Recreation Association of Victoria, formalised by a masters degree in landscape architecture (1987) focusing on children's independent exploration of local environments when they were at play. Jeavons continues her research and has lectured widely on PLAYGROUNDS. ML

JEKYLL, Gertrude (1843–1932), author, garden designer, plant enthusiast, and artist, was an influential English figure whose work related strongly to the ARTS AND CRAFTS movement and the ROBINSONIAN wild garden. She is principally noted for her collaboration with the architect Sir Edwin Lutyens, creating integrated house and garden designs in the 'Surrey School' style, derived from the vernacular buildings of Surrey, England, combined with strong axial layouts and softened by lavish planting. Edward Hudson's magazine *Country Life* became a major vehicle for publicity. In her garden, Munstead Wood, Jekyll experimented with ideas about colour and planting. She made great use of massed perennials, underplanted with bulbs for early colour, with late-flowering, tender bedding plants (such as dahlias) interspersed to lengthen the display. Her garden designs were complex, extensive, and demanded high levels of skilled labour.

In Australia her ideas found acceptance among wealthy Anglophiles. Reading her most important books *Wood and Garden* (1899), *Home and Garden* (1900), and *Colour in the Flower Garden* (1908) alongside those written later by Edna WALLING it is possible to discern her strong influence on the early development of the Australian designer and writer. Other Australian designers influenced by Jekyll were Elsie CORNISH and Jocelyn BROWN.

The resurgence of Jekyll's ideas following major restoration projects and exhibitions in England in the 1970s saw many of her books reissued, and several biographical works. Jekyll-influenced gardens were popularised internationally by influential English gardeners and writers such as Rosemary Verey and Penelope Hobhouse. In Australia, this influence caused a major shift in Australian garden style in the mid-1980s.

> Francis Jekyll, *Gertrude Jekyll: A Memoir* (London, 1934); Jane Brown, *Gardens of a Golden Afternoon: The Story of a Partnership: Edward Lutyens & Gertrude Jekyll* (London, 1982); Sally Festing, *Gertrude Jekyll* (London, 1991); Richard Bisgrove, *The Gardens of Gertrude Jekyll* (London, 1992); Michael Tooley and Primrose Arnander, *Gertrude Jekyll: Essays on the Life of a Working Amateur* (Witton-le-Wear, Durham, 1995)

TREVOR NOTTLE

JESSEP, Alexander William (1892–1991), horticulturist, educator, and botanic gardens director, was brought up on a dairy farm near Maffra, in Gippsland (Vic.). After serving in the AIF during the First World War, he returned to his studies at the University of Melbourne and completed a Master of Agricultural Science degree. He was appointed as science master at the School of Primary Agriculture and Horticulture, BURNLEY (1922), and succeeded Frederick RAE as principal of the school in 1926. He held the position until 1941, when he again succeeded Rae, this time as Director of MELBOURNE BOTANIC GARDENS. He was also appointed Government Botanist, holding both positions until his retirement in 1957. Widely recognised for his work in researching and growing CAMELLIAS and ROSES, Alex Jessep was especially interested in the varieties of camellias introduced to the Gardens by William GUILFOYLE from Sydney *c.* 1873. Soon after his appointment, Jessep planned a special area in the Gardens specifically for the growing of camellias. He vigorously opposed pressure from Melbourne City Council and the Victorian Government to use the Botanic Gardens for large outdoor public MUSIC concerts, finally forcing the Domain area to be used instead: construction of the Sidney Myer Music Bowl (1959) settled this lengthy dispute. Jessep visited the Seventh International Botanical Conference in Sweden (1950) and was a strong advocate for Australian horticulture and horticultural education.

LEE ANDREWS

JIMBOUR, near Dalby, Qld, retains a quintessential HOMESTEAD GARDEN, forming an enclosed oasis in the surrounding pastoral landscape. Gimba (Jimbour) run, stretching from the Bunya Mountains to the Condamine River, was sold to Thomas Bell in the mid-1840s and his son Joshua Peter Bell (1827–1881) took on its management, with Jimbour soon winning fame as one of the premier stations on the DARLING DOWNS. A two-storey bluestone house (*c.* 1870) replaced an earlier timber hut, but in 1874–76, Bell—by then a successful politician—erected the present grand homestead. Mature trees, including *Brachychiton rupestre* (Bottle Tree), and garden walling remain from this period. In 1923, after an interlude of bank ownership and land acquisition under the *Closer Settlement Act*, Jimbour was sold to Wilfred Adams Russell

The bloated girth and gnarled reptilian roots of *Brachychiton repestre* (Queensland Bottletree) form a dark shadow over the pleasure garden at JIMBOUR, near Dalby, one of the premier HOMESTEAD GARDENS of Queensland's DARLING DOWNS

(c. 1875–1932) and, by then fronting a redesigned garden including a circular rosary, was formally reopened with an open day in 1925. Charles Wilfred Russell (1907–1977) and his wife Hilary Maude (née Newton) carefully maintained the property and its extensive garden, continuing its tradition as a focal point of social life for the region.

    Charles and Hilary Russell, *Jimbour: Its History and Development* (Dalby, Qld, 1989)   RA

JOHN FORREST NATIONAL PARK, Greenmount, WA, declared a conservation reserve in 1898, is among the state's earliest NATIONAL PARKS. It was named in 1947 to honour the Western Australian political leader and explorer, Sir John FORREST, on the centenary of his birth. The park is located on the Darling Scarp east of Perth and covers approximately 2700 hectares. While most of the area is conserved *Eucalyptus marginata* (Jarrah) and *Eucalyptus calophylla* (Marri) woodland, there is a RECREATION area constructed by sustenance workers during the 1930s Depression. This focuses on a SWIMMING POOL formed by the damming of Jane Brook, which flows through the park. There are paths and steps elaborately edged with rock, walled gardens, and several early RUSTIC timber shelters. The park has traditionally been a popular PICNIC spot, particularly in spring, when the woodland plants flower in profusion.   PHILIP PALMER

JOHNS, Henry Isaac: see WILSON AND JOHNS

JOHNSON, Benjamin (1823–1879) and his brother **Stephen Johnson** (1825–1901), nursery proprietors, florists, and seed merchants, were assisted migrants who arrived at Port Phillip in 1853. Because of the high price of seed, they apparently grew and marketed their own vegetable and flower seed. By 1859 their Northampton Nursery at Thomastown—named for the Johnsons' county of origin—was supplying plants to other nurseries, such as Thomas LANG of Ballarat, and to the public through premises in Bourke Street. J.G. VEITCH, reporting on his 1865 visit, regarded the establishment as one of the largest in the colony (with Richard PERRY and John SMITH) for 'fruit trees and general out-of-doors stock'. The business became insolvent in 1877 but Stephen and his son (Thomas) George Hart Johnson (c. 1858–fl. 1901)—known as Stephen junior—soon opened the Southampton Nursery in Richmond, specialising in florists' flowers and plants, which were sold from the same Bourke Street premises and a stall at the Eastern Market.   GWEN PASCOE

JOHNSON, George William: see *COTTAGE GARDENER*

JOHNSON, Lawrence Alexander Sidney (1925–1997), taxonomic botanist and botanic gardens director, started work at the National Herbarium of New South Wales in 1948 and was Director and Chief Botanist 1972–85. He was subsequently appointed Honorary Research Associate and Director Emeritus (1985–97). He worked on the classification of a wide range of AUSTRALIAN PLANT groups, particularly within the families Juncaceae, Casurinaceae, Myrtaceae, Proteaceae, Oleaceae, Restionaceae, and Zamiaceae. However, he devoted much of his work to the classification of EUCALYPTUS, and with PRYOR published *A Classification of the Eucalypts* (1971). A special issue of *Telopea* (1996) was devoted to Dr Lawrie Johnson's career.   ML

JOHNSON, Roger Kirk Hayes (1922–1991), educator, civic designer, and architect, practised architecture in Britain and Kenya following graduation from Liverpool University and taught at the University of Cape Town, the Architectural Association (London), and the University of Rangoon, before coming to Australia in 1961 to join Gordon STEPHENSON in the planning and development of the University of Western Australia and, in 1966, in the establishment of the School of Architecture there. Appointed First Assistant Commissioner, Architecture and Urban Design at the National Capital Development Commission, Canberra, in 1968 he developed the 'National Place' plan for the PARLIAMENTARY TRIANGLE following the rejection of the lakeside site for Parliament House. The High Court and National Gallery, with their landscape settings, were built under his direction as the first elements in this radical new scheme. Disagreeing with the decision to site Parliament House on Capital Hill, he accepted the position of planner for Griffith University (Qld), where on a relatively untouched bushland site he was able to demonstrate his sensitive appreciation of the Australian landscape. His ideas for integrating urban and landscape design were set out in *The Green City* (1979). He was enticed back to Canberra in 1973 to establish a School of Environmental Design at the College of Advanced Education, where his objective was the combination of the teaching of the design disciplines. He persuaded Rex Fairbrother to leave England and become principal lecturer in landscape design. When he was unable to obtain agreement to the integration of landscape design with architecture and industrial design, he set himself the task of maintaining design excellence, pursuing this with great success until his retirement in 1987.   RICHARD CLOUGH

JOHNSON, Thomas (1821–1907), rose grower, arrived in Melbourne from Britain c. 1850. He purchased land in Hawthorn by 1853 and ran a rose nursery there in the 1860s and 1870s. Johnson's booklet *The Culture of the Rose* (1866)— the first Australian monograph on ROSES—gave detailed, if slightly idiosyncratic, instructions on propagation, culture, and exhibition on the show bench. The preface, written by Ferdinand MUELLER, praised the virtues of 'these noble flowers' as well as the useful directions 'offered by so observant a man as Thomas Johnson'. He won many prizes at HORTICULTURAL SHOWS, particularly for his roses, and supplied 'a fine collection of standard roses' to William GUILFOYLE for MELBOURNE BOTANIC GARDENS during 1874–75. Johnson's business folded around 1878, at the same time as he disappeared from the active—although somewhat controversial—role he had taken in the affairs of the local council. He worked with his son-in-law, Thomas Ellison, growing roses in Preston in the early 1880s. By 1894 he ran a florist's shop and nursery in Mentone and continued to grow roses: his 1895 catalogue was noted by the *Leader* for 'new seedling roses of his own raising'. This veteran rosarian died in 1907

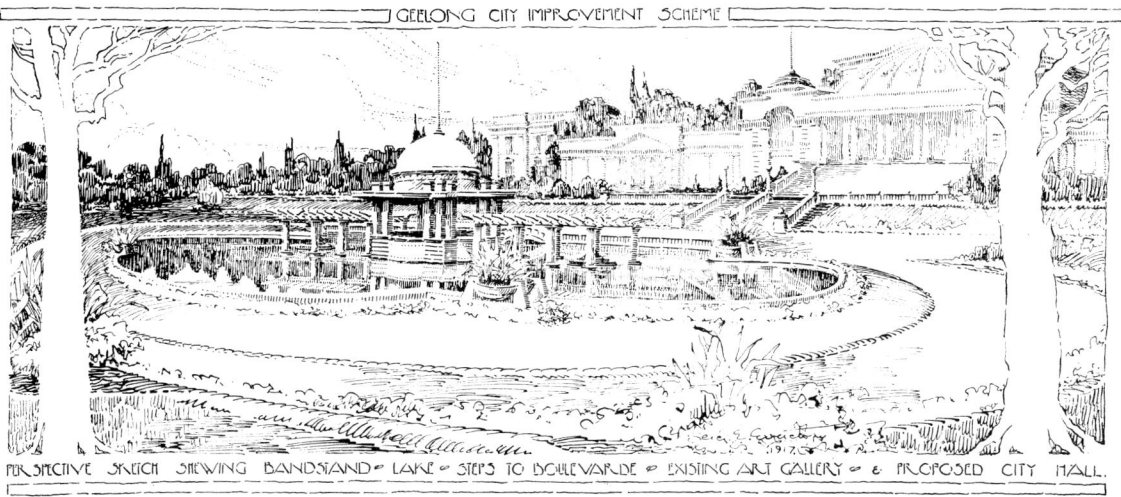

One of architect Percy Everett's evocative sketches (1917) of JOHNSTONE PARK, Geelong (Vic.), depicting the centrepiece of his CITY BEAUTIFUL scheme for the civic centre, based on the existing town hall, art gallery, and park, and further realised during 1919–26

and was buried in BOROONDARRA CEMETERY, for which he had been one of the first trustees. HELEN BOTHAM

JOHNSTONE PARK, Geelong, Vic., was set aside in 1848 by surveyor Robert Hoddle as a 'Reserve for Ornamental Ground, Gardens &c', and its subsequent development was influenced in large measure by its proximity to major civic facilities. In 1864, trees were planted at the behest of councillor Robert de Bruce Johnstone, and a committee of management was appointed in 1865. A year later an elm avenue, known as Maiden's Walk, was planted. Officially named in 1867, this central site was popular, even if its modest natural advantages were sometimes unfavourably compared with other reserves. A BANDSTAND (1873) and open air FERNERY (1886) provided embellishment, but it was the grand scheme initiated following the addition and enlargement of public buildings along its central BOULEVARD (1915–17) that marked its design apotheosis. In this premiated design in the CITY BEAUTIFUL manner (1916), architects Percy E. Everett, in association with Laird and Buchan, focused the garden on the Hitchcock Memorial Bandstand (1919) and Peace Memorial Foyer (1919–26). RA

JOLLY, Alexander (c. 1857–1925), landscape gardener, son of a Scottish farmer, migrated to Brisbane in 1878–79. During c. 1884–90 he was employed as head gardener on the Glen Lyon estate, Ashgrove (in Brisbane's western suburbs), and from c. 1917 until his death as landscape gardener for the Town of Ithaca (now part of Greater Brisbane). Using dry stone WALLING and exotic plants such as the sculptural AGAVE, Jolly transformed the recently made streets of hilly Ithaca, with elegant street ROCKERIES and embankment gardens. Tree planting aside, these were among the earliest street beautification projects in suburban Brisbane. A photographic display of Jolly's work, mounted at the Second Australian Town Planning Conference and Exhibition, Brisbane (1918), attracted interstate requests for photographs and plans of the Ithaca street improvements. Jolly's 'rare horticultural knowledge and technical skill' (Alderman Kaye, 1918) were greatly respected by the local community, including Governor Nathan, who in 1925 memorialised that Jolly's 'good taste has given constant pleasure to so many of us Ithaca residents'. Following Jolly's death, the Council renamed the Ithaca War Memorial garden, designed and laid out by Jolly c. 1922, as Alexander Jolly Park, 'in memory of one of the most esteemed men in the district, … a unique tribute … to the pick and shovel'. Remnants of Jolly's work survive in the suburbs of Red Hill, Kelvin Grove, Paddington, and Bardon. HELEN BENNETT

JOLLY, Norman William (1882–1954), forester, was born at Mintaro (SA), and made an outstanding contribution to the establishment of professional FORESTRY and to formal forestry education in Australia in the early twentieth century. Having gained a forestry diploma from Oxford, Jolly established the first professional forestry course in Australia at the University of Adelaide (1910–11). He was Queensland Director of Forests (1911–18), a New South Wales Commissioner in the three-member Forestry Commission (1918–25) and sole Commissioner (1926–33). Jolly is recognised for his establishment of softwood plantations in NSW and his work in managing and forecasting the yield from plantations. In 1954, the Institute of Foresters of Australia established the N.W. Jolly Medal—the highest honour bestowed by the Institute. Another memorial is the Norman Jolly Memorial Grove, a flora reserve in Moonpar State Forest, near Dorrigo (NSW). KEVIN FRAWLEY

JONDARYAN, on the DARLING DOWNS, Qld, was taken up by pastoralist Charles Coxen in 1842. Passing through a succession of owners, it was acquired (1858–63) from the Tooth Brothers by William Kent and Edward Weinholt, the resident manager being James White; the station has since remained in the hands of Kent and White descendants. The homestead, built in the 1850s (burnt and replaced 1937), with a surviving 1890s bedroom wing, overlooked the Oakley Creek, where Chinese gardeners once tended terraced vegetable gardens beneath ancient River Red Gums. Flanked by early outbuildings, the now-simplified garden forms a tight oasis of planting around the homestead, with lawns, shrubs, and a venerable *Brachychiton rupestre* (Bottle Tree). Jondaryan's labour history (1840–90) is analysed in Jan Walker's *Jondaryan Station* (1988); she observes that the station 'was a highly-structured and unequal society and exhibited many of the characteristics of a close-knit English village' and that in the 'Jondaryan Affair' of May 1890 the celebrated woolshed became 'a test case for the relative strengths of pastoral capital and newly federated pastoral labour'.

RA

JONES, James (b. 1839), gardener, trained at the Albert Agricultural Institution, Glasnevin, Dublin, during 1860. He worked as a gardener at Saumarez Park, Guernsey, Channel Islands during 1872–73 and in *Les Jardins de la Ville de Paris* following the main phase of park-making under Alphand; several of his French texts (including Du Breuil's *D'Arboriculture* and ROBINSON's *Parks, Promenades, and Gardens of Paris*, 1869) are inscribed from this period and survive in the library of the ROYAL BOTANIC GARDENS, SYDNEY. Jones became Overseer of the DOMAINS in Sydney in 1884 and his diary (1884–89) is an unusual surviving record of a gardener's working life. His post, described by MAIDEN as 'technical and very responsible', involved planning and supervising all outside work required by the NSW government in the city, suburbs, and country. This included all garden requirements of the Government Architect for RAILWAYS, police, and HOSPITALS in addition to laying out several municipal PARKS. He toured parks and gardens in Britain, France, and Italy in 1910 before retiring in 1913.

COLLEEN MORRIS

JONES, Paul Osbourne (1921–1997), botanical artist, was born at Bondi (NSW), into a family of various artistic talents. He determined to become a botanical artist, and left school aged 14 to attend Sydney art schools. Drafted into the AIF, he spent the war years in New Guinea; a bonus was his introduction to its forest flowers. A commission by Professor E.G. WATERHOUSE to paint CAMELLIAS established a long friendship. Work with his beloved flowers was his life, and he loved the contacts in the botanical art world. He earned his living painting and attracted several patrons. Jones was the artist for major publications including *Camellia Quest* (1947) and *Camellia Trail* (1952) with text by Waterhouse; and in Britain, *The Camellia* (2 vols, 1956–60), as well as *Flora Superba* (1971) and *Flora Magnifica* (1976)—the *Flora* books being among the great flower books world-wide. He carried his admiration for flowers into another art form, black-and-white photography; self-taught, he felt the prop of colour was not needed to make the viewer aware of the life of a flower.

Collections of botanical illustrations are, curiously, little appreciated in Australia, and it is not surprising to learn that most of Jones's work is held in renowned collections in the USA and England. Sir George Taylor, director of the ROYAL BOTANIC GARDENS, KEW, wrote (1971) of his paintings: 'They are technically astounding, scientifically exact and aesthetically so thoughtful and pleasing that, without risking hyperbole, I would rank them among the very finest achievements in the whole gallery of botanical art.'

CAROLINE SIMPSON

JOONDALUP CENTRAL PARK, Perth WA, was developed in 1991 and extends from the civic centre through the city and past a residential precinct to meet the Yellagonga Regional Park at the edge of Lake Joondalup. The park provides a range of experiences from NATIVE GARDENS to entertainment spaces and hard city squares. A particular focus of the park is the relationship with the Yellagonga Regional Park—a sensitive, protected area. This inner-city park incorporates new recreational spaces and water systems within a fragile, low-heathland bush setting. The extensive WATER gardens and lake feature sculptures of water creatures. The park was designed by TRACT landscape architects who worked closely with the community and with various artists.

ROSEMARY ROSARIO

JOURNAL OF HORTICULTURE OF AUSTRALASIA (1906–16) was published monthly in Melbourne as an offshoot of the *AUSTRALIAN CULTURIST*, under managing editor Harry DAVEY of the Horticultural Publishing Press of Australasia, assisted by R.E. BOARDMAN. The journal ambitiously aimed for, but never achieved, national coverage, giving prominence to news of HORTICULTURAL SOCIETIES—a useful barometer of readership—and information for keen amateur gardeners. Davey recruited interstate representatives, including Elizabeth LINTON (Tas.), Fred Caley SMITH (SA), and 'Daun Utan' (Sydney SKERTCHLY) (Qld), but advertising revenue outside Vic. remained low. In 1911 the subtitle *Home and Garden Beautiful* was added, and this was soon adopted as the main title, coinciding with an upgrading in production and an increased emphasis on building. This was the first combined use of the words 'home' and 'beautiful' in an Australian periodical title, foreshadowing the later success of MAGAZINES such as *AUSTRALIAN HOME BEAUTIFUL* and its home-making and lifestyle contemporaries. The upgraded journal was unable to maintain its high standard and ceased publication in 1916. The Horticultural Press (as it was known after 1923) returned to the market with the *(AUSTRALIAN) GARDEN LOVER* (1925).

RA

JOURNALS AND MAGAZINES: see GARDEN MAGAZINES

JOURNALS OF AGRICULTURE: see AGRICULTURAL GAZETTES

KAMESBURGH, Brighton, Vic., was developed (1872–74) for Scotsman William Kerr Thomson, a partner and managing director of the ironmongery James McEwan and Co. No expense was spared in the design and construction of his MANSION or the layout of its grounds. The pleasure garden, the work of an experienced (although unknown) garden designer, was entrusted to head gardener, George Kenner (sometimes spelt Kinnear) (c. 1818–1897), who had migrated to Vic. c. 1852. He was head gardener for Thomson first at Greenfields, Elsternwick (now Brighton) from c. 1865, then at Kamesburgh (c. 1874–87). The mansion sat on a crisply formed embankment, facing a picturesque lawn with centrally placed FOUNTAIN. To one side, the drive curved from a GATEHOUSE, shielded from the lawn by a shrubbery, while on the other, the formality of the house podium was reflected in a sunken rose garden. Thomson was president of the Brighton Horticultural Society from 1879, and his head gardener was a successful exhibitor. Kamesburgh became the Commonwealth Government's Anzac Hostel (1918–95), a home for totally and permanently incapacitated war veterans. It is now owned, with the loss of the service area, by Bayside City Council, which is committed to its conservation.

JILL ORR-YOUNG

KARRAKATTA GENERAL CEMETERY, six kilometres west of Perth, was established by the Western Australian Government (1897–99). The incentive was the declining condition of older cemeteries such as East Perth and Skinner Street, Fremantle, and increasing professional and community concern for improving conditions of public health. Karrakatta was enlarged, covering 263 acres (106 ha) by the 1930s, and was divided along denominational lines. Early improvements included a superintendent's lodge, waiting house, grave diggers' lodge, toilets, and shelters. Provision was also soon made for funeral trains. Karrakatta boasted several innovations including an extensive nursery from which it sold about 25 000 plants annually to relatives and friends looking after graves. For others, maintenance services were available for an annual fee. Innovative lease terms provided for fifty years for plots and ninety-nine years for vaults. Visitors approached burial areas through extensive gardens, and the whole site was landscaped—no mean feat in the extensive sandy soils. The PERTH WAR CEMETERY is adjacent.

ROBERT NICOL

KAWARRA AUSTRALIAN PLANT GARDEN, Kalorama, Vic., opened in 1971, occupies a two-hectare site in the

Glazed domes of ARTIFICIAL FLOWERS adorn a 1930s grave at Perth's Karrakatta Cemetery, demonstrating both a popular form of floral tribute and also the fragile nature of Australia's CEMETERIES and their constituent elements

Dandenong Ranges purchased by Lillydale Shire in 1965 and leased to Mount Dandenong Horticultural Society. Members spent two years cleaning up before beginning to plant in 1968. Ellis STONES' original design was never fully implemented and in 1978 designer Kathleen Deery (1912–1996) offered her services to the Society. A series of pools took advantage of the outlook over Silvan Reservoir and by 1984 meandering pathways and raised garden beds completed the picture. The Shire assumed control of the garden in 1989 and subsequent curators have added new dimensions to the design. The ORNAMENTAL PLANT CONSERVATION ASSOCIATION lists Kawarra as holding the *Boronia* Collection and *Telopea* Collection. Other genera of the Rutaceae are grown as well as large numbers of the Rhamnaceae and Sterculiaceae.

JOHN WALTER

KAY, Frederick Norman (*c.* 1863–*c.* 1917), gardener and horticulturist, was born the son of a gardener in Bedfordshire, England, and worked as gardener at Westella private hotel, Elizabeth Street, Hobart, at the beginning of the twentieth century. He gave frequent lectures and practical demonstrations on floriculture, and organised exhibitions for the Amateur Horticultural Society of Hobart from its inception (1900), although he could not become a member because of his professional status. He advised the Tasmanian Parliament during 1903 on the spraying of orchards to eradicate pests such as Codlin Moth and was widely regarded for his horticultural expertise. Kay ran the Carnation Nursery, Harrington Street, Hobart, and edited Walch's *Gardening in Tasmania* (several editions from 1907–17) based on the work first published in 1870, and updated to take account of new floricultural developments.

RA

KEENAN, Francis (Frank) (b. 1914), horticulturist and gardens superintendent, was born and educated in Vic. He was the first recipient of the CRONIN Memorial Horticultural Scholarship—established to encourage boys to pursue a gardening career—and he spent his first two years studying at the School of Primary Agriculture and Horticulture, BURNLEY. His third year was spent in the Melbourne City Council's parks and gardens department and he was the sole male graduate of his class in 1931. In that year he joined the department's staff, and apart from four years serving in the air force during the Second World War, worked there until his retirement in 1978. In 1954 he became assistant superintendent of parks and gardens, and succeeded Jack OWENS as superintendent (later director) in 1964.

Keenan was an enthusiastic member of the VICTORIAN TREEPLANTERS' ASSOCIATION, and together with other Association members was instrumental in having the certificate of competency in horticulture at Burnley upgraded to a diploma in 1958. Keenan was committed both to introducing the RECREATION movement to Australia and to integrating it with the HORTICULTURE profession. During 1975–78 he was the Australian councillor on the commission of the International Federation of Park and Recreation Administration. In 1980 he was awarded the prestigious Gold Veitch Memorial Medal by the ROYAL HORTICULTURAL SOCIETY.

ELIZABETH STEWART

KEEP AUSTRALIA BEAUTIFUL COUNCIL (1968–), administered until 1975 under the aegis of the NATIONAL TRUST OF AUSTRALIA (Victoria), was founded by community worker Dame Phyllis Frost (b. 1917) to combat littering and general despoliation of rural and urban environments. Building on several earlier initiatives in Vic. and SA, the Council became a national administrative body in 1971, with state and territory branches pursuing autonomous but complementary programs. The initial civic pride message, summarised in the slogan 'Don't Rubbish Australia' and memorably publicised by deployment of 'litter maids', has gradually broadened, and the Council has undertaken several important horticultural, gardening, and urban design initiatives. The NT branch, for example, has a unique role in remote and rural Aboriginal communities: it acts as an advisory and referral body for COMMUNITY GARDENING and beautification projects. In this, the Council aims particularly to promote responsible land conservation and management principles in Aboriginal communities as a way to improve community health and employment.

ANITA ANGEL

KELLY, Alexander Charles (1811–1877), Scottish-born surgeon and vigneron, established the foundations of the Southern Vales' VITICULTURE industry in SA at his five-hectare vineyard near Morphett Vale (1845) before establishing the Tintara Vineyard Company at MCLAREN VALE. While an excellent wine-maker, Kelly was a poor businessman, and had to sell his venture to Thomas HARDY in 1873. One of his sons, John Kelly (1859–1947), managed the vineyard for Hardy's from 1882. Dr Kelly wrote the important texts *The Vine in Australia* (1861) and *Wine-growing in Australia* (1867).

DAVID JONES

KELLY, Stanley (1911–2001), engine driver and self-trained botanical artist, was born in Ararat (Vic.), and the success of his first publication, *Forty Australian Eucalypts in Colour* (1949), inspired him to paint every species of EUCALYPT then described. His two volumes titled *Eucalypts* (1969 and 1978), incorporating 535 species and subspecies, were the culmination of that dream. When Stan Kelly started his thirty-year project, colour photography was inadequate for accurate reproduction of plant specimens, although his publications were intended to stimulate interest in eucalypts as much as providing a botanical record.

JOHN WALTER

KEMP, Edward (1817–1891), English landscape gardener, worked in the garden of the Horticultural Society of London at Chiswick (then under the direction of John LINDLEY) and subsequently at Chatsworth (under Joseph PAXTON). He laid out Liverpool's Birkenhead Park (1843–47) under the supervision of its designer Paxton, and was its superintendent for more than forty years. In a long review of Birkenhead Park (1847) in the GARDENERS' CHRONICLE (edited by Paxton and Lindley), Kemp's mentors wished their student well as he embarked on an independent career as a landscape gardener. Kemp designed many public landscapes including Anfield Cemetery, Liverpool (1856–63); Hesketh Park, Southport (1864–68); Grosvenor Park, Chester (1867); Stanley Park,

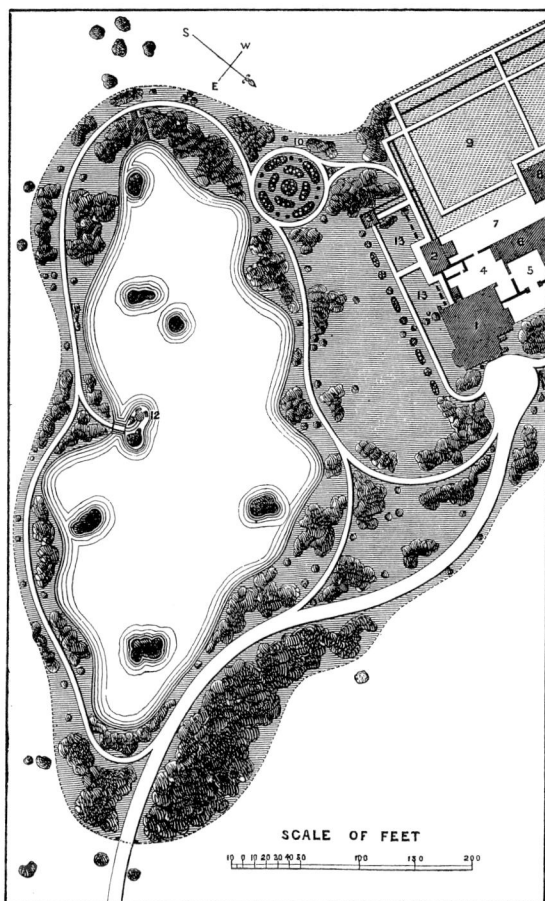

Edward KEMP's design for a garden at Thornton, Cheshire, England, illustrated in his *How to Lay out a Garden* (1858), with a LAKE as a principal feature of the pleasure garden—an arrangement imitated in Australian MANSION and HOMESTEAD GARDENS where wealth and natural topography permitted

Liverpool (1868–70); and Saltwell Park, Gatehead (1877) as well as private gardens he later used to illustrate his writings. His first foray into publishing came in this period with a modest pocket volume, *The Hand-book of Gardening*.

Kemp's major book, *How to Lay Out a Small Garden* (1850), met with great success (despite waspish allegations from Paxton of plagiarism, convinced his protégé had merely translated *his* practical ideas into print). Coinciding with Jane Loudon's edition of *The Villa Gardener* (first published by her husband in 1838), the two works covered similar ground, but for different audiences. Kemp aimed at the small landholder: his inexpensive, unillustrated volume suited the owners of quarter-acre allotments on the outskirts of English cities and towns. Stylistically, both books stressed the GARDENESQUE; Kemp saw it as a 'blending of Art with Nature ... Its object is beauty of lines, and general variety. Roundness, smoothness, freedom from angularity, and grace rather than dignity or grandeur are among its numerous indications' while by this late date Loudon's widow was also using the term as 'calculated for displaying the art of the gardener'.

With two subsequent editions (1858 and 1864), profusely illustrated and retitled *How to Lay out a Garden*, Kemp's book became a standard work in the Australian colonies. His ideas suited the emerging class of suburban landowners, especially in the crucial period following the discovery of gold, with its attendant rise of immigration, wealth, and urbanisation. His ideas were couched in a modern language—he acknowledged, for instance, the influence of railways on suburbanisation—although his instructions on the division of garden and domestic functions, appealing to those sections of society aspiring to emulate British class structures, were hardly calculated to inspire democratic social reform. But it was Kemp's instructions on garden STYLES that were most appealing, and these were reprinted (often unacknowledged) or paraphrased by many colonial authors including TRESEDER Bros. (1880) and William ELLIOTT (1897), bringing the Gardenesque to a new generation.

RA

KEMP, Herbert (1867–1941), horticulturist and nursery proprietor, born in Brandon, Norfolk, England, obtained his horticultural training in the Norfolk nursery of his father, Richard Kemp (1838–1919), before migrating to Adelaide in 1890. Around 1899 he founded Kemp's Nursery in Unley Park, the Kingswood Nursery (notable for its roses and carnations) in 1905, the Oaklands Estate nursery (specialising in roses and fruit trees) in 1920, and in 1929 purchased SEWELL's ALDGATE NURSERY. Following the onset of blindness (c. 1920) his assets were distributed among his sons, Jack, Bob, and Harry, but Kemp regularly supervised operations and walked the rows of the nurseries.

Herbert John (Jack) Kemp ('Grevillea') (1905–1963), horticulturist, undertook a three-year apprenticeship in the UK and France, and also trained in the Unley Park nursery. Jack Kemp, with his brothers, expanded the Kingswood nursery operations following his father's blindness until his own death. After he died his widow, Muriel Rosina (*née* Turnbull) (b. 1914), continued the nursery with his brothers. He initiated a landscape design service (engaging Max SHELLEY, Robin HILL, and Richard Massey to prepare plans), patented the tree wound paint 'Prunex', devised and marketed an innovative mist propagation system, and established Kemp's Garden Centre in the Myer Emporium (1953–72). Kemp regularly wrote under 'Grevillea' in the *Sunday Mail*, the *Chronicle*, and the *Advertiser*, and broadcast on ABC RADIO over a period of twenty-three years. He served as federal president of the Federation of Australian Nurserymen's Association (1946–47), president of the South Australian Nurserymen's Association (1943–47), chairman of the advisory committee of the South Australian Tree Planters' Association (1948–49), and a councillor of the Royal Agricultural and Horticultural Society of South Australia.

Robert (Bob) Frewer Kemp (1908–1972), horticulturist, took charge of the Aldgate Nursery. His son Peter Frewer Kemp (b. 1929) and Peter's wife Marjorie assumed management of this nursery in 1981. Peter served as president of the South Australian Association of Nurserymen (1970–72), president of the Federation of Australian Nurserymen's Associations (1972–73), and councillor of the Royal Agricultural and Horticultural Society of South Australia (1963–). Bob and Jack, with Barmera businessmen, established the Kemp's Murray Valley Nursery in 1945, to serve the RIVERLAND soldier settlements. The first nursery in the region, it specialised in propagating olives, citrus and other fruit trees, and today supplies virus-free vines.

Henry Kenneth Kemp (1912–1973), continued Jack Kemp's media commitments (as 'Garrya' and Arbor), while working for the Department of Agriculture. He later established an orchard at Balhannah. He served as a Member of the Legislative Council and retained an interest in the family nurseries.

DAVID JONES

KEMPE, (Friedrich Adolf) Herman(n), (1844–1928) was one the original Lutheran missionaries at Hermannsburg near Alice Springs. Arriving in 1877, he and other missionaries immediately established food gardens. Conditions for the MISSION GARDEN at Hermannsburg were harsh: scorching summers, freezing winter nights, and unpredictable rainfall. Some long-distance support was provided by Ferdinand MUELLER, who sent seed to the missionaries. In return Kempe reported on the garden's progress to Mueller, who published this information in his encyclopedic work on plant introduction, *Select Extra-tropical Plants* (1895). Judging from this book, the missionaries were able to provide themselves with an impressive variety of fruits and vegetables. One of their most successful plants was *Phoenix dactylifera* (Date Palm), which Mueller claimed to have introduced into Central Australia through Kempe.

P.A. Scherer and Adolf Hermann Kempe, *From Joiner's Bench to Pulpit* (Adelaide, 1973)

SARA MAROSKE

KENNERTON GREEN, Mittagong, is one of the grand gardens of the SOUTHERN HIGHLANDS, NSW. In the 1950s, Sir Jock and Lady Pagan slowly developed the garden surrounding the 1860s cottage, with camellia and rhododendron beds, a flowering cherry walk, deciduous trees, and an enclosed rose garden. A magnificent *Wisteria floribunda* 'Kuchibeni', a feature on the front lawn, was a gift from Dr Peter VALDER, as were many of the CAMELLIAS. Since 1988 the 3.5 hectare garden, under the guidance of Marylyn Abbott (b. 1942), author of *Gardening with Light and Colour* (1999), and well known for her rejuvenation of West Green House, Hampshire, England, has been further extended in a series of themed garden rooms. These include Una's Wood (a thick grove of silver birches, underplanted with bluebells), an ornamental vegetable garden (the theme of Abbott's latest book, *Gardens of Plenty*), a laburnum walk, an iris-rimmed lake, and a formal bay-tree parterre. Mature trees and sweeping lawns with hedges of cypress and box are a superb backdrop for the massed plantings of bulbs, roses, and perennials, at their peak in spring and early summer.

CHRISTINE REID

KERSLAKE, George Henry Tuck (1853–1911), florist and plant breeder, born in Teignmouth, Devon, England, the son of a farmer, migrated to Australia aged 20. He became the leading PLANT BREEDER in NSW at his Yukka Road property in Sydney's Potts Hill, during the 1890s–1900s. He raised many FLORISTS' flowers; bouvardias, CARNATIONS, gloxinias, herbaceous phloxes, penstemons, ROSES, and especially cactus and pompom DAHLIAS. While he propagated and distributed these himself, he also appointed others in the NURSERY trade as his agents. His plants were highly praised. In 1912 a correspondent wrote in the *Amateur Gardener*: 'I could not help feeling as I looked at this floral gem [Kerslake's Australian Beauty] that if the late honoured raiser had produced no other than this rose, he would have gained the approbation and thanks of all rosaries [sic] for all time'. 'Will we ever see his like again?' asked a knowledgeable contributor to the '*War Chest' Flower Book* (1917).

A company was formed to further his plant-breeding work, and when the nursery moved from Potts Hill to Blackheath, Thomas Ambrose Kerslake (1862–1923), landscape gardener and nursery proprietor, took over its management. Thomas was born at Teignmouth and at the age of 21 migrated to Sydney. Fourteen years later he moved to Blackheath as gardener to retailer John Pope (1827–1912) at Karaweera, a garden Governor Strickland thought one of the finest in the state. Pope, a partner in J. & W. Farmer & Pope (later Farmer & Co.), seemingly 'could not live without flowers', and introduced them into the workplace 'for the benefit of those who have too little of the perfume of flowers'. Kerslake established a nursery at Paddington, and in 1914 released a section of NOVELTIES raised by G.H. Kerslake, including dahlias, carnations, chrysanthemums, a new bouvardia, and a new climbing rose. Although further florists' flowers were released, the nursery changed to specialise in plants suited to gardens in colder parts of state.

RICHARD CLOUGH

KEW GARDENS: see ROYAL BOTANIC GARDENS, KEW

KEYLINE SYSTEM: see YEOMANS, Percival Alfred

KIDD, James (1801–1867), gardens overseer, was born in Fifeshire, Scotland. He was tried at Perth in 1830 for forging notes, and appears in the records as a gardener, married with four children. Transported to NSW for fourteen years, he arrived in Sydney late in 1830, and was assigned to SYDNEY BOTANIC GARDENS. A 'steady man', Kidd was strongly supported by Richard CUNNINGHAM, and became overseer in 1833. Allan CUNNINGHAM recommended him for a ticket of leave and, supported by references from leading Sydney worthies, this was granted in 1837. He was appointed assistant superintendent, and a conditional pardon came in 1843. Kidd worked industriously and effectively as 'a good practical gardener'. He declared his 'unrimitting [sic] exertions for the improvement of the Gardens' when successfully seeking remuneration for additional services rendered during the unsettled period 1842–44. Appointed acting superintendent from August 1844, he selected plants for the new GOVERNMENT HOUSE (1845), but was demoted (from September 1847) on the appointment of J.C. BIDWILL as director. Kidd then served as overseer for almost twenty more years.

Although Kidd sent 'excellent cases' of plants to Sir William Hooker, and was otherwise obliging, his former convict status caused some members of the scientific establishment in

The WALLED terrace at KILLYMOON, St Marys (Tas.) sets this outstanding early colonial residence on a substantial podium overlooking the landscape of the Break o'Day River flood plain

KEW and in Sydney to look askance at his position. He acquitted himself creditably at the enquiry into Charles MOORE's administration (1855), and ultimately gave faithful service to the Gardens for thirty-six years. James Kidd died in a Gardens cottage, and was buried amid some of Sydney's prominent citizens in the Camperdown Cemetery, where a handsome monument proudly declared that he was 'Late Superintendent of the Botanic Gardens, Sydney'—and that was true enough.
LIONEL GILBERT

KILLYMOON, St Marys, Tas., was one of Australia's most ambitious country houses of the 1840s. Irish and eighteenth-century in character, it is, however, nothing like its namesake in County Tyrone (a castle designed by John Nash c. 1803). Built for pastoralist Frederick Lewis von Stieglitz (1803–1866) on land acquired in 1829 (architect unknown), it is designed to command a broad landscape and looks out over the flood plain of the Break o'Day River. Completely symmetrical (two-storeyed above a semi-basement) it sits above a broad expanse of gravel and a high, bollarded retaining wall to separate it from the countryside. Balancing the façade at the side and beyond the principal rooms, brick garden walls with decorative gateways and niches shield the kitchen garden on the left and the flower garden on the right. At the back, the house looks across to the large stable yard with an intriguing and picturesque Gothic coach house.
CLIVE LUCAS

KING, Helena Elizabeth (Biddy) (1892–1964), garden designer, was born in WA, although she lived in England for twelve years. She studied garden design in England and continued her study under Australian conditions at BURNLEY, obtaining her qualification in horticulture (1940). She wrote several articles on 'Garden Planning' for the WEST AUSTRALIAN GARDENER in the 1940s, and regularly broadcast gardening advice on RADIO for the Australian Broadcasting Commission Women's Sessions in the early 1960s. Her 'vivacious and enthusiastic' nature saw her actively participate in the Guildford Tree Society and the Wildflower Society. King is known to have designed several private gardens in Perth, promoting the use of NATIVE PLANTS in the home garden. Her final commission (1964) was at Rowethorpe Retirement Village.
CAROLYN MIDDLEMIS

KING, Herbert John (1892–1973), naturalist and photographer, was a founding member of the Launceston FIELD NATURALISTS' CLUB (1949). His 1960 booklet on Tasmania's flora influenced Lord TALBOT de Malahide to organise the Endemic Flora project, for which King collected many specimens. Part IV of the *Endemic Flora of Tasmania* is dedicated to him. Winifred CURTIS named Tasmanian endemics *Euphrasia gibbsiae* var. *kingii* and *Ozothamnus rodwayi* subsp. *kingii* to honour him. King's photographs illustrate *Wildflowers of Tasmania* (1969) and *Guide to Flowers and Plants of Tasmania* (1981).
LINDEN GILLBANK

KINGS PARK AND BOTANIC GARDEN, Perth, is arguably the city's best-known tourist attraction and a popular icon of state identity and pride. Situated on Mount Eliza, little more than a kilometre from the city centre, this large urban PUBLIC PARK covers 400 hectares and is notable for its spectacular views and extensive bushland areas. A popular RECREATIONAL facility with generous PICNIC areas, children's PLAYGROUNDS, and nature trails, it is also a national shrine where most of the city's important monuments, including the State War Memorial, are located. Diverse in landscape character, the park is significant for Aboriginal cultural values, for the large area of urban bushland that occupies two-thirds of the park, and for its historic DESIGNED LANDSCAPES from the late nineteenth and early twentieth centuries.

Several hundred hectares were initially set aside for the establishment of the park in 1872; it was enlarged to its present extent in 1890. Development of Perth Park (renamed Kings Park in 1901) began with the symbolic planting of a Norfolk Island Pine by Premier John FORREST in 1895. Early works included the main scenic drives (now known as Fraser Avenue, Forrest Drive, and May Drive), the parklands along the ridge overlooking the city, the avenue of red-flowering gums along the main entrance road (replaced in 1938 with lemon-scented gums), and the terraced walks and gardens along Mounts Bay Road. Leading figures associated with this establishment phase were landscape gardener Alexander Campbell (1895–97), Government Gardener Daniel FEAKES (1897–1904), the first Superintendent, Jeremiah SHEATH (1904–13), and members of the Perth Park Board (later Kings Park Board), established in 1896.

The South African War Memorial (1901) was the first of many WAR MEMORIALS to be erected in the park—two of the most recent being the Vietnam Soldiers' Memorial (1989) and the Aboriginal and Torres Strait Islander War Memorial (2000). The State War Memorial, designed by architect and soldier Sir J.J. Talbot Hobbs (1864–1938), was unveiled in 1929; it is a prominent feature on the Kings Park skyline and a singular venue for the annual Dawn Service on Anzac Day. Also noteworthy are the honour avenues, planted along May Drive (1919–20) and LOVEKIN Drive (1932). Memorials commemorating historical figures include the Queen Victoria Statue (1903), Lord Forrest Memorial (1927), and Pioneer Women's Memorial Fountain (1968).

The 1960s marked a new phase in the development of the park, with the appointment of the first Director, Dr John BEARD (1961–70), the establishment of the seventeen-hectare BOTANIC GARDEN featuring the flora of WA, and construction of the innovative Arthur FAIRALL children's playground, broadwalk vista, and DNA observation tower. The 1970s saw the consolidation of Kings Park as a research and scientific institution, and in the 1990s management of the bushland areas became a special focus, along with recognition of the historic values of the park. Major upgrading and new wildflower display gardens as well as an education centre are proposed for the future.

OLINE RICHARDS

KINGSTON, George Strickland (1807–1880), architect, engineer, and surveyor, was born in Bandon, County Cork, Ireland. At 24 he was articled to the Birmingham civil engineer John Rofe, and in 1834 he began unpaid work for the South Australian Association (later the Colonisation Com-

The honour avenues in KINGS PARK, Perth, which serve as WAR MEMORIALS, now form fine features of the landscape where the closely spaced trunks of *Eucalyptus cladocalyx* (Sugar Gum) contrast with the surrounding bush plantings

mission) in London. He produced the renaissance plan for the colony's capital—with its terraces, SQUARES, and surrounding PARKLAND—and six months later (in March 1836) he embarked on the *Cygnet* as deputy surveyor-general. In December 1836 he discovered a site for Adelaide—later confirmed by LIGHT—and by the following March had laid out most of the town. Civil service politics forced his resignation in 1838, and he set up as a private architect, engineer, and surveyor. Kingston created Adelaide's first substantial public buildings and carried out numerous private commissions. Without specialised training, confidence, or imagination, he never developed a personal style, and despite auspicious beginnings, his practice simply faded. In 1839 Kingston and others unsuccessfully attempted to found a public BOTANIC GARDEN by subscription, and for ten years he petitioned the government to establish a garden 'of ornament and utility'. He showed an interest in VITICULTURE, becoming involved with the Agricultural and Horticultural Society of South Australia, acting as its secretary (1844–47). His coastal property at Marino, south of Adelaide, was the site of viticultural experimentation. A career in politics from 1851 until his death—mostly as speaker of the House of Assembly—gave him a leading role in establishing self-government for the colony.

Donald Langmead, *Accidental Architect* (Sydney, 1994)

DONALD LANGMEAD

KIOSK, a GARDEN BUILDING taking the form of a light, open, and generally ornamental PAVILION. The word's derivation from the French *kiosque* can be traced further back to Turkey and Persia (Iran), suggesting a close affinity with ISLAMIC architecture and gardens. Lightness of design and openness in plan are often achieved by use of hinged or demountable panels, leading to use of the term 'kiosk' for prosaic structures designed for occasional service of food, beverage, or other goods—for example at SPORTS or SHOWGROUNDS. RA

KIPPILAW, Goulburn, NSW, established in 1836 by the Chisholm family, has a rectilinear garden layout centred on an 1860s HOMESTEAD, approached by an axial oak-lined AVENUE underplanted with bulbs. The carriage loop ascends a stepped, grassy embankment dominated by a large *Cedrus libani* (Cedar of Lebanon), originally accented by cantilevered frames for roses and flanked by a pair of *Araucaria cunninghamii* (Hoop Pine). Of greater interest is the rare survival of kitchen (vegetable) and picking (flower) gardens to the north, formally enclosed by hedges of *Euonymus fortunei* and *Photinia robusta*, and separated by an arched arbour of galvanised pipe covered in wisteria. The picking garden has an elaborate geometric layout of beds bordered with terracotta tiles defining paths accented by four trellised Gothic iron arches, over which climb old-fashioned roses.

HOWARD TANNER

KIRKPATRICK, James Barrie (b. 1946), botanist and environmentalist, has worked in universities in California, Fiji, Melbourne, and Tas. (where he moved in 1972). Since 1988 he has been Professor of Geography and Environmental Studies at the University of Tasmania. His work has largely

Geometric tile-edged beds and trellised arches grace the PICKING GARDEN at KIPPILAW, Goulburn (NSW), where the intricate early layout has survived the threat of change that irrevocably altered many other HOMESTEAD GARDENS

been directed towards establishing a scientific basis for the reservation and management of plant species and communities. Kirkpatrick has published widely on the ECOLOGY and conservation of AUSTRALIAN PLANTS, particularly *EUCALYPTUS* species and ALPINE PLANT communities. He has been influential on government policy in biodiversity protection and enhancement, serving on many environmental and heritage committees and producing a range of critical reports on the environment. He has investigated environmental politics and the quantification of intangible values such as wilderness and scenery, and he acknowledges that his teaching 'takes advantage of the amazing natural laboratory called Tasmania'.

ML

KIRRIBILLI HOUSE, an 1850s Gothic residence situated on the northern shores of Sydney Harbour, adjoining ADMIRALTY HOUSE. Kirribilli has been used as the Sydney residence of the Australian prime minister since 1957. Set on 0.4 hectares of land with easterly views of Port Jackson, this well-maintained garden has changed little over the years, and is a fine example of a late-Victorian Sydney harbourside garden. Regrettably, it is rarely open to the public.

SILAS CLIFFORD-SMITH

KITCHEN GARDENS: see VEGETABLE GARDENS

KNEEN, Thomas Hugh (b. 1913), educator, was born and educated in Melbourne, and in 1935, following his university training in agricultural science and education, he joined the horticultural division of the Victorian Department of

Agriculture. After serving with the Second AIF in the Middle East and Papua New Guinea, Kneen continued to work in the Department as a senior horticultural instructor. In 1946 he was appointed principal of the School of Primary Agriculture and Horticulture, BURNLEY, and one of his first tasks was the training of Commonwealth Reconstruction Training Scheme students. One of Kneen's great interests was in furthering the status of horticultural EDUCATION; during his time at Burnley, supported by the Institute of Park Administration of Victoria (IPAV), he succeeded in having the Diploma of Horticulture introduced at Burnley (1958). He and college staff then worked hard to have the diploma recognised as a standard tertiary qualification, especially by the University of Melbourne, where many Burnley students pursued further studies.

Kneen was an active member of the IPAV (later the ROYAL AUSTRALIAN INSTITUTE OF PARKS AND RECREATION) and a founding member of both the Australian Institute of Agricultural Science and the AUSTRALIAN INSTITUTE OF LANDSCAPE ARCHITECTS. During 1967–74 Kneen served as principal of both Longerenong and Dookie Agricultural Colleges (Vic.), and from 1974 until his retirement in 1978 he held the position of chief of the Division of Agricultural Education of the Victorian Department of Agriculture.

ELIZABETH STEWART

KNIGHT, George William (1831–1923), horticulturist, vigneron, and nursery proprietor, was born into a London family of engineers, contractors, and stonemasons. Although trained as an architect and civil engineer, horticulture was an early enthusiasm. Aged 18, he built a CONSERVATORY adjoining his parents' dining room. Blocked in the family business, he and his elder brother, the architect and administrator John George Knight (1826–1892), migrated to Vic. G.W. Knight became a railway engineer on the Williamstown and Sunbury lines. He planted vineyards near Sunbury for himself and others along Jackson's Creek and soon left government service. He had pioneered the Sunbury region for VITICULTURE, but in 1870 sold his interests, complaining of the industry's unprofitability. He became Bendigo's building surveyor but took up as a nursery proprietor, orchardist, and vigneron instead, transforming barren mining-affected land into agricultural showplaces. In all, he established three nurseries in Bendigo and one at Epsom. He had an enduring enthusiasm for PALMS, and had more than 400 types of ORCHIDS, including New Guinean varieties. His most striking vine-breeding success was a large and delicious table grape (evolved from the Waltham Cross variety) exhibited at Melbourne's Centennial International EXHIBITION (1888–89). Admired by vice-regal visitors, it was henceforth known as the Centennial grape. A successful florist and supplier, Knight was a Fellow of the ROYAL HORTICULTURAL SOCIETY, a force in local politics, and a keen advocate of his adopted city's horticultural virtues. He was active almost until the last days of a long and creative life.

DAVID DUNSTAN

KNOX, Alistair (1912–1986), environmental designer, shared the view of Walter Burley GRIFFIN that a house should be at one with its landscape. In forty years of practice he produced numerous innovative mud brick buildings that seemed to grow from the earth and demanded gardens to suit. After working as a bank clerk and in the Navy he studied building at the Royal Melbourne Institute of Technology. In 1946 he designed his first house. By the early 1950s he was living in a bush environment in the outer Melbourne suburb of Eltham at the centre of a group of like-minded practitioners including Peter GLASS, Ellis STONES, and Gordon FORD. The gardens of AUSTRALIAN PLANTS that Stones and Ford designed at Knox's instigation around his houses were seminal to their own development in landscape design. Knox documented his philosophy in *Living in the Environment* (1975), *Alternative Housing* (1980), and *We are what we stand on* (1980). In the late 1960s he was a founding (affiliate) member of the AUSTRALIAN INSTITUTE OF LANDSCAPE ARCHITECTS. His honorary fellowship of that body and an honorary Doctor of Architecture degree from the University of Melbourne (1984) acknowledged his pioneering work in earth building and his early recognition of the aesthetic value of the Australian environment.

Alistair's wife, **Margot Knox (née Edwards)** (1931–2002), an artist who shared his landscape vision, worked for Ellis Stones in the early 1950s as a pavior and planter. Today her Mosaic Garden in Hawthorn (1993–) commands international attention for her application of ceramic tile fragments in Gaudiesque manner and her striking combination of plant form and colour.

ANNE LATREILLE

KOROIT BOTANIC GARDENS, Vic., was reserved in 1862 following agitation by local residents, William ANDERSON among them. The district's rich volcanic soil amply rewarded horticulture; a curator's cottage was erected (1869) and Ferdinand MUELLER sent a collection of pines and other conifers in 1870, but otherwise the site was little developed until Anderson persuaded William GUILFOYLE to redesign it. Guilfoyle visited in 1879, but the Minister for Lands sought to restrict his private commissions, and Guilfoyle was forced to subcontract the draughting of the plan to Robert WHITWORTH. The garden was steadily improved, and came to be renowned for its great beauty and horticultural diversity. In its heyday Edward Prior was a long-standing and dedicated curator (1878–95). Like other provincial BOTANIC GARDENS, Koroit's suffered post-war neglect; camping and caravanning intruded from the 1960s. The survival of Guilfoyle's GARDEN PLAN and growing community interest may yet spark a revival in the fortunes of this significant site.

HELEN DOYLE

KRAEHENBUEHL, Darrell Nairn (b. 1934), naturalist, botanist, and conservationist, is a self-trained plant enthusiast, former tutor in botany, and plant collector for the State Herbarium, who has made a major contribution to botanical identification and history in SA. A foundation member of the Nature Conservation Society of South Australia and the SOCIETY FOR GROWING AUSTRALIAN PLANTS (SA), he has written more than 140 publications about his research and botanical discoveries including the authoritative text *Pre-European Vegetation of Adelaide* (1996).

DAVID JONES

(1837–1921), had arrived in the district from Germany in 1862 and met his wife when both were working at Archibald Windeyer's property Kinross; her family were German vine dressers. William, a labourer and railway signalman, was a keen horticulturist (possibly through a friendship with Ernest BETCHE) and this interest was shared by many family members. Fred's son, Harry Lionel Krempin (1896–1970), juggled involvement in Krempin's Seeds with his own seedling nursery: Chinese MARKET GARDENERS formed an important clientele. His other son, John Lionel (Jack) Krempin (b. 1925), author and nursery proprietor, also worked in the family business (which ceased 1978) while specialising in exotic INDOOR PLANTS: his illustrated book *Decorative Plants* (1960) ran to many editions and brought this 'new rage' to post-war Australia.

RA

KRICHAUFF, Friedrich Eduard Heinrich Wulf (1824–1904), politician, farmer, and land agent, had a lifelong interest in scientific agriculture. Born into a German family in the Danish Duchy of Schleswig, Krichauff was educated locally at Husum (where he met Ferdinand MUELLER), at the University of Kiel (apprenticed to Ludwig FISCHER), and at the University of Berlin (studying horticulture). In 1848—a year after Mueller—he accompanied Fischer and his family to Adelaide, and later married Dorothea Fischer (1853). After district council experience, Krichauff was elected to the Legislative Assembly (1857) and spoke often on the subject of land use. In 1870 he initiated a select committee on the establishment and replanting of forest reserves (1870), a *Forestry Act* (1873), and a forest board (1875). Krichauff was appointed chairman of the Central Agricultural Bureau in 1888, and was a councillor of ROSEWORTHY AGRICULTURAL COLLEGE. Drawing on research and experimentation, Krichauff published widely on agricultural topics, including *Fertilising Field and Garden* (1901).

SARA MAROSKE

KURING, Peter Ernest (1951–1987), garden designer and decorator, was born at Windsor (NSW) and showed an early interest in horticulture while still at school in Melbourne. He fled to Sydney in the mid-1960s and became one of the last of the socialite gardeners (in the mode of English designer Russell Page) to work in Australia. Kuring was loved and admired by the many clients, customers, and friends for whom he created interiors, bought furniture and pictures, and created gardens of singular beauty and character. Starting out as a commercial florist, he gradually moved into creating gardens and trading Asian furniture. Kuring had no formal training in design or landscape construction but had a keen eye for design and detail, and a natural skill for planting composition: he typically worked without plans or specifications. Working with a rich palette and distinctive plants of strongly architectural form, the influence of Japanese gardens was strongly expressed in his urban projects, paralleling his developing taste for Asian furniture and decorative objects. Although his total output of gardens in Sydney and Melbourne probably numbered no more than twenty, Kuring was frequently in the pages of glossy magazines, where he was able to influence taste in garden design. He

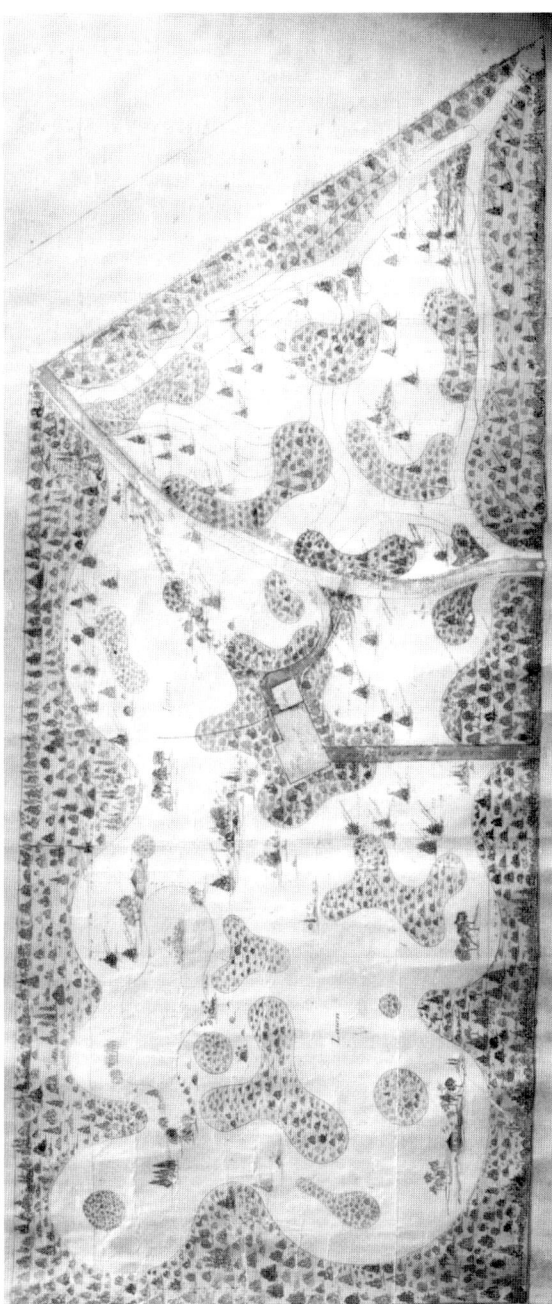

William GUILFOYLE's plan for KOROIT BOTANIC GARDENS (1879), drafted by Robert Whitworth, although only partly implemented, demonstrates many of Guilfoyle's design characteristics—in particular, sweeping lawns dotted with irregularly shaped flower beds and shrubberies to create a sense of containment as well as long vistas

KREMPIN, Frederick William (1869–1948), seed merchant, started in business *c.* 1892 in Newcastle (NSW). His father, Wilhelm Frederick Johan (William John) Krempin

Ku-ring-gai Wildflower Garden

Garden designer Peter KURING (left), pictured in the social pages of *Australian Women's Weekly* (1973) in 'Persian embroidered bolero with skivvy and flares', is joined by Lady Fairfax ('Jean Patou ruffled organza gown') and Liberace ('sequinned tuxedo and velvet pants') in Sydney's rich social melting pot

showed scant regard for contract documentation, but his inventive plant combinations and technical skill in composing hard landscape elements set a standard for domestic gardens that has rarely been equalled. Although many of his gardens have been dismantled or changed due to the tide of fashion, those remaining have held together in form and spatial quality with little intervention. IAN INNES

KU-RING-GAI WILDFLOWER GARDEN, St Ives, NSW, is located on 123 hectares adjoining Ku-ring-gai Chase National Park. In 1961, John WRIGLEY, on behalf of the SOCIETY FOR GROWING AUSTRALIAN PLANTS (North Shore Group), lobbied the local council for the formation of a WILDFLOWER garden. The site was selected in 1962 and in 1963 the name and objective of 'growing of plants from all parts of Australia for preservation and public display' were established. In 1968, after six years of work by governmental and private organisations and individual citizens, the Ku-ring-gai Wildflower Garden was officially opened. The garden featured a SHADE HOUSE filled with FERNS and ORCHIDS of the Central Coast District and many species from interstate were planted around the car parks and meeting rooms, the whole being offset by the natural beauty of the Hawkesbury Sandstone flora. Many NSW species not indigenous to the area were added to the understorey of the bush areas. Fire destroyed the entire garden a few weeks after opening; only the buildings were spared. Natural regeneration and continued efforts by the garden's managers (who adopted a more educational and conservation-minded direction) led to the removal of non-indigenous species from bush areas and the development of several walks providing access to the moist valleys, tall forests, rock formations, and hilltop plateaux of the garden. JOHN WALTER

KUWAHATA, Hideo (1864–1930), merchant and Japanese plant specialist, was born in Japan but for more than forty years conducted his business as ship provedore and indent merchant in Sydney. Two years before his death, in Nagasaki, he established the Mikado Farm nursery at Guildford (NSW), specialising in Japanese plants. Kuwahata had retail premises in Sydney's George Street and maintained a sideline in BONSAI model gardens, featured in the *Home* magazine in 1928. RA

LABILLARDIÈRE, Jacques-Julien Houtou de (1755–1834), naturalist, was born in Alençon, Normandy, France, the son of a lace merchant. After studies at Alençon's Collège Royal, he studied botany and medicine at Montpellier under Antoine Gouan (a correspondent of LINNAEUS) and then in Paris where he came under the influence of Louis-Guillaume Le Monnier, professor of botany at the Jardin du Roi. He visited England in 1783 and met Joseph BANKS. On his return to France, Labillardière travelled in the Alps with Dominique Villars and later Carolo Antonio Bellardi, both pioneers of Alpine botany. In 1787–88, with the assistance of Le Monnier and Foreign Minister Vergennes, he collected in Cyprus, Lebanon, Palestine, and Syria—travels that provided the foundations for his important early work on the botany of the Near East, *Icones plantarum Syriae rariorum* (1791–1812).

In 1791 Labillardière was selected as one of the naturalists of the d'Entrecasteaux expedition (1791–93) in search of La Pérouse, who had disappeared after visiting Botany Bay in 1788. Although d'Entrecasteaux failed to discover the fate of his compatriot and perished in the attempt, he made several significant geographical discoveries, including Recherche Bay and the D'Entrecasteaux Channel (Tas.), and Esperance Bay and the Archipelago of the Recherche (WA). In turn Labillardière's NATURAL HISTORY collections in these locations gave him an important place in the history of Australian botany and zoology. Labillardière was a republican, and after the disintegration of d'Entrecasteaux's expedition in the Dutch East Indies he suffered the indignity of internment and confiscation of his natural history specimens. Fortunately for posterity, these precious collections were returned through the gracious intervention of Banks.

Labillardière published an account of his voyage, *Relation du voyage à la recherche de La Pèrouse* (1800), which was soon translated into English and German. He then published the first flora of Australia, *Novae Hollandiae plantarum specimen* (1804–06), in which he coined the generic names for now-familiar Australian plants such as *Anigozanthus*, *Atherosperma*, *Calothamnos*, *Chorizema*, *Comesperma*, *Diplarrena*, *Exocarpus*, *Lepidosperma*, *Nuytsia*, and *Richea*. He also named seven new species of EUCALYPTUS: *E. amygadalina*, *E. cordata*, *E. cornuta*, *E. globulus*, *E. incrassata*, *E. ovata*, and *E. viminalis*. Labillardière later published the first flora of New Caledonia, *Sertum austro-caledonicum* (1824–25); unlike his earlier works, it was not organised on Linnean lines. In the wake of Napoleon's victories in Italy he was appointed a special commissioner by the Directory and was involved in the plunder of Italian museums and libraries for France. He was elected a member of the Institut de France in 1800. J.E. SMITH named the Australian genus *Billardiera* in honour of this great pioneer of Australian botany and the (now) widely planted grass *Poa labillardieri* is among more than two dozen plants that bear his name.

Edward Duyker, *Labillardière: A Naturalist's Life and Letters* (Carlton South, Vic., forthcoming, 2003)

EDWARD DUYKER

LA GERCHE, John (1845–1914), forester, was born in St Mary's Parish, Jersey, and arrived in Melbourne in 1865. By 1887 he had established a small nursery (later Victoria's second STATE FOREST NURSERY) and plantation at Sawpit Gully in the Ballarat–Creswick State Forest. Sawpit Gully Plantation was a pioneering experiment in reforesting denuded diggings with mixed species of CONIFERS and deciduous trees. His second son, Alfred Romeo La Gerche (1873–1948), architect, planned and designed Victoria's first model GARDEN CITY at Yallourn (1921) for the State Electricity Commission.

Angela Taylor, *A Forester's Log: The Story of John La Gerche and the Ballarat–Creswick State Forest 1882–1897* (Carlton South, Vic., 1998)

ANGELA TAYLOR

LA HAYE, Félix: see DELAHAYE, Félix

LAHEY, Romeo Watkins (1887–1968), engineer, timber merchant, and conservationist, from Pimpama (Qld), shared a vision with Robert Collins for the creation of a NATIONAL PARK in the McPherson and Main Ranges. He protested against the selections taken up by the O'Reilly family in 1911 and ran a campaign—through lectures, public meetings, and petitions—that culminated in 1915 with the gazettal of LAMINGTON NATIONAL PARK. Lahey's involvement continued with the design and construction of graded tracks (to minimise ecological disturbance), the establishment of Binna Burra Lodge in 1933, and donation of land. Lahey's belief in national parks became a lifetime commitment. In 1930 he was instrumental in forming the National Parks Association of Queensland, serving as president for thirty-one years. Lahey's contribution was recognised by the dedication of Kumuran Lookout in 1971 to his memory.

MARGARET COOK

LAIDLAW, William (*c.* 1866–1925), Scottish-born botanist, arrived in Vic. in 1908 following a university position in Canada. After work in the Department of Agriculture as a biologist, he was appointed Government Botanist and Director of MELBOURNE BOTANIC GARDENS—positions he held from 1924 until his death (with the positions united, as they had been from 1857 to 1873). He took a keen interest in plant pathology and AUSTRALIA FLORA, but his short tenure prevented major achievements in the Gardens.

LEE ANDREWS

LAKE HARRY, SA: see HERGOTT SPRINGS, SA

LAKES and other ornamental sheets of water such as ponds, pools, and dams, along with tanks and waterholes, are much used in gardens of various scales and treatments in Australia—one of the driest places on the planet. This use of water is associated with practical, aesthetic, and sometimes spiritual concerns.

Waterholes are permanent or seasonal places of water collection found in the indigenous environment. Some have social significance as meeting places and ceremonial places in Aboriginal and European cultures alike.

Lakes, dams, and tanks are more commonly associated with gardens, parks, and reserves or estates of a landscape scale incorporating a rural or once-rural context—for example, HOMESTEADS. Ponds and pools are associated with developments of a more intimate scale in any context, yet are to be found frequently as an element of the SUBURBAN GARDEN. Ponds and pools are also often associated with FOUNTAINS as a focal point, with either formal or informal placement in the water.

Natural lakes are found in areas where the water table is high; they have often been included in grand landscape compositions as borrowed scenic elements and as a focus for RECREATION. Dams suggests naturalness where the edges of the water reflect the contours of the containing land. Lake Burley Griffin, forming the GRIFFINS' water axis for CANBERRA, is a fine example, and possibly the largest designed water element forming an integral part of Australian URBAN DESIGN. Lake Burley Griffin is expressed as an informal element; some lakes and dams have more regular edges as a result of the imposed geometry of the architect, surveyor, or engineer. Such works can be seen in reservoirs and water supply sources created for urban and suburban development in nineteenth-century public works programs. Water bodies that were adapted as lakes and large ponds in the late nineteenth and twentieth centuries include Centennial Parklands, Prospect Reservoir, and Potts Hill Reservoir in Sydney, or Yuille's Swamp (Ballarat) and Eildon Reservoir in Vic. Possibly the grandest example in Australia is the lake system created as part of the Snowy Mountains Hydro-Electric Scheme in the 1950s.

Lakes and ponds have often been treated in a PICTURESQUE manner—islands lush with tropical foliage, rustic BRIDGES, and the illusion of naturalness—although occasionally they are rigidly formed into neatly edged banks with retaining walls or incorporate a mixture of both. Examples of picturesque treatment include lakes at the ROYAL BOTANIC GARDENS, MELBOURNE, RIPPON LEA, and MAWALLOCK in Vic. Perth's HYDE PARK has a rigidly contained lake surrounded by exotic trees and other introduced plants—formalised under the pressures of Euro-Australian occupation and the processes of civilisation, but once a natural lake fringed with drifts of paperbark trees and indigenous vegetation.

Ornamental sheets of water have been used as mirrors of reflection as well as commemorative elements and associated with areas of quiet contemplation. Larger-scale examples

The LAKE at the University of Melbourne, now paved as a courtyard, and porticoed medical school, long since demolished, give this nineteenth-century INSTITUTIONAL setting the air of a picturesque villa

include the War Memorial in Sydney's HYDE PARK and the Sculpture Garden at the National Gallery of Australia, Canberra. Smaller-scale water bodies appear in the domestic garden, where water and rocks may emulate the natural environment. Examples include some of the works of Ellis STONES and Bruce MACKENZIE, and the regular tanks often softened by stone edging and irregular planting in the works of Edna WALLING, Jocelyn BROWN, and Paul SORENSEN.

Plants are used around the edge of ornamental water bodies to break up the waterline and disguise seasonal changes of water levels due to the high rate of transpiration and evaporation as a result of the Australian climate. Aquatic plants are also used for foliage or flower effect or to help remove nutrient loads in the water body.

Moving water is frequently found in the form of fountains, cascades, and water jets. Fountains set in small ponds were often the centrepiece of the nineteenth-century urban park, and cascades have been used as a design element in both the nineteenth and twentieth centuries: examples can be seen at RIPPON LEA and ROSALIND PARK in Vic., the High Court of Australia forecourt in Canberra, and in Bicentennial Park, Darling Harbour, and Olympic Park, in Sydney.

Some lakes and ponds serve an intentional ECOLOGICAL function in their use of water—for instance as a central element in the Keyline system of P.A. YEOMANS or the design of farm dams to accommodate wildlife. The value of natural wetlands is increasingly recognised, as is reflected in a change of terminology from swamps (undesirable, required draining) to wetlands (ecologically desirable, recognised by international conventions). Designed wetlands are now a specialised part of landscape architecture and construction. They are important for filtering urban runoff through plants able to absorb heavy metals, and able to oxygenate water.   CRAIG BURTON

LAMINGTON NATIONAL PARK, Lamington Plateau, Qld, an area of 20 500 hectares on the southern end of the McPherson and Main Ranges, was gazetted as a NATIONAL PARK in 1915, after a long campaign begun in the 1890s and persistent advocacy by Romeo LAHEY and Robert Collins. Capitalising on increased visits to the region, selector (and later conservationist) Bernard O'Reilly established O'Reilly's Guest House on his selection by 1926. Alternative hiking and camping holidays were provided after 1933 at Binna Burra Resort by Queensland Holiday Resorts Ltd, formed by Arthur Groom and Romeo Lahey. By 1939 the resort comprised a lodge (brought from Cunungra), guest cabins (based on Victorian models), a vegetable garden (now Bellbird Clearing), and graded tracks. Supplies and luggage were transported by flying fox—another Lahey design—until 1947, when a road was constructed. A sawmill and Arthur Groom's house were added to the site; the house has been used as an Environmental Study Centre since 1977. A forestry camp was established at Green Mountains in the 1920s as a base for track construction. Much of the track network, supervised by ranger Gus Kouskos, was built by Depression labour. The park includes memorials to Lahey, Collins, and Kouskos. This World Heritage–listed subtropical rainforest is celebrated in paintings by Vida Lahey (Romeo's sister) and Lois Beumer; photographs; literary works by poet Rodney Hall, Arthur Groom, and Bernard O'Reilly (*Green Mountains*); song; and film (Harry Chauvel's *Sons of Matthew*).

J. Keith Jarrott, *History of Lamington National Park* (Brisbane, 1990)   MARGARET COOK

LANDCARE, a national program since 1989 following examples from the 'LandCare' movement, Vic., and 'land care' in WA (under the auspices of Land Conservation District Committees), includes practices associated with sustainable land use in rural Australia. Australia's Landcare program reflects Commonwealth government policy, articulated in July 1989 when Prime Minister Hawke, in his *Statement on the Environment*, signalled the need for ecologically sustainable development and launched the 'Decade of Landcare' with $360 million. Agreement between Rick Farley (National Farmers Federation) and Philip Toyne (Australian Conservation Foundation)—a radical alliance between agriculturists and conservationists—created a groundswell of support for a national program of land care. Landcare developed as a partnership between all levels of government, the community, and individuals to address land degradation. The National Landcare Program (NLP, 1982) amalgamated National Soil Conservation Program, the Resources Assistance Program, and community components of One Billion Trees, Save the Bush, and Natural Resources Management Strategy for the Murray–Darling Basin. In 1997 the NLP became the National Heritage Trust program.

Landcare is a community-based, participatory program involving many thousands of Australians. Some thirty per cent of Australian farmers are involved in Landcare activities. Initially, Landcare groups tended to be based on particular local issues such as salinity or noxious WEED control. However, evidence suggests groups develop expertise in property planning, local and regional vegetation management, and water catchment management activities. Establishing corridors of green between farms and regional conservation reserves, fencing out riparian strips, developing seed orchards, and extensive shelter belt and gully plantings, are some Landcare activities. Farmers estimate that their labour and supplies account for eighty per cent of costs in grant-funded projects. Landcare groups often coalesce to form Landcare Networks, providing lobbying and facilitation support. Funding support for Landcare projects is based on catchment priorities and grants from all levels of government. The Landcare concept of community, partnerships and environmental change has inspired Urban Landcare and international programs.

Landcare offers a powerful tool for creating a new Australian landscape vision. Ecosystem management is now recognised as the way to imagine and manage RURAL LANDSCAPES, and a program reinforcing the land management potential of local people is vital to our ability to sustain rural communities.   RUTH BEILIN

LANDSCAPE ARCHITECTURE is the conscious human manipulation of natural and modified elements of the earth for human use and pleasure. Considered as both an art form and an applied science, it involves the artistic arrangement of

Landscape architecture

The concept for Millennium Parklands, Homebush Bay (NSW), by Hassell, Peter Walker and Partners, and Bruce Mackenzie Design, reworking the site used for the 2000 Sydney Olympics, demonstrates the centrality of traditional plan representations in conveying complex LANDSCAPE ARCHITECTURE designs

unrefined soft materials—earth, water, plants—together with refined hard materials—stone, timber, concrete, steel, plastics—to create aesthetically pleasing and useful habitats for people and other living things. It ranges in scale from the design of small outdoor and indoor spaces to the planning of a total region. Unlike ARCHITECTURE, it is dynamic, constantly changing over time. No landscape design can ever be said to be finished: to remain viable it must be continually managed to ensure the living components are maintained and replaced as they mature. Landscape architecture therefore encompasses the theories and practices of planning, design, and management of the land.

The earliest recorded use of the term was by the Scottish author Gilbert Lang Meason in the title of his book *On the Landscape Architecture of the Great Painters of Italy* (1827). Fellow Scot John Claudius LOUDON subsequently used it in the title of his book *The Landscape Gardening and Landscape Architecture of the late Humphry Repton Esq.* (1840). In both instances the reference was to buildings in a landscape setting, not to the professional discipline. It was the American Frederick Law OLMSTED and his English partner, Calvert Vaux, who first adopted the title 'landscape architect' in 1863 (when they resigned their commissions overseeing the construction of their award-winning design for Central Park, New York City).

Landscape architecture comes to any civilisation only after a period of relative stability and affluence, and, although it first appeared in Australia in the form of private pleasure gardens and PUBLIC PARKS during the early 1800s, it was not recognised as a profession until the second half of the twentieth century. Given Australia's historic ties with Britain, it was inevitable that those first parks and gardens would be designed by LANDSCAPE GARDENERS and horticulturists trained in Europe and familiar with the landscape styles fashionable at that time. The first of these was Thomas SHEPHERD, who, after establishing himself as a nursery proprietor in Sydney, was invited to give public lectures on horticulture and landscape gardening—the first such lectures to be delivered in the colony. They were published posthumously as *Lectures on the Horticulture of New South Wales* (1835) and *Lectures on Landscape Gardening in Australia* (1836). Many of the directors of Australia's early BOTANIC GARDENS—Charles MOORE and Joseph MAIDEN (Sydney), William GUILFOYLE (Melbourne), George FRANCIS and Richard SCHOMBURGK (Adelaide), and Walter HILL (Brisbane)—in addition to laying out the grounds of their respective institutions, also advised on the design and planting of public parks, CEMETERIES, STREET TREES and AVENUES, and large private estates. All followed eighteenth-century English landscape and PICTURESQUE modes or nineteenth-century

GARDENESQUE design principles, into which were incorporated exotic and native plants.

The Chicago architect Walter Burley GRIFFIN was the first to officially use the title 'landscape architect' in Australia, when he won the design competition for the Federal Capital (1912). When he arrived the following year to take up the position of Federal Capital Director of Design and Construction, he brought with him the Beaux-Arts principles that were the essence of the North American CITY BEAUTIFUL movement, and these were enthusiastically embraced by many Australian architects and planners. Griffin's plan for CANBERRA resulted in the first major regional landscape design in this country, and, in spite of environmental shortcomings, the present overall visual effect is brilliant.

Canberra aside, most landscape design in Australia remained at the scale of public parks and large private gardens throughout the first half of the twentieth century. As a general rule, municipal parks were designed by council engineers, with park superintendents responsible for the planting, and there was considerable emphasis on SPORTING facilities and PLAYGROUNDS. During the inter-war years a number of talented landscape designers, including Edna WALLING (Vic.), Jocelyn BROWN and Paul SORENSEN (NSW), and Elsie CORNISH (SA), created some outstanding private gardens for wealthy clients. While several of these designers had training in horticulture, none had been educated in landscape architecture.

The period after the Second World War heralded a dramatic change in attitude towards the discipline of landscape architecture, which by then was well recognised overseas, with professional bodies being established in the USA (American Society of Landscape Architects, founded 1899) and Britain (Institute of Landscape Architects, founded 1929), and formal education programs being introduced at numerous universities. Seminal literature such as Christopher Tunnard's *Gardens in the Modern Landscape* (1938), Brenda Colvin's *Land and Landscape* (1948), Garrett Eckbo's *Landscape for Living* (1950), Peter Shepheard's *Modern Gardens* (1953), Thomas Church's *Gardens Are for People* (1955), and Sylvia CROWE's *Tomorrow's Landscape* (1956), became available in Australia and influenced a number of young architects and horticulturists who were interested in landscape architecture as a career change. Encouraged by their teachers, a growing band of these students undertook graduate studies in the discipline at British and American universities during the 1950s and early 1960s. After graduating, many stayed on to gain practical experience in landscape offices, and then completed the requirements for admission to the Institute of Landscape Architects (now the Landscape Institute). Well qualified, most returned to Australia to work as landscape architects in government departments, establish private practices, or teach in universities, which spawned the first graduate and undergraduate landscape programs in this country. There are now seven landscape architecture schools, and four of these include chairs of landscape architecture. The need for professional status equivalent to that of architecture, planning, and engineering was soon recognised, and, in 1963, a select group met in Melbourne to investigate the feasibility of forming an appropriate organisation; within four years the AUSTRALIAN INSTITUTE OF LANDSCAPE ARCHITECTS had been established.

The post-war years were also a period of increasingly large-scale developments in housing, mining, energy, transport, and tourism—all of which provided new opportunities for landscape architects to demonstrate their creative abilities. Enormous undertakings such as the Snowy Mountains Hydro-Electric Scheme, water storage dams in various states, the expansion of Canberra and other new towns, rural and urban freeways, hard-rock quarrying and sand mining, included landscape architects in the project teams. From the mid-1950s to the 1970s many government departments formed specialist landscape sections, and private practices expanded to meet the demand. The boom continued through the 1980s, catalysts including the 1988 Bicentenary and more recently the 2000 Olympics and Millennium celebrations.

Landscape architecture remains one of the few generalist design disciplines, and, because of their broad-based training, many landscape architects find they have much to contribute in the new specialist fields of URBAN DESIGN, heritage CONSERVATION, and resource management. In the present political climate, which embraces ecologically sustainable development, landscape architecture is one profession that can aspire to this ideal, and the related science of LANDSCAPE ECOLOGY is now emerging.

Norman T. Newton, *Design on the Land: The Development of Landscape Architecture* (Cambridge, Mass., 1971); Melanie Simo, *100 Years of Landscape Architecture: Some Patterns of a Century* (Washington, DC, 1999)   **ALLAN CORREY**

LANDSCAPE AUSTRALIA (1979–), the official journal of the AUSTRALIAN INSTITUTE OF LANDSCAPE ARCHITECTS (AILA), embraces LANDSCAPE ARCHITECTURE, land use planning, URBAN DESIGN, and landscape construction, thus covering a wide environmental spectrum. The journal was founded at the request of AILA by Ralph Neale (b. 1922), managing editor (1979–97). Neale adopted the name of the former AILA Quarterly Bulletin, *Landscape Australia* (1968–78), edited by Harold BLOOM; it had previously served as the Institute's newsletter. At the same time AILA relinquished ownership of that title, now owned by Landscape Publications (Aust) Pty Ltd.

While its focus is Australian, *Landscape Australia* frequently includes issues or projects of international interest. Contributors include many respected members of the profession, and the journal enjoys an interdisciplinary circulation and high professional regard. Understandably, the magazine showcases the achievements of AILA members—the biennial publication of the National Project Awards testifies to this—but more philosophical articles and opinions are also encouraged, although not always fully supported by conservative elements of the profession. The journal has also focused attention on garden design by sponsoring a number of successful conferences during the 1990s; they have attracted leading overseas personalities and local experts as speakers, which has lifted the profile of Australian gardens. With more than twenty years of continuous publication,

Landscape ecology

Landscape Australia is a valuable historical record of the development of landscape architecture in Australia.

ALLAN CORREY

LANDSCAPE ECOLOGY, recognised as a separate science since the early 1980s, bridges the established disciplines of LANDSCAPE ARCHITECTURE and ECOLOGY. Whereas landscape architecture emphasises visual and AESTHETIC qualities of the landscape, and ecology focuses on the interrelationships of geophysical and biophysical phenomena, landscape ecology takes a much more holistic approach involving a creative synthesis of all the physical components of landscape, together with cultural impacts and human perceptions.

It has long been the prerogative of geographers to study landscapes holistically, but taking little account of aesthetic variables. In the 1960s, however, landscape architecture academics, including Brian Hackett (UK) and Ian McHarg and Phil Lewis (USA), developed land-use planning methodologies based on ecological principles and utilising the new technologies of aerial photography and remote sensing. Many professions concerned with land use—urban and regional planning, forestry, soil conservation, for example—as well as the CSIRO Division of Land Use Research, adopted these methodologies, modifying them to suit their own individual needs. During the 1980s, European research focused on the dynamic equilibrium of natural, agricultural, and urban ecosystems, and the role of active human intervention in their management for long-term sustainability and aesthetic beauty. Management techniques such as controlled burning and grazing, controlled use of herbicides, selective harvesting, mulching, planting, and fostering natural regeneration were found to be more conducive to maintaining healthy, productive, economically viable and visually pleasing landscapes than many traditional methods. Landscape ecology is now widely accepted as part of regional planning and development in Australia; examples of its use can be seen in dune stabilisation, derelict land and mining reclamation, agroforestry, bush regeneration and LANDCARE, erosion control, and flood mitigation works.

ALLAN CORREY

LANDSCAPE GARDENING DOWNING credits English poet William Shenstone (1714–1763) with coining this term when in his posthumously published 'Unconnected Thoughts on Gardening' (1764) he divided gardening into three 'species': 'kitchen gardening, parterre gardening, and landskip or picturesque-gardening', likening landscape gardening to landscape painting. This conjunction was at the heart of the PICTURESQUE controversy, and when REPTON styled himself a landscape gardener, Uvedale PRICE accused him of 'assuming a title of no small pretensions'. The *Gardeners' Chronicle* (1867), clearly saw gardening and landscape gardening as distinct:

> the one being devoted to the culture of plants for use or ornament, the other entirely to the creation of tasteful and beautiful scenery—in a word, to the disposition of the ground, and the arrangement of the living materials by which it is decorated, which latter it is the gardener's business to tend with a loving hand.

In Australia, the publications of Thomas SHEPHERD and the design work of William GUILFOYLE exemplified this contemporary definition, although the term was freely used by many GARDENERS when dabbling in garden design. Later generations have preferred the term landscape designer, and the original scope of landscape gardening now often comes within the purview of LANDSCAPE ARCHITECTURE or landscape construction. Many involved in the 'design and construct' section of the industry use the term 'landscape gardener' to distinguish themselves from those who undertake garden MAINTENANCE.

RA

LANDSCAPE PLANT TYPES There is a confusing array of overlapping and generalised categories for PLANTS based on growth form and use. A BULB, for example, may also be a herbaceous PERENNIAL; there is no clear division between a woody SHRUB and a TREE; and a GROUND COVER could mean a rich understorey of plants in a natural setting or an ornamental monoculture with a height restricted to 300 mm. There is, however, a broadly accepted set of terms—widely used in horticultural practice and garden design—based on overall form, growth attributes, and life cycle.

The basic classification of trees as woody (forming wood) and perennial (growing for more than two years) may be subdivided into deciduous (shedding their leaves) and evergreen (maintaining leaves all the year). Non-woody plants, especially those in which the top dies down to the ground each winter, may be referred to as herbaceous. Herbaceous perennials, the mainstay of the HERBACEOUS BORDER, regenerate the following spring. ANNUAL PLANTS complete their life cycle in one year or growing season and a biennial does the same in two years or two consecutive growing seasons. CLIMBING PLANTS form another category based on their ability to climb—usually over a support structure, although many will grow over the ground. They use various mechanisms to climb but may be non-woody or woody and either evergreen or deciduous. Some growth forms are so characteristic that they form their own category: examples are the PALMS, CACTI and other succulents, FERNS, and GRASSES. Use categories for plants are also formed for edible groups such as HERBS, VEGETABLES, and FRUITS. These categories may contain many other divisions already mentioned, such as woody and non-woody plants, climbers, rainforest plants, bulbs and, alpine-like plants.

Ecologically based classifications may also be used. RAINFOREST trees are usually distinguished by their evergreen, glossy leaves with pointed drip tip. ALPINE plants naturally grow in alpine areas although, as with other categories, this has been broadened in horticulture to include alpine-like plants that are small in stature, but not necessarily from true alpine ecological communities. Many aquatic and bog plants, another ecologically based grouping, are able to oxygenate water and thus may also be described by their function—in this case as oxygenating plants, well known and marketed for ponds, but increasingly important for environmental restoration of waterways and streams.

Still further categories describe manipulated growth forms such as a HEDGE, usually formed from woody plants (which may be deciduous or evergreen), or a BONSAI—a plant kept small by restricting its growth. The setting for cultivated forms is yet another category; it includes INDOOR PLANTS, POT PLANTS, ROCKERY plants, and BUSH-HOUSE plants. These also relate strongly to different HORTICULTURAL TECHNIQUES for providing desirable conditions for growth.

Function as a landscape category for plants will become increasingly important and could include plants that are able to lessen energy consumption by reducing heat loads on buildings, or XERIC plants that decrease water usage and may assist with recovery from environmental degradation. The actions of plants—particularly those with a negative impact on gardens and the environment, such as WEEDS, or trees that produce suckers—also form separate categories. Many weeds are 'primary colonisers'—plants able to colonise disturbed ground. Such ecologically based functional groups assist in an understanding of plant growth in relation to its environment. ML

LAND SURVEY AND SALE When the European settlers arrived, the continent of Australia was largely uncharted, and its interior was completely unknown to them. One of the first tasks was to determine Sydney's exact latitude and longitude. For this, Lieutenant William Dawes (1762–1836) was appointed, and he built a small OBSERVATORY on the western side of Sydney Cove. From that time, the transformation of the Australian landscape began. The imposition of the surveyors' grid—a geometrical landscape—proclaimed a new conceptual environment, and one that relied on the legal doctrine of *terra nullius* (land belonging to no one)—a doctrine not seriously challenged until the *Mabo* decision in 1992 affirmed the existence of native title at the time of British colonisation (or invasion).

However, there was no firm direction, in Governor Phillip's instructions from the Colonial Office, about allotting land to prospective settlers. The colony, in those early years, was virtually a gaol, and there was no immediate need. The granting of land, however, assumed some importance when convicts' sentences had expired, and when some of the officers and marines elected to stay in the colony rather than return to England. Governor Phillip allowed four leases to be given before he departed: three were to officers who were married and had brought out their wives. Major Grose then allowed a further fourteen leases. Governor King realised that there was a pressing need to provide those who stayed with a sense of security. More leases were issued, seventy-four in all. Properties were also taken up and built upon by a system of 'permissive occupancy'. In 1804 a total of 580 households was recorded. It was Governor Bligh who, in his efforts to reorder the town allotments and redesign the Government DOMAIN, precipitated the resentments that led to the Rum Rebellion in 1807. It was a question of property rights rather than the control of the rum trade that turned the townsfolk against him.

Land grants then became common practice under Governor Macquarie. He adopted a sliding scale of grants; emancipists were allowed land equivalent to between twelve and forty hectares as farm land, with a small town plot in the nearest town. Officers and free settlers were given larger grants, between 80 and 120 hectares, and for a favoured few who could demonstrate they possessed capital to invest in and 'improve' their land, there was more. Provision was made

The allotment of this land selector at Gembrook (Vic.) clearly illustrates this mode of LAND SURVEY AND SALE, prevalent in Australia from the 1860s to the 1920s, when statutory 'improvements' such as clearing and FENCING transformed large sections of the Australian BUSH

also for grants for the support of a church and school house, and for sites for public buildings in the town. By the time Macquarie left, he had granted most of the land within the boundaries of the County of Cumberland.

It was not until 1829 that Governor Darling introduced the standard plan for towns in Australia. This standard plan had descended from the 'Grand Modell' devised in England by Lord Shaftesbury for use in the English colonial endeavours in Ireland and the Americas in the seventeenth and eighteenth centuries, where the town was a central component of the spread of settlement, and it was adopted widely by the Colonial Office. It allowed for a grid-plan to be placed over an area, preferably on the sea coast, with streets marked out, sites for public buildings, and allotments surveyed for householders. At the edge of the town, plots of ground were marked out for agriculture and town garden plots. Land was surveyed further out for larger farms. Even in the town itself, small gardens were possible on the allotments marked for private families. This was the pattern that was re-introduced in the Australian context in 1829, with the imposition of standard town blocks of ten square chains (4 ha) divided into twenty building allotments of half an acre (0.2 ha) between streets one chain (20 m) wide, with footpaths of nine feet (2.7 m) on both sides. The allotments were mostly one chain wide, with a depth of five chains (100 m).

The town plan was set within a larger Township Reserve, also carefully surveyed, which was to allow for several things: the expansion of the town sections, the designation of open space areas, and the establishment of institutions. Beyond that again, there were acreages for 'suburban' allotments, which could be from two and a half to twelve hectares. This was the basic structure that allowed for the cultivation of various sorts of gardens in NSW. It was also the planning pattern developed in the capitals and towns of the other colonies: Melbourne in particular has a clearly marked grid plan, while Adelaide, also planned in 1837, had a more sophisticated, articulated layout.

We see in these regulations the genesis of the small urban garden plot, the larger suburban garden at the edge of the town and, further out, the country garden—restricted only by the need for access to a good water supply. The permutations and combinations of these factors have resulted in a variety of garden shapes and sizes. Most of the gardens in Australian towns and suburbs are based on the original allotment size of approximately twenty metres of frontage to the street, and a depth of one hundred metres, fixed by the 1829 regulations. Later, in the inner city, they were subdivided for terrace houses with tiny backyards. Almost at the same time, in 1831, it was decided by the Colonial Office in London that land, both urban and rural, was to be sold, rather than 'granted' to applicants.

At this date, large swathes of rural land held by squatters were increasingly regulated; from 1837 by Governor Bourke as a series of licensed pastoral runs and then from 1846 by British government regulations in the form of leases. Purchase of one square mile or 640 acres (260 ha) under a right of pre-emption enabled squatters to acquire freehold tenure of some choice waterfront sites, often the nucleus of fine HOMESTEAD GARDENS. In NSW and Vic. the gold rushes overtook affairs, and legislation from the 1860s introduced land selection to enable smaller holdings to be settled with freehold following a stipulated licence period. Later forms of land selection included the settlement of 'irrigation colonies' and other rural areas under closer settlement and soldier settlement acts; these were attended with mixed success. Selection produced many distinctive Australian CULTURAL LANDSCAPES, ranging from irrigated arid-zone townships, to the archetypal selector's house and garden carved from the BUSH by Dad and Dave in *On Our Selection* (1899) by Arthur Hoey Davis ('Steele Rudd') (1868–1935).

In urban Australia, the development of the quarter-acre block was underpinned by the legal and conceptual framework of the 1829 regulations. While TOWN PLANNING in the twentieth century introduced different modes of land subdivision, only in the 1970s and 1980s did new forms of title, such as cluster titles (which incorporated jointly owned communal spaces) and strata titles (to give certainty to freeholds of high-rise developments), challenge long-established modes of land sale.

S.H. Roberts, *History of Australian Land Settlement (1788–1920)* (Melbourne, 1924; rev. edn 1968); Sharon Morgan, *Land Settlement in Early Tasmania: Creating an Antipodean England* (Cambridge, 1992)   HELEN PROUDFOOT

LANE POOLE, Charles Edward (1885–1970), forester, English-born, Irish-educated, and a graduate from the French Ecole Forestière, exerted a powerful but controversial influence on the development of Australian FORESTRY. His career marked the start of the Commonwealth's still contentious involvement in forestry, previously solely a state concern. He was a district forest officer in the Transvaal (1908–10) and conservator of forests for Sierra Leone (1911–16). He came to WA as conservator of forests in 1916 and addressed the problems of forest policy and legislation with characteristic energy. He resigned in 1921 when his proposal for greater control over the industry was not accepted by the government. Moving to the Commonwealth, Lane Poole surveyed the forest resources of Papua and New Guinea (1922–24). Believing in a strong national role, he advised the Commonwealth to establish the Forestry and Timber Bureau and the Australian Forestry School to train foresters to graduate level. He headed both from 1927. Lane Poole published numerous papers and reports on forest policy and resources. He was active in the formation of the Empire Forestry Association (1920) and the Institute of Foresters of Australia (1935). He retired in 1945 to practise as a forest consultant, and was still scrambling through the Kyogle forests with timbermen in his mid-seventies.

Lane Poole's career marked a change from the estate tradition and practical training of early foresters such as Ednie BROWN, which emphasised STATE FOREST NURSERIES, PLANTATIONS, and silviculture, to the imperial tradition, which emphasised policies for managing native forests to meet long-term national needs. It called for strong, centralised state forest services staffed by a cadre of forest officers trained in classic German and French forestry as transformed in INDIA and other parts of the Empire to suit imperial needs and colonial circumstances. It was predicated in the arrogant—if sometimes well-founded—belief that politicians should keep out of the forests: 'professional' foresters knew best.

The change was not smooth, nor was it always eased by Lane Poole. Experienced, intelligent, energetic and forceful as he was, he was also described as tactless, and his elite connections and national view did not sit easily in Australia's federal structure. Lane Poole drew strong, often opposing responses from people. Most notable was his long feud with E.H.F. SWAIN, the head of forest services in Qld and later NSW, over the conduct of the Australian Forestry School. Lane Poole disparaged the Victorian School of Forestry and foresters trained in the earlier tradition. By contrast, he readily acknowledged Charles WESTON's work in the ACT and was highly regarded by the Australian forester Maxwell Ralph Jacobs (1905–1979), who worked with and succeeded him. He formed long-lasting friendships with Sir Ronald Munro-Ferguson (Governor-General, 1914–20), and Sir Russell GRIMWADE.   JOHN DARGAVEL

LANG, Thomas (1815–1896), nursery proprietor and seed merchant, was born on Saint Croix, a Danish island in the West Indies. He and his brother Gilbert were taken to Scotland in 1821 to live with their grandmother in Irvine, Ayrshire, so that they could attend the Irvine Royal Academy. Hopes for a career in law were held for Thomas, but evidently botany was of greater interest; a book of botanical illustrations for the lectures of W.J. HOOKER at Glasgow University survives with Lang's name inscribed, but surviving university records have not as yet confirmed formal enrolment.

Thomas Lang went to Kilmarnock in 1832; he had an uncle there, Thomas Samson, who ran a long-established nursery. It is thought Lang worked for his uncle; by 1846 he is listed as a 'nurseryman' in the local directory. While in Kilmarnock he was a regular contributor to the local press, and issued a monthly circular with horticultural information. Against his name in the 1851 directory is written 'failed', and in 1853 the trustee of Lang's estate was selling off his extensive nursery stock, principally timber trees. As his name does not appear on the list of sequestrations in the Scottish Record Office, it is probable that he entered into a private arrangement regarding his debts.

In June 1854, leaving his family in Kilmarnock, Lang embarked on the *Great Britain* for Australia. He arrived in Ballarat in May 1855; his wife and five children arrived in Melbourne in November 1855 and proceeded to Ballarat. Initially Lang traded in general stores from premises in Bridge Street. In July 1857 he also had a small nursery by the Yarrowee Creek in Bridge Street, and by 1859 he advertised fruit trees, roses, and garden plants for sale. In October that year the Ballarat Horticultural Society was formed, holding its first show six weeks later. Lang was the Society's treasurer, a committee member, and highly successful exhibitor at shows. By 1860 he had a nursery of twenty acres (8 ha) at Warrenheip, near Ballarat, and William ELLIOTT of the Creswick Nursery had become a partner. By 1872 the nursery had doubled in size, with extensive stock; a large enterprise even by metropolitan standards.

Lang imported RHODODENDRONS quite early: in 1859 he imported 124 rhododendrons from England, the first of many imports and introductions. Lang began to market his own seeds in 1860, and that same year issued a catalogue listing 200 varieties of dahlia. He was soon also propagating large quantities of Cape bulbs, as well as hyacinths, tulips, crocus, and ranunculus. The nursery dominated the ROSE section at the Ballarat show for many years, and Lang imported many roses from celebrated English growers William Paul and Thomas Rivers. Lang was also an advocate for STREET planting, which initially engendered a certain amount of ridicule. HEDGE plants were an important stock item in a farming region developing in the wake of the land selection acts, and early on, Lang had available in quantity hawthorns, sweet briar, *Genista monspessulana* (Cape or Montpellier Broom), *Maclura pomifera* (Osage Orange), and *Ulex europaea* (Gorse). Among the many CONIFERS to capture the imagination in the nineteenth century was *Sequoiadendron giganteum*. SHEPHERD's Chatsworth Nursery in Sydney had this by 1860, as did Lang. The specimen planted in his nursery that year reached a height of 27 feet (8.2 m) after fourteen years.

Lang showed enterprise in importing vegetable seed from Shanghai for the benefit of the many CHINESE still in Ballarat. He also imported large quantities of fruit trees from England and North America: Thomas Rivers of Sawbridgeworth, Hertfordshire, supplied large orders for crab apples, thorn, pears, cherry, elm, and *Aesculus hippocastanum* (Horse Chestnut), and well as more specialised stock such as *Quercus cerris* (Turkey Oak), *Q. coccinea* (Scarlet Oak), and *Q. robur* 'Fastigiata' (Fastigiate Oak). The nursery was well known for the excellence of its fruit trees, particularly apples and pears. Apple growers were dogged by damage to trees by Woolly Aphis, and as early as 1864 Lang was using the resistant stock of Majetin or Northern Spy. Noted pomologist J.C. COLE, in his 1883 catalogue, recalled the prejudices encountered when blight-proof stocks were introduced by Lang, and called him 'friend and benefactor'.

By 1868 Lang had established a central Melbourne outlet and he moved to Melbourne *c.* 1875, taking over the Cremorne Nursery. His manager Sebastian Rennie (*c.* 1826– 1912), who had arrived in Melbourne by 1860, and later his son George Patrick Rennie (b. 1863), were left to run the Ballarat Nursery. In 1872 Lang was anxious to lighten his workload and retire from the nursery business. In 1880 Rennie bought the Ballarat Nursery, which continued to trade as Thomas Lang, Rennie and Co. At the same time the Cremorne Nursery was sold to Messrs LAW SOMNER and Co. Lang did, however, continue in the seed business, and he and his family resided in East Melbourne.

Lang's catalogues have extensive lists of all kinds of trees, shrubs, roses, bulbs and corms, fruit trees, stove and greenhouse plants, herbaceous plants, ferns and lycopods, flowers, and vegetable seeds, many of his own raising. Few nurseries could rival what he had to offer, and his catalogues, dated and numbered sequentially until his last issue (No. 52, published in 1887), now provide us with evidence of his extraordinary range of stock. Almost half his catalogues survive, and they represent a more extensive record than for any other nineteenth-century Victorian nursery. Lang had a distinguished career as nursery proprietor and horticulturist, and was praised for his comprehensive stock and numerous plant introductions by the likes of J.G. VEITCH and Charles MOORE (although few would now thank him for the success of Gorse and Cape Broom, major environmental WEEDS).

BARNEY HUTTON

LANGBECKER, Carl Conrad Emil Wilhelm (1881–1970), nursery proprietor, was born in Hamburg, Germany, and arrived at Fremantle (WA) c. 1910 with gardening experience, including time in Austria and Argentina. Langbecker worked as a miner while saving money and, following a gardening job in Melbourne, he established a nursery in 1912 near Brisbane. He relocated to Bundaberg in 1921 and issued his first mail-order catalogue a year later. Specialising in ROSES and fruit trees, the nursery developed steadily—its catalogues for the 1920s and 1930s are held by the ROYAL HORTICULTURAL SOCIETY's Lindley Library (London)—and by the mid-1950s, with 70 000 grafted citrus trees and 170 000 roses on the 100-acre (40 ha) site, the nursery was claimed to be Queensland's largest. Under the leadership of the second generation, Albert Wilhelm (b. 1924) and Edward Conrad Langbecker (b. 1919), and Roy Zielke (b. 1920), Langbecker's Drive-in Garden Centre was opened in 1962 on Logan Road, Mount Gravatt. Conducted on 'Super Market self-serve style of selling' and boasting 'a modern Showroom on departmental store style', fernery, courtyard, children's playground, landscaped setting, and 'a towering 40 ft. revolving, coloured sign', the venture was not a commercial success, perhaps introducing this North American concept to Australia before its time; the company thereafter specialised in mail-order sales until the business passed from family control.

RA

LANGDON, Raymond Forbes (b. 1916), botanist and horticultural journalist, studied at Gatton Agricultural College, and was with the Botany Department at University of Queensland (1940–81), apart from war service in New Guinea and New Britain as Commanding Officer of Radio Control. As a keen gardener with a scientific background, Langdon wrote a gardening column for the *Sunday Mail* for forty-one years (1956–97), enjoyed and appreciated for its practical approach and suitability to different regions in Qld.

JEANNIE SIM

LANGER, Karl (1903–1969), architect, planner, and landscape architect, was born in Vienna into the cultural ferment in the arts and social sciences that nurtured MODERNISM. His career exemplified the ideal of the *Gesamtkunstwerk*, of artistic integration across the spectrum of scales and disciplines. A perennial student, he progressed from basic architectural qualifications to work on ground-breaking social housing of the 'Red Vienna' years, concurrently attending the renowned Academy of Fine Art graduate master school of Peter Behrens (1868–1940), 'father of modern architecture'. Completing his studies in 1926, he joined Behrens to head his celebrated Vienna atelier, commencing sole practice in 1934. His designs, though disciplined and sophisticated, celebrated sense of

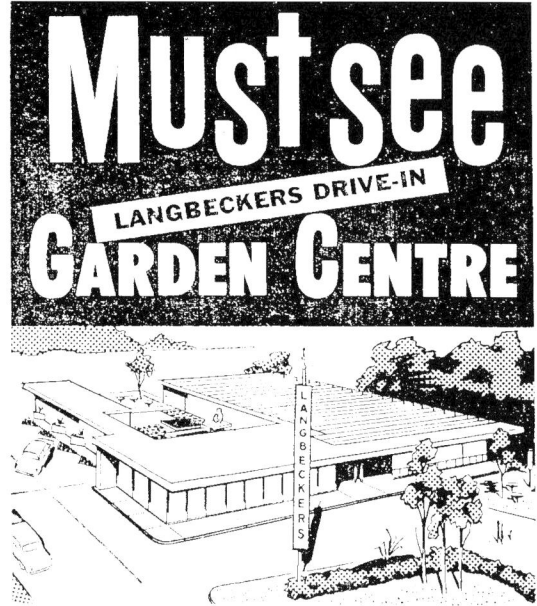

LANGBECKERS Drive-In Garden Centre, Mount Gravatt (Qld), one of Australia's earliest drive-in garden centres, was conducted along contemporary North American lines (1962), and introduced now-familiar features such as customer trolleys and supermarket-style checkouts to the retail NURSERY trade

place, recalling Balkan and Dolomite holidays studying landscapes, architecture, and their interactions. Some oil paintings in Greece explored the intricate forms and subtle colours of humble wayside shrubs and bracken. Langer then undertook doctoral studies in Fine Art at Vienna University, where he met Gertrude Freschel (1908–1984). They married in 1932 and received doctorates together in 1933.

A more hurried visit to Greece, thence Australia, occurred in 1938, following the annexation of Austria and anti-Semitic violence of the *Kristallnacht*. Soon after arriving in Brisbane in 1939 Langer, a reluctant citizen of the Third Reich, under wartime manpower regulations was mandated to Queensland Railways as a draftsman, and remained there, controversially, for the duration. Chafing in this unchallenging job, he kept busy with his researches. His sketchbooks annotate native plants and landforms. His influential *Subtropical Housing* (1944) called for energy-wise planning of suburb, house, and garden, and eschewed traditional highset 'Queenslanders' for ground-level houses, with gardens shading, screening, and extending living spaces. The Langers' St Lucia house (1950) demonstrated this elegant economy. On a small, sloping site it contrived total privacy, with a Japanese-influenced courtyard garden and a hand-grown RAINFOREST at the back, with 'borrowed' distant mountains. Both were important early examples, well researched from extensive garden studies in JAPAN and years observing rainforest ECOLOGY.

Langer's post-war practice attracted commissions Australia-wide. Of many designs for coastal RESORTS, few proceeded. One that did was Lennons Broadbeach Hotel (1956), stretching between (then) vast empty beach and bush hinterland. The first canal estates nearby were also his idea. He advised on Sydney's post-war planning, with broad terms of reference including cultural development. His most notable recommendation (1948) was for an opera house, sited on Bennelong Point: a masterly invocation of the *genius loci*. His cultural advocacy required much lecturing and committee work, and collaborative roles in establishing Qld chapters of what would become the Royal Australian Planning Institute and AUSTRALIAN INSTITUTE OF LANDSCAPE ARCHITECTURE, and a school of landscape architecture at Queensland Institute (now University) of Technology. He is commemorated by student awards and memorial lectures. IAN SINNAMON

LANYON, a grazing property of 1100 hectares near Canberra, retains an unusually intact HOMESTEAD complex established in the mid-1830s. Now operated by the Australian Capital Territory Government as a site museum, it demonstrates both continuity and change through five successive periods of ownership, and the conservation of the garden reflects this. Mature *Pinus radiata* (Monterey Pine) and *P. pinea* (Stone Pine) line the driveway, and a pair of *Araucaria bidwillii* (Bunya Pine) trees stand close to the house. A romantic lily walk has been re-created, and vegetable and picking beds appropriate to the period have been constructed in accordance with oral history evidence. Extensive lawns create restful open spaces, and although a *Crataegus monogyna* (English Hawthorn) boundary hedge provides a physical barrier on two sides, views to the mountains are preserved. Outside the garden, *Ulmus procera* (English Elm), *Robinia pseudoacacia* (False Acacia), and *Populus nigra* 'Italica' (Lombardy Poplar) of the 1860s share the paddocks with Paul SORENSON's 1960s paddock plantings of *Quercus robur* (English Oak) and *Fraxinus* 'Raywood' (Claret Ash). Stands of eucalypts are scattered through the paddocks and a planting program will ensure continuity of species.

Bruce Moore, *Lanyon Saga: A History of the Cunningham Family and the Lanyon, Tuggeranong and Wanniassa Estates in the A.C.T.* (Pearce, ACT, 1982); Elaine Lawson, *Lanyon* (Canberra, 1994)
ELAINE LAWSON

LASSCOCK, Edward Albert (1890–1956), nursery proprietor, gained an apprenticeship in KEMP's Nursery in Unley Park (SA), before establishing a nursery at Lockleys in 1908, in partnership with Percy Cowell (whom he bought out in 1909). Initially 'the kid nurseryman' supplied vegetable and flower seedlings at the Adelaide market. Ted Lasscock progressively moved into and developed specialities in carnations, roses, begonias, climbers, ferns, seedlings, and fruit trees, constructing extensive glasshouses and shade houses. The nursery was relocated in 1922 due to regular flooding by the River Torrens, and retail outlets were opened at Glenelg and Port Adelaide. Lasscock's wife, Effie (1894–1982) and son, John Roe Lasscock (b. 1919), continued to expand the business, opening reputedly the first 'Drive-In Garden Centre' in Australia (1958). Lasscock's Nurseries expanded to Modbury (1966) and Marion (1969), and supplied *Adiantum elegans* ferns—propagated from one environmentally controlled igloo house—throughout Australia via chainstores. New garden centres at Morphett Vale, West Lakes, and Elizabeth, were supplied from a plant farm at Callington established in 1978, and a wholesale nursery at Willunga. Progressively, sons Kim Genery Lasscock (b. 1951) took charge of the production and nurseries, and Ian McArthur Lasscock (b. 1945) managed the garden centres. Robin HILL provided a landscape design franchise at Lockleys (*c*. 1960–62), and the family acquired Tucker the Florist. DAVID JONES

LATHAM, John (*c*. 1841–1921), florist and seed merchant, was born in England, arriving in Hobart Town *c*. 1850. He was a chemist by profession, initially engaged as a dispenser; he subsequently carried on business at Battery Point. Latham showed an early interest in horticulture, being supplied with plants from the Royal Society's garden as early as 1863. He joined the committee of the Gardeners' and Amateurs' Horticultural Society, Hobart Town, in 1870, acting briefly also as secretary and collector, remuneration for these two offices being abolished in 1871 due to financial stringency. FLORICULTURE proved an irresistible attraction to him and from the early 1870s he carried on the business of florist and seed merchant. He was widely esteemed and respected, and was much sought after as a judge at shows: 'in making awards the commercial value of the exhibit always weighed most with him' wrote his obituarist in the *Mercury*. RA

LATREILLE (*née* DALRYMPLE), Anne Helen (b. 1946), is a Melbourne writer with a strong interest in gardens and the environment, developed through family traditions, extensive travel, and reading. She has worked as a journalist in Melbourne and London. Her weekly 'Environs' column in the Melbourne *Age* (1973–80) encompassed both the natural and the designed environment, including landscapes and buildings, publicly tackling issues that were then far from mainstream. Her empathetic and questioning style

Edward La Trobe BATEMAN's sketch, 'View of the larger rockery' (1854), depicts a richly planted, grotto-like ROCKERY at Jolimont, the East Melbourne residence of his cousin, the ardent horticulturist Governor Charles Joseph LA TROBE

earned her the Robin Boyd Environmental Award from the Royal Australian Institute of Architects (1980). She was gardening editor of the *Age* (1985–97), marshalling the talents of contributors such as Tommy GARNETT and Jean GALBRAITH in a page designed to give much more than mere horticultural advice. Her books include *The Landscape of the Streets* (1985), *The Natural Garden: The Life and Work of Ellis Stones* (1991), and *Kindred Spirits* (1999), which outlines the botanical correspondence between Galbraith and Joan LAW-SMITH. RA

LA TROBE, Charles Joseph (1801–1875), Superintendent of the Port Phillip District and Lieutenant-Governor of Victoria (1839–54), was a cultured gentleman rather than an administrator, 'a man of a thousand occupations', having been a tutor, traveller, and author of several books and of three reports to the British Government on education in the West Indies. He was interested in mountaineering, botany, geology, entomology, music, and poetry, and an active supporter of religious, cultural, and educational institutions. La Trobe was responsible for reservation of land for PUBLIC PARKS and reserves, including BOTANIC GARDENS at MELBOURNE (1846) and GEELONG (1848). He actively supported Melbourne Botanic Garden, appointing ARTHUR as the first superintendent and DALLACHY as the second. La Trobe appointed MUELLER as Government Botanist (1853) to facilitate the exchange of seeds and plants with KEW GARDENS and to explore Victoria's botanical resources. He also supported the Victorian Horticultural Society, reserving land for an exhibition ground and acting as patron.

This interest was not only official. Drawings by his cousin, Edward La Trobe BATEMAN, show La Trobe's cottage and garden situated on sloping land near the Yarra River. He was enthusiastic about NATIVE PLANTS, requested bulbs and seeds from 'home', and exchanged plants with friends nearby and interstate. La Trobe was especially interested in VITICULTURE; he distributed vine cuttings, showed how they should be planted, and encouraged the migration of SWISS vignerons: La Trobe and his wife had strong connections to Switzerland. The wine industry can be seen as his horticultural legacy, while the re-establishment (1956) of his cottage near Melbourne's Royal Botanic Gardens is symbolic of his botanical one.

Alan Gross, *Charles Joseph La Trobe* (Melbourne, 1956); *La Trobe and his Circle* (Melbourne, 1989); A.G.L. Shaw (ed.), *Gipps–La Trobe Correspondence 1839–1846* (Carlton, Vic., 1989); *Charles Joseph La Trobe: Landscapes and Sketches* (Melbourne, 1999)

GWEN PASCOE

LAUDERDALE, New Town, Tas., a large suburban estate at the mouth of Hobart's New Town Rivulet, occupies part of one of the original grants made to private settlers in 1804. By 1844 the grant had been subdivided and the present single-storey stone house built as a weekend retreat for publican John Mezger (*c*. 1790–1854). From a bridge over the Maypole Creek, a carriage drive encircles a plot of lawn and clipped cypress at the front of the house. Remnants of the Victorian garden include hawthorn hedging and an orchard of old apple varieties, with a greenhouse, fountain, and dovecote among the surviving structures. The estate is a remarkable and unusually large survivor in its present suburban context—formerly an area noted for its MARKET GARDENS and ORCHARDS.

LINDY SCRIPPS

LAW Laws regulate our society; they protect us and the things and places we value. Laws ensure that competing interests are guided so that conflict can be avoided. Laws provide the balance between private and public interests. Gardens are part of our everyday life: we enjoy them, pass through them, and need to manage them. Gardens contain things we want to keep and they may contain things that ought to go because they can cause harm. Laws are relevant to each of these aspects of gardens.

Laws may protect entire gardens, parts of gardens, or merely individual plants. In most instances, the heritage legislation in each state or territory contains the legal means to register significant gardens or trees within them. Owners of registered gardens or trees are usually required to obtain a permit from the relevant authority before significant alteration. At the national level, the AUSTRALIAN HERITAGE COMMISSION can register a significant garden for its heritage values, but listing at this level merely highlights the special nature of the garden, rather than providing actual protection. Commonwealth agencies must, however, give consideration to gardens registered on the national list when their actions might have an impact. In some states, planning laws may protect significant gardens or trees because the surrounding area contributes to urban character or a significant streetscape. Modification, such as land development, requiring destruction of special gardens or removal of significant trees will usually require a permit. Such laws balance the private and public interests in gardens. In many parts of Australia the local municipal authority has power to make local by-laws to protect garden trees above nominated sizes. 'Tree preservation orders' require the consent of the local authority before lopping or removal may occur.

In Australia there is no legal right to a view of another's garden, nor any right to require the retention of a garden that bestows benefits such as enjoyment or improved environmental amenity. This is despite the fact that property values may rise due to proximity to a desirable adjoining garden. However, a legal 'right' to argue for the retention of a garden near one's own property may arise under state planning law if the protection of neighbourhood amenity is a consideration.

The law provides for the safety and well-being of visitors to a garden. A visitor may, for example, include a workman, a friend, a water meter reader, or a stranger visiting a garden on show to the public. All reasonable efforts must be made to ensure that visitors are not harmed. The garden owner will be liable for unreasonably unsafe conditions even if visitors entered a garden on condition that they accepted risk for any damage to themselves—as is often the case when gardens are opened to the public. Careful garden management requires precautionary measures to be taken. These could include ensuring that watch dogs are restrained; ensuring that accessible paths are not so uneven that a visitor might trip; ensuring that access to poisonous plants is limited; and ensuring that fish ponds are not so accessible that visiting children might drown. Provided all reasonable precautionary steps are taken to avoid foreseeable problems, legal issues should not arise. Public liability insurance to protect the garden owner from visitors' claims is a prudent precaution.

The laws of nuisance and negligence apply throughout Australia. The way gardens are managed—or rather mismanaged—can give rise to liability. A myriad of possibilities may give rise to liability in a garden. Examples of liability in gardens have included neighbouring cattle being poisoned by eating a yew hedge around a garden; a swimming pool being cracked by tree roots; a roof being crushed by a falling tree; tree roots making a pathway dangerous for pedestrians; wild natural thickets becoming a fire hazard due to uncontrolled growth; fruit from an overhanging tree falling onto a neighbouring property causing drains to block so preventing drainage; neighbouring trees growing so large that soil moisture is so reduced that house foundations are destabilised; and the removal of vegetation cover causing increased runoff and water absorption resulting in property damage to neighbours.

In short, the law attaches liability where the blame for damage should reasonably rest. The ability to foresee the damage gives rise to potential liability. In some instances, even though a new owner took over a garden in which the cause of damage already existed (say an existing aged tree), if the law considers the owner ought to have been aware of the problem tree, then liability will rest with the new owner.

SIMON MOLESWORTH

LAWN AND TURF 'Turf' comes from the ancient Sanskrit word *darbha* (tuft of grass) and contemporary definitions cite turf as a surface layer of vegetation, consisting of earth and a dense verdure of GRASS and roots. Other synonymous terms include sod (a piece cut from this vegetative material with its adhering soil), sward (the grassy vegetation often used in association with pastures), grass (any plant belonging to the family Poaceae), a green (a smooth, uniform area used for sporting purposes), and lawn (a flat, and usually level, area of mown grass).

Turf has been appreciated not only for its aesthetic attraction but also as a valued medium on which games of various kinds may be played. References have been made to grass in the early scriptures, as well as in many early Persian, Chinese, Indian, and English landscapes. Natural grass surfaces have also played an important part in the development of many SPORT and RECREATION pursuits. For example, Akbar (1556–1605), the Great Emperor of Hindustan, played polo; the early American Indians played baggataway, an early form of lacrosse, over the grassed prairies; and many 'stick and ball' games were played by the shepherds of early Europe while tending their flocks on the lowlands. The naturally picturesque settings of the British village green were the forerunner of many of the grassed sports such as lawn BOWLS, TENNIS, CROQUET, cricket, hockey, and football. Similarly, wherever British people colonised other countries—India, Malaya, and Australia, for example—they often took with them the grasses and the sporting regulations.

Grassy swards not only civilised human settlement, but were a valued part of landscape scenery. For many years the lawn has been regarded as an essential element in the SUBURBAN GARDEN, particularly the FRONT GARDEN, where the lawn has been seen as a carefully manicured outside carpet. Grass in PUBLIC PARKS AND GARDENS has provided many city workers with a quiet resting place, and many thousands of tourists with pleasant places to visit and enjoy. Many institutional landscapes also rely extensively on lawn. For instance, ENFIELD CEMETERY, Australia's first lawn cemetery, was developed in 1945–47.

Lawn mower

The technologies associated with the management of lawns and turf have advanced greatly since the industrial revolution and the introduction of the first LAWN MOWER, based on Edwin Budding's design, in 1830. Before the widespread introduction of mowing machines, the making of a new lawn involved the striping of turf from a good pasture and maintaining it by animal or scythe to produce a satisfactory turf. The availability of reticulated water and the widespread introduction of HOSES AND SPRINKLERS during the mid- to late nineteenth century was perhaps the greatest boost to lawns in Australian gardens. Seed was imported and few FERTILISERS and PESTICIDES existed until the twentieth century. Today's maintenance programs have changed from heavy reliance on synthetic CHEMICALS to strategies that strive to work in partnership with nature.

Popular British introductions included *Cynosurus cristatus* (Crested Dogstail), *Festuca ovina* subsp. *tenuifolia* (Fescue), *Lolium perenne* (Ryegrass), and *Poa trivialis* (Rough Bluegrass), as well as *Trifolium repens* and *T. minus* (Dutch White Clover). *Stenotaphrum secundatum* (Buffalo Grass), with its distinctive flat stolens also made a great impact following its introduction in the 1860s, and in Australia it was particularly successful in hot areas. Today there are many improved warm- and cool-season cultivars and varieties suited to specific environments and functions. Some Australian native grasses, such as *Microlaena stipoides* (Weeping Grass), *Danthonia* spp. (Wallaby Grass), and *Bothriocloa macra* (Redleg Grass) have also shown potential as lawn grasses. Trends in the wider Australian landscape suggest a transitional change from the once intensively managed green lawn system to a much browner one that will make greater use of native, naturalised, and meadow grasses, and may also incorporate wild flowers and BULBS.

DAVID ALDOUS

LAWN MOWER Edwin Budding invented the lawn mower in England in 1830. His design was based upon a revolving knife or cutter that ran across a fixed blade. A roller was placed in front of the cutters to regulate the height of the cut and a box placed to the rear of the machine collected the grass clippings. Throughout the nineteenth century the art of lawn maintenance was refined in the quest for a perfect lawn. Shanks patented a horse-drawn machine (1842) and chain-driven models (1859), and huge steam-powered mowers were introduced by 1893. Other improvements included a petrol-driven engine (1899). Horse-drawn mowers were in use in Australian BOTANIC GARDENS during the 1880s but although the mechanisation of lawn mowers proved to be very popular the majority of gardeners continued to use scythes and hand-pushed mowers well into the 1920s.

A major development was the Australian-designed Victa lawn mower (1953), a light and inexpensive petrol-driven machine: 'Turns grass into lawn' was its proud boast as suburban gardeners in large numbers turned the Victa into an Australian gardening icon (paralleled only by the mass marketing of the rotary clothes hoist by Lance Hill). These mowers did not cut the grass with the scissor action of the original reel-type mowers, but instead tore it by high impact with a rotary action. The effect was a coarser cut but a more

Velvet Lawn strikes a blow for her sex in this LAWN MOWER advertisement—the use of female imagery in such advertising communicated both ease of use and a breakdown of tradition GENDER roles in the home garden

versatile machine. Mowing machine ownership was also encouraged as a form of exercise for the male member of the household. An Australian company, Scott Bonner Limited, had produced the first electric (battery) operated machine in 1919. Other lighter electric mowers were developed by Black and Decker during the 1960s; ease of operation of this new generation of electric mowers was invariably demonstrated by the depiction of women mowing in advertisements. The 'Flymo' was a revolutionary development; electric-powered, with blades spinning horizontally, and manoeuvred on a cushion of air, it was quick, economical, easy to operate in small spaces, and came into its own on steeply sloping sites.

Ride-on mowers have progressed from large tractor-drawn machines to purpose-built units designed for speed and manoeuvrability. Others, such as the flail mower, often tractor-pulled, have heavy-duty blades suspended on chains to cut long and rough grass.

Trees were planted singly over larger sites for many years, spaced so that the gang mower could be drawn comfortably between them, relegating design to horticultural technocrats. As late as the 1980s it was still difficult to persuade some park superintendents to plant informal groups of trees.

SUZANNE HUNT

LAW-SMITH (née DARLING), Joan (1919–1999), gardener and botanical artist, created an internationally acclaimed garden at Bolobek, near Macedon (Vic.). Even though open only occasionally to the public, it drew tens of thousands of visitors through the late 1970s and the 1980s. A garden of predominantly cool-climate exotic plants set in an Australian farming landscape, Bolobek, an intensely personal statement, was built on the bones of an earlier garden. In detail it was characterised by reticence and careful selection—pastel hues, white flowers, many shades of green, and species plants of modest demeanour. At a broader level its lines were clean, simple and strong.

Joan Law-Smith grew up in Toorak, then spent a formative period in England as a teenager. Here she happened across a primrose wood in full bloom—a sight she described as her personal epiphany. Here she saw flower paintings of the highest standard and decided that one day she would become a botanical artist. This ambition was interrupted by the Second World War and by marriage. In 1946 she and her husband, Robert Law-Smith moved to a farm near Coleraine in Victoria's WESTERN DISTRICT, where they raised three children and she made her first garden in tough conditions that did not suit the cool-climate plants she yearned to grow. The move in 1970 to the kinder situation of Bolobek enabled her to fulfil this part of her dreams. She had already set about becoming an expert painter of flowers, taking botany lessons in 1964 from Jean GALBRAITH—as recounted in *Kindred Spirits* (1999)—and painting lessons from Paul JONES.

Through the 1970s she worked unceasingly. Creating the garden at Bolobek brought a measure of solace after the death of a much-loved son. She wrote and illustrated books— *A Gardener's Diary* (1976), *Gardens of the Mind* (1979), and *The Uncommon Garden* (1983). All have become collectors' items. She exhibited her work in Adelaide in 1978, when the Australian National Gallery acquired a painting of a columbine.

Robert Law-Smith was knighted in 1979 for services to aviation, commerce, and industry, and through the 1980s, a time of fervent public interest in gardens and gardening, Lady Law-Smith assumed—albeit unwillingly for such a modest person—a pre-eminent position as exemplar and an (involuntary) arbiter of taste in the gardening world. She was also a generous benefactor to organisations such as the AUSTRALIAN GARDEN HISTORY SOCIETY, whose patron she was from 1989 until her death, the ROYAL BOTANIC GARDENS, MELBOURNE, whose guidebook she wrote in 1984, and the NATIONAL TRUST OF AUSTRALIA (Victoria).

Even in retirement her name resonated. In 1991 she published *The Garden Within*, the story of Bolobek (which she had left in 1990). In 1997 in Melbourne, a retrospective exhibition of her work publicly demonstrated her abiding love of Nature and her innate understanding of the garden plants she grew and loved.

ANNE LATREILLE

LAW, SOMNER AND CO. was formed *c.* 1864 by seed merchants William Law and William Somner, although in all subsequent advertising the firm claimed the establishment date of Law's business (1850).

William Law (*c.* 1820–1869) was born in York, England, and by 1853 was listed as a general produce merchant in Melbourne's Little Collins Street. Two years later he was listed as a seedsman at the same address. Law broadened his business interests and joined John Tanner in business at Geelong. The seed list issued by Law and Tanner in November 1854 was praised by the *Geelong Advertiser* as 'A small but very useful work. It is a very complete list of all plants that grow or are likely to grow in this climate, with a few hints as to the proper time for sowing or planting.' In March 1855, the same firm was advertising 'colonial seeds of every description on sale at O'Farrell and Son's Horse Bazaar … with gardening instructions for every month to be obtained free of charge'. At the first exhibition of the Geelong and Western District Agricultural and Horticultural Society (1855) the firm gained an honourable mention. Law and Tanner contributed monthly 'Gardening Directions' to the *Advertiser* and Tanner also published the *Victorian Gardener's Almanack* (1856) containing, in addition to the usual gardening calendar, 'choice and original instructions, for the entire management of the Vegetable, Flower, and Fruit Gardens' as well as a seed catalogue. In 1856 Law became a partner with James Gordon— Law, Gordon and Co. operated the Springfield nursery and seed farm at Brighton and city premises in Melbourne and Geelong, known under the name Colonial Seed Warehouse. The firm published a *List of Select Vegetable, Flower, and Agricultural Seeds, Fruit Bearing Trees, etc.* although later in 1856 the partnership was dissolved and debts were paid by Law.

By 1857 the Geelong experiment was over and William Law and Co., still trading as the Colonial Seed Warehouse, confined its operations to Melbourne, with Somner apparently joining as a partner. Law was elected a member of the Victorian Gardeners' Mutual Improvement Society in 1861 with an influential pair of nominators, Frederick SEARCH and Josiah MITCHELL. In 1862 his firm published *Tobacco, Its Cultivation and Management* and *The Osage Orange for Hedge Fences*; the *Yeoman and Australian Acclimatiser* noted that 'within the last three years' Law had brought into notice the merits of the *Maclura pomifera* (Osage Orange) as a HEDGE plant. A revised edition, *Live Fences: The Osage Orange and Other Hedge Plants*, was published in 1867. Immediately following his arrival in 1863 from Scotland, Thomas PURVES began his long career in the seed business as manager of Law's city store.

William Somner (*c.* 1833–1877) was born in Scotland, the son of Francis Somner, nursery proprietor of Kelso. He spent two years in NSW, after his arrival there *c.* 1855, before moving to Melbourne. In 1860 he was elected a corresponding member of the Victorian Gardeners' Mutual Improvement Society, also proposed by Search and Mitchell; by 1863 Somner was honorary secretary of the Society. The first *General Catalogue with Calendar of Gardening Operations* (1864) issued by Law, Somner and Co. gave business addresses in Melbourne, Sydney, and Dunedin (providing the business with an important supply of plants from NEW ZEALAND). Somner was noted in Melbourne directories during 1868–69 as being absent in Scotland, and it might be supposed that he was organising the supply of stock from Britain; from 1870 Edward Somner (perhaps a brother) was listed in the company's advertising as their 'English Agent'. Law, Somner and Co. published a *Handbook to the Garden for New South Wales* (1868), illustrated by a folding plate of *Swainsona damperii* (Sturt's Desert Pea)—a plant that exercised a fascination on the colonial mind. A similar volume was published as *A Handbook to the Garden for Victoria* (1870).

George ANDERSON was the Sydney partner; in 1873 he took over the Sydney branch, renaming the business Anderson, Hall and Co. In Melbourne, William Somner's widow disposed of the business in 1877 to Frederick Frith and Solomon LEVIEN, who continued to trade as Law, Somner and Co. They purchased the Cremorne Nursery from Thomas LANG in 1880, thus acquiring a source of nursery plants to join their seed stock. Palms, ferns, bulbs, succulents, pelargoniums, and roses were specialities among their comprehensive nursery stock, and agricultural business continued to form an important market for the company.

The Cremorne Nursery was closed in 1910 and, while maintaining prominent retail premises and head offices in the city, Law, Somner moved operations to the Orrong Nurseries, Armadale. By the late 1920s this had become the distribution depot for a new nursery further afield at Bayswater; a bulk seed store in South Melbourne continued this traditional line of business. During the heyday of the firm in the 1920s and 1930s, the managing director was C.P. Blott, who had worked for the company for more than forty years, and was recognised as an authority in the seed business, having trained with the large English house of Charles Sharpe and Co. of Sleaford. Law Somner Pty Ltd issued an impressive 'centenary catalogue' in 1950, but the firm never again reached the heights of the mid-Victorian or inter-war periods, and was ultimately taken over in 1978 by Hortico Ltd, extinguishing one of the most venerable names in Australia's seed and nursery trade. RA

LAWSON, Abercrombie Anstruther (1870–1927), botanist, was born at Hamilton, Ontario, Canada, to Scottish parents. He graduated (1898) from the University of California, Berkeley, and gained a doctorate (1901) for his botanical work at the University of Chicago. Following teaching posts in North America and at the University of Glasgow, he was appointed foundation professor of botany at the University of Sydney (1913). He worked in both field and laboratory: he stressed the didactic importance of field excursions and fought hard for adequate facilities, his efforts culminating in the erection of a purpose-built laboratory (largely to his design) attached to the MACLEAY Museum. He researched gymnosperms, introduced the study of ECOLOGY into his teaching (*c.* 1925), and was a strong supporter of the campaign that resulted in the *Wildflowers and Native Plants Protection Act* 1927 (NSW), giving popular extension lectures on AUSTRALIAN FLORA using his own hand-coloured lantern slides, which he gave to the university on his death. RA

LEADER (1856–1946), published weekly in Melbourne by the *Age* proprietor David Syme (1827–1908), included generous coverage of agriculture and horticulture—both having regular columns from 1867—with keen competition provided by the AUSTRALASIAN and later the WEEKLY TIMES. Syme was a radical reformer, espousing the overthrow of the squatter's monopoly in favour of the land selector: 'there are few who do not indulge in the hope of some day possessing a farm or a garden of his own. "Earth hunger" is universal …' (1867). Josiah MITCHELL was the *Leader's* knowledgeable agricultural editor during the early 1870s and William ELLIOTT was horticultural editor for twenty-five years from the 1870s to the 1890s—throughout the most influential period of its horticultural coverage. Reports of horticultural societies and shows, seasonal horticultural advice, extracts from overseas and intercolonial and state journals, and descriptive notices of gardens all filled the regular columns. Harold ALSTON was horticultural editor (and general editor of the paper) between 1941 and 1946. RA

LEAWOOD GARDENS, a nursery and TEA GARDEN located at Devil's Elbow within the ADELAIDE HILLS escarpment, was established in 1842 by George STEVENSON for his wife, Margaret Hutton (*née* Gorton) (1807–1874), to compete with John BAILEY. 'Stevenson's Garden' was planted with vines, figs, almond trees, and ornamental trees, initially with the advice of George MCEWIN. Francis Andrewartha, one of its lessees in 1861, introduced additional fruit, nut, and rubber trees, and along with a *Magnolia grandifolia* (Bull Bay), became 'famous for its camellias … [and] could be hired for private parties'. In Stevenson's obituary, the garden was credited as being 'so grand and extensive that it came to be known as the 'Botanical Garden of South Australia'. In 1874 Edwin SMITH acquired the lease to grow 'some of the more tender European and other trees' to supplement his nursery, and his son Henry Arthur Smith (1851–1930) continued the fruit tree plantings. From the 1920s the property declined, and was bequeathed to Stevenson's daughter Margaret DE MOLE (1844–1918); it remained in her family until 1928. In 1996 much of the CAMELLIA and RHODODENDRON collection was relocated to various Adelaide Hills gardens in anticipation of losses consequent on the Crafers Freeway project. DAVID JONES

LEE AND KENNEDY The Vineyard, Hammersmith—described by J.C. LOUDON (1822) as 'unquestionably the first nursery in Britain, or the world'—was founded in 1745 by James Lee (1715–1795) and Lewis Kennedy (1721–1782). Lee, classically educated, translated *Philosophia Botanica* of Linnaeus; published as *Introduction to Botany*, it did much to popularise the LINNEAN system of classification in Britain. The nursery was soon noted for rare and exotic plants, obtained by Lee through his many contacts and skilfully propagated by him. The most famous introduction was the FUCHSIA, of which Lee raised more than 300 from his first plant. Up to 1795, the firm introduced more than 135 plants into cultivation in Britain, twenty-four from Australia. Lee wrote *Rules for Collecting and Preserving Seeds from Botany Bay*

(1787) and received, in 1789, the first seeds from NSW (either through Joseph BANKS or Governor Phillip), including *Banksia serrata* and *Melaleuca armillaris*.

Little is known of Kennedy, but his son John (1759–1842) was horticultural adviser to the French Empress Josephine at Malmaison and The Vineyard supplied enormous amounts of material even during the Napoleonic War. The botanist to the Empress, Ventenat, named a group of Australian climbers, *Kennedia*, in his honour. Kennedy also introduced the standard rose to England from France and started a fashion in fancy PELARGONIUMS. The nursery, which trained many gardeners including Joseph PAXTON, and employed John CUSHING as a foreman, closed in 1894.

E.J. Willson, *James Lee and the Vineyard Nursery, Hammersmith, London* (London, 1961)   TONY CAVANAGH

LEHMANN, Johann Georg Christian (1792–1860), German botanist, librarian, and professor of natural history at Hamburg, named many AUSTRALIAN PLANTS and is commemorated in the names of some species. Much of his HERBARIUM is now in the Swedish Museum of Natural History in Stockholm, but some collections are at the National Herbarium of Victoria. He was editor (and author of sections on some families) of *Plantae Preissianae* (1844–48), in which several thousand plants collected by Ludwig PREISS were described, including many new species. The work remains a standard early reference on the flora of WA.

ALEX GEORGE

LEISURE was initially a luxury in Australia, confined to those with the requisite time and money. Working people had to be content with a few public holidays, and limited amusements that included drinking, dancing, and blood SPORTS, such as cock-fighting. Concern for the public good through the provision of public ground for was not an urgent priority, but nor was this amenity available in England until the 1830s; Sydney's HYDE PARK was an early exception. *Their Chastity was not too Rigid* (1979) by J.W.C. Cumes provides a useful overview of these early years.

By the mid-nineteenth century the spectacle of PLEASURE GARDENS and amusement parks was available to all classes. Visiting TEA GARDENS and PICNIC GROUNDS was also popular. Reduced working hours, including the Saturday half-holiday, made leisure time the preserve of the many rather than the few. Day trips to the seaside by steamer and riverside picnics could be enjoyed by all. With the advent of rail, travel trips to the beauty spots of the seaside and spa resorts also became popular forms of domestic tourism, examined in Davidson and Spearritt's *Holiday Business* (2000). PUBLIC PARKS AND GARDENS were a popular place for strolling and picnicking. MUSIC performances by local bands were common on a Sunday afternoon, as were open-air FILM screenings by the 1920s. BOTANIC GARDENS were established for both leisure and science. Although parks and gardens were intended to encourage fruitful use of leisure and RECREATION time, Victorian moral restrictions controlled the range of permitted activities on a Sunday. Speakers' corner in Hyde Park in Sydney and Jolimont in Melbourne attracted crowds to hear orators speak on all kinds of subjects.

Before the mid-nineteenth century it was unusual to find private gardens used solely for the purpose of ornament and leisure, since cultivation for food production was their essential role. Later, the extensive grounds, exotic plants, and large garden workforce needed to maintain private pleasure grounds kept them the preserve of the wealthy. Gardening became an increasing part of leisure, especially in the popularity of HORTICULTURAL SOCIETIES and their SHOWS. The rise of SUBURBAN development provided the BACKYARD garden. This has become an important part of the Australian home and lifestyle with lawn for games, cubby house or swing for the children's play, a BARBECUE, and an area for clothes DRYING.

Leisure and gardens continue to be closely associated. Gardening itself is one of the most common pastimes in Australia. Other leisure activities include FLOWER ARRANGING, and reading about gardens and gardening. In recent years GARDEN VISITING and NURSERY browsing have become popular.   RICHARD HEATHCOTE

LENNÉ, Carl: see HIRSCHI, Friederich

LE PLASTRIER, Constance Emily Mary (1864–1938), botanist, educator, and writer, was born into an affluent Melbourne family, although she moved to Sydney in 1900 following her conversion to Catholicism. An exceptional FIELD NATURALIST, Le Plastrier was senior mistress at Redlands School, Sydney, for twenty-two years. One of her pupils was Thistle HARRIS, whom Le Plastrier later introduced to the Naturalists' Society of New South Wales, of which she was the first woman president. Le Plastrier's presidential address of 1920 to the Society was an impassioned plea to the members to 'champion the cause of Nature'. Her friendship with architects Walter Burley and Marion Mahony GRIFFIN influenced their own appreciation for and protection of AUSTRALIAN PLANTS. Le Plastrier and Agnes Brewster wrote *Botany for Australian Students* (1916), in which the study of Australian plants in their environment was emphasised, in an effort to ensure that 'the local bush may become the laboratory of the pupils'. *The Story of Our Plants: First Steps in Australian Botany* followed in 1933.   JEANNINE BAKER

LETTERBOXES, or mailboxes, are such an integral part of the Australian landscape that people often take them for granted. Yet in both vivid and subtle ways they reflect many facets of Australian life and culture. The letterbox is among only a handful of remaining artefacts that many people still design and construct for themselves. It is not merely a practical container for the mail, however, but also the publicly accepted vehicle for unfettered creativity and self-expression in the built environment. It can take delightfully quirky forms—such as cannons, 44-gallon drums, milk cans, houses, fire alarms, koalas, petrol pumps, refrigerators, stoves, and teapots—which might reflect its owner's beliefs, dreams, fears, hobbies, occupations, or sense of humour. In fact, nearly every handmade letterbox has a story to tell. Prominently located on the boundary between the house and the street, usually in the FRONT GARDEN next to the gate, the letterbox

A tree-stump LETTERBOX in Brunswick (Vic.), artfully worked in concrete, with sunburst-pattern gate and companion poplar, in wrought iron, brought sylvan imagery to Melbourne's inner suburbs in the inter-war period

is the physical manifestation of everyday myths and rituals: the letterbox painted like an airmail envelope awaits the delivery of letters from loved ones overseas; a handyman has a tool box for his letters; a model train enthusiast makes his letterbox like a steam engine; and a dinosaur letterbox with its spiky mane, gaping mouth and sharp white teeth, threatens to bite the hand of anyone who dares to deliver 'junk mail'.

Derham Groves, *Mail Art: The Do-it-yourself Letterbox from Workshop to Gatepost* (Sydney, 1998); Bill Bachman, *Special Delivery* (Sydney, 1998)   DERHAM GROVES

LEVIEN, Benjamin (Goldsmidt) Goldsmith (1806–1890), nursery proprietor, born in England of French-Portuguese lineage, arrived in Melbourne in 1838, settling at Geelong in 1840. At Newtown he established a VINEYARD on leased land east of the Barwon River. The vines were soon replaced by fruit trees and by 1847 his Concord Nursery, stocked with trees, shrubs and other plants, was established: 16 500 trees were offered for sale when his nursery was closed in 1872. Levien ran a florist's shop in Geelong from 1863, his youngest son Solomon (1843–1923) becoming a partner until 1877, when he took sole control prior to establishing his Eden Park orchard at Buln Buln (formerly Brandy Creek settlement) in Gippsland (1881–96).

Jonas Felix Australia Levien (1840–1906), agriculturist and eldest son of Benjamin, born at Williamstown, was a 'seed-farmer' growing onions and potatoes on 640 acres (260 ha) near Drysdale (Vic.) from 1864. He was lessee of nearby Flat Island from where guano was gathered to overcome a phosphate deficiency on his farm, making it one of the most productive in the district. He, too, owned an orchard: Dwyerstead, located close to his brother's Eden Park.

A distinguished parliamentary career commencing in 1871 included the portfolios of mines and agriculture (1883–86). He was inaugural president of the Council of Agricultural Education and was on several investigatory committees; of significance was the select committee on Grape Phylloxera (1880).   GEORGE JONES

LEWIS-HICKMAN, Mary Francis: see XAVIER, Mary Francis

LIBRARIES comprising BOOKS, MAGAZINES, journals, and other information sources in the fields of GARDENING, HORTICULTURE, and BOTANY form indispensable aids to gardeners, professional and amateur alike, and have long been important in formal EDUCATION as well as self-directed learning. Yet the importance of the printed word was not always welcomed. Advocates of self-improvement such as J.C. LOUDON frequently editorialised on the merits of libraries for gardeners, yet for each blow struck for printed knowledge, there was a doomsayer who decried 'book knowledge' over empirical experience and tradition.

Private libraries were perhaps the earliest in Australia, carried by emigrants such as George BENNETT, William ARCHER, and Ronald GUNN, who maintained interests in natural history, botany, horticulture, and landscape gardening. Access to such collections was confined to the inner circle, but this range was increased by the establishment of subscription libraries such as the Australian Subscription Library, Sydney (1826), and collections of SCIENTIFIC SOCIETIES and public libraries. The Royal Society of Tasmania, for instance, included standard works by authors such as Loudon and PAXTON as well as a subscription to the *GARDENERS' CHRONICLE* by the mid-1850s. This range was mirrored by many mechanics' institutes during the mid- to late nineteenth century. Small, clearly focused collections were also formed by larger HORTICULTURAL SOCIETIES. Major public libraries with free access were established from the 1850s in capital cities and provincial centres, and books and periodicals aimed at the garden designer and practical horticulturist were commonly included in these collections. Specialised collections were established by government departments, with one of the earliest being formed by Victoria's Board of Agriculture (1860), later taken over by the Department of Agriculture. These were complemented by libraries attached to the various colonial parliaments, whereby parliamentarians could (yet rarely did) peruse works by REPTON and DOWNING (in Tas.), or an impressive retrospective collection of eighteenth-century titles (purchased from the private library of William Story) in Victoria's Parliamentary Library.

The large and specialised collections of BOTANIC GARDENS in metropolitan centres formed the largest collections in the nineteenth century, yet access to them was limited to employees and the serious enquirer. The tradition of exchanging publications between scientific societies—so important to the development of their collections and the free exchange of knowledge—was emulated to a limited extent by botanic gardens in the production of annual and other reports, and later journals. At the instigation of Ferdinand MUELLER,

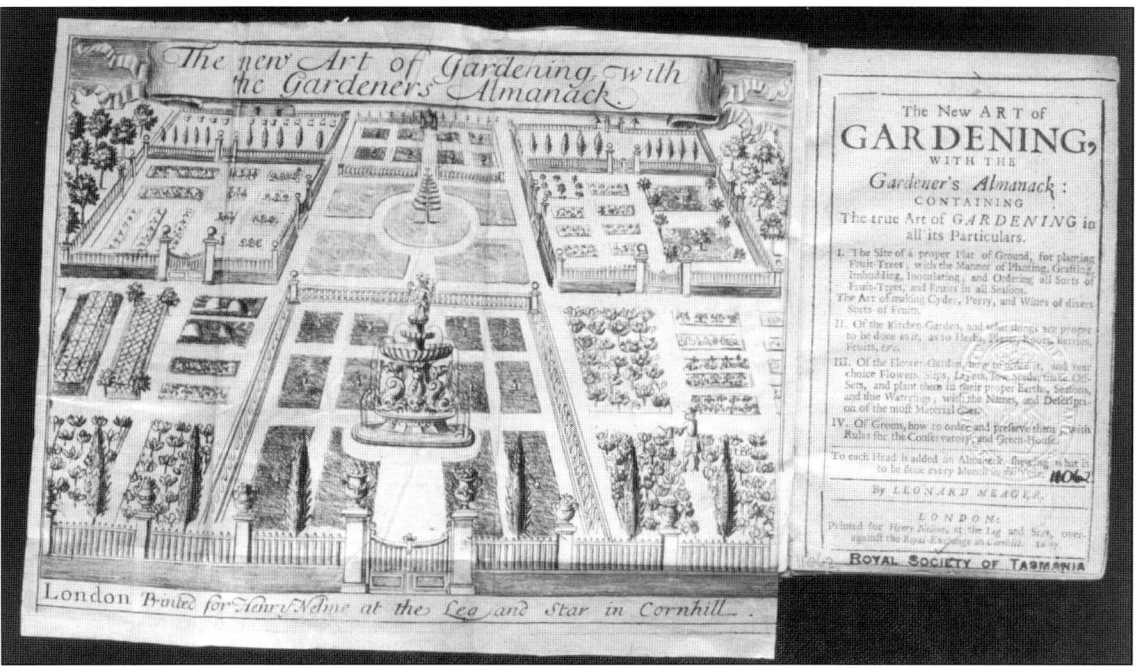

Leonard Meagher's *The New Art of Gardening* (1697), held in the collection of the Royal Society of Tasmania; such LIBRARIES now represent Australia's collective gardening memory and their conservation is a matter of the highest importance

Melbourne Botanic Gardens housed Australia's premier library of gardening, horticultural, and botanical works, many purchased from his own resources. F.M. BAILEY assembled a substantial botanical library at Brisbane Botanic Gardens, as did Charles MOORE and especially J.H. MAIDEN at Sydney Botanic Gardens.

University libraries began in Sydney (1851) and Melbourne (1856) but remained small for some years, and were accessible only to staff and students. As the study of botany, agriculture, and later horticulture became formalised, so library collections at AGRICULTURAL COLLEGES and horticultural institutions such as BURNLEY and RYDE developed. With an interest in conservation of historic gardens, new collections have also been formed by the various NATIONAL TRUSTS, and especially the Historic Houses Trust of New South Wales. Significant libraries have recently been amassed by private collectors such as Richard CLOUGH, Ross McKINNON, Trevor NOTTLE, and Diana POCKLEY, and the outstanding library of Australian gardening books collected by former university librarian Victor Crittenden has underpinned the compilation of his valuable bibliography and history of the subject. The printed word has recently been supplemented by the digitised word as a new array of sources derived from COMPUTERS, such as databases, CD-ROMS, e-books, and the Internet, embraces gardening, horticulture, and landscape design.

RA

LICH-GATE (or lych-gate) is derived from the Old English (*lic*) and Dutch (*lijk*) words for corpse (plus gate). Often applied to any covered gate, the term is more correctly reserved for those in CEMETERIES. It was a roofed structure under which the funeral bier or coffin was rested until clergy were ready for the burial service. A fine brick and timber lich-gate stands at the entrance to the old Catholic section at Sydney's GORE HILL CEMETERY, while the main drive into Goulburn General Cemetery (NSW) passes through an elaborate brick example. The structure was often adopted as an ornamental device over the pedestrian or vehicular entry to houses, particularly those of the late Victorian and Federation periods, where construction costs usually limited their use to grander residences.

CHRIS BETTERIDGE

LIGHT To appreciate and explore the three-dimensional effects of light in space is to make the most of a garden. Reflections, shadows, and light refraction change the spatial character as sunlight and moonlight moves up, down, and across the space, day and night. Australians garden in bright light. Large-foliaged exotic vegetation obscures light. Native vegetation filters it. Light striking foreground trees changes the scene through the day. An unencumbered view changes little. Determining the sun's path with every SEASON, from its rising to its setting is most fundamental to garden design; Roberto Burle Marx regarded light as 'the most important element that designers have to deal with'.

Shadows can have a profound effect on the garden's amenity and character. Shadow patterns of buildings and vegetation are critical design elements. Building shadows have less ultraviolet light than the same density cast by trees, and this affects plant growth. These patterns, and those of

Light

foliage shadow, translucent foliage, or a matrix of branchlets and twigs, are integral parts of the changing garden. Foliage colour and surface texture of shrubs and trees makes a difference to the apparent light. Hard-surfaced leaves such as *Castanospermum australe* reflect, or shine; furry-foliage plants such as *Thomasia macrocarpa* and *T. rhynchocarpa* absorb the light. Some plants demand light for growth, some thrive in shade. Those that thrive in both shadow and sun are some of the most valuable in horticulture.

Reflective surfaces—like the broad foliage of doryanthes—and blue foliage—like *Acacia argyrophylla*—pick up moonlight and ambient electric light, silvering the garden against the dark forms. Highlighted plants can be used to delineate pathways for safety. Designing for moonlight will add mystery, drama, or a little of the surreal. Reflections, as on the surface of a pond, add mood. A starry sky framed by tree silhouettes and distant hills can be exploited with imagination through shaping or strategic lighting. Backlight contributes to spaciousness. Light density and shade can be varied to create impact, magnify perspective, and invite the eye to enquire further as it travels through gradations of bright flooded surfaces to the darkest gloomiest shadows.

The use of garden light is now the province of lighting engineers, no longer the electrician or plumber as in the times of only a few gas or electrical fittings. The technology of low-voltage and low-energy lamps has made lighting accessible to modern gardens. Festoons of portable coloured lights and floods now give way to budding and washing of zones controlled by computers and sensors. Light ensures that gardens are never static or totally predictable. Using it to advantage has more exciting opportunities than ever.

PAUL THOMPSON

LIGHT, William (1786–1839), soldier and surveyor, unsuccessful in securing the post of South Australian governor, was consoled with the surveyor-generalship—for which he had no training—in February 1836. Colonel Light arrived in the colony in July and spent three months procrastinating over locating the capital. Forced to a decision by the arrival of the first colonists, he almost offhandedly confirmed the site recommended by his deputy, G.S. KINGSTON. Light remained in the survey office while Kingston and his staff laid out the town according to a plan Kingston (and perhaps others) had made in London in September 1835, three

Expressive imagery was a feature of the MALONEY and Walker BUSH GARDEN books (1966–67)—a silhouette of tree-fern fronds perfectly illustrates the effects of LIGHT and shade in the garden

months before Light returned to England from the Mediterranean. The extensive and celebrated ADELAIDE PARK LANDS were probably suggested by Matthew Hill, brother of the Colonisation Commission secretary, Rowland Hill. Because of political wrangling, Light resigned in July 1838, to become the silent partner in the surveying firm of Light, Finniss and Co.

Geoffrey Dutton, *Founder of a City* (Adelaide, 1971); David Elder (ed.), *William Light's Brief Journal and Australian Diaries* (Adelaide, 1984)
DONALD LANGMEAD

LINAKER, Hugh (1872–1938), landscape gardener, horticulturist, and tree planter, was born at Ballarat (Vic.) and gained his training and earliest work in that district. In 1901 he was appointed Curator of Parks and Gardens for the municipality of Ararat. Linaker set about landscaping the area later known as Alexandra Park, officially opened in 1907, when his work in transforming the previous wilderness of mullock heaps and a mining dam set against the unpropitious backdrop of Ararat Gaol was widely praised. His chance for promotion came when the Victorian Government advertised for an 'Ornamental Gardener' for the newly established Mont Park Hospital for the Insane. Linaker was appointed 'landscape gardener, Hospital for the Insane, on probation for twelve months' in 1912 and had his position as landscape gardener for the Lunacy Department confirmed in 1913.

Linaker's new position (of which he was the first incumbent) required him 'to give his expert advice at any of the other Hospitals for the Insane should he be required to do so'; these included the institutions at Yarra Bend, Kew, Ararat, Beechworth, Sunbury, Ballarat, and Royal Park, as well as the 'Kew Idiot Asylum'. Linaker set about his task with zeal and soon established a thriving plant nursery close to his departmental residence in Upper Plenty Road; during 1916, for instance, 10 700 plants were forwarded from Mont Park. Linaker regularly received praise from his superiors and initiated new landscaping or enhanced existing work at each of the hospitals under his control.

Linaker was a frequent lecturer and an inaugural member of the VICTORIAN TREE PLANTERS' ASSOCIATION (1926). He was keenly interested in tree-planting projects on main highways. His advice was sought by many municipalities for the planning of public parks and gardens. He advised on tree planting at the State Electricity Commission's model township at Yallourn (1925–31), his decorative approach often at odds with the formality sought by the architect Alan LA GERCHE. Other works with substantial input from Linaker were Buchan Caves (1929), Yarra Bend National Park (1930), MOUNT BUFFALO National Park (1920s), as well as the landscaping of numerous public buildings, especially police stations and prisons.

Around 1933 Hugh Linaker was appointed State Superintendent of Parks and Gardens, and invited to undertake the landscaping of the King's DOMAIN (1933). His plan took advantage of the curtailment of Government House grounds and the erection of the Shrine of Remembrance, although the criticism by WALLING of its masculine qualities was probably a gratuitous comment on Linaker's bold tree planting. A year later he designed the Pioneer Women's Memorial Garden in the Domain. His work for private clients included input into the two gardens of Alfred Nicholas: Carn Brea, Hawthorn (1928) and BURNHAM BEECHES (1930–34).

When he died at his Hawthorn home, Linaker was regarded by many as the leading landscape gardener of his generation in Victoria. In one sense, he was the successor to HODGKINSON and GUILFOYLE as the senior Victorian public servant with responsibility for horticulture and landscape design. Linaker's hallmark was his bold design ethos—he favoured 'planting for the future'—and his contribution to Australia's garden history is his pioneering landscape architectural work in a period before that profession was given due regard.
RA

LINCOLNE, Abraham (1815–1884), agriculturist, writer, and sketcher, emigrated from London after serving five years on a Suffolk farm. He arrived in Sydney in 1838 and his varied career is detailed in Humphreys' *Victorian Men of the Time* (1882). He formed the first farmers' debating society in NSW and after returning to England 1848–49 started a vineyard in SA on the Torrens. Lincolne relocated to Vic. in 1853, where his farming swung between success and failure at Moonee Ponds and on the Campaspe. He wrote the *Australasian Farmers' Guide* (1869) and, uniform with CLARSON's handbooks, the *Farm and Selection* (1878): both contained horticultural advice.
RA

LINDLEY, John (1799–1865), botanist and author, was born in Catton, near Norwich, England, son of a nursery proprietor. His early interest in botany was consolidated by his employment as assistant librarian to Sir Joseph BANKS (c. 1819). Lindley was appointed assistant secretary of the ROYAL HORTICULTURAL SOCIETY's new garden at Chiswick (1822), with superintendence of the collection of plants: his considerable achievement here were marred by financial difficulties of the Society, of which he was for many years a senior officer. He was the first Professor of Botany at the University of London (1829–60).

Lindley was conversant with colonial matters. He inscribed a copy of his *Introduction to Botany* (1835) in 1836 for Allan CUNNINGHAM 'in memorial of the many scientific obligations of his sincere friend' and played a key role in the Sydney appointment of Charles MOORE. He described plants in Thomas MITCHELL's *Three Expeditions into the Interior of Eastern Australia* (1838) and his *Sketch of the Botany of Swan River* (1839) summarised the first decade of intensive botanical exploration in WA (especially by DRUMMOND and MOLLOY). Lindley reported on shortcomings of KEW GARDENS in 1838 and with Joseph PAXTON founded the *GARDENERS' CHRONICLE* (1841). His *Theory of Horticulture* (1840)—credited with raising the standard of horticulture in England—was well known in the colonies, as was *The Vegetable Kingdom* (1846). Lindley was among Britain's pre-eminent nineteenth-century botanists, and his writings brought his expertise to a wide audience, from taxonomic botanists to gardeners and recreational lovers of nature.

William T. Stearn (ed.), *John Lindley 1799–1865: Gardener-Botanist and Pioneer Orchidologist* (Woodbridge, Suffolk, 1999)
RA

LINDNER, Albert Edward (b. 1915), farmer, naturalist, and pioneer grower of AUSTRALIAN PLANTS, was born in Horsham (Vic.), and as a child developed his love for Australian flora and fauna while exploring the banks of the Wimmera River. In 1937 he began planting a four-acre (1.6 ha) house garden, and soon extended his planting to a nearby sand-hill, where he was able to grow many sand-loving plants from Australia's ARID ZONES. 'Alby' Lindner was a close friend of both Edwin ASHBY and George ALTHOFER, and he frequently accompanied them on field collection trips. Ashby sent much of his seed to Lindner, who germinated it and established many specimens in his garden. Many plants were thus established before botanists had sighted and classified various species. The gardens and sand-hill contain many specimens planted more than sixty years ago, and provide an ideal location in which to see fully mature plants. Local botanists and authors have frequently visited this collection, eager to see and photograph the treasures of the West without having to cross the Nullarbor. JOHN WALTER

LINDSAY PARK, near Angaston, SA: see ANGAS, George French

LINNEAN SOCIETY OF NEW SOUTH WALES (1874–), was named after the Linnean Society, founded in London (1788) by J.E. SMITH and others. Both commemorated the great Swedish naturalist, Carl Linnaeus (1707–1778), ennobled as Carl von Linne, whose *Species plantarum* (1753) became the internationally accepted starting-point for all botanical nomenclature. It was Linnaeus also who introduced binomial naming for species: one generic name followed by a single, specific epithet. The influence of Linnaeus on Australia was felt even during his lifetime, when his talented student, Daniel SOLANDER, travelled on Cook's 1768–71 voyage as assistant to Joseph BANKS. Linnean works were held in many specialist Australian LIBRARIES and 'Ferdinando de Mueller' even published (in Latin) an *Index perfectus ad Caroli Linnæi species plantarum* (1880).

Foundation of the Linnean Society, devoted solely to NATURAL HISTORY, followed a visit to Sydney by the *Challenger* scientific expedition. William MACLEAY gave considerable assistance both financially and intellectually, and the Society soon established—and re-established following the disastrous 1882 Garden Palace fire—a fine LIBRARY and published *Proceedings* (1875–) that became a rich repository of information on the AUSTRALIAN FLORA. Key botanical contributors included MUELLER, F.M. BAILEY, MAIDEN, BAKER, BLAKELY, Cambage, CHEEL, and WOOLLS. Its natural history focus distinguished the Linnean Society of New South Wales from the colony's ROYAL SOCIETY, and, with its excursions, it functioned as a proto–FIELD NATURALISTS' SOCIETY. It has outlived many similar societies and annually offers the Linnean Macleay Fellowship for research.

A.B. Walkom (ed.), *The Linnean Society of New South Wales: Historical Notes of its First Fifty Years* (Sydney, 1925); *A Catalogue of the Works of Linnaeus issued in Commemoration of the 250th Anniversary of Carolus Linnaeus, 1707–1778* (Stockholm, 1957); Carl Linnaeus, *Species Plantarum: A Facsimile of the First Edition 1753, with an introduction by W.T. Stearn* (London, 1957)
LINDEN GILLBANK

LINTON (née LOWTHER), Elizabeth Helen (c. 1872–c. 1948), horticultural journalist, migrated to Tas. in 1882. Formerly from Cardiff, Wales, the Reverend William St George Lowther and family travelled aboard the *Potosi* armed with a Land Order Warrant issued by the Emigrant and Colonists Aid Corporation (Limited) London. Elizabeth ('under age') married a farmer, George Edward Linton, at Springfield (Tas.) in 1891 and the couple had four children (1892–98).

Elizabeth Linton apparently began her career as a horticultural journalist with an article entitled 'Rock gardens and stone borders: and what to plant in them' in the October 1907 issue of the JOURNAL OF HORTICULTURE OF AUSTRALASIA. She soon became the journal's regular Tasmanian correspondent, writing from Meldreth, Springfield, although as 'E.H. Linton, F.R.H.S.' her GENDER was rarely disclosed. Articles between 1907 and 1916 ranged over many subjects, including garden planning and planting, Australian flora, book reviews, and even church decoration. Her own book, *Some Good Climbers and Shrubs*, was reviewed in December 1907, but is only known today from surviving copies of a 1911 edition, entitled *Some Good Climbing Plants, and Shrubs—Usually Grown as Climbers: their culture, position, mode of planting, and of propagation, etc.* Extracts from a second book, *Beautiful Hardy Trees* (1908), were published in the *Journal*, but no copy of the complete work is known to survive. Linton's achievements as a journalist and as the first female author of a garden plant book in Australia belie her electoral-roll occupation of 'domestic duties'. RA

LIPSCOMBE, Frederick (1808–1887), nursery proprietor, seed merchant, publican, and politician, arrived in WA in 1829 on the *Gilmore* as part of the Peel expedition to establish a settlement at the Swan River. In 1831 he travelled to Van Diemen's Land and took up land on Brown's River Road, and later on the slopes of Sandy Bay. He was joined by his brothers **Henry Lipscombe** (1798–1873) and **Edward Lipscombe** (c. 1816–1887) and together they purchased land for their gardens and orchards. Henry's other great love was cricket; he played and promoted the game all his life. Showing little interest in public life, Edward spent his time in pomological solitude.

By c. 1840 Frederick owned two nurseries, The Grange—on land in today's Taroona—and Pine Apple Place Nursery, in Sandy Bay, which he rented to Edward. In 1840 Frederick advertised a 'Gardener's Kalendar' (to be published in the following year) to give advice on 'every circumstance worthy of note affecting the culture of fruit, vegetables and flowers in the neighbourhood of Hobart Town'. He also offered 'to visit different parts of the country, for the purpose of giving advice in laying out Gardens, Orchards, Shrubberies and Pleasure Grounds, or Land-draining or Irrigation'. By 1848 the Lipscombe brothers had established extensive gardens, were growing trees for export to SA and NSW, and were regarded as the best orchardists in the colony. Frederick made important improvements in apple strains and was seen as the father of the colony's fruit industry. He also owned the Beach Tavern and Tea Garden, was an initiator of the waterworks scheme of the Hobart City Council, and between 1859 an 1861 was a member of parliament. In 1861 he became insolvent, and was forced to sell most of his properties. At this time, while treasurer of the Gardeners' and Amateurs' Horticultural Society of Hobart Town, he retained some of their funds. Two years later it was ruefully reported that 'the sum of £32 0s 11d in the late Treasurer's hands is still unavailable for the purposes of the Society'. In 1867 Frederick advertised his business as a 'Nursery Seedsman and Salesman, Seed Grower and Collector of Indigenous Seeds and Plants', having issued a broadsheet catalogue (*c.* 1864) for his business at the New Wharf Market and the Derwent Nursery, Sandy Bay, where he died in 1887. Edward died a few weeks later, and his obituarist recalled that 'The three brothers were gardeners of the best type, and may be said to have done more than any other men in the colony for the development of its horticultural prosperity.'

Leslie John Lipscombe (1865–1929), son of Frederick, continued his father's nursery business. In 1915 he was appointed Superintendent of Reserves for the City of Hobart and planned or renovated many of the city's parks and reserves including Franklin Square and Fitzroy Gardens.

ANN CRIPPS

LIPTUS, Hugh K. (*fl.* 1920s), commentator on Australian flora, was a resident of Gisborne (Vic.) when in 1929 he took part in a spirited campaign over the selection of trees for the town's avenue of honour. Veteran nursery proprietor Walter Smith, son of John Smith of Riddells Creek, unsuccessfully advocated use of exotic tree species, while rival nursery proprietor and local councillor, James Railton, pushed the merits of eucalypts. Smith used the debate, conducted in the local press, to propose public plantings of exotic trees that would supply 'colour effects'—such as Scarlet Oak, Golden Poplar, and Golden Ash—and of existing street trees, though 'a good smart axeman, well directed, would accomplish much of what is necessary in a few days'. The 'gum avenue' of forty-four varieties was duly planted, and Liptus added a note of reason to the debate—now wildly out of control with claims and counter-claims involving the commemorative Sydney–Canberra avenue—by refocusing on more general urban design initiatives, his views accompanied by the plaintive but ultimately futile cry 'Enough of Gum Trees'.

RA

LISSNER PARK, Charters Towers, Qld, gazetted in 1883 as a recreation reserve, was named for local businessman and parliamentarian, Isidor Siegfried Lissner (1832–1902), who had campaigned for a park facility in this mining town. A formal axial plan is still evident in early plantings of figs, tamarinds, and palms, radiating paths, centrally placed fountain, timber bandstand, and iron kiosk. The kiosk (1910) was built to commemorate Boer War veterans: Francis Jorgensen, director of the technical college, won a design competition and Mayor S.H. Thorp boasted 'that every portion of it was the result of local industry'. The open kiosk has an unusual elongated plan with an inner and outer ring of cast-iron columns supporting a bell-shaped, corrugated-iron roof with three small, louvred, dormer windows on each side and encircling concave verandah, a distinctively tropical garden building.

JODI FRAWLEY

LITERATURE Gardens generally feature in early Australian fiction as an indicator of successful settlement. Indeed, some early poetry, fiction, and prose writing described the landscape as *already* like a garden or a gentleman's park, available and ideally suited to white settlement. Fidelia Hill's poem 'Recollections' (1840), written about Adelaide, describes these early perceptions: 'Park-like scenery/Burst on the astonish'd sight; for it did seem/As tho' the hand of art, had nature aided,/Where the broad level walks—and verdant lawns,/And vistas grac'd that splendid wilderness!'. In 'pioneer' fiction such as Alexander Harris's *The Emigrant Family* (1849), Charles Rowcroft's *Tales of the Colonies* (1843), and Henry Kingsley's *The Recollections of Geoffry Hamlyn* (1859), the settlers' gardens are a cultivated and sometimes hard-won barrier between domestic space and the threatening bush. Thornley, Rowcroft's hero, is satisfied in his old age by the ultimate fantasy of a stone house and a walled garden with a 'plot of English grass' and 'English' fruit trees. In other nineteenth-century fiction the garden is less a barrier against the 'new' environment than a zone of successful blending or adaptation, as in the garden in 'Iota's' *Kooroona* (1871), set in SA, where 'whispering shea-oaks and golden wattles bloom among green almonds, towering poplars, and shady willows'. Not surprisingly, gardens were significant thematic elements in the fiction works of the naturalists Louisa Atkinson in NSW and Louisa Meredith in Tas.

The 1880s and 1890s are commonly considered a crucial period in Australian writing. Most of the 'Bulletin school' writers, especially Henry Lawson, might be seen as making a point of the absence of gardens. The hut in 'The Drover's Wife' (1892) is the more desolate because it has 'bush all round—bush with no horizon', and in 'Water them Geraniums' (1901) the central theme is a pathetic attempt at a feminine garden, as doomed in the hostile bush as the woman who frets over it. Arthur H. Adams comments in his poem 'The Australian' (1899) that the Australian type is 'No flower with fragile sweetness graced—/[but] A land weed wrestling with the waste'. However, one of Lawson's earlier socialist poems, 'Freedom on the Wallaby' (1891), claims 'we have made the land/A garden full of promise'. The 'romance' fiction of the period, mostly, but not solely, by women is more positive in its representation of gardens—in novels such as Catherine Martin's *An Australian Girl* (1890), the large garden of the home station blends into the bush, and suggests a harmonious union of the native environment and the introduced. Here and elsewhere there is some suggestion that the garden is haunted by the memory of the displaced Aboriginal inhabitants.

In the field of children's literature the wild garden of Ethel Turner's *Seven Little Australians* (1894), where Judy scythes the grass in an attempt to ingratiate herself with her father (and in a metaphoric taming of her own wild self), is probably better remembered than that in her later novel *The Ungardeners* (1925), in which a walled garden becomes the focus of family dynamics and social reform. At the climax a hole is knocked through the wall to let the local slum children (but not their parents) benefit from its wholesome effects and NATURE STUDY lessons.

Heavily symbolic gardens, especially ROSE gardens, feature in many of the works of Patrick White, including *The Tree of Man* (1955), *The Eye of the Storm* (1973), and *The Twyborn Affair* (1979). In *Voss* (1957), the symbolic consummation of Laura and Voss's relationship takes place in the Bonner's bourgeois rose garden. In general, the formal exotic garden cannot overcome its locale: 'The science of horticulture had failed to exorcise the spirit of the place. The wands and fronds of native things intruded still'. Similar gardens feature in the works of 'M. Barnard Eldershaw' and Christina STEAD. Twentieth-century poetry such as Kenneth Slessor's 'Elegy in a Botanic Garden' (1932), and works by Judith Wright and Dorothy Hewett also make extensive use of the symbolic possibilities of the garden. Much Australian writing deals with mythological gardens, as for instance A.D. Hope's poems about the Garden of Eden. One of the divisions in poetry dealing with 'real' gardens is, as in fiction, an anxiety about whether the garden is representative of the natural world— generally, post-1910 depicted positively—or whether gardens represent artificial culture imposed on, or in opposition to nature and the bush. In John Shaw Neilson's 'You, and Yellow Air' (1909) the garden and nature are one. Judith Wright's poetry is more ambivalent in its representations. In her poem 'The Garden' (1949), the garden is in harmony with nature, and the gardener, '[w]alking slowly along her garden ways,/[is] a bee grown old at summer's end …'. But in '… And Mr Ferritt' (1955) the garden represents the unpleasant protagonist's artificial order battling nature, and in 'Brother and Sisters' (1949), the garden, like the title characters, is an artificial intruder in the bush that is gently erasing it.

Gardens in post-1900 Australian literature can invoke a positive longing for nature, as in Marjorie Barnard's 'The Persimmon Tree' (1943), or be caught up in the negative or ambivalent portrayals of Australian suburbia across the twentieth century, in which the SUBURBAN GARDEN is associated with middle-class uniformity and femininity, as in Lennie Lower's *Here's Luck* (1930), Hal Porter's *The Watcher on the Cast-Iron Balcony* (1963), Christos Tsiolkas's *Loaded* (1996), some of Peter Carey's fiction, and poetry such as Coral Hull's 'Liverpool' (1996). In Myron Lysenko's 'Living in Coburg' (1988) the protagonist's single life and untidy garden are a worry to his family-oriented 'Italian neighbours' who offer to 'mow my lawns/or at least the front one, please?/& maybe next week they could plant flowers/because flowers make a house look good; & if I'd like, they could turn my back yard/into a huge vegetable garden …'. Lee Cataldi's 'if you stay too long in the third world' (1990) has gardens as one of the indicators of 'first' world privilege. But gardens also feature more positively, as links between generations, cultures, and places in David Malouf's poem 'Early Discoveries' (1974), and Lisa Jacobson's 'The Mother Tree' (1995). In Murray Bail's novel *Eucalyptus* (1998), a bush garden is the fairy tale site for a courtship quest. Having with great difficulty established every species of EUCALYPT on his property, a father offers his beautiful daughter as the reward for the man who can correctly name them all. One might see a reversion to earlier alignments of the garden with the feminine in this tale, despite its twists.

A number of women writers have made extensive, and somewhat more positive, use of suburban and semi-rural gardens since the 1960s, for instance Barbara Hanrahan's mysterious and brooding gardens, Kate Llewellyn's semi-fictional garden diaries, and Thea Astley's and Janette Turner Hospital's mostly tropical gardens. Some recent writing, particularly that of Elizabeth Jolley and Drusilla Modjeska, has depicted the garden, in ways not unrelated to the colonial writings, as a site for negotiation with environment and sorting out national affiliations.

Michael Waters, *The Garden in Victorian Literature* (Aldershot, England, 1988)   SUSAN K. MARTIN

LITTLE MILTON, Toorak, Vic. was commissioned by the Moran family in the early 1920s. Built on the original driveway of the property, Whernside, the house is a small-scale

Sydney horticulturist John G. LOCKLEY was a great populariser of gardening and horticulture, especially through his magazine the *Amateur Gardener* and books such as *Rose Growing Made Easy* (1907)

replica of Great Milton, Oxfordshire, England. Edna WALLING was commissioned to design the garden in 1927, and it is now among the earliest of her designs to survive in an original state. Perusal of Walling's original watercoloured plan of the garden shows that it remains virtually intact in design, with its pergola, herbaceous border, and tennis court.

TRISHA DIXON

LOCKLEY, John Gilmore ('Redgum') (1865–1937), horticultural journalist, was born at Chippendale (NSW). He came to prominence in 1904 as the publisher and editor of the Sydney-based *Amateur Gardener* (1904–17). Appealing directly to urban and rural gardeners of modest means, Lockley concentrated on flower and vegetable gardens, with considerable space devoted to the most popular species—the rose, carnation, dahlia, bouvardia, and daffodil. He made a special effort to appeal to women gardeners with specific articles and in general editorial style; he included opinions of Gertrude JEKYLL and Mrs Earle, and reviewed books by Edith Wharton (*Italian Villas and their Gardens*) among others. He was an ardent nationalist, and this suffused his editorial policy—for example, he included poems by Henry Lawson: some well-known ('Waratah and Wattle'), others specially commissioned ('The Water', on irrigation and the basic rights of Australians to water, and 'The Water Lily', the tragic scene of a young mother reaching in her dreams for her dead child in a lily pond). Lockley published three books aimed at amateur gardeners: *Rose Growing Made Easy* (1907), *Dahlia Growing Made Easy* (1908), and *Carnation Growing Made Easy* (1914), the DAHLIA and CARNATION books being the first Australian monographs on their subject. An enlarged third edition of *Rose Growing* in 1927 included remarks on Australian-bred ROSES and lists of roses suited for various Australian towns and regions. Lockley contributed to the horticultural press as 'Redgum', gave regular RADIO broadcasts on 2FC, used his Killara garden for demonstrations, and conducted a library from his Sydney office, befitting his role as one of the great popularisers of Australian gardening in the first decades of the twentieth century.

RA

THE LODGE, Deakin, ACT, erected in 1926 as the official residence of the Australian prime minister, incorporated a 2.8 hectare garden. Created in a style typical of gardens associated with CANBERRA's Federal Capital–style architecture, it has lawns, shrubberies, and tree plantings with a few trees of fastigiate form for accent. The garden also included some existing eucalypts, a tennis court, and a croquet lawn. In 1968 the garden was reduced to 1.8 hectares with the loss of the orchard, fowl yard, and vegetable garden. A native garden in one corner was developed during the Gorton residency (1968–71) and since 1968, a swimming pool and pergolas have been added, and landscape upgrading undertaken. In its constant change of incumbents, this official residence shares attributes with GOVERNMENT HOUSES, and has many COMMEMORATIVE trees planted by prime ministers, their wives, and distinguished guests.

JULIET RAMSAY

LODGES: see GATES AND GATE LODGES

LONE PINE, a ridge at Gallipoli, Turkey, was named for a single specimen of *Pinus brutia* (Calabrian Pine) remaining after clear-felling for trench-construction timber by Turkish forces in the First World War. During the critical Battle of Lone Pine (6–9 August 1915) Australia lost 2273 soldiers in an area the size of only two soccer fields. Specimens of the Lone Pine, propagated from the original tree, have been planted in Australia at COMMEMORATIVE sites, such as WAR MEMORIALS, parks, and repatriation hospitals.

KAREN OLSEN

LONGLEY, George (1822–1899), botanic gardens curator, was born at Lowther, Westmoreland, England; he trained as a gardener at Lowther Castle, then subsequently worked for Lord Brougham. In 1853 he migrated to Vic. and was immediately attracted to the rich Ballarat diggings; he was present at the Eureka riots but, like many GARDENERS, sought to consolidate his wealth through his vocation. He was appointed to curate the newly created BALLARAT BOTANIC GARDENS in 1858, and died in the Gardens' cottage after forty-one years of continuous service. His skill and extensive experience were credited as major reasons for the success and high esteem of the Gardens, and the FERNERY was his chief pride. A son, William Robert Longley (1873–1914), was a gardener at TRAWALLA at the time of his father's death.

RA

LOOKOUTS and vantage points are places that entrance and exhilarate humans by capturing views and enabling people to experience vast expanses of landscapes. Lookout points for hunting and fishing, at places imbued with special meanings, and for 'looking at my country' have always been part of the environmental culture of Aboriginal Australians. In NATIONAL PARKS and scenic reserves, hundreds of lookout points such as Echo Point, BLUE MOUNTAINS (NSW), Mount Kosciuszko (NSW), and MOUNT BUFFALO (Vic.) are major destinations where people enjoy views of mountain ranges, forests, waterfalls, rivers, coasts, geological formations, or landscape panoramas. For cities with favourable topography, lookout points such as Mount Wellington (Hobart), MOUNT COOT-THA (Brisbane), and Castle Hill (Townsville, Qld) are valued community places. In CANBERRA, Mount Ainslie provides views of the major land and water axes within the NATIONAL TRIANGLE, and is itself a VISTA feature of the axial view from Parliament House. The structure of a lookout point is frequently unremarkable, often being a simple security fence, or a low wall; some, as at Mount Coot-tha, MOUNT LOFTY (SA), and Arthurs Seat (Vic.), are substantial summit structures. At a smaller scale, many gardens, particularly those in hills, frequently have lookout points integral with the garden design, such as the example at EVERGLADES.

In parks and gardens, vantage points use structures and seats to capture intimate and expansive garden views, VISTAS, borrowed scenery from the contextual landscape, and the ephemeral qualities of water sounds and light effects. Early Australian examples of lookout towers (also known as prospect towers or watch towers) survive at GLENARA and RIPPON LEA (Vic.). MODERNIST and Art Deco–styled towers

The MODERNIST design of this LOOKOUT overlooking Barwon Valley, Geelong (Vic.), brings the functionalist ethos of the inter-war period to the realm of garden architecture

were often constructed in concrete, with fine examples surviving at WOMBAT HILL (Vic.) and overlooking the Barwon River valley at Queen's Park (Geelong, Vic.). Water towers also served as lookouts, and in gardens such as ANLABY (SA) and PANSHANGAR (Tas.) these were architecturally distinctive and located to provide vertical landscape features as 'eye catchers'. Modern lookout towers such as Newcastle's foreshore park tower and the Treillage, in Homebush Bay Park (NSW), are distinctive focal points of their parkland settings.

Structures utilising vantage points such as gazebos, pavilions, temples, platforms, and seats vary in style from rustic to elegant and may reflect classical, picturesque, or eastern architecture. CATARACT GORGE (Tas.), NOOROO (NSW), and many other gardens have stylised gazebos. Peacock Point (NSW) utilises a series of timber platforms. The temples in the Chinese Garden at Sydney's Darling Harbour use garden vantage points to experience aesthetic qualities such as tumbling water. An enduring favourite is Mrs Macquarie's Chair, a traditional and popular public vantage point for viewing Sydney Harbour.   JULIET RAMSAY

LORD, Clive Errol (1889–1933), naturalist, was born in Hobart, scion of the Lord family of Richmond, and of the Watchorn family on his maternal side. He practised as an architect but also devoted his considerable energies to NATURAL HISTORY. He was a foundation member of the Tasmanian Field Naturalists' Club (1904), secretary of the Royal Society of Tasmania (1918–33), and director of the Tasmanian Museum and Art Gallery (1923–33). He was an ardent promoter of NATIONAL PARKS and as secretary for many years of the ROYAL TASMANIAN BOTANICAL GARDENS he assisted in their reorganisation in the early 1930s. A large collection of his books is housed in the Royal Society of Tasmania library, with Mawson's *Art and Craft of Garden Making* (1912) indicative of his design interests.   RA

LORD, Ernest Edward (1899–1970), horticulturist, landscape gardener, and educator, was born in London, and educated in England. He came with his parents to Australia in 1912 and obtained employment in Melbourne in the softgoods trade. Lord married in 1923 and took up horticulture and botany as a hobby. He was briefly honorary secretary of his local Bentleigh and Ormond Horticultural Society before accepting this position in 1933 with the vastly more prestigious Malvern and District Horticultural Society, then capable of attracting up to 400 to monthly meetings. He became curator of parks and gardens (1935–41) at Horsham (Vic.) and oversaw a rejuvenation of Horsham Botanic Gardens, partially implemented according to an 1880 design of William GUILFOYLE. Lord was the founding editor (1947–49) of the popular garden magazine *YOUR GARDEN*: he set a high editorial standard and keenly promoted Australian plants alongside more popular garden favourites. He served as treasurer (1943–50) and president (1950–52) of the Field Naturalists' Club of Victoria and was also closely involved with the management of MARANOA GARDENS.

Shrubs and Trees for Australian Gardens (1948) was his magnum opus, written, according to friends, over a decade as he commuted by train to the city—where, for a time, he worked with RAILTON. Impressively printed for LOTHIAN by the Hassell Press (Adelaide), the book, with its large quarto format and comprehensive coverage, was imposing, and set a new standard for Australian GARDENING BOOKS. AUSTRALIAN FLORA was given special coverage, aided by the photographs of Herbert Trethowan Reeves (1894–1963), and assistance from Ivo HAMMET, George ALTHOFER, and Garnet HATELEY. Describing himself as a landscape architect, Lord included observations on garden planning and—unusually for an Australian gardening book and with an eye to the local government market—he included a section on municipal tree planting that contained a chapter on TOWN PLANNING by Frank HEATH. The book ran through many editions; the sixth was revised by his friend and colleague Jim WILLIS.

Lord started a collaborative business venture c. 1950, titled 'Garden Art', to provide a garden design and construction service. He supplied plans and shrub selection, D.J.C. CHANDLER supplied and planted nursery stock, and others undertook rock walling, lawns, and pools. Lord's services as a garden designer were in keen demand, and his book *Your New Home Garden: Its Design, Plan, Construction and Planting* (1958) capitalised on the development of SUBURBAN GARDENS as Melbourne's post-war building industry boomed.

Lord travelled and lectured widely, and maintained an impressive international professional network. From 1953 he conducted a correspondence school in landscape gardening, capturing the market for part-time students and those who sought his expertise in plants. Gordon FORD was his first graduate and former students, Patricia Newton (b. 1924) and Edna Pollard (1931–2000), took over the school after his death. Lord was an idealist, a natural teacher, and he richly endowed Australian horticulture through his publications. RA

LOTHIAN, (Thomas Robert) Noel (b. 1915), horticulturist and botanic garden director, was born in Mont Albert (Vic.). He was the son of publisher **Thomas Carlyle Lothian** (1880–1974), who in 1912 had assumed management of his father's firm of publishers' representatives, established in 1905. As Thomas C. Lothian and Co. (and under subsequently restructurings) Lothian promoted the publication of Australian writers' works, including important garden titles. These included books by WOLLASTON, E.E. LORD, Noel Lothian, and, most recently, the multi-volume *Encyclopaedia of Australian Plants* (1980–) by ELLIOT and Jones.

Noel Lothian graduated from the BURNLEY School of Primary Agriculture and Horticulture in 1934, and then worked at Melbourne's FITZROY GARDENS and Christchurch Gardens, New Zealand (1935–36). Two years at ROYAL BOTANIC GARDENS, KEW, broadened his experience of plant varieties and cultivation techniques. War service in the Second AIF included a period in charge of a farm unit in New Guinea. He spent a further period in New Zealand as Senior Lecturer in Horticulture, Lincoln College, Christchurch, before being appointed director of ADELAIDE BOTANIC GARDEN in 1948.

In contrast to the nineteenth-century support for science by FRANCIS and SCHOMBURGK, emphasis in the Garden had turned to floriculture. Lothian re-established the scientific role, aided by the support of his board and Premier Playford. The herbarium and library were re-established; the important work of seed exchange was developed to international standards; traineeships for staff were established; a new catalogue of plants in the Garden produced (1955); and an advisory and technical service begun. The Schomburgk Range of glasshouses was developed, and a new building for the herbarium constructed. The potential range of plants was greatly expanded as Lothian became responsible for the new MOUNT LOFTY BOTANIC GARDEN (1952) and WITTUNGA BOTANIC GARDEN (1965). Lothian's establishment of experimental plantations in the country, and his support for the work of the tree advisory officer, enabled him to play a valuable role in encouraging farmers to revegetate and plant trees at a time when such endeavours received only limited popular support. Educational and scientific activities at the Botanic Garden both expanded dramatically during his tenure (1948–80).

Noel Lothian supported many community and civic groups embracing natural history, horticulture, education, and administration including the Field Naturalists' Society and Royal Society of South Australia, Royal Agricultural and Horticultural Society of South Australia, and Royal Institute for Public Administration. Lothian was president of the Kew Guild and later a life member. His *Practical Home Gardener* (1955) became a standard reference book and was followed by Lothian and Ivan HOLLIDAY, *Growing Australian Plants* (1965). His radio broadcasts, writing, and public speaking in both city and country helped to give amenity horticulture an enhanced public profile.

Stuart Sayers, *The Company of Books: A Short History of the Lothian Book Companies 1888–1988* (Melbourne, 1988)

PAULINE PAYNE

LOUDON, John Claudius (1783–1843), Scottish-born landscape gardener, horticulturist, author, and editor, and his wife **Jane Wells Loudon** (*née* **Webb**) (1807–1858), author and horticulturist, were prodigious in their literary output. J.C. Loudon's career as an author began in 1803 and his 'diffusion of useful knowledge' was well advanced when he enthusiastically reviewed an anonymously written three-volume science fiction novel (1828). Loudon met the young author, Jane Webb, well-educated but living in financially strained circumstances (1830). They married soon after, and she adopted the role of his amanuensis, amplifying his productivity—his right arm had been amputated in 1825—in addition to pursuing her own career as an author.

Loudon's career began after he moved to London in 1803; initially he adhered to PICTURESQUE principles as enunciated by Uvedale PRICE. Following a short but successful career as a farmer, including his Tew Lodge Farm, Oxfordshire (1808–11), he embarked on a number of tours to Europe, gathering information that culminated in the publication of his *Encyclopaedia of Gardening* (1822). From the mid-1820s, after reading an essay on aesthetics by French academician A.C. Quatremère de Quincy (1755–1849), Loudon promoted the idea that gardens should be recognisable as works of art—as opposed to wild nature—paving the way for a return to 'regular', or FORMAL gardens. In 1832 he coined the term GARDENESQUE, which emphasises the use of foreign plants to heighten the appearance of art—an aspect of his theory that had a lasting effect in Australia—and required plants to be spatially separate so that each could develop and be appreciated individually.

Loudon's links with the Australian colonies began long before his prominent publications. He was a friend of Sir Joseph BANKS, and Alexander MCLEAY proposed his election as a Fellow of the Linnean Society (1806). Loudon observed, in the first volume of his *Gardener's Magazine* (1826), that with the appointment of the 'new and enlightened colonial secretary', Alexander McLeay, there would be protection for olive and grape growing, important agricultural products of the colony. McLeay later wrote to Loudon on the state of agriculture and horticulture in NSW and encouraged Charles FRASER to submit a catalogue of fruits growing SYDNEY BOTANIC GARDENS for publication. Jane Loudon, in her account of her husband's life, described the *Gardener's Magazine* as 'the universal means of communication among gardeners … of incalculable benefit to them'—a resource appreciated by Georgiana MOLLOY in her letter to Captain MANGLES (1838). Other well-read publications included Loudon's *Encyclopaedia of Agriculture* (1825) and *Suburban Gardener and Villa Companion* (1838): designs and ideas published in the *Suburban Gardener* were often used as the basis for laying out the FRONT GARDENS of terrace houses and suburban VILLAS. His writings on CEMETERIES were also influential.

The first house design by a colonial architect to be illustrated in England was published by Loudon in his *Architectural Magazine* (1834). Sent by correspondent John THOMPSON, it was designed by Sydney architect and surveyor Mortimer Lewis (1796–1879), who produced many plans directly inspired by designs from Loudon's publications. Loudon's *Encyclopaedia of Cottage, Farm and Villa Architecture and Furniture* (1833) bears the imprints of 'Howe, Sydney; and Melville, Hobart Town', which attests to the perceived importance of his publications in the colonies. 'Communications' from, and references to, many colonists appeared in Loudon's periodicals. News from James ANDERSON was gleaned from Hugh Low of Clapton Nursery, London, for whom he collected. Frederick A. Meyer, a German who, when working at Clapton Nursery, contributed articles to the *Gardener's Magazine* (1828), migrated to NSW and laid out the first terraced vineyard in the colony for Sir John JAMISON (1830). Seeds and dried specimens were sent to Loudon by John McLean (c. 1797–1840), Assistant Superintendent of Sydney Botanic Gardens (1833) and from Hobart Town by William DAVIDSON (1834). Loudon also referred to William McGarvie (1810–1841), of *Sydney Herald* fame, as his correspondent.

Loudon promoted interest in the colonies, gleaning information from colonial newspapers, travellers' letters, and by reviewing publications by James BACKHOUSE, James BUSBY, Peter Cunningham, and Thomas SHEPHERD (some of whose published lectures exhibit significant similarities to extracts from Loudon's *Encyclopaedia of Gardening*). A friend of the liberal reformer, Jeremy Bentham, Loudon advocated EDUCATION as the key to the 'advance in the happiness of the lower classes' and his urban TOWN PLANNING ideas were far in advance of the time. He saw tremendous possibilities for progressive planning to be implemented in new settlements such as SA—a correspondent, Thomas ALLEN, having migrated

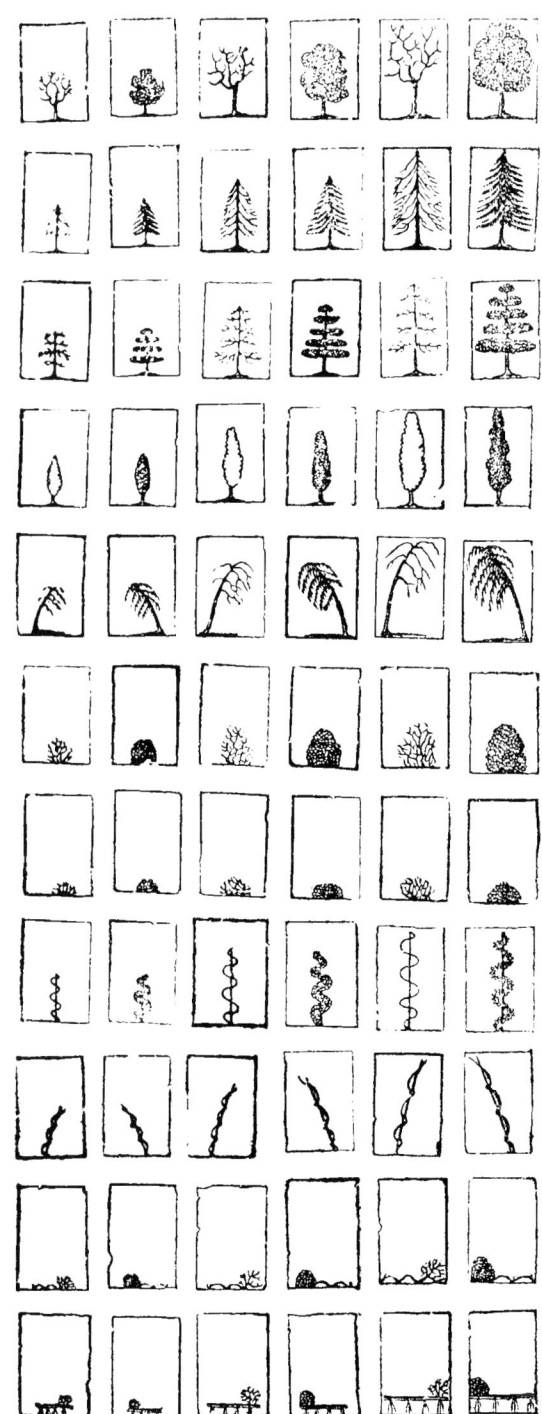

The matrix of plant shape symbols in LOUDON's *Arboretum et Fruticetum Britannicum* (1838) showing the habit of trees and shrubs (comprising round-headed, spiry-topped, fastigiate, drooping, twining, climbing, trailing, and creeping) perfectly captures the artifice of Loudon's GARDENESQUE style

to Adelaide. Loudon sent recommendations on the subject of village breathing-spaces and playgrounds to the editor of the *Hobart Town Courier* (1830). A long article on the Derby Arboretum, designed by Loudon, under the title 'Parks and Pleasure Grounds' in the *Launceston Examiner* (1842), indicates the colonial interest in PUBLIC PARKS AND GARDENS in his own lifetime. Although articles on this park were published in the *Civil Engineer and Architect's Journal* and other English sources, such local newspaper articles brought the example of Derby to a wider colonial audience. The many works by John and Jane Loudon held in Australian LIBRARIES, both public and private, attest to their usefulness in the colonies.

J.C. Loudon's periodicals were the first to deal with gardening and architecture exclusively. The inclusion of articles of international interest in the *Gardener's Magazine* (1826–44) and the *Architectural Magazine* (1834–39) set a bench-mark for later MAGAZINES. The family was almost ruined financially by Loudon's major work, *Arboretum et Fruticetum Britannicum* (1838), and he turned to publishing a volume of REPTON's complete works (1840), bringing these ideas to a new generation of readers. Although Jane Loudon shared most of her husband's views, many of her books and periodicals were written specifically for women—*Ladies' Flower-Garden* (1839–48), *Gardening for Ladies* (1840), *Ladies' Magazine of Gardening* (1841), and *Ladies' Companion to the Flower-Garden* (1841), for example. Her career continued after her husband's death. She was the first editor of the periodical *Ladies' Companion* (founded 1849), and her edited editions of J.C. Loudon's works, particularly his *Villa Gardener* (1850), reflected the progression of nineteenth-century values. Just as Loudon's books continued to be republished after his death, so did Jane's, with William ROBINSON revising and editing her *Amateur Gardener's Calendar* (1847) in 1870.

John Gloag, *Mr Loudon's England: The Life and Work of John Claudius Loudon and his influence on Architecture and Furniture Design* (London, 1970); Elisabeth MacDougall, *John Claudius Loudon and the Early Nineteenth Century in Great Britain* (Washington, DC, 1980); Melanie Louise Simo, *Loudon and the Landscape: From Country Seat to Metropolis* (New Haven and London, 1988). COLLEEN MORRIS

LOVEKIN, Arthur (1859–1931), English-born journalist, newspaper proprietor, parliamentarian, and public benefactor, settled in WA in 1886 and was soon a major figure in public life. KINGS PARK ranked highly among his many public interests. He was a member of the board from its inception (1896–1931), president (1918–31), and author of *The King's Park, Perth* (1925). Lovekin was the driving force behind the COMMEMORATIVE war memorial honour avenues in Kings Park, one of which bears his name.

OLINE RICHARDS

LUCAS, (Beryl) Llewellyn ('Chloris') (1898–1967), writer and horticultural journalist, was born at Harkaway (Vic.) and educated in Melbourne, Sydney, and London. She lived in Queensland's Moreton district before settling in Brisbane. She contributed verse and short stories to the *Bulletin*, the *Home*, and other journals, and (as 'Chloris') horticultural and music notes for the Brisbane *Courier* and its weekly, the *Queenslander* (1928–37). Under her writing name of Llywelyn Lucas she published a book of poems, *The Garden* (c. 1938).

Edith M. England, *Lost Kinship and other Poems: A Memorial to Llywelyn Lucas* (Brisbane, 1968). RA

LUEHMANN, Johann Georg (1843–1904), botanist, migrated to Australia *c.* 1862 and was one of several Germans employed while Ferdinand MUELLER was Director of MELBOURNE BOTANIC GARDENS. In 1869 he was appointed office assistant and custodian of Mueller's 'Phytologic Museum', where he managed the collections until his death. He could recognise not only the specimens but the handwriting on their labels. When attaching the specific epithet 'Luehmanni' to Australian plants and when introducing his *Iconography of Australian Species of Acacia* (1887) and his *Key to the System of Victorian Plants* (1888), Mueller acknowledged Luehmann's assistance in the HERBARIUM. He was one of Victoria's early Fellows of the prestigious Linnean Society of London. On Mueller's death (1896), Luehmann stepped quietly into his late mentor's taxonomic shoes and began describing new species from Herbarium specimens awaiting thorough examination—three acacias and two eucalypts in the *Victorian Naturalist*. Luehmann was acting curator of the Herbarium until 1900, when his title became Government Botanist and Curator of the National Herbarium, and his status—but not his salary—was raised from clerical to professional. At a FIELD NATURALISTS' CLUB of Victoria (FNCV) meeting in 1905, J.H. MAIDEN dedicated a beautiful new species of *Pultenaea* to the memory of his friend and colleague, and founding FNCV member, 'whose death, following too closely on that of Mueller, leaves a great gap in the sparse ranks of Australian botanical systematists'.

LINDEN GILLBANK

LUFFMAN(N), Charles (Bogue) (1862–1920), horticulturist and writer, was born at Cockington, Devon, England, and spent his early childhood in Knowle, Bristol. He was in Spain before 1890 and his writings suggest he had been in Australia prior to this time. He spent some time at the Cavello orchard of the Delius Brothers where he claims to have 'managed' the 1350-acre (550 ha) orchard. He walked through Spain during 1893 and this journey provided material for his first book, *A Vagabond in Spain* (1895). He was deeply influenced by George Borrow, whose *The Zincali: or An Account of the Gypsies in Spain* (1841) and *The Bible in Spain* (1842) created the romantic personality that he desired to emulate; thus he began to call himself Carl B. Luffmann and ultimately C. Bogue Luffmann.

He migrated to Vic. in 1895, and was joined by the woman who had encouraged him to write in England: Lauretta Caroline Maria Lane (1846–1929). They were married in 1895; Laura M. Lane (the name she used for her writing) was at this time 48, so their marriage echoed that of Borrow, who had married a woman older than himself. Luffmann was employed by the Victorian Government as an advisory instructor on raisin culture at Mildura. Following

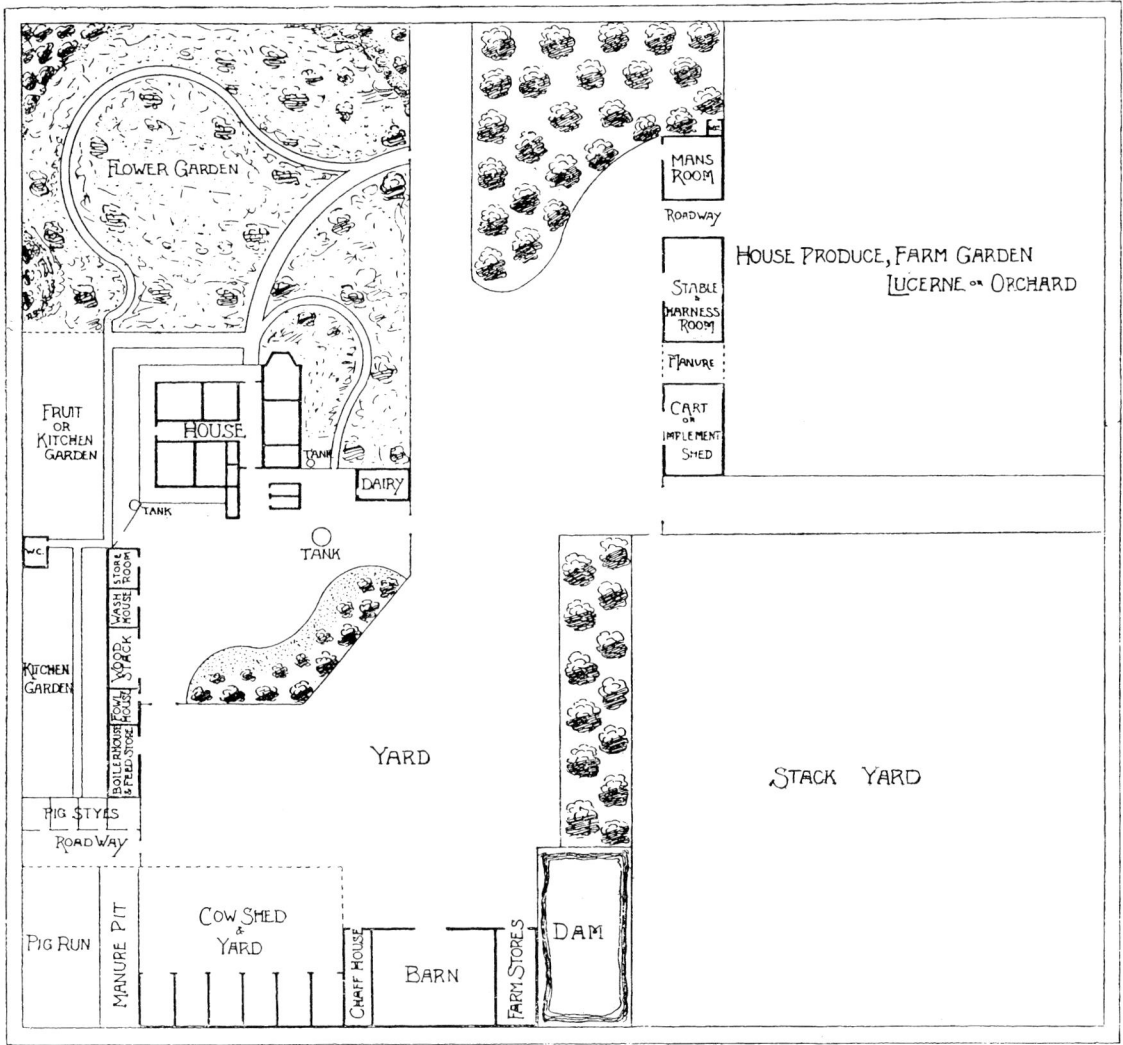

C. Bogue LUFFMANN's plan of a HOMESTEAD GARDEN, published by the Victorian Department of Agriculture (1905), brought his design ideas to the modest acreage of the farmer engaged in small-scale agriculture, rather than to the more expansive setting of the pastoralist

the financial collapse of the Mildura Settlement (1896), Luffmann provided evidence at the inquiry based on his experience of fruit cultivation in southern Europe. He was later praised for having organised and placed the dried fruit trade of Mildura on a sound footing, and for having encouraged the government to subsidise the settlement.

In 1897 Luffmann was appointed Principal of the BURNLEY School of Horticulture. He undertook an extensive remodelling of its garden and took the significant step of admitting WOMEN students—albeit for only two days each week. In 1900, as a witness before the Royal Commission on Technical Education, he stated 'I do not think horticulture is an affair of sex'. During his time at Burnley, Luffmann travelled to lecture to fruit growers and was given credit for much of the reform of the state's dried fruit industry. Luffmann and his wife separated in about 1902. The author Evelyn May Mordaunt (1872–1942) shared Luffmann's house at Burnley from 1903 to 1905, and several of her writings (as Elinor Mordaunt and E.M. Clowes) recall this period.

In 1903 Luffmann proposed to his London publisher, John Murray, that he should write a book about gardening in warm climes, to be based on a series of six lectures that he was about to give. *Principles of Gardening for Australia* (1903), published in Melbourne by the Book Lovers Library, was

Luffmann's most lasting contribution to Australian horticulture. In it he explained his approach to gardening and garden design—an approach that reflected that of William ROBINSON in Britain. Publication of his book brought Luffmann to the attention of the Royal Victorian Institute of Architects, and he was invited to debate Walter BUTLER on the design of gardens. Though Luffmann was ill on the night of the debate and unable to attend, Butler presented his paper, 'Garden Design in Relation to Architecture' on 30 June 1903: Luffmann's response, 'Garden Design in accord with Local Needs', was presented on 26 April 1904. Their argument reflected debate occurring in England at the same time between architect Reginald Blomfield (1856–1942), author of *The Formal Garden in England* (1892), and horticulturist William Robinson, who argued about the role of the garden designer and whether this was professionally the task of the architect or the horticulturist. In fact, in many respects Luffmann and Butler held similar views, for Luffmann abhorred the cultivation of flowers as collections, preferring to see them contributing to an overall design.

Luffmann was an early advocate of the use of the AUSTRALIAN FLORA in landscape design, advocating its use for the proposed Federal Capital of Australia in a paper contributed to a congress of engineers and others interested in the building of the capital (1901). His paper, 'The Agricultural Horticultural Sylvan Features of a Federal Capital', included the recommendation that the capital should contain 'a true botanic garden, representing Australian flora' and be a truly Australian city where 'native timber and all naturally attractive features should, as far as possible be preserved—If we must have symbols, let us typify our own'.

Of Luffmann's work little remains, though the free-form of Burnley's paths appears to have stemmed from his work. The Metropolitan Golf Club, Oakleigh (1908) seems to have been his largest project, though the plan has recently disappeared. Here Luffmann's use of *Acacia maidenii*, *Angophora costata*, *Banksia grandis*, *Callitris collumnaris*, *Eucalyptus ficifolia*, and other native shrubs led Edna WALLING to describe the site as 'the best collection of native trees and shrubs in Victoria'. A simple plan survives for the garden at Killamount, Wyuna East, where Luffmann's sweeping lawns, paths, and shrubberies may still be seen. A second garden by Luffman in this region was recently destroyed by subdivision.

In 1908 Luffmann resigned from Burnley, completing his work at Oakleigh before returning to Britain. He travelled through Spain intermittently during 1908–09, publishing *Quiet Days in Spain* in 1910. Work in the orange plantations of Florida provided Luffmann with sufficient funds to visit Japan. He prepared a book describing this journey, but the Great War prevented its publication. He worked at Wyke Regis in Dorset, England, training women apprentices in horticulture during the war, and published *The Harvest of Japan* in 1920.   JOHN PATRICK

LUTANA, Tas., was established in 1919 as a company village for the new Electrolytic Zinc Company works (1916), the first of its type in Tas. Its benevolent paternalism characterised other inter-war industrial workers' accommodation, including Cadbury Fry Pascall, Claremont (1922), Australian Paper and Pulp Manufacturers, Burnie (1936), and Australian Newsprint Mills (ANM), New Norfolk (1940) and **Maydena** (1947). In all cases, the housing was part of a company-sponsored social welfare system, producing an atmosphere in which unions co-operated to achieve above average conditions.

At Lutana, Walter BUTLER provided ARTS AND CRAFTS–inspired cottages in a GARDEN SUBURB setting, while at Claremont, under the direction of town planner Charles READE, a model village occupied the peninsula on the River Derwent. At these, as at New Norfolk and Maydena, landscape features including exotic avenues of trees were laid out. The envy of other workers, the Lutana housing project initially consisted of forty-two homes of concrete to suit 'artisan tenants', but hidden were poor work-place health standards. Enhanced facilities, including RECREATION facilities, partly offset complaints from residents. Such facilities were included in both the later ANM towns; at Maydena, company chairman Sir Keith MURDOCH was instrumental in facilitating planting of exotic trees in the midst of this eucalypt forest setting (from which his newsprint was manufactured). Today, although mostly freehold, these former company villages provide the amenity of mature landscapes
                                                PETER MacFIE

LYCETT, Joseph (*c.* 1775–1828), convict and artist, was raised in Staffordshire, England, and transported after conviction for forgery in 1811—a crime he again committed in Sydney in 1815, with confinement in Newcastle as his punishment. Granted a conditional pardon, he travelled throughout NSW and Van Diemen's Land during 1819–20, drawing PICTURESQUE landscapes that emphasised similarities between British prototypes and their Australian equivalents—particularly when they were private commissions. In 1820 Lycett drew plants collected by explorer John Oxley, and Governor Macquarie sent three landscapes, one of which was a large-scale *North View of Sydney*, to Earl Bathurst. With an absolute pardon, Lycett sailed for England in 1822, carrying the sketches used for his series of lithographs and aquatints, *Views in Australia* (1824–25), marketed to appeal to the growing British interest in the colonies and largely concentrating on the landscape settings of colonial houses. The original renditions and their modification for publication are among the best-known works of the early colony.

John Turner, *Joseph Lycett: Governor Macquarie's Convict Artist* (Newcastle, NSW, 1997)   COLLEEN MORRIS

LYNCH, Alfred (*c.* 1821–1887), amateur landscape gardener, probably arrived in Vic. (from London) in 1852. Although not initially a member of the Horticultural Society of Victoria, by 1860 Lynch held the important office of 'Collector' (of subscriptions—the tardy payment of which dogged many early horticultural societies). In that year the Society succeeded in obtaining a twenty-five-acre (10 ha) reserve in Richmond and an elaborate ITALIANATE plan, chosen in open competition (1861), was signed 'Plan of the/Experimental Gardens/of the Horticultural Society of Victoria—Survey Paddock/Richmond/Designed by Alfred Lynch Landscape Gardener Prahran'. By 1863, six acres (2.4 ha) had been laid out in an intricate geometric style 'unique to this country', although flood damage in 1864 caused the regrettable abandonment of Lynch's plan. Lynch achieved a second major success in 1861, when he won a competition sponsored by the ACCLIMATISATION Society for laying out Royal Park 'on a system of landscape gardening for zoological purposes'. His design has not been located, but it is quite possible that it formed the basis of the initial formal layout of the ZOOLOGICAL GARDENS. Apart from these two landmarks, little is known of his life. His appointment as 'collector' and his Prahran address point to his being the Alfred Lynch living in the Prahran/Windsor area by 1854, working as an inspector of weights and measures in 1870, and appointed by Prahran Borough Council in 1871 to a new position incorporating rate collector, valuer, receiver of the dog tax, collector of statistics, and kindred duties. RA

McALISTER, Edward James (b. 1942), horticulturist, was born in Northern Ireland, where he studied horticulture. He migrated to Australia in 1967 and initially worked at Jack Pike's nursery in Kellyville (NSW). In 1979, after completing a science degree at the University of New England, he was appointed horticultural botanist at the BOTANIC GARDENS OF ADELAIDE. In 1981 he was appointed Assistant Director of the Gardens, and since 1991 has been Director of Adelaide Zoo (with the added responsibility of Monarto Zoological Park). He is president of the Australasian Regional Association of Zoological Parks and Aquaria (1996–) and vice-president of the World Association of Zoos and Aquariums.

Ed McAlister's interests, while broadly based in environmental and ornamental horticulture, have centred on the development of plant collections, especially from ARID ZONES, for scientific and educational purposes in BOTANIC, ZOOLOGICAL, and trial gardens in SA. He has also served on a wide range of committees promoting horticultural EDUCATION and heritage CONSERVATION. He was an early member of the AUSTRALIAN INSTITUTE OF HORTICULTURE in SA and served on the state committee for many years, including executive positions; he also served on the Institute's national committee and was national president (1982–85). ML

MACARTHUR, John (1767–1834) soldier, entrepreneur, and pastoralist, was born at Plymouth, England, the son of a draper. Purchasing an ensign's commission in 1782, but placed on half-pay (1783–88), Macarthur acquired some farming knowledge in west Devon, where in 1788 he married Elizabeth Veale, a farmer's daughter. Transferring to the New South Wales Corps, he arrived in the colony with his wife and infant son in the Second Fleet (1790). A haughty, ambitious young lieutenant, Macarthur secured appointments that gave him extensive control over the colony's resources of materials and convict labour. In 1793 the family removed to 'a very excellent' brick house on **Elizabeth Farm**, Macarthur's first land grant of 100 acres (40 ha) on the river at Parramatta, which was soon under cultivation: the house was surrounded by a VINEYARD, ORCHARD, and a three-acre (1.2 ha) garden of 'most excellent vegetables'. Promoted to captain in 1795, Macarthur acquired properties in nearby districts, and by 1800 was one of the largest stock and landholders in the colony. Elizabeth Farm, which ultimately comprised more than 1000 acres (400 ha), was to remain John and Elizabeth Macarthur's principal residence; their seven surviving children—four sons and three daughters—inherited their parents' interest in horticulture.

Macarthur's driving ambition and abrasive personality inevitably led to conflict with successive governors of the colony. Sent to England under arrest in 1801 for duelling with the lieutenant-governor, Macarthur promoted the colony's fine wool potential, and through the influence of Lord Camden, Secretary of State, resigned from the army and returned triumphantly to NSW in 1805 with Spanish sheep from the Royal flocks, an order for 5000 acres (2025 ha)—subsequently selected at the Cowpastures, south-west of Sydney which he named **Camden Park**—and the promise of another 5000 acres if the fine wool venture succeeded.

Exiled from the colony between 1809 and 1817 as the 'leading Promoter and Instigator' of the deposing of Governor Bligh, Macarthur in England expanded his trading activities, oversaw the arrival and sales of his wool clip, and devised methods for its improvement. He toured France and Switzerland on foot in 1815–16, inspecting vineyards and investigating methods of agriculture. Permitted to return to NSW in 1817, Macarthur built a greenhouse on *Lord Eldon*'s deck to accommodate an extensive collection of plants comprising grape vines, fruit trees, and other plants, many new to the colony including the 'cork tree' (*Quercus suber*) and the China rose (*Rosa chinensis*).

Elizabeth Macarthur (née Veale) (1766–1850) endured her husband's enforced absences with resignation. With minimal support, she was left with the responsibility of their younger children, the family properties, the breeding of the valuable merino flock at Camden, and the export of its wool clip, contributing immeasurably to the wool industry in this critical phase. Her letters, written with clarity and insight on many aspects of the colony, reflect her admiration of native flora and the pleasure she derived from Elizabeth Farm's garden. The four Macarthur sons completed their education in England; Edward and John remained abroad for most of their lives. James and William accompanied their father to England in 1809 and to France and Switzerland 1815–16. They returned in 1817 and moved to Camden Park.

A man of 'violent passions', John Macarthur's mental stability deteriorated in the 1820s; during periods of lucidity he immersed himself in planning a family mansion at Camden

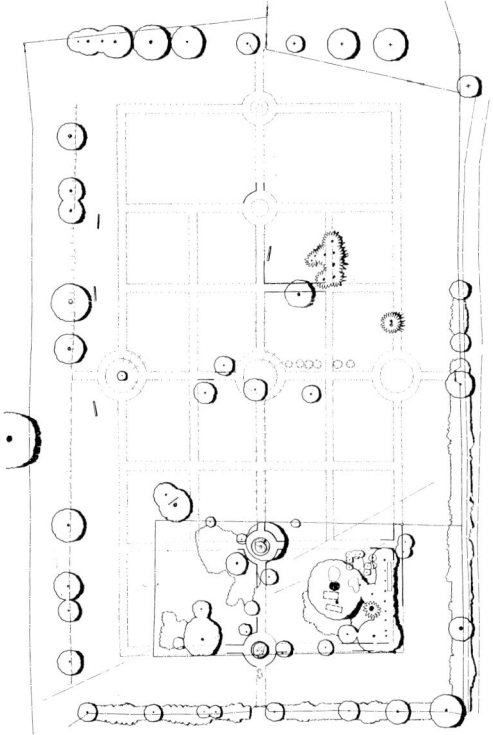

Reconstructed plan (1993) of the lower garden at Camden Park, the site of William MACARTHUR'S NURSERY, which is often overlooked as one of the most significant sites of Australian horticulture

and in building schemes for Elizabeth Farm, where his attention to the garden had not diminished. Thomas MITCHELL, a visitor in 1831, was impressed by the 'many interesting trees and plants which that most ingenious gentleman is endeavouring to propagate in the colony':

> I saw the first olive planted in Australia; the cork-tree in luxuriance; the caper, growing among the rocks; the English Oak; the horse-chesnut; broom; magnificent mulberry trees of thirty five years growth, umbrageous and green; great variety of roses in beds, also climbing roses, I saw Greek pirates at work training the vines to trellices [sic] which had just been erected according to the method of their country. The state of the Orange trees was remarkable …

John Macarthur, declared insane in 1832, died at Camden Park and was buried there on a rise within view of his unfinished mansion. Elizabeth Macarthur continued to live at Elizabeth Farm until her death.

Edward Macarthur (1789–1872), soldier and administrator, inherited the Elizabeth Farm estate. Sent to England in 1797 to be educated, and subsequently serving with the British army abroad, his visits to Elizabeth Farm were relatively brief. To his family the avenues of cypresses he planted there in 1806–08 were a constant fond reminder of one such visit. On another in 1824, Edward started the garden at The Cottage (now Hambledon), his residence on the estate, and presented a variety of trees to SYDNEY BOTANIC GARDENS.

Posted to Ireland in 1825, Edward dispatched plants to William at Camden: twenty varieties of roses, and a collection of 180 arbutus, elm, beech, and birch trees, some of which still embellish the garden. William relied on their brother, John junior (1794–1831), a London barrister, to act as the family's wool representative and to seek the most suitable pasture grasses, of which he sent vast quantities of seeds to Camden. After Edward's death in England, Elizabeth Farm estate was sold in 1881 and subdivided. A century later, the house and one hectare of its garden, still containing remnants of Macarthur plantings (including an olive (*Olea europea*) possibly planted by John Macarthur in 1805), were restored and opened to the public.

William Macarthur (1800–1882), horticulturist and plant breeder, and his older brother James (1798–1867) were lifelong companions. At Camden Park, where they lived from 1820 in the cottage and from 1835 in the newly completed mansion, they drew on their 1815–16 European experiences and observations to install innovative IRRIGATION systems for the orchards and vineyards, planted out with the collections brought back in 1817. Camden Park estate was increased to 28 000 acres (11 330 ha), developing like a feudal estate with tenant farmers and its own private township. The flocks were moved to more suitable pastoral leases on the Lachlan and Murrumbidgee rivers. William concentrated on wine production and the establishment of the Camden park nursery, which attracted many visitors and correspondents including J.C. BIDWILL and Ludwig Leichhardt, and from which many early donations of grafts and trees were made to Thomas SHEPHERD and Sydney Botanic Gardens. The Macarthurs' dire financial circumstances in the 1840s depression continued until the mid-1850s. Historian James Broadbent has suggested that William published the Camden Park nursery catalogues in 1843 and 1845 primarily to generate income from plant sales. These catalogues, and the 1850 and 1857 editions, remain a significant source of information on plants available in the colony.

William and James Macarthur both served as members of the legislature, as president of the Agricultural Society of New South Wales, and as trustees of cultural institutions. In 1855 William was Commissioner for NSW at the International Exhibition in Paris; he was awarded the *Légion d'honneur* and knighted in 1856. Emily, James Macarthur's wife, oversaw the running of Camden Park during the brothers' parliamentary absences and, like Elizabeth Macarthur, remained a stabilising influence in the family. William's nephew, Edward Macarthur BOWMAN, was the only member of the next generation to maintain a continuing involvement with plants, both as a breeder and then collector.

William Macarthur's voluminous horticultural and viticultural correspondence, papers, and plans record the breadth of his extraordinary contribution to Australia's horticulture and garden history. Using the pseudonym 'Maro' he published widely on viticulture. Multilingual, he corresponded and exchanged plants and bulbs with curators of botanic gardens, collectors, and botanists in England, Europe, and Asia. Invoices and correspondence spanning fifty years document his large purchases from London nurseries (usually Veitch and

Loddiges). Numerous notebooks record PLANT BREEDING successes and failures of fruit trees, CAMELLIAS, ROSES, ORCHIDS, and other plants; others record the orchards or vineyards; another provides a detailed inventory (*c.* 1833) of the lower garden at Camden Park, possibly laid out by Naismith ROBERTSON. Letters and sales books document the extensive mid-century distribution of Camden Park grape vines, plants, and bulbs to the four south-eastern colonies, directly or through nurseries. Camden Park employees included Edward BLAKE, Francis FERGUSON, and Silas SHEATHER; Ferguson and Sheather went on to establish successful nurseries, Sheather's on the Elizabeth Farm estate. Thomas REEDY, a long-term employee, was sent as a plant collector on the *Chevert* expedition in 1875. Such was the fame of the Camden Park garden that John Gould VEITCH claimed in an effusive review: 'The collection of plants and fruits at Camden is by far the best that I have seen in the colony. No means have been spared to obtain the best varieties in each case.'

Camden Park was inherited by James and Emily's only child, Elizabeth, who had married Arthur Onslow in 1867; the house is still occupied by her descendants. Phylloxera later destroyed the renowned vineyards. Well into the 1930s Camden Park was still a major supplier to exclusive Sydney florists. The Macarthur papers, an outstanding family archive, was presented by descendants to the Mitchell Library, State Library of New South Wales, and continues to contribute to Australian historiography. Rare nineteenth-century botanical books and journals from the Camden Park library are now held in public collections in Canberra.

M.H. Ellis, *John Macarthur* (Sydney, 1955); J.M. Ward, *James Macarthur: Colonial Conservative, 1798–1867* (Sydney, 1981); James Broadbent, *Elizabeth Farm: A History and a Guide* (Glebe, NSW, 1984); Joy Hughes, *The Macarthurs: A Brief Family History* (Glebe, NSW, 1984); Alan Atkinson, *Camden: Farm and Village Life in Early New South Wales* (Melbourne, 1988); Paul Fox, *Clearings: Six Colonial Gardeners and their Landscapes* (Carlton South, Vic., forthcoming, 2003) JOY HUGHES

McARTHUR (née EVANS), Kathleen Rennie (1915–2000), wildflower painter, and conservationist, was born in Brisbane. Her interest in the environment was awakened as a child when she explored her Queensland environs. She married in 1938 and withdrew into domesticity. Her introduction to flower painting came in 1950, when she began recording the native flowering plants of North Pine (where she was then living) with the help of Wilfrid Blunt's definitive text *The Art of Botanical Illustration*. Drawn to the Sunshine Coast by the beauty and abundance of its wildflowers, McArthur was to make the preservation of the coastal landscape her life's mission. In 1953 she set out to make a full year's record of the blossoming of the coastal wildflowers, resulting in the first of her books, *Queensland Wildflowers: A Selection* (1959). In recent decades she became a leader of the conservation movement in Qld; together with the poet Judith Wright and naturalist David Fleay, McArthur founded the Wildlife Preservation Society of Queensland (1962). She published eight books, including *Bush in Bloom* (1982) and *Looking at Australian Wildflowers* (1986). JUDITH McKAY

McCRAE, Georgiana Huntly (1804–1890), London-born artist and diarist, arrived with her children in Port Phillip in 1841, joining her husband, Andrew, and other members of the family who had migrated in 1839. She was well educated, a talented linguist and musician, and painter of award-winning portraits and miniatures. The family moved to Mayfield, near Abbotsford, in 1842, where she planted a substantial garden. Between 1845 and 1851, the family lived at the Arthurs Seat run (now a NATIONAL TRUST property), where she also gardened. After Andrew abandoned squatting to become a police magistrate, McCrae lived in Melbourne with her children. At both Mayfield and Arthurs Seat she drew and painted watercolours and miniatures. She represented refinement and taste to those with literary and artistic interests, yet was also extremely practical in her dealings with the indigenous people, droving cattle and horses, attending to medical emergencies, planting bulbs, or making gauze bags to protect the peaches from grasshoppers. Her journals, which were rewritten later in life (and published 1934), include entries on garden plants and techniques, and give a very personal sense of the way plants were enjoyed and shared in Port Phillip in the mid-nineteenth century.

Brenda Niall, *Georgiana: A Biography of Georgiana McCrae, Painter, Diarist, Pioneer* (Carlton South, Vic., 1994)
GWEN PASCOE

MACDONALD, Donald Alaster (1857–1932), naturalist and journalist, began preparing his reflections on nature and sketches of country life in 1881 for the daily Melbourne *Argus* (under his initials) and the weekly *AUSTRALASIAN* (as 'Gnuyang'). He wrote with nostalgia about the rural charm of Keilor (Vic.) where he had grown up, and described the valley's rhythms and rituals. A collection of his sketches was published as *Gum Boughs and Wattle Bloom* (1887). As the title suggests, he eschewed the use of taxonomic names, preferring popular names, which he felt were 'generally more expressive and appropriate'. One article, 'A Melbourne Garden', discussed with much poetic embellishment the MELBOURNE BOTANIC GARDENS. Early last century he began a popular new column, 'Nature Notes and Queries', in the Saturday *Argus*, later joined by 'Notes for Boys'. His *Bush Boy's Book* (1911) was an ideal handbook for the new scouting movement in Australia. He also wrote the columns 'Glimpses of Nature' in the women's magazine, *New Idea*, and 'Bush Notes' in the *Australasian*. He had an enduring interest in the sandy coastal heathlands at Black Rock, and following his death a small area, named Macdonald Park, was fenced as a sanctuary for the local birds and flora. Through his columns 'Mac' influenced many, young and old, to appreciate the joy and beauty of nature. LINDEN GILLBANK

McEWIN, George (1815–1885), landscape gardener, horticulturist, and fruit grower and preserver, was born in Galloway, Scotland, and worked in Liverpool, England, laying out several large gardens and estates before arriving in Adelaide via Melbourne in 1839. His botanist and gardening father, John Nash McEwin (1792–1855), a native of Kirkcudbright, Scotland, had migrated to Melbourne in 1838 and established a nursery at Heidelberg. George McEwin was immediately engaged by George STEVENSON to manage his North Adelaide and LEAWOOD GARDENS, and encouraged to write the *South Australian Vigneron and Gardeners' Manual* (1843). He worked for George Anstey (1814–1895) at Highercombe in 1843, before establishing his Glen Ewin property in the ADELAIDE HILLS near Houghton in 1844–45. In 1845 he planted a vineyard and in 1854 constructed winery facilities, which ceased production in 1891 in favour of jams. His jam production had begun in 1861 due to the volume of fruit cultivation, and was increased to meet demand (as its reputation grew) by importing fruits from throughout SA, Vic., and Tas.; McEwin's products gained medals in colonial and European exhibitions, and he steadily acquired more machinery and enhanced factory facilities.

McEwin was a prolific writer, and *A Classification of Plants in Scotland* (1833) earned him a fellowship from the Scottish Arboricultural Society; he won a gold medal for *The Natural Forests of South Australia* (1876) and a silver medal for *Arboriculture* (1877). He regularly contributed to the *Adelaide Observer*, *Farm and Garden*, and *Garden and Field*, and wrote *The Preparation of Dried and Preserved Fruits* (1872). Maintaining correspondence with Dr James Brown in Scotland, he was central to the appointment of John Ednie BROWN as conservator of forests. McEwin was also a proponent of scientific agriculture, lending support to Albert MOLINEUX and attempts to establish ROSEWORTHY AGRICULTURAL COLLEGE, and various horticultural and agricultural societies and boards. Mac's death was widely lamented, and obituarists hailed him as a pioneer of South Australian horticultural and forestry development.

Robert McEwin (1847–1929), son of George McEwin, carried on the jam-making business. One of George's brothers, Joseph Nash McEwin (1829–1914), settled in Karoola (Tas.) where a son, (Robert) Hamilton McEwin (1874–1954), wrote *The Fruitgrower's Handbook: A Practical Work on Australian Horticulture* (1910). DAVID JONES

MacGILLIVRAY, John (1821–1867), Scottish-born naturalist, was son of the ornithologist William MacGillivray, sometime Regius professor of natural history, Marischal College, Aberdeen, Scotland. He gave up his medical studies to serve as naturalist (from 1842) on HMS *Fly*, HMS *Rattlesnake* (with Thomas Henry Huxley as his assistant, and about which he published a *Narrative* in 1852), and finally HMS *Herald*, from which he was dismissed for drunkenness. From these voyages of exploration around Australia and the South PACIFIC he sent specimens of several hundred plant species to Sir William HOOKER. He married in Sydney (1848) but had difficulty making a living there as a scientist, so worked for five years in the South Sea Islands, having 'many strange adventures and hairbreadth escapes'. Returning to Sydney in 1861 he contributed papers on economic plants to Sydney's leading HORTICULTURAL SOCIETIES. He collected plants for influential members, such as John Thomas BAPTIST and Michael GUILFOYLE, especially after moving to Grafton (1864). He compiled Guilfoyle's 1862 catalogue and sought similar work from other nursery proprietors. In a sympathetic obituary Luke WOOFF wrote that 'being poor … much of his labours thus went before the public with an unknown or false signature'. RICHARD CLOUGH

McGOWAN, William (1858–1939), landscape gardener and parks superintendent, was born in Banffshire, Scotland, of a farming family. He served his apprenticeship at Ardoe House, Deeside, near Aberdeen, and was subsequently appointed outside foreman at Dunecht, the Scottish residence of the Earl of Crawford and Balcarras. He arrived in Launceston (Tas.), in 1882 and was appointed Superintendent of Parks and Reserves by the municipal council (1882–1937). In that capacity, he placed his stamp upon the major PUBLIC PARKS of the city, including CITY PARK, ROYAL PARK, CATARACT GORGE (including the Cliff Grounds), and, to a lesser extent, PRINCE'S SQUARE. He arranged the FERNERY at the entrance to the Launceston EXHIBITION (1891–92) with 'consummate skill', capturing the great popularity of this form of landscaping. From 1910 onwards, in response to a fashion for ROCKERIES, McGowan introduced rockwork to many Launceston parks, as well as in minor street reservations, utilising large uncut stones of local basalt, weathered brown in colour, and loosely placed. The *Cyclopaedia of Tasmania* (1900) praised his landscaping: 'so well and tastefully did he carry out the work that the "air lungs" of the city are now the pride of the residents and the admiration of visitors'. William McGowan (1887–1945) succeeded his father as superintendent. He was known as an authority on begonias and was responsible for the extensive planting of King Alfred daffodils in the Cataract Gorge Cliff Grounds, but otherwise remained very much in his father's shadow. ANNE NEALE

MACHATTIE PARK, Bathurst, NSW, named for medical practitioner and mayor, Richard Machattie (1813–1876), is a large, late nineteenth-century PUBLIC PARK in the centre of the city possessing a substantially intact layout and valuable plantings. It was laid out on a former gaol site, to the design of architect James Hine, in a basically geometric form with bisecting axes—one linking to the courthouse and the other through a cast-iron FOUNTAIN and timber BANDSTAND. Cross and diagonal paths subdivide the remaining space, intersecting at the various features and monuments, including a GREENHOUSE and the Queen Anne-style LODGE (1890), also designed by Hine, and the Munro Memorial DRINKING FOUNTAIN. The park incorporated some informal details, such as a free-shaped pond with adjacent walkways. Machattie Park was originally fenced, and the gates and elm plantings remain as a border. Other plantings include cedars, magnolias, and Bunya pines. BARBARA VAN DEN BROEK

McINNIS, Ronald Allison (1890–1982), surveyor and town planner, was born and educated in Mackay (Qld), and from the 1920s undertook a professional planning career in Qld, NT, and Tas. He was instrumental in the revival of the Queensland Town Planning Association and actively campaigned for a Greater Brisbane Council (established 1925). McInnis was responsible for planning and surveying Noosa (1929), regarded as 'the first Queensland town to be planned and zoned before settlement', and prepared a comprehensive town planning scheme for Mackay (1935). In 1944, as Brisbane City Planner (1935–45), he submitted a detailed zoning scheme for the capital city that included a permanent GREEN BELT on the urban fringe. By invitation of the Northern Territory Administrator, McInnis prepared a comprehensive Darwin Town Plan (1940), which he revised in 1944. Neither plan was realised. He was appointed Tasmania's Town and Country Planning Commissioner in 1945 when one of his roles was to sell the advantages of the *Town and Country Planning Act* (1944) to local councils. He retired in 1956, remembered as one of Australia's TOWN PLANNING pioneers. CHRISTINE GARNAUT

McINTOSH, Charles (1794–1864), Scottish-born landscape gardener, author, and horticultural journalist, succeeded his father as gardener at Abercairny, and then took management of the garden at Taymouth Castle. He was a correspondent of LOUDON, and *c.* 1829 became head gardener to Prince Leopold of Saxe-Coburg Saalfeld and his wife Charlotte (daughter of George IV), at their celebrated English seat of Claremont, Surrey, where he undertook numerous improvements. After the accession of Leopold to the Belgian throne in 1831, he also supervised remodelling of the garden at their Brussels residence.

McIntosh (often printed M'Intosh according to nineteenth-century convention) wrote his first book, *The Practical Gardener and Modern Horticulturist*, in 1828, and it was revised and reprinted many times. In it he devoted a special section to the Australian-House ('an object of interest and gratification') at a time when New Holland and Cape plants were popular in Britain. In *The Flower Garden* (1837–38) he codified four national styles—Italian, French, Dutch and English—asserting the superiority of rectilinear over rococo styles of bedding. *The Greenhouse, Hot House and Stove* (1838) was published in uniform style.

In 1838 McIntosh accepted the position of head gardener to the Duke of Buccleuch at Dalkeith Palace, south of Edinburgh. As one of Britain's leading horticultural authorities, McIntosh presided over the garden with untrammelled authority, and Dalkeith became a byword for excellence, sought by apprentice and aristocrat alike. Many gardeners who worked under McIntosh migrated to Australia, with some, like Josiah MITCHELL, achieving positions of pre-eminence in their adopted country. While at Dalkeith, McIntosh acted as horticultural editor of the *North British Agriculturist and Journal of Horticulture* (1849–51), and in its pages he showed himself to be a keen student of history—perhaps germane to his interest in the revival of formal geometric gardens. His major new illustrated work, the *Book of the Garden* (1853–55), was well received and, with KEMP's *How to Lay Out a Garden*, formed a bible for the post-Loudonian generation of emigrant gardeners, and was held by many colonial LIBRARIES.

McIntosh retired from Dalkeith in 1855 and was succeeded by William THOMSON. He then worked independently as a 'landscape gardener and garden architect', a successor to his compatriot, Charles H.J. SMITH, in this field. He also conducted the horticultural department of the *Scottish Farmer* for some years, before his death in Edinburgh. His high place in

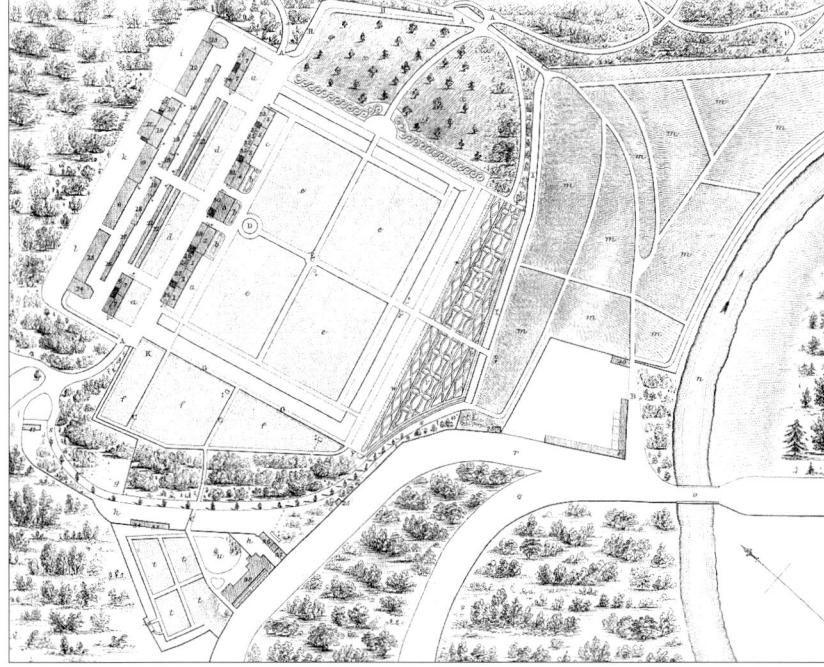

The KITCHEN GARDEN at Dalkeith, Scotland, laid out by Charles MCINTOSH in the 1840s and illustrated in his *Book of the Garden* (1853–55), was a formal training ground for many emigrant GARDENERS

MacIVOR, (Ralph Waldo) Emerson (c. 1856–1917), agricultural chemist and lecturer, was born at Leeds, Yorkshire, England, and educated in Scotland. He accepted an offer in 1876, from W.J. Clarke of RUPERTSWOOD, to deliver a course of lectures and demonstrations to Victorian farmers, at a time when scientific farming, including application of CHEMICALS, was emerging from an age of suspicion. Two books (1879), the *Chemistry of Agriculture* and *Agricultural Chemistry*, were based on the lectures and contained contributions on geology and water conservation by local experts as well as MUELLER's paper 'Creation, Maintenance, and Enrichment of Forests'. MacIvor moved to NSW, where he was the inaugural instructor in agriculture for the Board of Technical Education (1884–85), succeeded by Angus MACKAY. He returned to Britain in 1886. RA

MACK, Amy Eleanor (1876–1939), author and naturalist, was born at Port Adelaide and moved with her family to Sydney in 1882. Mack edited the *Sydney Morning Herald* women's page (1907–14) and published several collections of essays, including *A Bush Calendar* (1909), *Bush Days* (1911), and *The Wilderness* (1922), ruing the bushland destruction then rampant around her North Shore home. Her CHILDREN'S LITERATURE including *Bushland Stories* (1910) encouraged NATURE STUDY, using tales such as 'The Story of the Turpentines' (referring to the Australian tree *Syncarpia glomulifera*) and 'The Gallant Gum Tree'. RA

MACKAY, Angus (1834–1910), agriculturalist, politician, and instructor, was born at Wick, Caithness, Scotland. His career was varied—bridge worker in London, compositor on the *New York Tribune*, and overseer on a Georgia cotton plantation—before his return to London and migration to Qld (1863). He pursued journalism in the newly separated colony, and as the first editor of the QUEENSLANDER (1866) he emulated the weekly press of the southern colonies in the inclusion of horticulture. His great interest in horticulture and agriculture placed him at the forefront of the ACCLIMATISATION movement and he was a council member of the Queensland Acclimatisation Society. His writing in Qld included publications on cotton, sugar cane, and native grasses, and a comprehensive treatise, *The Semi-tropical Agriculturist and Colonists' Guide* (1875), with editions in the 1890s titled *The Australian Agriculturist*; all drew on his articles first published in the *Queenslander* and other weekly papers. He was a Queensland commissioner for the Centennial Philadelphia Exhibition (1876) and returned inspired by American technology and ideas he had witnessed. He represented South Brisbane (1878–80) as a Member of the Legislative Assembly.

Mackay moved to Sydney in 1880, editing the (AUSTRALIAN) TOWN AND COUNTRY JOURNAL—again devoting considerable space to gardening and horticulture—and instructing in agriculture at Sydney Technical College (1885–97). He continued his prolific publishing output with *Elements of Australian Agriculture* (1885), *Grazing, Farm, and Garden Soils* (1888), and *Helpful Chemistry for Agriculturists* (1894)—*Helpful Chemistry* being jointly published with the Orange Judd Publishing Co. (New York), which included many agricultural and horticultural titles in its list. He was also a frequent contributor to *Castner's Rural Australian*, his writings suffused with American ideas. Mackay retired to Scotland, where he became a journalist with the *Celtic Herald*. After his death at Portobello, Scotland, *Table Talk* lamented the passing of a man of such broad intellect and great energy. Among his contemporaries, his knowledge of and enthusiasm for North American agriculture and economic horticulture was without equal in Australia. RA

H.V. McKAY MEMORIAL GARDENS (formerly Sunshine Gardens), Sunshine, Vic., was developed from 1909 as an amenity for the workers of the Sunshine Harvester Works. Hugh Victor McKay (1865–1926) started to develop his factory in 1904, and by the end of the decade was employing 1000 people, many housed in his GARDEN SUBURB. The Sunshine Gardens, planned by landscape gardener Horsfall from Ballarat, incorporated RECREATION facilities alongside popular horticultural display. With long curatorships ensuring continuity of management, the Sunshine Gardens under inaugural curator S.G. Thompson (1909–27), James Willan (1930–39), and Harold GRAY (1939–50), became a showpiece for CHRYSANTHEMUMS and DAHLIAS, and a Mecca for workers, their families, and local residents. McKay died at his residence, RUPERTSWOOD, only a week after laying the foundation stone of Sunshine Presbyterian Church, set within the Gardens. Management of this early privately funded INDUSTRIAL GARDEN was handed to the newly established City of Sunshine in 1953, when the site was renamed. RA

MACKENZIE, Bruce Alexander (b. 1932), landscape architect, is known nationally for the design of some of Sydney's most innovative harbourside parks, notably Illoura Reserve (1970) and Long Nose Point (1976) in Balmain. Between 1968 and 1993 he directed Bruce Mackenzie and Associates, and now practises as Bruce Mackenzie Design, specialising in the industrial design of furniture for public places, but continuing to consult on prestigious projects such as Sydney's Millennium Park (2000).

Born in Sydney, he developed, through bushwalking and canoeing, a passionate love of natural environments, and this has been a continuing influence on his design philosophy, and is reflected in his use of natural structural materials and NATIVE PLANT species. With contemporaries Harry HOWARD and Bruce RICKARD, he was one of Australia's foremost practitioners in the 1960s to promote an approach to landscape design, which, while not based on rigorous ecological principles, nevertheless respected and harmonised with natural environments. Essentially self-taught—'At no stage was I influenced by the doctrines of a formal school of landscape teaching', he wrote in 1974—his design philosophy combines a personal romantic attachment to landscape aesthetics with a pragmatic approach to conservation resulting from years of prior experience in landscape construction. Both Illoura

Designed by Bruce MACKENZIE and illustrated in *Landscape Australia* (1981) with the sketches of Barry Mitchell, this PUBLIC PARK at Botany Bay (NSW) was shaped from sand along a reclaimed foreshore as 'a giant environmental sculpture ... inspired by the voluptuous forms of Nature's sandcoast'

Reserve and Long Nose Point were designed to give city dwellers an alternative to conventional parks, and, especially, to capture and establish the 'mood-experience of remote natural places within the confines of the city'. Their continuing popularity over twenty-five years, together with the fact that other designers have adopted the same basic ingredients, is testament to the enduring qualities of this philosophy.

The 1970s to early 1990s were Mackenzie's most productive years. Major commissions included William Balmain Teachers College (now University of Technology Sydney), Sir Joseph Banks Park, Sydney International Airport, and Coogee Beach Plaza in Sydney; Tuggeranong New Town and the Australian Defence Force Academy in the ACT; and, overseas, the Australian embassies in Bangkok and Paris.

Although not a founding member, Mackenzie was admitted to corporate membership of the AUSTRALIAN INSTITUTE OF LANDSCAPE ARCHITECTS in 1968, and has always played an active role in the Institute, serving on the National Council and elected National President in 1981. He has published a number of articles, chiefly about his design philosophy, in *Landscape Australia*. In 1981, together with the eminent American landscape architect Lawrence Halprin, he was one of the panel of judges for the Newcastle Foreshores Competition.

ALLAN CORREY

McKINNON, Ross David (b. 1949), horticulturist, curator, and media presenter, was born in Adelaide and trained at Adelaide Botanic Garden. He undertook further study in Brisbane and has been Curator of BRISBANE BOTANIC GARDENS (Mount Coot-tha) since 1983. He is a passionate horticultural educator and supporter of horticultural societies in Qld. He was a national board member of Australia's Open Garden Scheme (1996–98) and chaired the Heads of Australian Botanic Gardens Council (1999). His writings include a regular garden column in Brisbane's *Sunday Mail*. His RADIO and TELEVISION work includes popular gardening segments on the Australian Broadcasting Corporation and commercial networks.

JEANNIE SIM

McLAREN, Christine (*fl.* 1940–60s), horticultural journalist, is remembered today for her book *Everywoman's Gardening Book* (*c.* 1964)—the first Australian GARDENING BOOK to specifically address women in its title, and written with the conviction 'that most gardening is done, or at least planned, by women'. She lived for many years in western Qld before moving to Brisbane, where, with her family, she established a nursery and florist's shop. During the 1950s she contributed a gardening column to Brisbane's *Sunday Mail*, and compiled the *Sunday Mail Vegetable Gardening Book* and

Sunday Mail Gardening Book. She edited several editions of *Queensland Garden Annual* during the 1960s and contributed to the magazine *Queensland Garden*. RA

McLAREN VALE (or Southern Vales), SA, a valley to the south of Adelaide, is noted for its red and white wines, and ports. John REYNELL first planted vines at Reynella (1838), followed by Dr Alexander KELLY at Morphett Vale (1845) and at his Tintara Vineyards (1861) that were later acquired by Thomas HARDY, and George Manning at Hope Farm (1855), now called Seaview. Renewed interest in viticulture in the 1880s led to more plantings by Messrs Horn and Frampton at Glenroth, by Frederick Wilkinson at Ryecroft (1884), by William Hammond at Amery (1884), and at Pirramimma by A.C. Johnston (1892). While VITICULTURE dominates the character of the Vales, it is also known for its almonds, and intensive AGRICULTURE. Today, viticultural expansion is strongly regulated in the area due to water supply shortages. DAVID JONES

McLEAY, Alexander (1767–1848), public servant and entomologist, was born at Wick, a fishing village in Ross-shire, Scotland. He moved to London in 1786, marrying Elizabeth Barclay there in 1791. McLeay, who was employed in the civil service (1795–1817), was well known in British and European NATURAL HISTORY circles, having amassed by 1805 one of the most significant insect collections in Britain. He was elected a Fellow of the Linnean Society of London in 1794 and served as its secretary (1798–1825). He was elected a Fellow of the Royal Society in 1809. Robert BROWN, McLeay's close friend and suitor of his eldest daughter Fanny, a competent botanical artist, named the genus *Macleaya* in his honour. In enforced retirement from 1817 when his department was abolished at the end of the Napoleonic wars, McLeay's finances were stretched to support a large family (ten of seventeen children survived to adulthood), town and country residences, and his obsessive purchasing of insects. When assets had to be sold upon the collapse of his brother's private bank at Wick, in which he was a partner, he began in 1824 to borrow heavily from his eldest son, William.

McLeay accepted the position of Colonial Secretary of New South Wales, arriving in Sydney in 1826 and moving into the colonial secretary's house (fronting MACQUARIE PLACE) with his wife Eliza, their six surviving daughters, an extensive LIBRARY, and an insect collection then 'unparalleled in England' for its size, range, and number of type specimens. Three of the four surviving sons came later to NSW, of whom two—William and George Macleay—shared their father's natural history interests. (From the early 1820s the spelling Macleay was adopted; descendants of Alexander's brothers retained MacLeay or McLeay.)

On his fifty-four-acre (22 ha) grant at Elizabeth Bay, with its commanding views of Sydney Harbour, McLeay employed his horticultural expertise, assisted from the late 1820s by gardener Robert HENDERSON, to establish a private botanic garden with picturesque features of dwarf stone walls, rustic bridges, and winding gravel walks. Construction of **Elizabeth Bay House** began in 1835, and the family removed to 'the finest house in the colony' in 1839. The garden became known internationally through the letters and published accounts of local naturalists and visiting scientific expeditions:

> The drive to the house is cut through rocks covered with splendid wild shrubs and flowers of this country, and here and there an immense primeval tree … In this garden are the plants of every climate—flowers and trees from Rio, the West Indies, the East Indies, and even England. The bulbs from the Cape are splendid … you would not believe how beautiful the roses are here … Mr Macleay has also an immense collection from New Zealand.

To Joseph HOOKER in 1841, it was 'a botanist's paradise. My surprise was unbounded at the natural beauties of the spot, the inimitable taste with which the grounds were laid out and the number and rarity of the plants which were collected together.'

McLeay corresponded with and sent indigenous species to KEW, donated exotics to SYDNEY BOTANIC GARDENS, supplied trees to Thomas SHEPHERD, exchanged plants with William MACARTHUR, encouraged local naturalists, and promoted exploration. As a member of numerous public and charitable committees, he exerted considerable influence in the establishment of the Australian Museum, the Australian Subscription Library, and more particularly on policy at the Botanic Gardens.

McLeay, who had served diligently as Colonial Secretary, was ousted from office by Governor Bourke in 1837. The loss of salary added to his financial problems: British debts were unpaid; mortgages that had funded the lavish expenditure on both Elizabeth Bay and Brownlow Hill, his country house near Camden, were due; pastoral ventures failed in the 1840s depression. McLeay, whose bankruptcy was averted by his eldest son William, assigned ownership of Elizabeth Bay House and estate to him in 1845 as settlement of numerous previous loans, and bitterly moved to Brownlow Hill. McLeay was elected Speaker of the Legislative Council (1843–46). Injured in a carriage accident in 1846, and still suffering the effects, he died at Tivoli, Rose Bay, the home of one of his daughters.

William Sharp Macleay (1792–1865), public servant, scholar, and naturalist, and eldest son, inherited his father's renowned insect collection. **George Macleay** (1809–1891), pastoralist and explorer, and third surviving son, inherited his father's debts. Two contrasting personalities, William, a Cambridge classical scholar, controversial pre-Darwinian theorist, author and contributor to leading scientific journals, and recluse; George a pragmatist, and subsequently a peripatetic bon vivant; the brothers, individually and jointly, contributed to the colony's scientific and horticultural advancement. Both were involved with the Botanic Gardens, Australian Museum and, beginning with their father, maintained an unbroken connection with the Linnean Society of London (1794–1891).

The 1875 estate sale plan of MCLEAY's Elizabeth Bay Estate depicts the surviving PLEASURE GARDEN and ORANGERY of this celebrated early colonial garden amid subdivided allotments

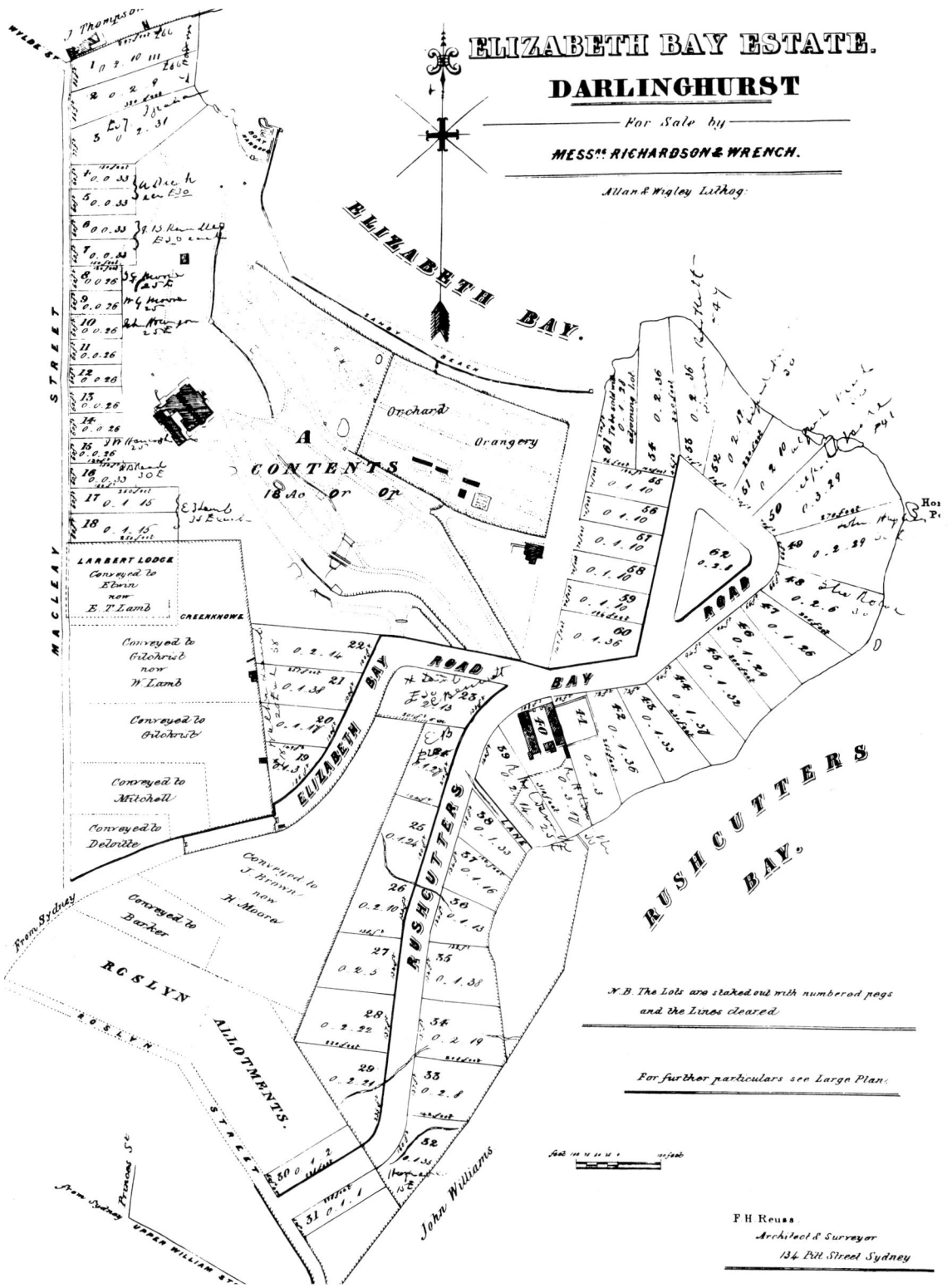

William arrived in NSW in 1839 with important collections of insects from South Africa (on which he published) and from Cuba where he was posted by the British Government (1825–36), as well as a large collection of plants. At Elizabeth Bay, two notebooks of plants and seeds exchanged, imported, or desired for its garden, which he compiled with his father, reflect the extent of their horticultural pursuits and provide vital records of this outstanding colonial garden. William was a corresponding member of the Royal Botanic Society of London. During his residency at Elizabeth Bay—with the family from 1839 and alone from 1845—the house continued as a favoured location for local and visiting scientists and Sydney's intellectual circle. William Sharp Macleay died unmarried, entailing the Elizabeth Bay estate to his brother George and leaving the insect collection to his cousin William John Macleay.

George Macleay had arrived in NSW in 1827 and moved to his father's property, **Brownlow Hill**, at Cobbitty near Camden, where, levelling the top of a small hill, he laid out the picturesque garden (with the assistance of Henderson) and in 1834 built a new residence, below which, at the entrance gates, he created a pond retained by a balustraded stone wall embellished with urns. Still redolent of the Macleays, both house and garden, owned by the Downes family since the 1860s, remain outstanding colonial examples. Accompanying Charles Sturt on his five-month expedition to the Murrumbidgee and Murray rivers (1829–30), George received the first of his pastoral grants. He inherited Brownlow Hill and its mortgages; his successful management of the property and other pastoral holdings enabled the trustees to finally settle his father's estate in 1859, after which George moved to England, acquiring Pendell Court, Surrey, where he propagated orchids between his frequent journeying to Europe and the Near East. Inheriting from William in 1865 a life interest in the Elizabeth Bay estate, George progressively subdivided and sold leaseholds of a substantial portion and leased the house to his cousin William John Macleay. He was knighted in 1869 and appointed KCMG in 1875; married twice and without issue, he died in France. A keen zoologist, he had donated specimens to his brother and to the Australian Museum; he presented the papers of his father and his brother William to the Linnean Society of London and through Charles Nicholson, Greek statuary to the University of Sydney.

William John Macleay (1820–1891), pastoralist, politician, patron of science, and nephew of Alexander McLeay, was born at Wick, came to NSW with his cousin William Sharp Macleay in 1839, and became a squatter with extensive pastoral runs on the Murrumbidgee whose profits would ultimately fund the scientific interests engendered by his uncle and cousins. He was a member of the Legislative Assembly (1856–74), a trustee of the Australian Museum (1861–77), and in 1862 helped found the Entomological Society of New South Wales. In 1865 William John inherited the insect collections of Alexander and William Sharp Macleay and leased Elizabeth Bay House, living there with his wife, Susan (née Deas Thomson), whom he had married in 1857.

William John employed collectors and sponsored collecting expeditions including that of the *Chevert* to New Guinea in 1875. Encouraging the study of botany, he was the first president of the LINNEAN SOCIETY OF NEW SOUTH WALES (1874). That year George Masters was engaged as curator of the burgeoning collections, which had expanded to include birds, marine animals, and reptiles. William Sharp Macleay had stipulated that the collections should ultimately pass to Cambridge University or the University of Sydney. William John decided on the latter, the government building a museum (1886–88) to which the collections were transferred from Elizabeth Bay House in 1889–90 together with some original collectors' cabinets, library, Macleay papers, and an endowment for a curator. William John was knighted in 1889, and died leaving substantial bequests to various institutions including the University of Sydney and the Linnean Society of New South Wales.

Elizabeth Bay House, entailed by William Sharp Macleay, passed, on the death of his brother George, to their sister Rosa's grandson, James Macarthur Onslow of CAMDEN PARK, and survives as a house museum, its garden destroyed by urban development. The Macleay Museum, University of Sydney, is open to the public. The Linnean Society of New South Wales presented the Macleays' early plant and seed books to the Mitchell Library, State Library of New South Wales.

Scott Carlin, *Elizabeth Bay House: A History & Guide* (Glebe, NSW, 2000); Lionel Gilbert, *Mr McLeay's Elizabeth Bay Garden: Plants, Privilege, and Power in Sydney's Early Scientific Community* (Canberra, 2000)   JOY HUGHES

McLEOD (née MATTHIES), Judyth Ann (b. 1944), educator and horticulturist, with her husband Keith, founded the Honeysuckle Cottage Nursery (1977–) at Bowen Mountain (NSW) and the quarterly magazine *The Cottager* (1986–97), both initiatives supporting the revival of COTTAGE GARDENS and 'heirloom' plants. McLeod obtained her PhD in plant ecology and taxonomy (1975) and has lectured at the University of Western Sydney (Hawkesbury) since 1977. She has worked and published widely in the field of horticulture, especially with HERBS and old-fashioned ROSES, and in garden and landscape history and restoration.

RA

MacMAHON, Philip (1857–1911), horticulturist, journalist, and teacher, was born in Dublin; his influence on landscape design in early Qld derives from his curatorship of the BRISBANE BOTANIC GARDENS (1889–1905), his written works, and his horticultural teaching activities. MacMahon was well respected in his adopted colony, with two major (and laudatory) biographical essays being published during his lifetime. His early life after Ireland was in England, where he worked for the large nursery Dickson and Son, Chester, and then gained a 'studentship' to KEW GARDENS. MacMahon, aged just 24, was appointed Curator of Hull Botanic Gardens, Yorkshire, on the recommendation of Sir Joseph Hooker, and held that position for five years. He next secured a position in India, in connection with 'tropical agriculture', but his health failed and he came to Vic. in 1888 to

Philip MacMahon, depicted against 'a frondacious palm branch' by the *Queenslander* (1896) in its series 'Men we Meet', was a great populariser of tropical horticulture and gardening, especially through his long curatorship of Brisbane Botanic Gardens.

a post with the *Daily Telegraph* writing on agricultural, economic, and scientific subjects.

In 1889 MacMahon was appointed as Curator of Brisbane Botanic Gardens; his tenure witnessed the worst and best of times, including major droughts, a devastating economic depression, and several disastrous floods. His personal losses from the 1893 floods included 'his valuable library, apparatus, photographs, etc., the collection of many years and wanderings'. Despite these traumatic and restraining situations, MacMahon's creativity and energy initiated several valuable design contributions. When the 1893 flood virtually destroyed the Gardens, MacMahon convinced the government that using unemployed men for the reconstruction work was a viable solution. Among his innovative creations were rustic shelter sheds, garden seats, and a coral-stone and clam shell fountain. He achieved increased visitor numbers, assisted by nine articles in the *Queensland Agricultural Journal* (1897–99), which contained colourful descriptions of the gardens and planting arrangements, mixed with encouragement about growing economic plants and other aspects of popular botany. MacMahon generally enthused about Qld as a most rewarding place to garden using plants from all over the world, Tropical or temperate in origin.

Corresponding with his fellow 'Kewites' in the *Journal of the Kew Guild* (1896), MacMahon wrote:

Tell the boys that there are many things to be learned beside gardening if they would hope to do anything out here. There are lots of openings, but we seldom get the right sort of men, most of those who come being almost always hampered by prejudices and fads and expecting things here to jog just as at home. The men who have built up these Colonies never heard of half the 'notions' English gardeners bring out with them, and have neither time nor inclination to listen.

As usual, MacMahon spoke his mind.

After losing half his staff and funding during 1904, MacMahon refused to continue at the Brisbane Botanic Gardens and took up the position of Director of Forests for Queensland (1905). This allowed him to satisfy a long-held passion for forest conservation. While on an inspection of Fraser Island in April 1911, MacMahon 'was suddenly taken ill, and died almost immediately', an untimely loss of one of Queensland's most genial and effective horticulturists.

JEANNIE SIM

McMAUGH (née BAKER), Judith Lesley (b. 1942), horticulturist and educator, graduated in agriculture from the University of Sydney (1963). She taught horticulture at the Ryde School of Horticulture (1967–84) where she specialised in plant production, plant identification, and plant culture. In 1984 she was appointed Principal Horticulturist (Ornamentals) with the Department of Agriculture in NSW, where she took primary responsibility for the garden advisory service and liaison with the horticultural production industry. Between 1991 and 1999 she worked for TAFE NSW in a variety of horticultural roles including Manager, Amenity Horticulture and Urban Pest Management Programs. Her book *What Garden Pest or Disease is That?* (1985) has become a standard work for horticultural students, professional horticulturists and amateur gardeners throughout Australia. Judy McMaugh has also made an enormous contribution to the development and promotion of the horticulture profession through her writing, involvement with professional seminars, and long association with the Australian Institute of Horticulture, serving as National President (1989–90). In 1989 she received the Australian Nursery Industry Award of Merit for outstanding service to the industry.

ML

McMILLAN, Thomas, see Handasyde, McMillan & Co.

MACOBOY, Kenneth Stirling (Bill) (b. 1927), author and photographer, was born in Vic. but grew up in Tas. He left school at 14 and worked in an advertising agency which, after he had spent a short time training to be a Japanese interpreter in Darwin in 1945, transferred him to the USA. He worked as a television producer in New York during 1952–53. His involvement with the production of drama and variety shows sharpened his appreciation of popular taste, and after his return to Australia he had a successful career producing television commercials. Alongside this work in the late 1960s he was supplying garden photographs to the *Australian Women's Weekly* and other magazines. Following a request from the publisher Paul Hamlyn, Macoboy produced a gardening book with a colour photograph of each plant described. *What Flower Is That?* (1969), an immediate success and much reprinted, set a trend for high-quality production, which the market now demands of GARDEN BOOKS. Sydney-based Macoboy has written more than twenty books, all featuring his photographs and his easy, informative writing style. *Macoboy's Roses* (1993) achieved world-wide success, particularly in the USA.

HELEN BOTHAM

MACPHERSON, Alexander (*c.* 1813–1894), experimental gardener and inventor, was born Kinglassie, Inverness, Scotland, and worked as game keeper for several highland noblemen and as a gardener for the Marquis of Abercorn before migrating to Moreton Bay. In 1864 the Queensland Acclimatisation Society appointed Macpherson park keeper and later, overseer, with duties to tend the animals and gardens at BOWEN PARK, Brisbane. His experience in constructing fences and aviaries was put to good use, but his creativity was best expressed in the splendid ornamental fountain he constructed. This rustic water feature consisted of a rough pile of rugged rocks (probably coral-stone from St. Helena Island in Moreton Bay) and giant clam shells used as catch-basins, set within a large circular basin of water. The rough construction was soon covered in ferns and mosses, and was greatly admired throughout the late nineteenth century. Arguably, this fountain design set a fashion among the richer settlers of Qld, and similar constructions proved immensely popular at the many international EXHIBITIONS in which the colony participated. By 1883 Macpherson had settled at Gotha Street, Fortitude Valley, as a self-styled 'experimental gardener', preparing award-winning exhibits of fibre plants for international exhibitions including Philadelphia (1876) and Paris (1878). William SOUTTER, in the *Queensland Horticulturist* (1893), praised the inventiveness of Macpherson's wood and wire weaving machine, which produced a material for covering SHADE HOUSES, VERANDAH screens, and FENCING. In his final years, Macpherson was employed as an attendant in the fledgling Queensland Museum.

JEANNIE SIM

MACQUARIE FIELDS HOUSE, NSW, was built *c.* 1830s–40s by John and Martha Hosking on land originally granted (1809) to surveyor James Meehan. Prominently sited on a knoll overlooking the once-rural Cumberland Plain, this remnant mid-nineteenth-century estate retains common features of HOMESTEAD GARDENS, including prominent ARAUCARIA plantings and olive boundary plantings, as well as a rare Australian example of an exedra (of brick construction, elliptical form, and taking advantage of distant VISTAS).

COLLEEN MORRIS

MACQUARIE PLACE, Sydney, an outstanding early urban SQUARE (of unusual triangular form), formed part of Governor Macquarie's grand vision for Sydney. Flanking the gate to (First) GOVERNMENT HOUSE and overlooked by four villas of leading colonial officials, Macquarie Place was formalised in 1816 with a 'very handsome stone obelisk in the centre … as an ornament … and also for the purpose for measuring the miles from all interior parts of the colony'. Now overshadowed by city buildings, Macquarie Place has survived the vicissitudes wrought by later improvers with a surprising degree of resilience.

COLLEEN MORRIS

MAGAZINES AND JOURNALS: see GARDEN MAGAZINES

MAIDEN, Joseph Henry (1859–1925), museum curator and botanic gardens director, was born in London. Developing a fondness for science at the London Middle Class School and at the Birkbeck Institution, he became associated with Professor Frederick Barff and with the popular science movement, before enrolling at London University in 1879. Ill-health caused him to suspend study and to take the almost mandatory sea voyage to a warmer climate.

Maiden arrived in Sydney in January 1881 and soon found part-time employment lecturing at the Technical or Working Men's College. After presenting himself, at Barff's suggestion, to Professor Archibald Liversidge of the University of Sydney, he was appointed curator of the recently formed Technological, Industrial, and Sanitary Museum in October. Soon becoming secretary of the Museum's committee of management as well as curator, Maiden worked tirelessly and effectively to assemble, categorise, label, and arrange an enormous and amorphous collection of material, largely obtained from the international EXHIBITIONS at Sydney (1879) and Melbourne (1880), from KEW GARDENS, and from manufacturers throughout the world. The young curator hoped to open the vast display in December 1882, and was devastated when the Garden Palace, adjacent to the Sydney Botanic Gardens—which contained the Museum, and much else—was destroyed by fire in September. With remarkable resilience and energy, Maiden and the committee amassed a new collection, which was housed in part of an exhibition hall in the Outer Domain, behind Sydney Hospital. Opened in December 1883, the Museum remained in what Maiden called 'the wretched tin shed' for ten years until removed to splendid new quarters in Ultimo. During that time, Maiden not only maintained an almost embarrassing flow of exhibits (many of which are now prized exhibits in the Powerhouse Museum), but also made his institution a centre of phytochemical research on which reports were published in scientific journals in 1887–88, and in his first book, *The Useful Native Plants of Australia* (1889). Retaining his Museum position, Maiden was made superintendent of the Technical Education Branch in 1894.

In May 1896 Maiden was appointed director of the SYDNEY BOTANIC GARDENS, succeeding Charles MOORE—who, like WOOLLS and MUELLER, had been one of his botanical mentors in Australia. During twenty-eight years as director, Maiden greatly improved the arrangement and content of the living collections in the Gardens, established an outstanding HERBARIUM, museum, and LIBRARY, made intensive studies of EUCALYPTS and ACACIAS, and wrote the massive *Forest Flora of New South Wales* (1904–24). Other special interests included reduction of sand erosion, promotion of wattle cultivation for the tanning industry, and control (or utilisation) of prickly pear. Maiden's diverse interests led him at different times to serve as secretary of the

distributing thousands of plants from the STATE (FOREST) NURSERY at Campbelltown to councils, schools, churches, hospitals, cemeteries, railway and police stations, war memorials, and other reserves. He declared that PUBLIC PARKS should be inviolable, advocated the reservation of additional parks and forests, and supported the GARDEN SUBURB movement. Some of his ideas were reflected not only in the Botanic and Palace Gardens, but also in the grounds of official residences: GOVERNMENT HOUSE, CRANBROOK, ADMIRALTY HOUSE, and, HILLVIEW.

After a staff member, T.C.G. WESTON, left the Campbelltown Nursery in 1913 to work on afforestation in CANBERRA, Maiden readily co-operated, sending hundreds of trees and shrubs. In 1919 Maiden visited Canberra to inspect the plantings and to write a report for the Commonwealth authorities. He commented on species likely to succeed, and urged careful experiment before choosing trees with unknown prospects.

Always the aspiring teacher, Maiden relished his university teaching and delivered lectures in both his institutions, which he considered places of instruction as well as recreation. His name became a household word through the press, his public pronouncements, evidence given to inquiries, and correspondence with a host of enquirers. Scores of articles in the *Agricultural Gazette of New South Wales* further ensured that his influence extended far beyond the city. Keenly interested in history, one of his greatest coups was arranging the transfer from London to Sydney of many specimens collected in 1770 by BANKS and SOLANDER; he also wrote a biography of Banks in 1909 and published numerous biographical memoirs of Australian botanists.

Meticulous, methodical, and with a strong sense of public duty tempered by a gentle sense of humour, Maiden was devoted to his work and family. He and his wife, Eliza Jane (Jeanie), stoically bore the loss at sea of their only son in 1905, and delighted in their four daughters, inevitably (and with good reason) dubbed 'the beautiful Maidens', of whom Mary illustrated some of her father's publications. Retiring to Turramurra in 1924, Maiden enjoyed a short time in his own garden, despite increasing disability, and continued work on his *Critical Revision of the Genus Eucalyptus*. With this great work unfinished, he died at his home and was buried in the leafy churchyard of St John's, Gordon. The vast number and diversity of mourners attested to the breadth and depth of his interests and influence. The genus *Maidenia* and species of *Eucalyptus*, *Acacia*, and *Amyema* (a wattle mistletoe) commemorate his name. He was also honoured by the bestowal of many fellowships and medals, and by being appointed a Companion of the Imperial Service Order (1916).

Lionel Gilbert, *The Little Giant: The Life & Work of Joseph Henry Maiden 1859–1925* (Armidale, NSW, 2001)

LIONEL GILBERT

The personal bookplate of Joseph MAIDEN, drawn by his colleague Margaret FLOCKTON, depicts the natural beauty of *Eucalyptus maideni* contrasting with cultural symbols of the designed landscape at SYDNEY BOTANIC GARDENS

(Royal) Geographical Society of Australasia, consulting botanist to the New South Wales Department of Agriculture and Forests, lecturer in agricultural botany and forestry at the University of Sydney, member of the Lord Howe Island Board, and trustee of the ROOKWOOD Church of England Cemetery. He also became an active office-bearer in the Royal and Linnean societies of New South Wales, the (Royal) Australian Historical Society, the WATTLE DAY League, the Horticultural Society and Horticultural Association, the Field Naturalists' Society, the Town Planning Association of New South Wales, and the AUSTRALASIAN ASSOCIATION FOR THE ADVANCEMENT OF SCIENCE. His expenditure of time and energy on meetings, correspondence, and research was phenomenal. He took a keen interest in his staff, defending the battler but chastising the loafer. Similarly, careful craft workers and efficient suppliers were warmly lauded, while slipshod workers and incompetent managers were roundly admonished.

Through his work and position, Maiden exerted a considerable influence upon gardens and gardeners. He made a feature of having displays of cut NATIVE FLOWERS in his institutions, and like his predecessor, was instrumental in

MAINTENANCE is an integral and accepted part of gardening but also, often, an unacknowledged factor in garden design. Within the industry, it is accepted that the future of any landscape project lies almost wholly in the hands of the person who will be maintaining it. Maintenance approaches strongly reflect technological and social factors. For LAWN,

Maintenance

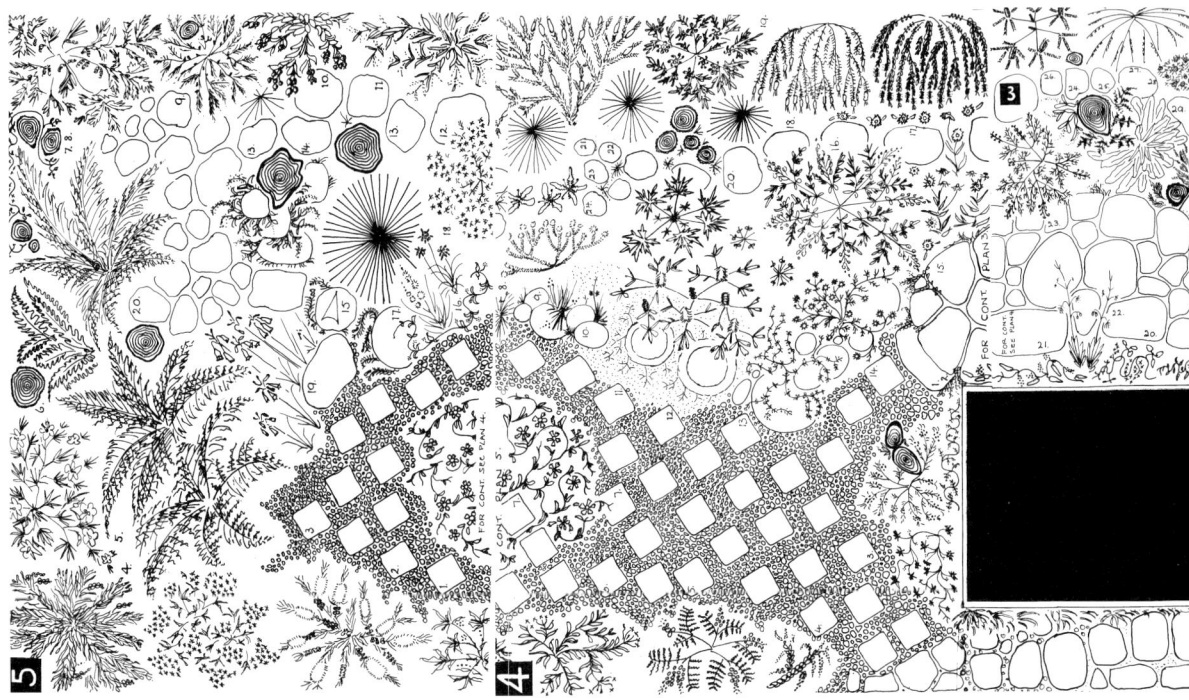

This expressive plan of Betty MALONEY's garden at Frenchs Forest (NSW), drawn by Jean Walker for their book *Designing Australian Bush Gardens* (1966), was spread over ten pages of the small-format paperback, necessitating destruction of the binding for those who wished to view the scheme in its entirety

the progression from grazing animals to TOOLS—the scythe, the motorised LAWN MOWER, the whipper snipper—encapsulates technological and ergonomic advances, while the move from careful disposal of clippings to their artless blowing-away from urban footpaths neatly expresses changing attitudes to garden maintenance, the individual, and society. Advances in biology are also reflected in the BREEDING of new grass cultivars that can better tolerate such demands as machine mowing, drought, and wear. Horticultural research has recently shown that practices such as the digging and hoeing of garden beds to open them up to annual precipitation are undesirable: they can damage plant roots, and instead of eradicating WEEDS actually spread perennial weeds and expose the soil seed bank for weeds. The use of mulch to improve moisture retention and control weed seed germination, has largely replaced this labour-intensive exercise. Burning deciduous leaves in autumn is now considered antisocial due to wider environmental concerns including the imperative for recycling—in this case to make COMPOST for organically enriching SOILS or for use as surface mulch.

Control over vegetation and the ideal of neatness have been a strong part of garden culture from Ancient Rome to the present. The GARDENESQUE style introduced in the early nineteenth century relied, in part, on maintenance for its implementation, and it was often described as reflecting the art of the gardener. Such gardens strove to maintain the high polish of the drawing room and clearly separated DESIGNED LANDSCAPES from natural scenery. Many public parks have adopted a technocratic approach, with their layout being more reliant on horticultural practice to provide ornamental display than on any strong design ideology. Even trees have been planted at sufficient spacings to allow tractor-drawn gang mowers to manoeuvre between them, rather than placing trees in more naturalistic groupings.

GARDENING BOOKS carry every instruction for culturing plants to reach their optimum growth capabilities, and while for many avid gardeners these practices are the essence of their art, craft, and enthusiasm, professional horticulture since the latter part of the twentieth century—especially in the management of PUBLIC OPEN SPACE—has sought to reduce these inputs in an attempt to form more self-sustaining landscapes. A greater appreciation of the role of ECOLOGY in the dynamics of garden vegetation has revised the maintenance process so that it potentially requires less input. The result is that a more NATURALISTIC approach is taken to both layout and planting. In REVEGETATION schemes, using local INDIGENOUS FLORA, design has again unwittingly become secondary to technical process (which is widely perceived to be the main ingredient for successful implementation). In these cases, individualistic design statements are also seen as antithetical to the reproduction of original settings. The dynamic nature of gardens provides a challenge in finding maintenance procedures that direct the growth change from implementation to maturity of a landscape, and recognise and sensitively manage over-maturity within acceptable resource limits. The public

veneration of TREES and the need for their ultimate replacement, for example, provides a constant reminder of the difficulties in successfully managing the maintenance of gardens and designed landscapes.

J.D. Hitchmough, *Urban Landscape Management* (Sydney, 1994)

ML

MALMSBURY BOTANIC GARDENS, Vic., set aside in 1857 and laid out in 1863 through the efforts of local doctor and councillor, Edward Davy, is among Victoria's earliest regional BOTANIC GARDENS. Located on the Coliban River, adjacent to the former town hall (1868), the design centres on a LAKE (with a fountain-bedecked island) and now-mature trees characteristic of late nineteenth-century gardens. A fine stone railway viaduct (1859–62) forms a distinctive backdrop. Rejuvenated in 1984–85, the garden remains a popular PICNIC venue.

FRANCINE GILFEDDER

MALONEY, Betty Florence (1925–2001), and **(Edith) Jean Walker** (b. 1922), bush garden proponents and sisters (*née* Brown), were born in Colac (Vic.). They studied art at Melbourne Technical College and later moved to Sydney, where they were captivated by the Hawkesbury sandstone landscape. Joining the SOCIETY FOR GROWING AUSTRALIAN PLANTS, each created a garden of entirely NATIVE PLANT species around their respective suburban houses—the Maloney garden was one of the earliest BUSH GARDENS to be classified by the NATIONAL TRUST. In 1964 they formed a landscape design consultancy and began designing gardens as abstractions of the Sydney bushland, planting only indigenous species and using local organic materials for construction. Their gardens were always consciously designed with an emphasis on aesthetic composition and human use, their stated philosophy being 'naturalness with order'. Maloney and Walker are best known for their books *Designing Australian Bush Gardens* (1966) and *More About Bush Gardens* (1967), which helped stimulate a wider interest in the preservation of native flora and the use and value of indigenous plants in suburban gardens. Designed and illustrated by the authors and based largely on their own gardens, they appealed to readers who found their ideas practical and easy to emulate. Walker's illustrations had a vivid visual texture bringing the plans to life and allowing the reader literally to use them as working drawings. In her last years, Betty Maloney concentrated on BOTANICAL ILLUSTRATION. Her eighty-six paintings for Alec BLOMBERY's *The Proteaceae of the Sydney Region* (1992) are held by the State Library of New South Wales.

ALLAN CORREY

MANAR (formerly Redesdale), near Braidwood, NSW, a HOMESTEAD GARDEN, has been in the Gordon family since 1841. The garden's founder, pastoralist Hugh Gordon (1816–1857), who renamed the property after his family home, wrote to his brother James in Scotland for seeds: 'all sorts of trees, firs, larches, ashes, oaks, hawthorns and beeches … do send me every kind of seed you can think of and put them in strong brown paper as that is the only way they can be taken across the sea'. The results can be seen in the many towering deciduous trees and conifers (including firs, Aleppo and stone pines) that remain a feature of this romantic garden.

TRISHA DIXON

MANGLES, James (1786–1867), English naturalist, horticulturist, and writer; his brothers Robert Mangles (d. 1860), horticulturist, and George Mangles (*fl.* 1830s), botanist, plant collector; and cousin Ellen Stirling (*née* Mangles) (1807–1874), wife of governor Sir James Stirling; with other members of the Mangles family, through their connections with the vice-regal establishment, were actively involved in the botanical, horticultural, and commercial life of Western Australia's early colonial period.

James Mangles, a retired Royal Navy commander and friend of J.C. LOUDON, visited WA in 1831, two years after the founding of the colony. During the 1830s and early 1840s he was a patron of botanical collecting in WA and instrumental in introducing numbers of Western Australian plants to British horticulture. Through his efforts, seeds supplied by such prominent local collectors as Georgiana MOLLOY and James DRUMMOND were distributed in England to an inner circle of horticulturists that included Robert Mangles, Joseph PAXTON, and various nursery proprietors. In return he sent consignments of useful and ornamental plants to WA, thus contributing to the development of horticulture in the fledgling colony. George Mangles, a member of Stirling's official party at the founding of the colony, was superintendent of government stock and botanised with Drummond on Rottnest Island in the early 1830s. James Mangles was author of *The Floral Calendar* (1839), a fellow of the Royal Society, and a founding member of the Royal Geographical Society. His letter-books containing correspondence from Molloy, Captain Meares, and others are held in the Battye Library (Perth). The names of several Western Australian plants honour members of the Mangles family, including the state's FLORAL EMBLEM, *Anigozanthos manglesii* (Mangles Kangaroo Paw) named for Robert, who grew the type specimen from seed in his English garden. OLINE RICHARDS

MANN, Beryl Vivienne (1911–1982), landscape architect, was born in Geelong (Vic.) and graduated in architecture from the Gordon Institute of Technology before completing the BURNLEY course in 1939. Her entry in the *Australian Home Beautiful* 'Garden Layout Competition' (1940) was highly commended and published; it was seen by Edna WALLING, who offered her work. Mann worked in various architectural offices, before joining Mockridge, Stahle, and Mitchell (1948–76). She specialised in large-scale site planning and landscapes, including Lake Ginninderra Parklands, Canberra (with Grace FRASER); Hotham Gardens Estate, North Melbourne; Australian Road Research Centre, Vermont (Vic.); H.C. Coombs Building, Australian National University; Janet Clarke Hall, University of Melbourne; the proposed Gunpowder arid-zone mining town; and primary schools in the ACT (1960–75). Her close working relationship with architects was unusual in an era when the landscape discipline was striving for independence. Mann lectured part time in landscape in the Department of Town and Regional Planning at the University of Melbourne (1964–73) and worked hard to develop LANDSCAPE ARCHITECTURE into a profession derived from sound academic education. She was a founding member of the AUSTRALIAN INSTITUTE OF LANDSCAPE ARCHITECTS (AILA), convenor of its education sub-committee (1968), and wrote its policy for undergraduate education (1972). With Grace FRASER, she organised the first AILA conference (1969) and published its papers as *The Landscape Architect and the Australian Environment* (1970). Her work now lives in the professionals she taught and inspired as students. RICHARD PETERSON

MANSION GARDENS are the cultivated grounds around grand houses and are essentially large VILLA gardens. They are characterised by compartmentalisation, the use of ornamental features, and stylish sophistication often linked by geometrical and axial planning. They include the notional ideals of retreat and self-sufficiency. Nineteenth-century scientific and technical advances combined to increase their botanical interest and reduce costs. In colonial Australia, where they reached their zenith in the 1880s, mansion gardens were derivative and reflected upper middle-class tastes and values. These qualities continued into the twentieth century on a reduced scale.

Mansion gardens differ across Australia because of climate and topography and, to a lesser extent, because of fashion and economics. In the nineteenth century they were designed invariably within the PICTURESQUE and GARDENESQUE idioms and they were overwhelmingly British in aspiration and largely ITALIANATE in influence. Other influences can be traced, notably from NORTH AMERICA, especially from the turn of the century. Professionals designed and maintained most mansion gardens in the nineteenth century in the more populous colonies, including Edward La Trobe BATEMAN, William SANGSTER, and William GUILFOYLE, but many were the work of unknown hands, perhaps involving a mix of the owner's personal direction and a professional supply of plants from an established nursery.

Few houses in Australia could truly be described as mansions. Rather, the larger houses of the upper middle-class followed the suburban villa form and its lifestyle: that is, they were houses with some architectural pretension, surrounded by gardens and set in and borrowing from the broader landscape. Usually sited on a rise or promontory, their aspect and prospect were critical. The sense of retreat and self-sufficiency associated with a villa estate was integral to the owner's lifestyle. The various GOVERNMENT HOUSES, themselves cast in the villa (rather than palace) mould, were models for any estate that aspired to the title and status of mansion. Their gardens are now also important survivors from the nineteenth century.

The gardens depicted in *Victoria's Representative Men at Home* (1904) and *Our Beautiful Homes* (*c.* 1904) give an especially revealing insight into mansions and their gardens in Vic. and NSW respectively. Paintings by artists such as William TIBBITS, and GARDEN PLANS such as those prepared for the various metropolitan sewerage authorities at the turn of the century, also provide vital evidence of layout and planning. Many mansions and gardens thus depicted, such as T.S. MORT's Greenoaks, have now been lost through subdivision and demolition, but RIPPON LEA in Elsternwick (Vic.) is an outstanding surviving example of an Australian suburban mansion garden.

The source of most mansion garden style and technique was Britain. The most pervasive influence, however, was Italy—both directly, and through an imperial filter. The Italianate style dominated later nineteenth-century domestic architecture and landscaping. It was within the Picturesque idiom, but still dignified by classical associations. It was easily adapted to formal and informal treatments. Gardens could be Italian-inspired even though the house might be Gothic. The similarity between the CLIMATE of southern Australia and the MEDITERRANEAN, already drawn by the first settlers, ensured a continuing Mediterranean influence into the twentieth century. A growing cross-influence from North America reinforced this. Mansion gardens in the twentieth century saw a major reduction in scale as well as a shift in stylistic inspiration—reflecting changing cultural, social, and economic values. They all but lost any notion of self-sufficiency. The USA, and especially Hollywood, as the source of glamour can be seen in Boomerang, at Elizabeth Bay in Sydney (1926), and in reworkings of other large gardens to introduce new features such as SWIMMING POOLS.

The principal residence, reached by an intriguing approach DRIVE, was always the focus of a mansion garden, but compartmentalisation allowed for a wide range of other functions. These included a formal area for PROMENADING along paths set in lawns, between flower beds, along terraces—and, in larger gardens, through a wilderness; a productive area for FLOWERS, FRUIT, VINES, VEGETABLES, poultry, and even a milch-cow; facilities for TENNIS, CROQUET, lawn BOWLING, and other sports; and a service area for propagation, composting, and other domestic services. Axial planning, usually by axes extending from the house and into the landscape, often united the various parts of the garden. The vertical axis created by a tower signalled a sense of proprietorship and domain. A porch, verandah, or CONSERVATORY might also link the house to the garden. GARDEN BUILDINGS, ranging from modest SUMMER-HOUSES and FERNERIES to a Burmese temple or the replica of a Pompeian fountain, acted as features and destinations within the garden. High walls, hedges, and natural defences provided privacy and security from without.

If mansion gardens were the urban or suburban equivalents of the rural HOMESTEAD garden, then their rate of survival has been far less impressive. Whereas homestead gardens might have declined through economic hardship or changed priorities, mansion gardens have been subjected to far more overwhelming pressure from subdivision. While this produced a fertile genre of new, smaller gardens in the inter-war period, subdivision of the post-war period was likely to result in a far higher density of development, and correspondingly less—often not a trace—of the original garden. The estates that have survived are therefore of great rarity.

Howard Tanner, *Converting the Wilderness: The Art of Gardening in Colonial Australia* (Sydney, 1979); Peter Watts and Margaret Barrett (eds), *Historic Gardens of Victoria: A Reconnaissance* (Melbourne, 1983); James Broadbent, *The Australian Colonial House: Architecture and Society in New South Wales 1788–1842* (Sydney, 1997)   **TIMOTHY HUBBARD**

MARANOA GARDENS, Balwyn, Vic., was developed between 1901 and 1926 by mercantile broker John Middleton Watson as a private garden composed entirely of Australasian flora. Watson purchased the bulk of the land in parcels between 1901 and 1912, and landscaped the site as an isolated rural campus, comfortably distant from his residence (and perhaps startled neighbours) in Canterbury. A member of the Field Naturalists' Club of Victoria, Watson incorporated lawns and large sweeping garden beds. When first opened to the public in October 1919, 500 visitors inspected a highly unusual garden, then perhaps comparable only to GUILFOYLE's Australian Border at MELBOURNE BOTANIC GARDENS or WATTLE PARK. Adjacent land on One Tree Hill was purchased by the City of Camberwell in 1916 and opened as Beckett Park a year later. Maranoa was acquired by the council on Watson's death (1926) and has since been maintained and developed as a public garden of AUSTRALIAN PLANTS, with input from enthusiasts such as Frederick Chapman, Charles FRENCH, E.E. LORD, and Arthur SWABY. Extensive work since the 1980s has enhanced ecological groupings, geographic coverage, and labelling in a site that is highly regarded by plant enthusiasts and students.   RA

MARATHON, Mount Eliza, Vic., the SUMMER residence of successful Melbourne businessman Harold William Grimwade (1869–1949), a brother of Russell GRIMWADE, was designed by Walter BUTLER in two major stages. The house, first built in weatherboard (1914), was later reworked as a more substantial Tudor Revival essay in roughcast and half-timbering in parallel to the renovation of the garden (1924). The foremost of Butler's surviving gardens, Marathon is distinguished by its use of natural materials in his favoured ARTS AND CRAFTS manner. Set on a sloping site, it retains the FORMAL character and much of the planting introduced from 1914 onwards, including ITALIAN-influenced planting with cypresses and clipped HEDGES, mature trees and shrubs, herbaceous perennials, and aquatic plants. Carefully considered structural elements include a series of descending terraces, paths, balustrading, steps, pools, pergolas, fountains, and statuary. The controlled, ARCHITECTURAL effect of the garden is heightened through the contrast afforded by its dramatic seaside and clifftop setting, with VISTAS within the garden juxtaposed against more distant views.   **BRYCE RAWORTH**

MARKDALE, Binda, NSW, is one of the few gardens in the state designed by Edna WALLING. This grazing property was established in 1836 and was purchased by the Ashton family in 1921. Walling began work on the garden in 1949; the stonework of local granite was constructed by Eric HAMMOND. The focal point in this two-hectare garden is a LAKE, reflecting the colonial revival homestead (redesigned by Professor Leslie WILKINSON in the 1950s). The watercoloured plan for Markdale is believed to be the last of Walling's distinctive coloured GARDEN PLANS.   **TRISHA DIXON**

MARKET GARDENS In the earliest days of European settlement, gardens around Sydney and Parramatta produced surplus vegetables for the Government Store, and many householders supplied some or all of their needs from their own VEGETABLE GARDENS. However, before long, much of the fledgling colony's vegetable requirements were supplied by the so-called 'dungaree settlers'—emancipists who took up land, often in conflict with Aboriginal people, along the fertile Hawkesbury River plain. Each new settlement was accompanied by the development of similar market gardens,

Market gardens

which were generally a part of small mixed farms also incorporating livestock, orchards, and sometimes cereal crops. They were usually established on the edge of swamps or rivers, where the soil was rich and there was easy access to water for summer IRRIGATION.

Anglo-Australians based their diet largely around meat, and were unadventurous when it came to vegetables, so commercial production was relatively small and centred on such standard fare as potato, cabbage, cauliflower, pumpkin, onion, root crops, peas, beans, and melons. Layout of the gardens was generally rectangular, with parallel raised beds one to two metres wide containing between two and four rows of vegetables. By the 1850s recommended equipment included two horses, dray and harness, a small plough and set of harrows, shovels, spades, forks, rake, hoes, dibble, string line and measuring tape, barrows, and watering pots. Buildings included a gardener's residence, stable and possibly other animal quarters, and an open-fronted wooden 'truck shed' where seed and TOOLS were kept and the loaded dray stored overnight before the early morning journey to market two or three times per week.

As non-farming populations increased in the towns and on the goldfields from the mid-nineteenth century, so too did the number of market gardens. In some areas, such as the 'sandbelt' of Melbourne's south-east, Anglo-Australian families built up substantial market garden holdings. However, the character of Australian market gardening was most dramatically influenced—at least in the short term—by the influx of CHINESE after the discovery of gold in 1851. The Chinese established gardens near all the gold towns, and as the gold rushes subsided, many returned to the major towns and set up market gardens there: during 1900–10 almost half of Victoria's market gardeners and two-thirds of those near Sydney were Chinese. The Chinese market gardeners were the subject of racist regulation, being prohibited, for example, from renting market stalls at Perth City Market until 1900. Local attitudes toward 'John Chinaman', 'Charlie', or the 'celestials' (as the Chinese gardeners were generally known) ranged from fear and suspicion to tolerance, and even geniality. Racism decreased as the twentieth century progressed, and although social barriers remained between the Chinese and the white community, the few gardeners who remained came increasingly to be regarded with the respect and gratitude they deserved.

The Chinese generally rented areas equivalent to between one and four hectares in the suburbs, or up to sixteen hectares further afield. They used labour-intensive techniques, and plots were worked by one person per half hectare on average, with additional labour hired seasonally. Water for the gardens was diverted from nearby lakes or rivers with a system of trenches and sluices or, where groundwater was close to the surface, drawn in twenty-litre buckets from wells about three metres square and about one and a half metres deep. Plants were watered individually from the buckets, which were hung from a wooden yoke and sometimes equipped with a bamboo spout and water rose. A variety of 'waste' nutrient materials were recycled in Chinese gardens, from animal manure and abattoir wastes to human faeces ('nightsoil'). The ground was prepared with fertiliser using simple wooden ploughs and spades, and weed control was carried out with hoes. Seedlings were planted in straight rows in long, raised, rectangular beds, with each plant being protected from the sun by a piece of bark or board. The Chinese were skilled and adaptable gardeners: even in the extreme heat and humidity of Darwin they produced a wide range of temperate and sub-tropical crops, including cabbage, lettuce, tomatoes, celery, beans, cucumbers, melons, sweet corn, and spinach. They sold their produce door-to-door from distinctive barrows and baskets, as well as at town and city markets.

The number of Chinese market gardeners declined from the 1920s, and the industry witnessed the increasing involvement of migrants from southern Europe, some of whom learnt their gardening techniques from the Chinese and, like the Chinese, suffered discrimination. Primarily Italian and Slavic, they often ran their enterprises as family affairs, with one member of the family in outside employment and children working before and after school. Many also included sidelines in poultry, pork, or dairying. The displacement of gardens by suburban residential development—a process begun in the nineteenth century—continued, and as pumping and irrigation technology improved, some gardeners relocated to areas away from lakes and rivers. Although much of the work was still labour-intensive, a few prosperous gardeners could afford to invest in new equipment, including scarifiers, sowers, sprayers, and sprinklers. In the 1920s and 1930s, trucks and tractors increasingly replaced horses, artificial FERTILISERS gradually superseded animal manure, and an increasing number of patent preparations were used to combat PESTS. As the amount of equipment and size of operations increased, market garden landscapes began to feature more buildings—predominantly corrugated iron sheds—with coolrooms and GLASSHOUSES appearing during and after the Second World War.

During the war, rationing, enlistment of labour, and the influx of American servicemen led to the spectre—and sometimes the reality—of vegetable shortages. The Australian Women's Land Army, internees, and prisoners of war all worked on market gardens to ease the labour shortage, and in the NT, ABORIGINAL GARDENERS worked on Army vegetable plots. New cultivating, harvesting, storage, and processing machinery was introduced from the USA, as well as new CHEMICALS—including DDT—for pest and weed control. After the war, small market gardens on the urban fringe remained dominant. However, as the new production technologies and better transport became more accessible, and competition demanded greater efficiency and economy of scale, growers tended to move further away from their traditional position within or near urban centres, to larger acreages of cheaper rural land. Although some of Australia's vegetables are still supplied by small periurban market gardens and organic mixed farms, and some are imported from gardens and farms world-wide, most are produced on highly capital-intensive vegetable farms that stretch over hundreds of hectares and are thoroughly reliant on synthetic fertilisers, chemicals, and specialised machinery.

Ronald Webber, *Market Gardening: The History of Commercial Flower, Fruit and Vegetable Growing* (Newton Abbott, Devon,

This extensive Chinese MARKET GARDEN on the foreshore of the area now occupied by central Darwin, photographed by Paul Foelsche in 1878, depicts a life of domestic self-sufficiency reminiscent of village life in southern CHINA.

1972); Michael Symons, *One Continuous Picnic: A History of Eating in Australia* (Adelaide, 1982); Robin Walker and Dave Roberts, *From Scarcity to Surfeit: A History of Food and Nutrition in NSW* (Sydney, 1988)   ANDREA GAYNOR

MARNOCK, Robert (1800–1889), landscape gardener and horticultural journalist, was (as his protégé William ROBINSON noted in a lengthy obituary) 'one of a group of remarkable young Scotchmen who soon took the foremost places in British gardens'. Marnock worked as gardener at Bretton Hall, Wakefield, England, before taking on the curatorship and design of Sheffield Botanic Garden in 1834. He edited the *Floricultural Magazine* (1836–42) and was horticultural editor of the *Gardeners' Journal* (1845–53), a weekly closely focused on the needs of the working gardener. Marnock promoted Australian emigration, both in his editorials and by the reprinting of letters from successful emigrant GARDENERS. LOUDON was impressed by the young man's work, and was instrumental in Marnock's appointment (1840) as curator and designer of the Royal Botanical Society's Garden in Regent's Park, London. Here he employed Charles MOORE as a foreman, and a near neighbour was Michael GUILFOYLE, both gardeners who later promoted a natural or picturesque style, of which Marnock was Britain's leading exponent. The notes accompanying his successful design in Regent's Park read as a manifesto: 'the garden must be attractively ornamental as well as scientifically useful ... excavations should be made for ornamental water, and eminences raised to break the present monotonous level ... Perhaps there is no other more effectual means of rendering the garden attractive than by diversifying the surface'. Marnock's landscaping was widely emulated; the work of his former colleague G.W. FRANCIS, at ADELAIDE BOTANIC GARDEN, was favourably likened to Regent's Park, and in William GUILFOYLE, Marnock had a talented young disciple of picturesque naturalism.   RA

MARRINER, George (*c.* 1834–1900), nursery proprietor, came from Middlesex, England, arriving in Geelong (Vic.) in 1857. He was a railway labourer for eighteen months before moving to Colac, where he was employed as a gardener by district pioneer Hugh Murray. In 1860 he was employed at a nursery at Colac East, two years later acquiring it and naming it Fulham Nursery (possibly after the London suburb, the site of many well-known nurseries). Catalogues were issued; that of 1877 contained an extensive listing of 'coniferae, shrubs, greenhouse plants, fruit trees, etc', including 196 named fruit trees. Marriner's eldest son, George Henry (*c.* 1854–1928), taxidermist, was interested in botany, which led to a friendship with MUELLER, who often visited the nursery. Marriner's second son, William (1861–1951), a skilled propagator and respected flower-show judge, worked at the nursery, taking over management in 1891. His catalogue that year was devoted chiefly to CHRYSANTHEMUMS, reflecting their greatly increased popularity. A seed and plant shop established in Colac in 1900 was closed in 1966.

On retirement *c.* 1902, William Marriner's three sons, Crial William (1889–1951), (Noel) Leonard (1900–1975), and (Van) Randall (1909–1997) Marriner, who had been taken into partnership, continued to manage the nursery before it passed, in 1985, to Randall's son Maxwell Randall

Marriner (b. 1938). Changed trading conditions brought a decision to close the nursery in 1996. For 134 years it had been conducted on the same site by four generations with unbroken family management—an achievement unlikely to be surpassed.   GEORGE JONES

MARRIOTT, Neil Reginald (b. 1951), conservationist and horticulturist, started his career in horticulture with the purchase in 1981 of White Gums Native Nursery, Stawell (Vic.). Two years before the sale of the nursery property in 1991, Marriott became a Regional Coordinator for the Wimmera–Grampians region with the Victoria Conservation Trust (now Trust for Nature). He is also actively involved with the promotion and use of AUSTRALIAN FLORA through the AUSTRALIAN PLANTS SOCIETY, and has been Victorian president (2001–). Marriott has lectured and written extensively on Australian plants, especially on the genus GREVILLEA.   ML

MARTIN, Joseph (1889–1958), head gardener, hybridist, and nursery proprietor, was born in Scotland and moved to Perth in 1921. He was employed by Subiaco Council as head gardener during the period 1926–42. He established the West Australian Treeplanters' Association in 1936 and was its inaugural president. His keen interest was in the education of CHILDREN in the joys of horticulture, and he assisted with tuition of teachers through the Teachers Training College at Claremont. He was also involved in adult education in 1945 through the University of Western Australia. As vice-president of the West Australian Horticultural Council (1936–51) he contributed extensively to the *WEST AUSTRALIAN GARDENER*, through articles and as an editorial committee member. He wrote the booklet *Rose Growing for Beginners* (1940s), and was vice-president and senior judge of the NATIONAL ROSE SOCIETY of Western Australia. As a HYBRIDIST, Joe Martin had a special interest in CHRYSANTHEMUMS, developing a cascading variety, well known throughout Perth in the 1930s for the magnificent displays at the SUBIACO MUNICIPAL GARDENS. He later established the Glen Afton Nursery at Forrestfield (1942–57).   CAROLYN MIDDLEMIS

MARYBOROUGH QUEENS PARK, Qld, was gazetted as a BOTANIC GARDEN in 1869; considered by Walter HILL to be a branch garden of the BRISBANE BOTANIC GARDENS it was called Queens Park to mark the distinction. Located in the town centre, the park was well frequented by local residents and praised as a healthy antidote to the crowded urban conditions experienced in port cities. Adjacent to the Mary River, the park was laid out perhaps as early as 1862 with paths and avenues of *Ficus benjamina* (Weeping Fig) and *Araucaria bidwillii* (Bunya Pine)—the pines being transplanted from the garden of John Carne BIDWILL, who had lived in the Maryborough area until his death. The decorative ROTUNDA (1890) was erected as a memorial to local businessman Andrew Wedderburn Melville from £500 generously bequeathed by his sister Janet. Despite periodic flooding, this park is well used, and with its many mature trees and other early features, remains one of the best examples of a nineteenth-century PUBLIC PARK in Qld.   JODI FRAWLEY

MARYLAND (originally Nonorrah), Bringelly, NSW, has a prominent hilltop location on land forming part of the 1815 grant of 3000 acres (1214 hectares) to engineer and manufacturer John Dickson (1774–1843). A fellow engineer, Thomas Barker (1799–1875), owned Nonorrah by 1854. Barker, a friend of Thomas SHEPHERD, sold Roslyn Hall, Darlinghurst, in 1859 and moved to Nonorrah—renamed Maryland—where he and wife Katherine undertook large-scale planting. Dense evergreen WINDBREAKS were established along with extensive VINEYARDS, ORCHARDS, and pleasure grounds. Their son, Thomas Charles Barker (1863–1940), inherited Maryland and married Emily Chisholm of GLEDSWOOD. Both Maryland and Gledswood gardens were romanticised by architect W. Hardy WILSON in his books. Since 1940 Maryland has been owned by the Thomson family, who maintain a Holstein dairy. A substantial collection of old plantings survive—ARAUCARIAS, *Pinus pinea* (Stone Pine), *Brachychiton populneus* (Kurrajong), *B. discolor* (Queensland Lacebark), furcraeas, clipped *Plumbago* hedging—along with an outstanding group of dairy and winery outbuildings and gatehouses. Callitris pines are also a feature.
   GEOFFREY BRITTON and COLLEEN MORRIS

MATTHEWS, David Reeves (1890–1969), gardens curator, served his apprenticeship with Ararat Council (Vic.) under Hugh LINAKER, continuing his mentor's work establishing the public gardens, recreation reserves, street plantings, and council nursery. This gentle and gifted gardener was chosen from seventy applicants for the position of 'working landscape gardener' of FOOTSCRAY PARK in 1916, which reached its horticultural zenith under his unremitting and skilful toil. He presided over these gardens until his retirement in 1964, during which time he also prepared plans for many other Footscray Council reserves, including Yarraville Gardens, the other major municipal showpiece. He was a friend and work colleague of W.H. NICHOLLS, orchidologist, field naturalist, and Footscray resident. Matthews was praised for his honorary work, including years of service to botany and agriculture, to the Somers, Shoreham, and Manyung camps, and Gilwell Park, and to the Save the Forests campaign.   RA

MAWALLOK, near Beaufort, Vic., was designed in 1909 by William GUILFOYLE for the Russell family, WESTERN DISTRICT pastoral pioneers. The residence—by architects Klingender and ALSOP—sits on a terrace overlooking spacious lawns with their edges irregularly shaped in Guilfoyle's characteristic manner. The surrounding farmland is effectively blocked, except for a long vista north to Mount Cole over a HA-HA and a LAKE, formed by engineer (Sir) John Monash from a small dam. PALMS, a fascination of Guilfoyle's mature years, once dotted the lawn. Mawallok is a fine example of his late work—its Russell family stewardship (until 1980) then careful rejuvenation by Peter and Jocelyn Mitchell, greatly aided by the survival of Guilfoyle's plan. Indeed, this garden served as an important stimulus and inspiration to Jocelyn Mitchell (b. 1937) during her capable chairmanship of the AUSTRALIAN GARDEN HISTORY SOCIETY

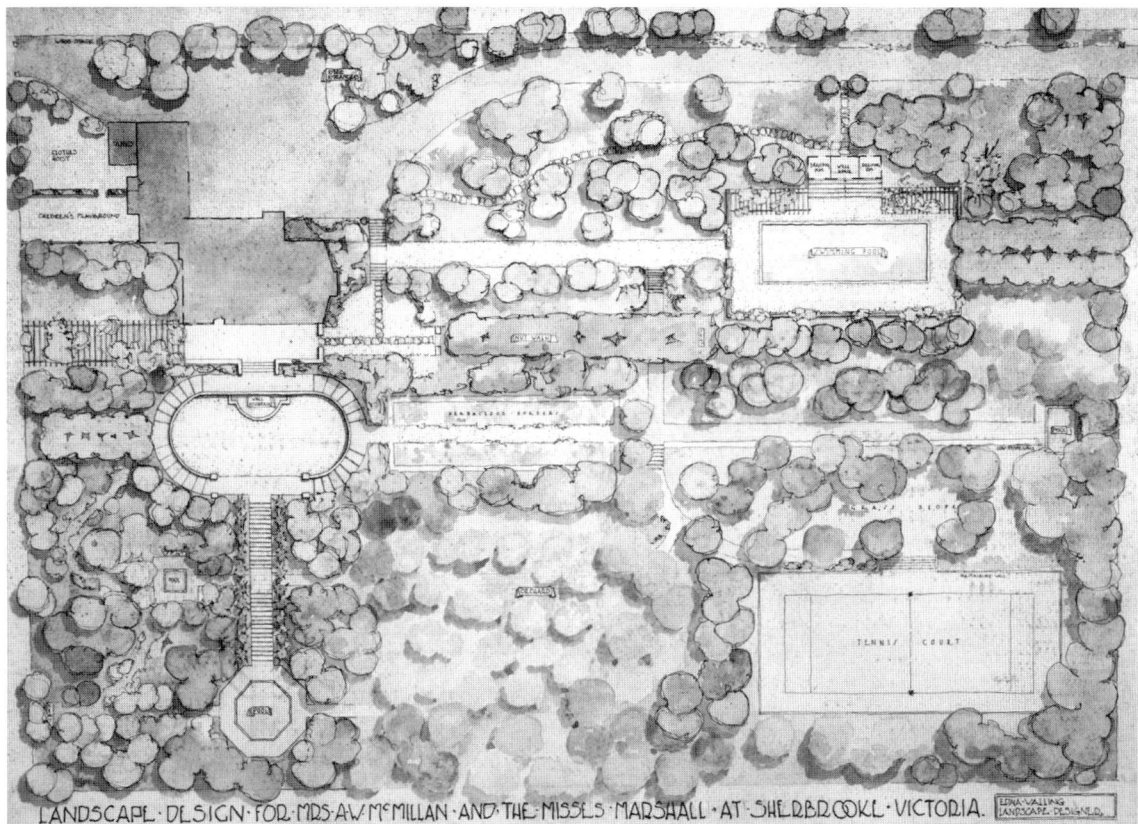

Edna Walling's GARDEN PLAN for MAWARRA, Sherbrooke (Vic.), is an outstanding example of her drafting and also a vital record of one of WALLING's most accomplished designs

(1984–90) and her early role in Victoria's (later AUSTRALIA'S OPEN) GARDEN SCHEME.   JOHN PATRICK

MAWARRA, Sherbrooke, Vic., an ITALIANATE-style garden set in the Dandenong Ranges outside Melbourne, was designed by Edna WALLING in 1932 for three sisters, the Misses Marshall and Mrs McMillan. Since 1960 Mawarra has been owned by Mr and Mrs Frank Walker. Curiously, the watercoloured plan, commissioned at the height of Walling's career, is monochromatic, and yet it illustrates her love of formality offset by wild secluded areas. Situated on a steeply sloping site, the two-hectare garden is extensively terraced with capped stone walls, flagged stone paths, and sweeps of steps leading to a broad central stairway descending to an octagonal reflecting pool. Walling's skilful use of stonework (constructed by Eric HAMMOND) and strong architectural framework is softened by massed shrubbery and the luxuriant growth produced by a high rainfall and rich volcanic soil. Walling described Mawarra—her finest formal garden—as 'not so much a garden as a symphony in steps and beautiful trees'.   TRISHA DIXON

MAWSON, Thomas Hayton (1861–1933), English-born landscape designer, achieved national and international fame in his chosen profession. He started a landscape design business in the Lake District in 1885, moving quickly from local commissions to prestigious projects throughout Great Britain and overseas. His major books, *The Art and Craft of Garden Making* (1900; 5th edn, 1926) and *Civic Art: Studies in Town Planning, Parks, Boulevards and Open Spaces* (1911), were influential on a generation of ARCHITECTS, town planners, and landscape designers, including those in Australia. These titles suggest his stylistic and practical concerns: from his early enthusiasm for the ARTS AND CRAFTS applied to domestic gardens to an increasing interest in TOWN PLANNING, especially the CITY BEAUTIFUL movement. Mawson planned a lecture tour of Australia in 1912 but a large (and unexpected) new commission in Greece precluded the visit.

The Life and Work of a Northern Landscape Architect: Thomas H. Mawson 1861–1933 (Lancaster, 1978)   RA

MAYDENA, Tas.: see LUTANA, Tas.

MAZE Topiary mazes became popular during the Renaissance, initially with low HEDGES outlining an intricate single path. Multiple-path puzzle mazes subsequently dominated. Most disappeared with the advent of the landscape style of gardening in the eighteenth century but persisted in

Mediterranean influences

PLEASURE GARDENS, and became popular again in large gardens during the high Victorian era, when the first mazes were recorded in Australia. With the popularity of informal planting, advocated by ROBINSON and JEKYLL, combined with increasing labour costs, the TOPIARY maze again lost favour. A renewed interest in geomancy and mysticism caused a rediscovery of the labyrinth motif, which was reincorporated into gardening tradition with a resurgence of maze building in the northern hemisphere from the 1970s onward. Australia followed this pattern, with a hiatus between 1902 and the 1980s apart from several isolated exceptions.

Nine hedge-puzzle mazes are known to have been planted in Australia in the colonial and Edwardian eras, although only one, at (BELAIR) NATIONAL PARK, SA (1886: *Cratageus laevigata*) survives. Generally, mazes were planted in the burgeoning BOTANIC GARDENS and PUBLIC PARKS of the period. The earliest examples were in Cremorne Gardens, Richmond, Vic. (c. 1863), a commercial pleasure garden, and Ballarat Botanic Gardens (1862: *Acacia paradoxa*). Others included Carlton Gardens, Melbourne (c. 1880), Geelong Botanic Gardens (1896: boxthorn, privet, and hawthorn), and a second maze at Belair (1902: *Dovyalis caffra*). The only known maze planted in a private garden in Australia was at DUNTROON, ACT (1871). This was replanted in 1965 with *Cotoneaster microphylla* and followed the popular Hampton Court pattern, as did the example in Carlton Gardens. The two at Belair were modelled on a maze in the Forest of Dean, Gloucestershire—a simple hedged-puzzle design popular in Europe in the sixteenth and seventeenth centuries. Few Australian mazes have used indigenous plant species.

Modern mazes have proliferated from 1980 in Australia, including forms with wooden walls, pavement style mazes, some colour coded, and one turf maze of Cretan design at Cockington Green, Gungahlin (ACT). All relate to tourist attractions, echoing the former pleasure gardens. Representative examples include Ashcombe, Shoreham, Vic. (1985: *Cupressus macrocarpa* 'Horizontalis') and Tasmazia, Promised Land, Tas. (1988), which has four examples including The Great Maze (a Hampton Court copy in *Viburnum tinus*). Currently most hedge mazes are to be found in Vic.   BARRY LONG

MEDITERRANEAN INFLUENCES The idea that parts of Australia bear some resemblance to the countries around the Mediterranean seems now so obvious that it is almost unremarkable. Unsure, and perhaps misled, settlers on the First Fleet brought both TROPICAL and subtropical seeds and plants from Rio de Janeiro, as well as those of the temperate and cool temperate zone from Cape Town, but it was soon apparent that Sydney possessed a maritime subtropical CLIMATE. However, a fuller understanding of the wet and dry SEASONS, and the times best suited to planting and harvesting, took many years.

With the benefit of several decades of experimentation, settlers at Swan River (1829) and Adelaide (1836) had better success in reading the local climate type. Their observations suggested strong physical similarities with parts of SPAIN and ITALY, particularly with the parts visited by those in the wine trade and frequented by artists and tourists on the Grand Tour. Apart from the general similarities of rolling hills, clear skies, and vegetation that resembled the distinct but associated Mediterranean types known as the *garigue* and the *maquis*, it was the weather patterns that confirmed their impressions. The pattern of cool, wet winters followed by a brief spring, and long, hot summers with an extended period of drought that concluded with a short autumn, were typical of those parts of coastal southern Europe where the climate was described by nineteenth-century physical geographers as 'Mediterranean'.

Early enthusiasts for ACCLIMATISATION and AGRICULTURAL diversification in SA and WA seized on the Mediterranean idea and advocated the potential for all manner of industries—from raising cochineal bugs for the production of a red colouring agent to the development of a perfume industry to rival that of Provence. Olive and almond groves, plantations of *Opuntia* sp. (to offer the cochineal insect a home), white mulberries for SERICULTURE, lavender, fields of *Pelargonium graveolens*, and many other plants were seen as having potential and were discussed by HORTICULTURAL and AGRICULTURAL SOCIETIES and through the pages of the horticultural press. Only a few such ideas were realised. It was from this start that olives naturalised in the ADELAIDE HILLS. The original intention was that the olive oil would act as the agent by which the essential oils of lavender, orange blossom, heliotrope, rose, and jasmine would be absorbed from the flowers and held ready for extraction. The quality of local perfumes was very high, and samples won prizes in European trade exhibitions; but the invention of cheaper synthetic perfumes killed the trade before it was soundly established. The olive groves were left untended and gradually they spread over considerable areas. Now that there is a strong demand for the oil for Mediterranean cookery, the groves have been rejuvenated and the old trees reworked with budwood of improved strains of olive. By a similar but more successful path, VITICULTURE and the wine industry were also established, the principal agents being some English gentlemen farmer-settlers keen on wine, and Prussian religious refugees whose passages to SA they sponsored.

Although there was much talk of the Mediterranean climate and the plants that would thrive in such conditions, the development of a Mediterranean garden style in Australia was only partly successful. The strong British influence mitigated against this, as did enhanced water supplies in urban areas during the late nineteenth century. There were exceptions—in both the fashion for dry ROCKERIES planted with CACTI and succulents so popular in the decades either side of 1900, and in the search for an Australian style of architecture during this period. While William Hardy WILSON sought this style in the Georgian architecture of the early colonists, other architects such as Walter BAGOT and Rodney ALSOP looked to the Mediterranean countries. Complementary architecture and landscaping was a key design ideal, but examples such as Bagot's Nurney House in North Adelaide were little emulated, and it was largely through the Spanish Mission influence of NORTH AMERICA that Australian architecture—

but rarely its associated landscaping—was influenced. Later twentieth-century revivals of Mediterranean style had more to do with an architectural fashion for Spanish and Hispanic-American (Tex-Mex) buildings than with any conscious awareness of integrating house and garden designs with the climate; thus architectural and exotic-looking plants with bold foliage were widely favoured rather than those with reliable drought tolerance.

At the end of the twentieth century another revival of Mediterranean-style houses and gardens has coincided with a change in lifestyle focus from indoor living to outdoor living, and with a strong push by water supply authorities to develop water-wise—or XERIC—approaches to gardening. To achieve successful and satisfying gardens within these parameters it seems a significant change in thinking will be required; gardens will no longer be made and remade at the whim of overseas fashions regardless of water consumption, but will be responsive to the natural patterns of rainfall and drought, and to the natural patterns of growth and rest of plants suited to those conditions.

Two possible types of plants seem well suited to this revival: those from similar Mediterranean climatic zones, and those that were popular garden plants before the availability of tap water permitted highly water-dependent gardens. Among the plants once popular are yuccas, agaves, aloes, echeverias, sedums, crassulas, agapanthus, belladonnas (*Amaryllis belladonna*), lavenders, rosemaries, PELARGONIUM species, and winter-growing South African BULBS such as watsonias, babianas, freesias, sparaxis, and ixias. Southern European bulbs such as NARCISSUS, tulip species, cyclamen species, and rhizomatous and bulbous irises are also drought-hardy old-timers. Drought-tolerant rose species and old-fashioned roses will be likely contributors to the floral display in water-wise gardens. Exotic shrub species that might contribute are Persian lilac (*Syringa* X *persica*), pomegranate (*Punica granatum* and vars.), oleander (*Nerium oleander*), duranta (*Duranta erecta*), lantana hybrids, pelargonium hybrids, plumbago, and mock orange (*Philadelphus* hybrids). To these will be added plants newly introduced to gardens that are native to coastal California, the Cape region of South AFRICA, and the 'Mediterranean' parts of Australia, such as ceanothus, proteas, BANKSIAS, correas, ACACIAS, and EUCALYPTS to name but a few of the most obvious genera. A telling factor in the maturation of the idea of Mediterranean-style gardens will be how successfully designers and nursery proprietors collaborate to create outdoor living spaces and gardens that are responsive to the climate using a palette of plants suited to the Mediterranean weather pattern. Important to the long-term success of these, however, will be the need to ensure that plants chosen for their low water use do not become environmental WEEDS, as so many from climatically similar locations have already become.

Mrs Phillip Martineau, *Gardening in Sunny Lands* (London, 1924); Hugo Latymer, *The Mediterranean Gardener* (London, 1990); Bob Perry, *Landscape Plants for Western Regions* (Claremont, USA, 1992); Heidi Gildermeister, *Mediterranean Gardening* (Palma di Mallorca, 1995); Trevor Nottle, *Gardens of the Sun* (Kenthurst, NSW, 1996)   TREVOR NOTTLE

MELBOURNE BOTANIC GARDENS: see ROYAL BOTANIC GARDENS, MELBOURNE.

MELBOURNE CRICKET GROUND, Jolimont, Vic.: see YARRA PARK, Vic.

MELBOURNE GENERAL CEMETERY, a product of community pressure to improve conditions for burial in the rapidly developing city, opened in 1853 on a sixteen-hectare site north of the city. It was extended in 1859, and currently covers forty-three hectares. Its nineteenth-century development was closely associated with three identities. First, architect Albert PURCHAS designed the original layout in 1852, using elements of both the picturesque and the formal geometric cemetery fashions of the day. He served as architect, surveyor, and secretary to the cemetery, retaining his position as architect until his death (1909). Secondly, from 1860, planting was heavily influenced by Ferdinand MUELLER. Like Purchas, he favoured formal evergreens, particularly pines and cypresses. Thirdly, after 1873 planting was directed by Clement HODGKINSON, who favoured a less-formal vista. However, the high-density grid pattern of burials and monumentation precluded a more romantic American-style development. Attempts to expand the site in the 1890s failed, leading to the redevelopment of many garden and border areas for burials, further increasing the dominance of monuments over planting. In the twentieth century there were major alterations to the original layout, and many more surviving nineteenth-century plantings were removed. The site contains a fine collection of built features including boundary fences and gates, entrance lodge, chapels, rotundas, and grotto, as well as monuments, though many other features were removed in an effort to find new burial space. The twentieth-century history of the cemetery has been dominated by declining revenue, neglect, malpractice, and corruption. All have had an impact on the site's integrity.

Don Chambers, *City of the Dead* (Flemington, Vic. 2001)
ROBERT NICOL

MELLOR (née HOLTTUM), Olive (1891–1978), horticulturist, landscape designer, and journalist, was born in Linton, England, and came to Melbourne in 1909. Her stepbrother, (Richard) Eric Holttum (1895–1990), was director of the Singapore Botanic Gardens (1925–42), and his work formed the basis of the orchid industry of Malaya. Olive Holttum enrolled at BURNLEY School of Horticulture in 1912, graduating with Certificate of Horticulture in 1913. She was the first woman to study horticulture full-time there, and possibly the first and only woman to graduate with the Diploma of Horticulture (1915). She was the first Instructress of Horticulture at Burnley from 1917 until 1919, when she married Alan Mellor, an orchardist from Wandin, who died in 1920 before their daughter Margaret was born. By the mid-1920s she had begun a garden maintenance business; later she was head gardener at a Toorak garden, and by the 1930s she was an established landscape designer and contractor. During the Second World War she was an early volunteer in the Australian Women's Land Army and was a field officer at the Instruction Depot, Mont Park, in charge of the vegetable garden and nursery.

Olive Mellor wrote for AUSTRALIAN HOME BEAUTIFUL from 1934 to 1970, increasingly taking space from Edna WALLING. Her early articles addressed garden design, but this changed by the 1960s to practical horticulture. Her books included the *Garden Lovers' Log* (1940), *Practical Gardening Illustrated* (c. 1950), *Your Flower Garden* (c. 1950), *Grow Your Own Vegetables* (c. 1950), and *Complete Australian Gardener Illustrated* (c. 1951), and she 'revised and adapted to Australian conditions' an English garden encyclopaedia, edited by Richard Sudell (c. 1900–1958), in *Australian Gardening of Today* (1943).

Comparing Mellor with Walling, her best-known contemporary, is difficult—their client base was different and there is virtually nothing left of Mellor's work. She designed for the average home owner, whereas Walling designed mainly for wealthier clients. Mellor was quiet and very practical: the antithesis of Walling's inventive flair. Walling's articles were often romantic, Mellor's mostly practical. Nevertheless, her contribution to gardens and horticulture was important. She assisted in opening areas of employment and education not previously offered to women; her voluminous writings served a broad and numerous readership; and she was a pioneering woman RADIO broadcaster—all major achievements for her time.

SANDRA PULLMAN

MEMORIAL GARDENS: see COMMEMORATIVE AND MEMORIAL GARDENS

MENINGOORT, Camperdown, Vic. Peter McArthur (1819–1897), a Scot, arrived at Port Phillip in 1839 and soon took up land beside Mount Meningoort with Nicholas Cole—a partnership that terminated in 1842. McArthur remained at this pastoral property, where a bluestone house of 1851 was further developed in 1886. Eugene von GUÉRARD's unusual 1861 view, looking over the house from the rear, accentuated a significant feature of the landscaping, a straight, double AVENUE on axis with distant Mount Leura. Possibly planted with wattles—now blue gums—the avenue terminated in front of the elevated house in a large turning circle, with steps to a terrace and thence the verandah—an unusual and early example of FORMALITY in the WESTERN DISTRICT landscape. To each side there were well-established trees, and a garden lay to one side of the house, but today only the axial bones survive.

GEORGE JONES

MENZEL, Ernst Wilhelm (1845–1917), landscape gardener and botanist, trained in Munich, Germany, and was engaged as head gardener at Forest Lodge for John BAGOT in 1890. He became 'one of the best known professional gardeners in this State ... [and] was recognised as a leading authority in South Australia on CONIFERS'. He was responsible for the design and management of several gardens in Adelaide and in the ADELAIDE HILLS, including The Conifers, Aldgate. In 1899 his sons, Bruno (*fl.* 1897–1902) and Oscar Ernst (*fl.* 1897–1906), established the Specialty Farm (ALDGATE NURSERY) with Fred Caley SMITH, before progressively ending their business interests with Smith. Oscar served as secretary of the Mount Lofty Gardeners Society (*fl.* 1890–1900), and contributed many plant specimens to the Adelaide, Melbourne, Sydney, Brisbane, Perth, Berlin, and Natal Herbariums. *Acacia menzelii* (Menzel's Wattle) was named by botanist J.M. BLACK in honour of 'the late Mr O.E. Menzel'.

DAVID JONES

MEREDITH (née TWAMLEY), Louisa Anne (1812–1895), author and artist, was influential in promoting the appreciation, preservation, and cultivation of AUSTRALIAN FLORA. She arrived in Australia in 1839, spending a year in NSW before moving to Tas., where she remained for most of her life, broken only by infrequent visits to Melbourne, and one journey back to the United Kingdom (1889–91). Before marrying her cousin Charles Meredith and moving to Australia, Louisa

Olive MELLOR reading *Spade Craft: or How to be a Gardener* (1914): a relaxed portrait made in her late twenties while she was employed as the first Instructress of Horticulture at Burnley

Louisa MEREDITH as illustrated in the sketchbook of Mary Morton ALLPORT (1856): homage paid by one artist to another in the elegant trellised surrounds of a colonial Tasmanian garden

Anne Twamley had earned a living as an artist and writer in Birmingham. The nature of her work was wide-ranging, but her books, *The Romance of Nature; or, The Flower Seasons Illustrated* (1836), *Our Wildflowers Familiarly Described and Illustrated* (1839), and *An Autumn Ramble on the Wye* (1839)—this last a late example of the PICTURESQUE travel genre, in the footsteps of GILPIN—prefigured her Australian interests.

Sympathetically disposed towards the local scenery, flora, and fauna from her earliest days in Australia, Meredith provided vivid written descriptions in a series of works beginning with *Notes and Sketches of New South Wales* (1844), *My Home in Tasmania* (1852), and *Over the Straits: A Visit to Victoria* (1861). Aimed primarily at overseas audiences, these works also contained critical commentary on colonial society—which did not always endear her to local readers. As well as describing the more striking elements of the local scenery, botany, and wildlife, and her own gardens, these works contain valuable descriptions of other gardens, now lost. Significant examples from *Over the Straits* include the original design for the grounds of the University of Melbourne by E.L. BATEMAN, the gardens of James Palmer's residence, Burwood, at Hawthorn; and the Bakewells' station on the River Plenty, near Melbourne (previously illustrated by Bateman). Among her subsequent illustrated publications, those depicting Tasmanian wildflowers were the most attractive and probably the most influential. *Some of my Bush Friends in Tasmania: Native Flowers, Berries and Insects Drawn from Life* (1860) and *Last Series: Bush Friends in Tasmania* (1891), both lavishly illustrated with chromolithographs, remain highly valued by collectors today.

Meredith's own taste in gardens tended towards the low-key elements of the picturesque, with VERANDAHS and other RUSTIC structures embowered in flowering climbers, and carefully chosen views of the best aspects of the local scenery. Exotics were happily combined with native plants, including blue gums, tea-tree, and native clematis. Meredith deplored the wanton destruction of native vegetation for short-term gain, publicly condemning such common practices of her day as the cutting of groves of fern-trees for the temporary decoration of a church or ballroom.

In the informed appreciation of Australian native flora and landscape scenery, Meredith found kindred spirits in figures such as Bateman, Georgiana MCCRAE, and the Godfrey HOWITT family in Vic., and Mary Morton ALLPORT in Tas. Bateman was responsible for the design of at least two of Meredith's books (the *Bush Friends* volumes): these, together with *Our Island Home* (1879), two works for children, *Loved, and Lost!* (1860) and *Waratah Rhymes for Young Australia* (1891), and two chromolithographed music covers, employed Australian native flora as the dominant motif of the binding designs.

Meredith regarded Jane LOUDON as a friend, and referred to several of J.C. Loudon's comprehensive works, including his encyclopaedias of agriculture (1825) and plants (1829). In preparing her English books she acknowledged her debt to the works of 'that excellent botanist, Mr SOWERBY'; her library included Dr Langhorne's *The Fables of Flora* (1804) and Priscilla Wakefield's *An Introduction to Botany* (1812).

Meredith was very aptly described as 'A poet in feeling, an artist by instinct, a naturalist by force of circumstances, a keen botanist, and an ardent lover of landscape scenery'. Through her work she encouraged many to place a higher value on Australian native flora.

Vivienne Rae Ellis, *Louisa Anne Meredith: A Tigress in Exile* (Sandy Bay, Tas., 1979)   ANNE NEALE

MICALAGO STATION, Michelago, NSW, taken up by Captain Francis Nicholas Rossi (1776–1851) in 1827, has remained in the Ryrie family since their purchase in 1859. The family developed the two-hectare homestead garden and extended the tree plantings into the surrounding landscape. Wide, wisteria-clad verandahs encircle the main homestead, altered by Professor Leslie WILKINSON in 1945. Framed by towering eucalypts and exotics, the garden comprises a series of garden rooms, bounded by slab and pisé outbuildings. A PERGOLA and low stone wall separate the main garden from the original drive, now the wild garden. Edna WALLING is reputed to have commented that Micalago Station possessed a garden that could not be improved.

TRISHA DIXON

MICHELL, George Howard (b. 1913), company director, and his wife, Christine (b. 1916), commissioned Edna WALLING to design their garden in Medindie (SA) in 1939.

Middle Eastern influences

A watercolour plan was prepared, and its laying out was personally supervised by Walling in 1940. It has many of her design traits, including s-shaped driveway, silver birches, palette-shaped front lawn, and typical underplanting species. Edwin and Patricia Michell, the present owners, maintain it in keeping with Walling's plan and have also acquired BURDETT's Wildflower Garden (1999) with a similar objective of stewardship.

John Alfred Michell (b. 1932) and his wife, Patricia Mary, commissioned Robin HILL, in conjunction with architect Peter Muller (b. 1929), to design their new residence in Medindie (1964). Reflecting NORTH AMERICAN Prairie School and Japanese ideas, it illustrates the influence of Garrett Eckbo's and Muller's ideas upon Hill in his use of paving and stone edgings, sculpting of an inner crescent-shaped garden, and the simplicity of textured plants.

DAVID JONES

MIDDLE EASTERN INFLUENCES The contribution of the Middle East—an extensive area of south-west ASIA and northern AFRICA, stretching from the MEDITERRANEAN to Pakistan, including the Arabian peninsula—and Islam to the gardens of the world has been magnificent, but has often been obscured by religious intolerance. This arose due to the fact that the supremacy of Islam was achieved at the expense of Europe, and in conflict with Christianity.

The system of irrigation used in farming, major water channels with minor channels leading off at right angles, gave form to Islamic gardens. Water channels were gradually widened into broad canals decorated with beautiful arrangements of fountain jets. In the Bagh-i-Iram in Shiraz (southern Iran) it is possible to experience the delight of coming from a hot, arid countryside where no trees grow, into a dark, shaded alley whose high walls are of deep-green cypress. Here one enters a secluded world of coolness and beauty—cooled by a murmuring water channel, and scented by the sharp tang of the cypress and the sweet perfume of roses growing in a border along the water course.

The Alhambra and Generalife in Granada (Spain) are widely recognised as the highest peak reached by Muslim garden art. The Alhambra is a superb landscape concept by reason of the juxtaposition of beautifully proportioned open spaces, courtyards, with enclosing areas of fine buildings, all placed in a subtle association with the surrounding country. The Generalife highlights include an avenue of high jets playing gaily along one of the large courts. This garden was completed in the fourteenth century, the Moorish style having been imported to SPAIN early in the eighth century.

Islamic gardens have had little direct influence on Australian gardens, but their general influence world-wide has been reflected in Australian landscape design in aspects of FORMALITY and also the notion of paradise gardens, where application of WATER in otherwise dry surroundings has produced an oasis-like quality. An interest in drawing environmental design analogies between Australia and the Middle East received prominence in landscape architecture in the 1970s and 1980s. Only in the post–Second World War period, with increased numbers of MIGRANTS from Middle Eastern countries, has direct influence been felt, and much of this has been in vernacular productive traditions rather than 'high style' gardens.

John and Ray Oldham, *Gardens in Time* (Sydney, 1980); Elisabeth B. MacDougall and Richard Ettinghausen, *The Islamic Garden* (Washington, D.C., 1976); John Brookes, *Gardens of Paradise: The History and Design of the Great Islamic Gardens* (London, 1987)

JOHN OLDHAM

MIDDLETON, William George Dyer (b. 1926) was forester-in-charge of the Forests Commission of Victoria nursery at Wail and the Dimboola Forest District (including the Big and Little Deserts) from 1959 until the early 1980s. The pioneering STATE FOREST NURSERY at Wail promoted dry-climate forestry and plants to local farmers and gardeners, and to visitors from all parts of Australia and overseas. Bill Middleton used every channel, particularly illustrated evening talks (averaging one a week over his twenty-three years in the district) and ABC RADIO (as 'the Western Victorian gardener'), to encourage landholders to plant more trees and protect remnant bush. An enthusiastic naturalist and ornithologist, in the 1980s he helped plan and supervise the innovative Potter Farmland Plan in western Victoria and has worked to secure protective covenants with landholders. He has been honoured for services to conservation, the environment, and land management.

ANNE LATREILLE

THE MIDLANDS, a favoured pastoral area in TASMANIA, north of Oatlands and south of Longford, and bounded by the Western Tiers, and a series of hills or 'mountains' (including Ben Lomond) to the east, contain a concentration of HOMESTEAD GARDENS and DESIGNED LANDSCAPES and form an outstanding CULTURAL LANDSCAPE. The undulating, grassy plains were well adapted for 'sheep walks', and patterns of land use and landscapes evolved from natural features such as watercourses, and imposed and designed elements such as land grant boundaries, hawthorn-hedged roads, a scattering of country residences (favouring elevated sites and characteristically surrounded by pleasure gardens), and modest, often picturesque townships and villages serving their immediate hinterland.

By the late 1820s much of the land along the main north–south route had been taken up under the generous land grant system (which prevailed until 1831). Originally sheep meat breeds predominated, but wool soon gained in importance, especially from highly successful sheep studs established from the 1820s, with the district becoming a major merino-breeding centre. Although wheat was an important crop between the 1820s and 1850s, most fortunes were founded on wool. The Midlands straddled the long-established divide between Hobart (south) and Launceston (north), with most social and commercial activity favouring the north. In general, the grand homesteads were built following some years' occupation in more modest houses, when fortunes and position were consolidated. Much building and garden-making took place in the 1830s, when landowners could take advantage of cheap convict labour and a booming economy. Well-known family names included von Bibra (BEAUFRONT), Cox (CLARENDON), Leake (ROSEDALE), and especially the ARCHER family, with properties (Brickendon, Panshanger, and Woolmers) concentrated around Longford. Woolmers received a substantial and sophisticated addition in 1845, reflecting overseas influences—but perhaps it was the development by Robert Quayle Kermode (1812–1870) of Mona Vale that set the stylistic and social pace. The early homestead of his father, the pastoralist and IRRIGATION pioneer William Kermode (1780–1852), had sat typically on a rise, but in 1865–69, the current house and garden was developed, an outstanding example of ITALIANATE influence. Other well-known homestead gardens were established at Winton (Campbell Town), Connorville and Saundridge (Cressy), Symmons Plains (Perth), and Somercotes and Wetmore (Ross).

COTTAGE GARDEN traditions have subsisted in town gardens, principally in Oatlands, Ross, Campbell Town, Evandale, and Longford, with distinctive designed landscapes such as CHRIST CHURCH GROUNDS, Longford and the treed hills of Ross, adding to the established landscape character.   RA

MIEGUNYAH, Toorak, Vic.: see GRIMWADE, (Wilfrid) Russell

MIGRANTS' GARDENS are expressions of the dislocating experience of migration, where early stages of settling involve establishing gardens both to grow familiar food and to connect with the new country by cultivating land. This phenomenon has been explored by Sam Bass Warner's *To Dwell is to Garden* (1987) in the COMMUNITY GARDENS in Boston, USA; however, Australian migrants' gardens differ in that they are associated with single dwellings and are generally hidden. British migrants predominated from the 1780s to the 1960s, and their gardens exemplified the majority taste in Australia. The other major nineteenth-century migrants were the CHINESE, whose MARKET GARDENS were established on the goldfields and in Australian cities from the 1850s. Early twentieth-century migrants' gardens were expressions of MEDITERRANEAN gardening, including Greek, Italian, and Lebanese. Australian writer David Malouf immortalised his Lebanese grandfather's East Brisbane garden in *12 Edmondstone Street* (1985). As personal expressions, migrants' gardens are often ephemeral, although intergenerational gardens exist in Italian families and also among Chinese market gardeners.

The major influx of European migrants occurred following the Second World War. European migrants in the 1950s were expected, under the policy of assimilation, to become 'New Australians'; as a result, migrants expressed cultural difference in the BACKYARD. Gardens of this era consisted entirely of vegetable beds containing aubergine, courgette, special beans, garlic, chives, basil, oregano, as well as lemon, fig, and olives—few of which were then grown in Australian gardens. Soap making and bread baking occurred near back fences, while small areas of concrete, shaded by grapevines, adjoined the backs of houses. In the 1980s—as a policy of multiculturalism took hold—Vietnamese migrants established two forms of garden: those reflecting a warrior's exile, and those embodying Taoist harmony. The warrior's garden was characterised by botanical experimentation, whereas the Taoist gardens contained Vietnamese fruit, herbs and vegetables along with fragrant flowers for shrines within the house. Both forms of garden incorporated beds of Vietnamese medicinal herbs.

As migrants settle, gardens go beyond the basic essentials with many incorporating hybridised cultural elements. Latvian gardeners in Brisbane have substituted Latvian apple blossom and *Syringa vulgaris* (Common Lilac) with *Bauhinia alba* (White Bauhinia) and *Lagerstroemia indica* (Crepe Myrtle). Some gardeners also grew plants associated with an antipodean—and often TROPICAL—Eden: olives juxtaposed against mangos, paw paws, bananas, and macadamias. Nostalgic plants were also evident—ORCHIDS for the Portuguese from Madiera, bay trees for Croatians, and walnuts and hazels beside the pizza oven for the Italians. Other gardeners, with increasing affluence after years of hard work, have created gardens that evoke qualities of their remembered gardens of their country of origin—often in the form of exuberant STATUARY, FOUNTAINS, and TOPIARY—reflecting the phenomenon of 'invented traditions' described by John Dixon Hunt in *Denatured Visions* (1991).   HELEN ARMSTRONG

MILES, William Wallace (1827–1908), nursery proprietor and florist, was born in Bedfordshire, England, and migrated to Geelong (Vic.) in 1849. In 1853 he established Mercer's Hill Garden, a nursery in Noble Street, Newtown, where he specialised in glasshouse plants, becoming noted for Regal Pelagoniums. A subsidiary business as seed merchant and florist in Ryrie Street, Geelong, began in 1868 in partnership with his son John Otway Miles (b. 1849), born at sea off Cape Otway. Their 1872 catalogue included seeds of thirty Australian plants. Miles was a foundation member (1855) and later a life member of Geelong and Western District Agricultural and Horticultural Society, and was active as a committee member, judge, and exhibitor of the Horticultural Improvement Association of the Western District from its foundation (1860). For thirty-five years from 1869 he was a Newtown and Chilwell councilor, and mayor on three occasions, taking a leading part as a trustee in the development of Queen's Park, Newtown.   GEORGE JONES

MILLIGAN, Joseph (1807–1884), surgeon and naturalist, was born in Dumfrieshire, Scotland. He graduated in 1829 and took up the post of surgeon at the Surry Hills establishment of the Van Diemen's Land Company in 1831. His later appointments included Inspector of Convict Discipline and Superintendent of Aborigines. In 1842 he accompanied Sir John and Lady FRANKLIN on their expedition to Macquarie Harbour. During his various appointments and travels around the island he collected botanical and geological specimens, including material for R.C. GUNN and W.J. HOOKER; his specimens are in the herbarium at KEW. He was Secretary of the Royal Society between 1848 and 1860, delivering lectures on a range of subjects including rainfall and palaeobotany. Milligan returned to Britain in 1860: he was described by J.D. HOOKER as 'one of the most indefatigable and able of Tasmanian botanists'. His contributions are recognised by the naming of several plants, including *Milligania*, a genus of native lily.

A. M. Buchanan, *The Tasmanian Collecting Localities of Ronald Gunn and Joseph Milligan* (Hobart, 1985)   LINDY SCRIPPS

MILTON PARK, Bowral, NSW: see HORDERN

MISSION GARDENS Church missions were established during the colonial period and early twentieth century, often located in remote areas, where self-sufficiency and practical gardening were essentials for survival. New Norcia, WA (1846), was one of the first to be established. The monastery building—with central COURTYARD garden, olive groves, and VINEYARDS—reflected the MEDITERRANEAN traditions of the founding Benedictine monks. Many missions and reserves were developed in the wake of the formation in 1836 of the Aborigines Protection Society. Devoted to the welfare of dispossessed or 'uncivilised' Aboriginals, these ranged from Coranderrk, Vic. (1863), and Hermannsburg, NT (1877), to Bathurst Island, NT (1911). Such settlements usually attempted some form of ornamental gardening around official residences and, importantly, in the quest for self-sufficiency, included extensive productive gardens tended by ABORIGINAL GARDENERS. In the Kimberley, in the wet-dry TROPICAL north of WA, the first of several missions was established at Beagle Bay (1890), where the Trappist monks developed flourishing gardens of tropical fruits, vegetables, rice, and sugar-cane. The Anglican mission on Forrest River (1913), now Oombulgurri, had a long ceremonial walk planted with *Adansonia gregorii* (Boab) trees, and at Kalumburu (1936) the gardens boasted ornamental plantings and lawns, as well as vegetable gardens, plantations of tropical fruits, citrus orchards, and avenues of coconut palms.

While New Norcia remains a Benedictine establishment, other former missions have become independent Aboriginal communities. A major change of official policy towards Aboriginal people came with the 1967 referendum, which formalised 'Aboriginal Affairs' as a Commonwealth responsibility. In the decades that followed, many missions formed the basis of self-governed Aboriginal communities, especially in the arid centre and tropical north of Australia, although many of these were distant from traditional homelands of dispossessed Aboriginal peoples.   RA

MITCHELL (née CHAUVEL), Elyne (1913–2002), writer, champion skier, and grazier-conservationist, daughter of military commander Sir Harry Chauvel, moved to Towong Hill (Vic.), a grazing property on the upper Murray in the foothills of the Snowy Mountains, after her marriage in 1935. Concerns for conserving the fertility of the earth and restoring an equilibrium in farming practices expressed in the third of Mitchell's thirty-one books, *Soil and Civilisation* (1946), were ahead of their time. *Australian Treescapes* (1950), with photographs by Harold Cazneaux, celebrated and popularised the AUSTRALIAN FLORA.   TRISHA DIXON

MITCHELL, Josiah (1822–1881), gardener, horticulturist, and agriculturist, was born in Whitehaven, Cumberland, England, and migrated to Vic. in 1853. He had been employed as a gardener to the Earl of Lonsdale, the Duke of Buccleuch, at the ROYAL BOTANIC GARDENS, KEW, and finally to T.G. Corbett of Elsham Hall. Upon arrival he was employed at the MELBOURNE BOTANIC GARDENS under John DALLACHY. After a short and unsuccessful visit to Forest Creek goldfields, Mitchell returned to Melbourne. There he superintended the laying out of MELBOURNE GENERAL CEMETERY to the design of Albert PURCHAS. He subsequently established a nursery at Fern Hill Gardens, Moonee Ponds, described in James SINCLAIR's *Gardeners' Magazine* (1856) as one of 'the most scientific practical gardens in the colony'. In 1857–58 Mitchell's nursery supplied trees, shrubs, and vines to Walter CLARK of Glenara. In 1859 he purchased twelve acres (5 ha) at Maribyrnong on the Saltwater River and planted an orchard. Mitchell was not merely a businessman; he was also fired by the philosophy of self-help of the Victorian age. In this guise, he was founding president (1860–62) of the Victorian Gardeners' Mutual Improvement Society. In his inaugural address Mitchell articulated an energetic and optimistic view of the colony as a place of limitless horticultural opportunity.

The year 1863 saw him lease the EXPERIMENTAL FARM in Melbourne's ROYAL PARK, where he conducted experiments relating to agriculture in the colony until 1871. Before taking up this appointment he had entered into a correspondence with T.C. COLE regarding the exhaustion of SOILS in the colony. Again Mitchell emerged as articulate and widely read, quoting LINDLEY's *Theory of Horticulture* to challenge his opponent's observations. During 1870–71 Mitchell was a member of the Board of Inquiry appointed to investigate and make recommendations regarding the administration and function of the Melbourne Botanic Gardens. As a proponent of the view that the gardens should demonstrate the practical aspects of horticulture, he was no supporter of the incumbent director, Ferdinand MUELLER.

On leaving the Experimental Farm, Mitchell pursued the practical benefits of AGRICULTURE in the Australian colonies. In 1874 he visited SA to judge flax harvesters, and in 1876 took charge of the Mount Derrimut shorthorn herd at Skelsmergh Hall, Carlsruhe (Vic.). In 1878 he visited the international show of cattle held in conjunction with the Paris EXHIBITION, while in 1880 he was the driving force behind the Vegetable Products Committee of the Melbourne Exhibition in his capacity as commissioner. Mitchell was a great disseminator of agricultural information to the wider colonial public. Between 1871 and 1874 he was agricultural editor of the *Leader*; in 1874 he wrote 'On Orange Culture' for the Agriculture Department of Victoria, and at the end of his life he was writing to the *Australasian* under the nom de plume 'Hodden-Cray'.

Mitchell also entered the political fray. He was a founder of the Victorian Farmers' Union (VFU) and in 1880 stood (albeit temporarily) for the Legislative Assembly seat of West Bourke, and unsuccessfully as the candidate for South Gipps-

Modernism

'On the way to work' at Notre Dame Abbey, Tarrawarra (Vic.), 1957, a purposeful and prayerful scene giving practical expression to the reverence for Nature as God's creation imbued in monastery and MISSION GARDENS

land on a platform that included VFU policies. Something of the personal attributes he brought to public discussion is captured in his obituary, where he was described as possessing 'good natured observations and unselfish views'.

Paul Fox, *Clearings: Six Colonial Gardeners and their Landscapes* (Carlton South, Vic., forthcoming 2003)   **PAUL FOX**

MITCHELL, Thomas Livingstone (1792–1855), surveyor-general, was born in Scotland, and in 1827, after a military career in topographical intelligence, arrived with his family in Sydney. He rose through the Survey Department, where he acknowledged draughtsman John THOMPSON a 'loyal lieutenant'. Mitchell's residence Craigend, Darlinghurst (1829), a very early essay in the Greek Revival, fused archaeological detail with PICTURESQUE sensibility. Conversant with the writings of PRICE, he was a veritable disciple of LOUDON, promoting Loudonian ideals for public spaces in the colony, manifest in schemes for the extension of Sydney's HYDE PARK. Mitchell's overland expeditions during the 1830s and 1840s—especially that through 'Australian Felix' (1836)—paved the way for pastoral settlement in Vic. where, enchanted, he described the countryside as being like an English gentleman's PARK. Mitchell returned to England (1837–41), where he published an account of his expeditions; once back in NSW he started to build Carthona, Darling Point (1841–44), modelled on Charles Fowler's 'Villa in the Old English Manner' (illustrated by Loudon). Parkhall, Douglas Park (1842–45), Mitchell's country seat south-west of Sydney, was based on a pattern in Goodwin's *Rural Architecture* (1835), described by Loudon as 'original, architectural and good'. Here Francis FERGUSON began his colonial career as Mitchell's gardener. Both Carthona and Parkhall demonstrated Mitchell's conversion to Romantic medievalism. A man of arrogant pretensions, his influence on his colleagues (including government architect Mortimer Lewis) and his broad-scale involvement in planning, made a lasting impression on the colonial landscape.

J.H.L. Cumpston, *Thomas Mitchell: Surveyor General & Explorer* (Melbourne, 1954); W.C. Foster, *Sir Thomas Livingstone Mitchell and his World 1792–1855* (Sydney, 1985); James Broadbent, *The Australian Colonial House: Architecture and Society in New South Wales 1788–1842* (Sydney, 1997)

COLLEEN MORRIS

MODERNISM, as derived from European avant-garde art and architectural movements of the 1920s, made only a fleeting appearance in Australian garden design before 1940. While gardens provided crucial visual counterpoints to the abstract forms of buildings such as Taylor Soilleux & Overend's Cairo flats, Fitzroy, Vic. (1935–36), and John Brogan and W.A. Crowle's Wyldefel Gardens, Potts Point, NSW (1935–36), these landscapes were rarely designed with the same stylistic consistency as the architecture. Exceptions were the brick planter walls of Dutch-influenced Modernist buildings and the Jazz-styled geometric paving and planting beds that were invariably accoutrements of the architecture itself.

Modernism in garden design was more frequently seen as accompaniment to 1930s house competition drawings by architects such as Arthur Baldwinson, who had worked for Walter Gropius and who, like many others, had a working knowledge of Christopher Tunnard's *Gardens in the Modern Landscape* (1938). Danish émigré landscape gardener Paul SORENSEN was the notable exception. The ROOF GARDEN for Feltex House, Sydney (1938), and pool terrace at EVERGLADES, Leura, NSW (1937), with which he was associated, were both examples of stylish flat planes contained by framing walls and pergolas. At Leura, the Australian bush that lay outside the architectonic garden framework contrasted with the severe modern forms of the architecture. A different but similarly progressive understanding of landscape design was a form of artless naturalism exemplified by the amoeba-shaped swimming pool for Miss E. Hughes-Jones, Olinda, Vic. (1939) designed by Edna WALLING. Such naturalism would find its apotheosis in the 1950s rock and bush gardens of Ellis STONES and find its greatest popularity in the Australian BUSH GARDENS of the 1960s–70s.

The Second World War dramatically refocused attention on the garden. Modernism shifted from aesthetics to aspects of economy, space-saving, and efficiency. In Qld, Austrian émigré architect and planner Karl LANGER argued for the complete integration of house and landscape. The garden was functionalised. In his *Homes in the Sun* (1945), Sydney architect Walter Bunning's proposed 'Suntrap Houses' were planned for sun, privacy, and maximum space with minimum means. For the aerial Modernist house, like Harry Seidler's Rose Seidler House, Turramurra, NSW (1947–50), the Australian landscape became a neutral backdrop, a site scraped clean for the house as sculptural object. The post-war house became the focus of a post-war lifestyle—outdoor living with the PATIO, the SWIMMING POOL, and the BARBECUE.

The glamorous Modern shapes and forms of Californian landscape designers Garret Eckbo and Thomas Church influenced garden designs by Ron RAYMENT first in Brisbane, then in Melbourne, and John OLDHAM in Perth—both architects who changed disciplines, later to become leaders of the new Australian landscape design profession. In *The Australian Roadside* (1952), Walling altered her plant preferences and design focus away from exotics, mirroring a new enthusiasm for AUSTRALIAN PLANTS, and especially their use in projects of modernity, such as post-war highways. Landscape designers such as Otto RUZICKA in Canberra and Ilmars BERZINS in Sydney brought sweeping curves and graphic shapes to the design of municipal and institutional landscapes. In the gardens of high-rise buildings, the low-maintenance biomorphic gardens of Brazilian designer Roberto Burle Marx provided inspiration for Melbourne landscape designer John STEVENS, who also incorporated abstract SCULPTURE, as in the garden of ICI House, Melbourne (1955–58). The provision of designed open space and a landscaped plaza at ground level enabled the breaking of the forty-metre height limit, and so began the visual transformation of the Australian city at ground level and at its skyline. Outside the cities, the new landscapes of mining towns, hydro-electric schemes, reservoirs, dams, and coastal tourism formed part of Australia's post-war economic recovery, and by the 1960s landscape was being engineered in the name of modernity rather than Modernism.

Dorothee Imbert, *The Modernist Garden in France* (New Haven and London, 1993); Jane Brown, *The Modern Garden* (London, 2000)

PHILIP GOAD

MOFFLIN, Horace Elgar (1867–1939), rosarian and wool merchant, was born in Auckland, New Zealand, and arrived in Perth in 1887. In 1922 he moved to Darlington, where he created a large rose garden of more than a thousand bushes, regularly opened for charity. Foundation president of the NATIONAL ROSE SOCIETY of Western Australia (1932–39) and regular prize winner at local agricultural and HORTICULTURAL SHOWS, his contribution is also recognised by the Mofflin Gate at Perth SHOWGROUNDS. CAROL MANSFIELD

MOIDART, Bowral, NSW, remains one of the finest inter-war gardens of the SOUTHERN HIGHLANDS. In 1930 shipping merchant James Burns (1881–1969) bought part of the Eridge Park estate, subsequently commissioning architect Laidley Dowling (1888–1981) to design a country home. House and surrounding gardens, particularly the south elevation, terrace, and sunken rose garden, are superbly integrated, suggesting a master plan by Dowling. A driveway winds gently to the front of the house, ending in a turning loop where a wide sweep of lawn is encircled by beds filled with white roses. The garden's form has remained largely unaltered, although plant growth has changed the emphasis in some areas. In spring, bluebells and daffodils are highlights, while in autumn deciduous trees, now seventy years old, are splendid. CHRISTINE REID

MOLINEUX, Albert (1832–1909), publisher and agriculturist, born in Brighton, Sussex, England, arrived in Adelaide in 1839, later becoming an advocate and practitioner of innovations in agriculture, economic forestry, horticulture, and gardening in SA. He worked variously as a farmer and a printing compositor before launching the GARDEN AND (THE) FIELD in 1875. Through this journal, which he edited until 1892, Molineux advocated establishment of EXPERIMENTAL FARMS, STATE FOREST NURSERIES and plantation trials, appointment of a professor of agriculture, establishment of AGRICULTURAL COLLEGES, creation of AGRICULTURE and FORESTRY departments, replacement of wheat monoculture with scientifically based and diversified agriculture, improved FERTILISERS and use of superphosphate, and establishment of butter factories. He disseminated technical information on fruit and vegetable canning, pickling advances, and insecticide and fungicide sprays. Molineux served as agricultural editor for the *Register* and ADELAIDE OBSERVER newspapers from 1875 to 1891. With his knowledge and acknowledged expertise, Molineux successfully proposed the establishment of a government Agricultural Bureau (1887) and served as its general secretary (1888–1902). He incorporated its *Journal of the Bureau of Agriculture* within *Garden and Field* (1894–97) before it was separately published as the *South Australian JOURNAL OF AGRICULTURE*. He also compiled a *Handbook for*

Olga Sharp's photograph of EVERGLADES, Leura (NSW), perfectly unites MODERNISM in the photographer's art and the garden designer's hand

Farmers and Gardeners in Australia (1893). While his desire was simply to increase communication between the farmer and the scientist, Molineux became known as the 'walking encyclopedia of miscellaneous information' in SA.   DAVID JONES

MOLLISON, Bruce Charles (Bill): see PERMACULTURE

MOLLOY (née KENNEDY), Georgiana (1805–1843), plant collector, was at the frontier of the first invasive wave of European settlers in the south-western corner of Australia. As indigenous people and plants were sacrificed to the god of British economic expansion, Molloy noted with increasing interest and affection the flora around her, and collecting plants for dispatch to England became her 'all consuming passion'. Newly married to Captain John Molloy, a veteran of the Napoleonic Wars, Georgiana Molloy arrived in the embryonic Swan River Colony in 1830. In search of available fertile land, they left the dust, flies, fleas, and mosquitoes of Perth and Fremantle for the cooler, moister, and unsurveyed jarrah forests east of Cape Leeuwin. Captain Molloy became the resident magistrate for the tiny community at the newly surveyed township site for Augusta.

In between bearing, rearing, and burying children, and shouldering manifold household and farm duties, often during her husband's absences, Georgiana Molloy somehow managed to find time and energy to cherish her garden of exotic flowers and to collect indigenous flowers from the encircling bush—'being in the Bush was one of the most delightful states of existence free from every household care'. She even named one of her daughters Flora. Her collecting was spurred by a request for Western Australian plants by Captain James MANGLES, who in return sent her English seeds and botanical books. Molloy's collecting was organised and thorough. She numbered each selection of SEEDS, carefully pressed HERBARIUM specimens, included information about growing conditions and locale, kept a set of duplicate specimens, and asked Mangles for their taxonomic names. She convinced 'Native Herdsmen' (local Nyungar people) and passing soldiers to bring her plants. Via Mangles, her seeds reached British gardens and her herbarium specimens reached William HOOKER and other British botanical authorities. Some were new to science. LINDLEY's *A Sketch of the Vegetation of the Swan River Colony* (1839) was based largely on Mangles' herbarium, which included many of Molloy's specimens. She invited the visiting botanist Ludwig PREISS to stay at the Molloy home on the Vasse River (near present-day Busselton) in 1839 and took him collecting. Preiss provided some plant names, but Molloy was disappointed with his 'rough and ungainly' preparation of herbarium specimens and his unfulfilled promise of further botanical information.

Following the difficult birth of her last baby, and a few weeks before her thirty-eighth birthday, Georgiana Molloy died—after thirteen years and eight pregnancies in WA. She was survived in Australia by her five daughters and husband,

and in Europe by strange and beautiful Australian plants pressed in herbaria and growing in gardens. She is commemorated by the beautiful *Boronia molloyae*.

> Alexandra Hasluck, *Portrait with Background: A Life of Georgiana Molloy* (Melbourne, 1955); William J. Lines, *An All Consuming Passion: Origins, Modernity, and the Australian Life of Georgiana Molloy* (St Leonards, NSW, 1994)

LINDEN GILLBANK

MOLYNEUX, William Mitchell (b. 1935), landscape designer and horticulturist, born in Footscray (Vic.), developed an affinity with AUSTRALIAN PLANTS through the basalt plains and Maribyrnong River near his home. Entering horticulture in 1969, he gained a certificate at BURNLEY COLLEGE, taking over Austraflora Nursery in 1972, and was later joined by his wife, Sue Forrester (b. 1945), a horticulturist and a contributor and assistant in much of his work. Bill Molyneux's output extends from landscaping using Australian plants for BP (Australia), REVEGETATION for mining companies, and vegetation planning for a South Australian expressway, to planting designs for private gardens, including some by Ellis STONES. An Honorary Research Fellow at La Trobe University, his botanical interests include *ACACIA*, *Callistemon*, and *GREVILLEA*. Plants bearing his name include *Grevillea molyneuxii* and *Eucalyptus molyneuxii*, in recognition of his involvement in saving its Little Desert habitat. Author or co-author of several books, Molyneux wrote for the *Age* newspaper (1979–98), and now concentrates on selecting and developing new varieties of Australian plants for horticultural use, and in the design and planting of wetlands.

JILL KELLOW

MONA VALE: see The MIDLANDS, Tas.

MONUMENT HILL (formerly Obelisk Hill), Fremantle, WA, overlooks the city and port of Fremantle and the Indian Ocean. In 1867 a stone OBELISK was constructed on the hill as a navigational aid for ships entering the port. After the First World War, the local community pressed for the erection of a WAR MEMORIAL on the site. This was designed by architects J.F. Allen and C.H. Nicholas, but due to financial constraints was not built until 1928. Since then, other smaller memorials have been added. Sustenance workers developed the grounds around the monument in the 1930s, implementing a restrained design that features formal paths and AVENUES of *Phoenix canariensis* (Canary Island Date Palm) and *Araucaria hetrophylla* (Norfolk Island Pine) trees, sweeping lawns, and well-maintained beds of flowering annuals.

PHILIP PALMER

MOOLERIC, situated on the basalt plains at the foot of Mount Gellibrand, Birregurra (Vic.), formed the north-eastern section of the Mount Gellibrand Station, taken up by pastoralists in 1841. It was purchased by brothers Robert Andrew (1869–1948) and Urquhart Ramsay (b. 1871) in 1899 and remained in family ownership until 1999. William GUILFOYLE, a close family friend, was invited to redevelop the garden that surrounded the original bluestone homestead (1871). The two-hectare garden, laid out under Guilfoyle's direction *c.* 1903–09, is an outstanding and relatively intact example of his mature landscape design. Entrance GATES flanked by ROCKERIES (planted with CACTI and succulents) head a winding drive that leads to sweeping lawns bordered by dense shrubberies, meandering perimeter walks, and an ornamental pond. The design incorporates striking SUBTROPICAL plants and includes such rarities as *Maytenus boaria*, *Prunus limonii*, *Aloe lettyae*, *Podachaenium eminens*, and *Phaedranthus buccinatorius*. Mooleric is enhanced by considerable surviving documentation, including Guilfoyle's plan, garden building designs, and planting lists held by the State Library of Victoria; letters and photographs are held by the family.

EVE ALMOND

MOORA PARK, Shorncliffe, Qld, set high above Moreton Bay, was a favoured Brisbane beach resort, especially after a rail link was opened (1882). Sandgate pier, a kiosk, amusement arcade, and sea baths were early facilities, later complemented by a bandstand (1897) and Spanish Mission–style kiosk (1928, demolished 1975). Donkey rides, outdoor films, and dancing on removable timber decks provided highlights for the holiday makers and daytrippers until the Second World War. Set on the high ground of Shorncliffe, Moora Park links with the Sandgate Esplanade via 'Lover's Lane' and around the cliffs south to Cabbage Tree Creek. The park remains a favourite destination and retains many early trees.

JEANNIE SIM

MOORE, Charles (1820–1905) botanic gardens director, was born into a farming family at Dundee, Scotland, the son of Charles Moir and Helen (*née* Rattray). In about 1828 the form Moore was adopted. Young Charles received elementary education at Dundee, but after his mother's death in 1832, was sent as an apprentice to Trinity College Botanic Garden, Dublin, where his eldest brother David (1808–1879) had been foreman since 1828. While training, Charles won several prizes, including, in 1835, the 'first premium' in the Horticultural Society of Ireland's annual examination for journeymen gardeners.

David Moore served as botanist to the Irish Ordnance Survey from 1834 until 1838, when he began a distinguished forty-one year career at Glasnevin Botanic Gardens, Dublin. Charles joined the Survey in May 1837, succeeding his brother as botanist until he resigned to go to England *c.* 1840. By October 1843, he had charge of 'perennial hardy plants in the botanical arrangement' at the Royal Botanic Society's garden in Regent's Park, London. In 1844 he revisited Ireland, collecting for this garden, where he was now foreman. Two years later he again travelled to Ireland, also to Scotland, and wrote a prize-winning essay on hybridisation. It has been recorded that Moore spent time at the ROYAL BOTANIC GARDENS, KEW. If so, the period must have been brief, whether he worked there or merely visited, for by 1847 he was at the centre of a classic bureaucratic bungle.

Following the resignation of Allan CUNNINGHAM (1838), the SYDNEY BOTANIC GARDENS deteriorated, owing to lack of professional care, drought, depression, and withdrawal of convict labour. When Governor FitzRoy arrived in 1846, there was concern in both Sydney and London at the insti-

The BANDSTAND (1897) at MOORA PARK, Shorncliffe (Qld), doubled as a refreshment kiosk; its exuberant architecture vividly conveyed the excitement of a seaside excursion

tution's reduced state and status. On local advice, FitzRoy appointed John Carne BIDWILL 'Government Botanist and Director of the Botanic Gardens', while Lord Grey, on advice from professors John LINDLEY and John Henslow (but not from Sir William Hooker of Kew) appointed Charles Moore. Despite local protests at 'Downing Street meddling', the imperial decision prevailed. Bringing five cases of 'rare and valuable Plants' from Glasnevin, Turnham Green, and Kew 'in excellent condition', Moore arrived in January 1848 and assumed control from Bidwill.

Young, tall, dignified, and 'a charming conversationalist', Moore encountered a somewhat hostile scientific community, and promptly received ample advice and instruction from Alexander McLEAY and other members of the Committee of Management. He responded quickly and creditably, restoring 'the Borders … and the Walks'; labelling the plants; establishing 'Botanical arrangements'; distributing seeds, cuttings and plants; compiling stringent rules of admittance and conduct; and, in 1849, submitting an informative report. William MACARTHUR, a Bidwill supporter, conceded that Moore speedily 'effected considerable improvements' and was 'most civil and obliging'. The new director pledged to make 'the Institution an object of interest and importance, as well for the study of Botany and Horticulture, as for … pleasure and recreation'. He began reclamation work in Farm Cove,

realigning its shoreline in a prolonged building project that was appropriately dubbed the 'Thirty Years' Wall'. In 1851, 'to introduce a taste for the science of Botany', he instituted popular lectures that continued intermittently until 1882.

In 1850 Moore collected in the Blue Mountains before joining HMS *Havannah* for the South Seas. From 1852 to 1854 he concentrated on the Castlereagh River and the Warrumbungle Mountains; travelled to Moreton Bay and Wide Bay (where he reported 'upon the plants left by the late Mr Bidwell' [sic] and collected for the Paris Exhibition); established a herbarium and a 'Public Botanical Library' of twenty-six works; and implemented sand-drift control at Newcastle. In 1855, Moore was relentlessly interrogated during an inquiry into 'the Management and Conduct of the Botanic Garden'. His qualifications, knowledge, accounts, lectures, and administration were all questioned, but the beleaguered director was defended by the Committee secretary, the Reverend George Turner, horticultural rector of Ryde, who had officiated at Moore's marriage to Elizabeth Bennett Edwards (1849).

Moore emerged from the gruelling examination chastened and chary, but grateful to Governor DENISON for rejecting moves to downgrade him. Another inquiry was held in 1861 to examine 'the present state and management of the Sydney Domain'. Surviving that ordeal also, Moore thereafter enjoyed general approbation for developing the vast reserves under his control. He became rather settled, even failing to furnish annual reports for one period of thirteen, and another of eighteen, years. In 1861 Moore collected timbers for the London Exhibition on the Richmond and Clarence Rivers, describing them in 'Woods Indigenous to the Northern Districts of the Colony'. He visited the Paris Exhibition (1867), where he met and travelled with William ROBINSON. In 1869, accompanied by surveyor-orchidologist Robert David FITZGERALD and Gardens collector William CARRON, he travelled to Lord Howe Island in the *Thetis*. In 1874 he joined brother David at the Botanical Conference in Florence.

Moore popularised the Jacaranda, Pepper Tree, and the 'gorgeous Hibiscus', and his introductions are said to have included *Howea forsteriana* (Kentia Palm) and *H. belmoreana* (Curly Palm) from Lord Howe Island. He is also remembered for establishing the celebrated Palm Grove in the Botanic Gardens (1862) and for having, as Robert Etheridge put it, a 'predilection for that scourge of gardens, the Moreton Bay Fig'. He compiled *A Census of the Plants of New South Wales* (1884) and, with the diligent aid of Ernst BETCHE, a *Handbook of the Flora of New South Wales* (1893) that remained the only such work for a century.

Moore's most significant and enduring work lay in developing Sydney's reserves, not only the Gardens and Domains, and the grounds of official residences, but also HYDE, VICTORIA, Wentworth, and CENTENNIAL Parks. He landscaped the lawns and gardens around the Garden Palace, and after it burnt down (1882), reclaimed the site as the Palace Gardens. In 1879 he advocated 're-foresting the country' and recommended the establishment of a government nursery. Two years later, twenty-two acres (8.8 ha) were reserved for this purpose at Campbelltown. Thereafter the distribution of plants to public reserves, institutional gardens, cemeteries, church, and school grounds, and railway stations was both wide and generous.

A Fellow of the Linnean Society, member of the Royal Botanic Society of London, and associated with the Philosophical (later Royal), Zoological, and Agricultural Societies, the Australian Museum and the (ROYAL) NATIONAL PARK south of Port Hacking, Moore became widely known. Seemingly indestructible, he enjoyed his public office and life in the Gardens residence until 1896, when the Public Service Board abruptly terminated his services and appointed J.H. MAIDEN. After a third trip to Europe, he retired to Myola, in Queen Street, Woollahra, where he died. Maiden was not the last to lament that Moore 'never committed to paper the horticultural and botanical reminiscences of his long official career'. He is commemorated by a handsome monument in the old Anglican section of ROOKWOOD CEMETERY, and by many plant species, including the remarkable *Nothofagus moorei* (Antarctic Beech). LIONEL GILBERT

MOORE, Gregory (b. 1952), educationalist, completed a PhD in botany (1982) after taking up a lecturing position at BURNLEY Horticultural College. He was appointed Principal in 1988 and was instrumental in the introduction of the first degree course in horticulture (1985) and subsequently a postgraduate program leading to a PhD. He has also promoted courses across a wide EDUCATIONAL range, from short introductory courses in horticulture to TAFE certificates able to be taken in the evening and higher education diplomas specialising in parks and gardens, nursery production, landscape construction, and arboriculture. He has a strong interest in ARBORICULTURE, writing and presenting many papers in local and international forums. He was inaugural president of the Australian Chapter of the International Society of Arboriculture (1997–98). ML

MOORE, Henry (*fl.* 1913–40), horticulturist and landscape gardener, came from Eaglehawk (Vic.) and was appointed the first Parks Superintendent for the Brisbane City Council (1913). His design work in Brisbane is significant and includes NEW FARM PARK, redevelopment of BOWEN PARK and NEWSTEAD PARK, and numerous additions to inner city PUBLIC PARKS. Another contribution was his novel method of constructing dry stone WALLS to create raised garden beds (or ROCKERIES) within streets (Kangaroo Point (1914) and Gregory Terrace (1916), Spring Hill) and within parks—YERONGA, Newstead, MUSGRAVE, and Lang parks. These were planted with a mixture of plants akin to a border and usually included flowering shrubs, perennials, and annuals tolerant of a SUBTROPICAL climate with an irregular rainfall and little maintenance. *Syagrus romanzoffianum* (Queen Palm) and poinsettias were particularly favoured by Moore in these beds. Moore's design work is yet to receive appropriate recognition. JEANNIE SIM

MORAL IMPROVEMENT and its connection with gardening has been a strong theme in nineteenth- and twentieth-century garden writing and thought. The roots of this association perhaps lie in the Judeo-Christian belief that cultivation of the soil was a God-given instruction. Acting on this became a mark of civilisation: gardens and gardening promoted home life and reflected a settled, domesticated society. In colonial Australia, where concerns about the moral fibre of the new country were heightened, gardens were seen as a mark of ownership, respectability, and order. In the wake of the turmoil of the gold rushes, men in particular were encouraged to garden in the hope that it would 'save them from many temptations'. Tending the garden would settle the souls of restless Australian men. Women could nurture their souls through rest and recreation in the garden. The working class—always at risk in the moral order—were a particular target in the promotion of gardening; those without gardens could visit PUBLIC GARDENS where their souls could be uplifted and their thoughts refined.

In the early twentieth century the concern to create a settled domestic life took on new dimensions. A new nation needed settled homes and good citizens, and gardens were crucial to both. As gardeners, citizens would be committed to creating beauty and valuing what was good. In the pages of GARDEN MAGAZINES and BOOKS, the 'citizen gardener' began to take on a particular identity: he was an earnest sort of chap who took seriously the task of beautifying his patch, growing vegetables to feed his family, and upholding the values of

This Picture represents a Neglected Garden.

"This, one of Mitchell's Favourites."

Melbourne seed merchant C.W. Mitchell's 1897 advertisement contrasted an axe-swinging harridan in her neglected garden with the MORAL IMPROVEMENT gardening could exercise—as shown in her conversion to an angelic young figure tending an orderly and productive plot

decency and moral order. He was an amateur, who may have taken much of his advice from BRUNNING's *Australian Gardener*, where the chapter on the 'Ethics of Gardening' issued strict instructions on the use of such things as manure, drains, and garden tools. Order, neatness, and even FORMALITY were to reign supreme—values reinforced through the numerous local gardening COMPETITIONS around the country.

The concern with citizenship, order, and compliance, inflected as it was with assumptions about race and class and GENDER, also found expression in the GARDEN CITY MOVEMENT. Gardens were necessary for a 'decent family life'. Walter Bunning, in *Homes in the Sun* (1945), observed that in inner city homes without space for gardens 'they grow sooty stunted flowers like their own withered lives'. Gardens provided lawns for children to play on, and educating CHILDREN in the love of gardening was a key strategy in their moral improvement. NATURE STUDY and gardening were thus taught in SCHOOLS in the hope that children would grow into public-spirited citizens. As the (AUSTRALIAN) GARDEN LOVER (1925) put it, 'The love of horticulture is of national significance, bringing with it a love of home life and pride of country'. Gardens had become a symbol of civilisation, respectability, and nationalism. In the twenty-first century, however, 'civilisation' is often closely linked to environmental destruction. CHEMICAL-free gardening is now promoted as the morally right and ecologically sustainable way to protect not only the national environment but also that of the globe.

KATIE HOLMES

MORLEY, Brian Derek (b. 1943), horticultural botanist and director of the ADELAIDE BOTANIC GARDEN (1980–2000), was born in Coventry, England. Author of *Wildflowers of the World* (1970), *Flowering Plants of the World* (1978), *Flowering Plants in Australia* (1983), and many technical papers, he enhanced the collections and resources of the Gardens. In particular, he facilitated restoration of the Museum of Economic Botany, Yarrabee House, and Palm House, development of the Bicentennial Conservatory (1989), and relocation of headquarters and HERBARIUM with the eastern expansion of the Gardens (1999). He supported the 'FRIENDS GROUP' established by Noel LOTHIAN and promoted the Gardens and Botanic Park for multicultural activities and events. A strong advocate of national and international collaboration, with experience in Britain, Jamaica, and Ireland, he was secretary-general of the International Association of Botanic Gardens (1984–94), a scientific adviser to the US National Tropical Botanical Gardens in Kaui, Hawaii (1989–93), and advised on the AUSTRALIAN ARID LANDS BOTANIC GARDEN.

DAVID JONES

MORRIS, Albert (1886–1939), horticulturist and botanist, was a pioneer of ARID-zone REVEGETATION ideas and practices in Australia. With his wife Ellen Margaret (*née* Sayce) (1882–1957)—who carried on after his early death—he initiated and guided development in the 1930s of revegetation plantations and parklands in and around Broken Hill (NSW), comprising an area of thirteen square kilometres called the Common. Morris concluded from his experiments that species grown from seed collected from local NATIVE FLORA withstood drought conditions better than introduced species. In 1936 Zinc Corporation Ltd consulted Morris, then working as an assayer, on suitable aesthetic treatment of nine hectares of new works areas. Tubestock and young sapling plantings of *Eucalyptus camaldulensis*, *E. largiflorens*, and *Atriplex nummularia* planted inside iron fences had a remarkable strike rate. Within nine months regeneration of native GRASSES, cassias, and various native colonisers was evident, proving his theory that 'if the land was fenced from stock and rabbits, the area would regenerate naturally'. This project led to the corporation establishing a nursery, and Morris successfully experimenting with simple wastewater IRRIGATION systems. With further success of these plantations—publicised to gardeners by E.E. LORD (1948)—the various mining companies enticed the Broken Hill Council to permit broadscale planting throughout the Common from 1937 'to control erosion and help prevent sand drift', as well as to physically define the township. Morris corresponded with ASHBY and BURDETT, amassed a large private HERBARIUM, and regularly exchanged seedstock world-wide.

Horace Webber, *The Greening of the Hill: Revegetation around Broken Hill in the 1930s* (Melbourne, 1992) DAVID JONES

MORRISON, (Philip) Crosbie (1900–1958), nature writer and broadcaster, completed a prize-studded zoological science degree at the University of Melbourne and post-graduate research—including six months on Australia's Great Barrier

Reef—before joining Melbourne's *Argus* newspaper as a cadet in 1926. He reported on a wide range of subjects under various pseudonyms, and helped Donald MACDONALD prepare his last nature columns. After Russell GRIMWADE convinced Sir Keith MURDOCH (of the Herald and Weekly Times Ltd) to publish an illustrated magazine on Australian NATURAL HISTORY, Morrison left the *Argus* to edit and prepare text and photographs for the monthly *Wild Life* (1938–54). It carried floral material by Ros GARNET, E. E. PESCOTT, and photographer Herbert Trethowan Reeves (1894–1963), and Morrison's persistent plea for nature conservation and better management of NATIONAL PARKS. For the centenary of MELBOURNE BOTANIC GARDENS he prepared a commemorative book funded by the new Maud Gibson (Gardens) Trust. *Melbourne's Garden* (1946) included chapters on the Gardens' origins, directors, lawns, lakes, birds, notable trees, recreational pleasures, and the National HERBARIUM. In a chapter on AUSTRALIAN FLORA, Morrison hoped that the beauty of the Gardens' Australian Border would encourage the taming of indigenous plants in other gardens. Declared Victoria's most popular RADIO personality (for his weekly nature program), he attracted a huge and far-flung listening and reading audience, and was Australia's 'Voice of Nature'.

Graham Pizzey, *Crosbie Morrison: Voice of Nature* (Melbourne, 1992)   LINDEN GILLBANK

MORT, Thomas Sutcliffe (1816–1878), businessman and horticulturist, was born at Bolton, Lancashire, England, and worked as a clerk, seizing the chance to migrate to Sydney in 1838 to bolster the family fortunes. In 1843 he set up as an auctioneer, becoming an innovator in wool sales. Pastoral interests included FRANKLYN VALE (Qld). By the end of the decade his fortune was made, but he restlessly pursued other projects, some ill-starred. His wealth facilitated his considerable horticultural ambitions. **Greenoaks** (later Bishopscourt), his Darling Point property, set the tone among the fashionable villas of this choice Sydney resort. Developing it from 1846, Mort employed the newly arrived Michael GUILFOYLE as his gardener and created a celebrated landscaped garden. In 1860 Mort acquired the Bodalla estate on the South Coast (NSW), where his gardener Michael Bell took up farm management in 1866, replaced at Greenoaks by George Mortimore. Both gardeners, like Guilfoyle and Mort, were active members of the Horticultural Society of New South Wales; Mort became its respected president in the 1860s and pursued HYBRIDISATION of CACTI in Sydney's premier garden.

Eirene Mort (1879–1977), whose father was T.S. Mort's nephew, was an accomplished artist and ARTS AND CRAFTS devotee, illustrating Florence SULMAN's *Wild Flowers of New South Wales* (1913–14).

Alan Barnard, *Thomas Sutcliffe Mort* (Melbourne, 1962)   COLLEEN MORRIS

MORTLOCK, James John (*c.* 1833–1909), London-born journalist and amateur florist, arrived in Sydney in 1882. He was a contributor to the *Sydney Morning Herald* and *SYDNEY MAIL*, and came to prominence through his book *Australian Amateur Gardening* (1895). This covered plants of contemporary popularity: ROSE, CHRYSANTHEMUM, FUCHSIA, CARNATION, PELARGONIUM, begonia, pansy, dahlia, bouvardia, primula, cineraria, CAMELLIA, azalea, auricula, gloxinia, and coleus, as well as FERNS and BULBS. On the arrangement of gardens, Mortlock cautioned against 'attempting too much'.   RA

MOSEL, Ken Lampert (1903–1971), head gardener at BROADLEES in the ADELAIDE HILLS (1925–48), laid out much of the garden, constructing the walls and fountains. He also established a small nursery that often supplied the plants the Waite sisters donated to projects in Adelaide. His brother, Crawford Lampert (Ted) Mosel (b. 1915), was a gardener at Yultewirra, Thorpe, and PANMURE in the Adelaide Hills, and in St Peters in the 1910s–20s. Their uncle, Albert Edward Mosel (1884–1971), was head gardener at GLENALTA in the 1910s–40s.   DAVID JONES

MOSS, Francis (*c.* 1834–1916), nursery proprietor and pomologist, arrived from England *c.* 1852 and established his business at Buninyong (Vic.) in 1853, capitalising on the demand for fruit and ornamental trees in the rapidly developing town gardens of Ballarat and hinterland farmsteads in the years following local gold rushes. By the 1870s, the Mossmount Nursery was not only a successful nursery but a popular place of resort during the summer months, with ten acres (4 ha) devoted to fruits, and seven acres (2.8 ha) to 'floral and arboricultural beauty'; close to the house was a 'large two-storey Swiss Arbor'.

With acumen, Moss foresaw the potential and demand for fruit trees in newly settled areas of South Gippsland, then being opened through land selection. He acquired land on the Tarwin River near Leongatha (*c.* 1888) and with capital derived from his Buninyong nursery, employed a gang of thirty scrub cutters to clear land for his new nursery; land was also leased at Ruby Creek. Between the wars, the grounds became a popular venue for sports meetings; community pressure in the 1940s (following sale of the site) resulted in the purchase by Woorayl Shire Council of a portion henceforth dedicated to public purposes. Mature trees from the nursery still ornament Moss Vale Park.

A.M. Blundell, *Francis Moss and Moss Vale Park* (Leongatha, Vic., 1956)   RA

MOSS, George William (1837–1923), nursery proprietor, was born in Worcestershire, England, and arrived in Brisbane in 1877. By 1887 he had established the Cemetery Nurseries, located in Sylvan Road, Toowong. Strategically close to the BRISBANE GENERAL CEMETERY, Moss specialised in ROSES, cut flowers, wreaths and crosses ('made to order on the shortest notice'), and 'all kinds of suitable trees'. He also advertised 'Graves Tiled, Planted and Attended to by the year'—a pioneer in this form of necropolitan landscaping.   RA

MOTT(E), Hamilton Charnock (1871–1963), journalist, newspaper proprietor, and sweet pea hybridiser, was born in Hamilton (Vic.) into a newspaper family. His father had migrated to Melbourne in 1853 before settling in Albury

An 1857 engraving of Thomas MORT's Greenoaks, Darling Point (NSW), shows the generous expanse of the pleasure garden at one of Sydney's most celebrated VILLA GARDENS

(NSW), where he established the *Border Post* (1856) before becoming part-proprietor of the *Hamilton Spectator* (1869–85) and, later, managing director of Gordon & Gotch. Hamilton Mott received his training on a family paper, the *Essendon Gazette and Flemington Spectator*, before he and two brothers moved to WA in the 1890s to try their fortunes. They started the *Western Argus* in Kalgoorlie, but early in the new century they returned to Vic.; Hamilton went to Albury, where he established the *Border Mail* (1903) against strong competition. His chief outside interest was gardening. He was one of several HYBRIDISTS who bred an early, winter-flowering strain of SWEET PEA, avoiding blooms being spoilt by the withering heat of Australian summers. He published his results widely, including articles in the English *Sweet Pea Annual* and the *'War Chest' Flower Book* (1917). His 'Motte' seeds—a spelling he adopted around this time in dealing with the sweet-pea world—were commercially developed with widespread success.   RA

MOUNT As artificial eminences, mounts developed as a post-medieval feature of European gardens, but followed precedents of artificial hills or mounds from much earlier cultures. From functional as well as decorative origins—providing different microclimates for plants and acting as LOOKOUTS—mounts also became symbols of power and dominance, especially in the rare instances they were constructed in Australian gardens. William SANGSTER included one (now-razed) in Victoria Gardens, Prahran (*c.* 1885), made from excavated soil from a sunken oval—perhaps a POLITICAL gesture of municipal aggrandisement. At RIPPON LEA (*c.* 1882), the best surviving nineteenth-century example was constructed from spoil from the lake enlargement—as the mounds at Liverpool's Birkenhead Park had been some decades earlier—and provided Sir Frederick Sargood with an unrivalled view across the flat topography to the bay. In rural situations, many early farmhouses were sited on natural mounts, or as at MONA VALE (Tas.), used an adjacent mount as a landscape feature.   RA

MOUNT ANNAN BOTANIC GARDEN, NSW, a branch of the ROYAL BOTANIC GARDENS, SYDNEY, displays the enormous diversity of the AUSTRALIAN FLORA and features many of Australia's 25 000 known plant species. Covering 416 hectares, it is Australia's largest BOTANIC GARDEN. Opened in 1988, Mount Annan features three themed gardens. The Bottlebrush Garden contains many species of the spectacular genus *Callistemon* together with their CULTIVARS and hybrids: the main flowering period is October–November. The Wattle Garden, devoted to the genus *ACACIA*, contains some 250 of the 900 known Australian species: the peak flowering period is July–August. The Banksia Garden has been planted with Australian members of the Proteaceae family including BANKSIAS, GREVILLEAS, and hakeas: the banksias flower mainly in May–June and the grevilleas in September. Landscaping is complemented by magnificent lakeside settings and panoramic views. Wildflower displays in September–October, the largest outside WA, are celebrated with an annual FESTIVAL. Mount Annan also contains significant natural areas, such as the threatened Cumberland Plain Woodland. Scientific work is carried out with rare and threatened species: *Wollemia nobilis* (Wollemi Pine), one of the world's rarest trees, is displayed. SEED banks within the garden provide storage under controlled conditions and play an important part in plant conservation.   PETER CUNEO

Mount Boninyong

MOUNT BUFFALO Chalet and its terraced garden under snow (1951)—a scene captured in numerous snaps over many decades at this popular RESORT

MOUNT BONINYONG, Scotsburn, Vic., was settled in 1839 by the Scott family, whose descendants built the present HOMESTEAD in 1884 on the site of the original slab hut. An 1845 notebook lists plants still found in the garden, making this one of the oldest surviving domestic gardens in Vic. The design is typical of the mid-nineteenth-century GARDENESQUE style. The main garden in front of the house, entered through elaborate timber gates, consists of concentric semicircular paths, many bordered with box hedging, some with small rocks, and others with terra cotta edging tiles. Flowers and shrubs in the beds include camellias, rhododendrons, and azaleas, and two *Magnolia grandiflora* (Bull Bay) listed in the 1845 notebook. A terraced lawn alongside the house, once used for CROQUET, is hedged with pittosporum and partly surrounded by an IRON FENCE brought from Scotland in 1884. An outer, less formal section of parkland—fenced off for grazing—where the original sweeping driveway can be seen, contains cedars, cypresses, and oaks. In 1989 the garden was damaged by a violent storm.

HELEN PAGE

MOUNT BUFFALO NATIONAL PARK, Vic. Ferdinand MUELLER collected at Mount Buffalo in 1853, drawing attention to its beauty, and in 1864 a celebrated depiction by Nicholas Chevalier (1828–1902) became the first Australian work purchased by the National Gallery of Victoria. Difficulty of access meant that for many years few visitors reached the plateau. It was declared a NATIONAL PARK (one of the first in Vic.) in 1898, a road opened in 1908, and a government accommodation house (forerunner of the present Chalet) was built in 1910. From that date it gradually became an important tourist RESORT, giving special emphasis to skiing, including Australia's first ski tow (1937). Since the 1930s, the Chalet grounds have also been an attraction, with both P.R.H. ST JOHN and Hugh LINAKER developing the landscape and gardens. Today both the Park and Chalet enjoy quality management, and it is easy to forget the long history of immense organisational and managerial conflict.

ELERY HAMILTON-SMITH

MOUNT COOT-THA: see BRISBANE BOTANIC GARDENS: *MOUNT COOT-THA*

MOUNT ELRINGTON, near Braidwood, NSW, an early pastoral HOMESTEAD GARDEN, dates from the late 1820s. Major William Sandys Elrington (1781–1860) established the garden when he resigned his army commission (after service in the West Indies and Spain) and brought with him many trees and shrubs from England. Around his original slab house he planted hedges of box, privet, and hawthorn, lilac bushes, a magnolia, and extensive orchard. James O'Brien, who purchased the property in 1866, installed a water race from Mount Creek to IRRIGATE the garden and paddocks. His descendants remain custodians of the garden, which retains many early plantings, including the HEDGES. The AUSTRALIAN GARDEN HISTORY SOCIETY has recorded this garden in a small gidebook.

TRISHA DIXON

(MOUNT FIELD) NATIONAL PARK, Tas., was officially opened in 1917 to retain a typical example of virgin forest for future generations and to serve as a sanctuary for flora and fauna threatened with extinction. Along with Freycinet, it is Tasmania's earliest NATIONAL PARK. Prior to establishment of the state's National Parks and Wildlife Service (1971), the park was administered by the Scenery Preservation Board, established in 1915 in response to community concern for the protection of scenic reserves and a desire to develop these resources as a tourist attraction. The park's best known attraction is Russell Falls, reserved in 1885. The national park has been enlarged from 10 800 hectares to encompass 16 265 hectares. A variety of habitats is represented, ranging from RAINFOREST in the lower part to ALPINE vegetation on the mountains. It contains some of the world's tallest EUCALYPTS, *Eucalypts regnans* (Mountain Ash).   LINDY SCRIPPS

MOUNT GAMBIER CAVE GARDEN, SA, a PUBLIC GARDEN laid out around a sinkhole in the town centre, became a focus in the late 1890s of community gardening activities under the leadership of horticulturist Paul Krummel (1875–1948). In 1925 William D. ROBINSON won a design COMPETITION and laid out his winning plan to create a picturesque GROTTO-like CAVE GARDEN, set within a GARDENESQUE civic green with large rose garden. He managed this civic showpiece until his death in 1945; his son, Robert Robinson (b. 1915), continued the intent of the design until 1965.
   DAVID JONES

MOUNT GAMBIER LAKES AREA, SA, recreation parkland dramatically sited within two volcanic craters with several lakes, includes the famed Blue Lake and the site of Adam Lindsay Gordon's celebrated poetic 'jump'. Originally an open woodland, its reliable water attracted Stephen Henty to erect a hut on Valley Lake edge in 1841. The Forest Board established the Leg of Mutton (STATE FOREST) NURSERY in 1876, under forester Charles BEALE; Conservators J.E. BROWN and Walter GILL developed it as the cornerstone of FORESTRY in south-east SA. By 1880 more than 100 000 exotic and native tree seedlings were under cultivation within an experimental ARBORETUM. With the erection of the Centenary Tower (1904) the area became a venue for major community plantings, resulting in the development of the Rook Walk and turret (1918), and culminating in the preparation of a master plan by William D. ROBINSON. He and his son progressively implemented the plan (1925–64) through ARBOR DAY and other organised plantings, resulting in the present vegetated landscape. The local council extended the recreational facilities during the 1970s.   DAVID JONES

MOUNT LOFTY BOTANIC GARDEN, SA, a branch of ADELAIDE BOTANIC GARDEN, occupies ninety-seven hectares in the Mount Lofty Ranges and has a more temperate climate than that of the Adelaide Plains. Since the first land purchase (1952), on the initiative of Noel LOTHIAN, and public opening (1977), plantings of northern and southern hemisphere temperate plants have been progressively made in the seven valleys that intersect this *Eucalyptus obliqua* (Messmate Stringy Bark) woodland. In accordance with an initial concept plan by Allan CORREY, each of the valleys is devoted to the cultivation of particular plant groups. Thus, Third Creek contains RHODODENDRONS, azaleas, and plants from the Himalayas and CHINA, while Sixth Creek forms the basis of a FERN gully. All the creeks converge on two purpose-built lakes; on their shores are collections of conifers and deciduous trees. The Garden affords extensive panoramas of the BAROSSA Ranges and Murray mallee country.
   BRIAN MORLEY

MOUNT MACEDON, Vic., contains one of Australia's most significant collection of nineteenth-century gardens. These lie on the southern slopes of Mount Macedon—mamelon of volcanic origin rising a thousand metres above flat basalt plains sixty kilometres north of Melbourne. Known to the local Wurrundjeri people as 'Geburrh' or 'Geboor', it is an area with steep terrain, a cool, damp CLIMATE, and deep SOIL.

Mount Macedon was first surveyed in 1836 by Major Thomas MITCHELL; pastoral settlement began in the 1840s south-east of the Mount. The earliest leases were issued to timber cutters: the ancient forests of Mount Macedon consisted of the most commercially valuable hardwoods in the world—in particular the stands of enormous *Eucalyptus regnans* (Mountain Ash) and *Acacia melanoxylon* (Blackwood). The demand for timber for developing Melbourne and, after 1851, the goldfields of Bendigo and Castlemaine, meant that by 1870 the mountain was virtually cleared of forest. Concern over this destruction and the need to develop new timber industries led in 1872 to the establishment in Macedon, of

Government Cottage, the vice-regal SUMMER RETREAT at MOUNT MACEDON, set in an expansive terraced garden, provided a contrast both climatically and in its relaxed style for incumbents of Victoria's more formal GOVERNMENT HOUSE

Mount Noorat

Australia's first STATE FOREST NURSERY, consolidating Mount Macedon's long connection with exotic and experimental horticulture.

In these years the newly wealthy of Melbourne established SUMMER RETREATS in its cool valleys. Many of the properties were established by community leaders, who developed their gardens—such as ALTON and HASCOMBE—in the spirit of scientific enquiry so typical of those times. Its fashionable status was confirmed when the governor took up residence in 1885. Similar to an Anglo-Indian HILL-STATION, the gardens created on Mount Macedon in the 1880s and 1890s were particularly well placed to take advantage of the new plant introductions coming from CHINA and JAPAN to the British Empire; in particular, the new species of RHODODENDRON and CONIFERS for which the climate and soil were so suited—well demonstrated at DURROL and DUNEIRA. Some of the first nurseries such as TAYLOR AND SANGSTER were responsible for early, exotic plant introductions and for laying out some of the most important gardens. Later, well-known garden designers such as Edna WALLING were associated with some of the gardens.

By the early twentieth century Mount Macedon had a busy tourist season, when it was considered healthful to escape the heat and pollution of a Melbourne summer, however the First World War followed by the Depression saw a decline in the popularity and affordability of large country estates and many properties became guest houses in this elevated RESORT. During this period the Memorial Cross was constructed (1935), financed by William Cameron of Cameron Lodge.

Mount Macedon's collection of gardens is now widely recognised and highly valued. Although some gardens were lost and much of the surrounding landscape was devastated by the 1983 bushfires, the surviving gardens remain a pre-eminent Australian collection of nineteenth-century landscapes, and contain an important range of mature and rare plants.

Marion Hutton, *Macedon and the Mount* (Mount Macedon, Vic., 1990); F.R. Moulds and H.B. Hutton, *The Macedon Ranges: Forests and People: A History of Change* (Mount Macedon, Vic., 1994)

PENNY DUNN

MOUNT NOORAT originally comprised the southern section of the squatting run Glenormiston, in Victoria's WESTERN DISTRICT, taken up in 1840 by Niel Black (1804–1880). Glenormiston was divided between its three owners in 1868 and Black reluctantly acquired this section. In an attempt to outdo Glenormiston's grandeur, he commissioned architect Charles Webb (1821–1898) to design an elaborate bluestone homestead at the foot of the Mount, which Black described as 'the crowning folly of my life'. Before building began, Black had planted out thirty-five acres (14 ha) with conifers and other exotics to create a picturesque setting of extensive landscaped PARKLAND. The homestead's elevation made it conspicuous from a distance and provided a majestic view outwards. A HA-HA wall enhanced the park-like quality. The homestead was demolished in 1941, although the picturesque GATE lodge and entrance gates remain, as do some ruins of garden buildings. Many of Black's trees survive, along with remnants of the once-grand ELM entrance AVENUE, ORCHARD, and HOMESTEAD GARDEN. A section of the property, developed by Black's son, later became DALVUI.

HELEN DOYLE

MOUNT TOMAH BOTANIC GARDEN, NSW, situated 1000 metres above sea level on a basalt peak in the BLUE MOUNTAINS, contains the cool-climate plant collections of the ROYAL BOTANIC GARDENS, SYDNEY. Mount Tomah was first surveyed by colonial botanist George CALEY (1804), who observed the richness of the native flora and the connection with its underlying geology. Development started in the early 1960s but was not completed to a stage enabling public access until 1987 (made possible by Commonwealth Bicentennial funding). Major landscape elements include a three-hectare scree-slope and ROCK GARDEN, a formal garden enclosed by walls and hedges of *Callitris*, *Nothofagus*, and *Prunus laurocerasus*, and the remnants of the Brunet's old home garden skilfully incorporated into the botanic garden layout. These are largely the work of designers James Pfeiffer (b. 1953) and Geoffrey Britton (b. 1956) and botanists Tony Rodd (b. 1940) and Ben Wallace (b. 1947), although they have been somewhat modified since completion in 1988. There is a distinct bias towards plants of the southern hemisphere—particularly where they illustrate the origin of AUSTRALIAN FLORA from the break up of GONDWANA—and the resultant close floristic links with plants of South America and New Zealand. There are also significant plantings of deciduous trees, shrubs, and herbaceous plants throughout the park-like setting. Various water features ornament the garden. Superb valley views towards Sydney are gained across large tracts of wilderness bushland.

The Mount Tomah Book (Sydney, 1987)

IAN INNES

MOUNT WILSON, NSW: see BLUE MOUNTAINS, NSW

MOWBRAY PARK, East Brisbane, a Brisbane City Council public park since 1925, was formerly the grounds of Riversdale, the residence of Rev. Thomas Mowbray, who settled there in the 1850s. After Mowbray's death (1867), his widow sold all but twelve acres (4.8 ha) around the house for redevelopment as suburban Mowbraytown Estate (later East Brisbane). Mowbray's son John sold the house lot to South Brisbane City Council in 1905 for use as a park and after demolition, sporting facilities were established, and a bandstand (1911: now demolished) and Brisbane's first Great War memorial (1917) were erected. Public baths (an enclosure in the river) inspired a life-saving club (1923), which merged in the 1930s with the then-struggling Burleigh Heads group. School boat racing regattas have been held here since the 1930s. Many of the mature structural planting survives, including a mixed tropical assortment of palms, figs, araucarias, jacarandas, and poincianas, which frame splendid views of the Brisbane River (Humbug Reach).

JEANNIE SIM

MUDD, Christopher (1852–1920), forester and botanist, was born in Cleveland, Yorkshire, England, and migrated to Vic. (*c.* 1883) from New Zealand. In 1887 he was appointed forester to the Ballarat Water Commission, and lived among the plantations between Kirk's and Gong Gong reservoirs. There he implemented a combined system of 'Conserved and Artificial Forestry': conserving every native timber tree, filling vacant spots with nursery trees, removing all 'injurious' undergrowth, and obtaining marketable timber by 'culling and not wholesale clearing'. He exchanged seeds with Ballarat–Creswick state forester John LA GERCHE. A practical forester with expertise in commercial timber trees, Mudd brought wide experience in FORESTRY to Victoria. As a boy, he had worked in plantations on the Yorkshire estates where his father William (1830–1879) had been forester. In 1875–76, as official botanist to H.R.H. the Prince of Wales (later King Edward VII), he visited INDIA and Ceylon, and observed Indian forestry. After botanical explorations in South AFRICA in 1877, he was engaged in large-scale tree planting in the Canterbury district of New Zealand from 1879. In evidence to the Victorian Royal Commission on Vegetable Products (1887), Mudd regretted the backward state of ARBORICULTURAL knowledge at the STATE FOREST NURSERY at Mount Macedon, where he had worked in the mid-1880s. He vigorously opposed *Pinus insignis* (now *radiata*, Monterey Pine), promoted by John Ednie BROWN's *Tree Culture in South Australia* (1881), as a valueless timber tree for Vic. Mudd advocated *Pinus austriaca* and *Pinus laricio* (Red and White Deal, both now subspecies of *P. nigra*, Austrian Pine) as valuable trees. 'The curse of all these colonies', he argued, was the damage done to forests by allowing novices to fell trees 'helter-skelter'.

ANGELA TAYLOR

MUELLER, Ferdinand Jakob Heinrich von (1825–1896), is principally remembered as Australia's pre-eminent botanist, although his contribution to nineteenth-century Australian gardening and horticulture should not be underestimated. Mueller was the first director of the MELBOURNE BOTANIC GARDENS and a leading figure in the ACCLIMATISATION movement. As such, he was not only in a position to introduce exotic plants into Australia, but also to display and distribute them widely. The best-known of the trees he was instrumental in establishing here was *Pinus radiata* (Monterey Pine), which he rated more highly as an ornamental than as a timber tree.

Born in the German state of Mecklenberg, Mueller was orphaned by the age of fourteen after his parents died of tuberculosis. His early passion for plants only became a vocation through diligence and single-mindedness—traits he carried through life, which could be faults as well as virtues. He became a qualified pharmacist and obtained a PhD from the University of Kiel in 1847. It was at Kiel that he saw his first scientific BOTANIC GARDEN, which was attached to the university. On visits to Hamburg he frequented its state garden, and also examined the curiosities of local nurseries. The only grand ornamental garden he is known to have seen was at Gravenstein in Denmark, which he visited on a scientific conference tour.

In Australia he was thought to be a typical GERMAN in his approach to landscaping—evidenced by his avenues of trees, and garden beds laid out in straight lines. While it is true that parts of Mueller's Botanic Gardens were very formal, it is

Ferdinand Mueller, awarded a doctorate by the University of Kiel in 1847, granted personal nobility ('von') in 1867 and hereditary barony ('Freiherr') in 1871 by the King of Württemberg, and knighted KCMG in 1879, is shown here in suitably splendid regalia

wrong to stereotype his entire approach to landscaping in this way. At Melbourne, Mueller inherited a garden established by two previous curators, ARTHUR and DALLACHY, but he was able to overlay their work with his own ideas. Local Germans who saw the results thought them remarkably free of the strict symmetrical presentation of genera that might be expected from a man of such great learning. The perception of Mueller as a Teutonic scientist persisted, however, and it became entrenched after he was removed as director in 1873.

The career path that led Mueller to Melbourne Botanic Gardens began in Australia at Adelaide, where he emigrated for the sake of his health in 1847. In 1852 he went to Vic. with the idea of setting up as a pharmacist, but was saved from this fate when the scientifically minded Lieutenant-Governor LA TROBE appointed him Government Botanist in 1853. Mueller spent much of the decade exploring the colony, with two years' service on Augustus Gregory's expedition in northern Australia (1855–56). Among Mueller's botanical discoveries were *Adansonia gregorii* (Baobab) and *Grevillea victoriae*.

Mueller was appointed Director of the Melbourne Botanic Gardens in 1857. He saw it as a place for the diffusion of botanical knowledge, the experimental introduction of foreign plants, and as a healthy locality for recreation. He did not regard the creation of a beautiful landscape as an object in itself. Believing plants to be naturally lovely, Mueller thought they could be as well arranged by scientists as gardeners (especially gardeners who were slaves to fashion). Mueller sought to educate the public though plant labels, and a SYSTEM GARDEN. He conducted research on living plants in the Gardens and on dried specimens in the HERBARIUM, seing the two institutions as inseparable. And while many citizens of Melbourne may have been unaware of these endeavours, they certainly helped to fulfil his third aim—recreation—by visiting the Garden in their thousands.

In the last year of his life Mueller recalled his proudest achievements at Melbourne as the geyser in the lake, the aviary, glasshouse, pinetum, the flowering of *Victoria amazonica* (Giant Water Lily), the living plant collection, and plant distributions. Mueller's successor, William GUILFOYLE, exploited the riches of Mueller's plant collection in a new design, but dismantled or reconfigured most of Mueller's other achievements. Rural Victoria was the main beneficiary of Mueller's distribution scheme, and it was only by determined indifference that any town or hamlet did not get plants (especially CONIFERS) free of charge for the ornamentation of their public spaces. Private citizens could obtain plants by exchange. Hundreds of thousands of seedlings were distributed in this way, much to the chagrin of those in the NURSERY TRADE, and this scheme was as responsible for Mueller's downfall at the Gardens as was discontent with his landscaping.

Mueller continued as Government Botanist after 1873; while locally he suffered the indignity of being increasingly marginalised in public affairs, overseas his reputation continued to grow. His honours and honorary memberships are too numerous to detail, but they included FRS (1861), 'von' (1867), Barony (1871), and KCMG (1879). These tokens of recognition were based on the reputation he gained from international distributions of AUSTRALIAN PLANTS (especially EUCALYPTS), his support for exploration, and for his publications, including George BENTHAM's *Flora Australiensis* (1863–78) in which he assisted substantially. The most notable book from a gardening point of view was *Select Extra-Tropical Plants* (1876), an encyclopaedic work on plant acclimatisation that appeared in eleven editions and four languages. He was an early promoter of the use of Australian plants for ornamental purposes, including the floristic *Rhododendron lochae* and *Telopea oreades*, which he named.

Despite some temptation to leave Melbourne after his dismissal, Mueller was a loyal British subject who saw Australia as his home. Although he cannot be remembered as a garden designer (despite some claims to the contrary), many individuals and communities had cause to thank him for his generosity with plants and planting advice. His ambitions for the Melbourne Botanic Gardens and Herbarium were unprecedented in Australia, and his death left a vacuum in botanical research for many years. Several biographers have attempted the extraordinary story of his life; the definitive account is currently being written as part of the Mueller Correspondence Project.

R.W. Home (ed.), *The Scientific Savant in Nineteenth-Century Australia* (Canberra, 1997); R.W. Home et al. (eds), *Regardfully Yours: Selected Correspondence of Ferdinand von Mueller. Volume 1: 1840–1859* (Bern, 1998), *Volume 2: 1860–1875* (Bern, 2002)

SARA MAROSKE

MUNDARING RESERVOIR, WA, was opened in 1903 as part of the Goldfields Water Supply Scheme, taking water from the Darling Range east to Coolgardie and Kalgoorlie. Landscaped gardens (overlooking the dam on the north ridge) catered for its many visitors. A bust (1907) of the project's brilliant engineer, Charles Yelverton O'Connor (1843–1902), by sculptor Pietro Giacomo Porcelli (1872–1943)— originally at the southern end of the dam wall—was relocated to the northern end when the wall was raised (1951). By the 1920s the gardens included a terraced walk of camellias leading to rose beds and exotic trees overlooking the dam. In the 1960s the native bushland below the dam was landscaped by John OLDHAM. Still a popular tourist venue retaining many beautiful mature trees such as *Cinnamomum camphora* (Camphor Laurel) and *Ficus macrophylla* (Moreton Bay Fig), the degraded gardens are now the subject of a conservation plan.

CAROL MANSFIELD

MURDOCH (*née* GREENE), Elisabeth Joy (b. 1909), is an icon of the gardening establishment, through her personal involvement and through her stewardship of one of Australia's finest gardens. Her marriage in 1928 to journalist and newspaper proprietor (Sir) Keith Arthur Murdoch (1885–1952) saw the creation of **Cruden Farm**, near Langwarrin (Vic.), using two noted design professionals in Harold DESBROWE-ANNEAR (house) and Edna WALLING (garden). Since then Walling's walled gardens have been developed and significantly embellished by the owner and her longtime gardener, Michael Morrison, who have also greatly extended the garden. In recent years Cruden Farm—much visited and regularly open to the public—has become an important landscape, with dramatic impact from the mature *Eucalyptus citriodora* (Lemon-scented Gum) trees closely planted along the curving drive, and lakes created in 1987 and 2000. Created DBE in 1963, Dame Elisabeth Murdoch's extensive community involvement—as participant, patron, or philanthropist—includes bodies such as the AUSTRALIAN GARDEN HISTORY SOCIETY, ROYAL BOTANIC GARDENS, MELBOURNE, and University of Melbourne (where the chair of LANDSCAPE ARCHITECTURE bears her name).

Anne Latreille, *Cruden Farm, Langwarrin, Australia: A Country Garden* (Langwarrin, Vic., 2002)

ANNE LATREILLE

MURDOCH, John Smith (1862–1945), Australia's first Commonwealth Government Architect (1904–29), was responsible for designing all large Commonwealth works and some important public squares and gardens. Born at Forres, Scotland, he arrived in Melbourne in 1885. Forrest Place, Perth (1912–24), was Murdoch's earliest scheme. Developed along American CITY BEAUTIFUL lines, a wide road, central strip of trees, and public seating formed a frontage to his monumental General Post Office (and other proposed government buildings). Similar principles were employed for the layout of ANZAC SQUARE, Brisbane (1916–28). The Parliamentary Gardens, Canberra, were laid out by Murdoch in the mid-1920s. Situated between Old Parliament House and the Secretariat Blocks (also to his design), the formal landscape was characterised by broad swards, avenues of trees, tennis courts and bowling greens, and borders of shrubs and flower gardens. While Murdoch's landscape proposals were few, those he initiated were of national significance. Indeed, these landscapes contributed to his quest for a unified image of government in the early twentieth century. DAVID ROWE

MURNDAL, an extensive pastoral run on the Wannon River in Victoria's WESTERN DISTRICT, was taken up in 1838 by Anglo-Irish colonist Samuel Pratt Winter (1816–1878). Winter sought to replicate at Murndal the style of European landed estates. He extended the original stone cottage by a series of extensions and lined the internal walls with ancestral portraits and the external walls with ivy. The garden, with its extensive PARKLAND of exotic trees, grand avenues, lawns, and lakes, also aspired to eighteenth-century traditions. Winter planted many English and other exotic species, including an oak grown from an acorn of the oldest in the world, and a cypress reputedly grown from seed taken from Italian specimens planted by Michelangelo. Imperialistic sentiment was also evident in the coronation avenue; a pair of oaks was planted for each new British monarch. Winter's nephew and successor, Samuel Winter Cooke, further extended the house in 1891 and 1906. HELEN DOYLE

MURPHY, Andrew (c. 1850–1930), seed collector, was born at St Albans (NSW) and without formal education worked as a timber-getter and market gardener. From his late teens he specialised in collecting SEEDS of Australian timber trees, one of very few in the late nineteenth century to make this a vocation. During the early 1890s, for example, his services were sought by J.H. MAIDEN, then curator of the Sydney Technological Museum and engaged on phytochemical research. Murphy collected seeds throughout Australia, and they were often exported for afforestation projects—with destinations including South Africa, North America, and India. Murphy possessed an exceptional knowledge of EUCALYPTS and ACACIAS. His *Descriptive Catalogue of Australian Timber Seeds* (1904), issued from Grandview, Woy Woy (NSW), is the earliest known catalogue exclusively devoted to the supply of AUSTRALIAN FLORA and included Qld seeds 'suitable for tropical climates'. RA

Though planted mainly with exotic trees and reminiscent of eighteenth-century English landscape gardens, MURNDAL, near Hamilton (Vic.), iis an unmistakably Australian RURAL LANDSCAPE

Museum Gardens

The former MUSEUM GARDENS, Bowen Hills (Qld), developed in the 1890s around the exhibition building erected on a portion of Bowen Park, included large BUSH-HOUSES, ROCKERIES, tropical SHRUBBERIES, and other staples of the Queensland colonial garden

Former MUSEUM GARDENS, Bowen Hills, Qld, located on land excised from the south-west corner of BOWEN PARK, once formed the grounds of the building erected for the 1897 Queensland International Exhibition. This building subsequently housed the Queensland Museum and Art Gallery until its relocation to South Brisbane (1986). The original semi-tropical garden design (attributed to William SOUTTER) included two 'classical' FOUNTAINS, very large interconnected BUSH-HOUSES (with 3000 epiphytes and 9550 potted plants), ROCKERIES (containing an eclectic mixture of bedding flowers, roses, and tropical herbaceous plants), and numerous PALMS. The surviving garden contains some early plantings (palms, shrubberies, and flower beds), rock structures, and one fountain. Although the bush-houses no longer remain, they were a star attraction in 1897:

> an enchanted bower of ferns, palms and orchids, so artistically arranged, so tastefully interwoven, that one can hardly credit that it was erected by human hands in the space of a few short weeks. It is nature made perfect.   JEANNIE SIM

MUSGRAVE PARK, South Brisbane, was among the first designated PUBLIC PARKS in Qld, with about twenty-three acres (9 ha) being set aside in 1850. Strong associations for the park by Aboriginal people included encampments recorded in 1855 and killings (and burials) in 1897, when legislation prohibited Aboriginal people from entering the Brisbane area. Recently, the opening nearby of the One People of Australia League hostel for homeless Aboriginal people is credited with renewed interest in the park as an Aboriginal meeting place. Originally South Brisbane Recreation Reserve (1865), it was renamed in 1885 to honour Governor Musgrave. Trustees (including A.J. HOCKINGS) managed the park between 1865 and the 1910s until South Brisbane Council assumed that role. Many sporting groups used the park, while a bandstand (1901) and circuses (1950s–60s) provided leisure usage. Early plantings included a formal St Andrew's Cross avenue pattern in the northern section (remnants remain), softened by tropical plantings of figs, *Cinnamomum camphora* (Camphor Laurel), *Albizzia* sp., and ARAUCARIAS. Henry MOORE added rockeries (*c.* 1914) along street boundaries for palms, shrubs, and flowering plants (removed 1960s).

Encroachments for Brisbane State High School (1923) and a swimming pool (1967) have reduced the area. In 1988, a former bowling clubhouse was renovated as the Jagera community Arts Resources Centre and in 1990 the Richard Randall Studio was relocated nearby. The Greek community holds its popular Panyiri Festival annually in the park, and several other ethnic groups, as well as Aboriginal people, claim an interest in Musgrave Park—evidence of Australian multiculturalism and diverse meanings assumed by parkland.

JEANNIE SIM

MUSIC, and its performance in Australian parks and gardens, has been a popular pastime since the early nineteenth century. The earliest European music heard on Australian shores was that of the military fife and drums of the First Fleet on an improvised parade ground in 1788. This tradition of military bands developed and diversified during the nineteenth century into brass bands and string orchestras, and performances extended into PUBLIC PARKS AND GARDENS—such as Sydney's HYDE PARK—as a popular LEISURE activity. Musical accompaniment often featured at early HORTICULTURAL SHOWS, adding a cultured air to what were often improvised tent venues. Australia's generally mild climates also encouraged garden parties in large VILLA and MANSION GARDENS, as well as INSTITUTIONAL sites, such as HOSPITAL GARDENS. Amateur and professional musicians contributed to the popularity of music performed in these outdoor venues. Many performances were aided by specialised GARDEN BUILDINGS such as BANDSTANDS and AMPHITHEATRES, which provided a visual and acoustic focus for performance in an outdoor environment. Some of Australia's earliest bandstands were located in BOTANIC GARDENS, although later in the nineteenth century William GUILFOYLE ensured that horticulture was not dominated by entertainment and permitted only one performance per annum—on Hospital Sunday—in MELBOURNE BOTANIC GARDENS. Music for the People concerts began in Melbourne Botanic Gardens in 1945, but with attendances peaking at 100 000 worried directors urged their relocation to a new dedicated venue; the Sidney Myer Music Bowl (1959) nearby in Melbourne's Domain is now the city's premier outdoor performance venue. In recent years there has been increased interest in using gardens for THEATRE, opera, and large orchestral and choral performances. They have ranged from exclusive operatic performances of Mozart's *Cosi fan tutte* at RAHEEN (Vic.) to well-attended amplified summer performances of operas in capital city DOMAINS, and esoteric contemporary music events and acoustic landscape installations.

AUSTRALIAN PLANTS have contributed in a distinctive and increasingly nationalistic manner to the country's music making, principally through the use of timber from native

The crowded BANDSTAND at Nhill (Vic.), located in the central road plantation of the town's main thoroughfare, demonstrates the obvious enthusiasm for MUSIC in PUBLIC PARKS and reserves during the nineteenth and early twentieth centuries

species. Aboriginal Australians have traditionally used wood to carve rhythm sticks and didgeridoos and European instrument-making traditions have also been transferred to Australia. Recent successes include the internationally renowned grand pianos of Stuart and Sons, incorporating Tasmanian Huon Pine, and a growing trend among instrument makers to use Australian timbers.

Songs composed in Australia provide GARDEN HISTORIANS with a rich, unexpected, and almost entirely neglected source. The use of native floral inspiration in titles was very popular in the late nineteenth and early twentieth centuries during the rise of nationalistic and patriotic pride, with the development of the Australian Natives Association and the move towards Federation. The decorative covers of sheet music also drew on plants and gardens for thematic inspiration. Thus *Tasmanian Waltzes* (1837), the first pictorial sheet music cover in Tas., features native plants, while the *Rupertswood Waltzes* and *Garden Palace Schottische* provide unusual or rarely seen views of these places.   GEORGINA BINNS

MYALL PARK BOTANIC GARDEN, Glenmorgan, Qld, see GORDON, David Morrice

MYILLY POINT HERITAGE PRECINCT, Darwin, comprises four rare examples of tropical-style houses built in 1938–39 to the design of architect Beni Carr Glynn Burnett (1889–1955) to accommodate senior public servants, and is set within distinctly landscaped TROPICAL gardens. Located on a promontory overlooking Darwin Harbour, the precinct has been managed and restored by the NATIONAL TRUST OF AUSTRALIA (Northern Territory) following a major heritage battle (1984). Despite the ravages of cyclones (1937, 1974) and defence force occupation during the Second World War, the precinct now interprets the development of garden styles in the Top End. These include pioneering 'container' gardens, featuring plantings common before the Second World War, and making use of tubs, galvanised-iron tanks, and hanging baskets on VERANDAHS, common in times of limited water supply; immaculately manicured gardens in the style of the 1950s and 1960s, with formal lawns, concrete paths, and neatly trimmed shrubbery; post-Cyclone Tracy 'urban jungle' gardens (with dense plantings of exotics); and modern XERIC gardens (with paving and features such as mulching and efficient irrigation).

Penny Cook, *Myilly Point* (Darwin, *c.* 1988)   ANITA ANGEL

NARCISSUS There are some fifty species of this genus of BULBS, occurring naturally—chiefly in cool temperate climates—for the most part round the MEDITERRANEAN, but including Britain. The vast majority of garden plants derived from the genus are, however, hybrids of mixed origins, known variously as DAFFODILS, narcissus, jonquils, or even pheasant-eyes. The ROYAL HORTICULTURAL SOCIETY (London) is the international registration authority and, from time to time, the Society issues a daffodil checklist of registered names and breeders. There are approximately 23 000 names on this list (1989), most of which have now disappeared. It is, for instance, extremely unlikely that the popular trumpet daffodil, 'King Alfred', bred by J. Kendall before 1899, still exists in its pure form. Classification methods vary from time to time; but in 1989, there were twelve classes, of which all but two were for bulbs of garden origin. These ten were Trumpets, Large-cupped, Small-cupped, Double, Triandrus, Cyclamineus, Jonquila, Tazetta (many flowers on the same stem), Poeticus (pheasant-eye, with a white perianth), and Split-corona. The remaining divisions included miscellaneous daffodils, wild variants, and wild hybrids. Flowers in these divisions are more precisely defined by measurement and by a colour code (white, green, yellow, pink, orange, and red).

The Great Daffodil Show held in Melbourne Town Hall on 24–25 August 1893 was perhaps the first show in the world devoted entirely to daffodils. The judge was an English actor, George TITHERADGE, who, in order to sort out nomenclature, had imported bulbs of all named species from Messrs BARR in England. Half of Titheradge's stock, on dispersal, was purchased by Tasmanian breeders and half by Alister CLARK of Glenara, who also, as a member of a British syndicate, imported named varieties. These he shared with his friend Leonard Buckland, whose variety, 'Pink 'un', illustrated in the *Daffodil Year Book* (1915), may have been the first of all daffodils with a pink trumpet—many years earlier than the English 'Mrs R.O. Backhouse'. Many people, however, believe that all daffodils should be yellow! Fashions in breeding change: of late years they have been directed towards miniatures and attempts to breed an all-pink trumpet daffodil, as well as to the refinement of shape and carriage.

Narcissus prefer full sun and damp ground, and have long been favourites in temperate parts of Australia, where they naturalise easily in grass. The flowering period—generally winter to spring—will depend on the local climate, but the *N. poeticus* varieties (strongly scented and whose red 'pheasant-eyes' are a magnet for slugs) are among the latest to flower.

T.R. GARNETT

NARROWS INTERCHANGE, Perth, a freeway interchange surrounded by parklands, was the first in Australia to be conceived as a PUBLIC PARK. The landscape scheme, by John OLDHAM (1967–73), followed community outrage over freeway construction on the edge of the Swan River, with the twenty-two-hectare landscaped area compensating

The pioneering nature of the landscaping of Perth's NARROWS INTERCHANGE has recently been recognised by the naming of a portion as the John OLDHAM Park to commemorate its LANDSCAPE ARCHITECT

for river infilling and loss of PUBLIC OPEN SPACE. The parkland, on largely reclaimed land, consists of undulating hills and valleys, streams, waterfalls, fountains, ponds, and islands, connected by paths, bridges, and underpasses. The water features, green lawns, and sheltering trees provide a surprisingly tranquil refuge for wildlife as well as city workers, joggers, cyclists, and picnickers.

CAROL MANSFIELD and PHILIP PALMER

NASH, Richard West (1808–1850), advocate-general, journalist, and agriculturist, was born in Dublin and studied law at Trinity College. In 1839 he migrated to the Swan River Colony, and supplemented his profession with farming and journalism He was honorary secretary of the Agricultural and Horticultural Society of Western Australia (1842–45) and edited the single volume of the Society's *Journal for 1842* (1843). He was also honorary secretary of the short-lived Perth-based Vineyard Society. Nash published *A Manual for the Cultivation of the Vine and Olive in Western Australia* (1845) before returning to London in 1849 to manage the Colonization Assurance Corporation, founded to sponsor emigration.

RA

NATIONAL PARKS The character of national parks has been contested throughout the history of the term, which was first used at Yellowstone in the USA (1872). Australia's first national park (now ROYAL NATIONAL PARK) was established at Port Hacking (NSW) in 1879, and was seen as a recreational area for the people of Sydney. It also provided for ACCLIMATISATION of introduced species of plants and animals, and a range of other, now-unacceptable uses. Many other important parks did not use the term 'national park', but were of very much the same character. The Jenolan Caves Reserve was established in 1866 for the protection of the CAVES, with conservation-based regulations being proclaimed in 1872. In WA the park at Mount Eliza (now KINGS PARK) was also established in 1872, and while serving many purposes, filled the same role as the park at Port Hacking and other near-city national parks.

The modern emphasis upon the role of national parks in environmental conservation tends to disguise the extent to which some were formerly seen as PLEASURE GARDENS. This perspective included the phenomenon that at areas rich in spectacular endemic flora, it was seen as appropriate for visitors to gather armfuls of flowers to fill their vases at home. At Port Hacking this was commonplace, facilitated by the park staff, who cleared less-attractive plants in order to create a more 'park-like' situation to both highlight and provide access to such species as *Telopea speciosissima* (Waratah), *Ceratopetalum gummiferum* (New South Wales Christmas Bush) and *Doryanthes excelsa* (Gymea Lily). At the Grampians in Vic. (not at that time a national park) special trains were provided to enable residents of nearby towns to collect their share of the *Thryptomene* and other popular flowers. Further, exotic species were often planted to 'beautify' the parks, particularly in near-city parks such as Port Hacking, Kings Park, and Ferntree Gully, and also BELAIR and Yarra Bend, which are no longer national parks. This was, of course, an expression of the acclimatisation movement and carried out with the very best of intentions.

However, there was an interest in conservation from the earliest times, even though this sometimes had limited impact upon early establishment and management. The romantic vision of the BUSH that was commonly expressed throughout the mid-nineteenth century did not seem to be translated directly into a movement for the establishment of parks or other protected areas. But certainly MUELLER and others, particularly the FIELD NATURALISTS' CLUB of Victoria, had a particularly significant influence in Vic. through their arguments for protection of the unique Australian flora and fauna. The modern conservation ethic was later developed with the leadership of various individuals, many of whom espoused a specific position. David STEAD of NSW focused upon wildlife protection issues. Romeo LAHEY and Arthur Groom of Qld argued for the protection of natural heritage in a pristine condition. Myles DUNPHY argued for wilderness or 'primitive area' preservation with a strong underlying vision of the importance of such areas for bush RECREATION.

Most national parks were managed by local committees of management, and so the quality of management was varied. The development of state-level park agencies was slow, and evolved over the period from 1956 (in Vic. and WA) to the present day. Initially, the focus on the pleasure gardens concept, already falling into decay, was phased out in favour of preservation, or even restoration, of the natural environment. But the demand for recreation continued, and management moved increasingly towards zoning as one means of achieving a balance between the pressures of recreation and the maintenance of pristine areas. The contemporary situation is characterised by economically motivated demands for activities such as grazing, mining, and logging to be allowed in specific areas of parks and for the development of accommodation and other tourism services within the parks. There is also growing contest over the potential role of commercialism in providing visitor services or even management of parks. Finally, the developing role of Aboriginal people in parks management is perhaps the most fundamental change and is already expressed in a range of ways.

Australia's 100 Years of National Parks (Sydney, 1979); Elery Hamilton-Smith (ed.), *Celebrating the Parks: Proceedings of the First Australian Symposium on Parks History* (Carlton South, Vic., 1998)

ELERY HAMILTON-SMITH

NATIONAL ROSE SOCIETY OF AUSTRALIA (1972–) was formed by the conjoining of the National Rose Societies in NSW, Qld, SA, Tas., Vic., and WA after the first Australian Rose Convention (Melbourne, 1967). The National Rose Society had been founded in London on 7 December 1876, and the first meeting of ROSE lovers in Melbourne—leading to the formation of the National Rose Society of Victoria—was symbolically held on this day in 1899. Richard ARDAGH, Herbert BRUNNING, Alister CLARK, Harry DAVEY, William Henry Moule (1858–1939), James Henry Simpson (1865–1935), James Sylvester Oliver (c. 1870–1943), and Thomas POCKETT were early supporters, with Davey honorary secretary. Moule was elected inaugural president in

'Planting his first standard rose', a gently humorous view of the need for a NATIONAL ROSE SOCIETY by cartoonist Percy Leason, published in the Society's *Australian Rose Annual* (1929)

February 1900 and the first general meeting was held in June. Davey's AUSTRAL CULTURIST was adopted as official journal and the Society's first show was held in 1901. James ALLAN, Samuel BRUNDRETT, Samuel Ernest Frederick (1883–1955), and B.V. ROSSI were successful early competitors. Alister Clark was the towering figure in the Australian rose world during the Society's first decades, and his assistance—including donation of royalties from newly bred roses such as 'Lady Medallist' (1912) and 'Sweet Seventeen' (1923)—was generous. 'Doc' THOMAS was the outstanding figure of the mid-century.

The National Rose Society of New South Wales (1913) was founded by William Herbert Ifould (1877–1969) and Edward Evans, with commercial growers George Wilkinson Kershaw (1861–1924), George Robert Knight (1879–1961), and Harry HAZLEWOOD prominent early members. The first *Australian Rose Annual* was issued in Vic. (1928–) under the editorship of T.A. STEWART, who set a high standard for this long-running publication: his contribution is recognised by the annual awarding of the T.A. Stewart Memorial Plaque (1948–), the Society's highest award for those 'who have given outstanding service to the rose in Australian and New Zealand'. The National Rose Society of South Australia (1929) founded by Alex ROSS and Dr Owen M. Moulden flourished during the post-war period following a recess (1942–51). The National Rose Society of Queensland (1930) drew together keen amateurs and commercial growers, such as Alfred WILLIAMS and John WILLIAMS, who struggled with TROPICAL conditions, long recognised by Hazlewood Brothers with 'Brisbane Zone' and 'Rockhampton Zone' in their pioneering CLIMATIC-zone recommendations (*c.* 1923). The National Rose Society of Western Australia (1932), instigated by Lieutenant-Commander George Prideaux (1871–1965), grew with the support of Charles Frost (1875–1964), C.C. HILLARY, Joe MARTIN, Horace MOFFLIN, and Charles Rhodes. The National Rose Society of Tasmania (1960) was inaugurated from the Hobart Gardening Club Rose Section.

The Societies promoted roses in their respective states, especially in PUBLIC GARDENS and, after the Second World War, MEMORIAL GARDENS such as the PEACE MEMORIAL ROSE GARDEN (WA). Nomenclature and reviews of NOVELTIES occupied much space in the *Annual*, known as the *Australian and New Zealand Rose Annual* (1943–63) following the formation of the National Rose Society of New Zealand (1931). Activities of the American Rose Society (1899) and its energetic journal editor (John) Horace McFarland (1859–1948) were also keenly monitored. Interest almost exclusively centred on Hybrid Teas until the early 1960s, when SA members Walter DUNCAN and Deane ROSS (and later David RUSHTON) promoted a revival of old-fashioned roses.

Christopher Heathcote (ed.), *A Century of Roses: A History of the Rose Society of Victoria 1899–1999* (Melbourne, 1999)

RA

NATIONAL TRIANGLE, Canberra, conceived in the 1911 GRIFFIN plan for the Federal (later AUSTRALIAN) CAPITAL TERRITORY as the physical and symbolic heart of Australia's national capital, is defined by Capital Hill, City Hill, and Mount Russell, and encompasses the Parliamentary Zone, the Central Basin of Lake Burley Griffin, and the parklands of Commonwealth Park and Kings Park. Although subject to numerous planning proposals, the integrity of Griffin's land and water axes has been maintained. The land axis is a landscaped central vista sweeping from Parliament House, on Capital Hill, across the waters of the lake and beyond the triangle, along Anzac Parade to the War Memorial and Mount Ainslie. Aligning with Black Mountain, the water axis traverses the lake and is accentuated by the vertical features of the Captain Cook Memorial Jet and the Carillon on Aspen Island.

The Parliamentary Zone was initially laid out during construction of Old (Provisional) Parliament House (1924–27) in front of the Camp Hill site proposed by Griffin. Terraces planted with evergreen and deciduous trees were formed under the direction of T.C.G. WESTON; hedged private gardens for the Senate and House of Representatives included rose gardens, tennis courts, bowling greens, and a cricket pitch. The National Rose Gardens (1933), designed by Rex HAZLEWOOD and developed by Alexander BRUCE, were laid out in front of the Old House. The adjacent Aboriginal Embassy (1972) was established as a focus for Aboriginal rights demonstrations. To the north-east the National Gallery of Australia includes a Sculpture Garden (1982), designed by Harry HOWARD and Associates, displaying sculpture in a setting of Australian plants, pools, marsh pond, fog garden, and a fern garden courtyard (1998) designed by Fiona Hall. To the north-west is the Peace Garden (1990) and to the north a formal lakeside promenade including the International Flag Display (1999). There are memorial plantings and spaces dedicated for future development.

A lakeside site planned for Parliament House (1958) was abandoned in favour of Capital Hill (1974). The gardens of Parliament House (1988), designed by Peter Rollands and Associates, include surmounting grass ramps, encircling Australian bush gardens, and a formal south-facing terrace garden, all with public access. Numerous internal courtyards, with limited public access, are embellished with trees, flowering plants, sculptures, and water features.

To the north of the lake lie the parklands of Commonwealth and Kings parks. COMMONWEALTH PARK includes a series of water gardens designed by Sylvia CROWE and a diversity of exotic trees planted by Lindsay PRYOR. Kings Park contains the restored Blundells Cottage and garden. Parkes Way (1961), a scenic urban parkway designed by Lord Holford, delineates the northern extent of the parklands.

DIANNE FIRTH and JULIE RAMSAY

NATIONAL TRUST OF AUSTRALIA, an independent, community-based organisation with branches in NSW (1945), SA (1955), Vic. (1956), WA (1959), Tas. (1960), Qld (1963), ACT (1976), NT (1976), coordinated through the Australian Council of National Trusts (1965), is dedicated to the CONSERVATION of both the cultural and the natural ENVIRONMENT. It has carried out surveys of historic gardens (and classified significant examples through its non-statutory but influential system of HERITAGE listings), compiled significant TREE registers, and published manuals on techniques for identifying and conserving historic gardens. As well as carrying out this conservation advocacy, the Trust owns and manages a large number of gardens. Major examples include RIPPON LEA (Vic.), Australia's most important surviving late nineteenth-century private urban garden—and perhaps its earliest successful conservation battle involving a garden (1963–72)—and EVERGLADES (NSW), a spectacular interwar HILL-STATION garden in the Blue Mountains. The portfolio, however, is widespread; it embraces the continent from north (MYILLY POINT HERITAGE PRECINCT with 1930s suburban gardens of public servants' houses in Darwin) to south (RUNNYMEDE, an early colonial garden in Hobart), and east (the Federation-era garden of Uskarty, the cottage adjoining Brennan and Geraghty's Store, Maryborough, Qld.) to west (the 1836 farm STRAWBERRY HILL, Albany, WA). Labourers' gardens—such as those at the Moonta Miner's Cottage (SA)—are included in this diverse portfolio alongside twentieth-century BUSH GARDENS—as at the GRIFFIN-designed Stella James House, Avalon (NSW). The Trust's approach to managing gardens has changed over the last forty years from an initial emphasis on decorous settings, to period houses, to more rigorously documented exemplars conserved within the spirit of the BURRA CHARTER.

Susan Marsden, *History of the National Trust in Australia: Significant Dates & Publications* (Canberra, 2000)

IAN STEPHENSON

NATIVE PLANTS/FLORA: see AUSTRALIAN FLORA

NATURAL HISTORY, as pursued in the eighteenth and nineteenth centuries, encompassed the study of natural

Douglas Annand's drawing of a typical colonial HOMESTEAD, published in Marjorie Barnard's *Macquarie's World* (1947), illustrated the *beau ideal* for many early members of the NATIONAL TRUST OF AUSTRALIA—a faraway place where top hats were worn in farmyards and fountains played to elegant, bonneted ladies

objects and phenomena, especially in the field. It is now commonly confined to field studies of animals, fungi, and PLANTS, but originally encompassed inanimate phenomena including CLIMATE, SOILS, and rocks (now GEOLOGY). Societies, magazines, museums, a medallion, and a university chair have all been dedicated to Australian natural history. But first came collectors, paid and unpaid. Invading and exploring Australia during the heyday of natural history, Europeans perceived it as a natural history wonderland of 'all things queer and opposite', and shiploads of specimens—inanimate and living—reached Europe for examination and description, enriching museums and HERBARIA, and provoking the elaboration and expansion of taxonomic systems. The peculiar AUSTRALIAN FLORA, much of it endemic, yielded plants of scientific and aesthetic interest, many being documented and cultivated at the ROYAL BOTANIC GARDENS, KEW.

In the nineteenth century, natural history was very popular. Some saw it as a means of understanding the great work of God: clerics, including John Lillie (1806–1866) and William WOOLLS, commonly collected specimens. It also sharpened the mind, fostered social intercourse, and rejuvenated the body with fresh air and exercise. Being mentally and MORALLY instructive, natural history was discussed and displayed at Mechanics' Institutes and Schools of Arts, common in mid-nineteenth-century Australian towns. In the late 1830s John FRANKLIN revived Van Diemen's Land Mechanics' Institute, and with its president, Lillie, and others, responded to British enquiries about Tasmanian natural history by establishing the Tasmanian Society. Jane Franklin organised its museum building, and its *Journal* provided an early antipodean literary vehicle for natural history. Since medical practice and prognosis required natural history, especially botanical, knowledge, medical men such as Joseph MILLIGAN commonly collected specimens and supported ROYAL SOCIETIES and other scientific societies. Colonial natural history museums were established, sometimes in association with these societies. While awaiting William MACLEAY's promised natural history collection, University of Sydney established Australia's only chair of natural history (1882–89); its professor, William John Stephens (1829–1890), was president of the LINNEAN SOCIETY OF NEW SOUTH WALES.

In the twentieth century, school NATURE STUDY prompted a proliferation of newspaper articles, magazines, and RADIO broadcasts on natural history. While several natural history societies came and went, FIELD NATURALISTS' CLUBS achieved longevity. It was this amateur tradition that fuelled much of Australia's interest in natural history during the twentieth century. Since 1940, the Field Naturalists' Club of Victoria's Australian Natural History Medallion has been awarded annually. Recipients including J.McC. BLACK, Crosbie MORRISON, Edith COLEMAN, J.B. CLELAND, Charles BARRETT, H.M.R. RUPP, James WILLIS, Norman Arthur Wakefield (1918–1972), Thistle Stead (*née* HARRIS), Winifred WADDELL, J. Ros GARNET, C.A. GARDNER, Jean GALBRAITH, (Alexander) Clifford Beauglehole (b. 1920), Alison ASHBY, Winifred CURTIS, Helen Isobel Aston (b. 1934), F.J.C. ROGERS, Enid L. Robertson (grand-daughter of Edwin ASHBY), Joan Winifred Cribb (*née* HERBERT), Rodger ELLIOT, Mary Patricia Cameron (b. 1925), and (Douglas) Malcolm Calder (b. 1933) have increased popular and scientific knowledge of Australia's flora and assisted in its protection and propagation.

C.M. Finney, *To Sail Beyond the Sunset: Natural History in Australia 1699–1829* (Adelaide, 1984); Ann Moyal, '*A Bright & Savage Land': Scientists in Colonial Australia* (Sydney, 1986); Colin Finney, *Paradise Revealed: Natural History in Nineteenth-century Australia* (Melbourne, 1993); Tom Griffiths, *Hunters and Collectors: The Antiquarian Imagination in Australia* (Cambridge, 1996)   LINDEN GILLBANK

NATURAL RESOURCES CONSERVATION LEAGUE OF VICTORIA (1944–) had its genesis in the Save the Forests Campaign, set up following disastrous Black Friday bushfires (January 1939). With parliamentarian Cyril ISAAC as a driving force, the Campaign linked the Forests Commission of Victoria, Education Department, and AUSTRALIAN FOREST LEAGUE. COMMUNITY FORESTS were instigated, and the Campaign's conservation strategy popularised Judge Stretton's memorable phrase (from the 1939 Royal Commission into Black Friday) 'The Inseparable Trinity' of forests, water, and soil. Incorporated in 1951 as the Natural Resources Conservation League of Victoria, its major activities included a tree nursery, a quarterly journal, *Victoria's Resources* (1959–), and an outreach program for children: the Junior Tree Lovers League (1962). Increased attention paid by governments to CONSERVATION and the ENVIRONMENT, and the success of national programs such as LANDCARE and GREENING AUSTRALIA, have permitted the League to concentrate on its nursery operations and farm-tree planting.

Libby Robin, *Building a Forest Conscience: An Historical Portrait of the Natural Resources Conservation League of Victoria (NRCL) 1944–1990* (Springvale South, Vic., 1991)   RA

NATURAL STYLES based on idealised nature have long formed a key theme in debate over garden STYLES, as for instance in the influence of Chinese garden traditions. In the early eighteenth century, to writers and garden designers such as Addison, Pope, and Kent, 'natural' often referred to the unchecked growth of plants in gardens in contradistinction to their modification by pruning. The new 'natural style' of their successors formed such a contrast with FORMAL styles of the past that the synonym 'modern style' persisted until well into the nineteenth century. Proponents of the English landscape movement invoked nature as the ideal that the gardener should follow. But what was nature, especially in a country such as England, where agricultural practices had altered the countryside known even to its medieval inhabitants? In Australia, many Aboriginal CULTURAL LANDSCAPES drew their inspiration from existing natural features: some of these were coincidently among the most admired landscapes by early colonists, especially due to their close resemblance to the English parkland ideal. SUBLIMITY in nature also inspired many Australian colonists.

Drawing on his British experience, Thomas SHEPHERD wrote of LANDSCAPE GARDENING in 1836 that it could be adjudged successful when it 'appears most simple, natural, and pleasing'. Yet he also conceded that 'landscape gardening is an art that improves upon nature', highlighting the complexity of the term 'natural style'. Shepherd felt that NSW was ripe for improvements that built on nature—although his remarks went unheeded by the majority of colonists. Throughout the nineteenth century 'natural' was also used loosely to mean PICTURESQUE but to some, such as James SINCLAIR, the natural or 'irregular' style was closely derived from the beauties of nature, which he regarded with a religious devotion. His idiosyncratic conception relied on groups of single plant species (rather than indiscriminate mixing of different plants), irregular outlines (preferably based on natural features) and avoidance of straight lines, low-intervention horticultural techniques (for example, disbudding in summer rather than heavy pruning in winter), disapproval of hybridisation to produce artificial forms, selective retention of indigenous vegetation, and due regard for natural factors such as soil, climate, and situation. He admired in 1856, for example, a Melbourne garden that featured pelargonium beds thirty-nine feet (12 m) in circumference and mesembryanthemums in a bed eighteen yards (16 m) in circumference: 'Art does much to beautify, but in this case Nature does much more, and in no one instance can this be better exemplified,' he wrote. Despite this extreme stretching of nature's bounds, many of his ideas were advanced—even to generations a century later—although they fell upon deaf ears among his contemporaries.

During the latter half of the nineteenth century the term had become so loosely used that it was ambiguous. Writers such as William ROBINSON, in espousing new principles, resorted to terms such as WILD GARDENING. A common theme was taking inspiration from nature, although this was not necessarily indigenous nature. Sinclair, for example, looked to the way 'the Creator' provided drifts of uniform planting rather than a GARDENESQUE arrangement of different plants. This drawing from nature was not always so literal: for example, in 1903 C. Bogue LUFFMAN felt that 'For studies in design, and the apportioning of trees and shrubs, and such materials as provide the outlines of gardens, nothing is so worthy of our notice as clouds, on what may be termed lazy evenings'. William GUILFOYLE's interpretation of nature included a judicious mix of native and exotic plants (for instance in his fern gully at Melbourne Botanic Gardens). J. H. MAIDEN, although strongly advocating the natural style for parks, demonstrated the artificiality of the term when he embarked on a program to give Sydney a more subtropical appearance through the widespread introduction of exotic palms.

The romance of the RAINFOREST in particular—and appreciation of the Australian BUSH more generally—formed an impetus to conserve nature, especially by reservation of NATIONAL PARKS. Many park advocates included NATURAL HISTORY enthusiasts who used AUSTRALIAN PLANTS with a deep understanding of their habits and characteristics. Edna WALLING (in her later native phase) and proponents of BUSH GARDENS, such as Betty MALONEY and Jean Walker, Ellis STONES, Gordon FORD, Alister and Margot KNOX, and more recently REVEGETATION enthusiasts have all introduced new manifestations of the natural style. An additional impetus has been a drive to reduce maintenance levels by creating more self-sustaining landscapes based on ECOLOGICAL principles.

COLLEEN MORRIS

NATURE STRIPS (also 'verges' or street lawns'), grassed strips of public land between the footpath and roadway, have been found in Australia from the mid-nineteenth century and were standard features of TOWN PLANNING by the time of the GARDEN SUBURB movement. Not only a space for underground services, overhead cabling, and STREET TREES, nature strips also act as a buffer between public and private space, offering a vital shard of green in the midst of the constructed environment. Fastidiously tended (a curious irony given the invocation of Nature), or unkempt and weedy, the nature strip—which commonly mirrors its adjoining FRONT GARDEN—can also become a contested site. For some it is symbolic of civic and personal pride, for others the strip becomes a bitter battleground as municipal councils and residents wage silent wars over responsibilities for appropriate maintenance and planting: removal (or replanting) of errant

'Why not make you footpath beautiful?' exhorted the *Australian Home Beautiful* (1929), illustrating one early form of beautification of the NATURE STRIP—a rare public pronouncement on this notoriously self-effacing ribbon of land

trees, flower beds, or even vegetable patches, can consume the resources of both parties. Nature strips remain an important icon of suburbia, complementing the quarter-acre block and the two-strip drive, a status apparent in the sometimes misrepresented rendition of Australia's national anthem: 'Our land abounds in nature strips/Of beauty rich and rare'.

ROWAN WILKEN and KAREN OLSEN

NATURE STUDY was part of a 'new education' which, in the late nineteenth and early twentieth centuries, aimed to replace rote learning with observation and thinking. Encouraging students to learn from plants and animals in the bush and garden, it was first introduced into an Australian SCHOOL curriculum in 1902 by Victoria's new Director of Education, Frank Tate (1864–1939), who wrote an enthusiastic introduction to *Nature Studies in Australia* (1903) by William Gillies and Robert Hall. School work was displayed at a 1905 nature study exhibition organised by Geelong FIELD NATURALISTS' CLUB, and in 1906 in Brisbane and Bairnsdale. Melbourne's much-publicised State Schools' Exhibition (1906) included displays of wildflowers and school garden produce. From 1905 John Albert Leach (1870–1929) taught nature study at Melbourne's Teachers' College and organised field excursions that attracted hundreds of teachers, many of whom were members of the Field Naturalists' Club of Victoria (FNCV); Leach also persuaded the Club to offer a new cheap membership for children. In 1906 he led an FNCV camp for teachers, with field studies and evening lectures. When Organizing Inspector of Nature-Study, Leach wrote *Australian Nature Studies* (1922) in time for the Schools' Exhibition, whose nature study section he organised. Students and teachers also enjoyed Leach's RADIO broadcasts and Donald MACDONALD's *Argus* articles.

As primary schools across Australia began teaching nature study, books, articles and broadcasts proliferated. From 1907 interstate teachers attended Leach's College lectures, and following his 1906 presentations at Victor Harbour, the SA curriculum included nature study. Alfred George Edquist (1873–1963), Supervisor of Nature Study for the SA Education Department, wrote *Nature Studies in Australasia* (1916) and, like Leach, *Education Gazette* articles. In the 1930s books abounded, including Melbourne's 'Sun Nature Books' and others by Charles BARRETT. Sydney's Shakespeare Head Press published the *Teacher's Nature Study Manual* (1934) by Ernest Breakwell and G.H. Wright, and 'Australian Nature Books' edited by David STEAD, including his *Tree Book* (1933), and *The Story of Our Plants* (1933) by Constance LE PLASTRIER. Many naturalists' clubs formed junior groups, and school nature study clubs were popular in WA. Crosbie MORRISON popularised post-war nature study through his Australia-wide school broadcasts and magazine *Wild Life*. By the 1960s, when Norman Arthur Wakefield (1918–1972) was lecturing, writing and broadcasting on nature, its study was being absorbed into the wider field of science in Australian school curricula.   LINDEN GILLBANK

NEATE, Ambrose (1815–1890) and son **Ambrose Charles Neate** (1843–1923), horticulturist and clerk of MELBOURNE BOTANIC GARDENS, respectively. Ambrose senior, a professional gardener, migrated with family members in 1852 to manage an ORCHARD at Barrabool (Vic.). In 1855 he briefly moved to Hobart to manage the orchard and VINEYARD of fruiterer Charles HOLLINSDALE, but subsequently joined the Melbourne firm of Smith and ADAMSON. While in their employ, family tradition suggests that he laid out the grounds of Bishopscourt, East Melbourne, residence of Archbishop Perry. Ambrose Charles, initially also employed with Smith and Adamson, went to MELBOURNE BOTANIC GARDENS in 1858 as an office boy under Ferdinand MUELLER. From the early 1880s until his retirement in 1903 he was the Gardens' senior clerk, and acting curator during William GUILFOYLE's absence in Europe (1890). In his later years Neate was an enthusiastic compiler of the early history of Melbourne Botanic Gardens, and contributed horticultural articles to the *Bankers' Magazine of Australasia*.   DARREN WATSON

NEILSON, George (1823–1897), horticulturist and curator, was born in Scotland and left school at an early age; by 1843 he was working as a gardener at Stirling Castle. He spent five years with Viscount Clifden in England and then three years as head gardener at Gowan Castle, the family's Scottish seat. He decided to emigrate in 1852, and his reference from Clifden's agent praised his skilful direction of labourers, his sobriety, honesty, and perseverance, and his versatile horticultural abilities. He had just finished designing and working out extensions and improvements in the flower and pleasure gardens, which had 'greatly added to the beauty of this place'. On arrival in Vic. he at once proceeded to the diggings, but a few years later, in partnership with his brother, Archibald, he started an orchard and fruit nursery at Fyansford. By 1865 he was employed at the Frogmore Nursery of Charles WYATT, and afterwards by Thomas LANG, at Ballarat. In 1872 he was one of two short-listed applicants for the curatorship of GEELONG BOTANIC GARDENS following the death of Daniel BUNCE, but the job went to John RADDENBERRY. Another chance came Neilson's way when William CLARSON resigned as honorary director of the Horticultural Society's garden at Burnley later that year; on the casting vote of T.C. COLE, he was appointed to the enhanced position of curator. POMOLOGY was his strong suit: Neilson was regarded throughout Australia as an authority. He developed a splendid collection of fruit trees at Burnley, and was an advocate of export trade with England. When the garden became part of BURNLEY SCHOOL OF HORTICULTURE (1891), Neilson was left in charge, but he resigned to become chief inspector under the new *Vegetable Diseases Act* in 1897, shortly before his death. Neilson was only the second Australian resident (after MUELLER) elected to the honorary membership of the ROYAL HORTICULTURAL SOCIETY.   RA

NELSON, David (d. 1789), plant and seed collector on James Cook's third voyage, trained as a gardener at KEW and was recommended to BANKS by James LEE. He was described by William Anderson, surgeon and naturalist on the voyage, as 'a person who understands botany'. In 1777 at Adventure Bay on Bruny Island, Van Diemen's Land, Nelson collected twenty-three lots of seed and the type material for *Eucalyptus obliqua* (from which the genus EUCALYPTUS was named by L'Héritier). *Acacia verticillata* from his collections, flowered in 1790, was the first published illustration of an AUSTRALIAN PLANT in colour. Nelson was later appointed botanist on William Bligh's ill-fated breadfruit expedition of 1788. At Adventure Bay, Nelson again collected specimens and planted fruit trees and vegetable seeds, none of which apparently survived. After the mutiny, Nelson remained loyal to Bligh and survived the open boat journey only to die of fever in Timor in 1789. He is commemorated in the genus *Nelsonia*.   TONY CAVANAGH

THE NETHERLANDS Dutch horticulturists have a long-standing reputation, especially as growers of nursery plants and flowers. Impact on Australian gardens from the Netherlands reflects this tradition and can be traced through three lines. The first of these is indirect, being the influence of Dutch horticulture on Britain, where Dutch plant breeders and growers have supplied plants for many centuries. Plant selections that originated in the Netherlands would thus have found their way to Australia through this means. The other impacts on Australia are more direct. Dutch nurseries have supplied plants, seeds, and bulbs directly to Australian gardeners. There is evidence of planting schemes illustrated in Dutch seed catalogues informing bedding schemes in Australia in the early part of this century. After the Second World War, migration from Europe to Australia included many Dutch nationals who used their expertise to establish horticultural enterprises here. Many of these businesses have gone on to become significant parts of the nursery, floriculture and related industries in this country. Names such as TESSELAAR, Slykerman, Koelewyn, and van der Staay are well known in their respective parts of the horticulture industry.

PETER MAY

NEW FARM PARK, Brisbane, was designed by Henry MOORE in 1913 and remains one of the city's favourite public parks. The Brisbane City Council purchased thirty-six acres (15 ha) of alluvial plain fronting the Brisbane River in 1913 and extensive landscape construction works were undertaken during 1914–15, including an elegant BANDSTAND and large KIOSK (with lessee residence) in a distinctively local timber idiom. Moore's vision for the park included 'A double line of jacarandas round the drive; a line of poinciana [*Delonix regia*] extending from Sydney Street to the river; a double line of bougainvilleas (eight varieties) bordering a walk 160 yards in length'. The park also included two ornamental lagoons (with islands), numerous palms, beds of massed tropical shrubs such as poinsettias, and hedges of acalyphas and hibiscus. By 1915 Moore had added a rose bed with more than 800 plants. New Farm Park's famous collection of ROSES—said in 1940 to number 20 000—was redeveloped several times: by Harry OAKMAN in 1948–53 and again in 1962; reconfigured in 1972; and in 1974, after the whole park was flooded, 4000 roses were replaced. This flood activated a deadly soil-borne fungal disease, noticed in 1991 after the loss of several jacarandas. A children's playground, established in 1955 and redeveloped several times since, includes very popular timber play structures laced through the branches and aerial roots of two huge *Ficus benghalensis* (Banyan) trees.

JEANNIE SIM

NEWMAN, Charles Frederick (1834–1899), nursery proprietor and florist, was born Carl Friedrich Neumann in Hamburg, Germany, and migrated to Adelaide in 1846. Following little success at the goldfields, he founded a nursery at Water Gully, near Houghton in the ADELAIDE HILLS (*c*. 1875) after acquiring the land in 1854 and progressively developing it. One observer, perhaps with some parochial license, claimed the nursery was eventually 'the largest in the southern hemisphere', enjoying 'a reputation overseas almost equal to that of the most famous in England and Europe'. Newman's Model Nursery, as it became known, imported and exported plants extensively in WARDIAN CASES, and regularly won show medals including 'nearly all the principal awards for floral designs, wreaths and bouquets, and swept the boards with a fine collection of orchids' in 1899. Newman

The Model Nursery of C.F. NEWMAN and Son, engraved for the firm's 1894–95 catalogue, illustrates the range of shade and hothouses for the propagation and growth of tender plants, and also the planted borders displaying the stock of this extensive NURSERY at Houghton (SA)

'was an enthusiast in all horticultural and floricultural matters, and was very widely known and respected'. Upon his accidental death, his wife Mary Ann Maria (née Bailes) (1838–1932), horticulturist, managed the business until severe floods and a hailstorm destroyed most of the nursery (1913). The property was sold upon her death.

Their first son, **Charles Lewis William Newman** (1858–1940), established C.F. Newman and Son at the Victoria Park Nursery in Perth, producing the first *Manual for the Garden, Orchard and Farm* (1905–06) in WA, 'for the guidance of those who may not have at their command the services of a professional gardener', and registering *Camellia* 'Charles Newman' and 'Jean Newman'. The firm was well known in WA for its roses, and Charles Newman is credited with the successful introduction of Fortuniana stock in WA. Their sixth son, Frederick Christoff Newman (1871–1955), managed the Model Nursery but in 1925 established his own nursery at Tea Tree Gully with his wife Doris (née Possingham) (1893–1988), building 'one of the largest bulb nurseries' in SA. Daughter Suzanne (b. 1924) and son-in-law Roger Hall (1925–1974) expanded the nursery upon the death of F.C. Newman into native and South African species, developing specialities in proteas, leucadendrons, leucospermums, and camellias; developing *Cupressus macrocarpa* 'Greenstead Magnificent'; promoting the Camellia Research Society; writing *Growing Camellias* (1969); being awarded six RHS Banksian medals; and developing *Camellia* cultivars including 'Just Sue' and 'Roger Hall'. Their third son, Jonathan (b. 1952), and his wife Dianne, continue the nursery under the long-established C.F. Newman and Son name.

DAVID JONES

NEWMAN, Francis William (*c.* 1796–1859), botanist and gardens superintendent, was gardener to surgeon and pastoralist James Bowman (son-in-law of John and Elizabeth MACARTHUR) at Lyndhurst, Glebe (NSW), when on the death of James ANDERSON (1842) he applied for the superintendent's position at SYDNEY BOTANIC GARDENS. Although unsuccessful, his botanical knowledge enabled him to secure the appointment in 1845 as superintendent of the gardens of the ROYAL SOCIETY of Van Diemen's Land (later ROYAL TASMANIAN BOTANICAL GARDENS). In his first years Newman introduced sixty new genera comprising 250 species, including new varieties of fruits, grains, and grasses. He also prepared a border for fifty plants indigenous to the colony. In 1848 the pond was made from a nearby creek, thus saving much expense in carting water from the town. With his botanical knowledge and practical experience in horticulture, the Gardens were enlarged, and greatly improved and beautified, which led to an increasing number of visitors. There was a great deal of plant exchange and members of the Royal Society were allowed plants from the Gardens to the amount of their subscription to the Society. In 1857 Newman published an extensive *Catalogue of Plants in the Royal Society's Gardens*. When he died in 1859 it was said that the Colony had 'lost a benefactor … for he laboured constantly and earnestly in importing every plant, tree, or shrub that was either useful, profitable, or ornamental'.

ANN CRIPPS

NEW SOUTH WALES Captain James Cook named the previously uncharted eastern portion of New Holland the territory of New South Wales, a mysterious choice and an intriguing counterpoint to the earlier naming of New North (and South) Wales in the 'Eskimaux Country' on Hudson's Bay. Phillip's account of the first years of Sydney (1789) was accompanied by a poem by Erasmus Darwin in which 'Hope stood sublime, and wav'd her golden hair'. The first farm was sited in an area encompassed by the present ROYAL BOTANIC GARDENS, SYDNEY, but by the time Phillip's account was published gardening as a serious enterprise had proved unviable in Sydney Cove and the government had shifted its agricultural focus further west to Parramatta. Initially the gardens were simple and geometric in style. In the mid-1790s even the grandest Sydney garden, the governor's, was essentially utilitarian, with the only hint of sophistication being two symmetrically placed circular beds in front of the house, and two larger beds, each containing a single orange tree, framing the central path leading away from the house. (Sir) Joseph BANKS, who, with Daniel SOLANDER, accompanied Cook in 1770, was to maintain an active interest in early botanising in the colony; his collector George CALEY and settler George SUTTOR were charged with caring for Banks's dispatch of plants for the colony (arriving in 1800).

Some early wealthy landowners developed estates where the gardens were geometric in form—such as George Johnston's Annandale Estate with its carriage drive lined by an AVENUE of Norfolk Island pines. Others began developing estates in the desired image of the wealthy landowners of Britain, picturesquely siting their houses on slopes above rivers or streams in a pastoral setting. The most notable was Elizabeth Farm, where John and Elizabeth MACARTHUR imported and planted fruit trees, olives, china roses, and CAPE bulbs. ORCHARDS, particularly of oranges, became a major industry by the 1850s, and the peach featured prominently on the farms of the Cumberland Plain. HEDGES of quince, lemon, and china rose were planted, with gardens embellished by agave, prickly pear, oleander, and pomegranate.

The arrival in 1810 of the fifth governor, Macquarie, ushered in a period of TOWN PLANNING, road-building, and expansion west of the Blue Mountains; the setting aside of the area for HYDE PARK in Sydney (1810), the construction of landmark public buildings, and the establishment of Sydney Botanic Gardens (1816) under Charles FRASER; Allan CUNNINGHAM, appointee of Banks as King's Botanist, arrived in 1816. The first AGRICULTURAL SOCIETY was founded at Parramatta under the patronage of Governor Brisbane (1822), evolving as the Agricultural and Horticultural Society (1826–36), with Sir John JAMISON as president. As a consequence of Commissioner Bigge's 1823 report, *The State of Agriculture and Trade in the Colony of New South Wales*, the growth of olives and wine grapes was promoted. During this period, the Botanic Gardens acted as an ACCLIMATISATION nursery, distributing excess plants to settlers with promising gardens. This practice meant that the early nursery proprietors in Sydney, Thomas SHEPHERD, Robert HENDERSON, and John BAPTIST encountered some difficulties in establishing a foothold, but as family businesses, they eventually

New South Wales

became the backbone of the NURSERY TRADE. Shepherd, who established his Darling Nursery in 1828, published several articles in the *Sydney Gazette* (1831) and delivered lectures on HORTICULTURE and LANDSCAPE GARDENING at the Mechanics' School of Arts, published in 1835–36.

Alexander MCLEAY arrived in the colony as its Colonial Secretary in 1826. The influence of the McLeay and Macarthur families, particularly William Macarthur, on gardening in the colonial period of NSW cannot be underestimated. Both families introduced a number of plants into NSW. William Macarthur's garden at Camden Park, established by the 1820s, evolved into a flourishing private nursery between the 1840s and 1860s, playing an important role in the field of HYBRIDISATION. During the 1830s Alexander McLeay developed a marine VILLA in a late REPTONIAN style at Elizabeth Bay, and his son George established Brownlow Hill at Cobbitty. McLeay's Elizabeth Bay garden—and that at Lyndhurst in Glebe—were described in Shepherd's final lecture on marine villas. Other examples occurred around Sydney Harbour and along the coastline: Nelson's Bay (BRONTE HOUSE), which typified the PICTURESQUE; VAUCLUSE HOUSE; Rose Bay Cottage; and the mansions of Darlinghurst—all exploited the views from their verandahs, their Regency gardens embellished with fashionable SHRUBBERIES, landmark plantings of ARAUCARIAS, FIGS, and clumps of giant BAMBOO, and lawns dotted with flower BEDS. Increasingly sophisticated houses and gardens were sketched and painted from 1835 by Conrad Martens (1801–1878). Prominent city gardens were often supported by their owners' pastoral pursuits beyond the Great Dividing Range, where a number established additional residences with impressive carriageways and extensive gardens. Early examples were in the Bathurst and Mudgee areas to the west, Goulburn and Braidwood areas to the south, and the HUNTER VALLEY, Port Macquarie, and New England areas to the north. The discovery of gold in the 1850s in the central west of NSW led to a general exodus of labour to the goldfields, but did not lead to the establishment of mansions and gardens to the same extent as occurred in Vic.

Charles MOORE became Director of Sydney Botanic Gardens in 1848, displacing J.C. BIDWILL, commencing a period of almost fifty years of shaping the designed landscape of NSW, laying out or providing plants for PUBLIC PARKS throughout the state (the most notable being CENTENNIAL

EXPERIMENT FARM, Parramatta (NSW), the site of Australia's first land grant (to convict James Ruse)—its plantings of agaves and araucarias, and its avenue of olives, are characteristic of early colonial gardens around Sydney and other early settlements of NEW SOUTH WALES

PARK), and either designing or advising on the gardens associated with HOSPITALS, gaols, churches, RAILWAY stations, and other public buildings in NSW. He expanded the Botanic Gardens in a predominantly GARDENESQUE style and was involved in the laying out of ROOKWOOD Necropolis. In the distribution of plants, Moore's preference for RAINFOREST trees, particularly *Ficus macrophylla* (Moreton Bay Fig), left an indelible mark on NSW. He introduced a number of plants from the PACIFIC ISLANDS into the Botanic Gardens. Many of these were collected by William GUILFOYLE for his father Michael GUILFOYLE's Exotic Nursery at Double Bay, who is reputed to have designed a number of Sydney gardens. Other nurseries that opened in the mid-nineteenth century were the Australia Nursery (Camden) of Francis FERGUSON and Camellia Grove (near Parramatta) of Silas SHEATHER, both previously gardeners for the Macarthur family, and Somerset Nursery (Harris Park, near Parramatta) of Samuel PURCHASE.

There were few local publications, apart from ALMANACS, the writings of James BUSBY on VITICULTURE, and Shepherd's lectures, to provide horticultural advice for settlers in the early colonial period. Horticultural articles occasionally appeared in the Sydney newspapers; for example, William Macarthur (as 'Maro') wrote on the vine in the *Australian* newspaper (1840s). Influential British publications included J.C. LOUDON's *Gardener's Magazine*, his encyclopaedias of agriculture and gardening, and the *Suburban Gardener and Villa Companion*, and later the widely read GARDENERS' CHRONICLE. The (AUSTRALIAN) TOWN AND COUNTRY JOURNAL provided descriptions of properties and gardening advice. Specialised information was disseminated through a number of short-lived professional and amateur horticultural societies. The SYDNEY MAGAZINE OF SCIENCE AND ART published the proceedings of the Australian Horticultural and Agricultural Society. Prominent member, Sir William Denison, NSW Governor (1855–61), was a great promoter of gardening and agricultural improvement. The *HORTICULTURAL MAGAZINE*, illustrated by Robert FITZGERALD, was published by the Horticultural Society of Sydney (reconstituted as the Horticultural Society of New South Wales in 1865), the membership of which consisted of Scottish- and English-trained professional gardeners, leading wealthy landowners (such as T.S. MORT), and enthusiastic amateurs. Gardeners such as Scottish-trained Alexander Stephen of the Walker family estate, YARALLA; Henry PARCEL from J.R. Young's Hereford House, Glebe; and Michael Bell of Mort's celebrated Greenoaks, described and discussed their latest accomplishments in the garden and GLASSHOUSE.

Increased interest in the local AUSTRALIAN FLORA, particularly FERNS, was encouraged by Louisa ATKINSON's newspaper articles, 'A Voice From The Country' (1860), and lectures, newspaper articles, and books by William WOOLLS. By the 1870s Sydney seed merchants Anderson, Hall and Co., had begun acting as publishers with LAW SOMNER's *Handbook to the Garden for New South Wales*, establishing a publishing trend among nursery proprietors such as TRESEDER, SEARL, YATES, and RUMSEY. The majority of works were published in Sydney although the Bathurst publication *A Treatise on the Orchards and Gardens of the Western Districts* (1877) indicated the growing need for more CLIMATE-specific advice.

The progressive urbanisation of country towns fostered the development of large public parks in towns such as Armidale, Bathurst, Deniliquin, Goulburn, Grafton, Newcastle, and Orange during the 1860s–90s. Street tree planting began to come into vogue from the 1870s, with Grafton's famous Jacarandas planted *c.* 1907–08 following mixed street-tree plantings from 1874. Gardens became increasingly ornamented and ostentatious in the city areas, and SUMMER RETREATS to the cooler areas of MOUNT WILSON and the SOUTHERN HIGHLANDS became fashionable following first the lease of Throsby Park near Moss Vale by the governor (1867) and the purchase of HILLVIEW in 1882 as the governor's summer residence. Wealthy industrialists created large country gardens planted with CONIFERS and cool-climate plants. Much of the rainforest around Mount Wilson was cleared of all but the stately, fashionable tree ferns. Horticultural advice was imparted by H.A. JAMES in the *Sydney Morning Herald*, and in 1893 'Mrs Rolf BOLDREWOOD' published *The Flower Garden in Australia*. The Agriculture Department was established in 1890 under the talented economic botanist Fred TURNER, and Hawkesbury Agricultural College at Richmond, opened in 1891, provided formal training and EDUCATION in all aspects of AGRICULTURE including BOTANY but not specifically HORTICULTURE.

In his role as Director (1896–1924), Joseph MAIDEN continued the influence that Sydney Botanic Gardens was already having on the NSW landscape. Whereas Moore's signature plant was the Moreton Bay Fig, Maiden's became *Phoenix canariensis* (Canary Island Date Palm). Numerous avenue and park plantings of this palm were undertaken from the 1910s to the 1930s after the success of the 1908 avenue planting in Centennial Park. New concepts in TOWN PLANNING were actively promoted from the 1890s, especially by architect John SULMAN. Gardening became focused on smaller suburban plots, with the ideal of the GARDEN SUBURB. The first was Haberfield, developed from 1902, followed from 1903 by Appian Way in Burwood with large Federation-style houses clustered around its exclusive, centrally placed TENNIS COURT. FLORICULTURE became the emphasis in gardening. SWEET PEAS enjoyed a revival in popularity, along with DAHLIAS and CARNATIONS, but the cultivation of the ROSE surpassed all.

During the inter-war period, plantings of MEMORIAL avenues, many of poplars, became common across the state. During this period significant government-funded work was undertaken in public parks and reserves by relief programs for workers affected by the Depression. The architect W. Hardy WILSON and his client E.G. WATERHOUSE led a revival in the appreciation of colonial architecture and gardens; others such as Leslie WILKINSON introduced a more MEDITERRANEAN style of architecture as suitable for the local climate, complemented by the dappled shade of angophoras, jacarandas, and *Brachychiton acerifolius* (Illawarra Flame Tree). Walter and Marion GRIFFIN created a new ideal at CASTLECRAG, where the emphasis for the garden was as a landscape setting of rock and native plants (surviving indigenous and planted), with the use of bright colour in flowers close to the houses as a foil in the overall scheme. Paul

SORENSEN established his practice in the Blue Mountains with major commissions throughout country NSW in the 1930s. Jocelyn BROWN created gardens that were formal—often symmetrical—to complement the Colonial Revival houses popular in the 1930s and influenced a wider audience through her articles in the HOME.

Author and educator Thistle HARRIS and nursery proprietor George ALTHOFER promoted the use of native plants for the garden from the late 1930s. With the formation of the SOCIETY FOR GROWING AUSTRALIAN PLANTS (1957) and the growing desire for a more ECOLOGICAL approach to gardening using native plants, the BUSH GARDEN movement had gained momentum by the 1960s, leading to the success of publications written for the home gardener by Betty MALONEY and Jean Walker. In the public sphere, work by Bruce MACKENZIE and Harry HOWARD reflected the same philosophy. Such gardens complemented the Sydney School of architecture, which advocated sympathetic and rugged design for the rocky, well-treed, sloping sites of the region. Three books evocatively summarised trends of the period from the 1960s to the 1980s: Rob Hillier's *Let's Buy a Terrace House* (1967) and *The Tiny Utopia* (1977) by Frances Kelly and Pauline Clements, which heralded and celebrated the inner-urban revival, with its courtyard and balcony gardens, and Don BURKE's *The Lazy Gardener* (1983), which epitomised the relaxed suburban ethos where gardening paralleled lifestyle choices promoted by the popular media. Since the 1980s the popularity of the Australian bush garden has been refined, and now more closely embraces local indigenous species, while an increase in the appeal of FORMALITY has seen COTTAGE GARDENS replaced by the Tuscan-style courtyard.

COLLEEN MORRIS

NEWSTEAD HOUSE AND PARK, Qld, illustrates the transformation of the natural landscape from its pre-European state, through residential estate development and conversion to a twentieth-century PUBLIC PARK of an intrinsically Brisbane character. DARLING DOWNS grazier Patrick Leslie (1815–1881) purchased the property in 1846 and fenced a portion of thirty-four acres (14 ha) for the establishment of his house, grounds, and food garden. Land fronting the house was grassed, establishing a strong visual connection to the Brisbane River—a link maintained today. The house, constructed in 1846, retains the layout developed in the 1870s by Brisbane entrepreneur, George Harris (1831–1891), who also planted Bunya and Kauri pines in the grounds as contrast to huge clumps of bamboo along the river bank. The land was subdivided in the 1890s and only the house block of four acres (1.6 ha) remained unchanged.

Brisbane City Council purchased the land in 1918 and Henry MOORE created the present park by removing all existing river bank vegetation and creating revetment walls, constructing paths, and planting additional trees in front of the house and, after purchasing all the remaining properties along Breakfast Creek Road (1926), by creating an entrance drive and stone entrance pillars. An act of parliament (1939) created a Trust to run the house as a historic museum. During the Second World War the house and park were taken over by the military; after the war, Harry OAKMAN reorganised the park layout and undertook some replanting. Mature trees suffered severe damage during storms in 1998 and affected areas are being replanted.

JANE LENNON

NEW ZEALAND and Australia share a similar colonial-imperial relationship with Britain, and therefore have much

The habourside setting of Sydney's early marine VILLAS was soon favoured by all who could garner even the smallest VISTA, but those with 'absolute frontage' enjoyed a privileged position and view, from balconies, summerhouses, and BOATHOUSES, which still resonates in contemporary NEW SOUTH WALES society

GARDEN HISTORY in common. When the first European settlers tilled New Zealand soil in the 1820s they were augmenting cultivation by the Maori, inheritors of East Polynesian agricultural traditions. The rich agricultural (and pastoral) potential of New Zealand was a great attraction to the British. Like Australia, New Zealand witnessed widespread migration and a corresponding transfer of agricultural and horticultural skills. New Zealand and the PACIFIC ISLANDS were much visited by Australian horticulturists, and the resulting introductions found their way into BOTANIC GARDENS, and through the NURSERY TRADE, into domestic gardens. In an age of maritime trade, the distances between Australian and New Zealand ports were comparable to—in some cases shorter than—those within the Australian colonies.

Phormium tenax (New Zealand Flax) attracted the attention of the Imperial powers for its economic properties in cloth manufacture, but increasingly it was the ornamental prospects of the New Zealand flora that attracted attention. *Cordyline australis* (Cabbage Tree) and *Metrosideros excelsa* (New Zealand Christmas Tree or Pohutukawa) became popular ornamental trees in Australia; Auckland artist Alfred SHARPE popularised the Pohutukawa in Newcastle (NSW) during the 1880s. Various forms of New Zealand Flax also became a staple of subtropical SHRUBBERIES, valued for their bold FOLIAGE. Private collectors, such as successive owners of ALTON at Mount Macedon (Vic.), purchased or imported many New Zealand plants and its garden, along with the New Zealand section of the ROYAL BOTANIC GARDENS, MELBOURNE, remain outstanding early examples of this interest. An interest in cultivating indigenous flora developed somewhat earlier in New Zealand than the corresponding local interest in AUSTRALIAN PLANTS, due in large measure to the influence of botanist Leonard Cockayne (1855–1934), and so New Zealand nurseries (such as Duncan & Davies and Nairn's), were well placed to export New Zealand plants. The trade in plants continued at all social levels until quarantine regulations at first made it difficult, later prohibited.

Australian plants were also popularised in New Zealand: *Hakea*, *Acacia*, and *Albizia lophantha* were cultivated for farm and garden hedges; *Eucalyptus globulus* (Blue Gum) was a popular ornamental tree of the 1850s and was later important as a farm shelter tree. EUCALYPTS were grown as ornamental street trees in most Waikato towns from the 1870s onwards, and during the 1930s *E. ficifolia* (Red-flowering Gum) was planted as a street tree in Napier's post-earthquake townscapes. Shared horticultural interests were also well demonstrated by joint societies such as the Australian and New Zealand Camellia Research Foundation, and publication of the *Australian and New Zealand Rose Annual* by the respective NATIONAL ROSE SOCIETIES.

Matthew Bradbury (ed.), *A History of the Garden in New Zealand* (Auckland, 1995); Winsome Shepherd, *Wellington's Heritage: Plants, Gardens, and Landscape* (Wellington, 2000)   JOHN ADAM

NICHOLLS, Robert Uriah (*c.* 1834–1910), nursery proprietor, was born in Devonshire, England, and migrated to Vic. in 1853. He landed at Geelong and, after visiting Van Diemen's Land, spent two years mining on the Ballarat diggings. In 1856 he set up in business as a nursery proprietor and seed merchant with William Rossiter, at first using leased land close to the diggings. One of his first contracts was laying out and planting the Ballarat Hospital grounds. The partnership was dissolved in 1858 and Nicholls started the long-running business bearing his name. At horticultural shows he was a successful exhibitor. He was a founding committee member of the Ballarat Horticultural Society (1859) and was involved in many other civic institutions. In conjunction with architect G.W. Clegg, he won the first prize for the best design for laying out Ballarat's Victoria Park (1889). Nicholls married Mary Hewitt in 1870 and several of their children, including George Henry (b. 1871–*fl.* 1920s), William Kelland (1878–1935), and Walter Hewett (b. 1887), worked in the family business. John Benjamin Nicholls (*c.* 1837–1914), brother of Robert, was also a horticulturist and nursery proprietor, and his three daughters became florists in Ballarat. R.U. Nicholls was one of a small group, with Thomas LANG and Francis MOSS, who dominated the nursery trade in Ballarat during the nineteenth century but whose influence was felt beyond the confines of the town. Nicholls stocked 20 000 each of *Pinus radiata* (Monterey Pine) and *Cupressus macrocarpa* (Monterey Cypress) in 1908, indicative of the size of his nursery.   RA

NICHOLLS, William Henry (1885–1951), orchidologist, was born and educated at Ballarat (Vic.). An enthusiastic walker and cyclist, and keen member of the Field Naturalists' Club of Victoria, Nicholls took to the bush with camera, journal, and sketchbook, garnering specialist knowledge of native ORCHIDS. He published many papers on the subject, but died before his monumental *Orchids of Australia* could be published: this appeared in one volume in 1969. Nicholls worked for many years as a propagator at FOOTSCRAY PARK during the curatorship of his friend David MATTHEWS.   RA

NIELSEN, (Mary) Fairie (b. 1926), farmer and gardener, was born in Sydney and came to Tas. as a child. Her garden at Pigeon Hill, Burnie, has been created since 1960 from natural, steep gullies into a woodland garden of native and exotic trees and shrubs, with a specialist collection of RHODODENDRONS. In 1985, as a member of the Australian Rhododendron Society, North-West Tasmanian Branch, she was one of the founders of the thirteen-hectare Emu Valley Rhododendron Garden, which has a collection of more than 12 000 plants. She is an enthusiastic promoter of gardens, and her involvement with the AUSTRALIAN GARDEN HISTORY SOCIETY, chairing the Tasmanian Branch (1987–96) and as a National Management Committee member (1987–96), did much to raise the Society's profile. Fairie Nielsen is an inspiration and role model to the many who have visited her garden or participated in her fondly regarded tours of Tasmanian gardens.
ANN CRIPPS

NINDOOINBAH, Beaudesert, Qld, was taken up as a pastoral run in 1842 and the first part of the present house was built in the late 1850s. Pastoralist William Collins purchased Nindooinbah in 1906 after a five-year lease and following an extensive honeymoon that included a visit to Japan. Talented Brisbane architect Robin Dods was employed to extend the house, and he gave advice on the extensive gardens developed by William's wife, Gwendoline Collins. The mix of formal and picturesque elements responded to the E-shaped plan of the house and its courtyards, and addressed the surrounding landscape with outlooks over the lagoon and to the distant hills. Red painted-timber gateways in the enclosing garden fence were designed in an ORIENTAL style. The restored and well-maintained gardens include a bush-house, grotto, fish pond, tennis court, and early plantings of *Ficus* sp., *Araucaria bidwillii* (Bunya Pine), and palm avenues. Additions (1984–85) include a Japanese-style tea house on a pond (both designed by artist Patrick Hockey), rose garden, and fernery.

CATHERINE BROUWER

NOBELIUS, Carl Axel (1851–1921), orchardist and nursery proprietor, was born at Tampere, Finland, eldest child of a horticulturist who had migrated from Sweden. Nobelius trained in horticulture and in 1871 arrived in Melbourne, where he was employed first in the Toorak nurseries of TAYLOR AND SANGSTER then by Joseph HARRIS in South Yarra. Harris was an important influence in forging close links with BRUNNING, RIMINGTON, CHEESEMAN and Nobelius: by 1900 this group controlled much of the NURSERY TRADE in Melbourne and was largely responsible for its successful combination of aggressive business drive, massive exports, strict quality control, and restless inventiveness.

Around 1886 Nobelius purchased land north-east of the present Emerald township, on which he established an orchard. He selected further land in 1890 and opened his business in 1892, trading as Gembrook Nurseries. He erected his residence, Carramar, overlooking the nursery and ceaselessly acquired adjoining land, ring-barking and clearing as his operations expanded. In 1898 the Gembrook Nursery comprised fifty acres (20 ha), of which fifteen acres (6 ha) was orchard, and in 1900 the total rose to eighty acres (32 ha). At this date the majority of his customers were in Tas., New Zealand, WA, and NSW. His son, Carl Oscar Nobelius (1879–1958), leased further land to increase the family holdings and by 1907, with the nursery employing fifty men, he was closely involved with the business. The new land was bisected by the narrow-gauge railway line that ran from Fern Tree Gully to Gembrook (opened 1900)—of which Carl Nobelius had been a strong advocate; from 1904, he had a siding and large packing shed there.

By 1914 Gembrook Nurseries held two million stock trees, produced large quantities of apples and pears, and conducted a huge export trade, both interstate and overseas, including New Zealand, South Africa, India, Japan, Europe and South America. The size of export is indicated by annual shipments of 400 000 tree stock to South Africa alone. Nobelius was a strong advocate of ornamental tree planting (including STREET TREE planting) and a major importer of ELMS.

After the death of Nobelius, the nurseries and orchards were sold to a Melbourne syndicate, which in the mid-1920s developed the **Emerald Country Club**—among the earliest in Vic.—on the northern portion of the site. A housing estate overlooked a GOLF COURSE and the old nursery track became Lakeside Drive, leading to the clubhouse (1929). For a time membership of the club was restricted to those who purchased land in the estate, and cottage designs were vetted by the committee to ensure that each had 'some distinctive quality of planning and building'—at a time when Edna WALLING was attaching similar conditions at BICKLEIGH VALE. Boundary fences were prohibited. Trees from the nursery were incorporated into the landscaping, and a former packing shed was converted c. 1928 for his own residential use by architect Reg Appleford (whose firm Cowper, Appleford, and Murphy was responsible for the design of the nearby clubhouse). The fortunes of the club wavered, but many of the early features remain.

In 1927 the Nobelius railway station opened, for passengers only, to cater for increasing tourist trade in the Dandenongs. A large portion of the former Nobelius nursery site was compulsorily acquired by the Shire of Fern Tree Gully in 1938–39, and this area (now known as Emerald Lake) was opened in 1941. Meanwhile the Nobelius nursery continued trading, managed by Clifford Leonard Nobelius (1893–1967), son of C.A. Nobelius. For a time in the 1930s the nursery was reputedly owned by Alfred Nicholas, who is said to have transplanted many trees and shrubs from there to his property BURNHAM BEECHES. During the 1950s the nursery was operated by Linton family members and in 1980–81 the remaining nursery site was purchased by the Shire of Sherbrooke. In 1993 a museum was opened at the Nobelius Heritage Park, adjacent to the former nursery packing shed on the narrow-gauge railway line.

RA

NOOROO, Mount Wilson, NSW: see VALDER, Peter George

NORGATE, Dennis Stephen (b. 1926), nursery proprietor, began growing vegetables at Bayswater (Vic.) and established Norgates Plant Farm in 1945. He moved to central Vic. following purchase of rich volcanic land at Trentham (1958), concentrating largely on perennials, always with a keen eye for a good plant or variety. He has maintained in cultivation a wide range of plants—some now extinct in Britain—and has issued numerous varieties bearing his own name. A working and generous gardener, with idiosyncratic views on many subjects, much of his trade is with clients from NSW, while visitors are advised to wear gumboots in wet weather, since they will find few frills such as brick or concrete paths. Though he issues a plain catalogue, many visitors select their own plants, which Norgate will dig for them himself as there are no potted plants available. Son Gordon (b. 1953) and his wife Annette have run the business since 1998.

T.R. GARNETT

NORTH, Marianne (1830–1890), botanical painter, was born in Hastings, England, into a family with contacts in the political, literary, musical, artistic, and scientific world. In this stimulating environment, North took lessons in flower painting during the 1850s. Following the death of her father

(1869) North determined to devote her life to painting flowers from nature; she had travelled in her youth and desired to paint in exotic places, especially in the tropics, and had sufficient means to achieve her aim on a grand international scale. During the 1870s and 1880s she travelled to all continents and accumulated a large collection of paintings of plants that had taken her fancy. These were mostly large and spectacular. North painted in oil on a specially prepared paper, and she set her subjects into their environment with most having a landscape background. Although her work lacked the finesse of the watercolourist and botanical illustrator, it usually carries broader messages, including recording biodiversity in its environmental context.

In 1880 North visited Australia and travelled widely from north Qld round to WA and on to Tas. It was during this trip that she met and influenced Ellis ROWAN. About this time North donated her collection and the funds to establish the Marianne North Gallery at the ROYAL BOTANIC GARDENS, KEW. Her work is still on exhibition—something that would have been impossible had she painted in water colour. The gallery contains more than 800 of her paintings and these include several Australian studies.

A Vision of Eden: The Life and Work of Marianne North (Exeter, England, 1980); Helen Vellacott (ed.), *Some Recollections of a Happy Life: Marianne North in Australia and New Zealand* (Melbourne, 1986)

HELEN HEWSON

NORTH AMERICA and Australia have much in common—both are vast continents with a great diversity of natural landscapes, both were formerly British colonies, both developed largely during the nineteenth-century industrial era, and each has adopted a similar frontier attitude to land and resource exploitation. While Australians initially looked to Europe for inspiration in horticulture and garden design, from the 1850s—chiefly as a result of the influx of Californian migrants during the gold rushes—North American influences, in the form of plants and design ideas, began to appear in Australian parks, gardens, and urban developments.

A wealth of new plants was discovered in North America by professional plant collectors such as David Douglas (1798–1834), who was employed by the (ROYAL) HORTICULTURAL SOCIETY from 1823. Many of these new species were cultivated by British nurseries, and wealthy Australian landowners ordered them for planting on their estates. Between 1843 and 1857, William MACARTHUR had published nursery catalogues of plants cultivated at his Camden Park estate, listing many North American species that became popular garden plants. Familiar examples included *Maclura pomifera* (Osage Orange), used extensively for rural HEDGES; *Cupressus macrocarpa* (Monterey Cypress), planted as rural WINDBREAKS; *Pinus radiata* (Monterey Pine), grown in huge monocultural FORESTRY plantations; and *Magnolia grandiflora* (Bull Bay), *Acer negundo* (Box Elder), *Liquidambar styraciflua* (Sweet Gum), *Quercus palustris* (Pin Oak), *Taxodium mucronatum* (Montezuma Cypress), and *Agave americana* (Century Plant), all of which were cultivated as ornamentals. Plant exchange was a two-way trade, and EUCALYPTS in particular, became popular in the USA. In 1860 Stephen Nolan, a Californian nursery proprietor, introduced *Eucalyptus viminalis* (Manna Gum), which was grown extensively around Santa Barbara, while *E. globulus* (Blue Gum), was widely planted in California in the late 1880s.

Another important influence came from the writings of Andrew Jackson DOWNING. In 1841 Jackson published *A Treatise on the Theory and Practice of Landscape Gardening Adapted to North America*, and, during 1846–52, edited a monthly magazine, the *Horticulturist*—both these publications were available and widely read in Australia, where Downing's precepts for improving estates in a tasteful manner were quite applicable.

Frederick Law OLMSTED and Calvert Vaux romanticised the North American wilderness in their designs for large urban PUBLIC PARKS, particularly Central Park, New York (1858), and Prospect Park, Brooklyn (1865). The same romantic influence and design principles are evident in Sydney's CENTENNIAL PARK (1888) in features such as exposed rock outcrops, wild lakeshore edges, and the Grand Drive with its horizontally separated pedestrian, equestrian, and vehicular

The intrepid flower-painting expeditions of Marianne NORTH inspired protégées such as Australia's Ellis ROWAN, caught here without a paddle in Queensland's tropical north during a trip in the early 1890s: a predicament she entitled 'Suspense!'

North America

Beach house at Aptos Beach, near Monterey, California (1948), illustrated by Thomas Church in his book *Gardens are for People* (1955) and then reproduced in AUSTRALIAN HOME BEAUTIFUL (1961) to accompany an article on PATIOS, demonstrates the nature of the influence of NORTH AMERICA on Australian design

routes. In addition to his urban parks, Olmsted was also involved in the establishment of North America's and the world's first state park at Yosemite, California (1864). This setting aside of a large tract of spectacular natural landscape for public enjoyment led to the American NATIONAL PARK movement, culminating in the establishment of Yellowstone as the world's first national park (1872). The NSW politician Sir John Robertson, impressed by the American national park ideal, campaigned for the establishment of Australia's first national park, ROYAL NATIONAL PARK, south of Sydney, which was designated in 1879, thus becoming the world's second park to adopt the title 'national park'.

Born in Canada, brothers George and William CHAFFEY had been successful citrus orchardists in California when invited to Australia by the Victorian politician Alfred Deakin in 1886. They designed and installed the first large-scale IRRIGATION systems in Australia, pumping water from the Murray River at Mildura (Vic.) and Renmark (SA). The Chaffey brothers formed a company that bought land, cleared it, and constructed irrigation channels. They then subdivided the land into four-hectare blocks, which they sold, and charged fees for the water used in irrigation. This successful venture was the beginning of large-scale Australian rural irrigation, which has brought prosperity to many rural communities in the short term, but has had disastrous long-term environmental consequences in the form of soil salination, degraded inland river systems, and the over-exploitation of WATER—the scarcest resource on the world's driest inhabited continent.

When Walter and Marion GRIFFIN came to Australia they brought with them many current American planning and design ideas. The Griffins incorporated CITY BEAUTIFUL ideals into the plan for CANBERRA and Riverside 'suburban village' principles into the 1930s subdivision at CASTLECRAG in Sydney. By this time MODERNISM in landscape design had become fashionable in the USA. Rejecting the traditional Beaux-Arts style, LANDSCAPE ARCHITECTS such as Thomas Church and Garrett Eckbo in California, and James Rose in

New York, experimented with free forms, abstract shapes, and new materials such as concrete, aluminium, nylon, and plastic. They saw the garden as both a work of art and as a functional outdoor living space—literally an extension of the house—and they wrote about their design philosophies and illustrated them with examples of their work in books and popular journals such as *Sunset Magazine*. Eckbo's *Landscape for Living* (1950), Church's *Gardens are for People* (1955), and Rose's *Creative Gardens* (1958) became seminal works in the literature of modern landscape design. During the 1960s and 1970s Australian landscape designers were influenced by these books, and many home owners who read *Sunset Magazine* began to demand more innovative ideas from designers and contractors. Today, the extensive use of concrete PATIOS, timber decks, railway sleeper retaining walls, brick paving, loose pebbles, glass screens, free-form pools, ground modelling, massed ground covers, and informal tree planting in Australian SUBURBAN GARDENS can be largely attributed to these American influences.

Both the profession and landscape architecture EDUCATION in Australia have been influenced by American practices and standards. To a large extent the AUSTRALIAN INSTITUTE OF LANDSCAPE ARCHITECTS has modelled its activities on those of the American Society of Landscape Architects, and teaching programs in Australian universities owe much to inputs from visiting American academics and to the fact that many Australians were themselves, educated in landscape schools in the USA. New philosophies expounded in Ian McHarg's *Design With Nature* (1969) and Anne Spirn's *The Granite Garden* (1984) have revolutionised the thinking of Australia's design professions.

> Liberty Hyde Bailey, *Cyclopaedia of American Horticulture* (New York, 1950 and later edns); U.P. Hendrick, *A History of Horticulture in America to 1860* (New York, 1900); Ann Leighton, *American Gardens of the Nineteenth Century* (Amherst, Mass., 1987); William H. Tishler, *American Landscape Architecture: Designers and Places* (Washington, D.C., 1989); Mac Griswold and Eleanor Weller, *The Golden Age of American Gardens: Proud Owners, Private Estates, 1890–1940* (New York, 1991); Peter Walker and Melanie Simo, *Invisible Gardens: The Search for Modernism in the American Landscape* (Cambridge, Mass., 1994); Edwinna von Baeyer, *A Selected Bibliography for Garden History in Canada* (Ottawa, 1987); *Sunset Magazine: A Centenary of Western Living 1898–1998* (Stanford, California, 1998); Charles A. Birnbaum and Robin Karson (eds), *Pioneers of American Landscape Design* (New York, 2000) **ALLAN CORREY**

NORTHERN TERRITORY gardens reflect in both form and planting the extremes of the natural environments in which they have been created, ranging from the TROPICAL Top End to the ARID desert centre. Historical remains of formal, ornamental gardens evidence late-colonial expansion (GOVERNMENT HOUSE), economically driven agricultural and horticultural endeavours by governments (DARWIN BOTANIC GARDENS), missionaries (MISSION GARDENS, ABORIGINAL GARDENERS), and the enduring threat of natural disasters, pests, and disease in the far north. European gardening and experimental agriculture in the NT was premised, as elsewhere in Australia, on the notion of ownership of land. However, since at least the 1970s, with the rise of the Aboriginal land rights movement and the creation of NATIONAL PARKS (including Kakadu and Uluru-Kata Tjuta), competing claims for exclusive ownership, native title, environmental protection, and rights of use and access, have highlighted the contentious nature of this premise in the context of garden history in the NT.

Subsistence gardens were first established on the northern coast at the (failed) British outposts of Fort Dundas, Melville Island (1824–29), Fort Wellington, Raffles Bay (1827–29), and Victoria Settlement, Port Essington (1838–49); remains of the last reportedly survived until at least the 1870s. Following the Territory's annexation to SA (1863), and GOYDER's 1868–69 survey of Darwin (originally Palmerston), new settlers found poor soil, an unreliable water supply, relentless heat, and insect pests a hindrance to establishing gardens for food production. William HAYES planted the first Government Garden on the foreshore of Francis Bay in 1869. Agricultural and horticultural experimentation was continued by Maurice and Nicholas HOLTZE, who established the site known today as Darwin Botanic Gardens. The discovery of gold in the early 1870s, and a general labour shortage in the nascent township and on the goldfields, led to CHINESE migration to the Territory. By 1888, the Chinese settlers outnumbered Europeans by four to one, and their traditional gardening skills and diligence produced the town's most successful MARKET GARDENS. The study of NATIVE PLANTS in the Top End, from the late nineteenth century until 1942, was championed by amateur botanist Flo BLEESER.

South Australia's misguided attempts to profitably exploit the Northern Territory's pastoral and agricultural potential ended in 1911, with the transfer of the Territory to Commonwealth Government control. The new administration inherited the unenviable task of developing a viable agricultural or pastoral economy for the north, and from this time until self-government (1978), an apparently endless stream of senior public servants—all answerable to Canberra—assumed, for the most part, temporary residence in the NT. In Darwin, despite poor soil, and restricted water supply (until the 1950s), many European residents planted gardens with palms and other exotic plants, thus re-creating the stereotypical image of a 'tropical outpost'. This trend was revived following Cyclone Tracy (1974), with denser planting, including shrubberies abutting residential walls to shield living space from direct sunlight, and minimal areas of lawn, giving rise to the modern 'urban jungle'. The Giese residence (formerly Audit House, 1938–39), now part of the MYILLY POINT HERITAGE PRECINCT, typifies this form. This precinct also features 'pioneer' or 'container' gardens, which prevailed in the post–Second World War period, when decorated containers, such as powdered milk tins (from supplies shipped to Darwin), were used for ornamental displays in undercrofts of elevated houses. The post-war rise in population also brought with it gardening trends then prevalent in typical Australian suburbs: formal lawns, concrete paths, and neatly trimmed shrubbery. Local gardening enthusiasts, including May FITZPATRICK and Nancy EDDY and, more recently, George BROWN were actively involved in the 'greening' of the

The tropical fruit and vegetable garden of Hugh CHRISTIE, head lighthouse keeper at Point Charles Lighthouse, cultivated in spite of the ravages of an extreme climate and a hostile environment for European plants, demonstrates an early phase of garden making in the NORTHERN TERRITORY

city and in encouraging practical gardening skills and botanical education through HORTICULTURAL SOCIETIES and community work.

Following the arrival of the railway (1929), Alice Springs developed as Central Australia's regional centre—for the pastoral and mining industries, for missionary societies located in the remote desert, and for the growing population. Today, the 1930s government housing precinct of Hartley Street retains many of its arid-zone garden forms. Following the Second World War, township growth led to extended urban planning, and new public and residential landscapes. Olive PINK dedicated her life to the creation of an arid-zone BOTANIC GARDEN, started in 1956. More recently, ALICE SPRINGS DESERT PARK has interpreted the region's landscapes, plants, and animals, and their traditional use and management by Aboriginal people.

David Carment, *Looking at Darwin's Past: Material Evidence of European Settlement in Tropical Australia* (Darwin, 1996); Alan Powell, *Far Country: A Short History of the Northern Territory* (Carlton, Vic., 1996); Graham Calley, *The Pumpkin Settlements: Agriculture and Animals in Australian's First Northern Colonies* (Darwin, 1998)

ANITA ANGEL and JAN SETO

NOTTLE, Trevor James (b. 1947), author, garden designer, and plant antiquarian, a resident of the ADELAIDE HILLS, is a leading advocate of MEDITERRANEAN gardening practices in Australia and in similar climates throughout the southern hemisphere, an international authority on old-fashioned ROSES, an expert on Australian COTTAGE GARDENING, as well as GARDEN HISTORY and its literature. His books include *Growing Old Fashioned Roses in Australia and New Zealand* (1982), *The Cottage Garden Revived* (1984), *Cottage Garden Flowers* (1988), *Roses for Every Garden* (1995), *Gardens of the Sun* (1996), and *The New Cottage Garden* (1997). Nottle received the Lester F. Harrell Award from the Trustees of the Huntington Library, California (1988), for internationally advancing knowledge about old-fashioned roses.

DAVID JONES

NOVELTIES, plants of recent introduction or HYBRIDISATION, were commonly offered by the Australian NURSERY TRADE from the 1870s, with an emphasis on boldness of form, habit, and colour. These were no shrinking violets, with 'Giant Wonders', 'Ne plus ultras', and 'Acmes of Perfection' abounding, not only in FLORICULTURE, but increasingly in the VEGETABLE seed trade. Many catalogues devoted special sections to novelty specimens, often printed on coloured paper, and advertising premium prices. Novelties have become a staple of the nursery industry, relying on a once-off annual impact to optimise profit. Their introduction was commonly associated with new or popular trends, such as the CHRYSANTHEMUM boom of the 1890s or the arcane world of the mid-twentieth-century ORCHID fancier. The vogue for novelties among suburban gardeners formed an egalitarian microcosm of the fashion for new and rare plants introduced into European STOVES in the wake of the colonisation and botanical exploration that occurred in the late eighteenth and early nineteenth centuries. Curiosity and one-upmanship were both satisfied. RA

NURNEY HOUSE, North Adelaide: see BAGOT, John

NURSERIES The plant nursery is an essential part of HORTICULTURE as the place where PLANTS are propagated and grown to the size required for their ultimate landscape destination. Nurseries were established from the earliest days of European settlement of Australia to receive plants, seeds, and cuttings imported on board ships principally from Britain, South America, and South Africa. The first horticultural plants imported were mostly fruiting species, but ornamental plants were added to nursery repertoires early. Today, surviving nursery catalogues are a major resource for GARDEN HISTORIANS and those in the HERITAGE industry.

Australian nurseries have influenced the development of landscape STYLES since they have been largely responsible for plant importation and evaluation. Much of the horticultural plant selection and BREEDING in Australia has also been done by nurseries, and this continues. The early nursery trade also influenced LANDSCAPE GARDENING with those such as Thomas ALLEN (SA), GUILFOYLE and SEARL (NSW), and TAYLOR AND SANGSTER (Vic.) offering design and construction services. While this service continues to be offered by some retail nursery businesses, specialist garden designers and LANDSCAPE ARCHITECTS now undertake most of this work. STATE FOREST NURSERIES have also been instrumental as a source of plants, especially AUSTRALIAN PLANTS, for rural gardens.

The vast majority of plants grown in nurseries were, until the twentieth century, grown in soil beds, in the open. When the plant reached its ultimate size it was dug up for shipment—a system known as field production. Plants grown in field beds can be dug for shipment in a number of different forms. In bare-root production BULBS are lifted when dormant; herbaceous plants are also generally lifted when dormant, with the soil adhering to the roots removed before transport. Bare-root transplanting is also used for woody plants, roses, and deciduous fruit trees, usually in smaller sizes. The other method of field production has the tree dug with a ball of soil retained around the roots, normally secured with a fabric wrap, often hessian. The American terminology 'balled and burlapped' (B&B) is often applied by Australian nurseries, and this mode of production tends to be used primarily for larger-sized trees and shrubs. A recent variant of this system is the Root Control Bag® where the tree is grown in a synthetic fabric bag in the ground and harvested with the bag.

A limitation of field production systems is the root system disruption that accompanies the harvest or transplant process. Roots are inevitably lost when the plant is dug and the older and larger the plant at the time of harvest, the greater the extent of this root loss. The term 'transplant-sensitive' refers to the capacity of a plant to survive field production and transplanting. Not all plants can tolerate the root loss of field harvesting, as is reflected in the relatively restricted range of tree species offered by field nursery growers.

One of the major technological changes in nursery production occurred during the twentieth century. This is the very significant adoption of container production by the nursery industry. In container production, the plant spends its life in the nursery in an above-ground container from which it is transplanted to a landscape destination. Because of the greatly reduced damage to root systems, transplant-sensitive species are especially suited to container production, thus greatly increasing the range of plants that may be offered by the nursery industry. In addition, the container allows easy transport and year-round planting, which has also changed the face of the industry. The retail garden centre is as much about the flexibility offered by container production as it is about the changes in society and consumption patterns of the later twentieth century. Another very important attribute of the container system is that it frees the nursery from the need to be located in an area of high-quality soils.

The adoption of container production has also brought challenges to the industry. The container itself has evolved considerably. The wood veneer tube or recycled jam or kerosene tin has become a plastic pot, often engineered to control and modify root development. The growing medium has developed from mixtures of SOIL and various additives, often formulated from forestry waste such as bark and wood chips. The nursery industry also had to change to high-technology FERTILISERS such as coated slow-release materials to overcome problems with fertiliser damage. There seems little doubt that container production is the future of the industry.

Apart from technological changes of the type outlined above, other changes have occurred to the way nurseries do business. Early Australian nurseries were almost always generalist in nature. There were relatively few nurseries and they were geographically widespread, necessitating a wide range of plant types to be offered. In many cases, the nursery not only propagated and grew-on the plants, but marketed them as well, either at the nursery gate or by mail. With time, nurseries have tended to specialise, either in the type of plants grown or in the segment of the market they occupy. This allows better exploitation of specialist skills or technology or of the attributes of the location. Increasingly, the grower is separated from the ultimate consumer with the grower selling to the retail garden centre. This is a world-wide trend, and for most plant buyers, the garden centre is now the source of most of their plant purchases. This change has had its own impact on the types of plants being grown in the nursery industry as an important selection criterion for the grower may not be ultimate landscape function but rather how the plant will look in the standard retail container size. Buyers looking for plants outside the range on offer in garden centres may have to find other avenues such as specialist mail-order nurseries or plant brokers. The importance of the retail garden centres as the ultimate outlet for most growers has seen other flow-ons from the marketing industry. These range from promotional labels and trade-marked plant names to intensive advertising campaigns for new plant products. Garden centres also form a permanent extension of the horticultural SHOW, often hosting speakers on garden design and horticultural techniques.

Rosemary Polya, *Nineteenth Century Plant Nursery Catalogues of South-East Australia: A Bibliography* (Bundoora, Vic., 1981); Robert F.G. Swinbourne, *Years of Endeavour: An Historical Record of the Nurseries, Nurserymen, Seedsmen, and Horticultural Retail Outlets of South Australia* (Adelaide, 1982); Margaret Brookes and Richard Barley, *Plants Listed in Nursery Catalogues in Victoria 1855–1889* (South Yarra, Vic., 1992); Noelle Weatherley and David Gordon, *Generations of Growth: A History of the Nursery Industry Association of Victoria* (East Malvern, Vic., 1999)

PETER MAY

OAKMAN, Henry Octave (Harry) (1906–2002), landscape architect, followed agricultural training in Sydney with work at a Pennant Hills flower nursery. This led to gardening work with Kur-ing-gai Municipal Council, laying the foundations for a career in local government service. While there, he attended the Sydney Technical College at night and obtained diplomas in agriculture and horticulture. In 1939 he moved to Newcastle City Council as second in charge of parks, then managed the parks department of Brisbane City Council (1946–63). He gained membership of the British Institute of Landscape Architects in 1947, making him the first LANDSCAPE ARCHITECT in government service in Qld.

Post-war Brisbane grew rapidly, and Oakman's distinctive TROPICAL design treatments in designing, building, and maintaining ornamental PUBLIC PARKS, SPORTS fields, CEMETERIES, and STREET TREES made an enduring contribution to the city's character. His objective was 'to make every major road throughout Brisbane colourful, bright and tropical'. Most of the city's older parkland received the Oakman treatment (including NEWSTEAD, NEW FARM, WICKHAM, and BOWEN PARKS, and BRISBANE BOTANIC GARDENS) as well as Queens Gardens (Brisbane) and TOWNSVILLE QUEENS PARK. Typically, this involved bright colours (foliage and flowers), massed plantings of shrubs or small trees (acalypha, hibiscus, frangipani, bauhinia), curvilinear beds and paths, and sometimes rockeries of boulders. Often a formal hedge (such as burgundy-coloured *Acalypha compacta*) was used as a backdrop to annuals. He gathered a talented support staff, including Arne Fink, Harry CAULFIELD, and George TRAPNELL, with Anne Voller, his able drafting assistant.

Oakman became Director of Landscape with the National Capital Development Commission (NCDC) in 1963. In Canberra his taste for colour was reflected in cool-temperate trees and his interest in ornamenting open spaces by his development of the lookouts at Red Hill and Black Mountain. He oversaw the change from landscape design by the NCDC and construction by the Department of the Interior to the employment of private consultants and contractors. He retired in 1972 and returned to Brisbane where he tended his own large garden at Moggill, on the Brisbane River.

Oakman's professional contributions were reflected by fellowships of the AUSTRALIAN INSTITUTE OF LANDSCAPE ARCHITECTS, Institute of Landscape Architects, and ROYAL AUSTRALIAN INSTITUTE OF PARKS AND RECREATION. Oakman was a prolific writer and photographer, widely known for his *Gardening in Queensland* (1958), revised as *Tropical and Subtropical Gardening* (1975); *Some Trees of Australia* (1962); *Colourful Trees for Landscapes and Gardens* (1967); *Garden and Landscape Trees in Australia* (1979); and *Shrubs for Tropical and Subtropical Gardens* (1990).

JAN SETO and JEANNIE SIM

OBELISKS appear in modest numbers in PUBLIC PARKS throughout Australia. Sydney, however, has had nine significant obelisks in its metropolitan area. Among them is the obelisk designed in 1818 by important convict architect Francis Greenway—the focal point of MACQUARIE PLACE near Circular Quay. A majestic HYDE PARK obelisk (1857) terminates the VISTA of Bathurst Street, while botanist Allan CUNNINGHAM is commemorated by an obelisk (1844) in Sydney's ROYAL BOTANIC GARDENS. There are more obelisks in Sydney than in their parent Egypt.

MICHAEL BOGLE

OBSERVATORY HILL, rising forty metres above the western side of Sydney Cove, supported Australia's first windmill (1796) but its strategic value soon saw construction of Fort

The public monument to commemorate Allan CUNNINGHAM, erected in 1844 in SYDNEY BOTANIC GARDENS, took the form of an OBELISK; in 1901, through the efforts of his successor Joseph Maiden, his remains were re-interred here

The PUBLIC PARK on Sydney's OBSERVATORY HILL still provides some sense of its original purpose, even if its panoramas and vistas have been profoundly altered since early European settlement

Phillip (1804–06). The hill formed part of a large military precinct stretching south to present-day Wynyard Park (dedicated 1887) and in 1825 a signal station was established on the eastern parapet of the fort. Phillip Parker King identified this in the early 1850s as the ideal site for a time ball, 'visible from all parts of the harbour and the city' and thus Sydney Observatory was developed here. In the 1870s the area was laid out as a PUBLIC PARK, initially Flagstaff Reserve but later Observatory Park (1887), its open lawns studded with *Ficus macrophylla* (Moreton Bay Fig). While Sydney's towering skyline has robbed the hill of its vertical prominence, it still provides splendid views of the inner harbour, north shore, Parramatta River estuary, and BLUE MOUNTAINS. In the 1930s, eastern views to the heads were destroyed by the construction of Sydney Harbour Bridge, although the bridge is now a spectacular landmark from the park. IAN STEPHENSON

OCEANIA: see PACIFIC ISLANDS

OLDHAM, John Bramston Russell (1907–1999), landscape architect, architect, planner, and conservationist, pioneered the profession of LANDSCAPE ARCHITECTURE in WA and was an influential figure in the field of landscape design, EDUCATION, and CONSERVATION in the state from shortly after the Second World War. John and his wife, Ruby Gertrude (Ray) Oldham (*née* McClintock) (b. 1911), historian and landscape architect, both born in WA, enjoyed a long collaboration promoting landscape architecture, campaigning for HERITAGE conservation, and writing. Together they wrote *Gardens in Time* (1980), a revisionary account of the world history of landscape design, and two books on Western Australia's architectural heritage: *Western Heritage* (1961) and *George Temple-Poole* (1980).

John Oldham trained as an architect during the 1920s, working for a period with Rodney ALSOP on the Hackett Memorial buildings at the University of Western Australia. During the volatile years of the 1930s, he established a graphic design business, and worked in architectural practices in Perth and Sydney. In the late 1930s he was in the Sydney office of architects Stephenson and Turner, where he designed the Australian pavilion and exhibition for the 1939 New York World Fair. He worked in the Ministry of Post-War Reconstruction during the 1940s, where he continued his success with exhibition design, followed by employment with the Snowy Mountains Hydro-Electric Authority, in charge of the architectural office at Cooma (NSW). It was there he became involved with the broader issues of environmental design, and on return to Perth in 1954 he embarked on a career as landscape architect, working in private practice and in the public service. Designs for the State Housing Commission flats in Subiaco and West Perth consolidated his status as a landscape architect. Appointment to the Public Works Department led to ground-breaking collaborative work with water supply engineers on a number of dams for the country and metropolitan water supply, and for the Ord River Irrigation Scheme in the Kimberley region. As senior landscape architect, he was also responsible for landscape projects for a wide range of public buildings, including schools, courthouses, hospitals, and extensions to Parliament House. His innovative landscape concept of urban parklands associated with the NARROWS INTERCHANGE and Mitchell Freeway in Perth, and his scheme for an integrated system of foreshore parklands surrounding Perth Water, are well known.

The Oldhams were founding members of the Tree Society of Western Australian (1956) and NATIONAL TRUST OF AUSTRALIA (Western Australia). John was foundation president of the Conservation Council of Western Australia (1967). His awards include an International Federation of Landscape Architects Citation (1982) and AUSTRALIAN INSTITUTE OF LANDSCAPE ARCHITECTS Award in Landscape Architecture (1984). OLINE RICHARDS

OLIVE PINK BOTANIC GARDEN, Alice Springs, NT: see PINK, Olive Muriel

OLIVER, John (1861–1942), garden curator, was born in Ballarat and served his apprenticeship at BALLARAT BOTANIC GARDENS (1875–80). He gained further experience at the BRUNNING nursery (c. 1883), and was later head gardener on the Devon Park Estate, Dunkeld (Vic.). He returned to Melbourne as a landscape gardener, and came under the notice of the McCracken family, whose garden he laid out. In 1890 he was appointed inaugural curator of QUEEN'S PARK, Moonee Ponds (Vic.); highly esteemed by fellow horticulturists, he gave five decades of devoted service to the Essendon City Council. Oliver's work included several local parks, beautification of Saltwater River and Mount Alexander Road, and local school grounds. He typified an influential generation of curators in the municipal sphere—alongside J.T. SMITH of Melbourne, Thomas POCKETT of Malvern (Vic.), and Joe MARTIN of Subiaco (WA)—whose voice was heard at HORTICULTURAL SOCIETIES, on the RADIO, through GARDEN MAGAZINES, and in the pages of the daily press. RA

OLMSTED, Frederick Law (1822–1903), is recognised as the founder of the LANDSCAPE ARCHITECTURE profession in NORTH AMERICA. Following a visit to England (1850) where he was greatly impressed by PAXTON's Birkenhead Park, he won (with DOWNING's former partner Calvert Vaux) the design competition for Central Park, New York City (1858). Olmsted relocated his extensive practice—which specialised in PUBLIC PARKS—to Brookline, Mass. (1883), where he successfully proposed the unified scheme for Boston's Back Bay and Fens, known as the 'Emerald Necklace'. Olmsted's influence on Australian parks can be seen in Sydney's CENTENNIAL PARK, where the separation of pedestrian and vehicular traffic is reminiscent of Central Park, and some open spaces reflect his 'Long Meadow' at Prospect Park, Brooklyn (commenced 1865–88). Olmsted's ideas were shared and disseminated by colleagues such as Charles Sprague Sargent, editor of *Garden and Forest*—an American journal that influenced J.H. MAIDEN in formulating his approach to park planning and design. Reverence for Olmsted's considerable achievements continues to grow among landscape architects, aided by several biographies and published volumes of his writings, and scholarship centred on the Olmsted archive at Brookline.

The Papers of Frederick Law Olmsted (Baltimore, 1977–97)
COLLEEN MORRIS

ORANGERY, in European gardens, was the term describing a building (see GREENHOUSE), dedicated to the reception of tubbed orange trees (or similar plants) to protect them from freezing temperatures during winter. In Australia, especially in the nineteenth century, the term was commonly used to describe an ORCHARD or smaller planting of orange or other citrus trees. RA

ORCHARDS comprise ordered arrangements of FRUIT trees, derived from the enclosures suggested by the Old English derivation *ortgeard* of the Latin *hortus* (garden) and 'yard'. Australia's varied CLIMATE allows for a great variety of fruits to be grown across the continent, including a vast range of tropical fruits. Fruit trees were likely carried by the First Fleet; they were certainly introduced to Van Diemen's Land at Adventure Bay on South Bruny Island by Bligh in 1788 and his records show that plants left there on Cook's earlier voyage had survived.

All early settlements included fruit orchards. Fruit trees were grown in the penal colonies; original trees or seedlings still grow in places such as the Richmond Gaol and PORT ARTHUR (Tas.). Early orchards had many failures because Australian soils and conditions were different from those in Europe. At times, up to seventy per cent of fruit crops was lost to diseases, frost, or drought. Fruits first introduced to Australia were popular varieties of the time, some of which are now considered 'heritage varieties' (such as Cox's Orange Pippin, Adams' Pearmain, and Sturmer Pippin apples). A typical one-acre (0.4 ha) home orchard may have contained as many as 100 fruit trees, and the remoteness of many areas of Australia meant that orchards were necessary for fresh fruit. By the 1890s, with population growth and urbanisation, many home owners with VILLA and MANSION houses on large blocks of land developed orchards, and even the gardens of small COTTAGES often included several fruit trees. Urban subdivision pressures have now all but eliminated orchards from the SUBURBAN GARDEN, although many older orchards survive in outlying areas. However, fruit-tree growing on a smaller scale continues to be important in Australian gardens. Many home gardeners are using ORGANIC and PERMACULTURE growing techniques and practise minimal watering, pruning, and cultivation management systems. Fruit trees are now often grafted to have multiple fruit types on the one tree and for pollination requirements. Trees such as apples are also ESPALIERED, thus providing ornamentation as well as fruit for small garden spaces.

Home orchards and fruit growing received considerable attention from early horticultural writers, and most early Australian GARDEN BOOKS gave the subject equal or greater weighting than ornamental gardening. By the mid-nineteenth century plant nurseries were able to supply the demand for fruit trees and other plants. LANG and NOBELIUS (Vic.), KEMP (SA), and SHEPHERD (NSW) all specialised in this branch of the business. In 1913 C.A. NOBELIUS and Sons at their Gembrook Nursery listed and described seventy-seven apple varieties. Many plant nurseries specialised in not only fruit trees but also advice on growing. The *YATES' Garden Guide* and BRUNNING's *Australian Gardener* became icons to many generations of fruit and vegetable gardeners. Books and magazine articles on fruit production in the home garden abound while TELEVISION and RADIO broadcasts service a growing home garden interest.

Commercial production of fruit began in Van Diemen's Land (Tas.) shortly after European settlement, and fruit trees were sent to other settlements in the Port Phillip District (Vic.) and to NSW. Fifty years after the settlement of Sydney an orchard industry including some citrus groves had also developed there. By 1911 a fledgling fruit export industry was

Orchards

Ancient walnut trees, remnants of the ORCHARD at Cambria, the Tasmanian property of Charles and Louisa MEREDITH, convey the beauty of fruit trees as an element of the designed landscape

developing, with Tas. shipping half the total Australian exports. Cooler areas of Vic., SA, WA, and NSW also grew large areas of stone fruits, while warmer northern areas—and irrigated inland areas—produced citrus and tropical fruits. About 270 000 citrus trees were grown in Australia in 1910. By 1995 there were approximately eight million trees producing more than 500 000 tonnes of fruit. Initially, fruit growers were protected by tariffs, but now growers compete in an open market with fears of competition offered by imports, especially citrus. Australian fruits have been relatively disease free, aided by strict quarantine regulations in an island continent. Although early settlers suffered heavy losses to PESTS, such as codlin moth, these have been controlled by improved pesticides. The fire blight scare in the apple industry (1997) and ongoing debate about quarantine measures have demonstrated both the significance of the fruit export industry to Australia and the rigours of international competition.

With mechanisation came more efficient packing, canning, and processing factories. Improved transport, shipping, and communication meant that products could be moved quickly and orchards became easier to manage. Refrigeration made possible long-term cool storage of fruit while the radio made weather forecasting accessible to growers. Chemical FERTILISERS produced healthier plants, and new CHEMICAL control agents prevented pest and disease outbreaks. All these contributed to increased fruit production, ease of management, and readier availability of fruit trees and materials for orcharding. Concerns about pollution have, however, led to deregistration of many harmful pesticides, weedicides, and other chemicals used in orchards. Integrated pest management and research into the use of biological control agents continues. Expanding exports and demand for quality have led to vast improvements in the quality of fruit packaged for export—particularly during the 1980s and 1990s—and led to quality assurance standards.

Government agencies and some private companies developed around the orchard industry, producing manuals on fruit culture, and providing advisory services. Each state agriculture department, together with the CSIRO, was responsible for the introduction of fruit varieties and technology. Introduced fruits, and results from research were available to commercial producers as well as to horticulturists and home gardeners. Most states established garden advisory services in the 1970s and 1980s, but most have since been closed due to funding cutbacks and restructuring. More recently, research has been oriented towards areas where private funding could be obtained, although funding bodies such as Rural Industries Research and Development Corporation evolved.

Fruit trees now available have come from BREEDING programs, and from selection. The commercially popular Granny Smith apple, for example, started as a chance seedling in a garden in Ryde (NSW). During the 1960s, virus-free budwood and scion material was developed, and the 'stud bud' system developed, growing virus-free fruit trees to supply buds to the fruit industry. In 1987 Australia introduced Plant Variety Rights, which enabled the importation of many fruit CULTIVARS from other countries, and its recent acceptance of Plant Breeder's Rights means that breeders can register cultivars world-wide and receive royalties for sale of intellectual property rights (or damages for their breach). Genetic engineering of fruit trees has allowed the breeding-in of resistance to pests and diseases, and can enable self-pollination, although debate over genetic modification continues world-wide.

Paul Baxter, *Growing Fruit in Australia* (Melbourne, 1981); L. Glowinski, *The Complete Book of Fruit Growing in Australia* (South Melbourne, 1991)   ALLEN GILBERT

ORCHIDS With more than 25 000 species world-wide, the orchid family is one of the largest and most highly evolved groups of flowering plants. Australia is estimated to have about 700 different species, sixty per cent growing in soil (terrestrial) and forty per cent growing on trees or rocks (epiphytes). Soon after the European discovery of Australia, botanists started collecting and classifying local species. The most important early finds were made by Robert BROWN but the later investigations of Ferdinand MUELLER, R.D. FITZGERALD, and Rev. H.M.R. RUPP were also noteworthy.

Early collections were exclusively composed of species plants, but by the end of the nineteenth century hybrid crosses increasingly began to appear. Most of these early hybrids were imported from England, and displayed as INDOOR PLANTS in CONSERVATORIES, tended by highly trained gardeners. Despite increased local knowledge in PLANT BREEDING and PROPAGATION, mass imports from England and the Indian subcontinent continued until the introduction of rigid quarantine restrictions in the 1950s. The 1930s saw a boom in the popularity of orchid growing. Increased knowledge about cultural requirements allowed more and more people the chance to grow orchids suitable for their climate. The orchid-fancier no longer had to be sufficiently wealthy to maintain a collection in heated STOVE-houses. At last, poorer Australians began to grow orchids in their own temples to Australian flora, the cheaply built BUSH-HOUSE. The Victorian Orchid Society was formed in the early 1920s and in 1933 orchid societies were established in Qld and NSW. The *Australian Orchid Review* (1936–) became an important vehicle for advice and opinion, and establishment of orchid societies continued nationwide during the following few years. This surge in interest was mainly due to the southern states' love affair with the easily grown Cymbidium orchid. Growers such as John BISSET organised several large orchid shows in the 1930s, which led to great public demand for Cymbidiums and other orchids, and the development of specialist nurseries around the country. The 1950s and 1960s were boom times for Australian orchid growing, with clubs and shows proliferating. The popularity of orchid growing in Australia arguably reached its peak with the hosting of the 6th World Orchid Conference in Sydney in 1969.

Interest in growing native orchids increased in the early 1960s, which led to formation of the Australian Native Orchid Society (1963). This interest has led to a regrettable increase in theft of wild plants by unscrupulous collectors, which, combined with destruction of habitats, has seen a decline in Australian orchid numbers. The Australian Orchid Foundation was set up in the late 1960s for study and conservation of this delicate component of the AUSTRALIAN FLORA.
SILAS CLIFFORD-SMITH

ORGANIC GARDENING utilises techniques that avoid inorganic GARDEN CHEMICALS, especially the pesticides and herbicides that increased in use during the nineteenth century. Concern about the effect of chemical residues in food and the environment increased after the Second World War, especially with widespread use of chemicals such as DDT. The year 1945 saw the founding of the Australian Organic Farming and Gardening Society, publisher of the journal *Good Earth*. Influential overseas writers included English Sir Albert Howard (1873–1947) in the early twentieth century, Americans J.I. Rodale, Leonard Wickenden, and Aldo Leopold during the 1940 and 1950s, and notably Rachel Carson's condemnation of chemical pesticides, *Silent Spring* (1962), which inspired a group of women headed by Dr Corona Adams to establish a branch of the (British) Henry Doubleday Research Association in NSW (1970). This organisation emphasises sustainable agriculture, waste management, and saving seeds of older vegetable varieties. The self-sufficiency journals *EARTH GARDEN* and *GRASS ROOTS* also began publication in the 1970s.

Events such as the 1987 rejection of a consignment of Australian meat due to unacceptable levels of chemical residues, together with appreciation of the increasing economic value of organically produced food, led to the establishment of the National Association of Sustainable Agriculture Australia, which first certified organic growers. The National Standard for Organic and Biodynamic Produce is set by the Organic Producers Advisory Committee, and more than thirty organic growers and gardeners' societies were listed in 1999. In recent years organic gardeners have been aided by the introduction of biological controls for plant diseases, PESTS and WEEDS.
JILL KELLOW

ORIENTAL INFLUENCES on Australian gardens have come largely through the importation of plants from ASIA,

Ornament

but also through more diffuse design influences indirectly from England. The Orient, derived from the Latin *oriens–entis* (rising, sunrise, east), encompasses the countries east of the MEDITERRANEAN, particularly East Asia. Its cultural construction and pervasive influence between the 1750s and the 1830s is analysed in Patrick Connor's *Oriental Architecture in the West* (1979). Early in the eighteenth century, Chinese ideas on natural philosophy and garden making created a revolution in garden design. In England in 1712 essayist Joseph Addison wrote in the *Spectator*: 'The Chinese laugh at the plantations of our Europeans, which are laid out by the rule and line, because they say anyone can place trees in equal rows and uniform figures. They choose rather to discover the genius in trees and in nature and therefore always conceal their art.' English garden designers William Kent and 'Capability' BROWN responded to this new oriental design philosophy, and launched the English School of LANDSCAPE GARDENING.

This new informality formed an underpinning—usually unstated or unacknowledged—of many early Australian gardens, although by the time this influence reached Australian shores, the English model rather than the oriental influence was paramount. More direct was the incorporation of oriental architectural references in GARDEN BUILDINGS: although much of this permeated via England, there was also direct contact between Australia and INDIA, CHINA, JAPAN, and other Asian countries through trade, travel, and EXHIBITIONS.

In the second half of the twentieth century LANDSCAPE ARCHITECTURE developed in Australia. This new profession built on the great landscape design tradition that was inherited from England but had blossomed in the Americas. The oriental garden once more inspired garden design, especially through a study of the historic landscape gardens of Japan. The philosophical integrity, restrained elegance, and microcosmic qualities of these gardens provided a strong influence, especially on domestic garden design and related fields such as FLOWER ARRANGING, INDOOR GARDENS, and architecture. In more recent years, oriental influence has been felt in TROPICAL gardens, especially through a lush RESORT landscaping style.

JOHN OLDHAM

ORNAMENT The earliest surviving garden ornament in Australia dates from the period of social change and economic prosperity of the 1830s. Although important earlier garden-makers, such as Elizabeth Macquarie, wife of the Governor, Captain John Piper of Henrietta Villa, and Sir John JAMISON of Regentville, constructed significant gardens in the first quarter of the nineteenth century, their ornamentation appears to have been restricted to relatively ephemeral GARDEN BUILDINGS and structures: SUMMER-HOUSES, AVIARIES, and arches of TRELLIS-WORK. From the 1830s, ornamentation of gardens, not only with architectural features and garden FURNITURE, but with POTS and urns, SUNDIALS, STATUES, ROCKWORK, and FOUNTAINS, proliferated. Brownlow Hill (NSW), the MCLEAY country house, has the finest range of garden furniture surviving from the period in Australia: English composition-stone and colonial-made stone urns, a sundial (*c*. 1836), a brick aviary, and massive rockwork.

Architectural ornament in Australian gardens has ranged from summer-houses and ARBOURS to arches, PERGOLAS, and even BARBECUES, although few gardeners, even rich ones in the late nineteenth century, were as ambitious as Sir James Martin in building at his house, Clarens, Potts Point (NSW), ITALIANATE balustraded terraces and a sandstone replica of the Choragic Monument of Lysicrates (now relocated to the ROYAL BOTANIC GARDENS, SYDNEY).

Arbours—built functionally for fruiting vines, or decoratively designed—have been a constant feature of Australia's gardens, particularly in the country. Contemporary tastes invariably influenced the design of the more decorative sort: trellis-work in the early nineteenth century, rustic woodwork and woven wire in the late nineteenth and early twentieth centuries, trellis-work again in Edwardian gardens, while pergolas in the 1920s and 1930s were often built of cast-concrete columns, rustic masonry, improvised columns of drainage pipes, or with frames of galvanised water-pipe. Welded pipe often replaced rotting wooden supports in the 1950s and 1960s. Summer-houses have usually been associated with larger or more pretentious gardens, but the major late twentieth-century contribution to garden features was the brick, stone, or concrete block barbecue: the backyard household-altar of Australian suburbia.

The earliest reference to plant containers in Australia is possibly for the sale of *Araucaria heterophylla* (Norfolk Island Pine) trees in barrels on Sydney wharves in the early 1800s, and half-barrels continue to be available from nurseries. They are one of the few garden ornaments without immediate connotations of class, place and time. It can be assumed that smaller earthenware pots were thrown by early potters in Sydney, but there is no surviving evidence of more elaborate containers being made earlier than the 1830s. The English composition-stone urns along the balustrade of the lily pond and the carved sandstone urn and pedestal in the flower garden at Brownlow Hill are possibly the earliest surviving Australian examples. Chinese ceramic pots also appear to have been imported, but no provenanced examples are known.

By the late nineteenth century, urns, either of vase or tazza form, were common in substantial gardens, most usually of cast cement (finished in imitation of stone or marble) or cast iron (finished in imitation of stone or bronze), but also of terracotta, elaborately moulded by local potteries. Marble was restricted to the most pretentious private and public gardens, and to funerary monuments. It was usual for urns to be raised on a balustrade or on pedestals, and their decline in popularity in the early twentieth century reflects changes in taste and the decline of the classical style in domestic architecture. Early twentieth-century plant containers, either in earthenware or cast in concrete, however, were often based on traditional Italian terracotta pots, decorated with masks and swags, or more restrainedly, with concentric bands.

The popularity of improvised containers continued through the twentieth century in suburban and country gardens and on railway stations. In the country, half-barrels were frequently replaced by cut-down galvanised-iron milk cans or half forty-four gallon drums; the popularity of tyre

Ornament

ORNAMENT, seen here in the form of balustrading and urns at Flemington House (Vic.) of the 1850s, often provides a note of FORMALITY and permanence in gardens, in contrast with the seasonal effects and varying growth habits of plants

urns, often of an elegant tulip-form, was widespread, although the use of hollow logs appears to have declined rapidly after the Second World War. Particularly between the wars, home-made planters and pots of concrete—often remotely Art Deco in design or cast and coloured in imitation of logs—were popular. A late twentieth-century innovation was the adaptation for pots of the spun metal or enamelled bowls from defunct washing machines.

Other ornaments varied in popularity at different times, but also extended over similar ranges of styles and materials. SUNDIALS, on baluster or column bases, of either natural or imported artificial stone, were popular among the richest colonists in the 1830s, particularly after Richard Clint began engraving and advertising brass dials. FOUNTAINS began to appear in large, fashionable gardens: Sydney's GOVERNMENT HOUSE and VAUCLUSE HOUSE, for example, boasted similar artificial stone tazza-form fountains by the 1860s. Basketwork edging to flower beds appeared in the early 1800s, together with rustic-work furniture. Concrete-modelled ornament was widely appreciated in the early twentieth century, usually in imitation of RUSTIC-WORK, but occasionally architectural. The newly opened Sydney Harbour Bridge (1932) inspired many planter-boxes, garden arches, and garden bridges. Bird baths, also in stone or cast concrete, increased in popularity with the twentieth century although in the later part of the century the principal ornament in the front garden of a suburban house was often a LETTERBOX, particularly distinctive forms being a metal box supported on a spiralling, welded chain, and pedestal boxes built of sandwiched layers of rusticated, highly figured sandstone slabs.

STATUES appear to have arrived in colonial gardens in the 1830s, although none appears to have survived from before the 1850s. Cast-iron or artificial stone, imported sculpted marble, or colonial sculpted stone figures were used in grander town and country gardens. The expected roll-call of classical Venuses, Mercurys, Wrestlers, and Floras that decorated grander late-Victorian public and private gardens had dwindled by the early twentieth century. With the taste for Japonaiserie, imported bronze cranes fashionably waded through late nineteenth-century and Edwardian ponds, and evolved into home-made concrete or were transformed into pink-painted flamingos in the mid-twentieth century. They were joined by a party of indigenous species: kangaroos, kookaburras and turtles. Frogs—in particular cast in concrete with eyes of glass marbles—were ubiquitously affordable, or easily home-cast, for perching on the sides of ponds or bird baths. These picturesque symbols of Australian suburbia's spurious sympathy with the bush were complemented by diminutive, spear-carrying Aborigines, cast in concrete, and black-painted.

The more eclectic garden decorators have continued, in a spirit of multiculturalism, to diversify the ethnic mix by populating their gardens with brightly coloured concrete GNOMES of mid-European extraction, engaging in their traditional occupations of fishing or wood-chopping, or, evidencing their assimilation both into the Australian garden and the late twentieth century, by pushing mini-Victas across smooth lawns. The most original ornament to have evolved for the twentieth-century Australian garden, however, was the TYRE SWAN. The diverse tastes in garden ornament in

Australia at the turn of the twenty-first century are exemplified by the choice for the terrace of an inner-city apartment of either a black or white-painted tyre swan, preferably with a provenance to a railway station, or a blue-painted ersatz *caisse de Versailles* from a garden boutique.

    Peter Hunt (ed.), *The Book of Garden Ornament* (London, 1974); George Plumptre, *Garden Ornament: Five Hundred Years of History and Practice* (London, 1989); John Davis, *Antique Garden Ornament: 300 Years of Creativity: Artists, Manufacturers, and Materials* (Woodbridge, Suffork, 1991)   JAMES BROADBENT

ORNAMENTAL PLANT CONSERVATION ASSOCIATION OF AUSTRALIA INC. (1988–), known prior to 2000 as the Ornamental Plant Collections Association, aims to 'maintain and increase the diversity of the garden plants by registering reference collections of related plant groups, where worthwhile ornamental plants can be documented, investigated and propagated'. Impetus for maintaining collections of cultivated plants came from a survey of plant CULTIVARS by the ROYAL BOTANIC GARDENS, MELBOURNE (1983). Research using early Australian nursery catalogues found that many useful cultivated plants had been lost, mostly by changes in fashion and closure of specialist nurseries. The Association adopted an approach to cultivated plant conservation similar to that adopted by the British National Council for the Conservation of Plants and Gardens (NCCPG). Members, including private collectors, NURSERIES, BOTANIC GARDENS, and PUBLIC GARDENS, hold living collections of particular groups of plants. Initially these were all in Vic., but collections are now held Australia-wide. Based at the Royal Botanic Gardens, Melbourne, the Association has now registered a wide range of specialist collections, both native and exotic, and with a range of plant life forms in various different geographic and climatic locations. An advantage of the collections—which display similar taxonomic groups in a common garden—is the ability to make direct comparisons of growth characteristics and thus identify superior forms for cultivation.   ML

OSBORN, Theodore George Bentley (1887–1973), botanist, ecologist, and academic, brought inspiration, innovation, and enthusiasm to the study of ECOLOGY and BOTANY. Born at Great Clacton, Essex, England, a student and teacher at Victoria University of Manchester, Osborn was appointed foundation professor of botany, vegetable pathology, and parasitology at the University of Adelaide (1912–26), working closely with Ralph TATE; professor of botany at University of Sydney (1926–37); and Sherardian professor of botany at the University of Oxford (1937–53). As 'father of Australian ecology', he developed the Australian plant ecology discipline, pointed to the dangers of ARID region overgrazing, established the Koonamore Vegetation Reserve, SA (1926), was awarded the Clarke Medal by the Royal Society of New South Wales (1958), and retired as emeritus professor, University of Adelaide.   DAVID JONES

OSBORNE, John (*c.* 1800–1878), gardener, nursery proprietor, and seed merchant, was born in England and following his arrival in Hobart (*c.* 1840) worked as a gardener. By the mid-1850s he was running a nursery, probably the Pine Apple Place Nursery established in 1840 by Frederick LIPSCOMBE. It was located in Montpellier Retreat (later Sandy Bay Road) and an 1860 advertisement called attention to its large and varied stock of fruit trees, evergreen shrubs, forest trees, hawthorns, roses, stove and greenhouse plants, hardy flowering plants, ornamental shrubs, and seeds. He was a long-serving member and an inaugural committee member of the Gardeners' and Amateurs' Horticultural Society, Hobart Town (1845).

Osborne was joined in business during the 1860s by his sons John Osborne [II] (*c.* 1840–1913) and Joseph Osborne (*c.* 1844–1884). John Osborne [II] became a committee member of the Gardeners' and Amateurs' Horticultural Society in 1862 and gave long service to Tasmanian horticulture, including appointment as an inaugural member of the Council of Agriculture (1903). His son, John Osborne [III] (b. 1864), joined the family business some years after the death of John Osborne [I] and was the Agriculture Department Fruit Expert (1905–16). Wilfred Wallace Osborne (1882–1950), son of John Osborne [II], worked as overseer of the Government House grounds (1905–17) and head gardener at the Hobart Botanic Gardens. He was later a member of the Tasmanian WATTLE DAY League for thirty years (secretary for half that time), a trustee of the Tasmanian Museum and Botanical Gardens, and for many years a public figure in Hobart (first elected an alderman in 1934, Lord Mayor 1946–48).   RA

O'SHANESY, John (1834–1899), gardener and nursery proprietor, was born in County Kerry, Ireland, and trained as a gardener in Ireland and Scotland. He arrived in Brisbane in 1861 and was employed at the BRISBANE BOTANIC GARDENS until 1864 (apart from a brief stint in Gympie following gold discoveries there). He moved to Rockhampton to lay out a large pleasure garden for John McGregor and in 1866 he started a nursery in Rockhampton. In 1870 he relocated to Kangaroo Park (Kabra), where he had selected a large area of land. Here he grew fruit as well as establishing his nursery. In 1876 he started farming, and continued the three businesses until his death. He collected grasses and other plants for MUELLER, with whom he was a regular correspondent. He wrote many articles on his experiments in agriculture for the Rockhampton *Bulletin*.

His brother, **Patrick Adams O'Shanesy** (1837–1884), gardener, botanist, and nursery proprietor, was born in County Kerry, Ireland, and trained as a gardener in Scotland. He left for Australia in 1864 and landed in Brisbane. He worked with his brother at his nurseries in Rockhampton and Kangaroo Park. In 1876 he entered into business on his own account. MAIDEN described him as 'an earnest student of botany of the Central District ... [who] gave considerable attention to the collection and arrangement of specimens of grasses and other plants'. He was also a constant correspondent of Mueller, and a Fellow of the Linnean Society. He made a fine collection of timbers for the Philadelphia Exhibition (1876) and wrote *Contributions to the Flora of Queensland, with an Epitome of Botany for Beginners* (1880), in addition to journal articles.   RA

The nascent mining township of Zeehan (Tas.), seemingly carved and reconstituted from the bush, was the site chosen in the early 1890s for the nursery of James OVERALL, an optimistic world away from his training ground of the Royal Exotic Nursery in London

OVERALL, James (1862–1946), nursery proprietor and seed merchant, began his training growing orchids at VEITCH's Royal Exotic Nursery in Chelsea, England. He came to Tas. in 1887 and in 1892 he laid out the first gardens in the west coast mining town of Zeehan, growing vegetables, small fruits, and flowers. The fast-developing mining areas opened new fields for botanical study and Overall began collecting specimens of the unique West Coast flora for KEW and Edinburgh Botanic Gardens. He established a reputation as a botanist and plant collector, sending plants and seeds to all parts of the world, in particular specimens of *Lagarostrobus franklinii* (Huon Pine), *Phyllocladus aspleniifolius* (Celery Top Pine), and *Richea pandanifolia* (Pandani). In 1909 James and his son Athol Overall (1894–1991) moved to Sulphur Creek, where they established one of Tasmania's largest nurseries on their fifty acres (20 ha) of land. Known as the Darwin Nursery, it had an extensive collection of herbaceous plants, trees, and shrubs. The growing conditions were ideal for seed production and this market flourished as traditional markets were closed as a result of war in Europe. James and Athol undertook many expeditions collecting native plants and seeds, including specimens of *Dicksonia antarctica* (Soft Tree-fern) for Kew. The Overalls are credited with pioneering the Australian spagnum moss trade, exporting the first consignment from Zeehan in 1906. Athol Overall's two sons, Jack (b. 1923) and Harry (b. 1926), worked in the business until it was sold in 1976.

James Overall was apparently not related to John E. Overell (*fl.* 1881–86), seed merchant, florist, and fruit importer and exporter, who operated from Elizabeth Street, Hobart.

ANN CRIPPS

OVERTON LODGE, Cottesloe, WA: see COTTESLOE WAR MEMORIAL TOWN HALL AND CIVIC CENTRE

OWENS, John Stanley (1899–1989), parks administrator, was born and educated in Vic. He began his working life as secretary to Melbourne's Lord Mayor, then began a long career with Melbourne City Council in 1922 as senior clerk for the Council's Parks and Gardens Committee. He became Director of Parks and Gardens (later Superintendent of the Parks, Gardens and Recreations Department) in 1947, a position he held until retirement in 1964. As a park administrator he supported innovative ideas such as the increasing use of sophisticated park maintenance equipment after the Second World War, and the introduction of RECREATION movement ideas to Australia in the late 1940s and 1950s.

Although not formally trained in horticulture, Jack Owens was concerned to see the standard of horticultural EDUCATION raised in Australia, and worked hard to increase the number and variety of courses in both horticulture and recreation. He was also keen to raise the status of horticulture as a career, and headed a successful campaign, in the late 1940s, to have the term 'curator' of parks changed to 'superintendent'. Many of his interests were pursued in his role as founding secretary, and later president, of the Victorian Tree Planters' Association. He was an honorary life fellow of the ROYAL AUSTRALIAN INSTITUTE OF PARKS AND RECREATION and, following a visit to the USA in 1946, was awarded a fellowship of the Institute of Parks and Recreation of America, a rare honour for an Australian.

ELIZABETH STEWART

PACIFIC ISLANDS Plants from the Pacific region, often known as Oceania or the South Seas in the eighteenth and nineteenth centuries, were prominent in early Australian gardens when there were fewer competing imports from further afield. The first came from Norfolk Island, which was occupied less than a month after the arrival of the First Fleet in 1788; some historians believe it was Cook's report on the plants he found growing on this island (1774) that was decisive in influencing the British Government to establish a settlement at Botany Bay. The 'flax plants' (*Phormium tenax*) and 'spruce pines' (*Araucaria heterophylla*) he reported growing there luxuriously were believed to be of great consequence to a nautical power. They were both soon readily available in Sydney, with Norfolk Island pines featuring prominently in early views of the new settlement. The potential economic value of Pacific region plants was also seen as a reason for developing Australian BOTANIC GARDENS.

Sydney became a clearing house for plants and seeds for the south-west Pacific. With the development of whaling, incursions were made into NEW ZEALAND, followed by missionary settlements that provided bases for botanists and plant collectors. In 1820 Charles FRASER listed fifty-three New Zealand plants growing in SYDNEY BOTANIC GARDENS, some with botanical names, some with Maori names, some with descriptions, and others without identification. The McLEAYS at Elizabeth Bay House regularly received plants and seeds from Norfolk Island, New Zealand, and Tahiti between 1835 and 1853. While Fraser only spent one day in New Zealand, both CUNNINGHAMS and BIDWILL collected there later; but the most popular New Zealand plants in Australian gardens had already been introduced. As early as 1820 HMS *Dromedary* had brought New Zealand plants to Sydney, heralding a long association between the Royal Navy and PLANT COLLECTORS in the Pacific. Richard Cunningham spent five months on HMS *Buffalo* (1833) while John MacGILLIVRAY served on HMS *Fly* (1842–46), HMS *Rattlesnake* (1846–50), and HMS *Herald* (1852–55).

In 1850 Charles MOORE joined HMS *Havannah* on a tour that included the New Hebrides (Vanuatu), New Caledonia, and the Solomon Islands. The plants he collected were remarkable for the form and COLOUR of their FOLIAGE, and were distributed to Sydney nursery proprietors: Michael GUILFOYLE offered eight of Moore's introductions for sale in the following year. John Gould VEITCH on HMS *Curacao* (1865) and William GUILFOYLE on HMS *Challenger* (1868) followed similar itineraries and collected similar plants. While they were grown in Australia to a limited extent, they reached the height of their popularity in the heated GREENHOUSES and winter gardens of Europe. The nursery trade joined in the search for new plants. John RULE's collector, William Duncan, discovered *Araucaria rulei* in New Caledonia in 1860, while William Guilfoyle's enthusiastic account of the plants he had discovered influenced BAPTIST in 1869 to send Henry PARCEL to collect in the same area, and his discoveries commanded a premium among British nurseries. Moore, William CARRON, and R.D. FITZGERALD visited Lord Howe Island in 1869 and brought back a collection of plants—the most significant being the 'Kentia' PALMS. These became generally available in the mid-1870s and one, *Howea forsteriana*, became—and still remains—the most widely used indoor palm world-wide.

Bernard Smith, *European Vision and the South Pacific 1768–1850* (Oxford, 1960)   RICHARD CLOUGH

THE PADDOCKS, Para Hills, SA, an integrated wetland and stormwater management system park, was designed in 1971–72 by landscape architect Barrie Ormsby, with assistance from Ray HOLLIDAY. A series of designed ephemeral and permanent wetlands control and filter stormwater pollutants and flood peaks amid a park-like setting of indigenous and salt-tolerant vegetation, with associated sporting ovals and picnic grounds, resulting in an exemplar for similar projects Australia-wide.   DAVID JONES

PALMS, in the strict sense, are plants of the monocotyledonous family Arecaceae (or Palmae in the older nomenclature). World-wide, the family comprises around 2700 species, of which more than ninety per cent are strictly TROPICAL, with greatest diversity in Central and South America, the Malay–New Guinea region, and Madagascar. Australia has only fifty-three native palm species in nineteen genera, the largest, *Livistona*, also showing the greatest diversity of habitat, with four of its sixteen species extratropical and some isolated populations in quite ARID regions—most notably central Australia's Macdonnell Ranges.

Prior to the mid-nineteenth century, palms were cultivated for utilitarian rather than ornamental purposes. Such palms, often included in early botanic gardens, included food

In ARID ZONES, the planting of PALMS became common from the mid-nineteenth century for productive purposes as well as ornament; they marked water holes, station homesteads, and MISSION GARDENS, as here at Hermannsburg (NT)

or fibre plants already long-cultivated; examples are the date, the coconut, the various sugar palms of tropical ASIA, and the oil palms of AFRICA and SOUTH AMERICA. A reluctance to see palms as garden subjects is curious, given that examples such as the date palms of biblical lands and the coconut palms of the Indies frequently appeared as elements in the 'picturesque' depictions of exotic landscape in the late eighteenth and early nineteenth centuries. This picturesque aesthetic is readily detected in Ferdinand BAUER's magnificent studies of palms in tropical Australian coastal settings, several of which were beautifully reproduced in the *Historia naturalis palmarum* (1833–50) of Carl Friedrich Philipp von Martius. But the picturesque style of garden design, popular in Australia's early colonial period, does not seem to have included palms.

Initially, the two palms most frequently grown were the NSW (and south Qld) natives *Livistona australis* (Cabbage Palm) and *Archontophoenix cunninghamiana* (Bangalow Palm). The emergence in European horticulture of palms and other exotic FOLIAGE plants as popular ornamental subjects began in the 1870s, gathering momentum in the 1880s and 1890s.

Coincidentally with this, two endemic palms of Lord Howe Island were introduced in 1870 by Charles MOORE and named, as *Kentia belmoreana* and *K. forsteriana*, by Moore and MUELLER; although given their own genus, *Howea*, by the great palm botanist Beccari in 1877, 'Kentia' was already entrenched, and has become their virtual common name. It was at much the same period as their introduction to Australian cultivation that the European craze for potted palms commenced. The two *Howea* species proved better suited for indoor decoration than almost any other palms, and the 1880s saw the start of Lord Howe Island's only export industry: collecting their seeds for European (initially Belgian) nurseries. This trade soon reached large proportions: in 1906, the first year for which records are available, the harvest totalled 3600 bushels (130 cubic metres), or more than twelve million seeds.

It was also in the period 1870–1900 that a larger range of palms was introduced to the BOTANIC GARDEN collections in Melbourne, Adelaide, Sydney, and Brisbane, and perhaps an even wider range to the tropical gardens in Rockhampton, Townsville, and Darwin. Both Moore in Sydney and William

GUILFOYLE in Melbourne saw the aesthetic possibilities of palms when planted in dense groves, and also used as solitary lawn specimens or in AVENUES. The fashion spread to the larger private gardens, though in these palms were often planted more haphazardly, resulting in some incongruous groupings as gardens matured. The southern cities were content with a limited palette of hardier palms, including the Chinese *Trachycarpus fortunei* (Chinese Windmill Palm, introduced to outdoor cultivation in Britain by Robert Fortune in 1849), *Chamaerops humilis* (Mediterranean Fan Palm), *Phoenix canariensis* (Canary Island Date Palm), *Jubaea chilensis* (Chilean Wine Palm), the southern-Brazilian *Butia capitata* (Jelly Palm), *Syagrus romanzoffiana* (Queen Palm), and the New Zealand *Rhopalostylis sapida* (Nikau). The two *Washingtonia* species (*W. filifera* and *W. robusta*) from western North America, newly discovered *c.* 1880, were also introduced and rapidly proved their vigour in cultivation. Some other hardy palms such as the eastern North American palmettoes (*Sabal*, *Serenoa*, *Rhapidophyllum*) appear to have been overlooked in the earlier stages, but began to appear around the turn of the century. Commercial date palm plantations were trialled in SA at HERGOTT SPRINGS and Lake Harry.

Palms were still generally regarded as too strange and exotic for deliberate inclusion in most late nineteenth-century domestic gardens, but an incidental result of their use as potted decoration was that many were planted out when they outgrew their pots. In harbourside suburbs of Sydney there are now many mature specimens of the slow-growing *Howea forsteriana* in the narrow front gardens and side passages of houses built *c.* 1890–1930. Houses of similar age in the cooler inland towns of NSW and Vic. occasionally retain old specimens of *Trachycarpus fortunei*, one of the most frost-tolerant palms. During the same period, *Phoenix canariensis* and the two *Washingtonia* species were widely planted as park and avenue subjects in coastal and in inland towns right across the southern half of Australia. Some of the finest plantings are to be found in the Victorian Murray River towns. In Sydney, horticulturist G.K. COWLISHAW promoted the merits of palms in *All about Palms: Australia's Native and Cultivated Species* (1929).

The middle of the twentieth century saw a decline in use of palms, but by the late 1950s they were again becoming available from nurseries. In Qld in particular there was a growing appreciation of the diversity waiting to be exploited, and the 1960s and 1970s saw the emergence of specialist nurseries, palm collectors, and palm societies. This new enthusiasm for palms had its origins mainly in the USA, where wealthy gardeners in Florida, southern California, and Hawaii were developing collections and a style of landscaping, initially taking their cue from older public gardens such as the Fairchild (Miami) and the Huntington (Los Angeles). In Australia, a debased form of this palm landscaping has become popular among affluent landowners in coastal areas, and may one day be viewed by garden historians as a period style. Mature palms, especially *Phoenix canariensis* and *Syagrus romanzoffiana*, are also being moved into new landscapes at great expense to form an instant effect. But there are also fine examples of well-designed, palm-dominated gardens, both public and private, mostly in coastal Qld and NT. The most extensive and diverse public palm garden is the Townsville Palmetum, developed since the 1980s.

TONY RODD

THE PALMS, Kalgoorlie, WA, a substantial residence in the Federation Queen Anne style (1901), was the private home of Effie and Sidney Hocking. Sidney Edwin Hocking (1859–1935), part owner of the daily *Kalgoorlie Miner* and a prominent member of the Kalgoorlie community, was a keen gardener. The garden, including palms and grape vines brought from their previous home, was established before the construction of the goldfields pipeline when gardens were not common in the town. The garden was watered by hand from a galvanised tank buried in the garden and filled with water delivered by a horse-drawn cart from the brewery (where it had been used for washing bottles), Hocking being the chairman of Kalgoorlie Brewing Company Ltd at the time. When the pipeline from MUNDARING WEIR was opened (1903), a garden COMPETITION was inaugurated (1904) as an incentive for residents to use more water. The Palms, tended by Tom Cunningham, won the competition for Section A (for gardens that employed a gardener). In 1966 the Palms was purchased by the Health Department of Western Australia, and it is currently an administrative centre. The garden remains substantially intact.

ROSEMARY ROSARIO

PANMURE (originally Berkley Vale), Stirling, SA, is one of the finest HILL-STATION gardens in the ADELAIDE HILLS. The garden, begun in the 1870s by Salvitor Wakefield, covered four hectares on a spur—the intended house site—and two small valleys. The layout included a rhododendron garden with serpentine paths, interspersed with camellias, magnolias, and Japanese maples, a grassy glen, stone walled terraces and a grand stone staircase, several areas of woodland, two ponded creeks with rills and small waterfalls, several other ponds and a large GROTTO cum SHADE-HOUSE. Before the intended house was built, the property was sold and the stables were converted to a house, and a tennis court was constructed on the proposed house site. The property changed hands many times between the late nineteenth century and 1970, when it was purchased by Chris and Tina Laurie; by this time all but half a hectare was derelict. Enthusiastic and knowledgeable rejuvenation saw the gardens significantly improved by tree surgery, weed control, water storage and irrigation, and many new plantings within the original strong framework.

TREVOR NOTTLE

PANSHANGER, near Longford, Tas.: see ARCHER, Thomas

PARAFIELD CEMETERY, ten miles (16 km) north of Adelaide, provided an extraordinary example of a fully developed public CEMETERY that was never used for burials. Intended to supersede Adelaide's main public cemetery at WEST TERRACE, the 1891 layout by Josiah Paull, of the Surveyor-General's Department, superimposed an elaborate road system over a grid burial plan. Within the eighty-three

The layout of Adelaide's PARAFIELD CEMETERY (1891) was strongly influenced by Sydney's ROOKWOOD CEMETERY, and although much of the landscaping was carried out, the site was never used for burials, and was abandoned in 1901

acre (34 ha) site there was provision for approximately 46 000 grave plots as well as areas for vaults, ornamental planting, and reserves. Paull's extensive planting included 3000 trees and 9000 hedge plants, and his choices provided a fine example of a nineteenth-century cemetery planting scheme. Public concern about the remote location, a campaign by undertakers questioning the site's suitability, and an economic depression led to the cemetery's abandonment in 1901 (despite expenditure exceeding £12 000). The site was given over to an experimental wheat farm and later a poultry farm. Regrettably, in the 1970s the mortuary station—then being used as an incubator room—was demolished.   ROBERT NICOL

PARCEL, Henry (c. 1828–1889), gardener and plant collector, was born in Hertfordshire, England, and numerous comments later published in the *Horticultural Magazine* indicate that he trained in English gardens. He arrived in Sydney in 1854 and was gardener during the 1860s to J.R. Young, Hereford House, Glebe (NSW), a garden that J.G. VEITCH greatly admired for its imported rarities, especially foliage plants. Sydney nursery proprietor John BAPTIST contracted Parcel in 1869 to collect plants and seeds in the South Sea Islands, and this PACIFIC expedition yielded many riches. A list in Parcel's hand survives in the Baptist papers (Mitchell Library) and includes crotons, pandanus, dracaenas, ferns, and orchids among others. *Ficus parcelii* (now *F. aspera*), one of several plants named for its discoverer, was handsomely illustrated in colour in *Flore des Serres et des Jardins de l'Europe* (1845–83). Following his return, Parcel was gardener for pastoralist James White at CRANBROOK, Rose Bay (NSW).   RA

PARKINSON, Sydney (c. 1745–1771), natural history painter, was born in Edinburgh, where he began his career as a woollen draper. He became interested in drawing plants and exhibited work in London after moving there with his widowed mother. Parkinson gained commissions from the exhibition, including one from James LEE to teach plant drawing to his daughter. This gained Parkinson a recommendation as a natural history artist to Joseph BANKS, who employed him in 1767 to illustrate fishes, birds and insects from his Newfoundland collection. The following year Parkinson joined Banks, Daniel SOLANDER, and anthropological artist Alexander Buchan as the natural history artist on James Cook's voyage to the Pacific (1768–71). When Buchan died in Tahiti (1769), Parkinson became the sole artist on board. His workload was such that it was no longer possible for him to make completed paintings. The best he could manage were pencil sketches with some colour-coded patches. As a result Parkinson did not complete any paintings of AUSTRALIAN PLANTS. When the expedition was plagued with dysentery and malaria in Batavia on the return journey, Parkinson was one of those who died at sea. Back in England, Banks proposed to produce a florilegium, with Solander providing the plant descriptions and several artists completing the artwork based on Parkinson's drawings and sketches. Unfortunately this was not completed; publication, by now of historic interest only, came (in black ink only) in Britten's *Illustrations of Australian Plants Collected in 1770* (1900–05) and Blunt and Stearn's *Captain Cook's Florilegium* (1973). Full sets of coloured impressions were issued by Alecto Historical Editions (1981–88).

D. Carr (ed.), *Sydney Parkinson: Artist of Cook's Endeavour Voyage* (Canberra, 1983); R. Joppien and B. Smith, *The Art of Captain Cook's Voyages* (vol. 1, Melbourne, 1985); Brian Adams, *The Flowering of the Pacific: Being an Account of Joseph Banks' Travels in the South Seas and the Story of his Florilegium* (Sydney, 1986)   HELEN HEWSON

PARKS and parkland had their most potent expression in the enclosed ('emparked') land, or DOMAIN, of eighteenth-century British country seats, especially those designed in the newly fashionable landscape style. Early settlers remarked frequently on the likeness of much of the open grassy country of south-eastern Australia to a vast 'gentleman's park'. Parkland in Australia was often an accompaniment to large pastoral HOMESTEAD properties, such as MURNDAL and many others in Victoria's WESTERN DISTRICT, and more generally in south-eastern Australia, including NSW and Tas. The term was often incorporated in naming (for example RETFORD PARK) and linked to other generic places, ranging from socially elite DEER PARKS to more egalitarian CAR and CARAVAN PARKS. PUBLIC PARKS were more widespread than their private counterparts in Australia, and from the 1840s, rapid urban development and TOWN PLANNING fostered their widespread creation. This coincided with agitation in Britain and NORTH AMERICA for provision of public parks, NATIONAL PARKS, and other PUBLIC OPEN SPACES for LEISURE, RECREATION, and SPORT.   RA

PARKS AND LEISURE AUSTRALIA (1998–) was formed as the result of a merger between the Australian Leisure Institute (ALI) and the Royal Australian Institute of

Parks and Recreation (RAIPR). The ALI was formed in 1993 from the merger of various local RECREATION groups in Vic., while the RAIPR has a history stretching back to 1926, when it originated as the Victorian Tree Planters' Association (VTPA). It was during Melbourne's annual Garden Week FESTIVAL in April 1926 that J.T. SMITH, Curator of Parks and Gardens at the Melbourne City Council, called a meeting of nursery proprietors and park curators to discuss common problems, including the need for increased tree planting and the provision of PUBLIC PARKS in urban areas. The need for an association to take on an advisory role on these matters became apparent, and the VTPA was formed. One key founding member was Jack OWENS, a curator working under Smith, who was secretary (1926–47), then president (1947–65). The Association's annual conference became a pivotal event for members, enabling them to exchange ideas and information, and form networks of those concerned with parks and recreation throughout Australia.

In 1955 all references to tree planting were removed from the Association when its members voted to adopt a new name, the Institute of Park Administration of Victoria. The name change reflected the views of younger members, such as Frank KEENAN and Tom KNEEN, eager to see the organisation adopt new trends in the planning of parks, including the growth of the recreation movement. A natural progression of this trend was another name change, in 1962, to the Australian Institute of Park Administration, to reflect the Australia-wide nature of the membership and its interests. This period saw the establishment of the journal **Australian Parks (and Recreation)** (1964–). In 1966 members included the term 'recreation' included the Institute's title, so it became the Australian Institute of Parks and Recreation—with Royal status granted in 1977—reflecting the impact that the recreation movement was having on the Australian way of life.

Throughout its history, members have pursued a variety of concerns, but two persistent issues have been to raise the profile of the profession of horticulture as a career, and to raise the status of horticulture and recreation EDUCATION. Members lobbied hard to achieve these goals and produced some significant results. These included helping to establish the Diploma of Horticulture at the BURNLEY Horticultural College (1958), having gardening recognised as an apprenticeship trade in Vic. (1966), and establishing a long-running summer school of park management at the (now) University of Canberra (1971).

Elizabeth Stewart, *Places in the Park: A Sixty Year History of the Royal Australian Institute of Parks and Recreation 1926–1986* (Dickson, ACT, 1991)   ELIZABETH STEWART

PARLIAMENTARY TRIANGLE, Canberra: see NATIONAL TRIANGLE, Canberra

PARONELLA, José (1888–1948), tourism promoter, was born in Catalonian Province, Spain, and came to Qld in 1913, returning to Spain in 1924–24 where he married Margarita (née Soler). Between 1929 and 1935 the family developed **Paronella Park**, a tourist RESORT in a five-hectare valley set between rainforest and sugarcane fields near Innisfail (Qld). Paronella's self-constructed designs for the resort buildings were fanciful interpretations in stone, stucco, and concrete of Spanish castles. Facilities set in the informal gardens included a cottage residence for the family, castle tower (folly), ballroom–cinema-hall, café–kiosk, picnic areas, tennis courts, hydro-electric generator house, 'tunnel of love', fountains, urns, bridges, and balustrading. The nearby Mena Falls were part of the experience, as were the rambling paths through the rainforest. TROPICAL gardens complemented the buildings. Paronella's wife and children carried on the resort after his death, adding a CARAVAN PARK in 1958. Paronella Park changed owners several times from 1977 and, following ravages of fire, storm, and vandals, has recently been reopened.

Dena Leighton, *The Spanish Dreamer: A Biography of José Paronella* (Wollongong, NSW, 1997)   JEANNIE SIM

PARRAMATTA PARK, NSW, comprising ninety hectares of the former governors' DOMAIN, is closely associated with the beginnings of rural settlement in Australia and includes Old GOVERNMENT HOUSE (1790–1857), the former observatory (with important VISTAS), former convict huts, and farm buildings. It is also significant as an Aboriginal heritage place and for its contiguity with a precinct of early INSTITUTIONAL sites. The early change from government farm to picturesque PARKLAND, with plantings of stone pines and oaks, was initiated by Governor Macquarie. Provisions for a PUBLIC PARK were enacted by the *Parramatta Domain Act* 1857 and improvements included AVENUES and plantings of *Ficus macrophylla* (Moreton Bay Fig) and ARAUCARIAS. Gazetted as a NATIONAL PARK in 1917, the park has since performed the role of regional park with more recent controversial excisions for social and SPORTING uses. A recent addition, by the Heritage Rose Society, was the RUMSEY rose garden.   COLLEEN MORRIS

PARRY, Henry Griffith (1886–1971) nursery proprietor and cut flower producer at Floralands, Kariong (NSW), took up land near Gosford in the early 1900s, applying for a crown grant in 1910. The property contained a large stand of *Ceratopetalum gummiferum* (New South Wales Christmas Bush), which Parry soon discovered was in demand among Sydney FLORISTS. By 1914 he was planting new seedlings at Floralands, becoming one of the first to cultivate AUSTRALIAN FLORA for the cut-flower trade. **Percival Joseph Parry** (1901–1986) joined his brother in 1915 and took over Floralands in 1925 when Henry's health forced him to take on lighter duties.

Perce Parry married keen local botanist Olive Kari Olsen (1906–1987) in 1929 and completed the purchase of Floralands from Henry the same year. The *Wild Flowers Protection Act* 1927 banned public transportation of wild flowers, preventing access to Sydney markets. This was amended in 1932. The Parrys fought a proposed total ban on the sale of wild flowers in 1944, arguing that cultivation would reduce demand on bush-picked plants, and they were instrumental in the introduction of a licence system for growers and landholders (1945). Local species such as *Telopea speciosissma*

(Waratah), *Blandfordia grandiflora* (Christmas Bell), *Eriostemon australasius* (Wax Flower), and *Actinotus helianthi* (Flannel Flower) were produced along with many Western Australian species. By the late 1940s, waratahs at Floralands were yielding 20 000 to 30 000 blooms a year. Floralands was also a nursery, with demand growing steadily from the mid-1960s, and the range of plants increasing to more than 2000 species. Percival's son, Brian Parry (b. 1942), took over management of Floralands in 1973 until its sale in 1999.   JOHN WALTER

THE PARTERRE GARDEN, Sydney-based garden design consultancy (1985–), with related shops (Woollahra 1986, Mosman 1993), was established by Annie Wilkes (b. 1949) and Richard Haigh (b. 1962). Both were graduates of the RYDE Horticultural School. Wilkes first trained in art, and gained experience in her parents' plant nursery. She was determined to provide sophisticated designs that drew on FORMAL northern hemisphere traditions, adapted to suit Australian conditions. Initially Wilkes and Haigh produced large TOPIARY shrubs: with the first garden commissions came a need for appropriate architectural planting tubs, FOUNTAINS, and GARDEN FURNITURE, which were marketed through the shops. Early designs for city COURTYARDS featured a crisp, ordered use of paving, ground covers, HEDGING, and usually a WATER accent. Commissions for larger country gardens ensued: major examples are at Broke, Mudgee, and Yarramalong Valley (NSW). The firm's trend-setting formal planning is typically highly architectural, emphasising simplicity and massed planting.   HOWARD TANNER

PARTERRES, especially in their early manifestation as *parterres de broderie* (ornamental plantings of box separating coloured earth), had fallen from favour by the time of Australia's European settlement. Derived from the French *par terre* (on the ground), the term also referred to a flower garden, particularly adjoining the house, laid out in a regular ornamental manner. In Australia, during the nineteenth century, this meaning was extended—perhaps ironically—to refer more generally to the FLOWER GARDEN. In the spirit of its original usage, the parterre in late nineteenth- and early twentieth-century Australian gardens generally referred to hard-edged, geometric flower BEDS cut in LAWN. The most prominent examples were to be found in INSTITUTIONAL GARDENS and PUBLIC PARKS.

Robin Whalley and Anne Jennings, *Knot Gardens and Parterres: A History of the Knot Garden and How to Make one Today* (London, 1998)   COLLEEN MORRIS

PASADENA, Kalamunda, WA, a two-acre (0.8 ha) garden high in the Darling Range, was designed and planted in 1929 by Thomas Price (1865–1955), retired orchardist and horticulturist. Price had trained at the VEITCH nursery in London before arriving in WA in 1891, where, for a brief period, he became partner in the Woodbridge Nurseries of *WESTERN MAIL* proprietor, Charles Harper. After thirty years as a highly successful orchardist Price retired to Pasadena, named after that fertile district in California. The property was laid out and planted in the manner of a paradise garden, with running water, rustic bridges, curving pathways, and rock-edged garden beds. Roses and exotic trees and shrubs were imported from nurseries in the eastern states, many being rare at that time in WA. Until the 1960s the garden was regularly opened for charity; recently refurbished, it still retains much of its original design and plantings.

Eric T. Price, *Thomas Price of Illawarra* (Adelaide, 1985)
CAROL MANSFIELD

PATHS, while primarily a functional element in gardens, also provide a framework for design and may provide complementary texture, permanent COLOUR, and patterned effects to planting. Most garden STYLES, including FORMAL and more PICTURESQUE curvilinear arrangements, have drawn on paths as key design elements, and path layouts also assist in charting hybrid layouts in GARDENESQUE examples, especially during the Federation–Edwardian period. Paths can be designed to direct pedestrians through a landscape, or be based on desire lines for natural pedestrian flows; when ramped or linked to steps, they can provide access to different levels. Many different materials have been used for paths, including local gravels, cut stone, asphalt, concrete, and various concrete and brick unit pavers, generally sympathetic to the style of garden they serve. Paths can also be of mown LAWN, such as those through the area of rough grass with herbaceous plantings in Walling's garden at BOORTKOI (Vic.).

Detailed plans prepared prior to sewering Australia's major cities between the 1890s and the 1930s provide an outstanding document of garden paths, especially in the widespread absence of individual GARDEN PLANS. With their resolute objectivity, the plans of the Melbourne and Metropolitan Board of Works are especially worthy successors to the British Ordnance Survey tradition, and provide vital evidence for GARDEN HISTORIANS.   ML

PATIO, a Spanish word, indicates a COURTYARD enclosed within a dwelling yet open to the sky. The cooling patio evolved in response to the hot, dry, climate of MEDITERRANEAN countries. The Imperial Romans introduced patios to the Iberian Peninsula, adapting the peristyle (or columned space) that they had borrowed from the Greeks. Later, Muslims, who controlled parts of Spain for nearly 1000 years, enhanced the patio as family life focused on it. The patio was the place at the centre of the house where residents interacted, and were insulated from the clamour and dirt of the street. The Muslims introduced plants to the patio, and water features. The patio concept came to Australia largely from NORTH AMERICA, the south-western portion of which once formed part of the Spanish Empire. An important means of transfer was the *Sunset Patio Book*, first published in California in 1952, and widely available in Australia. Today, the word patio is often used in Australia instead of 'terrace' to refer to an open, paved, outdoor eating or lounging space attached to a building.   CLIVE SORRELL

PATRICK, John William (b. 1951), landscape designer, educationalist, horticulturist, and media personality, migrated

PATHS at GOVERNMENT HOUSE, Sydney, lined in the 1870s by urns, flank the raised shrubbery, where they define boundaries between garden compartments; they also change levels by means of carefully placed steps, and define points of entry for garden visitors

from England in 1980 to lecture in amenity horticulture at BURNLEY Horticultural College. Appointed senior lecturer in 1981, he was instrumental in forming the new degree program in horticulture and a revitalised curriculum in amenity horticulture focusing on PUBLIC OPEN SPACE management and garden design. He left in 1988 to pursue consultancy work for private and government clients in design, heritage, and horticultural advice. A versatile and accomplished speaker, he has lectured widely and broadcast on both RADIO and TELEVISION, initially for the ABC in Vic. on 3LO and more recently for several commercial stations, including 3AK and the Nine Network's BURKE'S Backyard. Through his association with the ABC he helped initiate Victoria's (now AUSTRALIA'S) OPEN GARDEN SCHEME and was responsible for writing its first guide books. His other books include *The Australian Garden* (1985). He has served on many garden and landscape committees and was a foundation board member of the ROYAL BOTANIC GARDENS, MELBOURNE. Through his many varied activities Patrick has both spanned and linked amateur and professional horticulture. ML

PATTERSON, Alfred Andrew (*c.* 1859–1932), surveyor and gardener, was born in Drottningholm, Sweden and graduated from Uppsala University. Aged only 18 he was appointed lecturer at Hamburg University, Germany, and afterwards left for England. He migrated to Australia, working variously as surveyor on the Mount Bischoff railway (Tas.) and the Nyngan–Byrock railway (NSW), interspersed with botanical collecting in Qld. Following a severe illness he worked as gardener for merchant James Dalton, at Duntryleague, Orange (NSW), an 1870s mansion set in magnificent grounds. Through Dalton's influence he became the inaugural gardener at COOK PARK, Orange, and he was subsequently head gardener at MACHATTIE PARK, Bathurst, for twenty years of a formative period in its development. He spent the remainder of his career as a shire engineer in country NSW. RA

PAVILION is an inclusive term taken to include a range of GARDEN BUILDINGS, especially those with qualities such as elegance, lightness, and ephemerality, and floating, peaked, or tent-like forms, relating to the etymology of the term from the Latin *papilio–onis* (butterfly, tent). Fine examples with these characteristics include the PICNIC shelter at BALLARAT BOTANIC GARDENS, Vic. (1908), the Fairfax pool pavilion, Bowral, NSW (1969) by architect Guildford Bell, and the sculptural SUMMER HOUSE at HEIDE, Bulleen, Vic. (1991) by architect Greg Burgess.

The term also includes buildings used for entertainments, especially when combined with a viewing function at SPORTS grounds. Here the banqueting TENT ethos was often combined with the architecture of simple inns or public houses (having gables to the main facade and an elongated verandah) to form a composite building, the grandstand. RA

PAXTON, Joseph (1803–1865), English gardener and architect, started working at the garden of the (ROYAL) HORTICULTURAL SOCIETY at Chiswick in 1823. While there, he apparently impressed the Duke of Devonshire, from neighbouring Chiswick House and was appointed head gardener at CHATSWORTH in 1826. Paxton set to work immediately, marshalling his staff with creative energy; he was soon aided by the efficient managerial flair of his wife Sarah (née Bown). He developed an arboretum, installed much-praised rockwork, designed the estate village Edensor, and experimented with glasshouses, culminating in his Great Conservatory (1836–39). Paxton maintained a private practice from 1842, especially designing PUBLIC PARKS. Prince's Park (1842) and Birkenhead Park (1843), both near Liverpool, stamped him as an influential innovator in this new garden type, so recently pioneered by LOUDON at the Derby Arboretum (1840). Later projects included People's Park, Halifax (1857), by which date his protégés Edward Milner, John Gibson, and Edward KEMP were forging influential careers. Paxton also channelled energy into writing, editing the *Horticultural Register* (1831–34) and *Paxton's Magazine of Botany* (1834–49), jointly founding the GARDENERS' CHRONICLE (1841), and writing a treatise on the dahlia (1838) and a *Pocket Botanical Dictionary* (1840). His magazines were widely read and quoted in the colonies, and his tutelage was a highly regarded credential for emigrating gardeners.

Paxton became fascinated by railways, both as a speculator and company director. It was through railway connections that his famous sketch design of the Crystal Palace (1850), utilising the ridge and furrow glazing developed at Chatsworth, was adopted for the 1851 Great Exhibition in London's Hyde Park. It was the subsequent re-erection of the building at Sydenham that produced Paxton's influential Crystal Palace Garden (1852–56), with its immense formal terraces recalling Baroque splendour. By this date, Paxton was a wealthy man; yet Donald BEATON, deferentially describing Paxton's loyalty to his profession, wrote in 1853 'although he is now rich enough to pay for a passage to Australia for all the gardeners he ever knew … [he] never thinks of separating himself, at … public meetings, from his old friends'.

Violet R. Markham, *Paxton and the Bachelor Duke* (London, 1935); G.F. Chadwick, *The Works of Sir Joseph Paxton 1803–1865* (London, 1961); John Anthony, *Joseph Paxton: An Illustrated Life of Sir Joseph Paxton 1803–1865* (Princes Risborough, Buckinghamshire, 1973) RA

PAYNE, Frederick Cyril (1893–1972), nursery proprietor and promoter of AUSTRALIAN PLANTS, established his specialist nursery in Torrensville (SA) in the 1940s. Growth in trade prompted him to re-establish as Payne's Nursery (affec-

Joseph PAXTON's Crystal Palace Garden (1852–56), at Sydenham, south of London, was a training ground for several emigrant gardeners and also a commonly invoked exemplar of the formal ITALIANATE garden style

tionately known as 'The Sanctuary') with an extensive wildflower garden. His nursery, later renamed the Athelstone Wildflower Garden and Nursery, was acquired by Campbelltown City Council (1963) and Ray HOLLIDAY appointed as manager (1963–72). In 1974 the state government acquired the property and incorporated it within the Black Hill Native Flora Park Trust (to a design by Lindsay PRYOR). Several popular cultivars of Australian plants had their origins in Payne's nursery. DAVID JONES

PAYNE, Thomas (b. c. 1816), gardener at the Royal Palace Gardens, Kensington, and the Spring Gardens, near Exeter, England. He arrived in Qld in 1855 and worked as overseer at the newly established BRISBANE BOTANIC GARDENS. Between 1858 and 1861 (and possibly later) he leased an orchard where he conducted an ORANGERY and nursery, claiming long experience in the 'rearing and cultivation of tropical and semi-tropical productions in conservatories and hot-houses in the old country'. He wrote on oranges for *Pugh's ALMANAC* (1859). RA

PEACE MEMORIAL ROSE GARDEN, Nedlands, WA, was developed following an appeal launched by Charles Frost, president of the NATIONAL ROSE SOCIETY of Western Australia. Nedlands Road Board's architects, W.G. Bennett and Associates, drew up the design, which incorporated 5000 rose bushes. On 22 October 1950 the Memorial Rose Garden was dedicated as a WAR MEMORIAL to the 'glorious memory of all who sacrificed their lives on active service in their country's cause'. Most of the original plantings have been replaced, though not always with the original variety. This MEMORIAL GARDEN is currently maintained by Nedlands City Council; the National Rose Society holds annual rose pruning demonstrations there on the first Sunday in July.

CAROLYN MIDDLEMIS

PEATE (née WAGNER), Natalie Florence (b.1931), nursery owner, plant propagator, and horticultural writer, was director from the early 1970s until 1998 of Plant Growers Australia, leading growers of garden plants and introducers of new CULTIVARS. Melbourne-based, Peate has been influential on many industry bodies, including the Nursery Industry Association of Victoria, serving as president (1985–86). She was a co-opted member of Council of the Victorian College of Agriculture and Horticulture (1985–92), serving as vice-president of Council in 1992. She is a member of the International Plant Propagators' Society, the Australian Plant Society, the Australian Daisy Study Group, and the Plant Breeders' Rights Consultative Committee. Peate has pursued her long-term interest in the development of Australian plants through her BREEDING and improvement of paper daisies (*Rhodanthe* spp.). She has written many books, including (as co-author) the *Grow What Where* series. JAMES WILL

PEJAR PARK, near Goulburn, NSW: see BLIGH (née GORDON), (Rosemary) Beatrice

PELARGONIUMS AND GERANIUMS Geranium is the popular name for the large range of hybrid pelargoniums grown in Australian gardens or in pots for CONSERVATORIES and PATIOS. However, the genus *Geranium* also represents a large number of species in garden use—such as *Geranium endressii*, *G. cinereum*, *G. ibericum*, *G. phaeum*, *G. pratense*, and *G. sanguineum*. There are also several Australian native geraniums; several of these, such as *Geranium australe*, have been used for ornamental garden planting; others have been included in indigenous plantings such as Australian GRASSLAND reconstructions.

Pelargoniums take a wide range of forms, and are placed within different groups depending on appearance and form; groups include zonal pelargoniums (including the variously marked VARIEGATED types much planted in Victorian times), ivy-leaved pelargoniums (including trailing forms used in hanging baskets, window boxes, and on terraces and balconies, but also found in Australian gardens trailing over embankments, dead tree stumps, and over arched gateways, particularly in COTTAGE GARDENS), and show or regal pelargoniums (including forms with large and showy blooms in a range of colours).

Pelargoniums have been widely grown in Australian gardens; their ease of propagation and robust constitution made them early favourites, especially in POTS on VERANDAHS, and in cottage-style gardens. In recent times, with the increase in balcony gardens in inner-city townhouse developments, their popularity for pot culture has been revived. Another group with renewed popularity, especially from the interest in cottage gardens in the 1980s, is the scented-leaved pelargoniums: lemon and peppermint SCENTED types are commonly planted. ML

PELLOE (née SUNDERCOMBE), Emily Harriet ('Ixia') (1878–1941), journalist, botanist, artist, and humanitarian, was born in Melbourne, arriving in WA with her parents in 1901. Well known to readers of the *West Australian* as 'Ixia', under which name she edited the lively 'Women's Interests' weekly page (1923–34), her first love was horse-riding though the BUSH and painting WILDFLOWERS. Having studied botany in Perth she subsequently published three illustrated books on Western Australian wildflowers: the most significant and scholarly was *Wildflowers of Western Australia* (1921). Claimed to be the first book in English to deal exclusively with that flora, it included seven of her own brilliantly coloured plates. An enthusiastic and prolific artist of wildflowers and landscapes, forty of her watercolours are held by the Lawrence Wilson Art Gallery, and 400 smaller paintings by St Catherine's College (both within the University of Western Australia). CAROL MANSFIELD

PELZER, August Wilhelm (1862–1934), landscape gardener, trained in a nursery at Erfurt and at the Royal Horticultural College in Geisenheim, Germany. He worked for local authorities in Berlin and Hamburg and in a nursery at St Albans near London before migrating to Adelaide, where he designed and planted several private gardens. He served as gardener to the City of Adelaide (1899–1934), including management of ADELAIDE PARK LANDS. He provided design and planting advice for VICTOR HARBOR SOLDIERS' MEMORIAL GARDENS. DAVID JONES

PENFOLD, Christopher Rawson (1811–1870), medical practitioner and vigneron, born in Steyning, Sussex, England, migrated to Adelaide in 1844 with his wife Mary (*née* Holt) (1816–1895). Bringing select vine cuttings, principally the cultivar Grenache, from France, he acquired land at Magill near Adelaide, and started producing ports and sherries before specialising in clarets and Rieslings. The Penfolds' cottage was called Grange, a name later adopted in the famous Grange Hermitage wine label (1951). Penfold believed that wine was a useful medicament, and while his medical practice was profitable, viticultural activities soon dominated his life, and that of his wife. Upon the death of 'the first scientific vigneron of Australia', Mary continued the business with Thomas Francis Hyland, taken into the partnership of Penfold and Co. in 1863.

Joseph Gillard (1823–1901), appointed winery manager in 1881, moved the winery into dry table wines, and became principal manager in 1884. Gillard's appointment signalled a boom in the development of facilities at Magill, the 'largest vats in the colonies', and some fifty-seven hectares under cultivation, becoming the second largest wine maker in the colony after Thomas HARDY. Penfold and Co. continued expansion with vineyard purchases in the HUNTER VALLEY (1904), MCLAREN VALE (1910), and the BAROSSA VALLEY (1911–12). The last vintages were crushed at Magill in 1972–73, before the vineyards were sold for subdivision, and operations shifted to Nuriootpa (1993); the original cellars, cottage, and some five hectares of vineyards were retained to perpetuate the Penfold's Grange name. The company has since established vineyards in the Clare Valley, COONAWARRA, and Koonunga Hill, and is now part of the Southcorp group.

DAVID JONES

PENGILLY (PENGELLEY), William (1825–1911), gardener, horticulturist, and amateur geologist, was born in St Ives, Cornwall, England, and migrated to Adelaide in 1849. Working first as a stonemason, he was appointed gardener to the City of Adelaide (1867–83), a position he held until dismissal following problems with the supervisor of the ADELAIDE PARK LANDS, John Ednie BROWN. He then established a prominent nursery and orchard in Fullarton (SA), specialising in roses, vegetables, fruit trees, and seeds.

DAVID JONES

PERENNIAL This term may apply to any plant that lives for more than two years, to distinguish them from ANNUALS (which complete their life cycle within one year or growing season) and biennials (which do this within two years, or two consecutive growing seasons). Various plant types such as TREES and SHRUBS are perennials, although the term is usually applied to soft-wooded perennial plants such as *Agapanthus*, and includes many Australian plants such as those within the genera *Anigosanthus* (Kangaroo Paw), *Brachyscome*, *Conostylus*, *Dampiera*, and *Dianella*. Many of the exotic soft-wooded perennials are now serious environmental WEEDS. The term also includes herbaceous perennials, such as anemone, asters, delphiniums, echinacea, shasta daisies, and phlox, in which the top part of the plant dies off each winter and regenerates the following spring. These form the mainstay of the HERBACEOUS BORDER, but are also often grown in mixed SHRUBBERIES to add colour and texture throughout the summer months. A number of short-lived perennials, such as stocks and pansies, flower best in their first season and are therefore treated as if they were annuals, and removed after one flowering.

ML

PERGOLAS were known in Roman and Renaissance gardens: 'pergola' is an Italian term derived from the Latin *pergula* (projecting roof), defined in 1675 as 'an arbour or covered walk formed of growing plants trained over trellis work'. This garden structure has been a popular subject in Australia, initially taking the form of an ARBOUR made of RUSTIC tree trunks or boughs, supporting flowering vines and climbing roses. This evolved into a system of substantial, squared hardwood posts and beams encompassing a pathway. Nineteenth-century interest in ironwork also produced light arched frames supporting wire trellises; RIPPON LEA's rose garden had a hybrid example by 1875. *Domestic Architecture in Australia* (1919) revealed an Edwardian preference for heavy, circular rendered piers with square capitals supporting paired beams. The interest of architects such as Leslie WILKINSON and Marcus Martin in MEDITERRANEAN and Georgian styles introduced more classical forms with slender whitewashed columns. Today, metal frames often provide a contemporary expression, especially as lightweight additions to ROOF GARDENS, where CLIMBING PLANTS can provide a mass of foliage without heavy masses of soil. Used with deciduous plants next to buildings they can also reduce heat loads throughout summer by shading, yet allow sun to infiltrate during the winter.

Paul Edwards and Katherine Swift, *Pergolas, Arbours, and Arches: Their History and How to Make Them* (London, 2001)

HOWARD TANNER

PERMACULTURE is the name Bill Mollison gave to his self-sustaining, ECOLOGICAL system of AGRICULTURE, based on perennial food crops grown in 'food forests'. **Bruce Charles (Bill) Mollison** (b. 1928) was born in Stanley (Tas.) and left school aged 15. His philosophy—developed from the late 1950s—grew from his comparison of traditional farming methods with the self-sustaining and flexible natural systems of the Tasmanian forests. He established his first permaculture garden, in Tas., in 1973, and in 1978 published *Permaculture 1: A Perennial Agricultural System for Human Settlements*. Mollison's philosophy became a world-wide movement, based on sustainable design for all systems supporting humans, including food, fibre, water, waste, energy, and finance. There are more than 4000 'grass roots' projects in more than 100 countries, and Mollison has received numerous national and international awards for his work. Permaculture groups exist throughout Australia; the Permaculture Institute, a non-profit educational trust, operates from Tas., and the Permaculture Research Institute, founded by Geoff Lawton, is based at Tagari Farm in northern NSW.

JILL KELLOW

PERRIN, George Samuel (*c.* 1849–1900), forester, was born in England, and migrated with his parents to Vic. in

The PERGOLA at MICALAGO STATION (NSW), basking in the strong midday sun, demonstrates the effects of LIGHT and shade so characteristic of Australian gardens

1853. He gained his FORESTRY training with the Woods and Forests Department of South Australia, under energetic conservator of forests, John Ednie BROWN. Perrin was appointed acting ranger to Mount Burr Forest in 1880, promoted to forester in 1881, and became chief forester at WIRRABARA in 1885. After two years as Tasmania's forests conservator, in 1888 Perrin was appointed to Vic. as Conservator of Forests, the position he held until his untimely death. From Ferdinand MUELLER Perrin learnt much about the ACCLIMATISATION of exotic trees and the growth of Australian forest flora. An outspoken advocate of 'forest conservancy', Perrin argued that when government reserved a state forest, its 'duty was not to let a single acre become diverted from its legitimate purposes'. Forestry critics derided him as a 'crank' who 'would make Collins-street a forest if he had his way'. Perrin's spirited efforts to establish sound, systematic management of Victoria's state forests, two decades before the creation of an autonomous Forests Department (1908), were constantly thwarted by the Lands Department's predominant ethic of land alienation, and Mines Department concessions to miners. Nevertheless, Perrin laid the foundations of systematic forestry in Vic. by implementing thinning operations and fire protection schemes, controlling cattle grazing, reintroducing a limited royalty system on sawmillers, and expanding STATE FOREST NURSERIES and plantations. The Royal Commission on State Forests and Timber Reserves (1897) convincingly vindicated Perrin's complaints about government neglect of forestry.

ANGELA TAYLOR

PERROTT family, well known in the Qld NURSERY TRADE, is descended from Thomas Perrott (d. 1897) and his wife Ellen (*née* Turnbull), who were married in Brisbane.

One son, Thomas Perrott (1888–1955), and his wife Daisy (*née* Gemmill) (*c.* 1891–1975), founded a family of nursery proprietors and florists in Brisbane in 1919. Thomas had worked from 1903 with Lawrence SUMMERLIN and T.F. Wood, and Daisy came from a nursery and florist's family. After the death of Thomas, his sons Douglas and Thomas Robert Perrott (b. 1912) looked after the nursery at Enoggera, while daughter Dorothy Daisy Elle Perrott (b. 1914) and her mother were florists at Herston. Children of Douglas now run retail nurseries at Enoggera and Deception Bay. Perrotts Florists passed from family control in 1991.

A second son, (Albert) Victor Perrott (1889–1976), timber merchant and SWEET PEA specialist, and his wife Clara Sophie (*née* Clayphan) (1894–1977), were long-time members of the Royal Queensland Horticultural Society, and for more than forty years judged in Qld agricultural and HORTICULTURAL SHOWS.

JEANNIE SIM

PERRY, Richard (d. 1867), nursery proprietor, married Elizabeth Ann Cock (d. 1865) at Fulham, England, in 1819 and they had nine children. The family migrated to Melbourne in 1849 and established a farm, VINEYARD, MARKET GARDEN, and NURSERY on 105 acres (42 ha) at Fulham Grange, Alphington. They also leased and purchased pastoral land at Spring Plains near Heathcote, and at Wild Duck Creek. The Spring Plains property was run by the younger Richard Perry (1825–1904). William (1827–1885) and George Perry (b. 1829) assisted their father with the management of Fulham Grange, and ran it after his death. William was also in partnership with George Symon(d)s, as auctioneers and commission agents, in Collins Street West, and plants were among the material auctioned. The partnership was dissolved in 1860, but receipts show that the Collins Street business continued under William until at least 1862. A surviving Perry catalogue (1870s) lists a wide range of shrubs, conifers, greenhouse plants, camellias, fruit trees, vines, oranges, and lemons. Fulham Grange was the site of many enterprises: 100 000 sets of hop plants from Tas. were planted in 1868; cut flowers, including violets, were grown for the market; and produce was processed into jams, jellies, bottled fruit, tomato sauce, and chutney. William left Fulham Grange in 1880, with the property being sold and subsequently subdivided. Eugene von GUÉRARD's painting *The Farm of Mr Perry on the Yarra* shows Fulham Grange in 1855, an outstanding document of the early nursery trade in Vic.

GWEN PASCOE

PERTH WAR CEMETERY and the adjacent Dutch War Cemetery and Garden of Remembrance adjoin KARRAKATTA GENERAL CEMETERY. The War Cemetery, established by the Australian Army in 1942 and ceded to the Commonwealth War Graves Commission in 1946, contains graves of both First and Second World War casualties. Graves are marked by granite headstones surrounded by continuous flower beds of roses in manicured lawns. The records building houses a cremation memorial. The Dutch War Cemetery contains the remains of twenty-six Dutch evacuees from Java, relocated from Broome (where they died in tragic circumstances). The Garden of Remembrance was opened in 1966, extended in 1977, and reopened in 1997. From the main entrance, a central pathway leads to a gazebo that contains a dedication plaque. From the gazebo, a feature wall is visible with the inscription 'Their Name Liveth for Evermore'.

ROSEMARY ROSARIO

PESCOTT, Edward Edgar (1872–1954), horticulturist, naturalist, and author, was born at Geelong (Vic.), son of a builder whose great love of nature was transmitted to his large family. In 1888 he was appointed a junior teacher, and taught successfully at Watta Wella, Willenabrina East, Cannum West, Chilwell, Brit Brit, and Tahara Bridge, all in western Vic. He received medals from the Geelong Field Naturalists' Club for work on GRASSES and FERNS. While head teacher at Jarrahmond, near Orbost, he explored the Snowy River 'jungle', and the collected flora is now in the National Herbarium, Melbourne. In 1901 Pescott was encouraged by Charles Hamilton FRENCH to join the Victorian Department of Agriculture as an inspector of the ORCHARD branch. At Shepparton he met Violet Jane, daughter of John Furphy; they were married there in 1906. In 1938 Pescott co-operated with Kate Baker to produce *The Life Story of Joseph Furphy*, his wife's uncle, the celebrated writer.

Appointed principal of the BURNLEY SCHOOL OF HORTICULTURE in 1909, Pescott introduced several innovations; he resigned in 1916, but continued to lecture in botany until 1939. In 1917 he became government POMOLOGIST and seed tester, and was closely associated with the Pomological Committee of Australia. He contributed regularly to the *Journal of the Department of Agriculture*, *Stock and Land*, and other journals and newspapers. An authority on native ORCHIDS,

Pescott made weekly RADIO broadcasts on NATIVE FLORA from the early 1920s and directed the Wildflower and Wild Nature shows in Melbourne during this time. He was elected fellow of the Linnean Society of London as a result of a study published as *Census of the Genus Acacia in Australia* (1914). He retired from the Department of Agriculture in 1937.

Pescott was associated with many NATURAL HISTORY organisations. In the Australian WATTLE DAY League, he was secretary of the Victorian (1910–20) and Australian (1913–22) movements. He was president of the Victorian Horticultural Society (1912–17) and was elected a fellow of the ROYAL HORTICULTURAL SOCIETY. Secretary of the Field Naturalists' Club of Victoria from 1920 and president in 1926–28, Pescott was made a life member in 1947. During his presidency the Victorian parliament passed the *Wildflower and Native Plant Protection Act*. During 1915–46 he made thirty-two contributions to the *Victorian Naturalist*; *The Orchids of Victoria*, which first appeared therein, was published as a book in 1928. In addition to his many writings for scientific journals, Pescott wrote *The Native Flowers of Victoria* (1914), *The Dahlia in Australia* (1920), *Bulb Growing in Australia* (1926), *Gardening in Australia* (1926), *Rose Growing in Australia* (1928), *Wild Flowers of Australia* (1929) and, with Charles BARRETT, *New Way Gardening* (1933). First issued in a special number of the *Victorian Historical Magazine*, his study *Pioneers of Horticulture in Victoria* (in which he acknowledged his debt to W.R. HAWKINS) was published in 1940.

E.E. PESCOTT's bookplate of a reading bushman draws together his love of the Australian BUSH and the way he, as author, communicated the joys of its NATURAL HISTORY to a wide audience

An interest in natural history led to Pescott's wider interest in Australian history and the collection of an extensive private library of natural history works and Australiana. He contributed a chapter, 'Victoriana', on his collection in Barrett's *Across the Years* (1948). Pescott's collection of articles and desiderata on Ferdinand MUELLER, entitled 'Reliquae Muelleriana', is in the National Herbarium, Melbourne; he contributed 'Notes on Mueller's Literary Work' to the *Victorian Naturalist* (1922). Most of his library was divided among his family, but many items were offered for sale by N.H. Seward in 1956. His horticultural papers are held by the State Library of Victoria. A nephew, R.T.M. PESCOTT, was director of the National Museum of Victoria (1944–57) and of the ROYAL BOTANIC GARDENS, MELBOURNE (1957–70).

IAN F. McLAREN

PESCOTT, Richard Thomas Martin (1905–1986), entomologist, museum director, and botanic gardens director, was born in Melbourne and graduated from the University of Melbourne in 1929 with a Master of Agricultural Science degree. He was entomologist to the Victorian Department of Agriculture for fifteen years, and as one of the Department's expert staff, he taught at the School of Primary Agriculture and Horticulture, BURNLEY. In 1944 he was appointed to the position of Director of the National Museum of Victoria.

Pescott became the Director of the ROYAL BOTANIC GARDENS, MELBOURNE, in 1957, following a succession of former Burnley principals: John CRONIN, Frederick RAE, and Alexander JESSEP had between them, except for a period of two years, held the directorship of the Melbourne Botanic Gardens since 1909, each having left his position as principal of the school to do so. In addition, R.T.M. Pescott's uncle, E.E. PESCOTT, also a principal at the school, had served as relieving director of the Gardens during Cronin's illness (1921–22). When R.T.M. Pescott took over, his role was to continue the maintenance program needed to retain William GUILFOYLE's concept of the Gardens, adding new local and overseas material to the plant collections as it became available. He retired as director in 1970 and undertook historical research to prepare two major books: a biography of Guilfoyle (1974) and a history of the Royal Botanic Gardens, Melbourne (1982).

LEE ANDREWS

PESTS AND DISEASES In horticulture, the term 'pest' typically refers to insects but may also refer to mites, slugs and snails, millipedes, slaters, and even WEEDS. Diseases are caused by some fungi, bacteria, mycoplasmas, viruses, and nematodes. Problems created by adverse growing conditions, such lack of nutrients, are often referred to as non-pathogenic diseases. In Australia there are hundreds of pests and diseases of crops and gardens. Problems vary with geographical location because factors such as CLIMATE and SOIL type influence pest and disease growth and development. The damage and frequency of occurrence is generally greater in commercial production than in home gardens.

Most major pests and diseases have been introduced into Australia, usually by accident in association with their host plants. This probably began with the First Fleet, and continued unchecked for more than a hundred years until federal plant quarantine legislation was first enacted in 1908. Thousands of pests and diseases present in other countries are not yet found in Australia. Many pests native to another country cause more damage in Australia than in their country of origin because their numbers can increase more easily

By 1949 the use of 'death-dealing' DDT to combat PESTS AND DISEASES in the garden was trumpeted as a human triumph over nature—a view increasingly challenged in succeeding decades as the wider effects of such CHEMICALS came under closer scrutiny

in the absence of their natural enemies and severe winters. Australia has strict quarantine laws to limit further introductions. AUSTRALIAN NATIVE PLANTS have many associated native insects, fungi, and other organisms. Relatively few of these cause problems with introduced food crops or ornamentals. Some notable exceptions are Queensland fruit fly, lightbrown apple moth, leafeating ladybird and cutworms, armyworms, and locusts.

Pests and disease-causing organisms enter and spread in gardens in various ways. For example, insect larvae and pupae may be transported in soil; nematodes may be transported in infested bulbs or leaves; fungal spores and insects, usually tiny ones such as aphids and thrips, are spread by wind; bacteria are commonly spread in running and splashing water; and viruses may be spread by feeding aphids or thrips. Control is easier to achieve using knowledge of pest and disease biology. It often involves the use of pesticides but non-CHEMICAL methods such as alteration of planting dates and trapping are increasingly favoured.   JUDY McMAUGH

PETER FRANCIS POINTS ARBORETUM, near Coleraine, Vic., contains the largest known collection of EUCALYPTUS species world-wide. A disused quarry site was selected by the Wannon Shire Council in 1966 for planting as a reserve. Community volunteers led by Mary Hope assisted, and chief among these was Peter Francis (1907–1989), who retired from contracting in 1968 due to ill health and spent the next twenty-one years establishing this ARBORETUM. Approximately one-third of the arboretum was destroyed by fire in 1983, leading to extensive replanting, now extended to thirty-seven hectares, with more than 20 000 native trees and shrubs covering more than 2000 species. This includes the *Eucalyptus* collection of 540 species and subspecies recognised by the ORNAMENTAL PLANT CONSERVATION ASSOCIATION. Management was handed to the state government in 1984 in order to secure permanent funding, and the Friends of the Points was formed. In 1999 a Eucalyptus Discovery Centre was opened in Coleraine as an extension to the arboretum.   JOHN WALTER

PEWSEY VALE, SA, near the BAROSSA VALLEY, was established by Joseph Gilbert (1800–1881) in 1839 with a homestead erected in 1843. Extensive vineyards were first planted in 1847 and old cellars remain on the property. The park-like setting of conifers and deciduous trees includes a prominent *Pinus pinea* (Stone Pine) on Pewsey Peak, a reservoir for the gardens, orchard, and homestead 'village', and originally included a DEER PARK. The HOMESTEAD GARDEN features a front garden of herbaceous perennials and large fountain with rustic rockwork centre-piece. The garden was remodelled when Walter BAGOT reconstructed the house in 1939, including relocation of pines.   DAVID JONES

PFEIFFER, Andrew Anthony Frederick (b. 1949), Sydney-born landscape designer, gained inspiration from family properties in Sydney and southern NSW before training at Kalmthout Arboretum (Belgium), ROYAL BOTANIC GARDENS, KEW, and on large estates in Britain and France. Now based in Sydney and London, he undertakes commissions internationally. His design philosophy and oeuvre are illustrated in his books *Australian Garden Design* (1985) and *A Sense of Place* (1999), the latter title suggestive of Pfeiffer's desire 'to create gardens that suit their own environment'.   RA

PHILLIPS GARDENS, Maryborough, Vic., was transformed from a municipal dam reserve in this mining town to a public garden after its reservation in the 1870s. Laid out to a 'rough sketch' by Messrs Farquhar and Mackenzie, the garden featured a LAKE with central island (planted with willows), coniferous and deciduous theme planting, and ornamental shrubs. Although the tree collection today is largely dominated by post-1945 plantings, the garden retains a jewel-like quality in its diminutive scale, lake reflections, autumn foliage, and Tuberous Begonia display.

JILL ORR-YOUNG

PHOTOGRAPHY from its inception in 1839 embraced the decorative aspects of nature, demonstrated by the publication of English co-inventor Fox Talbot's *Pencil of Nature* (1844–46). In colonial Australia, nature in its cultivated state did not capture the daguerreotypist's eye. The garden had to await the invention in 1851 of the collodion process before it began to be recorded by amateur photographers. Even then gardens were more often incidental to family portraits, buildings, or townscapes.

Following the 1850s gold rushes, a desire to record new property tempered by taste, saw the photographing in the 1860s of newly formed VILLA gardens. It was to be a representation of the garden that lasted for decades, reaching its apogee in the turn of the century publication *Representative Men at Home*, which recorded the domiciles and gardens of men of influence. Perhaps the most resonant of these type of garden photographs was the album of 1880 photographs of RIPPON LEA house and garden that accompanied its owner, Frederick Sargood, to England as a (successful) aide in finding a wife.

In the age of the sketchbook, when language was poetic and the weekly horticultural press descriptions assumed a familiarity with rare plants growing in colonial gardens, the role of photography was secondary in disseminating gardening information. It was not until the rise of photographically illustrated periodicals in the late nineteenth century that the balance shifted in favour of photography. Until then, photographs of plant specimens remained few—and when used, were likely to be for overseas audiences, as in the illustration of *Dicksonia antartica* taken from a photograph of Mount Wellington (Tas.) after a snow storm, published in *Select Ferns and Lycopods* (1868) by London nurseryman B.S. Williams. Colonial nursery proprietors also used photography to convey to their British counterparts new plant discoveries. For example, in 1870 BAPTIST sent photographs of thirteen Pacific plants to VEITCH in London. By 1885 plants were being photographed in situ on the Royal Geographical Society of Australasia's expedition to New Guinea, while in 1893 William GUILFOYLE was sending to the *Gardeners' Chronicle* in London photographs of Indian azaleas growing in Melbourne

Botanic Gardens. Guilfoyle continued to use photography when he engaged Nicholas Caire (1837–1918) to illustrate his *Australian Plants* (1909). Similarly, wealthy garden owner Russell GRIMWADE photographed plant specimens in his Melbourne garden Miegunyah to illustrate his *Anthography of the Eucalypts* (1920).

An important change occurred in the inter-war period. With the publication from the 1920s of AUSTRALIAN HOME BEAUTIFUL, which featured contributions from Edna WALLING, the photograph created a new visual literacy about gardens. So, too, did the 1920s catalogues of nurseries such as Law Somner. It was Walling's genius to capitalise on this in *Gardens in Australia* (1943) and *Cottage and Garden in Australia* (1947), where full-page black-and-white photographs were as important as the writing in creating the work's ambience. If periodicals of the inter-war period associated the garden with the feminine space of the home, this continued after the war when Helen BLAXLAND's *Flower Pieces* (1946) featured photographs by Olive Cotton and Max Dupain of floral arrangements; while Norman SPARNON's books on Japanese flower arrangement continued the imaging of the cut flower as well as new economic realities of post-war Australia. By contrast the 1960s BUSH GARDEN books of Betty MALONEY and Jean Walker, with their spare, grainy, and often elegant black and white photographs, recall a different gardening aesthetic and cultural preoccupation centred on AUSTRALIAN FLORA.

By the 1970s the availability of cheap Asian colour printing saw Australian publishers, especially the Paul Hamlyn Group, introduce colour photographic plant companions on a scale previously unknown in Australia. The large-format coffee table book meanwhile favoured the publication of the pioneering *The Great Gardens of Australia* (1976) by Howard TANNER with photography by Jane Begg. Since that time, the alliance between printing and photography has allowed for an increasing number of gardening titles characterised by such photographic lusciousness (jokingly known in the trade as 'horto-erotica') that one could ask whether the contemporary GARDENING BOOK is just an up-market GARDENING MAGAZINE in hard covers.
PAUL FOX

PICKING GARDEN: see FLOWER GARDEN

PICNIC GROUNDS, public reserves especially adapted for outdoor eating, catered for a LEISURE pursuit that had become popular in Britain in the early 1800s; but the term itself, from the French *picque-nique*, has older and more obscure origins, perhaps best explained as 'to peck' (*piquer*) with the tooth (*nique*: child's tooth). This had evolved by the 1700s into an informal communal meal to which guests brought their own food, or paid for themselves at a restaurant, but which increasingly took place outdoors.

In Australia, a favourable climate, ample public land, and diverse scenery, saw camping and eating outdoors become standard aspects of Australian leisure. Picnics reunited families and friends, school and church groups, trade unions, and others. They became an almost compulsory sideline to outdoor sporting events, and country 'picnic races' derive from this. Fireplaces for BARBECUES, water pumps, outdoor FURNITURE, shelters, and PAVILIONS were installed in many PUBLIC PARKS and gardens to cater to growing picnicking demands. Purpose-built picnic grounds became more elaborately landscaped in the 1920s and 1930s, with rustic and 'log-cabin' style shelters and furniture, using natural timber and stone construction. Children's PLAYGROUNDS also became a feature. Picnic grounds proliferated in the 1950s and 1960s with increased motor car ownership. While originally favoured for their 'natural' attributes, many became highly developed, providing a range of public amenities, kiosks, and adjunct leisure activities. In the countryside and the BUSH, less-frequented picnic spots have often better preserved their idyllic quality.
HELEN DOYLE

PICTURESQUE is one of the more confusing terms encountered in GARDEN HISTORY. It was used in the eighteenth century in a rather general sense to describe natural and designed landscapes that would make good Romantic landscape pictures in the manner of seventeenth-century artists such as Claude Lorrain (*c*. 1604–1682). Consequently a wide range of English eighteenth-century landscape gardens could be termed picturesque, from architecturally laden and artfully contrived compositions rich in symbolism, to the minimalist designs of 'Capability' BROWN and his followers, utilising little more than sweeping lawns, placid water, and clumps and belts of trees. Landscape scenery, not consciously designed but more or less modified by human intervention, might also be described as picturesque, and analysed according to its capacity to make a good landscape picture. The published works of William GILPIN encouraged travel in search of the picturesque, and the development of sophisticated critical faculties in the appreciation of its finer points. The pervasive nature and occasional absurdity of this activity were satirised in William Coombe's *Dr Syntax in Search of the Picturesque* (1812), and in some of the works of Jane Austen (1775–1817), notably *Northanger Abbey* (1797/1818).

As a formal AESTHETIC category, however, the Picturesque was not defined until 1794, in a published controversy between two Herefordshire squires and erstwhile friends, Uvedale PRICE and Richard Payne Knight (1750–1824). The two were united in their intense dislike of the Brownian landscape, but differed in their understanding of the Picturesque. Price, in *An Essay on the Picturesque* (1794), argued that there were intrinsic characteristics by which the Picturesque might be defined, following on from the work of Edmund Burke (1729–1797). In 1756 Burke had published an *Inquiry into the Origin of Our Ideas of the Sublime and the Beautiful*. By SUBLIME, Burke meant that which tends to cause awe or even terror, either by its intrinsic nature, by obscurity, by solitude, or by vastness. The Beautiful, by contrast, was connected with smoothness, gentle curves, polish, and delicacy. Thus the awesome, terrifying nature of something beyond control, was contrasted with what was pretty, elegant, and refined. The Picturesque, Price suggested, was a third aesthetic category, a middle way between these two extremes, characterised by such qualities as roughness, 'sudden variation' (implying movement, variety, and surprise), irregularity, and intricacy. As with the Beautiful and the Sublime, it was felt that these qualities, which could be found in Nature, might also be re-created, more or less successfully, in Art. Knight's view, first outlined in *The Landscape: A Didactic Poem* (1794), was that an appreciation of the Picturesque was far more subjective, dependent upon both an appreciation of landscape painting, and the notion of Associationism, as developed by his mentor Archibald Alison (1757–1839) in his *Essay on the Nature and Principles of Taste* (1790). This concept of Associationism was to do with the ideas that might spring to mind in viewing a particular object or scene. It was somewhat dependent upon the culture and education of the viewer: the associations of a ruined Roman temple would obviously be more complex for one educated in the classics, for example. While Knight disputed Price's theory on the Picturesque, the pair of illustrations prepared for *The Landscape* by Thomas Hearne—showing a landscape 'improved' in the Brownian manner, contrasted with the same landscape in desirably Picturesque garb—serves equally well to illustrate the views of both men.

From earliest days of British exploration, there is evidence of a Picturesque sensibility in viewing the Australian landscape. It may not be mere coincidence that New South Wales was so named when, shortly before Cook's voyage, Joseph BANKS had visited the famously Picturesque scenery of Persfield and the Wyndcliff, on the Wye River in south WALES. Thomas MITCHELL brought the eye of an artist, as well as military surveyor, to his explorations, and appreciated and named newly discovered landscapes accordingly. Other educated travellers, such as Louisa Anne MEREDITH, viewed the scenery of NSW, and later Tas. and Vic., in terms of the Sublime, the Picturesque, and Romantic Associationism, and wrote about it in such terms for her English readers. Likewise, early artists such as Thomas WATLING and Joseph LYCETT were evidently conscious of Picturesque aesthetics, both in selecting and composing their scenes, and in seeking to market them to the British public. Not surprisingly, this Picturesque sensibility can be traced in the work of most nineteenth-century Australian landscape artists; it also crept into more mundane areas of life, exemplified by a suburban gully in West Hobart that still rejoices in the appellation 'Salvator Rosa Glen'.

The introduction of Picturesque aesthetics into the theory and practice of LANDSCAPE GARDENING in Australia was heralded by Thomas SHEPHERD, in his *Lectures in Landscape Gardening in Australia* (1836). In his descriptions of estates such as that of Alexander MCLEAY at Elizabeth Bay, Shepherd was very appreciative of the Picturesque qualities of the natural scenery and vegetation, but also advocated its improvement where appropriate, indicating, for example that:

> At the extremity of [the] beautiful shrubbery and mowed-grass lawn, wood walks will commence, winding through thickets of trees naturally grouped among picturesque rocks. Here also rustic chairs and rustic caves are placed, and the river is seen from them through a rich foreground of natural trees and beautiful creepers.

A naturally Sublime landscape might be tamed or suitably enhanced to render it acceptably Picturesque: this was arguably the case with Knight's famous Downton estate, and it can be seen in Australia in examples such as Launceston's CATARACT GORGE. Similarly, any designed landscape might conceivably *become* Picturesque through many years of neglect, as REPTON had recognised in his scathing reference to 'the new system of Improvement by Neglect and Accident'. In practice, the successful design, from scratch, of a truly Picturesque landscape was probably quite rare—all the more so in Australia, where wild and unimproved Nature was often immediately at hand.

Most of the nineteenth-century Australian designed landscapes described by modern authors as 'Picturesque' are, in reality, either Beautiful scenery resembling an English park (such as PANSHANGER, Tas., of the 1830s), or GARDENESQUE, in either the particular sense of LOUDON, or the more general meaning of KEMP. While these landscapes may well contain elements that are products of the Picturesque, such as an irregular layout, rough rockwork, or rustic timber structures, their overall design and particularly their intended planting was designed to display the gardener's improving hand, rather than to be mistaken for the work of unassisted Nature.

By the late nineteenth century in Australia, as elsewhere, the term 'picturesque' had become debased by popular usage and had come to mean little more than 'attractive' or 'scenic'. As an aesthetic theory, the true meaning of the Picturesque was rediscovered by Christopher Hussey in the 1920s, but it languished under the pervasive shadow of MODERNISM for many decades. However, in recent years the Picturesque has become not only the subject of scholarly studies in garden history, but also a fashionable topic for theoretical discussion in the design disciplines more generally.

Christopher Hussey, *The Picturesque: Studies in a Point of View* (London, 1927, 1983); David Watkin, *The English Vision: The Picturesque in Architecture, Landscape, and Garden Design* (London, 1982); Malcolm Andrews, *The Search for the Picturesque: Landscape Aesthetics and Tourism in Britain 1760–1800* (Aldershot, Hampshire, 1989; John Dixon Hunt, *Gardens and the Picturesque: Studies in the History of Landscape Architecture* (Cambridge, Mass., 1992); Malcolm Andrews (ed.), *The Picturesque: Literary Sources & Documents* (Mountfield, East Sussex, 1994)   ANNE NEALE

PINETUM, a specialised ARBORETUM forming a collection of CONIFERS arranged according to botanical classification or for artistic effect, was popularised in the mid-nineteenth century. The pinetum reflected the interest in recent introductions such as NORTH AMERICAN conifers, and the enthusiastic advocacy of J.C. LOUDON, especially in his espousal of the GARDENESQUE, which valued foreign plants as one mode of introducing art over nature in the garden. Other books, such as William Barron's *The British Winter Garden* (1852) and VEITCH's *Manual of the Coniferae* (1881), helped promote the fashion, as did the horticultural press.

The pinetum was a feature of many large nineteenth-century Australian gardens, especially in Tas. and Vic., including BOTANIC GARDENS; ARAUCARIAS formed prominent notes, especially in NSW and Qld. MUELLER began a pinetum at MELBOURNE BOTANIC GARDEN in 1858 with 'lines of Aleppo pine, rows of Moreton Bay and Norfolk Island

Araucarias and groups of miscellaneous conifers': in 1873 this feature formed the palette for GUILFOYLE as he relocated hundreds of these trees to become focal points in his extensive landscaping. BUNCE established a pinetum in GEELONG BOTANIC GARDEN in 1861, and remnants of pineta remain at WARRNAMBOOL, CASTLEMAINE, and WILLIAMSTOWN BOTANIC GARDENS. Interest declined during the century as it became apparent how much space was required to retain shapely specimens, and because the mixed species varied in soil and climatic requirements. ROCKHAMPTON BOTANIC GARDEN contains a late example, begun in 1935 by George Simmons, specialising in *Cupressus* and *Chamaecyparis* species.

GWEN PASCOE

PINK, James (*c.* 1836–1923), gardener and nursery proprietor, worked during the 1870s in Sydney, where his floral BEDDING designs were praised in the horticultural press. He then worked as gardener at BOWEN PARK for the Queensland Acclimatisation Society and at BRISBANE BOTANIC GARDENS before assuming the role of Head Gardener at the latter in 1881 (upon the removal of Walter HILL). During his time in charge, in the period when there was no director or curator, Pink's duties of maintenance included some design input, such as opening the VISTA through the giant BAMBOOS across the old Alice Street lagoon towards Parliament House, devising intricate bedding and ribbon border displays in the upper Queen's Park area, clearing all understorey vegetation along river, and asphalting the gravel paths throughout. Pink suffered permanent physical damage in an accident to his left arm in 1882 but remained active nonetheless. He published several horticultural articles on lawn grasses (*Planter and Farmer*, 1882), plant hybridisation (*Proceedings of the Royal Society of Queensland*, 1884), gardening advice (ALMANACS by Pugh and Thorne, 1880s), and fruit culture (Alfred Midgley's *Queensland Illustrated Guide*, 1888).

Pink left the Brisbane Botanic Gardens in 1886. He started an ORCHARD on his land at Wellington Point near Brisbane and in 1890 set up Badgers Nursery with Alexander COWAN, specialising in fruit trees and roses. Their new enterprise of plant, seed, and cut-flower production, advantageously located on the rich red volcanic soils of the Redland Bay district and served by the Cleveland railway line, was glowingly described by William SOUTTER in the *Queensland Horticulturist*. The partnership lasted about five years, after which Pink and his family carried on the business, with Mrs Pink continuing the seed sales into the late 1920s.

JEANNIE SIM

PINK, Olive Muriel (1884–1975), artist, Aboriginal rights activist, anthropologist, and gardener, was born in Hobart. Her interest in INDIGENOUS FLORA grew from her love of art and childhood sketching expeditions in the bush around Hobart. She specialised in watercolour paintings of flowers. As an anthropologist she carried out research among the Arrernte and Warlpiri peoples during the 1930s, collecting and sketching plants as she did so. With almost no income, in 1938 she moved to central Australia, spending four years camped at Thompson's Rockhole before moving into Alice Springs (NT). There, she established a domestic garden around her hut on Gregory Terrace, growing fruit, vegetables, and flowers for sale. When conflict with the neighbouring firefighters led to her eviction, she started again on what is now the nineteen hectares of the Olive Pink Botanic Garden (gazetted in 1956 with the help of (Sir) Paul Hasluck). Her concept for a garden devoted to the indigenous flora of the ARID regions was unique at the time. She established a domestic garden to supply her own needs, surrounding it with protective CACTI. For the public garden, she dug watering channels to support the mulga alley, gums, bean trees, and flowers she grew from seed. She was more than seventy when she began this work, and became increasingly reclusive. When

Ferdinand MUELLER's uncompromisingly regimental PINETUM in the MELBOURNE BOTANIC GARDENS and adjoining domain was planted with earnest zeal, although when William GUILFOYLE relandscaped the area (pictured here from Government House tower) many of the trees were thinned or relocated to conform to more picturesque ideals

John JAMPIJINPA came to work with her she had found the ideal assistant. When he died, Pink carried on alone. She was a woman of great courage and perseverance.

Julie Marcus, *The Indomitable Miss Pink: A Life in Anthropology* (Sydney, 2001)   JULIE MARCUS

PLANS: see GARDEN PLANS

PLANT To some, plants represent the essential component of gardening, while to others—often those fond of the term 'plant material'—they are merely elements within an overall design scheme. Nonetheless, whichever role they play, plants are fundamental to the concept of a GARDEN. Different selections and combinations of plants often earmark certain periods in garden culture—especially through new plant introductions as a result of PLANT COLLECTING and BREEDING—and may reflect attitudes to changing STYLES. Vast numbers of plants have been used in Australian gardens by incorporating exotic, native and indigenous floras: native and indigenous plants form the major basis of contemporary approaches to planting styles. The use of such a wide range of plants follows an inherited British emphasis on gardens as collections of plants for display—rather than the CHINESE and JAPANESE approaches, for example, which subordinate plant selection to traditional design ideals.

The celebrated English landscape designer Russell Page (1906–1985) stated in his book *The Education of a Gardener* (1962) that since the eighteenth century 'I would say that in Europe plant material has been of far more importance than style in the evolution of gardens'. In Australia, the result of this approach has been to produce gardens with unique and distinctive combinations of plants that, for the most part, distinguish them from the European models they intended to emulate. In addition to a base of familiar European garden subjects, native AUSTRALIAN PLANTS, SUCCULENTS, exotic and native PALMS, and various other selections from parallel CLIMATIC zones—especially SOUTH AFRICA and the MEDITERRANEAN—have been brought together to form an expanded garden flora. This shift in floristic composition is made even more pronounced by the exclusion of a range of plants traditionally cultivated in European gardens, such as many of the maples, magnolias, and rhododendrons, from all but the few cool-climate locations (such as those where HILL-STATION gardens became established).

In an attempt to cultivate a wide range of plants, the boundaries restricted by climate and edaphic factors are expanded by manipulation of the growing conditions. For example, the application of WATER to overcome drought has been essential to grow many plants under optimal conditions. The skill in gardening in Australia has therefore traditionally been to change the conditions to grow as many plants as possible, rather than to select plants that will tolerate the limitations of an existing environment. On the other hand, a large number of introduced plants well suited to existing conditions have become environmental WEEDS.

Biologically, plants are placed in the Kingdom Plantae. Originally, biological organisms were divided between plants and animals, although this division was refined after it became clear that plants actually consisted of a wide diversity of organisms difficult to group together in a single category. Thus, the array of organisms was subsequently divided into five kingdoms, with the old plant group essentially being divided into four: Blue-green Algae (Kingdom Monera), other Algae (Kingdom Protista), Fungi (Kingdom Fungi), and mosses, ferns, and seed-bearing plants (Kingdom Plantae). This is not completely satisfactory, however, as some of these groups are now thought to contain certain assemblages from different evolutionary lines. The fungi, for example, have been further divided into three Kingdoms: Protoctista, Chromista, and Eumycota.

Divisions within the plant kingdom follow a formal taxonomic, hierarchical classification system. One of the main divisions occurs between plants that produce seed, and non-seed-bearing organisms such as the FERNS. Further division is made in seed-bearing plants between the Gymnopermae (plants with naked seeds, including the widely cultivated CONIFERS) and the flowering plants or Angiospermae (with enclosed seeds). The flowering plants are additionally divided between the monocotoledonae (monocots), with one seed leaf (they often have strap-like leaves), containing a large number of the BULBOUS plants, ORCHIDS, GRASSES, BAMBOO, and palms—and dictotyledonae (dicots) with two seed leaves (containing the majority of the trees, shrubs, and herbaceous plants cultivated in gardens). While this formal system is used to name plants scientifically, divisions of plants used in gardens and horticulture are less clear.

In addition to the above groupings, overlapping form and life-cycle categories are used: for example ANNUAL, PERENNIAL, HERBACEOUS, SHRUB, TREE, CLIMBER, deciduous, and evergreen; these now form widely accepted LANDSCAPE PLANT TYPES. Typical categories used in nineteenth-century Australian plant catalogues were: select ornamental trees (often large deciduous trees); conifers; ornamental shrubs; bulbs; herbaceous plants; climbers; palms; ferns; succulent plants; edging plants; trees that were both useful and ornamental (including FRUIT trees such as the loquat, which produced fruit but also had large bold and textual foliage); VEGETABLES; HERBS; and specimen trees (trees usually planted in a lawn as the single display feature). In addition, successive catalogue editions usually devoted a section to NOVELTIES containing new and sometimes bizarre introductions to cultivation. Many of these new introductions come under the formal taxonomic classification of a CULTIVAR (cultivated variety) to distinguish them from variants below the species level that might be recognised in the wild. These variants are either raised in cultivation or perpetuated to maintain a selected form in cultivation. Many of these variants are differentiated by characteristic differences such as flower doubling, flower or foliage colour changes, variegation, differences in growth rate (such as dwarfing), and overall form variations that produce weeping, spreading, and upright habits. A wide range of cultivars is listed in Australian catalogues; many have been raised locally. Large groups that have traditionally been cultivated include CAMELLIAS, NARCISSUS, RHODODENDRONS (including azaleas), and FUCHSIAS. The Australian flora has also provided a rich source of new cultivars, especially since the rise in interest in Australian plants for cultivation in the 1960s and 1970s. Some species that hybridise readily, such as the GREVILLEAS, have produced large numbers of variants formally recognised in cultivation. These cultivars are registered by the Australian Cultivar Registration Authority based at the AUSTRALIAN NATIONAL BOTANIC GARDENS.

While cultivation of a wide range of plants continues, especially in SUBURBAN GARDENS, more recently there has been a strong interest in raising indigenous plants for ECOLOGICAL restoration and REVEGETATION schemes in an attempt to produce more sustainable landscapes and to overcome environmental degradation. ML

PLANTATION was often used in Australia in its widest sense to denote a group of like plants, particularly economic plants or crops (such as sugar-cane or commercial wood lots). In the lexicon of LANDSCAPE GARDENING, it was more commonly used to denote, as LOUDON observed (1822), 'Assemblages of Trees'. He classified the extent of these in ascending order as groups, clumps (if compact) or thickets, masses, and woods (natural or artificial) or forests (natural only). Further subdivision was provided by outline: rows or lines; clumps (round), platoons (square), or stripes, screen, or belts (oblong); and thickets or masses. Disposition of trees included rows, squares, parallelograms, quincunx, groves, woods, copses, or AVENUES. Whereas a plantation usually implied a single species (such as a WINDBREAK of *Eucalyptus cladocalyx*) or group of similar plants (for instance, a geographically themed ARBORETUM), a SHRUBBERY encompassed a more promiscuous range of plant types. Modern plantations touch upon diverse aesthetic, commercial, ecological, legal, and philosophical concerns. RA

PLANT BREEDING The production of new useful and ornamental garden plants by artificial means was developed in Europe during the first decades of the nineteenth century and soon became popular both with amateurs and in the NURSERY trade. J.C. BIDWILL introduced plant breeding to Australia. He arrived in Sydney in 1838 from Exeter, England, where he had raised a number of new plants. His hibiscus, 'Sydneyi', a hybrid between two Australian species, was released in 1843. He co-operated with William MACARTHUR, Edward Macarthur BOWMAN, and others in raising new varieties of *Amaryllis, Camellia, Crinum, Erythrina, Gladiolus, Hippeastrum, Ixia, Nerium*, and *Passiflora*, as well as ROSES. Nursery proprietors then began distributing plants of Australian origin, with bouvardias, CAMELLIAS, DAHLIAS, pelargoniums, ROSES, and verbenas being especially popular. It is not possible in most instances to say whether they were raised in Australian nurseries or merely marketed by them, or whether they were produced artificially or were chance seedlings or sports.

At the turn of the century G.H. KERSLAKE of Sydney was a most versatile and successful plant breeder who raised new and greatly admired bouvardias, carnations, chrysanthemums, dahlias, gloxinias, pentstemons, and roses. Other horticulturists were more selective. T.W. POCKETT in Melbourne concentrated on raising CHRYSANTHEMUMS, and his new yearly releases soon attracted favourable attention both here and in Europe and North America. The Australian visit of Peter BARR stimulated the interest of Leonard Buckland (1872–1930), Alister CLARK, George TITHERADGE, and others in the raising of new DAFFODILS and this pursuit became popular, especially in Tas. and Vic., with many important varieties being produced. Clark, described as 'our greatest rose hybridist', set out to raise roses suited to Australian climatic conditions. He released his first introduction, 'Lady Medallist', in 1912 and in 1948, the year before his death, he published the names of the best 118 roses selected from the thousands of seedlings he had raised.

As well as roses, new carnations and dahlias were raised in all states by a large number of enthusiasts. SWEET PEAS were favoured in NSW where the discovery in 1904 by W.H. Young of an early-flowering Sweet Pea growing among his 'Spencers' led to the development of the world-famed Australian early-flowered strain over the next thirty years. Another annual to be improved was the Iceland Poppy, when in the 1920s Mrs J.S. Oliver of Coonara, Essendon (Vic.), bred the 'Coonara Pink' strain with pastel colours and the 'Coonara Giant' strain with large blooms and long stems. The early plant breeders had raised new GLADIOLI—Henry PARCEL for instance had raised seedlings in the 1860s—and interest in them continued. By the early 1920s Vic. had become the centre, with the ERREY Bros. of Camperdown the leading breeders. Each year until the mid-1960s they released gladiolus NOVELTIES, and from the early 1930s also released new bearded irises bred by them. With irises being increasingly popular, STINTON's Claremont Nurseries of Geelong (Vic.) and William P. Aylett of Mangoplah (NSW) regularly listed novelties of their own. While watsonias were never as keenly sought as gladioli or irises, John CRONIN of Melbourne Botanic Gardens, who was a keen plant breeder, worked to improve them, introducing 'a number of pretty shades into these elegant bulbous plants'. In 1939 an amateur, Roy Wallace of Warburton (Vic.), produced a hybrid *Lilium* he named 'Jillian Wallace'. This has become widely known and acclaimed throughout the world, and is certainly one of the greatest triumphs of Australian plant breeding.

A number of local trees and shrubs, mostly propagated from chance seedlings, have been used in our gardens. *Erica* 'Webbleyana' raised at Malvern in the early 1900s, was locally popular, while *Prunus* 'Pollardii', said to have originated at Creswick (Vic.) *c.* 1904, is internationally known. So too is *Fraxinus angustifolia* ssp. *oxycarpa* 'Raywood', distinguished by its autumn foliage colour. Found growing at SEWELL's Nursery, Aldgate (SA), it was purchased by T.C. WOLLASTON and planted at his property, Raywood, then first released by the Ray Nursery in 1928. A great improvement in the size of Crepe Myrtle flowers was brought about first by the raising in Brisbane in the 1880s of *Lagerstroemia* 'Matthewsii' (now *L. indica* 'Rubra') and the further breeding done by S.H. EAVES, the Brisbane nursery proprietor who produced *L.* 'Eavesii' *c.* 1915. *Prunus* 'Elvins' was discovered in Hawthorn (Vic.) in the 1940s, and is noted for its exceptional pink flowering. A hybrid *Crataegus*, considered the best of the large red-fruited sorts, appeared at the

Plant collecting

Yarralumla Nursery, Canberra, in the 1920s. It was selected by J.P. Hobday and issued as *Crataegus* 'Smithiana' and *C.* 'Smithii'. Confusingly, a Melbourne-raised *Crataegus* had been given similar names. A *Tecoma*, thought to have been a hybrid raised in Melbourne, was introduced to Britain in 1889 to considerable acclaim and named *Tecoma* 'Smithii' after its putative raiser (but has since been identified as a species, *T. alata*).

In Britain in the nineteenth century, many cultivars of AUSTRALIAN NATIVE PLANTS (then popular in GREENHOUSES) were raised, while in Germany, Erbritch, a plant breeder of Erfurt, produced a strain of giant annual helichrysums in 1856. In Australia where special forms of plants were found growing wild they were introduced into gardens. In 1869 for instance a double flowered form of *Epacris* was exhibited in Sydney. This may be the same plant that received a First Class Certificate from the ROYAL HORTICULTURAL SOCIETY in London in 1880. It was the 1940s before Australian plant breeders, including nursery growers and hobbyists, began experimenting with the local flora to any extent. Although other plants were selected, *Grevillea* attracted early interest. Leo HODGE selected Australian plants from his Victorian farm gardens for his Poorinda cultivars. Other selectors of *Grevillea* included Bill CANE, whose *G. rosmarinifolia* selections are especially noted, and David GORDON, whose *G.* 'Robyn Gordon' (a garden hybrid, *G. bipinnatifida* X *G. banksii*) is widely planted. F.C. PAYNE raised *Hakea* 'Paynei', *Melaleuca* 'Paynei', and *Thryptomene* 'Paynei', while George ALTHOFER, E.M.M. BODDY, and others commenced the development that has led to the wide choice of CULTIVARS of Australian plants now available. Bill MOLYNEUX is prominent for *Grevillea* selections labelled 'Austraflora', and he and Sue Forrester are significant selectors of many Australian plants including *Acacia*, *Banksia*, and *Eucalyptus*.

Controlled breeding of Australian plants began with *Anigozanthos* hybrids produced by M. Turner in Monbulk (Vic.). His many hybrids, 'Bush Gems', were produced from the late 1970s onwards and include the well-known 'Bush Ranger'. Many of these hybrids have been exported as cut flowers. Professor M. Sedgley in Adelaide is recognised for breeding and development of *Banksia* as cut flowers. Most notable is 'Waite Orange' (*B. hookeriana* X *B. prionotes*). Also in SA, T. Loffler at Waikerie has selected *Dodonea* and *Maireana* for cut flowers. Selections of *Chamelaucium* and hybrids of *Anigozanthos* have been produced by B. Jack in WA; these include *A.* 'Big Red' and a range of cut flower *Chamelaucium*. N. PEATE and A. Salmon at Plant Growers Australia in Melbourne have produced hybrids of *Brachyscome*, including 'Lemon Twist' and 'Pink Haze', and are successfully exporting these through Outback Plants Pty Ltd. Dr D. Beardsell, of the Victorian Institute for Horticultural Development, is recognised for 'elite' selections of Australian plants for street trees, selected from controlled-pollination orchards. The Australian Daisy Study Group is important for many Brachyscomes from wild and garden selections.

Specialty food crops have been bred in Australia, with many important fruits being the subject of breeding to suit local conditions. Australia is a world leader in genetic engineering of non-crop plants. In 1986, Calgene Pacific Pty Ltd was established to develop cut-flower varieties using genetic engineering. Their goals included use of additional 'blue' genes to give blue roses, carnations, chrysanthemums, and gerberas, as well as the insertion of an anti-ethylene gene to prolong cut flower vase life. The anti-ethylene gene has been successfully manipulated in carnations to produce a long-lived flower in vases. Florigene Pty Ltd, as the company is now known, has not produced true blue flowers, but has instead released strong purple carnations under the name of 'Moon Dust'. Molecular genetics has become significant in developing plant breeding strategies and understanding native plant populations. These molecular techniques are widespread, used by all plant research institutions in Australia.

RICHARD CLOUGH and JAMES WILL

Hybridisation to produce varieties suited to Australian conditions was a principal objective of much PLANT BREEDING, and some of the NOVELTIES that resulted were a striking success among their target audience

PLANT COLLECTING for scientific study, cultivation, and economic and medicinal exploitation has a long tradition. In the field of BOTANY, taxonomic botanists base their studies mostly on dried HERBARIUM specimens collected in the field, while horticulturists and economic botanists have long hunted far and wide for live plants, seeds, and cuttings. A number of plants were introduced to Europe by the Romans and, later, by the Crusaders of the twelfth and thirteenth centuries, although records of plant collecting expeditions date back to ancient Egypt. For the Europeans, this pursuit was most intense in the seventeenth, eighteenth, and nineteenth centuries, when new lands were opened up by exploration and colonisation. Trophies from the natural world were returned to the major cities of Europe, whose citizens were hungry for the beautiful, the curious, and the new. Collectors included amateurs as well as those trained at BOTANIC GARDENS or employed by prominent NURSERY proprietors such as the James VEITCH.

Many popular garden plants were originally brought into cultivation by the activities of avid collectors, and eventually found their way to Australia. Among the most prolific collectors—many of whom are commemorated by plant names—were Pierre d'Incarville (1706–1757, China), Carl Thunberg (1743–1822, South Africa and Japan), Friedrich Humboldt (1769–1859, Central and South America and Mexico), Aime Bonpland (1773–1858, Central and South America), Nathaniel Wallich (1782–1854, the Himalayas, Malaysia, and Indonesia), Ecklon (1795–1868, South Africa), David Douglas (1798–1834, North America), Zeyher (1799–1858, South Africa), Robert Fortune (1813–1880, East Asia), Joseph HOOKER (1817–1911, the Himalayas), Augustine Henry (1857–1930, China), George Forrest (1873– 1932, China and the Himalayas), Frank Kingdon-Ward (1885–1958, China and Tibet), and Ernest Henry Wilson (1876–1930, China).

The AUSTRALIAN FLORA was a great enticement to Europe's wealthy gentry, prominent nurseries, and government scientists: more than eighty per cent of the species are endemic, and they display many unique and spectacular features. After an initial surge of interest, however, Australian plants generally faded from favour in the greenhouses of Europe, where the CLIMATE was not suitable for many plants and their cultural requirements were not understood. This understanding is vital if plants are to be ACCLIMATISED when they are taken from their natural habitat. In more recent times, places with MEDITERRANEAN climates have searched out our native plants. EUCALYPTS and ACACIAS in particular have proved successful, for example, in California.

The rigours and deprivations involved in collecting, storing and transporting specimens from difficult environments tested human ingenuity. Many means of fending off insects, damp, mould, and salt spray were devised, and the remarkable sealed glass WARDIAN CASE was invented for sea travel. Nevertheless, the collectors' success rate was generally dismally low.

Early collectors were mostly on government business, but a few were professional collectors: they usually visited briefly and confined their activities to the coast. Abel Tasman is known to have made collections as early as 1642; he was followed by the privateer William DAMPIER, some of whose specimens were collected in the north-west in 1699. Perhaps the most famous collectors were Joseph BANKS and Daniel SOLANDER with Cook in the *Endeavour*; their successes were celebrated in the change of the name of Stingray Harbour to Botany Bay. Banks remained influential for many years, and he encouraged collectors to sent material to him in England. Other prominent early collectors of this period include George CALEY, Allan CUNNINGHAM, Robert BROWN and Archibald Menzies (1754–1842, Britain); Karl HUGEL and Johann PREISS (Germany); Jaques-Julien LABILLARDIÈRE and Jean-Baptiste Leschenault de la Tour (1773–1826, France); and Franz Sieber (1789–1844, Czechoslovakia).

From the 1830s the focus shifted from sending specimens overseas to retaining them within Australia. Collectors were now residents—often interested amateurs—rather than visitors on official business, and they began to collect from inland regions. Botanists arrived and laid firm foundations for the future, encouraging Australian clergymen, geologists, amateur and professional botanists, and various explorers to send them specimens to be retained in Australian herbaria. Pre-eminent among the botanists was Ferdinand MUELLER, himself a remarkable explorer and prodigious worker, who collected in inland regions prior to major settlement.

Contemporary botanists still collect plants for herbaria to supplement their studies and to improve our knowledge of plant variation and classification, although little collecting for horticulture continues. Specimens of vascular plants are collected in the field: notes of their location and characteristics are kept in collecting books. The specimens are then pressed completely dry between newspaper and cardboard so they can be stored for future reference, virtually in perpetuity, in herbaria. Collecting is, however, strictly controlled, and a government permit is required for collecting in most areas. Seed is now accumulated in gene banks in preparation for future needs, most notably the revegetation of natural areas with plants that are indigenous to a particular locality. Plants that are rare, or threatened in the wild, are maintained in (PLANT) CONSERVATION collections.

Early enthusiasm for live plant introductions has been tempered by the unintended introduction of environmental WEEDS and potentially devastating PESTS AND DISEASES. Many parts of Australia have, for example, become infested with South African plants of the Iris family, while South Africa has vast tracts of land blanketed by Australian hakeas, wattles, and melaleucas. Greed in collecting has reduced many plants to extinction, and legislation has been enacted to attempt the protection in the wild of popular horticultural groups such as ORCHIDS, CACTI, and CYCADS. Collecting has become more selective, with collectors searching for plants with provenances of special value for horticulture and forestry: specially adapted forms with improved aesthetic potential or functional attributes useful on difficult sites. Australia's flowering plants, CONIFERS, and FERNS are now well documented, except for parts of northern Australia, and the scientific focus is shifting to the less well known elements of the flora: bryophytes, fungi, and algae. More controversially, plant prospecting for pharmaceutical products is under way worldwide; dividends may be promised to local communities, but this form of collecting (bioprospecting) has raised complex moral and intellectual property issues.

Kenneth Lemmon, *The Golden Age of Plant Hunters* (London, 1968)

ROGER SPENCER

PLANT CONSERVATION has become a vital activity for many organisations and individuals involved in land management, as large losses of vegetation through human activity occur apace worldwide. An estimated 60 000 plant species—about a quarter of the known species—will become threatened over the next few decades. Reductions in plant diversity on this scale not only cause the destruction of many animal species, reliant on a diverse habitat for survival, but human survival itself will also become seriously jeopardised. In addition to human reliance on plants for food, fuel, clothing, shelter, and medicine, plant diversity is also essential to maintain ENVIRONMENTAL balance.

Plant conservation programs dealing with natural communities can be divided into two main components. *In situ* conservation—conservation in wild localities—is considered of primary importance, and in Australia is undertaken largely as a result of government policy at all levels and by government agencies or related organisations such as GREENING AUSTRALIA, Trust for Nature, and LANDCARE groups. For gardens, *ex situ* conservation—cultivation of plants in gardens, beyond their wild localities—has become an important backup to *in situ* conservation. The cultivation of rare and endangered plants—those considered to be under threat in the wild, or that exist in drastically reduced numbers—has become an essential part of the work of BOTANIC GARDENS and ARBORETA, which together implement a worldwide Plant Conservation Strategy. The formation of SEED banks to establish a repository of genetic diversity, with storage under ideal conditions to maximise longevity, is also part of this strategy. Seed banks are also maintained by other agencies involved in conservation work, some for the practical purposes of REVEGETATION using INDIGENOUS PLANTS. The success of the *ex situ* program has not only been in the collection and rescuing of endangered plants by establishing them in cultivation, but also in the rediscovery of plants already in cultivation that were thought to be extinct, or at least rare in the wild. For example, *Sophora toromiro* was thought to be extinct, but was found in cultivation in the Royal Botanic Gardens, Melbourne, as a direct result of the international network set up as part of the Botanic Gardens Conservation Strategy. This plant is now being PROPAGATED to increase its numbers for reintroduction into its wild locality.

Garden plants have also been actively conserved in recent times. Collections of cultivated plants are held by garden enthusiasts either individually or through dedicated groups. Plants in cultivation can also be lost, often as a result of changing fashions, or simply because a nursery that propagated a certain group of plants ceases operation. Interest in the conservation of 'old fashioned' or 'heirloom' plants developed with the rise of COTTAGE GARDENS in the 1970s and 1980s and from managers of HERITAGE PLACES in growing appropriate plants for a particular period. Organisations such as the ORNAMENTAL PLANT CONSERVATION ASSOCIATION OF AUSTRALIA have facilitated the establishment and maintenance of collections in various geographic locations for a range of plant groups. Perhaps the most compelling justification for the conservation of cultivated plants comes from those concerned with maintaining collections of traditional fruit and vegetable CULTIVARS, anxious to maintain quality and diversity in taste and form against modification brought about by PLANT BREEDING and gene manipulation to better suit mass cultivation, transport, appearance, and shelf life. ML

PLANTER AND FARMER (1882–90s) was established in Brisbane, edited and published monthly by pioneering journalist and ALMANAC compiler Ebenezer Thorne. Styled on the *Southern Cultivator* (Georgia, USA), the *Planter and Farmer* sought to inform and promote dialogue among agriculturists and horticulturists in Qld. Considerable space was given to horticulture, especially ACCLIMATISATION of fruit and other plants for the TROPICAL garden. In 1885 the *QUEENSLAND AGRICULTURIST* was incorporated, its editor, Theodore WRIGHT, taking charge of the revamped journal. RA

PLAYGROUNDS The setting aside of areas specifically for CHILDREN's play is of comparatively recent origin, with examples dating from about the 1880s in Europe and the USA. The earliest public playgrounds in Australia were established in the Sydney DOMAIN and CENTENNIAL PARK. According to J.H. Maiden's paper 'The Parks of Sydney' (1902), these were 'an innovation for Australia' and followed overseas examples of gymnasia 'with swings, trapezes, see-saws, parallel and horizontal bars, and ladders of rope and wood'.

Playground design has generally reflected society's attitude to childhood. Middle-class reformers, such as Maybanke ANDERSON (NSW) and Mary Josephine BEDFORD (Qld), saw playgrounds as vehicles for helping the poor and for lifting the moral tone of the community. The playgrounds they encouraged were fenced to exclude undesirable outside influences, and were supervised by a trained supervisor. There was space for organised play and separate areas for boys and girls.

Between the wars supervised and unsupervised playgrounds were constructed. Generally the design of playgrounds changed little—metal pipe equipment replaced timber—but the emphasis was still firmly on the acquisition of physical skills and the release of surplus energy. This was widespread in Australia until the 1970s, and in some cases well beyond, with the typical playground consisting of several fixed pipe structures—swings and slides, with perhaps a steamroller, on level and cleared sites, with minimal consideration of landscape elements such as trees, gardens, and landform.

The late 1960s saw various changes in playground design in Australia due to a combination of factors: overseas influences, such as the development of adventure playgrounds in Europe; the environmental movement of the 1960s and the preference for natural materials; the increasing employment of designers, such as LANDSCAPE ARCHITECTS and playground designers; and the greater stress on the importance of play. Although very few so-called adventure playgrounds in Australia followed the European precedent of a supervised playground, where waste construction materials were available for children to develop their own play spaces, there was considerable innovation. The National Capital Development Commission developed a number of pioneering playgrounds in CANBERRA, for example: Weston Park in Yarralumla

Pleasure gardens

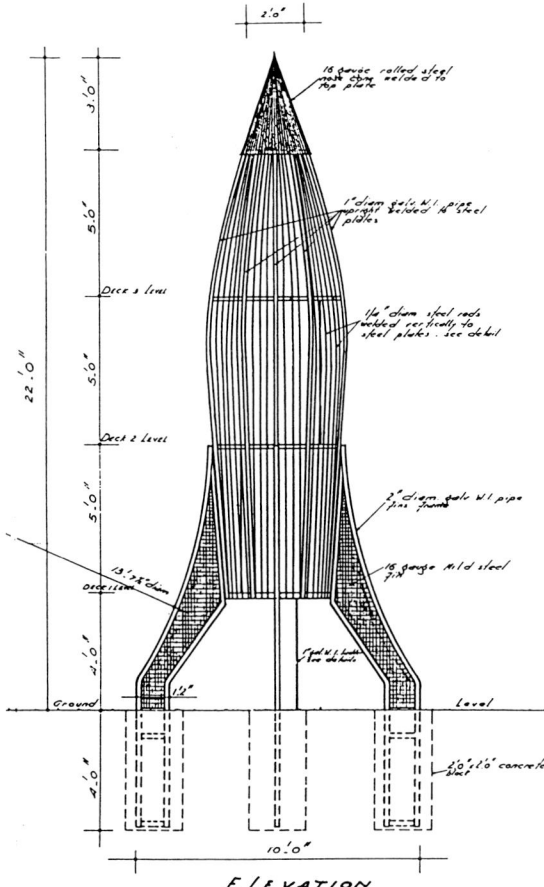

This proposed rocket ship (1963) for the PLAYGROUND at Erskineville (NSW) captured a contemporary fascination for space travel, and was soon popular in playgrounds across the country

(planned 1968, completed early 1970s) used a combination of log-climbing equipment, a cave, forts, TREE HOUSES, and a shallow lake for paddling.

More recently there has been a strong emphasis on safety. This has resulted in the removal of equipment considered unsafe—such as rockets and boat swings—and its replacement with catalogue equipment of often limited appeal to older children. Yet a number of innovative playgrounds that encourage creative play in attractive surroundings have been developed, often in conjunction with community groups.

BARBARA VAN DEN BROEK

PLAZA, although not a term widely used in Australia, usefully encompasses a range of urban spaces that recall its origins in SPAIN as an open communal space. In early LAND SURVEYS of townships, reserves for market places, small ornamental parks, gardens, or plantations, and even some forms of watering place—a spring, well, or bore, for example—were set aside, often in hope rather than expectation of development. Grander residential SQUARES, with their private commitment to development (at least on the frontages), often fared better than state-owned reserves, although local government in many instances developed urban spaces that now engender considerable community attachment. In the late twentieth century, the plaza has again attracted attention as part of URBAN DESIGN, whether as a high-rise forecourt or pedestrian mall (common from the 1970s) with commercial objectives, or more sophisticated community or institutional spaces such as Melbourne's Federation Square (2002). RA

PLEACHING, a technique dating from the seventeenth century, means to entwine, interlace, tangle, or plait, and in the horticultural context usually refers to interlaced and plaited boughs of a tree forming an arch or ARBOUR. This usually involves tying the young tree to a trellis or frame. The upright branches are then pruned, and horizontal branch growth is encouraged or trained along the support and interwoven or plaited to give the pleached effect. Upright branches must be continually pruned to prevent the shading of the pleached boughs, and to allow light to reach the leaves of the framework. The technique is known to work well with beech, hornbeam, apple, pear, and peach trees, but can also be used with other plants such as grapes and wisteria. In an appropriate landscape the effect can be stunning.

GREG MOORE

PLEASURE GARDENS, often later known as amusement parks, were popular in Australia from the 1850s. Like London haunts such as Vauxhall, Surrey Gardens, and Cremorne, these summer amusements became notorious for the activities of pick-pockets and prostitutes. In Adelaide, theatre manager George Selth Coppin (1819–1906) advertised in 1851 that he had laid out the grounds of his Semaphore Hotel 'after the plan of Surry [sic] Zoological Gardens'. More successful were Cremorne Gardens established in Melbourne and Sydney. Melbourne's Cremorne was started in 1852 by bankrupt caterer James Ellis (1812–1874), creator of London's Cremorne. Ellis developed land formerly owned and landscaped by Henry GINN at Richmond on the Yarra; a steamboat, the *Gondola*, ferried patrons from Melbourne. Attractions included an elaborate dancing ROTUNDA, the Pantheon Theatre, a 'Swiss Tree House', tight-rope performances above the lake, and firework displays over a huge modelled and painted panorama. Australia's first successful balloon ascent occurred there in 1858. Cremorne was managed by Coppin between 1856 and 1863, until his insolvency necessitated its sale to the proprietor of a private mental asylum. Ginn's original landscaping had been elaborated over the years, and Coppin placed imported plaster copies of classical STATUES amid the ARBOURS. Some of these statues were later moved to Melbourne's FITZROY GARDENS.

Sydney's Cremorne Gardens was established in 1856 at Mosman Bay on the north shore of Sydney Harbour. People travelled to Cremorne by ferry, and *bals masqués* and PICNICS were the main activities. Not as elaborate as its Melbourne namesake, the gardens nevertheless remained a popular summer amusement until the 1870s. The name Cremorne

The Sir Joseph Banks Hotel, developed at Botany Bay (NSW) from 1844, incorporated an extensive PLEASURE GARDEN with landscaped grounds, a menagerie, and even play equipment for children and the young at heart—a uniquely Australian commemoration of botany's great patron

Gardens was later used for outdoor amusements in Perth (1890s), Kalgoorlie (1910s–20s), St Kilda (1910s–20s), and the Cremorne Theatre, Brisbane (1910s–54). Other Sydney pleasure gardens included Vauxhall at Randwick, Athol near Bradleys Head, and Sir Joseph Banks Hotel at Botany. Amusements included balloon flights, dancing, quoits, and even ZOOLOGICAL exhibits.

Private pleasure gardens were also popular on the goldfields, where amusement was based on a mix of ORCHARDS, VINEYARDS, SPORTS facilities, and BEER GARDENS. This form of COMMERCIAL GARDEN was often an extension of a hotel or nursery, and examples include establishments run by John CHEYNE (Qld) and Friedrich HIRSCHI (Vic.), and also the garden at BELMONT (Vic.).

Early twentieth-century outdoor entertainments were influenced by the NORTH AMERICAN Coney Island style where concrete, chicken wire, and painted timber were the main landscape components. In Melbourne (1904–1909), Princes Court near the Yarra (now part of the Victorian Arts Centre site) was the first of the amusement parks where mechanical rides were the main attraction. Dreamland, which opened at St Kilda in 1908, was followed by the long-lived Luna Park on the same site from 1912. Sydney followed a similar pattern of beach-side amusements, with Wonderland at Waverley (1906–11), White City Gardens, Rushcutters Bay (1913–18), and Luna Park at Milsons Point (1935–). There was also a short-lived Luna Park at Glenelg, near Adelaide, in the late 1920s; collectively, these parks were forerunners to THEME PARKS of the late twentieth century.

The term pleasure garden, or more commonly pleasure grounds, also described the ornamental grounds attached to a residence (in contradistinction to the productive areas of the KITCHEN GARDEN). MIMI COLLIGAN

PLUCK, Patrick Joseph (d. 1903), was gardener to Andrew Lang Petrie (1854–1928), scion of the well-known Brisbane family of builders. Petrie's residence (Mooloomburram) overlooked Albion Park, speculatively developed as a major amusement centre, but on which Petrie lost £20 000 in a forced sale in 1891. With his employer's move to modest premises, Pluck started the Albion Nursery and worked as a landscape gardener, specialising in 'The formation of TENNIS Grounds' to capitalise on this newly fashionable sport. RA

PLUMRIDGE, Frederick John (1814–1857), was born at Holyport, Berkshire, England, and worked as a gardener, probably for Edward Sugden at Boyle Farm, Thames Ditton, Surrey. His services as secretary of the Long Ditton United Gardeners and Land Stewards' Mutual Instruction Society were rewarded by certificate in 1846. Plumridge emigrated with his family, arriving at Port Phillip in 1849. His two sons, Frederick John jnr (1840–1887) and Henry Edward (1842–1910), continued the family horticultural tradition, with Henry and his son, Hector Harold Plumridge (1877–1971), running a florist's business based at South Brighton (now Moorabbin). Charles Louis Plumridge (1878–1961), a son of Frederick jnr, was a long-serving curator for the City of Kew and well-known member of Melbourne's horticultural community, while a grandson, Arthur John (Jack) Plumridge (1901–1990), was a long-time staff member at Burnley and from 1958 was a pioneering RADIO broadcaster on the ABC. RA

POCKETT, Thomas William (1857–1952), chrysanthemum specialist and parks curator, was born near Cheltenham, England, and aged 10 went to work in the Ireton House gardens. Over the next eleven years he gained experience in a London nursery, at Mereworth Castle (Kent), and as a foreman to J.H. Elwes at Colesbourne Park (Gloucestershire). Migrating to Melbourne in 1878, he went to Kerang (Vic.) where his activities were unsuccessful financially. Forced to return to gardening he spent eighteen months at a garden in Hawthorn and then seven years at Kenley, Toorak, working for successive owners T.K. Scott (of MOUNT BONINYONG) and W. Leonard. In 1888 the plans he prepared for Malvern Public Gardens were accepted and he was engaged to carry them out, a prelude to thirty-one years spent as curator of parks for Malvern Council. During this time he designed PUBLIC GARDENS for other municipalities, including Hawthorn Gardens and Caulfield Park.

In 1882, while working at Kenley, he began growing and exhibiting CHRYSANTHEMUMS—having obtained scions from BURNLEY GARDENS. Four years later he moved to Hatherley, Malvern Road, and started raising them from seed. At this time he was also BREEDING new roses and water-lilies, but soon devoted his time solely to chrysanthemums, erecting a glasshouse (1888) in which to grow them for exhibition. With the help of his family—sons and daughters—he raised between three and five thousand seedlings a year, selecting 200 for further trial. Of these he would then name and release about a dozen each year. Two of his earliest successes were 'Nellie Pockett' and 'John Pockett' (1898), and he went on to concentrate on the production of 'Chinese' and 'Japanese' exhibition varieties, until by the time of his death 'most of the big giants seen on the show benches ... were of his raising'. By the 1920s, recognising the 'increasing demand for single chrysanthemums of decorative quality that remain in good condition over a length of time', he started raising varieties 'for cut flower work and garden decoration'. In the 1930s his 'William Turner' was grown commercially 'in larger numbers than any other in large cut flower centres in Holland, France, England and the United States'.

In 1898 W. Wells of Merstham, Surrey, began marketing Pockett's chrysanthemums in England, where they won seven Awards of Merit from the ROYAL HORTICULTURAL SOCIETY. In 1903 C.H. Totty became his North American agent, listing at times more than sixty of Pockett's CULTIVARS. In Australia, eldest son William Pockett had exclusive rights to his father's introductions after establishing his nursery in 1912. This arrangement lasted until they were given to his brother J.B. Pockett, in the early 1920s, who continued marketing them until after his father's death. For twenty years after being recognised internationally for his plant breeding Pockett was in full-time employment as parks superintendent. He did, however, obtain leave to visit England in 1901 and 1912 before he retired in 1918. He then moved to Healesville and continued to raise new chrysanthemums until his death.

William Pockett (1879–1958) was apprenticed to CHEESEMAN's Nursery, Brighton, in 1894. After working as a gardener in SA and Vic. he established his own nursery at Canterbury, moving in 1940 to Dandenong. While at first he concentrated on growing and exhibiting chrysanthemums, later he also issued CARNATION, DAHLIA, and SWEET PEA catalogues.

John Bayliss Pockett (1894–1981), after working for the Melbourne and Metropolitan Board of Works, moved to the Malvern Council where he worked first under his father and then under J.T. SMITH. Induced by his father to establish his own nursery, he moved to Healesville and in 1924 began testing his father's new seedlings at his Cowley Nursery, exhibiting and distributing his NOVELTIES. In 1958 he published *Chrysanthemums*, an account of his father's life and work.

RICHARD CLOUGH

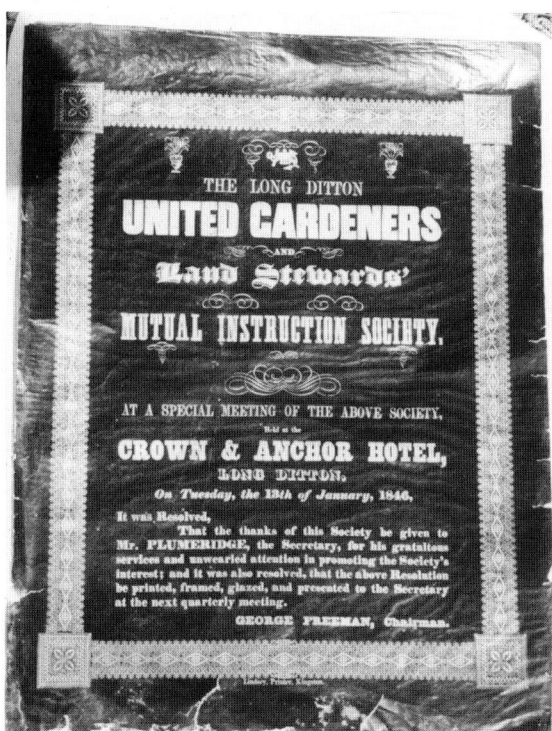

The illuminated address presented to Frederick PLUMRIDGE by the Long Ditton United Gardeners and Land Stewards' Society (1846) recalls the thirst for EDUCATION and earnest debate of the post-Loudonian generation of GARDENERS, many of whom brought these qualities to newly adopted colonial situations

POCKLEY, Diana (b. 1913), a gifted and committed gardener, born in Devon, England, founded the NATIONAL TRUST OF AUSTRALIA (New South Wales) Garden Committee (1964). The role of the Committee—ably chaired by Pockley—was to design and maintain Trust gardens and raise funds for their upkeep. Most notable under their care were Lindesay, Experiment Farm Cottage, and Old GOVERNMENT HOUSE. She also established the Garden Committee's reference LIBRARY, collecting books and pamphlets relating to nineteenth- and twentieth-century horticulture in Australia, as well as a wide range of practical aspects of gardening. This valuable collection, although disbursed in 1993, has been reassembled and generously presented to the State Library of New South Wales as the Diana Pockley Horticultural Library (1998).   CAROLINE SIMPSON

POINTS ARBORETUM, near Coleraine, Vic.: see PETER FRANCIS POINTS ARBORETUM

POLITICS Power is strongly drawn to display. In the days when political power was closely associated with wealth, that display commonly took the form of large and elaborate gardens and PARKLAND. From the Hanging Gardens of Babylon to the Versailles of Louis XIV, the Medici villas at Florence, the surrounds of the aristocratic homes of Britain, and even early landowners in Australia, political power for centuries has put itself on display through magnificent gardens.

In more democratic times the power of the people tends to be evinced in the public ownership of parkland and gardens, which are indeed by far the most highly treasured areas of public land. Australia has greatly profited from the fact that nearly all of its cities and towns were planned from the beginning, and no town plan was in the least acceptable without proper areas of public parkland—and in most cases, large reserves for police horses, which later became available as PUBLIC PARKS. A love of gardens and open space is indeed a prominent part of our heritage, and is thus closely linked to our political thought. BOTANIC GARDENS are a feature of most large Australian cities, and provide free access to many thousands, especially families. They are indeed part of the Australian experience and lifestyle, and have been regularly supported, maintained, and developed by public funds, with bipartisan support.

For another reason, politics in Australia is strongly influenced by gardening. A predominantly middle-class community such as Australia's will always be directly interested in the cultivation of flowers, and of fruits and vegetables for the table—and indeed gardening is by far the preferred LEISURE and RECREATION activity of Australians, far ahead of golf, or swimming, or football. Thus the private garden is an important factor for TOWN PLANNERS and for political management at all levels. True, there is increasing interest in inner-city apartment living, but this is often associated with weekday jobs and a seaside or country weekender, with garden. In any case, the preferred home for most Australians is still the suburban VILLA on the quarter-acre block, which governments ignore at their peril.

CLIMATE is of course the major determining factor in gardening, and this is especially the case in Australia. First, because our land incorporates virtually all the growing conditions of the globe, ranging from about one-third of the country in the TROPICS to the temperate climate of southern Tas., in the same latitude as large parts of Europe. Thus, all the plants, fruits, and vegetables of the globe can find compatible growing conditions here. Australia's first importance, before the discovery of minerals, was as a producer of food and fibre: its political life in the early colonial period was dominated by the interests of the wool grower and grain cropper. Secondly, because of its long physical separation from other lands, Australia has an enormous range of unique trees and plants, especially evergreens, that are of great interest, and in some cases, great value, to other parts of the world. The indigenous population of Australia, being largely nomadic, directly relied on the native fruits of the bush and wetlands for their sustenance and developed a close and devoted relationship with the land that persists to this day among Australia's Aboriginal peoples. As Australians learn more about ABORIGINAL ENVIRONMENTAL MANAGEMENT, there is growing political sentiment towards recognising and valuing these skills.

Politics in a democracy must reflect the life of the people. The climate of Australia is broadly conductive to outdoor living, to enjoyment of open space, and to the development of gardens, both public and private. It is in response to a strong community interest in the flora and fauna that vast areas throughout Australia have also been permanently reserved as NATIONAL PARKS, state or coastal parks, and nature reserves. Even as early as 1881 the Victorian Government, followed later by other colonies, permanently reserved as public land the water frontages to our streams, bays, inlets, and ocean BEACHES that to this day provide free access to a system of coastal and inland parks of the utmost importance. It was in recognition of this preoccupation that the State of Victoria elected to be known proudly as the 'Garden State'. This imperative must also be reflected in any plans for the growth and development of our cities. For instance, in the late 1960s the plan for Melbourne called for growth corridors, separated by areas of open space, mostly along river valleys, to provide 'lungs' for the growing city, and enjoyment and recreation for its citizens. It also by implication demanded the buy-back of large areas already alienated and their conversion into riverside parks. This has not always been the case. In the nineteenth century, large sections of public parkland were sold off for housing (and to allow colonial governments to replenish their coffers) without strong public protest. Likewise, intruders, and notably BOWLING CLUBS and even GOLF CLUBS, were permitted exclusive occupation of portions of some public parklands.

The political impact of Australia's passion for gardens is widespread. Local governments spend a substantial part of their rate revenue on maintaining their public parks and flower beds, on planting and nurturing STREET TREES, and on the provision of PUBLIC OPEN SPACE for the recreation of their citizens. In many municipalities, the felling of any tree, even on private land, requires a permit. State and federal governments proudly trumpet any addition to the national parks system and expect public acclaim for their policies.

The growing political power of the 'Greens' is quick to condemn on environmental grounds any invasion or loss of public parkland or native forest, often exercised out of proportion to representation in Australian parliaments, particularly where they hold the balance of power. However, environmental issues are assuming a rapidly growing importance in the public consciousness, and political parties of all colours ignore this factor at their peril. Our history and our geography, both geological and recent, allied with contemporary concerns about our air quality and our waterways, have all conspired to produce a close alliance in Australia between gardening and politics, which will certainly endure, and indeed intensify, as the new millennium develops.

G. Cranz, *The Politics of Park Design* (Cambridge, Mass., 1982); Martin Hoyles, *The Story of Gardening* (London, 1991); Nigel Everett, *The Tory View of Landscape* (New Haven and London, 1994); Martin Hoyles, *Bread and Roses* (London, 1995)

RUPERT HAMER

POLLARDING involves severe annual PRUNING of one- to two-year-old branches of a tree to approximately the same place; this is normally done at the terminal of a branching framework that has been developed over many years. Sometimes it is undertaken to a branching framework of between four and seven major branches, which may be restricted to a metre or so in length. Occasionally pollarding terminates at a mass of buds in the main trunk or axis of the tree. In more recent times, pollarding has been undertaken less frequently, and may be done on a cycle of three to five years. In this case, the resulting growth can be substantial, and there is the possibility of branch shedding and subsequent damage. Pollarding is usually done to restrict the size of the canopy of trees or to achieve a specific landscape purpose—such as the cultivation of *Erythrina crista-galli* (Coral Tree). While the technique was once common throughout Australia, especially with plane trees and ELM species growing under powerlines, it is costly and labour-intensive, and so is rarely practised in modern horticulture.

GREG MOORE

POMOLOGY, from the Latin *Pomum* (fruit), is specifically concerned with the apple section of the rose family (including apples, pears, quinces, medlars, and loquats), but often refers to the general study and practice of FRUIT growing. Research attempts to produce new and improved varieties suited to the soil and climate of a district, while development aims to establish the cultural methods that will give the best possible commercial results with the least possible outlay, for example different styles of PRUNING (ESPALIER, vase, trellis, or pyramid), which will produce shapes best suited to particular methods of cultivation.

Nomenclature has formed an important component of pomology, and different varieties were recorded and maintained in collections held by private nurseries and ORCHARDISTS, in horticultural society gardens, and in wax models (such as those held by Melbourne's Scienceworks Museum). British pomologist Robert Hogg (1818–1907), whose book *The Fruit Manual* (1860) ran to many editions, was the international authority. Historically, familiar or promising varieties were introduced by nursery proprietors, orchardists, and individual horticulturists. Some new varieties resulted from deliberate cross-pollination—for example, the Packham's Triumph pear was bred by Charles Henry Packham of Parramatta (NSW), from Uvedale's St Germain and Williams' Bon Chrétien (1896)—while others were recognised among chance seedlings—for example, the Granny Smith apple, noticed at Ryde (NSW) in 1862. An important advance in Australian pomology was the discovery by Thomas LANG that woolly aphids, which had been inadvertently imported from Van Diemen's Land by Thomas ADCOCK in 1849, did not attack the roots of Northern Spy apple. The industry was saved from possible extinction by the introduction of grafting onto Northern Spy rootstocks.

Allen Gilbert, *All About Apples* (Flemington, Vic., 2001)

GWEN PASCOE

POOLE, George Thomas Temple: see TEMPLE-POOLE, George Thomas

POOLS: see LAKES

PORT ARTHUR, Tas. Within six years of its inception in 1830 as a penal station for secondary offenders, the site's dominant landscape features were in place, contributing then as

As late as the 1950s apples still featured prominently in Tasmania's fertile heartland, the bosom of Australian POMOLOGY

now to the sense of a 'prison in a park'. Private gardens extended the status of senior officials, who, as members of the ROYAL SOCIETY, enjoyed privileged access to plants from the Society's gardens. Prison staff were allocated convict gardeners for private vegetable plots, and prisoners also worked large productive gardens. Diarist and colonial official Thomas James Lempriere (1796–1852) recalled the white-washed timber cottages of officers, 'overgrown [with] … the Macquarie Harbour vine, the deep green of its leaves giving a clean and neat appearance', while the garden of the Commandant's House (1831) was 'filled with fruit trees, gooseberries, currants and almost every plant to be found in an English garden'. A 'handsome gateway' led to the church (1836) where 'on either side of the walks is a beautiful border of flowers, interspersed with native shrubs and … young oaks, elms and ash trees'. During the 1840s a government garden was added, adjacent to the church and centred on a fountain. Government Cottage (1854), built for visiting dignitaries, overlooked this garden and featured a 'sweet embowering arch of the multi-flora rose in full bloom' while around were 'walks bordered with the rarest shrubs and flowers of our native land'. James Boyd, commandant during 1853–71, who corresponded with MUELLER on establishing industrial plants (particularly flax), modified the landscape, including a new avenue leading to the asylum (1857), and a row of blue gums along the reclaimed foreshore. By 1874 the Commandant's House possessed an 'incredibly sweet smelling garden' with a mature Norfolk Island pine, and 'English honeysuckle, [and] yellow jasmine'.

The post-convict tourist and fishing village of Carnarvon (1877) developed its own gardens, retaining the site's large trees and formal elements, but added a distinctive First World War memorial avenue of *Cupressus macrocarpa*. With later administration by the state's National Parks Department (1971–79), former vegetable gardens became lawns. Following a conservation project (1979–86), and new management authority (1987–), aspects of the site's historic gardens have been reconstructed, particularly the fountain garden. After the 1997 massacre of thirty-seven visitors and staff by a lone gunman, a MEMORIAL GARDEN (1999) was developed featuring a reflective pool surrounded by plantings of young native trees and shrubs.

Jane Collins and Rosemary Harrington, *A Garden Guide to Port Arthur Historic Site* (Port Arthur, Tas., 1992)

PETER MacFIE

PORTLAND BOTANIC GARDENS was one of the first three BOTANIC GARDENS developed in Vic. The original thirteen-hectare site (now reduced to just over three) was reserved in the early 1850s and developed by William ALLITT from 1858 to a plan designed and set out by Alexander ELLIOTT in 1857. The design, still reflected in the surviving path system and placement of major features, such as the rose and dahlia beds, was based on the traditional squared FORMAL layout of EXPERIMENTAL and SYSTEMATIC GARDENS. The picturesque curator's cottage at the entrance to the gardens dates from 1859. The garden contains a number of unusual rare plants including *Wigandia caracasana*, the largest *Cordyline australis* (remnant of a former AVENUE) in a Victorian garden, *Rhus viminalis* (African Sumach), and *Ceonothus pinetorum*. The garden has a collection of 300 different varieties of ROSE and the 170 varieties of DAHLIA and bedding displays remain popular features.

PAMELA JELLIE

POTS AND CONTAINERS have played a significant role in Australian gardens because of the dependence on them for the transportation of plants for our imported horticulture. These ranged from relatively unsophisticated boxes to glazed WARDIAN CASES, which carried plants both to and from our shores. The first Australian NURSERIES, dependent on contemporary British practice, used terracotta pots for seed raising and rooting cuttings as the main techniques of propagation, and amateur gardeners followed the British fashion for growing flowering plants in pots—also doubtless influencing early brickworks and potteries to produce garden pots. While few identifiable Australian-made pots survive from the early days of settlement, garden pots here have followed the traditional European models, from the tiny and fragile thumb pots to elegant Long Toms and weighty tree-sized pots. As the nursery industry and the cultivation of FLOWERS became more popular, an extensive range of pots was developed, based on the needs of specialised groups of plants such as ORCHIDS.

Containers, such as jardinières, were vital for INDOOR PLANTS and decorative examples from many periods are now greatly valued, particularly those glazed examples of art pottery from the 1920s with distinctly Australian motifs such as gumnut clusters. A little later RUSTIC home-made pots of cement and alpine troughs of mock 'tufa' were popularised by Edna WALLING and made by other economically minded gardeners who followed the directions provided in GARDENING MAGAZINES. Since the Second World War, with its campaign of austerity, the range of commercially produced pots made in Australia has generally been reduced.

Many pots and containers formed conspicuous ORNAMENTS, and gardeners in both COTTAGE GARDENS and more QUIRKY GARDENS have developed their own naive approach to containers for flowering plants, using all manner of found objects, especially hollow logs, and discarded household objects to create useful pots. Strictly utilitarian holed cooking pots and pans, enamel washing machine drums and basins, cracked crockery, and used food tins may stand alongside containers crafted from old rubber tyres, wooden fruit crates, polystyrene vegetable boxes, and cut-down oil drums and kerosene tins. Wine barrels, old ceramic kitchen sinks, tin bathtubs, and galvanised-iron and concrete wash troughs have all been utilised for containers. The use of potted plants has been a feature of VERANDAH GARDENING, and in ARID ZONES container gardening has suited both frugal WATER regimes and the transient lifestyles of many, especially those who worked in the NT and on remote settlements such as MISSION stations.

Gardening in containers has taken on a whole new life with the expansion of townhouses and balcony gardens. A number of artisan potters produce fine terracotta pots sold through art galleries and garden decor shops and one or two commercial potteries have successfully countered the importation of cheap pots from South-East Asia, Mexico, and Italy. Garden fashions for MEDITERRANEAN and TROPICAL garden styles have also created markets for all manner of pots from traditional southern European *pithoi*, amphorae, jardinières, lemonières, and kraters to celadon-glazed Thai fish-sauce jars and mosaic-covered containers as vivid as any Burle Marx garden.   TREVOR NOTTLE

POULTER, Robert Henry (*c*. 1865–1944), carnation specialist, was born at Frimley, Surrey, England; he arrived in Australia in 1888 with experience in gardening. After a year in Qld he established his first nursery on a suburban allotment in Wentworth Avenue, Canterbury (Vic.), growing carnations, roses, and cut flowers under the trade name Frimley. The business rapidly extended and in 1919 he relocated to Burwood; his three sons Bertie Albert (b. 1892), Robert Henry (b. 1894), and Arthur Edward (b. 1899) all joined the business. Poulter achieved international fame as a carnation BREEDER and was pre-eminent among Australian enthusiasts. Copies of almost all Poulter catalogues issued during 1908–56 are held in the RHS Lindley Library (London), a major resource for the history of the CARNATION in Australia.   RA

POWELL, Brian Martin (b. 1926), naturalist and horticulturist, born at Reynella, near Adelaide, is a pioneer of ARID-land horticulture in SA. While managing Partacoona Station near Quorn (1963–76), he nurtured pioneering research on the Yellow-footed Rock Wallaby, salt-tolerant agricultural strategies, 4000–8000 ppm saline water cultivation of vegetation, and native vegetation propagation trials. While working for GREENING AUSTRALIA (1988–98) he promoted arid land planting activities at numerous station properties across SA. This built on successful native and exotic vegetation propagation trials using 4000 ppm saline water irrigation that Powell and his wife Fay (b. 1929) had undertaken from 1974 at their property Endilloe, near Quorn. The garden includes quandongs, carobs, almonds, pistachios, figs, Chinese dates, wild desert limes, and wine grapes, and incorporates some 12 000 NATIVE PLANTS.   DAVID JONES

PREISS, (Johann August) Ludwig (1811–1883), German naturalist, arrived in the Swan River Colony in 1838, to collect NATURAL HISTORY specimens. Although he made extensive collections of animals, ethnographic materials, and geological specimens, he was primarily a PLANT COLLECTOR. Collecting widely from north of Perth to Cape Riche (east of Albany) until he returned to Germany in 1842, Preiss amassed a vast HERBARIUM including approximately 2500 species from 850 genera. He was in many ways ahead of his time: his labels gave accurate details on locality, date, flower colour, Aboriginal usage, and habitat. His collections, including numerous new species, were published by LEHMANN and twenty-one co-workers in *Plantae Preissianae* (Hamburg, 1844–48). He also collected SEEDS of more than 300 species, which were distributed for cultivation in Europe. Preiss is, therefore, among the foremost of original contributors to the exploratory phase of Australian systematic BOTANY.

GREGORY and BRONWEN KEIGHERY

The undercrofts of many houses in TROPICAL regions were favoured locations for growing plants in POTS AND CONTAINERS, affording both shade and shelter; in this Darwin residence, recycled tins housed a makeshift containerised garden in the 1950s

PRICE, Uvedale (1747–1829), English landowner and writer, is remembered for his book *An Essay on the Picturesque* (1794) and his central role in the ensuing debate over what constituted the PICTURESQUE, especially in LANDSCAPE GARDENING. In reaction to the smooth landscapes of 'Capability' BROWN, neighbouring Herefordshire squires Price and Richard Payne Knight (1750–1824) sought to codify the writings of William GILPIN into an abstract AESTHETIC theory. Knight maintained that the Picturesque was a matter of association, conditioned by painters—a concept later developed by Archibald Alison—whereas Price sought to categorise its intrinsic objectives as roughness, sudden variation and irregularity, in the manner that Edmund Burke (1729–1797) had earlier defined the Beautiful and the SUBLIME. Price and Knight earnestly quarrelled in essays and letters over the next decade; Price's collected *Essays on the Picturesque* (1810), especially the 1842 edition edited by Thomas Dick Lauder, found its way into many colonial

Prime Minister's lodge

Prince's Square, Launceston (Tas.), an outstanding urban square dating from the 1850s, had its formal design qualities enhanced by the erection of a splendid fountain (1857) at its centre—a commemoration of the town's new reticulated water system

libraries—William Guilfoyle's included—with his ideas suffusing much local debate over garden design.   RA

PRIME MINISTER'S LODGE, Canberra: see The Lodge

PRINCE'S SQUARE, Launceston, Tas., is an outstanding and intact Victorian urban square. The park, laid out under the supervision of Thomas Wade, was formally opened in 1859. Known prior to 1863 as Church Square or St John's Square, the site was levelled for use as a parade ground in 1843 and functioned as a civic square. Here rowdy public elections took place in 1851, and more circumspect mass rejoicing in 1853 celebrating the cessation of convict transportation. The main impetus for enclosing the square was the completion of a reliable, reticulated, municipal water supply (1857) and a fountain was an obvious article of commemoration. The large central fountain (1859) of bronzed cast iron, made to order and imported from France, closely resembled one exhibited at the Paris Exhibition (1855). Its decorative imagery on aqueous themes vied with congratulatory aldermanic commemoration.

The square, which occupies an entire city block, has maintained its original formal layout. Corner entrances with diagonal paths lead to the circular fountain plaza. Other paths run parallel to the boundaries, separated from the fence by shrubberies. Seating faces the fountain and this inward focus is emphasised by heavy boundary planting. The original timber picket fence (1859) was replaced by the present dwarf stone wall, iron railings, and gates in 1898. Large exotic trees are located along the main paths. Originally principally ash and poplar, with a few oaks, these were supplemented by commemorative oaks planted for the wedding of the Prince of Wales (1863), a visit by the Duke of Edinburgh (1868), and Queen Victoria's diamond jubilee (1897).   ANNE NEALE

PROMENADE, from the French *promener* (to walk), describes both a place and an activity. The walk (or drive) might be undertaken for exercise or recreation, amusement or display, or as a form of social ceremony. Examples in Germany (and France) from as early as the seventeenth century, occasionally set on town fortifications, constituted a place where all classes could mingle (*Volksgarten*), while the Italian *Corso* was linked with festival and display. Australian examples have often taken the form of esplanades, boulevards, plazas, or squares. In public parks and gardens, botanic gardens, and domains, promenades have included formal paths (which, combined with their formal bedding displays and architectural features, Shirley Hibberd nicknamed the 'promenade style'), serpentine walks or drives, or a combination of these. Areas of scenic beauty, such as Launceston's Cataract Gorge, were often made accessible for public promenading, especially in combination with a tea garden or lookout destination. Promenades have generally been linked with town planning (especially the City Beautiful movement), urban design, and exhibitions, seen recently at Darling Harbour, Sydney, and Southgate (in both Brisbane and Melbourne).   RA

PROPAGATION When the First Fleeters landed in 1788 they discovered a landscape that, for at least 60 000 years, had been occupied by people who were adept at manipulating their environment in order to increase the supply of a few required plants. ABORIGINAL ENVIRONMENTAL MANAGEMENT included fire-stick farming, used to enhance the spread of edible plants. This use of FIRE represented active intervention in the natural fire regime for the express purpose of plant multiplication.

The First Fleet was remarkably ill-prepared for survival in the new colony. While it was reasonably well equipped with agricultural tools and carried a small quantity of seed, little thought had been given to the composition of the convicts sent on that first fleet. There were a few farm labourers, but only one young gardener. Propagation and PLANT BREEDING expertise increased rapidly through migration when gold was discovered in the 1850s and a vibrant NURSERY TRADE and BOTANIC GARDEN network developed.

Plant propagation requires an understanding of plant structure and function, knowledge of the various techniques and, most importantly, an appreciation of the suitability of those techniques to the plant being propagated. It can be neatly classified as either propagation by seed—where a transfer of genetic information ensures variation—or asexual plant propagation, where the resultant plants are genetically identical.

Propagation by seed required a suitable germination environment as well as overcoming any seed dormancy. In the case of AUSTRALIAN NATIVE PLANTS, dormancy is sometimes associated with the widespread presence of fire as an environmental variable. This might mean that seeds are produced with a hard coat requiring some form of scarification in order to initiate germination. Alternatively, smoke may provide a chemical trigger for germination.

All asexual propagation techniques—for example budding and grafting—depend on the fact that all living cells contain all of the genetic information required to reproduce the entire plant. In the case of stem cuttings, the stem section is required to produce an adventitious root system. Cells within the stem start multiplying—but not generating stem tissues. They now begin producing roots, which rupture the stem tissues and emerge into the surrounding medium. Clearly it is important at this stage to minimise water loss from transpiration. Modern propagation facilities use intermittent mist or fog units in the propagation house to reduce transpiration losses. Propagators who are budding or grafting rely on the two components of the graft—the scion and rootstock—to produce callus. The callus tissue merges together to produce a bridge, physically joining the graft. Differentiation of vascular tissue then occurs.   ROSS HALL

PRUNING is a traditional gardening technique used to manipulate PLANT growth, especially of woody plants. Reasons for pruning include reduction of overall growth; to direct growth forms; removal of dead, diseased, or poor growth; promotion of increased flower production and fruit; removal of spent flowers; and to prolong aesthetic-functional life. Specialist techniques include BONSAI, ESPALIER, PLEACHING, and POLLARDING.

Pruning to renew growth works by overthrowing the apical dominance of a branch to release into growth dormant buds below and to allow the infiltration of light necessary for new growth. The many methods detailed in horticultural and gardening books are tailored in both technique and timing to the needs of individual plants. Some of these operations are critical for good growth and to obtain the form desired, but others are optional procedures reflecting traditional practice. In contemporary landscape and garden MAINTENANCE, interference should be kept to a minimum; detailed pruning of a wide selection of plants using these techniques is in any case not feasible.

The pruning of native AUSTRALIAN PLANTS has, in the past, not been strongly advocated other than by specialist growers. Australian plants were promoted in the 1970s as requiring low maintenance, and were perceived to require little pruning if at all. Much of the Australian flora suffers canopy removal in the wild to a greater or lesser extent, especially by FIRE but also due to animal grazing, insect attack, and drought. A large number of plants have the ability to regenerate vegetatively from canopy removal, and therefore respond well to clipping and light pruning (pinching back) to maintain or improve density, and even severe pruning back to the ground (or coppicing) to completely rejuvenate a particular aesthetic or functional form. Many other plants that do not respond in this way regenerate from SEED. The BANKSIAS, for example, consist of forms that regenerate vegetatively after fire and those that are killed and regenerate from seed. Tree species cannot be renewed by coppicing, as this method forms weak

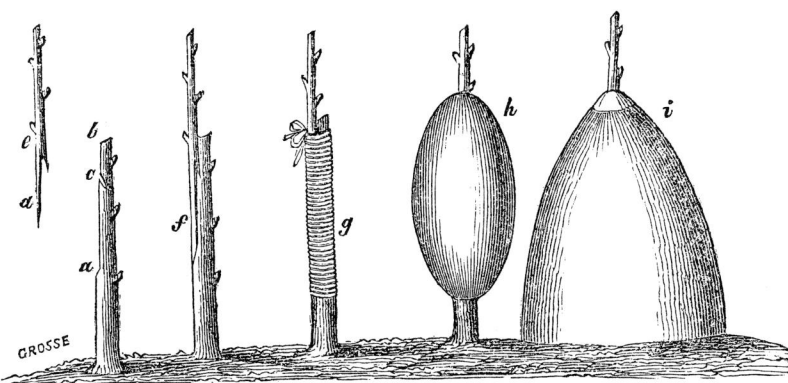

These diagrams of grafting using bast matting and well-wrought clay mud mixed with cow dung, published in the Melbourne-based *Journal of Australasia* (1856), and among the earliest horticultural illustrations to be published in the colony, demonstrate the importance of PROPAGATION techniques to Victoria's early horticulturists

branching in the mature specimen, although it is often carried out to maintain a range of EUCALYPTUS spp. in a shrubby form to prolong their interesting juvenile FOLIAGE, used in the cut-flower trade. ML

PRYOR, Lindsay Dixon (1915–1998), landscape architect, horticulturist, forest scientist, and botanist, was born at Moonta (SA). He graduated in 1935 from the University of Adelaide and Australian Forestry School, Canberra. Between 1944 and 1958 he was the National Capital's Director, Parks and Gardens—a position held previously by Charles WESTON, Alexander BRUCE, and John Hobday (1879–1944). The youthful Pryor acted decisively to build on Weston's foundation city planting of the 1920s. During a time of rapid city expansion, he successfully unified central CANBERRA with large-scale plantings of mixed exotic and indigenous trees and shrubs. In addition he mechanised many landscape management tasks, thereby enabling him to cope with the rapidly expanding area under his control. He introduced new and genetically superior Australian and exotic trees and shrubs.

Pryor had an enormous influence over Canberra's GARDEN CITY landscape. Parks and streets were planted in the suburbs of Acton, Ainslie, Braddon, Deakin, Forrest, Fyshwick, Griffith, Kingston, Manuka, Narrabundah, O'Connor, Red Hill, Reid, Turner, and Yarralumla. Other landscape developments included the Australian War Memorial, parts of Central (now COMMONWEALTH) PARK, several schools, and indigenous plantings in Westbourne Woods ARBORETUM. He shifted the emphasis of major AVENUE plantings from exotic to indigenous species, including in Northbourne Avenue and Captain Cook Crescent. In 1945 he founded the HERBARIUM of the future AUSTRALIAN NATIONAL BOTANIC GARDENS and began work on the Gardens itself. He wrote a popular local guide on tree and shrub planting (1962), which went through several editions, the final one being co-authored with John Banks as *Trees and Shrubs in Canberra* (1991).

Pryor also pursued other landscape interests. He contributed to the founding of a landscape design course at the University of Sydney, teaching in it in the early 1950s. He designed landscapes for several new Australian UNIVERSITY CAMPUSES including La Trobe University (Vic.), Flinders University (SA), and the Australian National University (ACT). He researched the genetics and breeding of EUCALYPTS between 1949 and 1958, leading to the award of Doctor of Science, University of Adelaide. From 1958 to 1976 he was foundation Professor of Botany, Australian National University. He continued with his taxonomic and breeding research and was in demand nationally and internationally as an adviser on eucalypts and poplars. He published prolifically, including five important books, and was awarded the Mueller Medal at the 47th AUSTRALIAN AND NEW ZEALAND ASSOCIATION FOR THE ADVANCEMENT OF SCIENCE Congress (1976). His professional recognitions were many, and included several fellowships and an honorary science doctorate from Flinders University. Pryor was recognised particularly for his highly successful landscaping of Canberra. He also made a significant contribution nationally and internationally to botanical science, principally through his work on tree breeding and taxonomy. JOHN GRAY

PUBLIC ART: see SCULPTURE

PUBLIC OPEN SPACE is an inclusive term embracing a wide diversity of PUBLIC PARKS AND GARDENS, RECREATION reserves and SPORTS grounds, BEACHES AND FORESHORE RESERVES, ESPLANADES, SQUARES, PLAYGROUNDS, bike paths and trails, nature reserves, and can, in the prosaic bureaucratic mind, even refer to the recreational attributes of BOTANIC GARDENS. It can also extend to private land with (controlled) public access, such as COMMERCIAL sites. Spawned by the professionalisation of disciplines such as TOWN PLANNING, LANDSCAPE ARCHITECTURE, and HORTICULTURE, especially at a local government level, its bald connotations can often be valuable when development POLITICS intrude into matters of public land management. RA

PUBLIC PARKS AND GARDENS developed expressly for the free enjoyment and RECREATION of all members of society was a concept just starting to form at the time Europeans settled Australia. Some royal parks had been opened to the general populace, such as London's Hyde Park in the 1630s, and a number of public PROMENADES had been created. In the 1820s J.C. LOUDON was among the first to campaign for the provision of recreation grounds within Britain's overcrowded industrialised cities. They were viewed as improving living conditions and people's health, as well as instructive places where all levels of society could mix, thereby promoting harmonious relations between classes. In 1848 A.J. DOWNING began the same campaign in NORTH AMERICA.

The first formal move towards providing such an amenity in Australia occurred in 1810 when Governor Macquarie announced that the area known by such various names as The Common, Exercising Ground, Cricket Ground, and Racecourse was 'intended in future for the recreation and amusement of the inhabitants' of Sydney, and directed that it be named HYDE PARK. The following year Macquarie set aside the Sydney Common as pasturage for town animals, part of which was turned into CENTENNIAL PARK later that century. BOTANIC GARDENS with their scientific and economic imperatives often preceded the development of public gardens, as happened in Sydney where Australia's first botanic garden was initially closed to the general public. By the time Colonel LIGHT surveyed Adelaide in 1837, provision of PARKLAND was seen as an integral part of TOWN PLANNING. Melbourne was particularly fortunate. Lieutenant-Governor LA TROBE reserved large areas from sale during the 1840s, often at the request of the City Council and local residents. As the century advanced, country towns as well as cities and suburbs were furnished with what was by then considered an indispensable adjunct to civilisation. BEACH AND FORESHORE RESERVES were also developed for recreation, while CEMETERY design incorporated many features of public parks.

In the 1850s and 1860s the largest and wealthiest cities, Sydney and Melbourne, led the way in developing their reserves. Other places, which did not have a reticulated WATER supply or the means to develop and maintain gardens until late in the century, followed more slowly. European

Public parks and gardens

The great popularity in the Edwardian period of postcards depicting PUBLIC PARKS AND GARDENS such as Perth's QUEENS GARDENS, shown here, mirrored society's wider respect for these leisure and recreation amenities

models influenced park design, although this was as dependent on available resources and prevailing conditions as on celebrated examples by designers such as Joseph PAXTON. Clement HODGKINSON, designer of Melbourne's FITZROY GARDENS, remarked that 'strict adherence to the rules of landscape gardening, with regard to the grouping of trees, &c., had to be abandoned' because of summer heat, dust, and a shortage of water and skilled labour. Nineteenth-century park plans, which frequently formalised earlier tracks across a reserve rather than incorporating any more deliberate design, were rarely the province of professional landscape designers. More often they were prepared by engineers, architects, botanists, and horticulturists, for whom the creation of these landscapes was only a minor aspect of their work. They frequently had to contend with difficult terrain, as land set aside for recreation was often unfit for subdivision and sale. The early parks and gardens varied greatly in STYLE and content depending on size (ranging from less than a few hectares to more than 200), community wealth, the designer's taste and experience, CLIMATE, and use. Although many accommodated football and cricket, until the twentieth century less attention was paid to developing parkland for SPORT than to creating ornamental settings for other LEISURE activities. All had perimeter fences to exclude wandering stock (or in some instances to confine agisted animals), some had carriage DRIVES, the more elaborate were ornamented with STATUARY, BANDSTANDS, PAVILIONS, FOUNTAINS, and ponds, a few included ZOOLOGICAL GARDENS, and many contained staff LODGES. A favourable climate, and heightened interest in botany and horticulture during the nineteenth century, ensured that most recreation grounds brought together plants from all over the world, a practice that has continued to the present.

Continual social, physical, and technological change influenced the perception, design and use of the many parks and gardens created during the twentieth century, and resulted in modifications to existing reserves. Fences were removed as they were increasingly seen as restricting free access to public property—a concept originating in the USA, as was the establishment of children's PLAYGROUNDS. AUSTRALIAN FLORA had always been included among exotics, but with a burgeoning national consciousness and appreciation of Australia's natural heritage, heightened by Federation and the creation of NATIONAL PARKS, Australian plants were given greater prominence. Yet at the same time, improved IRRIGATION techniques and larger LAWN MOWERS

Public parks and gardens

resulted in more extensive and manicured lawns. Parkland benefited from schemes to provide work during the Depression, and many ornamental gardens attained a high level of development and maintenance in the inter-war period. The parking of motor cars in parkland also began at that time. Although there has been no more contentious issue in the sphere of POLITICS and gardens than use of 'free' parkland for government-sponsored projects, CAR PARKING has been an insidious form of alienation.

After the Second World War, ornamental gardens were simplified to save money. Paths and garden BEDS were grassed over, labour-intensive plants were replaced with shrubs, decorative features allowed to decay, and in many instances inappropriate community facilities introduced to avoid the cost of land acquisition. Simultaneously, substantial resources were diverted into upgrading ovals and developing sports facilities to satisfy a rapidly increasing population with more leisure than ever before. Public interest in growing Australian plants and concern over loss of indigenous vegetation escalated in the 1960s, leading to the formation of suburban reserves devoted to Australian species, in particular species indigenous to the locality. In recent years, reclamation of former industrial sites has led to new recreation spaces, as at Brisbane's Southbank, which often combine traditional park characteristics with commercial elements. While their perceived role has changed to some extent over the years, and the nature of appropriate development is at times hotly debated, public parks and gardens remain a highly valued part of Australian life.

G.F. Chadwick, *The Park and the Town* (London, 1966); R. Wright, *The Bureaucrats' Domain: Space and the Public Interest in Victoria 1836–84* (Melbourne, 1989); Hazel Conway, *People's Parks: The Design and Development of Victorian Parks in Britain* (Cambridge, 1991); G. Cranz, *The Politics of Park Design: A History of Urban Parks in America* (Cambridge, Mass., 1982); Elizabeth Close and David Beaver (eds), *Urban Parks of Heritage Significance: A Collection of Essays on the History, Conservation and Management of Urban Parks* (Sydney, 1993); Hazel Conway,

The professionalisation of PUBLIC PARK management during the mid-twentieth century encouraged a band of (mainly male) curators for whom MAINTENANCE was of paramount importance and overshadowed issues of design

Public Parks (Princes Risborough, Buckinghamshire, 1996); Georgina Whitehead, *Civilising the City: A History of Melbourne's Public Gardens* (Melbourne, 1997)

GEORGINA WHITEHEAD

PURCHAS, Albert (1825–1909), architect, civil engineer, and surveyor, was born in Chepstowe, Monmouthshire, Wales, the son of a civil engineer. On his arrival in Melbourne (1851) his first work appears to have been as a contract surveyor for Surveyor-General Robert Hoddle (1794–1881). His appointment as architect and surveyor for the MELBOURNE GENERAL CEMETERY (1852) was in line with current overseas trends to establish garden CEMETERIES whose layout and plantings were an integral part of their function and management, and his innovative design set the tone for many Victorian cemeteries. Purchas joined civil engineer Charles Swyer in partnership (*c.* 1855–62) and a major domestic commission was Glenara (1857) for Walter CLARK, with the firm superintending laying out of the garden. The first connection of Purchas with the Melbourne ZOOLOGICAL GARDENS was in 1858, when he arranged for the fencing and clearing of the grounds for the Acclimatisation Society. He maintained a long connection with the Melbourne zoo and designed an elephant house (1891) among several commissions. In 1864 he took on the role of trustee at BOROONDARA CEMETERY, and although the grounds were already laid out, Purchas was responsible for commissioning fences, rotunda, entrance gates, lodge, office, and boardroom. As his first act as trustee he installed garden seats for the comfort of mourners and visitors, strengthening the Trust's moves to create a garden cemetery. In providing rotundas to shelter visitors at Melbourne General Cemetery and at Boroondara, Purchas also encouraged the use of the cemetery as a place of RECREATION.

FRANCES O'NEILL

PURCHASE, James (1842–1911), nursery proprietor, was born at Parramatta (NSW), among the earliest colonial-born members of the NURSERY trade. His nursery at Parramatta had 'not been long established' when John Gould VEITCH visited in 1864; in his account of colonial horticulture in the *Gardeners' Chronicle* (1866) Veitch praised the site and described oranges and other fruit trees as the 'chief portion of the stock'. Purchase was then also importing much general stock from England. His brother, **Samuel Purchase** (1848–1902), was also born at Parramatta and took over the Somerset Nursery *c.* 1871, increasing its range of stock. This was housed in a massive BUSH-HOUSE graced by a central dome and watered, as early as 1878, by an intricate reticulated HOSE system. Purchase maintained a city seed depot and established a wide network of country agents, notably in Qld.

COLLEEN MORRIS

PURVES, Thomas (1840–1911), seed merchant, was born in the Lothians, Scotland, and in 1863, after learning the art of farming, migrated to Melbourne. He found immediate work with LAW, SOMNER AND CO. as the manager of their city store. William Somner proposed his membership of the

The plan for MELBOURNE GENERAL CEMETERY by Albert PURCHAS, published in the Cemetery's *Rules and Regulations* (1854), was influential in Victorian CEMETERY design as an exemplar of the garden cemetery style

Victorian Horticultural Improvement Society in 1863 and within six months Purves was elected honorary secretary. In 1876, following the death of William ADAMSON, Purves took over as manager of Adamson's seed company and continued in this role after the company was purchased by George BRUNNING and ultimately renamed F.H. Brunning Pty Ltd. This industrious and genial Scot increased the business from a staff of one in 1876 to thirty by the time of his death. The *Journal of Horticulture* described him as the 'presiding genius of the firm', attributing his success to a 'clear head and far-seeing capabilities'. His son, Thomas jnr., succeeded him as managing director of the business.

RA

Australia's outstanding nineteenth-century postal network, where even the most remote settlements usually enjoyed at least weekly deliveries, ensured that seed merchants (such as William PURVES) and NURSERY proprietors could supply their stock across the country by mail order

PURVES, William John (1855–1920), seed merchant, was born in Richmond (Vic.) and trained with David RAILTON prior to establishing his own business in 1875. In addition to city premises, he established a large mail-order clientele for vegetable, flower, grass, forage, and Australian tree and shrub seeds. Purves conducted extensive business with MARKET GARDENERS and in their comprehensiveness his catalogues rivalled those of larger firms. His 1892 catalogue even included a special section for the 'Vegetarian Diet', with beans and lentils prominent. A case brought by a market gardener against a failed crop, and decided against Purves Seeds, resulted in seed merchants drafting conditions of sale limiting liability to the purchase price only. RA

PYE, James (1801–1884), pioneering orchardist, was born at Toongabbie (NSW), son of John Pye, who began growing oranges at Seven Hills c. 1810. Acquiring large ORCHARDS at North Parramatta, Baulkham Hills, and Seven Hills, James Pye was a founding member of the Cumberland, Camden and Cook Agricultural Society (1843); the Cumberland Agricultural Society (1857); and vice-president, trustee, and committee member of the Agricultural Society of NSW (1860s). He became an authority on fruit-growing, giving evidence to a Legislative Assembly select committee (1865) after groves in NSW were attacked by rot, and was entrusted with propagating new resilient varieties of oranges collected by Charles MOORE in Europe. An active politician, he was a member of the first NSW Legislative Assembly (1856) and served on Parramatta council. Until the death of James Pye at his main estate, Rocky Hall, tourist guides recommended Pye's orchard as an essential stopover in Parramatta.

COLLEEN MORRIS

QUARRELL, Alfred James (1876–1940), horticulturist and journalist, 'one of the best-known gardening authorities in South Australia', was garden editor for the *Sunday Mail* and *South Australian Homes and Gardens* during the period 1925–40. He favoured flowering annuals and rock gardens, and was a SWEET PEA enthusiast and propagator, editing the *Australian Sweet Pea Annual* (1918–19) while secretary of the Carnation and Sweet Pea Society of South Australia. Quarrell was a leading horticultural and garden judge and a frequent exhibitor at Royal Adelaide Show and many South Australian country AGRICULTURAL and HORTICULTURAL SHOWS.

DAVID JONES

QUEENS GARDENS, formerly East Perth Park or Brickfields Reserve, is located on former clay pits used between 1860 and 1880 for brick making. Concerns in the 1880s over the site's derelict condition led the Perth City Council to develop the reserve as PUBLIC GARDENS, coinciding with a period of colonial prosperity and civic pride. Named in honour of Queen Victoria's diamond jubilee (1897), Queens Gardens opened in 1899, soon becoming a popular venue for social events. The gardens retain their original picturesque design by A.W. Farris, a Sydney landscape gardener specialising in GROTTOES and rockwork, and J.G. BRAITHWAITE, with a chain of ponds (the old clay pits) filled with waterlilies and crossed by bridges, verdant lawns, and flower beds, all enclosed by dense, luxuriantly foliaged trees. Elegant iron gates guard the main entrance. The caretaker's cottage (1905) was continuously occupied by gardeners until 1998. A cherished feature, especially for children, is the statue of Peter Pan (1929).

PHILIP PALMER

QUEENSLAND The Aboriginal peoples of north-east Australia had managed the environment for thousands of years before the Europeans first settled in the south-east of Qld at Moreton Bay—a British penal settlement established on the Brisbane River in 1825. The first gardens in Brisbane were VEGETABLE, FRUIT, and cereal plots, vital to the survival of the colony and included one main Government Garden and several small gardens associated with the officers' residences, soldiers' barracks, and HOSPITAL. Until 1842, the penal settlement was contained by a fifty-mile (80 km) exclusion zone, into which no free settler could enter. The DARLING DOWNS, more than 110 kilometres west of Brisbane, on a well-watered upland plateau over the Great Dividing Range, were discovered by Allan CUNNINGHAM in 1827 journeying north from NSW. The following year, he found a passage east through the range (Cunningham's Gap). It was not until 1840, however, that the first squatters arrived in Qld; Patrick, Walter, and George Leslie brought nearly 5000 sheep from the New England district to the Condamine River, where they established the homesteads Canning Downs and Toolburra.

While convicts and guards laboured in Brisbane until 1849, when deportation ceased, botanists such as Cunningham were discovering many INDIGENOUS PLANTS. Their collections were sent back to KEW and later to southern BOTANIC GARDENS (Melbourne and Sydney). The establishment of local botanic gardens was part of the concerted effort given by colonial governments towards locating and exploiting economically valuable plants for food, timber, dyes, fabric, and drugs. The first botanic garden in Qld was established in the area of the original Government Garden and was proclaimed in 1855 as the BRISBANE BOTANIC GARDENS under the management of WALTER HILL. Other regional botanic gardens—often known as Queens Parks—at COOKTOWN, CAIRNS, TOWNSVILLE, ROCKHAMPTON, Mackay, MARYBOROUGH, TOOWOOMBA and Warwick were established in the 1870s–90s, thus extending the climatic range of testing grounds. Hill was appointed Government Botanist in 1859, followed by F.M. BAILEY, J.F. BAILEY, and C.T. WHITE as directors of the QUEENSLAND HERBARIUM. Knowledgeable amateur botanists such as L.A. BERNAYS and Anthelme THOZET added to this experimental phase of ACCLIMATISATION.

In 1859, Qld was proclaimed a colony separate from NSW, but struggled to establish a stable government and a healthy economy—due in part to unfamiliar and unreliable climatic factors. The widespread perception among newcomers was that the natural landscape was alien and threatening, and required hard work to conquer. The RAINFORESTS—or 'Scrubs'—were particularly difficult to remove, but clearing bushland was a prerequisite for the development of agricultural settlements. Finding reliable supplies of water for humans, stock, and garden use was the first step in the selection of properties. The next step in siting house and garden was to avoid damage from floodwater or storm water. Initial European settlements entailed productive or 'survival' gardening for fruits, vegetables, cereals, and herbs. In warmer coastal areas, gardening entailed experimenting with strange

Queensland

The bandstand and dance floor at Lennon's Broadbeach Hotel, Surfers Paradise, QUEENSLAND, designed by Karl LANGER (1956), combine with other sculptural elements of the landscape to create a MODERNIST paradise, now regrettably demolished

tropical plants as much as testing the viability of familiar temperate favourites. Even these early gardens featured a small ornamental component—flowers (particularly roses) were preferred. Plants that provided a dual function—ornament and food—were naturally very popular; for example grape vines provided shade to verandahs, bore fruit, and in the winter, dropped their leaves to let in warming sunshine. Gaining knowledge of local CLIMATES and conditions was a constant theme in early Qld: the frosts of the inland and uplands excluded many of the tropical plants of the coast.

The spread of pastoralism was extensive during the early 1860s, with almost half the colony being taken up within five years. In the 1870s, the competition between squatters and selectors intensified. Steele Rudd's witty stories of 'Dad and Dave' were located on the Darling Downs, and gave voice to the battling selector. Within the urban areas (such as the hilly inner-Brisbane suburbs), the elevated sites were taken up first by wealthy buyers and remain today as the locations most likely to yield a significant historic residence and garden. These prominent urban positions often featured ARAUCARIAS and *Syagrus romanzoffiana* (Queen Palm), which provided distinctive silhouettes against the sky, while settlers inland favoured *Araucaria bidwillii* (Bunya Pine), a tall marker on flat plains. Rare pockets of good soil—such as that at Laidley Plains, Redland Bay, and Toowoomba—were the prized locations for the NURSERY trade, MARKET GARDENS, small multi-purpose farms, and occasionally, a large MANSION estate. To support the town or country settler in making gardens, commercial nurseries and seed merchants were vital, and the earliest local businesses were established by A.J. HOCKINGS, S.H. EAVES, and Carl HARTMANN, followed by A. WILLIAMS, L. SUMMERLIN, Matthew RIGBY, G. SEARLE, the CHEYNE family, the brothers O'SHANESY and GULLIVER, PINK and COWAN, J. WILLIAMS, LANGBECKERS, and the PERROTTS (to name only the most prominent). Many of these offered services in design and construction (as landscape gardeners). A semi-public garden and nursery was established by the Queensland Acclimatisation Society in 1863 at BOWEN PARK in Brisbane. This establishment rivalled the Brisbane Botanic Gardens in the testing and provision of seeds and plants for (subscribing) settlers. Some of the early horticulturists (Hockings and W. SOUTTER) and curators (Hill, P. MACMAHON, and E.W. BICK) provided horticultural and garden design advice through newspaper articles or garden manuals. Large nursery operators from southern Australia also offered produce and advice (albeit usually climatically unreliable). HORTICULTURAL SOCIETIES (including agricultural interests) were formed throughout the colony and provided much needed support for newcomers.

By the 1880s, a maturing body of horticultural experience and botanical knowledge had developed, culminating in 1887, with the establishment of the Department of Agriculture. The department took over Brisbane Botanic Gardens and set up an AGRICULTURAL COLLEGE at Gatton (1897), making it the first tertiary education institution in Qld. The new discoveries and attitudes expressed by agriculturists and horticulturists of NORTH AMERICA were greatly admired at this time, championed particularly by Angus MACKAY, A.J. BOYD, and E.M. SHELTON, often via the widely distributed *Queensland Agricultural Journal*. While increasingly 'science' was the catch-cry of farmers and professional gardeners in the late nineteenth century, there was also a growing aesthetic and sentimental appreciation for natural landscapes. Along with the seaside, the scenic views of ancient forests and waterfalls, such as those found on the LAMINGTON Plateau, were being promoted as tourist destinations, abetted by the development of railways and published photographic views. Travel and recreation grew in popularity and the influence of the natural environment on garden design included using FERNS, staghorns, ORCHIDS, and NATIVE TREES (many from rainforests) on VERANDAHS, and in BUSH-HOUSES, SCHOOL GARDENS, and PUBLIC PARKS, and the collecting of wildflowers.

Government surveyors using standard guidelines laid out towns in the nineteenth century with reserves set aside for RECREATION and PUBLIC PARK purposes, favouring the edges of rivers and the seashore. As local government developed, many reserves were developed as a public focus for horticulture. Annual AGRICULTURAL and HORTICULTURAL SHOWS, established in almost every district by the end of the nineteenth century, continued the striving for excellence in plant-culture; concern for garden design was less evident. Garden COMPETITIONS (especially for RAILWAY GARDENS, schools, and private residences) emphasised ANNUAL plants, with only scant attention given to their overall arrangement and long-term garden character, despite criticism from judges.

With the new century, Queenslanders had gained some two or more generations of gardening experience in local conditions and climates. They were becoming familiar with the opportunities and constraints of gardening in the sub/tropics (coastal and inland). Professional landscape gardeners such as H. MOORE (Brisbane City Council) created outstanding public gardens, many of which survive. However, the effects of WEEDS such as the Prickly Pear, world wars, and economic depressions stifled gardening practices in the state in the first half of the new century. After the First World War, the universal expression of grief was the construction of WAR MEMORIALS, with ANZAC SQUARE, Brisbane (1930) being Queensland's national war memorial. Motor transport increased from the 1920s and led to an expansion of recreational opportunities. The seaside, the mountains, and the countryside were all destinations for caravanning travellers and day-trippers alike. Tourism became a serious industry, made possible by the rich variety of natural resources in Qld. Guesthouses and hotels with lush tropical garden settings were typical in these RESORT destinations.

Gardening in the middle of the twentieth century was centred on TROPICAL GARDENING. Native plants and old-fashioned European favourites were incorporated, but the general idea was to create an eclectic mixture of bold, bizarre, colourful, and mostly tropical plants. This was true of the coastal regions. In the colder areas such as Stanthorpe, Warwick, Toowoomba, and Tambourine Mountain, gardeners continued to make traditional English gardens (formal arrangements or COTTAGE GARDENS). In the 1950s and 1960s, the writings of D.A. HERBERT, Harry OAKMAN, and Christine MCLAREN offered horticultural advice that had been missing for decades. Design advice was even scarcer with professional garden designers almost unknown. LANDSCAPE ARCHITECTURE began in Qld after the Second World War, especially through the efforts of Karl LANGER and Oakman. The AUSTRALIAN INSTITUTE OF LANDSCAPE ARCHITECTS was established in the late 1960s, with tertiary training in the field provided from 1968 at the Queensland Institute (now University) of Technology.

The rise in popularity of the native plants was marked during the 1970s with ideas of BUSH GARDENS, low-maintenance gardening, and water-wise (XERIC) approaches. The SOCIETY FOR GROWING AUSTRALIAN PLANTS and other specialised plant collectors began the slow process of experimentation and publication of findings, spreading their intimate knowledge to the public. This period also witnessed the rise in popularity of decks at the back of old timber houses: the newest version of the verandah, which allowed 'living outside'—a local catch-cry. The boom times of the 1980s meant rapid development of tourist resorts, GOLF COURSES, hotels, and THEME PARKS, designed by landscape architects in a formulaic international idiom highlighting a formal arrangements of PALMS, hedges of tropical shrubs, and massed groundcovers, using a limited plant palette. By the 1990s, landscape architecture began to develop more sophisticated approaches to planting and unified design concepts, such as in the urban design schemes of central Brisbane or university campuses. On the home garden front, large home and garden shows and garden centres now promote the latest plant releases and design fashions, reflecting the immense business that gardening has generated. At the start of the twenty-first century, garden design in Qld is at its most diverse: wild cottage gardens vie with Tuscan or Mediterranean-themed formal gardens, while rainforest gardens sit beside bushland regeneration schemes. But learning how to garden in the tropics continues, although increasingly it is people rather than plants being acclimatised.

Jeannie Sim and Jan Seto, *Inventory of Historic Cultural Landscapes in Queensland* (Manly West, Qld, 1996)   JEANNIE SIM

QUEENSLAND AGRICULTURIST (1879–85) was established in Toowoomba by the proprietors of the *Darling Downs Gazette*. It was modelled on weekly broadsheets (such as the AUSTRALASIAN) and also agricultural newspapers of NORTH AMERICA, and considerable space was devoted to horticulture. Its capable proprietor and editor, Theodore WRIGHT, attracted generous contributions from specialists in Qld, especially from those based in the 'Garden of Queensland', the DARLING DOWNS. The paper later merged with the *Australian Tropical Planter* and was incorporated into the *PLANTER AND FARMER* in 1885.   RA

QUEENSLANDER (1866–1939), a weekly newspaper with a strong country readership, was published in Brisbane by the proprietors of the daily *Brisbane Courier* (later *Courier-Mail*). A variety of regular and occasional columns on horticultural, agricultural, and forestry matters provided 'a practical and useful aid to the Country Settler'. From the 1880s numerous illustrations (engravings and photographs) were featured. Walter HILL contributed gardening notes from his *Pugh's* ALMANAC contributions during the 1860s and 1870s, as well as series on forest conservancy during 1879. The use of pseudonyms was a common practice, and regular horticultural writers for the *Queenslander* included 'Agricultural Reporter' (A.J. BOYD, the paper's agricultural editor 1874–97), 'Coolibar' (William SOUTTER, 1900–25, weekly during 1905–22), 'Hortulanus' (1925–30), 'Chloris' (Llewellyn LUCAS, weekly 1928–37), 'Spinifex' (1929), and 'Panicum' (articles on poisonous plants, 1930). Topics covered by these writers included vegetable, fruit, flower, and bush-house gardening, and the beauty and usefulness of native plants both for the home garden and for public plantings.   JEANNIE SIM

QUEENSLAND HORTICULTURIST (1892–95), was official monthly organ of the Queensland Horticultural Society (established 1887), edited by William SOUTTER. Topics included landscape design, horticulture for all parts of Qld, and communication among professional horticulturists, this latter emphasised by the addition to the title, after the first volume, of the phrase 'and Fruit-growers' Journal'. This broadening perhaps highlights the limited demand for landscape gardeners in Qld at this time; most of professionals were involved in either commercial fruit or market gardening, operated plant nurseries, or worked as gardeners in government employ. An important contributor was E.W. BICK, who provided landscape gardening design advice. The *Queensland Horticulturist* fulfilled an important, yet precarious publishing role, taking over from the PLANTER AND FARMER and its antecedents, but unable to match the might of the weekly QUEENSLANDER.   JEANNIE SIM

QUIRKY GARDENS, through their appearance and the motivation of their creators, lie outside the usual expectations for domestic gardens. They do not fit into the vernacular tradition of neat suburban FRONT GARDENS that is now part of Australian folk culture. Nor do they share neighbourhood values or aesthetics—often displaying extreme exaggerations of the decorative aspects of standard garden forms that go well beyond the bounds of accepted taste. Quirky gardens are characterised by the expressions of their owners' remarkable bold individuality. Through the use of unusual materials—humorous or grotesque statuary and structures (often homemade), eccentric spatial organisation, and often-thematic collections of containers, plants, and knick-knacks—brave statements of personal taste have been and continue to be made.

While the components of a quirky garden may be considered as folk objects—TYRE SWANS and GNOMES, for example—the way these have been presented within the garden constitutes their main claim to quirkiness. The presentation of objects may take the form of an informal art environment or a collection, a creation of fantasy and 'extravagant visions' as described by Gordon Taylor and Guy Cooper in *Garden of Obsession* (1999), or passionate acquisition of items often discarded by others. Quirky gardens often make ecological statements and consciously recycle materials. The makers of quirky gardens indulge their all-consuming passions by continuously developing their eccentric visions within the confines of an otherwise restricted domain.

Jennifer Isaacs, *Quirky Gardens* (St Lucia, Qld, 1995)
   DEBORAH MALOR

Australian iconography is reflected in this QUIRKY GARDEN embellished with shell-encrusted ORNAMENTS at Wolseley (SA)

RACECOURSES for horse-racing have formed a major part of Australian SPORT since the early nineteenth century, initially transplanting English turf traditions. The first courses at HYDE PARK (Sydney) and New Town (Hobart Town) were little more than paddocks, but with the development of Randwick (Sydney), Victoria (Adelaide), and Flemington (Melbourne) racecourses in the 1830s and 1840s, the trappings of modern courses, such as grandstands and landscaped settings, began to evolve. Professional designers such as R.C. BAGOT assisted in this process, and by the start of the twentieth century, courses such as Ascot (Perth), Doomben and Eagle Farm (Brisbane), and at countless country centres (often associated with SHOWGROUNDS), were catering for this nationally popular LEISURE pursuit. Racecourses often boasted extensive floral displays—a particular feature of spring carnivals—ranging from roses at Flemington to BEDDING displays of annuals and stridently coloured cannas at Perth's Ascot. Trees have also formed features of racecourses, be they PLANTATIONS at small country courses or the grove of plane trees at Ascot under which bookmakers plied their trade.

PHILIP PALMER

RADDENBERRY, John (1820–1898), horticulturist and botanic gardens curator, was born in Devonshire, England, the son of a gardener. Soon after migrating to Vic. in 1853 he became a partner in Smith, Raddenberry and Co., successfully exhibiting at the Victoria Industrial Exhibition in 1856. That year Raddenberry became a member of the Horticultural Society of Victoria foundation committee. He also joined the Victorian Horticultural Improvement Society in 1859. It was not long before Raddenberry transferred to the Ballarat district. In 1862 he leased thirty acres (12 ha) in the Parish of Scarsdale 'for the cultivation of the vine, olive, mulberry and hop', although by 1867 he was insolvent.

Raddenberry went to Geelong in 1872, having successfully applied for the position of Curator of Parks and Gardens—one of twenty applicants in a strong field. When the Corporation of Geelong replaced the Victorian state government in the management of the GEELONG BOTANIC GARDENS and surrounding Eastern Park (1874), Raddenberry was soon thinning out trees, replanting, and changing some of the walks. He visited the botanic gardens in Sydney and Adelaide, returning with significant plants for Geelong. In 1884 he advised Hawthorn Council to follow Geelong in planting elms as STREET TREES. A huge fernery designed by Raddenberry was constructed in the centre of Geelong Botanic Gardens in 1885–87, the building and its planting being praised by J.H. VEITCH during his visit in 1893. Raddenberry had an interest in PLANT BREEDING, an abutilon (Chinese lantern) bearing his name being released in 1886. He may also have been the raiser of two show verbenas, one with his name (c. 1883), the other 'Mrs Raddenberry' (c. 1884). Margaret BROWNE ('Mrs Rolf Boldrewood') in her book *The Flower Garden in Australia* (1893) included the violet 'John Raddenberry' in her list of 'very good new varieties'.

The onset of senility became apparent in about 1894, and Raddenberry resigned from the Corporation two years later. He gained wide recognition as curator of the Geelong Botanic Gardens, especially for his skilful adaptation of the formal layout of his predecessor BUNCE, into an immensely popular centrepiece of Eastern Park.

GEORGE JONES

RADIO, to use the American term, or wireless, the British, was established in Australia in 1923 and regulated by the federal government in 1924. Eight A-class (government funded) stations were on air by 1925, twelve B-class (commercial) stations by 1926, and by 1932, when the government-controlled Australian Broadcasting Commission was formed, broadcasts were an everyday part of Australian life. By 1935 national networking on the ABC was functioning and although individual commercial stations were established in each state, it was not until 1938 that the Macquarie Network, based on the model of American commercial networking, was established.

The earliest known broadcast specifically targeting gardeners, from January 1925 on Fridays between 9 p.m. and 10 p.m., was Leslie BRUNNING's 'Gardening Notes' on 3LO, one of the Melbourne A-class stations. Its competitor (and later ABC sister station), 3AR, broadcast a weekly 'Garden Talk' by R. Standley Haines of Brunnings on Friday nights and 2FC (Sydney) ran a program of the same title on Saturday mornings. By 1926 specialist talks were also being broadcast on 4QG (Brisbane). These were all rudimentary affairs, broadcast live from a studio. Often, as in the case of 'Tecoma' on 4QG, a transcript was printed by the horticultural press, and many early broadcasters were experienced print journalists. The first known horticultural 'actuality' broadcast took place in Melbourne on 13 April 1926, when 3LO broadcast the

The immediacy provided by RADIO, after its introduction in an era of leisured communication, gave S.H. HUNT and his colleagues in the pioneering field of garden broadcasting a huge popular following, and the commercial potential this offered was quickly realised by the nursery trade

opening of the second annual Garden Week FESTIVAL, and later that week many talks were also broadcast live.

In Sydney, George Cooper (Superintendent of Parks for the City of Sydney) broadcast regularly on 2BL from 1926 and by 1931 so too did 'Redgum' (J.G. LOCKLEY) on 2FC and S.H. HUNT on 2UW. During the 1930s most of the commercial stations included some form of gardening program, and Hunt for instance, was soon broadcasting on 2UW, 2GB, 2UE, 2SM, 2KA, and 2GZ. Other early broadcasters included George L. Gellatly (2KY), Anthony Antonio and G.R. Gould (3AR), Herbert KEMP (5CL), H.A. Corbett (6WF), and John OSBORNE (7NT), with Friday nights and Saturday mornings favoured time slots. Radio was an excellent marketing and advertising medium for horticultural products, but also did much to publicise events in the gardening community, such as HORTICULTURAL SOCIETIES and SHOWS, and supplemented the role of GARDENING BOOKS and MAGAZINES in the dissemination of practical information. The early dominance of the NURSERY industry in broadcasting was soon supplemented by other 'expert' presenters, such as local government parks and gardens curators or Agricultural Department staff. From the 1950s, national networking increasingly brought gardening programs to interstate audiences.

The immediacy, intimacy, and ease of access provided by radio, especially in a pre-television era, captured devoted listeners. The eloquent naturalist Crosbie MORRISON retained a spot on 3DB/3LK from 1938 to 1958 to publicise his magazine *Wild Life*, and a 1943 survey showed his program had a seventy-eight per cent audience share. By 1947 his talks were broadcast by twenty-three commercial stations, influencing a generation of conservationists. The advent of TELEVISION in Australia (1956) provided an alternative electronic medium for gardening shows, but the simultaneous introduction of portable transistor radios and the immediacy of live 'talk-back' between listener and presenter were two areas that offered distinctive differences. Some presenters later straddled both media, especially with a state-based radio show and a national television presence (such as Don BURKE on 2WS, 2UE and the Nine Network, and Peter CUNDALL on 7ZR/7NT and ABC TV). Despite the allure of television to advertisers, radio remains a low-key but powerful force in Australian home gardening.

K.S. Inglis, *This is the ABC: The Australian Broadcasting Commission 1932–1983* (Carlton, Vic., 1983); Lesley Johnson, *The Unseen Voice: A Cultural Study of Early Australian Radio* (London, 1986); John Potts, *Radio in Australia* (Kensington, NSW, 1989)

RA

RAE, Frederick James (1883–1941), horticulturist and botanic gardens director, was born at Blackwood (Vic.). He was educated at the University of Melbourne where he completed several degrees, including a Bachelor of Agricultural Science. He served with the AIF (1915–18), and became Principal of the School of Primary Agriculture and Horticulture, BURNLEY, in 1921. He is best remembered as Government Botanist and Director of the MELBOURNE BOTANIC GARDENS, a position he held from 1926 until his death. During his directorship Rae made significant improvements to the Gardens, including the building of a new HERBARIUM and the landscaping of the Huntingfield Lawn. He took a keen interest in the development and improvement of private gardens, and he was often called upon to serve as a judge in garden and horticultural COMPETITIONS. Rae was a founding member of the VICTORIAN TREE PLANTERS' ASSOCIATION.

ELIZABETH STEWART

RAHEEN, Kew, Vic., erected for brewer Edward Latham (1870s, extended 1884), was sold to barrister and politician Henry Wrixon (1888), then to the Catholic Church (1918)—occupied by Archbishop Daniel Mannix between 1918 and 1963—before again passing into private hands (1981). The towered mansion has an intact formal ITALIANATE GARDEN, with a grand, grassed terrace replete with steps and urns, and a polished-granite fountain centred on the main eastern arcade. A large cedar dominates the less-formal south garden. Paddocks and riverside frontage were lost through mid-twentieth-century subdivision.

MICHAEL LEHANY

RAILTON, David Balderston (*c*. 1834–1892), seed merchant and florist, was a native of Scotland who received training and managerial experience with several Dundee seed houses. He arrived in Melbourne in 1865, and established his own seed business in Swanston Street the following year. By 1867 Railton was acting as the city agent for J.C. COLE's Richmond Nursery and, although primarily catering to MARKET GARDENERS, also dealt in native Australian plant seeds for export. In 1876, however, he sold both the seed firm and a hat business he owned, the former to Peter WATTERS and James Jones. These continued to trade under the name Railton & Co., and Railton himself maintained an interest at least through his ownership of the firm's city premises. Well respected in Melbourne horticultural circles, Railton was elected a member of the Victorian Horticultural Improvement Society in 1866, and was credited with training many aspiring seed merchants and nursery proprietors.

By the time of his death Railton's sons, Thomas (1867–1942) and **James Railton** (1872–1951), were also associated with Railton & Co. In 1893 they joined with John Stevens Smith to found Railton Bros., leaving the former company entirely in the hands of the Watters family. With Smith's departure in 1898, and the retirement of Thomas in 1901, James Railton became the sole proprietor of the firm. This now catered for a substantial retail as well as wholesale market, and incorporated a nursery in Raglan Street, Preston, together with offices in Swanston and Elizabeth streets, Melbourne. When nominated as an employer representative on the Gardener's Wage Board in 1926 (initiating a lengthy term on both it and the succeeding Nurserymen's Board) his establishments encompassed a staff of forty-five. Railton was a keen advocate for Victorian horticulture, particularly through his positions as president and committee member of the Nurserymen and Seedsmen's Association of Victoria. He was influential in the founding and management of the Garden Week FESTIVAL, serving as chairman (1927–33), was a founder of the VICTORIAN TREE PLANTERS' ASSOCIATION, and played a leading part in the establishment of the CRONIN Memorial Horticultural Scholarship (1926). He was also actively involved in the Mount Dandenong ARBORETUM and Geelong Road plantation scheme. After his death, James Railton's city business was taken over by Lewis & Waller.

DARREN WATSON

RAILWAY GARDENS developed in Australia following the introduction of this new transport mode in the 1850s. The network, initially private but increasingly state-run, soon covered vast distances and every town on the line had a railway station and many major centres had locomotive depots or railway workshops. Staff levels were high and there were often long hours between trains when employees could beautify their often harsh surroundings. The railway station was regarded as the 'front door' of the town, and station gardens exemplified the fraternity among garden lovers and those who wish to make their own and their workmates surroundings 'pleasant and uplifting'. Queensland Railways first employed a gardener in 1876, and the garden tradition has continued at Brisbane's Roma Street Station and at Kuranda on the Atherton Tableland, where the station is festooned with lush tropical growth. At Spring Bluff, on the ascent to the DARLING DOWNS near Toowoomba, local garden enthusiasts maintain spectacular displays of spring flowers and specimen trees. At important early railheads such as Goulburn (NSW), the station and railway were integrated into the town's grid street pattern and marked with avenue planting.

The New South Wales Railway Institute ran a HORTICULTURAL SOCIETY that held its first flower show in 1896. The Institute's journal, *Railway Budget*, carried gardening articles redolent of MORAL IMPROVEMENT. In 1899 the New South Wales Railways Commissioners launched an annual railway station garden COMPETITION, with categories including the most improved garden and the best bouquet of flowers. Plant species recommended for consideration by staff included AGAVES, *Doryanthes excelsa* (Gymea Lily), *Livistonia australis* (Cabbage Tree Palm), *Cortaderia* spp. (Pampas Grass), cannas, and GERANIUMS. In 1903 railway staff were encouraged to use *Rhagodia hastata* (Saltbush) not only for topiary but also for hedging: it was considered useful for catching dust on its leaves, thereby 'saving the curtains and the house'. TOPIARY was once a feature of many railway gardens, the most spectacular being the extensive display at the Flemington Car Sheds, just west of Sydney. Significant among prize-winning railway gardens in NSW were those on the Blue Mountains and on Sydney's North Shore line, where some (such as Killara) were developed and maintained by the local communities, with mass displays of flowering shrubs. Native plants, especially staghorns and bird's nest ferns, adorned many railway gardens from the 1920s—a fine example being Murwillumbah, on the far north coast of NSW. Important railway plant nurseries were established at Homebush, NSW (1923) and Port Augusta, SA (1947). Small parks were sometimes located adjacent to railway stations and representative gardens survive at Footscray and Ripponlea (Vic.). The railways attempted to revive community involvement in gardens briefly in the early 1990s during the Life: Be In It health awareness campaign.

CHRIS BETTERIDGE

RAINFORESTS are forest systems with closed canopies, dense tree spacings, and generally a complex species mix with no one species or genus being dominant. Located along Australia's east coast from TROPICAL north Qld to Tas., the temperate southern rainforests are distinguished from their tropical counterparts by a simpler floristic mix as well as an absence of significant buttressing at the tree base, and lack of woody lianas (climbing and twining plants). Only small pockets of rainforest remain after rapacious clearing during the nineteenth century of a resource that was already greatly confined in area on the Australian land mass prior to European settlement.

The 'exotic' nature of rainforest in a country dominated by open, predominantly EUCALYPT forests has served as an inspiration for garden design since the mid-nineteenth century. BOTANIC GARDEN curators such as Charles MOORE (Sydney), Walter HILL (Brisbane), and William GUILFOYLE (Melbourne) all had first-hand experience of the vegetation, and within their landscape designs extended its collective use beyond the earlier fascination for single plant species. However, most interest still lay in the exploitation of rainforest and the 'challenge' of clearing it, especially in northern NSW and Qld; the devastation of *Toona australia* (Red Cedar) symbolises this era. Later a more rigorous appraisal by botanists such as W.D. FRANCIS led to a growing scientific interest, even if still aimed at commercial exploitation. Nonetheless, such work underpinned conservation initiatives that emerged in the 1960s. In 1986–94 the Central Eastern

Rainforest Reserves of Australia were inscribed on the World Heritage List.

In the southern states, visits to cool mountain retreats and their fern gullies to escape the summer heat provided another strong design influence, evident in the general popularity of FERNS AND FERNERIES in gardens. In the early decades of the twentieth century, native plants such as Sweet Pittosporum, Lilly Pilly, and Kurrajong became popular garden subjects, with their habit, leaf shape and colour sitting easily within existing garden styles. This provided a comfortable transition to a more widespread adoption of AUSTRALIAN PLANTS and landscape character in garden design. The success of the BUSH GARDEN movement led to a wider interest in other Australian plants, including a revival of many rainforest species that had not been available from nurseries for many years.

Rod Ritchie, *Seeing the Rainforests in 19th-century Australia* (Sydney, 1989)

NIGEL LEWIS

RANICAR (née BARRETT) Betty Russell (1909–1991), plant enthusiast, was born in Melbourne although began gardening in India, where she lived with her husband, a tea planter. Here, she also collected and sketched the local flora. On retirement the Ranicars migrated to Tas., eventually settling at Red Hill Farm, Deloraine, in 1951. It was here that Betty created what came to be regarded as one of Tasmania's leading gardens. Although not formally trained in horticulture, Betty Ranicar collected and successfully grew many rare plants from all over the world. She helped many others in their horticultural endeavours, including John and Corrie Dudley of the Elizabeth Town Nursery. They discovered in a nearby garden a double white hellebore, which they propagated and named *Helleborus orientalis* subsp. *gattatus* 'Mrs Betty Ranicar'. Her skill, knowledge, and generous nature endeared her to many throughout the gardening world.

ANN CRIPPS

RANKIN GARDENS, Subiaco, WA: see SUBIACO MUNICIPAL GARDENS

RAPHAEL, Thomas Davidson (1904–1987), horticulturist, was born in Northern Ireland and worked in the FRUIT industry in Britain, before migrating to Tas. where he joined the Department of Agriculture in 1927. His qualifications, Master of Agriculture and Diploma of Horticulture, were gained at Cambridge University. Raphael worked in the area of apple, berry, and vegetable research and wrote a number of handbooks for the industry. During the Second World War he undertook valuable work that led to an increase in the production and processing of vegetables for the armed forces. He was also a keen gardener and flower judge, and for many years gave regular gardening sessions on RADIO and TELEVISION. In 1969 Raphael retired from his position as senior research horticulturist and wrote *Gardening in Tasmania*, a handbook suited to local conditions, which was first published in 1972.

ANN CRIPPS

RAWSON, Mina (c. 1853–1933), as 'Mrs Lance Rawson', wrote the *Australian Enquiry Book of Household and General Information: A Practical Guide for the Cottage, Villa, and Bush Home* (1894) based on two decades of pioneering farming experience near Mackay, Maryborough, and Rockhampton (Qld). Reflecting the variety of skills required for frontier living, she included guides to cookery, interior decoration, 'scientific' agriculture, and gardening (practical and ornamental). While her gardening advice was not extensive, her recommendations for experimentation set important standards for smallholders and newcomers to Australia.

JEANNIE SIM

RAYMENT, Ronald Clarence (b. 1930), architect and landscape architect, was born at Cheltenham (Vic.) and following architectural training in Melbourne (1946–51) worked in Brisbane, Stockholm, London, and Wellington (1952–64) and Melbourne (1965–69). His Swedish experience (1953–55) provided great inspiration, particularly the holistic architecture and landscaping of its new towns. He undertook further training in horticulture and landscape design, and worked briefly with Ellis STONES in the landscape practice Stones and Rayment (1970–71) before starting his own company, Rayment Associates (1972–95). His landscape work included major institutional and industrial projects in Vic., Tas., and NSW, and included the South Lawn (roof of underground car park), University of Melbourne; macropod display, Melbourne Zoo; Deakin University campus master plan, Waurn Ponds (Vic.); and Alcoa head office and works, Point Henry (Vic.). Much of Ron Rayment's later work concentrated on environmental impact statements and expert witness briefs, and since 1995 he has pursued advanced academic research in the field of object-oriented modelling and a genetic basis for style in design.

RA

RAYWOOD, Bridgewater, SA: see WOLLASTON, Tullie Cornthwaite

READE, Charles Compton (1880–1933), was appointed Adviser on Town Planning to the South Australian Government in 1916, and, from 1918, Government Town Planner, the first in Australia. Driven by socialist conviction and a personal ambition to seek improved living and working conditions for the poorer classes, Reade abandoned a journalistic career to pursue voluntary employment with the London-based Garden Cities and Town Planning Association (GCTPA). Untrained in TOWN PLANNING or any related profession, he familiarised himself with the aims and influence of Ebenezer Howard and the GARDEN CITY movement and learnt the craft of the town planner through travel in Britain and Europe, *in situ* investigations of residential developments 'on garden city lines', and two years' service in the GCTPA offices. A New Zealander by birth, Reade arrived in Australia in 1914 as organiser and co-lecturer of the Australasian Town Planning Tour conducted under the auspices of the GCTPA. He became the Association's chief propagandist and spokesperson for the garden city message in Australia.

As well as promoting the social, economic, aesthetic, and cultural benefits of planning 'on garden city lines', Reade demonstrated practical application of the garden city idea in

Recreation

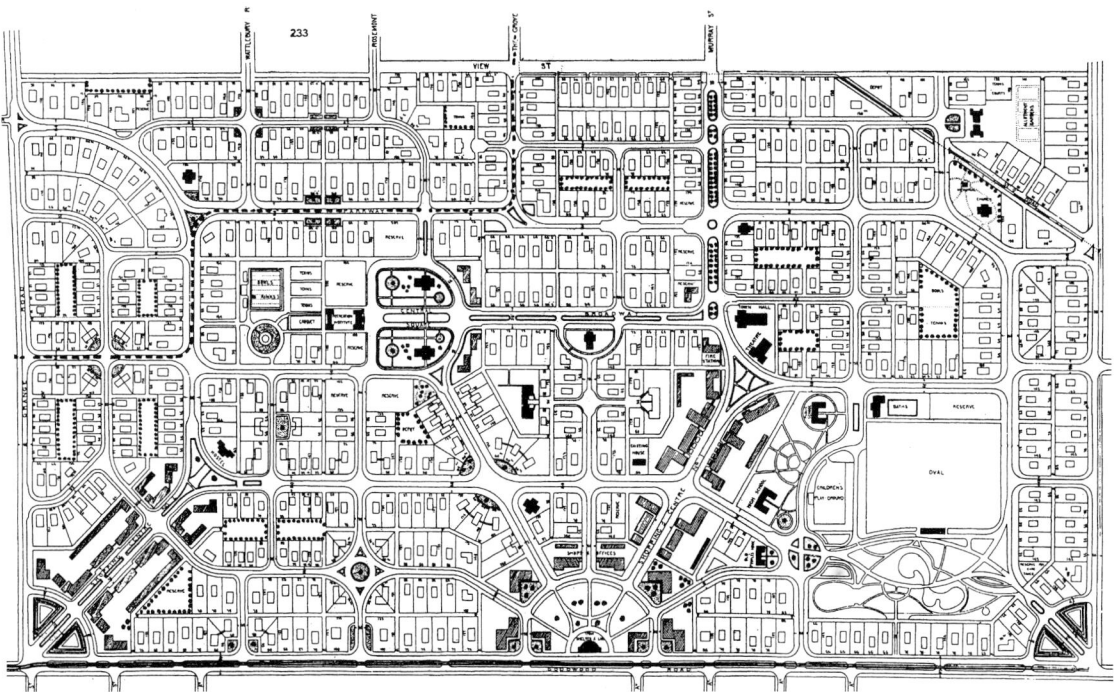

Charles READE's plan of Colonel Light Gardens (SA), designed in 1917 and established from 1921, covered an entire suburb of Adelaide and became a model example for proponents of the GARDEN CITY MOVEMENT in Australia

designs for residential subdivisions in Adelaide and rural towns including the RIVERLAND. His most significant achievement was the model garden suburb at COLONEL LIGHT GARDENS. His comprehensive plan, drawn in 1917, included PUBLIC OPEN SPACE in the form of recreation areas, parks, and formal gardens. An ordered arrangement of paths, hedges, and flower beds was proposed for public gardens and, where appropriate, a rotunda or shelter shed. Existing trees were retained and new ones, planted in avenues of like-species, were intended along the wider streets, in rows to define the perimeter of the larger parks and the children's PLAYGROUND, as well as the suburb's boundaries.

Reade carried over the notion of comprehensive planning into his landscape architecture commissions, undertaken from 1916. These included improvements to Morialta Reserve (1916); Adelaide's West Terrace and Port Pirie's children's playgrounds (1917, 1918); recreation grounds for the District Council of Prospect and Thebarton Corporation (1917, 1918), and the Victor Harbor Soldiers' Memorial Gardens (1918). Typically, plans for his projects combined formal garden beds and tree plantings, existing natural features, and design elements appropriate to the site's function. His immediate successors emulated Reade's comprehensive approach and relied on a similar repertoire of design components.

Reade left Adelaide in 1920 for a position as Government Town Planner in the Federated Malay States. Following the termination of that appointment he advised on town planning in Northern Rhodesia and South Africa before his untimely suicide in Johannesburg. He is internationally regarded as one of the pioneers of the early twentieth-century town planning movement.   CHRISTINE GARNAUT

RECREATION in Australia is mainly an outdoor activity due to the mild CLIMATE and availability of PUBLIC OPEN SPACE. In the nineteenth century, fresh air was regarded as a tonic for health, and pleasant natural surroundings were considered beneficial. Gentle exercise—involving greater exertion than LEISURE—for both sexes was achieved through walking, boating, horse-riding, or cycling.

PUBLIC PARKS AND GARDENS, recreation reserves, and SPORTS grounds provided space for a range of sporting activities, which were enjoyed for their recreational value as well as for serious competition. TENNIS COURTS, and CROQUET and lawn BOWLING GREENS, were marked out from the 1870s to the 1980s, and accompanying PAVILIONS and seating areas built. Sea-bathing was popular at many BEACHES AND FORESHORE RESERVES from the 1850s, and in the twentieth century, especially the 1920s and 1930s, SWIMMING POOLS were constructed by local councils, or built into lakes and river beds. Many recreational areas were adorned with garden features, such as the rose beds at city RACECOURSES; some adjoined or were part of BOTANIC GARDENS, such as the cricket grounds at Benalla and Port Fairy (Vic.). Recreational activities were often associated with outdoor eating, either at a PICNIC GROUND, where outdoor furniture, fire-places, and later BARBECUES, were provided, or at one of the many tearooms and KIOSKS that serviced parks and gardens, race-tracks, and the public boating ramps at LAKES and riverbanks. Professional interest in the North American 'recreation movement' was reflected in the establishment of the (ROYAL) AUSTRALIAN INSTITUTE OF PARKS AND RECREATION (1966).

In the late nineteenth century, the natural environment was increasingly promoted for outdoor recreation. Bushwalking tracks—especially in NATIONAL PARKS—were made more amenable with steps, scenic LOOKOUTS, seating, shelters, and signage. Alpine skiing became popular in the 1920s, and by the 1950s and 1960s ski resorts were operating in Vic., NSW, and Tas. Camping and CARAVAN PARKS were serviced with modern facilities, often at the expense of the older garden settings in which they had been first established. HELEN DOYLE

REDLEAF, Double Bay, NSW, developed from 1863 by merchant William Benjamin Walker, is a large ITALIANATE mansion and harbourside estate. Surviving 1860s landscape features are the original estate boundaries, terrace and bank formations, and sandstone walling, piers, and steps. Subsequent owners included pastoralist and politician William Busby (1813–1887)—whose father-in-law, Thomas Woore, provided detailed 1870s watercolours of the grounds—and merchant and horticultural provider Frederick Lassetter (1828–1911), who transformed the old service terrace into lush gardens where a line of *Howea forsteriana* (Kentia Palm) remain. Surviving nineteenth-century trees include FIGS (*Ficus* sp.), ARAUCARIAS, *Podocarpus elatus* (Brown Pine), and *Pinus roxburghii* (Chir Pine). Remarkably, an old colony of *Xylomelum pyriforme* (Woody Pear) survives, despite 140 years of site development. An extensive panorama remains across Sydney Harbour with views of Carthona, Lindsay, St Mark's (Darling Point), and BABWORTH HOUSE. GEOFFREY BRITTON

REDOUTÉ, Pierre-Joseph (1759–1840), Belgian-born botanical artist, worked as a decorator before settling in Paris in 1782. He was drawn to the Jardin du Roi and mingled there with botanists and artists. The amateur botanist Charles-Louis L'Héritier (1746–1800) recognised his ability and employed Redouté, teaching him the art of botanical illustration. Some of this work was carried out in England, where Redouté met Francesco Bartolozzi (1727–1815), who taught him the art of stipple engraving. Redouté went on to become a master of the technique and illustrated works for Empress Josephine, including *Jardin de la Malmaison* (1804–05), and on his own account, his celebrated works of coloured stipple engraving, *Les Roses* (1802–16) and *Les Liliacées* (1817–24): AUSTRALIAN PLANTS were included in the *Malmaison* volume and *Les Liliacées*. Of a more scientific nature was LABILLARDIÈRE's *Novae Hollandiae plantarum specimen* (1804–06), which illustrated 370 Australian plants, many by Redouté. Indeed, Redouté was a prolific artist of AUSTRALIAN PLANTS during the heyday of BOTANICAL ILLUSTRATION in the early nineteenth century.

Jill, Duchess of Hamilton, *Napoleon, the Empress & the Artist* (East Roseville, NSW, 1999) HELEN HEWSON

REEDY, Thomas (1842–1929), gardener, was born in Tipperary, Ireland, and as a child arrived with his parents in Sydney. Aged just 12 he started work at the MACARTHUR estate, Camden Park, where his father was employed. As a garden boy under Edmund BLAKE, he progressed to become a trusted assistant to William Macarthur, versed in all aspects of the garden, from hybridisation of orchids to orchard management. Reedy participated in the *Chevert* expedition, sponsored by his employee, to the Fly River, New Guinea (1875), and amassed valuable tropical plants, including a Croton that was named for him. He became orchard manager at Camden Park and served for more than seventy years on the estate (spanning three generations)—a remarkable and presumably unsurpassed record for horticultural longevity. RA

REGENERATION: see REVEGETATION

REGISTER: see *Adelaide Observer*

REPTON, Humphry (1752–1818), English landscape designer, was educated in Norwich, Norfolk, and in Holland, a country having close trade links with East Anglia. Young Repton showed an early love of drawing, although he was set up in a mercantile business. Upon the death of his parents he used his inheritance to establish a country estate, which formed the basis of his practical experience. Around 1788 he determined to set up as a LANDSCAPE GARDENER and most early commissions were from local gentry: filling a void caused by the death of 'Capability' BROWN (1783), he soon became the leading English practitioner.

Repton's *modus operandi* included the preparation of 'Red Books', so-called for their red morocco leather bindings. By skilful use of watercoloured sketches with hinged flaps he presented clients with visions of mature landscape schemes, aided by descriptive (and often flattering) text. Repton's schemes were often modest, and his attention to comfort and convenience—by linking the residence to the park through a garden setting, often incorporating a terrace, discrete compartments for embellishments such as a rosary,

The 'Red Books' of Humphry REPTON enabled clients to view 'before and after' scenes of his landscape schemes by the use of flaps and overlays, illustrated and hinged so as to reveal his major proposals against a backdrop of retained elements

trellised flower garden, or conservatory—perhaps coincidentally bridged the gap between the Brownian park and the modest villa garden. These ideas were expounded for public consumption in books such as his *Sketches and Hints on Landscape Gardening* (1795), *Observation on the Theory and Practice of Landscape Gardening* (1803), and *Fragments on the Theory and Practice of Landscape Gardening* (1816). These lavish productions were republished by J.C. LOUDON in an inexpensive format (1840), and in this way were made widely available to colonists.

Repton joined architect John Nash in business between 1795 and 1800 (for whom NSW architect Francis Greenway apparently worked during 1800), an arrangement that also involved his talented son and sometime collaborator, John Adey Repton. This close link between architecture and landscape architecture was one that Loudon also espoused and, especially with his addition of GARDENESQUE concepts, its influence can be found in countless Australian MANSION, HOMESTEAD, and VILLA GARDENS of the nineteenth century.

> Dorothy Stroud, *Humphry Repton* (London, 1962); George Carter, Patrick Goode, and Kedrun Laurie, *Humphry Repton: Landscape Gardener 1752–1818* (Norwich and London, 1982); Stephen Daniels, *Humphry Repton: Landscape Gardening and the Geography of Georgian England* (New Haven and London, 1999)

RA

RESORT GARDENS Gardens emerged as an important setting for coastal and mountain accommodation establishments in the latter part of the nineteenth century. While the grand city hotels might be opposite public garden reserves they rarely had their own garden setting. But many large Victorian and Edwardian guesthouses—Erskine House (Lorne, Vic.), Greenmount (near Coolangatta, Qld), MOUNT BUFFALO CHALET (Vic.), and Caves House (Jenolan, NSW)—all had spectacular settings and carefully planned gardens. In the era before surf bathing became either legal or popular, these gardens were a primary attraction for visitors. In the case of CAVES and alpine areas the scenery itself was considered the primary attraction, so the gardens and vegetation complemented the accommodation complex. But in coastal and HILL-STATION settings, including Marysville (Vic.) and Mount Victoria (NSW) the gardens often included SPORTING facilities, especially CROQUET and TENNIS. The garden of the Imperial at Mount Victoria even had its own ZOO.

The term 'resort'—long used in travel promotion, especially for mountain areas and natural springs—became commonplace in the inter-war years, when almost every state tourist bureau included the term 'holiday resorts' in their tourist guides and accommodation directories. The Karri Bank resort in Western Australia's Porongorup Range was carved out of natural BUSH. Its grounds consisted of a tennis court, railings (to keep the dairy cattle at bay), and stray gum trees that survived the original frenzy of clearing.

The coming of mass air travel, predicted in the 1950s and a reality by the 1960s, enabled large new resorts to be built in isolated coastal areas and on the islands of north Qld. In these resorts the developers were often able to acquire large sites abutting BEACHES. Sometimes the sites had been degraded by sand-mining or poor environmental management, so an integral part of development was to drain and landscape the site, especially if mangroves or sand dunes were involved. The Mirage Resorts at the Gold Coast and Port Douglas (Qld), along with similar resorts at Maroochydore (Qld), Coffs Harbour (NSW), and Broome (WA), all involved grand landscape creation, special plantings (usually of TROPICAL species), and provision for tennis courts, SWIMMING POOLS, and other recreational necessities, from floating bars to bicycle tracks. The resorts simultaneously offered access to the beach while using landscape and vegetation devices that emphasised their exclusivity. Just a little inland another category of resorts was developed around GOLD COURSES, including Coolum, Sanctuary Cove, and in the backblocks of Cairns (Qld). Aimed at the convention trade and the Asian market—especially the Japanese for whom such large golf courses were a real luxury—the garden layouts were usually entrusted to LANDSCAPE ARCHITECTS, often multinational firms.

One of the hallmarks of resort development is that lessees and proprietors are forever having to upgrade their facilities to keep pace with both consumer expectations and changing fashions. In the 1960s, all the Whitsunday Island resorts installed swimming pools. A 1966 report on Queensland's islands remarked that pools were becoming an 'essential amenity' even where sea bathing was readily available. The pool, surrounded by landscaped tropical gardens, provided a setting for drinking, swimming, and socialising, while the beach and the sea were reserved for romantic forays or real oceanic experiences.

A handful of large COMMERCIAL resort gardens were developed in both the nineteenth and twentieth centuries as RECREATIONAL areas. They did not offer accommodation, and were distinct in concept to amusement parks, ZOOLOGICAL GARDENS and THEME PARKS. Deriving ultimately from PLEASURE GARDENS of the 1850s and early TEA GARDENS, the Oasis at Sunnybank, an outer suburb of Brisbane (1950s), was one example and included PLAYGROUND equipment, three swimming pools, manicured hedges, pines relieved by tropical trees and shrubs, and 'aviaries with gaily coloured birds'. Near the Pacific Highway, and serviced by Pioneer buses, it offered morning and afternoon teas and light luncheons.

Modern watering techniques and access to groundwater have enabled the development of resort gardens in ARID ZONES. Modest gardens can be found around hotels in IRRIGATION areas but much more spectacular has been the establishment of glamorous gardens within the resort accommodation at Uluru (NT). These gardens are frequently used in advertising campaigns, with oblique aerial photographs showing the starkness of the central Australian landscape against the oasis landscaping of the resort itself.

> Jim Davidson and Peter Spearritt, *Holiday Business: Tourism in Australia since 1870* (Carlton South, Vic., 2000)

PETER SPEARRITT

RETFORD PARK, Bowral, NSW: see HORDERN

REVEGETATION is the practice of artificially encouraging or facilitating the rapid re-establishment of vegetation, usually with plants common to the area. It is distinguished from regeneration, which is the natural (or only minimally assisted) re-establishment of indigenous vegetation. Revegetation is more than replanting. It may involve WEED and PEST control, the use of FIRE, appropriate fencing, and stock management techniques. Revegetation can be a rural or urban activity and can be undertaken at any scale from a small suburban allotment to vast tracts of rural land.

Initially, revegetation was seen as predominantly the realm of the FORESTER, and was primarily for replacing tree species for potential future commercial use. Many early foresters were conservationists at heart, and often saw that appropriate plantings replaced those removed in forestry operations. URBAN FORESTRY was another influence, although not as potent in Australia as in the USA.

While the idea of revegetation—and some notable examples of it, such as the areas of planting around Broken Hill pioneered by Albert MORRIS—had been around for some time, revegetation received greater attention from the 1970s onwards. There was a recognition that the wholesale clearing of land undertaken since European settlement had caused environmental damage that could be stabilised and reversed to some degree by revegetation. Initially, revegetation was seen as replanting of predominantly the dominant storey of vegetation using Australian native plants. There was little comprehension of the diversity of genetic material within a genus or species and also little concern for the understorey species, particularly forbs and GRASSES.

A strong influence in shifting views on revegetation from the replanting of a broad range of species to restoration of the indigenous bushland was the work of the BRADLEY sisters in Sydney from the late 1960s. They developed principles such as working from good areas towards bad ones, keeping the soil deeply mulched, and allowing regeneration to dictate the rate of clearing. They developed weeding techniques and management regimes to hold the areas in their restored states. The BUSH GARDEN movement was another influence, developing theory and practice in relatively small areas, which could be extended to larger areas such as farmland and open land.

The Potter farmland plan, developed in Victoria's WESTERN DISTRICT during the 1980s, was a benchmark project that saw a new approach to the revegetation of farmland. It demonstrated that there were financial as well as habitat and soil conservation gains to be had from revegetation. It also developed techniques for dealing with large areas that could be effectively transferred to other large areas other than farms. It was largely responsible for the increase in interest in revegetation and was a forerunner of the widely accepted LANDCARE movement, which provides the community focus for revegetation today.

Today, revegetation ideally involves the use of plants of local provenance, a management regime tailored to the site, and some use of design concepts where replanting is undertaken. A burgeoning literature, which includes authors such as Buchanan, Bradley, and Denton, describes different aspects of revegetation.

JAN SCHAPPER

REYNELL, John (1809–1873), pastoralist and vigneron, was a major proponent of VITICULTURE in SA. Born in Ilfracombe, Devon, England, he took up land at Reynella Farm (between Adelaide and McLAREN VALE) in 1841, establishing a successful vineyard. Before migrating to Adelaide (1838), Reynell's observations in Italy and southern France convinced him that

Since the 1970s, REVEGETATION has become a major means of halting or mitigating environmental damage, especially that caused by industrial activity or other past land degradation, as is demonstrated here by plantings for Alcoa at Anglesea (Vic.) in 1977

the vine, fig, and olive could be cultivated in SA. Reynell was a founding member of the Agricultural and Horticultural Society of South Australia.   DAVID JONES

RHODODENDRONS, although introduced into British gardens in the seventeenth century, did not make an impact on gardens until the early nineteenth century—especially after Joseph HOOKER's introductions from the Himalayas in 1849. The first rhododendron to be recorded in Australia was *Rhododendron ponticum*, introduced in 1836 to Alexander MCLEAY's garden at Elizabeth Bay House in Sydney from the MACARTHUR's Camden Park garden. (The first azaleas recorded in Australia, 'Azalea sinensis' and 'Azalea phoenicea', were obtained by McLeay from Loddiges nursery in 1836.) *R. ponticum* was shown at the Launceston Horticultural Show in 1843 and it was available in Adelaide by 1845. In Melbourne it was shown by J.J. RULE at the Horticultural Society's show in 1850.

The availability of species and varieties gradually increased. Camden Park had six species in 1843 and in his 1862 catalogue Michael GUILFOYLE listed ten species as well as seedlings from Sikim seed. Thomas LANG's Ballarat Nursery became a major source for rhododendrons in the late 1860s and early 1870s. In Launceston (Tas.), nursery proprietor Frank WALKER imported twelve 'good varieties' in the 1870s that he used as stock plants, propagating all his plants by layers. His nursery became an important source of supply, with large quantities being sent to Melbourne and Sydney. In 1872 rhododendrons found a place among exhibits at the Horticultural Society of Victoria's show and had a permanent place thereafter.

The advent of HILL-STATION gardens in Australia from the 1870s, with their cool-climate locations and rich soils, greatly stimulated interest in rhododendrons. When TAYLOR AND SANGSTER established their MOUNT MACEDON nursery in 1876 it became particularly notable for its rhododendrons. In NSW, the opening up of the BLUE MOUNTAINS led to rhododendrons being extensively grown there—Mount Wilson being particularly noted for these shrubs. In the ADELAIDE HILLS, rhododendrons also formed popular garden subjects. Many of the rhododendrons were imported but D.E. WHIBLEY, formerly gardener to Sir Edward STIRLING, set up as a nursery concentrating particularly on rhododendrons.

With increasing development of Victoria's Dandenong Ranges during the inter-war period, many nurseries became established there, and several (such as BOULTER's) later specialised in rhododendrons. The Australian Rhododendron Society was formed in 1958, an offshoot from the Ferny Creek Horticultural Society (Vic.). The Society's Victorian branch established the National Rhododendron Gardens at Olinda from 1960: forty hectares in extent, and now a major attraction in spring. During the 1970s, the Society also began establishing gardens in NSW at Mount Pleasant (Illawarra) and Blackheath (Blue Mountains).

Still a garden favourite, although only suited to a relatively small area of the continent, rhododendrons are a major feature of gardens in the cooler parts of SA, Vic., Tas., and NSW. Since the 1980s, interest has increased in the Australia native *Rhododendron lochae*, and other plants of the Vireya group, endemic to South-East ASIA (from northern Australia to the Malay peninsula).   BARNEY HUTTON

RICHARDSON, John Matthew (c. 1797–1882), gardener and horticulturist, convicted of larceny at the Sussex Assizes, England, in 1816, and sentenced to seven years' transportation, arrived in Sydney in 1817. Possessing some nursery experience, he was employed in SYDNEY BOTANIC GARDENS under Charles FRASER, through whose probable agency he participated in at least one of John Oxley's exploratory expeditions from 1818 to 1820. In 1821 the botanical specimens gathered in those explorations afforded the recently pardoned Richardson an opportunity for repatriation, he having been charged by Governor Macquarie with the care of botanical and geological collections being shipped back to England. A year later, however, Richardson reappeared in the Sussex Assizes charged with housebreaking, and was sentenced to transportation for life.

Richardson arrived back in Australia at Hobart Town in 1822, and was assigned to William Jemott, of Macquarie Street, Hobart Town, as a gardener. In the following year he once again came into contact with Fraser, to whom he was reassigned as a servant. He returned with Fraser to Sydney, and to the position of overseer in Sydney Botanic Gardens. In early 1826, together with his new wife and child, Richardson took passage for Melville Island, having been appointed to oversee horticultural activities at the fledgling settlement in return for a salary of £25 per annum. He sailed from there to Timor later that year and returned with plants and seeds presented by the Dutch administrator. With the abandonment of the Melville Island settlement Richardson returned to Sydney in 1829, where he was granted a ticket-of-leave. This privilege was later cancelled in 1831 on account of embezzlement, drunkenness, and insolence, and the ensuing three years saw Richardson undergo a total of 100 lashes for incidents of absconding. Nevertheless, he was appointed to Major Thomas MITCHELL's 1836 expedition as plant collector, and impressed Mitchell sufficiently for him to recommend a conditional pardon from the governor (duly granted in 1837). Richardson subsequently moved to Patrick Plains (Singleton), and died at Newcastle.

DARREN WATSON

RICKARD, Bruce Arthur Lancelot (b. 1929), educated in architecture at the Sydney Technical College (1954), was the first Australian to gain a Master of Landscape Architecture degree (University of Pennsylvania, USA, 1957). He taught courses in LANDSCAPE ARCHITECTURE in the Department of Town and Country Planning, University of Sydney (1958–59), before establishing his own Sydney practice in 1959, to date the longest continuous landscape architecture practice in Australia. Although best known for his domestic architecture, Rickard has always considered the siting of buildings and their associated landscape setting an integral part of his design process, and, with contemporaries Bruce MACKENZIE and Harry HOWARD, he became an advocate for the use of NATIVE PLANTS. His most productive years were the 1970s and 1980s, foremost among his landscape projects being the overall planning and design for the Ocean Shores Resort at Brunswick Heads (NSW), part of the University of Newcastle campus (NSW), West Lakes development (SA), and the grounds of numerous high schools in NSW and the ACT. A founding member of the AUSTRALIAN INSTITUTE OF LANDSCAPE ARCHITECTS, he was a member of the interim council in 1966–67.   ALLAN CORREY

RICKETTS, William (1898–1993), conservationist and artist, developed a SCULPTURE GARDEN at Olinda (Vic.), on a bushland site purchased in 1935. Amid the tree ferns, bracken, and towering gums, he built winding paths and rocky GROTTOES, and fashioned terracotta clay models of Aboriginal people, and plants and animals. Ricketts revered the BUSH as a sacred place to be preserved as a sanctuary of life, SPIRITUALITY, beauty, and peace. Drawing mainly on Dreaming beliefs from Central Australia, Ricketts used the Aboriginal sculptures to depict his fundamental philosophy: the interconnectedness of all life. He donated the site to the Victorian Government in 1962; it operates as a PUBLIC PARK, gallery, and nature reserve.

Peter Brady, *Whitefella Dreaming: The Authorised Biography of William Ricketts* (Olinda, Vic., 1994)   HELEN DOYLE

RIETHMULLER, Francis Lewis (1885–1966), bookkeeper and rosarian, was born in Toowoomba (Qld) and on his retirement (*c*. 1945), in Turramurra (NSW), he developed a keen interest in rose BREEDING. A number of his ROSES remain popular with gardeners, including 'Titian' (1950), 'Spring Song' (1954), 'Gay Vista' (1957), 'Honeyflow' (1957), 'Carabella' (1960), and 'Claret Cup' (1962). Frank Riethmuller was awarded the T.A. STEWART Memorial Award of the NATIONAL ROSE SOCIETY in 1959.   TREVOR NOTTLE

RIGBY, Matthew (d. 1896), started in business in the late 1860s as a fruiterer in Brisbane. He soon diversified as a seed and plant merchant, by 1876 claiming special vice-regal appointment. The *Townsville Times*, reviewing *Rigby's Queensland Gardener's Guide and Catalogue* (1876), thought the book 'generally useful' but 'more suitable for Southern than for Tropical Queensland'. The 1881 edition survives, one of only a handful of extant pre-1920s catalogues for Qld; its comprehensive range indicates that Rigby was at the forefront of the colony's NURSERY trade. A son, John Bennett Rigby (b. 1874), succeeded to the business.   RA

RIMINGTON, George (*c*. 1847–1925), nursery proprietor, was born in Lincolnshire, England, and according to a company history was apprenticed to VEITCH and Sons. E.E. PESCOTT records that he also trained in the gardens and glasshouses of the Earl of Chesterfield and Sir Edward Mosely. Rimington arrived in Vic. in 1871 aboard the *Great Britain*, accompanied by a consignment of Regal Pelargoniums destined for George BRUNNING, thus forging a long friendship. Almost immediately on his arrival, he was engaged as a propagator for Joseph HARRIS at his South Yarra Nurseries, working alongside C.A. NOBELIUS. Rimington left to establish his Park Hill Nurseries at Kew in 1877, specialising in Regal Pelargoniums and palms. The business expanded, with Rimington and his five sons shareholders. The original nursery was increased during the 1930s by an additional site at Clarinda, on the outskirts of Oakleigh, and for the purpose of growing advanced exotic trees, a further area at Mount Dandenong. Expansion continued with acquisition of a large new site at Toolangi for tree stock. Suburban encroachment overtook the original site in the 1950s and in 1975 both the Clarinda and Toolangi nurseries were sold. George Rimington was a leading and highly esteemed member of the Nurserymen and Seedsmen's Association of Victoria, as were members of the second and third generations of this long-established business.   RA

RIPPON LEA, Elsternwick, Vic., developed between 1868 and 1903 by merchant and politician Frederick Thomas Sargood (1834–1903), remains perhaps the largest and most intact nineteenth-century private garden in Australia and is exceptional for the quality of its landscaped garden. The self-sufficient estate of twenty-seven hectares included pleasure grounds, service areas with kitchen gardens, orchards, paddocks, and a rifle range. The grounds were originally laid out in the GARDENESQUE mode but in 1882, following major refurbishment to the residence, which transformed the polychrome brick VILLA into a substantial city MANSION, William SANGSTER was hired to make extensive landscape changes. He introduced a more PICTURESQUE style, sweeping away the previous FORMALITY of geometric beds and paths, introducing a serpentine carriage drive and garden paths. The new landscape, with enlarged LAKE, MOUNT, LOOKOUT tower, GROTTO, and GARDEN BUILDINGS, provided grounds suited to public entertaining and functions increasingly held at the property.

Sargood was a keen horticulturist, ably supported by Adam Anderson (1848–1926), his Scottish head gardener, who had served his apprenticeship at CHATSWORTH, England, and worked at Haddo, the Duke of Aberdeen's Scottish estate, before being recruited by Sargood in London. Sargood established the largest collection of exotic ORCHIDS in colonial Australia and maintained many specialised environments, including a vast SHADE-HOUSE of an elegant double-cusped configuration for his FERN collection. To sustain a garden of this scale, especially with its lake and waterfalls, a sophisticated WATER management system was installed (1870s), and its unique subterranean IRRIGATION and DRAINAGE system continues in use.

Benjamin Nathan (1864–1935), businessman and owner between 1910 and 1935, also used Rippon Lea as a private estate open on occasions to the public. Nathan had a particular passion for orchids and boldly erected a huge display house (1916) opposite the front door, supported by twenty-four glasshouses. Stanley Orchard, an English orchid specialist, was his head gardener. Louisa Jones (1894–1972), eldest daughter of Nathan and last private owner, inherited in 1935 and added a Hollywood-style SWIMMING POOL complex (1938–39). During the 1960s she strenuously fought government plans to compulsorily acquire the main garden to extend neighbouring ABC television studios. Jones worked closely with the NATIONAL TRUST to secure Rippon Lea's

The patchwork of RIVERLAND orchards and vineyards near Berri (SA) highlights the orderly DESIGNED LANDSCAPES associated with Australia's vast IRRIGATION schemes, while the remnant bush in the background hints at the uncertain environmental balance they have created

place in Australian CONSERVATION history as the first property to be saved specifically for its garden.

Mary Ryllis Clark and Celestina Sagazio, *The Story of Rippon Lea* (Melbourne, 1995) RICHARD HEATHCOTE

RIVERLAND, a major IRRIGATION region along the River Murray in SA, first had its potential identified by George GOYDER, and the government encouraged the CHAFFEY brothers to establish an irrigation colony in the mallee scrubland at Renmark in 1887. The venture proved a success —particularly with fruits, olives, sultanas, and currants—until the 1893 bank crash, whereupon the *Renmark Irrigation Trust Act* was gazetted. Olivewood in Renmark (1887), a property linked to Charles Chaffey, younger brother of George and William, was planted with olives, oranges and other fruit trees, and *Washingtonia filifera* (Cotton Palm); these palms were planted along Renmark's main avenue. The Chaffeys used the latest irrigation technology, installing pumps and extensive channels; fruit-growers were guided and settlers encouraged in *The Australian Irrigation Colonies* (1887). Thirteen co-operative villages, including Lyrup, were established in 1899 to deter emigrants to Paraguay and to reduce unemployment in Adelaide. The government fostered extension of the irrigation areas, partly through soldier settlements, between 1908 and 1925, extending the irrigation system, water storages, and pumping stations, and commissioning Charles READE to design Waikerie (1919), Berri (1919), and Barmera (1920), as GARDEN CITIES. Mature palms were replanted from LAKE HARRY at Barmera and Berri in the 1920s, and the KEMP family established the Murray Valley Nursery to provide trees and virus-free vines. The Bookmark Biosphere Reserve was established in the region in 1993. DAVID JONES

RIVER TORRENS LINEAR PARK, SA, along thirty kilometres of river corridor and dissecting the ADELAIDE PARK LANDS, is the largest integrated stormwater management and linear park project in Australia. Envisaged in the 1960s and designed (1975–79) by Hassell, it was completed (costing $34 million) in 1998. Reversing years of abuse, the park integrates nature conservation and recreation planning with innovative low-cost flood mitigation measures, responding to the increasing urban development and run-off in its catchment, in an area of great historic, cultural, and environmental value. DAVID JONES

ROBERTS, James Fountain (1829–1894), landscape gardener and nursery proprietor, was born in Yorkshire, England, son of James Roberts, gardener at Bretton Hall, near Wakefield. His father accepted the prestigious position of gardener to the Duke of Cleveland, at Raby Castle, Durham, at the time his son was completing his schooling. Here James Roberts jnr. began his career as a gardener. He progressed to the seats of Sir Walter Trevelyan (Como, Northumberland), the Duke of Northumberland (Alnwick Castle, with a park by 'Capability' BROWN), and was head gardener to the Dowager Duchess of Cleveland. In 1850 he undertook work at Tunbridge Wells and in 1851 became head foreman of the Chelsea Physic Garden, London, where he was also assistant to LINDLEY in his lectures on materia medica.

Roberts migrated to Victoria in 1852 and entered a partnership in a Prahran nursery. Personal misfortune dogged his early years in the colony, and in 1856 he went overland to Adelaide. He was credited in *Victoria and its Metropolis* (1888) as the originator of the lake in the ADELAIDE BOTANIC GARDENS. He worked in SA as a horticulturist and also in well-sinking for squatters. He had returned to Melbourne by 1863, and in the 1870s opened the York Nursery at Kew, specialising in FLORISTS' flowers, ORCHIDS, and, in later years, fruit trees, as well as laying out and planting gardens. He botanised in New Caledonia in 1886 and was involved in a failed venture to export orchids from New Guinea. E.E. PESCOTT recalled Roberts as the 'Beau Brummel' of the nursery trade, always attending flower SHOWS wearing a white vest and a belltopper hat. After one show opening by Sir Henry Loch, the governor reportedly turned to the committee men and said, 'Now, where are the orchids?'. 'Ah', exclaimed Roberts, 'That's the Governor we want'. RA

ROBERTSON, Enid Lucy: see ASHBY, Edwin

ROBERTSON, Naismith (c. 1784–1844), gardens superintendent, was born in Kilmany, Fifeshire, Scotland. Arriving in Sydney as a steerage passenger in 1829, he soon obtained employment with the MACARTHUR family at Camden Park, where he became principal gardener, entrusted with 'the chief direction of their extensive gardens and vineyards'. After the death of SYDNEY BOTANIC GARDENS superintendent, James ANDERSON (1842), Robertson applied to succeed him. Supported by Alexander MCLEAY, William Macarthur, and noted naturalist–explorer Rev. William Branwhite Clarke (1798–1878), Robertson was selected by the committee of management for the post, to the disappointment of other applicants, including naturalist Ludwig Leichhardt (1813–c. 1848) and James KIDD. Robertson, who was 'not a scientific Botanist, but simply a good practical Gardener', was deemed to be 'considerably advanced in years' (aged 58) and was 'to be called Superintendent of the Botanic Gardens—not Colonial Botanist'. Late in 1842 he travelled to Bathurst and the Bargo area to collect seeds, and returned for more the following year. However, when Leichhardt visited him in 1844 at the behest of Helenus Scott of Glendon, he found that 'the poor man seems to lie on his deathbed'. Naismith Robertson (sometimes named as William Naismith, Nasmyth, or Nasmith), recently delighted by the receipt of a diploma as Fellow of the Royal Academy of Botany in Stockholm for 'transmitting a choice collection of valuable and rare seeds and plants to Sweden', died in his Gardens cottage, his passing 'much regretted by his friends and the numerous and respectable members of his own profession'. He was buried in the Devonshire Street Cemetery not far from fellow botanical Scots Allan CUNNINGHAM, James ANDERSON, and Thomas SHEPHERD. LIONEL GILBERT

ROBERTSON, Neil Roderick Goldsbrough (b. 1955), gardener and bibliophile, worked at the Margareta Webber bookshop in Melbourne (1974–80), building Australia's most comprehensive GARDEN BOOK list. After experience in the London West End bookshop, G. Heywood Hill, he returned to purchase and run Webber's business (1981–86). As National Executive Officer of AUSTRALIA'S OPEN GARDEN SCHEME (1992–), Robertson travels throughout Australia overseeing selection and co-ordination. His office is situated in his garden, Westport, New Gisborne (Vic.), where a large stretch of ornamental water reflects nearby MOUNT MACEDON. He is a noted lecturer, broadcaster, and writer, having recently co-authored *The Open Garden* (2000). TRISHA DIXON

ROBINETTE, Charles (1841–1921), grotto and horticultural builder, was born in Moulton, Lincolnshire, England, and in 1875, following work as a gardener in Yorkshire, he migrated to Adelaide. He first advertised his services in *Garden and Field* in 1881 as 'designer and builder of rockeries, grottoes, ferneries, and all kinds of horticultural structures'. He constructed rockeries 'of fantastic design' at Montefiore (North Adelaide), and The ACACIAS, which William GUILFOYLE visited in 1887, perhaps influencing the expansion of these features in the MELBOURNE BOTANIC GARDENS. The grottoes and rockeries at Montefiore were praised as a triumph 'of nature, art, and practical convenience … The whole is as natural-looking as if it had been carved *in toto* from the side of a mountain stream'. In 1886 Robinette shifted to Melbourne to undertake several public GROTTO and ROCKERY projects, initially under Guilfoyle's patronage, in the Melbourne Botanic Gardens, DOMAIN, ZOOLOGICAL GARDENS, and MELBOURNE GENERAL CEMETERY (recently converted into an Elvis Presley shrine). Other projects were at Malvern Gardens, Darling Gardens (Collingwood), and rockeries at Flemington Racecourse ('in connection with the apartments set apart for the governor'), his last known work (1899). DAVID JONES

ROBINSON, William (1838–1935), Irish-born gardener, horticultural journalist, and author, trained in private gardens and at Glasnevin Botanic Gardens, Dublin, before joining the staff of the Royal Botanic Society's garden in Regent's Park, London (1861). As foreman of the herbaceous department he filled a similar role for the Society as Charles MOORE had, a decade and a half earlier: the two men formed a lasting friendship through Moore's illustrious brother David, Robinson's mentor at Glasnevin. Robinson began his writing in the 1860s, initially through journalism. He spent much of 1867 in FRANCE, studying the horticulture of that country and attending the Paris Exposition Universelle, reporting for the *Times*, the *Field*, and the *GARDENERS' CHRONICLE*. He published his views in *Gleanings from French Gardens* (1868) and *The Parks, Promenades & Gardens of Paris* (1869), especially highlighting advances in fruit and vegetable gardening, and ornamental plants. This latter was also the subject of his influential book *The Subtropical Garden* (1871), which helped popularise BEDDING of plants with bold or ornamental foliage in picturesque groupings, in reaction to massed annual flower bedding. Many plants featured, such as *Wigandia caracasana*, were available in the Australian nursery trade, and extensively used by William GUILFOYLE and Charles Moore to create bold foliage effects. *Alpine Flowers for English Gardens* (1870), *The Wild Garden* (1870), and *Hardy Flowers* (1871) resulted from particular interests of the author, especially in promoting a NATURAL STYLE of gardening. Robinson's writings were well known in Australia, through reviews in the weekly horticultural press, as well as circulation of the *Gardeners' Chronicle* and the books themselves.

The grotto-like ROCKERY at MELBOURNE GENERAL CEMETERY, built by Charles ROBINETTE, is pictured here c. 1892 as his initial bold-foliaged plantings are beginning to take effect

Robinson founded the *Garden* in 1871, a weekly journal he edited until 1899, and he also established several other periodicals. The *Garden* became a mouthpiece for the MARNOCK group, who were keen to reassert the virtues of an informal style of flower gardening. Robinson's major work on FLORICULTURE, *The English Flower Garden: Style, Position, and Arrangement* (1883), ran to many editions and in Australia was perhaps the best known of his books. This gave general advice on his naturalistic style as well lengthy cultural notes on his preferred 'Flowers of the open air'. Robinson entered the debate against formal revivalists in the 1890s and through the work of his friend Gertrude JEKYLL his advocacy of naturalism over formality was brought to new generations and audiences.

Mea Allen, *William Robinson: Father of the English Flower Garden* (London, 1982)   RA

ROBINSON, William Denham (1868–1945), floriculturist and landscape gardener, was born in Pickering, England, and migrated to Melbourne before settling in SA. Trained as a landscape gardener while working in an English plant nursery, he applied these skills and knowledge, particularly with ROSES, and became head gardener at Bythorne in the ADELAIDE HILLS. In 1920 Robinson moved to Mount Gambier and established the Sunnyside Nursery, becoming pre-eminent in CARNATION cultivation and distribution throughout Australia. Known locally as the 'Carnation King of Australia', he developed the popular 'Cheerio' and 'Pink Pearl' cultivars and advocated the establishment of an Australian carnation society. Robinson, as Mount Gambier City Gardener (1928–45), also designed and developed MOUNT GAMBIER CAVE GARDEN (1925), Vansittart Park (1926), and numerous private town and HOMESTEAD GARDENS in the district. He also prepared and supervised the execution of a REVEGETATION master plan for MOUNT GAMBIER LAKES AREA (1925–45). His son Robert William Robinson (b. 1915) succeeded him as City Gardener (1945–64).

DAVID JONES

ROCHLITZ, Julius Albert (Béla) (1824–1886), was born in Hungary and arrived in Australia in 1852, trained as a civil engineer. After an unsuccessful stint on the Victorian gold fields he turned to professional photography at Ballarat. In 1856 he inconclusively responded to the Victorian Government's advertisement for competitive designs to lay out park lands around Melbourne and began working in Beechworth (Vic.), as a photographer. His only known garden plan—for a pleasure ground at Beechworth (1856) —was an imaginative, although unexecuted *tour de force*. Illustrated in Tanner's *Converting the Wilderness* (1979) the plan epitomised the bold idealism of Victoria's gold-rush period. His career as an itinerant photographer, illustrator, and teacher is traced in Joan Kerr's *Dictionary of Australian Artists* (1992).   RA

ROCKERIES and rock gardens and in Australia have been characterised not only by traditional cool-climate plantings but also by plants that grow on dry rocky surfaces with relatively little WATER. Popularised in Britain from the late eighteenth century onwards, rock gardens allowed horticultural enthusiasts to display plants recently discovered from the world's ALPINE regions and other small plants (often not strictly alpine) difficult to display in standard garden beds. JAPANESE and CHINESE gardeners have for centuries used rocks to re-create the geological landscape in miniature; in recent years several Australian public gardens in Australia have been developed in an ORIENTAL style.

In the late nineteenth and early twentieth centuries rockeries and ROOTERIES containing eclectic mixes of rocks, roots, driftwood, SHELLS, and plants were popular features in Australian gardens. At MELBOURNE BOTANIC GARDENS, William GUILFOYLE was prominent among BOTANIC GARDEN directors who developed rock gardens and rockeries as a way of displaying rock-loving plants. Optimum growing conditions required a range of rock sizes and pockets of particular soil types to suit the special requirements of many alpine and other rock-loving (lithophilous) plants for acid or lime soils. Rockeries provided nooks and crannies for many prostrate and creeping plants, and shelter for mosses and lichens. In shady spots these features might be planted with FERNS, ground ORCHIDS, and violets. In more exposed sites they were likely to be planted with CACTI and succulents such as aloes, agaves, mesembryanthemums, sedums, portulacas, echeverias, furcraeas, and yuccas.

In the inter-war period and the 1950s, landscape gardener Paul SORENSEN created rockeries in his BLUE MOUNTAINS gardens often using the hard, weathered ironstone found on the exposed ridge tops of the mountains for displays of alpine plants such as *Aubretia*, *Gentiana*, and *Phlox subulata* (Alpine Phlox). In Vic., Edna WALLING used rock walls as a habitat for trailing plants and the spaces between paving stones for growing ground covers. BUSH GARDENS of the 1960s and 1970s gave rocks new prominence as landscape features, often scattered rather than grouped. Ellis ('Rocky') STONES was especially noted for his placement of rocks, displaying an appreciation of strata and geological character often absent from earlier examples (but stressed in garden books from the mid-nineteenth century). Notable recent examples of rock gardens in botanical gardens are those at the AUSTRALIAN NATIONAL BOTANIC GARDENS and MOUNT TOMAH BOTANIC GARDEN. At Mount Tomah massive blocks of stone have been used to provide a suitable habitat for southern hemisphere cool-climate plants including lobelias, senecios, and proteas.

Rockwork is a feature of many private gardens and public landscapes, often as a means of handling changes in level or of retaining soil. The work of Murdo McLennan (fl. 1893–1912) and Peter Mulheran (fl. 1882–1905) on the walking tracks in the BLUE MOUNTAINS of NSW includes many fine examples of dry stone walls and stone-cut steps. Dry stone walls are also a feature of some RURAL LANDSCAPES, particularly the area around Kiama, on the Illawarra coast of NSW, and in Victoria's WESTERN DISTRICT.

Artificial rockwork—often actual rocks joined or augmented with textured cement render—was used extensively in the late nineteenth and early twentieth centuries for GROTTOES, in both private and public gardens and as shrines in convents, monasteries and other church properties. Specialist grotto builder Charles ROBINETTE, who created many fantastic rockeries, was the Australian pioneer of this art form. Artificial rock made of concrete was also used extensively in ZOOS, such as Sydney's Taronga Zoo, to create enclosures and naturalistic habitats for rock-dwelling animals. Increasingly, artificial rock has been formed from moulds of *in situ* outcrops; in the Tropical Centre at the ROYAL BOTANIC GARDENS, SYDNEY, for example, artificial rockwork was created from casts taken from places such as Kakadu National Park. Sculptures and installations described as stone gardens are a feature of the recent work by artists including Julie Collins, Jill Peck, John Davis, and Andy Goldsworthy on Herring Island in Melbourne's Yarra River. CHRIS BETTERIDGE

ROCKHAMPTON BOTANIC GARDENS, Qld, gazetted in 1869 as a BOTANIC GARDENS reserve, is located on the western slopes of the Athelstone Range on the shores of Murray Lagoon. James Scott EDGAR, appointed inaugural curator in 1873, undertook extensive ACCLIMATISATION experimentation. Only ten acres (4 ha) was intensively cultivated initially, close to the lagoon and therefore easily watered. Edgar's successors were father and son Richard Simmons (1902–31) and H. George Simmons (1931–57), who were also keen naturalists. Early development included recreational and horticultural display facilities: kiosks (1881, replaced 1911) adjacent to a celebrated *Ficus benghalensis* (Banyan), shelter sheds, walks, glasshouse, BUSH-HOUSE (rejuvenated in 1939 as the Hugo Lassen Fernery), and a ZOOLOGICAL collection. Plant distribution to the district reached its peak in the 1920s, with numbers of fruit trees exceeding those of shrubs and ornamental trees. There was also keen demand for bush-house plants and seedling annuals. A WAR MEMORIAL was constructed within the Upper Gardens in 1924. In 1930, Simmons planted out a row of *Araucaria cunninghamii* (Hoop Pine) interplanted with bougainvillea between the Upper and Lower Gardens. During the 1930s, rock-lined drainage channels, road-making, and clearing improvements were undertaken by relief work schemes. Natural disasters such as floods, droughts, and cyclones (1918 and 1949) have caused great losses. Ken C. Baker, appointed manager in 1957, compiled descriptive booklets and a history (1969). Today, the garden is noted for its PALM collection, PINETUM, kiosk under the Banyan, FLORAL CLOCK, and the entry AVENUE of *Araucaria bidwillii* (Bunya Pine) and bougainvillea planted by George Simmons.

K.C. Baker, *The Garden Story: An Historical Review of a Century of Development at the Rockhampton Botanic Gardens* (Rockhampton, Qld, 1969) JEANNIE SIM

RODWAY, Leonard (1853–1936), botanist, migrated from his native Devon, England, to Tas. in 1880, where he practised as a dentist. As a hobby he travelled widely in Tas. to collect plants, unusually among Australian botanists becoming knowledgeable in flowering plants, mosses, liverworts, and fungi. He was honorary botanist to the Tasmanian Government (1896–1932). He lectured widely and wrote

As early as 1910 a huge specimen of *Ficus benghalensis* (Banyan), one of the FIGS popular in tropical regions of Australia, was a feature of ROCKHAMPTON BOTANIC GARDENS (Qld)

extensively on the island's flora, most notably *The Tasmanian Flora* (1903), *Ferns of Tasmania* (1905), *Some Wildflowers of Tasmania* (1910), and *Tasmanian Bryophyta* (1914–16). His collections are housed mainly in the Tasmanian Herbarium and the National Herbarium of Victoria. He named a number of new species, including flowering plants and agarics (toadstools), and several plants are named after him.

ALEX GEORGE

ROE, John Septimus (1797–1878), British naval officer, surveyor, and explorer, had undertaken extensive surveys in eastern Australia when offered the position of surveyor-general at the new Swan River settlement. He arrived on the *Parmelia* in 1829. Roe was first and foremost an explorer and surveyor, with botanical collecting a subordinate activity. He undertook sixteen carefully documented expeditions into the interior of WA where he made botanical collections used at KEW by George BENTHAM in writing *Flora Australiensis*. He was associated with LAND SURVEY of many town lots in Perth and Fremantle, including reservation of the future KINGS PARK reserve.   GREGORY and BRONWEN KEIGHERY

ROGERS, Frederick James Charles (1927–1996), teacher, botanist, and horticulturist, was born in Horsham (Vic.) and became a strong advocate for AUSTRALIAN FLORA. He willingly shared his knowledge, through his books *A Field Guide to Victorian Wattles* (1968), *Growing Australian Native Plants* (1971), and *Growing More Australian Native Plants* (1978), as well frequent lectures on propagation and cultivation of Australian plants. He also founded two of the largest Victorian district groups (Maroondah and Wimmera) of the SOCIETY FOR GROWING AUSTRALIAN PLANTS.   JOHN WALTER

RONA, Bellevue Hill, NSW, a large landscaped estate, was formed *c.* 1883 by sugar magnate Edward William Knox (1847–1933), around a neo-Gothic sandstone house, sheltered by WINDBREAKS of *Cinnamomum camphora* (Camphor Laurel), *Ficus* sp., and pine, beyond which were cow paddocks. A drive of crushed brick and stone led up to a carriage sweep ringed with camellias and azaleas. The house sat on a grassed plateau with VISTAS to Sydney Harbour framed by ARAUCARIAS, *Agathis robusta* (Kauri Pine), *Magnolia grandiflora* (Bull Bay), and clumps of giant BAMBOO, and with lower grassy slopes accented by sweeps of South African bulbs. Indented in to the hillside, the quarry for the house became a terraced garden, its cliff faces garlanded with wisteria. The original circumstance is well conveyed in Helen Rutledge's *My Grandfather's House* (1986); today only the immediate setting of the house and its major trees survive.

HOWARD TANNER

The flats at Domain Park Towers, South Yarra (Vic.), designed during 1960–61 by architect Robin Boyd, incorporated a rudimentary ROOF GARDEN but the powerful imagery of high-rise living his drawing conjured was the focus of landscape innovation in succeeding decades

RONALDS, Nathaniel (c. 1840–1898), nursery proprietor and florist, born in Staffordshire, England, migrated to Australia in 1848 with his father, Alfred Ronalds (1802–1860), and five of his six siblings. Many ancestors were in the nursery and seed trade, most notably his uncle Hugh Ronalds (1759–1833), author of *Pyrus Malus Brentfordiensis* (1831). Ronalds gained experience at his father's market garden, the Wendouree Nursery Gardens (Ballarat, Vic.), at Excelsior Nursery (Richmond Park), and as head gardener to W.R. Virgoe at the Old CHATSWORTH Nursery (Brighton). He was also contracted to lay out ST VINCENT GARDENS in 1869. He purchased land in New Street, Brighton (c. 1876), to set up his own nursery and florist's business. His principal business was in cut flowers for bouquets, which averaged 800 per month in 1878. Among general stock, the Brighton nursery stocked some 400 species and varieties of ORCHIDS. In c. 1887 he established Ronalds Central Florist in Swanston Street, which soon gained a reputation as one of the finest in Melbourne. About this time he acquired nine hectares of the Riddell Estate in MOUNT MACEDON to supply flowers at all seasons as well as growing large quantities of alpine flowers and FERNS.

In 1891 Ronalds experienced severe financial difficulty, and the bank foreclosed on his Macedon and Brighton nurseries. The florist's business continued under the direction of his daughter Maria Emily Ronalds (1870–1942) and a Miss W.M. Fawcett, maintaining its reputation for floral excellence. In the late 1920s, another daughter, Mary Ellen ('Mollie') Ronalds (1891–1976), purchased seven hectares opposite the original Macedon site as a nursery and to supply material to the florists, as did sons Lindsay (1896–1956) and Ralph Nathaniel Ronalds (1898–1958) in nearby Governors Drive and Brougham Road respectively. Daughters Lily Agnes (1892–1981) and Ivy Ronalds (1894–1979) opened Kays Florist in Flinders Way, Melbourne. Ivy later taught floral art at the Emily McPherson College and established her own floral art school in 1945. Despite succumbing to ill health and financial problems before his death, Nathaniel Ronalds displayed considerable entrepreneurial spirit and indefatigable industry to achieve both success and notoriety in his chosen fields.

A.F. Ronalds, *The Ronalds Family of Australia* (North Balwyn, Vic., 1985)

JACKIE COURMADIAS

ROOF GARDENS do not have a long tradition in Australia as a popular form of garden or landscape design. This is possibly due to the perceived spatial expansiveness of the physical environment, with its generous suburban landscape, where residential allotments were regulated by setbacks from the street frontage dictated by local governments. Indeed, there has been an inherent suspicion of flat roofs—a prerequisite for roof gardens—since their introduction to Australia at the start of the twentieth century by architect George Sydney Jones. The use of the roof as an extension to the living areas of domestic buildings was promoted by Walter and Marion GRIFFIN in some of their designs for buildings at Sydney's CASTLECRAG estate in the 1920s. An attempt was made to create not only alternative living space but LOOKOUT vantage points and to reduce the visual impact of pitched tiled roofs and the scale of the buildings to create the illusion of living in the BUSH.

Early commercial roof gardens were created atop Farmers Building (later Grace Bros.) (1912) and Feltex House (1930s), both in Sydney. Many Australian roof gardens were found in the commercial realm, almost as novelty items or special marketing features, reflecting contemporary overseas fashions set by such commercial premises as Derry & Tom's department store, Kensington, London (1931–33), Geoffrey Jellicoe's simulated moonscape roof garden for Harvey's Store, Guildford, England (1956), and examples at the Festival of Britain, London (1951). American precedents and influences included the work of Roberto Burle Marx in South America and Thomas Church in California during the 1930s and 1940s respectively.

Roof gardens as extensions to domestic living areas were emphasised from the late 1960s. In Sydney, The Penthouses development, Darling Point (1968), a collaboration between architect Ken Woolley and landscape architect Bruce MACKENZIE, expressed a stepped series of planted terraces overlooking Sydney Harbour. This project revived and stimulated a series of roof garden designs in Sydney during the 1970s using native plants, many designed by Bruce Mackenzie and Associates; notable examples including Readers' Digest Building, Surrey Hills (1969), Ku-ring-gai College of Advanced Education, Lindfield (1971–73), and Oatley College of Advanced Education (1981). Roof gardens for office blocks and residential units were also designed by Bruce RICKARD, James Mitchell, and Stuart Pittendrigh in the early to mid-1970s. Perhaps the most extravagant gardens were those constructed as part of the Cameron Offices, Canberra (1974–76), to the collaborative design of John Andrews and Don Sigsby. In the same period an extensive roof garden was designed and built under the supervision of the New South Wales Government Architect's Office for the extension to Parliament House. Harry HOWARD designed the roof garden at the High Court of Australia, Canberra (1979). Hotel development also resulted in roof gardens such as Sydney's Wentworth and Hyatt hotels.

The National Gallery of Victoria and Art Gallery of New South Wales both integrated roof gardens with SCULPTURE GARDENS. The idea of the roof garden as both sculpture and outdoor room had its precedents in the works of Antonio Gaudi in Spain and Le Corbusier in France. This has been taken up by the office of Marsh Freedman in the rooftop design of the State Bank building in Martin Place, Sydney (1987), where sculptural form and colour are manipulated to create a rooftop to be viewed from above.

The lack of plants in some contemporary examples follows from practical issues of avoiding extra building structure to support the high loads created by soil and planting containers, and the sometimes unfavourable microclimate created by tall buildings in the urban environment. One of the most influential recent examples has been the University of Melbourne underground car park, where mushroom-headed columns contain tree planters—an elegant means of reclaiming urban open space. The new Parliament House, Canberra is a significant recent example, with its turf roof and extensive courtyard gardens, designed using sand-based construction methods and controlled slow-release fertiliser techniques.

CRAIG BURTON

ROOKWOOD CEMETERY, sixteen kilometres west of Sydney at Haslems Creek, was opened in 1867 following extensive landscaping and development of the large site extending over several years. Like Springvale (Vic.) it was called a 'necropolis', or city of the dead, and was the largest and most ambitious of the nineteenth-century Australian CEMETERY schemes. It also came closest to J.C. LOUDON's 1843 precept, where 'a general cemetery ... properly designed, laid out, ornamented with tombs, planted with trees, shrubs and herbaceous plants, all named and the whole properly kept, might become a school of instruction in architecture, sculpture, landscape gardening, arboriculture, botany and those important parts of general gardening, neatness order and high keeping'. Its style and layout were PICTURESQUE with winding avenues and paths leading visitors from a central circuit to the various denominational compartments. There was an impressive attempt to incorporate natural water courses in an elaborate serpentine DRAINAGE system with ponds and fountains, and as the site was developed and extended, a variety of chapels, gazebos, covered walkways, and family mausolea were added. A notable feature was connection to the main railway line with fine mortuary stations designed by government architect James Barnett at either end. Funeral trains were in regular use until 1948. Planting at Rookwood drew on a diverse range of traditions. In some compartments, an attempt at GARDENESQUE formality was achieved with exotics and specimen plantings. In others, native vegetation mixed with cypresses and pines gave a more informal appearance, while in large areas an English garden effect was created with buildings and monuments alike mimicking traditional follies and 'surprising' the visitor. Several significant figures had a hand in the planning and subsequent development of Rookwood, including Charles MOORE and Simeon Henry Pearce (1821–1886), a trustee and manager of the Necropolis. Loudon and the early planners would have been proud of the fact that the cemetery became a popular place for Sydneysiders to stroll and relax in the late nineteenth century.

David A. Weston, *The Sleeping City: The Story of Rookwood Necropolis* (Sydney, 1989) ROBERT NICOL

ROOTERY Although now seldom encountered, the rootery (or stumpery, as it was sometimes termed) was a feature of many mid-Victorian gardens, especially those of a naturalistic or informal character. Roots were often used in ornamental structures in eighteenth-century British gardens and during the nineteenth century great interest attached to the ornamental value of living tree roots. Alfred Young in the *New South Wales Gardener* (1880s) described the rootery as a substitute for the ROCKERY and integral to the 'RUSTIC attraction of the WILD GARDEN':

> a very bold effect may be produced by the use of crooked and knotted limbs of trees, stumps, and curiously-shaped roots. Stumps and roots should be embedded in an inverse position, so that the hollows and interstices may be utilized by planting in them Ferns and Orchids, or other small plants.

A fine example at RIPPON LEA dated from the 1870s. As late as 1905 LUFFMANN was still recommending inclusion of a rootery or rockery in the farm garden, and urging use of local materials. The best surviving British examples are at Biddulph Grange, Staffordshire, where one dead tree trunk, planted upside down (with its roots forming a canopy), is known colloquially as the 'Australian tree'.

RA

ROSALIND PARK, fronting Bendigo's Pall Mall, is one of Victoria's most impressive PUBLIC PARKS. Dedicated as a recreation reserve in 1861 (on the site of a government camp), the park was developed during 1870–1910 and encompasses an upper reserve (Camp Hill), lower reserve, fernery, Conservatory Gardens, Queen Victoria Gardens, and extensive areas devoted to government buildings and SPORTS facilities. The twenty-five-hectare reserve straddles Bendigo Creek and from a poppet head on the highest point of the sloping site a fine regional panorama is obtained. A reconstructed cascade highlights the steep topography. The Conservatory Gardens, laid out in 1886 by curator Samuel Gadd, houses a fine CONSERVATORY (1897), while the open-air FERNERY was praised in 1891 'by competent authorities in the neighbouring colonies as the finest fernery in Australia'. Annual bedding displays in the Conservatory Gardens and seasonal displays of indoor plants in the conservatory are a major attraction. The Queen Victoria Gardens (1901) contains display beds of *Canna* and other shrubs. The park's numerous AVENUES are of oak, elm, *Pinus canariensis* (Canary Island Pine), *Cedrus deodara* (Deodar), and *Brachychiton populneus* (Kurrajong). Unusual trees include *Prunus ilicifolia* (Holly Leaved Cherry), *Ulmus glabra* (Wych Elm), *Umbellularia californica* (Californian Bay Tree), *Flindersia australis* (Australian Teak), *Phoenix reclinata* (Senegal Date Palm), *Podocarpus falcatus* (Outeniqua Yellowood), and *Brachychiton rupestris* (Queensland Bottle Tree).

FRANCINE GILFEDDER

ROSEDALE, Campbell Town, Tas., is Australia's most archetypal VILLA estate of the early Victorian period, conforming very much to the 'beau ideal' laid down by such architectural writers as J.C. LOUDON. The original bungalow was built in 1828 for pastoralist John Leake (1780–1865), who in 1847 engaged architect James Blackburn (1803–1854) to aggrandise the house, and 'who from a plain cottage has converted it into a beautiful villa in the Italian style' (wrote H.B. Stoney in 1856). Seen against distant hills, Rosedale looks out over the fertile flats of the Elizabeth River. The drive comes in from the side, skirts the pleasure garden, and before the house is a gravelled sweep edged by a curving wall. From the old carriage road it is a remarkable piece of antipodean theatre. Behind are farm buildings dominated by imposing stables and against the linking wall is a heated vinery.

CLIVE LUCAS

ROSÉN (*olim* PERSSON), Lars (Archie) (1862–1951), nursery proprietor, was born at Bjarsjolagard, Skane, Sweden, into a family of tenant farmers. After working in English nurseries he set out in 1890 to migrate to New Zealand, but having lost his passage money gambling on board ship was forced to stay in Australia and seek employment. Persson adopted the surname Rosén and worked in nurseries at Ermington and Rydalmere (NSW), before becoming manager of VOLLMER's Mount Tomah Nursery. After leaving there in 1901 he established the Fernhill Nursery at Carlingford, moving several times to virgin land (as was the contemporary practice for nurseries raising citrus trees). He developed an extensive trade in citrus plants, regularly exporting them to California. While his 1907 catalogue dealt primarily with fruit trees, roses and ornamental shrubs were also included. Rosén was especially interested in advances in technology and marketing and used his expertise in these to develop a long and successful business.

In 1908 Rosén's Copenhagen-born second cousin, John Will Edgard Larsen (1887–1977), arrived from Denmark. He worked in the nursery, eventually marrying Rosén's daughter Edith. Son Conrad Wilfred Rosén (1892–1932) joined the firm, subsequently L.P. Rosén and Son, and on his father's retirement (1926) assumed its management in partnership with Larsen. Following Conrad Rosén's early death Larsen ran the nursery until it was sold to ANDERSON and Co. (1942).

RICHARD CLOUGH

ROSES are likely to have been imported to Australia in the late eighteenth century, but a precise date of introduction is not known. A happy coincidence of a strong cultural tradition of rose growing transposed from ENGLAND and a benign CLIMATE has brought roses to pre-eminence as garden flowers in Australia. While they do not prosper equally across the continent, roses are everywhere desired and popular garden plants, even to the point of frustration for gardeners in the northern tropical zone. In the settled southerly areas of WA, SA, NSW, ACT, Vic., and Tas., roses flourish.

Free settlers accompanying the First Fleet may well have attempted to transport rose cuttings and small plants from gardens at the Cape of Good Hope. The gardens maintained there by the Governors of the East India Company, and the private gardens of farmers and townspeople contained many old European roses essential to the manufacture of homoeopathic remedies for eye diseases and for home-made toiletries. It is known that settlers in the First Fleet bought plants in Cape Town and on nearby farms to bring with them on the last leg of their long journey. While the CAPE was probably the primary source of roses brought to Australia in the late eighteenth century, some may also have come directly from nursery gardens in trade stations on the coast of CHINA. With free trade unimpeded by quarantine regulations, individual entrepreneurs interested in ACCLIMATISATION had free rein to introduce whatever they wished. The common yellow *Rosa banksiae* 'Lutea' (Lady Banks Rose), a Chinese garden rose, was introduced to England in 1825 from plants purchased in the vicinity of Canton by plant hunter John Parks. It was well established in Sydney gardens by the 1840s—planted as early as 1825 according to Charles FRASER—as was another Chinese rose *R. bracteata*. Alexander MCLEAY of Elizabeth Bay House obtained roses from Loddiges nursery (London) and directly from China, but most came from William MACARTHUR.

From the few varieties listed in McLeay's garden the number of roses available in Australia rapidly increased as new hybrids flooded onto the market from breeders in FRANCE, England, and GERMANY. The mid-nineteenth-century gold rushes and pastoral booms boosted demand for drought-tolerant and decorative garden flowers; roses were among the most popular of all garden plants. Nursery catalogues of the late nineteenth century list many hundreds of new rose NOVELTIES as well as hundreds of established garden roses. New classes of repeat flowering roses such as Hybrid Perpetuals and Tea roses displaced older, less frequently flowering kinds of roses: Bourbons, Noisettes, and the old-fashioned once-flowering European roses.

Garden fashion dictated formal rose gardens laid out with PERGOLAS and walks with strong axial lines and, most likely, a central FOUNTAIN or pool. Private and public gardens aspired to extensive collections of roses displayed separately from other parts of the garden, and in the case of large country gardens these 'rosaries' could be dominant garden features. At the turn of the nineteenth century, the rose garden at ANLABY, Kapunda (SA), was reported to be the largest in the southern hemisphere, containing thousands of roses each with its own cast-bronze name tag. As well as bush roses there were extensive plantations of climbing roses and pillar roses trained on ropes, rose 'maypoles', against buildings, and on trellis-work screens.

Alister CLARK, a gentleman farmer of Glenara, Bulla (Vic.), was a keen amateur rose grower who used his leisure and income to pursue a personal goal of BREEDING garden roses that would flower repeatedly and prolifically in the warm, dry conditions of Australian summers. His dedication resulted in the introduction, between the 1920s and the 1940s, of more than 135 roses. Many of these have been collected and conserved by Susan IRVINE and John Nieuwesteeg (b. 1946), among others. More recently, rose breeders such as Sister XAVIER, Lilia Weatherly (b. 1927), and Richard Walsh (b. 1945) have continued Clark's vision, breeding and selecting garden roses that perform well in Australia.

Since the mid-nineteenth century, significant public rose collections have been maintained at BOTANIC GARDENS such as those at Adelaide and Melbourne, and in PUBLIC PARKS in

The popularity of the large rose garden at ADELAIDE BOTANIC GARDEN, a showpiece of Richard SCHOMBURGK's curatorship, demonstrated the high public esteem ROSES attracted in the late nineteenth century, and have retained for more than a century

cities and towns. Collections of modern and heritage roses have been conserved and displayed in restored formal rose gardens at WERRIBEE PARK (Vic.) and at CARRICK HILL (SA). At URRBRAE HOUSE (SA) a collection illustrating the development of the rose through HYBRIDISING adds an important historical focus. A collection of species roses has been made at MOUNT LOFTY BOTANIC GARDEN in the Adelaide Hills, and another has recently been established at the Orange Botanic Gardens (NSW). These are displayed in an informal shrubbery that offers a contrast to the formalism dominant in other gardens.

Groups such as the NATIONAL ROSE SOCIETY and Heritage Roses—Australia (1979–) flourish in most states, dedicated to popularising all kinds of roses from those used for exhibition purposes to the species and old-fashioned kinds. These societies support many educational programs, display gardens and activities. The Roy and Heather RUMSEY Memorial Rose Garden at PARRAMATTA PARK in Sydney is one such garden that honours two prominent commercial rosarians. At Kojonup (WA) is a garden of heritage roses including many unknown garden roses that have been found and propagated by enthusiasts such as Rose Marsh (b. 1939). The influence of garden fashions has seen a revival of COTTAGE GARDENS in which informal mixed plantings of roses, flowering shrubs, perennials, herbs, bulbs and annuals has displaced more formal design. Roses, however, still tend to be predominant.

The tradition of large privately owned country gardens where roses are a strong feature continues in gardens such as HUGHES PARK near Watervale in the Clare Valley (SA) and in the extensive rose collection of David RUSTON at Renmark (SA). The advent of AUSTRALIA'S OPEN GARDEN SCHEME has stimulated interest in roses as plants that have a long flowering season and thereby enable garden owners to maintain a degree of floral continuity from early summer until early winter; a feature of roses that has always endeared them to gardeners across the country. TREVOR NOTTLE

ROSEWORTHY AGRICULTURAL COLLEGE, SA, was the first AGRICULTURAL COLLEGE in Australia. Established in 1883 following advocacy by various individuals, including Albert MOLINEUX and George GOYDER, Roseworthy led major innovations in agricultural and VITICULTURAL education and research in Australian for many years. Professor John Daniel Custance (1842–1923), its first professor, laid out the ARBORETUM with advice from John Ednie BROWN, who provided the first BOTANY and ARBORICULTURE classes. The grounds and arboretum were maintained by Bill and Keith Fairlie during 1919–67.

> Geoffrey C. Bishop, *Australian Winemaking: The Roseworthy Influence. The Contribution of Alan R. Hickinbotham and Roseworthy Agricultural College to Winemaking in Australia* (Hawthorndene, SA, 1980) DAVID JONES

ROSSER, Celia Elizabeth (b. 1930), botanical artist, was born in Melbourne and had art training at the Royal Melbourne Institute of Technology before moving to east Gippsland where she taught art and raised her family. While there Rosser became inspired by the local flora and began painting plant subjects. This led her to exhibit work in Melbourne, and in turn to her 'discovery' by the botanical world. In 1970, Rosser joined the staff of Monash University as the Faculty of Science artist, initially preparing illustrations of mosses for *The Mosses of Southern Australia* (1976). In 1974 she was appointed Monash University Botanical Artist, and in this singular role she embarked upon the task of painting all species of BANKSIA, published in the three magisterial volumes, *The Banksias* (1981–2000), with text by Alex GEORGE. Rosser has emerged as the greatest artist to paint this genus—one that is technically very challenging.

Rosser works in the minutest detail. The mosses were captured in pencil and other subjects are painted in water colour. The thoroughness with which each species has been captured is extraordinary, from her field observations through to design, delineation, and execution. Apart from books, she has also painted for commissions, for postage stamps, and for exhibition. Rosser was awarded the Jill Smythies Award (1996) by the LINNEAN SOCIETY of London and an honorary Doctorate of Laws (2000) by Monash University in honour of her internationally significant contribution to BOTANICAL ART. HELEN HEWSON

ROSSI, Benvenuto Vincenzo (1860–1953), lithographer, nursery proprietor, and rosarian, was born at Casale-Monferrato near Asti, Piemonte, Italy. He trained as a lithographer in Turin and worked in that capacity in Egypt for three years, before leaving Port Said in the German ship *Salier* bound for the USA. He arrived in Melbourne in 1887 en route and settled there, initially living at Fitzroy. Following his marriage in 1892 he purchased land at Coburg; in 1898, having been introduced to the 'Queen of Flowers' by Melbourne rosarian Frederick Buzaglo, he started a carnation and rose nursery while working as a lithographer with Troedel & Co. Rossi's earliest catalogue (1900), which he lithographed in hand-written form, listed more than 150 varieties of ROSE. Widowed in 1910, Rossi and his son, Julius Vincent Rossi (1893–1959), moved to Ivanhoe, where in 1912 he established his celebrated Roseland nursery. Fond of Gorgonzola cheese and the poetry of Dante (which he translated), Rossi—known as the 'Rose Wizard'—brought an Italian exuberance to the stuffy Melbourne rose world. He was a prolific exhibitor and prize winner, especially among the ranks of the NATIONAL ROSE SOCIETY OF VICTORIA. J.V. Rossi took over Roseland in 1926—by then a Mecca for garden lovers—and in retirement at his Ivanhoe house, Sunny South, B.V. Rossi published his very popular book *Modern Roses in Australia* (1930). He was a prolific contributor to horticultural journals and in popular demand as a lecturer. The nursery closed during the 1950s. RA

ROSS ROSES, a long established family nursery in SA specialising in roses, was commenced by **Alexander Ross** (1895–1983), son of Guernsey-born emigrant George David Ross (1860–1959), who had grown fruit trees at Norton Summit (SA) from 1902. Ross began growing roses for sale at his parents' home and nursery at Montacute on the Adelaide

Plains c. 1915 and after a series of partnerships set up on his own at Torrensville in 1936. Continuing growth in business saw several moves within the suburb of Edwardstown until 1964 when further room for expansion necessitated a move to Bedford Park, at that time on the southern outskirts of the city. Here, on the banks of Sturt Creek, Alex was joined by his son **Deane McLaren Ross** (1930–1993), who brought to the business a keen interest in old-fashioned roses, which he imported from Graham Stuart Thomas, then at the Sunningdale Nursery in England. He was also able to secure a license to grow and sell roses introduced by the famed Meilland family of France. Deane established a large DISPLAY GARDEN but continued growth of the business—and of the suburbs—compelled a move further south to farmland near Willunga. Here Deane and his wife Maureen (b. 1935) and son Andrew (b. 1962) continued to build the business. Ross Roses still trades as a family nursery from the Willunga site despite Deane's untimely death. His outstanding contribution to growing old-fashioned roses is commemorated in the Deane Ross Memorial Award, given biennially to a person or persons who have advanced heritage roses in Australia.

TREVOR NOTTLE

ROTUNDA, a garden building (especially a TEMPLE) with a circular ground plan or hall, particularly one with a dome. Ancient models were found in classical Roman architecture and the naming is from the Latin *rotondo* (*camera*), round (chamber), the feminine gender of *rotundus* (round), perhaps furtively invoking the plump connotations of the English word rotund. The rotunda was revived during the Renaissance and thence found its way into eighteenth-century LANDSCAPE GARDENS. Australian examples are rare, but rotundas were used to evoke ITALIANATE imagery, as at Melbourne's FITZROY GARDENS (1873). William GUILFOYLE's Temple of the Winds (1901) at MELBOURNE BOTANIC GARDENS cleverly evokes a glorious past, in this case Victorian rather than classical, by wittily using Australian Stag Fern capitals on his rotunda columns to help commemorate C.J. LA TROBE and his founding role in the Gardens. The term was also often applied to BANDSTANDS (especially circular ones) and is now indiscriminately used to describe small SUMMER-HOUSES or gazebos.

RA

ROUSE HILL estate, NSW, was begun in 1813 by Richard and Elizabeth Rouse, who arrived in NSW as free settlers in 1801. The Rouse family's taste was conventional, as demonstrated by their Georgian-style house and landscape improvements. While later generations of the family explored most of the gardening fashions of the nineteenth century, they remained within Richard Rouse's uncompromising rectilinear garden composition. Some of their nineteenth-century exotic plantings survive. Now reduced from almost 500 hectares to a garden and modest paddocks of ten hectares, Rouse Hill's unbroken chain of family occupancy has preserved its major landscape features from 1825 to the present. Its ARBOURS, Chinoiserie SUMMER-HOUSE, fencing, locally obtained ironstone gravel paths, and regionally thrown ceramic containers provide a case study for the development of garden practices in this low-rainfall region of the Hawkesbury district. The Rouse Hill estate is now a property of the Historic Houses Trust of New South Wales.

MICHAEL BOGLE

ROWAN, (Marian) Ellis (1848–1922), wildflower painter, was born in Melbourne, daughter of Charles Ryan, pastoralist and later stock and station agent, and creator of the celebrated garden Derriweit at MOUNT MACEDON. Rowan's maternal grandfather, John Cotton (1802–1849), was a pioneer naturalist in Vic. Following her education in Melbourne, Rowan visited England and probably took art lessons, though she claimed to have been entirely self-taught as an

The Italian flag flies over the gate of Roseland, B.V. ROSSI's nursery in Ivanhoe (Vic.) during the First World War while a collection box for the Italian Red Cross stands prominently in the office—both obvious indicators of his proud heritage

The Victorian SUMMER-HOUSE at ROUSE HILL, located at the periphery of the early squared garden plots, brings an unmistakable ORIENTAL INFLUENCE to its design—perhaps unconsciously echoing the rich treasures in the garden originating from the Orient

artist. She began exhibiting her watercolour paintings at about the time of her marriage in 1873 to Frederic Charles Rowan, a British army officer then serving in New Zealand and later a successful businessman of Melbourne.

Ellis Rowan took up a career of travel and adventure after meeting the world-travelling English flower painter, Marianne NORTH, at Albany (WA) in 1880. Following North's practice of recording subjects in their native habitats, she travelled to remote parts of Australia: to northern Qld in 1887 and 1891–92, and WA in 1889. Rowan first came to Qld with the goal of collaborating with her friend Ferdinand MUELLER on a serial edition on Australasian flora, but the proposal did not proceed. A woman of indomitable will and courage, she forsook her husband and young son to pursue her travels, and returned to Melbourne only shortly before the untimely death of her husband (1892). Thereafter Rowan extended her travels: to New Zealand (1893–94), London (1895–96), the USA and the West Indies (1897–1903), and later to SA, NSW, and back to Qld and WA. Travelling in Papua New Guinea from 1916 (then in her late sixties), she contracted malaria, which eventually led to her death.

In a career spanning fifty years, Ellis Rowan produced well over 3000 paintings and won numerous medals at intercolonial and international EXHIBITIONS of art and industry. She subsidised her travels with exhibitions held throughout Australia and as far afield as London (1896) and New York (1902). Her Sydney exhibition of 1920 set national records in its size (more than 1000 exhibits) and its takings (over £2000). Rowan's efforts to raise public appreciation of the AUSTRALIAN FLORA extended beyond her prodigious painting. Also a skilled writer and publicist, she recounted her travels in the popular press and in her books *A Flower-Hunter in Queensland and New Zealand* (1898) and *Bill Baillie: His Life and Adventures* (1908).

While portraying herself as a neglected artist, Ellis Rowan was able to sell large collections of her paintings to the governments of NSW, SA, and Qld, and in later life had a 'memorial' committee lobbying the Federal Government to purchase her remaining collection. The collection of 947 paintings was purchased in 1923, and is now housed in the National Library of Australia. Rowan's bold, close-up compositions set her apart from other Australian flower painters of her era, as did her public success. In the words of art historian Joan Kerr, 'the fact that a colonial woman could make an international reputation from the despised female "hobby" of flower painting … was a considerable achievement'.

H.J. Samuel, *Wild Flower Hunter: The Story of Ellis Rowan* (London, 1961); Margaret Hazzard, *Australia's Brilliant Daughter: Ellis Rowan, Artist, Naturalist, Explorer, 1848–1922* (Richmond, Vic., 1984); Judith McKay, *Ellis Rowan: A Flower-Hunter in Queensland* (Brisbane, 1990) JUDITH McKAY

ROYAL AUSTRALIAN INSTITUTE OF PARKS AND RECREATION: see PARKS AND LEISURE AUSTRALIA

ROYAL BOTANIC GARDENS, CRANBOURNE, Vic., is an annexe of the ROYAL BOTANIC GARDENS, MELBOURNE. The initial 160-hectare site, purchased in 1970 by the Victorian Government to grow and display native AUSTRALIAN PLANTS, has been increased to more than 360 hectares. Natural heathlands, swamplands, and woodlands are to be complemented under a 1995 master plan by landscaped zones. The most important of these will be an Australian Garden designed by landscape architects Taylor and Cullity in association with Paul THOMSON to form a twenty-five-hectare self-contained exhibit garden located in a former sand quarry. Although an important natural refuge and now within a rapidly developing urban growth corridor, the project has to date been poorly funded since the original purchase. It has, however, had consistent support (including land purchases) from the Maud M. Gibson Trust. The site is also home for the Australian Research Centre for Urban Ecology. ML

ROYAL BOTANIC GARDENS, KEW, one of the most important BOTANIC GARDENS in the world, is situated beside the River Thames in Richmond, a suburb of London. Kew is a Mecca for visitors who, while admiring the beautifully maintained and colourful displays, are largely unaware of the scientific basis and horticultural expertise that underpin those displays. Occupying 120 hectares of sandy and gravelly riverflats, Kew nevertheless boasts a collection of living plants exceeding 40 000 taxa representing about 25 000 species. An annexe, Wakehurst Place, situated fifty kilometres south of London in Sussex, was acquired in 1968. With its higher rainfall and better soil, Wakehurst Place offers a dramatically different environment, permitting an increased range of plants to be grown. Here is the *Nothofagus* collection and many species of Australian Proteaceae are growing outdoors. The Kew HERBARIUM of more than six million specimens is rich in type specimens, particularly of Australian species, while the LIBRARY contains an unparalleled collection of books and periodicals plus extensive collections of botanical art and archival material.

Originally a private garden belonging to the royal family, Kew became a scientific centre after 1772, when Joseph BANKS assumed its management at the request of his friend George III. From this position, and enjoying as he did the presidency of the ROYAL SOCIETY, Banks exercised all his influence and entrepreneurial skills in encouraging the study of BOTANY, the systematic collection of plants from all over the world, and the practice of HORTICULTURE. Australia's connection with Kew was firmly established under the aegis of Banks, tangible evidence of his abiding interest in the continent whose botany he did so much to elucidate. This was epitomised by the famous Botany Bay House, which from 1788 to 1856 was generally bursting with species from New Holland. To further the study of the unique AUSTRALIAN FLORA Banks sent botanical collectors to NSW, notably George CALEY, who was in the colony 1800–10, and Allan CUNNINGHAM whose rich herbarium of Australian plants collected 1816–37 is now lodged at Kew. By 1789 Banks had 5600 species in cultivation at Kew, many of them Australian, all enumerated in *Hortus kewensis*, an unprecedented inventory of the collections prepared by its superintendent, William Aiton (1731–1793).

Within fifteen years of the death of Banks in 1820 Kew had fallen into such a state of disrepair and lassitude that concern was expressed as to its continuance. A commission of inquiry headed by botanist John LINDLEY concluded that the royal property should be either abandoned or appropriated to the state and converted into a powerful means of promoting national science. The latter course was chosen. In consequence **William Jackson Hooker** (1785–1865) became Director of the Royal Botanic Gardens, Kew, in 1841 after a distinguished career as Professor of Botany at Glasgow University. Under his management Kew was restored to the scientific eminence it enjoyed under Banks. Hooker was not without his problems, however, suffering from the persistent efforts of his civil service masters to turn Kew into a PUBLIC PARK. This is symptomatic of the consistent failure of bureaucrats to comprehend the scientific and educative nature of botanic gardens. In 1865 William was succeeded as Director by his son **Joseph Dalton Hooker** (1817–1911) who, for the next twenty years, continued his father's work in establishing Kew's pre-eminent position. Widely travelled, a first-class taxonomic botanist, and pioneer in the study of the geographic distribution of plants, Joseph shared with Banks a lifelong interest in the Australian flora arising from his visit to Van Diemen's Land during 1840–41, which also resulted in his *Flora tasmaniae* (1855–60).

Both William and Joseph Hooker were convinced that Kew was the botanical centre of the Empire, just as Whitehall was its political and administrative centre. This guiding principal underlay Kew's dealings with colonial botanists and garden administrators. The unwritten rule whereby curators and directors of colonial botanic gardens should be men trained at and nominated by Kew went a long way in ensuring that these botanists were of a suitable calibre to curate the gardens to Kew standards and to act as PLANT COLLECTORS for Kew. Australia proved the exception. With the appointment by the local authorities of such luminaries as Ferdinand MUELLER, Richard SCHOMBURGK, and Joseph MAIDEN it is clear that the influence of Kew was somewhat tempered in Australia, a circumstance of some regret at Kew.

The roles Kew has undertaken have been many and varied. One of the most important has been the encouragement of AGRICULTURE. Under the direction of Kew, economically important species were subject to intense cultivation in countries other than those to which they were native. Largescale translocation of industrial crops such as quinine, rubber, and sugar was facilitated by Kew in furtherance of the industrial enterprise of the Empire. Australia, however, played little part in this process. The facilitation of exchange of information has remained a cornerstone of Kew's activities. Since William Hooker's time, Kew has published books and periodicals that set the standard in horticultural and taxonomic publications. Australian plants often found their way into Europe by way of Kew, either through the distribution of propagating material or by their inclusion in the living collections at Kew. The Temperate House (1859–63, extended 1895–97) has always been used for the display of warm-temperate species such as *Araucaria* and *Podocarpus* from Australia and New Zealand. These plants would not survive the winter outdoors in Britain. More recently the Australian House (1952) was built for the better display of Australian plants.

PLANT CONSERVATION issues have assumed an increasing importance in Kew's programs as we become more aware of the necessity to preserve our environment. A new undertaking is the Millennium Seed Bank which by 2010 will store seed from ten per cent of the world's species. SEEDS will be wild-collected and stored in conditions such that they are not killed by the freezing or drying processes. Major objectives of this project are to promote the reintroduction of endangered species into the wild and increase public awareness of the importance of biodiversity conservation. Kew houses the headquarters of the Botanic Gardens Conservation International, an international organisation of botanic gardens that monitors and promotes the conservation of the world's flora.

Mea Allan, *The Hookers of Kew 1785–1911* (London, 1967); Ray Desmond and F. Nigel Hepper, *A Century of Kew Plantsmen: A Celebration of the Kew Guild* (Richmond, London, 1993); Ray Desmond, *Kew: The History of the Royal Botanic Gardens* (London, 1995); Ray Desmond, *Sir Joseph Dalton Hooker: Traveller and Plant Collector* (Woodbridge, Suffolk, 1999)

HELEN M. COHN

ROYAL BOTANIC GARDENS, MELBOURNE, founded with great foresight in 1845 at the instigation of Superintendent (later Lieutenant-Governor) LA TROBE, initially comprised approximately five acres (2 ha) beside a Tea-tree swamp on a curve of the Yarra River, and have expanded to thirty-six hectares of world-renowned landscaped grounds. Developed under two Scottish-trained superintendents, John ARTHUR (1846–48) and John DALLACHY (1848–57), the Melbourne Botanic Gardens—as they were known until 1958, when the Royal epithet was granted—gained an early reputation in the growing capital as a pleasure resort, probably planned by Henry GINN. From 1853, with the appointment of Ferdinand MUELLER as Government Botanist and establishment of the National Herbarium of Victoria, the institution also became the pre-eminent HERBARIUM and centre for botanical research in Australia—a reputation that lasted throughout the nineteenth century, and laid the basis for an ongoing research focus.

Mueller, appointed Director in 1857, and his successor, William GUILFOYLE (1873–1909), stand out in the establishment and development of the Gardens. Mueller increased the area of the site to embrace a north-facing declivity, and linked his scientific expertise with horticulture in the creation of a SYSTEM GARDEN, a PINETUM and other themed plant groupings (including some in glasshouses), settings for ZOOLOGICAL exhibits, and a vast ARBORETUM in the adjoining DOMAIN. Mueller explored the scientific and economic potential of plants, and used the nursery at the Gardens as a plant warehouse to supply countless public reserves across the new colony. Guilfoyle, appointed following public and political disquiet with Mueller's direction, rearranged and augmented the plants in a major redesign implemented over several decades. He softened functional aspects, and the linear design, with major renovations including realigning the Yarra River, relocating mature trees, and adding ornamental structures. His landscape style explored the natural landform and features by using curved paths, and emphasising bold foliage, strong colours, and textures of subtropical foliage.

Under subsequent directors, including John CRONIN (1909–23), William LAIDLAW (1923–25), Frederick RAE (1926–41), Alexander JESSEP (1941–57), and Richard PESCOTT (1957–70), the landscape was consolidated with a general respect for its outstanding nineteenth-century design. Since 1970, INTERPRETATION has become a major factor in management, and plant collections are now integrated within the historic landscape to explore ecological, evolutionary, geographic, botanical, horticultural, and conservation themes. In 1970 the Gardens were complemented by the acquisition of a 363-hectare satellite native plant garden at CRANBOURNE. Commerce has also increasingly challenged traditional modes of management since 1992, when the Gardens became administered by an independent Board after almost a century and a half of government departmental control. Recent developments include the Observatory Gate Precinct (1999), a major new entrance to the Gardens.

Numerous publications have been devoted to the Gardens' history, including Pescott's standard work (1982) and a special issue of the *Victorian Historical Journal* (1996), as well as considerable material generated by the Mueller Correspondence Project and a forthcoming history of the National Herbarium of Victoria by Helen Cohn.

R.T.M. Pescott, *The Royal Botanic Gardens Melbourne: A History from 1845 to 1970* (Melbourne, 1982)

ROGER SPENCER

ROYAL BOTANIC GARDENS, SYDNEY In 1912, J.H. Maiden truly maintained that 'our Botanic Gardens "growed"—like Topsy—following at first the economic requirements of a Colony formed under peculiar circumstances'. Governor Arthur Phillip established cultivations beside a small creek that flowed into 'Woccanmagully', which was named Farm Cove. The '9 Acres in Corn' coaxed into growth by July 1788 formed the genesis of the thirty hectares (75 acres) that now comprise Sydney's Royal Botanic Gardens.

The abiding influence of Joseph BANKS ensured that the new colony would be a prime source of 'botanical novelties' for KEW and other grand gardens, and a brisk traffic in seeds and potted plants developed. By 1789 Phillip had found more promising farmland at Parramatta. The first cultivations languished, and land around Farm Cove was leased, contrary to Phillip's intentions, for he planned to reserve a large area extending east to Woolloomooloo Bay 'for the Crown and for the use of the Town of Sydney'.

A strong link between the dispatch of desirable plants and the receipt of official approbation became apparent, and the Farm Cove cultivations, however unpromising, became an entrepôt for the establishment and ACCLIMATISATION of useful exotic plants, and for the assembly and preparation of unusual INDIGENOUS PLANTS for export. Governors Bligh and Macquarie took firm measures to reclaim much of the land Phillip had reserved, thereby ensuring that there was a 'governor's demesne' (or DOMAIN) for privacy and for fruit and vegetable production.

Under Macquarie, land exploration and plant discovery flourished, and Charles FRASER was appointed the governor's or 'colonial' botanist. A carriageway, 'Mrs Macquarie's Road', constructed around Farm Cove to Anson's Point (Mrs Macquarie's Chair) and back to (First) GOVERNMENT HOUSE, helped to delineate the expanding Gardens which, by the time the road was completed on 13 June 1816, comprised three large garden plots and an extensive nursery. Maiden established this date as the 'official birthday' of the Gardens.

The ROYAL BOTANIC GARDENS, SYDNEY, captured in the early years of the twentieth century in this postcard view, boasted an array of garden ORNAMENT more commonly associated with contemporary VILLA GARDENS, highlighting the delicate balance between science and pleasure in Australian BOTANIC GARDENS

After Fraser, the Botanic Gardens was developed, despite disputes over perceived policy and purpose, by Richard and Allan CUNNINGHAM and by a succession of superintendents, until J.C. BIDWILL was appointed first 'director' in 1847 only to be superseded by Charles MOORE. During Moore's long incumbency (1848–96), extensive land reclamation, addition of the Garden Palace EXHIBITION grounds, and embellishment with monuments and statuary transformed the site, although during his term the scientific function was not highly developed. His successor, Joseph Henry MAIDEN, worked vigorously and effectively during 1896–1924 to develop the HERBARIUM, the LIBRARY, and the scientific reputation of the institution, a tradition that has been strongly maintained. The directorships of both Moore and Maiden established a tradition of planting native plants of NSW, especially RAINFOREST and other SUBTROPICAL species suited to the intensively modified site.

Until 1962, the Royal Botanic Gardens, Sydney—which received the Royal epithet in 1959—had an adjoining harmonious backdrop provided by the Domain of thirty-four hectares, but the construction of the Cahill Expressway destroyed that pleasing unity, to the bitter disappointment of director, R.H. ANDERSON. At the opening of the new herbarium building (1982), the then director, Dr L.A.S. JOHNSON declared: 'a Botanic Garden of world standard, which this I hope is, although … in need of and undergoing improvement in most spheres, is not a glorified park … It is a scientific institution set in surroundings of beauty and catering for peaceful recreation.' Johnson's comments remain valid, especially in the face of increasing public usage. During the 1990s there was a shift in focus towards using the living collections of the Gardens as a medium for INTERPRETATION, which balances public education with ornamentation. The Royal Botanic Gardens, Sydney, is imbued with a remarkable and idiosyncratic sense of place, the result of exquisite combination of site, plant science, and landscape art.

Lionel Gilbert, *The Royal Botanic Gardens, Sydney: A History 1816–1985* (Melbourne, 1986)   **LIONEL GILBERT**

ROYAL HORTICULTURAL SOCIETY (1861–), previously the Horticultural Society of London (1804–61), was established for 'the improvement of horticulture', with Sir Joseph BANKS among the seven founding members. This aim was furthered through publications; an experimental garden at Kensington (1818) and, more significantly, Chiswick (1821); training of gardeners; plant collecting expeditions; meetings and lectures; exhibitions and shows; awards; and distribution of plants to its members, initially drawn from the aristocracy and landed gentry. Financial mismanagement led in 1859 to the sale of the Society's library, a loss subsequently repaired by acquisition of long-serving secretary John LINDLEY's collection, which formed the nucleus of the outstanding Lindley

Library housed in the Society's Vincent Square premises. A new centrally located garden in South Kensington in the ITALIANATE style (1861–88) was soon derided as inappropriate for the society and, under reformed management, this function was transferred to rural Wisley (1903–).

Several emigrant gardeners, such as John DALLACHY, trained at Chiswick, which, with the ROYAL BOTANIC GARDENS, KEW, and the Royal Botanic Society's garden at Regent's Park, formed an important training ground. After reform of the Society in the 1880s, many Australian horticulturists and gardeners became Fellows of the Royal Horticultural Society (FRHS), a splendid-sounding category of membership for which nomination was required and an annual fee payable. During the twentieth century, the Society's publications and its annual show at Chelsea (1913–) have been an important British influence for the dedicated Australian gardener.

Harold R. Fletcher, *The Story of the Royal Horticultural Society 1804–1968* (Oxford, 1969)   RA

ROYAL NATIONAL PARK, SYDNEY, initially 18 000 acres (7300 ha) and now doubled in size, was established at Port Hacking in 1879. It was the first site in Australia named 'NATIONAL PARK'. While its general purpose was to provide a healthy escape for the people of Sydney, the government and the trustees were unclear about how to achieve this. It was used for RECREATION, ACCLIMATISATION, and various commercial exploitation purposes. The *Official Guide*, first published in 1893 (with many later editions), charts this early history and usage. It remained extremely popular as a recreation venue, but from the 1920s until the establishment of the New South Wales Parks and Wildlife Service (1967), it was the subject of continuing conflict between the 'anything goes' administration of the trustees and the growing conservation movement.   ELERY HAMILTON-SMITH

ROYAL PARK, Launceston, Tas., planted from *c.* 1900 and laid out from 1910 by William McGOWAN on land sweeping down to the Tamar River, was in its heyday a large and attractive PUBLIC PARK. It now incorporates mature exotic trees and a COMMEMORATIVE rose garden (1975), as well as the city's WAR MEMORIAL (1924) and a bronze statue of King Edward VII (*c.* 1917). The creation of massive flood levees (1960s), separating the park from the river, and subsequent roadworks, have destroyed much of McGowan's design.

    ANNE NEALE

ROYAL PARK, Melbourne, was part of a large area reserved from sale by Superintendent C.J. LA TROBE in the 1840s that included Princes Park, MELBOURNE GENERAL CEMETERY, and the University of Melbourne. By 1854 about 280 hectares was known as Royal Park, although it had no legal standing as PUBLIC PARKLAND. This area was reduced by the EXPERIMENTAL Model Farm, ZOOLOGICAL GARDENS (1862), and subdivision and sale, to its current 180 hectares. Pines were planted initially, but eucalypts had more enduring popularity, particularly the indigenous *Eucalyptus camaldulensis* (River Red Gum). Clement HODGKINSON and Ferdinand MUELLER joined the board of trustees, established in 1862 to manage the park. They were forced to rely on grazing fees until cricket and football began to generate more funding shortly before Melbourne City Council assumed control (1934). Council accelerated development, concentrating on sports facilities until 1977, when four hectares designed by Grace FRASER (displaying AUSTRALIAN PLANTS) was opened. Recent development has been guided by a master plan by landscape architects Brian Stafford (b. 1943) and Ron Jones (b. 1959)—selected through a 1984 design COMPETITION—which aims to balance provision for SPORT and casual RECREATION, and evoke the spacious indigenous landscape that European colonists encountered.

    GEORGINA WHITEHEAD

ROYAL SOCIETIES and their precursors, which often preceded NATURAL HISTORY societies, included AUSTRALIAN PLANTS in their purview. Royal societies in SA and Qld had FIELD NATURALISTS' sections, and those in WA and Tas. developed from natural history societies, the latter having a unique horticultural history. In the 1820s and almost a decade after establishment of Sydney's Philosophical Society of Australasia, which rarely discussed plants, Dr John Henderson (*c.* 1790–1836) established another ephemeral society, the Van Diemen's Land Society, 'in imitation of Royal and other literary and scientific societies'. Members discussed Tasmania's flora and other aspects of natural history, but its museum never expanded beyond its cupboard and a projected EXPERIMENTAL GARDEN remained unplanted. In the 1830s similar societies flourished outside Hobart, and in 1837–38 John FRANKLIN helped establish the Tasmanian Society, whose *Tasmanian Journal of Natural Science, Agriculture, Statistics, &c.* (1841–49), then the only Australian scientific periodical, intended to include all known and newly 'discovered' indigenous Tasmanian plants. It carried James BACKHOUSE's catalogue of edible fruits and roots (with Ronald GUNN's additions), and Joseph HOOKER's work on Tasmanian CONIFERS. In 1843 the Society was hijacked. Ex-officio president, Lieutenant-Governor Eardley-Wilmot, convened a meeting to convert it into a society to manage the Government Garden. When most of the surprised members left angrily, he established the Horticultural and Botanical Society of Van Diemen's Land and in 1844 this became the Royal Society of Van Diemen's Land for Horticulture, Botany, and the Advancement of Science—the first royal society outside Britain. It concentrated on the Garden (later the ROYAL TASMANIAN BOTANICAL GARDENS), held HORTICULTURAL SHOWS, and from 1846 supported shows of the new Hobart Town Gardeners' and Amateurs' Horticultural Society's shows. Meanwhile, under Secretary Gunn, who believed that science was republican rather than royal, the Tasmanian Society met in Launceston and continued publishing the respected *Tasmanian Journal*.

Royal societies were born as philosophical societies in NSW, SA, Vic., and Qld in the 1850s, and as a natural history society in WA in 1891. At their meetings diverse speakers ranged across the sciences, including BOTANY, and by

Royal societies

The prize-winning landscape master plan for Melbourne's ROYAL PARK (1984) was enhanced by pencil sketches of proposed effects, evocatively conveying the planting scheme of AUSTRALIAN FLORA, which ranged from native grasses to indigenous tree species

exchanging their periodicals with other societies they developed substantial scientific LIBRARIES rich in botanical information. In 1889, for instance, the Royal Society of New South Wales sent its *Journal and Proceedings* to 350 groups. Scientific journals became rich repositories of indigenous plant taxonomic and ecological information, thanks to contributors including MAIDEN, BAKER, and Cambage (NSW), F.M. and J.F. BAILEY, and BANCROFT (Qld), TATE (SA), BEARD, GARDNER, and HERBERT (WA), and MUELLER, EWART, and WILLIAMSON (Vic.). Before and after Victoria's Philosophical Institute was granted a Royal Charter (1859), Mueller used the society's *Transactions* to name and describe many new species of AUSTRALIAN PLANTS and suggested useful plants for cultivation. A long-standing member and office bearer of the Royal Society of New South Wales, Maiden described new species in the Society's *Journal* and included two horticultural suggestions in his 1912 presidential address—a state horticulture council appointed by HORTICULTURAL SOCIETIES (to keep an official record of Australian horticultural creations with coloured illustrations officially marked as types) and a horticultural hall (for exhibits including illustrations of flowers, plants, gardens, horticultural methods and appliances, and garden architecture and plans) where horticultural societies could hold meetings and exhibitions free of charge. Despite the establishment of numerous other specialist scientific societies,

Royal Tasmanian Botanical Gardens

Australian royal societies continue to foster discussions about botanical science.

Australian royal societies and their precursors

New South Wales
- 1821–22 Philosophical Society of Australasia
- 1850–55 Australian Philosophical Society
- 1856–66 Philosophical Society of New South Wales
- 1866– Royal Society of New South Wales

Tasmania
- 1829–31 Van Diemen's Land Society
- 1838–49 Tasmanian Society for the Promotion of Natural Science, Agriculture, Statistics, etc.
- 1843–44 Botanical and Horticultural Society of Van Diemen's Land
- 1844–55 Royal Society of Van Diemen's Land for Horticulture, Botany, and the Advancement of Science
- 1855–1911 Royal Society of Tasmania for Horticulture, Botany, and the Advancement of Science
- 1911– Royal Society of Tasmania

South Australia
- 1853–80 Adelaide Philosophical Society
- 1880– Royal Society of South Australia

Victoria
- 1854–55 Victorian Institute for the Advancement of Science
- 1854–55 Philosophical Society of Victoria
- 1855–59 Philosophical Institute of Victoria
- 1859– Royal Society of Victoria

Queensland
- 1859–83 Queensland Philosophical Society
- 1883– Royal Society of Queensland

Western Australia
- 1891–95 Natural History Society
- 1897–1903 Mueller Botanic Society
- 1903–09 West Australian Natural History Society
- 1909–14 Natural History and Science Society of Western Australia
- 1914– Royal Society of Western Australia

Australian Capital Territory
- 1930– Royal Society of Canberra

LINDEN GILLBANK

ROYAL TASMANIAN BOTANICAL GARDENS, Hobart, established in 1818 as a Government Garden, was expanded after the arrival of Lieutenant-Governor Arthur in 1824. Following William DAVIDSON's appointment as superintendent (1828–34), the Garden was developed, including native plants collected on Mount Wellington, a flued brick wall, and a superintendent's house. Prison labour worked the initial twelve acres (5 ha), a reliance continued until recent years. The Garden played a pivotal role in furthering HORTICULTURE and FLORICULTURE in Van Diemen's Land, with plants collected, propagated, and distributed. Donors included Charles FRASER from SYDNEY BOTANIC GARDENS, who supplied Norfolk Island pine and acacia seeds.

Under the influence of John and Jane FRANKLIN and Lieutenant-Governor Eardley-Wilmot, control of the Gardens transferred to the ROYAL SOCIETY of Van Diemen's Land in 1844. With F.W. NEWMAN as superintendent (1845–59), a gate-keeper's cottage was erected, a public drive through the DOMAIN laid out, and the Gardens divided into three sections, illustrating botanical, medicinal, and horticultural plants 'useful for the colony', while a large pond, established in 1848, saved the expense of carting water. The Society attracted new members due to their privileged access to plants from the Gardens. With the removal of an entrance fee, visits became popular, particularly when garrison bands entertained, visitor numbers growing from almost 2300 in 1847 to more than 15 000 in 1859. A new GOVERNMENT HOUSE adjoining the Gardens was erected during the 1840s and 1850s, where Eardley-Wilmot erected a second extensive brick wall in 1845. ACCLIMATISATION of FRUIT trees and GRASSES was trialled and by 1856 more than twenty acres (8 ha) was in cultivation. Through the Society, the Gardens exchanged plants world-wide including with the HOOKERS, BACKHOUSE, and MUELLER, and with local collectors including GUNN and ARCHER. Plants were shared with the local community and with commercial horticulturists such as DICKINSON and LIPSCOMBE.

During the superintendency of Francis ABBOTT (1859–1903) the Gardens developed a new FORMALITY, with strong emphasis on CONIFERS. In 1885 responsibility for the Gardens passed back to the government, with the superintendent reporting to the Director of the Tasmanian Museum and Botanical Gardens. The directorships of Alex Morton, Clive LORD, and Leonard RODWAY exercised a strong influence on the Gardens, with its scientific reputation enhanced by establishment of a HERBARIUM (1928).

During the 1930s Superintendent Ira Thornicroft's design emphasised vistas with lawns and large-scale planting of flowers. An access road to the new trans-Derwent bridge (1943) cut the Gardens from its riverside frontage. Post-war, grounds were extended behind the second wall, a Japanese garden (1985) and gardens for the disabled were developed, and the Gardens took on a renewed public profile. The tea-rooms (1954) have recently been converted to house an educational centre. Today staff contend with a serious outbreak of root fungi and varied public expectations on a limited budget.

Marcus Hurburgh, The *Royal Tasmanian Botanical Gardens 1818–1986: A History in Stone, Soil and Superintendents* (Sandy Bay, Tas., 1986)

PETER MacFIE

RULE, John James (*c.* 1831–1887), nursery proprietor, was born at Buenos Aires, Argentine Republic, South America, and migrated in 1835 with his Cornish-born parents to Van Diemen's Land. The family relocated to the Port Phillip District, arriving in Melbourne in 1840, where his father, James Rule (*c.* 1796–1872), established himself as a builder in Bourke Street.

Rule started his Victoria Nursery, Richmond, in 1850—or so he claimed in his 1857 catalogue—and in 1854–55 he joined his brother, James Henry Rule (1833–1915), in a Bourke Street drapery business, from where his nursery catalogues could be obtained. Between 1854 and 1856 George BRUNNING managed the Victoria Nursery, and when James

Sinclair described Melbourne's gardens in 1856 he proclaimed 'there is perhaps not another so richly stocked with flowering plants, fruit trees, native and foreign, with greenhouses and stoves for their culture, and a great deal more that we could mention'. Rule appointed William McDonald ('late of Duncan and McDonald') as his town agent—his business was next door to Rule's drapery—and also advertised 'Gardens laid out and planted, Greenhouses and Conservatories built and stocked'. Rule's 1855 catalogue is one of the earliest known nursery catalogues for the colony and it reveals his interest in trees, especially CONIFERS. In 1858 Rule established his own seed warehouse in Elizabeth Street but within two years had relocated to his former Bourke Street premises. He published *Rule's Economical Gardening for Cottagers; Being Concise Directions for Cultivating Useful Culinary Vegetables* (1859), written by Thomas McMillan. By 1860 Rule's letterhead advertised 'Gardens, Orchards, Vineyards, &c., Laid out and Stocked' and in that year he provided 700 vines and a substantial quantity of trees for Glenara, the celebrated estate of Walter Clark. Rule engaged William Duncan to act as a botanical collector in New Caledonia and in 1861 the *Gardeners' Chronicle* announced that Duncan had discovered a new species of *Araucaria*, named *A. Rulei* by Mueller. Rule was also credited by the *Leader* with importation of the parent tree of *Cupressus macrocarpa* 'Horizontalis' (c. 1855–57), much planted as a WINDBREAK and still a distinctive feature of the Victorian rural landscape.

Rule was a pioneering nursery proprietor in Victoria and E.E. Pescott drew attention to the Victoria Nursery as a training ground for many nursery and garden workers. Rule was actively involved with the Victorian horticultural world; in 1853 he was present at a meeting held in Henry Ginn's office to revive the Victorian Horticultural Society and he was a founding committee member of the Horticultural Society of Victoria. When Rule's nursery was plotted on James Kearney's *Plan of Melbourne and Suburbs* (1855) it sat amid scattered cottages, but intensification of inner suburban development necessitated its early closure in the 1870s. Rule's brother continued in drapery but after 1866 pursued a successful career in mining at Maldon (Vic.), where J.J. Rule died and was buried. RA

RUMSEY, Herbert John (1866–1956), seed merchant and author, was born at Leamington, Warwickshire, England, and brought to Sydney by his family in 1872. After various jobs unconnected with horticulture he started a nursery and seed business on his father's selection at Barber's Creek, Marulan (NSW), in 1895, and later took over seed merchants G. Hemsley and Co. of Moss Vale. In 1901 he moved to Dundas (NSW) and continued his business from there for the rest of his life. He began his career as an author contributing articles to the *Agricultural Gazette of New South Wales* in 1897. He published his first book, *ABC of Australian Vegetable Growing*, in 1910, which remained in print through many editions. He also wrote *Australian Book of Berries* (1918), *A to Z of Australian Fruit Growing* (1921), *Australian Garden Fair* (1923), *Australian Nuts and Nut Growing in Australia* (1927), and *Australian Tomato Book* (1927). He visited North America in 1915 and Britain several times, presenting a paper on the progress of HORTICULTURE in Australia to the IX International Horticultural Congress (London, 1930), in which he described the improvements he had affected in cape gooseberries by selection over a twenty-five-year period. He sent his sons overseas to further their training, Anthony to the USA and Roy to England, before taking them into partnership, the firm becoming Herbert J. Rumsey and Sons in 1930. He remained general manager until his death. In 1966 Rumsey's Seeds Ltd was sold to Arthur Yates and Co.

Roy Henry Rumsey (1909–1995) attended Hurlstone Agricultural High School then worked for Hazlewood Bros for four years before going to England in 1929. After working for the noted nursery of Hillier and Sons at Winchester for a year he became a student gardener at the Royal Botanic Gardens, Kew. On completing his training he returned to Australia in 1932, joining the family firm. In 1946 he left to manage Rosèn's nursery for Anderson and Co. Rumsey had married (Eva) Heather (*née* Nankivell) (1913–1995) in 1936 and although keen to start their own nursery, this did not occur until 1950, when they purchased forty acres (16 ha) at Dural. They soon began to specialise in Rose plants with Heather becoming interested in miniature roses and old-fashioned varieties. Such was their esteem that following the death of Harry Hazlewood they took over reviewing new releases for the *Australian and New Zealand Rose Annual*. Heather Rumsey published *Old-Fashioned Roses for Australian Gardens* (1990). The Rumseys' nursery, the premier supplier of old garden roses and miniature roses in NSW, was not closed until shortly before their deaths. RICHARD CLOUGH

RUNNYMEDE, New Town, Tas., was built for lawyer Robert Pitcairn (1802–1861) in the early 1840s, one of a cluster of villas then comfortably distant from Hobart Town. The general layout of the garden, which survives in a truncated form, is likely to date from this period. Bishop Francis Nixon (1803–1879) purchased Cairn Lodge in 1850 and renamed it Bishopstowe: his photographs document the early garden. Plants, including two Norfolk Island pines, were supplied to his wife Anna by the Royal Society of Tasmania in 1857. Charles Bayley (1813–1875), master mariner, whaler, and ship owner, purchased the estate, which he renamed Runnymede (after one of his ships), in 1864. It passed to his brother James (1823–1894)—who expanded the estate—and subsequently to his daughter Harriet Louisa (1861–1931), who lived there with her husband Henry Bayly and their young family. Two single Bayly daughters, Hally (1886–1971) and Emma (1890–1993), remained at Runnymede until old age: their decision in 1963–65 to sell to the state government safeguarded this early VILLA GARDEN, now managed by the National Trust. RA

RUPERTSWOOD, Sunbury, Vic., an extensive country estate, was developed by William John Clarke (1831–1897) on part of the vast holdings his father, pastoralist William John Turner Clarke (c. 1801–1874), had taken up on Melbourne's north-west fringe in 1850. The fifty-room mansion was erected in 1874–76 and William Sangster was engaged to

RUNNYMEDE, New Town (Tas.), pictured during the occupancy of Bishop Nixon (1850–64), retains many early garden elements and recalls the early colonial period when New Town was a favoured location for gentlemen to develop their VILLAS far from the bustle of central Hobart

landscape the grounds, twenty-five hectares in extent. He used the site's dramatic topography to create one of the most important nineteenth-century PICTURESQUE gardens in Vic. Features included a tree-lined drive sweeping down a hill to a scenic lake, before climbing the ridge to the rocky promontory upon which the mansion was carefully sited. The principal garden of expansive lawns and curved shrubberies was laid out on the slopes to the south-west of the mansion. Other attractions included a fern gully, a tennis lawn, and a bowling green. Extensive use was made of conifers as well as flowering shrubs, particularly camellias and rhododendrons. Sangster also developed an extensive kitchen garden and orchard on the rich alluvial flats of Jackson's Creek. Rupertswood became a centre of social activity in the 1870s and 1880s. The great cricketing legend of The Ashes was born there after a social game of cricket between the visiting English cricket team (staying at the mansion during Christmas 1882) and a local side.

Rupertswood was sold by the Clarke family in 1922 to H.V. MCKAY, who replaced over-mature plantings, added a 'wattle lawn', and installed a nine-hole golf course for his weekend guests. Following his death in 1926, the property was subdivided and the mansion, grounds, and 340 hectares were acquired by the Salesian Brothers for use as a school. Tantalising remnants of the original landscaping survive.

Michael Clarke, *Clarke of Rupertswood, 1831–1897: The Life and Times of William John Clarke, First Baronet of Rupertswood* (Melbourne, 1995)

EVE ALMOND

RUPP, Herman Montague Rucker (1872–1956), clergyman and botanist, was born at Port Fairy (Vic.), the son of a Prussian-born Anglican clergyman. At Geelong Grammar (1885–91) while his uncle, the naturalist John Bracebridge Wilson, was headmaster, Rupp flourished academically and athletically, and pursued NATURAL HISTORY. In 1891 his first botanical paper, 'Orchids', appeared in the school's *Quarterly*. More than 250 others would be published during the next sixty-four years in diverse newspapers and journals, often spiced, like his enormous botanical correspondence, with impish humour. Rupp saw the study of botany as 'an essential department of the study of Life', and his *Guide to the Orchids of New South Wales* (1930) and *The Orchids of New South Wales* (1943) promoted this view.

With a scholarship to Trinity College and a letter from Wilson to MUELLER, Rupp went to Melbourne in 1892. Unusual subject combinations embracing science, the humanities, and theology led to his ordination (1901). For forty years he worked in country parishes in Vic., Tas., and NSW, and on roving assignments for the Australian Board of Missions. Wherever he travelled, he maintained the search for native ORCHIDS, and on moving to a new rectory, he would coax astonished parishioners to find a few light posts for a BUSH-HOUSE where orchids could be assembled, tended, studied, and propagated.

At R.H. ANDERSON's behest Rupp served in retirement as curator of orchids at the National Herbarium of New South Wales (1939–56). Rupp's influence on the appreciation, conservation, cultivation, and classification of indigenous orchids was profound. He was honoured by the ROYAL SOCIETY of New South Wales with its Clarke Medal (1949), and the Australian Natural History Medallion (1954). The specific epithets of some orchids, an *Acacia*, and a *Boronia* commemorate his name.

Lionel Gilbert, *The Orchid Man: The Life, Work and Memoirs of the Rev. H.M.R. Rupp 1872–1956* (Kenthurst, NSW, 1992)

LIONEL GILBERT

RURAL AUSTRALIAN (1875–98), began publication in Sydney as *Castner's Monthly and Rural Australian* and each of its three series (1875–88; 1889–91; 1892–98) included horticulture within its purview. Founding publisher and proprietor John L. Castner often looked to North America for inspiration and included many reprinted articles from this source. Designs for 'rural architecture' by F. Reuss jnr; frequent contributions by Angus MACKAY; farm, garden, poultry, kennel, apiary, and household advice; and a strong agricultural content all distinguished this widely distributed journal. RA

RURAL LANDSCAPES, especially those associated with rural dwellings, have since European settlement achieved an iconic status in Australian cultural life. These CULTURAL LANDSCAPES often sat within a wider natural setting, or themselves contained more intensive DESIGNED LANDSCAPES such as gardens. The dramatic conjunctions of dwelling, garden, paddock, and BUSH have been documented in LITERATURE and ART since the late eighteenth century, and since the 1850s by PHOTOGRAPHY. The Australian pastoral and bush dwelling is a pivotal theme in nineteenth-century rural settlement and has resulted in an accepted vernacular grammar of rural building, enclosing, and landscaping. Early land tenure was most often achieved by grant or squatting, and the earliest work of the land owner or manager was in FENCING and subduing the landscape in order to suit pastoral or agricultural purposes, all of which challenged traditional notions of ABORIGINAL ENVIRONMENTAL MANAGEMENT. Only then was a dwelling and garden landscape created.

The grandest of these landscape assemblages were centred on HOMESTEADS, exemplified by those in the MIDLANDS (Tas.), WESTERN DISTRICT (Vic.), DARLING DOWNS (Qld), and the Riverina (NSW). Defining features of homestead landscapes included a long approach DRIVE (often a treed AVENUE terminating in a carriage loop), water features (such as a LAKE), a PLEASURE GARDEN (often with FLOWER GARDENS, SHRUBBERIES, LAWNS, and extensive tree and boundary plantings), VEGETABLE GARDENS, and a complement of outbuildings (such as stables, carriage sheds, and shearing sheds), all set within fenced enclosures against the open paddocks. Especially in the west of NSW and Qld, large pastoral stations were marked by one or more tall trees—commonly *Araucaria bidwillii* (Bunya Pine)—which 'located' the homestead complexes on the otherwise featureless plains.

Land Selection Acts of the 1860s attempted to open up the country to smaller 'selections'; this mode of LAND SURVEY AND SALE profoundly altered the Australian rural landscape. The dwellings and pastoral landscapes of these selections were smaller in scale but were created within the vernacular framework common to the larger properties. COTTAGE GARDENS also had their place within these broad acreages, as did VINEYARDS, ORCHARDS, MARKET GARDENS, and NURSERIES.

Then, as now, the key characteristics of rural dwellings and their landscapes were generated by CLIMATE, GEOLOGY, availability of WATER (especially through IRRIGATION), and other functional imperatives. In the twentieth century the phenomena of closer settlement, corporate ownership, and the

Squatter–artist Duncan Elphinstone Cooper (c.1813–1904) plotted the transition of his Challicum Station (Vic.) from the unmodified RURAL LANDSCAPE of the early 1840s to the cultural oasis on the WESTERN DISTRICT plains, as painted in 1850

rural dwelling as an urban escape made new contributions to an evolving rural landscape. But it has been responses to degraded landscapes, manifest in groups such as LANDCARE and GREENING AUSTRALIA, and attendant REVEGETATION projects, that signal the greatest force for change.

J. Freeland, P. Cox, and W. Stacey, *Rude Timber Buildings in Australia* (London, 1969); Philip Cox and Wesley Stacey, *The Australian Homestead* (Melbourne, 1972); D.N. Jeans and Peter Spearritt, *The Open Air Museum: The Cultural Landscape of New South Wales* (Sydney, 1980); Peter Freeman, *The Homestead: A Riverina Anthology* (Melbourne, 1982)

PETER FREEMAN

RURAL MAGAZINE (1855), with the subtitle 'A Monthly Journal of Farming, Gardening, Natural History and Domestic Economy', was published in Melbourne during the unsettled period of the early gold rushes. Internal evidence suggests that the editor was possibly nursery proprietor Thomas MCMILLAN, who claimed the lion's share of editorial and advertising space. SUBURBAN and MARKET GARDENERS were the principal beneficiaries of advice on VEGETABLE growing, FLORICULTURE, and INDOOR GARDENING. The lack of HORTICULTURAL SOCIETIES in Vic. was lamented and AUSTRALIAN PLANTS received sympathetic editorial treatment. James SINCLAIR was among the advertisers and his *Gardener's Magazine* filled the void left by the demise, after only eight issues, of the *Rural Magazine*. RA

RUSSIA, and the former Union of Soviet Socialist Republics, share many spatial factors with Australia in their large land mass embracing geographic extremes with grouped population centres skewing influence to the periphery, yet their climatic and political differences have mitigated against close horticultural links. Peter the Great (reigned 1682–1725) and Catherine the Great (reigned 1762–1796) both fostered Russian interest in gardening, the latter discussed in Dimitri Shvidkovsky's *The Empress and the Architect* (New Haven and London, 1996). This flourishing of LANDSCAPE GARDENING was brought to a British audience (and so to a colonial one) through the writings of J.C. LOUDON, who travelled through Russia for several months during 1813–14: he devoted several pages of his *Encyclopaedia of Gardening* (1822, with many later editions) and many notices in his *Gardener's Magazine* (1826–44, especially one leading article in 1827) to Russia.

First-hand knowledge of Russian gardens was brought to Australia by gardener James SINCLAIR, who had worked on the Crimean estates of Prince Mikhail Semenovich Vorontsov, and Maurice W. HOLTZE worked in Russia 1862–64 before his arrival in Australia in 1872. MUELLER corresponded with Russian colleagues, including those from botanic gardens in St Petersburg and Moscow. After the Revolution of 1917, interest in the Soviet Union was principally shown in the gardening world by those of leftist interests, with attention in some (limited) quarters in collectivisation and production methods. The works of hybridist Ivan Vladimirovich Michurin (1855–1935) circulated in Australia and Alan EDMUNDS in his book *Espalier Fruit Trees* (c. 1946) quoted from Soviet publications, observing wryly of great state horticultural triumphs: 'After the Russian espaliered lemons I'm ready for anything, even trained bananas!'. RA

RUSTIC-WORK Australia in the early nineteenth century was, generally, too rude an environment to foster an appreciation of deliberate, PICTURESQUE rusticity. In the second quarter of the nineteenth century, a requisite contrast with the wilderness, together with a prospering society, led to more NATURALISTIC as well as fashionable forms of landscaping in colonial Australia, including a taste for the 'rustic', although before 1850 this seldom went further than a seat of gnarled branches or a SUMMER-HOUSE. Rarely, as at Louisa Anne MEREDITH's Tasmanian house, was there a verandah or porch made from tree trunks. Sir Thomas MITCHELL's possession of T.J. Ricauti's *Rustic Architecture* (1840) in 1841 forms an early documentation of the growing fashion in colonial NSW, and the rusticated ORNAMENT, cut from living rock in the GROTTO at ELIZABETH BAY HOUSE in the mid-1830s was exceptional.

By mid-century, owners of suburban VILLAS were divorced sufficiently from the BUSH to appreciate rustic FERNERIES, and garden furnishings and FURNITURE, such as plant stands, benches, and tables. Much of this was ephemeral, but the increasing use of cast iron in the second half of the century has left a legacy of cast-iron garden ornament imitating rustic twigwork, ranging from the substantial bridges at Melbourne's RIPPON LEA (c. 1885), to the hundreds of garden and park benches sold well into the twentieth century by mail-order firms such as F. Lassetter & Co., Sydney. Specialist grotto manufacturers such as Charles ROBINETTE also found a ready market for their specialised rustic constructions.

The Aesthetic Movement of the last quarter of the nineteenth century, in which—for the first time—artiness, fashion, and improvisation coalesced, fostered an enthusiasm for rustic-work, particularly in the country, where genteel taste and a few contorted branches gathered from the bush fashionably and happily overcame a lack of cash.

The taste for the rustic probably reached its zenith in Edwardian Australia. Although it was rarely employed architecturally for more than summer-houses, it pervaded private gardens, public parks, and scenic pleasure grounds such as CATARACT GORGE, Launceston (Tas.), not only with furnishings of branches and twigs (natural or of cast and modelled terracotta), but also with fountains, retaining walls, arches, and grottoes of imitation ROCKWORK, exemplified by the original decoration of Sydney's Taronga ZOO. Many late nineteenth- and early twentieth-century memorials of sculpted marble rockwork or tree trunks are to be found in suburban and country cemeteries.

Rustic furnishings of chairs and tables of intertwining branches and pots improvised from sections of hollow tree trunks (standing or hung from the rafters) also spread from verandahs (and railway station platforms) into the house itself where terracotta jardinières could mimic the form of rustic fences (complete with kookaburras) and dining tables commonly sported a display of white ceramic 'Lilianware' posy vases in the form of hollow logs, stiles, fences, and miniature baskets of twigwork. In the early twentieth century an active

This RUSTIC-WORK gate at Hamilton Botanic Gardens, probably dating from the turn of the century, demonstrates an exuberant form of construction and decoration

sideline—possibly made in their own time by employees—of factories manufacturing earthenware pipes was the improvisation of these, by scoring, contorting them, or adding knots and branches, into log-like pots and jardinières. More sophisticated moulded and cast terracotta pieces—even tables and chairs, following English designs—were produced commercially.

Stick or twigwork verandah tables, usually of asymmetrical tee-pee or tripod form (for stability and ease of construction) with tops of salvaged deal from packing cases, were often made at home or by itinerant workers between the wars although, by the 1930s, the elaborate Edwardian cement fondue work had developed into home-made concrete rustic-work imitating hollow logs and, sometimes, twigwork. The concrete was reinforced with chicken wire and coloured 'naturalistically' (usually with green and ochre pigments). The scale of this work ranged from bird baths and flower pots, fences and gate-posts to transmogrifications of the Sydney Harbour Bridge into twigwork arches or plaster boxes to whole facades of motor garages. This work continued well into the third quarter of the century and has proved more resilient to weather (if not to taste) than natural wooden rustic-work, although the porosity of the concrete and the resulting rusting of the reinforcing has caused damage to many larger examples.

Modern taste did not encourage the improvisation of 1950s and 1960s materials such as steel, plastics, and rubber into rustic forms and the taste for, and appreciation of, the rustic. It was revived, in a limited way, by the romantic revivalism of the late twentieth century.

Jean Stone, *The Rustic Garden* (London, 1992)

JAMES BROADBENT

RUSTON, David William (b. 1930), rosarian, florist, and nursery proprietor, developed a strong interest in roses as a youth, especially their exhibition and propagation, and developed this interest into a successful business and a life devoted to promoting ROSES. From his large garden, formerly an irrigated fruit block developed by his father at Renmark (SA) in the RIVERLAND, he supplies cut roses to the Australian florist trade, and offers a very extensive and varied range of budwood to commercial rose growers. His DISPLAY GARDEN—the largest private rose garden in the southern hemisphere—covers eleven hectares and includes more than 50 000 rose plants representing 4000 varieties, among thousands of perennials, bulbs, trees, shrubs, and climbers.

Ruston is widely known for his expertise as a floral arranger and demonstrator, and an instructive and entertaining lecturer. He has distinguished himself in Australia and internationally through his services to horticulture, especially commercial rose growing and amateur rose organisations. He was president of the World Federation of Rose Societies (1991–94), president of the Rose Society of Australia (1986–91), and inaugural president of Heritage Roses—Australia (1992–93). His many awards and honours include the T.A. STEWART Memorial Award (1966) of the NATIONAL ROSE SOCIETIES of Australia and New Zealand, the Deane M. ROSS Award (1997) of Heritage Roses—Australia, and the Dean Hole Medal (1994), the highest honour bestowed by the Royal National Rose Society (UK) and regarded internationally as the highest honour possible for rosarians.

TREVOR NOTTLE

RUZICKA, Otakar (Otto) (1920–1996), garden designer, was born in Pilsen, Czechoslovakia, and received his education in garden design at Weihenstephan, Bavaria, Germany. In 1949 he migrated to Australia, introducing the sophisticated urbane approach to gardening developed in central Europe by the influential German garden designer and author Otto Valentien (b. 1897) and others. From 1952, when appointed to the parks and gardens section of the Department of the Interior by Lindsay PRYOR, he designed many CANBERRA gardens. These included the rhododendron garden at GOVERNMENT HOUSE, the AUSTRALIAN NATIVE PLANT garden at the Prime Minister's LODGE, gardens for several embassies (including Sweden and Germany), a number at the Australian National University (including the ROOF GARDENS at the John Curtin Medical School and the COURTYARD at the Institute of Anatomy), and projects within the AUSTRALIAN NATIONAL BOTANIC GARDENS (including the lower ponds). His work, illustrated by attractive drawings, was characterised by the sensitive grouping of plants, use of ground-shaping and rocks, and at times of WATER and SCULPTURE.

RICHARD CLOUGH

RYAN, Stephen Godfrey (b. 1955), nursery proprietor and plant enthusiast, is the principal of Dicksonia Rare Plants, a

Ryde School of Horticulture

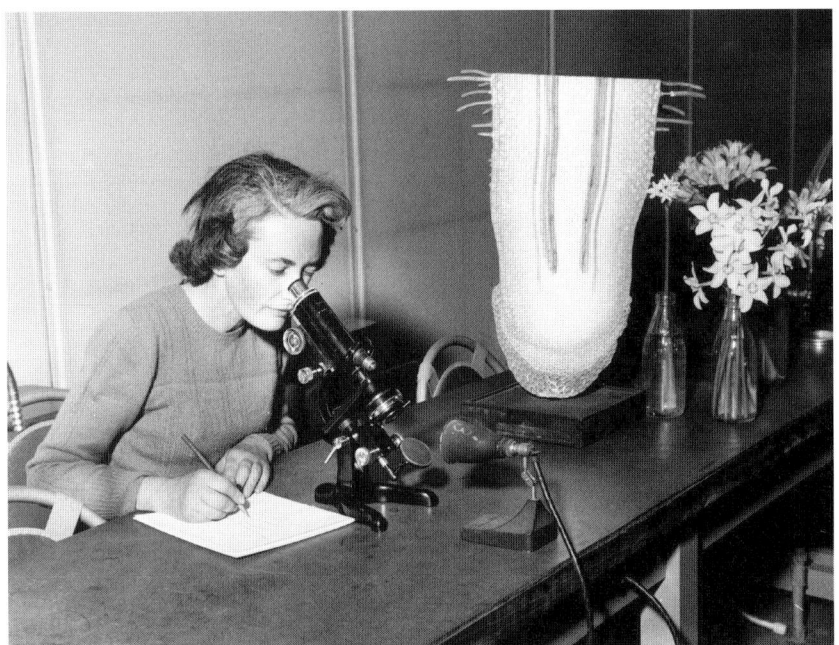

With the establishment of RYDE SCHOOL OF HORTICULTURE in the post-war years, formal horticultural EDUCATION in NSW received a major boost

specialist nursery in MOUNT MACEDON, Vic. Through his collection of rare and specialist plants, Ryan has been able to establish Dicksonia as one of the premier rare plant NURSERIES in Australia. He has a special interest in the genus *Cornus*, and holds the Dogwood collection for the ORNAMENTAL PLANTS CONSERVATION ASSOCIATION. A knowledgeable and enthusiastic lecturer—and an entertaining presenter—he is active in many gardening organisations throughout Vic. In 1999, Ryan published *Exceptional Plants*, a volume outlining 100 rare woody plants of garden merit. He has also written widely for both the specialist press and the popular horticultural press. JAMES WILL

RYDE SCHOOL OF HORTICULTURE, NSW, part of the state's technical and further education system, is a well-respected centre for EDUCATION in ornamental and urban horticulture and over many years has trained leaders in all areas of HORTICULTURE. The ten-hectare site was purchased in 1946 as an annexe to Sydney Technical College. The first classrooms were built in 1955 and all horticultural teaching transferred there by 1957. It has steadily grown from two full-time teachers and around 200 students to a full-time teaching staff of forty (assisted by 150 part-time teachers) and 3000 students. The grounds have permanent plantings for teaching purposes, and areas for practical classes and seasonal displays. The original buildings were replaced in 1975 and in 1988 there was a considerable enlargement and upgrade of facilities, including the provision of a retail garden centre, state-of-the-art glasshouses, and purpose-built landscape construction areas. JUDY McMAUGH

SACKVILLE-WEST, Victoria (Vita): see SISSINGHURST

ST AUBINS, south of Scone, in the Hunter Valley, NSW, was redesigned by Jocelyn BROWN in 1940 and is her most formal garden. The house was a fine Victorian mansion, built in 1888 by William Bakewell, owner of the Bakewell Pottery and Terracotta Works at Macdonaldtown, NSW, as his country retreat. It was already surrounded by a complex of buildings and an existing garden when Brown made her design, which provided a strong FORMAL framework for various garden spaces around the homestead in the style of English Edwardian gardens in the ARTS AND CRAFTS manner. Notable is the WALLED rose garden with brick paths and a terracotta bust of Captain James Cook. Various fine terracotta urns are used as garden ORNAMENTS.

HELEN PROUDFOOT

ST DAVIDS PARK, Hobart, a semi-formal PUBLIC PARK of about two hectares was designed by Hobart City Council's Superintendent of Reserves L.J. LIPSCOMBE and opened in 1926. It occupies the site of Hobart's first burial ground (1804–72). The more historically significant and elaborate monuments remain *in situ* at the north-east corner of the park but the remainder of the gravestones were moved, some to be used in the construction of the three PERGOLA-like gateways and the central ROTUNDA (used for band recitals). The surviving gravestones were incorporated into memorial walls (1982). The park features undulating lawns criss-crossed with paths, shrubberies, and mature exotic trees underplanted with fuchsias and azaleas. Significant trees include two massive *Sequoiadendron giganteum* (Giant Redwood), planted in 1937 to COMMEMORATE the coronation of George VI and Queen Elizabeth.

LINDY SCRIPPS

ST JOHN, Percival Reginald Harry (1872–1944), botanist and EUCALYPT authority, worked for fifty-four years at MELBOURNE BOTANIC GARDENS. A taxidermist's son, he began aged 11 as seedsman's assistant under GUILFOYLE. Rising through positions of painter and label writer to head gardener (1917–24) and classifier (1924–37) he developed an authoritative and encyclopaedic plant knowledge, especially of AUSTRALIAN PLANTS, and under CRONIN greatly extended the Australian Border. His meticulous work as classifier was horticulturally important. He botanically surveyed Wilsons Promontory (1908–10) with AUDAS and during FIELD NATURALIST and walking club excursions collected many specimens for the Gardens' Economic Botany Museum. Passionately interested in the horticulture and economic value of native plants, he advised on planting of the Metropolitan Golf Links at Oakleigh with Australian plants, investigated eucalyptus oils, and provided eucalypt information to Russell GRIMWADE, who sponsored his 1938 survey of the Buffalo Plateau flora. St John's HERBARIUM collection survives at MOUNT BUFFALO Chalet.

LINDEN GILLBANK

ST KILDA BOTANIC GARDENS, Vic., was gazetted in 1860, a year after the newly established council had sought the site. A design competition (1860) was won by Tilman Wilhelm Gloystein (*c*. 1817–1894) and his formal design was progressively, though incompletely, implemented over succeeding decades (shown on a Melbourne and Metropolitan Board of Works plan of 1897). Originally with bay views, the flat site was little-treed, and Gloystein's design turned the focus onto horticultural embellishment, with an axial parterre as the intended centrepiece for a carriage drive and a diamond arrangement of paths within the rectangular site. Gloystein was appointed to lay out the garden, but in 1861 local nursery proprietor George BRUNNING was contracted as gardener. Many plants were supplied by Ferdinand MUELLER through the nursery at MELBOURNE BOTANIC GARDENS. A gravel pit was filled in (1900) and Gloystein's diamond arrangement was gradually replaced with curved paths. A major alteration came with development of the Alister CLARK Memorial Rose Garden (1949–50), designed by superintendent Norman Thomas Scoble (1899–1966) and planted by A.S. THOMAS. A CONSERVATORY and collection of plants indigenous to the region are recent additions. With WILLIAMSTOWN, St Kilda was one of two suburban BOTANIC GARDENS in Melbourne, and part of an outstanding network of such garden in Vic. mixing horticulture with leisure. The garden retains a large collection of mature trees, and its formal design is an unusual survival.

RA

ST OMER, near Braidwood, NSW, is an early surviving HOMESTEAD GARDEN. Captain George Bunn was granted St Omer in 1827, and his descendants planned and tended the garden; fifth-generation owners have been responsible for its rejuvenation in recent years. The basic layout has remained unchanged since its beginnings in 1852, with a line of Italian cypress leading to the front gate, where an ancient privet hedge bounds the garden. Beyond the garden is a wilderness of *Robinia pseudoacacia* (False Acacia) and massive willows (*Salix* sp.) that line St Omer Creek. In restoration of the garden (1990s), the original curved carriageway has been redefined, box hedges trimmed, and pathways uncovered. The largest tree in the garden is a *Cupressus goveniana* (Gowen Cypress), a rare and endangered species.

TRISHA DIXON

ST VIGEANS, Stirling, SA, a HILL-STATION estate in the ADELAIDE HILLS, was established in 1880 by (Sir) Edward STIRLING and became internationally renowned for its RHODODENDRON collection and HYBRIDISATION program. The garden, developed by head gardener Douglas Searle (1854–1894) in 1882, following instructions from Stirling, swept down a valley, past a large pool and large shade houses on the north-eastern slope, overlooked by a two-storey residence (1883). It was planted extensively with deciduous trees, palms, and conifers, together with camellias, maples, azaleas, and rhododendrons mostly imported from England. Waterer's nursery in England named a rhododendron cultivar, 'Mrs E.C. Stirling', in honour of Stirling's patronage. The garden was photographed at its height in the 1910s by Stirling's daughter, Ada Florence (1879–1939), and his nephew, Collingwood 'Cherry' Ingram, stayed at St Vigeans en route from collecting cultivated forms of *Prunus* sp. in Japan. Alfred FAIRHALL followed Searle as head gardener, before David WHIBLEY was engaged in this role and started the first successful graftings of the Rhododendron CULTIVARS 'Pink Pearl', 'Mrs E.C. Stirling', 'Alice Sapphire', and several unnamed cultivars planted elsewhere in Adelaide Hills gardens. St Vigeans stayed in the Stirling family until 1936, whereafter it was sold and progressively subdivided, while respecting the broad outline of the garden structure, including the woodland and lily pond areas.

TREVOR NOTTLE and DAVID JONES

ST VINCENT GARDENS, Albert Park, Vic., is the central focus of the St Vincent Place residential estate, a spacious urban SQUARE planned by Clement HODGKINSON in 1857. The gardens, which date from 1868 (following an earlier unexecuted scheme attributed to Edward La Trobe BATEMAN) were designed by Hodgkinson about a central east–west axis with symmetry expressed in the layout and planting (including dominant ARAUCARIAS). The flat site was perfectly suited to the FORMAL layout, floral displays, and the 1869 incorporation of a BOWLING GREEN and CROQUET LAWN (later converted for TENNIS). In 1870, a tender for the laying, planting, and maintenance of the gardens was let by contract to gardener Nathaniel RONALDS, although from 1871 a permanent gardener was appointed. Despite alterations over successive curatorships, much of the garden layout and collection of mature trees—and the surrounding Victorian terrace houses, which provide a sense of enclosure—have survived.

JILL ORR-YOUNG

SALISBURY COURT, south of Uralla, NSW, is one of the oldest HOMESTEAD GARDENS in the New England region, having been established following a land grant of 1844. The HA-HA, believed to be among the earliest in Australia, dates from the 1840s and allows uninterrupted views of the billabong and paddocks, planted with elms, oaks, poplars, and hawthorns. The house and garden have benefited from single-family ownership and current custodians Sir Owen and Lady Croft have further developed the garden, building dry stone walls, softening and extending the planting and creating a formal herb parterre on the original tennis court.

TRISHA DIXON

SALMON PONDS, Plenty, Tas., constructed in 1862, was based on Scotland's famous Stormontfield Ponds on the River Tay, plans of which were brought to the colony by Curzon Allport, brother of barrister, naturalist, and keen ACCLIMATISER Morton ALLPORT. After years of enthusiastic effort but considerable difficulty finding a suitable transportation medium, Atlantic salmon and trout ova were successfully transported to Tas. from England during 1864 in special wooden boxes layered in moss, charcoal, and ice. In anticipation, members of Tasmania's Salmon Commission had selected a suitable hatchery site on the banks of the Derwent River at Robert Read's property Redlands. The Ponds quickly became a tourist attraction, and by 1869 the grounds had been laid out with 'English and Australian' trees; an AVIARY with an emu, parrots, cockatoos, and pheasants; and an ornamental garden surrounding the keeper's cottage. The large collection of mature ornamental trees contains some rare CONIFERS.

FRANCINE GILFEDDER

SANDGATE CEMETERY, NSW, opened in 1881, remains one of the state's largest cemeteries and is particularly notable as the only Australian CEMETERY to retain an integrally designed railway branch line. For most of the twentieth century the cemetery was well vegetated, based around a *Pinus radiata* (Monterey Pine) avenue along the branch line, providing Newcastle with an impressive PUBLIC PARK and gardens. Surviving plantings include *Magnolia grandiflora* (Bull Bay), *Harpephyllum caffrum* (Kaffir Plum), *Hibiscus rosa-sinensis* (Rose of China), *Podocarpus falcatus* (Outeniqua Yellowwood), and numerous PALM species. Sandgate Cemetery contains a rich variety of monuments (including imported sculptures and some from the 1840s relocated with the closure of early Newcastle cemeteries) and some notable buildings (including a fine brick gatehouse).

GEOFFREY BRITTON

SANGSTER, William: see TAYLOR AND SANGSTER

SANGWELL, William (c. 1811–1885), gardener, a native of Berkshire, England, arrived in Hobart Town in 1855 with his wife and large family. He was also accompanied aboard the *Fortitude* by fellow bounty passengers, the gardeners William CHANDLER and James Axton, both bonded to John Leake of ROSEDALE. Sangwell was 'Working Gardener in charge' at Hobart's CORNELIAN BAY CEMETERY from 1876 until his death, a formative period in the cemetery's development.

ACCLIMATISATION at SALMON PONDS, Plenty (Tas.) embraced both fauna and flora, with Atlantic salmon and trout ova hatched in the ponds, and an arboretum including many English trees lining its banks and surrounding grounds

Several members of the Sangwell family took up gardening professionally. William's eldest son Jesse Sangwell (c. 1834–1907) had worked as an agricultural labourer in England, but by the time of his marriage in 1859 he gave his occupation as gardener. The second son, Alfred Henry Sangwell (c. 1844–1921), was working in Hobart as a gardener by 1864, although he later moved to Melbourne. His break came in 1886 with a commission from the local council to lay out his plan for Benalla Gardens. He became its first curator and was joined at Benalla by his son, Joseph Samuel Sangwell (1865–1942), perhaps assisting his father in the public garden. J.W. Sangwell—perhaps Jesse or Joseph—was gardener during the 1880s for Edward HENTY's family at their Melbourne residence, Offington, and detailed research would doubtless yield further horticultural exploits of this family of emigrant gardeners.

Svetlana Karovich, *The Benalla Gardens* (Benalla, Vic., 1988)

RA

SARGEANT, Harold John ('Anthos') (1882–1973), journalist and horticulturist, was born at Geelong (Vic.) and started his journalistic career with the *Stawell Times*. He then worked on newspapers in Launceston (Tas.) and Adelaide, before joining the Melbourne *Herald* in 1912. He was chief sub-editor for ten years, then motoring writer, editor of the *Herald Road Guide*, and manager of the Touring Club until 1928. Sargeant was assigned to the gardening section of the *Herald* to 'help out' for a few weeks and four decades later retired from writing the gardening column that made his pen-name, 'Anthos', a household word to Victorian gardeners. His *Flowering Trees and Shrubs* (c. 1934) drew on the 'quickening interest in permanent features of the garden'. He instanced the thousands of trees and shrubs planted by home gardeners as a result of the *Herald* garden COMPETITION, which he managed, and his comments that this would 'yield and sustain interest throughout the year … surrounding … homes with permanent beauty' challenged prevailing preferences for bedding of annuals to create floral interest. Greatly enlarged and revised editions of his book appeared in 1951 and 1968. Sargeant retired in 1948 but continued to write his gardening column until 1968, when he was aged 85 and venerated by two generations of garden lovers. RA

SAVIGE, Thomas James (1913–1999), camellia expert, was born in Bonalbo (NSW) and, towards the end of his life, lived near Albury (NSW). An aeronautical engineer, his job took him to San Diego, USA, where he became interested in CAMELLIAS. Back in Australia he built a house in suburban Melbourne (at Canterbury) and began planting and raising camellias in its garden. In 1956 he joined the Australian and New Zealand Camellia Research Society and for the rest of his life was involved in national and international organisations, culminating in the presidency of the International Camellia Society (1977–82). The Camellia Society became the authority for the registration of cultivar names of the genus *Camellia* in 1962. Having a special interest in nomenclature, Savige was appointed registrar in 1980. He took over the work already done and with great enthusiasm masterminded the work of many experts, resulting in the publication the *International Camellia Register* (1993) and a supplement (1997). The 1993 volumes contained 32 000 CULTIVAR names (including synonyms and errors) and the Chinese and Japanese names of 9000 oriental cultivars. A regular contributor to Australian and overseas horticultural journals, he was the author of *Camellias in Australian Gardens* (1967), and, with Peter Longhurst as illustrator, *The Camellia* (1982). In 1993 the ROYAL HORTICULTURAL SOCIETY awarded him the VEITCH Memorial Gold Medal and in 1994 the University of Sydney the degree of Master of Science *honoris causa* for his outstanding work on camellias.

RICHARD CLOUGH

SAYCE, Joseph (*c.* 1815–1876), amateur horticulturist and landscape gardener, arrived in Melbourne from London in 1852. A banker by profession, Sayce was employed by the Bank of New South Wales and, from 1856, the Bank of Victoria. In 1867 he became the first manager of the latter's branch in the burgeoning gold-mining town of Walhalla. Returning to Melbourne in 1871, Sayce quit the bank the following year, his financial status assured by judicious mining investments.

In 1860 Sayce had joined the Victorian Gardeners' Mutual Improvement Society, and acquired a local reputation as an amateur horticulturist and landscape designer. Nonetheless, it was only by accident that he learnt in late 1872 of indecision surrounding the laying out of Victoria's GOVERNMENT HOUSE grounds and adjacent DOMAIN. A government design COMPETITION, held in August 1872, had garnered only mediocre entries—three of these (all by professional landscape gardeners and civil engineers) were eventually judged equal winners, but no single one was considered of sufficient merit to implement in its own right.

At this point, Sayce stepped forward to freely offer a plan of his own devising. Broadly PICTURESQUE in style, its features included an extensive system of lakes, an AMERICAN GARDEN, and a classical 'Temple of Eolus' overlooking the Yarra River. Sayce was familiar with the published work of KEMP, and his design had similarities with Sefton Park, near Liverpool, England (1867: landscape designer, Edouard André). The Board overseeing the project quickly assessed this as superior to anything previously submitted, and, after some simplification, it was formally adopted in January 1873. Work started immediately, but the foreman proved lacking in technical expertise, and Sayce was asked to supervise the implementation of his plan, taking over as temporary curator from 14 March. In the ensuing months he was largely engaged in forming the driveways, this progress being sustained by an advance of £4000 in funds. His superiors baulked, however, at his request—subsequently withdrawn—for an extravagant rise in his pay should his services be retained after 30 June. Undaunted, Sayce's official report of 1 June confirmed his expectation of being retained in the position of curator, and of lavish future government spending on the project (he was wont to cite the more than £300 000 expended on Sefton Park as a yardstick). On 31 May, however, Assistant-Commissioner of Lands and Survey Clement HODGKINSON had penned a report of his own that affirmed the government's decision to abandon Sayce's 'costly design' in favour of a 'well-arranged public park'. Sayce was formally advised of the termination of his position on 14 June. After defending his work through a sympathetic press he withdrew, embittered. Meanwhile, control of the Government House grounds and Domain passed to the newly appointed director of the adjacent Botanic Gardens, William GUILFOYLE. Sayce retired to his residence Edenthorpe, Caulfield, and remained active in amateur horticultural circles until his death.

DARREN WATSON

SCANDINAVIA, comprising Norway, Sweden, and Denmark, and having strong historic and cultural links with Finland and Iceland, has a strong tradition of botany, horticulture and landscape design. Swedish botanist Carl LINNAEUS (1707–1778) exercised profound influence on BOTANY through his system of binomial nomenclature, linked to Australia through his Uppsala student Daniel SOLANDER, who accompanied Cook and BANKS on the *Endeavour*. A later graduate of Uppsala was Andrew PATTERSON, whose German career exemplified the strong historical and cultural links between these European regions. Indeed, the state of Schleswig-Holstein veered between Danish and German control: it was here that Ferdinand MUELLER and his compatriot Friedrich KRICHAUFF spent their early years. Carl NOBELIUS (born in Finland) and Lars ROSÉN (born in Sweden) both made significant contributions in Australia (to the NURSERY trade), as did Danish-born landscape gardener Paul SORENSEN. Scandinavian MODERNISM, especially through the influence of architects Alvar Aalto (1898–1976) and Gunnar Asplund (1885–1940) was felt in Australia, and this was intensified with the presence of Danish architect Jørn Utzon, working on the Sydney Opera House from 1957 to 1966. By the 1970s, an uncluttered Scandinavian look was embraced not only in architecture but more generally, in domestic interior and landscape design.

RA

SCARTH-JOHNSON, Vera (1912–1999), botanical collector, artist, and farmer, was born in Morley, near Leeds, Yorkshire, England, and after completing a horticultural course at Hertfordshire Institute of Agriculture, started a piggery and market garden. She migrated to Australia after the Second World War and settled in Bundaberg (Qld.), where she purchased a thirty-hectare property. Voluntary plant collecting for the ROYAL BOTANIC GARDENS, KEW, took her to many parts of Australia. In the evenings she sketched and painted flowers, and after her move north to Cooktown (1972)—inspired by the beauty of the Endeavour River and by the early botanical work of BANKS and SOLANDER—she set out to paint 200 local plants. The onset of Parkinson's disease brought the project to a close at 175 paintings; in 1990 Scarth-Johnson gave these to the people of Cooktown to be housed locally. Her name is commemorated in the shrub *Argophyllum verae*.

JUDITH McKAY

SCENTED PLANTS can be divided largely into those with perfumed flowers and those with aromatic foliage. Many plants, including exotic shrub groups such as the ROSES and lilacs, and individual subjects such as *Luculia gratissima*, *Michelia figo* (Port Wine Magnolia), *Philadephus* spp. (Mock Orange), *Daphne* spp. (Daphne), *Chimonanthus praecox* (Winter Sweet), and *Osmanthus fragrans* (Sweet Osmanthus) have been traditionally valued in Australian gardens for their highly scented flowers, although BREEDING practices in some cases have produced new forms lacking scent. A range of AUSTRALIAN PLANTS produce scented flowers; some such as the *Pittosporum undulatum* (Sweet Pittosporum)—now regarded as a WEED in some locations—release their intense perfume in the evening. *Boronia megastigma*, although often fickle in cultivation, has long been grown in Australian gardens and releases its scent when flowers are open. Used in the cut flower trade, this species is largely harvested from the wild in WA for essential oil production. An Australian perfume industry was even advocated in the late nineteenth century, but initiatives such as the Government Scent Farm, at Dunolly, Vic. (1891–99), were soon abandoned. Lavender farming has, however, witnessed a recent resurgence of interest. Other groups are valued for their aromatic foliage, usually activated when this is bruised or brushed. Plant leaves high in volatile oils, such as in the families Lamiaceae (for example *Lavandula*) and Myrtaceae (such as *Eucalyptus*, *Leptospermum*, and *Melaleuca*), can be strongly aromatic and are often selected for landscape planting for this quality in addition to overall aesthetic appeal; the *Eucalyptus citriodora* (Lemon-scented Gum) provides a fine example. Scented plants are essential subjects in SENSORY GARDENS and their aroma is a vital aspect of many HERB GARDENS. ML

SCHOMBURGK, Richard Moritz (1811–1891), botanist, horticulturist, and botanic gardens director, was born in Freyburg on the Unstrut in Saxony, son of an assistant Lutheran pastor. The family had a background in civic and court responsibilities. All four sons had notable careers. The eldest, Robert, joined a family business in Leipzig; the second son, Otto studied at Halle University; Richard was apprenticed as a gardener at Merseburg; and the fourth son, Julius, was apprenticed as a goldsmith and silversmith. At the time, a gardening apprenticeship provided many opportunities for a young man from an educated background; German gardeners held positions of note throughout northern Europe. After national service in the Royal Guard and work in the famous gardens at Sanssouci, Richard joined an expedition to British Guiana (1840–44) led by his brother Robert for the British Government and the Royal Geographical Society. Richard travelled on behalf of the Prussian Government as botanist and historian. Surviving yellow fever, he returned to Berlin to carry out further research with assistance from leading scientists of the day, and to publish his travels as *Reisen in Britisch Guiana* (1847–48).

The palm house that Richard SCHOMBURGK imported from GERMANY for ADELAIDE BOTANIC GARDEN was among the most horticulturally and architecturally sophisticated glasshouses in Australia during the nineteenth century, and perfectly displayed Schomburgk's vision uniting science, education, and recreation

Richard and Otto supported the liberal cause in 1848 and were advised by their mentor, Alexander von Humboldt, to leave Germany. With educationalist and pastor Muecke and teacher Listermann they formed a colonisation society, embarking with some 180 people from Hamburg on the *Princess Louise* and reaching Adelaide in 1849.

The brothers and their wives took up land at Buchsfelde, near Gawler, north of Adelaide, where they farmed, planted vines and an orchard, and become active in local civic affairs. Richard had married Pauline Henriette Kneip, daughter of a Potsdam builder and timber merchant. Following the death of Otto, Richard successfully applied in 1865 for the position as director of the ADELAIDE BOTANIC GARDEN, established in 1855 by his predecessor G.W. FRANCIS. The move enabled him to provide better educational and social opportunities for his son and five daughters.

Schomburgk was in a strong position. The British Guiana expedition had given him an international reputation. Sixteen years at Buchsfelde provided practical experience of the problems of managing vines, orchard, and farm under Australian conditions. He had experienced the demands of army life and the harsh conditions of British Guiana, been trained to work for clients as an apprentice, and learned to work with British officials and committee members. He was not academically brilliant but was capable, enthusiastic, and could combine vision with pragmatism. He also had good communication skills.

A balanced approach saw him start by improving the rosary and tropical plant displays, develop animals houses and aviaries, while also working on experimental plots of pasture grasses and other utilitarian plants. The site was not large and rather flat. Landscape features to enhance the gardens included an avenue of *Ficus macrophylla* (Moreton Bay Fig) that combined European traditions with the use of AUSTRALIAN PLANTS. He was careful to leave the scientifically important but aesthetically bland class ground (or SYSTEM GARDEN) until more popular features were developed. He took care to maintain good relationships with the local NURSERY trade.

An early coup was to persuade his government to grant funds for a Victoria House; the Schomburgk brothers were associated with the naming of the Giant Water Lily, then known as *Victoria regia* (now *V. amazonica*). The venture was a huge success attracting extraordinary attention, with hour by hour newspaper descriptions of flowers opening and with visitors visiting during their lunch-breaks. Schomburgk's continued success with the lily over the years was a matter of parochial pride. Up to 300 000 visitors per year were recorded when the population of the whole colony was about 163 000.

In the prosperous decade of the 1870s, such success enabled Schomburgk and his board to import a tropical palm house, opened in 1877. Prefabricated of wrought iron and cast iron and at the forefront of technological design for its time, the palm house (or CONSERVATORY) was designed by Gustav Runge and manufactured by Bremen's Höper and Co. Now the only one of its kind extant outside Europe, it has recently been restored. In 1884 a solidly constructed museum of ECONOMIC BOTANY in classical style opened to display specimens of economic plants and to house Schomburgk's HERBARIUM.

Modelled on that at KEW, the museum is unique in Australia. The original display cases and stencilled ceiling decoration still survive. Plant material used for cordage, dyes, fibres, timber, grain, resins, oils, beverages, and medicines, including plants used by Aboriginal people were displayed, paralleled by plants in the EXPERIMENTAL GARDEN, sent from all over the world. Trees and cuttings were given away to farmers and civic bodies: up to 12 000 trees were given away annually.

Schomburgk's great success lay in the balance he maintained between the scientific, educational, and recreational roles of the botanic garden. Visitors enjoyed the walks, vistas, statues, and parterre plantings while learning what could be grown under South Australian conditions. Lengthy annual reports included agricultural and viticultural advice. People could send specimens from remote parts of the colony for identification and advice. The world-wide exchange system included not only the British Empire but Java, Russia, and the USA. This was a multi-purpose institution that included pleasure garden, crop research institute, and herbarium.

Schomburgk received honours from European dignitaries but above all was honoured locally as 'the people's pet'. The Garden was known as 'Dr Schomburgk's gardens'. He lived to see his children take their place in Anglo-Australian society. Like so many successful middle-class German migrants, he had joined the Church of England and was an active member of his Masonic Lodge. His publications had ranged from his *Reisen in Britisch Guiana* and two catalogues of plants in the Botanic Garden to papers on pasture grasses, forestry, phylloxera, flower farming, sericulture, rust in cereals, and an overview of possible crop plants for the colony.

PAULINE PAYNE

SCHOOL GARDENS were first planted and tended by pupils as a formal part of their NATURE STUDY lessons in the early 1900s. As a movement, it appears to have been born of two quite different impulses. The first came from countries like the USA, Britain, and Germany, where school gardens were already well established. It sought to reduce the negative effects of modern city life by keeping city and suburban children in touch with the beauty and wonder of nature, and by instilling notions of self-discipline, co-operation, duty, and pride. This broadly Progressive aim was also behind the institution of ARBOR DAY and the foundation of the PLAYGROUND movement.

The other main impulse—very strong in Australia—was to civilise and beautify the barren monotony of 'the BUSH': to make of the country a place of cultivation, in every sense of the word. English-born George Brown, then foreman of Melbourne's FITZROY GARDENS, a founder of the school garden movement in Vic., made no secret of the fact that he found the houses and schools of Australian bush communities to be quite uninspiring, even desolate. Writer Mary Gilmore's serialised reminiscences of life as a teacher in small country schools popularised the view of the country as harsh, spare, and lacking in refinement and even basic amenities. According to Education Department bureaucrats (especially Victorian inspector of schools and, from 1902, director of education, Frank Tate) and doyens of various hor-

From the temperate south—as in Jeetho (Vic.), where, by 1911, staff and pupils of the local state school had developed an impressive formal plot carved from the bush—to the tropical north, SCHOOL GARDENS provided an important introduction to gardening and horticulture for many CHILDREN

ticultural societies, school gardens could fix this problem. Gardens would transform the physical environment with colour, beauty, and bountiful produce, creating in country children an appreciation of the more refined pleasures of life. On a more practical note, experimental plots for agricultural crops, common at rural schools, would benefit farmer and pupil alike. In other words, the bringing together of children and gardens, in city and country, would turn out valuable future citizens and contribute to future prosperity.

The establishment of the first school gardens was not without problems. At many inner-city primary schools there was no space for proper playgrounds, let alone gardens. Education departments addressed this problem by acquiring many new school sites over the next decade or two. At country schools, grounds were often unfenced, and the new gardens were soon overrun by rabbits. It was often up to teachers and parents to carry the expense of wire netting. At private schools, this was more likely to be the province of a paid staff, in the manner of other INSTITUTIONAL gardens.

After a slow start in some states (notably Tas. and WA), the school garden movement took off, in some states aided by specialist HORTICULTURAL SOCIETIES, publications, and COMPETITIONS, reaching its peak in the 1920s and 1930s. After the Second World War, interest waned or was displaced into related areas. For example, schools in Qld replaced horticulture with forestry and sugar cane cultivation, while in NSW, gardening was nudged out in favour of new activities such as physical education and drama. In Vic., children continued to participate in school gardening activities up to about 1980, due largely to the support of the State Schools Nursery. With the advent of the Information Age, the idea of using gardening as a tool for moral and economic advancement has become passé. In its stead, excursions to natural habitats and wider environmental discussions have provided an alternative stimulus, often expressed in REVEGETATION schemes within the broad LANDCARE movement.

ANGELA CARTLAND

SCHUBERT, Bernhardt Edlewyn (1914–2002) and **Dulcie Lillian (née Corrie)** (1918–1990), nursery proprietors, born at Rupanyup and Stawell (Vic.) respectively, were among the earliest growers to devote a commercial nursery entirely to the production of AUSTRALIAN PLANTS. They began propagation at the Arbor Vista (later Wondaree) Nursery, East Oakleigh (Vic.), in 1947, moving temporarily to the Victorian Grampians before settling at Noble Park in 1952, where the nursery still thrives, run by son Bernard (b. 1949). Unhampered by a nursery background—Bernhardt had been a carpenter—they experimented with many methods of propagating native species and developed a number of very successful techniques. The 'Schubert method' of landscape planting utilised a 300-mm layer of hardwood sawdust covered with a thin layer of river sand, with the paths compacted slightly lower than the planted areas. Plants were then placed in a hole opened in the sawdust and backfilled with soil. As the sawdust aged and became covered with leaf litter, the garden developed a NATURAL appearance. To display many relatively unknown Australian species and to demonstrate how they could be used to create bush-like and semi-natural settings, the Schuberts established a wonderful DISPLAY GARDEN next to the nursery. This garden—now removed although well recorded in photographs—proved to be an inspiration to many landscape designers determined to work with Australian plants in a natural manner, far removed from European horticultural influence.

GLEN WILSON

SCIENTIFIC SOCIETIES: see AUSTRALIAN AND NEW ZEALAND ASSOCIATION FOR THE ADVANCEMENT OF SCIENCE;

Field Naturalists' Clubs and Societies; Linnean Society of New South Wales; Royal societies

SCOBORIO, Charles (1827–1912), botanic gardens curator, was born in Cornwall, England, of Italian paternity. He trained under Lindley at the (Royal) Horticultural Society's garden at Chiswick and also on the Continent. Scoborio arrived at Warrnambool (Vic.) in 1857, working initially as a draper while also advertising that he would lay out gardens. He was appointed as gardener to establish the Warrnambool Botanic Gardens in 1859, but after six fruitless years the site was abandoned, and Scoborio subsequently took up the position of head gardener—reputedly for James William Manifold Aitkin at Ellerslie, and later for Joseph Ware at Minjah. He returned as curator of the Warrnambool Botanic Gardens (at its current site) in 1872 and spent a productive career planting and nurturing this Guilfoyle-designed garden and other council reserves, until his retirement in 1906. RA

SCOTLAND, the northern section of the geographic land mass of Great Britain and, since 1707, united politically and economically with England and Wales, has exercised a major influence on Australian gardens. Although Scotland is still under-researched in garden history terms, as a nation it did not always follow English stylistic trends, but developed its own 'language' and absorbed influences at different times from Europe. It maintained a fierce social and cultural independence much in common with Ireland and Wales, transmitting this to Australia through its export of hardy and resourceful Scottish gardeners.

Why did Scots make such an impact? Independence, born of political struggles over centuries; caution, forethought, diligence, thrift, resourcefulness, and indomitable perseverance, stemming in large measure from the extremes of climate and geography; widespread education; and mobility were all critical factors. Education through the apprenticeship system was widespread in Scotland by the early nineteenth century, and a journeyman gardener was not expected to stay in a situation longer than one year. Experience at the celebrated seats of Hamilton Palace, Dalkeith, and Drumlanrig, and at the Edinburgh Botanic Gardens was especially highly regarded. Mutual help among gardeners was reflected educationally, manifest in self-improvement through reading from private libraries, garden visiting, and meetings, either informally or organised through horticultural societies (often encouraged by employers as a means of moral improvement), as well as in social welfare matters, as for instance, in the Free Gardeners movement. Walled gardens were climatically unnecessary in Australia, but the Scottish reputation for neatness and order was emulated, often in habits as much as gardens. These qualities found in gardeners from 'North Britain'—as Scotland was often known during the late eighteenth and nineteenth centuries—were widely recognised, even in England.

It was through emigration of Scots that the most profound influence was felt in Australia. Highland clearances resulting in a displaced agricultural workforce initially provided the labour for Australia's pastoral industry, particularly in Tas. and in Victoria's rich Western District. Here Scottish pastoralists, such as John Lang Currie of Titanga, employed kith and kin, linkages forming raw material for historians Margaret Kiddle in *Men of Yesterday* (1961) and Philip Brown (ed.) in *Clyde Company Papers* (1935–71). Scottish-born or trained gardeners among the earliest generations of migrants became superintendents or head gardeners of Australia's earliest Government Gardens and Botanic Gardens, including (with dates of arrival in Australia) Charles Fraser (1816), Naismith Robertson (1829), James Drummond (1829), James Anderson (1832), John Arthur (1839), John Dallachy (1848), and Charles Moore (1847). Several had worked in private gardens before their appointments, and yet others remained in private situations. Several, including Robert Henderson (*c.* 1825), Thomas William Shepherd (1827), John and George McEwin (1838–39), and Francis Ferguson (1849), went into the nursery business, or had trained in Scotland (or elsewhere in Britain), and then established the trade in Australia.

During the early gold-rush period, especially 1852–56, when demand for labour was high, many Scottish-born or trained gardeners were attracted to Australia (principally NSW and Vic.). Distinguished among these were William Adamson (1852), Walter Hill (1852), George Neilson (1852), John Smith (1852), William Sangster (1853), William Law (by 1853), Josiah Mitchell (by 1853), Joseph Graham (1853), Gilbert Handasyde (1853), Thomas Lang (1853), Robert Hughan (1854), James Sinclair (1854), Alexander Sturrock (1854), Thomas McMillan (by 1855), William Hyndman (1855), William Somner (*c.* 1855), Alexander Elliott (1856), and William Taylor (1856). Many possessed English or British colonial experience, generally seeking fortunes through the nursery trade (which they came to dominate) rather than mining. Numberless others just hoped for regular employment and an enhanced situation for their family. A second wave of post–gold rush migrants from the 1860s to the 1880s was attracted to a prosperous and stable society: prominent among these were Angus Mackay (1863), Thomas Purves (1863), Alexander Macpherson (by 1864), David Railton (1865), James Fern (1860s), Alexander Grant (1878), Alexander Jolly (late 1870s), William McGowan (1882), Charles Bisset (1883), and William Soutter (by 1885).

Apart from migration, influence was felt among gardeners from Scottish (or Scottish-born) horticultural writers and landscape gardeners: Walter Nicol, John Claudius Loudon, Charles H.J. Smith, Charles McIntosh, Robert Marnock, Donald Beaton, Robert Thompson, and William and David Thomson all reached a wide audience, with the indefatigable Loudon seen to exemplify Scottishness. To earlier generations, William Gilpin's *Observations on the Highlands of Scotland* (1789) had fuelled an appetite for the Picturesque; his nephew William Sawrey Gilpin drew on this tradition in several Scottish projects. The planting character of Scotland changed radically during the major period of emigration, with widescale evergreen (especially conifer) planting transforming the countryside. The influence of this Scottish tree planting was felt in early Australian FORESTRY and ARBORICULTURE, especially through the agency of John Ednie BROWN and Charles WESTON. Proud nostalgia also bestowed Scottish appellations on landscape features such as Arthur's Seat, the Grampians, the Esk River, and Cora Linn.

Twentieth-century links have been far less profound. Isolated migrant gardeners such as Joseph MARTIN (1921) continued beneficial Scottish influence. Temperate AUSTRALIAN PLANTS now find a place in gardens on the west coast of Scotland, such as Logan Botanic Gardens, warmed by the Gulf Stream, and Scotland remains important for research and development of RHODODENDRONS, for ALPINE and ROCKERY plants, and in conifer conservation.

> J. Holloway and L. Errington, *The Discovery of Scotland: The Appreciation of Scottish Scenery Through Two Centuries of Painting* (Edinburgh, 1978); A.A. Tait, *The Landscape Garden in Scotland 1735–1835* (Edinburgh, 1980); Malcolm D. Prentis, *The Scots in Australia: A Study of New South Wales, Victoria and Queensland, 1780–1900* (Sydney, 1983); Don Watson, *Caledonia Australis: Scottish Highlanders on the Frontier of Australia* (Sydney, 1984); *Historic Scotland and Scottish Natural Heritage: An Inventory of Gardens and Designed Landscapes in Scotland* (Edinburgh, 1987); Tim Buxbaum, *Scottish Garden Buildings: From Food to Folly* (Edinburgh, 1989); Forbes W. Robertson, *Early Scottish Gardeners and Their Plants 1650–1750* (East Linton, East Lothian, 2000)   RA

SCOTT, James (1819–1879), florist and nursery proprietor, was born in Northumberland, England, and after his arrival in Vic. established his business in 1853 (according to evidence in the firm's 1889 catalogue) and a year later purchased land in Burwood Road, Hawthorn; Scott's was consistently claimed to one of the oldest nurseries in Melbourne. He was elected to the first Hawthorn Council (1860) and was active in local civic affairs. He provided plants for MUELLER at the Melbourne Botanic Gardens during the early 1860s; Mueller's young colleague Charles FRENCH trained with Scott. St James Park, opposite the nursery, was laid out in 1861 by Scott, using trees distributed by Mueller. Scott was a member of the Horticultural Society of Victoria, and in 1863 he moved a successful resolution 'that practical gardeners, or persons employed as gardeners, be admitted as members on payment of an annual subscription of 10s 6d'; his nursery was conveniently close to the Society's gardens at BURNLEY. The nursery received patronage during the 1867 visit of the Duke of Edinburgh and was henceforth known as the Royal Nursery. Scott maintained a large stock and the firm's 1880 catalogue offered 400 varieties of FERNS (compared with SANGSTER's 200 at the same date). He introduced several ROSES, was at the forefront with DAHLIAS, and in 1886 the nursery was said to contain the oldest *Schinus molle* (Pepper Tree) in the colony.

Around the time of his father's death, Thomas Sherbourne Scott (c. 1849–1889) joined the business, but operations were curtailed. A nursery had been established at Nunawading for growing heavy stock and the Hawthorn nursery was chiefly devoted to the growth of pot plants, cut flowers, and the more valuable kinds of ornamental trees and shrubs. After the death of Thomas jnr. his widow, Mary Annie Scott (*née* Kelly) (c. 1856–1945), continued the business for several years.   RA

SCOTT, James W. (*fl.* 1820s–30s), was among the earliest commercial seed and plant collectors in Australia. LOUDON reprinted an 1829 article, stating that 'No resident of Hobart Town, either passing or permanent, should omit visiting Mr Scott, the industrious and well-informed seedsman of Brisbane Street. In his garden there will be found a most interesting collection of almost all the indigenous plants of our island, and many others of foreign origin.' Melville, in his 1831 *Van Diemen's Land Almanack*, claimed that Scott was the only person in the colony then making his living from botany, 'having discovered the method by which he is enabled to guarantee plants and seeds that may be required in the northern hemisphere'.

Scott advertised in Melville's 1833 *Almanack* as 'Seedsman, and Collector of Indigenous Plants, of the Island of Van Diemen's Land', offering for sale to 'neighbouring Gentlemen, Merchants, and others … a choice collection of Seeds, accompanied by Specimens and Dried Plants, that he can recommend as worthy of notice, and warranted for Exportation, together with instructions as to the nature and culture of the Plant'. Melville—who judged Scott 'a very meritorious Individual'—instanced 'deservedly high encomiums from several persons of distinction, who have had opportunities of viewing his Specimens, and of making trial of the admirable manner in which he not only preserves them, but ensures, by a process peculiar to himself, their retaining all their original beauty, in whatever climate they may be placed'. Scott was mentioned in the 'Index Plantarum' of James BACKHOUSE and Ronald GUNN (1834) as 'the collector', presumably to distinguish him from several colonists of the same name.   RA

SCULPTURE Egyptian sphinxes, lions, and copies of classical sculpture imported from ITALY were commonly used as decorative features in nineteenth-century PUBLIC GARDENS throughout Australia, establishing a fashion that continues with the ubiquitous cheap cement casts still seen in private gardens. Although classical **statuary** was strategically placed in the BOTANIC GARDENS in Sydney, Adelaide, and Ballarat, none was found in Melbourne's—and this absence contrasted with European counterparts. But whereas virtually all the marble statues originally in the ROYAL BOTANIC GARDENS, SYDNEY, were destroyed by weather or vandalism, Ballarat continued to acquire sculpture for both BALLARAT BOTANIC GARDENS and for the wide BOULEVARD plantation in Sturt Street. During the nineteenth, and for the first half of the twentieth century, public parks and gardens were seen as suitable places to erect monuments COMMEMORATING explorers, kings, queens, military leaders, and politicians, as well as WAR MEMORIALS. Charles Woolner's monument to Captain Cook, in Sydney's HYDE PARK (1879), was one of the earliest in a long line of such academic works by British sculptors or Australian artists, who had generally trained in Britain.

During the 1980s a number of gardens throughout Australia were modified to become public sculpture parks, specifically for the display of contemporary sculpture, usually by Australian artists. Some of the most notable include Melbourne's Museum of Modern Art at HEIDE; Adelaide's CARRICK HILL; Brisbane's King Edward Sculpture Park; McClelland Art Gallery, Langwarrin (Vic.); and more recently the Evandale Sculpture Walk, Gold Coast (Qld) and Herring Island, Melbourne. The Sculpture Garden at the Australian National Gallery, Canberra, on the other hand, was specifically and imaginatively designed by Harry HOWARD as a foil for the major collection of European, American, and Australian sculpture. Using AUSTRALIAN PLANTS, a series of individually designed spaces were established for specific works, encouraging spectators to meander through the garden, discovering the sculpture as they proceed. Sculpture is increasingly seen as a way of bringing additional—and permanent colour—into the landscape rather than using plants alone.

FOUNTAINS were frequently used as focal points in nineteenth-century gardens, as with the Exhibition Fountain (1880), modelled by German-born Josef Hochgurtel for Melbourne's EXHIBITION Building. Other notable fountains of a sculptural nature are situated in gardens throughout Australia, such as the Art Deco Archibald Fountain (1927) by the French sculptor François Sicard, in Sydney's HYDE PARK; Margel Hinder's abstract arrangement of sculptural forms and water at Newcastle (NSW), to commemorate Captain Cook (1961–66); and the remarkable Antipodean Voyage Fountain (1972) in the ROYAL TASMANIAN BOTANICAL GARDENS, Hobart, constructed of Huon Pine by Stephen Walker.

A number of sculptors, ranging from Norman Lindsay at SPRINGWOOD, William RICKETTS at Olinda, Inge King (b. 1918) at Warrandyte, and May Barrie (b. 1918) at Calderwood have used their gardens to display their work. There are, however, very few private collections of sculpture in Australia, and therefore even fewer gardens where sculpture has been used to any extent, the one major exception being the beautifully designed garden and the superb collection of Geoffrey and Gael Cousins at Mittagong (NSW).

During the 1980s and 1990s Australia saw a rapid development in **public art**, including sculpture, sometimes community-based, at other times carried out by professional artists. Venues have ranged from commercial and civic sites to parks and motorways, while the works have varied from light-hearted entertainments to the extraordinarily impressive *Gateway* by the architects Denton Corker Marshall on Melbourne's Tullamarine Freeway. The most ambitious of all these projects was the 2000 Olympics site at Sydney's Homebush Bay of nearly 800 hectares, where $7.5 million was committed to public art.

Ken Scarlett, *Contemporary Sculpture in Australian Gardens* (Sydney, 1993); Michael Hedger, *Public Sculpture in Australia* (Sydney, 1995)   KEN SCARLETT

SEALE, Allan John (1919–2001) horticulturist, author, and media presenter, was born in Sydney. Having had some experience at a nursery, when he returned from his war duties as an anti-aircraft gunner he opened a MARKET GARDEN in Pennant Hills (NSW), specialising in cut flowers and vegetables. He joined YATES as a sales representative in the early 1950s and during twenty years with the company, he rewrote *Yates' Garden Guide*. He presented the daily Yates

Bold foliage and textures complement SCULPTURE in the Lewers garden, (NSW)—an unusually sophisticated and visually satisfying integration of natural and cultural materials

gardening segments on Channel 9 in Sydney when television started in 1956, and his program 'In Your Garden' was seen on ABC television for more than fifteen years. He left Yates when his media commitments—TELEVISION, RADIO, and newspaper and magazine articles—increased; from 1976 until the late 1980s, his ABC radio talkback program was enduringly popular with gardeners in NSW. His many popular books gave detailed practical advice on varied aspects of gardening, and his sincerity and practical knowledge made him a highly respected member of the horticultural industry. With Kevin HEINZE, he was an inaugural recipient of the Horticultural Media Association's Hall of Fame Silver Laurel (2000).   HELEN BOTHAM

SEARCH, Frederick (c. 1819–1895), horticulturist and journalist, was born in Cirencester, Gloucestershire, England, and migrated to Vic. in the wake of the gold rushes. On his arrival he established himself in the NURSERY trade in the Flemington area, and by 1862 he was a committee member of the Melbourne-based Apiarian Society. In 1871 he became editor of the 'Yeoman department' of the *AUSTRALASIAN*, which included the important agriculture and horticulture portfolios. He assembled a talented array of contributors, including William SANGSTER ('Hortensis') and Joseph HARRIS (horticultural editor from 1885), and during his tenure the paper published *The Australasian Farmer* (1885). When failing strength compelled him to relinquish the arduous duties of agricultural editor, he continued to provide regular notes on fruit and flowers, his special love.   RA

SEARL, Frederick Rutt (c. 1818–1891), founder of the celebrated Sydney firm of florists, Searl and Sons, was born in Essex, England, and travelled the world as a steamer steward, marrying Louisa Derepas, of Scottish origins, in China before arrival in Australia c. 1848. A coach-builder by trade, he established a nursery in Parramatta (NSW) soon after arrival, and by 1853 he had a market stall in Sydney selling plants and cut flowers. Two sons, **John Thomas Searl** (1853–1937) and **Frederick Henry Searl** (1856–1920), worked in the garden from an early age, and the business took the name Searl and Sons c. 1867. By 1870 the family had moved to Newtown, and in 1875 to Petersham. Operations centred on the Blair Athol Nursery (Petersham), soon supplemented by a rose ground in Ashfield for cut flowers (1885) and an extensive nursery at Botany (1887). Searl died at Leighton, Essex, and was mourned by the *Rural Australian* as 'our pioneer florist … eminently distinguished for his skill, taste, business capacity and sterling integrity'. In 1872 his skill had been rewarded by Sir Hercules Robinson with vice-regal appointment, an honour continued by successive NSW colonial governors.

The partnership between John and Frederick Searl ceased in 1906 with the younger brother (and his sons) continuing in business as seed merchants, nursery proprietors, and florists. Additional suburban land for roses was acquired and in 1907 a large nursery was established at Exeter in the SOUTHERN HIGHLANDS for cool-climate plants and bulbs. Searl and Sons offered 'Landscape Gardening in all its branches, including

This beguiling sketch advertising the patent asphalt compound 'Paval' (for garden paths and drives), published by SEARL and Sons in their *Key to Australian Gardening* (1922), deftly captured the contemporary image of the 'home beautiful'

the laying out of new and renovating of old gardens, the making of lawns, tennis courts, croquet lawns … erecting bush houses and glass houses, and furnishing of same'. The firm published a general horticultural handbook, *Searl's Key to Australian Gardening* (1922), and a popular journal, the *Garden Magazine* (1923–26). Family business difficulties prompted a takeover in 1931, with the new firm Searl and Jeans later becoming Searls Limited, and finally ceasing business in the 1980s.   RA

SEARLE, George (1845–1927), seed merchant and nursery proprietor, was born at Sussex, England, and landed at Brisbane in 1869. After several years there, he moved to the Darling Downs as gardener on the Clifton and Pilton stations. In 1889 he started his nursery business in Toowoomba, joined later by several of his sons. His obituarist in the *Queenslander* described him as 'a man of remarkable energy', recognised as an authority in his profession throughout southern and western Qld. He contributed a chapter 'The Grape-vine and its Cultivation in Queensland' in Alfred Midgley (ed.), *The Queensland Illustrated Guide* (1888), and a 'Garden and field calendar' for *Groom's Darling Downs Book Almanac* (1898). The family business later traded as George Searle and Sons Ltd.   RA

SEASONS Vivaldi could never have written *The Four Seasons* if he had lived in Australia. Although the earth tilts on its axis without regard for hemispheres, Australia's latitudinal and geographical position between three oceans and her relatively smooth surface produce few of the vegetational attributes that those from the northern hemisphere associate with the seasons. Although, by convention, the names winter (June, July, August), spring (September, October, November), summer (December, January, February) and autumn (March, April, May) are given to portions of the year, few Australians

Seasons

garden where snow provides both moisture and a covering blanket for dormant plants, where plants grow slowly to flowering and decay, followed later in the year by spectacular displays of colour from deciduous leaves. Red cedar was virtually the only tree to be deciduous in what northerners regarded as the 'normal' way. The predominant EUCALYPTS dropped their leaves in summer when there was not enough moisture to sustain them. This, of course, did not stop the homesick invaders from importing and attempting to ACCLIMATISE plants that nourished their illusions that the familiar four seasons continued to exist.

In fact, moisture—mostly as rainfall—is the primary determinant of Australian seasons. Temperature is the next most important. The TROPICAL north has two seasons—the dry and the wet (which is itself divided into two periods). A few areas, for instance, near Tully (Qld), have enormously heavy rainfall, while areas inland of the Great Dividing Range may be without rain for a year or more, a period sometimes followed by floods. The Pacific Ocean phenomenon known as *El Niño*, occurring at irregular intervals, produces terrible droughts in eastern Australia—from which south-western Australia, deriving its weather patterns from the Indian Ocean, is free, though cyclones strike further north. South-eastern Tas. has the most equable CLIMATE for gardeners. There are frosts, of course, but they are seldom severe, and neither penetrate deep nor persist for long. They do, however, extend further north than many realise: the north gets its rain in summer, the south in winter. Central Qld can be bitterly cold, and in many places there is daily a steep temperature gradient. Many on the coast, especially in big cities, never experience a frost, with all the consequences that absence entails. Many Australian plants flower in winter, when they get their rain, while in the ARID ZONE, colourful annuals hurry into flower after the first rain.

Australian seasons, therefore, can be described not by calendar months but in sequence—fairly cold, fairly warm and

S.T. GILL's well-known painting *Spring* (c.1847), from his series depicting the SEASONS, shows an industrious scene of traditional horticultural techniques and garden styles transplanted to the colonies

sunny, hot, very hot, cooler—with the rainfall grid imposed on top. Aboriginal peoples often defined the seasons by available resources, such as Bogong moths or the seeds of *Araucaria bidwillii* (Bunya Pine), available for food.

T. R. GARNETT

SEDDON, George (b. 1927), professor, environmental planner, writer, and gardener, is a perceptive and wry commentator on Australian gardening STYLES and practices past and present. He is to Australia what W.G. Hoskins is to Britain and J.B. Jackson is to the USA: the country's most distinguished landscape essayist. His work makes strong connections between gardening and environmental history, arguing that 'gardeners are one of the most important groups of land managers in the country'. Born in Berriwillock (Vic.), he kept moving, geographically and academically, first as the son of a peripatetic bank manager and later as an interdisciplinary and international academic. He has been a Professor of Geology (Oregon), History and Philosophy of Science (NSW), Environmental Studies (Melbourne), and English Literature (UWA). Wherever he has lived, he has cultivated the soil and put down roots. 'I'm a catchment boy,' he says, 'I like to know where the rivers run'. And the home gardens he created have had the same mixture of influences he carries himself: broad and respected historical traditions, a dash of international style, and a determination to revive and display intimate native associations, and to foster gardening habits that are frugal, ECOLOGICAL, and local. His intensive regional studies are his gardening writ large—he has written path-breaking books on Perth (*Sense of Place*, 1972, and *A City and its Setting*, 1987), the Swan River (*Swan River Landscapes*, 1970), and the Snowy River (*Searching for the Snowy*, 1994). They are the big backyards of his urban existence. Some of his finest essays (including several on gardening) were collected in *Landprints* (1997) and his account of his Fremantle home and surrounds is in *A House, A Cottage and A Shop* (1993).

Places rather than people or books have been Seddon's chief intellectual influence. He is a connoisseur of landscape, of its surface forms, the arrangement of its features, its felicitous routes of passage, yet he is able also to plumb its depths and mysteries, to analyse it formally and technically. His vision is deeply practical—he has been an active consultant for government and business and has served on many committees concerned with environmental design, gardens, and landscape evaluation, particularly in Vic. and WA. He aims to unite 'good science, good planning, good design, and good communication'. Whereas his work was first received as a novel contribution to environmental planning, historical geography, or LANDSCAPE ARCHITECTURE, it later became valued as an Australian precursor of environmental history—with gardening, quite unusually, in the national narrative.

TOM GRIFFITHS

SEEDS are complex and wonderful structures that provide a plant with four important adaptive features: the production of a new generation, the re-sorting of genetic material through pollination and fertilisation, a means for dispersal, and a life stage that generally is much more resistant to environmental extremes than its parents. A viable seed consists of a living embryonic plant that is surrounded by various protective layers. These layers can include nutritive tissue, the seed coat, and, in some cases, part or all of the fruit and other plant structures such as sepals and bracts. At maturity, the seeds of most species are very dry and, in such a state, they are much more resistant to environmental extremes than their parents. Seeds that do not dry at maturity, such as those of some species from RAINFORESTS and other moist environments, cannot be stored readily and will die if they are not able to germinate immediately.

The primary requirements for seed germination are water, air, a suitable temperature regime, and, occasionally, specific conditions of light or darkness. Complex seed dormancies (failure to germinate) are seldom encountered in those seed-grown horticultural species having a long history of cultivation, but they are common in species recently introduced into horticulture from the wild. While many of Australia's native species germinate readily, particularly after a few months of dry storage, others possess a challenging range of dormancies. Traditional dormancy-breaking treatments such as scarification, stratification, and leaching will overcome dormancy in many of these species, but numerous other species require more research. The recent discovery of the role of soluble components from plant-derived smoke in the germination of seeds from various environments, including many Australian species, has added a powerful new technique to the horticulturist's armory.

A less positive contribution from seed plants to Australia's environment is the burgeoning WEED problem that is seriously affecting urban, rural, and bush vegetation. Many of these exotic, invasive plants are of garden origin. The seeds of most traditional garden plants are produced overseas, imported to Australia and repackaged as high-quality, easily germinated retail products. Under national quarantine laws, only species that are considered not to have serious weed potential are allowed into Australia.

Processed seeds are staple foods in most human societies and they are an easily stored and transported means for propagating large numbers of plants for food, fibre, timber, and ornamental use. Seeds play a vital part in PLANT CONSERVATION.

JOHN DELPRATT

SENSORY GARDENS The particularities of place are formed and remembered principally through the sensory qualities of the nature and structure that its vegetation imparts. The fragrance of wattle blossom and the foliage of the eucalypt can characterise perceptions and memory of Australia. SCENTED GARDENS, too, can reinforce fond memories of homelands. The sight of vast open space has stimulated containment in many country gardens just as a desire is found in constricted cities for recreational escape to the country. Urban garden design is dominated by a lush green oasis aesthetic that offers freshness and abundance. Recognition of COLOUR, such as the subtle grey–green and gold of the indigenous landscape is increasingly manifest in public and rural landscapes. Here the practical purpose reinforces the original aesthetic. Rustling leaves are seasonally common in other countries with deciduous vegetation. Here that sound is always with us along with the crackling bark, the snapping of twigs, and foliage that lies as mulch. The elements of an indigenous aesthetic appear to be a fundamental part of the subconscious memory of its inhabitants. This memory has spread to an exploration of the culinary possibilities of our flora. The 'bush tucker' practices of the indigenous peoples and early settlers are now mainstream. Touch in Australian gardens can disclose an infinite diversity, from prickles that repel to furry foliage that conserves moisture. Textures and shapes are used by designers more for the way they look rather than their feel. The exception is with the specialist designers who design sensory gardens that heighten experience, educate and raise awareness, and provide equal access for young, old, and disabled people, often as a conscious part of GARDEN THERAPY.

PAUL THOMPSON

SEPPELT, Joseph Ernst (1813–1868), vigneron, was born in Wustewaltersdorf, Silesia, and became head of a family business in liqueur and cordial production. Migrating to Adelaide in 1849, he settled near Greenock (1851) and established the first viticultural plantings at Seppeltsfield in the BAROSSA VALLEY. His eldest son, **(Oscar) Benno Pedro Seppelt** (1846–1931), drawing upon a flair for invention and promotion, transformed the family business into a major concern, establishing Grenache, Mataro, and Palomino vines at Seppeltsfield, and Cabernet Sauvignon nearby at Dorrien. Benno acquired further vineyards at Rutherglen, Vic. (1915), Château Tanunda in the Barossa Valley (1916), and GREAT WESTERN, Vic. (1918). Benno and his family enhanced Seppeltsfield, especially by AVENUES of *Phoenix canariensis* (Canary Island Date Palm) planted in the 1930s along many local roads, and a stepped *allée* of *Pinus halepensis* (Aleppo Pine) that leads up a rise to the family mausoleum (reminiscent of a Greek temple) surrounded by a garden. The 'village' of Seppeltsfield is a cluster of offices, huge stores, cellars, plants, and buildings, together with the original 1851 homestead in an extensive terraced garden.

The House of Seppelt 1851–1951 (Adelaide, 1951)

DAVID JONES

SERICULTURE, or silk cultivation, has met with limited success in Australia. Mulberry trees, on which silkworms grow, were first planted in NSW in the 1790s, and some attempts to develop the industry were made in the early nineteenth century. Interest grew in the 1850s and 1860s, especially in cool-temperate viticultural regions where mulberry trees grew best. Raising silkworms and skeining their fine thread were considered genteel activities, and women were particularly active in early developments. Mrs Bladen Neill founded the Victorian Ladies' Sericultural Company in 1873 and was later granted land at Castlemaine for this purpose, while Ann Timbrell, 'prize sericulturist', ran a silk farm in suburban Collingwood (Vic.). Margaret Davenport imported the 'Ailantus' (Ailanthus) silkworm into SA, and with her husband Samuel DAVENPORT formed the Silk Association in Adelaide in the 1870s. Developments in the late 1880s and 1890s were short-lived. The New South Wales Government established a silk farm in 1891, and offered instruction. Sericulture continued to be promoted as suitable work for women and children, but high labour costs, inadequate knowledge, unsuitable soil, and disease impeded development. Failing to attain commercial success, sericulture has remained a specialist pursuit.

HELEN DOYLE

SERPENTINE DAM, Jarrahdale, WA: see WELLINGTON DAM, Collie, WA

SEWELL, Henry (1847–1926), nursery proprietor and horticulturist, was born in Thame, Oxfordshire, England, and gained his training in the nurseries of James Meares and John Walker in London. He migrated to Adelaide and in 1868 gained employment with Richard SCHOMBURGK in the ADELAIDE BOTANIC GARDEN. In 1871 he established his Payneham Nursery (which ceased as a wholesale business in 2000). By 1881 this two-hectare nursery was one of the biggest on the Adelaide plains, with the city's largest glasshouse, lathed shade house, and propagation facilities. With this complex, Sewell gained a reputation for his supplies of flowering climbing vines, palms, cycads, flowering perennials and annuals, camellias, and species of *Dracaena*, *Hibiscus*, *Erythrina*, *Eucalyptus*, *Agathis*, *Aloe*, and *Arbutus* genera. He also offered *Petunia*, *Pelargonium*, and *Coleus* cultivars, which he propagated. In 1885 he established a shopfront business in central Adelaide, and in 1887 established the West Marden Nursery on four hectares that specialised in almonds and other fruit trees, vines, and olives, together with a wide selection of callistemons, poplars, melaleucas, and roses. Through these three outlets Sewell influenced much of Adelaide's interest in and selection of typical Victorian-era plants, and its fondness for palms, camellias, roses, vines, and fruit trees. Perceiving a burgeoning interest in temperate-garden plants, he acquired four hectares near the ALDGATE NURSERY in 1897 and developed the former orchard and market garden with roses, fruit trees, camellias, rhododendrons, carnations, heaths, palms, and ferns. In 1899 this nursery hosted more than 15 000 trees and shrubs with shade houses and glass pits cultivating the latest conifers, lilies, narcissus, hyacinth, and daffodils.

In 1908 Sewell toured England and Europe, returning with numerous plants and seeds. His nurseries also became a significant training ground for the nursery trade, including the Bowels, COPAS, and Sever families. Sewell was influential in promoting professionalism in the nursery community, was well known interstate, and served as an original member of the Gardeners' Mutual Improvement Society (later the South Australian Gardeners' Society), as president of the South Australian Horticultural Society, as member of the Acclimatisation and Zoological Society, and as a vice-president of the Australian Nurserymens' Association in 1909. While his only son, Henry Reginald Spencer Sewell (1882–1948), took over the city operations in 1907, the Sewell nurseries were sold following his death to the Bowels and KEMP families.

DAVID JONES

SEXUALITY and its connections to gardens can be found in many traditions and cultures. In classical Rome,

Priapus was god of the garden and a symbol of sexuality. In the Judeo–Christian tradition, the garden contains the 'tree of knowledge of good and evil', and the Song of Songs eulogises: 'let my beloved come into the garden and eat his pleasant fruits'. The Hindu deity Krishna is frequently pictured making love in a garden, and Indian gardens of love celebrate the association between fertility and erotic love.

Gardens are evoked as fertile, sensuous, and erotic, as sites for (illicit) sexual encounters. Often equated with a woman's body, especially her genitals—fecund, perfumed, enclosed—the design of gardens can augment such associations: the high hedges of the Baroque garden heightened the eroticism within its walls, courtyard gardens were often equated with virginity, while the 'landscaped park' of the English garden made it a meeting place for the sexes. The private garden of the nineteenth-century English middle class was also the place where women were to be found, wooed, and seduced. Those too poor to have their own garden relied upon PUBLIC GARDENS for such purposes, often prompting authorities to restrict opening times on Sundays. There were other concerns. The secluded areas of gardens offered useful cover for illicit lovemaking, but they also provided camouflage for acts of rape and other violence. Homosexual activity in public gardens also raised alarm. Recently, the 'romantic garden' style has made a resurgence, as ruthlessness and pragmatism give way to romance and imagination.

Plants themselves can be seen to carry sexual meaning, their extracts and perfumes to act as aphrodisiacs: the flower of the broad bean is said to cure impotence, while the early purple orchid makes a potent love potion. The Linnean system of classification identified plants according to their reproductive features; under such a system, botany proved to be a useful way for young middle-class women to learn the secrets of reproduction. Flowers particularly have been equated with female sexuality, be they metaphors for virginal innocence or 'deflowered' beauty. Their scent can be intoxicating; the facial expression of a woman as she savours it supposedly resembles that when making love. Other plants can be seen to resemble male genitalia, and in 1931 the journal *Garden and Home Maker of Australia* playfully accused men of wanting to reduce all growth to six inches above the ground.

Painters, sculptors, and writers have made much of the relationship between gardens and sexuality. In eighteenth-century Europe statues of Priapus adorned parks and gardens, replete with enlarged genitals, which in Protestant countries were often cut off by offended passers-by. Georgia O'Keeffe's paintings of poppies erotically evoke a woman's vulva, while Brett Whitely depicted the Australian landscape in the form of a woman's body. In LITERATURE, Australian novelists have also milked the garden for its erotic possibilities: Ada Cambridge, Barbara Hanrahan, and Patrick White to name a few. In art as in life, the garden is literally and metaphorically a place for sex.   KATIE HOLMES

SHADE HOUSE: see BUSH-HOUSE

SHANNON, Mollie Glen: see BEGG AND SHANNON

The cemetery shelter (1883) at Maryborough (Qld), although found in a seemingly innocent situation, offers vigorous evidence that metaphoric references to SEXUALITY abound in our gardens and designed landscapes

SHARP(E), Alfred (1836–1908), landscape artist, was born in Cheshire, England, and while living in Birkenhead was impressed by the creation of Joseph PAXTON's public park (1843–47). In 1887 he arrived in Australia via New Zealand and, writing under pseudonyms to the *Newcastle Morning Herald*, persistently advocated many public landscape improvements. Sharp is credited with designs for Islington, Wickham, Hamilton, King Edward, and Lake Macquarie parks, and for introducing *Metrosideros excelsa* (Pohutukawa or New Zealand Christmas Tree) to Newcastle (NSW).

Roger Blackley, *The Art of Alfred Sharpe* (Auckland, 1992)
GEOFFREY BRITTON

SHEATH, Jeremiah (c. 1850–1915), landscape gardener and horticulturist, was born on the Isle of Wight, England. He trained as a horticulturist, possibly at the ROYAL BOTANIC GARDENS, KEW, and was also employed as a landscape gardener on private estates in England, before coming to WA, recruited to take charge of the grounds of GOVERNMENT HOUSE, Perth. Among his testimonials was a recommendation from James VEITCH and Sons of the famous Royal Exotic Nursery, Chelsea. Sheath arrived in 1885, with his wife and young son, Herbert; three daughters were added to the family in WA, the youngest being named Eucharis Lilian, after Sheath's favourite flower, *Eucharis grandiflora* (South American Eucharist Lily).

Sheath was employed at Government House between 1885 and 1890, and while the grounds were well established when he arrived, in the decade 1887–97 major redevelopment occurred. Throughout the 1890s Sheath worked as an independent landscape gardener, numbering many of the colony's leading citizens among his clients. He was appointed inaugural superintendent at KINGS PARK in 1904, remaining until his retirement due to ill-health in 1913, during a significant period in the Park's development. According to anecdote, the Eucharist Lily, grown by Sheath while resident at Kings Park, in time became a naturalised plant in the park.

Like other nineteenth-century emigrant horticulturists, Sheath's horticultural tastes were eclectic and included enthusiasm for growing the local flora. While at Kings Park he propagated Western Australian species from seed sent to him from different parts of the state. *Eucalyptus sheathiana*, a eucalypt from the wheat belt of WA, was one such plant, named after him by J.H. MAIDEN, and described from the plant cultivated by Sheath at Kings Park. Another plant from WA, *Gyrostemon sheathii*, was named for his son, Herbert Edmund Sheath (1879–1910), who collected the original specimen at Torbay, on the south coast of WA.

OLINE RICHARDS

SHEATHER, Silas (*c*. 1823–1906), nursery proprietor, was born in Sussex, England, and in 1838 accompanied his family to Sydney on the *Royal George*, the ship bringing William Sharp MACLEAY to Australia. After landing at Redbank early in 1839, Sheather, a sixteen-year-old youth with little formal education, went to Camden Park where William MACARTHUR employed him in the garden for eight years. During this period Macarthur issued plant catalogues in 1843 and 1845 and the proceeds from plant sales were divided between Edmund BLAKE, Francis FERGUSON, and Sheather. He moved to Elizabeth Farm, Parramatta, where he worked for Macarthur's brother-in-law, Henry Watson Parker, for three years, and then to Newlands, Parramatta.

Following marriage, Sheather acquired three acres (1.2 ha) of land in 1852 on the Parramatta side of Subiaco, south of the river, and established a MARKET GARDEN and NURSERY specialising in the propagation of citrus trees, which he sold in large quantities to other nurseries. He also specialised in growing CAMELLIAS for sale as cut flowers and as plants, naming his nursery Camellia Grove. While not issuing catalogues, he advertised in Fuller's *Sydney Handbook for 1877* that 'having been devoted to the cultivation of Camellias for the last thirty years he has now one of the largest and most recherché collections in the world'. His stock included many varieties not previously recorded, some of which are still popular. That these resulted from the continuation of the breeding program begun at Camden Park would seem obvious were it not that his son Arthur stated his father did not practise HYBRIDISATION. His nursery, once one of the principal sights of the district, has given its name to the suburb Camellia.

RICHARD CLOUGH

SHELLEY, Max Robert (1895–1954), garden designer, landscape architect, plant supplier, and contractor, was active in Sydney between 1926 and 1930. He designed and laid out the lush grounds of Boomerang, music mogul Frank Albert's Spanish Mission mansion in Elizabeth Bay (1926–29). Shelley contributed articles to the *Garden*, the *Home*, the *Commonwealth Home*, and *Garden Gossip*, promoting a relatively formal style and a wide range of plants, native as well as exotic. Three other gardens by Shelley are known to have been laid out at Hunters Hill and Grose Wold. From 1930 until 1939 he appears to have refocused on floristry and interior decoration.

STUART READ

SHELLS as they appear in Australian gardens are but a faint echo of their use in seventeenth- and eighteenth-century GROTTOES. Although they were more commonly available and less expensive in Australia than in Europe, they still carried exotic overtones. The use of clam shells in colonial gardens probably dates from early trading with the islands of the East Indies, and PACIFIC ISLAND sources. They were documented by the mid-nineteenth century—at the MCLEAY property Brownlow Hill, for example—where they often appeared ornamenting steps and prominent spots in the garden. Their use in gardens peaked in the 1920s, by which time they were used as bird baths and under taps. Shells generally appeared as casual ornaments and embellishments to QUIRKY GARDENS, in which shell mosaic work was revived as embellishment to concrete garden ORNAMENTS, but generally they declined in fashion between the 1930s and the 1960s.

MICHAEL LEHANY

SHELTER BELTS: see WINDBREAKS

SHELTON, Edward Mason (*c*. 1847–1928), instructor in agriculture, was born in Huntingdonshire, England, but was raised and educated in North America. After a government position in Japan (1871) his returned to the USA as director of the experimental station at Kansas State Agricultural College (1874). In 1890 he came to Qld as the inaugural Instructor in Agriculture in the newly established Department of Agriculture. His duties included travelling the colony providing advice, participating in farmers' conferences, encouraging ARBOR DAY activities, and writing papers for publication. The most interesting of these, in terms of design, *Tree Planting for Shade and Ornament: Suggestions for Teachers and Others Interested in the Planting of Trees* (1892), concerned the use of INDIGENOUS TREES in school grounds. Shelton quoted DOWNING, included a manifesto for the 'modern or natural style', and illustrated the booklet with plans for SCHOOL GARDENS. Professor Shelton—as he was always titled—was also the founding principal of the Queensland Agricultural College, Gatton (1897–98). Upon retirement, Shelton returned to USA, living and working in Seattle.

JEANNIE SIM

SHEPHERD, Thomas (*c*. 1779–1835), landscape gardener and nursery proprietor, was born in Kemback, Fifeshire, Scotland, where he grew up and was educated. His father was Principal Gardener to the Earl of Crawford and Lindesay at his property Struthers, where the young Shepherd received his earliest horticultural education. He then trained in all aspects of LANDSCAPE GARDENING and worked for the practice of Thomas White (*c*. 1736–1811) and his son Thomas White (*c*. 1764–1836) before setting himself up as a practising landscape gardener in both Scotland and England. In his work in England he came in contact with Humphry REPTON, and in his writing criti-

This FOUNTAIN of clam SHELLS, the centrepiece of Queensland's contribution to the Colonial and Indian Exhibition (1886) and engraved for the *Illustrated London News*, captured contemporary enthusiasm for RUSTIC garden ornament

cised some of Repton's methods. Shepherd eventually established a nursery at Hackney (London) to support his landscape business. Widowed (*c*. 1821–22) and then remarried (1823), and faced with an unprofitable landscape and nursery business in the period after 1815 at the end of the Napoleonic Wars, Shepherd took a position with the New Zealand Company. As Principal Superintendent he was charged with the establishment of a colony on Stewart Island, New Zealand, with the intention of cultivating flax.

With a band of colonists, mainly Scots, he sailed in 1825 with his new wife Jane Susan (*née* Henderson) and young family for the South Pacific. Unsuccessful in finding a suitable place for a settlement in either Stewart Island or the rest of New Zealand, they arrived in Sydney early in 1827. With the encouragement of Governor Darling, Shepherd established the first commercial NURSERY garden in Australia near Grose Farm (1827), which he named for his patron. Progress was difficult because of the unprepared nature of the land he was allocated and he began with a vegetable garden. This was gradually expanded into the Darling Nursery with the help of stock from SYDNEY BOTANIC GARDENS, as well as from Alexander McLEAY at Elizabeth Bay House and William MACARTHUR at Camden Park. Little is known of his landscape design work but, having established himself in the colony, Shepherd gave two sets of lectures at Sydney Mechanics' School of Arts during 1834–35, for which (in their published form) he is now chiefly remembered.

Shepherd's first published writings were on VITICULTURE (1831) and he was an early supporter of James BUSBY. Shepherd's *Lectures on the Horticulture of New South Wales* (1835) addressed practical matters, such as the growing of vegetables in a colony with a different CLIMATE and SOILS to those of Britain and complete turnabout of the SEASONS. The vital need for water in hot Sydney summers was also stressed in this, Australia's first GARDEN BOOK. *Lectures on Landscape Gardening in Australia* (1836), of which only the first was able to be delivered due to Shepherd's death, was the first Australian book to address garden design, and preceded by five years the first major NORTH AMERICAN text on landscape gardening (by A.J. DOWNING). At first sight conservative in their aesthetics, the lectures drew rhetorically on the BROWNIAN tradition of the English landscape garden, albeit tempered by local circumstance and contemporary thought. He deplored the indiscriminate destruction of timber and instead advocated selective thinning and tasteful arrangement and disposition of exotic trees to create 'pleasing effects [and] … improved scenery'. He addressed a range of garden types—MANSION, VILLA, and COTTAGE—and garden STYLES—SUBLIME, PICTURESQUE, and Beautiful—an inclusive approach in a colony of only modest population. His advice on EDUCATION for young GARDENERS had strong overtones of J.C. LOUDON, and many of the later lectures borrowed from his writings. On Shepherd's early death, his widow was assisted in management of the Darling Nursery by Robert HENDERSON, husband of Elizabeth Joslyn (*née* Shepherd) (b. 1813), Thomas Shepherd's daughter from his first marriage.

Shepherd's second family eventually carried on their father's tradition in their continued involvement in Australia's nursery trade and horticulture. **Thomas Shepherd** jnr (1824–1884)—who later added William as a middle name—was born in Hackney (London), and subsequently took on management of the nursery with his brothers. He was responsible for the firm's 1851 catalogue and after he left the nursery, his botanical and horticultural skills served him well in a career in journalism. He wrote many articles on native plants for the *SYDNEY MAGAZINE OF SCIENCE AND ART* (1857–58) for instance, and for many years was 'agricultural and botanical editor' of the *(AUSTRALIAN) TOWN AND COUNTRY JOURNAL*. **David Shepherd** (1826–1911), born at sea in New Zealand waters, joined his brother in management of the Darling Nursery, as did their youngest brother, **Patrick Lindesay Crawford Shepherd** (1831–1903). The firm, now Shepherd and Co., had by the 1860s bought land at Rooty Hill (which became its CHATSWORTH Nursery) as various parts of the original site were sold. By this stage the nursery had become a large business, sending trees and plants to all parts of the continent. The Chatsworth Nursery was run by David while Patrick remained at the Darling Nursery.

In 1881 Shepherd and Co. leased the Baptist Nursery in Bourke Street, Surry Hills, paying John BAPTIST £200 for his nursery stock. Taking full possession in 1882, David and Patrick handed the business over to their sons Thomas R. (b. 1885) and Lindesay (b. 1858) respectively, and moved into a semi-retirement. In 1884 the family business was reorganised, with David (in association with his son Thomas and F.M. Creswick), continuing as Shepherd and Co. in Ashfield and Redfern, while Patrick (in association with his son Lindesay) formed P.L.C. Shepherd and Son, a separate and subsequently well-known firm of seed merchants. Patrick later acquired land at Bowral in the SOUTHERN HIGHLANDS, and became well known in the region. In 1904 a report on P.L.C. Shepherd and Son, the *Australian Nurseryman*, noted

William Macdonald's Mount Adelaide estate (1833–37) at Darling Point (NSW) is the only known landscape design that can confidently be attributed to Thomas SHEPHERD—a terraced vineyard overlooking an ornamental fishpond with Sydney Harbour as a backdrop

that the Darling Nursery had 'fallen into our hands, and is being carried on by us'. The business contracted to that of seed merchants and ceased during the 1940s. The Shepherd dynasty had been one of the most important influences in the development of gardening in NSW—and to some extent in the rest of Australia—in the colonial period, not only as a provider of plants, especially of trees and shrubs, but also for the reputation the published lectures secured for its head, Thomas Shepherd.

Una Shepherd Price, *My Family of Shepherds* (Scone, NSW, 1988); Victor Crittenden, *A Shrub in the Landscape of Fame: Thomas Shepherd, Australian Landscape Gardener and Nurseryman* (Canberra, 1992)   VICTOR CRITTENDEN

SHERWOOD ARBORETUM (now Sherwood Forest Park), fifteen hectares of parkland planted with Queensland NATIVE PLANTS, was commenced in 1922 at the initiative of C.T. WHITE with support from scientific, natural history, forestry, public health, and horticultural groups. An AVENUE of seventy-two *Agathis robusta* (Kauri Pine) was planted at the official opening (1924) by leading Brisbane citizens. Subsequent ARBORETUM plantings by local school children (1925) were supplemented with more than 600 planted by E.W. BICK, appointed curator with the change of management to Greater Brisbane Council (1925).   JEANNIE SIM

SHOOBRIDGE, William (1781–1836), carpenter and pioneer hop-grower, was born in Tenterden, Kent, England, of a farming and hop-growing family. In 1822 he migrated to Van Diemen's Land with his family, several of whom (including his wife) died on the voyage. In Hobart Town he was appointed superintendent of the Government timber yard and received a grant of twenty acres (8 ha) at Providence Valley (now the suburb of Mount Stuart). He established hop-fields with the sets he had brought with him from Kent and in 1825 produced his first marketable crop. Although he is often credited with introducing hops to the island, there had been earlier experiments with growing the crop. He established a hop-growing dynasty continued by his son, Ebenezer Shoobridge (1820–1901), who pioneered the industry in the Derwent Valley at Plenty and at Turiff Lodge, New Norfolk, in the 1840s before purchasing the now well-known hop-growing properties of Valleyfield (1852) and Bushy Park (1863).

Eileen Brammall, *The Shoobridges in Australia: A History* (Glenora, Tas., 1985)   LINDY SCRIPPS

SHOWGROUNDS As AGRICULTURAL AND PASTORAL SOCIETIES proliferated in Australia from the 1820s, showgrounds were set aside for exhibitions of farming and horticultural produce and associated educational, commercial, and entertainment activities. Every state capital has a large showground, managed by its 'Royal' agricultural society. Melbourne's showground at Ascot Vale (1883) is the oldest metropolitan site still in use after Sydney's Royal Easter Show relocated from the Moore Park Showground (1882) to Homebush Bay in 1998. Some 650 agricultural societies now manage showgrounds throughout Australia.

The central focus of any agricultural show—and hence showground—is the arena. At metropolitan showgrounds, the arena is surrounded by 'streets' lined with numerous buildings, many of heritage interest: pavilions (including horticultural halls), livestock sheds, administration blocks. Rural showgrounds, in contrast, may have only a couple of permanent structures, adjoining a tree-ringed oval. Historically, showgrounds have been utilised as military camps during WARTIME, temporary hospitals, and campsites for the unemployed in the 1930s Depression. Showground facilities are generally leased to community and SPORTING groups, and the arena often doubles as a RACECOURSE or trotting track.

KATE DARIAN-SMITH

SHOWS: see HORTICULTURAL SHOWS

SHRUB is a term usually applied to a woody plant that forms multiple trunks or shoots from its base and is distinguished from a TREE by not having a dominate shoot. This is an inclusive descriptive term, however, and there is no clearly agreed distinction between shrubs and trees. Some woody forms, such as a mallee eucalypt with multiple stems from the base, may for instance be referred to as a tree. Shrubs have been a mainstay of the Australian garden, especially used collectively in the SHRUBBERY, forming the middle level in height, and (often in association with trees) a permanent framework within which more ephemeral plants such as ANNUALS and PERENNIALS may be added. Exotic and Australian native shrubs have been widely used in Australian gardens.
ML

SHRUBBERY The shrubbery developed in the mid-eighteenth century from the English concept of 'the wilderness' and became, along with the flower garden, an essential component of the Regency pleasure ground. Scottish horticulturist Walter Nichol viewed the shrubbery as both useful and ornamental, promoting its function of screening the offices or kitchen garden from the house, or for connecting the house with the garden or orchard (1810). English gardener Henry Phillips, in *Sylva Florifera* (1823), described it being 'as peculiar to the British nation as landscape-planting' and recommended that it be planted for general effect, the most beautiful SHRUBS occupying the most prominent places. His shrubbery included some elevation and detachment from the house, so as to not cast too much shadow over the dwelling, a concept implemented *c.* 1845 at Sydney's new GOVERNMENT HOUSE. Discussed by authors along with the flower garden, by the mid-nineteenth century, some defined the shrubbery as the link connecting the mansion and lawn to the flower garden, although Jane LOUDON simplified it to 'a walk bordered by shrubs and trees with some flowers in front' (1841). Clearly, not all agreed with this practice, with William FERGUSON stating that 'to plant flowers among trees and large flowering shrubs shows a decided want of taste, and such practice is right to be carefully avoided' (1863).

In the eighteenth and early nineteenth centuries, height gradation played a major role: Daniel BUNCE advised 'Pay attention to the habits of growth, height, &c, planting the tallest at the back of the Shrubbery, and the shortest in front; the back ones five feet apart, & those in front not less than three' (1837), a commonly prescribed formula. This was the likely mode of planting used at ELIZABETH BAY HOUSE to produce the 'polished shrubberies' abutting the 'ornamental lawns', described by Thomas SHEPHERD (1836), and clearly separate from the planned 'wood walks'. By 1880 TRESEDER brothers wrote of this as an 'old-fashioned' method of planting, preferring trees and shrubs of mixed heights.

Delineation between FLOWER GARDEN and shrubbery was blurred. A flower garden consisted chiefly of BEDS of flowers and often included shrubs, while the shrubbery always contained flowering shrubs, and usually some dark, evergreen trees. Shepherd referred to this aspect of the projected shrubberies at Lyndhurst, Glebe (NSW), remarking that they would 'darken the glow of light which is produced by the expansion of the water'. Few authors differentiated between a shrubbery and a PLANTATION, many interchanging the terms.

The shrubbery became a standard part of the Australian garden: W.H. ELLIOTT stated 'Shrubs constitute a large portion of all gardens' (1897). BRUNNING's *Australian Gardener* (1924) proclaimed it one of the most effective and enduring features of the garden: 'The Shrubbery should consist of a uniform belt of trees or shrubs surrounding a lawn, irregular in outline, with easy and graceful curves, prominent projections, and deep recesses, the more prominent parts being in contiguity to separate groups and single specimens on the lawn' and, displaying Ferguson's 'decided want of taste', recommended filling the spaces of the developing shrubbery with annuals, a practice common in Australia often for reasons of quick effect.

Mark Laird, *The Flowering of the Landscape Garden: English Pleasure Grounds 1720–1800* (Philadelphia, 1999)

COLLEEN MORRIS

SILVICULTURE: see FORESTRY

SIMONS, Phyllis Frazer (b. 1923), landscape designer and teacher, influenced by Thistle HARRIS, became a convert to the 1950s conservation movement, joining the SOCIETY FOR GROWING AUSTRALIAN PLANTS at its first meeting. Lecturing in environmental design in WA, Tas., and Vic., Phyl Simons inspired students with her knowledge and energy. Her work included the Western Australian Institute of Technology campus, Tasmanian College of Advanced Education campus, and parklands and coastal regeneration along the Derwent estuary (Tas.). She was a founding member of the AUSTRALIAN GARDEN HISTORY SOCIETY and her publications include *Historic Tasmanian Gardens* (1987), a pioneering study of 290 early gardens.

GEORGINA WHITEHEAD

SINATRA, James Benedict (b. 1942), educator, landscape architect, and emeritus professor, studied at Georgia State and Pennsylvania Universities before being appointed foundation Head and Professor of Landscape Architecture at Royal Melbourne Institute of Technology (1981–98). Jim Sinatra, co-author of *Landscape for Health* (1997) and *Listen to the People, Listen to the Land* (1999), practises as Sinatra • Murphy, particularly in Victoria's WESTERN DISTRICT, and at numerous indigenous communities, specialising in community planning, sustainable landscapes, and environmental art.

DAVID JONES

SINCLAIR, James (1809–1881), landscape gardener and horticultural journalist, was born in Morayshire, Scotland. His father was reputedly head steward to Sir William Gordon Cumming, whose estate Altyre, near Forres, possessed a noted garden. Landscape gardener Donald BEATON worked at Altyre (becoming head gardener *c.* 1819) and his *Autobiography* (1854) provides useful details of Sinclair's early life. He recorded that 'Jamie Sinclair, the garden-boy, and a natural genius, played the violin. Lady Cumming had this boy educated by the family tutor, sent him to London, where he was well known in 1836–7–8 for his skill in drawing and colouring.' His drawing, including orchids and other novelties, was apparently undertaken for Joseph Knight (*c.* 1777–1855), a partner with Thomas A. Perry in the Exotic Nursery, King's Road, Chelsea. According to family tradition, his London training also included landscape gardening.

Sinclair's first book, with collaborator J. Freeman, was *A History and Description of the Different Varieties of the Pansey or Heartsease*, published in monthly parts between 1835 and 1838—the first book solely devoted to the pansy and favourably reviewed in the *Floricultural Cabinet* (1837). Sinclair later claimed authorship of a *Treatise on the Dahlia*.

In 1838, aged just 29, Sinclair was engaged by Prince Mikhail Semenovich Vorontsov (1782–1856) to manage his estates on the Crimea and he left London for Russia. Beaton credited Knight for the introduction and described Sinclair's work for 'Prince Woronzoff': 'He laid out those beautiful gardens which the Allies so much admired the other day; had a thousand acres of vineyards belonging to the Prince; was well known to the Czar, who often consulted him about improvements, and who gave him a "medal of merit", and a diploma, or kind of passport, by which he was free to pass from one end of the empire to the other, and also through Austria and Prussia. I have seen these instruments.'

Sinclair returned to London in 1851, with his English wife, Mary (née Cooper), and their Russian-born daughter, Malvina Anne. His book, *The Beauties of Nature: and how far they Transcend those of Art, in Landscape Gardening. A Poem*, was published in London in 1852. Sinclair intended his epic poem 'to introduce a new era in the art of Landscape Gardening' which he termed the NATURAL system: 'parallel lines … are totally disused … the object here, is to point out a method of blending together large or small masses of wood, gravel, lawn, or water, so as to produce a beautiful picture, having order and regularity reigning in every part.' He drew on the inspiration of a divine Creator and also examples by the hand of man not only in England and Scotland 'but also on the mountains and plains of Spain, Portugal, Greece, Turkey, Tartary, South Russia, Moldovia, Wallachia, Transylvania, Hungary, Croatia and Bohemia; and by the cities of Constantinople, Odessa, Vienna, Dresden, Berlin, Potsdam, Magdenburgh, Hanover, Colnge [sic], Brussels, Paris, &c.' giving some idea of his recent travels. The work was, however, that of a poetaster:

Go to the mountain peak ye lovers here / Of true variety, and there look down / Upon wild Nature's robes, that do appear / Not like to man's fair planting, is her own; / She never has her works around o'er done / With numerous species, that confusion makes …

Critical reaction to this obtuse design manifesto was damning: the *Gardeners' Chronicle* wrote 'We cannot but distrust the judgement of one who spends his time so unprofitably as the author of this most unhappy attempt of winning fame'. Sinclair had just been engaged with a London publisher with a three-year contract when the Crimean War erupted: 'Menschikoff found the Turks too hot … the Russians then made up for blows, and Mr Sinclair was more dangerous for them in London than Lord Aberdeen. He was the only foreigner who was ever allowed to see all that was done in and about Sebastopol, and all over the Crimea; the Czar, however, took care that Sinclair could not join the 'Allies'; but where he is, and what he is about, I must not tell until the war is over; except that he is not in Russia, and that he will never play first fiddle in Morayshire.'

By the time Beaton wrote, Sinclair was on the other side of the world, starting his career anew in Melbourne. In 1855 he was working as a seed merchant and contributing to the first number of the RURAL MAGAZINE, also advertising to 'Landed Proprietors and others that he is ready to prepare plans for laying out grounds for Villa Residences, in illustration of the principles laid down in his Beauties of Nature, and how far they transcend those of art in Landscape Gardening. Terms:– Five Guineas'.

Sinclair saw himself as an antipodean LOUDON. During 1855–56 he edited twelve issues of his *Gardener's Magazine and Journal of Rural Economy* (named after Loudon's hugely successful journal), copying many features of its namesake, even to the extent of styling himself 'The Conductor'. He pointed to the relevance of the southern European climate in which he had worked but gave idiosyncratic advice. A major feature was his series of descriptive notices, later compiled in a manuscript volume entitled 'The Beauties of Victoria in 1856' describing approximately 130 Melbourne gardens. Sinclair reissued individual copies of the *Gardener's Magazine* with variant titles and also issued bound volumes of the magazine as *Everyman His Own Gardener*, this title ingenuously appropriated from Abercrombie and Mawe's standard work.

Sinclair claimed in the introduction to the *Gardener's Magazine* that he had 'left some fair traces of his handiwork on the South coast of the Crimea', yet by this date even his old friend Beaton was starting to doubt the claims. Sinclair exhibited plans for Melbourne's parks at the 1858 Exhibition of the Victorian Industrial Society, but no examples of his

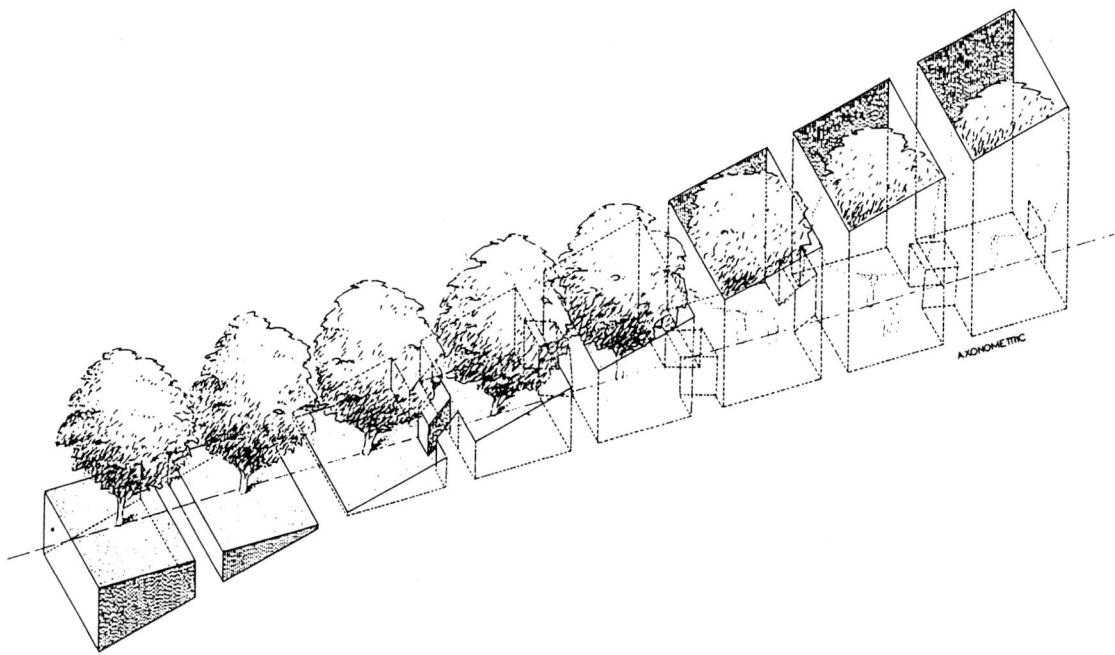

Vladimir Sitta's *Garden of Emergence* (1987), designed for a setting in France and demonstrating his innovative style, which combined landscape design and environmental art, captures the intellectual edge that distinguishes Sitta's approach to design

design work have yet been documented. Later that year he accepted the position of gardener at Fitzroy Gardens upon resumption of control by the Lands Department from the Corporation of Melbourne. BATEMAN's scheme of 1856–57 was largely abandoned and during the ensuing decades a new design, the basis of the current plan, was implemented by Sinclair. He lived in the Gardens—by family tradition in the building now known as Sinclair's Cottage—but his modest annual salary makes clear he was part of the workforce rather than a key decision maker.

In 1865 Sinclair published *The Australian Gardeners' Chronicle or Calendar of Operations for every Month of the Year in the Kitchen Garden*. The Sinclairs had two further children, and after Mary's death, James married her friend Ellen Roberts, who helped him complete botanical drawings when his ageing hands were crippled with rheumatism.

No one has yet adequately considered the life of this enigmatic figure, whose training promised so much, but whose colonial career stalled. Hattie Knight, a descendent, writing in the *Victorian Historical Magazine* (1940) gave a warm and congratulatory account, based on family documents and pride. More recently, Rex Swanson (*Melbourne's Historic Public Gardens*, 1984), Ray Wright (*The Bureaucrats' Domain*, 1989), and Georgina Whitehead (*Civilising the City*, 1997) have taken advantage of close reading in Lands Department correspondence to transfer Knight's design attribution of Fitzroy Gardens from Sinclair to Clement HODGKINSON, and to draw attention to Sinclair's relatively modest status within the Department. For all this, he remains an enterprising landscape gardener whose life history encapsulates experiences scarcely to be found in the collective lives of a dozen of his contemporaries. The absence of personal papers is the more regretted when one considers the paucity of biographies in the literature of Australian GARDEN HISTORY.   RA

SISSINGHURST, Kent, England, the garden created in the years either side of the Second World War by writer and gardener **Victoria (Vita) Sackville-West** (1892–1962) and her husband Harold Nicolson, was arguably the most-visited English property by Australian gardeners during the last decades of the twentieth century. Through visits and publications, its fascination continues unabated. Under antipodean skies it is not so much a place as an idea or a state of mind, characterised by close reading of Sackville-West's books, the pilgrimage, a cool-climate plant palette, a degree of formality (especially enclosed 'rooms'), good breeding, and above all a White Garden. BOLOBEK and KENNERTON GREEN pay skilful homage.

Anne Scott-James, *Sissinghurst: The Making of a Garden* (London, 1975); Jane Brown, *Vita's Other World: A Gardening Biography of Vita Sackville-West* (Harmondsworth, Middlesex, 1985)   RA

SITTA, Vladimír (Tom) (b. 1950), landscape architect and urban designer, has made an outstanding contribution to Australian environmental design since the early 1980s. Originally from Brno, Czechoslovakia, Sitta studied at Brno University and quickly established a reputation for innovative work that combined landscape design and environmental art. He was twice awarded the prestigious Lenné

Prize (for URBAN DESIGN) in West Germany. After coming to Australia in 1981 Sitta has been responsible for design projects as diverse as theatre sets and street furniture, though it is his work in landscape design that is more widely known, particularly several remarkable private gardens that are distinguished as much by their poetic affinities as their intellectual preoccupations, innovative use of materials, and concern for precise detail. Built projects have been balanced by an ongoing interest in major national and international design competitions, in which he has regularly won first prizes. Sitta's work has been frequently published in international journals and landscape monographs, where he is included with other designers of international significance. He has also influenced, generously supported, and encouraged many students and younger practitioners through his Sydney office (Terragram) and as a part-time tutor at the University of New South Wales.

Since 1985 Sitta has collaborated with Perth-based landscape architect, artist, writer, and academic Richard Weller (b. 1963). Their firm, Room 4.1.3, has produced some important environmental designs such as the national competition-winning landscape scheme for the National Museum of Australia, Canberra. Weller has also had considerable experience in Europe—including working with Daniel Libeskind in Berlin—and has played a prominent role in establishing an innovative course in landscape architecture at the University of Western Australia. GEOFFREY BRITTON

SKERTCHLY, Sydney Barber Josiah (1850–1926), scientist, horticulturist, and journalist, was born at Ansty, Leicestershire, England, trained at London's Royal School of Mines and worked in Egypt and England as a geologist. He knew Lyell, corresponded with DARWIN, and entered a fruitful phase in his career with publications and society memberships. Following a serious accident, Skertchly travelled in France and Italy, then worked in California, Borneo, and China. He was appointed Professor of Botany in Hong Kong but the Sino–Japanese war led him to move in 1891 to Brisbane. Between 1895 and 1897 he was assistant government geologist. In 1906 he was inaugural president of the Field Naturalists' Club, he served as president of the Royal Society of Queensland, lectured widely, and wrote for the *Brisbane Courier* on nature subjects. From 1906 he regularly contributed (as 'Daun Utan') to the JOURNAL OF HORTICULTURE OF AUSTRALASIA. 'Professor' Skertchly—as he was invariably styled—was a man of wide talents, adding cosmopolitan lustre to Queensland horticulture. RA

SMITH, Charles Hope Johnston (1810–1895), landscape gardener and garden architect, was born East Lothian, Scotland; his father, James Smith, was head gardener to the Earl of Hopetoun at Hopetoun House, Queensferry (1823–50), and both Charles and his brother John trained in horticulture under their father's tutelage. Charles H.J. Smith started on his own account as a landscape designer and garden architect *c.* 1834 and soon attracted an influential clientele. The two brothers contributed to Patrick Neill's *The Fruit, Flower and Kitchen Garden* (1840): John on the pineapple and the flower garden, and Charles the various building designs (his specialty), including a large house for New Holland plants. By 1850 the *North British Agriculturist* could describe Charles Smith as 'the principle [*sic*] garden architect in Scotland', while two years later the *Gardeners' Chronicle* described him as an 'experienced landscape gardener, and a man of much good sense'.

It was Smith's book *Parks and Pleasure Grounds; or, Practical Notes on Country Residences, Villas, Public Parks and Gardens* (1852) that brought his name to a wide audience. It was reprinted in Philadelphia (1852) and published in new editions for the North American market with commentary by Lewis Allen (1853 and 1856). Its scope was a direct reflection of Smith's client base: baronial seats (often remodelling existing layouts), large villas, and institutional gardens. He showed himself to be a disciple of Whately, PRICE, and GILPIN, aiming 'to popularise their principles, and to simplify and extend their processes in practice'. The PICTURESQUE ethos espoused by Smith was enthusiastically adopted in the colonies, but it was Edward KEMP's book *How to Lay out a Garden*, with its more modest ambit, which captured the market.

For reasons as yet unknown, Smith migrated to Vic. in 1855, aged 45, and settled in Kyneton: perhaps having made his fortune, he sought warmer climes, or was attracted by the potentialities of the gold-rich colony. He appears to have lived a modest life in the country, within easy access to Melbourne, but without troubling himself to seek major commissions. Surveyor-General Andrew Clarke sought his assistance in 1856 regarding landscaping of the proposed new government house, but the project was aborted. He offered suggestions (unheeded) on the competition for the landscaping of the current GOVERNMENT HOUSE, but expressed little faith in those responsible for Melbourne's PUBLIC PARKS. Smith found recreational pleasure in APICULTURE and in his old age enjoyed a cordial meeting with Victoria's governor, the 7th Earl of Hopetoun, with whom he exchanged reminiscences of their Hopetoun House boyhoods, two generations apart. RA

SMITH, Farquharson: see ADAMSON, William

SMITH, George (1828–1896), nursery proprietor and seed merchant, was born in Warwick, England. He was apprenticed to a Mr Deakin, head forester and gardener at Eastnor Castle, the seat of Earl Somers in Herefordshire, and studied under William Hooker at KEW GARDENS. For four years Smith had charge of a department at the Royal Fruit and Flower Garden, then in the process of formation at Frogmore, near Windsor Castle. He emigrated in 1853 and following several successful years on the Ballarat diggings established a seed and nursery business on the north side of Lake Wendouree (1860), later with a retail outlet in Armstrong Street North. The naming of Smith's Royal Exotic Nursery recalled his English training. He was a foundation committee member of the Ballarat Horticultural Society (1859) and in 1862 published *The Cottage Gardener*, a booklet addressing kitchen, fruit, and flower gardens. He was elected a city councillor in 1874 and took a lively interest in STREET tree planting, the BALLARAT BOTANIC GARDENS, and the water commission reserves. Smith's horticultural expertise was recognised by Fellowship of the ROYAL HORTICULTURAL SOCIETY, proposed by MUELLER. RA

SMITH, James Edward (1759–1828), British botanist, was born in Norwich, England, and studied medicine at Edinburgh University, specialising in botany under John Hope, an advocate of the Linnean method. Joseph BANKS in 1783 recommended his purchase of the natural history collections and library of Carl LINNAEUS, an acquisition that was to determine his future career, as Smith now devoted himself to the study of botany and writing. He was elected Fellow of the Royal Society, and in 1788 founded the Linnean Society, being annually elected president until his death.

While Smith was prolific in his botanical writing, he was also noted for the clarity of his scientific descriptions and his accuracy. Though less well known than his thirty-six volume *English Botany* (1790–1814) and *Flora Britannica* (1800–04), his *Specimen of the Botany of New Holland* (1793–95) with its sixteen coloured plates by SOWERBY and descriptions of twenty-seven new species, was the first book solely devoted to AUSTRALIAN FLORA. Most of the plates were made from specimens and drawings sent by Surgeon-General John WHITE. Through other works such *Exotic Botany* (1804–08)—which included illustrations of thirty-seven Australian plants—and his many papers to the Linnean Society, Smith did much to make the Australian flora better known. TONY CAVANAGH

SMITH, John (1803–1886), nursery proprietor and pomologist, was born in Scotland and trained in London, Edinburgh, and at the Fairfield Nurseries near Liverpool. He arrived in Melbourne in 1852 and worked as manager for the nursery of Smith (no relation) and ADAMSON.

Smith selected land *c.* 1863 at Riddells Creek (Vic.), on which he developed an orchard, vineyard, and nursery garden. By 1869 he had ten acres (4 ha) planted with fruit trees, including seventy-one kinds of desert apples and eighty varieties of pears. In a long report of this date, the *Australasian* correspondent sang a pomological paean: 'this private firm have done more towards the cultivation and reliable nomenclature of hardy fruits suited to this climate than all the horticultural societies in Victoria put together'. This fine reputation for fruit trees was rewarded with a prize at the Vienna International Exhibition (1875) for the apple Newton Wonder—all Smith's apples were on blight-proof stock by 1876. Smith was an expert in 'crossing' and HYBRIDISING. His verbenas, petunias, and pansies won many prizes at Victorian HORTICULTURAL SHOWS and were much sought after for floral BEDDING. The nursery soon widened its interests to ornamental trees, shrubs, and herbaceous plants, and was well placed at the foot of MOUNT MACEDON to compete with TAYLOR AND SANGSTER as Melbourne's elite developed their HILL-STATIONS. In 1871 the nursery had twenty species of oak as well as varieties of elms. The nursery is reported to have imported the first Golden Oak (*Quercus robur* 'Concordia') to the colony, one of which was planted near the bridge over Riddells Creek, where it can still be seen.

On Smith's death, his two sons, **Thomas Smith** (*c.* 1840–1898) and **Walter Joseph Smith** (1854–1938), carried on the business. At this time, the nursery had fine collections of camellias, rhododendrons, and ericas. Many RHODODENDRONS were raised from their own seed, with Thomas as hybridist. Thomas also had a special interest in ORCHIDS: the nursery is credited by the *Australasian* as the first in Vic. to start their cultivation, having fifty-three species and varieties in 1883, as well as a special list of eighty additional choice varieties, most of which were new to the colony. In the last decade of the nineteenth century Walter Smith was a key populariser of CHRYSANTHEMUMS and DAFFODILS in Victoria. He raised many varieties at the Riddells Creek Nursery, gave lectures extolling their merits, and published a pamphlet, *The Culture of Chrysanthemums for the Production of Exhibition Blooms*. Very few different narcissi were available until late in the century; by 1898 Smith had over a hundred varieties growing. Walter Smith was a leading spirit in the early shows and conferences, including the first Daffodil Conference in Vic. (1884). Both Smith and his friend, actor George TITHERADGE, did much to promote their cultivation, leading in 1891 to the first BULB show held by the Royal Horticultural Society of Victoria.

After Thomas died, Walter carried on the business. In 1902 he sold much of the orchard section of the nursery. A bad flood in 1906 greatly damaged the nursery; three years later a worse flood completely ruined it. The Smith family, apart from their considerable horticultural innovations, were very active in local affairs. They did much to beautify the township of Riddells Creek with donations of trees for the streets and the reserve. BARNEY HUTTON

SMITH, John Thomas (1878–1950), horticulturist, achieved renown as head of Melbourne City Council's Parks and Gardens Department. He served his apprenticeship at Turner's Royal Nurseries, Slough, England, and was employed on large British estates before migrating *c.* 1912 to Vic. Smith was head gardener at WERRIBEE PARK, and then at Glenbervie, the Toorak residence of wealthy merchant E.L. Yencken, who recommended him as 'hardworking and free of all d—— trades Hall nonsense'. After several years as curator at the City of Malvern, he was appointed curator of Melbourne's public reserves in 1921.

Smith's gardening style, with its 'wonderful displays of chrysanthemums, zinnias, and dahlias', was greatly admired, and he was lauded by many for transforming Melbourne's TREASURY, FLAGSTAFF, and FITZROY GARDENS into highly cultivated reserves. However, his preference for sweeping lawns scattered with specimen trees brought him into conflict with some, including Edna WALLING, who castigated his 'aesthetic appreciation' and injudicious removal of the old trees. Skilled in raising plants under glass, his arrangements of orchids, poinsettias, and the like for the Lord Mayor's ball and other civic functions contributed to his acclaim and influence. As a founder and prominent member of the VICTORIAN TREE PLANTERS' ASSOCIATION, he promoted debate of parkland issues. During the 1920s and 1930s he judged the *Herald* garden COMPETITION with Alex JESSEP and Frederick RAE. The Royal Horticultural Society of Victoria staged its Autumn Show, opened by Lady GOWRIE in Melbourne Town Hall, as a tribute to Smith when he retired in 1943.

GEORGINA WHITEHEAD

SMITH, Samuel (1812–1884), vigneron and gardener, born in Wareham, Dorset, England, worked as a brewer before migrating to Adelaide in 1847. He served as head gardener for George Fife ANGAS at Lindsay Park before founding Yalumba Vineyards (1849) at Angaston, in the BAROSSA VALLEY. His eldest son, vigneron Sidney Smith (1837–1908), who married Eleanor Jane Caley (1837–1925) in 1862, carried on the winery, establishing its reputation in Shiraz and fortified wines, and gaining international awards; Yalumba is still maintained by descendants of Sidney Smith.

Fred Caley Smith (1864–1913), seed merchant and nursery proprietor, was born at Yalumba, a son of Sidney Smith. After employment in Adelaide he returned to the Angaston district for health reasons, managing the orchards and cannery, and specialising in fruit disease eradication. He embarked on a six-month tour in 1893 of America, Europe, India, Singapore, and Java in order 'to obtain information with regard to the diseases &c. of fruit-trees, and the best markets for the fruit and wines of this colony'. By 1899 he advertised from Angaston in the *Gardeners' Chronicle* as a seedsman, offering principally Western Australian perennial flowering plants 'suitable for pot culture'. Each collection was accompanied by a pamphlet, *The Cultivation of Australian Plants*, perhaps the first individually published horticultural work on AUSTRALIAN FLORA. What the British public made of 'drought-resisting fodder plants' (such as Saltbush) is not known, but in 1899 he started the Speciality Farm, or ALDGATE NURSERY, with Oscar and Bruno MENZEL, concentrating on the hybridisation and propagation of bulbs, flowers, and cool-climate plants. The partnership lasted until 1906, after which he traded alone, specialising in dahlias, petunias, delphiniums, gladioli, aquilegias, and CARNATIONS, and contributed (as the South Australian expert) to the *JOURNAL OF HORTICULTURE*.

In 1910 Fred married **(Myra) Coralie Hill** (1882–1920), a grazier's daughter from Scott's Creek (SA). The Caley Smiths—as they preferred to be known—enjoyed a brief marriage and after her husband's early death, the young 'Mrs Fred Caley Smith' took on management of the nursery, described in *Everylady's Journal* (1918) as Australia's only woman 'nurseryman'. While the claim was slightly misleading, she did employ three female gardeners, citing their superiority in all tasks except deep cultivation. During her management the nursery propagated and exported 'thousands of seedlings and bulbs' nationally and internationally. After her untimely death from typhoid the property became Mrs Barclay's Tearooms and Gardens in the 1920s–30s.

DAVID JONES

SMITH AND ADAMSON: see ADAMSON, WILLIAM

SMYTH, Arthur Bowes (1750–1790), surgeon, travelled to Botany Bay with the First Fleet and his journal (published 1979) described the voyage and his short stay in NSW. He recorded a geranium in flower in his cabin (5 January 1788), two weeks before arriving in Botany Bay. Also mentioned were grape vines 'which flourish', and myrtles and bananas brought from Rio de Janeiro. He illustrated a grass tree or 'Blackboy' from which he collected 'balsam [with] … medicinal virtues', which he used successfully to treat pulmonary disorders, claiming it had a 'Fragrant and aromatic Taste & smell'. Smyth mentioned James Smith, the only non-convict civilian on the First Fleet, being given land, a tent, and seeds to establish a garden in Sydney.

VICTOR CRITTENDEN

SNAPE (née HODGSON), Diana (b. 1937), teacher, artist, gardener, and Australian plant enthusiast, was born at Croydon (NSW), and, now based in Vic., continues a lifelong passion that led her to initiate the Garden Design Study Group (1993) of the AUSTRALIAN PLANTS SOCIETY. She periodically contributes to Melbourne's *Age* newspaper, *Landscape Australia*, and other journals, especially promoting an Australian garden STYLE based on use of plants that form part of the local environment. Her book *Australian Native Gardens: Putting Visions into Practice* (1992) describes thirty inspirational Australian plant gardens.

RODGER ELLIOT

SOCIETY FOR GROWING AUSTRALIAN PLANTS was formed by Arthur SWABY in 1957, with 187 people attending the inaugural meeting held in Melbourne on 12 March. By April 1958, Regional Councils had been formed in all mainland states and a National Council was established in 1962. The Society's motto, 'Preservation through Cultivation', is best explained in Swaby's words: 'We exist to cultivate, improve and to preserve our flora in gardens and in the bush.' After four decades the Society has more than 6000 members and 100 District Groups, making it one of the largest HORTICULTURAL SOCIETIES in Australia. The groups meet monthly to exchange information and plants, and many hold annual flower shows or plant sales for the public. A recent name change to **Australian Plants Society** has been adopted in NSW, SA, Tas., and Vic. Along with branches in the ACT and Qld, and the Wildflower Society of Western Australia, these groups are linked through the Association of Societies for Growing Australian Plants, a national administrative body that also takes up issues beyond state and territory boundaries.

The Society's quarterly journal **Australian Plants** was first published in December 1959 with William Herbert Payne (b. 1926) as Managing Editor. Bill Payne is still editor forty years on and the journal is recognised world-wide as a source of information on the cultivation of AUSTRALIAN FLORA. The Society has also published a wide range of books and local flora guides, and has assisted, both financially and as a source of information, in the publication of many major works. The Society's membership list contains many botanists, authors, landscape designers and constructors, and nursery proprietors who have become recognised for their work with Australian native plants. A quick survey of people prominent in native plant circles since the 1950s and the pioneer growers before them would find that most are either former or current members of the Society.

The Society established its first areas of special study in 1958 and this has grown to more than thirty Study Groups covering a wide range of plant genera as well as speciality subjects such as garden design or container plants. Many study groups have been successful in introducing difficult species into cultivation and a large range of publications has also been produced, for example *The Grevillea Book* (1994) and *Australian Brachyscomes* (1995). The Society has also taken on an important role by providing advice and volunteers to propagate plants now rare in the wild, thus aiding PLANT CONSERVATION. The Society was recognised as the official body for dealing with the international registration for cultivars of Australian endemic plants in 1962 and this led to the formation of the Australian Cultivar Registration Authority (1963). The Society also played a major role in the establishment of the Australian Flora Foundation, and has established a world-class web site on the Internet to take Australia's flora to the world.

As a grassroots organisation, the Society has probably had more influence on Australian gardens than the majority of designers and has probably been the most important means of the acceptance of native plants by the gardening public, especially through its publications and well-attended shows. Many public and well-known native gardens throughout Australia began as the dream of a member who was able to gain knowledge and plants from the Society.

JOHN WALTER

SOILS and related growing media are an essential for PLANT growth and therefore for gardens. Plants absorb nutrients and water from soil and it is the space where plant roots grow. Australian soils are generally very old (geologically) and very poor, often in terms of both physical (air, water) and chemical (nutrient supply, acidity or alkalinity) attributes. The native vegetation of each region is well adapted to the soil in which it grows but many horticultural plants require enhanced growing conditions, some being quite specific. As is the case with CLIMATE, good horticultural practice requires selection of plants on the basis of their tolerance of prevailing site soil conditions. Increasingly the wider landscape is being designed using those principles. For the gardener, however, the desire to grow a particular plant often means that extant soil conditions have to be modified—by cultivation, importation of new soil, drainage modification, increasing soil organic matter levels, changing soil pH, or adding extra plant nutrients—for successful growth.

Inevitably, the urbanisation of Australia has meant that natural soils of high quality may not be available on site for garden developments. One solution has been to mine soils and then sell them as a commodity to the gardening trade. Environmental concerns and problems of supply have meant that 'good' soils have become very difficult to supply and soil merchants are forced to use lower grade materials or to make up blends of soil and other components to supply the market. These soils and soil blends have been extremely variable. An attempt to provide guidelines for the production and use of landscape soils has been made by Standards Australia in *Soils for Landscaping and Garden Use* (AS 4419–1998).

HORTICULTURE also has a number of specialist soil applications. When container production became a very important element of the NURSERY industry the choice of growing medium for use in containers rapidly became a critical decision for growers. Early media were based on soils with organic and inorganic amendments. Common problems with these mixes were variability, poor aeration and drainage, and weed and pathogen contamination. In Australia, local growers used versions of overseas systems of the 1930s–50s to formulate their own media. The work on pinebark-based media undertaken at Victoria's Knoxfield Horticultural Research Institute in the late 1970s was critical in developing a local response to shortages of good-quality soils and the cost of imported peat. Throughout the 1980s and 1990s Kevin HANDRECK of the CSIRO Division of Soils in Adelaide did an enormous amount of research into growing

Australian Plants, since 1959 the journal of the SOCIETY FOR GROWING AUSTRALIAN PLANTS, provided the first forum devoted to the horticultural use of the AUSTRALIAN FLORA

media—research that is encapsulated in Kevin Handreck and Neil Black, *Growing Media for Ornamental Plants and Turf* (1994) and as the Australian Standard for *Potting Mixes* (AS 3743–1996). Some horticulturists have sought to avoid perceived problems with soil and grow plants in soil-less HYDROPONIC systems.

The other area of significant research into soil performance has been the development of specialist TURF soil profiles. These have had their greatest impact in the construction of GOLF and BOWLING GREENS but more recently the principles have been also applied to larger scale construction such as major football grounds in Melbourne and Sydney, and RACECOURSES. These specialist soil profiles are based on the use of carefully specified sands. The construction of cricket squares is a counterpoint to the sand-based turf problem. Constructed from a plastic, cracking clay the cricket square is a highly specialised soil profile with rigorous specifications and maintenance requirements.

> Peter E.V. Charman and Brian W. Murphy (eds), *Soils: Their Properties and Management* (South Melbourne, 2000); Kevin Handreck, *Gardening Down-Under: A Guide to Healthier Soils and Plants* (Collingwood, Vic., 2001)   PETER MAY

SOLANDER, Daniel (1733–1782), naturalist, was born in Pitea, Sweden, and *c.* 1749 went to Uppsala to study medicine and NATURAL HISTORY under Carl LINNAEUS. He travelled and collected in Lapland in 1753–55. In response to requests made of Linnaeus by several British naturalists, Solander travelled to England in 1760 to give instruction in Linnean methods. He quickly befriended most of the leading botanists and nursery proprietors in London. He had an important role in the naming of the *Gardenia* and published a detailed description in 1762. He was soon appointed Assistant Keeper at the fledgling British Museum. Throughout this period, he also led a double life as a Swedish agent.

Solander, the first Swede to circle the globe, was one of the founders of Australian botany and ecology. This resulted from his friendship and scientific partnership with Joseph BANKS, who invited him to join the *Endeavour* expedition (1768–71). Their rich botanical harvest included 110 previously unknown genera and 1300 new species. In 1772 he travelled to the Hebrides, Iceland, and Orkney with Banks. In addition to Banks's HERBARIUM, Solander catalogued the Duchess of Portland's natural history collection, provided William Aiton with plant classifications for KEW GARDENS, helped revise Alexander Russell's *Natural History of Aleppo* (1756), and assisted leading British naturalists such as Fothergill, Collinson, Pennant, Lightfoot, Bartram, and Garden. Solander died suddenly of a stroke, and although Banks failed to publish the botanical results of the *Endeavour* voyage, Solander's descriptions (and some manuscript names) were appropriated by other naturalists.

> Edward Duyker, *Nature's Argonaut: Daniel Solander 1733–1782: Naturalist and Voyager with Cook and Banks* (Carlton South, Vic., 1998)   EDWARD DUYKER

SOMERCOTES, Ross, Tas., originally granted to Samuel Horton in 1823, is marked by a long and straight entrance avenue of mixed conifers and deciduous trees, clearly visible from the Midland Highway. The small west-facing front garden blends unobtrusively into the extended rural scenery, separated from surrounding farmland by an original three-bar wrought-iron fence in the English landscape manner. A number of garden spaces, including a walled courtyard for security against bushranger attack, surround the accretion of buildings on this historic property.   CHRISTINE REID

SOMNER, William: see LAW, SOMNER AND CO.

SORENSEN, Paul Edwin (1891–1983), horticulturist, nursery proprietor, and landscape gardener, was born in Copenhagen, Denmark, where according to his biographer, Richard Ratcliffe (1932–1999), he trained at the Hørsholm Teknisk Scole and by working at the Hørsholm Plantescole

Hardenbergia violacea, collected by Joseph BANKS and Daniel SOLANDER at Botany Bay (NSW) in 1770, engraved from a drawing by Sydney PARKINSON and published in *Illustrations of Australian Plants Collected in 1770* (1900–05)

under the direction of Lars Nielsen, a prominent horticulturist credited with the design of many Copenhagen parks. Ratcliffe records that after qualifying he worked for short periods in Germany and France, then spent four years working in Zurich, Switzerland, for Mertens Brothers, leading landscape designers and contractors. As war approached, Sorensen, a dedicated pacifist, decided to migrate to Australia, arriving in Melbourne in 1915. After a period of unsatisfactory work in Vic. he moved to the BLUE MOUNTAINS (NSW), where he became gardener at the Carrington Hotel. He set up his own nursery business in Katoomba at the end of 1917, which he moved in 1920 to land he had purchased in Leura. While at the Carrington, Sorensen met Anestina Hillenberg and they were married in Sydney in 1919; they had three sons, Derrick (b. 1920), Neville (b. 1922), and Ib (b. 1928).

At first the major source of income was from garden maintenance, particularly for guesthouses, with the rest of his time taken up with the establishment of the nursery. The earliest recorded garden laid out by Sorensen was Sylvan Mists (1920) in Katoomba, followed by Mount Edgecombe in the same year. In 1923 he established Gabo in Leura for Judge Edwards, and from then on at least two or three gardens were started each year for the rest of the decade. All of these were in the Blue Mountains but in 1932 he was commissioned to undertake a garden at Heaton Lodge, Mudgee, for the Loneregan family. This was to be the first of many gardens in the country starting in the Bathurst–Orange district but later in other areas, especially around the SOUTHERN HIGHLANDS (NSW).

In 1928–29 he was involved with adjoining gardens in Leura; Dean Park for R.J. Wilson and Cheppen for Ernest Trigg. Wilson introduced Sorensen to Henri Van de Velde, a prominent Sydney businessman who in 1932 purchased land nearby on which to build his house and garden; Sorensen claimed EVERGLADES as his masterpiece. In 1933 Van de Velde and Sorensen entered into a verbal agreement for the construction of the garden and the work continued uninterrupted, except for the Second World War, until Van de Velde's death (1947). The agreement was never formalised and Sorensen at no stage put any designs on paper. Everglades showed mastery in articulation of spaces, an appreciation of scale and texture, immaculate craftsmanship in the stonework of retaining walls that divide the garden into terraces, and an extensive understanding of plants and their requirements. Other major gardens laid out by Sorensen in the pre-war years included INVERGOWRIE, Exeter, for Cecil Hoskins; Gleniffer Brae, Wollongong, for Sidney Hoskins; and Redlands, Mittagong, for Cedric Rouse. He also was commissioned by Hoskins to design the grounds of the Hoskins Memorial Church, Lithgow, and the Mount Kiera Scout Camp near Wollongong.

Both Derrick and Neville Sorensen lost their lives in service with the RAF in Europe. After the war Ib joined his father in the business. As Paul Sorensen grew older he increasingly relied on Ib for the construction of his garden designs and there is no doubt that without his son's assistance he could not have achieved as much as he did.

Immediately after the war Sorensen's gardens again tended to be local and small. Neubeck House at Lidsdale near Lithgow was the first larger post-war country garden; it was quickly followed by Pine Hills, Bathurst; Ballantyre, Cassilis; and Bethune, Orange. Blackrock and Pitlochry, both at Merriwa, were built in 1954–55. The 1960s were the busiest period of Sorensen's career, with large gardens spread over country NSW from Boogadah near Binnaway to Merewoth, Berrima; Calleen near Cowra; and FERNHILL, Mulgoa; as well as his largest city project, Mahratta, in the northern Sydney suburb of Warrawee. At the same time he was working on Blue Mist, Leura, and the Proctor garden, Wahroonga, as well as many smaller gardens. He was to continue working right up to the time of his death, although by that time he was only providing design input with Ib responsible for all of the physical work.

Paul Sorensen's gardens were based on the idea of creating outdoor rooms defined by the use of large trees and shrubs or with walls and changes of level. He was not particularly interested in smaller flowering plants, which he considered as furniture to his rooms; he left these very much to the taste of the garden owner, whom he always seemed to be able to enthuse with his ideas. Wherever possible he would borrow views from outside the garden to expand its boundaries but was always conscious that the scale of some scenery, such as in the Blue Mountains, was such that these borrowed views had to be achieved with great care to avoid conflict of scale between nature and the garden. He did not believe that good design could be done on paper, preferring to carry all of his ideas in his head and virtually design the garden on site. He never wrote about his work and his design philosophies can only be appreciated through his surviving gardens and the memories of those associated with them. With more than forty known gardens in the Blue Mountains and at least thirty more around other parts of NSW and the ACT, his was an important contribution to landscape gardening in Australia. His style, although influenced by the ideas of Mertens Brothers of Switzerland and possibly by Thomas MAWSON of England, was distinctive, being more closely attuned to modern LANDSCAPE ARCHITECTURE than to the garden design ideas of his age.

Richard Ratcliffe, *Australia's Master Gardener: Paul Sorensen and his Gardens* (Kenthurst, NSW, 1990)   RA

SOUTH AFRICA: see AFRICA

SOUTH AMERICA and Australia were originally joined as part of GONDWANA, so some members of ancient plant families such as Araucariaceae, Fagaceae, and Proteaceae are indigenous to both continents. South America was also one of the sources of the first exotic plants cultivated in Australia. The First Fleet called at Rio de Janeiro, Brazil, and took on board living plants of banana, coffee, citrus species, and prickly pear, all of which were planted at Farm Cove in 1788. For decades afterwards, many ships sailing from Europe to the Australian colonies called at Rio and collected seed and plants of many South American species, which were brought on to Australian ports. Among these were species from TROPICAL, cool temperate, and ARID regions as the South American continent embraces as great a range of climate zones as does Australia. For this reason, many species adapted well to Australian conditions—some too well. Jacaranda, *Lantana montevidensis* (Trailing Lantana), bromeliads, aroids, and begonias, for instance, have proved useful ornamentals, while prickly pear, pampas grass, *Schinus molle* (Pepper Tree), and *Lantana camara* (Lantana) have become troublesome WEEDS. Jacaranda, now a fashionable garden and street tree, is thought to have been introduced into Qld by Walter HILL and into NSW by Charles MOORE in the mid-1850s. The spectacular designs created by Brazilian landscape architect Roberto Burle Marx (1909–1994) featuring broad patterns of colourful tropical plants have influenced some Australian designers, particularly those involved in designing private gardens and tourist RESORTS in tropical Australia.

ALLAN CORREY

SOUTH AUSTRALIA Gardening traditions in SA are based upon sustenance and experimentation. Sustenance underpins the long COTTAGE GARDENING tradition, promoted by colonial publications, and supported by the generations of English, Irish, German, Cornish, and Welsh migrants who sought to transpose European practices upon a landscape with poor alkalinity and often nutrient-deficient soils, a low rainfall, and a semi-ARID climate. Assisted by numerous experienced German and English scientists, nursery proprietors, and gardeners, who migrated to the colony, experimentation involved the testing of northern hemisphere and MEDITERRANEAN plants and economic crops. This was exhibited in agricultural, VITICULTURAL, silvicultural, and horticultural trials, particularly during the 1870s and 1890s and again in the 1920 and 1930s.

Even before Adelaide was surveyed by William LIGHT in early 1837, Thomas ALLEN and Sons had advertised their services in the first edition of the *South Australian Gazette and Colonial Register*, published in London on 18 June 1836. The *Register*, under editor George STEVENSON, promoted gardening and horticulture—advice he demonstrated at his North Adelaide and LEAWOOD GARDENS properties. Gardens were generally sustenance-based in philosophy, geometric in design, and emphasised food plants, with only limited use of herbaceous annuals and perennials. John BAILEY, appointed Colonial Botanist in 1839 by public and government subscription, attempted to establish a BOTANIC GARDEN and after this venture failed, due to inadequate financial support, he established the Hackney Nursery. The earliest plants and seeds imported from Europe during this time included vines, date palms, olives, figs, and bougainvilleas, together with a wide spectrum of vegetables, fruit, and nut trees, and annuals and perennials.

The period 1840–90 was marked by rapid advances and innovations in gardening and horticulture; activities, policies, and discoveries; and the foundations of a distinctive gardening culture. While small, sustenance-based geometric-styled gardens were common, many prosperous owners attempted to establish GARDENESQUE designs on the Adelaide Plains, in the ADELAIDE HILLS, and around rural HOMESTEADS, assisted by the advent of reticulated water and several years of plant and tree cultivation trials. Significant gardens, such as THE ACACIAS, CARMINOW, FOREST LODGE, Marble Hill, GOVERNMENT HOUSE (Belair), and the ADELAIDE BOTANIC GARDEN, all illustrated these stylistic characteristics.

This was a period when the private NURSERIES of Bailey at Hackney, Stevenson at Leawood Gardens, Elisha and Walter HACKETT at Marryatville, Charles Ware at Clifton Nursery, Charles GILES at Kent Town Exotic Nursery and Grove Hill, Ernst HEYNE at Beulah Park, Henry SEWELL at Payneham and ALDGATE, George McEWIN at Glen Ewin, and Charles NEWMAN at Water Gully were established, undertook extensive plant trials, and imported significant plant collections from Europe, NORTH AMERICA, and South Africa (particularly fruits, vines, olives, ROSES, CONIFERS, FERNS, PALMS, and SUCCULENTS). Stevenson commissioned his gardener, the horticulturist George McEwin, to prepare *The South Australian Vigneron and Gardeners' Manual* (1843) and Heyne subsequently prepared *The Amateur Gardener for South Australia* (1871), both significant and influential texts.

In the public sector, the scientific, agricultural, and silvicultural ideas of George GOYDER, Albert MOLINEUX, and Friedrich KRICHAUFF were translated into the establishment of a Forest Board, an Agricultural Bureau, and the monthly horticultural periodicals FARM AND GARDEN (1858–63) and GARDEN AND FIELD (1875–1940), all innovative early initiatives. John Ednie BROWN, under the Forest Board, established nurseries and FORESTRY plantations at WIRRABARA, BUNDALEER, Belair, and MOUNT GAMBIER. George FRANCIS established the ADELAIDE BOTANIC GARDEN in 1855, which Richard SCHOMBURGK later crafted into a major landscaped garden. During this period Goyder also refined Light's attributed parkland town model. Friendships between Ferdinand MUELLER, Krichauff, Brown, Schomburgk, and Heyne—redolent of the strong GERMAN contribution to SA—enabled an exchange of plants and seeds with MELBOURNE BOTANIC GARDENS and prominent nurseries and botanic gardens in Britain and Germany.

The Federation period witnessed a boom in housing development around Adelaide, and in the Hills. Pride in Federation fostered a renewed patriotic interest in English plant traditions, especially in roses, CAMELLIAS, and RHODODENDRONS. Individuals such as Frank Snow, Langdon Bonython, and Edward STIRLING expressed this interest in specialist displays and propagation experiments at their Hills properties, and so too did nurseries including those of Herbert KEMP and Ted LASSCOCK. Properties such as CARMINOW, ST VIGEANS, WILLYAMA, BEECHWOOD, and WAIROA became major social and display venues in Adelaide, aided by the wide plant selections promoted by the major nurseries and importation by plant enthusiasts.

The post-Federation period, which led into the Californian Bungalow stylistic period, resulted in further urbanisation in Adelaide and further redevelopment of the late nineteenth-century HILL-STATION gardens. A fascination with English ARTS AND CRAFTS gardens and architecture, American

South Australia

This float depicting an idealised COTTAGE GARDEN, drawing strongly on local traditions, represented the town of Clare in a 1936 pageant to commemorate the centenary of European settlement of SOUTH AUSTRALIA

house and garden literature, ITALIANATE influences, and the CITY BEAUTIFUL philosophy were predominant influences.

Gardens strongly influenced by English fashions, especially cottage gardens, and the ideas of Edna WALLING, Elsie CORNISH, and Gertrude JEKYLL, were exemplified by places such as ANLABY, Arbury Park, CARRICK HILL, Dulwich House, Eringa, GAMBLE COTTAGE, GLENALTA, HUGHES PARK, LINDSAY PARK, Mount George, PANMURE, and URRBRAE, and at the Pioneer Womens' Garden in the ADELAIDE PARK LANDS. Walling was commissioned to design the MICHELL garden, while Cornish guided the Waite sisters in their JEKYLL-inspired BROADLEES. Roses, rhododendrons, camellias, the Claret Ash, and display annuals were the popular plant species, promoted by nurseries run by BURDETT, ASHBY, LASSCOCK, Kemp, Osborn, WOLLASTON, and Heyne, and complemented by the use of slate, concrete slab, and crazy paving.

While the romantic American style was applied in several HOMESTEAD GARDENS, such as HILL RIVER STATION, other owners adopted Italianate design ideas or adhered to traditional English geometric display or cottage garden interpretations. Walter BAGOT promoted Italian ideas at Nurney House and Forest Lodge, and Cornish applied this approach at the University of Adelaide.

GARDEN CITY ideas received political commitment from the Labor Vaughan administration with the appointment of Australia's first government town planner, Charles READE,

Australia's first TOWN PLANNING conference, and the development of COLONEL LIGHT GARDENS, Springfield, and VICTOR HARBOR SOLDIERS' MEMORIAL GARDENS. Waikerie and Berri were designed by Reade and his principal successor Walter Scott Griffiths (1863–1929). Garden design advice was promoted through the magazine (SOUTH) AUSTRALIAN HOMES AND GARDENS (1923–53) and numerous specialised nursery catalogues and planting guides.

The Playford period (1938–65) witnessed expansive industrialisation and large-scale housing developments. John DWIGHT's *Gardening Handbook* (1957) was issued to every South Australian Housing Trust resident to provide horticultural and design advice. The progress imperative, veiled in a strong affinity with English traditions, displayed little concern for the natural environment. While roses, camellias, and rhododendrons dominated there was an interest in Australian and Mediterranean-style vegetation and local materials including timber railway sleepers, stone, and slate. *Eucalyptus leucoxylon* (Yellow Gum or South Australian Blue Gum), *E. citriodora* (Lemon-scented Gum), and *E. sideroxylon* (Ironbark) were used by Richard Massey, Robin HILL, Allan CORREY, and Ray HOLLIDAY against conventional practices in public sector organisations. Landscapes at Stangate House and Elizabeth reflect the former, while the Athelstone Wildflower Garden and Nursery, Michell garden, Art Gallery of South Australia Sculpture Court, Highways Department forecourt, and Wittunga reflect the latter. Noel LOTHIAN, as Director of the Adelaide Botanic Garden, was an influential figure in gardening and horticultural matters, writing *The Practical Gardener* (1955), *Growing Australian Plants* (1964) with Ivan Holliday, and engaging Correy to master plan the MOUNT LOFTY BOTANIC GARDEN. It was a time when the AUSTRALIAN INSTITUTE OF LANDSCAPE ARCHITECTS was formed and promotion of LANDSCAPE ARCHITECTURE was guided by Gavin WALKLEY and other professionals.

The late twentieth century displayed an attuned awareness in environmentalism, particularly under the Dunstan administration (1967–79), and several innovative projects were initiated. These projects, including the new town Monarto, South-Eastern Freeway, West Lakes, Rundle Mall, RIVER TORRENS LINEAR PARK, THE PADDOCKS, and Leigh Creek South, were envisaged as integrated environmental and socio-democratic experiments devised by individuals including Ray Holliday, Barrie Ormsby, Ian Barwick, Chris Wren, Rodney BEAMES, Ellis STONES, and Geoff Sanderson together with numerous allied design and scientific professionals. Adelaide hosted the second AILA National Conference (1972) in association with the Australian Conservation Foundation, under Walkley's guidance. Major projects of the 1980s–90s included the Bicentennial Conservatory, Regent Gardens, and the AUSTRALIAN ARID LANDS BOTANIC GARDEN. Interest in English exotic plants and European design traditions continued in the garden but an increasing awareness of Australian and Mediterranean plants, and landscape sustainability have influenced attitudes leading into the twenty-first century.

R.O. Beames and J.A.E. Whitehill, *Some Historic Gardens in South Australia* (Adelaide, 1981); Robert F.G. Swinbourne, *Years of Endeavour: An Historical Record of the Nurseries, Nurserymen, Seedsmen, and Horticultural Retail Outlets of South Australia* (Adelaide, 1982); David Jones, *Designed Landscapes of South Australia* (Adelaide, 1997); David Jones and Pauline Payne, *Gardens in South Australia 1840–1940* (Adelaide, 1998).

DAVID JONES

SOUTH AUSTRALIAN CHRONICLE (1858–1975), with minor variations to title and frequency, was published weekly by the proprietors of the *Advertiser* and from 1931 absorbed the rival ADELAIDE OBSERVER. The *Chronicle* provided extensive reports on agricultural, horticultural, literary, rural, and social issues and events throughout SA. It included regular profiles of select pastoral properties and was a strong advocate for VITICULTURE. Widely read, it contained regular columns by Albert MOLINEUX, Henry SEWELL, and George MCEWIN.

DAVID JONES

SOUTH AUSTRALIAN HOMES AND GARDENS (1931–53), previously *Australian Homes and Gardens* (1925–31), a prominent monthly social magazine published in Adelaide, was influential in advocating and advising on fashions in architecture, interior design, and garden and landscape design in SA. A successful parochial competitor to AUSTRALIAN HOME BEAUTIFUL and strongly influenced by Sydney Ure Smith's stylish magazine *The HOME*, each issue profiled a prominent SA house and garden, and provided detailed social notes. Edited by Joyce Noel Warren and M. Irvine Smith, gardening advice was contributed by Alfred QUARRELL (1940–53) and Edna WALLING.

DAVID JONES

SOUTH AUSTRALIAN HORTICULTURIST (1856), edited by J.F. Wood, consisted of just four monthly issues, yet was a pioneering publication, one of the earliest Australian HORTICULTURAL MAGAZINES. The first issue of the *South Australian Horticulturist and Magazine of Agriculture, Botany, and Natural History* (to quote its full title) stated its intention of supplying colonists with information on 'everything connected with rural and domestic economy' including fruit, vegetables, flowers, and agricultural plants and seeds. It achieved this through feature articles, advice on garden operations, and notes from local HORTICULTURAL SOCIETIES.

John Frederick Francis Wood (1806–1883), horticulturist, born in Nottingham, England, was the editor (for eight years) of the English *Midland Florist and Suburban Horticulturist*. In SA he served as secretary to the South Australian Horticultural and Floricultural Society, and started the Evandale Nursery at Angaston (with a retail outlet in Adelaide), before establishing his property Woodlands at Kyneton. He was a prolific contributor to South Australian journals and newspapers, including *FARM AND GARDEN* and *GARDEN AND FIELD*.

DAVID JONES

SOUTH AUSTRALIAN REGISTER: see ADELAIDE OBSERVER

SOUTHERN HIGHLANDS, NSW, described by Governor Lachlan Macquarie in 1820 as a 'fine, extensive pleasure ground', forms part of the Woronora sandstone plateau, 650–860 metres above sea level. Mount Gibraltar ('The Gib') and Mount Gingenbullen are major landmarks as is the lush Kangaroo Valley on the south-eastern escarpment. Early settlers in the area included surveyor and explorer John Oxley (*c.* 1785–1828) at Camden and Bowral; surveyor Thomas MITCHELL laid out roads; bridges were built over Medway Rivulet and Wingecarribee River; and Bowral, Mittagong, and Moss Vale became permanent settlements. Oldbury Farm, Newbury, and Throsby Park survive from this early period.

The district's popularity and social prestige increased with the coming of the railway to Moss Vale in the late 1860s and the leasing of Throsby Park, as a SUMMER RETREAT for the governor (1865–72). A permanent summer vice-regal residence, HILLVIEW at Sutton Forest, was acquired in 1882. Wealthy city dwellers, such as the retailing HORDERN family, built grand country estates as retreats for the summer months. Retford Park, a mansion in the ITALIANATE manner set in a PARKLAND of exotic trees, remains a superb example of this genre.

A new impetus for building country retreats by industrialists came in the 1930s, after the Depression. The Burns family built MOIDART with its sunken rose garden; INVERGOWRIE, once owned by the YATES family, was newly landscaped by Paul SORENSEN; Milton Park (1915) was extensively remodelled by Mary Hordern; shipping magnate Howard Smith built Mount Eymard. Exotic deciduous and evergreen trees, and flowering shrubs such as rhododendrons, flourished in the cool climate, giving the area its distinctive character. Gardens created post-war, such as KENNERTON GREEN, continued the tradition of exotic plantings.

Local identities of influence have included Claude Crowe (1914–1999) and his Berrima Bridge nursery, supplying trees and shrubs to local gardeners for more than fifty years from 1943. At Frensham School, Mittagong, Winifred West (1881–1971), pioneer educator, created gardens where 'young growing minds could find the quietness necessary for inner growth'. The tranquil, secluded surroundings of wisteria-covered pergolas, may (*Spiraea* sp.) hedges, and sunken gardens have been influential on generations of Frensham students. Through the 1950s, winners in the prestigious *Sydney Morning Herald* country garden COMPETITIONS were consistently from the area.

Tourism, particularly GARDEN VISITING in spring and autumn, is now a major activity and the image of the Southern Highlands as a 'gardening Mecca' is reinforced by the annual Tulip Time FESTIVAL, held for more than forty years. In the past decade, many new gardens (such as Greenbriar Park, Gowan Brae, and Comfort Hill) have been created amid the area's mature stands of pines, cypresses, and massed deciduous trees. The intriguing drives to hidden villages and homesteads, and mixture of grand estates and cottage gardens make the Southern Highlands one of Australia's premier gardening districts.

Jane Cavanough, Anthea Prell, and Tim North, *Gardens of the Southern Highlands, New South Wales, 1828–1988* (Bowral, NSW, 1988); Ann Hawker, *Echoes of Dreamland* (Toowoomba, Qld, 1992)

CHRISTINE REID

SOUTTER, William ('Coolibar') (*c.* 1851–1925), horticulturist and horticultural journalist, was born in Aberdeen, Scotland, and attended Aberdeen University studying medicine (but never taking a degree). Soutter, with his wife Martha and young son Richard, came to Queensland to take up a position as gardener at CRESSBROOK Station, in the Brisbane Valley. In 1885 Soutter was appointed overseer at BOWEN PARK for the Queensland Acclimatisation Society and, after 1887, as the Society's secretary; he remained there until 1898. His scientific experimentation was matched by keen horticultural skills and design sense that made Bowen Park a favourite place for visitors and a thriving, well-respected EXPERIMENTAL ground. ECONOMIC PLANTS and ornamentals were tested; from hibiscus to pansies, sugar cane to potatoes. The results were often displayed in shows and international EXHIBITIONS to spread the knowledge among the colonists. The highlight of the Queensland Exhibition (1897) was a huge BUSH-HOUSE created by Soutter to link the main building to the annexes. Here 3000 elkhorn and staghorn ferns (from the Bunya Mountains) decorated posts and walls, while 9550 potted plants replicated a tropical forest. An elaborate RUSTIC coral, stone, and shell ornamental FOUNTAIN amid this bush-house was another Soutter creation, following a tradition in Qld dating back to the 1870s at least.

Soutter's influence was also felt through his publications. He was founding editor of the QUEENSLAND HORTICULTURIST (1892–95) and contributed many articles reflecting his strong knowledge of garden design as well as gardening experience in the subtropics. His optimistic belief in the future of Qld and the standing of the horticultural profession was often revealed: 'Gardeners, you are nearer than any to the great secret of the

The BUSH-HOUSE at Bowen Park, landscaped under the direction of William SOUTTER for the 1897 Queensland International Exhibition, capitalised on the popularity of ferns and other bold-foliaged plants in the setting of a large shade house

principle of life … Gardeners, awake to your possibilities, and also be sure of this, the better gardener the better patriot'. Soutter also contributed to E.M. SHELTON's *Tree-Planting for Shade and Ornament* with a list of indigenous shade trees for four climatic districts in the colony—southern coast lands and inland, central, and northern Qld. Between 1895 and 1898 he prepared the 'Gardening and Farming Calendar' for *Thorne's Queensland Almanac*. Perhaps his most influential literary contribution was under the pseudonym 'Coolibar' in his monthly 'Field and Garden Reminders' for the QUEENSLANDER (1900–25); his regular gardening advice was a rich combination of design and practical horticultural knowledge.

Beween 1898 and 1901 Soutter was Inspector of State Farms for the Department of Agriculture and Stock, travelling all over Qld providing advice. He was also well respected as a horticultural judge, helping many societies across the state under the auspices of the National Association. After leaving the Department he set up a farm, first at Sandgate, and later at Sunnybank. His son, Richard Ernest Soutter (1878–1955), whom he introduced to botany, became a leading agricultural scientist with expertise in wheat breeding, and managed the Roma State Farm (1906–35). William Soutter served the horticultural development of Qld for more than forty years.

JEANNIE SIM

SOWERBY, James (1757–1822), botanical illustrator, was born in London and trained as an artist and engraver at the Royal Academy School. As a botanical illustrator he teamed with James Edward SMITH in describing plants in many publications, of which *A Specimen of the Botany of New Holland* (1793–95) was devoted entirely to AUSTRALIAN PLANTS. He illustrated numerous Australian plants in other works, in many undertaking both the drawing and engraving.

HELEN HEWSON

SPAIN, and its impact on Australian horticulture, are usually ignored because of a prevailing focus on the cultivated plants and garden styles of England, France, and Italy. Gardens and dwellings of Spain too have terracotta plant containers, water reflecting from dishes and pools, canaries in cages, citrus trees, olives, and grapes; typical of the countries surrounding the MEDITERRANEAN Sea. This only describes the sunny southern and eastern parts of Spain. Northwards, Spain fronts the Atlantic Ocean and the Sea of Cantabria. Here, the provinces are moist, steeply hilly, and green. The plants are different also, for Spain contains one of Europe's most diverse and numerous flora. From its north, Spain has given Australia *Antirrhinum*, *Helleborus*, *Digitalis*, and *Castanea sativa* (Spanish Chestnut), and is a home to beech, walnut, birch, alder, and elm.

Throughout history, Phoenecia, Carthage, Athens, and Rome brought into Spain their plants and horticulture. Eventually, under Islam, and later still when the country was united under Ferdinand and Isabella, Spain surpassed the rest of Europe in horticulture, for now came the plants of empire and via Spain to the rest of the world went citrus, tomatoes, sunflowers, corn, potatoes, dahlias, and *Phytolacca dioica* (Ombú) and other trees from the New World. One such tree, *Schinus molle*, is so ubiquitous as 'the peppercorn tree' in parks and gardens of southern Australia, that it is believed to be native. Australian horticulture has always utilised Spain's indigenous plants: *Arbutus*, *Lavandula*, *Cistus*, *Narcissus*, *Thymus*, *Dianthus*, *Juniperus*, *Pinus*, and *Quercus*. Yet some of Spain's indigenous flora have become WEEDS in parts of Australia: *Genista*, *Cytisus*, *Olea*, and *Pinus*. In return, Spain is concerned about the spread there of Australian *Acacia*, *Eucalyptus*, and *Hakea*. Three species of Spain's oaks, *Quercus suber*, *Q. ilex*, and *Q. canariensis*, stand as fine, old, specimens in various parts of Australia, and are still popular for planting. The PATIO too came to Australia from Spain via California, formerly part of Spain's American empire.

C.M. Villiers-Stuart, *Spanish Gardens: Their History, Types, and Features* (London, 1929); Marquesa de Casa Valdes, *Spanish Gardens* (Woodbridge, Suffolk, 1987) CLIVE SORRELL

SPARNON, Norman James (1913–1995), Australian Ikebana master, was born in Melbourne and studied Japanese there. As a result of his spoken and written proficiency in the language, he was seconded to General Macarthur's Japanese headquarters following the Second World War; during these years (1945–58) he gained an insight into Japanese culture, including FLOWER ARRANGING. Following his return to Sydney, Sparnon became a top-ranking master of both the classical Ikenobo and the modern Sogetsu schools. His first book, *Japanese Flower Arrangement: Classical and Modern* (1960), set out basic principles. His 'Creative Ideas for Japanese Flower Arrangement' series included *The Beauty of Australia's Wildflowers* (1967), *The Magic of Camellias* (1968) jointly written with E.G. Waterhouse, and *The Poetry of Leaves* (1970), all handsomely designed by Meredith Weatherby. His small book *A Guide to Japanese Flower Arrangement* (1969) capitalised on the burgeoning popularity of Ikebana in Australia. For Sparnon, 'Just as within strict verse some of the world's greatest poetry has been written, within the basic and sometimes strict principles of Ikebana the greatest, and freest, and most creative flower arrangements find their inspiration.' RA

SPARROW, George (1854–1913), gardener and horticulturist, was born in Stowmarket, Suffolk, England, and received his training in a Suffolk nursery and on several estates. He migrated to Adelaide in 1884 to design and lay out Monalta for Alexander George Downer (1839–1916). Sparrow established a farm at Aldgate in the ADELAIDE HILLS and was engaged (c. 1888–1913) by W.A. Horn to design and plant the garden of WAIROA. This included laying out intricate bedding designs to feature rhododendrons, camellias, and Japanese maples; building rustic timber arbours and seats; and design of the reticulated water system.

DAVID JONES

SPENCER, Roger David (b. 1945), horticultural botanist, joined the garden staff at the ROYAL BOTANIC GARDENS, MELBOURNE, in 1972 after the completion of studies at the Universities of Wales (Aberystwyth) and Melbourne. He soon moved from garden to HERBARIUM, where he established a specialist group in horticultural botany responsible for developing the Gardens' plant records and for researching and recording Victoria's cultivated flora. The resulting information base is the most important source of information about the history and nomenclature of cultivated plants in the state and has culminated in Dr Spencer's multi-volume *Horticultural Flora of South-Eastern Australia* (1995–), soon to be completed. This was preceded by published writings (some co-authored) on topics including cultivated plants, silver- and grey-foliaged plants, ELMS, plant nomenclature, and heritage landscapes. He has contributed to various state Floras and is on the committee of the Australian CULTIVAR REGISTRATION AUTHORITY and the ORNAMENTAL PLANT CONSERVATION ASSOCIATION OF AUSTRALIA. Spencer also manages the Greenlife Database™ listing all plants available in the Australian nursery industry, which cross-references common, scientific, commercial, and legally protected names. ML

SPIRITUALITY In the increasingly complex and unpoetic world of today, people seek, as ever, the sanctuary of a GARDEN to provide the needed counterpoise. This universal basic instinct has not altered throughout the centuries—a characteristic of all societies and all religious beliefs. In Nature's cloth are we not all close-knit with creatures, plants, and trees of creation, because we are all part of the same life cycle of birth, life, and death?

Human beings have a need to express themselves creatively and a garden is one way to fulfil that need, for in the act of tending the earth we are all drawn closer to the spirits of other natural things—with birds in song and flowers in bloom, which, by their beauty, seem to take us into another world than this, a place where earth and heaven meet.

The garden designer Russell Page wrote: 'Remember that one of your aims must be to lift people, if only for a moment, above their daily preoccupations. Even a glimpse of beauty will enable them to make a healing contact with their own inner world.' A gardener, Phyllis Coate Stratford, wrote: 'And in the lovely presence/Of such miracles as these,/It seems most meet/To dig the earth/In quiet on my knees'.

Many years ago I had an unforgettable experience, alone in some gardens in Kyoto; they were numinous in mood, expressing what the Japanese people term *yugen* (tranquillity). Although only lightly touching the road where Buddhist feet had trod, through this serenity I glimpsed another path to God.

A sonnet by Michelangelo ends: 'Ravished by all that to the eyes is fair,/And hungry for the joys that truly bless,/My soul can find no stair/To mount to heaven, save earth's loveliness'. The plant kingdom is a treasurehouse of inspiration for poets, artists, and composers, whose souls Nature touches so deeply. Through their harmonies, the composers convey the same effect gardeners seek. All unconsciously pay homage to the Giver of all they express.

Thomas Hardy, in his poem 'The Year's Awakening', asks: 'O vespering bird, how do you know?'. Another poet, Muriel Stuart, ends verses entitled 'The Seed Shop' with: 'And in my hand a forest lies asleep'. In those seeds there lies eternity. In echoing the writers' sense of wonder we question, ever without answers, the mysteries that surround us; but these earthly miracles are surely reassurance enough and give us hope beyond our earth-homed eyes.

It is not possible to single out one flower most sacred to all people. In the literature of both East and West so many differing flowers are regarded with reverence. I like to think that the ones you choose to plant and care for in your garden assume a deeper significance, hallowed, in a sense, by the joy they give and the beauty they impart to others and to you.

JOAN LAW-SMITH

SPOONER, Peter (b. 1919) landscape architect and educator, obtained his diploma in architecture from the Sydney Technical College in 1941 and spent time in the army and in practice before he joined the architectural staff of the College (1949). He later transferred to the University of Technology (now University of New South Wales). Receiving the Byera Hadley travelling scholarship in 1955 he studied LANDSCAPE ARCHITECTURE in the postgraduate course at the University of Durham, England, returning there as a lecturer in charge of the course while Brian Hackett, the professor, was teaching in the USA (1960–61). In 1964 he inaugurated a two-year postgraduate diploma course at the University of New South Wales and then in 1974, having been appointed Professor of Landscape Architecture, with an enrolment of fifteen students he began the first undergraduate course to be established in an Australian university. Spooner took an active role in the formation of the AUSTRALIAN INSTITUTE OF LANDSCAPE ARCHITECTS and in 1968 became its first president. In practice he carried out an impressive range of large-scale works as consultant to the Department of Main Roads (1960–69) and to the Metropolitan Water Sewerage and Drainage Board (1964–76). From 1962 to 1966 he was landscape consultant to his UNIVERSITY, and he designed there the boardwalk (now destroyed) that provided its memorable main entrance, the vice-chancellor's garden, and the chancellor's courtyard. He retired in 1979, and has since lived in England and France.

RICHARD CLOUGH

SPORT Australian PUBLIC PARKS, more speedily than formal 'gardens', have lost space to sportsgrounds. Private suburban gardens might be more mundanely described as the surrounds of the BACKYARD cricket pitch or football ground. At the same time some sports, golf and thoroughbred horseracing in particular, have sought to give their courses a formal garden setting.

Horseracing was one of the first sporting intruders into public parks with Sydney's first race meeting held in HYDE PARK in 1809. The first Australian Rules football match was held in Melbourne's YARRA PARK in the 1850s, and now this park is little more than a CAR PARK for the two enclosed sporting arenas that take up most of its space, the Richmond and Melbourne Cricket Grounds. The site of Australia's pioneer GOLF COURSE, the Australian Golf Club, took up a part of the original Moore Park in Sydney in 1882. Sometimes golf courses erased more utilitarian gardens—Woollahra golf course was sited on a former Chinese market garden. The Adelaide Cricket Ground stands in a key location within the city's GREEN BELT, as does one of the city's racecourses.

Springfield

Suburbs and country towns have speedily sacrificed public space to sports—in Melbourne's west, at Footscray, the municipal botanical reserve was gradually encroached upon by the Western Oval, home to the Footscray cricket and football clubs. Now a few forlorn botanical specimens struggle to survive between parking for players and officials.

CROQUET and BOWLING GREENS, TENNIS COURTS, and netball courts were often included, by permissive occupancy, in suburban public gardens. Melbourne's FLAGSTAFF GARDENS is home to the Melbourne Bowling Club and public netball courts. SWIMMING POOLS too are proud interlopers in public gardens, as seen most spectacularly in the Boy Charlton Pool, sited above the harbour and at one entrance to the Royal Botanic Gardens, Sydney. Such facilities often form focal points for private RESORT gardens.

Designers of RACECOURSES and golf courses have made some attempts to bring a planned-garden quality to their courses. The Castlecove Golf Course in Sydney, for example, was designed by Walter Burley GRIFFIN in 1924, as a partner to the CASTLECRAG residential development. At Flemington Racecourse, visitors to the track descend into a green bowl, lined with magnificent exotic trees. Bookmakers and punters gather under 'The Elms' each Melbourne Cup Carnival, and after the great race, the winning horse is led back to the mounting yard through an avenue of carefully tended ROSES. Other racecourses boast garden entrances and ornamental lakes as well as pavilions and equine garden statuary. Some sportsgrounds even boasted BANDSTANDS and many incorporated distinctive PAVILIONS and grandstands. In the country, ovals were often used as the local SHOWGROUND.

The most recent wave of sports stadia has emphatically departed from garden settings, with their retractable roofing and artificial surfaces. Yet they still, as in the naming of the home of the Australian Open Tennis Championship, Melbourne (originally Flinders) Park, seek to maintain some semblance of sport's traditional link to PUBLIC OPEN SPACE. Meanwhile, the balance in public land management between RECREATION and LEISURE use and facilities for organised, often team-oriented, sport remains a major point of debate.

Wray Vamplew, Katharine Moore, John O'Hara, Richard Cashman, Ian Jobling (eds), *The Oxford Companion to Australian Sport* (Melbourne, 1994)   CHRIS McCONVILLE

SPRINGFIELD, Goulburn, NSW, conveys nineteenth-century pastoral prosperity and the continuous ownership of the Faithful/Maple-Brown family. The 1859 towered Italianate front of the HOMESTEAD is based on a design in J.C. LOUDON's *The Suburban Gardener and Villa Companion* (1838) for 'A Suburban Villa, with the House in the Italian Style and the Ground laid out in the picturesque Manner', and the broad planning of the garden may derive from this source. The Goulburn Plains are windswept grassland, and belts of pine trees and hawthorn hedges shelter the garden, which was celebrated in the nineteenth century for its flowers. The drive is lined by lilacs and crabapples, underplanted with iris. Near the house are mature specimen trees: oaks, a celtis, and *Arbutus unedo* (Irish Strawberry Tree). The garden was considerably simplified in the 1950s and 1970s to achieve a manageable entity.   HOWARD TANNER

A Geelong football team of the Edwardian period poses for the camera at Queen's Park, Newtown (Vic.), illustrating a link between SPORT gardens through the siting of sports facilities PUBLIC PARKS AND GARDENS—an increasingly contested realm as facilities become ever more specialised

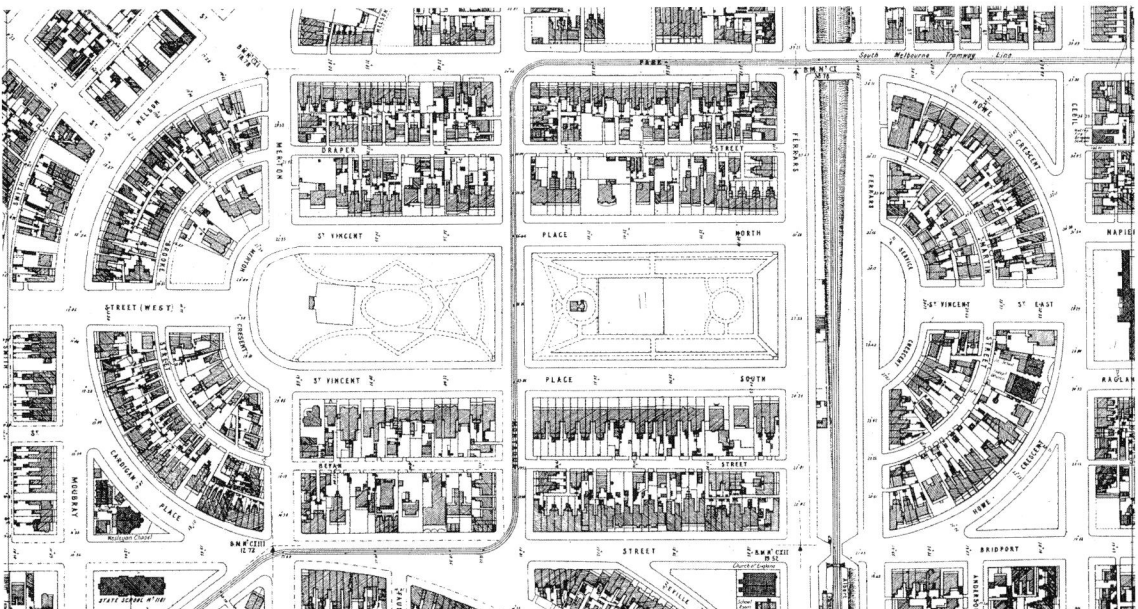

St Vincent Place, Albert Park (Vic.), set out in the 1850s and little changed from this plan of the 1890s, remains one of Australia's most complete examples of an urban SQUARE; it relies for much of its amenity on the central reserve of ST VINCENT GARDENS

SPRINGWOOD, NSW, in the lower BLUE MOUNTAINS, retains a distinctive contribution to Australian gardening through the property (named after the nearby township) of artist Norman Lindsay (1879–1969). In 1912, Lindsay's lover and model, Rose Soady, purchased a forty-two acre (17 ha) bush block from the Foys, a well-known retailing family. Over the next twenty years Lindsay transformed the estate into an antipodean Olympus by adding classical colonnades and a roman COURTYARD to the house and embellishing the grounds with FOUNTAINS and SCULPTURES of nymphs and satyrs, all ingeniously wrought from cement. It was his imagined realisation of Hyperborea, the mythical ancient Greek utopia. Situated on a knoll surrounded by dense bush, the garden's cypress-lined walks lead into a landscape that is purely Australian. The transition is exhilarating. Springwood's garden is a three-dimensional realisation of Lindsay's pictures. The property is now a museum run by the NATIONAL TRUST OF AUSTRALIA (New South Wales).

Ursula Prunster, *The Legendary Lindsays* (Sydney, 1995)

IAN STEPHENSON

SQUARES There are no consistent design themes in the early squares and PLAZAS of Australian urban cities. They were mainly inspired by British examples, but by contrast with those on the great leasehold estates of London they were all developed by government rather than by private owners, they were rarely FENCED, and they were never restricted in access.

The first two designed urban spaces were long narrow strips leading down to a waterfront, and might be classified as parade grounds, but bear comparison with later English examples such as Brunswick Square, Brighton. In each case a GOVERNMENT HOUSE was proposed to be at the head or landward end, and the houses of the principal officers were spaced out along either side. One, planned for Sydney (1788), was never implemented, and the other, at Sydney Cove, Norfolk Island (c. 1793), lasted about two decades until the settlement was abandoned.

In his rationalisation of Hobart in 1811, Governor Macquarie could not achieve a truly rectangular grid, and he reserved a trapezium between Macquarie Street and the government buildings on the waterfront, and called it Georges Square. In the following year his architect, Francis Greenway, prepared a scheme for a major square at the (then) south end of the town of Sydney. It was to measure 180 by 90 metres, in the form of an elongated circus (inspired by Wren's proposals for St Paul's, London) and to have St Andrew's Cathedral as the focus of the south end, and the sides surrounded by public buildings in a classical style. This, Sydney's second attempt at an urban space, was aborted by the intervention of Commissioner J.T. Bigge.

Perth and Adelaide, neither under the administration of NSW, achieved something better. At Perth, Surveyor-General J.S. ROE reserved Church Square (c. 1829–30) on top of a hill, and straddling the intersection of two main streets. Although meant as a church site rather than a public square, it nevertheless was envisaged as being an open site around the church building. Similar church squares were reserved in Fremantle and Guildford soon afterwards, but in Perth the Church of England rejected the site, and the original square, reduced in size, was subsequently occupied by St Mary's (Catholic) Cathedral.

Colonel William LIGHT gave Adelaide the most innovative TOWN PLANNING layout of any Australian colony, including a large central square and four smaller ones disposed about it on the diagonals, each one straddling a street intersection. At first sight the arrangement was reminiscent of James Oglethorpe's design for Savannah, Georgia (1733), but whereas his squares were simply a diagonal grid, intended to be extended indefinitely, Light's scheme was a quincunx centralised on the large space, and incapable of extension because of the GREEN BELT with which he constrained the town. The precedent—if not necessarily the source—was an idealised town design in Pietro di Giacomo Cataneo's *l'Architettura* (Venice, 1567).

In the planning of Melbourne, Robert Hoddle (1794–1881), a surveyor of little imagination, provided occasional squares by dropping out a block or so of the town grid. But when Hoddle was replaced in 1853 by Lieutenant (later Sir) Andrew Clarke (1824–1902), several innovations were introduced. The grandest was a scheme for the suburb of Merriville (near today's Clifton Hill), which had a pair of circuses and, leading from these, an axial sequence of geometric spaces: a hemicircus off the Heidelberg Road and then two spaces with segmental sides. The whole scheme was unmistakably inspired by James Gleeson's design for the Moray Estate in the New Town of Edinburgh, but unfortunately it was never implemented. Clarke's executed designs are less interesting. The most successful was ST VINCENT PLACE, Albert Park (Vic.), though it underwent some modification during the development stages. It was conceived as a space one block long with semicircular ends, probably based upon George Gutch's plan for Tyburnia on the Paddington Estate, London (1838). After the St Kilda railway line was surveyed, severing one of these ends, the square was extended to two blocks, still with curved ends. Despite the insertion of a bowling green and a tennis court—more common than not in such spaces—it is surrounded by some of Melbourne's grandest terrace housing, and remains one of the finest nineteenth-century urban spaces in the country.

MILES LEWIS

STAER, John (1850–1933), botanical collector, seed merchant, nursery proprietor, and pioneer AUSTRALIAN PLANT specialist, was born Johann Ernst Ferdinand Stähr in Crossen, Prussia (now Krosno Odrzanskie, Poland), and aged eight migrated to Adelaide with his father. He spent twenty-seven years in Adelaide and four in Melbourne before moving to Sydney. Staer opened a nursery at Wahroonga and later operated from Blackheath (1914–26). An experienced botanical collector, J.H. MAIDEN thanked him in 1899 for supplying HERBARIUM specimens to SYDNEY BOTANIC GARDENS and later named *Eucalyptus marginata* var. *staeri*, later redescribed as *E. staeri* (Albany Blackbutt), from the type specimen collected by Staer in 1911. He also worked with Gardens' staff sending Australian plants overseas. Staer's 1908 catalogue listed seeds and plants of more than 850 Australian trees, shrubs, herbaceous plants, conifers, orchids, cycads, palms, ferns, and club mosses (including fifty-nine acacias, seventy-four eucalypts, thirty grevilleas, and thirty-two hakeas). These came from all states, with a high proportion from WA—West Australian botanist William Vincent Fitzgerald (1867–1929) is thought to have been in partnership with Staer.

RICHARD CLOUGH

STATE FOREST NURSERIES have provided large quantities of young trees for state FORESTRY plantations and have provided trees and shrubs for official and private plantings. State plantations followed early trial plantings with trees from BOTANIC GARDENS. The first state forest tree nursery was set up at MOUNT MACEDON in Vic. (1872). John Ednie BROWN set up the second at BUNDALEER, SA (1876), and was instrumental in those set up at Gosford, NSW (1887), and Drake's Brook, WA (1899). Small nurseries were established in Qld on Fraser Island (1882) and near Cairns (1902), mainly for Red Cedar, and a large nursery at Imbil (1918) for Hoop Pine. A nursery for state plantations was set up in Tas. in 1922. Smaller district nurseries were also established in several states to reduce the distance seedlings had to be transported.

The range of species needed for the major state forestry plantations was gradually reduced to concentrate on *Pinus radiata* (Radiata or Monterey Pine) in southern Australia; *P. caribaea*, *P. elliottii*, and *Araucaria cunninghamii* (Cuban, Slash, and Hoop Pine) in Qld; *P. radiata* and *P. pinaster* (Maritime Pine) in WA; *Eucalyptus grandis* (Flooded Gum) in NSW; and recently on *E. globulus* (Blue Gum), *E. nitens* (Shining Gum), and *E. regnans* (Mountain Ash) in Tas., Vic., and WA.

Techniques were developed to grow large numbers of seedlings cheaply and transport them in good condition. Most of the CONIFERS and northern hemisphere trees were grown as open-rooted stock. EUCALYPT seeds were sown into earth-filled bamboo tubes in which the seedlings were grown and planted. SA established areas of *Arundo donax* (Spanish or Giant Reed) for the tubes. Qld used metal tubes which were removed immediately prior to planting. Tube systems were replaced by fibre and moulded polythene pots.

The nurseries also grew a wide range of species for state, municipal, and state-supported INSTITUTIONS, and for ARBOR DAY and SCHOOL plantings. Northern hemisphere oaks, ashes, elms, sycamores, walnuts, poplars, and willows were grown from the beginning. For example, the Gosford nursery was growing 159 species of trees and shrubs by 1890.

Some states encouraged planting on farms by distributing free or cheap trees from their nurseries. Private NURSERY proprietors opposed this but were too expensive. SA had the largest program, which distributed eleven million free trees to 63 000 landowners between 1881 and 1924. Opposition and state managerialism eventually defeated state programs and the Mount Macedon nursery closed in 1995. The NATURAL RESOURCES CONSERVATION LEAGUE developed a large nursery from 1949 and numerous small community-based nurseries evolved during the 1990s to support planting by farmers, LANDCARE, and kindred groups encouraged by GREENING AUSTRALIA.

JOHN DARGAVEL

STATION GARDENS: see HOMESTEAD GARDENS

STATUARY: see SCULPTURE

STEAD, David George (1877–1957), marine biologist, naturalist, and conservationist, studied zoology at Sydney Technical

College after leaving school aged 12, but by 1902, his expertise in the area of marine studies led to his being appointed a scientific assistant in the New South Wales Fisheries Commission. He was a key figure in the New South Wales Naturalists' Society from his youth, and in 1898, at age 21, became a member of the LINNEAN SOCIETY OF NEW SOUTH WALES. Later, in 1910, when elected a fellow of the Linnean Society (London), he was said to be the youngest person ever elected to that favoured position. Stead's most important contribution to Australian conservation was as co-founder in 1909 of the **Wild Life** (later Wildlife) **Preservation Society**, the first conservation body in Australia and still a viable society at the start of the twenty-first century. His daughter, Christina (1902–1983), a well-known author, was born to Stead's first wife, Ellen (d. 1904): her autobiographical novel, *The Man who Loved Children* (1940) contains intense reflections of her childhood. Stead had six more children by his second wife, Ada, and on her death in 1951, married botanist Thistle HARRIS. David Stead was one of Australia's most talented pioneer naturalists and conservationists, considered by some to be largely responsible for the ideals and philosophy behind the Australian environment movement.

JOAN WEBB

STEELE, Richard (*fl.* 1790s), was the author of *An Essay Upon Gardening, Containing a Catalogue of Exotic Plants for the Stove and Green-houses of the British Gardens* (1793), the earliest known GARDENING BOOK to discuss plants from New Holland, New Zealand, and New Caledonia. Steele lived in Yorkshire, England, at Sion-hill (near Thirsk) and wrote from experience, although the novelty of plants from NSW was evident in his (erroneous) advice to propagate EUCALYPTS from cuttings. He included lengthy 'Observations on the Stove, the Hot-House, &c.', gave 'Directions for the preservation of seeds' (by covering in bees wax), and among New Holland plants he listed 'Casuarina Torulosa' (*Allocasuarina torulosa*, Rose She-oak), 'Casuarina Stricta' (*A. verticillata*, Drooping She-oak), *Eucalyptus obliqua* (Messmate Stringybark), and 'Mimosa verticillata' (*Acacia verticillata*, Prickly Moses) in his catalogue. Steele implored his dedicatees to 'cherish and preserve those great curiosities of the vegetable kingdom, which the bold and adventurous have, with extreme hazard and difficulty collected'. A second issue of the *Essay* was published in 1800.

RA

STEPHENSON, Gordon (1908–1997), English-born architect, planner, and academic, had a distinguished professional and teaching career in England, Canada, and Australia before settling permanently in Perth in the early 1960s. His humanist approach to TOWN PLANNING and URBAN DESIGN earned him the accolade of 'practical idealist'. He is best known in WA as co-author of the *Plan for the Metropolitan Region Perth & Fremantle* (1955), from which extensive open space reservations along the coastline, foreshores of the Swan and Canning rivers and the Darling Scarp are an enduring legacy. A strong landscape design ethos is central to his campus plans for the University of Western Australia (UWA, 1954–65), Murdoch University (1973), and the Joondalup Regional Centre (1977).

Stephenson also designed campus plans for Adelaide, Flinders, and James Cook Universities. He was consultant to the National Capital Development Commission for projects in Canberra, a member of the National Capital Planning Committee (1967–73), and was foundation Professor of Architecture at UWA (1965–72).

OLINE RICHARDS

STEVENS, John Martin (b. 1920), landscape architect, graduated from BURNLEY School of Primary Agriculture and Horticulture in 1938 and worked as a garden designer with Melbourne landscape contractors R.P. Knight and Co. After serving in the Australian Army (1940–45), he graduated with a Bachelor of Agricultural Science degree from the University of Melbourne (1949). For the next three years he was assistant to Professor Sir Samuel Wadham, President of the Royal Agricultural Society of Victoria, and also served as the Society's secretary.

In 1952, on the advice of architect Roy Grounds (1905–1981), Stevens began his own LANDSCAPE ARCHITECTURE firm, the first such office in Vic. and one of the first in Australia. His clients included leading architects of the day: Grounds, Robin Boyd, Stephenson and Turner, Bates Smart and McCutcheon, and Godfrey Spowers. The scope and variety of projects, especially for high-rise office buildings, INDUSTRIAL sites, and UNIVERSITIES, set new standards for non-residential garden design in Australia. Early projects such as the Vacuum Oil Refinery, Altona (1953), and Shell Refinery, Corio (1955), were carried out in association with landscape designer Emily GIBSON. Inspired by the dramatic shapes and colours of landscapes by Brazilian designer Roberto Burle Marx, his most innovative gardens were for skyscrapers, notably ICI House, Melbourne (1955–58). The inclusion of SUCCULENTS, FOUNTAINS, and abstract SCULPTURE made these collaborative projects a distinctive MODERNIST contribution to the post-war city. Other important projects included landscape designs for Wilson Hall, University of Melbourne (1956), Southgate Fountain, Melbourne (1958–59), ETA Factory, Braybrook (1958–59), Mobil House, South Melbourne (1960–61), Chadstone Shopping Centre (1961), and South British Insurance Co., Melbourne (1961). Stevens was instrumental in formulating landscape master plans for Monash University, Clayton (1960–63) and the Memorial Park Crematorium, Altona North (1958–62).

Stevens was Visiting Lecturer in Landscape Design at the University of Melbourne (1954–64), through which he influenced a generation of architecture and TOWN PLANNING students. In 1964 he left private practice to become landscape architect to the Australian National University (1964–87); during that time its grounds came to be nationally acclaimed as one of the country's most beautiful institutional landscapes. In 1977 Stevens returned to private practice in Melbourne. He was a founding member of the AUSTRALIAN INSTITUTE OF LANDSCAPE ARCHITECTS and active in the field of HERITAGE conservation.

PHILIP GOAD

STEVENSON, George (1799–1856), editor and horticulturist, was born at Berwick upon Tweed, Northumberland,

England, and following a varied career was appointed editor of the London *Globe* (1835). In 1836 he was appointed secretary to Governor Hindmarsh and clerk of the council in the new province of SOUTH AUSTRALIA, and also founded and edited the *South Australian Gazette and Colonial Register*. He arrived in SA later that year and continued his fiery journalism, resulting in antagonism and libel cases. Through the *Gazette* (and other newspapers with which he was later associated) he advocated and advised on gardening and horticulture, and helped form the Natural History Society. His detailed lectures on horticulture in 1840 were the first on this topic in SA. In 1838 he employed George MCEWIN as gardener at his North Adelaide residence to create 'the best garden in Adelaide', growing both ornamental and economic plants, and commissioned McEwin to write the *South Australian Vigneron and Gardeners' Manual* (1843), the first GARDENING BOOK published in SA. This garden was influential in cultivating perhaps the first vines and almonds in SA. He also founded 'Stevenson's Garden' or LEAWOOD Nursery in 1842, long known for its camellias, and fruit and nut trees (including figs and almonds), and as an important social venue for parties, suppers, and teas. On his death, the REGISTER recorded his ability to 'foster the love of gardens' and his well-earned designation as 'Father of Horticulture in South Australia'.

DAVID JONES

STEWART, Thomas Adams (1871–1946), accountant and rosarian, was born in Melbourne and joined the NATIONAL ROSE SOCIETY of Victoria soon after its foundation. A keen judge of ROSES, he occupied the Society's presidential chair for several terms and was for many years a member of the executive. It was, however, his position as foundation editor (1928–46) of *Australian Rose Annual* that distinguished his service to Australian horticulture. Under his guidance the yearbook stood confidently alongside its British and North American companions, and his high standards continue to exert a beneficial influence over this long-running publication. He is commemorated in the T.A. Stewart Memorial Award (1948–) for 'outstanding service to the rose in Australia or New Zealand'. His son, Thomas Gerrard Stewart (1901–1969), commenced a well-known rose nursery at Box Hill in the early 1930s.

RA

STINTON, William (*c.* 1847–1931), nursery proprietor, was born in England and arrived in Geelong (Vic.) in 1854 accompanying his parents. Following an apprenticeship at the Kardinia Nursery of Thomas ADCOCK he established a nursery at Belmont in 1880. He transferred to Newtown in 1888, a further move coming in 1906 to Fairview (later Stinton) Street, Newtown. Here in 1910 the Claremont Nursery was established and his son Frederick William Stinton (*c.* 1889–1957) joined him. William's wife, (Sarah) Louisa Stinton (née Nash) (*c.* 1856–1918), conducted a successful florist's shop in Geelong, providing a valuable publicity showcase. Fred studied with noted American plant breeder Luther Burbank during 1918–19, thereafter developing ranunculus as a prime product. Additional ground at Moolap was procured and selective breeding produced

Louisa STINTON's 1895 advertisement in *The Wombat* (1895), published by the associations at the Gordon Technical College, Geelong (Vic.), is an uncommon public acknowledgment of female involvement in the nineteenth-century NURSERY trade

excellent results. Many BULBS, including a large proportion of Leonard Buckland's daffodil collection, were also grown. Administration and the mail-order department were transferred to the Moolap bulb fields in 1959, but the widely admired business closed in 1965.

GEORGE JONES

STIRLING, Edward Charles (1848–1919), surgeon, scientist, and politician, son of Edward Stirling (1804–1873)—after whom two South Australian towns are named—was director of the South Australian Museum (1884–1912). An ardent horticulturist, he argued for the reservation of Flinders Chase National Park and developed ST VIGEANS in the ADELAIDE HILLS into a significant RHODODENDRON garden. English nursery proprietor J. Waterer honoured him with the rhododendron 'Mrs E.C. Stirling'. His brother, John Lancelot Stirling (1849–1932), supported many agricultural and zoological societies, and was a trustee for the STRATHALBYN SOLDIERS' MEMORIAL GARDENS Endowment Fund

DAVID JONES

STIRLING GARDENS (formerly Stirling Square), at the corner of St Georges Terrace and Barrack Street, Perth, was proclaimed a PUBLIC GARDEN in 1845. Initially utilised as a leased market garden, it was given over to public use in 1858 and used for PROMENADES, recreation, and band concerts. In the late nineteenth century it also served as an ACCLIMATISATION and BOTANIC GARDEN for WA, and for meteorological observations. The site has variously been known as the public gardens, government gardens, botanic gardens, and Treasury Gardens, and is named after Governor Stirling. Over the years, the site has housed a small glasshouse, fernery, drinking fountain, and a memorial to the public benefactor Charles McNess (1852–1938). Today council house (1962) is sited here, plus an 'ore obelisk' (1971), public memorials, a water feature with kangaroo sculptures, and many century-old specimens of palms, pines, oaks, and a giant bamboo clump.

JOHN VISKA

STONES, Ellis ('Rocky') (1895–1975), was a self-taught landscape designer whose outstanding talent was the use of ROCK, stone, or huge mossy boulders in simple landscapes of great naturalness and beauty. 'It is a rare thing this gift for placing stones, and strange that a man possessing it should bear the name Stones', Edna WALLING wrote in *Australian Home Beautiful* in 1938.

Stones did not enter the field until he was 40. Working on a building site in Heidelberg, where Walling was creating a garden, he offered to construct a rock wall for her. She recognised his innate ability and said she would give him work. She was Victoria's 'name' garden designer of the day, so this was a considerable opportunity—in terms of general experience, and of introductions to clients who could afford to spend money on garden design.

Stones soon began securing work on his own account, but in this initial stage he built many FORMAL landscape features such as WALLS, steps, and paving for Walling, as well as informal outcrops and pools, which were something quite new in the 1930s. Uncharacteristically Walling, whose specifications were always precise, gave him free rein in the design of these NATURAL-looking elements, which he executed with such sureness of touch. An outstanding collaboration was the Hughes-Jones swimming pool at Olinda (1939). For the next twenty-five years Walling continued to recommend him to clients who wanted this kind of work. He always acknowledged her seminal influence on his career.

Born in Wodonga (Vic.), Ellis Stones had grown up in the outer Melbourne suburb of Essendon, which in those days was more country than city, and he trained as a carpenter before fighting in the First World War. A severe wound sustained at the Gallipoli landing saw him invalided home. For the rest of his life he walked with a limp and suffered acute pain—which he did not discuss—in one leg. Although incapacitated he would not accept a pension, and worked as a carpenter and builder in outback NSW and country Vic. through the 1920s and the early Depression years. He returned to Melbourne with his wife and young family around 1932. Battling illness and lack of opportunity, eking out a living from odd jobs, his meeting with Walling was fortuitous. He never looked back.

Stones had an artist's eye, and an intuitive awareness of the contours and details of the natural landscape. As Walling said after their first meeting, he was a 'natural'. He built his own gardens, but he did not draw plans until the late 1960s, when clients started to demand them. But although he made his reputation with gardens, his broader mission was to bring a flavour of the country to the city, to soften the incursions of bricks and asphalt, to allow people to re-create around their homes spaces that evoked the atmosphere of the BUSH as an antidote to the stresses of modern life. He was one of Victoria's first and most vocal conservationists, and his enduring crusade was the protection of Melbourne's Yarra River and its tributary creeks and billabongs. Many of his most beautiful gardens had frontages to the river, particularly the Tanner garden (substantially altered) in Templestowe (1961) and the Hawthorne garden (demolished) in Hawthorn (1963–64).

Stones served in the Civil Construction Corps during the Second World War, then built up his business through the 1940s to early 1960s. Many of his employees, such as Margot KNOX, Gordon FORD, Bob Grant, and Beverley Hanson, went on to make their own names in the field. For a time he ran a nursery near his home in Ivanhoe (a stone's throw from the Yarra River) as a source of plants for his gardens. In the mid-1950s he was a co-founder of the Save the Yarra League. From 1962 he was involved in moves to establish a professional institute for landscape architects. A special membership category was established for practitioners such as Stones, Ford, Alistair KNOX, and Bruce MACKENZIE, who lacked formal qualifications. He became an affiliate of the AUSTRALIAN INSTITUTE OF LANDSCAPE ARCHITECTS in 1967, an honorary fellow in 1975.

Most of his large commissions were private gardens and it was not until the mid-1960s, when Stones was at retiring age, that broad-scale recognition arrived. Important designs in the public arena included a lake and outcrop at COMO, South Yarra (mid-1960s), median planting in Springvale Road, Nunawading (1965), an outcrop in the ROYAL BOTANIC GARDENS, MELBOURNE (1966), and the Wilson Reserve playground, Ivanhoe (1968). His advancing years and indifferent health were no deterrent—he was thrilled at being able to promote his beliefs to the public at large.

A further prized commission gave him an even wider canvas. In 1965 the exciting new project housing firm, Merchant Builders, put Stones in charge of gardens and public spaces around their architect-designed houses. This exposure to the mass market made him a household name and resulted in one development, Elliston at Rosanna, being named for him. Between 1970 and 1975 he wrote a regular column in *Australian Home Beautiful* (for which he had also written in 1946). His book *Australian Garden Design* (1971) sold 50 000 copies; a posthumous publication, *The Ellis Stones Garden Book* (1976), went to two editions. Up to the end of his life he worked 10 and 12-hour days, which often finished with an evening lecture to a community group about garden design or conservation. His enthusiasm was contagious. 'I can't slow down', he would say. 'They won't let me.' He died after a day spent placing rocks along a reach of Salt Creek at Rosanna (1975).

Stones used AUSTRALIAN PLANTS in his gardens from the late 1930s, searching out sources such as SCHUBERT's Noble Park nursery and ALTHOFER's Nindethana mail-order service. He was a fervent advocate of native plants, loving them for their delicacy and strength, and because they fitted so well with his preferred elements of stone, river pebbles, timber, and WATER. But he did not force them on his clients. Gardens, he maintained, were for people, and a client's preferences were important.

Like Thomas Church, the American landscape architect whose writings he sought out in the 1950s, he saw gardens as extensions of the houses they surrounded. His gardens always had 'special' spots—a secret corner where children could hide, a place for a housewife to shell the peas. He liked curving paths, hidden boundaries, and 'borrowed' elements such as neighbouring trees. His plant palette was not broad; 'repeat and repeat', he would say. His maxim was 'be bold', and all his life he stressed that nature was the greatest teacher. When people complimented him on an effect he had achieved he would say; 'Take a walk down any bush track and you'll see that God does it a whole lot easier and a whole lot better'.

The ITALIANATE formality of the terraces of STONNINGTON, Malvern (Vic.), contrasted with the more picturesquely informal lawns and shrubberies that bounded and framed the house and its garden

After his death an appeal was begun in his name to raise funds for a chair of landscape architecture at the University of Melbourne. While the chair does not bear his name, the Ellis Stones Memorial Award is presented biennially for an outstanding piece of student work.

Anne Latreille, *The Natural Garden: Ellis Stones: His Life and Work* (Ringwood, Vic., 1990)   **ANNE LATREILLE**

STONES, (Elsie) Margaret (b. 1920), botanical artist, was born at Colac (Vic.) and studied at Swinburne Technical College and the National Gallery Art School. In 1946 she began painting plants while confined to bed with tuberculosis, sketching wildflowers brought by friends. In 1951 she left Melbourne for England and the ROYAL BOTANIC GARDENS, KEW, where she worked on various Floras and produced more than 400 plant portraits (1958–83) for *CURTIS's Botanical Magazine*, becoming its principal contributing artist. Commissioned in 1961 by the Commonwealth Art Advisory Board for twenty watercolours of Australian flowers, she visited Australia, where she received Lord TALBOT's request for drawings of Tasmanian plants. This grew into *The Endemic Flora of Tasmania* (1967–78). She quickly and accurately captured the beauty of fresh specimens air-freighted from Tas., and sent annotated sketches of magnified sections to Winifred CURTIS to facilitate taxonomic classification and specimen pieces to the Royal Botanic Gardens, Kew, for propagation. Her exquisite botanical drawings of 254 endemic Tasmanian plants hang in the Queen Victoria Museum and Art Gallery, Launceston (Tas.). She also executed commissions for the ROYAL HORTICULTURAL SOCIETY, London; the Moreton Arboretum, Illinois; Lousiana State University; and the Maud Gibson Trust, Melbourne. She received honorary Doctorates of Science from Lousiana State University (1986) and the University of Melbourne (1989) for her contributions to botany. Her exceptional artistic skill and botanical insight bring the beauty of distant and little-known plants to the eyes of gardeners everywhere.

Irena Zdanowicz, *Beauty in Truth* (Melbourne, 1996)
LINDEN GILLBANK

STONNINGTON, Malvern, Vic., now comprises the core of an 1890s MANSION estate, developed by coach proprietor John Wagner (1827–1901), and later used as Victoria's GOVERNMENT HOUSE (1901–30). The garden combines picturesque and geometric themes, best exemplified by the eastern terrace with its impressive balustrade and sweeping steps, which extend the architecture of the house into the landscape. Other features include the original cast- and wrought-iron entry gates and iron palisade fence, curving drive, sweeping main lawn, and mature trees, shrubberies, and garden beds. Notable trees remaining from the nineteenth century include a large *Cedrus atlantica* f. *glauca* (Blue Atlas Cedar), a pair of large *Quercus canariensis* (Algerian Oak) flanking the terrace stairs, *Trachycarpus fortunei* (Chinese Windmill Palm), *Cedrus deodara* (Deodar) on the main lawn, and a stand of mature ARAUCARIAS—(including the uncommon *A. columnaris*, Captain Cook's Pine), which strategically screen the residence from the entrance gates. Now a campus of Deakin University, its significance is reflected in the naming of the City of Stonnington (1994). CARMEL McPHEE

STORY, George Fordyce (1800–1885), medical practitioner, botanist, naturalist, and plant collector, travelled to Van Diemen's Land in 1828 as surgeon on the *Mary* with his childhood friend Francis Cotton (1801–1883). In 1829 Story was appointed assistant surgeon at Waterloo Point Military Station on the East Coast, where he ultimately settled with the Cotton family on their grazing property Kelvedon. A keen observer, he kept regular meteorological records for the ROYAL SOCIETY of Van Diemen's Land, sent minerals and bird skins to the FRANKLINS, ferns to James BACKHOUSE, and botanical specimens to MUELLER. He was briefly Secretary of the Royal Society and Superintendent of their gardens (1844–45) but returned to his medical practice when the government grant was not renewed. His meticulous notes reveal his keen scientific interest in the development of the Kelvedon garden and include *Flora Tasmaniensis* (1850), an impressive catalogue (with comments) of more than 1000 plants of the colony.

SALLYANN DAKIS

STOVE, in European gardens, was a heated and generally glazed building providing a specialised environment for the growth of plants requiring considerable heat. Often utilising dry heat from flues or hot beds (of bark, dung, or other fermenting substance), the term was used with less discrimination after the advent of steam and, later, hot-water heating. In Australia this more general usage of the term stove was common in the nineteenth century to describe a heated GREENHOUSE or HOTHOUSE. RA

THE STRAND, Townsville, Qld: see ANZAC PARK, Townsville, Qld

STRATHALBYN SOLDIERS' MEMORIAL GARDEN, SA, a civic garden on a sweeping bend on the River Angas, was developed from 1869 through spirited community initiatives led by father and son, Joseph (1833–1883) and Joseph William Elliott (1859–1939), and with design advice and plantings from Richard SCHOMBURGK, John F. BAILEY, and Harold GREAVES. The installation of a bronze bas-relief memorial monument by C. Douglas Richardson (1853–1932), and the official opening as the Soldiers' Memorial Garden (1921), followed erection of a cast-iron bandstand (1913) and concrete Childrens' Bridge (1919).

DAVID JONES

STRAWBERRY HILL, Albany, WA, was the location in 1827 of the first land to be farmed in WA as a government farm. Captain Richard Spencer (1779–1839) purchased land, including the cleared Strawberry Hill farm, before arriving as the Government Resident in 1833, bringing out his family and agricultural workers as well as plants and animals. In 1889 the reduced site was bought by architect Francis Bird, who set about restoring the house and outbuildings, developing the gardens, and establishing croquet lawns. The early two-storey stone house and agricultural worker's cottage are extant, and pear trees from the Spencer era still grow in the orchard. Some original plantings along the drive survive, including two aged *Araucaria heterophylla* (Norfolk Island Pine), as do indigenous eucalypts that survived early clearing. The property was vested in the NATIONAL TRUST OF AUSTRALIA (Western Australia) in 1964.

JOHN VISKA

STREET AND ROADSIDE PLANTING in Australia has evolved from a number of influences, including eighteenth-century utopianism about the Antipodes as a 'Garden of Eden' and interest in AUSTRALIAN PLANTS, as well as British models for colonial TOWN PLANS, characterised by wide streets in grid layout, planted with shade trees. The intense interest in Australian plants was a significant impetus to settle NSW and PLANT COLLECTORS had an important influence on the progress of settlement. The early governors collected plants, and official plant collectors became explorers who opened up the hinterland. The plants collected were initially ACCLIMATISED in the SYDNEY BOTANIC GARDENS, shade trees being used later for the early public AVENUES.

The species used and the form of the urban avenue in nineteenth-century Australia resulted from the sources of trees, and the influences of key individuals and horticultural developments. Initially these influences came from HORTICULTURAL and philosophical or ROYAL SOCIETIES where trees for town design were discussed. Later the influences came from the directors of BOTANIC GARDENS and FORESTRY departments. The early avenues to private estates included oaks, pines, olives, and citrus, collected from botanic gardens at Rio de Janeiro and Cape Town. After twenty years the EXPERIMENTAL GARDEN within the Sydney Botanic Gardens was propagating an extensive range of rainforest species collected by Allan CUNNINGHAM and Charles FRASER. In 1847 the first public avenue of *Ficus macrophylla* (Moreton Bay Fig) was planted in Sydney's Outer DOMAIN from trees propagated in the experimental garden. In 1848 Charles MOORE became Director of the Sydney Botanic Gardens and during his directorship he influenced the choice of trees used in the streets of Sydney and country town in NSW. He mainly recommended and supplied pines and RAINFOREST trees, such as *Grevillea robusta* (Silky Oak) and the Moreton Bay fig. By the 1870s, due to the climatic variations, the cold tableland towns were using deciduous exotic trees, particularly in the south, influenced by the Director of MELBOURNE BOTANIC GARDENS, Ferdinand MUELLER. To the west of NSW and later in WA, trees were recommended and supplied by the South Australian Conservator of Forest, John Ednie BROWN. These were mainly *Eucalyptus cladocalyx* (Sugar Gum) and *Schinus molle* (Pepper Tree).

The condition of the roads between the towns acted against roadside planting, but the poor road conditions encouraged the development of local government. During the 1870s some of the larger towns responded to their municipal status by planting street trees outside important buildings such as

Street and roadside planting

These details of STREET TREE planting in John Ednie Brown's *A Practical Treatise on Tree Culture in South Australia* (1881) were published at a time of increasing urbanisation of Australia's cities, and embraced the expansive vision that characterised TOWN PLANNING of the mid-nineteenth century

town halls, or along fast-developing BOULEVARDS (such as Ballarat's Sturt Street, Vic.). By the 1880s, concern about the issues of rural deforestation and urban sanitation resulted in initiatives to plant trees in the countryside and in the towns, culminating in 1889 in ARBOR DAY. The trees were generally supplied by STATE FOREST NURSERIES. Between 1890 and 1893 more than 300 000 trees were planted in the streets, and parks of NSW country towns alone. Moore's successor, J.H. MAIDEN, wrote prolifically on many topics, including street planting. He recommended PALMS, in particular the *Phoenix canariensis* (Canary Island Date Palm), to be planted centrally in wide streets.

Individuals and issues had more influence on street planting than events such as the centenary and Federation, which did not promote extensive planting. Both world wars resulted in the planting of MEMORIAL avenues, often of poplars or *Brachychiton populneus* (Kurrajong) and the coronation of King George VI (1937) initiated a program of street and roadside planting. The most significant roadside planting in NSW resulted from the Department of Main Roads roadside tree program during the 1930s, which involved extensive tree planting along roadsides over the state. Vic. had similar roadside planting programs, encouraged by the VICTORIAN TREE PLANTERS' ASSOCIATION, and later the writings of enthusiasts such as Edna WALLING, who also strongly advocated the retention of existing vegetation in her book *The Australian Roadside* (1952). The advent of services in the street, the needs of the car, and stormwater drainage affected the amount of street and roadside planting from the 1920s to the 1960s, especially on NATURE STRIPS.

By the 1970s, rural deforestation and urban pollution again initiated intense tree planting, including street trees. There was a resurgence of interest in Australian trees, although not as a civic design response but instead as an ECOLOGICAL response to the ENVIRONMENT movement. As a result, the trees selected were predominantly EUCALYPTS, she-oaks, paperbarks, and bottlebrush, often planted in simulated bush settings. By the 1980s, much of the 1970s tree planting was in conflict with overhead utilities and, due to their evergreen habit, were interfering with solar access to energy-conscious housing. This resulted in an interest in smaller deciduous trees. In the mid-1980s enthusiasm for HERITAGE issues revealed an interest in reinstating nineteenth-century avenues.

Street and roadside plantings show similarities, due to the sources of trees and influences on tree planting, but there are also regional differences. Similarities reflect different historical eras and although the early oak and pine avenues have gone, there is still evidence of the subsequent historic eras of street planting. Some Moreton Bay fig avenues remain in Sydney, Melbourne, and Adelaide. Central rows of Canary Island palms are still found in rural towns. Poplar approach avenues from the 1930 roadside tree program also persist in many areas. Memorial avenues of poplars and kurrajongs also exist in many towns.

Regional differences in street and roadside planting mainly result from the effects of CLIMATE and SOILS. This is particularly evident in the arid central regions of Australia and along the coast, where both regions have harsh conditions for tree growth. Street and roadside trees in the different regions in eastern Australia can be baldly summarised as *Eucalyptus torquata* (Coral Gum), pepper trees, and *Tamarix* spp. (Tamarisk) in the dry regions; sugar gums, pepper trees, *Melia azedarach* (White Cedar), and kurrajongs on the western slopes of the divide in the south eastern states; pines, ELMS, *Platanus* X *acerfolia* (Plane Tree), and pin oaks on the tablelands; *Araucaria hetrophylla* and *A. bidwillii* (Norfolk Island Pine and Bunya Pine), FIGS, *Lophostemon confertus* (Brush Box), jacarandas, *Cinnamomum camphora* (Camphor Laurel), and coral trees along the coast. In WA, brush box and *Agonis flexuosa* (Weeping Peppermint) have also been popular choices.

HELEN ARMSTRONG

STUART, Charles (1802–1877), gardener and botanical collector, started collecting seeds and plants for Ferdinand MUELLER shortly after the Mueller's arrival in SA. Stuart, assisted occasionally by William ARCHER, also collected in Van Diemen's Land (1848–52), Vic., and NSW. He donated plants to the MELBOURNE BOTANIC GARDENS (1859) and Mueller named *Helipterum stuartianum* (now *H. floribundum* var. *stuartianum*) and *Polyclymma stuartii* (now *Myriocephalus stuartii*) for him. Stuart seemed resigned to an impecunious life, often ill and 'plunged into poverty'. After a decade-long correspondence and friendship Mueller learnt some 'unfavourable episodes' of his history and requested BENTHAM not to publish any notes on Stuart in *Flora Australiensis* (but Mueller later spoke with concern for his colleague's welfare). RA

STUCKEY, Kenneth John (1910–1991), horticulturist and AUSTRALIAN PLANT cultivator, established 'Stuckey's Folly' at Furner, near Millicent (SA) *c.* 1960. This comprised an extensive collection of Proteaceae, including numerous GREVILLEAS, BANKSIAS, hakeas, isopogons, and dryandras. An avid collector, he corresponded with LINDNER, GORDON, ALTHOFER, and Alf GRAY, and pioneered the cultivation of banksia flowers and dryandra foliage for export to Japan in the 1980s. DAVID JONES and JOHN WALTER

STURROCK, Alexander Corsar (*c.* 1829–1909), gardener and seed merchant, was born at Arbroath, Scotland. Giving his occupation as 'mechanic', he arrived at Port Phillip in 1854 as an unassisted passenger. In 1861 he was elected a member of the Victorian Gardeners' Mutual Improvement Society, proposed by William ADAMSON and seconded by Joseph HARRIS; Sturrock was then living in Brunswick and gave his trade as gardener. His advertisement in *The Australian Gardener* (1862) was more specific: 'A.C. Sturrock, Jobbing Gardener, &c. Gardens Laid Out and Planted, or kept by Contract. Order at Smith & Adamson's, 71 Collins Street West. Punctually Attended to.' When Smith and Adamson dissolved their partnership in 1862, Sturrock was a witness to the documents, and by 1866 he was working with Adamson in his nursery. He 'revised and corrected' the ninth edition of Adamson's *The Australian Gardener* (1875), the year of his mentor's death. Sturrock compiled a rival book, *The Australian Gardeners' Guide: An Epitome of Horticulture for the Colony of Victoria* in 1879, marking the commencement of his own Melbourne seed business; the book title paid unsubtle homage to the commercial success of its long-established rival. Sturrock died at his residence in Blyth Street, Brunswick, aged 80, respected as one of the last surviving members of the horticultural world who had emigrated in the immediate wake of Victoria's gold discoveries. RA

STYLES of GARDENS and other DESIGNED LANDSCAPES in Australia are generally based on an accepted international taxonomy, but categorising individual gardens requires an understanding of complex factors varying with time, climate, location, original design intent, and subsequent interventions. Classifying design into 'styles' is a well-established practice and has been applied to all forms of human artistic or creative endeavour. Style and fashion are not the same: fashion refers to the fluctuating preferences that carry social prestige—style, like taxonomy, is a particular classification approach. The field of stylistic analysis is dynamic, constantly absorbing and reflecting the theoretical and philosophical developments of the changing times. Hence, there is no single definition of style as a concept, no static framework into which works of art and design are classified. Even the word describing the concept of classifying design has changed— beginning with 'manner' in the sixteenth century, 'taste' in the eighteenth century, and arriving at 'style' in the nineteenth century. The word derives from both the ancient Greek *stylos* (pertaining to the orders of architecture) and the Latin *stilus* (writing instrument) and its subsequent meaning in literature as a manner of writing involving the doctrine of *decorum* (appropriateness of style to the occasion). One of many dictionary meanings of 'style' is a 'mode or form of skilled construction, execution, or production … determined by manner of composition or construction, or by outward appearance'. For the keen observer of garden design, there is more to the nature of style than its outward appearance.

For stylistic categories to exist, there must be an agreed designation of the particular characteristics or common determinants upon which differences in style are judged. In art, these determinants are differences in the use of conventions, materials, techniques, motifs, relationships between forms or motifs, and qualities of expression. For garden and landscape design, these determinants can be summarised as the differences between components (built and plant features), arrangements (layout), and characters (ambience and visual qualities), which are all concerned with form. The other key determinant is content—the philosophies, beliefs, ideas, and intentions behind these forms.

Australian architectural historians Richard Apperly, Robert Irving, and Peter Reynolds, in *A Pictorial Guide to Identifying Australian Architecture* (1989), perceived three assemblages of styles: *contrived* ('high styles', by architects); *popular* (when 'elements of one or more contrived styles are borrowed and used—sometimes naively, anachronistically, incorrectly, incompletely or out of context'); and *vernacular* ('stable, self-sufficient communities where choice is severely limited and where sound architectural solutions have been evolved by trial and error'). These authors also devised a binomial system for describing architectural design in Australia consisting of a historical period name and a stylistic epithet (such as Victorian Gothic or Interwar Classicism). No binomial system or assemblages of styles has been devised for garden design in Australia, although the options are currently being explored by those interested in achieving such a system.

Existing terms show the immense influence of British garden design in Australia, especially during the nineteenth and early twentieth centuries. Styles such as the English Landscape School, with its emphasis on such elements as beauty and smoothness, the PICTURESQUE and SUBLIME, GARDENESQUE, and various FORMAL and NATURAL styles, were well adapted to Australia. Many of these incorporated stylistic components such as BEDDING (including carpet

Australian's PUBLIC PARKS AND GARDENS included a wide range of garden types and styles, ranging from highly maintained and well used public gardens such as SUBIACO MUNICIPAL GARDENS (WA) to reserves in smaller centres that were bypassed in the rush towards prosperity—all are now vital public assets under considerable pressure from economic rationalism

bedding), ALPINE GARDENS, and ROCK GARDENS, which through their distinctive constituent elements also formed specialised stylistic categories.

Whatever stylistic categories are used to describe garden and landscape design in Australia, there is a fundamental classification that prevails overall. This is the three-fold design system of informal (irregular, romantic), formal (regular, classical), and utilitarian (perhaps the only form of vernacular design in this country). For instance COTTAGE GARDENS and BUSH GARDENS mark the informal end of the spectrum, while ITALIANATE and CITY BEAUTIFUL designs are mostly formal. ARTS AND CRAFTS gardens may combine elements of both extremes. Traditional KITCHEN GARDENS, ORCHARDS, and FORESTRY plantations all draw upon utilitarian design arrangements. These overall stylistic groups can be traced to the writings of LOUDON (and his contemporaries), who classified gardens styles as either 'ancient' (formal, geometric) or 'modern' (informal, naturalistic). Similarly, KEMP classified design into three styles: 'geometric', 'gardenesque' ('the mixed, or middle style'), and 'picturesque' (naturalistic). Sometimes, individualistic approaches to garden design are grouped under headings such as QUIRKY GARDENS, or plant-enthusiasts' gardens.

Some recent theorists (including some modernists, post-structuralists, and post-modernists) have questioned whether style is a creditable concept. However, in both architectural and landscape architectural spheres, the recognition of stylistic categories as worthwhile concepts is gaining credence again. The Modernist approach to functional design incorrectly concluded that styles were merely the result of fashion and not founded in good design. Now, such ideas are considered to be another stylistic philosophy (MODERNISM or International Style) and newer landscape design movements have arisen, including post-modernism, deconstructionism, avant-garde, and an ecological style. The eclecticism in style of the nineteenth century returned in the late twentieth century. Whether in architecture, interiors, furniture, landscapes, or gardens, design as an artform is more than just solving problems (the traditional functionalist approach). Perhaps, when current design attitudes recognise the relevance of stylistic concepts, design will have a sound theoretical foundation and be expressive again—reflecting changing social structures, customs, beliefs, attitudes, and technological development. The recent awakening of interest in the meanings attached to 'place' (including landscapes and gardens) may help provide this depth of understanding. There is also a powerful influence from science (biology and related disciplines) in providing scientific and technological inputs particularly relating to an ecological understanding of landscapes.

One way of describing garden design is to combine design style (visual form, arrangement, and character) with the process of gardening (practices) and the designer's attitudes or intentions (strategies). This approach provides a greater understanding of the diversity inherent in gardens and the dual roles of gardener and designer in influencing the end result.

J. Mordaunt Crook, *The Dilemma of Style: Architectural Ideas from the Picturesque to Post-Modern* (London, 1989); Jeannie Sim, *Landscape Design Theory Primer: Explorations and Expectations in Landscape Design* (Brisbane, 2001)   JEANNIE SIM

SUBIACO MUNICIPAL GARDENS (now Rankin Gardens), WA, was laid out in 1899 by Irish-born Danny Regan, and included a BOWLING GREEN at the Hamersley Road end. These formal-style gardens (renamed c. 1914 after Town Clerk Alexander Rankin) had rose beds, formal BEDDING, and a rotunda where bands played regularly. Extremely popular with the public, the Gardens remained open until 10 p.m. during the summer months from 1914. Joe MARTIN became head gardener in 1926 and continued to develop and maintain the gardens to a high standard. A water tower was used to support mass displays of the cascade chrysanthemums, 'colour and blending beyond any description'. A SHADE HOUSE and palm house contained TROPICAL and semi-tropical plants. Bush roses were arranged in a circular layout, while climbing roses were festooned along the fence.

CAROLYN MIDDLEMIS

THE SUBLIME was the term given to the pleasurable feeling in viewing grand yet sometimes fearful aspects of Nature. By 1788 the Sublime was triumphant all over Europe and landscape features that prompted the emotional response also came to be called 'sublime'. Snow-capped mountains, majestic forests, cataracts, fast-flowing rivers, or an expanse of ocean typified 'sublime' scenery. The extensive grounds of parks and gardens of the eighteenth-century English landscape movement gave scope for their design to include 'sublime' elements; streams and waterfalls, dense groves of trees, large rocks, or even small artificial mountains or volcanos. The Sublime was codified in 1756 by English philosopher Edmund Burke (1729–1797) as an AESTHETIC concept in a manner that Uvedale PRICE later used to categorise the PICTURESQUE.

In Australia, the Sublime continued to influence garden design well into the second half of the nineteenth century. Thomas SHEPHERD followed the aesthetic terminology of contemporary landscape scenery and divided garden styles into sublime, picturesque, and beautiful. His second lecture on landscape gardening (1836) offered advice to owners wanting sublime gardens: plant 'lofty spreading trees in deep glens', with 'close embowered dark walks' within hearing of 'a high waterfall, or abrupt cascade hurling down with fury'. He suggested 'high precipices overhung by monstrous-sized rugged rocks with deep recesses and natural or artificial caves'.

The early gardens of Sydney's marine villas ran down exposed sandstone slopes to weathered rocks at the water's edge. The steep sites of MORT's Greenoaks and MITCHELL's Carthona at Darling Point provided a naturally sublime setting for these romantic Gothic mansions and beyond were the spectacular waters of Sydney Harbour. The original grounds of Nelsons Bay (BRONTE HOUSE) were fortunate to include a waterfall and a deep gully of native plants. Inland at Mount Wilson and the BLUE MOUNTAINS, dense ravines and precipitous cliffs surrounded the cultivated gardens of the 1870s houses and lent a wildly sublime backdrop to their elevated sites. Undulating land was shaped into extensive vistas, native trees grouped into 'wilderness' plantations, and river and mountain views exposed. RIPPON LEA (Vic.) lacked suitable natural features so a hill of boulders was constructed with tunnels and waterfall.

CONIFERS and pines were first among several species of trees considered sublime. Native pines, *Araucaria bidwillii* and *A. heterophylla* (Bunya Pine and Norfolk Island Pine), graced the skyline of nineteenth-century CEMETERIES, calling to mind the sublime and spiritually uplifting idea of an afterlife. BROWNLOW HILL's drive was planted with *Pinus pinea* (Stone Pine) and passed by an artificial lake, equally sublime in the dark brooding water of its still surface. By employing the two plants believed to be the most ancient of species, William GUILFOYLE invoked the awe and wonder of the Sublime in his design of the PALM and FERN gully in MELBOURNE BOTANIC GARDENS. It was surpassed in Sublime concepts only by his 1876 remodelling of a section of the Gardens to represent a series of extinct volcanos with a lava flow carving channels towards the redesigned lake.

MARY MACKAY

SUBTROPICAL GARDENS: see TROPICAL GARDENS

SUBURBAN GARDENS According to conventional wisdom, the most popular hobbies in Australia are gardening and fishing. While the accuracy of this homespun belief may be hard to establish, there is strong evidence to support its likelihood in the case of suburban gardening. Gardening is highly popular, and most Australians live in suburbs.

The numbers who flock to open gardens each weekend as well as a glance through TELEVISION guides attest to this popularity, while a visit to a newsagency or bookshop will disclose shelves of GARDENING MAGAZINES and BOOKS. Gardens are one area in our culture in which the GENDER divide has never been clear-cut. While heavier work is traditionally the province of the male, the inspiration, creation, and tending of gardens has ever been as much a part of the woman's world. It has formed a sort of gender no-person's land between women's domain (the home) and the male domain (the outside world), a space where a couple could meet, blend, or pursue their own paths. Perhaps this is part of its appeal.

For more than a century the majority of Australians have been urban dwellers in cities and towns, with a substantial proportion living in suburbs circling our cities and towns. By 1901, for example, the percentages in each state living in capital cities were SA (45%), Vic. (41%), NSW (36%), Qld (24%), WA (20%), and Tas. (20%). By becoming suburbanites Australians fulfilled one of the great national goals—occupation of their own residence on their own block of land and with their own garden.

Australian urban entities developed rather different characteristics from those in Britain and Europe. In particular, they were much more geographically spread and less densely populated, and with far fewer tenements, terraces, and other forms of high-density housing. There were many reasons for this, but principally the relative cheapness of the land and the high disposable income and standard of living enjoyed by a large proportion of Australians. These brought within the reach of many urban dwellers the occupation of a suburban residence; in the late nineteenth and early twentieth centuries owner-occupation ranged from more than fifty per cent in middle-class suburbs to under forty per cent in working-class suburbs, which was somewhat higher than the norm in Europe.

Proprietorship, or even tenancy, of a piece of suburbia frequently results in a desire to garden in order to fulfil a variety of utilitarian, personal, and cultural needs. It satisfies a desire for creativity, it caters to a love of plants, it appeals to inherited European aesthetic concepts of beauty, and may be a manifestation of social success. Possession of a garden suggests fresh air, a healthy environment, and a place for recreation and privacy.

From the earliest decades of our history some people have needed or wished to grow their own food. Normally this has taken place in the BACKYARD—which was where one cultivated FRUIT and VEGETABLES, alongside clothes DRYING, a DRIVE and garage for the motor car, and later a BARBECUE and PATIO or other place for entertaining. By contrast, the

Suburban gardens

The suburban garden provided an endless source of inspiration for artist Howard Arkley, and in *Family Home: Suburban Exterior* (1993) he reworked a familiar scene in a richly patterned celebration of its design and details—termed 'featurism' by architectural critic Robin Boyd

suburban FRONT GARDEN is essentially aesthetic and is traditionally where one's personality is likely to shine through. It betrays to passers-by one's aesthetic tastes, social pretensions, horticultural knowledge, income, and whether one has sufficient interest in gardening to bother mowing the LAWN or pulling the weeds. Traditionally in Australia the house is placed towards the front of the block, creating a larger gardening and private recreational space in the rear, and a smaller show garden at the front.

Nevertheless, there is an enormous diversity in the suburban gardens Australians have created, chronologically, spatially, socio-economically, climatically, and geographically, not to mention stylistically and horticulturally. Over time, gardens have been greatly influenced by the availability and fashion of various species, but generally they have exhibited some variation on the exotic species and styles that Australians of European origin found more aesthetically pleasing, such as COTTAGE GARDENS and the GARDENESQUE. A notable turning point was the surge in popularity of native species in the 1960s with the BUSH GARDEN movement, although exoticism has again dominated in more recent years.

Apart from those who choose to live in APARTMENTS with a few potted plants, the size of one's garden has traditionally been a significant major socio-economic indicator. Suburban gardens range from the tiny plots of the inner-suburban terrace, through the slightly more generous space of the worker's cottage or bungalow and the quarter-acre or so of the VILLA garden, to the somewhat grander sweep of the MANSION lawn. However, contemporary trends cut across this pattern. In recent decades average block sizes have shrunk as city populations have climbed into millions and land prices have become much higher. In some new and expensive suburbs large, squat monsters with rows of columns take up so much of the tiny modern blocks that little space is left for the concrete paths and feature shrub. In former working-class suburbs, the gardens of terrace homes and cottages are being overcome by gentrification, disappearing beneath extensions that accommodate the new kitchen, family room, and spa. By contrast, the outer ring of suburbia is occupied by the one-to-five-hectare set whose properties boast sweeping lawns and formal garden beds that fight for space with the three-car garage, tennis court, and horse paddock.

CLIMATICALLY and geographically there is a vast gap between Hobart and Darwin, and between Alice Springs and Townsville; this gap produces fundamental differences in what can be grown, from ROSES to poinciana, from maples to

SUCCULENTS. In most regions a major factor in the development of the suburban garden has been the availability of WATER in dry periods in this driest of continents, and the capacity to deliver it to the plants. The establishment of urban reticulated water systems from the mid-1850s and the development of rubber garden HOSES AND SPRINKLERS later in the century have been fundamental for the creation and survival of the ever-thirsty lawns and gardens of suburbia. Suburban gardens are major consumers of domestic water and therefore a principal factor in the manipulation and damming of rural water systems and the consequent environmental impact. For suburban gardens to maintain their importance in Australian cities and towns our society will need to rethink future water supplies and the nature of those gardens.   DON GARDEN

SUCCULENTS: see CACTI

SULMAN, John (1849–1934), architect and town planner, was born in Greenwich, Kent, England, and from *c.* 1864 he received architectural training in London. He soon established a busy office and was prominent in his profession. A keen artist, he travelled widely in Europe, sketching and observing buildings and their settings; his observations in Italy were especially influential in his ensuing Australian career.

Sulman, now married with two children, arrived in Sydney in 1885 and entered a partnership with architect C.H.E. Blackmann, soon terminated by the latter's flight overseas with a Sydney barmaid. Between 1889 and 1908 he practised with Joseph Porter Power and lectured part-time in architecture at the University of Sydney (1887–1912), his opinions frequently sought publicly and privately. Sulman and Power specialised in INSTITUTIONAL buildings, giving him ample scope to implement his ideas on landscape design. His Women's College, University of Sydney (1890–94), was emphatically ITALIANATE, axially planned (though not fully implemented) with a generous loggia and COURTYARD. His masterpiece was the Thomas Walker Convalescent Hospital (1890–93), pleasingly sited on the Parramatta River at Concord and approached from the water through a striking BOATHOUSE or 'Water Gate', which terminated the axial site planning. The landscaping responded strongly to the axis: formal close to the buildings, and picturesque on the margins of the peninsula. Taking his inspiration from Italian courtyards, particularly ones he sketched in Genoa, Sulman predicted these would 'afford a charming resort for the patients alike when rain is falling or the sun is too hot for exercise'.

Sulman was a pioneer of TOWN PLANNING in Australia. His 1890 lecture 'The Laying-out of Towns' to the AUSTRALASIAN ASSOCIATION FOR THE ADVANCEMENT OF SCIENCE marked the beginning of town planning as a formal discipline in Australia and in later lectures, publications, and expert pronouncements he was an influential advocate for the movement. He was foundation president of the New South Wales Town Planning Association (1913–25), and later chaired both the New South Wales Town Planning Advisory Board (1918–28), and Federal Capital Advisory Committee (1921–24) at a time when GRIFFIN's plan for CANBERRA was being implemented and pragmatically refined.

Sulman's wife Sarah died in 1888 and he remarried, in 1893, Annie Elizabeth (*née* Masefield)—a childhood friend of Sulman's later patron (Dame) Eadith Walker. Annie was a talented nature photographer and published two series of booklets entitled *Some Familiar Wild Flowers* (*c.* 1914–17), in which she acknowledged the assistance of her step-daughter Florence, and botanist Edwin CHEEL. **Florence Sulman** (1876–1965), an active member of the Naturalists' Society of New South Wales, is best remembered for her *Popular Guide to the Wild Flowers of New South Wales* (1913–14), illustrated by Eirene MORT and Dorothy Watkins. Dedicated to Amy MACK, and acknowledging the assistance of J.H. MAIDEN, R.T. BAKER, and Cheel, her book disseminated information on AUSTRALIAN PLANTS then rarely found outside the covers of the various Floras. The works of both Annie and Florence Sulman captured contemporary sentiment for the NATURAL HISTORY of the Australian BUSH, and especially the translation of this by enlightened gardeners and landscape architects, such as the Griffins, into a landscape design ethos.
   COLLEEN MORRIS

SUMMERHOME, Moonah, Tas., sits on land granted to Henry Hopkins (1787–1870) in 1844. Hopkins and his wife Sarah arrived in Hobart Town in 1822, where he established a mercantile partnership, initially buying and selling produce. His business, in ironmongery and wool, prospered and in 1835 he built Westella, one of the colony's most substantial town houses. In 1842, by now with family pastoral interests in the Port Phillip District and fresh from three years in England, he established his SUMMER RETREAT on Hobart's northern outskirts. Summerhome had been erected by Robert Wilkins Giblin (1780–1845) and used as an academy for boys during the 1830s. Hopkins enlarged the house, and views of the 1850s by pioneering amateur photographer John Smith (1821–1885) show the house and garden much as it is today, confirming the significance of the surviving PARTERRE-style pleasure garden as one of the oldest documented examples in Australia. An intricate geometric pattern formed by box hedges contains beds of roses and perennials, with paired *Cordyline australis* (Cabbage Tree) framing the central entry axis. The front garden is encircled by a drive, while CONIFER plantings contain vistas over the Derwent valley. A fine early GLASSHOUSE sits adjacent to the main residence and outbuildings. H. Butler Stoney's 1856 description of Summerhome as 'very pretty … nestling under the hill side amid luxurious gardens' still perfectly captures the atmosphere of this remarkable survivor.   RA

SUMMER-HOUSE, a GARDEN BUILDING that permits enjoyment of the outside especially as a cool shady retreat during fine weather, is known from mid-eighteenth-century British examples. In Australia the VERANDAH arguably fulfilled many of the purposes of the summer house. Nonetheless, the summer-house was affordable by a wide range of people and graced PUBLIC PARKS, BOTANIC, HOMESTEAD, HILL-STATION, MANSION, and VILLA GARDENS. Architecturally, summer-houses were often fanciful—from the exaggerated RUSTIC and picturesque to the overweeningly formal. As decorative

The intricate patterns of box-edged BEDS at SUMMERHOME, Moonah (Tas.), like many long-vanished counterparts, were designed to be appreciated from the drawing room and verandah, as well as through a leisured walk or drive

garden features they often took on the role of 'eye catching' follies, occasionally terminated VISTAS, or formed gazebos, from where a prospect or panorama might be gained in the manner of a (truncated) LOOKOUT tower. Most summer-houses incorporated seating and enclosed walls (of varying permeability, but sufficient to provide shade). Formal examples might take on the form of a ROTUNDA or other classically derived source, while picturesque examples were likely to resemble PAVILIONS. Others, although rarer, were bare, adopting open-sided TENT forms. Octagonal plans resulted in pointed hipped roofs (straight or curved like a tent, often topped by a finial or embellishment) providing an ideal landscape focus.

The Gothick smoking house at WOOLMERS (Tas.) is among Australia's earliest extant examples. The ROYAL BOTANIC GARDENS, MELBOURNE and RIPPON LEA (Vic.) retain several nineteenth-century summer-houses of the restrained rusticity promoted by Edward KEMP, while many examples elsewhere, such as Philip MACMAHON's shelters, chairs, and tree-surrounds at the BRISBANE BOTANIC GARDEN (1893), have disappeared due in large measure to the vulnerability of the predominantly timber construction of Australian summer-houses.

JEANNIE SIM

SUMMERLIN, Lawrence (1851–1938), seed merchant, was born in Bedfordshire, England, and arrived in Brisbane in 1872. He was first included in trade listings in 1882 in Woolloongabba, and he later established nurseries at Mount Gravatt and Toowoomba. In 1885 Summerlin opened a new seed shop in the city, well-stocked with his specialty, pot plants. The *Queenslander*, following a visit to the nursery of Summerlin and WHITTLE in 1888, commented that the potted daisies 'have had an extensive sale, the demand for the plants having been virtually created by Mr Summerlin himself'. Summerlin published *Seeds and How to Grow Them* (1888), and a copy of *Summerlin's Seed Catalogue and Amateurs' Guide for 1891* is one of the earliest known catalogues for Qld., representative of a leading member of its seed and nursery trade. His son, Robert Lawrence Summerlin (1880–1961), also worked as a nurseryman.

RA

SUMMER RETREATS In Australia commercial and industrial activity winds down over Christmas (in the middle of summer) and the population is free to indulge in a long holiday, at the beach or in the hills. This has been reinforced by the concentration of Australia's urban development on the fringe of the continent, in easy reach of both coastline and mountains.

In India, Malaya, Ceylon, and other colonies, British expatriates retreated to the high country to escape the heat. In the late nineteenth century, high-ranking civil servants (especially those who had served in other colonial outposts), governors, parliamentarians, gentlemen scientists, and those with wealth from commerce maintained this HILL-STATION tradition. These were concentrated in the high country of southeastern Australia, predominantly in the BLUE MOUNTAINS and the SOUTHERN HIGHLANDS (NSW), MOUNT MACEDON and the Dandenongs (Vic.), and Mount Lofty and the ADELAIDE HILLS (SA). A smaller exodus took place to Toowoomba (Qld) and Kalamunda (WA).

Summer retreats in the hills were of two main types: guest houses accessible to the public, offering large and complete accommodation, good mountain air, tennis, and walking, or private homes, euphemistically known as 'cottages', but more often built on a grand scale and luxuriously appointed. At Mount Macedon the vice-regal seal of approval was given when the government bought a 'cottage' for the purpose of providing the governor with a summer residence for his family and entourage on the cool southern slopes.

At these retreats, rich soils, high rainfall, and moderate temperatures provided the conditions needed for a thriving horticultural industry, often cool-climate outposts of city NURSERIES. The gardens owed much of their charm to their BUSH setting; tall forest trees providing either framework for, or backdrop to, the garden. An army of gardeners was needed for initial development and maintenance, and a diverse horticultural industry developed. Plants were imported, nurtured, ACCLIMATISED, propagated, and exchanged. The late nineteenth-century passion for BOTANY, HORTICULTURE, and FORESTRY greatly increased the quantity and variety of available plants. Collectors vied with each other to acquire rare and beautiful plant specimens. Certain gardens were known for various horticultural and landscape specialties, such as their CONIFERS, RHODODENDRONS, dry stone WALLS, WATER features, and the like. As the twentieth century progressed, American country club–style estates based on GOLF COURSES were also developed.

With the advent of better and more accessible transport, particularly the motor car, the summer retreat was democratised. BEACHES became the preferred retreat for many people, although the casual lifestyle this setting promoted resulted in simple gardens, ranging from semi-cleared bush to easily maintained swards of LAWN surrounded by and dotted with heat- and salt-tolerant plants. A shift to RESORT-style accommodation as the twentieth century progressed is charted by Davidson and Spearritt in *Holiday Business: Tourism in Australia since 1870* (2000). JAN SCHAPPER

SUNDIAL is an instrument showing the time by the shadow of a pointer (gnomon) cast by the sun on to a graduated disc. In the garden setting, the sundial has all but lost its practical time-telling function. Now its primary role is as a garden ORNAMENT, highlighting a point of strong visual interest such as the terminus of an axis, or the centre-point in radial or other formal schemes. As a garden ornament, a sundial is often visible from a garden chair or bench, particularly in a setting in which time is idled away. Thus, if sundials have retained their time-telling function in any sense, it is in marking the passing of leisure time. The sundial's vegetal manifestation may well be the FLORAL CLOCK.
ROWAN WILKEN and KAREN OLSEN

SUNK WALLS: see HA-HA

SUN PICTURE GARDENS, Broome, WA, was opened in 1916, following commissioning in 1913 of architect Claude Hawkes by Broome pearler Edmund Harold Hunter. Some of Hawkes' drawings survive, but there are no records of the original garden layout. The site, in Broome's Chinatown, comprises a hall with street verandah that opens into a rear garden, developed over the past twenty years and comprising a central lawn with perimeter planting, a seating area, and film screen. Deck-chair seating spills from the covered areas out into the rear gardens. The screen doubles as the east facade of a new building and the peaked roof that projects over the screen imparts a tropical West Indian flavour to this rare surviving example of a 'picture garden'. ROSEMARY ROSARIO

SUNSHINE GARDENS, Vic.: see H.V. MCKAY MEMORIAL GARDENS, Sunshine, Vic.

SUTTOR, George (1774–1859), settler and Banksian collector, was born in Chelsea, near London, the son of a Scottish botanist and gardener who had trained under James LEE. Suttor started working in his father's MARKET GARDEN at 14, was an avid reader, and although initially drawn to the theatre, became interested in settling in Sydney. His father's former employer George Aufrere, uncle of Sir Joseph BANKS, provided a letter of introduction to Banks in 1798. Needing a custodian for eighteen boxes of useful plants to be dispatched to the colony, Banks appointed him honorary Botanical Collector, to tend the collection, including grape vines, apple and pear trees, and hop bushes, which Suttor helped assemble at KEW.

Suttor befriended George CALEY and, after several false starts, arrived in Sydney in 1800. Many of the plants did not survive the journey and some were replaced at the CAPE. Suttor selected a grant at Baulkham Hills, established Chelsea Farm, and planted lemons grown from seed and three young orange trees (a gift from Colonel William Paterson). He was the first in Australia to propagate and advertise a variety of fruit trees for sale (1804) and by 1807 sent loads of oranges to market but was struggling financially at a time when the colony was in turmoil over the rebellion against Governor Bligh, whom Suttor supported. In 1810 Suttor returned to England as a witness for Bligh against the rebel leader Colonel Johnston, taking the opportunity to approach Banks for help. Impatience caused him to petition the Colonial Office himself, an endeavour that failed. He returned in 1812 with 'valuable plants' including olives and date palms, to an improved orangery and considerable debts. Suttor's friend Reverend Samuel Marsden suggested he take over as superintendent of the Lunatic Asylum at Castle Hill, a post he accepted (1814) but in which he was unhappy. Proclaimed to be neglectful in his duties, he was dismissed from his position in 1819 and he returned to Chelsea Farm.

A caterpillar plague encouraged him to seek pastures beyond the BLUE MOUNTAINS at Bathurst and he applied for a grant in 1822, established Brucedale, and lived there for several years before returning to restore his orangery at Baulkham Hills. Suttor prospered and moved to Elizabeth Street, Sydney (1834), botanist Allan CUNNINGHAM residing with him and his family. Between 1839 and 1844 the Suttors lived in England and toured the Continent, where he studied VINEYARDS and winemaking. While in London, he published *The Culture of the Grape-Vine, and the Orange, in Australia and New Zealand* (1843) and was elected a member of the Linnean Society. After the death of his wife (1844) Suttor returned to live at Bathurst, a pioneer of Australian ORCHARDING.

George Mackaness (ed.), *Memoirs of George Suttor F.L.S.; Banksian Collector (1774–1869)* (Sydney, 1948).

COLLEEN MORRIS

SWABY, Arthur James (1887–1979), botanist, and school teacher, was founder of the SOCIETY FOR GROWING AUSTRALIAN PLANTS (1957). He contributed a regular column, 'Know Your Natives', in YOUR GARDEN (1954–60), which became a focal point for native plant enthusiasts in the days when AUSTRALIAN FLORA was only grown by 'eccentrics'. Swaby's desire to pool and then widely share experiences led him to call for an association of growers, which has since successfully promoted the thoughtful use of native plants in Australian gardens.

JOHN WALTER

SWAIN, (Edward) Harold Fulcher (1883–1970), forester, was born in Sydney and made a significant contribution to the establishment of professional FORESTRY in Australia in the early twentieth century. He had a vision of an 'Australian' forestry adapted to the characteristics of the Australian forests, and founded on a sound scientific and economic base. In this, he was influenced by NORTH AMERICAN 'wise use' conservation ideas. He opposed European influences, symbolised in his view, by the Australian Forestry School and its (acting) principal, C.E. LANE POOLE. Swain was head of the Queensland Forest Service (1918–32) and a New South Wales' Forestry Commissioner (1935–48). These periods were characterised by a striving for efficient timber utilisation, establishment of appropriate silvicultural procedures, and adequate forest reservation. On the basis of Swain's mapping of areas of similar CLIMATE throughout the world, *Pinus elliottii* (Slash Pine) and *Pinus taeda* (Loblolly Pine) from Florida, USA, were chosen for planting on the coastal sand-plains of south-east Qld. He was closely involved in the establishment of the Eastern States Timber Industry Stabilisation Conference in 1943, and after retirement in 1948 served as a forestry adviser to Ethiopia. In 1963 he was awarded the JOLLY Medal for his 'outstanding contributions to Australian forestry'. Believing that all great cities should have a forest, Swain was instrumental in setting aside Cumberland State Forest at West Pennant Hills (NSW). In the 1920s, on the banks of the Brisbane River behind his home in Chelmer (Qld), he established a plantation of native *Araucaria cunninghamii* (Hoop Pine), which is now a mature stand.

KEVIN FRAWLEY

SWAINSON, William (1789–1855), zoological lithographer and natural history journalist, enjoyed a successful career in London before migrating to New Zealand. Needing money he visited Australia seeking employment in BOTANY, of which he knew little. Engaged by the Victorian Government, he spent the year of his engagement doing little but complain. His 1853 botanical report was greeted as imaginative nonsense. Swainson left Australia, ridiculed for his botany, but highly respected as a zoological artist.

HELEN M. COHN

SWANE'S NURSERY, specialist ROSE growers, was established in 1919 at Ermington, an outer Sydney suburb. Brothers Edgar Norman (Ted) (1892–1974) and Harold Rudyard Kipling (Tim) Swane (c. 1899–c. 1965) began growing fruit trees for orchardists on their father's property; Ermington, on the Parramatta River, was then known for its market gardens, orchards, nurseries, and small farms. The Swane brothers registered their business as Enterprise Nurseries and grew roses and citrus, with vegetables as a cash crop while waiting for the other plants to mature. Early in the 1920s Ted visited Melbourne to contact nursery growers, including C.A. NOBELIUS, and establish new markets. By 1941 the Swane brothers had sold hundreds of thousands of citrus trees to Victorian nurseries and growers.

At the outbreak of war, production was curtailed; Tim left the business, leaving Ted to run the nursery. Innovations during the inter-war period included purchase of a 1921 Model T Ford for speedy delivery of vegetables, use of the motorised Howard rotary hoe, and the technique of 'growing-on' plants in large containers.

In 1945 Edgar Norman (Ben) Swane (b. 1927) joined his father, Ted, at the nursery, followed by brother and sisters Valerie Gwendoline (1926–1993), Geoffrey Duncan (b. 1933), and Elwyn Lettitia (b. 1935). By the early 1960s, the company, with restricted space at Ermington, moved rose and fruit tree growing to Dural. A larger holding (53 ha) at Narromine, near Dubbo (NSW), was purchased soon after and is used for rose production. More than 400 000 roses are now grown annually. On Ted Swane's death, Valerie became managing director of the company, and her high professional standing helped further establish the name and reputation of Swane's. Through her books, newspaper articles, and RADIO broadcasts, Valerie was a generous contributor to Australian horticulture and gardening, and widely honoured.

The Dural nursery, with its flowering trees, shrubs, and landscaped gardens with 5000 bush roses, continues to attract thousands of visitors weekly; each year the company mails

Secret men's business being conducted at the Adelaide SWEET PEA trials in Kensington Gardens (1918) as the judges take note of improved strains

out 15 000 catalogues with more than 250 roses listed. Swane family involvement continued into the third generation prior to the sale of the business in 2000. Swane's introduced and developed a special yellow rose, 'Australia's Olympic Gold Rose', to commemorate the Sydney 2000 Olympics.

CHRISTINE REID

SWEET, Robert (1783–1835), horticulturist, nursery proprietor, and author, was born at Cockington, Devonshire, England, and started work as a gardener aged 16, holding a succession of positions as partner or foreman in some of the best known London nurseries. He was elected Fellow of the Linnean Society in 1812 and in 1818, wrote his first book, *Hortus Suburbanus Londinensis*, a catalogue of plants cultivated in gardens around London. At Colvill's Nursery he wrote the five-volume *Geraniaceae* (1820–30) based on their holdings, the first of the series of large, illustrated works with which his name is associated. *The Botanical Cultivator* followed in 1821, a manual of cultivation advice for HOTHOUSE and GREENHOUSE plants, many of them Australian. In all, Sweet wrote ten major works in a little over twelve years, the best known featuring AUSTRALIAN PLANTS being *Flora Australasica* (1827–28). This had fifty-seven hand-coloured plates illustrating plants found in London nurseries and gardens, many of them raised from seed collected by William BAXTER, Allan CUNNINGHAM, and Charles FRASER. Like most of Sweet's work, it provided cultivation information as well as botanical descriptions and was intended for the wealthy who maintained large gardens and hothouses rich in Australian plants. Sweet's frantic energy and an unstable personality led to a mental breakdown in 1831, from which he never recovered. He is commemorated in the small South American leguminous genus *Sweetia*.

TONY CAVANAGH

SWEET PEAS (*Lathyrus* sp.) were popular subjects in Australian gardens during the nineteenth century, especially after English hybrids appeared during the 1860s and 1870s. Henry Eckford bred many new cultivars but it was the raising of a sweet pea with waved standards and wings (1900), by Silas Cole, gardener to Earl Spencer at Althorp Park, Northamptonshire, and introduced to the trade by Robert Sydenham of Birmingham as Countess Spencer, that led to a surge of interest in Australia. The Carnation and Sweet Pea Society of South Australia was formed in 1903, followed closely by the Carnation, Dahlia, and Sweet Pea Society of Victoria. In 1904 William H. Young of Yarrawa, Summer Hill (NSW), raised an early-flowering sweet pea that flowered in eight or ten weeks from planting—against many months for the conventional, late-flowering varieties. YATES marketed the Yarrawa strain in 1911, followed by SEARL and Co. with hybridist William H. Hatcher of Brookvale (1913), and ANDERSON and Co. with Hamilton MOTTE of Albury (1915). Sweet peary in Australia reached new sophistication with the publication of two volumes of the *Australian Sweet Pea Annual* (1918–19) under the editorship of leading South Australian grower Alfred QUARRELL. Since then the flower has enjoyed modest popularity, although it is now regarded as an old-fashioned subject mainly confined to COTTAGE GARDENS.

RA

SWIFTS, Darling Point, NSW, was developed by Sydney brewer Robert Lucas-Tooth (1844–1915) when in 1882 he aggrandised an earlier dwelling, intending to eclipse GOVERNMENT HOUSE. Swifts was sold in 1900 to German-born brewer Edmund Resch (1847–1923), and passed through his family to the Catholic Church (1964–86), and then to private owners. The garden, planned and laid out by Alexander GRANT (c. 1882), has suffered remarkably little

Swimming pools

Many SWIMMING POOLS installed in residential properties during the 1930s and 1940s, such as this 1939 example in Toorak (Vic.), created dramatic MODERNIST interventions in established garden settings

diminution in size or layout. Its compartments include many characteristic features of MANSION GARDENS, with a large lawn fringed with flower beds, a serpentine drive climbing to the house platform, pleasure garden, and dense shrubbery borders along the boundaries. A retaining wall with quatrefoil balustrade defines a terrace around the ballroom. Further ornament is provided by bronzed cast-iron sculptures of classical subjects, possibly added by Resch. Now the largest harbourside mansion to survive with its garden intact, Swifts contains some of Sydney's most notable *Ficus macrophylla* (Moreton Bay Fig) among its conspicuous trees.

MICHAEL LEHANY

SWIMMING POOLS Australia's climate has generally encouraged swimming, although government prohibition on daytime public bathing in urban areas, the moral dilemma of mixed sex bathing, and issues of public decency over costume coverage delayed its emergence as a popular form of RECREATION and SPORT until well into the twentieth century. Bathing—rather than swimming—was confined to segregated baths, set on piles over BEACHES AND FORESHORE RESERVES, tightly enclosed against the outside and protected by close boarding (against voyeurism) and submarine grids (against sharks). Municipal beach baths or rock pools were first constructed at Bronte, NSW (1887), typical of many that were to edge rocky, coastal outcrops along the Sydney shore. BATH HOUSES on dry land catered for those with a taste for the exotic or seeking recuperative benefits. Surf bathing (and surfing) rose greatly in popularity during the 1920s and 1930s, as resorts such as Bondi and Manly (NSW) and Coolangatta (Qld) were developed to capitalise on the free attraction of the sea. Open-air public swimming pools were developed from the 1920s and especially when incorporating garden settings, such as that found at Malvern Baths, Vic. (1927), public pools became places of leisure as well as recreation. (Renamed the Harold Holt Memorial Swimming Centre in 1969, this Malvern pool remains a unique commemoration of a drowned prime minister.).

Incorporating swimming facilities into private gardens as a landscape feature has occurred in various ways. Gardens such as GLENARA (Vic.) used the natural rock formations of Deep Creek to provide both picturesque views and a swimming hole. Private swimming pools began to be constructed in Australian gardens in the 1920s, encouraged by publications such as *AUSTRALIAN HOME BEAUTIFUL* and the *HOME*, and NORTH AMERICAN influences derived from magazines such as *Beach and Pool* (established 1924). Among the earliest Australian examples was that at COOMBE COTTAGE (1924). By the 1930s, fashionable architects incorporated pools as a matter of course in larger domestic commissions, and MODERNISM set the seal on rakish horizontal lines and crisp white colour schemes. Likewise Art Deco and 'moderne' styles favoured nautical overtones, Hollywood or American west coast ambience, and bold integration of swimming pools and gardens as outdoor living areas, epitomised by the pool at Beverley Hills apartments, South Yarra, Vic. (1935), and RIPPON LEA, Elsternwick, Vic. (1938–39). The swimming pool at Mooramong near Skipton, Vic. (1938), was created for Scobie Mackinnon's wife, Clare, who had been a star of the silent movie screen in Hollywood before moving to Australia. Landscaping of pools provided a new sphere of activity for designers; the Mackinnons commissioned Edna WALLING to provide a landscape scheme including the pool surrounds, while at Glenara, Ellis STONES designed landscape facilities for a new in-ground pool (1973). In smaller gardens, a demountable pool set in the BACKYARD or built-in to a PATIO is a more common response. Pools have also become a feature of RESORT GARDENS, mostly to focus commercial gain, but occasionally in northern Australia as a pragmatic refuge against crocodile-infested waters.

RICHARD HEATHCOTE

SWINBOURNE, Robert Frederick George (b. 1936) horticultural botanist, has done much to assemble the GARDEN HISTORY of SA. His book *Years of Endeavour* (1982) is a comprehensive survey of the NURSERY trade of SA since 1836 and his manuscript 'Lost Gardens' (edited and awaiting publication) details many gardens now destroyed by urban development and rural depression. He has described and registered many Pelargonium hybrids, particularly those introduced by Ted Both (1900–1962), including the now-famous 'Both's Staphs' R. Swinbourne (*Pelargonium* X *palmatifolium*). His study *Sanseverias in Australia* was published by the ADELAIDE BOTANIC GARDEN.

TREVOR NOTTLE

SWITZERLAND Swiss influence on Australian gardens revolves around general influences—such as the SUBLIMITY of its landscape, its importance as a source and inspiration for ALPINE plants and gardens, and the occasional reference to typical Swiss architecture in GARDEN BUILDINGS—and the knowledge of migrants such as Jacob HAWTER, Charles LA TROBE, and vignerons Hubert DE CASTELLA and Friedrich HIRSCHI, who made a significant contribution to Australian VITICULTURE.

RA

SYDNEY BOTANIC GARDENS: see ROYAL BOTANIC GARDENS, SYDNEY

SYDNEY MAGAZINE OF SCIENCE AND ART (1857–59), edited by Joseph Dyer and published monthly, contained 'by authority' the proceedings of the Australian Horticultural and Agricultural Society and the Philosophical Society of New South Wales. Presumably named after the English Department of Science and Art formed in 1853 in the wake of the Great Exhibition (1851), the magazine contained much of horticultural and agricultural interest. The *First Report* and *Second Report of the Australian Horticultural and Agricultural Society* are generally found bound with the two volumes.

RA

SYDNEY MAIL (1860–1938), published weekly in Sydney by John Fairfax and Son, proprietors of the *Sydney Morning Herald*, included much of horticultural and agricultural interest. John Fairfax (1804–1877) and his son James assembled a talented editorial group for his newspapers, and this extended to the choice of contributors: Louisa ATKINSON, for instance, regularly contributed 'A Voice from the Country' (1860–71). The *Mail* was a keen observer of Charles MOORE's progress with enlargement and planting of SYDNEY BOTANIC GARDENS during the 1860s and 1870s, and regularly reported on activities of HORTICULTURAL SOCIETIES. A local rival was the *(AUSTRALIAN) TOWN AND COUNTRY JOURNAL*.

RA

SYSTEM GARDENS All botanic gardens have an EDUCATIONAL role, primarily through plant labels that give scientific names and their author, common names, and country of origin. A system garden—sometimes called a class ground or teaching garden—is a specialised botanic garden designed as a gigantic teaching aid, a HERBARIUM of living plants arranged according to the principles of botanical classification.

The system garden at the University of Melbourne was designed in 1856 to illustrate 'all the natural Classes, Orders and most of the Families and many of the Genera of plants, arranged with the systematic precision of the leaves of a book and fully labelled', for the benefit of students and interested members of the public. This chamomile-edged arrangement of three concentric circles with radial paths leading to a central octagonal CONSERVATORY surrounded by a moat, was laid out by Edward La Trobe BATEMAN, and occupied about four acres (1.6 ha) in the north-west corner of the university grounds. It was planted to illustrate the botanical classification devised by John Hutton Balfour (1808–1884) of Edinburgh University. Frederick McCoy (1817–1899), foundation Professor of Natural Science,

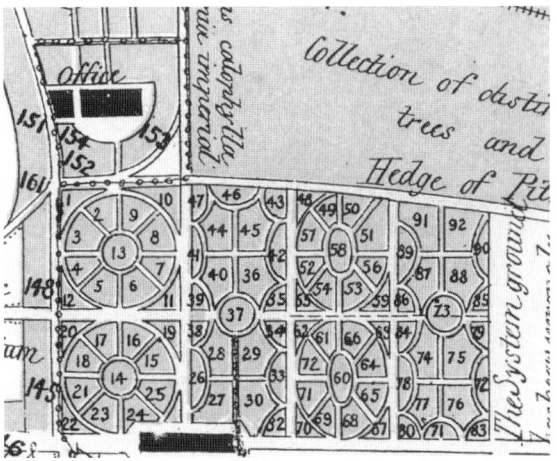

Detail of the plan of MELBOURNE BOTANIC GARDENS, prepared by E.B. HEYNE and published in 1865, showing Ferdinand MUELLER's SYSTEM GARDEN, in which the geometric formal layout complemented the systematic arrangement of plants

System gardens

claimed his design was original, and this apparently referred to the inclusion of everything from seaweeds to GRASSES, from CONIFERS to FERNS. (It would appear that earlier system gardens, such as those at Uppsala and Cambridge, had displayed herbaceous plants.) The garden gradually declined in importance after the 1880s. A small area remains, with the central tower of the conservatory as its focus.

From 1854, MELBOURNE BOTANIC GARDENS included a 'classground' of about three acres (1.2 ha), planted according to the 'Natural System' in a parterre design. Ferdinand MUELLER hoped that it would 'be a still greater source of instruction to the botanical enquirer' than the general garden, but it was removed by William GUILFOYLE in 1874. The ROYAL SOCIETY of Tasmania considered establishing a system garden in Hobart c. 1880, but decided against it for reasons of expense, maintenance, and lack of public interest. In ADELAIDE BOTANIC GARDEN, Richard SCHOMBURGK laid out a 'class ground' in 1873 (where the rose garden now grows). It was 'in the shape of a hippodrome with two serpentine walks and a fountain in the centre for water plants'. In 1881 Schomburgk wrote that his garden followed the sequence of botanist Adrien de Jussieu (1797–1853). Planting included monocotyledons along both sides of the main axis. Adelaide Botanic Garden still has a 'classground' set out in a rectangular format and displaying the classification system of Adolf Engler (1844–1930) and Karl Prantl (1849–1893). GWEN PASCOE

TALBOT, Milo John Reginald (1912–1973), 7th Baron Talbot de Malahide, British diplomat and plant enthusiast, acquired a garden—around Malahide Castle at Fingal near Dublin—with his barony in 1948, and developed his horticultural interests and the garden with passion and skill. He also owned the Malahide estate at Fingal (Tas.). His impressive Irish garden and horticultural writing stimulated British horticultural interest in AUSTRALIAN PLANTS and his Tasmanian visits stimulated his interest in Tasmania's endemic plants. He commissioned Margaret STONES to draw a full set for the lavish iconography *The Endemic Flora of Tasmania* (1967–78) and persuaded Winifred CURTIS to write the text. He occasionally provided specimens from his Irish garden and sometimes accompanied enthusiastic collectors in Tasmania's bush. His appendices on cultivation, in successive parts of the *Endemic Flora*, chart horticultural progress of subject plants in Australia and Britain. On his death his sister Rose, who now tends Tasmania's Malahide garden, oversaw the completion of the *Endemic Flora* project.

LINDEN GILLBANK

TALINDERT, Camperdown, Vic., built for pastoralist James Chester Manifold (1867–1918) in 1890, possessed a much admired HOMESTEAD GARDEN with extensive lawns, shrubberies, herbaceous borders, vegetable garden, orchard, and a flowering cherry avenue. Outstanding was a ROSE garden laid out *c.* 1893 by William Jack Adamson (1865–1944), Manifold's Scottish-born head gardener (1893–*c.* 1923). A rose fancier, he bred here the exceptionally successful climber 'Miss Marion Manifold' released by Samuel BRUNDRETT in 1913. Another hybrid perpetual rose, 'Mrs J.C. Manifold', followed in 1915.

GEORGE JONES

TANNER, Howard Napier (b. 1946), architect, lecturer, and writer, was born and educated in Sydney. He joined Philip Cox in a joint architectural practice (1974–83), which evolved into his own Sydney-based practice. Tanner's student interest in gardens and GARDEN HISTORY, stimulated by family friendship with Beryl GUERTNER, and encouraged by fellow student James BROADBENT, flourished in the 1970s–80s, culminating in his book *The Great Gardens of Australia* (1976) and his curatorship of the seminal travelling exhibition *Converting the Wilderness: The Art of Gardening in Colonial Australia* (1979), the catalogue of which has long provided the best historical overview of Australia's colonial gardens. His *Towards an Australian Garden* (1983) synthesised this research into a garden design manifesto, demonstrated in Tanner's own works by strong use of spatial and architectural elements, reflected in large gardens he has master planned at Goulburn, Mittagong, and Scone (NSW). As Chairman of the Heritage Council of New South Wales (1993–96) he encouraged the protection of surviving colonial gardens.

RA

TASMANIA European settlements were first established in what was then Van Diemen's Land in 1803. Land was cleared and VEGETABLE GARDENS established within days of the landings at Risdon Cove and Port Dalrymple. The early camps were soon abandoned in favour of more suitable locations at George Town in the north and Sullivans Cove in the south. In the early years the settlements were often in danger of starvation through crop failure and drought, and the non-arrival of supply ships from Sydney. Land and work had to be geared to feeding the population. However, as houses replaced tents and the population became more settled, ornamental plants began to be introduced. As early as 1815 the chaplain at Hobart Town had ROSES growing in his garden.

Despite the initial clearing of native vegetation for the purpose of cultivation, and the importation of exotic plants as reminders of Home, NATIVE PLANTS were incorporated into ornamental gardens. In 1819 the commissary official George Hull planted two gum saplings in his garden at Hobart to commemorate the birth of a son. In the 1820s the sprawl of Hobart Town was likened to an English village but with native evergreens mixed with exotics such as roses, wallflowers, stocks, geraniums, and vines. Tasmania (as it was known from 1855) experienced the late Victorian craze for FERNS and in 1877 they were said to be the most popular plant then grown. Enthusiasts were advised to visit the fern gullies on Mount Wellington to enable them to reproduce the natural habitat of the plants.

In the countryside the early settlers soon established hedgerows of briar roses, hawthorn, and blackberry. These had a practical purpose—to prevent stock straying—as well as an aesthetic one in recalling the hedgerows of England. Many visitors to the island commented on the Englishness of the landscape through the widespread use of these plants, particularly in the MIDLANDS. Some of these hedgerow plants, and another early favourite, gorse, carefully nurtured

Tasmania

The Archer property Brickendon, near Longford, was typical of early colonial gardens in TASMANIA in its incorporation of the glazed protection provided by a CONSERVATORY, considered a necessity for the growth of tender plants from 'home'.

by settlers, have adapted so well to the Tasmanian climate that they now create major problems for land managers as environmental WEEDS.

Initially settlers relied on English gardening books, taking into account different CLIMATIC conditions and the reversal of SEASONS. This was often a matter of trial and error. Horticultural information was occasionally provided in the columns of the *Hobart Town Gazette* and from 1824 ALMANACS also provided horticultural notes, often in the form of a gardening calendar but with little guidance on the subject of landscape design. A more comprehensive book was Daniel BUNCE's *Manual of Practical Gardening* (1837–38). Again, landscaping information was incidental but Bunce recommended the use of native plants in mixed SHRUBBERIES, provided sufficient attention was paid to their size and habits of growth. The favoured edging plant, English box, then not being readily available, he suggested several indigenous substitutes. Manuals were subsequently produced by James DICKINSON (1855) and by J. Walch and Sons, printers and publishers, from 1870. From 1877 to 1935, the weekly *TASMANIAN MAIL* also published horticultural notes.

Exotic plants were introduced by interested individuals who exchanged seeds and plants with their friends and neighbours. Many of these were medical men whose scientific interests went beyond their professional domain, men such as Dr Robert Espie of Bagdad, who is credited with being the first to introduce moss roses and *Magnolia grandiflora* to the colony in 1830. Some settlers such as Adolarius William Henry Humphrey (c. 1782–1829) of Humphreyville near New Norfolk and Thomas ARCHER of Woolmers near Longford had extensive private nurseries from which they could supply hundreds of plants, principally useful but also ornamental.

Commercial NURSERIES are not recorded until the 1830s, although James SCOTT advertised as a collector and exporter of the SEEDS of indigenous plants. In 1836 Daniel Bunce acquired the HOTHOUSES and gardens of Thomas Lightfoot in North Hobart and opened for business as the Denmark Hill Nursery. Bunce subsequently produced the first nursery catalogue in 1836, and the first Australian GARDENING BOOK to deal with the flower garden as well as the fruit and vegetable garden. His business failed in 1839, but another nursery was established further up the street by Valentine Marshall (c. 1814–1887), who visited England in 1844–45 and returned with several new varieties of FUCHSIA and greenhouse plants that he offered for sale by public auction. Nursery proprietor James Dickinson advertised a wide range of stock including 200 varieties of flower seeds and the preparation of native species for export. He was also a LANDSCAPE GARDENER, advertising that he would lay out and plant gardens. Garden design and planting was also offered by Edward LIPSCOMBE, who had established a nursery in

Sandy Bay by the 1840s. The middle decades of the century saw the beginning of a number of dynasties in the nursery trade including the ALLENS of Longford, the Lipscombes of Sandy Bay, and the CHANDLERS, who are still in business in Sandy Bay.

By the turn of the century, the nursery trade was well established; the southern centres were Hobart city and the suburb of Sandy Bay. Launceston was also well served, and there were nurseries at Hadspen, Longford, Ulverstone, and Zeehan. Regulations of the period intended to prevent the introduction of PESTS dangerous to the important FRUIT industry also affected the importation of ornamental plants with nursery proprietors considering the risk of plant loss during the required fumigation with hydrocyanic gas to be too great.

HORTICULTURAL SOCIETIES were also an important source of gardening information and new plants. The Launceston Horticultural Society, established in 1838, was the first such society in the colony. At its gardens, now known as CITY PARK, the society aimed to carry out research on native plants as well as to collect and distribute valuable and ornamental plants. The Hobart equivalent was the Royal Society of Van Diemen's Land for Horticulture, Botany, and the Advancement of Science (later the ROYAL SOCIETY of Tasmania), which took over the management of the Government Garden on the DOMAIN in 1844. The Government Garden (later the ROYAL TASMANIAN BOTANICAL GARDENS) had been established by William Sorell in 1818. The Royal Society had its origins in the Tasmanian Society promoted by Sir John and Lady FRANKLIN. Lady Jane Franklin had a particular interest in the native flora and purchased land in the suburb now called Lenah Valley where she intended to create a native garden called Ancanthe. However, the Franklins were recalled before much progress had been made and her plans were not realised.

Experiments with the ACCLIMATISATION of useful plants were also carried out in the gardens at the PORT ARTHUR Penal Settlement. The officials of that establishment each enjoyed the perk of a garden for the raising of vegetables to supplement their government rations and for ornamental plants. A garden planted with deciduous trees for the recreation of the officials and their families was established in the 1830s and further developed in the 1840s by William Thomas Napier Champ (1808–1892), the then Commandant and a keen gardener.

Landscape gardening fashions followed trends in Britain and Europe. By the 1830s–40s, the settlers of Van Diemen's Land were replacing the primitive houses of the early years with substantial VILLAS, MANSIONS, and HOMESTEADS to cement their status among the colonial gentry. The approach to the house with sweeping drives, tree-lined avenues, and impressive entrance gates was designed to create the impression of established position. At Panshanger the grounds were laid out like the PARKLANDS so typical of the English landscape movement, and complete with imported DEER.

FOUNTAINS and other garden ORNAMENTS were typically imported from Britain and the local production of flower POTS and garden tubs was sporadic. Between the 1830s and 1950s, the pottery at Port Arthur produced pots for GOVERNMENT HOUSE and the botanic gardens as well as for the general market. During the 1870s the Campbell and McHugh potteries in Launceston and Waller's brickworks at New Town produced plain and fancy pots, and ornamental garden edging.

The well-to-do had long had their PLEASURE GARDENS, but around the turn of the century similar resorts became available to the masses in the form of TEA GARDENS. Most of these RESORTS were located at the end of tram routes and in Hobart there were several in the foothills of Mount Wellington. Massed floral displays, fern glades, RUSTIC summer-houses, and water features formed an eclectic style that remained popular until the Second World War.

During the First World War there were several proposals to establish garden suburbs in Tasmania along the lines of English GARDEN CITIES. The housing estates established for the workers of the Electrolytic Zinc Company at LUTANA near Hobart and the Cadbury's factory at Claremont were only a partial realisation of these proposals. At Claremont the horticultural efforts of the employees were encouraged through a Floricultural Society and regular floral SHOWS.

ROCKERIES, stone walls, and crazy paving were a feature of many gardens in the 1920s and 1930s, the necessary building materials available from a supplier at Kingston. Local landscape gardener and florist Kitty HENRY had a particular interest in rockeries and rock garden plants and acknowledged the influence of Gertrude JEKYLL and Edna WALLING. Professional garden landscape design, by reason of economy and scale, was slow to develop in Tas. A tradition of owner–designers persisted until the rise of LANDSCAPE ARCHITECTURE in the 1970s. Barry McNeill instituted Australian's first tertiary department of environmental design at Tasmanian College of Advanced Education (1972) and in recent years, landscape practitioners such as Jerry de Gryse (b. 1952) have linked ECOLOGICAL concerns with high-quality design and land management. REVEGETATION has played an increasing part in this approach, building on an initial boom of interest in native plants for ornamental purposes and more recently tending towards the use of local indigenous plants for both ecological and ornamental reasons.

Plant enthusiasts, embracing both indigenous and exotic tastes, have found a secure niche in Tas. Specialist nurseries such as those of Ken GILLANDERS and Rod BARWICK have received international recognition. Since the 1980s there has also been widespread interest in historic gardens, many of which have now been restored, often strongly influenced by the concurrent fashion for COTTAGE GARDENS. Tourism in Tasmania is now strongly focused on gardens and the wider landscape.

Phyl Frazer Simons, *Historic Tasmanian Gardens* (Canberra, 1987); Sharon Morgan, *Land Settlement in Early Tasmania: Creating an Antipodean England* (Cambridge, 1992)

LINDY SCRIPPS

TASMANIAN MAIL (1877–1935), 'A Weekly Journal for Tasmania of Politics, Literature, Science, Agriculture, News & Notes', was published by the proprietors of the Hobart *Mercury*. From the first issue, a regular column entitled 'The

Gardener' brought seasonal advice, as well as notes on landscape gardening, descriptive notices of gardens, and reports of HORTICULTURAL SOCIETIES and SHOWS. Editorials occasionally broached subjects such as FOREST conservancy, STREET TREE planting, and enhanced provision of PUBLIC PARKS. As illustrations came to grace its pages (1894) gardens were regularly featured. The paper became the *Illustrated Tasmanian Mail* in 1921.   RA

TATE, Ralph (1840–1901), botanist, zoologist, and geologist, was born in Alnwick, Northumberland, England, and educated at the Royal School of Mines, London. In 1874 he was appointed to the inaugural Elder chair of natural science at the University of Adelaide, and became an influential contributor to Australian science through his research, NATURAL HISTORY fieldwork, publications, lecturing, and advocacy. In 1877 he founded the first continuing scientific journal in SA (which became the *Transactions and Proceedings of the Royal Society of South Australia*) and in 1880 reformed the comatose Adelaide Philosophical Society into the ROYAL SOCIETY of South Australia. He participated in several exploratory investigations of the NORTHERN TERRITORY. Tate's botanical research (much assisted by MUELLER), culminating in his *Handbook of the Flora of Extratropical South Australia* (1890), formed the foundation of botanical records in the colony (including its Northern Territory). While controversy accompanied his advocacy initiatives, his critical documentation of discoveries and patterns portray him as a pre-eminent proponent of scientific advancement in Australia. He was also a key promoter of its scientific societies (especially the AUSTRALASIAN ASSOCIATION FOR THE ADVANCEMENT OF SCIENCE).   DAVID JONES

TAYLOR AND SANGSTER, arguably the leading nursery proprietors and landscape designers in Vic. in the nineteenth century, combined the talents of two Scots, although Taylor remains a somewhat obscure figure in the partnership. **William Taylor** (1826–1892), born in Edinburgh, migrated to Australia in 1856 and was for some years gardener at GOVERNMENT HOUSE (then Toorak House), until he established the Vice-Regal Nurseries in Toorak. In his 1865 catalogue he claims to have 'graduated in some of the most extensive Nurseries and Private gardens in the United Kingdom'.

William Sangster (1831–1910), born in Inverness, worked in the celebrated gardens of Hamilton Palace in Scotland before migrating to Melbourne. By mid-1853 he was working at MELBOURNE BOTANIC GARDENS under fellow Scot John DALLACHY. In March 1854 he went as gardener to a Mr Dickson at Mount Pleasant but in December returned to Melbourne, where he noted: 'entered into my duties as gardener and overseer, Como Estate', where three men were employed at day labour. The COMO gardens were extensive: the Sangster papers detail the large and varied array of fruit trees, vegetables, and flowers, including ninety different ROSES as well as bulbs, tubers, and perennials. William Sawrey GILPIN through his book *Practical Hints upon Landscape Gardening* (1832) was an influence on Sangster. Among Sangster's papers are passages copied from this work. He probably had in mind advice on approaches when planning the new carriage DRIVE at Como and his later design for RUPERTSWOOD, Sunbury (1875): 'An approach should appear to be an unstudied road to the house and its character should vary with that of the house and its character.'

Sangster left Como in mid-1856 to join William Taylor, whose nursery was thereafter known as Taylor and Sangster's Nursery, an area of two acres (0.8 ha) in Toorak. There is no evidence that William Taylor did any landscaping. He carried out the major work of propagating while Sangster was involved in landscaping (when not working also in the nursery). Some of the gardens known to have been designed by him include Como, Manderville Hall, Devorgilla, Studley Park, Victoria Gardens (Prahran), alterations at RIPPON LEA (1883), the rearrangement of the Exhibition (CARLTON) GARDENS (1880), and a scheme for WOMBAT HILL, Daylesford (1884). A beautifully drawn plan for this latter survives: the fern gully is similar to the one he created at Rupertswood, and the accompanying notes refer to his use of the GARDENESQUE style, a surprisingly rare reference in relation to his work. On MOUNT MACEDON he was responsible for ARD CHOILLE and Braemar House on the northern slopes, and on the southern side Tieve Tara, Hohewarte (now Camelot), and supplied the early plantings for ALTON. He was not only a private designer, but also a member of the Board of Inquiry into the Administration of MELBOURNE BOTANIC GARDENS (1870–71), which resulted a greatly enhanced emphasis on landscape design at the Gardens.

Over many years the Toorak nursery was a major prize winner at the Horticultural Society of Victoria's SHOWS, being outstanding for its collections of CONIFERS, azaleas, and cut flowers, which often numbered fifty varieties. In the 1870s the nursery began showing CAMELLIAS with great success. It was in the 1870s also that SUMMER RETREATS began to be developed on Mount Macedon and in 1874 Taylor and Sangster commenced clearing a nursery site as a cool-climate extension of their Toorak nursery. Each year Taylor came up for extended periods to do the propagating. In the original plantings a decision to build up stocks of RHODODENDRONS must have been taken as lists show sixty-four choice rhododendrons mostly in bud were imported, as well as 124 choice hybrid seedlings and 200 two-year-old plants. Large imported plants of Ghent azaleas are also mentioned in the initial plantings. A large variety of conifers was listed, reflecting contemporary interest in them. In 1893 J.H. VEITCH was impressed with the variety and growth of these conifers. In 1900 Peter BARR remarked he had not seen 'better grown or so choice a variety as at this place'.

After Taylor's death Sangster evidently thought running both nurseries too burdensome, particularly with the depressed economic situation. An attempt to lease the nursery failed so staff cuts were made. A capable foreman, Gavin Fleming, took over the propagating formerly done by Taylor. In the ensuing years the nursery became famous for its rhododendrons and in the early 1900s large quantities were exported to New Zealand. Though Taylor's son William and his daughter Margaret inherited Taylor's share of the nursery, they had no interest in being directly involved. William

Taylor jnr. had already, in 1883, with J.J. Rushton, taken over the Melbourne branch of the seed business of CRESWELL and Co. The windows of the shop in Swanston Street were used for displaying seasonal flowers from the Toorak and Macedon nurseries until about 1893 when William Taylor moved to Shepparton. After Sangster's death his share of the nursery went to his daughter Jane Yates Sangster, who acquired the whole of the nursery in 1912 and continued to run it successfully until 1930.

Sangster's obituary stated that he was 'for many years the leading landscape gardener in the state', and with William GUILFOYLE his only rival in the design field, the claim has some justification, especially given Sangster's extensive list of clients. Sangster also wrote about gardens; articles of his appeared under the name 'Hortensis' in the *Australasian*. These articles have been gathered together in John FOSTER's book *Victorian Picturesque* (1989), which also contains an introductory essay on Sangster's life and work.

BARNEY HUTTON

TEA GARDENS were usually privately operated PLEASURE GARDENS that incorporated the commercial provision of light refreshments. Drinking tea and other non-alcoholic refreshments beneath bowers and ARBOURS had become popular for the leisured class in late eighteenth-century England, a development influenced by JAPANESE traditions. Unlike English BEER GARDENS, tea gardens traditionally upheld genteel behaviour and delicate manners. By the nineteenth century, when tea gardens were established in Australia, they were geared more towards mass appeal. Essentially they comprised a tea PAVILION set in a scenic or picturesque location; authentic Japanese models were extremely rare. Landscaping was generally minimal and often blended with the natural environment. Commonly sited by a lake or river bank or at the seaside, tea gardens formed an adjunct to LEISURE activities, such as boating and river cruises or simply strolling and PROMENADING. They reached the height of their popularity in the Edwardian period, when they were a favoured destination on Sundays and public holidays, and when music and dancing could be enjoyed on summer evenings. With the growth of mass tourism in the twentieth century, tea gardens gradually made way for kiosks, better equipped PICNIC GROUNDS, and mobile refreshment vans. Banjo Paterson asked cynically of Henry Lawson how he intended to civilise the bush: 'Would you make it a tea garden and on Sundays have a band / Where the "blokes" might take their "donahs" and a "public" close at hand?'.

HELEN DOYLE

TEESE, Arnold James (b. 1920), horticulturist and nursery proprietor, grew up on the family farm near Warragul (Vic.), where he was encouraged to garden. Aged just 12 he was breeding award-winning dahlia varieties and importing seeds, bulbs, and tubers. An avid plant collector, Teese instructed in horticulture and taxonomy at the School of Primary Agriculture and Horticulture, BURNLEY (1945–52), and was subsequently in charge of plantings at the Metropolitan and Commonwealth golf clubs and managed the Yarra Farm Bulb Company. Then followed a long period as the propagator at BOULTER's nursery in Olinda. Teese was a foundation member of the International Plant Propagators' Society Australian Region and friendships developed through overseas travel assisted him in introducing many rare and unusual plants into Australia. Teese became both foundation member and secretary (later president) of the Australian Rhododendron Society (1960). In 1954 Teese and his wife, Elizabeth, established Yamina Rare Plants Nursery, Monbulk, now run by sons Peter and Don.

ROSS HALL

TELEVISION, not unlike RADIO, has an immediacy that has generally excluded self-examination, and nowhere is this more evident than in the paucity of archival documentation of its programs. Internationally, television was a major social and cultural force in the post-war period: three English-speaking countries, Britain, the USA, and Canada, provided key organisational and technical precedents when Australian television was 'switched on' in time for the 1956 Melbourne Olympic Games. As with radio, a dual system of government and commercial stations was instituted in Australia, with the existing Australian Broadcasting Commission (later Corporation) and commercial media owners securing licences.

The first televised horticultural event in Australia—at least, as far as can be determined—was a rose planting demonstration in Melbourne by 'Doc' THOMAS and Mrs R.A.P. Worth, broadcast live on ABV2 on 1 February 1957. The earliest regular gardening programs can now only be traced through published television guides and hazy recollections. In Sydney, Allan SEALE (TCN9 for YATES) and Ted Gattenby (ATN7 for ANDERSONS Seeds) were both broadcasting on commercial channels in 1957. HSV7 in Melbourne presented 'Green Fingers' in 1957 by Danny Webb and John Sunnyman (John STEVENS), replaced during 1959–60 by 'Your Garden' with presenter Martha Gardner. These programs followed the pattern adopted for radio of strong cross-linkages between horticultural providers (especially the NURSERY industry) and commercial programs, with a

Television's 'Master Gardener', Ted Gattenby of ANDERSONS Seeds, and *Your Home* personality, Miss Del Cartwright, front the cameras of Sydney's ATN7 in 1957 during the first years of TELEVISION in Australia

more sober presentation of information on the ABC. Initially gardening programs were relatively short, rarely lasting longer than fifteen minutes.

Jack PLUMRIDGE commenced a gardening program on ABV2 in 1958 with other states having similar local programs. ABN2 commenced its 'In Your Garden' program by 1960, compered in its early days by Cam Tucker and Stan Peck, and later by Allan Seale. The well-known program 'Sow What' on ABV2 commenced in 1967, compared by John Butterworth with panel members Eric Prohaski and Helen Wiltshire. Kevin HEINZE soon took over as its host; by the time of his departure in 1988 he was revered in the garden world. In 1989 these and other state-based ABC programs were replaced by a national program, 'Gardening Australia', still presented by Peter CUNDALL.

With the advent in 1984 of 'Burke's Backyard', devised and hosted by Don BURKE, gardening was increasingly presented on television as a lifestyle choice rather than a horticultural pursuit. That is not to say that programs such as 'Better Homes and Gardens' do not incorporate meaningful garden content, but that it is aimed at consumers with all the skill that marketing consultants can muster, and is commonly linked to tandem products such as magazines or retail items. Plants are generally treated as mass-produced products—often disposable ones at that—rather than as natural organisms imbued with decades or even centuries of tradition in cultivation. 'Backyard Blitz' (2000) and 'Ground Force' (2000) take this approach to even greater lengths, and commonly dispense with all semblance of horticultural didacticism in the pursuit of entertainment. Television and garden centres have become the horticultural societies and horticultural shows of the new century, with the old social order that underpinned these precedents replaced by a new, and less attractive, ethic.

K.S. Inglis, *This is the ABC: The Australian Broadcasting Commission 1932–1983* (Carlton, Vic., 1983); Stuart Cunningham and Graeme Turner (eds), *The Media in Australia* (St Leonards, NSW, 1993)   RA

TEMPLE, a small GARDEN BUILDING derived from Egyptian, Greek, and Roman architecture (or its revival during the Renaissance), and also—often named pagoda—from buildings dedicated to Hindu and Buddhist gods. The term is ultimately derived from the Latin *templum* (open or consecrated space), although it was the general allusion to an ancient past (perhaps to a figure such as Flora or Pomona) rather than specific religious associations that saw their incorporation in gardens. Craigend, Thomas MITCHELL's Greek-revival house (*c*. 1829–33), 'introduced an exact copy of the Parthenon for the portico … [and] may almost be considered the Acropolis of Sydney'. An 1834 BATH HOUSE proposal for Alexander MCLEAY took the form of an octagonal temple. Circular planned temples—ROTUNDAS—were also occasionally used for garden buildings, William GUILFOYLE's Temple of the Winds (1901) being the supreme example. A fine early example of square plan was the BANDSTAND (1864) in Melbourne's FITZROY GARDENS. Two structures displayed at the 1880 Melbourne Exhibition, one a Burmese temple and the other a pagoda of Western Australian timber, were re-erected in local gardens. The temple form was also appropriately used for large monuments, notably the Springthorpe Memorial (1901) at BOOROONDARA CEMETERY, and elsewhere in large nineteenth-century CEMETERIES such as ROOKWOOD.   RA

TEMPLE-POOLE, George Thomas (1856–1934), architect, engineer, and leading TOWN PLANNING advocate, was educated in England and migrated to WA in 1885 following his appointment as Superintendent of Public Works. He retired from professional life in 1897 to pursue his interest in engineering and minerals. During 'retirement', he actively promoted town planning, lecturing regularly on the subject: one of his best-known addresses, 'Perth as it should be' (1911), critically assessed the results of the city's haphazard development. He set out a remedial plan that hinged on relocating the central railway station and yards and replacing them with civic buildings, gardens, and squares, ordered on CITY BEAUTIFUL lines. He also called for the reservation of a green girdle of unimproved land around the capital. Temple-Poole was a founding member of the Western Australian Town Planning Association (1916), chair of the committee that developed KINGS PARK from 1890 and designer of the park's original layout, and a founding and long-serving member of the Kings Park Board (1895–1934).

Ray and John Oldham, *George Temple-Poole: Architect of the Golden Years 1885–1897* (Nedlands, WA, 1980)

CHRISTINE GARNAUT

TENNIS COURTS have been a feature of large Australian gardens since the mid-1870s, when the game was brought to the colonies by British visitors and returning residents. As in England and the USA the game in Australia found its first home on the private LAWNS of wealthy families; William Clarke for instance installed private courts at both his country property, RUPERTSWOOD, and his town house, Cliveden, in East Melbourne. Lawn tennis sets were sold in England and included a net, posts, four racquets, and six hollow red India rubber balls. The Melbourne Cricket Club owned a set in 1877 but did not install a court until 1879. The game was taken up in vice-regal circles and lawn courts were established in the various colonial GOVERNMENT HOUSE grounds from the late 1870s. Often the site of the court occupied a prominent position in the landscape, as at Perth and Sydney, with a PAVILION for spectators as well as wire fencing to enclose part or all of the playing area.

Tennis required a large, flat area approximately the size of the current rectangular court (24 by 11 metres) with either an asphalt or lawn playing surface. In England the game soon became more popular and competitive, especially after the introduction of the cloth-covered India rubber ball and the promotion of a tournament by the All England Croquet and Lawn Tennis Club at Wimbledon in 1877. The Melbourne Cricket Club constructed four lawn courts in 1880 and used them to hold the first lawn tennis tournament in Australia. There quickly followed tournaments in NSW (1885), Qld (1889), Tas. (1893), and WA (1895). In the early twentieth

This Sargood family portrait (c. 1885) set in front of the tennis pavilion at RIPPON LEA, Elsternwick (Vic.), demonstrates the degree of informality that the sport of TENNIS introduced to Australian society during the 1870s and 1880s

century Australian players increasingly gained international success and recognition, first winning the Davis Cup in 1907, the same year that Norman Brookes became the first Australian to win Wimbledon. Tennis clubs began to be formed in towns and suburbs, either acquiring land independently or attaching themselves to PUBLIC PARKS OR GARDENS.

The size of the court, the upkeep of turf (if used), and the need for a level site precluded the spread of courts to smaller gardens, but many gardening books, such as Brunning's *Australian Gardener* (1916) still found room to advise on this garden feature. New all-weather playing surfaces, such as clay or *en-tout-cas*, were introduced after the Second World War; improved technology for automatic irrigation systems soon followed, reducing the labour-intensive requirements of lawn courts. Synthetic turf on a sand base is the most recent innovation. RICHARD HEATHCOTE

TENTS are commonly associated in the Australian mind with camping holidays, yet they have many links with Australian parks and gardens where they were commonly used in the nineteenth century. Their light construction and floating forms often recall garden PAVILIONS and their portable form—the UMBRELLA—is well suited to garden settings.

Portability and demountability were both attributes well suited to sports venues, where uses ranged from small tents for shade and shelter for summer sports (such as tennis) to marquees for entertaining at larger sporting and recreational venues. Tents were commonly used for HORTICULTURAL SHOWS although for many HORTICULTURAL SOCIETIES the 'tent debt' was often a crippling impost on struggling finances. Once purchased, though, tents were often rented out to recoup costs. The popularity of PATIOS and decks, and increasing concern over harmful ultraviolet radiation from the sun have recently promoted the use of sail-like covers to shade outdoor areas, while shadecloth has all but replaced the use of timber laths for BUSH-HOUSE walls and roofs. RA

TEPPER, Johann Gottlieb Otto (1841–1923), Prussian-born entomologist and botanist, arrived in Adelaide in 1847 with his parents. He taught in country schools between 1867 and 1883 while actively pursuing NATURAL HISTORY research and publication. During 1883–1911 he served with the South Australian Museum, principally as a collector and entomologist, and made significant contributions to its natural history collection. In 1888 he advocated legislation for the 'Better Protection of our Fauna and Flora'. He was an active participant in local HORTICULTURAL and SCIENTIFIC

SOCIETIES, and a regular contributor to local and German scientific publications and newspapers (including *Garden and Field*) on botanical and entomological instruction and advancement, and regularly spoke on these topics at meetings in Adelaide.
DAVID JONES

TESSELAAR, Cornelius Ignatius (Cees) (1912–1996), nursery proprietor and tulip grower, left his father's bulb farm in Beverwijk, Holland, on his wedding day in 1939 with his wife, seeking a new life growing BULBS in Australia. He purchased land in Ferntree Gully (Vic.) and started growing his beloved tulips, moving in 1944 to Silvan. His fame as a pioneering tulip grower spread and the business expanded, with the annual Tesselaar Tulip FESTIVAL (1954–) attracting thousands of visitors each spring. Having established a tradition of supporting others in the industry, in 1982 Tesselaar was awarded the Dutch Government's highest civilian award for his contribution to the well-being of those from the NETHERLANDS coming to and living in Vic. and Australia. On his seventieth birthday Cornelius Tesselaar handed the running of the Padua Bulb Nurseries to his sons Kees (b. 1941), Henk (b. 1943), Anthony (b. 1947), and John (b. 1954). Today, second-and third-generation Tesselaars continue to run the flourishing business.
HELEN BOTHAM

TETRATHECA, Basket Range, SA: see BISHOP, William James

THEATRE Dramatic performances have been presented with varying degrees of sophistication in both private and public gardens in Australia. Military parades and fireworks were early forms, and with the rise of PLEASURE GARDENS in the 1850s the theatrical aspect was considerably heightened. In MANSION GARDENS from the late nineteenth century, fetes and theatricals, such as the open-air Shakespearean performances held at RIPPON LEA (Vic.) in the early 1900s, were a popular form of entertainment. Privately, much was happening in the gardens of bohemian or artistic families, such as the Lindsays, where masques and plays—often written by the participants—were performed using the garden environs as settings for their accomplished but amateur enterprises.

Use of gardens by professional theatre companies was revived in the 1990s following isolated performances of works such as Suzanne Spunner's pioneering *Edna for the Garden* (1989), a play tracing WALLING's career, and presented in Melbourne's FITZROY GARDENS. Glenn Elston's pioneering productions of Shakespeare in Australia's capital city BOTANIC GARDENS have marked the renaissance of the art form of environmental or locational theatre. Children's theatre has also thrived in garden settings, with such productions as *Wind in the Willows* now well established in the summer season. These productions often just used gardens as single back drops to the play but innovation emerged in the 1990s with groups such as Performing Arts Projects (Melbourne), which presented adaptations of literary pieces, such as D. H. Lawrence's *Lady Chatterley's Lover*, moving the audience to different locations around a garden and capitalising on the varying moods and visual impact of landscape settings.
RICHARD HEATHCOTE

THEME PARKS first opened in Australia in the 1960s. The first parks were pioneer villages, influenced by Disneyland (opened 1955) and American heritage and village sites, including Colonial Williamsburg (1926) and Old Sturbridge Village (1946). The first heritage theme parks in Australia, Swan Hill Pioneer Village, Vic. (1964) and Sovereign Hill, Ballarat, Vic. (1970), both involved the moving of structures from elsewhere; but Swan Hill was a complete re-creation, whereas Ballarat at least had some real mines on its site. Recreational and leisure parks pre-dated these two, but were not seen at the time as theme parks, but as 'fun fairs' or AMUSEMENT PARKS. The Luna Parks in Melbourne (1912) and Sydney (1935), had spectacular but restricted sites. Swan Hill, Sovereign Hill, and Old Sydney Town (1975), an extraordinary attempt to re-create the Sydney Cove of *c*. 1810 on farmland near Gosford (NSW), were much more elaborate undertakings, with major earthworks, streetscapes, and plantings of native trees and shrubs. During the mid-1980s Sovereign Hill, in particular, acknowledged horticultural authenticity in reconstructed garden settings for its houses, aided by detailed local research.

In the 1970s and 1980s, with the rise of Queensland's Gold Coast as Australia's premier coastal RESORT, huge theme parks including Dreamworld, Wet n' Wild, Sea World, and Warner Brothers Movie World were opened. Owing more to Disneyland and EuroDisney, than any Australian examples, these parks used local and exotic vegetation to create themed landscaped precincts within the overall site. These resort-influenced theme parks owe a debt to a vegetal pioneer at Nambour (Qld), the Big Pineapple (1971), and its progenitor at Coffs Harbour (NSW), the Big Banana (1964).
PETER SPEARRITT

THOMAS, Alfred Strickland (1900–), medical practitioner and rosarian, grew up at Mudgee (NSW) and as a boy exhibited roses from his father's garden (1915–17). He studied medicine at the University of Sydney (1918–23) before commencing practice at Bentleigh (Vic.) in 1924. Here he grew roses, initially without success due to the unfamiliar climate and conditions, but he was soon one of the leading amateurs. He joined the NATIONAL ROSE SOCIETY of Victoria in 1930 and accepted the presidency in 1938; his youth contrasted sharply with the previous long-serving incumbent James ALLAN (who died in office in 1936) and his duty-bound replacement Alister CLARK. Thomas wrote *Introduction to Rose Growing* (1944) and *Better Roses: Rose-growing for Everyone* (1950). A dominant presence among Australian rosarians, he received the Dean Hole Medal (1952), the Veitch Memorial Award (1962), and the first Gold Medal of the World Federation of Rose Societies (1979).
RA

THOMAS, William (*c*. 1815–1884), gardener, native of Glamorgan, Wales, sailed for Hobart as a bounty migrant on the *Conway* with his wife and children, arriving in 1855. Within two years he was employed as landscape gardener laying out the grounds of the new GOVERNMENT HOUSE, HOBART, aided by eighteen convicts. By 1860 he was secre-

The Gosford Dinosaur (1963) at Eric Worrell's Australian Reptile Park, Gosford (NSW); THEME PARKS in Australia cover a wide spectrum from nature to culture, and offer experiences midway between fantasy and reality

tary of the Gardeners' and Amateurs' Horticultural Society of Hobart Town and he held this paid position until 1864 when financial stringency forced the society to revert to an honorary officer, a role he accepted in 1871. He was then well established in Sandy Bay as a 'Pomological Nurseryman, Landscape Gardener, &c.', catering for a burgeoning market of orchardists. Thomas was prominent in local friendly societies and an accomplished musician. On his death, the *Mercury* mourned the loss of a 'Well-Known Colonist … who, from his many excellencies, was universally respected as a man and prized as a friend'. RA

THOMPSON, John (*c.* 1800–1861), land surveyor, 'pictorial draughtsman', and 'student of Landscape Gardening', practised in London during the 1820s, advertising an ability in drawing up plans for villas and estates. A friend of J.C. LOUDON, he contributed to the *Gardener's Magazine* during 1826 with remarks on the effect of the 'Lombardy Poplar in Park Scenery' and the 'Cedar of Lebanon in Landscape', indicating a close knowledge of Blenheim, Sion House, and the Botanic Garden at Chelsea; Loudon repeated their substance in his *Arboretum Britannicum* (1838). Thompson's third article, 'Design for Improving the Parks, by Extending Kensington Gardens, and Continuing the Serpentine River into Green Park, &c.' (1826) drew lengthy and favourable comments from Loudon.

Thompson arrived in NSW in 1827 and, on his appointment as an assistant surveyor, was placed in charge of maps, surveys, and other graphic records that had accumulated over a period of years. These he arranged and classified, in addition to drafting the results of the fieldwork by Surveyor-General MITCHELL. As Loudon's 'esteemed' correspondent, his first letter from Sydney (1830) refuted the general claim that the foliage of Australian forest trees was ugly, declaring that there were 'beautiful spots' ready for 'improvement', and Loudon's 'lessons and laying out have not been lost upon me even here', having used his skills to design a plan (location unknown) for laying out and planting HYDE PARK. Despite ill health precluding his participation in survey work, he was instrumental in establishing a new drafting school in the survey department and in 1835 became chief draftsman. Continuing to correspond with Loudon, he provided informed observations on the intellectual climate in Sydney, a plan by Mortimer Lewis for a proposed dwelling for Charles Windeyer (Thompson's father-in-law), and contemporary descriptions of the progress in gardening in the colony, especially at ELIZABETH BAY HOUSE. With a keen interest in horticulture, landscape gardening, and architecture, but of modest income, Thompson based the simple plan for his own house on a design for 'a small Roman Villa' from Loudon's *Encyclopaedia of Architecture* (1842 supplement), which he adapted for the Australian climate.

When Captain Perry retired (1853), Thompson became deputy surveyor-general (1854) and acting surveyor-general during the absence of Sir Thomas Mitchell. On Thompson's retirement in 1859, his fellow officers presented him with a silver flower vase, crafted in Sydney. The trunk of an ancient Australian forest tree 'overlaid with vines and parasites' formed the stem of the vase from the cup of which descended a 'graceful festoon of the staghorn fern giving it an appearance at once light and unique'. COLLEEN MORRIS

THOMPSON, Paul (b. 1945), landscape designer, was born in Melbourne and in 1970 commenced his own design and construction firm, specialising in using AUSTRALIAN PLANTS. His large output ranges from small private gardens to sizeable industrial and rural estates. In 1973 he completed the landscape master plan for Yarran Dheran Reserve in Mitcham (Vic.). A notable commission (in association with landscape architects Taylor and Cullity) has been the master plan and design development for ROYAL BOTANIC GARDENS, CRANBOURNE (1995), recognised at state and national levels by AUSTRALIAN INSTITUTE OF LANDSCAPE ARCHITECTS awards. His planting design for the Forest Gallery (1997–2000), with Taylor Cullity Lethlean, is the centrepiece for the new Melbourne Museum and he has had major involvement in the planting design of Melbourne's riverside park (2000). Thompson's designs are noted for their individuality and plant diversity; he has never been shy of utilising little-known or untried species and cultivars, often after animated and enthusiastic discussion with clients. He lectures regularly and has written *Water in Your Garden* (1991). RODGER ELLIOT

THOMPSON, Robert (1798–1869), Scottish-born horticulturist and pomologist, trained in the gardens of noted Scottish seats such as Skene, Haddo House, and Dunottar Castle. In 1824 Thompson came to London to the newly established garden of the London Horticultural Society at Chiswick. Among his compatriots at Chiswick was John DALLACHY, who had also progressed through the gardens at Haddo and was later to return as head gardener. Thompson was at once placed in the fruit department and during a forty-four year career at Chiswick 'made pomology his special and passionate study'; his *Catalogue of Fruits Cultivated in the Garden of the Horticultural Society of London* formed the foundation of modern pomological eponymy. He was a prolific contributor to horticultural journals and his best-known book, *The Gardener's Assistant* (1859, revised 1878, 1902), was well known in Australia; its wide scope embraced both garden design and practical horticulture, and Thompson was one of many writers to discuss the GARDENESQUE style, which he defined as the 'free symmetrical' style—a useful descriptive epithet. RA

THOMSON (née COMRIE-SMITH), Estelle (1894–1953), naturalist and wildflower painter, was born in Glasgow, Scotland, her parents keen naturalists. She was a teacher of physical culture and eurhythmics before her marriage in Glasgow in 1917 to an AIF surveying engineer. In 1919 the couple settled on a farm at Eight Mile Plains, south of Brisbane; the then unspoilt bush made a lasting impression on Thomson, who was to spend the rest of her life awakening public appreciation of Australian wildflowers. An active member of the Queensland Naturalists' Club from the 1920s, she contributed flowers, paintings, and drawings to its annual wildflower shows and also to the Arts and Crafts Society of Queensland. Thomson produced *Flowers of Our Bush* (1929), describing and illustrating coastal species. From 1929 to the 1930s she ran a weekly 'Wildflowers' column in the *Brisbane Courier,* followed until *c.* 1950 by 'Nature's Ways' in the Brisbane *Telegraph*. During the 1940s she gave a series of children's talks on wildflowers on the ABC. Her delicately hand-coloured lantern slides used for lectures are now held by the John Oxley Library, Brisbane. JUDITH McKAY

THOMSON, William (1814–1895) and his brother **David Thomson** (1823–1909), Scottish-born gardeners and horticulturists, in their parallel careers had a wide influence on many young gardeners, including some who migrated to Australia. William trained at Bothwell Castle, then took charge of Wrotham Park outside London, where he made his mark as a grape-grower, experience shared in his *Practical Treatise on the Culture of the Grape Vine* (1862). Here he remained sixteen years before taking charge in 1855 of Dalkeith for the Duke of Buccleuch—arguably Scotland's leading garden of the time—upon the retirement of Charles McINTOSH. He retired from Dalkeith in 1871 but continued in horticulture. Thomson's obituary spoke of his influence on 'a brood of gardeners hailing from Dalkeith that has well maintained the prestige of that practical school of learning'. David Thomson also worked at Bothwell then proceeded to Regent's Park, London, where he worked alongside Charles MOORE. He briefly worked for his brother at Wrotham then took charge of remodelling the garden at Dyrham Park, Gloucestershire. His reputation was made at Archerfield, East Lothian, and then, at the peak of his career, he took charge of the Buccleuch estate, Drumlanrig. Here Charles WESTON received his tutelage under Thomson. His best-known book was his *Handy Book of the Flower-Garden* (1868), which was widely consulted in the Australian colonies. At various times, the brothers edited the *Gardener* and the *Scottish Gardener*. RA

THOZET, Anthelme (*c.* 1826–1878), botanist and experimental gardener, was born near Lyons, France, but little is known of his early life. A republican and member of the National Assembly formed in 1848, he fled after the *coup d'état* of 1851 to England where he became a naturalised British subject. He was again affected by upheavals in France when in 1870, on his only return visit, he nearly starved in the Siege of Paris, a final stage of the Franco-Prussian war.

In the mid-1850s Thozet and his wife Marie Isabella (*née* Berthold) migrated to Australia. He worked as a gardener at SYDNEY BOTANIC GARDENS (1856–58), then went to the Port Curtis goldfields in Qld and settled in Rockhampton. His aim to establish a secure financial future by running a hotel met with early success and, after leasing out the hotel, he devoted the rest of his life to botany and horticulture. Thozet earned an international reputation as a collector of plant specimens, most of which he sent to Ferdinand MUELLER at MELBOURNE BOTANIC GARDENS. He also prepared specimens of woods and edible plants for display at EXHIBITIONS in London and Paris. Particularly significant was a collection of edible NATIVE PLANTS. The booklet accompanying the specimens, *Notes on some of the Roots, Tubers, Bulbs, and Fruits, used as Vegetable Food by the Aboriginals of Northern Queensland, Australia* (1866), described the plants, warned which parts were poisonous, and explained how to prepare the edible parts of these ABORIGINAL FOOD PLANTS. Profits from the sale of this booklet supported one of his cultural projects, the Rockhampton Museum Building fund. His status as a botanist was acknowledged by election to Fellowship of the Linnean Society of London in 1867.

Thozet is most remembered for Muellerville, his extensive EXPERIMENTAL GARDEN at Kalka, North Rockhampton. There he cultivated trees and plants, many not usually grown in TROPICAL climates, in order to determine their ECONOMIC value and suitability for the Qld climate. These included cotton, coffee, sugar-cane, cereals, tobacco, grapes, and a number of tropical fruits, such as bananas, new to Rockhampton. The much-praised garden, created on scientific principles and concerned with the utility of plants, contrasted with the nearby recreational Cremorne Gardens established by his fellow countryman and former associate in the hotel business, Bernard Pene.

Thozet was buried at Muellerville, and the garden was continued under the care of his wife, and son Auguste. Madame Thozet, who shared her husband's botanical and civic interests, collected lichens and played a leading role in local moves to resist federation in the 1890s. Thozet is commemorated in the names of a genus, *Thozetia* (now *Marsdenia*), and various species including *Jambosa* (now *Syzgium*), *Ixora*, *Acacia*, *Eucalyptus*, and *Aristolochia*.

MONIKA WELLS

TIBBITS, Wiliam Taylor Smith (1837–1906), artist, was born at Flecknoe, Warwickshire, England. From the 1860s he operated from Ballarat (Vic.), travelling the central goldfields painting watercolours to commission. Each work presented a property, mine, shop, hotel, cottage, or residence in meticulous detail. In 1875 Tibbits moved to Melbourne from where he enlarged the class and territory of his clientele. He moved to Adelaide (1897) and then Sydney (1898), painting there until his death. Many works are of interest to the GARDEN HISTORIAN for their detailed depictions of gardens, ranging from simple COTTAGE GARDENS of miner's cottages to more ambitious GARDENESQUE arrangements of VILLAS and pastoral HOMESTEAD estates. COMO, MELBOURNE BOTANIC GARDENS, and WAIROA were representative subjects. Tibbits consistently claimed his work had 'No Connection with PHOTOGRAPHY', yet his output forms a fascinating parallel to this technique. His works are in the State Library of Victoria and in the state's regional galleries, but the larger number are individually held in private ownership.

George Tibbits, *William Tibbits 1837–1906: Cottage, House and Garden Artist* (Parkville, Vic., 1984); *Portraits in the Landscape: The House Paintings of William Tibbits 1870–1906* (Sydney, 1984)

GEORGE TIBBITS

TITANGA, Lismore, in Victoria's WESTERN DISTRICT, has a splendidly intact HOMESTEAD GARDEN, laid out in 1872 by Alexander Buchanan behind his new basalt residence. The design took into account distant views and wind protection, and the low rainfall and lack of reticulated water also greatly influenced the design, consisting of a large gravelled carriage circle, ornamental garden with wide box and rosemary edged paths, orchard (now a tennis court), and vegetable garden. Significant WINDBREAKS of *Eucalyptus globulus* and *E. cladocalyx* were trialled by Buchanan (1875) and second owner John Lang Currie (1889). Currie's descendants, the Lang family, have since 1898 continued the tradition of tree planting using Australian species especially in an ARBORETUM along the driveway, which contains hundreds of mature trees, predominantly EUCALYPTS. In 1938, a small, grassed area with a lily-pond was added to the garden when dam water became available.

PAMELA JELLIE

TITHERADGE, George (1853–1916), English Shakespearean actor and bulb enthusiast, met the nursery proprietor and daffodil enthusiast Walter SMITH at a pub in Riddell's Creek (Vic.) in the 1890s. Given a few BULBS, he found

Watercolour view (1879) by William TIBBITS of the Fairfax property Ginahgulla, Bellevue Hill (NSW), commissioned only a decade after this prolific painter of houses and gardens began his career with depictions of cottages and mines on the Victorian goldfields

himself committed (thanks to Smith) to giving a lecture on DAFFODILS to a group presided over by the governor's wife. Hooked on daffodils—already popular in Victoria—he imported, in order to settle disputes about nomenclature, from Messrs BARR and Sons of Covent Garden, London, a collection of named varieties. On his return to England in 1898, he sold all his bulbs, including a number of South African ones, half of which were purchased by Alister CLARK and formed the basis of Clark's breeding program, initiated in the same year. Other bulbs went to Tasmanian gardens.

T.R. GARNETT

TOOLS for garden use, such as iron spades and forks, were brought to Australia with the First Feet to aid the production of essential food crops, vital for survival in the new colony. Ornamental flower gardens, a slightly later refinement, saw further importation of tools as new settlers arrived and permanent dwellings were established. Technical innovations in England during the nineteenth century dramatically improved both the availability and variety of devices used in gardening, especially garden MAINTENANCE; two important inventions, the LAWN MOWER and HOSES made from rubber, were to revolutionise the way gardens would be developed and maintained into the twentieth century. The most notable change, however, was the explosion in both the number and range of tools produced.

All types of garden work were catered for. A typical catalogue advertisement might contain illustrations of thirty different pruning knives and several different varieties of secateurs, shears, and clippers. The shapes of many spades, forks, cultivators, and rakes were custom designed for specific tasks, such as the onion hoe and fern trowel. Tools were often described by the number of prongs or style of head and neck such as 'swan' or 'goose'. Many of these had double-ended heads such as the combination hoe and rake. Ladies' and CHILDREN's sets were also popular. The refinement of manufacturing techniques to produce high-quality tempered steel meant that tools were lighter and very durable; stainless steel was very expensive and utilised for only a limited range of goods. Wooden shafts of varying lengths were fitted with either 'Y', 'T', or 'D' shaped handles. Wooden wheelbarrows were superseded by longer lasting galvanised trays fitted with pneumatic rubber wheels for ease of handling. Spray pumps used in the control of PESTS AND DISEASES were made of brass and copper and were hand-held, carried on the shoulder as a backpack, or foot-controlled. The scale of nineteenth-century garden tool design was staggering.

The Australian public was informed about the latest trends and fashions in garden equipment through GARDEN BOOKS and MAGAZINES that increasingly flourished during this period, and by the many newspaper articles written about the subject. Advice regarding the most appropriate tools to use for PRUNING, COMPOSTING, mulching, spraying, tilling, aerating, seeding, or trenching was given as well as useful tips about care and maintenance. Most of the tools available were imported from England and France. Distribution was organised through agents located in all the capital cities and sold through ironmongers, hardware stores, seed merchants, and NURSERIES. Local blacksmiths made hand tools and small skilled workshops produced a range of equipment such as axes, picks, mattocks, pruning knives, secateurs, wire sieves, and sprinkler fittings. The tools of trade used in gold and tin mining also found currency in gardening, in particular the long-handled shovel with a pointed blade, specifically used by the Cornish.

Competition from imported goods (mainly English) and the unavailability of machinery able to forge large shovel blades and fork tines restricted the mass machining of these tools in Australia. Higher tariffs introduced by the Federal Government during the 1930s to protect locally made goods provided the opportunity for Trojan Ltd to successfully design and build machinery capable of this type of production between 1935 and 1937 and in the 1950s Cyclone Forgings Pty Ltd in Vic. formed a trade agreement with the English firm Brades Pty Ltd to assist the local firm with expertise in hot pressing and roll forging. A shortage of imported English goods and the necessity to produce vegetable crops from the home garden during the Second World War did for a short time foster a viable climate for locally manufactured tools.

Production in Australia was originally undertaken by a small number of companies situated in the larger manufacturing states of NSW and Vic. From the 1920s to the 1960s the main tool makers were Tulloch Ltd, Mintern Tools, and Trojan Ltd (formally Scott and Sons). These companies operated as separate entities until the late 1950s. As a result of several company takeovers, there is now only one major company, Cyclone Hardware (a division of Pioneer Industries, which also markets the brand name 'Trojan Hytest'), that manufactures mass-produced garden tools in Australia. The monopolisation of the garden tool industry is a world-wide phenomenon. Today, retail outlets encompass large chain stores as well as local hardware stores and plant nurseries, and England, once the largest exporter of tools to Australia, competes in the market place with Asia.

The range of tools produced from the 1950s onwards became standardised and more 'user friendly'. Moulded plastics were introduced as a cheap and lighter alternative to heavier metals, particularly in the design of rakes, small implements, and wheelbarrows. Welded steel and aluminium construction techniques were employed in the production of some specialised goods, and the mechanisation of tools such as rotary hoes and cultivators reduced the heavy work of tilling the soil. Tools have also become more versatile recently; for instance, handles and poles can be fitted with different detachable heads and some are specially made for people with disabilities, or are being ergonomically designed to prevent injuries associated with bending or lifting.

SUZANNE HUNT

TOOWOOMBA QUEENS PARK, Qld. The original botanic garden site, bounded by Mackenzie, Margaret, Mary, and Herries streets (gazetted 1861), was considered too far from the work and residences of Toowoomba's working classes, who would benefit most from the establishment of a PUBLIC PARK. In 1869 the colonial government exchanged this site for a camping reserve east of Hume Street and closer

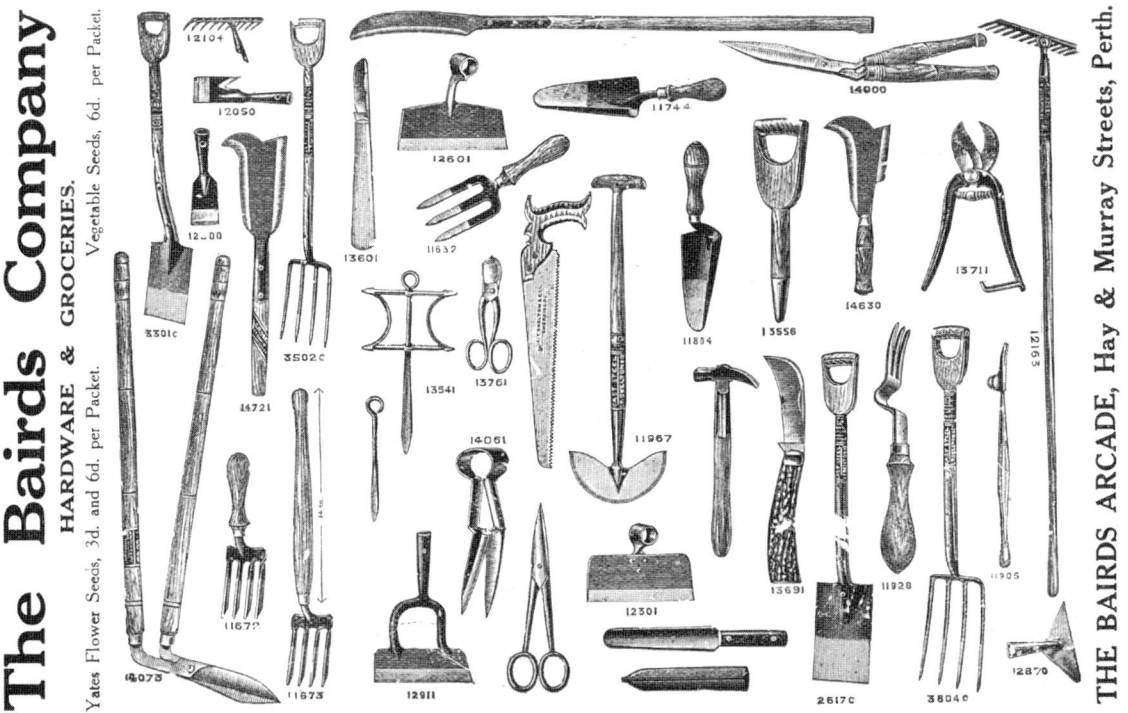

This small selection of catalogue illustrations (1916) indicates the great variety of specialist gardening TOOLS and implements that were available to both professional and amateur gardeners

to the heart of the city. Queens Park included a BOTANIC GARDEN, the first section to be laid out and developed. By 1886 the garden had received or exchanged 4800 plants. The initial planting of RAINFOREST trees around the perimeter and avenues of *Cinnamomum camphora* (Camphor Laurel) provided shade but more importantly filtered the air. Richard Ross Harding, the second curator, argued that 'they purify the atmosphere, counteracting the effects of animal life, and various processes of decomposition'. The late nineteenth-century change from pastoral to agricultural economy for the DARLING DOWNS was supported by trial work carried out in the garden. Experiments were conducted on fodder crops, native and exotic GRASSES, wheat, and fruit suitable for the local conditions. The emphasis elsewhere in Queens Park was on RECREATION, including municipal BATHS (1874), BANDSTAND (1896), and SPORTING facilities, which complemented earlier strolling paths and passive LEISURE features.

JODI FRAWLEY

TOPIARY, the art of clipping and PRUNING shrubs and trees into ornamental, usually three-dimensional, shapes, exemplifies its origins as *topia opera* or 'fancy gardening'. Adapted in Australia from the traditional influences of European *parterres de broderie*, and also, more recently, from Japanese landscaping techniques, this art is generally practised by home gardeners in its simplest forms of sphere, box, and cone, forming specimen plantings in the neatly trimmed environs of a SUBURBAN GARDEN and LAWN. Topiary art is also associated with the whimsical and QUIRKY, such as retail nursery esoterica where specimens are cut to form rings, love hearts, and miscellaneous animal shapes such as emus and reindeer. Idiosyncratic examples, such as a tree-fern dinosaur in Noojee (Vic.) or the monumental temporary Sydney installation, 'Puppy' (1996) by international artist Jeff Koons, may well test the more conventional boundaries of topiary.

ROWAN WILKEN and KAREN OLSEN

TOWN PLANNING The emergence of modern town planning ideology after Federation concatenated various reform impulses: city improvement, civic design, tree planting, pro-reservation and anti-alienation of parkland, subdivision and building regulation, and the democratisation of the SUBURBAN ideal. The Federal Capital project lent a distinctive character to what was an international movement. Capital city–based town planning associations offered leadership with ex-London architect John SULMAN assuming national figurehead status. Major conferences were held in Adelaide (1917) and Brisbane (1918). Early idealism hardened into technical prescriptions and lobbying for legislation. Depression and war were setbacks, but post-war reconstruction saw a decisive refocusing on issues of planned redevelopment, community planning, local land use control, and metropolitan strategies. Under the stimulus of the Commonwealth Housing Commission, the mid-1940s was a crucial legislative phase for the establishment of planning systems in the states. Through the 1950s planning was professionalised. Guided by aesthetic and

Town planning

technocratic MODERNIST ideals, master plans, zoning schemes, and labyrinthine procedures were institutionalised. In the 1970s a raft of unpopular redevelopment proposals politicised planning processes, exemplified by the GREEN BAN movement. The response was greater emphases on public participation, HERITAGE conservation, and environmental protection. Planning continued to be remade in the 1990s, shaped by myriad forces: economic rationalism, deregulation, privatisation, entrepreneurialism, CONSERVATION, and URBAN DESIGN. The spatial locus has shifted from greenfields to brownfields development, and the social imperative towards defence of the public realm.

PUBLIC PARKS, gardens, and related open spaces as 'the lungs of the city' bestowing benefits of health and beauty have endured as major preoccupations of planning. A seminal statement was Sulman's *The Laying Out of Towns* (1890) which foreshadowed GREEN BELTS, planting schemes, and statutory provision of parkland. In his *An Introduction to the Study of Town Planning in Australia* (1921), the scope of space planning was broadened to encompass SHOWGROUNDS, ZOOS, RACECOURSES, GOLF COURSES, even aerodromes. The desired design of PUBLIC OPEN SPACES varied from formalistic urban parks through more naturalistic suburban treatments out to reserves of native BUSH. A.J. BROWN and H.M. Sherrard's *Town and Country Planning* (1951, revised 1969) introduced a new consciousness of landscape design to transcend 'gruesome eccentricities of the untutored mind'. Brown's wife Jocelyn was a leading educator and practitioner of DESIGNED LANDSCAPES. The professional links between landscape architecture and planning were solidified by others such as Rex HAZLEWOOD, John OLDHAM, and Frank HEATH (who contributed in 1948 to E.E. LORD's *Shrubs and Trees for Australian Gardens*). As planning discourse became increasingly fragmented from the 1970s, growing recognition of the intrinsic environmental value of urban green space provided one unifying theme. Non-urban zones became a mosaic of ecological communities and not just a green fence to the city, open space systems were adapted for multiple uses including stormwater DRAINAGE and IRRIGATION, bushland remnants were conserved, biodiversity valued, and environmental sustainability became a further rationale for planning.

The major achievement of the nineteenth century was the reservation of large tracts of open space for commons, public DOMAINS, BOTANIC GARDENS, and government farms. The most memorable and still substantially intact parklands encircle Adelaide, a legacy of William LIGHT's 1837 plan. The parkland towns of SA and western Vic. are a distinctive regional variation. The laying out of major spaces such as Sydney's CENTENNIAL PARK (1888) introduced synoptic visions that emphasised the value of pre-planning at larger scales. However, the breakthrough to the American park system idea was

'Proposed Remodelling of Queen's Square', looking north from Sydney's HYDE PARK—this (unexecuted) proposal shows Elizabeth and Macquarie Streets widened and planted as part of the TOWN PLANNING suggestions contained in the report of the 1909 Royal Commission on Sydney Improvement

not made, because of local government fragmentation. The real battle was retention of community open space in the face of subdivision and re-subdivision pressures.

From the early 1900s, CITY BEAUTIFUL and GARDEN CITY movements codified the complementary thrusts of planning towards the enhancement of public spaces and reform of residential standards. The former linked aesthetics and growth via new parks, BOULEVARDS, and street beautification. The latter endorsed 'one house—one family—one garden', usually in the guise of the garden suburb, a planned physical and social entity of detached houses, trophy FRONT GARDENS, tree-lined streets, and generous open spaces. An outstanding showpiece was Adelaide's COLONEL LIGHT GARDENS (1921), designed by Charles READE. CANBERRA synthesised garden city and city beautiful aspirations. Thomas WESTON played the crucial horticultural role in realising both the framework of Walter Burley GRIFFIN's grand manner 1912 scheme and Sulman's garden suburb interventions from the early 1920s.

The planned suburb went into mass production in the 1920s. From the 1950s public housing estates set high technical standards for site planning, although financial restrictions meant that the full panoply of community facilities and planted reserves and NATURE STRIPS was not delivered. Open spaces in public and private housing estates became the responsibility of cash-strapped local authorities. Influenced by American standards, the standard of one-tenth of subdivided area for parkland was accepted even before the Second World Ward as a yardstick. Later, population density norms were introduced but in practice quotas were often negotiated as development control shifted from strict minimum to performance standards of provision. Cluster and community titles legislation since the 1970s has provided new types of common green areas in planned residential developments. In the strengthening policy push towards compact cities via urban consolidation, a critical challenge is retention of the character of traditional house-and-garden streetscapes.

The distribution of open spaces emerged as a major planning theme in the inter-war years. Animated by propagandists such as Charles Edwin Woodrow Bean (1879–1968) in Sydney, J.W. BARRETT in Melbourne, and W.E. BOLD in Perth, parks and PLAYGROUND associations campaigned for more equitable access. In the 1930s progress was made through beautification, reclamation, and improvement schemes carried out under unemployment relief. In the 1940s metropolitan green belts conserving rural, scenic, and recreational resources were advocated to contain 'promiscuous suburbanisation', later giving way to more trend-friendly 'green wedges'. Post-war metropolitan strategies have targeted the consolidation and expansion of regional open space systems, a process that continues through land acquisition, landscaping, and access improvement initiatives, often by state–local joint ventures. The era of big park creation is not over, with the development of the Millennium Parklands at Sydney's Homebush Bay tied to the staging of the 2000 Olympics. Rehabilitation and redevelopment of former industrial, port, and railway land made surplus by economic restructuring has provided ongoing opportunities and new challenges for park and garden design.

Robert Freestone, *Model Communities* (Melbourne, 1989); Stephen Hamnett and Robert Freestone, *The Australian Metropolis: A Planning History* (Sydney, 2000)

ROBERT FREESTONE

TOWNSVILLE QUEENS PARK, Qld, was laid out by its first curator, William Anderson, in 1878. Italian-born chemist and druggist Pio ARMATI assisted Anderson in the early design and remained actively involved as a member of the original board of trustees. The dramatic backdrop of Castle Hill complemented the placement of trees, shrubs, and decorative bedding plants. Trees were donated by Rockhampton plant hunter Anthelme THOZET, the Queensland Acclimatisation Society, and Walter HILL. Remnant nineteenth-century plantings include a large variety of RAINFOREST species with large *Ficus benghalensis* (Banyan) trees located in the centre of the gardens. After the retirement of Anderson in 1900 the park was treated as a pleasure ground, with charges levied by the Townsville City Council for PICNICS and musical entertainment. In 1950, Harry OAKMAN's assistant, Alan Wilson, was commissioned to redesign a section within the bounds of Queens Park. Upon completion it was renamed Queens Garden to commemorate Queen Elizabeth II.

JODI FRAWLEY

TOYNE, Gilbert (1888–1983), inventor of the all-metal rotary clothes hoist, was born at Batesford, outside Geelong (Vic.), and advertised his distinctive addition to the DRYING GROUND as early as 1924. With its defining features of two cross arms supporting wires and central post with winding mechanism (facilitating raising and lowering to suit the user), the original crown wheel and pinion mechanism was apparently machined at Ballarat railway workshops. Toyne patented his invention in 1923. Initially located in Carnegie, the manufacture of Toyne's All Metal Rotary Clothes Hoist moved to Mont Albert in the late 1920s, when the company was acquired by Archibald James McKirdy (1874–1933). A hydraulic model was introduced in the late 1930s. When production of 'non-essential' goods began again after the Second World War, Adelaide-based **Lancelot Leonard Hill** (1902–1986) produced a hoist that in almost all respects replicated Toyne's original. While many companies produced rotary clothes hoists in the post-war era, the 'Hills Hoist' in time dominated the market and became an Australian BACKYARD icon.

PETER CUFFLEY

TRACT (1973–), a consultancy set up in Melbourne by David YENCKEN, was among the earliest independent professional LANDSCAPE ARCHITECTURE offices to be established in Vic. and its achievements represent an approach and standard now mirrored in numerous practices around the country. Partner Howard McCorkell (b. 1940) was soon joined by Dr Rodney Wulff (b. 1947) and Stephen Calhoun (b. 1943)—the key design partner—and later followed by George Gallagher (b. 1950) and Michael Stokes (b. 1953). Early projects included private and institutional commissions, international in scope from 1977. A national reputation was established in 1981 with the firm's win in the Newcastle foreshore development competition. From the early 1980s campus planning, housing, cemetery development, and strategic development commissions increased, aided by new offices in Perth (1985), Sydney (1988) and Brisbane (1990). RA

TRAPNELL, (Walter) George (*c.* 1919–1998), horticulturist, field botanist, ecologist, and nursery proprietor, began work as a gardener at BRISBANE BOTANIC GARDENS in the late 1950s after Harry OAKMAN persuaded him to leave tailoring. There, with Harry CAULFIELD, he developed a RAINFOREST garden under trees planted by Walter HILL, and carried out Oakman's design changes. Over four decades he made numerous plant collecting expeditions into all parts of Qld with his friend Keith WILLIAMS, bringing many new species (including *Callistemon* and *Melaleuca*) into cultivation and making numerous contributions to the Queensland HERBARIUM. As amateur naturalists and members of the Queensland Naturalists' Club these men spread the word about cultivating NATIVE PLANTS. Together they set up the 'Save the Trees Campaign Research Nursery' at Zillmere in the 1970s (now disbanded). Williams was a major influence on the fledgling AUSTRALIAN INSTITUTE OF LANDSCAPE ARCHITECTS and its members in Qld through his wise counsel on selecting and growing native plants. JEANNIE SIM

TRAWALLA, near Beaufort, Vic., is approached by a long drive lined with *Pinus radiata* (Monterey Pine), then elms and oaks, while the rear drive passes through a fine stand of *Eucalyptus camaldulensis* (River Red Gum) and indigenous grassland. Although the 1840s homestead remains with remnants of its original garden, the nearby brick two-storey homestead (1891) is the focus for eleven hectares, of which about two hectares is intensively gardened. The remainder, known as The Policies (after the Scottish term denoting the ornamental planting surrounding a large country house, generally embracing the PLEASURE GROUNDS and PARKLAND), consists of oaks, pines, other woodland trees, and naturalised bulbs. The garden, little changed since the 1890s, includes sweeping lawns, shrubberies, fine specimen trees, a pergola covered in ornamental grapes, and rose, kitchen, and picking gardens. A key feature is 'Diana's Walk', an avenue of oaks underplanted with bluebells, daffodils, and grape hyacinths terminating at a statue of Diana. A fine working CONSERVATORY is attached to the 1891 homestead. HELEN PAGE

TREASURY GARDENS, Melbourne: see FITZROY GARDENS, Melbourne

TREE It would seem a simple matter to define a thing as lovely and as common as a tree. However, definitions are neither as easy nor as simple as they might seem. The word 'tree' is of Old English origin; meaning a plant having a self-supporting woody main stem or trunk and growing to considerable height and size. In light of considerable debate about the technical aspects of such definitions, there is consensus that trees are long-lived woody perennial plants greater than three metres in height, with one or relatively few stems or trunks.

Since trees are large and long-lived PLANTS their successful growth and cultivation is a major part of HORTICULTURE and they make a significant contribution to GARDENS and broader DESIGNED and CULTURAL LANDSCAPES. They provide a sense of scale that no other plant can contribute, and the right tree planted in the right place at the right time can influence a landscape not just for decades but centuries. Their management and manipulation often require specialist treatments that involve ARBORICULTURE, TREE SURGERY, and FORESTRY.

There are many different types of trees, and while most are considered to be woody, undergoing secondary growth, this does not apply to all trees. Among the plants that make up the group of trees are CONIFERS, most of which have distinctive cones, and are often described as softwoods. The large flowering trees are part of the angiosperm group and are often described as hardwoods. The PALMS are a distinctive group that are not woody (as they do not exhibit secondary growth), and are known for their tall, slender stems of near-uniform diameter.

The pleasure garden at TRAWALLA, near Beaufort (Vic.), photographed in the early years of the twentieth century, featured a large and intricate arrangement of beds prominently sited near the homestead and backed by extensive shrubberies and tree plantings

The life-spans of trees can range from a few short years or decades to centuries and even millennia. Among the longest-lived trees are the redwoods of California (3000 years), the Bristle-cone pines of the Sierra Nevada (4000 years), and Australia's own Huon pines (2000 years). Eucalypts are much shorter lived, with species such as *Eucalyptus camaldulensis* (River Red Gum) achieving ages of 500–700 years. The tallest specimens can exceed 100 metres in height, with some of the conifers and EUCALYPTS being among the tallest and largest living things on the planet. *Sequoiadendron giganteum* (Giant Redwood) and *Eucalyptus regnans* (Mountain Ash) are respectively the tallest softwood and hardwood species.

Many of the genera of trees are well known to gardeners and horticulturists. Among the conifers, the genera *Pinus* (pines), *Cupressus* (cypress), *Cedrus* (cedars), and *Abies* (spruces) are well known, while among the AUSTRALIAN FLORA, hardwoods such as EUCALYPTUS (eucalypts), ACACIA (wattles), GREVILLEA (especially *Grevillea robusta*, silky oak), and *Ficus* (FIGS) are as well known as their exotic counterparts *Ulmus* (ELMS), *Quercus* (oaks), and *Liquidambar*. Among the PALMS the genus *Phoenix* is probably the best known.

Trees can be found in many different places. They are an important part of BOTANIC GARDENS, PUBLIC PARKS AND GARDENS, and CEMETERIES, as well as many private gardens from SUBURBAN to large HOMESTEAD and HILL-STATION GARDENS. STREET TREES form AVENUES in many thoroughfares, where they contribute to the ambience of a city and its suburbs. Sometimes a special collection of trees may be established, known as an ARBORETUM (if there is a diverse range of tree species and genera), PINETUM (for a specialised collection based on pines and other conifers), or ORCHARD (fruit trees). Some of Australia's finest trees are recognised by listing on the NATIONAL TRUST Register of Significant Trees. Symbolic and folkloric aspects are evocatively demonstrated by Peter Solness in *Tree Stories* (1999).   GREG MOORE

TREE HOUSES utilise the elevation provided by their host tree for varied purposes. Cubby houses in the form of tree houses have traditionally permitted children to be free from adult occupation, re-creating a domestic environment or 'house in miniature' in a garden setting. Often makeshift in materials and construction, tree houses have generally been situated atop the main fork of a large BACKYARD tree. For the child-occupant of the tree house, the aerial position affords both protection from the (adult) world and surveillance of the surrounding garden 'wilderness'. Tree houses in the manner of LOOKOUT towers have also formed distinctive GARDEN BUILDINGS. In the 1890s, photographer and ethnographer J.W. Lindt recaptured memories of New Guinea with rustic shelters midway up trunks of giant *Eucalyptus regnans* (Mountain Ash) at his HERMITAGE. Hollow trunks of giant eucalypts also occasionally provided makeshift houses to struggling selectors in Gippsland (Vic.) in the late nineteenth century.

ROWAN WILKEN

TREE OF KNOWLEDGE, Barcaldine, Qld, a 300-year-old *Eucalyptus papuana* (Ghost Gum), is considered the birth place of the Australian Labor Party. Tension between pastoralists and shearers over living standards and employment of non-white and intercolonial labour in the 1880s prompted the formation of the Central Queensland Labourers' Union in 1889 at Barcaldine. Turbulent negotiations ensued, culminating in strikes, with camps established at the railway terminus of Barcaldine. This tree became the meeting place. The 1891 shearers' strike was a watershed in political history, triggering the transformation of workers' movements into a significant political force.   MARGARET COOK

TREE SURGERY is a term that is applied to a number of specialist techniques that are carried out on woody plant species. The most common of these techniques is PRUNING, particularly of large limbs. However, other techniques such as the filling of hollows and cavities, and the cabling or bracing of major limbs also come within the ambit of the tree surgeon's craft. In recent years, tree surgery has often involved the use of elevated platform vehicles or travel towers and buckets, and chainsaws. Sophisticated rope and harness techniques are used for gaining access to various parts of the TREE without causing damage to the tree's structural integrity. Once considered a specialist remedial aspect of HORTICULTURE, tree surgery is now seen as a significant component of ARBORICULTURE. Many of its techniques, such as canopy thinning and formative pruning, are seen as proactive techniques, which reduce the risks of canopy deformity or tree failure.   GREG MOORE

TRELLIS-WORK The earliest recorded uses (1810s) of ornamental trellis-work in Australia are probably the cruciform ARBOURS in the Governor's DOMAIN, Sydney, and the garden porch (later known as Lady Gipps's Bower) attached to the breakfast room at GOVERNMENT HOUSE, Parramatta. Both were probably instigated by the Governor's wife, Elizabeth Macquarie. By the 1830s architectural wooden treillage for verandahs was fashionable, but simpler trellis-work, including RUSTIC-WORK formed of branches and twigs, was recorded on garden structures, fences, and garden seats. This taste continued into the twentieth century, but by the late nineteenth century trellised WIRE-WORK provided a more delicate and more durable alternative to wooden laths. In early trellis-work the wooden laths tended to be widely spaced; later, equal spacing was more common, or, in the late nineteenth century, herringbone arrangements of closely spaced parallel laths. In the early twentieth century the traditional diagonal lattice-work patterns were often replaced by square designs. Rustic-work was little used between the wars, but improvised materials, such as water-pipe frames with chicken wire, or woven flat iron straps salvaged from packaging, were popular. These vernacular practices continued into the 1950s–60s with the innovative weaving of the flexible steel slats used in venetian blinds, and the practical substitution of woven wirework by sheets of welded steel concrete reinforcing mesh. In the last quarter of the twentieth century, with the fashion for nineteenth-century design, came a revival of traditional wooden lattice, much of it ready-made, little of it as substantial or well-designed as the original.

JAMES BROADBENT

TRELOAR, Henry (*c.* 1873–1932), a native of Redruth, Cornwall, England, migrated and established a MARKET GARDEN at Townsville, Qld. In 1913 he published *Cottage Gardening in Queensland*, an idiosyncratic guide for the small landholder. The 1915 edition, with a self-confessed 'unconventional calendar of the season's operations', included a novel offer to readers who correctly answered '1. On what date do you predict the great European War will end? 2. Who do you predict will be the victors? 3. In what capital do you predict the Peace Treaty will be signed?'. He exhorted readers to hear the cry for food of Europe's starving and to increase production. He also decried Chinese market gardeners—'a *yellow* blot [that] has run and splattered far and wide'—preaching his white, Eurocentric message to a community divided about the merits of Asian and islander labour. The 1920 edition, in more muted tones, stuck closely to the theme of the title, his journalistic bent satisfied by conduct of a regular gardening column (as 'Eucalyptus') in the *Townsville Daily Bulletin*. RA

TRESEDER, John Garland (*fl.* 1830s–90s), and his brothers **Thomas Garland Treseder** (*fl.* 1880s) and **Stephen Treseder** (*c.* 1833–1909), nursery proprietors and seed merchants, were active in NSW in the second half of the nineteenth century. Of Cornish ancestry, their father was a landscape gardener and nursery proprietor in Truro (where the brothers trained). Stephen Treseder resided in Australia and New Zealand *c.* 1856–70 before commencing a nursery business specialising in roses at Cardiff, Wales. William Treseder (*c.* 1829–1893), a well-known Cardiff nursery proprietor, was possibly an elder brother. John Treseder married at Orange (NSW) in 1866 while Thomas married at Concord (NSW) in 1880. The brothers leased the Dobroyde Nursery at Ashfield and by 1880 advertised as 'Plant & Fruit Tree Growers, Contract Planters, Landscape Gardeners', with their nursery supplemented by a Pitt Street seed store. They also advertised 'Parks and Gardens Designed and Planted'; their work at Woollahra House, Rose Bay, was praised by *Casteners's Monthly and Rural Magazine* (1885) as 'one of the most conspicuous examples of high art in landscape gardening'. John Treseder purchased an established garden at Ashfield where he ran the Underwood Nursery, named after the previous owner. Treseder (possibly Thomas) traded as Treseder and Bartlett during the mid-1880s, and the city retail business was sold *c.* 1888 to Pearce Brothers.

The most enduring legacy of the Treseder Brothers was their handbook *The Garden* (1880). Stylistic comments were taken directly from KEMP's *How to Lay out a Garden*, but there was much original material on COTTAGE GARDENS, seaside gardens, SUBURBAN GARDENS, town and window gardening, bush-houses, and rockeries. FLOWER GARDENS were described with the aid of two plates ('The Flower Garden' and 'The Rosary') and buffalo LAWN was recommended. Revised editions were published in 1884 and 1890. RA

TREVASKIS, Percival (1903–1991), gardener, was born in Cornwall, England, and served his apprenticeship (1923–25) at Aldenham Park, residence of Vicary Gibbs, who was responsible for the fine garden with its notable arboretum famous in the early twentieth century for its variety and extent. Trevaskis received training at the nurseries of BARR and Sons, in the rock and alpine gardens at the ROYAL BOTANIC GARDENS, KEW (1925–27), and at the Imperial Bureau of Entomology. He was introduced to Alfred Nicholas in 1929 at the Chelsea Flower Show—Nicholas required a landscape gardener for his new HILL-STATION, named BURNHAM BEECHES, in Victoria's Dandenong Ranges. Trevaskis was duly appointed and recalled that 'Prior to leaving for Australia, about once a week I would receive a letter from Mr. Nicholas … requesting that I inspect various gardens he had seen during his stay and his travels'. Trevaskis was head gardener throughout the formative period of the garden and was responsible for much of the ROCKWORK and the ALPINE rockery, superintending the planting, and transplanting of many shrubs and trees. He lived in the grounds and remained at Burnham Beeches until 1936, when he joined the staff at the School of Primary Agriculture and Horticulture, BURNLEY, as garden supervisor and as later demonstrator in horticulture. Trevaskis was appointed superintendent of parks for the City of Brighton (1944–50) and ultimately State Superintendent of Parks and Gardens in the Public Works Department (1950–64). Percy Trevaskis was a committee member of the Royal Horticultural Society of Victoria and a life member of the Kew Guild. RA

TRIGGS, (Harry) Inigo (1876–1923), English architect, garden designer, and descendent of architect Inigo Jones (1573–1653), was an authority on the history of FORMAL gardens in Britain, brought to an Australian audience through his *Formal Gardens in England and Scotland* (1902). This and other books, including *The Art of Garden Design in Italy* (1906), *Town Planning, Past, Present and Future* (1909) and *Garden Craft in Europe* (1913) demonstrated his ARTS AND CRAFTS sympathies, which found receptive ears in the colonies.

In 1892 Inigo's brother, Arthur Bryant Triggs (1868–1936), married Maria Sophie Ritchie (*c.* 1868–1897). Triggs had arrived in Australia aged 19 and become a successful pastoralist. His father-in-law, James P. Ritchie (*c.* 1835–1878), owned Linton, North Yass (NSW), which Triggs subsequently acquired. Triggs remarried in 1901 and from 1907 spent two decades renovating the house at Linton. Following trips back to England in 1922–26, parts of the garden were reworked in an Arts and Crafts manner, with walled and gated 'rooms' arranged around an axial plan, and garden ornaments such as statues, urns, and stone seats. JULIET RAMSAY

TROPICAL GARDENS occur in those parts of Australia with warm temperatures and summer rains and include those subtropical areas with a minimum temperature of 3°C and no ground frosts. These essential CLIMATIC qualities, found along coastal regions of northern NSW, Qld, NT, and northern WA, ensure rapid plant growth and provide strikingly different plant, foliage, and colour combinations to gardens in temperate regions.

Ancient American, Asian, and African cultures have been gardening in the tropics for thousands of years, and from the sixteenth century, colonial and post-colonial settlements have combined the gardening experience and aesthetic values of Europe with new possibilities and challenges of the tropics. Early Australian garden writers often overlooked tropical gardening, but with the rise of horticulture in Qld from the 1860s, writers such as A.J. HOCKINGS, William SOUTTER, Henry TRELOAR, Llewellyn LUCAS, D.A. HERBERT, and Harry OAKMAN specifically addressed its special requirements, as did BOTANIC GARDEN directors commencing with Walter HILL and Maurice HOLTZE. From the 1870s, the fashion for BEDDING using subtropical FOLIAGE received considerable attention in Australia, particularly through the work of Charles MOORE and William GUILFOYLE.

Significant international publications began with *Tropical Planting and Gardening with Special Reference to Ceylon* (many editions from 1910) by Hugh Fraser Macmillan (1869–1948). Hawaiians Lorraine E. Kuck and Richard C. Tongg presented the views of landscape architects in *The Tropical Garden* (1936) with important and innovative design ideas, although they did not then detect a distinct 'tropical style of gardening'. Their *Modern Tropical Garden* (1955) extended their earlier 'living outside' theme. Kuck and Tongg maintained that tropical gardens should embody a jungle-like character with these three distinctive components: lush density of planting, large-leaved plants, and lianas or creepers scrambling up tree trunks.

What can be discerned in the early twenty-first century is that tropical landscape character has been applied to various stylistic arrangements: informal/irregular, formal/regular, and utilitarian traditions. Other typical features of tropical gardens include an 'exotic' aspect in the deliberate mixture of native and foreign plants; 'iconic' tropical species with visually striking forms (PALMS, BAMBOO, tropical FIG trees, and RAINFOREST vines and epiphytes—ORCHIDS, staghorn ferns, and bird's nest ferns); masses of bold, bright COLOURS in flowers and/or foliage (poinciana, jacaranda, frangipani, bauhinia, acalypha, coleus, croton, canna, and bougainvillea); and tropical shade gardening practices in the BUSH-HOUSE and VERANDAH GARDENING. In nineteenth-century Qld, a bizarre note was sometimes observed to creep into tropical gardening with RUSTIC constructions of giant clam shells and coral-stone, and strange GARDEN ORNAMENTS—whale-bones and nautical *objets trouvés*.

Later influences on local gardens came from Brazilian landscape architect Roberto Burle Marx (1909–1994) in his personal version of MODERNISM. Most memorable were his broad sweeps of massed colourful foliage ground covers (alternanthera, coleus, and bromeliads) and unusual feature trees. He also invented a column of epiphytes for interior gardens, which was repeated at the 1998 World Expo (Brisbane) by Landplan Studios. From the 1970s, tropical versions of BUSH GARDENS were formed in Qld and northern NSW, based on the re-creation of native rainforests. By the 1990s new tropical gardens in South-East ASIA, especially the work of Australian-born Made WIJAYA centred on Bali and popularised in photographic books by Warren and Tettoni, began having an impact on Australia. Asian traditions meet the irregular, prolific planting of English COTTAGE GARDENS in this latest wave.

William Warren and Luca Invernizzi Tettoni, *The Tropical Garden* (London, 1991)

JEANNIE SIM

TROUETTE, Jean-Pierre (1833–1885), viticulturist and agricultural worker, and much-travelled, came from the south of France. In 1857 he took over a small vegetable garden at Great Western (Vic.). Trouette had married Anne-Marie Blampied, also French, who with her younger brother, Emile, had been attracted to Australia by the gold discoveries. Trouette secured freehold to twenty-seven acres (11 ha), which he named St Peter's, grew fruit and vegetables, and sold them to local gold miners and communities. In

This Edwardian tableau under banana trees at DARWIN BOTANIC GARDENS, its participants complete with bonnets, gloves, and parasols, illustrates the way even rudimentary and remote TROPICAL GARDENS provided leisured moments to rival those in the larger and more splendidly landscaped gardens of the populous and temperate south

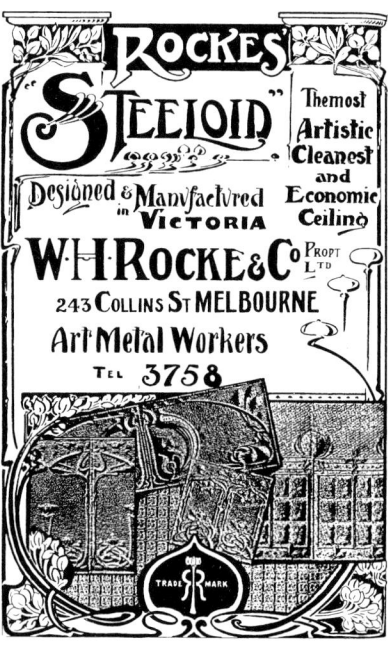

The First Australian Exhibition of Women's Work (1907), of which Mrs Arthur TUCKETT chaired the Horticultural Section, gave exhibitors and sponsors a fine opportunity to highlight the use of native timbers in craftwork and also to promote more generally the use of AUSTRALIAN FLORA in DECORATIVE ARTS

1863 he planted a vineyard for fruit but in 1866 made his first wines and sent samples to Melbourne's intercolonial EXHIBITION. They established Trouette's reputation as a grower and maker, and that of Great Western as a VITICULTURAL area. By 1878 the partnership of Trouette and Blampied had forty-five acres (18 ha) under vine and had created an outpost of French provincial life described charmingly by Hubert DE CASTELLA in *John Bull's Vineyard* (1886). Trouette was the pioneer of Great Western as a viticultural area and his success inspired others, such as the BEST brothers. **DAVID DUNSTAN**

TUCKETT (née GIBSON), Margaret Thomas (1860–1938), horticulturist, was born in Melbourne and married Arthur Helton Tuckett (1857–1934) at St Kilda in 1884. Tuckett's father, Joseph Richardson Tuckett, had entered into a long-established auctioneers business with Hugh M.C. Gemmell in 1867, and was responsible for many notable Melbourne sales, including the RIPPON LEA sale in 1904, following the death of Sir Frederick Sargood. Margaret and Arthur Tuckett were both keen horticulturists; Margaret was a judge at one of the earliest shows of the NATIONAL ROSE SOCIETY (1901) and she chaired the horticulture committee of the first Australian Exhibition of Women's Work (1907).

The Tucketts lived at Omama, Neerim Road, Murrumbeena, *c.* 1899–1910, 'planned and laid out more than a quarter of a century ago', according to the *Australian Home Beautiful* (1932), 'by Mrs Arthur Tuckett, one of our best amateur gardeners, in conjunction with Mr Guilfoyle, of Botanic Gardens fame, and a visiting English expert'. It was this property that 'Mrs Arthur Tuckett' described in *A Year in my Garden* (1905). The book—possibly styled on Mrs Earle's highly popular *Pot-pourri from a Surrey Garden* books of the 1890s, especially in its practical monthly arrangement of chapters, its handsome illustrated format, and disarming prose—was only the second Australian gardening book, after Mrs Rolf BOLDREWOOD's *The Flower Garden in Australia* (1893), written by a woman. When the *Journal of Horticulture of Australasia* finally reviewed *A Year in my Garden* in 1907, its use of adjectives such as 'original', 'valuable', and 'enthusiastic' signalled that a literary approach had seldom been adopted in the overwhelmingly practical canon of Australian GARDEN BOOKS. **RA**

TURF: see LAWN AND TURF

TURKEITH, Mount Gellibrand, Vic., a pastoral property with an 1860s bluestone homestead, was purchased by Robert and Urquhart Ramsay and their cousin Tom McKellar, in 1903. The Ramsay brothers bought out their cousin in 1907; Urquhart and his new bride went to live at Turkeith while Robert and his widowed mother remained at adjoining MOOLERIC. The Guilfoyle and Ramsay families were very close and family diaries record visits of William GUILFOYLE to both Mooleric and Turkeith and detail his plant lists. Guilfoyle appears to have redesigned the Turkeith garden between 1905 and 1907 in a similar style to that of Mooleric. Notable features include the drystone WALLS along the original carriageway, sweeping lawns, dense shrub borders, and perimeter walks. Unlike Mooleric, the Turkeith garden was not continuously maintained, although it is being restored by the present owners, the Gordon family, descendants of the Urquhart Ramsays. **EVE ALMOND**

TURNER, Fred (1852–1939), horticulturist and economic botanist, was born at Burton Salmon, Yorkshire, England, the son of a gardener. Developing his early botanical interests in nurseries in Yorkshire and London, Turner botanised widely in Europe, and visited the CANARY ISLANDS and South Africa. In 1874 he left London's Royal Vineyard Nursery to join the staff of BRISBANE BOTANIC GARDENS, where he worked energetically under Director Walter HILL, winning parliamentary approbation. He travelled extensively, collecting 'upwards of 10 000 specimens', including the Fraser Island creeper, *Tecomanthe hillii*, which he declared 'the rarest Australian plant'. In 1879, Turner became curator of BOWEN PARK, but in 1880 joined the SYDNEY BOTANIC GARDENS where Charles MOORE gave him charge of the grounds around the Garden Palace. The next year, Turner was invited 'to re-design and beautify HYDE PARK, Sydney'. He replaced many *Ficus macrophylla* (Moreton Bay Fig) with *Phoenix canariensis* (Canary Island Date Palm) and various deciduous and evergreen trees, being complimented in the press for his 'taste and diligence'.

In 1890 Turner was appointed ECONOMIC BOTANIST in the new Department of Agriculture. Now in his element, he continued writing not only for the *(AUSTRALIAN) TOWN AND COUNTRY JOURNAL* but also for the Department's *AGRICULTURAL GAZETTE*, to which he contributed nearly 150 articles (1890–93). Receiving 'over 2000 letters' in 1892, Turner answered a remarkable variety of pastoral, agricultural, and horticultural enquires. He encouraged appreciation 'of our beautiful flowering NATIVE PLANTS' and was credited with introducing the 'CARPET style of gardening to Australia'. In mid-1893 during the depression, Turner was retrenched amid protests that this was 'a public calamity'. Bitterness did not still his pen. During 1891–1922 he contributed more than 100 papers to the LINNEAN SOCIETY of New South Wales, and frequently wrote for the Sydney press. His *Census of the Grasses of New South Wales* (1890) and *Forage Plants of Australia* (1891) were followed by *Australian Grasses* (1895) and *Australian Grasses and Pasture Plants* (1921). By mid-1907, Turner had produced three *Manuals* for ANDERSON and Co. on *The Farm*, *The Flower Garden and Shrubbery* and *The Vegetable Garden and Orchard*. These brought congratulations from the publisher and praise from the printer, who considered Turner's script 'the acme of perfection and neatness, characteristic no doubt of the man'. Well known to his botanical contemporaries, the doughty Yorkshireman clashed with J.H. MAIDEN and agronomist Ernest Breakwell, charging them with plagiarism. A fellow of the ROYAL HORTICULTURAL SOCIETY (1888) and of the Linnean Society of London (1892), Turner succeeded MUELLER as consulting botanist to the West Australian government (1896). He frequently addressed HORTICULTURAL SOCIETIES and was president of the Carnation and Picotee Society.

In 1925, Turner wrote an autobiography. Essentially an apologia, it reflected the bitter disillusionment of a vigorous traveller and collector, practical horticulturist, and prolific writer whose work, despite the award of sundry medals and diplomas, had, in his view, been inadequately recognised. A northern Qld tree, *Pygmeum turnerianum*, named by F.M. BAILEY, commemorated this vigorous contributor to Australian horticulture.

LIONEL GILBERT

TURNER, John Stewart (1908–1991), botanist and educator, was born in Middlesborough, England, and completed his education at Cambridge. He was Professor of Botany and Plant Physiology at the University of Melbourne (1938–73) and made a profound contribution in training a generation involved, during the 1950s and 1960s, with major land-use decisions in Vic. For more than thirty-five years he was involved with various aspects of conservation, especially ecological research on the high mountain catchments. His passion also encompassed the CONSERVATION of DESIGNED LANDSCAPES. For more than twenty years he guided the management of the COMO garden for the NATIONAL TRUST OF AUSTRALIA (Victoria) and encouraged landscapers such as Edna WALLING and Ellis STONES. He was a foundation member and chaired the Maud Gibson Trust, established in 1945 to assist the work (including research) of the ROYAL BOTANIC GARDENS, MELBOURNE, and the National Herbarium. He was enthusiastically involved with CRANBOURNE BOTANIC GARDEN and BUDA.

H.T. Clifford (ed.), *Cambridge to Castlemaine: A Tribute to John Stewart Turner on the Occasion of his 80th Birthday* (Brisbane, 1989)

GWEN PASCOE

TYRE SWAN The ornithology and habitat of this endangered species is, as yet, improperly studied. Until verified sightings are recorded in Europe, Asia, or the Americas, it must be presumed to be an indigenous species (both black and white) of mainly coastal Australia, ranging in latitude

TYRE SWANS, rising like mythical characters from a lost Australia on lawns or in beds and borders, may soon only exist in the imagination or memory if urgent steps are not taken to safeguard this endangered species

Tyre swan

from Tas. to northern Qld. Sightings in WA have yet to be confirmed. Its habitats appear more to be determined by their eco-systems: open, largely treeless gardens within mining communities or related to road haulage activities. The species, perhaps a subspecies, often inhabited RAILWAY STATIONS, but these are now rarely seen owing to the incompatibility of the swan's native habitat with the modern corporate image. The change in construction of the modern tyre, with steel reinforcing, is a principal reason, apart from the hugely virulent disease of gardening good taste, for the near extinction of the species, making procreation difficult. Recently attempts have been made by a few enlightened gardeners to establish tyre swanneries within modern HERBACEOUS BORDERS. Unfortunately this has had little success and possibly Australia's only indigenous garden ORNAMENT is in danger of extinction.

JAMES BROADBENT

UMBRELLA (or umbrello), a light, usually circular or polygonal, screen of fabric in collapsible form over radial ribs, was popular in eighteenth- and early nineteenth-century European gardens. A fine iron-framed example (*c.* 1895) in this early tradition survives at WAIROA (SA). The etymological derivation from the Latin *umbre* (shade) tells of the usefulness umbrellas can play in the Australian CLIMATE, and their close relation to TENTS. They gained a new following with the rise in popularity of outdoor living following the Second World War; to some eyes no BACKYARD can now be regarded as complete without this accoutrement of the café society.
RA

UNALLA, Peppermint Grove, WA, a double-storeyed residence (*c.* 1903), was designed by architect Charles Lancelot Oldham (1865–1920) for wool merchant Henry Rischbieth (1869–1925) and his wife Bessie Mabel (*née* Earle) (1876–1967), a significant campaigner for women's rights at both a national and international level. The garden of this suburban VILLA is well recorded in photographs of the 1920s. Bronze Japanese temple lanterns, bought in 1911 by the Rischbieths, flanked the front steps. A FERNERY, TENNIS COURT, and stables formed features.

CAROLYN MIDDLEMIS

UNITED STATES OF AMERICA: see NORTH AMERICA

UNIVERSITY CAMPUSES have undergone a variety of landscape designs reflecting different eras, from the Victorian values of the nineteenth century to more contemporary expressions of the late twentieth century, as well as the crucial influence of different individuals on their layout and structural organisation, architectural character, and landscape character. Often the campuses were the result of a collaboration between planners, architects, landscape architects, gardeners, grounds staff, grounds committees, and interested academics.

Three main eras of campus development can be identified; different trends in the overall layout and landscape treatment are reflected in each but are not necessarily exclusive to any one. These trends include symmetrical or formal arrangement and the development of axial alignments to link major open spaces; horticultural embellishment of boundaries; outdoor 'rooms' and courtyards of varying scale; planting clumps (often in constricted spaces); designs for special gardens areas; and a gradual shift from exotic to Australian plantings.

The first distinct era, the period up to the First World War, included Australia's earliest university campuses, at Melbourne and Sydney (1850s), which followed traditional English collegiate architecture with quadrangles, linear entry drives, formal plantings, expansive grounds with public access, and specialised garden features (such as the University of Melbourne's SYSTEM GARDEN). Until rapidly increasing building development of the early to mid-twentieth century, these early campuses were planted in a similar manner to other INSTITUTIONS, and often resembled large, poorly maintained public parks. Located in major urban centres, subsequent development of the eclectic Victorian landscape character of the older universities tended to create an urban setting rather than the initial vision of a picturesque landscape.

During the inter-war period, development of the University of Western Australia marked a new era in which a 'civic design' approach drew on contemporary TOWN PLANNING principles. Buildings of a romantic Mediterranean character contrasted with an equally romantic landscape treatment of clumped plantations of rainforest flora, grassed areas, and eucalypt plantings to soften the larger landscape setting. The campus was developed, like many other Australian campuses, over many decades. At the University of Adelaide, developed between the 1920s and 1960s to a master plan by Walter BAGOT, northern Italian design ideas influenced the red-brick Classical-styled buildings and spatial layout, including Italian Poplars that embraced a central pedestrian spine and rivulet. Leslie WILKINSON produced master plans for the University of Sydney, University of Western Australia (Crawley), and the University of Tasmania (Hobart); that at Sydney was implemented over a long period in conjunction with Professor WATERHOUSE. At Newman College (University of Melbourne), Walter Burley GRIFFIN provided an important early use of AUSTRALIAN FLORA in an institutional garden setting. Griffin also prepared a master plan for the University of Sydney and a competition entry for the University of Western Australia master plan (won by H. DESBROWE-ANNEAR, but not implemented).

The post-war era was marked by a sharp rise in the number of new universities, all developed to overall master plans that included integral landscape plans. Two main groups

Urban design

stand out. The first had an external focus, as at La Trobe University (Bundoora, Vic.), while the second sought to integrate into their urban settings, as at Macquarie University (North Ryde, NSW). Both groups drew extensively, particularly from the 1960s, on the use of Australian native plants to provide either an overall landscape character or to achieve an integrated and unified approach within an urban context. Examples from this period include the Australian National University (Canberra), Curtain University of Technology (WA), Flinders University (SA), and Griffith University (Qld.). Many of the professionals involved, such as Griffin, Wilkinson, Gordon STEPHENSON, John OLDHAM, Lindsay PRYOR, John STEVENS, and Richard CLOUGH, had input to the planning and design of more than one campus. Parallel to these new campuses, expansion of the older universities continued and although landscape treatments were often used to unify disparate elements, cohesion was sometimes sacrificed by a tendency to appoint new designers for each project.   CRAIG BURTON

URBAN DESIGN aims to improve the public realm of cities and towns as a setting for cultural and commercial activities. It involves aspects of TOWN PLANNING, LANDSCAPE ARCHITECTURE, civil engineering, HORTICULTURE, and allied professions. In Australia, establishment of government departments and university programs specifically dealing with urban design commenced in the 1980s. Despite the discipline's recent formalisation, concentration of Australia's population around a few urban centres has promoted 'urban design' since European settlement.

Nineteenth-century town plans were typical of those in NORTH AMERICA and other European colonies. A carefully proportioned street grid aligned to a river was often surveyed over a large area, anticipating growth, although capital cities soon expanded beyond these plants into less regular north-oriented grids, sprawling along highways. Central Sydney and Hobart were exceptions, with organic plans derived from their earlier foundation as penal colonies and the rugged terrain of both harbourside cities. CANBERRA represented a unique transfer of American CITY BEAUTIFUL planning principles. PUBLIC PARKS AND GARDENS were an integral part of Adelaide's city design, recalling London's and Philadelphia's SQUARES, but parks were more often located at the periphery of towns. Typical features included CEMETERIES and reserves for government and INSTITUTIONAL buildings (such as UNIVERSITIES), often set in ornamental landscapes and associated with public gardens as at Adelaide's North Terrace.

Engineering works frequently drove civic improvement schemes. Highways were sometimes formed into broad tree-lined BOULEVARDS. Flood mitigation works on Melbourne's Yarra River included a PROMENADE and gardens designed by the government engineer, Carlo CATANI. However, this integration of concerns was often absent from projects of the later twentieth century, whether freeways, public housing estates, or the monumental cultural centres that were built in most capitals. Some recent urban projects have aimed to achieve a better balance of mechanical, social, and aesthetic concerns in areas affected by such single-purpose works. Transport and industrial changes have also led to redevelopment of riverfronts and harbour ESPLANADES, where new PUBLIC OPEN SPACES, such as PLAZAS, have been created.

There is little control of private landscapes as an aspect of urban design. In most commercial and older residential areas, buildings form walls enclosing the streets, focusing controls on this interface. Canberra's prohibition of FENCES, to maintain a type of streetscape characteristic of American suburbs, is an unusual Australian example of regulation. Conservation controls have expanded since the 1980s from an initial focus on buildings to now address streetscapes and gardens, as well as tree protection (especially in urban fringes). The orientation of activity towards streets makes them the most important of public spaces, and the focus of many projects. Drastic interventions into street design, such as pedestrian malls, exist in many cities but have become less favoured than more widespread improvement by planting STREET TREES, modestly widening footpaths, and installing FURNITURE and PUBLIC ARTWORKS.   RONALD JONES

URBAN FORESTRY is frequently used as a synonym for ARBORICULTURE, especially in NORTH AMERICAN literature. However, while arboriculture has as its focus the management and cultivation of a single specimen tree, urban forestry deals with urban trees as a group or 'forest'. This is sometimes extended to collectively include management of trees growing within, affected by, or influencing an urban population. The density of such tree canopy cover may range from as low as ten per cent to as high as thirty per cent. In Australia the term usually implies the application of FORESTRY techniques to a large group of trees growing in an urbanised area, such as mass plantings of trees on industrial sites, significant remnants of native forests, or large parks and gardens. In many instances an implied production value (such as fruit, timber, or foliage) is associated with management practices, but urban forestry can address aesthetic, recreational, or other non-utilitarian issues.   GREG MOORE

URRBRAE HOUSE, SA: see WAITE AGRICULTURAL RESEARCH INSTITUTE

VALDER, Peter George (b. 1928), botanist, horticulturist, and lecturer, was born in Sydney and developed an early interest in gardens and plants. He graduated in agriculture from the University of Sydney and obtained his PhD at the Botany Department in Cambridge. Returning to Australia in 1956, he worked as a plant pathologist in the New South Wales Department of Agriculture and as a botanist and mycologist at the School of Biological Sciences at the University of Sydney, retiring in 1988. While he has been a populariser of Australian botany and horticulture throughout his career, his TELEVISION and RADIO appearances, writing, and lecturing have increased since his retirement, and since the sale of Nooroo in 1992 he has written *Wisterias* (1995), the first book in any European language about the genus *Wisteria*, and *The Garden Plants of China* (1999), documenting the history, use and occurrence of more than 400 plants grown in CHINESE gardens. In recognition of his support and voluntary work for the ROYAL BOTANIC GARDENS, SYDNEY, he was made its first Honorary Horticultural Associate in 1995.

The house at **Nooroo** was built and the garden planted in 1880 by William Hay (1816–1908), the owner of Boomanoomana, on land at MOUNT WILSON (NSW) bought in 1870 for a SUMMER RETREAT. Valder's grandfather purchased Nooroo in 1917 and on returning from the First World War, his father, horticulturist George Ernest Valder (1896–1976), was the first to live there year-round. He commenced transforming the garden, which had been laid out on typically formal lines, establishing an orchard and introducing unusual plants obtained from gardens and nurseries in NSW and Vic. Peter Valder's involvement commenced in 1950 when he started importing plants from Britain, Holland, Japan, and the USA and propagating others found in old gardens at Kurrajong Heights and the Blue Mountains. The renaissance of the garden, which had become overcrowded, began in 1965 when a heavy snowstorm brought down trees and caused other extensive damage. He sought advice from his friend Richard CLOUGH, whose guidance improved the house setting, provided a new plan of circulation, and developed VISTAS within the garden and to the native vegetation beyond. The SUMMER-HOUSE (1980), commemorating the centenary of the garden, provided a principal focal point for the composition and assisted in renewed interest in their construction in Australian gardens. The reorganisation of the garden continued with a series of informal spaces, one flowing into another. In these, Valder's collections of plants were displayed, integrated with the tree ferns and eucalypts from the original vegetation and the deciduous and evergreen trees planted in 1880. On his visits to Indonesia, Malaysia, Thailand, Burma, China, and Japan he collected plants from the wild, sharing them with botanic gardens and interested parties world-wide. Notable are the RHODODENDRON species and cultivars and the collection of different wisterias.

In 1958 Valder and his mother formed a small committee to organise the opening of five Mount Wilson gardens for one weekend in October of that year for fund-raising purposes. The aid of garden writers and broadcasters was enlisted, and the event proved an astonishing success, with thousands of visitors descending on the district. This event drew attention to the potential in Australia of garden opening as a means of both raising funds and giving pleasure. It was followed by the organisation of such events as the Leura Gardens FESTIVAL and the blossoming of GARDEN VISITING in general. Nooroo was then opened every spring and autumn and, because of numerous enquiries for the plants it contained, a small nursery was started to meet the demand. Between the 1960s and 1980s this nursery had a pronounced effect on the composition of gardens in the BLUE MOUNTAINS, SOUTHERN HIGHLANDS, and even Sydney.

ALLAN McNEISH

VAN DEN BROEK (*née* WHITMAN), Barbara Ruth (1932– 2001), architect, landscape architect, town planner, and lecturer, moved from Auckland (New Zealand) to Brisbane (1956) then Sydney (1983). She won the competition to design the grounds around the University of Queensland (1963), where she later inspired a younger generation of students. Subsequent projects included the settings of the Queensland Cultural Centre and Art Gallery, Brisbane; Waigani government centre and parliament building, Port Moresby; Civic Square, Alice Springs (NT); and Olympic Basketball Stadium, Blacktown (NSW). Van den Broek was an active member of her chosen professions and a respected mentor.

COLLEEN MORRIS

VARIEGATION is caused by the inability of some tissue to produce chlorophyll, thus removing green pigmentation in this portion of the PLANT. The loss of chlorophyll reduces the ability for photosynthesis in variegated plants and thus growth is generally less robust than it is in the non-variegated forms. Examples are found among a wide range of plants, including PELARGONIUMS, CROTONS and other TROPICAL plants, and CACTI and succulents. Most of these need to be cloned, traditionally by cuttings, as the variegated effect will not reproduce via seed.

Plants with unusual size, shape, or COLOUR of FOLIAGE (especially those with bicoloured or tricoloured variegations either regularly or irregularly arranged) became popular in the second half of the nineteenth century. Enthusiasm for them reached a peak in the 1870s when they featured in many publications. In Europe, where their value was first recognised, they were used INDOORS as potted plants, especially in CONSERVATORIES. Outdoors they were employed in carpet BEDDING and to a lesser extent as HARDY garden plants. Most of the ornamental leaved plants introduced by Australians came from the PACIFIC ISLANDS, with PLANT COLLECTORS supplying nursery proprietors who then distributed them world-wide. The fashion for foliage plants declined and they were little used during the early decades of the twentieth century. The increase in the number of people living in flats and working in open-plan offices after the Second World War led to a revival of interest in indoor plants with many varieties with ornamental variegated leaves being brought back into use. At the margins of conventional taste, variegated plants have attracted strong opinions and can form bold accents in the gardener's palette.

RICHARD CLOUGH

VAUCLUSE HOUSE, NSW, the estate established in 1827 by politician William Charles Wentworth (1780–1872) and his wife Sarah, comprised 208 hectares of picturesque terrain on the shores of Sydney Harbour. The setting for their Gothic-style marine VILLA was characterised by rugged sandstone escarpments, seasonal watercourses, and small isolated beaches including Milk Beach, Shark Beach, and Vaucluse Bay. It was resumed by the state government in 1910, making it one of the nation's earliest historic site museums. The Historic Houses Trust of New South Wales has managed the surviving ten hectares of the estate since 1981.

Within the immediate view of the house, the surrounding bushland provided a setting for Wentworth's 'park' of grazing paddocks. Within this park, the family created two fine views. A carefully designed VISTA looked north-east to the sandstone outcrops of nearby Parsley Hill. Another outlook, framed by a long V-shaped avenue of native trees, looked north by north-east. This was gardening on a grand scale. A winding carriageway separated the parklands from the pleasure grounds. In the later nineteenth century these garden boundaries were marked by iron estate fencing (since restored). The inner pleasure garden, with its original layout of rolling lawn, shrubbery, and meandering gravel paths, has survived. To the rear of the house, stock fences, service yards, and an extensive vegetable garden were reconstructed in the 1990s. Completing the estate, the Wentworth Mausoleum and its iron-palisade fence in nearby Chapel Road was conserved in the mid-1990s. Original plantings of *Lophostemon confertus* (Brush Box) survive within the site. The estate's bushland setting is being conserved through a bush regeneration program.

Michael Bogle, *Vaucluse House* (Glebe, NSW, 1993)

MICHAEL BOGLE

VEGETABLE GARDENS were the earliest European gardens in Australia; one was begun at Sydney Cove just days after the First Fleet arrived in January 1788. With limited supplies and a minimal understanding of ABORIGINAL FOOD PLANTS, the newcomers understandably placed a high priority on growing vegetables, and although disappointed with the quality of the soil, within three months the colonists had established three vegetable gardens. Eight months from the landing Governor Phillip reported that vegetables had become plentiful and the Governor's garden contained 'excellent cauliflowers and melons'. Despite Phillip's enthusiasm, however, the colony struggled to provide itself with sufficient food and the threat of starvation loomed large until at least 1792. Even subsequently, whenever crops were threatened by flood, fire, or drought, **kitchen gardens** (as domestic vegetable gardens were often known) became of vital importance: on two occasions in 1806 and again in 1809 when floods on the Hawkesbury decimated the season's cereal crops, the governor threatened to dispossess Sydney householders of their land if they would not grow vegetables. By 1803 Governor King could report that the colony was producing twenty-six different vegetables, although the botanist George CALEY, who arrived with King in 1800, reported that potatoes, pumpkins, melons, and cabbages were the most common.

Although the rectangular vegetable beds in front of the first GOVERNMENT HOUSE were replaced by ornamental landscaping in the 1810s, gardens well-fenced against wandering stock and dominated by vegetable beds remained common in the major towns until later displaced by higher-density development (with limited suitable space for vegetable production), or SUBURBAN GARDEN layouts (with ornamental FRONT GARDENS and utilitarian, potentially productive BACKYARDS). Evidence relating to small-scale vegetable gardening in the emerging cities is scant, but the garden layouts of many existing nineteenth-century country HOMESTEADS and stations, and suburban VILLAS and MANSIONS, show that for these classes of property at least, the kitchen garden remained a common feature throughout the nineteenth century, and even well into the twentieth.

The inconvenience, or in some cases impossibility, of procuring fresh vegetables outside cities and towns meant that farm houses were quite likely to have a vegetable garden until wartime petrol rationing ceased in the 1950s. Available evidence also suggests that the vegetable 'patch' has been an important component of suburban backyards throughout the later nineteenth and much of the twentieth centuries. In GARDENING BOOKS and MAGAZINES of this period, the home vegetable garden was constantly promoted as a valuable or even essential part of the back garden, as it was variously seen to provide a satisfying hobby that provided healthy fresh-air exercise, a means of stretching limited incomes, and produce that was cheaper, cleaner, fresher, and available in greater variety than that offered for purchase. While information on the

Vegetable gardens

During the WARTIME GARDENING conditions of the Second World War, government advertising encouraging the cultivation of VEGETABLE GARDENS reflected and intensified lessons learnt from the First World War

planning of the vegetable garden and cultivation of particular vegetables has been a consistent feature of popular gardening books and magazines, vegetable gardening has certainly been more popular at some times than others. Although apparently taking a second place to flower gardening in the 1920s, there appears to have been considerably more interest in it during the years of the Depression, the effects of which were mitigated to some extent where people had secure access to land on which to grow food.

During the Second World War, domestic vegetable growing received a major boost as rationing decreased the availability of meat, a decline in the availability of farm labour led to decreased commercial vegetable production, and civilian supplies were diverted to the military. These factors converged in sporadic, informal campaigns to encourage home food production as early as 1941. In that year, a major survey of Melbourne households revealed that where people had access to a yard of reasonable size vegetable cultivation was very common, being carried out by up to eighty-eight per cent of households in some areas. It is likely that the number of households producing their own vegetables increased even further in 1943, when the Commonwealth Department of Commerce and Agriculture initiated a nation-wide 'Grow Your Own' campaign in which home gardeners were strenuously and frequently encouraged, via FILM, RADIO broadcasts, public demonstrations, competitions, posters, newspaper advertisements, brochures, and stickers, to grow their own vegetables as a patriotic duty.

The literature generally advised 'amateurs', or from the 1920s 'home gardeners', to give priority in the vegetable garden to items with poor keeping qualities—a factor that was particularly important before domestic refrigeration became widespread in the 1950s and 1960s. The contents of Australian vegetable gardens have also varied with changes in diet, as well as regional variations in climate and soil type. Gardens in north Qld, for example, were more likely to produce sweet potato and snake beans than the common white potato and French beans more prevalent in southern gardens. The ethnic background of the cultivator has also influenced the content and form of vegetable gardens. MIGRANTS from ASIA and southern Europe in particular have often cultivated highly productive gardens—back and front—containing traditional vegetables and seasonings as well as more standard fare. Other migrants from these regions operated MARKET GARDENS which supplied most of the vegetable requirements of Australian cities and towns.

Traditionally, vegetables in home gardens were grown in rows in an area set aside from the rest of the garden. This area was either left undivided or contained small, well-defined beds (normally rectangular and often raised where drainage was poor), separated by paths and sometimes edged with boards, bricks, or HERBS. Climbing vegetables such as beans and chokos were often grown on fences or over poultry coops, and pumpkin vines provided a productive way to disguise the 'rubbish' (COMPOST) heap. In the wake of Rachel Carson's pivotal book *Silent Spring* (1962), a growing number of home gardeners began to eschew the use of synthetic CHEMICALS in their vegetable gardens in favour of techniques including companion planting (using particular combinations of vegetables, herbs, and flowers to reduce the depredations of insects and other PESTS). Although this approach was often applied to traditional vegetable garden layouts, it also found a place in PERMACULTURE gardens, which usually featured vegetables, interplanted with perennial ornamental, utility, and fruiting species. Since the 1970s, some vegetable gardening has moved out of the backyard (or occasionally front yard) and into COMMUNITY GARDENS and city farms.

ANDREA GAYNOR

Veitch

VEITCH family–operated nurseries in Exeter and London for more than a century epitomised all that was outstanding in the NURSERY trade. John Veitch (1752–1839), a Scottish landscape gardener, established his second Exeter nursery in 1832, run with his son, James (1792–1863). In 1853 James purchased the Royal Exotic Nursery of Knight and Perry in Chelsea and sent his son, James (1815–1869), to manage it. James jnr made many improvements to Chelsea but in 1864 severed all connection with the Exeter branch, which continued until the 1960s. Commemorated in the Veitch Memorial Medals of the ROYAL HORTICULTURAL SOCIETY, James jnr was renowned for his skill as a cultivator, his business acumen, and his support of PLANT COLLECTORS whose work introduced hundreds of new plants to the Veitches. James jnr's sons John Gould (1839–1870) and Harry James Veitch (1840–1924) supervised the London nurseries, which became a huge national and international organisation until their closure in 1914.

The Veitch family was principally associated with Australia through its plant-hunters ('travellers') and their purchases and exchanges, through AUSTRALIAN PLANTS cultivated by them in England, and through emigrant nursery proprietors trained by them (who included Eugene FITZALAN, George RIMINGTON, and W.R. WARNER). From 1840, when they sent William Lobb to South America, the Veitches sponsored twenty-two plant-hunters, three members of the family collecting in Australia—John Gould, Peter (1850–1929), and James Herbert Veitch (1868–1907). John Gould left his impressions of a visit during 1864–65 in a series of articles in the *Gardeners' Chronicle* (1866) and presented a detailed picture of gardens and nurseries in Australia. He was pleased to find 'many plants in the wild state which I had previously known under greenhouse culture in England'. His main collections were ferns, orchids, and palms from north Qld, including three species of *Dendrobium* and the first large importation of *Dendrobium biggibum*. Peter visited clients of the firm and made excursions during 1875–77. Some material reached England but he was shipwrecked off northern Australia in 1877, and most was lost. James Herbert visited South-East Asia and Australia and New Zealand in 1891–93, recording his journeys in *A Traveller's Notes* (1896). He described most of the BOTANIC GARDENS in Australia but provided few details of plants he sent home. He found seed collecting in WA much more difficult than anticipated but observed 'there is strong evidence that we already have the best things from King George Sound'.

Although *CURTIS's Botanical Magazine* featured 422 plates of Veitch introductions to cultivation, very few were Australian. Perhaps the most noteworthy were the golden form of *Blandfordia grandiflora* ('Blandfordia aurea') in 1869, several ORCHIDS (including a large-flowered form of *Dendrobium biggibum*), and, most spectacular of all, *Swainsona formosa* (Sturt's Desert Pea), which they first flowered in 1850 and which won for Veitches the Silver Medal of the Horticultural Society of London.

James H. Veitch, *Hortus Veitchii* (London, 1906)

TONY CAVANAGH

VERANDAH GARDENING, including potted and trellised plants and described by tropical horticulturist H.F. Macmillan as an 'essential feature of horticulture in the tropics', drew on European traditions of window and INDOOR gardening (especially in CONSERVATORIES). Gardening in POTS, either free-standing, on a stepped framework, or hanging baskets from verandah rafters, provided both decoration for the living spaces and a virtual bush-house effect for the plants. The BUSH-HOUSE provided a continuous supply of these potted plants in peak condition, a public showcase for the gardener's skills.

Verandah favourites included PALMS, FERNS, dracaenas, coleus, and crotons, although climatic variations greatly influenced plant selections. The verandah was often augmented or extended by use of TRELLIS supporting CLIMBING PLANTS and providing privacy and shade. The Mediterranean tradition of using grape vines was continued in suitable parts of Australia over PERGOLAS, often connected to the verandah or forming an unroofed version. In temperate areas, *Wisteria* and climbing ROSES were also favourites, while in the tropics, bougainvillea and *Pyrostegia venusta* (Orange Trumpet Creeper) were common. Water gardening was also possible on verandahs, using old wooden tubs and waterlilies.

Institutional sites, such as RAILWAY station platforms and hospital balconies, commonly featured potted plants, while the use of tropical herbaceous plants for decorative purposes was a well-established component of local EXHIBITIONS by the 1870s. By the late 1880s, however, Queensland garden writers were advising against the rampant growth of creepers on verandahs (especially over the roof), due to problems with leaves in gutters and the harbouring of vermin. Perhaps it was the delightful wild and picturesque aspect of such creepers that has encouraged the continuous resurgence in popularity of this gardening practice. Verandah gardening links the garden and the house, and offers lushly decorated spaces for semi-outside lifestyles. It also caters for those with restricted garden space or limited mobility. With the growth of APARTMENTS AND RESIDENTIAL FLATS, balcony gardens have also become a popular manifestation.

Philip Drew, *Veranda: Embracing Place* (Pymble, NSW, 1982)

JEANNIE SIM

VERSCHUER (née SLATYER), Jean (b. 1926), landscape architect, was born at Rockhampton (Qld), but moved to Perth aged five. After seven years nursing, and her marriage in 1952, she studied horticulture and related subjects. Starting private practice in 1959, she undertook a wide range of landscape projects, including Mason's Gardens (Nedlands), School of Mines (Kalgoorlie), Nickel Refinery (Kwinana), and the mining township of Kambalda (1969–73), 700 kilometres east of Perth. With a population of 2000 and an annual rainfall of only 200 mm, she aimed to blend the town into the natural landscape and to achieve minimum maintenance. She was consultant to a number of Perth architects, government agencies, and the University of Western Australia (1970–73), where during 1974–81 she worked as staff landscape architect. From 1963 she worked for the formation of the AUSTRALIAN INSTITUTE OF LANDSCAPE ARCHITECTS, repre-

VERANDAH GARDENS were popular in all areas of Australia, especially in TROPICAL areas, where they took advantage of cooling breezes—as in this Darwin residence of the 1920s—and hot, dry areas, where wide shade verandahs were a climatic necessity

senting it on the International Federation of Landscape Architects (1967–77), and in 1977 becoming the first woman president. Now married (1978) to Sir Laurence Brodie-Hall, she continues to serve on advisory bodies including that on GOVERNMENT HOUSE grounds, Perth.   RICHARD CLOUGH

VESSEY, Charles Eustace: see VOLLMER, Martin Frederick

VICTOR HARBOR SOLDIERS' MEMORIAL GARDENS, SA, were established on the foreshore; the original two gardens were developed in 1913 around several *Araucaria hetrophylla* (Norfolk Island Pine). The gardens were planted in memoriam of First World War soldiers (and officially named in 1917) following design and planting advice from Mayor William Northey and August PELZER. Charles READE was commissioned in 1918, following passage of the *Victor Harbor Foreshore Act* (1917), to plan the extension of the gardens towards the causeway and to prepare a master plan for development.   DAVID JONES

VICTORIA The short-lived settlement at Sorrento (1803) and the permanent European settlement at Portland (1834) formalised a process of coastal and inland exploration that had taken place in preceding decades; of these, the settlement of Port Phillip (later Melbourne) (1834–35) and the overland journey through western Victoria by Thomas MITCHELL (1836) were the most significant. In Melbourne early gardens were clustered along water courses, with river banks often exploited for picturesque effect or utilised for MARKET GARDENS. Verandahs were a necessity in the new colony and their floral decoration was a high priority for both aesthetic and functional reasons. The cottage of Superintendent LA TROBE, especially as depicted in the drawings of Edward La Trobe BATEMAN, was the archetypal early colonial garden, with lawns dotted with floral shrubberies, and borrowed vistas over the growing city shaped by clumps and belts of trees, both planted and retained.

The founding of BOTANIC GARDENS at Melbourne (1845–46) and Geelong (1851), the allocation of a generous government DOMAIN, and the surveying (and subsequent landscaping) of urban SQUARES all assisted in laying the foundation for landscape design in Vic. Educational, scientific, and recreational objectives underpinned these early public landscapes, which were complemented by increasingly sophisticated private gardens. Horticultural expertise in this early period was imported from neighbouring colonies and from overseas.

While Melbourne and Geelong developed, pastoral settlement by squatters in the hinterland and especially in the WESTERN DISTRICT (Mitchell's 'Australia Felix') provided a source of wealth with which to shape new landscapes. Following an uncertain tenure, land sale by auction with a right of pre-emption for the squatter to purchase one square mile or 640 acres (260 ha) led to the creation of an

Victoria

The ROYAL BOTANIC GARDENS, MELBOURNE, have been a focus for horticulture in VICTORIA, especially through the plant distribution activities of Ferdinand MUELLER from the 1850s to the 1870s, the influence of William GUILFOYLE's landscape gardening during the late nineteenth century, and the Gardens' sustained popularity during the twentieth century

extraordinary wealth of HOMESTEAD GARDENS and designed land- scapes. Early primitive huts soon gave way to more substantial basalt homesteads with extensive gardens. A common pattern was for the pastoral property to be complemented by a MANSION and garden in Melbourne, and perhaps a coastal SUMMER RETREAT.

The earliest GARDEN BOOKS included locally published ALMANACS and books brought from Britain, although from the 1850s Australian gardening books and nursery catalogues became available. Influential British and North American books included those by LOUDON, DOWNING, MCINTOSH, and KEMP. In the realm of GARDEN MAGAZINES, by far the most influential British titles were the *GARDENERS' CHRONICLE* and *COTTAGE GARDENER*; the local publishing scene briefly flourished in the 1850s with the *RURAL MAGAZINE* and *VICTORIAN FARMERS' JOURNAL AND GARDENERS' CHRONICLE* as well as magazines edited by James SINCLAIR and Samuel HANNAFORD.

Wealth generated by gold mining from the 1850s profoundly stimulated LAND SURVEY AND SALE and TOWN PLANNING. An influx of gardeners, horticulturists, and botanists—including such well-known names as ADAMSON, BRUNNING, and LANG—came from ENGLAND and SCOTLAND. Chinese market gardeners also arrived in Vic. with the gold rushes. There was a significant GERMAN influence on Victorian horticulture, dominated by Ferdinand MUELLER, who undertook extensive distribution of plants from MELBOURNE BOTANIC GARDENS to suburban and provincial sites, stirring jealously within the nursery trade, but benefiting countless CEMETERIES, parks, provincial botanic gardens, and government reserves across the colony.

With the ACCLIMATISATION movement came the debate over the extent to which Vic. possessed MEDITERRANEAN characteristics. Would the orange grow in Melbourne, for instance? What were suitable trees for plantings in local gardens, and for street plantings of dusty towns? CONIFERS achieved an early popularity and they defined boundaries across the colony, playing a major part in the creation of distinctive DESIGNED LANDSCAPES—a role similar to that played by PALMS from the turn of the century. FORMALITY in the design of landscapes was not confined to the cognoscenti, but suited the miniature plots of inner-suburban terraces houses, springing up in suburban Melbourne from the 1850s. The influence in the new colony of PICTURESQUE theory was strong—although, freed from the dictates of fixed taste, garden designers faced an almost bewildering freedom in the choice of style. The GARDENESQUE style was soon transformed from a concentration on the perfection of individual plants into a more popular style generally highlighting the art of the gardener.

The advent of responsible government and the introduction of local government in the 1850s provided the infrastructure necessary for funding and maintaining PUBLIC PARKS AND GARDENS, many designed by Clement HODGKINSON. Mueller's design efforts at the Melbourne Botanic Gardens had meanwhile earned the scorn of an influential section of the metropolis, eager for a pleasure ground rather than a scientific garden. William GUILFOYLE soon transformed this and other botanic gardens. He was matched in the private domain by William SANGSTER, who designed numerous large gardens including RIPPON LEA, RUPERTSWOOD, and estates at MOUNT MACEDON, and like Guilfoyle skilfully combined exotic and Australian plants into picturesque compositions, fully exploiting topography and vistas.

One of the major themes of Victorian (and indeed Australian) history in the mid-century was the call to 'unlock the lands'—to break the stranglehold of the squatters and permit smaller land selections. During the 1860s a series of Land Acts was introduced and, combined with the concurrent geodetic survey, a square grid of land holdings was imposed over much of the colony. Fencing and 'improvement' of holdings underpinned the regulations and, combined with irrigation and later Closer Settlement Acts, this pastoral and agricultural influx introduced a new wave of homestead gardens, generally less ostentatious than their squatting cousins but tended with no less care and pride.

The weekly AUSTRALASIAN and LEADER newspapers gave prominence to horticulture from the 1860s, and were especially influential in the absence of local gardening magazines. The economic value of horticulture was an oft-repeated theme and promoted the establishment of a Department of Agriculture (1872). Fruit growing was encouraged, especially with advances in refrigeration and IRRIGATION. VITICULTURE spread north from its previous strongholds in river valleys around Melbourne and Geelong to the newly irrigated areas.

Urbanisation saw the rise of domestic gardens in towns and suburbs. The land boom of the 1880s fuelled extravagant development, and villa gardens now marched across the eastern suburbs. A new wave of suburban parks catered for Melbourne's increasing population. Increasing land values forced nurseries to move from inner suburbs to the periphery of suburban development. As land became available for selection in the Dandenongs during the 1890s, shrewd nursery proprietors established large holdings on newly cleared land. Productive gardens were no longer feasible on expensive suburban real estate and a concentration of market gardens became centred on the sand belt south of Brighton, and orchards to serve the metropolis were clustered in the outer east and on Mornington Peninsula.

The land boom came to an abrupt halt in 1893 with the closure of many financial institutions, and a period of austerity placed the focus on creation of smaller suburban gardens. FLORICULTURE dominated and cult followings attended the CHRYSANTHEMUM, DAHLIA, CARNATION, and SWEET PEA. ROSES had never lost popularity and this interest consolidated with the formation of the NATIONAL ROSE SOCIETY of Victoria. Specialist nurseries catered for these favourites, including those of ERREY, ROSSI, BRUNDRETT, and POCKETT.

The gradual economic recovery following the bank crashes of the 1890s, the euphoria of Federation (1901), and a perception of international status following participation in the Boer War (1899–1902) were matched by new architectural and horticultural ideas. Horticultural training had commenced in 1891 at BURNLEY, with the government taking over the former Horticultural Society experimental garden. With the charismatic C. Bogue LUFFMANN as principal, the school soon attracted a wide range of students, including many women. Walter BUTLER, Walter Burley GRIFFIN, and Harold DESBROWE-ANNEAR promoted the involvement of architects in landscape design, and new stylistic trends derived from the ARTS AND CRAFTS and GARDEN CITY movements achieved some popularity, especially among the design professions. The deaths of Guilfoyle (1910) and Sangster (1912) ended a heroic era in Victorian landscape gardening. The gap was filled by many, but in institutional circles a major government appointment was that of Hugh LINAKER as landscape gardener for the Lunacy Department (1912). The influence of large-scale INSTITUTIONAL landscaping was reflected at a slightly later date by the formation of the VICTORIAN TREE PLANTERS' ASSOCIATION.

The Great War (1914–18) had a profound effect on Australian society, and on horticulture in particular. Opportunities for women in horticulture were provided by the absence and tragic loss of many men. This opportunity was seized by Edna WALLING, who rose to prominence with confident articles in the *Australian Home Beautiful*, influential commissions, and a fine sense of design and plant selection. Other women prominent in gardens and horticulture included BEGG AND SHANNON, Emily GIBSON, Olive MELLOR, and Jean GALBRAITH.

The formation of the Melbourne and Metropolitan Board of Works (1891) and Melbourne Town Planning Commission (1929), and the active involvement of local councils in zoning and other regulatory measures, led to a widespread professional interest in town planning. In the 1920s and 1930s, Melbourne's suburbs expanded, particularly to the east, fuelled by electrified railways, tramways, and increasing use of the motor car. The creation of new suburbs with large quarter-acre blocks created a demand for gardening. Membership of suburban and specialist horticultural societies soared. New monthly magazines, including the AUSTRALIAN GARDEN LOVER, AUSTRALIAN HOME BEAUTIFUL, HOME GARDENER, and JOURNAL OF HORTICULTURE catered for amateur gardeners. While AUSTRALIAN PLANTS had been used in landscaping from the earliest days of colonisation, the new fervour surrounding the wattle fostered a climate in which nature conservation became allied to horticulture; Charles BARRETT and Edward E. PESCOTT became great popularisers of this movement. Later, Cyril E. ISAAC orchestrated the SAVE THE FORESTS CAMPAIGN.

In Vic., architectural styles were profoundly challenged and altered by what Robin Boyd dubbed 'The 1934 Revolution'. In reality, Boyd's 1934 represented the date of popular knowledge of MODERNISM, since local architects had absorbed this stylistic influence some years earlier. The profound effect of the First World War and the economic depression of late 1920s introduced an age where enlightened gardeners were receptive to modernist ideas. Modernist landscaping received a boost with post-war reconstruction, when architects and town planners led the charge. At the suburban garden level, ideas filtered slowly; there was an increasing acceptance of courtyards, pergolas, enhanced use of hard paving, sculptural use of trees, and stridently coloured, bold-foliaged plants. The Second World War focused economic and horticultural interest on vegetable gardens, but in the post-war 1950s outdoor living was in the ascendant and Americanisms such as the barbecue and swimming pool made their way into the designer's palette. Although community facilities were well used, the recreational spotlight was focused on the individual home in a manner not previously seen. Post-war migration brought further diversity in gardens with Greek and Italian migrants wreaking havoc to long-cherished Anglo-Saxon mores in the unashamed use of front gardens for productive fruit and vegetable crops, introduction of exotic vegetables, and unrestrained use of colour.

New magazines aimed at the home gardener, such as *YOUR GARDEN* and *AUSTRALIAN HOUSE AND GARDEN* supplemented existing titles especially at a time when homemaking was starting to embrace landscaping as an integral component in a lifestyle. Department stores such as Myer and Coles expanded their garden departments while the BODDY and SCHUBERT nurseries catered for enthusiasts of Australian plants, who had banded together in 1957 to form the SOCIETY FOR GROWING AUSTRALIAN PLANTS. Many landscape architects, and other key individual voices such as Alister KNOX and Gordon FORD, enthusiastically embraced the BUSH GARDEN concept, and with the publication of MALONEY and Walker's *Designing Australian Bush Gardens* (1966) this enthusiasm was transferred to the suburban gardener.

The 1960s heralded a rise in the profession of LANDSCAPE ARCHITECTURE and with the formation of the AUSTRALIAN INSTITUTE OF LANDSCAPE ARCHITECTS the profession at last found a unified voice after a long alliance with the nursery and horticultural trades. Introduction of tertiary courses in landscape architecture and horticulture also fostered a rise in professionalism. The building boom of the 1960s brought new opportunities for landscaping of high-rise offices, apartments, freeways, and other accoutrements of an expansive economy.

As the twentieth century drew to a close, the catchcry of 'think globally, act locally' brought issues such as the ENVIRONMENT, ECOLOGY, and PLANT CONSERVATION to the attention of gardeners, with consequent interest in REVEGETATION, plant species indigenous to local areas, water and soil conservation, and responsible use of CHEMICALS.

> Peter Watts and Margaret Barrett (eds), *Historic Gardens of Victoria: A Reconnaissance* (Melbourne, 1983); R. Wright, *The Bureaucrats' Domain: Space and the Public Interest in Victoria 1836–84* (Melbourne, 1989); Georgina Whitehead, *Civilising the City: A History of Melbourne's Public Gardens* (Melbourne, 1997)
> RA

VICTORIA GARDENS, East Perth, is a small PUBLIC PARK with frontages to the Swan River and the newly created Claisebrook Cove in the East Perth Redevelopment Area. The place has historic associations for the Aboriginal community and with the colonial history of WA. On his 1827 expedition along the Swan River, Captain James Stirling explored the area and named Claise Brook. By mid-century, the site—which formerly spanned both sides of the freshwater creek—was occupied by the government abattoir. The land was developed as a public park in the 1870s and later vested in Perth City Council (1880). Named Victoria Park, it had a chequered history: following popularity during the 1880s it declined as new parks were developed elsewhere in the city. By the early 1900s the site was used as the council nursery and depot, and until 1936 housed the city's sewage treatment plant. Araucarias and exotic trees planted in the late nineteenth and early twentieth centuries remain as dominant elements in the redeveloped Victoria Gardens, established in the mid-1990s. Public art works and symbolic rock sculptures commemorate the Aboriginal and colonial history of the site.
OLINE RICHARDS

VICTORIAN AGRICULTURAL AND HORTICULTURAL GAZETTE (1857–61), published monthly by Heath and Cordell in Geelong (Vic), was edited by Samuel HANNAFORD. Later claimed to be 'the first of its class in the Australian colonies'—it pre-dated regular coverage of its topic by the mainstream weekly press and was paralleled only by the FARM AND GARDEN—the *Gazette* was designed to advance AGRICULTURE and HORTICULTURE by circulating information 'from any intelligent person who has had sufficient experience of our soil and climate to entitle his opinion to respect'. The editor also sought reliable information on money-saving 'scientific apparatuses' for farmers. A section on gardening catered for the 'kitchen, fruit, and flower garden'. Reports on agricultural and HORTICULTURAL SHOWS were a prominent feature. Items of interest were also reprinted from local newspapers (such as the daily Melbourne *Argus* and weekly LEADER), and British journals (such as the *Literary Gazette*, *Illustrated London News*, and GARDENERS' CHRONICLE). Its diverse topics included soil chemistry, fertilisers, early rising, *Cordyline australis*, the labour market, alpacas, blight, the moon's influence on vegetation, *Victoria regia*, and food adulteration. The publication span covered a period of great change in Vic., including the amalgamation of NURSERIES and the extension of others into outer suburbs, an interest in NATIVE PLANTS, and the proliferation of AGRICULTURAL SOCIETIES and shows.
GWEN PASCOE

VICTORIAN FARMERS' JOURNAL AND GARDENERS' CHRONICLE (1859–64), a weekly tabloid published by Ebenezer and David Syme, proprietors of the Melbourne *Age*, was closely modelled on the British agricultural press. The *Journal* included many abridgments from overseas journals, especially the GARDENERS' CHRONICLE and GLENNY's *Midland Florist*, but original material, including reports of HORTICULTURAL SOCIETIES, was strongly featured. The *Journal* was incorporated in the *Weekly Age* (1864–68) and from 1867 the LEADER assumed the mantle of horticultural mouthpiece for Syme.
RA

VICTORIAN TREE PLANTERS' ASSOCIATION: see PARKS AND LEISURE AUSTRALIA

VICTORIA PARK, NSW, adjacent to the University of Sydney and once part of Grose Farm on the Parramatta Road, was formed as a PUBLIC PARK when the land was given to the university (1854). The original design, a long walkway (aligned with the towered quadrangle) through a *Ficus macrophylla* (Moreton Bay Fig) AVENUE was augmented under the direction of Charles MOORE with a more complex GARDENESQUE scheme (1877–78) plotted by James JONES. This is now being partially reinstated after being swept away by a 1930s design in which the main entrance to the university was relocated, truncating the earlier avenue approach.
HELEN PROUDFOOT and COLLEEN MORRIS

VILLA GARDEN The term villa was first used in England in the early seventeenth century, partly from the Latin and

Villa garden

Italian 'country-house, farm', perhaps derived from the stem of *vicus* (village). The villa was a country mansion or residence, together with a farm, farm-buildings, or other house attached, built or occupied by a person of some position and wealth. It was taken to include a country seat or estate and later a residence in the country or in the neighbourhood of a town, usually standing in its own grounds. From this it was appropriated by the middle of the eighteenth century to mean a residence of a superior type, in the suburbs of a town or in a residential district, such as that occupied by a person of the middle class, and also a small, better-class dwelling house, usually detached or semi-detached.

The term villa garden was used in the context of Hobart and Sydney residences in the 1830s, and if near the coast or harbour, the appellation 'marine villa' was often applied. Australian origins probably date from the grant conditions applied to Sydney's Woolloomooloo Hill (1827), which obligated the construction of villas fulfilling certain conditions. Historian James BROADBENT (*The Australian Colonial House*, 1997), invokes the 1825 definition of English architect John Buonarotti Papworth, 'its insulated form, its garden-like domain, and external offices for stables and domestic economy', to typify the early colonial villa, such as RUNNYMEDE, BURSWOOD, and BELEURA, along with numerous Sydney examples (albeit often with subdivided gardens).

Many gardens of nineteenth-century villas followed GARDENESQUE conventions, with garden ORNAMENTS often complementing the architecture of the house. The term had acquired such widespread usage by the 1850s that when Jane LOUDON issued a new edition of her husband's *Suburban Gardener and Villa Companion* (1838) she merely entitled the revised work *The Villa Gardener* (1850). This coincided with a growing period of SUBURBANISATION in Australia and the consequent fostering of the NURSERY trade, whose members often advertised 'Designs for Villa Gardens furnished and superintended'. BUDA and CINTRA both typify this mid- to late nineteenth-century villa garden.

By the 1880s, descriptions of Australian villas implied sufficient room for a lawn on two or three fronts of the residence. By the 1920s, a garden attached to a large suburban house (such as CALTHORPES' HOUSE) was often described as a villa garden and this usage was applied to ordinary suburban

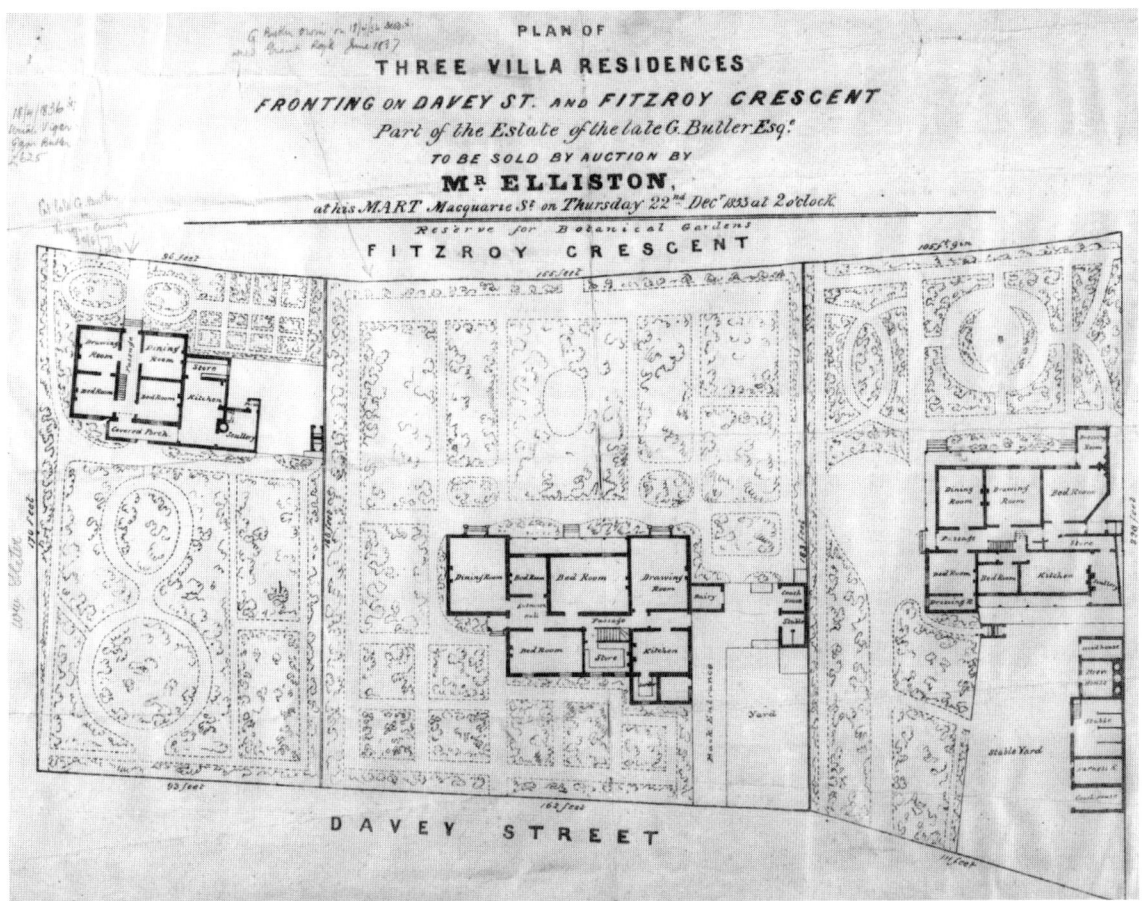

The plan (c.1836) of these three VILLA GARDENS overlooking Hobart's FITZROY GARDENS is a rare and evocative record of an early and important phase of garden making in Australia

Vineyards

allotments with small side gardens, although this usage reflected a certain amount of ironic wishful thinking. Especially after the Second World War, the term villa was rarely used and its contemporary equivalent, perhaps a large architect-designed residence on half an acre (0.2 ha), was usually more prosaically described as a large home, house, or residence. The term villa was chiefly used in Australia to describe a suburban residence rather than a rural one, so the term 'suburban villa' is largely a tautology.   RA

VINEYARDS: see VITICULTURE

VIRTUAL GARDENS refers most commonly to COMPUTER-generated landscapes created solely in the abstract realm of cyberspace. Pioneers of the virtual realm, like their terrestrial forebears, are intent on cultivating the landscape they inhabit. As cyber-philosophers Esa Saarinen and Mark C. Taylor assert, the living space of our world 'is as much electronic as natural. The matrix in all its embodiments must be cultivated'. Virtual gardens (also known as 'terminal gardens') differ primarily from their physical cousins in being created from data rather than dirt. A key, early creation was Australian media artist Jon McKinnon's CD-ROM *Turbulence*—a self-making digital landscape populated by strange, pulsating triffid-like species (1995). 'Virtual gardens' can also refer to three-dimensional rendered GARDEN PLANS and 'walk through' reconstructions of existing (or, indeed, forgotten or lost) gardens, as well as the abstract, labyrinthine spaces of LITERATURE and the mind (as in Jorge Luis Borges' 1956 short story *The Garden of Forking Paths*).   ROWAN WILKEN

VISTAS, controlled views to distant objects or scenes, form a key design feature of many gardens in Australia. This is especially true of HOMESTEAD GARDENS—where the surrounding rural scenery often provides rich prospects—and in urban gardens set in dramatic locales. Vistas are usually contrived as part of a design: panoramic views from LOOKOUTS generally exploit the grandeur of a scene rather than the drama associated with vistas. The idea of a distant view through a narrow opening is closely aligned with the theatre, and controlled planting or other landscape devices often parallel theatre sets. Vistas have generally focused on natural features (a gully with craggy rocks, or a slice of ocean framed by cliffs—the more dramatic the better) although occasionally architectural features (such as a church spire in the case of CAMDEN PARK) provided a focus. In this, vestiges of the PICTURESQUE could be detected. In the absence of features of perceived value, selectively cleared native vegetation, or carefully arranged PLANTATIONS or AVENUES could create vistas. An extreme example of this was implemented by American metallurgist Robert Sticht at Queenstown (Tas.), when in the 1890s he cut a vista through a mountainside, terminating on the smelter chimney. The need to plant or artificially frame vistas was especially strong in small gardens, where vistas may have been contained within limited grounds. Vistas were commonly associated with or directed by other garden features. For instance, the principal axis of the FORMAL terrace at GOVERNMENT HOUSE, Sydney, directed the viewer to the harbour, while GARDEN BUILDINGS were sometimes used as optimum vantage points from which to partake of a vista. Many smaller gardens often terminated an internal vista on a structure, statue, urn, or other garden ORNAMENT.

Vistas discussed thus far were directed outwards from the observer (whether in house or garden), although in some cases the reverse was true. For instance, much effort was expended in levelling the brow of the hill on which Victoria's GOVERNMENT HOUSE sat, as much for the benefit of the governed as the governor, with the seat of imperial power made clearly visible from Melbourne city's principal southern intersection. The 1830s DRIVE at FERNHILL provided the visitor with vistas to the house, controlled by its serpentine alignment as it ascended the foothills of the BLUE MOUNTAINS through gullies and plantings of *Angophora costata* (Smooth Bark Apple Myrtle), a colonial echo of the English landscape movement. Vistas were often a feature of the approach drive of homestead gardens, well demonstrated by many WESTERN DISTRICT gardens in Vic.

TOWN PLANNING schemes introduced many FORMAL vistas, especially those influenced by the CITY BEAUTIFUL movement, as at CANBERRA where outstanding use of the natural topography, especially the dominant hills, provided key axial nodes of the GRIFFIN plan. The vista to the Shrine of Remembrance along Melbourne's St Kilda Road, controlled legislatively by height limits, is an example of the powerful potential of vistas, yet many similar town planning opportunities in Australia—often seen as anti-democratic and redolent of unwanted POLITICAL power—have met with suspicion and remain unrealised. As spaces have been lost to commercial development, so too have many opportunities for vistas. The scale of Australian cities has in that sense shrunk, as spaces are filled and vistas have narrowed or vanished.

MICHAEL LEHANY

VITICULTURE Australia's sunny climates seemed to perceptive early settlers to beg for the cultivation of vineyards and agricultural industries along MEDITERRANEAN lines. The French botanist François Péron (1775–1810), who accompanied Baudin's expedition (1800–04), believed that Australia would, eventually, enable Britain to stop buying wine from SPAIN, Portugal, and FRANCE altogether. Vines were among the cargo of the First Fleet (1788); obtained from the Cape of Good Hope, they were planted at Farm Cove (later to become SYDNEY BOTANIC GARDENS). Probably, this was the small vineyard Governor Phillip reported on in 1791 but fungal diseases spread by Sydney harbour's humid subtropical climate destroyed the young shoots and leaves. With survival paramount and viticulture not a tradition of British agriculture, the foundation vineyard was neglected. Later, in 1800, Governor King had two French prisoners of war he believed were expert vignerons grow grapes and make wine, but with poor results. Thereafter, grape growing was left to individual settlers; many of them did plant vines in their KITCHEN GARDENS, but mainly for fresh fruit.

At Brush Farm, near Eastwood, settler Gregory Blaxland (1778–1853) sought to discover blight-resistant varieties, considering himself successful with the 'Constantia' and later the 'claret' grape (although this may have been Shiraz). In 1816 he sent Governor Macquarie some wine and shipped a barrel to London in 1822, for which he was awarded a silver medal by the Society for the Encouragement of Arts, Manufactures and Commerce. James BUSBY was an early and influential activist and writer. His collection, gathered systematically in Europe, provided a wide and reliable source of wine and fruit cultivars. Busby distributed upwards of 20 000 cuttings himself and claimed credit for the general appearance of vineyards in NSW dating from 1830. Vineyards were successfully developed inland, by the MACARTHUR family at Camden, and also on the river flats of the lower HUNTER VALLEY, where the white grape Semillon and Shiraz (Hermitage) proved successful. The innovative Hunter River Vineyard Association (formed 1847) promoted the use of the names of vineyard properties—Dalwood, Kaludah, Kirkton, Cawarra—to identify wines produced.

Viticulture was boosted by the migration of skilled vignerons, nursery proprietors, and agricultural workers, and by ideas of ACCLIMATISATION. The migration of Swiss to Port Phillip and Germans to the Albury district of NSW supported grape growing; as did that of Silesians to SA, particularly the BAROSSA VALLEY. The DESCHAMPS family were Burgundian Swiss experts who established vineyards in Victoria's upper YARRA VALLEY. But there were far-sighted individual English, Scots, and Irish pioneers of the vine as well, notably John REYNELL, George ANGAS, and Joseph Gilbert (1800–1881) in SA. The Victorian gold rushes increased demand for fresh fruit and small-scale farming was embraced as an ideal; mining towns Great Western, Bendigo, and Rutherglen all became viticultural areas. The 1860s saw a dramatic increase in plantings and moves away from traditional European practices of deep trenching for new vineyards and close spacing of vines as unnecessary. The writings of J.I. BLEASDALE and A.C. KELLY illuminate this period, which saw the emergence of most of Australia's traditional viticultural areas. Typically, these were close to centres of population or nearby in hinterland districts. Many vineyards, especially in Melbourne and Adelaide, were swallowed up when the cities expanded.

The appearance of the vine PEST Grape Phylloxera (*Dactylasphaera vitifoliae* syn. *Phylloxera vasterix*) in Geelong district vineyards in the late 1870s meant a new era of quarantine, restrictions on vine importation and, for a time, the ruthless destruction of affected vineyard districts in Vic. and NSW. From the 1880s, exports and government-sponsored bonuses boosted plantings, in north-east Vic. especially, and reflected a trend towards warmer climate viticulture, and richer and fortified styles of wine. The combined effects of industry trends, phylloxera, economic depression, and the removal of tariff protection saw the near collapse of the Victorian industry by the turn of the century. The creation of IRRIGATION colonies along the Murray River in NSW, Vic., and SA, and later the Murrumbidgee Irrigation Area (NSW), saw 'blockers' growing grapes for fresh and dried fruit and for brandy production, with Sultana and Doradillo varieties. Soldier settlement later boosted plantings in these

Australia's vineyards have a wide geographical spread and embody many universal visual characteristics associated with VITICULTURE, but in their landscaping—as here, in the hinterland of Perth—the presence of mature Australasian trees lends a distinct antipodean character

parts. Eventually, these 'warm climate' regions would turn to fortified and table wine production and become the great engine houses of Australian wine and brandy production. An interesting southern offshoot of these developments was COONAWARRA.

By the turn of the century, most of the colonial governments employed viticultural experts whose job it was to advise governments and disseminate expertise among growers. Arthur James Perkins (1871–1944) was the architect of South Australia's quarantine legislation and taught at ROSEWORTHY AGRICULTURAL COLLEGE. Francois DE CASTELLA was instrumental in the reconstitution of phylloxerated vineyards in Vic. and a leading ampelographer when confusion reigned as to the nomenclature of different—and in some cases the same—CULTIVARS.

Australia now boasts a standardised nomenclature of grape varieties and a system of preferred synonyms. Vine improvement programs and improved rootstocks and methods of grafting have been beneficial. Strict quarantine regulations still control the movement of vine stocks both into and within parts of Australia and most new vineyards source their stocks from commercial nurseries. There is a keen interest in new varieties, and in viticultural research. Allan ANTCLIFF bred new varieties; in 1965 Dr John Gladstones identified a new area, Margaret River in WA, as suitable for vines (now one of Australia's best-known regions); and in the 1970s Dr Andrew Pirie, Australia's first PhD in viticulture, researched Tasmania's potential for cool-climate viticulture. Viticulture is now seen as an important dimension of wine quality. The research and writings of Dr Richard Smart, formerly with Roseworthy College but now a consulting viticulturist, have advocated exposure of grapes to sunlight and a new systems of trellising. Italian varieties (such as Nebbiolo and Barbera) and the Rhone varieties (Grenache, Mourvedre, Viognier, and even Shiraz) are being seen in a new light. Some new discoveries have, in fact, been old ones. Chardonnay, brought into Australia in the Busby collection in the 1830s, survived in old vineyards at Mudgee and the lower Hunter Valley until discovered and propagated in the modern era.

Grape vines appeared in the BACKYARDS of inner-city properties soon after MIGRANTS from southern Europe arrived in the years immediately after the Second World War. Undoubtedly, they contributed to the astonishing contemporary increase in interest in wine among Australians. In the 1960s–70s, city professionals began establishing hobby vineyards alongside their weekenders, only to find themselves drawn into a challenging and absorbing agricultural pursuit. More recently, farmers have been drawn to professional grape growing to diversify and in some cases to save their investment. The current success of Australian wine, especially on international markets, has made for buoyant development of new regions and varieties, dramatic increases in plantings, and a booming tourist industry.

David Dunstan, *Better Than Pommard! A History of Wine in Victoria* (Kew, Vic., 1994); Jancis Robinson (ed.), *The Oxford Companion to Wine* (Oxford, 1999)   DAVID DUNSTAN

VOGUE LIVING (1967–), a monthly (initially quarterly) lifestyle magazine spawned by *Vogue Australia* (1959–), has provided gardening commentary from an early date, firstly in a series of articles by English-born writer Carol Parker (1972–77) and subsequently in regular columns provided by Sydney-based garden designer Gay Stanton (1980–94) and Melbourne-based John PATRICK (1994–99). From 1999, Sydney-based writer Robin Powell has provided regular articles. Expansive garden features in each issue have included Dame Elisabeth MURDOCH's Cruden Farm, historic Edna WALLING–designed MARKDALE, composer Peter Sculthorpe's city courtyard, and others designed by leading garden designers, such as Paul BANGAY. A two-page section, Garden Notes (1992–99), subsequently Gardener, has been a regular feature. A separate spring supplement, *Gardens Today*, has been published since 1997. *Vogue Living* has provided a consistent benchmark for sophisticated living and gardening in Australia.   HOWARD TANNER

VOLCKERS, Henry August (1835–1911), seed merchant and nursery proprietor, was born in Holstein, Germany, and arrived at Moreton Bay in 1856, working initially as a miner. Leaving mining in 1869 he moved to Grafton (NSW) and, having a particular interest in botany, opened a business there as a seed merchant and nursery proprietor. He introduced many fruit trees and vines to the area, and as his business expanded he established two other nurseries. He was involved with the planting of many of the trees in Grafton, and in the late 1870s recommended that jacarandas be planted as STREET TREES, now such a conspicuous feature of the town. He was for a time a council member of the Clarence Pastoral and Agricultural Society, and also successfully exhibited at its shows.   HELEN BOTHAM

VOLLMER, Martin Frederick (*c.* 1846–1916), nursery proprietor, worked in a large seed firm in his native Germany before migrating to Australia in the 1880s. After a short time at Kurrajong (NSW), he moved to the Mount Tomah Nursery at Mobbs Hill—the first nursery in the Epping area—where he produced fruit trees for the ORCHARDS being developed in the district. As fresh land was required for the production of good citrus plants, nurseries raising them had to move frequently and Vollmer moved to East Carlingford in the early 1890s where he employed L.P. ROSÉN to run the nursery while he managed the office. In 1901 Rosén left either as a result of differing attitudes to the Boer War or because he was denied a partnership. **Charles Eustace Vessey** (d. 1937), a rose specialist who had managed the Royal Nurseries, Homebush, one of Sydney's leading nurseries, became a partner. He expanded the range of stock to include ornamental plants—in 1911 their stock boasted upwards of 100 000 palms—and in 1912 became sole proprietor. The Vollmer and Vessey Mount Tomah Nursery continued under that style until Vessey announced in the 1916 catalogue that henceforth 'only my name will be used'. He retired in 1919 and his son F.C. (Fred) Vessey took over. The nursery moved to Eastwood in 1920 and closed some time after C.E. Vessey's death.   RICHARD CLOUGH

VON ARNIM, Elizabeth, see ARNIM, Mary Annette (Elizabeth) von

VON GUÉRARD, (Johann Joseph) Eugen(e): see GUÉRARD, (Johann Joseph) Eugen(e) von

VON HÜGEL, Carl (Charles) Alexander Anselm: see HÜGEL, Carl (Charles) Alexander Anselm von

VON MUELLER, Ferdinand Jakob Heinrich: see MUELLER, Ferdinand Jakob Heinrich von

WADDELL, Winifred (1884–1972), English-born, Melbourne-based mathematics teacher, loved AUSTRALIAN PLANTS. In 1949 she formed a wildflower preservation group within the FIELD NATURALISTS' CLUB of Victoria (whose Australian Natural History Medal she received in 1964). In 1952 this became the Native Plants Preservation Society of Victoria, and as its indefatigable secretary she helped establish wildflower sanctuaries around the state. Jean GALBRAITH's *Wildflowers of Victoria* (1950) was written at her suggestion. In 1976 Galbraith edited articles Waddell had written for the 'Junior Age' (in the early 1960s) into the posthumous tribute, *Wildflower Diary*. ANNE LATREILLE

WADE, Thomas D. (b. c. 1825), gardener and nursery proprietor, was superintendent of the Launceston Horticultural Society Gardens (later CITY PARK) c. 1858–63. In 1859 he was invited to lay out the new PRINCE'S SQUARE, Launceston. Wade was also secretary of the Launceston Gardeners' and Amateurs' Horticultural Society for their fiftieth show, held in 1862. His business in Pomona Place and Brisbane Street, Launceston, Tas., imported from Europe and the Australian colonies fruit trees, shrubs, and choice vegetable and flower seeds. In 1884 he was entrusted with the preparation of a greatly expanded second edition of the *Hand-Book of Garden and Greenhouse Culture in Tasmania*, published by J. Walch and Sons. In 1890, as a 65-year-old widower and 'gardener' he married Ann Rofe (or Nofe), a 52-year-old widow and 'housekeeper' at her Launceston home using Primitive Methodist forms. Ann Wade, 'gardener's wife', died in 1896 but nothing further is known of her husband. ANN CRIPPS

WAIROA, Stirling, in the ADELAIDE HILLS, SA, was purchased in 1883 by mining director William Austin Horn (1841–1922) and developed into a Victorian HILL-STATION garden under head gardener George SPARROW. Enclosed by a conifer forest, the garden is entered past a gatehouse along a tree-lined drive that arcs towards the two-storey residence (1893). The garden retains a circuitous path and bedding layout that descends into a valley with a series of levels—one accessed by a rare cast-iron staircase—and small meadows,

Watercolour of WAIROA, Stirling (SA) by William TIBBITS (1897) depicting the garden layout—a panoramic view that is now difficult to appreciate due to the mature plant growth in this favoured ADELAIDE HILLS location

planted with annuals, massed camellias, rhododendrons and azaleas, and specimen deciduous trees. A large GROTTO featuring original sculptures by Horn is topped by an unusual early UMBRELLA structure. Robert Barr Smith (1824–1915) acquired the property in 1896 on behalf of his son, Thomas Barr Smith (1863–1941) and his wife (Mary) Isobel (née Mitchell) (1863–1941), and it passed to their daughter Joanna Lang (1887–1965), wife of James Hay Grosse (1876–1952), in 1941. Wairoa was acquired by Marbury School in 1972. While Thomas commissioned William TIBBITS to depict the garden in watercolours (1897), it was Isobel and Joanna, assisted by their head gardeners, who extended the rhododendron, camellia, conifer, and maple collections, and added a picking garden in the style of Gertrude JEKYLL.

DAVID JONES

WAITE AGRICULTURAL RESEARCH INSTITUTE, nestled in the foothills of Adelaide at Urrbrae, was established in 1924 following a bequest to the University of Adelaide by pastoral pioneer Peter Waite (1834–1922). Waite Institute has established an international reputation for excellence in research and teaching in agriculture, horticulture, and environmental sciences. Horticultural research has included work on the reproductive biology of eucalypts, and the development of banksia CULTIVARS, acacias, and other Australian natives for cut FLOWERS and FOLIAGE. Based around Waite's **Urrbrae House** (1891), the grounds include the thirty-hectare Waite Arboretum, which comprises more than 2200 labelled trees and shrubs from all over the world, grown under natural rainfall. Special collections include EUCALYPTS (360 species), BANKSIAS (55 species), ornamental pears (26 species), and oaks (70 species). The garden is being redeveloped in collaboration with artists: the rose garden includes 200 varieties important in rose breeding during the twentieth century and a fine collection of heritage roses; a SENSORY GARDEN delights sight, taste, and touch; while SCULPTURES in the Mallee Garden make reference to Waite, his pastoral pursuits, and the Australian landscape. Through innovative art works the Garden of Discovery and its science discovery trail will celebrate seventy-five years of scientific achievements at the Waite Institute.

V.A. Edgeloe, *The Waite Agricultural Research Institute: The First Fifty Years (1924–1974)* (Adelaide, 1974)

JENNIFER GARDNER

WALES The Welsh, particularly after large-scale migration to colonial goldfields in the mid-nineteenth century, made a contribution to the arts in Australia that outweighed their numerical strength. In gardening, however, influence was diffuse and initially related to Wales as the cradle of PICTURESQUE tourism in the late eighteenth century. A tour of the Wye Valley rivalled the Lake District or the Scottish Highlands, all destinations popularised by the books of William GILPIN. Among those who settled in New South Wales, the writings of naturalist George BENNETT betrayed him as a disciple of Gilpin's Wye tour; the affection of Louisa Anne MEREDITH (née Twamley) inspired *An Autumn Ramble by the Wye* (1839). In the twentieth century, Welsh gardens (such as Bodnant and Powis) with their fine collections from the Orient, have attracted many visitors, Australians included. The power of the Wye Valley has now dimmed for all but the keen student, and a Welsh pilgrimage is more likely to focus on the purchase of garden books at Hay-on-Wye than to lead to exclamations of surprise and delight at Monmouth or Chepstowe.

Elizabeth Whittle, *The Historic Gardens of Wales* (London, 1992)

RA

WALKER, Frank (*c.* 1854–1941), nursery proprietor, seed merchant, and florist, trained at the VEITCH nursery and migrated in 1874 to Tas. from Kent, England. In 1876 he established a nursery and florist's business in Wellington Street, Launceston, and later bought land for a nursery at Sandhill. In the early 1890s he established fruit farms and nurseries at Lalla, growing rhododendrons, azaleas, roses, heath, and boronia. He revised and expanded the third edition of the *Hand-Book of Garden, Greenhouse and Fruit Culture in Tasmania* (1892) published by J. Walch and Sons. Walker's four sons and three daughters worked in the expanding business, which propagated stock for the nursery and cut-flower trade throughout Australia. The firm grew and donated thousands of trees that were planted in the AVENUE between Hobart and Launceston, completed in 1935. The eldest son, **William Alexander George Walker** (1889–1969), was responsible for the management and development of the Lalla complex, which supplied fruit trees for orchards in Tas. and overseas. The firm worked on the improvement of apple strains and exhibited at fruit shows, gaining first prize at the international fruit exhibition in London (1937). William Walker also became an authority on RHODODENDRONS, introducing many new varieties; many can still be seen at the W.A.G. Walker Rhododendron Reserve on the site of the early nursery at Lalla. William's eldest son, **(William) Frank Walker** (1914–1985), chief horticulturist in the Tasmanian Department of Agriculture for many years, had a particular interest in urban horticulture. He was president and later a life member of the International Society for Horticultural Science and in 1984 was awarded the Veitch Memorial Gold Medal of the ROYAL HORTICULTURAL SOCIETY.

ANN CRIPPS

WALKER, (Edith) Jean: see MALONEY, Betty Florence, and (Edith) Jean Walker

WALKLEY, Gavin (b. 1911), architect and educator, was influential in establishing the design and planning professions in SA as well as holding the Chair of Architecture at the University of Adelaide. Born in Adelaide, he studied architecture at the University of Adelaide and Clare College, Cambridge, before being appointed Head of the School of Architecture at the South Australian Institute of Technology (1951–76). He instigated courses in planning, interior design, and landscape architecture; developed these professions in SA; and served as national president of the Royal Australian Institute of Architects (1965–66), Royal Australian Planning Institute (1964–66), Australian Institute of Landscape Architects (1971–73), and as the inaugural president of the Australian Institute of Urban Studies (1968–69) in an attempt to realise a unified environmental design institute and profession. DAVID JONES

WALLCLIFFE HOUSE, Margaret River, WA, was built by pastoralist Alfred Bussell (1816–1882) in 1865 after three decades in the Swan River Colony. The approach to the house is dominated by a huge clump of *Agave americana* while old yuccas line the back driveway. Two symmetrically placed *Melia azedarach* (White Cedar) trees—one of which survives—framed the VISTA to the river from the house. Since 1987 Mark and Cate Hohnen have redeveloped the garden using a formal layout with stone walls and hedges.

COLLEEN MORRIS

WALLING, Edna Margaret (1895–1973), landscape designer, conservationist, writer, and photographer, was born in Yorkshire, England, and spent her early years in Devon before migrating with her family to New Zealand (1911) and later to Australia (1914). One of the first women to attend the full-time course at Melbourne's BURNLEY School of Horticulture, the young Edna Walling was soon to become the single most important person in the metamorphosis of an Australian garden style.

Graduating from Burnley in 1917 as one of the best-performing students, Walling worked with little enthusiasm as a 'jobbing gardener' until the pivotal day she came upon a stone WALL supporting a semicircular terrace. This was to be the turning point in her career. 'I shall build walls', Walling wrote of this incident. From then on, gardens became the means to carry out the architectural designs 'wizzing around in my head, not places where one slaved for too many boring hours of the precious days'. Without hesitation, Walling visited the architect brother of a friend and asked if she could design the garden for one of his houses. 'He had no objection—gardens didn't interest him anyhow. So one of his clients was persuaded to let me design his garden. As luck would have it the man I got to build my first wall made a splendid job of it and on we went from garden to garden building walls, always building walls.' These walls were to be her *leitmotif* and by 1927 Walling was being hailed as 'Melbourne's famous landscape gardener' and 'a genius at her job'.

As William ROBINSON had done in the 1870s, Walling too railed against the uninspiring mass displays of annuals and horticultural 'brilliance' being extolled by the popular press. Drawing on her love of the natural countryside, childhood memories of walks across the moors in the Devonshire countryside, and the writings of Gertrude JEKYLL, Walling developed a distinctive landscape style, and used Australian plants with great effect. One of her earliest gardens was Cruden Farm, Langwarrin (Vic.), designed for Keith and Elisabeth MURDOCH in 1929. In one of her most brilliant plantings, she chose *Eucalyptus citriodora* (Lemon-scented Gum) to line the long DRIVE leading to the house.

Unlike Jekyll, Walling's greatest creative era was in her twenties and thirties—Jekyll did not start designing until well into her fifties—and Walling's plans were works of art, compared to Jekyll's, which were only ever intended as working copies. Beautifully rendered in ink and watercolour on

The young Edna WALLING, pictured in *Australian Women's Mirror* (1925), at the start of her rise to prominence as a garden designer and journalist

Whatman's handmade paper, remarkably, and a testament to their quality, approximately one-quarter executed by Walling throughout her career survive today. Many of these are held by the State Library of Victoria and in private collections in Tas., SA, NSW, and, principally, Vic.

Early plans from the 1920s and 1930s show a strong architectural framework with low stone walls, wide PERGOLAS, and PATHS—always softened with a mantle of greenery. In later years, she was to use boulders, rocky outcrops, and indigenous plants in a more naturalistic style—drawing inspiration from the Australian BUSH. Walling believed landscape design to be 'the art of dealing with land in such a manner that the hand of man is practically unseen'. Even in her more formal designs, there was a subtle understated simplicity and an extraordinary grasp of space as a third dimension. This was particularly important in small SUBURBAN GARDENS, where she would create garden 'rooms', making each garden appear far larger than it actually was.

'Funny things, gardens. I think they like to be *discovered*, not shown off', wrote Walling in one of her many articles that appeared between the 1920s and the 1970s. It was through her writings that Walling became known to the gardening public. Here she expounded simplistic philosophies that would change the evolution of gardening in Australia.

Walling's first foray into writing for the general public was in the HOME magazine in 1924. Within a year, Walling was to start contributing a garden column to the AUSTRALIAN HOME BEAUTIFUL, which continued for almost a quarter of a century. Her chatty writing style, impressive landscape plans, and evocative photographs made her name a byword in gardening circles.

Throughout her career, Walling lived at BICKLEIGH VALE, the village she created on the outskirts of Melbourne. Purchasing 1.2 hectares of bushland at Mooroolbark in 1921, Walling built her own home, Sonning. She later purchased an adjoining 7.4 hectares and embarked on a subdivision scheme, unique in that she actually approved prospective purchasers and then designed both home and garden. 'Bickleigh Vale is definitely *not* to be a GARDEN SUBURB with neatly shaped lawns and regularly spaced trees', she wrote, 'not one thing have I had to do with this completely satisfying landscape scene—except to LEAVE WELL ALONE. Ah! How important that can be.' Leaving well enough alone was to become a recurring theme through her writings.

With the hope of creating a similar type of village on the slopes of Buderim in tropical Qld, Walling left Bickleigh Vale in 1967 and moved to Bendles, at Buderim. Here she created more gardens, although the village concept did not progress. Despite suffering a number of strokes before leaving Vic., Walling continued to write prolifically, rewriting manuscripts, sending streams of Letters to Editors on environmental issues, and trying to republish her books, *Gardens in Australia* (1943), *Cottage and Garden in Australia* (1947), *A Gardener's Log* (1948), and *The Australian Roadside* (1952).

Walling died at Buderim. Her legacy lies as much in her garden philosophies, expressed in her writings and her exquisite watercolour plans, as in her few remaining gardens. Passionate about the preservation of Australia's native vegetation she was equally resolute in creating harmonious relationships between garden and landscape. A number of books published since her death pay tribute to an extraordinary vision.

Peter Watts, *The Gardens of Edna Walling* (Melbourne, 1981); Trisha Dixon and Jennie Churchill, *Gardens in Time: In the Footsteps of Edna Walling* (Sydney, 1988); Trisha Dixon and Jennie Churchill, *The Vision of Edna Walling: Garden Plans 1920–1951* (Hawthorn, Vic., 1998)   TRISHA DIXON

WALLIS, Alexander Robert (1848–1928), Victoria's first Secretary for Agriculture, was born in Gazipur, India, and educated in England and Germany. He migrated to Melbourne in 1871 and was appointed Secretary in November 1872. Among many duties, Wallis was given responsibility for the development of Melbourne's DOMAIN. He delegated key structural works to head gardener W.L. Homeyer who, to the consternation of Melburnians, misaligned driveways and felled trees unnecessarily. Wallis suspended him and personally took charge. He made good progress in laying out driveways but in April 1873, pleading overwork, relinquished control. Wallis remained Secretary until 1882, when his services were dispensed with. He migrated to New Zealand in 1887, where he worked as an estate manager and timber merchant, and died in Dunedin. The contributions of Wallis to Victorian agricultural education, viticulture, and forestry were significant, although his bequest as a gardener was modest.

Ray Wright, *'Dispensed With': A.R. Wallis, First Secretary for Agriculture in Victoria, 1872–1882* (Melbourne, 1982)
RAY WRIGHT

WALLS AND WALLED GARDENS The European tradition of terracing, to make ground practical or useful, and of walled enclosures, to secure land or to protect young or sensitive plants, is evident from the earliest days of Australian colonial settlement. First GOVERNMENT HOUSE, Sydney (1788–89), had a walled terrace or parade ground before it, while Governor Macquarie's improvements (1816) to the Botanic Gardens site in the Sydney DOMAIN included a stone wall to reduce the exposure of the Middle Garden to winds and sea spray. Similarly, Hobart's Government Garden had, by 1826, a high protective wall to the Derwent, heated by flues and with a compact GLASSHOUSE set against its northern face. Later, utilitarian gardening walls often supported ESPALIERED fruit trees.

By the 1830s, grander mansions such as ELIZABETH BAY HOUSE (NSW) had an oval forecourt retained and edged by a decorative stone wall. Beyond the immediate 'pleasure grounds' an enclosure for the kitchen and picking garden was often constructed. At WOOLMERS (Tas.), the pleasure grounds were contained by encircling brick walls, while at BEAUFRONT (Tas.), stone walls defined the KITCHEN GARDEN. Such an estate required effective public presentation, and GATES, pillars, and a handsome wall and related FENCING usually accented the road frontage, as at MACQUARIE FIELDS HOUSE (NSW). Early garden walls were generally of stone, finely chiselled or rusticated where sandstone or limestone, more random or fieldstone in arrangement where basalt or granite prevailed. Brick walls were also used where suitable clay was available or economy dictated.

The irregular terrain occupied by many of Sydney's nineteenth-century marine VILLAS was transformed by massive terrace structures. Handsome balustrades and stairs accented the levels, and introduced soil enabled lusher planting. A similar pattern was later found at MARATHON (c. 1914) at Mount Eliza (Vic.), an unusually formal design with four distinct terraces, contained by hedging and with viewing platforms along the clifftop, all overlooking Port Phillip Bay. It was designed by fashionable architect Walter BUTLER, whose ideas accorded with those of English ARTS AND CRAFTS architect J.D. Sedding, with whom he had trained. British taste continued to influence Australia garden design during much of the twentieth century, especially through publications associated with *Country Life*. The Arts and Crafts ideal of a strong structural framework underlying the garden plan and involving walled enclosures, retaining walls, solid balustrades, and axial arrangements of stairs and walls can be found in work of Butler and Edna WALLING, in particular in her gardens at MAWARRA, ARDGARTEN, and DURROL, and in later walled rose gardens by others, such as ST AUBINS (c. 1940) and BOLOBEK (c. 1980).

The most remarkable twentieth-century use of fieldstone walls is found in the work of Paul SORENSEN. The primary example, EVERGLADES (c. 1935), has beautifully crafted walls of irregularly shaped pieces of ironstone, occasionally punctuated by stylish wrought-iron work in the Art Deco style. There was a vogue for walls of shallow horizontal bands of stone, often married into a setting of natural stone outcrops, existing eucalypts, and freely shaped lawns: examples in NSW include the Arthur McElhone Reserve at Elizabeth Bay (1953) and the Pacific Club at Palm Beach (c. 1956).

Modern public landscapes often feature sheer blade divisions (Federation Square, Melbourne) and canted masonry retaining walls (VICTORIA GARDENS, East Perth) ensuring bold spatial modelling, with plantings as sculptural accents. Architectural road walls, along freeways, are also providing new expressions for walling.

HOWARD TANNER

WALLSEND PARK, NSW, gazetted in 1883, is an important early PUBLIC PARK in the Newcastle area. Formerly part of a wetland system draining into Ironbark Creek, the area was infilled from 1875 by employees of the Newcastle–Wallsend Coal Company. Government grants in the 1880s and 1890s enabled landscape improvements. Surviving older plantings include Newcastle's best AVENUES of *Araucaria bidwillii* (Bunya Pine) and *A. cunninghamii* (Hoop Pine), along with *Ficus* spp. (FIGS) and *Cinnamomum camphora* (Camphor Laurel).

GEOFFREY BRITTON

WALSH, Richard Bruce (b. 1945), teacher and rosarian, commenced hybridising roses in 1980 and has introduced a number of miniature cultivars commercially, raised in his Woonona (NSW) garden, including 'Autumn Kiss', 'Love Me', and 'Mini Magic' (1994). 'Wollongong Gold', a cluster flowered yellow rose awaiting introduction, celebrated the fiftieth anniversary of the City of Wollongong. Other roses are being assessed for release as fund-raisers for charities. He has had a long association with the National Rose Society of New South Wales, including the offices of president and editor of *New South Wales Rose*. He has also served as the Illawarra and Southern Highlands Co-ordinator for Heritage Roses—Australia. Walsh was a delegate for Australia at the 1997 World Federation of Rose Societies conference and in 1996 he was awarded the T.A. STEWART Memorial Award by the NATIONAL ROSE SOCIETIES of Australia and New Zealand.

TREVOR NOTTLE

WARD, Edward Naughton (1871–1934), gardener, was born in Yorkshire, England, and trained at the BACKHOUSE nursery. He migrated to Australia c. 1896 and worked in Vic. as a Department of Agriculture inspector. In 1897 he joined the fruit inspection branch, New South Wales Department of Agriculture. After a stint as head gardener of CRANBROOK, he became overseer then superintendent (1914) of the SYDNEY BOTANIC GARDENS. On the death of J.H. MAIDEN, he became curator of the Botanic Gardens and CENTENNIAL PARK (1924–34). Ward's obituarist described him as 'an artistic landscape gardener' and claimed that 'Many of Sydney's most attractive private gardens were laid out under his direction … He also acted as gardening adviser to many municipal councils and hospitals'. Ward was a great

WARDIAN CASES, with their enclosed and protective atmosphere, were an ingenious means of transporting plants during long sea voyages, and were also popular for decorative indoor use, as illustrated here in E.B. HEYNE's *The Amateur Gardener* (1881)

proponent for *Ficus microcarpa* var. *hillii* (Hill's Fig): 'the beautiful street specimens in the eastern suburbs of Sydney are a living memorial to [his] great work'.

COLLEEN MORRIS

WARDIAN CASE Transporting plants around the world safely was an almost insurmountable difficulty until the 1830s when English physician and naturalist, Nathaniel Bagshaw Ward (1791–1868), perfected a 'closely glazed frame', a kind of miniature GLASSHOUSE built around a strong wooden framework with fitted wooden slats on the outside to protect the glass from damage, and tightly sealed to retain soil moisture. The idea was to recirculate the soil moisture by containing the process of evaporation and condensation inside the case. After several years of experimentation, beginning in 1829, Ward successfully trialled his invention in 1833 by sending two cases of plants to Sydney, filled on their return with AUSTRALIAN PLANTS bound for Loddiges nursery in Hackney (London).

Ward's success followed many earlier attempts—attended by varying degrees of success—of transporting plants to and from foreign countries, but was the first to perfect a concept and persuade a prestigious nursery to back his trial shipments. His idea was published in HORTICULTURAL JOURNALS and also in his book *On the Growth of Plants in Closely Glazed Cases* (1842), whose title indicated another major use of the Wardian case, growth of plants as part of INDOOR GARDENS, especially in polluted cities. Wardian cases were quickly accepted as the best means of transporting plants across the oceans and many plants destined for the Australian NURSERY trade were received by this means, and a strong return flow of native plants was sent to England, and elsewhere, for scientific study and introduction as CONSERVATORY plants.

TREVOR NOTTLE

WAR MEMORIALS became a feature of the Australian landscape after the First World War (1914–18), recording the devastating impact of war on a newly federated nation. Some 60 000 Australians lost their lives from a population of four million, representing one in five of those who served. By 1925 most communities across the nation had a memorial, a highly visible expression of grief that cut across class, ethnic, and other divisions of Australian society. State and federal memorials took longer to realise, and culminated in the opening of the Australian War Memorial, Canberra, in 1941. To those who erected them, war memorials were as sacred as grave sites, substitute graves for the Australians whose bodies lay in battlefield cemeteries in Europe and the Middle East.

Typically, the memorials took the form of stone soldiers, obelisks, ornamental gates, and the like, supplied by local monumental masons. They bore the names of all who served from a community—the 'returned' and the 'fallen'—for Australians were proud that their first great national army, unlike other belligerent armies, was composed entirely of volunteers. Funded by public subscription, the memorials were sited in public places and became the focus of annual Anzac Day (25 April) observance. WAR TROPHIES and flagstaffs were often positioned nearby, as were kerbing, fences, paths, and symbolic planting. These MEMORIAL GARDENS had a linear manifestation in AVENUES OF HONOUR.

No other war has made such an impact on the Australian landscape, hitherto almost devoid of public monuments. Though the Boer (or South African) War (1899–1902) brought Australia its earliest war monuments, they were rare and typically erected by war veterans in less prominent places, such as CEMETERIES. Further, the Second World War (1939–45) brought utilitarian memorials, such as parks and buildings, in preference to monuments; often new generations of names were added to the old monuments. During the 1980s, more memorials and inscriptions have been erected to acknowledge more recent conflicts, notably Vietnam (1965–72), or mark sites of significance to the Second World War. The involvement of Aboriginal Australians in war, both at home and abroad, is also being acknowledged.

K.S. Inglis, *Sacred Places: War Memorials in the Australian Landscape* (Melbourne, 1998)

JUDITH McKAY

WARNER, William Richard (*c.* 1883–1961), nursery proprietor, was born and educated at Old Windsor, England, and after an apprenticeship gained further experience at the Chelsea nursery of James VEITCH and Sons, and in other English gardens (including Windsor Castle). He migrated to Melbourne in 1913 and commenced a florists' nursery at Auburn in 1914, soon expanding his business to Camberwell and becoming well known in the NURSERY trade. He was a founding contributor to *HOME GARDENER*, gave weekly RADIO broadcasts on 3AR, enthusiastically supported the Canterbury Horticultural Society and VICTORIAN TREE PLANTERS' ASSOCIATION, and was Mayor of Camberwell for several terms. He also served as president of the Nurserymen and Seedsmen's Association of Victoria and of the Garden Week FESTIVAL committee. Sons Jack (1922), Geoffrey (1931), and Robert (1946) joined the business, located in Burwood from 1938. The founder retired in 1951, the same year that his youngest son Arthur, and grandson Max entered the business. As further members of the third (and later fourth) generation joined the business, the firm incorporated as Warner's Nurseries Pty Ltd (1979) and henceforth restricted its business to wholesale trade, building on a market commenced by the firm in 1948. Further expansion on new sites in Melbourne's south-east corridor has consolidated Warner's Nurseries as a major producer of advanced evergreen trees and shrubs. Family members have also built on the lead provided by William Warner as generous contributors to Victoria's nursery industry.

RA

WARRNAMBOOL BOTANIC GARDENS, Vic., was established in 1858 with seeds and plants supplied by Ferdinand MUELLER to the care of gardener Charles SCOBORIO. The ten-acre (4 ha) site, overlooking the Hopkins River, proved unsuitable, however, and in 1864 Scoborio and local market gardener William Clutton (*c.* 1829–1864) selected the current site for 'for its proximity to the town, the undulating and romantic nature of its conformation and the quality of its soil'. Clearing of dense vegetation and fencing was undertaken in 1866–67. Charles Hortle (*c.* 1834–1881), linked by marriage to the ARCHER family of Tasmania, was appointed gardener in 1869, and a year later a well and gardener's cottage were constructed. Scoborio returned as curator in 1872 and set about establishing WINDBREAKS (including a PINETUM on the south-west frontage) and ROCKERY beds near the main entrance and cottage. A new plan by William GUILFOYLE (1877) realised the site's potential for a 'natural and picturesque design'. His plan for the sloping site incorporated Scoborio's earlier works and remnant *Eucalyptus viminalis* subsp. *pryoriana* (Coast Manna Gum), while planning broad sweeping pathways and lawns defined by SHRUBBERIES and a LAKE with two islands. His unfolding spatial arrangement incorporated short VISTAS, and long views linked by repeated plantings of *Washingtonia filifera* (Cotton Palm). His SUBTROPICAL plant palette introduced a lush, exotic effect and botanical diversity into Scoborio's CONIFEROUS setting. Guilfoyle's approach was essentially broad brush, left to the curator to implement, sometimes resulting in a GARDENESQUE style in the spacing and pruning of individual plants. Subsequent long-serving curators contributed distinct features, but the period 1866–97 saw the defining elements established. This BOTANIC GARDEN remains among the best and most intact of Guilfoyle's collaborative works.

JILL ORR-YOUNG

WARTIME GARDENING, most relevant in Australia during the First and Second World Wars, involved profound shifts in horticulture and left distinctive legacies. During the First (or Great) War (1914–18), German horticultural supplies were cut off, *Rosa* 'Frau Karl Druski' was briefly renamed 'Snow Queen' (in a fit of patriotic and xenophobic pique), VEGETABLE GARDENING received a huge boost, GARDEN VISITING and fetes in mansion gardens aided patriotic causes, and, significantly, the GENDER balance in horticulture and gardening was altered (as opportunities for woman were provided by the absence and tragic loss of many men). In the public landscape, impetus was given to AVENUES OF HONOUR, and WAR MEMORIALS and WAR TROPHIES took pride of place in public parks and gardens. The Second World War (1939–45), which involved action much closer to Australia, again saw huge patriotic gestures. New vegetable plots, ranging from vice-regal acres to small backyards, carried a strong message of self-sufficiency, thrift, and collective effort, and at a government level, the Australian Women's Land Army engaged in large-scale productive horticulture (where respected horticulturists such as Olive MELLOR played a leading role). AIR RAID SHELTERS were carved from public parkland and suburban backyards. The post-war era witnessed significant migration from war-torn Europe, bringing important strands of MODERNISM to Australia. Just as MIGRANTS' GARDENS of the post-war period transferred rich traditions, so conflicts in our region have more recently brought migration and consequent enrichment to our horticulture.

RA

WAR TROPHIES, mostly cannon from the Crimean (1853–56) and Boer (1899–1902) Wars, were occasionally placed in Australian PUBLIC PARKS and BOTANIC GARDENS during the nineteenth century, but it was trophies from the First World War (1914–18)—field guns, trench mortars, and machine guns—that were most widely distributed. In 1919 State Trophy Committees were established to control the distribution of the great quantities that had been collected. Allocation was determined by population: towns with a population of more than 3000 received at least one field gun; smaller towns, one machine gun. Conditions included appointment of three trustees (including an AIF member); permanent housing in a public park, garden, or building; and conduct of a simple ceremony. Many guns sat next to or were part of newly unveiled WAR MEMORIALS. In deciding to accept the trophies, communities saw in them conflicting sentiments—weapons of destruction, reminders of suffering or of heroism, symbols of victory, or the lessons of war. Now those trophies that remain, including a sprinkling from the Second World War (1939–45), sit as relics of an antiquarian military past.

K.S. Inglis, *Sacred Places: War Memorials in the Australian Landscape* (Melbourne, 1998)

JAN BRAZIER

WATER The CLIMATE and physiography (land forms) of Australia determine its water resources. Climatic variation, especially in predominant rainfall SEASONS—winter in southern temperate areas, summer in northern TROPICAL areas, and prolonged absences in central ARID ZONES—has a major effect on landscape design. Australian's physiography also exhibits great contrasts, generating great diversity in the landscape. River systems are also an important influence on DESIGNED LANDSCAPES since they provide a water source and are often associated with fertile lands. Many areas in Australia also have groundwater resources, although not always suitable for horticultural use. IRRIGATION has considerably redistributed the available water to areas of low rainfall, which has sometimes led to increased salinity. Australia has extensive plains, of which lakes (sometimes ephemeral) are often a feature, and frequently a backdrop, to designed landscapes. Australia also has a vast and richly varied coastline ranging from sandy BEACHES and reefs to steep rocky cliffs; a common focus for early European settlement in these areas is the choice of a coastal location combined with a river mouth.

Much of Australia's infrastructure development since European settlement has been directed at gathering and directing water, from early dams and irrigation schemes to sophisticated systems of reticulated supply in urban centres.

Russian guns, WAR TROPHIES from the Crimean War (1853–56), were installed in the MELBOURNE BOTANIC GARDENS in 1858 but relocated to nearby Victoria Barracks (where they still sit) in 1867, following a change in British government policy on the display of such trophies

The cost of undertaking and maintaining this supply is not always measured. Costs increase daily and when combined with the unreliability of rainfall across much of the continent, water conservation is now a major force in gardening, horticulture, and landscape design. XERIC GARDENING is no longer an enforced practice for 'dry' areas; it is a widely promoted imperative for many areas with reticulated water supplies. The Leigh Creek township (SA) reduced its consumption in 1985–86 by forty-seven per cent and so became a model for other places. Popular literature and promotion by once-profligate authorities are slowly contributing to this essential cultural change.

After a long and widespread promotion of irrigation, the work of innovators such as P.A. YEOMANS has influenced a new attitude to water conservation. Irrigation of crops currently accounts for almost three-quarters of available national water while ten per cent is used domestically (including water for gardens). The breakdown of this domestic usage varies from a high of almost two-thirds in Perth and Canberra for garden use to a low of one-third for Melbourne and Sydney. GEOLOGICAL factors are at work here. Perth has porous, sandy soil with a low moisture content, and consumption for gardens is high. Soil that is dense and impermeable, as in Canberra, results in little readily available moisture. Loam needs to be watered more frequently than clay, as the holding capacity of clay is greater. These conditions, together with a high evaporation rate, are part of the explanation for high water use on gardens.

Regulating rainfall by seepage or irrigation relies on interpreting the SOIL and specific PLANT needs. Xeric gardens develop more slowly than fully irrigated schemes yet are better adapted for survival. Since the mid-1980s sprinkler, dripper, and micro-jet spray use has increased and is expanding. Carefully targeted irrigation replaces evaporated or transpired soil moisture, especially for new planting establishment, by gradually reducing water until a minimum is used. Another responsible course involves a change from traditional, often British-based, gardening practices to methods that utilise vegetation adapted to fluctuations in dry and wet conditions. MAINTENANCE and HORTICULTURAL TECHNIQUES such as mulching can greatly assist in this.

Rainfall needs to be retarded in its progress to the drain to increase the stored soil moisture necessary for plant growth. Yet adequate DRAINAGE is also required to maximise the water-carrying capacity of the soil while still allowing it to drain. The use of ponds, pools, dams, and naturalistic wetlands has increased in rural, public, and domestic landscape since the rise of the environment movement in the 1970s. This has not only been generated by a BUSH GARDEN aesthetic, but for conservation purposes in storm water control and utilisation, such as in Glen WILSON's award-winning work at Ainslie Village (ACT).

Water features in many ornamental ways in landscape design, through LAKES and pools (and associated islands and BRIDGES), FOUNTAINS and jets, reflecting ponds, and wetlands. The work of Sydney-based water sculptor Robert WOODWARD always maximises effect while minimising water use. This is an appropriate message for Australia in an era when even continued public ownership of this life-sustaining natural resource is not assured.

David Ingle Smith, *Water in Australia: Resources and Management* (Melbourne, 1998)   PAUL THOMPSON

WATERHOUSE, Eben Gowrie (1881–1977), garden and landscape designer, camellia expert, writer, and lecturer, developed a love of gardens, AUSTRALIAN NATIVE PLANTS, and the BUSH in his youth. After graduating from the University of Sydney he became a language teacher and in 1906 made the first of many trips overseas. He spent more than two years in Europe studying and travelling and in 1912 returned for a further six months, devoting part of his time to the study of art, architecture, and gardening. Back in Sydney he met leading painters and architects and so, when he came to build his own house, was able to choose an architect, William Hardy WILSON, responsive to the progressive ideas he had developed overseas.

Eryldene in McIntosh Street, Gordon—the house and garden resulting from their collaboration—was finished in 1914. Wilson, influenced by contemporary work in England and North America, developed a style based on the early colonial buildings of NSW and Tas. Groups of native trees retained on the site provided a background for the formal symmetrical elevation of the house. The materials, detailing, and colours of the house were carried into the garden, defining and articulating the space between house and street, creating the first of the garden rooms for which Eryldene became noted. In 1921 extra land was purchased and the garden enlarged. The building of the garden study allowed four new spaces, stepping up the slope, to be created. After Wilson returned from a visit to CHINA in 1927 the tea house facing the tennis court was built, combining in its design elements from classical and Chinese architecture. With minor alterations the property assumed its present form; the planting, however, under Waterhouse's expert direction, was continually modified as plants were removed and replaced, shaped and pruned. The significance of the garden was soon recognised. It was illustrated and described in the *Home* by Waterhouse (1926) and Jocelyn BROWN (1940), and after Waterhouse died the Eryldene Trust was established to manage and preserve it.

Appointed to the staff of the University of Sydney in the early 1920s when a number of buildings designed by Professor Leslie WILKINSON were nearing completion, Waterhouse gradually assumed responsibility for the design of the landscaping. He first designed the 'Pleasaunce' of the University Union and this was so successful that he was invited to design the Main Quadrangle, the Vice Chancellor's Quadrangle, the Botany Courtyard, and the McMaster Laboratory. He then redesigned the older areas, creating a unified landscape setting for the first time. He was also invited to take control of the grounds of Royal Prince Alfred Hospital and designed the landscape setting for the newly built Gloucester House (1937). Having received a Carnegie grant to study UNIVERSITY landscaping, after visiting Europe in 1934 he returned via the USA and inspected the grounds of twenty-nine educational institutions, holding discussions with their

The garden of E.G. WATERHOUSE at ERYLDENE, Gordon (NSW), provided not only a fine setting for the distinguished architecture of William Hardy WILSON but also a field for horticultural experimentation by Waterhouse

designers, including Beatrix Farrand, one of the founders of the American Institute of Landscape Architects. He claimed on his return that 'the landscape treatment of the parkways in the Eastern states and the Campus treatment of some of the American Universities and Colleges reach a level of beauty unknown and undreamed of in Australia'. He recognised the need for professionally qualified landscape architects and sought, unsuccessfully, to have a school of LANDSCAPE ARCHITECTURE established at the University of Sydney. In 1946 he retired from the chair of German; however, he stayed on at the university as curator of grounds until the end of the decade.

While both Waterhouse and Wilson were influenced by the layout of colonial gardens, they also developed a special appreciation of the plants that survived in them. Waterhouse became increasingly interested in CAMELLIAS. He planted six at Eryldene in 1914 and gave a further six to Wilson. After learning to propagate them from cuttings he built up his collection, growing all the CULTIVARS he could find from old gardens. He then turned to the task of establishing their current names. As interest in camellias grew he saw the need for a specialist nursery and in 1939 established the Camellia Grove Nursery at St Ives, which was managed by his son Gordon until sold in 1946. With camellia enthusiast A.O. Ellison he organised an exhibition of camellias at the Macquarie Gallery in 1939, when sixty-two varieties were shown. This was followed in the next year by one containing 100 varieties. As interest in camellias became Australia-wide he corresponded with camellia enthusiasts in all states and after attending the Camellia and Magnolia Conference organised by the ROYAL HORTICULTURAL SOCIETY in London in 1950 his circle of correspondents became worldwide. In 1952 the Australian and New Zealand Camellia Research Society was formed with Waterhouse as honorary secretary and editor. Ten years later the International Camellia Society was established with Waterhouse as its first president, an office he held until his death. His work in connection with camellias and his service to horticulture in Australia were recognised by the award of the VEITCH Gold Medal by the RHS in 1966.

Waterhouse was an influential writer and lecturer. In 1926 he contributed an article, 'Gardening as an Interpretive Art', for the *Home*, in which he dealt with the aesthetics of gardening, a subject he developed in lectures given for the University Art Club, the University Extension Board, and the (then) Australian Broadcasting Company. These were printed in the *Sydney Morning Herald* and the *Union Recorder*. The issues relating to private gardens received expanded treatment in his 'Domestic Gardening as an Art' in W.A. Shum's *Australian Gardening of Today* (1943). Other issues dealt with public landscaping, with STREET TREES, with bush retention, especially the preservation of native trees in newly developed urban areas, and with urban open spaces. He even pressed for the large-scale landscaping of the newly erected Harbour Bridge. He raised landscape CONSERVATION issues, writing for the press on tree removal and the alienation of parkland. The campaign he led against the building of laboratories for the Department of Agriculture in the SYDNEY BOTANIC GARDENS resulted in the work being halted and that already built being removed. His article 'The Return of the Camellia', published in the *Home* (1941), was the first of many on his favourite plants. His *Camellia Quest* (1947) and *Camellia Trail* (1952) were published by Sydney Ure Smith, a fellow trustee of the National Art Gallery of New South Wales and a fellow council member of the Australian Limited Editions Society. The first was illustrated by Adrian Feint and Paul JONES, and the second by Jones. They are arguably the most beautiful garden books published in Australia and clearly demonstrate Waterhouse's concern for GARDEN HISTORY.

Mary Amati, *E.G. Waterhouse of Eryldene* (Sydney, 1977); Zeny Edwards, *The Grecian Pagoda and the Architecture of Eryldene* (Sydney, 1995)   RICHARD CLOUGH

WATLING, Thomas (c. 1762–c. 1814), painter, was born in Dumfries, Scotland, and trained to be a professional landscape artist. Tempted to apply his skills to forgery, he was caught and transported to NSW in 1792. He was appointed to work for surgeon John WHITE, depicting the NATURAL HISTORY and landscape of the colony. The paintings were sent to England along with collections made by White, among the first to make their way into science from the colony. Some of the collections and the accompanying Watling paintings were used by James SOWERBY to prepare the paintings and engravings for James SMITH's *A Specimen of the Botany of New Holland* (1793–95). Watling received an absolute pardon in 1797 and left the colony for India and Scotland. He is Australia's only early convict artist known to have had his work used in the compilation of the published scientific botanical record.

Thomas Watling: Dumfries' Convict Artist (Dumfries, 1988)   HELEN HEWSON

WAT(T)ERS, John (c. 1820–1901), gardener, left a private gardening position in Lincoln, England, for Australia in 1852. In November that year he was employed in MELBOURNE BOTANIC GARDENS, and the following January accompanied Ferdinand MUELLER on a short expedition to the Dandenong Ranges (of which an account by 'John Walters' was published in the *Gardeners' Chronicle*). In 1856 he was engaged in collecting specimens for Mueller at Wilsons Promontory, and it is probable that Watters is synonymous with the 'Mr Waters' who represented the gardeners of the Melbourne Botanic Gardens before the Royal Commission into the Victorian Public Service (1872), pleading for permanent status in the public service. At the time of his retirement from the Gardens (1885), Watters was in charge of the fernery and greenhouse. His sons, Thomas (1859–1917) and John (b. 1859) were a gardener and seed merchant respectively.

Peter Watters (c. 1832–1915), gardener and seed merchant, brother of John, was employed as a gardener at COMO (1864) and by the Victorian governor (1870) prior to his co-purchase of Melbourne seed merchants Railton & Co. from D.B. RAILTON in 1876. There is evidence that the Railton family retained an interest in the firm until 1893, after which Peter and wife Christina became the sole proprietors. Their sons, Thomas (1869–1929) and Andrew Alexander Watters (1872–1936), succeeded to the business upon their father's death, and from 1920 traded under the name Watters & Sons. Their departure from the firm in 1929 ended any direct family connection, although the business continued until 1970.

DARREN WATSON

WATTLE DAY The Wattle Blossom League, a women's auxiliary of the Australian Natives Association, was formed in 1889–90 in Adelaide. The League aimed to encourage national sentiment as symbolised by the wattle (ACACIA spp.), a native flower, and by celebrating Wattle Day on 1 September. The movement was fostered by enthusiasts such as William J. Sowden and Tullie WOLLASTON (SA), A.J. CAMPBELL (Vic.), and J.H. MAIDEN (NSW). The first Wattle Day celebrations did not occur until 1910. In Adelaide and Sydney, trees were planted, seeds sown, and sprigs of wattle were worn. A gathering in Melbourne was rained out. By 1911 Wattle Day was celebrated in provincial towns such as Broken Hill (NSW) and Castlemaine (Vic.). In Broken Hill students heard addresses on patriotism and unity. In 1912 Wattle Day was first celebrated in Hobart: wattle was tied to the mastheads of vessels in the harbour.

In the years following 1910, sales of wattle trees and seeds to private and public gardeners increased greatly. Nursery proprietors also reported a much wider variety of trees available. Wattle gathered by country children was freighted free of charge by rail to depots for distribution in city streets by women wearing wattle-trimmed hats. Concerns were raised that demand was damaging trees in rural districts. After the First World War, Wattle Day's focus changed from national sentiment to charities, as sprigs and badges and ribbons featuring wattle were sold. In 1925 Wattle Day sales were consolidated to a charity benefiting children. Since 1978 celebrations have been run by the Wattle Day Child Care Society.

Although popular, Wattle Day did not succeed as a truly national day. It could not be celebrated on a single day; wattles are not at their best in each state at the one time. Anzac Day may have provided a focus for national sentiment.

Maria Hitchcock, *Wattle* (Canberra, 1991)   AMANDA BEDE

A.J. Campbell's *Golden Wattle* (1921), published to capitalise on the fervour surrounding WATTLE DAY, transcended the mere collection of wattle sprays from the bush by recommending the growing of ACACIAS (such as *Acacia maidenii*) in the home garden

WATTLE PARK, Burwood, Vic., was opened by the Hawthorn Tramways Trust in 1917. Located at the outer suburban terminus of the Trust's electric tramway from Melbourne, the fifty-five-hectare reserve was modelled on contemporary NORTH AMERICAN 'trolley parks', which promoted tram travel and provided public LEISURE and RECREATION facilities. After taking over the Trust's operations in 1920 the Melbourne and Metropolitan Tramways Board planted thousands of wattles and other trees, and developed and promoted the park. New features included a large reception venue called The Chalet (1928), an ornamental lake, and SPORTING facilities. Ornamental fencing was fashioned from old cable tramway cables, and redundant cable tramcars became quaint PICNIC shelters. Special tree plantings have been a regular feature since the park's inception, including a LONE PINE (1933) to honour members of the 24th Battalion First AIF. A nine-hole GOLF COURSE was opened in 1937. ROBERT GREEN

WATTS, Peter Roy (b. 1949), architect, landscape architect, and museum director, was born and educated in Vic. Research commenced while a student led to his widely praised book *The Gardens of Edna Walling* (1981). Working for the NATIONAL TRUST OF AUSTRALIA (Victoria) he was actively involved in landscape issues and the Trust's properties (1976–81). During 1978–79 he undertook a pioneering survey of Victoria's historic gardens: this was published as *Historic Gardens of Victoria: A Reconnaissance* (1983) and led to his proposal to found an AUSTRALIAN GARDEN HISTORY SOCIETY, of which he was inaugural secretary (1980–84) and founding editor of *Australian Garden History* (1989–90). Appointed the first Director of the Historic Houses Trust of New South Wales (1981), he assembled a talented staff and forged one of Australia's leading museum organisations, its dynamic management providing a lead for kindred bodies. Many culturally significant gardens are managed by the Trust—including ELIZABETH FARM, GOVERNMENT HOUSE, ROUSE HILL, and VAUCLUSE HOUSE—and conservation policies for each reflect his sharp intellect and meticulous eye for detail. Watts co-curated *An Exquisite Eye*, an exhibition of Ferdinand BAUER's drawings of Australian plants (1997). RA

WAVERLEY CEMETERY, NSW, sited on the Pacific coast of Sydney's eastern suburbs and possessing a backdrop of rugged sandstone cliffs and pounding ocean, enjoys one of the most spectacular settings of any Australia CEMETERY. In 1868, after a public campaign, the New South Wales Government provided £1200 for its establishment. The first burial took place in 1877 and by 1885 the cemetery was fenced and laid out with drainage trenches, roadways, and tree plantings. The first Mayor of Randwick and sometime secretary of ROOKWOOD CEMETERY, Simeon Henry Pearce (1821–1886), of Blenheim House, Randwick, has been credited with the plan. The harsh coastal environment proved unsuitable for many of the introduced plant species, but remnant early twentieth-century plantings survive. Lines of *Araucaria hetrophylla* (Norfolk Island Pine) follow the northern and southern boundaries and extensive use has been made of sandstone quarried on the site. ROBERT NICOL

WAY, Edward (c. 1825–1881), gardener, was born in Devonshire, England, and trained during the 1840s in the well-known London nursery of A. Henderson & Co. He arrived in Sydney c. 1851, where he was head gardener to Thomas Ware Smart (1810–1881) at Mona, Darling Point. In 1854 he arrived in Moreton Bay and commenced his South Brisbane Nursery, initially obtaining stock from SHEPHERD's Darling Nursery in Sydney. He imported seeds from his former employer Henderson and also from Garaway, Mayes & Co. (Bristol). Way advertised his services 'for drawing Plans, laying out Grounds, and superintending Orchards, Shrubberies, and Plantations, after the most modern and improved systems, as adopted in the first grounds in England'. He was an active member of the short-lived Moreton Bay Horticultural Society, gaining prizes for dahlias in 1856. Way was the first curator (c. 1874–81) of TOOWOOMBA BOTANIC GARDENS, implementing its early development and planting, and using it as an EXPERIMENTAL GARDEN. RA

WEATHERLY, Lilia Margaret (b. 1927), Hobart-based rose breeder, has introduced several roses that have achieved international distribution, including 'Pink Iceberg' (1995), 'Brilliant

Pink Iceberg' (1999), and 'Light Touch' (1997). She hybridises across a wide range of rose groups and has developed several outstanding hybrids of 'Macrantha', including a fine double named 'Margaret Bushby' (1999). She was Heritage Roses—Australia Co-ordinator for Tasmania (1991–97).

TREVOR NOTTLE

WEBLEY, Daniel (1829–1891), horticulturist, nursery proprietor, and landscape gardener, was born in England, and after reputedly training at KEW GARDENS and being associated with the Clapton (possibly Clapham) Nurseries in London, he arrived in Vic. in the 1850s. He laid out the garden at Thomas Chirnside's homestead, Point Cooke, which still bears evidence of his enthusiasm for local SHELLS. Webley is reputed to have worked on the Yan Yean Reservoir gardens and he probably laid out the HOMESTEAD GARDEN (c. 1865) at WERRIBEE PARK; he was certainly living and working on this Chirnside property when the main garden was under way in 1877 as his son Harry died there from the effects of corrosive sublimate after falling into the sheep wash. The RUSTIC stone fountain pool, the rockwork GROTTO covered with succulents and lined internally with shells applied in geometric patterns, and the use of heaths and camellias reveal his hand.

The Werribee tragedy probably led the Webleys to move to Malvern in 1878; in the following year the ratebooks listed Webley as a landscape gardener, owning a house and small nursery. He propagated camellias; pioneered the introduction of CACTI and other succulents into Vic.; and hybridised many well-known ericas—including the white, pink-spotted 'Webleyana', 'Hentyana', and 'Mackinnoniana' (named for Toorak clients), and 'Charsleyana' (commemorating Fanny CHARSLEY). Following his death the nursery was carried on by his wife, Sarah Webley (d. 1920), with the help of the Williams brothers—Webley is said to have adopted James and Jack Williams, possibly sons of James WILLIAMS—until 1904, when it was rented and later sold to the Williams.

JESSIE SERLE

WEEDS are the bane of every gardener's existence whatever our horticultural predilections—they overtake or destroy desirable plants, compete for moisture, light, and nutrients, and make gardens unsightly. They may cause health problems (such as hay fever) or are prickly or otherwise irritating. Approximately 2500 weed species are known from Australia and the most weedy areas, in terms of numbers of species, are those with the longest, most intense history of European settlement—south-eastern and south-western Australia. Some were introduced at an early date while others regularly appear as 'new', never having been recorded before.

It is convenient—because it aids in understanding their origins and impacts—to recognise three types of weeds, though categories are by no means mutually exclusive; **weeds of gardens** and disturbed areas, **noxious weeds** affecting agriculture and horticulture, and **environmental weeds**. Here we focus on environmental weeds because of their conservation significance and the role of HORTICULTURE in their introduction and spread. Environmental weeds are exotic species that invade natural vegetation, jeopardising flora and fauna, as well as ecosystem processes such as nutrient cycling and fire regimes, over varying time scales. In ways that will be immediately comprehensible to gardeners—the processes are essentially identical—invading environmental weeds out-compete indigenous plants for crucial resources, killing them and preventing their regeneration or recruitment. In the worst instances exotic plant invaders completely eliminate indigenous vegetation and its dependant fauna.

Environmental weed invasion is a global phenomenon. Though scarcely recognised as such, it is the most serious of conservation problems, notwithstanding well-publicised crises such as forest destruction, climate change, and pollution. It is best documented in Australia, South Africa, New Zealand, and the USA. Millions of hectares of Australia have been invaded by environmental weeds and especially in the TROPICAL north, many weed species are also agricultural weeds; most parts of the country are invaded and probably none are immune to invasion—mangrove communities, saltmarshes, forests, woodlands, grasslands, rangelands, tropical savannahs, rainforests, alpine herbfields, and wetlands.

Environmental weeds come from all parts of the world and embrace the full life-form spectrum, for example trees, shrubs, vines, aquatic plants, annuals and perennials, bulbous and cormous perennials, and succulents. AUSTRALIAN PLANTS are far from blameless and some of the worst weeds are indigenous elsewhere in the country. Many (*Hakea* and *Acacia* for instance) are catastrophically invasive in South Africa where, for example, the fynbos vegetation with its superb endemic *Protea*-rich flora is threatened. Conversely, Australia has a subset of the South African flora that is devastatingly invasive. Weeds are relentlessly opportunistic travellers, readily accompanying products and goods as contaminants. However, of the several thousand weed species in Australia, at least seventy per cent (eighty-three per cent in the USA) were deliberately introduced. Rarely, weeds were introduced before European invasion, such as *Tamarindus indicus* (Tamarind) introduced to the NT by Macassan mariners.

The number of environmental weed species in Australia, more than 1250 species, is large; in Vic. alone 586 kinds were listed in 1992. Horticulture has a central role in enabling or facilitating weed invasion: most environmental weeds come directly from ornamental horticulture. At least forty-three per cent of Victorian environmental weed species are available in the NURSERY trade. Legions more potential weeds can be introduced without legal restriction. Inevitably some newly introduced or long-present species will jump the garden fence and become invasive. Notable garden-escapee environmental weeds in Australia include *Acacia nilotica* (Prickly Acacia), *Asparagus asparagoides* (Bridal Creeper), *Chrysanthemoides monilifera* (Boneseed or Bitou Bush), *Cortaderia* spp. (Pampas Grass), *Cryptostegia grandiflora* (Rubber Vine), *Cytisus scoparius* (English Broom), *Eichhornia crassipes* (Water Hyacinth), *Hedera helix* (Ivy), *Lantana camara* (Lantana), *Macfadyena unguis-cati* (Cat's-claw Vine), *Mimosa pigra* (Giant Sensitive Plant), *Opuntia* spp. (Prickly Pear), *Salix* spp. (Willow), and *Watsonia* spp. (Watsonia).

Although seemingly out of control, this situation is slowly changing. Horticultural industries have until recently been mostly very reluctant to accept responsibility, but the evidence is as incontrovertible as it is damning, facts now well recognised by the Australian Quarantine Inspection Service, the government agency controlling plant introductions. Clearly a radical change is necessary. It must also be remembered that only a small fraction of horticultural species are weedy or potentially so. As horticulturists of any persuasion, we have a compelling environmental responsibility not to import, cultivate, or promote known or potential weeds. Indeed we have a strong vested interest because horticulture depends on the botanical riches available in breeding programs. We now know that globally, one in every eight plant species faces extinction; the overwhelming threat to this bio-diversity in many part of the world is environmental weed invasion.

G.W. Carr, J.V. Yugovic, K.E. Robinson, *Environmental Weed Invasions in Victoria: Conservation and Management Implications* (Melbourne, 1992); Q.C.B. Cronk and J.L. Fuller, *Plant Invaders: The Threat to Natural Systems* (London, 1995); N.M. Smith, *Weeds of Natural Ecosystems: A Field Guide to Environmental Weeds of the Northern Territory, Australia* (Darwin, 1995); Tim Low, *Feral Future: The Untold Story of Australia's Exotic Invaders* (Ringwood, Vic., 1999)   GEOFF CARR

WEEKLY TIMES (1869–) was established by the proprietors of Melbourne's *Daily Telegraph* (1869–92) under the general banner 'The Liberal Deviseth Liberal Things'. Regular columns such as 'Farm and Homestead' appealed strongly to the land selector and small holder, and the horticultural column became a feature of the newspaper, though perhaps not so prominent or influential as its competition in the AUSTRALASIAN and the LEADER. Gardening is still covered, although the proliferation of illustrated garden magazines has taken over much of this role.   RA

WELLINGTON DAM, Collie, WA, was the first site to be landscaped by John OLDHAM in his pioneering position as LANDSCAPE ARCHITECT to the Western Australian Public Works Department. In 1959 a picnic area, with lawns and shade trees, was created in the quarry (from which the material for the dam wall was taken), with a zigzag road to the valley below the dam. This use of natural local materials was further developed by Oldham in the landscaped areas of the **Serpentine Dam**, Jarrahdale, which were designed to harmonise with the native bushland. Completed in 1961, stands of mature native jarrah and marri trees were retained, with granite from the site used for hard landscaping features. Panoramic views of the dam have been exploited, with lawns, picnic places, and a parterre (1961) reflecting the Aboriginal legend of the mythical snake, Mundan.

CAROL MANSFIELD

WELLINGTON NURSERY, Perth: see BARRATT, Enoch

WENTWORTH, Charles (*c.* 1849–1909), pansy and carnation specialist, and nursery proprietor, was born at Finchley, Middlesex, England, and sailed with his parents to Vic. in 1849. His father, Emmet Charles Wentworth (1809–1881), established an orchard in Canterbury Road, Boroondara (now Canterbury) on land astutely purchased in 1859. Charles Wentworth had established a nursery in this locality by the early 1880s and carried on business as a florist, specialising in greenhouse plants and the pansy. He enjoyed vice-regal patronage; Lady Loch admired thousands of pansies on one visit in the mid-1880s. Wentworth concentrated his attention on CARNATIONS from the late 1880s and hybridised many varieties popular both in the garden and on the show bench, mostly perpetual flowering carnations, so suited to Australian conditions. His fame was such that in 1886, without a hint of irony, the *Australasian* described him as 'facile-princeps among professional pansy-growers'. Wentworth's Shenley Nursery was situated close to the Outer Circle Railway, a notorious product of Melbourne's land boom, which opened as Melbourne's suburban development was confidently moving eastward in the years immediately prior to the bank crashes of the 1890s. Wentworth speculated in land with his Hawthorn Park Estate, and the well-located Shenley railway station was named after his nursery. Wentworth Avenue, Canterbury, now marks the site of his nursery.   RA

WERRIBEE PARK, Vic. Thomas Chirnside (1815–1887), a lowland Scot, had been 'taming' the Werribee plains for more than thirty years before building Victoria's finest country house in the 1870s with his brother Andrew (1818–1890). The ITALIANATE mansion set in twenty-five acres (10 ha) of rectangular pleasure garden was bounded by plantations, which were substantially in place by 1861. The design for this oasis of greenery, set jewel-like on a treeless plain, was almost certainly by William GUILFOYLE. The long, tree-lined carriage drive, floral PARTERRE, croquet lawn, rustic fountain and pond, bush-house and glasshouses, expansive lawns, contrived vistas, sinuous paths, and lake with island GROTTO encompassed the full panoply appropriate to the owners with a 93 000 acre (37 600 ha) freehold. In 1877 the head gardener, Daniel WEBLEY, who had probably designed the HA-HA walled garden of the earlier homestead (1865), oversaw work as thousands of loads of black soil were carted from the nearby Chirnside homestead, Point Cooke, which also provided SHELLS to line the domed, candle-lit interior of the grotto. An abundant water supply pumped from the Werribee River and the Chirnsides' keen interest in ACCLIMATISATION resulted in a collection 'of ornamental plants … as full and varied as that of any botanic garden'. The garden—now managed by Parks Victoria—retains enough original form and content to make it among the most significant publicly accessible privately built gardens in Vic. It has survived Edwardianisation, neglect, partial rescue by the Catholic Church, and some loss of integrity due to intrusive adjacent developments.   JESSIE SERLE

WEST AUSTRALIAN GARDENER (1932–58, 1969–98), a monthly magazine published in Perth, was the official organ of the Western Australian Horticultural Council (whose affiliated societies numbered twenty-one in 1934 and seventy-five in 1998). The *West Australian Gardener*, 'devoted entirely to horticulture', aimed to remedy the lack of topical local information on horticultural advances. In its first two decades, the focus was on seasonal horticultural advice and techniques, new plant introductions to WA, and garden COMPETITIONS and HORTICULTURAL SHOW results. Articles were contributed by members of the affiliated societies, many of them professionals in the horticultural industry. However, during the early 1950s content was increasingly borrowed from interstate publications. The journal ceased in 1958 due to lack of advertising revenue and new subscribers. The Council resumed (quarterly) publication in 1969, revitalising the magazine and boasting 'purely Western Australian in content' as it again tapped into the local market.

CAROLYN MIDDLEMIS

WESTERN AUSTRALIA The coast of WA had been known to Europeans for two centuries before the first British settlers arrived at Swan River in 1829. Dutch, British, and French mariners and scientists had explored and charted the area and important collections of the AUSTRALIAN FLORA had been made. Colonists encountered a PARK-like landscape shaped by thousands of years of ABORIGINAL ENVIRONMENTAL MANAGEMENT. They were soon to discover the ancient soils were largely infertile and the equable MEDITERRANEAN climate, so conducive to a casual, open-air lifestyle, made gardening more difficult, and consequently, less ambitious, than on the east coast where more favourable conditions for horticulture prevailed.

The port at Fremantle, the capital at Perth, and the inland market town at Guildford, were established in the first year of settlement. Modest cottages and gardens were developed overlooking the scenic waters of the Swan River at Perth and on the alluvial soils at Guildford where every cottage was 'ornamented with a garden'. Diaries, such as that of G.F. Moore (1884), recorded the earliest experiments with horticulture, and authors, such as Mrs Millett (1872), provided contemporary impressions of Perth, with its riverside gardens sloping to the water's edge, resplendent with 'luxuriant creepers', bamboos, figs, oranges, oleanders, and geraniums.

Food production remained a primary consideration during the early settlement phase, but ornamental gardening was not overlooked, and seeds and cuttings of favourite plants were included in the goods brought to the colony by the pioneering settlers. DAHLIAS and CHRYSANTHEMUMS arrived with the official party in 1829, part of nine boxes of plant stock donated by the (ROYAL) HORTICULTURAL SOCIETY in London. Delight in the richness and beauty of the Australian flora, particularly the spectacular Western Australian wildflowers, went hand-in-hand with the desire to grow the familiar plants of the Old World. Settlers retained the local EUCALYPTS, BANKSIAS, zamias, and grass trees in their gardens, collected seed, and transplanted wildflowers from the BUSH. Seeds and specimens of the Australian flora were exchanged with enthusiasts in England and the Continent, where they were successfully cultivated. In England in the late 1880s, Western Australian ORCHIDS were said to be the fashionable plants of the day.

A wide range of temperate and semi-tropical plants—imported from the northern hemisphere, South AFRICA, Mauritius, Malta, and INDIA—was tested in the local conditions (although the success of some caused them to become environmental WEEDS). Those best suited to the MEDITERRANEAN climate were favoured, leading one observer to describe Perth as 'the land of the olive and the vine'. Indeed the 'mania' in the 1840s for growing grapes, on trellises and covered walks, persisted as a feature of SUBURBAN GARDENS well into the twentieth century. Where WATER was scarce, whether in the towns, suburbs, or on farms, VERANDAH GARDENS with plants in pots or kerosene tins, and creepers trained on posts and wires, satisfied a fundamental need to enhance the home environment. The phenomenon of the 'winter garden' was another manifestation of the local conditions, where plants came to life after being dormant through the dry months of summer.

The East Perth Cemeteries (1830), with symbolic plantings of cypresses and pines; GOVERNMENT HOUSE Domain (1834); STIRLING GARDENS (1845), originally called the Government Gardens; and the Benedictine Mission (1846) at New Norcia are important historic landscapes that survive from this early colonial period.

WA continued to be a focus of botanical exploration and discovery throughout the nineteenth century, with major collections being made by colonial botanists, amateurs and professionals, such as DRUMMOND, MOLLOY, MUELLER, ROE, and visiting Europeans HÜGEL and PREISS.

The granting of self-government in 1890, and the opening up of the rich inland goldfields in the 1890s, heralded a period of optimism, confidence, and rapid expansion. The

The *WEST AUSTRALIAN GARDENER* (1946) filled a gap among GARDENING MAGAZINES by providing information specific to conditions found in the West—a point made clear on the cover of the earliest issues, which carried the words 'Received by hundreds as filling a definite need'

Western Australia

Edward Keane's residence in the Perth suburb of Keane's Point (c.1898), demonstrates the use of VERANDAH GARDENS, an important early phase of gardening in WESTERN AUSTRALIA.

long-awaited rise in Western Australia's fortunes coincided with economic hardship elsewhere in Australia. The resulting massive migration of people to the West—with most coming from the eastern colonies, among them architects and horticulturists—boosted the population and local expertise. New government agencies came into existence, including the Bureau of Agriculture (1894) and Woods and Forests Department (1896), and an ambitious program of public works was undertaken. The desire for a new civic image, influenced in part by British and North American GARDEN CITY and CITY BEAUTIFUL ideas, inspired the creation of amenities such as KINGS PARK (1895), the ZOOLOGICAL GARDENS (1898), and a number of smaller municipal PUBLIC PARKS AND GARDENS in the city, suburbs, country towns, and on the goldfields. The old colonial cemeteries at East Perth, an anachronism in the progressive climate of the time, were closed and a new metropolitan CEMETERY was established at KARRAKATTA (1899).

STREET TREE planting, begun in a small way in Perth in the late 1850s, was pursued in earnest at the end of the century with 3000 trees of various kinds, including EUCALYPTS, planted throughout the city. At Cottesloe, the first *Araucaria heterophylla* (Norfolk Island Pine) were planted in 1905, setting in train a tradition that gave this seaside suburb its distinctive visual identity.

The small-scale local NURSERY industry, which had been operating since the 1860s, came into its own with the establishment of new enterprises in the 1890s and early 1900s, such as Roselea Nursery, C.F. NEWMAN and Son, WILSON AND JOHNS, and DAWSON and Harrison, all of which remained household names well into the post–Second World War era. The government nursery at HAMEL (1897), with a policy of free distribution of trees to municipal authorities, schools, institutions, and the farming community, was instrumental in encouraging the widespread planting of trees, particularly in the agricultural and dry, inland, mining areas. ARBOR DAY planting was inaugurated at this time by government conservator, John Ednie BROWN, to be later enshrined in the *Forests Act* (1919).

The expansion of the reticulated water supply in the metropolitan area around the turn of the century, and generous use of ground-water on larger sites, meant gardens were easier to establish and maintain. Buffalo grass became an alternative to couch for the prized LAWN surrounding the house. Residential properties in the more affluent riverside suburbs, such as Killowen (now St Anne's Hospital), Mount Lawley; Knutsford (now Christ Church Grammar School), Claremont; The Bungalow, Keane's Point (now Royal Freshwater Bay Yacht Club); and The Cliffe at Peppermint Grove, had extensive grounds often embellished with GATE LODGES, BUSH-HOUSES, FERNERIES, SHRUBBERIES, and the ubiquitous TENNIS COURT, and in many cases were cared for by live-in gardeners.

New industries associated with this period of expansion were the Cyclone Fence Company (1902) with popular and affordable metal gates and FENCES, which became the hallmark of early twentieth-century suburban gardens, and the pottery works of C.R. Courtland at Rivervale, manufacturers of earthenware garden products (1904–96).

The inter-war period saw the relocation of the University of Western Australia from Perth to Crawley, and the first major development of the campus, with important plantings such as the Great Court rainforest and Somerville Auditorium cathedral of trees. WAR MEMORIALS, invariably a simple stone obelisk, were erected in suburbs and towns across the state, and honour AVENUES—a new form of memorial—were planted not only in Kings Park, but in the suburbs and country towns, such as Albany and Collie. ROSE growing, which had always been popular if problematical, was boosted with the formation of the NATIONAL ROSE SOCIETY of Western Australia (1932) and by the widespread adoption of *Rosa* X *fortuniana* rootstock. Rose gardens became a feature of public parks; those at Stirling Square, Guildford, attracted crowds of sightseers from across the metropolitan area to view the spectacle of the roses in full bloom. ARALUEN (1930s), the Young Australia League's holiday RESORT in the hills south of Perth, was another popular destination where day-trippers could enjoy the spring displays of tulips and flowering shrubs in a picturesque bushland setting.

Until the 1930s the main source of horticultural advice for the home gardener had been through local newspapers and the weekly *WESTERN MAIL*, with few other publications available dealing specifically with Western Australian conditions. The *WEST AUSTRALIAN GARDENER*, published by the Horticultural Council of Western Australia, was launched in 1932 and became the first successful GARDENING MAGAZINE to fill this void.

Street tree planting in the suburbs was given new energy with the introduction of the state's first TOWN PLANNING legislation (1928) and the formation of the Tree Planters' Association (1936). *Lophostemon confertus* (Brush Box) was planted extensively throughout the metropolitan area—and in the city along St Georges Terrace—giving Perth's suburban landscapes a monotonous uniformity, not redressed until the post–Second World War period when jacaranda plantings became popular.

The period of post-war expansion and major resource development from the 1950s onwards coincided with a revitalised environmental consciousness; the emergence of the profession of LANDSCAPE ARCHITECTURE; and the introduction of formalised horticultural training and apprenticeships. John OLDHAM was appointed government landscape architect and landscape design became an integral part of major public works, including the Ord River project in the Kimberley and major dams in the South-West. New mining towns were established in the Pilbara with public and residential gardens designed to attract workers and their families to these remote ARID-ZONE locations The development of the Botanic Garden at Kings Park (1963–65) dedicated to the flora of WA, and the establishment of specialist native plant nurseries, contributed to a burgeoning enthusiasm for BUSH GARDENS. In the 1990s, as water conservation has become increasingly important, the ethos of water-wise or XERIC GARDENING provides a new horticultural direction.

Oline Richards, *Theoretical Framework for Designed Landscapes in Western Australia* (Como, WA, 1997) **OLINE RICHARDS**

WESTERN DISTRICT, Vic., one of the largest volcanic plains in the world, extending west of Port Phillip Bay to the South Australian border, was a key area of Australian pastoral expansion and provided the wealth to underwrite extensive HOMESTEAD, garden, and estate development. Its 'Men of Yesterday'—as described by historian Margaret Kiddle—were mainly Scottish lowland farmers who established squattocracies that grew substantially on the profits of the 'golden fleece', leaving lasting DESIGNED and CULTURAL LANDSCAPES.

Geelong was the departure point for the pastoral expansion westwards on the lightly timbered grass plains, although the HENTY brothers had crossed from Van Diemen's Land in 1834 and established the first settlement in the District at Portland. In the 1830s–40s licensed pastoral runs were taken up but dwellings were makeshift, outbuildings rudimentary, and gardens utilitarian until tenure of crown leases was proclaimed in 1847. Funds were then invested in modest dwellings and infrastructure such as fencing rather than embellishments.

With the escalation of wool prices in the 1860s and 1870s and greater fleece quality, pastoral fortunes peaked and homestead building flourished. Many of these structures adhered to Gothic-revival architectural styles, with gardens influenced by English and Scottish PICTURESQUE planning principles, resulting in PARKS, HA-HA walls, dry-stone WALLING, gates and GATE LODGES, and AVENUE-lined drives. Representative examples included ERCILDOUNE, Glenormiston, MENINGOORT, MOUNT NOORAT, Narrapumelap, TALINDERT, and TITANGA. Variants were the park-like landscape at MURNDAL, the timber village of Warrock, the garden designs of Edward La Trobe BATEMAN at Wooriwyrite and CHATSWORTH House, and the small GARDENESQUE expressions at residences such as BURSWOOD. Essentially the planting was to shelter the residence, and to provide a kitchen and flower garden. Many landowners commissioned landscape artists Eugene von GUÉRARD, Thomas Clark (*c.* 1814–1883), and Abram-Louis Buvelot (1814–1888) to record their estates or features in the landscape.

In regional towns BOTANIC GARDENS benefited from the activities of Ferdinand MUELLER, who distributed plants for ACCLIMATISATION, and from the 1870s William GUILFOYLE contributed to the design of gardens at Camperdown, COLAC, HAMILTON, KOROIT, and WARRNAMBOOL. PORTLAND also established a botanic garden.

Increases in fleece prices in the mid-1880s ensured additional homestead, woolshed, and garden developments, mainly in classically derived architectural styles and pleasure grounds in the Gardenesque mode, although not at the scale of the earlier decade. CONSERVATORIES and rusticated timber structures were occasionally added as features, as at TRAWALLA, Marida Yallock, and BARUNAH PLAINS. Late in his career Guilfoyle was sought to design private gardens, including BANONGIL, DALVUI, MAWALLOK, MOOLERIC, and TURKEITH. Tree plantings included WINDBREAKS of *Eucalyptus cladocalyx* (Sugar Gum) by Alexander Buchanan and later J.L. Currie around Lismore and Titanga. The extensive use of sugar gums, *Pinus radiata* (Monterey Pine), and cypresses, mostly *Cupressus macrocarpa* (Monterey Cypress), is now a distinctive feature of the Western District. Closer settlement schemes following both world wars were widespread and significant for their increased windbreak planting and the introduction of improved pastures.

The first decades of the twentieth century saw a reaction against the high Victorian garden and many gardens (and residences) were altered in keeping with the latest trends, drawing on ARTS AND CRAFTS principles or bolder American modes. Purrumbete and Ercildoune typified the former, as did gardens by Edna WALLING at ARDGARTEN, BOORTKOI, and Willaroo, while Mooramong drew on elements of each.

In more recent times the Western District has witnessed a deterioration of its pastures and mature trees, and the ravages of salinity and erosion. Numerous attempts at LANDCARE and whole farm management, such as by the FENTON family, are displaying a renewed understanding of the fragility of this landscape. Many owners are also looking at their fine historic gardens and houses to supplement farm revenue, through tourist and other commercial opportunities. Maintenance and rejuvenation of ageing gardens also engages a wide spectrum of expertise, from owners and gardeners to consultants and volunteers.

Margaret Kiddle, *Men of Yesterday* (Parkville, Vic., 1961); David Conley and Claire Dennis, *The Western Plains: A Natural and Social History* (Parkville, Vic., 1984); George Jones, *Growing Together: A Gardening History of Geelong, extending to Colac and Camperdown* (Belmont, Vic., 1984)   DAVID JONES

WESTERN MAIL (1885–1955), a weekly illustrated news magazine aimed at rural readers but also with a metropolitan circulation, included a regular horticultural column, monthly calendar, and articles on gardening. It was published in Perth by Charles Harper (1842–1912), politician, agriculturist, and nursery proprietor, and John Winthrop HACKETT, joint proprietors of the *West Australian*. In 1905 Harper engaged **(William) Catton Grasby** (1859–1930), educator and former principal of ROSEWORTHY AGRICULTURAL COLLEGE, SA (1894–96), as its agricultural editor, a position he occupied with authority for almost twenty-five years.

OLINE RICHARDS

WESTON, (Thomas) Charles George (1866–1935), horticulturist, arboriculturist, and landscape gardener, was born at Poyle, England. He left school aged 13, working initially at two gardens near London. His next appointment (*c*. 1889–96) was in Dumfriesshire, Scotland, at the vast estate and gardens of Drumlanrig Castle, the seat of the Duke of Buccleuch. Under head gardener David THOMSON, one of Britain's most respected horticulturists, the foundations of Weston's extensive horticultural knowledge and skills were laid. Carrying a glowing letter of recommendation from Thomson, Weston migrated to Australia in 1896.

For the next seventeen years he worked at horticultural posts in the Sydney area. In 1898 he joined the staff of SYDNEY BOTANIC GARDENS, reporting directly to its director, Joseph MAIDEN. His initial appointments were head gardener at ADMIRALTY HOUSE (1898–1908) and GOVERNMENT HOUSE (1908–12). Under four British admirals and two governors-general he maintained and improved the grounds at each, and provided indoor floral displays.

While in Sydney Weston expanded his knowledge of horticulture and related fields through extensive reading and experimentation. He was an exhibitor at HORTICULTURAL SHOWS and was keenly interested in PLANT BREEDING, becoming well known for his creation of five hybrid *Watsonias*. He was in demand as an adviser to the Commonwealth and during 1911–12 he visited, on five occasions, the recently created Federal (later AUSTRALIAN) CAPITAL TERRITORY to provide advice and establish an experimental nursery. Impressed with his breadth of knowledge and skills Maiden promoted him in 1912 to Superintendent, STATE (FOREST) NURSERY, Campbelltown. However, in 1913 he accepted appointment as Officer-in-Charge, Afforestation (later Parks and Gardens) Branch at the remote, bare, windy, rabbit-infested, and degraded federal capital site.

The emphasis of Weston's work between 1913 and 1920 was on reversing land degradation, and ameliorating the windiness of the federal capital site through planting, regeneration, and fencing. In this period he also laid out the grounds of (Old) Canberra House, the administrator's official residence. His work was conducted in an environment of severe financial restraint, differences of opinion with landscape architect, Walter Burley GRIFFIN, and political uncertainty. In 1914 he founded the forty-hectare Yarralumla Nursery for plant production and the 120-hectare Westbourne Woods ARBORETUM for testing the performance of different exotic and indigenous tree species. By 1920 some 45 000 trees had been planted in the latter while the nursery had supplied 780 000 trees and shrubs to afforestation projects, largely on hills surrounding the city site. His successful *Pinus radiata* (Monterey Pine) plantings on Mount Stromlo proved to be the beginning of today's large pine plantation estate in the ACT.

From 1921 to 1926, the emphasis of Weston's work moved towards city landscaping as part of the establishment of the federal parliament in Canberra, which was being developed as a GARDEN CITY. In the absence of Griffin (who had resigned), Weston controlled this work. He grouped exotic and indigenous tree and shrub species into formal and informal arrangements to create massed colourful seasonal effects. His surviving plantings include the grounds of (Old) Parliament House, Canberra and Kurrajong Hotels, Telopea Park School, and Prime Minister's LODGE; Commonwealth, Kings, Ainslie, and Sydney Avenues; City Hill and Haig, Telopea, and Collins Parks; STREET TREES and small PARKS in Braddon, Kingston, Forrest, and Yarralumla; and Westbourne Woods (now Royal Canberra Golf Course). The grounds of Yarralumla (now GOVERNMENT) HOUSE were upgraded. In the period 1921–25, nearly 1 200 000 trees and shrubs were planted in the ACT, mostly in city areas.

Disciplined experimentation with indigenous and exotic species to test their suitability to Canberra conditions was an important feature of Weston's work. He consulted closely with Maiden, who maintained a continuing interest in this work. In 1919 Maiden made public Weston's achievement as the first in Australia to produce hybrid eucalypts 'by the direct action of the plant breeder'. In the 1920s Maiden pro-

Charles WESTON, armed with a roll of plans while surveying newly planted trees at CANBERRA (c.1925), was a major contributor to the landscaping of the federal capital as a GARDEN CITY

posed to the Royal Society of New South Wales the names *Acacia westoni* (now *A. pycnantha*) and *Eucalyptus* X *westoni* for new species Weston had discovered.

When Charles Weston died in Sydney, he was recognised and honoured principally for his success at the federal capital site. A street and park in Yarralumla are named after him. His remarkable achievements at such a large scale, unequalled in Australia to that time, mark a significant point in Australian garden history. His pioneering work continues to have a major influence on the continuing evolution of Australia's best-known garden city.   JOHN GRAY

WEST TERRACE CEMETERY (originally Adelaide Public Cemetery), sited in the south-west ADELAIDE PARK LANDS in William LIGHT's 1837 plan, was shown by him as a thirty-two-acre (13 ha) oval with serpentine walks. A member of Light's survey team was Robert Thomas, who later designed Newport Cemetery, Wales. Other influences came from surveyors G.S. KINGSTON, Edward Charles Frome (1802–1890), and Arthur Henry Freeling (1820–1885). It was Freeling who in 1854 imposed a simple grid pattern to bring some order to a chaotic and poorly managed site. Problems included inadequate fencing, inadequate surveying and record keeping, and poor drainage, exacerbated by divided management when discrete Anglican, Jewish, and Quaker divisions were established (1843–55). In 1845 an adjacent but separate Catholic Cemetery with its own entrance was established.

Early planting schemes had little impact due to theft and lack of water. From 1861 orderly management and development was gradually introduced, particularly once public health officials turned their attention to the site. They advocated grave mounding and extensive use of native trees rather than 'the gloomy and melancholy cypress and yew' previously favoured. An 1870s campaign to close the cemetery failed, but the site remained a subject of periodic public complaint. At the turn of the century new surveys and layouts were prepared by Josiah Paull (designer of PARAFIELD CEMETERY) and the cemetery was progressively extended over the next two decades to the west. Paull's designs introduced terraces and a series of concentric circles to the additions. In 1920 a war cemetery was added.   ROBERT NICOL

WESTWOOD, Betty Rutherford (b. 1917), matron, native plant propagator, and conservationist, known as 'The Tree Lady' of SA. Inspired by the words of the original 'Man of Trees', Richard St Barbe Baker (1889–1982), she looked 'at the treeless wastes [of Strathalbyn] and knowing how this overcleared land had become so degraded, I thought I should do something on my own doorstep' and from 1955 onwards encouraged replanting. Westwood had earlier established the Anzac Garden (1937) in the STRATHALBYN SOLDIERS' MEMORIAL GARDEN.   DAVID JONES

WETTENHALL, (Henry) Norman Burgess (1915–2000), consultant paediatrician, ornithologist and advocate for history and the natural environment, was born in London and then lived on the family property in Toorak (Vic.). Both sides of his family were from the land and keen gardeners: opportunities for farm holidays led to concerns about destruction of the Australian landscape and the ENVIRONMENT. Wettenhall's interest in history was allied to an interest in the countryside, derived from an appreciation of the work of the English NATIONAL TRUST. Just as one needed to know about history to understand human modification of the environment, he argued, so an appreciation of GEOLOGY, BOTANY, and ornithology—this last a great passion—could provide clues to longer term changes to biodiversity. An instigator or foundation member of the Australian Conservation Foundation, Victoria Conservation Trust, and Landscape Preservation Committee (of the Victorian National Trust), his work as a benefactor continues to lay foundations for ongoing investigation and monitoring of the environment.   RA

WHIBLEY, David Francis (1878–1961), gardener and nursery proprietor, was a son of David Whibley (1847–1891), who headed a remarkable family of gardeners and was for twenty-two years head gardener at Shurdington (now Boode House) in the ADELAIDE HILLS. D.F. Whibley served as a gardener at ST VIGEANS, grafting and naming many of its significant RHODODENDRON cultivars, while establishing his own nursery and sending cultivars to MOUNT MACEDON gardens. He worked at FOREST LODGE, and also for Stirling District Council, laying out many of their gardens, including planting in the main street of Stirling, using stock from his nursery. He was engaged by industrialist Essington Lewis in 1945 to propagate *Carya ovata* (Hickory) for Broken Hill Proprietary's forestry operations. D.F. Whibley's son, Godfrey

Leslie (1906–1965), worked at BEECHWOOD for nine years. His grandson, David John Edward Whibley (b. 1936), author of *Acacias of South Australia* (1980) and honoured by *Acacia whibleyana* (Whibley Wattle), worked for the BOTANIC GARDENS OF ADELAIDE for thirty-five years.

David Whibley's other sons included Arthur George (1864–1946), head gardener at Cheltenham Racecourse; Henry Leonard (1869–1963), head gardener at Bythorne in the Adelaide Hills; Herbert James (1869–1938), gardener for the City of Adelaide and at Craig-Ard (now Drapers Hall) in the Adelaide Hills; and Frederick Henry (b. 1870), noted for his floral arrangements. DAVID JONES

WHITCOMBE'S AUSTRALIAN GARDENING HANDBOOKS, a series of popular and inexpensive handbooks aimed at the amateur gardener, published by Whitcombe & Tombs Limited, Melbourne, was the first substantial GARDEN BOOK series published in Australia. Titles included *Gardening in Australia* (1926), *Bulb Growing in Australia* (1926), and *Rose Growing in Australia* (1928), all written by E.E. PESCOTT; and *Vegetable Growing in Australia* (c. 1931), by E.F. COOK. The first two titles were released during Melbourne's Garden Week FESTIVAL in April 1926 and signalled the strong commercial push of this publishing venture, which was both a popular and critical success. The series had its genesis in the company's earlier Australian Practical Handbooks series, which included Pescott, *The Dahlia in Australia* (1920); G. Seymour, *Potato Growing in Australia* (1920); and Fred TURNER, *Australian Grasses and Pasture Plants, with Notes on Native Fodder, Shrubs and Trees* (1921). Other horticultural books published by this company included W.R. GUILFOYLE, *Australian Plants Suitable for Gardens, Parks, Timber Reserves* (1911); David TANNOCK, *Manual of Gardening in Australia* (c. 1916); R.G. ELLIOTT, *The Australasian Rose Book* (1920); and J.W. AUDAS, *Native Trees of Australia* (1934). RA

WHITE, Cyril Tenison (1890–1950), government botanist, the third member of his family to hold this position for Qld, was employed as pupil assistant to his maternal grandfather, F.M. BAILEY, from 1905 and succeeded his uncle, J.F. BAILEY in the position in 1918, which he retained until his death. He was born at Kangaroo Point (Qld), an only child. His family moved to Rockhampton when he was five, but returned to Brisbane where he completed his schooling. While pupil assistant to his grandfather, White drew the 970 illustrations for F.M. Bailey's *Comprehensive Catalogue of Queensland Plants* (1912). This acquainted him with a wide variety of indigenous species and doubtless laid the foundation for his facility of identifying plants by sight. White was very interested in ECONOMIC BOTANY, especially native GRASSES and other fodder plants, poisonous plants, and WEEDS. During 1918–19 he spent several weeks collecting in New Guinea and in 1919 was appointed to the committee of the Bureau of Science and Industry, which was making a complete survey of weed pests of the Commonwealth. After an approach by the director of Boston's Arnold Arboretum, White collected woody plants, especially CONIFERS, from New Caledonia and he also identified a collection from New Guinea, published in the *Journal of the Arnold Arboretum* (1929). Unfortunately his request to the Department of Agriculture to study Australasian collections held at KEW was refused in 1925 and his eventual trip there in 1939 was curtailed by the outbreak of the Second World War.

White had a wide interest in science, horticulture, and nature conservation issues and was an active member of many local and national societies. He served the Royal Society of Queensland as president, and was an active member of the Queensland Naturalists' Club, Horticultural Society of Queensland, Orchid Society, and Royal Geographical Society of Australasia (Queensland). He made a large contribution to the knowledge of the floras of Qld, north-eastern NSW, New Guinea, New Caledonia, and the Solomon Islands, adding well over 13 000 specimens to the Queensland and other HERBARIA. He wrote and illustrated more than 300 botanical papers and prepared two textbooks, *An Elementary Textbook of Australian Forest Botany* (1922) and *Principles of Botany for Queensland Farmers* (1941). White was awarded the MUELLER Medal for his distinguished service to Australian NATURAL HISTORY (1946) and was granted an honorary Master of Science by the University of Queensland (1948), where he had lectured on forest botany for more than twenty years. JUDITH DEPPELER-HAGAN

WHITE, John (c. 1756–1832), surgeon-general to the First Fleet and the settlement at Port Jackson, was possibly the most significant of Australia's first resident naturalists. He forwarded his journal of the voyage and the first ten months of settlement along with NATURAL HISTORY specimens to London, where Thomas Wilson, a minor naturalist, prepared White's *Journal of a Voyage to new* [sic] *South Wales* (1790), with botanical notes by J.E. SMITH. White investigated the medicinal properties of AUSTRALIAN PLANTS and in 1788 sent a quart of EUCALYPTUS oil to Wilson. He continued to compile his journal and to collect natural history specimens and drawings. Thomas WATLING, the convict artist, was assigned to him soon after his arrival in 1792 and he contributed to White's collection. In 1794 White left Sydney and sought the assistance of botanist Aylmer Bourke Lambert (1761–1842) in the preparation of a further section of his journal. While this failed to appear, the specimens and drawings of plants that accompanied it were used by Smith in his publications. The so-called 'Watling Collection' of 512 drawings now in the British Museum (Natural History) is considered to be that assembled by White. RICHARD CLOUGH

WHITTLE, Robert (d. 1918), nursery proprietor, trained at the ROYAL BOTANIC GARDENS, KEW, leaving in 1882. By 1888 he was working in Brisbane, when 'SUMMERLIN and Whittle's Florist's Nursery' was favourably reviewed by the *Queenslander*. His role was not specified and by 1892 he advertised as a fern specialist and nursery proprietor at Hamilton (Qld). He listed the BRISBANE BOTANIC GARDENS as his address in the 1897 issue of the *Journal of the Kew Guild* but during 1905–18 conducted a nursery at Ascot, where he employed fellow Kewite William Leslie. RA

WHITWORTH, Robert Percy (c. 1832–1901), journalist and garden draftsman, was born in England and settled in Melbourne in the 1860s where he became a well-known journalist, novelist, playwright, and member of the local literati. While working for the publishing firm of F.F. Bailliere, he wrote the bulk of that firm's first *Gazetteer* for Victoria (1865). Whitworth was an intrepid traveller and spent time in New Zealand. In 1880 he advertised guided 'upcountry tours' to Gippsland, which he considered the most PICTURESQUE part of the colony.

Whitworth's first association with landscape designer William GUILFOYLE appears to have been in 1879, when he assisted in drawing up Guilfoyle's plan for the KOROIT BOTANIC GARDENS. The municipal council had commissioned Guilfoyle to redesign the garden, but his superiors in the Lands Department prohibited him from preparing the plan; as a result he appointed Whitworth for the task. While Whitworth signed his own name to the plan it seems probable that the design itself was Guilfoyle's work, and that Whitworth merely drafted the plan to satisfy a ministerial regulation that Guilfoyle not receive payment for it. Guilfoyle's plan for the Horsham Botanic Gardens, which carries the inscription 'Designed by W.R. Guilfoyle, Drawn by Robert P. Whitworth, 1880', was produced according to a similar arrangement and bears striking similarities to that for Koroit. Their collaborative work in western Vic. also included a plan for the Stawell hospital gardens (1880).

In his *Official Guide to Victoria* (1880), specifically designed for visitors to the Melbourne International EXHIBITION, Whitworth offered descriptions of the PUBLIC PARKS AND GARDENS in major towns across the colony. Brief as they were, they provided an unusually comprehensive picture of the extent of development of public gardens in Vic. The same work also included a plan and lengthy description of the MELBOURNE BOTANIC GARDENS, which acknowledged Guilfoyle as the major source of information.

HELEN DOYLE

WICKHAM PARK, Spring Hill, Qld, is a steeply sloping park that forms, with ALBERT, Observatory, and King Edward Parks, a verdant ridgeline behind the central city. Gazetted in 1876, it was placed into the care of the Brisbane Municipal Council in 1887 and named for John Clements Wickham (1798–1864), first government resident. The TROPICAL tree assortment includes six *Ficus* spp., *Agathis robusta*, *Araucaria bidwilii* and *A. cuninghamii*, *Podocarpus andinus* (from Chile), and PALMS (*Syagrus romanzoffiana*, *Phoenix* spp., and *Livistona* spp.). From 1913, Henry MOORE added the bandstand with an amphitheatre of simple timber benches, more than 700 metres of rockeries for shrubs, and, edging the Upper Albert Street boundary, 300 red poinsettias. In the 1950s Harry OAKMAN added Mount Coot-tha bluestone rockwork planted with pandanus, purple bougainvillea, agave, and *Phoenix roebelenii*. A monumental bluestone retaining wall (dubbed the 'Fort') was constructed in 1983 to prevent further erosion and is now being covered by different coloured bougainvillea.

JEANNIE SIM

WICKS, Henry (1854–1939), horticulturist and nursery proprietor, obtained an apprenticeship at Sutton's Nurseries, Kent, England, before migrating to Adelaide. He acquired Charles Pitt's Felixstow Nursery (1887) and established the Riverside Nurseries in Payneham. With his two sons Leonard John (1887–1967) and (Hubert) Norman David Wicks (1889–1974), he developed the Balhannah Nurseries (1905) in the ADELAIDE HILLS, specialising in ROSES, fruit and nut trees, and vines. Norman served on the South Australian Advisory Board of Agriculture for forty years. The family recently sold their interest in the Balhannah Nurseries. Leonard established the Freshford Nursery in 1915 at Highbury, specialising in roses, and fruit and nut trees (often supplying the RIVERLAND), introduced *Pyrus calleryana* (Callery Pear) into SA, and first propagated the Freshford Gem walnut and 'Prunus wicksoni': his family continue the business.

DAVID JONES

WIJAYA, Made (b. 1953), landscape designer and writer, born Michael White in Melbourne, has lived in Bali, Indonesia, since 1971 and operates throughout South-East ASIA. Writing for the *Sunday Bali Post* under the pen-name 'Stranger in Paradise', Wijaya (meaning 'victory') has described his TROPICAL gardening experiences. His home, Villa Bebek, established in Sanur in 1988, is an experimental ground for his designs. Wijaya combines tropical plants and Balinese gardening and spiritual traditions with English cottage garden traditions to create an Arts and Crafts look described by Tim Street-Porter as 'Tropical Cotswolds'. His entrepreneurial skill, artistry, and deep appreciation of Balinese culture have produced more than 350 gardens. His commissions include major hotels and private residences (including David Bowie's Carribean house on Mustique). Through his publishing arm, Wijaya Words, he has published *Stranger in Paradise* (1974), based on his newspaper columns, *Balinese Architecture: Towards an Encyclopaedia* (1984), and *Tropical Garden Design* (1999).

JEANNIE SIM

WILDFLOWERS: see AUSTRALIAN FLORA

WILD GARDEN, a concept flowing from early nineteenth-century English and American Romanticism, was popularised in the mid-nineteenth century by writers such as William Wordsworth (1770–1850) and John Ruskin (1819–1900), and horticulturally codified by William ROBINSON in *The Wild Garden* (1870). The 'wilderness' in Baroque gardens had been little more than a plot of shrubs and trees with an irregular path system, but its contrast to formality elsewhere was stark. Native plants were not essential to the Robinsonian concept but rather an ability to thrive without constant care. William GUILFOYLE sketched an idealised tropical wild garden dominated by palms at Villa Pallavicini, near Genoa, Italy (published 1897–98) and his FERN gully at MELBOURNE BOTANIC GARDENS was a tangible manifestation. Walter BUTLER, at Warrawee, Toorak, Vic. (c. 1910), used a wild garden to contrast with formal terraces. Robinson's ideas were refined by Gertrude JEKYLL, who greatly influenced Edna WALLING and many of her contemporaries. The

William GUILFOYLE's 1890s sketch of Villa Pallavicini, near Genoa, Italy, captured his conception of the WILD GARDEN, attained by 'just ... so much art as will exactly assimilate to nature, and that whatever is beautiful, graceful and pleasing in nature may be adopted, and whatever is extravagant and bizarre may be avoided'

'return to nature' envisaged by the Transcendentalist poets of North America, such as Henry David Thoreau (1817–1862) and Ralph Waldo Emerson (1803–1882), influenced American landscape architects well into the twentieth century and lay behind many early proposals for NATIONAL PARKS. OLMSTED, for instance, combined this philosophy with Robinson's concept in his designs for parks. The wild garden later found expression in Australian BUSH GARDENS of the 1960s–70s and occasionally reached new sophistication with REVEGETATION projects in the 1980s–90s. In *Bold Romantic Gardens* (1990), the American designers Oehme and van Sweden synthesised these strands into a romanticised ECOLOGICAL image.

COLLEEN MORRIS

WILDLIFE PRESERVATION SOCIETY OF AUSTRALIA: see STEAD, David George

WILHELMI, (Johann Friedrich) Carl (1829–1884), botanical collector and seed merchant, migrated from Dresden to SA in 1849. Within weeks of arriving, while on an expedition to the Bugle Ranges, he became acquainted with Ferdinand MUELLER. Between 1849 and 1855, despite being hampered by financial difficulties, Wilhelmi made excursions to Lake Alexandrina and the lower reaches of the Murray River, Eyre Peninsula, and Kangaroo Island. Besides collecting botanical specimens Wilhelmi studied Aboriginal use of NATIVE PLANTS. He collected a number of plants, named by Mueller, which proved to be endemic to SA. In 1855 Wilhelmi moved to Melbourne and, in Mueller's absence on the North Australian Exploring Expedition, was appointed Acting Government Botanist. Wilhelmi continued his botanical excursions, travelling throughout Vic. On Mueller's resumption of his duties as Government Botanist (1857), Wilhelmi remained as his deputy.

Wilhelmi was an intrepid explorer and skilled bushman. His letters, published papers, and specimens in the National Herbarium of Victoria show him to have been an acute observer and botanical collector. He was the first collector to publish a detailed account of the flora of the Grampians and the first since Robert BROWN to explore systematically the botany of Eyre Peninsula. In late 1868 Wilhelmi decided to return to Germany: he established a seed business but it did not flourish and he lost most of his savings. Of his last years nothing is known.

HELEN M. COHN

WILKINSON, Leslie (1882–1973), professor of architecture, was born and trained in London, where he won scholarships to tour England, France, Italy, and Spain. A superb draftsman, he was strongly influenced by MEDITERRANEAN architecture and landscapes. When he arrived in Sydney in 1918 to take up the first chair in architecture at the University of Sydney, William Hardy WILSON persuaded him to contribute to *Domestic Architecture in Australia* (1919). Wilkinson wrote:

> In a house set in a beautiful garden, simplicity can hardly be carried too far. A well placed feature or two, tastefully designed and of perfect craftsmanship, may be all sufficient, and in place of overloading the building with unnecessary ornament, a few garden furnishings, a tank, a fountain, a sheltered seat may well complete the scheme.

While Wilkinson was not a plantsman, his designs consistently formed elegant outdoor spaces—with stone flagged paths, classical PERGOLAS, and VISTAS to FORMAL gateways and decorative flèches—usually as an adjunct to a carefully proportioned façade. His own house, Greenway, Vaucluse (1923), was approached through a series of garden 'rooms', accented by a FOUNTAIN and GATEWAYS. Sandstone outcrops were integrated into the design, and the house colour-washed to reflect the tawny-pink trunks of *Angophora costata* (Smooth Bark Apple Myrtle). Samuel Hordern's house at Bellevue Hill (1936) featured a WALLED COURTYARD paralleled by an arcaded loggia. Important country projects with designed garden settings included Hazeldean, Cooma (1937), and MICALAGO (1948–60). Wilkinson is perhaps best remembered for his imposing buildings and spaces at the University of Sydney, and the related gardens realised with Professor E.G. WATERHOUSE.

David Wilkinson, *Leslie Wilkinson: A Practical Idealist* (Sydney, 1982)

HOWARD TANNER

WILLIAM RICKETTS SANCTUARY, Olinda, Vic.: see RICKETTS, William

WILLIAMS, Alfred (*fl.* 1877–1905), was first listed in Brisbane directories in 1877 with a nursery at Eight Mile

Plains. His Green Hill Nursery specialising in ROSES—a hobby of the proprietor—and fruit trees rapidly assumed a position of pre-eminence in the NURSERY TRADE in Qld. He was an advocate of deep DRAINAGE for orchards, a frequent contributor to the local horticultural press, and in 1879 he sent coffee, Chinese date plums, pineapples, mangos, guavas, and citrus to Sydney's International Exhibition. RA

WILLIAMS, George Richard (b. 1940), graduated in architecture (University of Queensland, 1965) and landscape architecture (Newcastle-on-Tyne, England, 1967). He joined the Queensland State Works Department, becoming head of section 1971–72 and from 1969 taught part time at the new landscape architectural postgraduate course at Queensland Institute (later University) of Technology. In 1973, he began teaching full time and set up the undergraduate program, continuing to coordinate or contribute to both courses until retiring in 1996. He joined the AUSTRALIAN INSTITUTE OF LANDSCAPE ARCHITECTS in 1969 and served as national president (1979–81). JEANNIE SIM

WILLIAMS, James Belton (*c.* 1870–1942) landscape gardener, nursery proprietor, and bowling green expert, worked at the Dublin Botanic Gardens before coming to Australia in 1888. He was employed by LAW SOMNER at their Cremorne Nursery, Richmond (Vic.), before becoming head gardener to a South Yarra resident and later setting up on his own account as a LANDSCAPE GARDENER with an extensive workforce. He ran the old-established Webley nursery in Malvern, initially in collaboration with Sarah WEBLEY and after 1904 as her tenant. In 1910 he purchased twenty-one acres (8.5 ha) at Kallista, devoted to rhododendrons, azaleas, kalmias, andromedas, Japanese maples, camellias, shrubs, and bulbs, managed by his son John Theodore Austin Williams (1896–1975), which from *c.* 1959 supplied the Myer Emporium plant department. In 1921 Williams purchased another nursery in Oakleigh, where he specialised in roses and dahlias. JESSIE SERLE

WILLIAMS, John (1858–1928), gardener and nursery proprietor, was born in Wales. He served an apprenticeship in the garden of Viscount Harberton (under head gardener Joseph Powell) and then after training as an 'improver' with seed merchants Sutton and Son of Reading (*c.* 1873–75), he returned to Wales as foreman for Lord Llanover, at Llanover near Abergaveny (*c.* 1875–78), responsible for sixteen gardeners. He arrived in Sydney in 1879, working under Charles MOORE at SYDNEY BOTANIC GARDENS (and alongside James PINK). He attracted the attention of William MACARTHUR and *c.* 1880 was in charge of the hothouses at Camden Park. Pink moved to take charge at BRISBANE BOTANIC GARDENS and in 1881 he appointed his friend Williams as propagator, a position of considerable importance in an experimental phase of tropical horticulture in Qld. By 1889 he had established a nursery at Mount Cotton and in 1896 he commenced the Broadwater Nursery, Mount Gravatt, specialising in citrus trees and ROSES. His rose 'Penelope' was awarded a ROYAL HORTICULTURAL SOCIETY certificate (1906), the first Australian-bred rose to obtain such a valued distinction, although due to marketing difficulties in Europe his cultivar was released by others before he could profit. The rose 'Star of Queensland' was another of his introductions. Williams later established his nursery at Sunnybank. RA

WILLIAMS, Keith Alfred Walter (b. 1916), photographer, amateur naturalist, and environmentalist, wrote and published the four-volume *Native Plants of Queensland* (1979–99). These were compiled from his extensive journeys into the bush, usually with long-time friend George TRAPNELL. With his keen eye for plant form, brilliant photographs, and non-academic descriptions, this series has became a major reference for amateurs and professionals alike. It has fostered garden use of Queensland's NATIVE PLANTS (encompassing approximately 8000 species) on a wide scale, concurrently promoting a strong environmental message. JEANNIE SIM

WILLIAMSON, Herbert Bennett (1860-1931), naturalist and botanist, encouraged an appreciation and understanding of Victoria's INDIGENOUS PLANTS and became a leading taxonomic authority. While teaching in primary schools scattered across Vic., he observed the local flora and shared his love and learning with students, teachers, and fellow members of the Field Naturalists' Club of Victoria (FNCV). An FNCV member from 1901, he became its assistant secretary and librarian in 1921, the year before becoming a Fellow of the LINNEAN SOCIETY, London. Especially after retiring (1925) he led many FNCV excursions and presented impressive systematic floral arrangements at FNCV wildflower shows. He collected many plants in the Grampians, one of which MUELLER used to name *Grevillea williamsonii*. MAIDEN and WILLIS named *Pultenaea* species and BLACK a *Pimelea* after him. With many beautiful Australian trees and shrubs introduced by Williamson, Hawkesdale State School's grounds were prizewinning. His schools became NATURE STUDY centres and he stimulated and supported regional FIELD NATURALISTS' CLUBS. He dealt with botanical contributions to the *Victorian Naturalist*, then the main literary vehicle for Victorian plant taxonomy, including his own on Victorian ferns (1926), lilies (1928), and other plants. He welcomed his 1929 appointment as honorary keeper of the HERBARIUM of the University of Melbourne's Botany School because it gave him 'more scope for passing on advice and material gratis'. LINDEN GILLBANK

WILLIAMSTOWN BOTANIC GARDENS, Vic., was set aside in 1856 and developed from 1858 according to a sophisticated GARDENESQUE design of Edward La Trobe BATEMAN, laid out by local surveyor William Bull. Based around the 'axis of symmetry' (propounded by LOUDON in 1840), Bateman's design was symmetrical along both cardinal axes. The northern half formed a PLEASURE GROUND and the southern half a PINETUM (initially grown with ACACIAS to shelter rarer plants from the exposed seaside frontage). The east–west symmetry was defined by an avenue of *Cordyline australis* (Cabbage Tree), replaced *c.* 1910–15 with *Washingtonia robusta* (Thread Palm), with the intersection of the paths punctuated by the statue of a local worthy (1891). Minor paths encircled lawns or garden beds. The path layout and

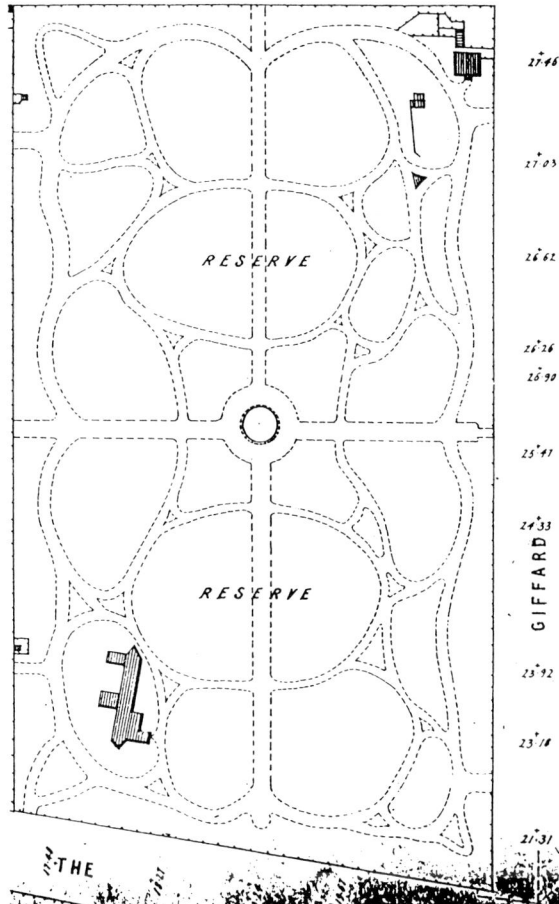

The sophisticated GARDENESQUE layout (1856) of WILLIAMSTOWN BOTANIC GARDENS (Vic.), attributed Edward La Trobe BATEMAN, forms the basis of the existing layout of this outstanding suburban BOTANIC GARDEN

boundary plantings of *Pinus halepensis* (Allepo Pine) and the remnants of the pinetum assist in an appreciation of this earliest phase of development. Two extensions to the west (1865–75) catered for sport, thereby sparing the garden this intrusive form of development. Curator Thake (incumbent 1899–1912) rejuvenated the garden into an Edwardian showpiece, establishing a lake (1904), new curator's cottage (1907), and redesigned the north-east entrance on the former cottage site (1907). This latter was fitted with handsome iron gates, cast in Scotland and relocated from Fairlie, South Yarra: their favourable price was seen as coup by the West over its richer and more salubrious cousins across the bay. The Williamstown gardens are among the earliest of Victoria's regional BOTANIC GARDENS and among its most evocative Edwardian landscapes. RA

WILLIS, James Hamlyn (1910–1995), botanist, spent his childhood in Stanley (Tas.), with secondary schooling in Melbourne, before he gained a scholarship to the Victorian School of Forestry, Creswick. Awarded a diploma in 1930, he worked in the Victorian Forests Commission before his transfer to the National Herbarium of Victoria in 1937 and a science degree at the University of Melbourne. Like MUELLER, Willis was a consummate collector-trekker. Collecting plants comprehensively in Vic. and widely across Australia, he established sixty new plant species. From 1943 he was secretary of the FIELD NATURALISTS' CLUB of Victoria's reconstituted Plant Names Subcommittee. In 1947 his 'Australian Flowers for Australian Gardens' appeared in *Wild Life*, and he was commissioned to prepare a successor to EWART's *Flora of Victoria*. His protracted and painstaking research at the British Museum and the ROYAL BOTANIC GARDENS, KEW, as well as Australian HERBARIA and in the bush, culminated in *A Handbook to Plants in Victoria* (1962–72), which allowed the ready identification in field and garden of Victoria's indigenous and naturalised vascular plants. In 1972 he retired from his decade-long position as Assistant Government Botanist; during the last year he was also Acting Director of the ROYAL BOTANIC GARDENS, MELBOURNE, and National Herbarium. During a busy retirement of trips, talks, and taxonomy, Willis revised LORD's classic *Shrubs and Trees for Australian Gardens* (1982). A great chronicler of Australia's botanical and horticultural history, Jim Willis was honoured by many awards and plant names. For his *Handbook* and other publications, he was awarded a Doctorate of Science from the University of Melbourne (1974). LINDEN GILLBANK

WILLYAMA, Medindie, SA, was redeveloped in 1890 by Broken Hill Proprietary Company director Charles Rasp (1846–1907) and his wife Agnes. German-born Rasp had arrived in Melbourne in 1869, pruned vines amid a varied career, then amassed a fortune from silver discoveries. The Rasps extended the large suburban house and garden and added several formal COURTYARDS, creating brick-lined interconnecting paths with sculptural accents or trees crowning axes. Agnes (later Countess von Zedtwitz) continued developing the courtyards, installing a cast-iron fountain and a CONSERVATORY, and nurturing the garden, which remains relatively intact. DAVID JONES

WILSON AND JOHNS George Harmston Wilson (1869–1951), florist and nursery proprietor, was born and trained in Lincoln, England, before migrating to Vic. in 1890 where he worked on a MOUNT MACEDON estate. He arrived in Perth by 1897 and was employed as a gardener in the government gardens. In 1898 his nursery was established on land purchased on Albany Highway, Cannington. By 1901 he had a site at the Perth markets in Wellington Street and by 1902 in Hannan Street, Kalgoorlie (which continued until the 1920s). In 1903 he commenced a partnership with **Henry Isaac Johns** (*c*. 1873–1948), seed merchant of Kalgoolie, establishing city premises in Perth's Barrack Street. From 1917 an annexe was developed at Carmel in the Darling Ranges, where roses, fruit trees, and hardy plants were raised, while pot plants, palms, and ferns were grown at Cannington. In the mid-1930s a Fremantle branch was opened in High Street and another production site came into operation at Spearwood from the 1950s. The firm produced *The Western Australian Gardening Guide* (1924, revised

1936), suited to local conditions and among the earliest Western Australian GARDENING BOOKS. Initially Wilson and Johns produced their own ornamental, vegetable, and fodder seeds, specifically developing the Spearwood brown and white onion varieties. George Wilson's sons, Lincoln, Leslie, Don, and Lionel, entered the business, which continued to trade until 1967. Don Wilson (1913–1979) was for two decades a popular and pioneering RADIO and TELEVISION broadcaster on the ABC (as 'Greenfingers').   JOHN VISKA

WILSON, Glen Wordsworth (b. 1927), landscape designer, spent his childhood in SA before shifting to Melbourne, where he honed his creative and technical skills in the printing industry as a toolmaker. His interest in NATIVE PLANTS developed in the 1950s through contact with Bernhardt and Dulcie SCHUBERT. Wilson was attracted to the writings of Edna WALLING and in 1956 became her student. He then wrote on design and native plants for the *Australian Garden Lover*. The landscape contracting firm of E.H. HAMMOND took on Wilson as a supervisor and designer (1962–70), leading to two collaborative designs with Walling, one in Merricks and the Freiberg Garden in Kew. The Squibb courtyard in Clayton, built with Hammond, was an outstanding piece of design for the time. Wilson was a founding member of the AUSTRALIAN INSTITUTE OF LANDSCAPE ARCHITECTS and lectured at Oakleigh Technical College (1967–73) and in the post-graduate course in LANDSCAPE ARCHITECTURE at Royal Melbourne Institute of Technology. In 1972 for Gladesville Developments Wilson developed a co-ordinated Australian landscape for their 300-hectare waterway development at Patterson Lakes (Vic.), a revolutionary scheme for its time. Wilson's pivotal book *Landscaping with Australian Plants* (1976) was published while he was lecturing in landscape technology at Canberra College of Advanced Education (1975–82), where he provided a major influence. His book *Amenity Planting in Arid Zones* (1980) was the result of six months' sabbatical in Israel. Wilson has written widely on planting design and the Australian landscape, including articles for the *Age* newspaper and *Landscape Australia*, and is one of the most influential writers on landscape issues in Australia. The Ainslie Village project in Canberra (1987–96) has been a fine demonstration of his commitment to people, conservation, and the Australian landscape.   PAUL THOMPSON

WILSON, (William) Hardy (1881–1955), architect and artist, was born at Campbelltown (NSW), his mother's grandfather being Thomas SHEPHERD. Upon his return to Sydney in 1910 from an architectural grand tour through Europe and North America he determined to seek out Australia's early architecture. With the architect's pencil, the author's pen, and the artist's eye, Hardy Wilson recorded the beauty of buildings in NSW and Tas. In the countryside about Sydney, along the Cow Pasture Road from Parramatta to Camden, Wilson saw the established gardens of such celebrated houses as CAMDEN PARK, BROWNLOW HILL, Harrington Park, HORSLEY, DENBIGH, and GLEDSWOOD. He was introduced to their trees and plants—all most suitably chosen by the early settlers for the soil and climate—which led to his interest in the gardens for houses designed by his firm. His study, undertaken during 1912–22—and which he described as the pleasantest years of his life—culminated in *Old Colonial Architecture in New South Wales and Tasmania* (1924), a large book of his beautiful drawings. Alongside the hard and tight architectural drawings, his admiration was held by the play of shadows on sunlit walls from the foliage of surrounding trees and plants. As no such record of our early houses and gardens had been attempted previously, Wilson's work undoubtedly promoted their conservation as well as introducing their charms into the twentieth century.

During the years of the First World War, his architectural firm Wilson, Neave, and Berry closed their office in Sydney. Wilson took the opportunity to concentrate on his study of colonial architecture and landscape and to design his own house at Warrawee. Purulia was a long, low house with white walls, broad twelve-paned windows with apple-green shutters, wide plastered eaves, and shingled roof—a fashionable prototype. Around the boundaries Wilson planted oleanders with tall poplars and fruiting olives, circled around the house were oranges, mandarins, and camellias, and along the flagged path bordered with box, were diosma, rosemary, lavenders, red China roses, and purple flag irises. As the motor car age dawned he thought of a spacious side garden with room for a drive and a garage or a pergola covered with ornamental grape vine. Wilson used his favourite trees and plants in many gardens around houses built by his firm. At ERYLDENE (1913), he chose the single white *Rosa laevigata* 'Cherokee' to grow over the Moon Gate. Ever conscious of Sydney's sea breezes, a sheltered courtyard at Barford, Bellevue Hill (1931), planted with pomegranates and mandarins, was covered with the ornamental grape vine; a drive bordered with clipped African olive hedges circled a fine Chinese elm. His garden interest was strongly demonstrated by his contribution to a special edition of *Art and Australia* on 'Domestic Architecture in Australia' (1919).

Caroline Simpson (ed.), *William Hardy Wilson: A Twentieth Century Colonial 1881–1955* (Sydney, 1980); Zeny Edwards (ed.), *William Hardy Wilson: Artist, Architect, Orientalist, Visionary* (Surry Hills, NSW, 2001)   CAROLINE SIMPSON

WINDBREAKS or shelter belts, less commonly breakwinds (chiefly nineteenth century), form distinctive features of many Australian DESIGNED and CULTURAL LANDSCAPES. Composed of tree PLANTATIONS in the form of belts, commonly to the south and west to provide shelter from prevailing winds, the windbreak is to the RURAL LANDSCAPE what the HEDGE is to the garden. Conifers, especially pines, were favoured in the mid-nineteenth century: *Pinus radiata* (Monterey Pine) windbreaks still define many early holdings in south-eastern Australia, as do those of Monterey Cypress, especially the low spreading form *Cupressus macrocarpa* 'Horizontalis'. Cypresses could also be clipped to form high dense hedges sheltering HOMESTEAD GARDENS and outstanding examples survive in Victoria's WESTERN DISTRICT. *Eucalyptus cladocalyx* (Sugar Gum) also formed distinctive windbreaks, and Alexander Buchanan and J.L. Currie's broadcast sowing of these in ploughed furrows at TITANGA,

This pot plant stand at ROUSE HILL (NSW) demonstrates a typical nineteenth-century garden application of WIRE-WORK, where plant and stand provide a complementary ornamental union

Lismore (Vic.), from 1875 formed a pioneering use of this method and an early use of AUSTRALIAN NATIVE PLANTS for this purpose. Twentieth-century developments included prescriptive planting designs by government departments of environment and even wind tunnel testing by CSIRO of new planting designs. It is important that the windbreak is slightly pervious to the wind and not a total barrier: *Allocasuarina* and *Casuarina* (She-oak) have been found to be especially useful for this, and are now widely used.   RA

WINTON, Campbell Town, Tas., contains many fine plantings of exotic trees by members of the Taylor family, who began breeding Saxon Merino sheep in the district in the 1820s. These trees include ELMS lining the entrance driveway, a magnificent single elm, the central feature of the horse paddock, planted to commemorate the coronation of Edward VII (1902), and fruiting trees. Mulberry, apple, and pear trees survive in the original ORCHARD. Century-old *Buxus sempervirens* (Box) hedging delineates the foundations of the original *pisé* house (1821) and these beds are planted with hybrid tea roses. A wooden Edwardian summer-house survives in this rose garden. Nineteenth-century Taylor family diaries record tree plantings and changes in the garden.

CHRISTINE REID

WIRE-WORK formed an important embellishment, for garden ORNAMENTS and FENCING. Popularised during the Regency period, its delicacy was particularly recommended for FLOWER GARDENS, where it formed edging to beds, garden arches, pot plant stands, and fountain surrounds. Manufactured in Australia from the 1860s, it reached a wide market after Federation in the form of crimped wire fencing, and later as Cyclone fencing. Neglected ornamentally for much of the twentieth century, wire-work is again inspiring artistic expression in the garden.   COLLEEN MORRIS

WIRRABARA FOREST NURSERY, SA, a STATE FOREST NURSERY and PLANTATION, was established in 1877 by forester Robert Lucas (1833–1897), as part of Forest Board initiatives under George GOYDER and Conservator John Ednie BROWN. It was a major trialling base, in conjunction with BUNDALEER FOREST NURSERY, for economic forestry initiatives in SA. *Pinus radiata* (Monterey Pine) were felled and milled (for fruit boxes) at Wirrabara, under Conservator Walter GILL, as early as 1902.   DAVID JONES

WIRRA WILLA ('place of green trees'), Armadale, WA, originally open eucalypt forest but now within Perth's urban spread, is a romantic 1.4-hectare garden. It was planted in the 1930s by tenants (and owners between 1940 and 1962) Barbara Whitehead and Evelyn Broadley with an interesting collection of exotic trees and shrubs such as *Calodendron capense* (Cape Chestnut) and *Cinnamomum camphora* (Camphor Laurel). The resultant cool micro-climate has provided ideal conditions for subsequent owners to increase the range of unusual plants. Narrow paths lined with subtropical plants, as well as azaleas, camellias, and rhododendrons, lead to areas of lawn with VISTAS over Neerigen Brook, a valuable source of water. The now-mature trees create a sense of enclosure, offering a welcome retreat during the sometimes-inhospitable Western Australian summer.   CAROL MANSFIELD

WITTUNGA, Blackwood, SA: see ASHBY, Edwin

WOLLASTON, Tullie Cornthwaite (1863–1931), opal dealer, horticulturist, and nursery proprietor, born at Lake Hamilton (SA), practised as a surveyor before becoming an international dealer and proponent of opals. His book *Opal: the Gem of the Never-Never* (1924) was written for the British Empire Exhibition in London. His early years at Lake Hamilton imbued in him a love for flora and fauna and all natural things. In 1904 he bought land at Bridgewater in the ADELAIDE HILLS, where he developed his property **Raywood**. Planting extensively with native and exotic trees and shrubs, including palms, roses, and Japanese species, he created an ARBORETUM where he propagated the first Claret Ash (*Fraxinus angustifolia* subsp. *oxycarpa* 'Raywood'). He developed the nineteen hectares adjoining Raywood as Ray Nursery and in 1928 he obtained the services of E. R. Beckett (d. 1932), formerly a propagator at the ROYAL BOTANIC GARDENS, KEW, and manager of SEWELL's ALDGATE NURSERY. Wollaston sought to encourage planting of NATIVE FLORA, which endeared him to like-minded colleagues such as ASHBY, BURDETT, and MORRIS. His books *The Spirit of the Child* (1914) and *Our Wattles* (1916) articulated his love of Australia's natural beauty and its flora. *Our Wattles*, with a preface by William J. Sowden, president of the Australian WATTLE DAY League, advised on identification, propagation, and cultivation of ACACIAS and was published partially mindful of an audience of Australian soldiers serving overseas.

Wollaston's opal dealings entailed extensive travels overseas, enabling visits to nurseries and botanic gardens to collect and exchange seeds. His close friend Dr Arthur W. Hill of the Royal Botanic Gardens, Kew, stated that Wollaston 'has made a garden which is the admiration of every British gardener who has seen it'. Ray Nursery was acquired by his son Morton George Wollaston (1903–1978) in 1932, and he operated the nursery until 1945. Raywood, the original cottage and land, was acquired by (Sir) Alexander Downer in 1933 and renamed Arbury Park. In 1964 part of this land was resumed by the state government for the South Eastern Freeway.

Raywood Nursery was established in 1958 by Quentin Tullie Wollaston (b. 1938) at Piccadilly in the Adelaide Hills, growing ornamental plants. In 1975 he and his family moved to Delamere on the Fleurieu Peninsula. Here they have created a place of distinction in the bushland, with Quentin displaying the same gifts of innovation and experimentation, and love of growing things, as his grandfather, T.C. Wollaston.

> Donovan H. Wollaston, *From Now to Domesday with the Wollastons* (Thebarton, SA, 1975); Kath Crilly, *Raywood in the Adelaide Hills: The Magnificent Garden of T.C. Wollaston* (Glenelg, SA, 1995)

DAVID JONES

WOLLONGONG BOTANIC GARDENS, NSW, at the foot of Mount Keira (which provides a dramatic backdrop), was officially opened in 1970 by industrialist Sidney Hoskins, who donated the site (1954). Initially based on a 1963 plan by Peter SPOONER, this BOTANIC GARDEN includes remnant indigenous RAINFOREST and from 1977 was developed by director Deane Miller to display plants in natural habitats. Enlarged to an area of twenty-seven hectares in 1978 by the acquisition of Hoskins' adjacent house, Glennifer Brae (1928, now Wollongong Conservatorium of Music), its SORENSEN-designed garden formed the nucleus of a CONIFER section. Prominent features include an ornamental LAKE, stands of indigenous turpentines, the outstanding Mercury Fountain by Robert WOODWARD, and the vista to its multiple cascades from the Northfields Avenue entrance. COLLEEN MORRIS

WOLSTON HOUSE, Wacol, Qld, was established in 1852 by Dr Stephen Simpson, Commissioner for Crown Lands, on a 640-acre (260 ha) pastoral property overlooking the Brisbane River. Surveyor William Pettigrew (1825–1906) was commissioned to design an extensive garden and orchard. Although extended to 2000 acres (810 ha) in 1860, when acquired by the Department of Agriculture and Stock (1960) the estate had dwindled to 117 acres (47 ha). Faced with demolition, Wolston House was purchased by the NATIONAL TRUST in 1965. Early plantings of *Ficus macrophylla* (Moreton Bay Fig), palms, and bougainvilleas survive.

Ian Sharp, *The Wolston Story* (Brisbane, 1998)

MARGARET COOK

WOMBAT HILL BOTANIC GARDENS, Daylesford, Vic., reserved as a PUBLIC GARDEN in 1862 on a former police reserve, sits atop the most prominent local landmark. CONIFEROUS tree massing reinforces the vertical dominance and provides a dark contrast to the deciduous ELM avenues and oaks, which include one of two 'Royal Oaks', *Quercus robur* (English Oak), planted in 1863. Specimens of *Pseudotsuga menziesii* (Douglas Fir), *Pinus ponderosa* (Western Yellow Pine), and *Sequoiadendron giganteum* (Big Tree) survive from the early 1870s, a legacy of Ferdinand MUELLER's plant distribution network, and the cool climate and volcanic soils. A FERN gully was the only constructed feature from William SANGSTER's 1884 plan (which survives as a rare example of his documentation). In the era of rail travel, the gardens became a popular tourist destination. Early postcards illustrate a bandstand and large timber shade-house. The Tuberous Begonia display, introduced by curator Gascoigne in the late nineteenth century, continues as a popular tradition.

JILL ORR-YOUNG

WOMBAT PARK, Daylesford, Vic., was settled in 1851 by gentleman scientist and parliamentarian William Edward Stanbridge (1821–1894), and by 1859 its garden was being described in glowing terms in the local press. The Stanbridge homestead was demolished when the present Rodney ALSOP–designed residence was built (1908). Among the outstanding features of the 'old' garden are the collection of mature exotic trees including a multi-trunked *Chamaecyparis lawsoniana*, rare trees such as the *Pinus cembroides* (Mexican Nut Pine) planted by Stanbridge, remnant box, cherry laurel, crataegus, holly, and Portuguese laurel hedging, a camellia walk, and a conifer avenue. The adjacent 'new' garden was established c. 1910 by Gavin Fleming of TAYLOR AND SANGSTER. The elm-lined driveway, now providing a stunning entrance to the garden, perimeter planting, cedar forest, and arboretum parkland, were planted in 1910–16. A crenellated HEDGE, and two tapestry hedges of green, golden, and silver hollies, cherry laurel, Portuguese laurel, arbutus, box, viburnum, and green and variegated pittosporum remain in fine condition. A croquet lawn, retaining wall, deciduous forest, sunken path, and the driveway's sweeping turning circle are also notable. Many of the shrubs, perennials, and bulbs are a feature in spring while the wide range of deciduous trees make a stunning autumn display. The entire garden is significant for its retention of many features from both the nineteenth and twentieth centuries, and forms a fine complement to nearby WOMBAT HILL, a garden in which Stanbridge took a keen interest. HELEN PAGE

WOMEN GARDENERS: see GENDER

WOOD, John Frederick Francis: see SOUTH AUSTRALIAN HORTICULTURIST

Robert WOODWARD's El Alamein Fountain (1960–61) in Sydney's Kings Cross, was the seminal work by this internationally renowned designer of FOUNTAINS and has become an icon of Australian MODERNISM

WOODWARD, Robert (b. 1923), trained as an architect (University of Sydney, 1952) and enjoys an international reputation as a designer of FOUNTAINS. Initially educated in the technical school system, he completed university after war service. He then moved to Helsinki, where he worked with renowned Finnish architect Alvar Aalto (1898–1976) before returning to Australia (1955). His first major fountain was designed for a 1959 competition for Kings Cross, Sydney (constructed during 1960–61), to commemorate the El Alamein action of the Second World War. Among his many commissions are the High Court, Canberra, ACT (1980), Lyric Theatre, Brisbane (1984), Parliament House, Canberra (1988), and Darling Harbour, Sydney (1988). Bob Woodward's large-scale work is characterised by meticulous attention to the minute effects of the movement of light and water. While his earliest work is characterised by technical brilliance (Kings Cross), mid-career training in LANDSCAPE ARCHITECTURE produced more physically integrative projects (High Court and Darling Harbour). MICHAEL BOGLE

WOOF(F), Luke (c. 1832–1906), gardener, following his migration to NSW, commenced working in SYDNEY BOTANIC GARDENS (1857–58), his first job being the 'rooting out of the BUSBY grape vines'. While gardener at Craigend (c. 1861–77)—formerly Thomas MITCHELL's residence—he was closely involved with the Horticultural Society of New South Wales as a committee member. He gave many papers to meetings during the 1860s and 1870s, where he demonstrated extensive botanical knowledge in promoting an appreciation of science among gardeners. Recognised (with William WOOLLS) as a major and 'talented contributor' to the HORTICULTURAL MAGAZINE, his papers included 'Advantages to be Derived from Horticulture', 'On Gases, Their Importance to Animal and Vegetable Life', 'Hedge Plants', 'Teratology or Morphology of Plants', 'Native Fruits', 'Cultivation of the Vine', and 'Neglected Plants'. A prominent exhibitor and prize winner at HORTICULTURAL SHOWS in the 1860s, he specialised in GREENHOUSE plants; his hybrid 'Coleus Wooffii' was given to John VEITCH, who introduced it in England as 'C. Gibsonii' (1867). Wooff was a park ranger (1886–87) before becoming caretaker of VICTORIA PARK (1889–1900). At the time of his death he was the affiliated representative of the ROYAL HORTICULTURAL SOCIETY of London for the Horticultural Association of New South Wales, the latter making him a life member shortly before his death. COLLEEN MORRIS

WOOLLS, William (1814–1893) teacher, clergyman, and botanist, was born at Winchester, England, the nineteenth child of Edward and Sarah Woolls. By the time he was orphaned at 16, a succession of clergymen had steeped him in classics, literature, history, and theology. Not receiving a cadetship from the East India Company, Woolls joined the brig *Grecian* and arrived in Sydney in 1832, with an introduction to Governor Bourke. He declined the Governor's offer of 'a Clerkship' in the Female Factory, Parramatta, to become a junior master at The King's School. After experience at King's (1832–36) and at Sydney College (1838–39), Woolls conducted his own academy at Parramatta (1841–72). Repeatedly urged to take holy orders, he finally did so in 1873 and served as rector of Richmond for ten years.

Woolls 'first imbibed a taste for Australian botany' during the 1840s from the Reverend James Walker, then headmaster of King's and rector of All Saints, Parramatta. This led to correspondence with Ferdinand MUELLER that lasted thirty-six years. In 1856 he began a lengthy series of popular articles in the *Sydney Morning Herald* dealing with medicinal and poisonous plants, and major plant families. Special interests developed in some lower plant groups such as algae, lichens, mosses, and FERNS, as well as in ORCHIDS and EUCALYPTS, which he declared were 'very perplexing'. Mueller considered Woolls possessed 'unrivalled knowledge of the Eucalypts of New South Wales'. Woolls wrote frequently for the *Horticultural Magazine*, *Victorian Naturalist*, and *Proceedings of the Linnean Society of New South Wales*, and became the respected correspondent of a large circle of professional and amateur botanists, including Henry Deane (1847–1924), Robert FITZGERALD, Louisa Calvert (née ATKINSON), F.M. BAILEY, William Sharp MACLEAY, Fred TURNER, and a number of clergymen–botanists. J.H. MAIDEN and Walter Scott Campbell, Chief Inspector of Agriculture, both willingly acknowledged indebtedness to him.

Through his studies and observations, teaching and public lectures, and his publications and prolific correspondence, Woolls promoted a wider understanding and appreciation of the NATIVE FLORA. A pioneer conservationist, he attacked overstocking of pastures and described wholesale ring-barking as a 'murderous process', a 'practice of a slovenly and greedy kind' that would be later deplored. In 1856 he declared that 'owing to changes … taking place … the "native botany" will soon become a matter of history'. Even over-enthusiastic collecting

Woolmers

The KITCHEN GARDEN in the Frogmore Royal Gardens at Windsor, England, illustrated in Charles MCINTOSH's *Book of the Garden* (1853–55), was the training ground for Charles WYATT before his emigration and success in the colonial nursery trade at the Frogmore Nursery, Fyansford (Vic.)

for annual flower shows caused bushland devastation, and he saw his concept of economy and equilibrium in nature being replaced by an imbalance. Whereas Aboriginal peoples had adapted to the Australian BUSH, Europeans destroyed it.

George BENTHAM acknowledged Woolls' specimens more than 500 times in *Flora Australiensis*, volumes of which Mueller inscribed to 'a most generous and disinterested supporter'. Of Woolls' own works, *A Contribution to the Flora of Australia* (1867), *Lectures on the Vegetable Kingdom* (1874), and *The Plants of New South Wales* (1885) attested to his passionate interest and enthusiasm. Predeceased by two of three wives and all three of his children, William Woolls—the man who once met Allan CUNNINGHAM—was commemorated by a window in St John's, Parramatta, and by species of orchids, a tree-fern, a rare forest climber, *Sloanea woollsii* (the Yellow Carabeen of the rainforests), and the monotypic genus *Woollsia*.

Lionel Gilbert, *William Woolls, 1814–1893: 'A Most Useful Colonist'* (Canberra, 1985)   **LIONEL GILBERT**

WOOLMERS, near Longford, Tas.: see ARCHER, Thomas

WRIGHT, Theodore (*c.* 1835–1904), horticulturist, agriculturist, and journalist, apparently arrived at Moreton Bay in the mid-nineteenth century, although details of his early career are not known. Wright established the QUEENSLAND AGRICULTURIST in 1879 and served as agricultural editor of the QUEENSLANDER (1882–85). He relinquished proprietorship of the *Agriculturist* in 1885, but following its merger with the PLANTER AND FARMER, retained editorial control of the new amalgamated paper. Wright included a regular column in his agricultural papers entitled 'Phrenological and Mesmerical'; his obituary noted that he 'was very prominently associated with the theosophical and astrological movements'.

In 1882 he was awarded a prize by the Queensland National Association for a horticultural treatise, published the following year as *Fruit Cultivation in Queensland … Together with a Complete Calendar for Field and Garden Operations, Adapted for all Queensland*. This work, based on his colonial experience, was only the second locally published book on the subject (after that by A.J. HOCKINGS) and it drew together material originally published in the *Queenslander*, much of which was also reprinted in *Thorne's Queensland Almanac* (1884–90) and regional ALMANACS. Wright was awarded a five guinea prize in 1883 by the Wide Bay and Burnett Pastoral and Agricultural Association for the best essay on orange culture. His two prize essays formed the basis of *The Queensland Horticulturist and Gardener's Guide* (1886), which he considered a second edition of his earlier book. Wright's long and successful experience well qualified him as the author of 'a brief digest of the capabilities of Queensland horticulture' published for the Colonial and Indian Exhibition in *Queensland: Its Resources and Institutions* (1886).   **RA**

WRIGLEY, John Walter (b. 1934), horticulturist and botanic gardens curator, was Curator of the AUSTRALIAN NATIONAL BOTANIC GARDENS, Canberra (1967–81) before moving to Coffs Harbour (NSW). He promoted the idea of small regional BOTANIC GARDENS—such as those at Coffs Harbour and Tamworth (NSW) and Mildura, Vic. (for which he was a design consultant)—located throughout the country in different CLIMATIC zones that could carry collections suited to the prevailing conditions. His strong interest in the propagation and cultivation of AUSTRALIAN PLANTS has resulted in many publications on both general and specialist groups within the flora, with several produced in conjunction with illustrator and photographer Murray Fagg (b. 1943), who worked with Wrigley at the National Botanic Gardens as Education-Display Officer. Their major work, *Australian Native Plants: A Manual for their Propagation, Cultivation and Use in Landscaping* (1979) was published when interest in growing and landscaping with AUSTRALIAN PLANTS had reached a high point, and its huge sales of many editions supports the claim, made by John Simmons, Curator of the ROYAL BOTANIC GARDENS, KEW, in the foreword that 'in compiling this book … a standard work of reference has been produced'. The publications of Wrigley and Fagg have also been widely consulted overseas for information on Australian plants. Wrigley has been involved in many organisations, including a term as National President of the SOCIETY FOR GROWING AUSTRALIAN PLANTS. He has also presented many papers on the management of Australian plants and landscapes at national and international conferences and was responsible for landscaping the Australian pavilion at Expo70 in Japan. ML

WYATT, Charles (1823–1885), nursery proprietor and grazier, was born in Hampshire, England, and trained in horticulture at the Frogmore Royal Gardens at Windsor. He migrated from London, arriving at Port Phillip in 1847. He acquired properties at Fyansford, on the Barwon River near Geelong, in 1856. Here in 1859 he established a plant nursery which he named Frogmore. The earliest known (undated) catalogue preceded an enlarged 1874 catalogue in which he claimed to have 'the largest, healthiest, and best grown stock of fruit and forest trees, hedge and edging plants, plants for avenue and street planting, conifers, and flowering plants, in Victoria'. He imported extensively from countries throughout the world. The range of plants offered was very impressive but with grape vines (fifty-one varieties listed), importing proved disastrous. In 1877 the American vine pest Grape Phylloxera was discovered in the Geelong region. Next year the twelve acres (5 ha) of vines at Frogmore and at three other vineyards were the first in the region to be compulsorily destroyed. Floods were occasionally experienced on his 1200 acres (485 ha) of rich agricultural land, but despite these setbacks, while he was in charge the nursery continued to be one of the most extensive and well patronised in the colony. Visiting Wyatt's 'peculiarly neat and well kept' nursery in 1865, J.G. VEITCH 'was astonished to find an establishment in a remote part of Australia which might bear favourable contrast with any English provincial nursery'.

GEORGE JONES

WYNSTAY, Mount Wilson, in the BLUE MOUNTAINS, NSW, was developed by Sydney merchant Richard Wynne (1822–1895), who had been influential in encouraging the government to survey the area following a visit in 1867.

The Turkish BTHHOUSE at WYNSTAY, Mount Wilson (NSW), survives as a most unusual example of this GARDEN BUILDING type

Wynstay

Wynne purchased his land in the early 1870s, the largest landholding in Mount Wilson at the time and occupying a dominant position at the end of The Avenue. His intention was to create an English rural estate with grand architecture but this was not fully achieved in his lifetime. He built a small Gothic cottage in 1875 and soon constructed a larger weatherboard cottage. A description of the Wynstay garden in the 1880s appeared in W.H. Suttor's *Australian Stories Retold and Sketches of Country Life*. Early plantings included an avenue of *Cupressus macrocarpa* (Monterey Cypress) and specimen trees such as *Abies nordmanniana* (Caucasian Fir), *Picea smithiana* (Himalayan Spruce), and *Sequoiadendron giganteum* (Giant Redwood). The many deciduous trees, including different forms of beech, oak, maple, chestnut, magnolia, cherry, and dogwood, provide a colourful autumn display. Shrubs surviving from the early period include cultivars of camellia, deutzia, hydrangea, ilex and viburnum. In the early 1890s a stone gatekeeper's lodge, hexagonal in plan, was built beside the main gates. The original carriageway is lined with crenellated dry stone walls which match the parapets of the stone stables. One of Wynne's more eccentric features was an Italianate-style Turkish BATH HOUSE in polychrome brick. Wynne's grandson built the present house at Wynstay in 1923 on the site reserved for Richard Wynne's grand residence.

DAVID BEAVER

XAVIER, Mary Francis (1910–1975), rosarian, born Mary Francis Lewis-Hickman in Devonshire, England, arrived in Australia in 1914. She subsequently became a nun of the Presentation Order at St Finn Barr's Convent, Launceston (Tas.). Sister Xavier bred 'Iced Parfait' (1972) and several other roses. 'Nano Nagle', a double, dark red rose raised by her and named to honour the founder of the order, which is dedicated to teaching children, is awaiting introduction.

TREVOR NOTTLE

XERIC GARDENS, from the Greek *Xeros* (dry), promoting water-efficient horticulture, have tended to be the exception in Australia, rather than the rule. The earliest gardens were for the production of food and other useful items and it was quickly learnt that supplementary watering would be needed to ensure successful results with the traditional crops grown. Similarly, the first ornamental gardens mostly featured plants that needed watering in the dry months. Some drought-tolerant species survived where others failed and their success and broad use has turned many into icons of Australian gardens. Examples include Agapanthus, geraniums, *Schinus molle* (Pepper Tree), and *Cupressus macrocarpa* (Monterey Cypress). The ability to survive without IRRIGATION has turned some, such as Lantana, into serious WEEDS.

The nineteenth-century obsession with scientific discovery and fascination with all things exotic saw a boom in plant collecting and exhibiting. Displays of weird and wonderful xerophytic plants were set up in numerous public and

The planting and maintenance of this recent coastal garden on Victoria's Mornington Peninsula reflects contemporary trends in XERIC GARDENING, wholly appropriate to this exposed and informal setting

Xeric Gardens

private gardens, often placed among grotesque ROCKERIES, also popular in this period. Notable examples survive in the ADELAIDE BOTANIC GARDEN and the ROYAL BOTANIC GARDENS, MELBOURNE.

By the early twentieth century reliable reticulated WATER had reached most urbanised areas and coincided with a domestic garden style of annuals and verdant lawns involving high water usage. In areas without plentiful water gardens continued to use a palette of survivors, determined mostly from experience. A few private collectors continued accumulating xerophytic plants, notably CACTI and other succulents, and several DISPLAY GARDENS were established.

The second half of the twentieth century saw a growing awareness of the AUSTRALIAN FLORA. Writers such as Edna WALLING, Betty MALONEY, and Jean Walker promoted the use of native plants as low water users and encouraged BUSH GARDENS, while quite sophisticated NATURAL Australian gardens with minimal water input were created by people such as Ellis STONES and Glen WILSON. Native plant collections established by enthusiasts such as David GORDON and Olive PINK formed the genesis of two xeric BOTANIC GARDENS, Myall Park Botanic Gardens (Glenmorgan, Qld) and the Olive Pink Botanic Garden (Alice Springs, NT). Later in the twentieth century at least two other botanic gardens in ARID ZONES were established with a xeric theme, the AUSTRALIAN ARID LANDS BOTANIC GARDEN (Port Augusta, SA) and the AUSTRALIAN INLAND BOTANIC GARDENS (Mildura, Vic.).

More recent xeric gardens have arisen from a growing awareness of the finite nature of our water resources and a number have been established as demonstration water-efficient gardens with the co-operation of water authorities. A recent movement towards MEDITERRANEAN-style gardens has also seen the creation of many domestic gardens less reliant on supplemental watering. Contemporary xeric gardens are rarely exclusively of native plants, and nowadays generally feature flora from parallel climates such as the Mediterranean, South Africa and the south-eastern USA.

Kevin Walsh, *Water-Saving Gardening in Australia* (Chatsworth, NSW, 1993)

KEVIN WALSH

YALLUM PARK, near Penola, SA: see COONAWARRA, SA

YANCHEP NATIONAL PARK, WA, containing natural lakes and limestone CAVES, was an important source of ABORIGINAL FOOD PLANTS—'Yanchep' is derived from the Aboriginal *yanget* (bulrush). The area was vested in the Caves Board in 1905 'for the preservation of flora and for a health and recreation resort'. During the 1930s Depression, sustenance workers developed the cultivated gardens with lawns, introduced trees, flower beds, and paths. Parts of the lake were dredged for boating, and the construction of a hotel and guest house, provision of lighting to the caves, and introduction of a koala population added to its great popularity during the inter-war years as a venue for social events and picnics within easy access of Perth. Declared a NATIONAL PARK in 1969, it is now valued for its conservation of flora and fauna, while retaining reminders of its RESORT past.

PHILIP PALMER

YARALLA, Concord, NSW, was developed on the Parramatta River from the 1850s by merchant Thomas Walker (1804–1886). His massive Italianate 'cottage' (1857–59: architect Edmund Blacket), possessing 'all the necessary appliances applicable to a marine villa, viz. bathing house and splendid jetty and boathouses', was set off by spacious lawns and shrubberies. Head gardener Alexander Stephen claimed in 1865 to have introduced ribbon BEDDING to the colonies in Walker's garden. Stephen had served 'a considerable portion of his time in the gardens' of the celebrated Scottish seat Dalkeith under William THOMSON. Gardener Alexander GRANT was also employed at Yaralla. Later developments included a formal ITALIAN garden; a 'fine, well-grown specimen of Cedrus Deodara', noted in 1865, still graces the turning circle of the driveway. Walker left £100 000 from his considerable estate for the building and support of the nearby Thomas Walker Convalescent Hospital (1890–93: architects SULMAN and Power). His daughter Edith Campbell Walker (1861–1937) inherited Yaralla and her extensive travels were reflected in the garden by Norwegian and Swiss cottages, Japanese lanterns, an Indian House, and a rustic GROTTO (*c.* 1910). A salt water SWIMMING POOL with wave-making machine brought aquatic splendour. This splendid estate had few rivals in Sydney, although gradual erosion of detail followed its later conversion to the Dame Edith Walker hospital.

BARBARA VAN DEN BROEK

YARRALUMLA, ACT: see GOVERNMENT HOUSES: *Australian Capital Territory*

YARRA PARK, Melbourne, and adjacent Flinders Park, were established in the 1850s. Originally an unbroken swathe of open woodland between the city, East Melbourne, and the Yarra River, it has been dissected by railways and roads, with large areas given over to SPORTING and entertainment facilities. The earliest was Melbourne Cricket Ground (1853), now the city's largest stadium and sporting icon. It hosted the 1956 Olympic Games, with events held in a purpose-built complex—renamed Olympic Park—overlooking the river. More recent excisions include the National Tennis Centre (1986), and a multi-purpose stadium and tramway (1999). Melbourne City Council manages the remaining fifty-six hectares comprising open parkland with mature exotic and Australian trees. Speakers Cornet, a remnant of Flinders Park once used for public debating, has been combined with land reclaimed from road and railway uses to create a 'new' eight-hectare riverside park, Birrarung Marr, its first stage of construction completed in 2002.

Keith Dunstan, *The People's Ground: The MCG* (Kew, Vic., 2001)

GEORGINA WHITEHEAD

YARRA VALLEY, Vic., was the location of early European exploration (1803) by surveyor Charles Grimes, accompanied by convict gardener James FLEMING. The city blocks of Melbourne were laid out parallel to the river's northern bank (1837) and the site of MELBOURNE BOTANIC GARDENS (1845), chosen on the recommendation of Lieutenant-Governor LA TROBE, formed a favourable north-facing declivity leading to the river. The adjoining area, later Melbourne's DOMAIN, was noted on early surveys as 'Hilly forest land, thin of Trees.' Large suburban allotments with frontages to the Yarra and to Gardiner's Creek (later Toorak) Road, sold in 1840, permitted the creation of MANSION GARDENS (now represented, albeit in a subdivided state, by COMO). Further upstream, past Dight's Falls, the expansive river valley can still be appreciated in the former grounds of Abbotsford House and St Hellier (later the Abbotsford Convent). In its upper reaches, the Yarra provided fertile plains for agriculture at Yarra Glen (recalled by the NATIONAL TRUST's Gulf Station estate): Victoria's VITICULTURE industry began in the undulating upper Yarra Valley. La Trobe's watercolour sketches vividly convey this early landscape, and his SWISS background was mirrored by pioneering local vignerons, the DE CASTELLA and DESCHAMPS families. During the mid- to late nineteenth century other gardens—including Cremorne PLEASURE GARDENS, Yarra Bend National Park, the nursery of T.C. COLE, the BURNLEY Gardens of the (Royal) Horticultural Society of Victoria, and numerous TEA GARDENS and VILLA GARDENS in South Yarra, Toorak, and Hawthorn—took advantage of the Yarra and its valley as a source of water and favourable soils, and for its picturesque qualities. A project to alleviate downstream flooding by straightening a section of the river, directed by Carlo CATANI, was begun in 1896: this created a boulevard (Alexandra Avenue), with AVENUES of trees and subtropical ROCKERIES (built by Charles ROBINETTE) so striking that one contemporary commentator likened it to the 'Paris of the South'. Work further upstream on the Yarra Boulevard commenced during the Depression; this roadway can still be followed, with early sections of landscaping remaining in Richmond Park. Other town planning, urban design, and horticultural projects have since had the Yarra as their focus, most recently the new riverside PUBLIC PARK, Birrarung Marr (2002), the naming of which recognises the vital importance of the river to the original Kulin people.   RA

YATES, Arthur (1861–1926), seed merchant, was born in Manchester, England, son of seed merchant Samuel Yates (1831–1901). In 1826 Arthur's grandfather, George Yates (1804–1879), had opened a seed store in Stockport, followed in 1843 by a branch in nearby Manchester. Three years later the young Samuel was put in charge of the Manchester branch store and it soon eclipsed the original store and larger premises were sought. Samuel joined his father in partnership in 1855 and assumed sole control in 1885. Samuel's sons, Harry, Arthur, William George, Ernest, and Percy successively joined the firm, and it was Arthur who established kindred businesses in New Zealand and Australia.

Arthur Yates entered the family business in 1877, but owing to poor health it was decided that he should go to New Zealand. He arrived there in 1879 and initially worked as a station-hand and shepherd on pastoral runs in the Otago and Hawkes Bay districts. Sensing an opportunity for supplying seeds, Yates opened a modest seed shop in Auckland in 1883, travelling on horseback through the Waikato farmlands seeking orders. He visited Australia in 1886 and travelled extensively along the eastern coast. Working initially through a commercial agent, Arthur commenced a branch in Sussex Street, Sydney, in 1887. He was joined in partnership by his brother Ernest in 1889, with Arthur choosing the preferred climate of Sydney, and Ernest running the Auckland business. Arthur Yates married in 1888, and sons Harold (b. 1890), Arthur (Max) (b. 1891), Guy (b. 1898), and Philip (b. 1904) all subsequently joined the family business.

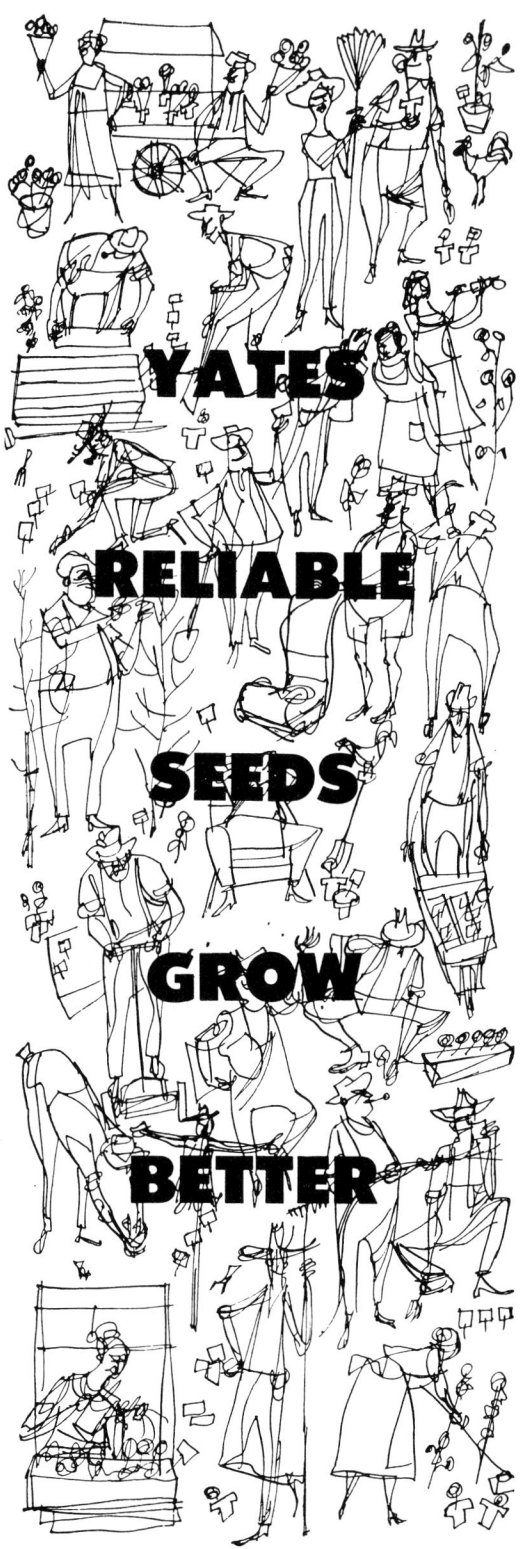

From mowing to hoeing, this YATES seed advertisement (1955) captures the seasonal pleasures of the SUBURBAN GARDEN

By 1893 Arthur Yates and Co. had launched a range of packet seeds for home gardeners and in 1895 Arthur Yates wrote and published the first edition of *Yates' Gardening Guide for Australia and New Zealand*, initially provided to customers 'gratis on application'. Bearing the subtitle 'Hints for Amateurs', the guide concentrated on FLORICULTURE and VEGETABLE growing, unashamedly aimed at purchasers of Yates seeds. More modest in ambit than ADAMSON's (later BRUNNING's) rival *The Australian Gardener*, Arthur Yates made a timely entry into the market in a period when home gardening, especially floriculture, was growing in popularity. *Yates' (Seed) Annual*, a lavish yearly catalogue, provided a regular supplement to the guide, and by the early 1900s was joined by separate farm seed catalogues, and catalogues of roses, fruit trees, and nursery stock, although seeds continued to be the company's mainstay. Sales were conducted by travelling salesmen servicing a vast network of retail storekeepers who acted as agents, and also increasingly through postal sales. The company had purchased land at Exeter (NSW) by the turn of the century for a seed and bulb farm, and later established trial and breeding grounds at Concord, near Sydney, where the famous Yarrawa strain of SWEET PEA was commercially trialled. A Tasmanian seed farm was also established in 1916 on the Derwent River near New Norfolk.

Both the Auckland and Sydney businesses prospered and in 1897 Arthur Yates erected a six-storey seed warehouse in Sussex Street, doubled in size in 1903, and again in 1910. The partnership arrangement lasted until *c.* 1907, when Arthur and Ernest formed two distinct firms, but preserving the old name and acting conjointly in all matters of mutual interest. In 1910 both firms were converted to limited companies and the 1926 issue of *Yates' Annual*, which included a useful history to celebrate the centenary of the parent business, outlined the advantages:

> Thus there were three businesses—one in Manchester, one in Auckland, and one in Sydney—each distinct, each developing along its own lines untrammelled by outside control but conducted co-operatively in the growing, buying and selecting of stocks, to their great mutual benefit.

On the death of Arthur Yates in the firm's centenary year, his sons took over management. Harold, who had joined the company in 1905 and spent a two-year apprenticeship with the English company, became a director in 1911 and was subsequently general manager. Outsourcing of seed production to contract farmers was established and close links with the New South Wales Department of Agriculture assisted in the trialling of farm seeds. Harold Yates was a member of the National Vegetable Seeds Committee, established in 1942, and his company's publications stressed the benefits of cultivating vegetables and flowers for the war effort. By this date a separate New Zealand edition of *Yates' Garden Guide* was being published. The Australian edition was progressively revised, reflecting the increasingly crowded book market catering for home gardeners in the post-war period. After Harold's death, his brother Philip became managing director and on his retirement in 1964 this role was taken by Harold's son, Peter Yates (b. 1915). In 1967 new premises were acquired at Milperra in Sydney's outer west. The centenary edition of *Yates' Garden Guide* (1995) was marked by the inclusion of a short company history, prepared by Deirdre O'Donnell and Wendy Hucker. Recently the company has diversified into the garden care business with franchised gardeners, marking one of the first major departures from the core business, established in 1826, of selling 'Yates' Reliable Seeds'. RA

YENCKEN, David George Druce (b. 1931), environmental planner and academic, was born in Berlin to Australian parents. After graduating from Cambridge University he returned to Australia to pioneer motel development, memorably at Merimbula (NSW) with the Black Dolphin Motel (1958–62: architect Robin Boyd). He then founded Merchant Builders (1965), whose houses prominently featured landscaping by Ellis STONES. He also founded the firm of TOWN PLANNERS and LANDSCAPE ARCHITECTS, TRACT CONSULTANTS, acting as managing director of both firms. He was an author of the seminal *Report on the National Estate* (1974), which led to the establishment of the AUSTRALIAN HERITAGE COMMISSION, which he then chaired (1975–81). Yencken headed Victoria's Ministry for Planning and Environment (1982–87), presiding over major URBAN DESIGN and planning initiatives in Melbourne. He held the post of Elisabeth MURDOCH Professor of Landscape Architecture and Environmental Planning at the University of Melbourne during 1988–97. During this time he also chaired the Design Committee of the Australia Council for the Arts and was president of the Australian Conservation Foundation. His advocacy for planning, design, and ENVIRONMENTAL issues is wide-ranging and his contribution has been recognised by many peer awards. RA

YENGO, Mount Wilson, in the BLUE MOUNTAINS, NSW, was purchased in the early 1870s by Jesse Gregson (1837–1919), general superintendent of the Australian Agricultural Company. The cottage, built from locally quarried sandstone, was completed by 1881 and the garden was developed over the ensuing years. Gregson, a keen amateur botanist, stocked the garden with a diverse range of exotic specimen trees, receiving advice from both Charles MOORE and Joseph MAIDEN. From the imposing gates, a gravel drive passes through a dense shrubbery before arriving at the cottage. An expansive lawn area extends east from the house with an outstanding *Thuja plicata* (Western Red Cedar) as its focal point. CONIFERS such as *Sequoiadendron giganteum* (Giant Redwood), *Cedrus deodara* (Deodar), and *Cupressus sempervirens* (Italian Cypress) provide contrast to the many deciduous trees. The Pigott family purchased Yengo in the mid-1960s and have embellished the garden with many new plants, a walled garden, laburnum walk, ponds, and SCULPTURE. Bronze statuary by renowned English sculptors Judith Holmes Drewry and Lloyd le Blanc is a major feature. DAVID BEAVER

YEOMAN AND AUSTRALIAN ACCLIMATISER: see *AUSTRALASIAN*

YEOMANS, Percival Alfred (1905–1984), mining geologist, agricultural planner, and inventor, born in Harden (NSW), discovered that 'off contour cultivation'—which he

This cover illustration from YOUR GARDEN (1954), titled 'Last Sunday morning', captures the joys of the Australian BACKYARD and hints at a one important group of readers of this popular and long-running GARDEN MAGAZINE.

called The Keyline—provided a sensitive form of WATER manipulation in AGRICULTURE. Many of his ideas were formed following the purchase of 400 hectares at North Richmond (NSW) in 1943. Yeomans devised a sustainable agricultural system based upon storage of water run-off for IRRIGATION, creating within soils a biological environment to increase fertility and minimise use of CHEMICALS, use of tillage equipment with tines, and application of cultivation predicated upon soil fertility enhancement and on-farm water storage. His Keyline System combined development of deep, biologically fertile soil in a systematically designed landscape enabling increased rainfall absorption complemented by stored run-off fed to gravity-powered irrigation. His concept tackled soil erosion and salinity, and increased soil productiveness. His ideas were published in *The Keyline Plan* (1954), *The Challenge of Landscape* (1958), and *Water For Every Farm* (1965), and presented at the Habitat Forum of the United Nations Conference on Human Settlements (1976) in Vancouver, Canada. *The City Forest* (1971) promoted application of his ideas to the urban environment. Yeomans' Keyline Plough received the Prince Philip Design Award (1974). Sons Allan James (b. 1931) and Kenneth Bruce Yeomans (b. 1947), agricultural technologists, continue his ideas and technological innovations.

DAVID JONES

YERONGA PARK, Qld, was gazetted in 1882 as a recreation ground but development did not commence until after the First World War, when part of the land was resumed for soldier settlement. Honour Avenue, an uncommon form of WAR MEMORIAL in Qld, was planted in 1917–19, each tree commemorating a fallen hero from the Stephens district. As part of a rising community awareness of LEISURE time, sporting groups began to apply for leases within the park from the 1920s and a wide range of SPORTS and RECREATION facilities was subsequently established. JODI FRAWLEY

YOUR GARDEN (1947–), published monthly in Melbourne, commenced with foundation editor Ernest E. LORD reflecting on the quickening tempo of Australian life after the war:

> Never before in its history has this country been faced with such a program of expansion of home building. The complement of every home is its garden; but without reliable and simple guidance, much labour is often misdirected. It is the purpose of this journal to supply such guidance.

The magazine's modest octavo size rapidly increased to quarto and, as it incorporated the *Royal Horticultural Society of Victoria Journal* and saw off Melbourne competitor, the *HOME GARDENER*, its horizons expanded to achieve national coverage. The magazine drew on many talented contributors, including leading horticulturists of the period: Jean GALBRAITH, George ALTHOFER, Thistle HARRIS, Edith COLEMAN, Arthur SWABY, and Les Fuaux (on CACTI), with Lord contributing many articles on garden design and maintenance. Australian plants received considerable attention, as Lord had a special interest in promoting their use. In the 1950s dryandras gave way for a time to dahlias as editor William COMEADOW steered the magazine to the majority taste. *Your Garden* consolidated its position in the market during the 1950s and by the 1970s was wearing down its older rival, *AUSTRALIAN GARDEN LOVER*. During the 1950s–70s the back cover sported different colour illustrations of 'another E.H. HAMMOND construction', a marvellous record of this landscaper. *Your Garden*, among the most long-lived Australian garden magazines, acts as a barometer of middle-class taste for those exploring the SUBURBAN GARDEN. RA

ZOOLOGICAL GARDENS Australia's major zoos are defined today by their contribution to the unified objectives of the international community of zoos and wildlife parks. Together the zoo community supports animal conservation and preservation on a global basis as well as providing popular recreational venues. The Australian zoos in this category are Melbourne Zoo, Adelaide Zoo, Sydney's Taronga Zoo, Perth Zoo, and Territory Wildlife Park (NT), together with their outlying properties at Werribee and Healesville (Vic.), Monarto (SA), and Dubbo (NSW).

London Zoo was the model for zoos all over the world. The Zoological Society of London opened their exotic menagerie in 1828 to provide its members with live specimens for scientific study. Soon the curiosity value of exotic animals in a PLEASURE GARDEN setting drew large crowds of members and their friends. Although the immense popularity of London Zoo lasted only ten years, the concept of an urban zoological garden spread. The origins of the Australian zoos followed the international pattern in most respects. Civic leaders established zoos to provide a venue that combined RECREATION, LEISURE, and education. They relied to varying extents on government assistance for land and financial support. In several cases the animals were initially kept in BOTANIC GARDENS. Despite access to a local fauna that was of great interest to scientists in Europe, in Australia scientific study of the animals was not promoted. One unusual feature of the origins of Australian zoos was their close links with the ACCLIMATISATION movement, the purpose of which was to import animals that were not already part of the existing native wildlife or domestic stock. In Melbourne's case, the Zoological Society of Victoria evolved into the highly active and wealthy Acclimatisation Society of Victoria for a number of years before returning to develop a traditional zoo. In Adelaide, Sydney, and Perth the acclimatisation societies came first but their focus quickly shifted towards building zoos.

Two families shaped the early Australian zoos, the Le Souefs and the Minchins. The Le Souef family began its association in 1870 when Albert Alexander Cochrane Le Souef (1828–1902) was appointed secretary (later director) to Melbourne Zoo, and ended in 1939 when his son (Albert) Sherborne (1877–1951) retired from Taronga Zoo; between those dates, two other sons, (William Henry) Dudley (1856–1923) and Ernest Albert (1869–1937), were directors of Melbourne Zoo and Perth Zoo respectively. The Minchins confined themselves to Adelaide, where three generations of the family ran the zoo during 1883–1940.

In their early years, Australian zoos displayed native fauna and exotic animals that were easy to acquire. Lions, tigers, bears, and small monkeys could be purchased from enterprising ships' captains and other travellers at the docks. Other species such as elephants, orang-utans, and giraffes had to be ordered specially and were expensive. Yet by 1920 all of the large species that were available on the market had been displayed in Australian zoos. Side shows and the gardens were as important as the animals in creating a zoo. Elephant, train, and cart rides, refreshments, and even small circuses raised extra funds and drew repeat visits. Flower beds, trees, shrubs, and PICNIC GROUNDS created pleasant walks around the sometimes smelly enclosures. Colourful garden displays also disguised a lack of excitement in the animal collections during lean times.

By the 1920s, the four major Australian zoos were firmly established. Then, like many other zoos around the world, they moved into a period of stagnation. Illustrated publications and greater access to zoos and circuses reduced both the excitement value and the educational role of zoos. In addition other urban attractions were now competing for the attention of families. In the post–Second World War years, only Taronga Zoo was in a position to take advantage of the sudden availability of large numbers of popular African and Asian animals. As the other zoos languished in poverty, there was growing public disquiet with the conditions in which the animals were kept and there were questions about the continued justification for zoos.

In the 1960s, leading zoo administrators opened communications to examine fundamental issues concerning their institutions on a global basis. They identified four objectives for maintaining a public zoo—education, conservation, recreation, and research. Since then, these objectives have given Australian zoos a renewed purpose, popularity, and appearance. The educational function developed quickly with the establishment of successful zoo schools in Adelaide, Taronga, and Melbourne in the late 1960s. Volunteer organisations (such as 'FRIENDS GROUPS') that promoted adult participation followed. Enclosures are now designed to provide information about the animals. Even the selection of animals has shifted as butterflies, meerkats, and other small

Zoological gardens

Inclusion of the word 'garden' in the term ZOOLOGICAL GARDENS reflects the origins of zoos, and whether as ornamental planting (such as this example at South Perth in the 1920s) or more recently as habitat for animals, horticulture forms a major part in zoo management

animals are given prime locations and expensive enclosures. Despite early scepticism about how the zoos could support conservation and research, these objectives have since settled on several levels. High-profile projects attract attention while, behind the scenes, staff contribute to the international information network concerning animal species in their care and environment. Many of the animals on display are considered to be part of a global breeding pool, theoretically removing price tags, and eliminating competition between zoos.

The major zoos have extended beyond their urban property. Wildlife parks and sanctuaries, some pre-existing, have been developed to display animals in different environments. The enclosures are often large and bear a resemblance to the animals' natural habitats, and rely on considerable horticultural expertise. The collections associated with one zoo authority can be distributed through the properties to manage breeding programs and to provide the public with a different—and for some a more acceptable—version of the day out at the zoo.

New South Wales The Zoological Society of New South Wales (established 1879) opened Moore Park Zoo in 1883 on a seven-acre (3 ha) site known as Billy Goat Swamp. The site proved too small and insanitary; in 1902, bubonic plague was detected in the kangaroos and the zoo was closed for four months while feed and building materials were burnt. Rather than persist with that site, plans were made to move the zoo. In 1912, the beautiful harbour site was selected and management of the zoo transferred to Taronga Zoological Park Trust. In 1916 Moore Park Zoo closed when Taronga Zoo was officially opened. Several of Taronga Zoo's earliest enclosures, including that for the lions, were influenced by the innovative barless designs of zoo showman Carl Hagenbeck (1844–1913). In the mid-twentieth century Edward Hallstrom, the refrigerator manufacturer, sponsored collection trips to Africa and other continents, making the zoo's animal collection the most exotic in Australia at the time. Again, however, space became a problem, and in 1977 the Zoological Parks Board of New South Wales (which succeeded the Trust in 1973) opened Western Plains Zoo on a 300-hectare site in Dubbo. This allowed it to display large animals in spacious, moated enclosures. Exhibits now include the African elephant and a breeding group of Black Rhinoceros.

Northern Territory The region's public zoo, Territory Wildlife Park, Darwin, was opened in 1989 by the Territory Conservation Commission. The zoo, set in 400 hectares of bushland, displays only native animals. The magnificent network of habitat-based aviaries is one of its great features, allowing visitors to view birds at tree-top level or by the edge of a swamp. The aquarium is particularly popular as it includes an underwater view of a 3.4 metre saltwater crocodile. Territory Wildlife Park is now managed by the Northern Territory Parks and Wildlife Commission. ALICE SPRINGS DESERT PARK is a recent development.

Queensland Queensland's zoo tradition is based on privately owned sanctuaries that display native animals. Lone Pine Koala Sanctuary was established in 1927 and has since expanded its collection from koalas exclusively, to include kangaroos, wallabies, emus, and other native animals. Currumbin Sanctuary started in 1946 when Alex Griffiths began feeding rainbow lorikeets to distract them from his garden beds. The sanctuary grew from there and in 1976 it was gifted to the National Trust of Queensland. Fleays Wildlife Park, Burleigh, was created in 1952 by David Fleay, formerly from Healesville, and is noted for its platypussary and ornithological displays. It is now government owned. While the Queensland sanctuaries promote contact with animals to appeal to tourists, behind the scenes they contribute significantly to the regional conservation and preservation programs.

South Australia Adelaide Zoo was opened in 1883 by the Royal Zoological Society of South Australia (established 1878). Situated on the River Torrens in the ADELAIDE PARK LANDS, this site retains many fine landscape and architectural features dating from the nineteenth century. Monarto Zoological Park, about seventy kilometres east of Adelaide, was opened in 1993 by the Royal Zoological Society of South Australia.

Tasmania The state's major public zoo was Hobart Municipal Zoo. It was opened in 1922 in the Queens DOMAIN, near GOVERNMENT HOUSE, with a native collection acquired from the estate of Mary Roberts. An elephant, lions, bears, and other traditional zoo animals were added. The Zoo closed in 1953 for financial reasons but its reputation continues as the home of the last thylacine (which died in 1936) to be held in captivity.

Victoria Victoria's network of zoos began with the opening of Melbourne Zoo in 1861 at ROYAL PARK by the Acclimatisation Society of Victoria, formerly the Zoological Society of Victoria (established 1857), which housed its first collection in MELBOURNE BOTANIC GARDENS. Great emphasis was placed on the beauty of the gardens and this tradition has been maintained. In 1937 the management was transferred to the Zoological Board of Victoria. But the mid-century was a difficult period and even the gardens deteriorated. A major modernisation program was begun in the 1960s and since then the Zoo has adopted the 'landscape immersion' enclosure style that uses vegetation rather than concrete to define exhibits. In 1975 the Board established a wildlife park near WERRIBEE PARK to display African savanna species. It was officially opened in 1983 and is now called Victoria's Open Range Zoo at Werribee. The scope of the collection has been extended to include grassland animals from Australia and abroad. The Board expanded its responsibilities in 1978 when it took over the management of Healesville Sanctuary, formerly the Sir Colin MacKenzie Sanctuary (established 1934). The sanctuary specialises in Australian flora and fauna, displaying a range of regional animals in the lush bushland setting. It is internationally renowned for its association with the platypus, a reputation further enhanced by the successful breeding of a pair of platypus in 1999. The three Victorian properties are now managed by the Zoological Parks and Gardens Board of Victoria.

Western Australia Perth Zoo was opened in 1898 by the Western Australian Acclimatisation Committee (established 1897). The fine gardens and landscaping, integral to the Zoo's early history, were developed by Harry Steedman. The magnificent PALM collection was begun then and the Zoo now has forty-five different species, many of great age. Today Perth Zoo is managed by the Zoological Gardens Board of Western Australia.

Catherine de Courcy, *The Zoo Story* (Ringwood, Vic., 1995)

CATHERINE DE COURCY

ZWAR, John (b. 1951), horticulturist, has established a significant role in arid lands amenity horticultural practice and research in SA. Trained at the ADELAIDE BOTANIC GARDEN, he worked at Leigh Creek coalfield, served as curator, National Botanic Garden, Lae (Papua New Guinea), established the City of Port Augusta's Parks and Gardens Department (1975), and, following a Churchill Fellowship, helped establish the AUSTRALIAN ARID LANDS BOTANIC GARDEN (1981). He is now involved in environmental management at Olympic Dam and Roxby Downs for Western Mining Corporation.

Simon Schama, *Landscape and Memory* (London, 1995)

DAVID JONES

Illustration Acknowledgments

All illustrations are taken from the collection of Richard Aitken unless otherwise specified.

Alphabetical headpieces from *Catalogue of the Melbourne Public Library* (1880), State Library of Victoria

p. 3 photograph by Richard Aitken

p. 4 Wynne Evans Collection (PH0063/0021), Northern Territory Library

p. 7 *Adamson's Australian Gardener* (1896)

pp. 8–9 photographs by Richard Stringer (4157/36, 37), (courtesy Howard Tanner)

p. 11 National Trust of Australia (Victoria) collection (courtesy Australian Garden History Society)

p. 13 *Prospectus of the Queensland Agricultural College* (1897), Gatton College collection (courtesy Jeannie Sim)

p. 14 *Air Raid Precautions: Advice to Householders* (1941)

p. 17 Andrew Bent, *Van Diemen's Land Pocket Almanack* (1824), Royal Society of Tasmania collection

p. 19 photograph by Richard Aitken

p. 20 Anderson, Hall & Co., *Seed and Plant Catalogue* (1875), National Agriculture Library, Beltsville, Maryland, USA (courtesy Barney Hutton)

p. 23 *Architecture* (October 1930), (courtesy Jeannie Sim)

p. 25 *School Paper* (1956) from Brian McKinlay (ed.), *School Days* (1985)

p. 27 photograph by Richard Stringer (3403/52), (courtesy Howard Tanner)

p. 29 photograph by Richard Stringer (3524/09), (courtesy Howard Tanner)

p. 31 photograph by John Zwar

p. 32 Fiona Hall, 'Grapefruit (*Citrus paradisi*)' from *Paradisus Terrestris* (1989–90), Australian National Gallery

p. 35 Louisa Atkinson, 'Todea barbara' (detail), Mitchell Library (PXA 4498), State Library of New South Wales

p. 36 James Wales Audas, *Native Trees of Australia* (1934)

pp. 38–9 G.H. Knibbs (ed.), *Federal Handbook, prepared in connection with the eighty-fourth meeting of the British Association for the Advancement of Science* (1914)

p. 40 Watling 19, The Natural History Museum, London (courtesy Historic Houses Trust of New South Wales)

p. 42 Sharkey Collection (SH1433), Government Printing Office, New South Wales (courtesy Historic Houses Trust of New South Wales)

p. 44 *Victorian Architectural Students Society Journal* (April 1911), State Library of Victoria

p. 46 *Yates' Seed Book of What & When to Sow* (c. 1944)

p. 48 photograph by Richard Aitken

p. 50 oblique aerial photograph (c. 1920s)

p. 53 photograph by Jaime Plaza, Royal Botanic Gardens, Sydney (courtesy Wildlight Photo Agency)

p. 55 *Wild Flowers of Australia* (c. 1929) and associated ephemera

p. 57 Glen Wilson, *Landscaping with Australian Plants* (1975)

p. 59 *Australian Home Beautiful* (May 1935)

p. 60 *Australian House and Garden Annual* (1957)

p. 63 Small Picture File (Hobart, Tas.— Parks and gardens—Domain, 1895), Mitchell Library, State Library of New South Wales

p. 65 *Australian House and Garden* (December 1951)

p. 67 photograph by Richard Stringer (3519/21), (courtesy Howard Tanner)

p. 69 Richard T. Baker & Henry G. Smith, *A Research on the Pines of Australia* (1910)

p. 70 *Journal of Horticulture and Cottage Gardener* (15 January 1874), (courtesy Royal Horticultural Society Lindley Library)

p. 72 George Suttor, *Memoirs Historical and Scientific of the Right Honourable Sir Joseph Banks* (1855), Richard Clough collection

p. 74 Val and John Moss, *International Barbecue Cooking* (1973)

p. 77 Edward La Trobe Bateman, 'Plan of Fitzroy Square in the City of Melbourne, Victoria' (detail), 1856–57, VPRS 8168/P1, Unit 157, Plan No. Melb RL 8 (reproduced with the permission of the Keeper of Public Records, Public Record Office Victoria, Australia)

p. 79 Bauer Botanical Number 225, The Natural History Museum, London (courtesy Historic Houses Trust of New South Wales)

p. 81 photograph by Richard Stringer (4138/05), (courtesy Howard Tanner)

p. 83 Small Picture File (Melbourne— Parks and gardens—Exhibition Gardens), Mitchell Library, State Library of New South Wales

p. 85 Watkin family collection (courtesy Australian Garden History Society)

p. 86 George Bennett, *Gatherings of a Naturalist* (1860), Richard Clough collection

p. 89 *Australian Home Beautiful* (November 1930)

p. 90 James Wales Audas, *Native Trees of Australia* (1934)

p. 93 Helen Blaxland, *Flower Pieces* (1946)

p. 94 *Parks and Wildlife* (April 1979)

p. 96 Rippon Lea Estate, National Trust of Australia (Victoria)

p. 99 C.G.S. Hirst, 'Part of the Botanical Gardens at Toowoomba' (1879), reproduced by permission from the City Collection of the Toowoomba Regional Art Gallery

Illustration Acknowledgments

p. 101 Florence Sulman, *Popular Guide to the Wild Flowers of New South Wales* (1913–14)
p. 102 photograph by Richard Aitken
p. 105 photograph by Matt Irwin
p. 107 photograph by Richard Stringer (4159/03), (courtesy Howard Tanner)
p. 109 Royal Society of Tasmania collection
p. 111 T.W.H. Leavitt (ed.), *The Jubilee History of Victoria and Melbourne* (1888), (Barney Hutton collection)
p. 113 Buda collection (P.532), Buda Museum, Castlemaine (Vic.)
p. 115 Geelong Heritage Centre Collection (courtesy George Jones)
p. 117 C. Bogue Luffmann, *Report of the Principal of the School of Horticulture* (1899), courtesy National Trust of Australia (Victoria)
p. 119 Charles Barrett, *From Range to Sea* (1907)
p. 120 *Illustrated Sydney News* (18 May 1878), National Library of Australia (courtesy Barney Hutton)
p. 121 *Building* (June 1910)
p. 123 *Agricultural Gazette of New South Wales* (September 1898)
p. 125 Historic Places ACT
p. 127 Keith Winser, *Australian Caravan and Touring Manual* (1961)
p. 129 Carrick Hill collection
p. 131 Tasmaniana Library (AUTAS001125641449), State Library of Tasmania
p. 133 Mitchell Library, State Library of New South Wales (courtesy Australian Garden History Society)
p. 137 Joyce Gilbert Collection (PH0048/0057), Northern Territory Library
p. 139 *Chinese Australian Herald* (1910), (courtesy Richard Clough)
p. 141 *Royal Commission on the Improvement of Sydney and its Suburbs* (1909), (courtesy Robert Freestone)
p. 143 La Trobe Collection (LTA 715 f.13), State Library of Victoria
p. 147 A.F. [sic] Cole, *The Bouquet: Australian Flower Garden Guide* (c. 1914)
p. 150 photograph by Chris Bell (courtesy Torquil Canning)
p. 152 photograph by Richard Stringer (5334/03)
p. 155 Photo 23/6A, Eastern Goldfields Historical Society Inc., Kalgoorlie (WA)
p. 156 photograph by Richard Stringer (3524/22)
p. 158 National Trust of Australia (Victoria) collection (courtesy Rippon Lea Estate)
p. 161 David Dunstan collection
p. 163 Holtermann Collection (ON 4, Box 10, No. 70154), Mitchell Library, State Library of New South Wales
p. 165 photograph by Lynette Zeeng
p. 167 *Australian Home Beautiful* (April 1934)
p. 169 photograph by Richard Aitken
p. 171 William Curtis, *Lectures on Various Subjects* (1805)
p. 173 photograph by Richard Aitken
p. 174 William Dampier, *A Voyage to New Holland, &c. In the Year 1699* (1703), Mitchell Library, State Library of New South Wales
p. 177 Foelsche Collection (Series F399, item 25), Northern Territory Archives Service
p. 178 Garden Clubs of Australia Inc. collection
p. 181 photograph by Richard Aitken
p. 183 Myer family collection (courtesy Stella Barber)
p. 186 C. Cartwright, 'Plan of the Governor's Demesne Land' (1816), Mitchell Library (Z M3 811.172/1816/1), State Library of New South Wales
p. 189 photograph by Richard Stringer (3914/39), (courtesy Howard Tanner)
p. 190 *Australian Home Beautiful* (September 1924)
p. 192 John Dwight, *Gardening Handbook* (1957)
p. 195 PIC/3010/1-70 LOC Album 939, National Library of Australia
p. 197 Alan Edmunds, *Espalier Fruit Trees* (c. 1946)
p. 199 printed postcard (c. 1910)
p. 201 [engraving after Edward Hopley], 'A Primrose from England' (1858), National Trust of Australia (Victoria) collection (courtesy Rippon Lea Estate)
p. 205 Labillardière, *Relation du voyage à la recherche La Pérouse* (1800), Richard Clough collection
p. 207 Mitchell Library, State Library of New South Wales
p. 210 La Trobe Collection, State Library of Victoria
p. 213 *Niven's Guidebook and Souvenir of Ballarat* (1885), La Trobe Collection, State Library of Victoria
p. 214 *Ballarat Begonia Festival Souvenir Pictorial* (1966)
p. 217 reproduced from *Australian Horticulture* (September 1986)
p. 218 Arthur H. Davis ('Steele Rudd'), *On Our Selection* (1899)
p. 219 Ferdinandus de Mueller, *Fragmenta Phytographiae Australiae* (vol. VII, 1869–71)
p. 221 National Library of Australia
p. 222 published photograph (c. 1960s)
p. 225 Norman Sparnon, *The Poetry of Leaves* (1970)
p. 227 PIC/3010/1-70 LOC Album 939, National Library of Australia
p. 228 photograph by Trisha Dixon
p. 230 photograph by Richard Aitken
p. 233 Botanic Gardens of Adelaide Archive Collection
p. 235 photograph by Richard Aitken
p. 237 Australian Publicity Council, *Liquid Gold: Australia* (1959)
p. 238 *Illustrated Catalogue of Goods Manufactured and Supplied by W. Cooper* (1893)
p. 239 *Australian House and Garden* (July 1954)
p. 241 Jean Galbraith, *Garden in a Valley* (1939)
p. 245 photograph reproduced from *Australian Garden Journal* (May/June 1983)
p. 246 Robert Freestone collection
p. 249 J.H. Maiden, *A Guide to the Botanic Gardens, Sydney* (1903)
p. 251 *South Australian Horticulturist* (March 1856), State Library of South Australia
p. 253 Mark McWha and Associates
p. 255 *Australian Builders and Contractors News* (13 April 1889), State Library of Victoria
p. 257 *Yates Garden Guide* (1960)
p. 259 E.B. Heyne, *The Amateur Gardener* (1881)
p. 261 S.T. Gill (Australia 1818–1880), 'Prospect House, the seat of J.B. Graham, Esq., near Adelaide, South Australia' (1850), watercolour and gouache on paper, 40.3 x 68.2 cm, Gift of Mrs F.M. Graham and family, 1947, Art Gallery of South Australia
p. 263 photograph by Richard Aitken
p. 267 Federal Parliamentary Visit 1912 (PH0100/0041), Northern Territory Library
p. 269 photograph by Richard Stringer (3301/06), (courtesy Howard Tanner)

Illustration Acknowledgments

p. 271 photograph by Richard Stringer (1861/41)

p. 273 Small Picture File (BM), Mitchell Library, State Library of New South Wales

p. 276 Eric Nicholls collection (courtesy Marie Nicholls)

p. 278 photograph by Richard Stringer (3888/29), (courtesy Howard Tanner)

p. 279 Howard Tanner collection

p. 281 Royal Botanic Gardens Melbourne collection

p. 282 *Garden Gazette* (December 1902), Royal Botanic Gardens Sydney collection

p. 287 Hamilton Art Gallery (Vic.)

p. 291 photograph by Richard Stringer (3512/02), (courtesy Howard Tanner)

p. 293 Buda collection, Buda Museum, Castlemaine (Vic.)

p. 294 National Trust of Australia (Victoria) collection

p. 297 Desmond Herbert, *Gardening in Warm Climates* (1952)

p. 299 La Trobe Collection (H94.23), State Library of Victoria

p. 300 E.B. Heyne, *The Amateur Gardener* (1881)

p. 302 artist unknown, 'Highfield, Circular-head', Allport Library and Museum of Fine Arts, Hobart

p. 303 JOL 46967, John Oxley Library

p. 305 Albert John Hockings, *Queensland Garden Manual* (1865), Mitchell Library, State Library of New South Wales

p. 307 B.C. Mettam Collection (PH0429/0128), National Territory Library

p. 309 Frederick Kruger (born Germany 1831, arrived in Australia 1860s, died 1888), 'A view of the You Yangs from Lara Plains', albumen silver photograph, 18.4 x 27.3 cm, Gift of Mrs Beryl M. Curl, 1979, National Gallery of Victoria

p. 312 9779P, courtesy Battye Library

p. 314 artist unknown, 'Opening of the Launceston Horticultural Fete' (1847), watercolour on paper 9.4 x 13.3 cm, 1976/75/18, Queen Victoria Museum and Art Gallery, Launceston (Tas.)

p. 318 *Home Gardener* (January 1927)

p. 321 E.A. Hughes, *Every Amateur's Gardening Guide* (c. 1931)

p. 322 Conrad Martens, 'Cressfield' (1862), Simpson family collection (courtesy Caroline Simpson)

p. 327 SRA Photo 974/10 NID, State Rail Authority of New South Wales (courtesy Chris Betteridge)

p. 329 *Buzacott's Gates & Fences* (c. 1918)

p. 331 printed postcard (c. 1910)

p. 333 photograph by Richard Stringer (4155/02), (courtesy Howard Tanner)

p. 335 H.A. James, *Handbook of Australian Horticulture* (1892), Richard Clough collection

p. 337 photograph by Richard Aitken

p. 339 Geelong Heritage Centre Collection

p. 341 photograph by Richard Aitken

p. 343 Edward Kemp, *How to Lay out a Garden* (1858)

p. 345 photograph by Richard Stringer (4136/23), (courtesy Howard Tanner)

p. 346 photograph by Oline Richards

p. 347 photograph by Richard Stringer (3535/29), (courtesy Howard Tanner)

p. 349 Moyne Shire (courtesy Helen Doyle)

p. 350 *Australian Women's Weekly* (18 April 1973), reproduced by courtesy of the *Australian Women's Weekly*

p. 352 La Trobe Collection (H10765), State Library of Victoria

p. 354 Hassell Pty Ltd

p. 357 Small Picture File (Bush life—Victoria), Mitchell Library, State Library of New South Wales

p. 360 Langbecker family collection

p. 362 Edward La Trobe Bateman, 'View of the larger rockery' (1854), La Trobe Collection (H98.135/11), State Library of Victoria

p. 364 lawn mower brochure for Ogden Industries Pty Ltd, Huntingdale (Vic.) (c. 1960)

p. 368 photograph by Richard Aitken

p. 369 Leonard Meagher, *The New Art of Gardening* (1697), Royal Society of Tasmania collection

p. 370 Betty Maloney, Jean Walker, and Barbara Mullins, *All About Australian Bush Gardens* (1973)

p. 374 John G. Lockley, *Rose Growing Made Easy* (1907), Tasmaniana Library, State Library of Tasmania

p. 376 photograph by Richard Aitken

p. 378 J.C. Loudon, *Arboretum et Fruticetum Britannicum* (2nd ed., 1844)

p. 380 *Victoria: The Year Book of Agriculture* (1905)

p. 384 Plan drawn by Michael Lehany for the Public Works Department of New South Wales

p. 387 Charles McIntosh, *Book of the Garden* (1853–55)

p. 389 drawing reproduced from *Landscape Australia* (November 1981)

p. 391 Mitchell Library, State Library of New South Wales (courtesy Historic Houses Trust of New South Wales)

p. 393 *Queenslander* (6 June 1896), John Oxley Library (courtesy Jeannie Sim)

p. 395 Royal Botanic Gardens Sydney collection

pp. 396–97 Betty Maloney and Jean Walker, *Designing Australian Bush Gardens* (1966), (courtesy Jean Walker)

p. 401 Foelsche Collection (Series F399, item 36), Northern Territory Archives Service

p. 403 courtesy Trisha Dixon

p. 406 Peggy Hicks collection, Birmingham, England (courtesy Sandra Pullman)

p. 407 Mary Morton Allport, 'Mrs Meredith 1856' (1856), Allport Library and Museum of Fine Arts

p. 411 Helen Doyle collection

p. 413 Elyne Mitchell, *Australian Treescapes* (1950)

p. 415 John Oxley Library

p. 417 William Elliott, *Cole's Australasian Gardening and Domestic Floriculture* (1897)

p. 419 *Australian Picture Pleasure Book* (1857), National Library of Australia

p. 420 Aitken family collection

p. 421 La Trobe Collection (H31045/84), State Library of Victoria

p. 423 La Trobe Collection (H5057), State Library of Victoria

p. 425 photograph by Brian Hatfield, National Trust of Australia (Victoria) collection

p. 426 John Oxley Library (courtesy Australian Garden History Society)

p. 427 cabinet photograph (c. 1910)

p. 429 John and Ray Oldham, *Gardens in Time* (1980)

p. 431 *Australian Rose Annual* (1929)

p. 432 Marjorie Barnard, *Macquarie's World* (1947)

p. 434 *Australian Home Beautiful* (June 1929)

p. 436 C.F. Newman and Son catalogue (1894–95), reproduced from Robert F.G. Swinbourne, *Years of Endeavour* (1982)

p. 438 National Trust of Australia (New South Wales), (courtesy Colleen Morris)

Illustration Acknowledgments

p. 440 Mitchell Library, State Library of New South Wales
p. 443 Ellis Rowan, *A Flower-hunter in Queensland & New Zealand* (1898)
p. 444 *Australian Home Beautiful* (February 1961)
p. 446 B.C. Mettam Collection (PH0429/0046), Northern Territory Library
p. 449 Rex Nan Kivell Collection (NK9593/10), National Library of Australia
p. 450 photograph by Richard Aitken
p. 452 photograph by Richard Stringer (4145/22), (courtesy Howard Tanner)
p. 455 La Trobe Collection (H35065), State Library of Victoria
p. 457 Mitchell Library (ML PXA 609/155), State Library of New South Wales
p. 460 Hermannsburg Historical Precinct Collection, Hermannsburg (Ntaria) Council
p. 462 Robert Nicol collection
p. 465 Sharkey Collection, Government Printing Office of New South Wales (courtesy Historic Houses Trust of New South Wales)
p. 466 cabinet photograph (*c.* 1866)
p. 469 photograph by Richard Stringer (3892/12), (courtesy Howard Tanner)
p. 470 E.E. Pescott bookplate (*c.* 1930s)
p. 471 *South Australian Homes and Gardens* (January 1949)
p. 475 Holtermann Collection, Mitchell Library, State Library of New South Wales
p. 478 Blue Dandenongs Gladioli Farm, *Striking Gladioli* (1953)
p. 481 Sydney City Council Archives (CRS 684 P445/5), (courtesy Colleen Morris)
p. 482 Royal Society of Tasmania collection
p. 483 Plumridge family collection (courtesy Helen Botham)
p. 485 *Fourth Annual Mersey Valley Apple Festival* (1959), Tasmaniana Library, State Library of Tasmania
p. 487 photograph by Donald Seto (courtesy Margaret and Jan Seto)
p. 488 Community History Department (QVM:1983:P:1080), Queen Victoria Museum and Art Gallery, Launceston (Tas.)
p. 489 *Journal of Australasia* (July 1856)
p. 491 printed postcard (*c.* 1907), Silas Clifford-Smith collection

p. 492 *Australian Parks*, February 1969
p. 493 National Trust of Australia (Victoria) collection
p. 494 W.J. Purves, seed catalogue (1899)
p. 496 *Architecture and Arts* (April 1957)
p. 498 photograph by Richard Aitken
p. 500 S.H. Hunt, *Gardening Simplified* (1934)
p. 503 Christine Garnaut collection
p. 504 Humphry Repton, Red Book for Compton Place, Sussex, England (1803), Chatsworth House, Derbyshire, England, photograph by Richard Aitken (finger courtesy Nicola Spasoff)
p. 506 Wolfgang Sievers, [Man planting trees], Alcoa Anglesea (Vic.), (1977), PIC P1511/2, National Library of Australia
p. 509 *South Australian Homes and Gardens* (July 1948)
p. 511 La Trobe Collection (H39357/154), State Library of Victoria
p. 513 *Queenslander* (5 March 1910), John Oxley Library
p. 514 *Architecture and Arts* (October 1960)
p. 517 Richard Schomburgk, *Catalogue of the Plants under Cultivation in the Government Botanic Garden, Adelaide, South Australia* (1878), Burnley College Library
p. 519 Rossi family collection (courtesy Lois Gothard)
p. 520 photograph by Ray Joyce (courtesy Historic Houses Trust of New South Wales)
p. 523 printed postcard (*c.* 1912), Silas Clifford-Smith collection
p. 525 drawing by Ron Jones
p. 528 Francis Nixon, *The Cruise of the Beacon* (1857), extra-illustrated copy, Allport Library and Museum of Fine Arts
p. 529 Duncan Elphinstone Cooper, 'View from window of hut, Challicum, 1850', PIC R304, National Library of Australia
p. 531 Robert Oliver Collection, Hamilton Historical Society (Vic.)
p. 532 Mitchell Library (GPO2-14477), State Library of New South Wales
p. 535 Mitchell Library (ML PXA 609/131, State Library of New South Wales
p. 537 photograph by Richard Aitken
p. 539 Education History Unit, Department of Education and Training, Victoria

p. 542 photograph by Richard Stringer (4184/01), (courtesy Howard Tanner)
p. 543 *Searl's Key to Australian Gardening* (1922)
p. 544 S.T. Gill, 'Spring' (*c.* 1847), PIC R3304, National Library of Australia
p. 546 photograph by Richard Stringer (2669/4)
p. 549 *Illustrated London News* (28 August 1886), State Library of Victoria (courtesy Australian Garden History Society)
p. 550 Mitchell Library (ML Z PDX 390), State Library of New South Wales
p. 553 drawing by Vladimir Sitta (courtesy Australian Garden History Society)
p. 557 *Australian Plants* (June 1961)
p. 558 James Britten, *Illustrations of Australian Plants Collected in 1770* (1900–05), Richard Clough collection
p. 561 *Pictures of the Floral Pageant held in connection with S.A. Centenary Celebrations 1836–1936* (1936)
p. 563 *Queenslander* (19 June 1897), John Oxley Library (courtesy Australian Garden History Society)
p. 566 Geelong Heritage Centre Collection
p. 567 Baillieu Library, University of Melbourne
p. 570 *The Wombat* (August 1895)
p. 572 private collection
p. 574 John Ednie Brown, *A Practical Treatise on Tree Culture in South Australia* (1881), Richard Clough collection
p. 576 Subiaco Museum (courtesy Australian Garden History Society)
p. 578 Howard Arkley, *Family Home: Suburban Exterior* (1993), synthetic polymer paint on canvas, 203 x 254 cm, Monash University Collection (courtesy Monash University Museum of Art and Kalli Rolfe Contemporary Art), © Estate of Howard Arkley
p. 580 photograph by Richard Stringer (3503/14), (courtesy Howard Tanner)
p. 583 *Australian Sweet Pea Annual* (1918)
p. 584 *Journal of the Royal Victorian Institute of Architects* (December 1939–January 1940)
p. 585 Ferdinand Mueller, *Annual Report of the Government Botanist and Director of the Botanic Garden* (1865)
p. 588 Archer family collection (courtesy Richard Archer)

Illustration Acknowledgments

p. 591 *Andersons Garden Book and Catalogue* (1957)

p. 593 Brian Webster collection (courtesy National Trust of Australia (Victoria), Rippon Lea Estate)

p. 595 *Eric Worrell's Australian Reptile Park* (1975)

p. 597 William Tibbits, 'Ginahgulla' (1879), John Fairfax Ltd (courtesy Historic Houses Trust of New South Wales)

p. 599 Lady [Deborah] Hackett (ed.), *The Australian Household Guide* (1916)

p. 600 *Royal Commission on the Improvement of Sydney and its Suburbs* (1909), (courtesy Robert Freestone)

p. 602 La Trobe Collection (LTAF 5, p. 32D), State Library of Victoria

p. 605 Greenwood Gillstrom Collection, National Library of Australia

p. 606 *Catalogue of the First Australian Exhibition of Women's Work* (1907)

p. 607 photograph by Richard Aitken

p. 613 AA CA 6843, C2829/1, Australian Archives (courtesy Andrea Gaynor)

p. 615 Roy Edwards Collection (PH0274/0617), Northern Territory Library

p. 616 photograph by Richard Aitken

p. 619 Archives Office of Tasmania

p. 621 photograph by Richard Aitken

p. 623 William Tibbits, 'Wairoa' (1897), Marbury School, Stirling (SA), photograph by Richard Stringer (3520/27)

p. 625 *Australian Women's Mirror* (21 July 1925)

p. 627 E.B. Heyne, *The Amateur Gardener* (1881)

p. 629 Small Picture File (BM), Mitchell Library, State Library of New South Wales

p. 631 photograph by Richard Stringer (2949/01), (courtesy Howard Tanner)

p. 633 Archibald James Campbell, *Golden Wattle* (1921)

p. 636 *West Australian Gardener* (April 1946)

p. 637 Barbara Evans Collection (courtesy Oline Richards)

p. 640 Weston family collection (courtesy John Gray)

p. 643 *Bankers' Magazine of Australasia* (1897–98), Royal Botanic Gardens Melbourne collection

p. 645 Baillieu Library, University of Melbourne

p. 647 photograph by Richard Aitken

p. 649 printed postcard (*c.* 1968)

p. 650 Charles McIntosh, *Book of the Garden* (1853–55)

p. 651 photograph by Richard Aitken

p. 653 photograph by Simon Griffiths

p. 656 *Australian House and Garden Annual* (1955)

p. 658 *Your Garden* (May 1954)

p. 660 Photo No. P121-32, Perth Zoo Collection (courtesy Oline Richards)

Index of Gardens

Abbotsford House, 655
Abercairny, 387
Aberfeldie, 18
Aberglasslyn, 321
Abney Park Cemetery, 132
Acacias, The, 4, 510, 560
Adelaide Botanic Garden, 5, 7, 8, 10, 34, 43, 51, 66, 67, 68, 80, 82, 98, 114, 118, 124, 131, 158, 161, 178, 192, 195, 196, 198, 232, 233, 250, 259, 261, 263, 268, 307, 377, 383, 389, 401, 417, 421, 460, 509, 517, 537, 538, 541, 546, 560, 584, 585, 654, 661
Adelaide Cricket Ground, 565
Adelaide Festival Centre, 80
Adelaide Oval, 10, 160
Adelaide Park Lands, 4, 9, 10, 28, 107, 114, 161, 185, 198, 249, 269, 272, 371, 467, 468, 509, 561, 600, 640
Adelaide Public Cemetery, 640
Adelaide Zoo, 10, 383, 659, 661
Admiralty House, 10, 19, 269, 347, 395, 639
Aeolia, 10
Ainslie Village, 630, 646
Albert Park, 14, 642
Albion Park, 482
Albury Botanic Gardens, 14, 98, 282
Aldenham Park, 604
Aldridge Lodge, 16
Alexander Jolly Park, 339
Alexander Park, 150, 235
Alexandra Avenue, 101
Alexandra Gardens, see Domain (Melbourne)
Alexandra Park, 371
Alfred Nicholas Memorial Gardens, 116
Alhambra, 408
Alice Springs Airport Garden, 30
Alice Springs Desert Park, 15, 30, 49, 57, 446, 661
Alnwick Castle, 509
Altdorf Botanic Gardens, 259
Althorp Park, 583
Alton, 18, 116, 156, 291, 422, 441, 590

Altyre, 80, 552
Amalgamated Wireless of Australia Gardens, 151
Ancanthe, 234, 283, 589
Anfield Cemetery, 342
Anlaby, 22, 376, 517, 561
Annandale Estate, 437
Anzac Highway, 272
Anzac Hostel, 341
Anzac Memorial Avenue, 88
Anzac Parade, 141, 146
Anzac Square, 22, 141, 425, 497
Appian Way, 439
Araluen, 24, 638
Arbury Park, 561
Archerfield, 596
Ard Choille, 28, 29, 590
Ardgarten, 29, 626, 639
Ardoch, 23
Ardoe House, 386
Argyle Place, 280
Argyle Square, 323
Arnold Arboretum, 641
Arrowfield, 321
Art Gallery of New South Wales, 515
Arthur McElhone Reserve, 87, 627
Arthurs Seat, 375, 385
Arundel Model Farm, 208
Ascot Garden Suburb, 310
Ascot Racecourse, 499
Ashcombe, 404
Ashton Park, 104
Athelstone, 280
Australian Arid Lands Botanic Garden, 30, 31, 48, 51, 57, 99, 417, 562, 654, 661
Australian Defence Force Academy, 389
Australian Embassy, Bangkok, 389
Australian Embassy, Paris, 389
Australian Inland Botanic Gardens, 30, 61, 99, 654
Australian National Botanic Gardens, 48, 56, 62, 92, 96, 99, 100, 477, 490, 512, 531, 650
Australian National Gallery Sculpture Garden, 542

Australian National University, 398, 490, 531, 610
Australian Reptile Park, 595
Australian Road Research Centre, 398
Australian War Memorial, 490, 628
Avenue of Honour (Ballarat), 150, 153

Babworth House, 239, 277, 310, 504
Bagh-I-Iram, 408
Ball Green, 19
Ballantyre, 559
Ballara, 69
Ballarat Botanic Gardens, 68, 69, 70, 82, 159, 187, 200, 213, 214, 223, 263, 375, 404, 451, 465, 541, 555
Ballarat Hospital, 441
Banongill, 73, 638
Banool, 282
Barmera, 509
Barn, The, 89
Baroona, 175, 321
Barragunda, 78
Barton Vale, 89
Barunah Plains, 76, 638
Basildon New Town, 146
Basin Banks, 278
Bathurst Island, 410
Battersea Park, 82
Beagle Bay, 410
Beaudesert, 128
Beaufront, 81, 409, 626
Beaumont, 81, 144, 177
Bebeah, 81, 94
Beckett Park, 399
Bedervale, 240
Beechwood, 8, 83, 158, 560, 641
Beechworth Cemetery, 83, 132
Belair National Park, 9, 66, 84, 107, 144, 272, 304, 404, 430
Belair State Forest Nursery, 560
Beleura, 84, 619
Bella Vista, 84
Belltrees, 321
Belmont Park, 332
Belmont, 85, 482
Belmore Park, 20, 141

Index of Gardens

Belodun Point, 263
Benalla Botanic Gardens, 503, 535
Bend, The, 174
Bendles, 626
Bendora Dam, 146
Benwell, 178
Berkeley Vale, 8, 461
Berlin Botanic Gardens, 259
Berri, 509, 561
Bethune, 559
Beverley Hills, 584
Bicentennial Park, 150, 353
Bickleigh Vale, 19, 33, 61, 88, 89, 442, 626
Biddulph Grange, 187, 516
Big Banana, 594
Big Pineapple, 594
Binna Burra Resort, 351, 353
Birkenhead Park, 342, 419, 451, 466, 547
Birksgate, 83
Birrarung Marr, 655, 656
Bishopscourt (Sydney), 418
Bishopscourt (Melbourne), 121, 332, 435
Bishopstowe, 527
Black Dolphin Motel, 657
Black Hill Native Flora Park, 467
Blackrock, 559
Blaise Castle, 289
Bleak House, 331
Blenheim House, 633
Blenheim, 595
Blue Lagoon Caravan Court, 127
Blue Mist, 559
Blue Mountains National Park, 94, 95
Bodalla, 418
Bodington, 253
Bodnant, 624
Bold Venture, 260
Bolobek, 365, 553, 626
Bontharambo, 96, 97, 154, 229
Boode House, 8, 640
Boodjamooling, 322
Boogadah, 559
Bookmark Biosphere Reserve, 509
Boomanoomana, 611
Boomerang, 164, 399, 548
Boortkoi, 97, 464, 639
Boroondara Cemetery, 97, 132, 339, 493, 592
Borrinyallock South, 73
Botanic Park, 5, 7, 10, 417
Bothwell Castle, 596
Bougainvillea Gardens, 101
Bourke, 247
Bowen Park, 5, 13, 67, 86, 88, 101, 102, 105, 207, 394, 416, 425, 426, 449, 475, 496, 563, 606
Bowood, 211

Boxford, 52
Boyce Gardens and Rainforest, 103, 175
Boyle Farm, 482
BP Administration Building, 235
Braemar, 18
Braemar House, 590
Braemark, 61
Bramford Hall, 159
Brest Botanic Gardens, 231
Bretton Hall, 401, 509
Brickendon, 25, 27, 409, 588
Brickfields Reserve, 495
Brisbane Botanic Gardens, 5, 14, 41, 43, 49, 67, 68, 87, 88, 98, 103, 104, 105, 131, 158, 164, 185, 234, 247, 263, 267, 302, 303, 315, 325, 369, 375, 389, 392, 393, 402, 449, 456, 460, 467, 475, 495, 496, 580, 602, 606, 641, 644
Brisbane Crematorium and Gardens of Remembrance, 293
Broadlees, 9, 66, 106, 161, 418, 561
Broadmeadows Army Establishment, 179
Brockenhurst, 106
Brompton Cemetery, 132
Bronte House, 106, 438, 577
Brookvale, 583
Broome Courthouse Garden, 106
Brownlow Hill, 40, 390, 392, 438, 454, 548, 577, 646
Bryant and May Gardens, 151
Buchan Caves, 132, 371
Buda, 64, 112, 113, 293, 325, 607, 619
Bundaleer, 80
Bundaleer Forest Nursery, 114, 560, 568, 647
Bungalow, The, 637
Bungaree, 114
Burlington, 26
Burnham Beeches, 19, 116, 371, 442, 604
Burnley Gardens, 12, 13, 116, 144, 147, 207, 229, 235, 316, 381, 435, 483, 541, 656
Burrendong Arboretum, 18, 25
Burrundulla, 164
Burrungurroolong, 117
Burswood, 76, 117, 296, 619, 638
Burswood Park, 117
Burwood, 407
Bushy Park, 15
Bythorne, 8, 511, 641

Cairn Lodge, 527
Cairns Botanic Gardens, 98, 124, 216
Cairns State Forest Nurseries, 568
Cairo flats, 23, 411
Calcutta Botanic Gardens, 325
Callan Park Mental Asylum, 319

Calleen, 559
Calthorpes' House, 14, 52, 124, 619
Camberwell Girls Grammar School, 235
Cambria, 452
Camden Park, 40, 41, 73, 92, 103, 118, 123, 125, 147, 211, 261, 309, 383, 385, 392, 438, 443, 504, 507, 510, 548, 549, 620, 644, 646
Camelot, 590
Cameron Lodge, 422
Cameron Offices, 515
Campbelltown State (Forest) Nursery, 395, 639
Camperdown Botanic Gardens, 282, 638
Canberra, 51, 63, 124, 140, 146, 168, 247, 275, 352, 355, 431, 444, 490, 601, 610, 620
Canberra Airport, 178
Cape Arid National Park, 254
Cape Don Lighthouse, 139
Cape Town Botanic Gardens, 573
Carlton Gardens, 78, 83, 127, 231, 279, 323, 404, 590
Carminow, 8, 127, 560
Carn Brea, 371
Carngham, 76
Carrick Hill, 128, 129, 518, 542, 561
Carrington Hotel, 95
Carthona, 411, 504, 577
Cascade Brewery Gardens, 151
Cascade Tea Garden, 129
Castle Hill, 375
Castlecrag, 19, 45, 119, 129, 130, 246, 247, 276, 439, 444, 515, 566
Castlemaddie, 16
Castlemaine Botanic Gardens, 130, 187, 475
Catani Gardens, 80
Cataract Gorge, 130, 131, 376, 386, 474, 488, 530
Caulfield Park, 483
Centenary Place, 133
Centennial Park, 133, 134, 135, 150, 231, 249, 352, 416, 438, 439, 443, 451, 480, 490, 600, 627
Central Park, 354, 443, 451, 490
Chadstone Shopping Centre, 569
Challicum Station, 529
Charlton, 121
Chatsworth (Brighton, Vic.), 135
Chatsworth (Derbyshire, England) 78, 135, 186, 201, 211, 273, 342, 508
Chatsworth House, 135, 638
Chelsea Physic Garden, 509, 595
Cheltenham Racecourse, 641
Cheppen, 559
Cheshunt, 26
Chestnuts, The, 9

669

Index of Gardens

Chislehurst, 310
Chiswick, 173, 201, 342, 371, 466, 523, 524, 540, 596
Chiswick House, 466
Christ Church Grounds (Longford), 139, 409
Christchurch Gardens, 377
Church Missionary Society Mission, 4
Church Square, 488, 567
Churston, 287
Cintra, 140, 619
Circular Quay, 150, 204
City Beach, 310
City Botanic Gardens, 105
City Park, 141, 187, 296, 314, 315, 386, 589, 623
Claremont, 142, 151, 247, 381, 387, 589
Clarendon, 106, 142, 409
Clarens, 454
Cleland Conservation Park, 144
Clendon, 23
Cliff Gardens, 22
Cliff Grounds, 386; see also Cataract Gorge
Cliffe, The, 637
Clifton, 543
Clifton Park, 231
Cliveden, 160, 224, 592
Cliveden Mansions, 23
Cloudehill, 296
Cockburn Sound, 179
Cockington Green, 404
Coffs Harbour Botanic Gardens, 650
Colac Botanic Gardens, 114, 146, 282, 638
Colesbourne Park, 483
Collingwood, 106
Collingwood Community Garden, 153
Collins Park, 639
Colonel Light Gardens, 149, 247, 503, 561, 601
Colonial Williamsburg, 594
Comfort Hill, 563
Commonwealth Avenue, 110
Commonwealth Park, 51, 152, 168, 431, 432, 490
Como, 11, 153, 154, 175, 509, 571, 590, 597, 607, 655
Coney Island, 482
Conifers, The, 406
Connorville, 409
Coochin Coochin, 158
Coogee Beach Plaza, 389
Cook Park, 159, 465
Cook's Cottage, 134
Cooktown Botanic Gardens, 159
Coolibah, 107, 159
Coolmore, 321

Coolringdon, 159
Coolum, 505
Coombe Cottage, 84, 121, 159, 160, 584
Coonawarra Fruit Colony, 160
Co-operative Flats, 23
Coranderrk, 410
Corin Dam, 146
Cork Botanic Garden, 189, 328
Cornelian Bay Cemetery, 132, 160, 534
Cornerways, 89
Cottage, The, 384
Cottesloe War Memorial Town Hall and Civic Centre, 163
Craig-Ard, 641
Craigend, 411, 592, 649
Craigow, 165
Cranbrook, 165, 166, 266, 395, 462, 627
Cranlana, 165, 167, 182, 183
Cremorne Gardens, 118, 332, 404, 656
Cremorne Gardens (Kalgoorlie), 482
Cremorne Gardens (London), 481
Cremorne Gardens (Melbourne), 481
Cremorne Gardens (Perth), 482
Cremorne Gardens (Rockhampton), 597
Cremorne Gardens (Sydney), 481
Cressbrook, 166, 234, 563
Cressfield, 322
Cross, The, 298
Cruden Farm, 425, 622, 625
Crumpford, 18
Crystal Palace, 91, 133, 206, 292
Crystal Palace Gardens, 82
Crystal Palace Grounds, 186
Currumbin Sanctuary, 661
Curtin University of Technology, 610

Daceyville, 247
Dalkeith, 310, 387, 540, 596, 655
Dalvui, 174, 282, 422, 638
Dalwood, 321
Darling Gardens, 510
Darling Harbour, 353, 376, 488
Darwin Botanic Gardens, 3, 15, 98, 106, 176, 177, 193, 196, 292, 307, 308, 314, 445, 460, 605
Darwin Town Plan, 387
Dawson's Cactus Garden, 124, 179
Deakin Avenue, 101
Deakin University, 502
Dean Park, 559
Décor Corporation Factory, 228
Delatite, 180
Delhi Square, 289
Delhi Villa, 112, 325
Denbigh, 181, 646
Denham Court, 110
Dennarque, 94, 182

Derby Arboretum, 78, 466
Derriweit Heights, 41, 282, 519
Derry & Tom's Department Store, 515
Devon Cottage, 89
Devon Park Estate, 451
Devonshire House, 78
Devorgilla, 590
Disneyland, 152, 594
Domain (Brisbane), 105, 267
Domain (Hobart), 1, 185, 589, 661
Domain (Melbourne), 18, 63, 130, 141, 150, 154, 167, 185, 187, 223, 268, 337, 371, 427, 510, 536, 626, 655
Domain (Perth), 185
Domain (Sydney), 40, 63, 108, 126, 186, 267, 340, 357, 415, 416, 480, 526, 573, 603, 626
Domain Park Flats, 23, 514
Doogallook, 309
Dookie, 12
Doomben Racecourse, 499
Downderry, 89
Downton, 474
Drake's Brook State Forest Nursery, 568
Drapers Hall, 641
Dreamland, 482
Dreamworld, 594
Drumlanrig, 540, 596, 639
Dublin Botanic Gardens, 644
Dulwich House, 561
Dunecht, 386
Dunedin, 241
Duneira, 190, 422
Dunottar Castle, 596
Duntroon, 51, 191, 404
Duntryleague, 465
Durham Hall, 191
Durrol, 191, 422, 626
Dutch East India Company Botanic Garden, 10
Dutch War Cemetery, 470
Dyeworks Park, 149, 253
Dyrham Park, 596

Eagle Farm Racecourse, 499
Eaglemont, 276
East India Company's Garden, Calcutta, 265
East Perth Cemeteries, 636
East Perth Park, 495
East Point Reserve, 193
East Sale RAAF Base, 179
East Talgai, 193
Eastern Beach, 193
Eastern Freeway, 287
Eastern Park, 256, 499
Eastnor Castle, 554
Echo Point, 375

Index of Gardens

Edensor, 466
Edrington, 18
Eildon Reservoir, 352
Elder Park, 4, 10, 71, 80, 198
Elizabeth, 192
Elizabeth Bay House, 19, 40, 78, 106, 125, 128, 139, 142, 158, 170, 230, 238, 239, 295, 390, 392, 438, 459, 474, 507, 517, 530, 549, 551, 595, 626
Elizabeth Farm, 158, 163, 325, 383, 384, 385, 437, 633
Elizabeth Gardens, 187
Ellensville, 211
Ellerslie, 540
Ellerston, 321
Ellington, 295
Elliston, 571
Elsham Hall, 410
Elvaston Gardens, 219
Emerald Country Club, 442
Emerald Necklace, 451
Emu Valley Rhododendron Garden, 441
Endilloe, 30, 487
Endowment Lands Perth, 310
Enfield, 133
Enfield Cemetery, 200, 363
Ercildoune, 136, 203, 638
Eringa, 561
Eringa Hyde Park, 161
Erskine House, 505
Eryldene, 138, 164, 208, 311, 630, 631, 646
ETA Factory, 569
Eulinya, 121
Eurilla, 8
Evandale Sculpture Walk, 542
Everglades, 45, 95, 206, 375, 412, 413, 432, 627
Evergreen Memorial Park, 200
Experiment Farm Cottage, 92, 484

Fairbairn Gardens, 182
Fairchild Botanic Garden, 461
Faire Knowe, 16
Fairlie, 645
Fairview, 182
Farmers Building, 515
Fawkner Cemetery, 132, 209, 293
Fawkner Park, 14, 78
Federation Square, 481, 627
Feltex House, 412, 515
Fernberg, 88, 185, 268
Ferndale, 91
Fernhill, 41, 213, 559, 620
Ferntree Gully National Park, 430
Fiona, 249
First Fleet Park. See Circular Quay
First Government House Place, 28

Fitzgerald River National Park, 254
Fitzroy Gardens, 63, 71, 76, 77, 78, 82, 87, 141, 187, 217, 220, 221, 230, 235, 276, 277, 306, 323, 373, 377, 481, 491, 519, 538, 553, 555, 592, 594, 619
Flagstaff Gardens, 221, 306, 555, 566
Fleays Wildlife Park, 661
Flecker Botanic Gardens, see Cairns Botanic Gardens
Flemington Car Sheds, 501
Flemington House, 41, 78, 212
Flemington Racecourse, 67, 499, 510, 566
Fletcher Jones Gardens, 76, 151, 222
Flinders Park, 566, 655
Flinders University, 146, 490, 569, 610
Flinders Way, 110
Floreat Park, 310
Florida Mansions, 23
Footscray Park, 17, 227, 272, 402, 441
Footscray Railway Station, 501
Forest Lawn Cemetery, 133
Forest Lodge, 8, 66, 406, 560, 561, 640
Forestry Commission Nursery, Perth, Tas.135
Forrest Place, 141, 425
Forrest River, 410
Fortuna, 230
Fountains, 107
Fragrant Garden (Erina), 253, 254
Franklin Square, 234, 268, 373
Franklyn Vale, 234, 418
Frankston Golf Course, 235
Fraser Island State Forest Nursery, 568
Frogmore Royal Gardens, 554, 650, 651
Fulham Grange, 469, 470
Fülling, 228

Gabo, 559
Gallop Botanic Reserve, 159
Gamble Cottage, 9, 242, 561
Garden City, 247
Garden of Friendship, 138
Garden Island, 71, 251
Garden of Remembrance, 470
Garden of St Erth, 255, 300
Gatton Agricultural College, 12, 68
Geelong Botanic Gardens, 42, 114, 213, 229, 256, 362, 404, 435, 475, 499, 615
Geelong Road Plantation, 501
Generalife, 408
Georges Square, 567
Giessen Botanic Gardens, 259
Gilwell Park, 402
Ginahgulla, 597
Glasgow Botanic Gardens, 231, 234
Glasgow Necropolis, 132

Glasnevin Botanic Gardens, 328, 414, 510
Glebe Park, 52
Gledswood, 263, 264, 402, 646
Glenalta, 264, 418, 561
Glenalva, 335
Glenara, 6, 117, 142, 143, 208, 229, 332, 375, 410, 429, 493, 517, 527, 584
Glenbervie, 555
Glencairn, 89
Glendon, 510
Glenholme, 264
Gleniffer Brae, 559, 648
Glenormiston, 422, 638
Glyn, 18
Golden Gate Park, 54
Golfhill, 76
Gondwanaland, 152
Good-A-Meavy, 89
Googong Dam, 146
Goomburra, 175
Gordon Reserve, 231
Gore Hill, 132
Gore Hill Cemetery, 266, 369
Gostwyk, 175
Goulburn General Cemetery, 369
Government Garden (Perth), 185, 189, 210, 570, 636
Government Gardens (Brisbane), 104
Government Gardens (Launceston), 141, 524, 626
Government House (Adelaide), 268, 269
Government House (Belair), 84, 268, 560
Government House (Brisbane) 105, 132, 185, 194, 267, 418
Government House (Canberra), 266, 269, 639
Government House (Darwin), 267
Government House (Hobart), 268, 326, 594, 661
Government House (Melbourne), 63, 135, 185, 268, 575
Government House (Mount Macedon), 421
Government House (Parramatta), 185, 603
Government House (Perth), 269, 592, 615, 636
Government House (Sydney), 185, 186, 266, 269, 465, 551, 592, 612, 620, 626, 639
Government Scent Farm, 537
Governor's Garden, 170
Gowan Brae, 563
Gowan Castle, 435
Gracemere, 270, 271
Grantham, 175

671

Index of Gardens

Green Park, 595
Greenbriar Park, 563
Greenfields, 341
Greenmount, 274, 505
Greenoaks, 280, 398, 418, 419, 439, 577
Greenwood Cemetery, 160
Greenwood, 107, 274
Grevillea Park, 275
Griffith, 330
Griffith University, 338, 610
Grong Grong, 121
Groote Eylandt, 4
Grosser Garten, 259
Grosvenor Park, 342
Grove Hill, 260, 261
Gulf Station, 655
Gums, The, 150
Gunpowder, 398
Gurrawarra, 209

H.V. Mckay Memorial Gardens, 151, 388
Haberfield, 439
Haddo House, 173, 508, 596
Hambledon, 384
Hamburg Botanic Garden, 218
Hamel Government Nursery, 286, 637
Hamilton Botanic Gardens, 212, 282, 286, 287, 320, 638
Hamilton Palace, 540, 590
Hamilton Park, 547
Hampton Court, 179, 191, 404
Hanging Gardens of Babylon, 484
Harlaxton Manor, 159
Harleston, 276
Harold Boas Gardens, 95, 289
Harold Holt Memorial Swimming Centre, 584
Harrington Park, 646
Harrow, 175
Harvey's Store, 515
Hascombe, 291, 422
Hatherley, 483
Hawkesbury, 12
Hawthorn Gardens, 483
Hazeldean, 164, 643
Healesville Sanctuary, 661
Heaton Lodge, 559
Heide, 245, 294, 465, 542
Heights, The, 294
Henrietta Villa, 40, 454
Hereford House, 439, 462
Hergott Springs, 108, 298, 461
Hermannsburg, 30, 344, 410, 460
Hermitage, The, 299, 603
Heronswood, 78, 299, 301
Herrenhausen Royal Gardens, 259, 307
Herring Island, 512, 542
Hesketh Park, 342

Hever Castle, 187
Hidcote Manor, 71, 115, 149
High Court of Australia, 353, 515
Highfield, 301, 302
Highgate Cemetery, 132
Highlands, 310
Hill River Station, 304, 561
Hill View, 19, 266, 304, 395, 439, 562
Hobart Airport, 178
Hobart Botanic Gardens, see Royal Botanic Gardens, Hobart
Hobart Town Public Cemetery, 160
Hobart Zoo, 661
Hohewarte, 590
Homebush Bay Park, 376
Hopetoun House, 553
Hopewood House, 310
Horsham Botanic Gardens, 282, 376, 642
Horsley, 311, 325, 646
Hortus Palatinus, 259
Hotel Canberra, 50
Hotham Gardens Estate, 398
Hughes Park, 190, 209, 320, 321, 518, 561
Hull Botanic Gardens, 392
Humphreyville, 588
Huntington Botanic Garden, 461
Hurst, 89
Hyatt Hotels, 515
Hyde Park, 20, 41, 87, 141, 150, 229, 231, 322, 352, 353, 367, 411, 437, 541, 542, 565
Hyde Park (London), 466, 490
Hyde Park (Sydney), 416, 426, 449, 490, 499, 595, 600, 606
Hydro Majestic, 95

ICI House, 235, 287, 412, 569
Illoura Reserve, 388, 389
Imbil State Forest Nursery, 568
Imperial Gardens (St Petersburg), 307
Invercauld, 107
Invergowrie, 255, 328, 559, 562
IPEC Building, 302
Ipswich Queens Park, 303, 328
Islington Park, 547
Ithaca War Memorial Garden, 339

James Cook University, 569
Japanese Garden (Cowra), 336
Japanese Garden (Toowoomba), 175
Jardin des Plantes, 231
Jardin du Roi, 180, 351
Jena Königsberg Botanic Gardens, 259
Jenolan Caves, 92, 95, 131, 430, 505
Jervis Bay, 62
Jimbour, 175, 337
John Forrest National Park, 338

John Knight Park, 52
Johnstone Park, 71, 141
Jolimont, 76, 362
Jondaryan, 175, 339
Joondalup Central Park, 340
Joondalup Regional Centre, 569
Joseph Harris Park, 290

Kagoshima Park, 117
Kakadu National Park, 445, 512
Kalbarri National Park, 254
Kalgoorlie Arboretum, 30
Kalgoorlie–Boulder Native Garden, 30
Kalmthout Arboretum, 472
Kalua, 310
Kalumburu, 410
Kambalda, 30, 614
Kamerunga State Nursery, 164
Kamesburgh, 341
Kamillaroi, 121
Kapunda Reservoir, 107
Karaweera, 344
Karrakatta General Cemetery, 132, 285, 341, 470, 637
Karri Bank, 505
Katanga, 182
Kawarra Australian Plant Garden, 341
Kelvedon, 573
Kenley, 483
Kennerton Green, 344, 553, 563
Kensal Green Cemetery, 132
Kensington, 523
Kensington Gardens, 583, 595
Kentville, 91
Kevin Heinze Garden Centre, 295
Kew Gardens, see Royal Botanic Gardens, Kew
Kiddell Gardens, 182
Kiel Botanic Garden, 423
Killalpaninna, 30
Killamount, 380
Killara Railway Station, 501
Killowen, 637
Killymoon, 345
Kilmory, 164
King Edward Park, 542, 547, 642
Kings Park, 48, 56, 80, 99, 100, 185, 190, 209, 210, 223, 230, 231, 285, 345, 346, 379, 430, 431, 432, 513, 547, 548, 592, 637, 638
King's School, 146
Kinross, 41, 349
Kippilaw, 347
Kirkton, 118
Kirribilli House, 347
Knutsford, 637
Koonamore Vegetation Reserve, 456
Koonamore, 51

Index of Gardens

Koort-Koort-Nong, 278
Koroit Botanic Gardens, 21, 282, 329, 348, 349, 638, 642
Kuitpo, 107
Kuranda Railway, 501
Ku-ring-gai College of Advanced Education, 515
Ku-ring-gai Wildflower Garden, 350
Kyneton Botanic Gardens, 272

Labassa, 170
La Cima, 88
Lake Burley Griffin, 146, 152
Lake Ginninderra, 146, 235, 398
Lake Harry, 298, 461, 509
Lake Macquarie Park, 547
Lamington National Park, 351, 353
Lamington Plateau, 497
La Mortola, 143
Lanark, 211
Lang Park, 416
Lanyon, 51, 361
La Trobe University, 19, 146, 188, 490, 610
Lauderdale, 362
Launceston Airport, 178
Leawood Gardens, 9, 181, 366, 386, 560
Leeton, 330
Leg of Mutton, 80, 107, 421
Leigh Creek South, 30, 562
Leinster, 30
Leipzig Botanic Gardens, 259
Lennons Broadbeach Hotel, 361, 496
Letchworth, 246
Lewer's Garden, 542
Lilianfels, 94
Lincoln Square, 323
Lindesay, 92, 484, 504
Lindsay Park, 21, 556, 561
Linton, 604
Lissner Park, 373
Little Milton, 374
Llanover, 644
Llewllyn, 104
Lodge, The (Canberra), 375, 531, 639
Lodge, The (New Town Park), 52, 277, 375
Logan Botanic Gardens, 541
London Zoo, 659
Lone Pine, 375
Lone Pine Koala Sanctuary, 661
Long Nose Point, 388, 389
Long Water Holes, 76
Longerenong, 12
Loreto College, 4
Lowther Castle, 375
Luna Park (Adelaide), 482
Luna Park (Melbourne), 482, 594

Luna Park (Sydney), 482, 594
Lutana, 151, 247, 380, 589
Luxembourg Gardens, 118
Lyndhurst, 73, 103, 437, 438, 551
Lynton Lea, 61, 89

M.H. Baillieu Garden, 68, 165, 182, 183
Macarthur New Cities, 161
Macarthur Square, 323
Macclesfield, 177
Macedon State Forest Nursery, 272
Machattie Park, 386, 465
Mackay Town Plan, 387
Macquarie Fields House, 394, 626
Macquarie Place, 390, 394, 449
Macquarie University, 146, 610
Madrid Botanic Gardens, 131
Main Street, Bairnsdale, 101
Malahide, 587
Malahide Castle, 587
Malmaison, 54, 180, 231, 367, 504
Malmsbury Botanic Gardens, 397
Malvern Gardens, 483, 510
Manar, 93, 397
Manar, The, 23
Manderville Hall, 590
Manoah, 8
Maranoa Gardens, 56, 216, 236, 376, 399
Marathon, 121, 399, 626
Marble Hill, 268, 560
Marida Yallock, 638
Maritimo, 117
Markdale, 399, 622
Martindale Hall, 217
Maryborough Cemetery, 547
Maryborough Queens Park, 303, 402
Maryland, 402
Mawallok, 18, 76, 282, 286, 352, 402, 638
Mawarra, 229, 287, 403, 626
Maydena, 380, 381
Mayfair, 23
Mayfield, 385
McClelland Art Gallery, 542
McGeorge House, 182
McKay Memorial Gardens, 217
Melbourne Aids Memorial Garden, 71
Melbourne Botanic Gardens, see Royal Botanic Gardens, Melbourne
Melbourne Crematorium, 293
Melbourne Cricket Ground, 67, 287, 565, 655
Melbourne General Cemetery, 132, 209, 293, 306, 405, 410, 493, 510, 511, 524
Melbourne Museum, 596
Melbourne Park, 566
Melbourne Teachers Training College, 282

Melbourne Zoological Gardens, 493, 502, 510, 524, 659, 661
Memorial Park Crematorium, 569
Mena Hotel Gardens, 179
Meningoort, 278, 406, 638
Mereworth Castle, 483, 559
Metropolitan Golf Club, 380, 533
Micalago Station, 310, 407, 469, 643
Miegunyah, 277
Mildura Botanic Gardens, 650
Mildura, 134, 330
Millennium Park, 150, 388, 601
Milton Park, 310, 562
Minimbah, 321
Minjah, 540
Mistover, 89
Mitchell Freeway, 450
Mobil House, 569
Moidart, 412, 562
Mona, 633
Mona Vale, 135, 332, 409, 419
Monarto City Centre, 307
Monarto Zoological Park, 383, 661
Monash University, 178, 228, 235, 569
Monsoon Tropical Botanical Gardens, 99
Montefiore, 510
Montpellier Botanic Gardens, 118, 231
Monument Hill, 414
Mooleric, 282, 283, 414, 606, 638
Mooloomburram, 482
Moonta Miner's Cottage, 432
Mooramong, 584, 639
Moora Park, 414, 415
Moore Park, 6, 21, 551, 565
Moore Park Zoo, 660, 661
Morialta Reserve, 503
Mosaic Garden, 348
Moscow Botanic Gardens, 530
Mosman Park Picture Gardens, 217
Mount Adelaide, 310, 550
Mount Ainslie, 375
Mount Annan Botanic Garden, 49, 57, 419
Mount Boninyong, 420
Mount Brown, 80
Mount Buffalo, 130, 174, 371, 375, 420, 505
Mount Burr, 107
Mount Coot-tha Botanic Gardens, see Brisbane Botanic Gardens
Mount Dandenong Arboretum, 25, 501
Mount Eagle, 212
Mount Edgecombe, 559
Mount Elrington, 330, 420
Mount Eymard, 562
Mount Field National Park, 420

673

Index of Gardens

Mount Gambier Cave Garden, 131, 421, 511
Mount Gambier Lakes, 80, 421, 511
Mount Gambier State Forest Nursery, 560
Mount George, 9, 561
Mount Gingera, 62
Mount Kosciuszko, 375
Mount Lawley Estate No.3, 310
Mount Lofty Botanic Garden, 8, 9, 49, 99, 161, 200, 375, 377, 421, 518, 562
Mount Lofty House, 8
Mount Macedon State Forest Nursery, 212, 421, 422, 423, 568
Mount McIntyre, 107
Mount Noorat, 174, 255, 422, 638
Mount Tomah, 21, 49, 99
Mount Tomah Botanic Garden, 95, 422, 512
Mount Wellington, 375
Mount Yule, 282
Mowbray Park, 422
Mrs Macquarie's Chair, 376, 522
Muellerville, 596, 597
Mulberry Hill, 182
Mundaring Reservoir, 424, 461
Munich Botanic Gardens, 259, 262
Munstead Wood, 336
Murchison Square, 323
Murdoch University, 569
Muresk, 12
Murndal, 41, 159, 329, 424, 425, 462, 638
Museum Gardens (Brisbane), 102, 425, 426
Musgrave Park, 306, 416, 425
Myall Park, 266, 654
Myilly Point Heritage Precinct, 3, 427, 432, 445

Naracoorte Caves, 131
Narrandera Memorial Gardens, 231
Narrapumelap, 638
Narrows Interchange, 429, 450
Nassenheide, 31
National Gallery of Victoria, 515
National Library of Australia, 146
National Museum of Australia, 553
National Rhododendron Gardens, 507
National Rose Gardens, 51, 110, 313, 431
National Sculpture Garden, 52
National Triangle, 52, 152, 319, 375, 431
National Tropical Botanical Gardens (Hawaii), 417
Neotsfield, 174
Nestlé Gardens, 151
Neubeck House, 559

New Farm Park, 416, 436, 449
New Guinea National Botanic Garden, 661
New Melbourne General Cemetery, 209
New Norcia, 410, 636
New Town Racecourse, 499
Newbury Park, 562
Newman College, 275
Newport Cemetery, 640
Newstead House and Park, 102, 416, 440, 449
Newstead Reserve, 187
Newstead, 284
Nindooinbah, 441
Nonorrah, 402
Nooroo, 46, 94, 146, 376
Noosa, 386
Norman Jolly Memorial Grove, 339
North Coast Regional Botanical Garden, 99
North Parramatta Cemetery, 292
North Terrace, Adelaide, 101
Northam Cottage, 88
Northbourne Avenue, Canberra, 101
Nunhead Cemetery, 132
Nurney House, 66, 164, 333, 404, 561
Nymphenburg Botanic Gardens, 218, 259

Oasis, The, 505
Oatley College of Advanced Education, 515
Obelisk Hill, 414
Observatory Hill, 449, 450
Observatory Park, 642
Ocean Shores Resort, 508
Ockerby Gardens, 187
Offington, 535
Old Admiralty House, 93
Old Sturbridge Village, 594
Old Sydney Town, 594
Oldbury Farm, 34, 35, 562
Olive Pink Botanic Garden, 3, 30, 336, 475, 654
Olympic Dam, 661
Olympic Park, 353
Olympic Village, 69
Omama, 606
Oombulgurri, 410
Orange Botanic Gardens, 518
Ord River Irrigation, 450
Osborne House, 332
Overton Lodge, 163
Oxford Botanic Gardens, 98

Pacific Club, 627
Paddocks, The, 307, 459, 562
Padua, 98

Palms, The, 461
Panmure, 8, 418, 461, 561
Panshanger, 26, 376, 409, 474, 589
Parafield Cemetery, 132, 461, 462, 640
Parc de la Villette, 232
Parkes Place, 146
Parkes Way, 432
Parkhall, 411
Parliament House (Canberra), 110, 164, 425, 515
Parliament House (Melbourne), 282
Parliament House (Perth), 210, 450
Parliament House (Sydney), 515
Parliamentary Triangle, 338
Paronella Park, 463
Parramatta Park, 78, 185, 267, 463, 518
Partacoona Station, 487
Pasadena, 464
Patterdale, 32, 264
Patterson Lakes, 646
Peace Memorial Rose Garden, 431, 467
Peacock Point, 376
Peake, The, 66
Peerewur, 309
Pejar Park, 93
Pendell Court, 392
Penola Fruit Colony, 160
Penthouses, The, 515
People's Park, 466
Percyville, 280
Père Lachaise, 132, 160
Persfield, 474
Perth Airport, 178
Perth Endowment Lands Scheme, 272
Perth Park, 346
Perth War Cemetery, 341, 470
Perth Zoo, 637, 659, 660, 661
Peter Francis Points Arboretum, 25, 471
Pewsey Vale, 471
Phillips Gardens, 472
Pigeon Hill, 441
Pilton, 543
Pine Grove, 332
Pine Hills, 559
Pinnacles, The, 127
Pioneer Women's Garden, Adelaide 150
Pioneer Women's Memorial Garden, 10, 18, 150, 161, 371, 561
Pisa, 98
Pitlochry, 559
Plenty Station, 76
Point Charles Lighthouse, 139, 446
Point Cooke, 634, 635
Point Henry Alcoa, 502
Poorinda, 306
Port Arthur, 63, 151, 451, 485, 589
Port Campbell National Park, 80

Index of Gardens

Port Fairy Botanic Gardens, 272, 294, 328, 329, 503
Port Road, 107
Portland Botanic Gardens, 16, 117, 154, 173, 199, 229, 294, 296, 486, 638
Potts Hill Reservoir, 352
Powis, 624
Prince Alfred Park, 65, 207, 280
Prince's Court, 482
Prince's Park, 78, 282, 466, 524
Prince's Square, 230, 386, 488, 623
Prospect House, 226, 261
Prospect Park, 443, 451
Prospect Reservoir, 352
Punchbowl Reserve, 187
Purrumbete, 278, 332
Purulia, 646

Queen Victoria Gardens, 130, 150
Queens Gardens, 491, 495
Queens Park (Brisbane), 105, 449, 566
Queens Park (Cooktown), 495
Queens Park (Mackay), 495
Queens Park (Maryborough), 495
Queens Park (Moonee Ponds), 451
Queens Park (Newtown), 409
Queens Park (Rockhampton), 495
Queens Park (Toowoomba), 495
Queens Park (Townsville), 495
Queensland University, 611
Quorn Hall, 277

Raby, 40
Raby Castle, 509
Raheen, 170, 427, 500
Randwick Racecourse, 499
Rankin Gardens, 576
Ratisbon Botanic Gardens, 259
Ravensworth, 90, 103
Raywood, 9, 15, 647
Readers' Digest Building, 515
Red Hill Farm, 502
Redesdale, 397
Redlands, 534, 559
Redleaf, 504
Regent Gardens, 562
Regent's Park, 16, 126, 201, 211, 232, 401, 414, 510, 524, 596
Regentville, 40, 454
Remembrance Driveway, 150, 292
Renmark, 134, 330
Retford Hall, 310
Retford Park, 310, 462, 562
Retreat, The, 319
Richmond Gaol, 451
Richmond Park, 656
Rintel Botanic Gardens, 259
Rio De Janiero Botanic Gardens, 573

Rippon Lea, 27, 28, 78, 95, 96, 104, 120, 123, 134, 158, 170, 175, 187, 213, 250, 254, 331, 352, 353, 375, 398, 419, 432, 468, 472, 508, 516, 530, 577, 580, 584, 590, 593, 594, 606, 616
Ripponlea Railway Station, 501
River Torrens Linear Park, 80, 305, 509, 562
Rockhampton Botanic Gardens, 98, 196, 460, 512, 513
Rockhampton Queens Park, 303
Roma Street Railway Station, 501
Rona, 513
Rookwood Cemetery, 132, 187, 250, 395, 416, 439, 462, 515, 592, 633
Rosalind Park, 158, 231, 263, 353, 516
Rose Bay Cottage, 438
Rose Hill, 63
Rose Seidler House, 412
Rosebank, 124
Rosedale, 26, 332, 409, 516, 534
Rosemount, 21
Roseworthy Agricultural College, 12
Roslyn Hall, 402
Rossbank, 1
Rotherwood, 175
Rottnest Park, 164
Rouen Botanic Gardens, 231
Rouse Hill, 11, 37, 106, 239, 519, 520, 633
Roxby Downs, 30, 661
Royal Agricultural Showground, 223
Royal Botanic Gardens, Cranbourne, 49, 57, 99, 520, 522, 596, 607
Royal Botanic Gardens, Dresden, 259, 300
Royal Botanic Gardens, Edinburgh, 88, 110, 234, 270, 302, 457, 540
Royal Botanic Gardens, Kew, 3, 5, 15, 71, 72, 76, 78, 80, 86, 90, 93, 97, 98, 109, 114, 118, 124, 126, 141, 164, 169, 189, 195, 196, 201, 202, 207, 210, 231, 232, 234, 262, 265, 302, 340, 345, 362, 371, 377, 390, 392, 393, 394, 409, 410, 414, 432, 435, 443, 457, 472, 495, 513, 521, 524, 527, 536, 538, 547, 554, 558, 572, 581, 587, 604, 634, 641, 645, 647, 648, 650
Royal Botanic Gardens, Melbourne 1, 5, 25, 28, 32, 33, 36, 41, 42, 43, 63, 68, 75, 78, 82, 93, 98, 110, 113, 123, 125, 131, 140, 142, 144, 157, 167, 173, 178, 185, 187, 199, 212, 217, 221, 231, 235, 250, 255, 262, 268, 277, 283, 290, 295, 300, 301, 323, 330, 331, 332, 337, 338, 352, 362, 365, 369, 379, 385, 399, 410, 418, 423, 425, 426, 434, 435, 441, 456, 460, 465, 471, 474, 475, 480, 500, 510, 512, 519, 520, 522, 533, 541, 560, 564, 571, 573, 575, 577, 580, 585, 590, 596, 597, 607, 615, 616, 629, 632, 642, 645, 655, 654, 661
Royal Botanic Gardens, Sydney 5, 6, 10, 20, 21, 31, 37, 41, 43, 68, 71, 73, 79, 80, 82, 86, 87, 90, 91, 92, 93, 98, 110, 118, 125, 126, 128, 134, 135, 139, 147, 150, 158, 161, 170, 176, 182, 185, 186, 212, 217, 222, 231, 234, 238, 239, 247, 248, 249, 250, 260, 263, 280, 281, 291, 323, 338, 340, 344, 369, 377, 378, 384, 390, 394, 414, 419, 422, 437, 438, 439, 449, 454, 459, 460, 507, 510, 512, 522, 523, 526, 541, 549, 566, 567, 573, 585, 596, 606, 611, 620, 627, 632, 639, 644, 649
Royal Botanic Gardens, Tasmania, 1, 43, 98, 178, 185, 223, 247, 268, 316, 376, 437, 524, 526, 542, 589
Royal Children's Hospital, 235
Royal Horticultural Society Gardens, 82
Royal Mint, Melbourne, 255
Royal National Park, 180, 270, 416, 430, 444, 524
Royal Palace Gardens, Kensington, 467
Royal Parade, 200
Royal Park (Launceston), 524
Royal Park (Melbourne), 5, 207, 228, 235, 381, 386, 410, 524, 525, 661
Rundle Mall, 562
Runnymede, 432, 527, 528, 619
Rupertswood, 143, 255, 256, 388, 527, 590, 592, 616

Sale Botanic Gardens, 282
Salisbury Court, 286, 534
Salmon Ponds, 534, 535
Saltwell Park, 343
San Donato, 54
Sanctuary Cove, 505
Sandgate Cemetery, 132, 534
Sandringham Garden, 87, 150
Sanssouci, 259, 537
Santa Barbara Botanic Gardens, 62
Saumarez Park, 340
Saundridge, 409
Schönbrunn Botanic Gardens, 218, 259
Schloss Augustusburg, 259
Schlossgarten, 259
Scienceworks Museum, 19
Scrivener Dam, 146
Sculpture Garden (National Gallery of Australia), 319, 353, 431
Sea World, 594
Sefton Park, 78, 536
Serpentine Dam, 635
Sheffield Botanic Gardens, 401

Index of Gardens

Shell Refinery, 569
Sherwood Arboretum, 88, 550
Shrine of Remembrance, 141
Shrubland Park, 81
Shurdington, 640
Silent Hearts Memorial Garden, 150
Singapore Botanic Gardens, 405
Sion House, 595
Sir Joseph Banks Hotel, 482
Sir Joseph Banks Park, 389
Sissinghurst, 149, 202, 553
Skene, 596
Soho Square, 53, 72
Somercotes, 409, 558
Somerleyton Hall, 111
Sonning, 626
South Brisbane Recreation Reserve, 425
South British Insurance Co., 569
South Kensington, 524
Southbank, 105
South-Eastern Freeway, 562
Southgate Brisbane, 488
Southgate Fountain, 569
Southgate Melbourne, 488
Sovereign Hill, 594
Spring Bluff Railway, 501
Spring Gardens, 467
Spring Hill Playground, 82
Springfield, 561, 566
Springside, 277
Springvale Necropolis, 209
Springwood, 542, 567
St Aubins, 107, 321, 533, 626
St Davids Park, 533
St Heliers, 118, 655
St James Park, 16, 541
St John's Square, 488
St Kilda Botanic Gardens, 143, 154. 482, 533
St Kilda Cemetery, 187
St Kilda Road, 141, 620
St Ninian, 78
St Omer, 533
St Petersburg Botanic Gardens, 530
St Vigeans, 8, 209, 534, 560, 570, 640
St Vincent Gardens, 78, 124, 514, 534, 568
St Vincent Place, 567, 568
St Wilfreds, 83
Stangate House, 9
Stanhill, 23
Stanley Park, 342
State Bank Building, 515
Stella James House, 432
Stirling Castle, 435
Stirling Gardens, 189, 210, 269, 570, 636
Stirling Square (Guildford), 638

Stirling Square (Perth), 185, 570
Stonnington, 255, 301, 572
Stony Range Flora Reserve, 94
Stormontfield Ponds, 534
Strand Park, 22
Strand, The, 204
Strathalbyn Soldiers' Memorial Gardens, 272, 570, 573, 640
Strathspey, 209
Strawberry Hill, 432, 573
Struthers, 548
Studley, 23, 121
Studley Park, 590
Sturt Street, 101, 102, 230, 574
Stuttgart Botanic Gardens, 259
Subiaco Municipal Gardens, 402, 576
Summerhome, 579, 580
Sun Picture Gardens, 217, 581
Sunshine Gardens, 272, 388
Surrey Gardens, 481
Swan Hill Pioneer Village, 594
Swifts, 583
Sydney Botanic Gardens, see Royal Botanic Gardens Sydney
Sydney Common, 490
Sydney International Airport, 389
Sylvan Mists, 559
Symmons Plains, 409
Syon House, 118
System Garden University of Melbourne, 78

Talgai East, 175
Talindert, 587, 638
Tally Ho, 152
Tamworth Botanic Gardens, 650
Tarban Creek Asylum, 319
Taronga Zoo, 119, 161, 223, 512, 530, 659, 661
Tasmanian College of Advanced Education, 551
Tasmazia, 404
Taymouth Castle, 387
Telopea Park, 51, 164, 639
Tennant Creek Preschool Centre, 137
Terraces, The, 104
Territory Wildlife Park, 659, 661
Tetratheca, 91
Thanes, 121
Theodore, 247
Third Swamp Reserve, 322
Thomas Park, 101
Thomas Walker Convalescent Hospital, 95, 164, 579, 655
Thornton, 343
Thorpe, 8, 418
Throsby Park, 439, 562
Tieve Tara, 590

Tintern Church of England Girls Grammar School, 235
Titanga, 203, 540, 597, 638, 646
Tocal, 12
Tomago, 321
Toorak House, 268, 332, 590
Toowoomba Botanic Gardens, 99, 633
Toowoomba Queens Park, 175, 303, 598
Tower Hamlets Cemetery, 132
Tower Hill Reserve, 278
Townsville Queens Park, 31, 449, 460, 601
Towong Hill, 410
Trade Offices, 164
Trawalla, 76, 375, 602, 638
Treasury Gardens, 221, 282, 306, 555, 570
Tree of Knowledge, 603
Trentham, 201
Trevallyn Reserve, 187
Trinity College Botanic Garden, 328, 414
Trinity College Grounds, 282
Tubbo, 142
Tuggeranong New Town, 389
Tuggeranong Town Park, 52
Tullamarine, 178
Turanville, 321
Turkeith, 282, 606, 638
Tutuila, 8
Twyford, 148

Ulinda, 375
Ulm Botanic Gardens, 259
Uluru, 505
Uluru–Kata Tjuta National Park, 157, 169, 445
Umpherston Cave, 131
Unalla, 609
University of Adelaide, 80, 161, 561, 609
University House, 164
University of Kiel's Botanic Garden, 218
University of Melbourne, 134, 199, 352, 398, 502, 515, 524, 569, 585, 609
University of New South Wales, 565
University of Newcastle, 508
University of Sydney, 146, 164, 579, 609, 630, 643
University of Tasmania, 609
University of Western Australia, 19, 285, 338, 569, 609, 638
Urrbrae House, 518, 561, 624
Uskarty, 432

Vacuum Oil Refinery, 569
Vansittart Park, 511
Vaucluse House, 26, 230, 438, 455, 612, 633

Index of Gardens

Vauxhall Gardens (Sydney), 481, 482
Veitshöchheim, 259
Versailles, 180, 484
Victor Harbor Soldiers' Memorial Gardens, 467, 503, 561, 615
Victoria Gardens, 419, 590, 618, 627
Victoria Park (Ballarat), 441
Victoria Park (Perth), 618
Victoria Park (Sydney), 416, 618, 649
Victoria Racecourse, 499
Victoria Square (Windmill Hill), 187, 232
Victoria's Open Range Zoo, 661
Villa Bebek, 642
Villa Pallavicini, 642, 643

Waikerie, 509, 561
Wail Forest Commission Nursery, 47, 95, 272, 408
Wairoa, 8, 277, 560, 564, 597, 609, 623
Waite Arboretum, 200, 624
Wakehurst Place, 521
Walden Pond, 75, 298
Wallcliffe House, 11, 625
Wallsend Park, 627
Walsham, 148
Wanilla, 80
Warley Place, 143
Warner Brothers Movie World, 594
Warrawee, 121, 642
Warrnambool Botanic Gardens, 628, 475, 156, 638, 282, 540
Warrock, 638
Warwick Farm Racecourse, 292, 293
Water Works Park, 223
Watiparinga Reserve, 34
Wattle Park, 399, 633
Waverley Cemetery, 132, 633
Wellington Dam, 635
Wellington Caves, 131
Welwyn Garden City, 106
Wembley Downs, 310
Wentworth Hotel, 515
Wentworth Park, 21, 416
Werribee Park, 136, 158, 277, 286, 326, 518, 555, 634, 635, 661

West Green House, 344
West Lakes, 307, 508, 562
West Princess Street Gardens, 223
West Terrace Cemetery, 132, 461, 640
Westbourne Woods, 51, 52, 639
Westella, 579
Westerfield, 182, 277
Western Australian Institute of Technology, 551
Western Plains Zoo, 661
Western Suburbs Memorial Park, 235
Westmead Children's Hospital, 319
Weston Park, 480
Westport, 510
Wet 'n' Wild, 594
Wetmore, 409
Whernside, 374
White City Gardens, 482
Wickham Park, 449, 547, 642
Wilhelmshöhe, 259
Willaroo, 639
William Balmain Teachers College, 389
Williamstown Botanic Gardens, 78, 156, 475, 533, 644, 645
Williamstown Dockyards, 179
Willow Glen, 137
Willyama, 560, 645
Wilson Reserve, 571
Wilsons Promontory National Park, 36
Wimbourne, 89
Windsor Castle, 628
Winster, 18
Winton, 409, 647
Winty, 89
Wirra Willa, 647
Wirrabara State Forest Nursery, 107, 114, 262, 469, 560, 647
Wirrimbirra, 290
Wirriwa, 93
Wisley, 524
Wittunga Botanic Garden, 8, 33, 34, 377
Woden Town Park, 52
Wollemi National Park, 24
Wollongong Botanic Gardens, 99, 100, 648
Wollongong Civic Plaza, 80

Wolston House, 648
Wombat Hill Botanic Gardens, 250, 376, 590, 648
Wombat Park, 18, 293, 648
Wombeyan, 131
Wonderland, 482
Woolldunga, 107
Woollahra House, 604
Woolmers, 26, 27, 28, 332, 409, 580, 588, 626
Woomargama, 175
Wooriwyrite, 78, 638
Wörlitz, 259
Wotonga, 10
Wrotham Park, 596
Wurrook, 76
Wyldefel Gardens, 23, 411
Wyndcliff, The, 474
Wynstay, 78, 94, 650, 651
Wynyard Park, 450
Wyperfeld National Park, 255

Yalla-y-Poora, 278
Yallourn, 151, 247, 351, 371
Yallum Park, 160
Yanchep National Park, 655
Yandilla, 175
Yaralla, 82, 270, 277, 278, 311, 332, 439, 655
Yarra Bend National Park, 371, 430, 656
Yarra Boulevard, 101, 656
Yarra Park, 67, 78, 565, 655
Yarralumla, 19, 51, 266
Yarran Dheran Reserve, 595
Yarrangobilly Caves, 131
Yarraville Gardens, 402
Yarrawa, 583
Yellagonga Regional Park, 340
Yellowstone, 430, 444
Yengo, 94, 657
Yering, 159, 175
Yeronga Park, 416, 658
Yosemite, 444
Yuille's Swamp, 352
Yultewirra, 9, 418

Index of Names

Aalto, Alvar, 536, 649
Abbot, Marylyn, 344
Abbott, Francis (1799–1883), 1
Abbott, Francis (1834–1903), 1,43, 526
Abbott, Hilda, 267
Aberdeen, Earl of, 173
Acheson, Frederick, 97
Adams Corona, 453
Adams, Arthur H., 373
Adamson, William, 6, 7, 41, 43, 111, 148, 218, 236, 244, 289, 493, 540, 555, 575, 587, 616, 657
Adcock, Edward, 7
Adcock, George Henry 7, 12
Adcock, Thomas, 7, 265, 485, 570
Addison, Joseph, 433, 454
Agostini, Isadore (Jack), 176
Ahlfeld, (Gustav F.) Werner, 14, 56, 251
Aitkin, James William Manifold, 540
Aiton, William (1731–1793), 71, 521, 558
Aiton, William (1766–1849), 109, 169
Akbar 363
Allan, James, 15, 431, 594
Allen, (née Cox) Catherine, 15
Allen, (Edith) Mervyn, 191
Allen, Charles Ernest Frank, 15, 176
Allen, J.F., 414
Allen, Joseph 15, 589
Allen, Lewis, 554
Allen, Stanley Anketell 191
Allen, Thomas, 15, 16, 378, 447, 560
Allen, Trevor, 106
Allitt, Elizabeth, 16
Allitt, William, 16, 294, 329, 486
Allport, Joseph, 16, 184
Allport, Mary Morton, 16, 407
Allport, Morton, 16, 534
Alphand, Adolphe, 206, 231
Alsop, Rodney, 17, 18, 28, 33, 227, 332, 404, 450, 648
Alston, Harold, 18, 112
Alston, Peter, 18, 47
Althofer Peter, 18
Althofer, George, 18, 34, 45, 56, 291, 372, 376, 440, 478, 571, 575, 658

Althofer, Hazel, 18
Ancher, Mortlock Murray and Woolley, 23
Ancher, Sydney, 319
Anderson and Co., 94, 139, 292, 527, 583, 591
Anderson, (née Mason), Ethel Campbell Louise, 19, 267
Anderson, (née Selfe) Maybanke Susannah, 20, 21, 480
Anderson, Adam, 508
Anderson, George, 19, 20, 41, 366
Anderson, Hall and Co., 439
Anderson, James, 20, 378, 510, 540
Anderson, Joan, 160, 299
Anderson, Robert Henry, 21, 523, 528
Anderson, William (1828–1909), 21, 348, 435, 601
Anderson, William, 73
André, Edouard 78, 536
Andrewartha, Francis, 366
Andrews, Edward William 209, 243
Andrews, John, 515
Andrews, Malcolm, 262
Angas (née Good), Gwynnyth Fay, 21
Angas, George Fife 21, 74, 556, 621
Angas, George French, 21, 86
Angas, John Howard 304
Angas, John Keith 21
Angove, Thomas Carlyon, 22
Angove, William Thomas, 22
Annand, Douglas, 432
Annand, George, 6
Antcliff, Allan, 22, 621
Apperly, Richard, 575
Appleford, Reg, 442
Archer, Charles, 270
Archer family, 41, 139, 409, 628
Archer, Joseph, 26
Archer, Thomas, 26, 27, 588
Archer, William (1788–1879), 27, 588
Archer, William (1818–1896), 270
Archer, William (1820–1874), 26, 28, 53, 332, 368, 526, 575
Archibald, Alison, 474, 487
Ardagh, Richard, 28, 329, 430

Argyll, Duke of 32
Arkley, Howard, 32, 578
Armati, Pio, 30, 31, 601
Armit, William Edington de Margrat, 31
Armstrong, John, 266
Armytage, Charles and Caroline 11, 153
Arne, Fink, 449
Arnim (née Beauchamp), Mary Annette (Elizabeth) von, 31
Arnim-Schlagenthin, Graf Henning August von, 31
Arthur, George, 185, 526
Arthur, John, 32, 33, 173, 362, 423, 522, 540
Ashby, Alison Marjorie, 34, 433
Ashby, Arthur Keith, 34
Ashby, Edwin 9, 33, 45, 115, 372, 417, 433, 561, 648
Ashby, Esther, 33
Ashby family, 56
Asplund, Gunnar, 536
Astley, Thea, 374
Aston, Helen Isobel, 433
Atkins, Richard, 52
Atkinson, James, 34
Atkinson, Louisa, 34, 35, 56, 308, 373, 439, 584
Atyeo, Sam, 294
Audas, James Wales Clarendon, 35, 56, 641
Aufrere, George, 581
Austen, George Thomas (1847–1921), 36
Austen, George Thomas (1875–1947), 36
Austen, Jane, 473
Auteriello, Guglielmo, 244, 335
Axton, James, 534
Ayers, Henry, 66
Ayers, Lucy Josephine, 66
Aylett, William P., 477

Bacchus, William Henry, 309
Backhouse, Alfred Paxton 65
Backhouse, Benjamin Joseph, 65, 526
Backhouse, James, 17, 54, 65, 114, 201, 283, 319, 378, 524, 541, 573
Backhouse, Thomas, 65

Index of Names

Bagot, Charles Hervey, 66
Bagot, John, 9, 66, 406
Bagot, Robert Cooper, 67, 499
Bagot, Walter, 21, 22, 28, 43, 45, 66, 67, 106, 107, 161, 164, 332, 333, 404, 471, 561, 609
Bail, Murray, 374
Bailey family, 56
Bailey, Frederick Manson, 41, 43, 53, 67, 68, 207, 215, 216, 369, 372, 495, 525, 607, 641, 649
Bailey, John Frederick, 8, 68, 105, 268, 495, 525, 573, 641
Bailey, John Rayer, 68, 105
Bailey, John Rodger, 68, 298
Bailey, John, 67
Bailey, John, 81, 366, 560
Baker, Euphemia Eleanor (Effie), 68
Baker, Jeannie, 138
Baker, Ken C., 512
Baker, Richard St Barbe, 640
Baker, Richard Thomas, 43, 56, 69, 180, 196, 223, 372, 525, 579
Bakewell, William, 533
Baldwinson, Arthur, 28, 412
Balfour, John Hutton, 585
Ball, Erica Margery Jane, 69
Ballerstedt, Christopher and Theodore 230
Bancroft, Joseph, 70, 525
Bangay, Paul, 71, 622
Banks, John, 490
Banks, Joseph, 37, 53, 54, 73, 78, 71, 72, 79, 97, 108, 109, 118, 124, 125, 139, 159, 169, 171, 201, 215, 222, 250, 265, 351, 367, 371, 372, 377, 395, 435, 437, 462, 474, 479, 521, 522, 523, 536, 555, 558, 581
Banks, William, 71
Baptist, John Thomas, 19, 34, 41, 73, 74, 280, 386, 437, 459, 462, 472, 549
Baracchi, Pietro, 130
Barber, Josiah 'Daun Utan' see Skertchly, Sydney
Barff, Frederick, 394
Barillet-Deschamps, Jean-Pierre, 206, 227, 232
Barker, Thomas Charles, 402
Barker, Thomas, 402
Barkly, Henry, 5
Barley, Anita, 98
Barnard, Marjorie, 374, 432
Barnett, James, 515
Barr, Peter, 75, 104, 136, 142, 143, 202, 429, 477, 590
Barr Smith, Robert, 66, 624
Barr Smith, Tom, 83
Barramundi Charlie, 3

Barratt, (Frederick) Walter, 75
Barratt, Albert William, 75
Barratt, Edward James, 75
Barratt, Enoch Pearson, 75
Barratt, James Enoch, 75
Barrett, Charles, 56, 75, 119, 433, 435, 470, 617
Barrett, J.W., 44, 601
Barrie, May, 542
Barron, William, 219, 474
Barry, Charles, 229, 332
Barry, Redmond, 323
Barsby, Edward, 76, 117
Barsby, Thomas, 76
Bartolozzi, Francesco, 504
Barton, Charlotte, 138
Barwick, Ian, 562
Barwick, Rodney Lyndon, 76, 589
Basedow family, 75
Basedow, M.P.E., 259, 300
Bateman, Edward La Trobe, 41, 76, 78, 127, 135, 220, 229, 299, 320, 323, 362, 398, 407, 534, 553, 585, 615, 638, 644, 645
Bateman, John Frederic, 76, 552
Bates Smart and McCutcheon, 569
Bauer, Ferdinand, 37, 53, 72, 78, 79, 97, 109, 633
Bauer, Franz, 79
Bauer, June, 176
Bauerlen, Wilhelm, 53, 290
Baxter, William, 54, 55, 79, 583
Bayer, Ernest, 66
Bayley, Charles, 527
Bayley, Harriet Louisa, 527
Bayley, James, 527
Bayly, Emma, 527
Bayly, Hally, 527
Beale, Charles, 80, 114, 421
Beale, Lance, 80
Beale, Thomas, 139
Beames, Rodney Owen, 80, 562
Bean, Charles Edwin Woodrow 601
Bean, William Jackson, 80
Bean, William, 202
Beard, John Stanley, 57, 80, 346, 525
Beardsall, David, 205, 478
Beaton, Donald, 80, 162, 202, 270, 466, 540, 552
Beauglehole, (Alexander) Clifford, 53, 216, 433
Becker, Ludwig, 98
Beckett, E.R., 15, 647
Bedford, Mary Josephine, 82, 480, 504
Begg, Elizabeth Mary (Betty) 59, 84, 116, 160
Begg, Jane, 473
Begg and Shannon, 617

Behrens, Peter, 360
Bell, Fannie Eliza, 193
Bell, Gertrude, 158
Bell, Guildford, 465
Bell, James, 158
Bell, Joshua Peter, 337
Bell, Michael, 418, 439
Bell, Thomas, 337
Benjamin, Nathan, 508
Benko, Andrew, 200
Bennett, (Alexander) Carr, 85
Bennett, Charles, 85, 140, 199
Bennett, George, 131, 170, 262, 368, 624
Bennett, Henry, 85
Benson, Albert Herbert, 86
Bent, Andrew, 16, 17
Bentham, George, 53, 54, 85, 86, 98, 201, 219, 234, 424, 513, 575, 650
Bentham, Jeremy, 378
Bernays, Lewis Adolphus, 5, 6, 41, 86, 202, 290
Berry, John, 308
Berthelot, Sabin, 126
Berzins, Ilmars, 87, 412
Best, David, 87
Best, Henry, 87
Best, Joseph, 87, 606
Best, Marion Hall, 164
Betche, Ernst, 87, 349, 416
Beumer, Lois, 353
Beuzeville, James, 179
Beyer, Joseph, 15
Bibb, John, 28
Bicheno, James Ebenezer, 87
Bick, Ernest Walter, 68, 88, 105, 128, 268, 496, 498, 550
Bickford, Ernest John 88, 316
Bickford, Nicholas Moysey, 88, 220, 279
Bidencope, Joseph, 89
Bidwill, John Carne, 24, 56, 72, 89, 90, 103, 344, 384, 402, 415, 438, 459, 477, 523
Bigge, J.T., 437, 567
Bird, Francis, 573
Bischoff, (née Dietrich), Charitas, 184
Bishop Tony, 180
Bishop, Douglas Alan, 91
Bishop, Geoffrey Charles 91
Bishop, William James, 91
Bisset, Charles Begg, 91, 540
Bisset, John William (Jack), 91, 453
Black, Alan, 12
Black, John McConnell, 34, 53, 91, 98, 198, 221, 406, 433, 644
Black, N.D., 288
Black, Neil, 558
Black, Niel, 174, 422
Blackall, William E., 53

679

Index of Names

Blackburn, James, 516
Blacket, Edmund, 10, 655
Blackmann, C.H.E., 579
Blackwell and Cala, 289
Blackwell (née Peake), Marion Isabel, 57, 91
Blackwell, Tony, 92
Bladen, Neill, Mrs 546
Blake, Edmund, 73, 92, 211, 385, 504, 548
Blake, Russell, 209
Blake, Stanley T. 53
Blakely, William Faris, 56, 92, 372
Blass family, 75
Blaxland, Gregory, 620
Blaxland (née Anderson), Helen Frances, 92, 93, 225, 473
Blazey, Alan, 299
Blazey, Clive and Penny, 299
Bleasdale, Joseph Ignatius, 93, 621
Bleeser, Florenz August Karl, 93, 445
Bligh (née Gordon), (Rosemary) Beatrice, 93
Bligh, Francis Leonard, 93
Bligh, Hugh, 93
Bligh, Michael, 93
Bligh, William, 72, 195, 357, 435, 451, 522, 581
Blombery, Alexander Morris, 94, 245, 397
Blomfield, Reginald, 33, 121, 182, 202, 380
Bloom, Harold, 20, 94, 355
Bloomfield, Douglas, 193
Blore, Edward, 267
Blott, C.P, 366
Blunt, Wilfrid, 385, 462
Boardman, Ralph, 59, 95, 177, 340
Boas, Harold, 95, 289
Boddy family, 56
Boddy, (Edward) Morton Murray 95, 478
Boddy, Mollie, 95
Boddy, Ralph, 47, 95, 618
Boden, Robert William, 62, 96
Bogie, Alex, 235
Bold, William Ernest, 44, 96, 140, 310, 601
Boldrewood, Mrs Rolf, see Browne, Margaret Maria
Bolton, Geoffrey, 137
Bonaparte, Josephine, 54, 180, 231, 367
Bond, Richard W. 75
Bonpland, Aime, 479
Bonython, Langdon, 127, 560
Borges, Jorge Luis, 620
Bosisto, Joseph, 97, 276, 277
Both, Ted, 584
Boulter, Frank John, 101

Boulter, Geoffrey Edmund, 101
Boulter, Victor John, 101, 507, 591
Bourke, Richard, 86, 247
Bowels family, 546
Bowen, Diamantina, 268
Bowen, George, 5, 185, 193
Bowie, David, 642
Bowie, James, 170
Bowman, Edward Macarthur 90, 103, 477
Bowman, James, 90, 103
Boyce, Henry, 103
Boyce, Leslie, 103
Boyce, Margaret, 103
Boyd, (William) Alexander Jenyns, 12, 103, 497, 498
Boyd, James, 486
Boyd, Robin, 28, 514, 569, 578, 617, 657
Boyle, Robert, 103
Brace, Emmeline Marcia, 103
Bradley, (Henry) Burton, 104, 290
Bradley, Eileen Burton, 57, 104
Bradley, Henry Houghton Burton, 104
Bradley, Joan Burton, 57, 104
Bradley, Rolfe, 61
Bradley, William, 159
Bradshaw, Ernest R., 121
Bragato, Romeo, 12, 104
Braithwaite, Henry Norman, 104
Braithwaite, J.G., 104, 495
Breakwell, Ernest, 435, 606
Brewster, Agnes, 194, 367
Brisbane, Thomas, 78, 125, 437
Britten, James, 462
Britton, Geoffrey, 422
Broadbent, James, 106, 142, 250, 384, 587, 619
Brogan, John, 411
Brooke, J.H. 212
Brookes, John, 202
Brookes, Norman, 593
Brown, Alfred John, 106, 600
Brown, George, 106, 176, 445, 538
Brown, James, 107, 386
Brown (née Giles), Jocelyn, 45, 106, 159, 161, 253, 274, 308, 332 321, 337, 353, 355, 440, 533, 600, 630
Brown, John, 153
Brown, John Ednie, 10, 12, 41, 44, 84, 107, 198, 221, 228, 249, 262, 270, 279, 298, 386, 421, 423, 468, 469, 518, 541, 560, 568, 573, 574, 637, 647
Brown, Lancelot, 40, 108, 201, 454, 473, 487, 504, 509, 549
Brown, Philip, 540
Brown, Ray, 275
Brown, Robert, 37, 53, 71, 72, 78, 79, 97, 108, 124, 170, 390, 453, 479, 643

Browne, Margaret Maria, 43, 85, 110, 146, 245, 257, 439, 499, 606
Browne, Thomas Alexander, 110, 308
Bruce, Alexander, 51, 110, 313, 431, 490
Brundrett, Allen Ambrose, 110
Brundrett, Bruce Alister, 110
Brundrett, Samuel, 43, 110, 431, 587, 617
Brunet, Alfred and Effie 21
Brunn, Theodore Herman, 110, 135
Brunning, George Edward, 111
Brunning, George, 7, 18, 41, 43, 44, 45, 111, 112, 198, 202, 227, 236, 244, 290, 292, 321, 417, 442, 493, 508, 526, 533, 551, 616, 657
Brunning, (Frederick) Hamilton 6, 7, 111, 112, 262, 493
Brunning, Herbert John, 111, 112, 430
Brunning, John, 111
Brunning, Leslie Herbert Ashley, 112, 499
Brunning, William, 111
Buchan, Alexander, 462
Buchan, Laird, 260
Buchanan and Cowper, 22
Buchanan, Alexander, 597, 638, 646
Buchanan, Barbara, 319
Buckland, Leonard, 143
Budding, Edwin, 364
Buhot, John, 302
Buik, William, 9
Bulcock, Robert, 113
Bull, William, 16, 644
Bunce, Daniel, 113, 115, 146, 148, 187, 223, 244, 248, 256, 289, 325, 435, 475, 499, 551, 588
Bunjoey (Susan), 159
Bunn, George, 533
Bunning, Walter, 412, 417
Burbank, Luther, 146, 570
Burbidge, Nancy, 51, 114
Burbury, Ronald William, 115, 123
Burdett (née Walker), Elsie May, 115
Burdett, May, 115
Burdett, William, 9, 34, 45, 115, 269, 408, 417, 561, 648
Burge family, 75
Burgess, E.J. 160
Burgess, Greg, 28, 465
Buring family, 75
Burke, Donald William, 60, 115, 440, 465, 500, 592
Burke, Edmund, 473, 487, 577
Burle Marx, Roberto 278, 412, 487, 515, 560, 569, 605
Burman, Nicolaas Laurens, 53, 116
Burnett, Beni Carr Glynn 427
Burnham, Daniel, 140
Burns family, 562

Index of Names

Burns, James, 412
Burton, David, 37, 54, 71, 118
Burton, Pritchard John, 118
Busby, James, 40, 118, 231, 244, 321, 378, 439, 549, 621, 649
Busby, William, 504
Bussell, Alfred, 625
Butchart, James, 84
Butler, Richard, 121
Butler, Walter Richmond, 18, 23, 28, 33, 45, 121, 122, 160, 182, 379, 381, 399, 617, 626, 642
Butterworth, John, 592
Buvelot, Abram-Louis, 638
Buzacott and Co., 329
Buzaglo, Frederick 518
Byrnes, T.J., 133

C.D. Young & Co., 329
Cadell, Francis, 283
Cahill, Patrick, 3
Caire, Nicholas, 473
Calder (née Wright), Winifred Braithwaite, 124
Calder, (Douglas) Malcolm 433
Caley, George, 37, 53, 71, 109, 124, 195, 422, 437, 479, 521, 581, 612
Caley Smith, Mrs 15, 173, 556
Calhoun, Stephen, 601
Calvert, James Snowden, 35
Calvert (née Atkinson), Louisa, 649
Calvert, Louise Snowden, 35
Cambridge, Ada, 547
Cameron, Mary Patricia, 433
Cameron, William, 422
Camfield, Julius Henry, 126
Campbell, Archibald George, 126
Campbell, Archibald James, 126, 146, 632, 633
Campbell, George, 191
Campbell, Marianne, 191
Campbell, Robert, 191
Campbell, Walter Scott 219, 649
Campion, Jane, 217
Candolle, Alphonse, 126
Candolle, Augustin Pyramus de, 126
Candolle, Casimir, 126
Cane, William Lancashire, 56, 126, 478
Carey, Peter, 374
Carlyle, Thomas, 65
Carne, Walter Mervyn, 215
Carr, Geoffrey William, 49, 128
Carrington, Lord, 133
Carron, William, 128, 219, 416, 459
Carson, Rachel, 48, 136, 453, 613
Carter, Paul, 229
Cartwright, C. 185, 186
Cartwright, Del, 591

Cartwright, Julia, 333
Casey, James Joseph, 281
Caslake, Charles Robert, 129, 166, 256
Castner, John L. 529
Cataldi, Lee, 374
Catani, Carlo Georgio Domenico Enrico, 101, 130, 333, 610, 656
Caulfield, Harold William, 105, 131, 449, 602
Cavanilles, Antonio José, 131, 173
Cazneaux, Harold, 308, 410
Cecchi, Ettore, 130
Chadwick, Edwin, 132
Chaffey, Benjamin William, 134
Chaffey Brothers, 30, 330, 444, 509
Chaffey, George, 134
Challinor, Henry, 328
Chambers, (Thomas) Carrick, 134
Champ, William Thomas Napier 589
Chandler, Alfred Elliot, 134
Chandler, David James William, 134, 375
Chandler, Edward Charles, 135
Chandler, Gilbert Lawrence, 134
Chandler, Gregg William, 41, 134, 135, 589
Chandler, Harold Cecil, 135
Chandler, Herbert Theodore Septimus 134
Chandler, Thomas David 134
Chandler, Thomas Herbert (John), 134
Chandler, William (1818–1883), 46, 134
Chandler, William (1844–1911), 134
Chandler, William Charles (c. 1835–1915), 15, 135, 534
Chandler, William Charles (1863–1944), 135
Chandler, William Charles (1895–1978), 135
Chandler, (Lawrence) Wreford, 134
Chapman Frederick, 399
Charsley, Fanny Anne, 98, 135, 634
Chatto, Beth, 202
Chauncy, Nan, 138
Cheel, Edwin, 92, 135, 372, 579
Cheeseman, Colin Harvey, 136
Cheeseman, Henry Albert (Harry), 136
Cheeseman, Richard, 135, 290, 292, 442, 483
Chenery, Alfred, 181
Chenery, George, 181
Cherry, Robert John, 34, 136
Cheung, Alan, 336
Chevalier, Nicholas, 76, 420
Cheyne, John, 137, 482, 496
Chippendale, George McC. 53
Chirnside, Andrew 136, 635
Chirnside, Thomas, 634, 635
Chisholm family, 347

Chisholm, James and Elizabeth 263
Chisholm, James Kinghorne 264
Chisholm, Nerine Neil, 139, 198
Christie, Hugh Watson, 139, 446
Church, Frederic, 319
Church, Thomas, 47, 302, 355, 412, 444, 445, 515, 571
Churchill, David Maughan, 140
Churchill, Jennie, 185
Clark, Alister, 15, 44, 45, 75, 110, 142, 150, 208, 224, 243, 255, 331, 429, 430, 477, 517, 533, 594, 598
Clark, Annie (née Cooper), 142
Clark, George John Edwin 193
Clark, Thomas, 638
Clark, Walter, 6, 142, 410, 493, 527
Clarke (née Snodgrass), Janet Marion 143
Clarke, Andrew 554, 567
Clarke, Francis Grenville (Frank), 143
Clarke, Frank, 150
Clarke, William Branwhite 510
Clarke, William John 143, 527
Clarke, William John Turner, 388, 527, 592
Clarson, William, 17, 41, 116, 144, 202, 244, 371 435
Clegg, G.W. 441
Cleland, George Fullerton, 53, 144
Cleland, John Burton, 144, 433
Clements, Pauline, 440
Clint, Richard, 455
Clough, Richard, 52, 61, 146, 266, 369, 610, 611
Clowes, E.M. 380
Clucas, Evan, 57
Clutton, William, 628
Cobham, Mary, 78
Cockayne, Leonard, 441
Coffee, John Francis, 146
Cohen family, 140
Cohn, Helen, 522
Cole, A.E. 120, 146
Cole, Charles Frederick 148
Cole, Edith Marion, 147
Cole, Edward William, 146, 147, 200
Cole, George, 148
Cole, George Graham, 148
Cole, George Ward 78
Cole, Henry Ungerford, 148
Cole, J.C., 359, 500
Cole, John, 147
Cole, John Charles 148
Cole, Silas, 583
Cole, Thomas Cornelius (1810-1889), 41, 118, 147, 244, 410, 435, 656
Cole, Thomas Cornelius (c. 1836–1879), 148

681

Index of Names

Coleman, Edith, 148, 298, 433, 658
Collins, David, 209
Collins, Gwendoline, 442
Collins, Julie, 512
Collins, Robert, 351, 353
Collins, William, 441
Colville, James, 54
Colvin, Brenda, 161, 228, 355
Comeadow, William Austin, 45, 149, 658
Conabere, Betty, 98
Conarty, James, 155
Connolly, John, 319
Connor, Patrick, 454
Cook, Albert, 274
Cook, Edward Frances George James, 159, 641
Cook, James, 24, 37, 53, 54, 71, 97, 215, 437, 451, 459, 533, 541, 542
Cooke, Graham Roger 296
Coolibar see Soutter, William
Coombe, William, 473
Cooper, Daniel, 256
Cooper, Duncan Elphinstone 529
Cooper, Ellwood, 20
Cooper, George, 500
Cooper, Guy, 498
Copas family, 160, 546
Copas, Henry, 160
Copas, Henry Walter 160
Copas, Keith, 160
Copas, Peter Raymond 160
Coppin, George Selth, 118, 332, 481
Corbett, H.A. 500
Cornish, Elsie, 10, 45, 66, 106, 150, 161, 269, 337, 355, 561
'Correa', see Galbraith, Jean
Correia De Serra, José Francisco, 108, 109
Correy, Allan Dale, 9, 47, 80, 161, 421, 561
Corrie, Dudley, 502
Costermans, Leon Francis, 161
Cottew family, 29
Cotton, Francis, 573
Cotton, John, 309, 519
Cotton, Olive, 93, 473
Cotton, Susannah 309
Cousins, Gael, 542
Cousins, Geoffrey, 542
Cowan, Alexander Menzies, 105, 164, 475, 496
Cowell, Percy, 361
Cowley, Ebenezer, 164
Cowlishaw, George Keith, 45, 56, 164, 244, 308, 461
Cowper, Appleford, and Murphy, 442
Cowper, Charles, 256
Cox, Catherine, see Allen, Catherine

Cox, Edward, 81, 212, 213
Cox, Eliza, 142
Cox family, 409
Cox, James, 142
Cox, Paul, 217
Cox, Philip, 587
Coxen, Charles, 339
Creswell, Charles Frederick (c. 1826–1895), 41, 166, 591
Creswell, Charles Frederick (1858–1916), 166
Creswell, Harvey Strathmore, 166
Creswick, F.M. 549
Crew, Gary, 138
Cribb, Alan Bridson 298
Cribb (née Herbert), Joan Winifred, 298, 433
Cribb, John George, 166
Crichton, David Alexander, 166, 223
Crittenden, Victor, 110, 369
Croft, Owen, 534
Cronin, John, 116, 167, 173, 342, 471, 477, 522, 533
Cronin, Maurice, 167
Crowe, Claude, 563
Crowe, Sylvia, 51, 61, 146, 152, 161, 168, 202, 295, 355, 432
Crowle, W.A. 411
Cruickshank, Alan, 244
Cubbitt, William, 262
Cuffley, Peter Leonard, 168, 236
Cumes, J.W.C. 367
Cumming, William Gordon 552
Cundall, Peter, 169, 500, 592
Cunningham, Allan, 20, 31, 37, 40, 53, 54, 56, 72, 90, 104, 169, 185, 215, 234, 344, 371, 414, 437, 449, 459, 479, 495, 510, 521, 523, 573, 582, 583, 650
Cunningham, Peter, 378
Cunningham, Richard, 169, 344, 459, 523
Cunningham, Tom, 461
Curnow, (William) John Jenkins 114
Curr, Edward, 1
Currie, Alan, 203
Currie, J.L. 203, 540, 597, 638, 646
Curtis (née Gemmell), Dorothy, 266
Curtis, William, 37, 79, 97, 98, 171, 201, 248, 572, 614
Curtis, Winifred Mary, 47, 171, 345, 433, 572, 587
Cushing, John, 171, 367
Custance, John Daniel 518
Cuthbert family, 264

Dahl, Andreas, 173
Daintree, Richard, 210
Daintrey, Edwin, 10

Dallachy, John, 53, 147, 173, 199, 325, 362, 410, 423, 522, 524, 540, 590, 596
Dalton, James, 159, 465
Dampier, William, 53, 97, 174, 479
Dangar, Albert Augustus 175
Dangar, Henry, 174
Dangar, William, 174
Dangerfield, Barry, 105
Daniell, Hilda, 84
Dardel, James Henry, 175
Darley, Frederick, 94
Darling (née Anderson), Margaret, 58, 80, 175, 358
Darling, Ralph, 10
Darwin, Charles Robert, 176, 219, 553
Darwin, Erasmus, 437
Davenport, Margaret, 546
Davenport, Samuel, 81, 176, 300, 546
Davey, Harry H. 52, 95, 177, 340, 430
David, T. Edgeworth, 138
Davidson, Jim, 581
Davidson, William, 177, 378, 526
Davis, Arthur Hoey 175, 358, 496
Davis, John, 512
Davis, Margaret, 150, 178, 313, 314
Davis, Mervyn Twynam, 47, 178
Davy, Edward, 397
Dawes, William, 357
Dawson, George, 179
Dawson, George Russell, 179, 637
Dawson, Thomas Henry, 179
Dawson, (Russell) William, 179
de Bernales, Claude Albo, 163
de Beuzeville, Wilfred Alexander Watt, 56, 179
de Castella family, 656
de Castella, Francois Robert, 179, 621
de Castella, Hubert, 585
de Castella, Paul 159
de Caux, Isaac 33
d'Entrecasteaux, J.A.R. Bruny, 37, 53, 180, 351
de Gryse, Jerry 589
d'Incarville, Pierre 479
de Jussieu, Adrien 585
de Malahide, Talbot, 216, 329, 345
de Mestre, Roi 19
De Mole, Fanny Elizabeth, 98, 181
De Mole, Harriet Jane 181
De Mole, Margaret 181, 366
de Quincy, A.C. Quatremère, 248
de Soissons, Louis 106
de Vandes, Comtesse, 79
de Vlamingh, Willem 53
Deakin, Alfred, 69, 134, 444
Deakin, Pattie, 69
Deane, Henry, 219, 649
Deans, William C., 179

Index of Names

Dechaineux, Lucien, 180
Deery, Kathleen, 342
Delahaye, Félix, 180, 231
Dell, Edgar, 98, 181, 254
Dellit, C. Bruce 323
Denham, Ilma (Elma), 128, 181, 245
Denison, William Thomas, 182, 266, 415, 439
Denton Corker Marshall, 28, 542
Derham, John, 318
Desbrowe-Annear, Harold, 28, 45, 68, 84, 165, 167, 182, 183, 229, 425, 609, 617
Deschamps family, 621, 656
Deschamps, Joseph Clement, 183
Despeissis, Adrian Jean Marie, 12, 183, 231
Di Giacomo Cataneo, Pietro, 568
Dickinson, James, 23, 41, 124, 128, 148, 173, 184, 244, 264, 526, 588
Dickson, B.T. 62
Dickson, John, 402
Diels, Ludwig, 53
Dietrich (née Nelle), (Konkordia) Amalie, 53, 184
Dietrich, Wilhelm, 184
Dixon (née Burkitt), Patricia Annesley, 185, 250
Dixon, Kingsley Wayne, 185
Docker, Joseph, 97
Dodd, Henry, 185
Dods, Robin, 33, 234, 442
Domin, Karel, 53
Doran, Philip, 130, 186
Doubleday, Henry, 453
Douglas, David, 443, 479
Douglas, Neil, 294
Dowling, Laidley, 412
Downer, (Sir) Alexander, 648
Downer, Alexander George 209, 564
Downer, James Frederick 264
Downer, John William 264
Downing, Andrew Jackson, 187, 254, 277, 333, 356, 368, 443, 451, 490, 548, 549, 616
Dowse, Frank Robert, 187
Drake, Sarah, 97
Drewry, Judith Holmes 657
Drummond, James, 53, 188, 189, 203, 269, 328, 398, 371, 540, 636
Dryander, Jonas, 109
Du Faur, (Frederick) Eccleston 304
Dudley, John, 502
Duncan, Geoffrey, 582
Duncan, John Gordon 321
Duncan, John Grant 321
Duncan, John James (1845–1913), 321
Duncan, John James (1913–1997), 321

Duncan, Walter Hughes, 190, 321, 431
Duncan, William, 459, 527
Dunphy, Milo Kanangra 191
Dunphy, Myles, 94, 95, 191, 430
Dunstan, Don, 562
Dupain, Max, 308, 473
Dürer, Albrecht 182
Dutkiewicz, Ludwick, 98
Dutton, Frederick Hansborough 22
Dutton, Frederick Hugh 22
Dutton, Geoffrey, 22
Dwight, (Horace) John De Fraine, 192, 561
Dwyer, R.E.P. 297
Dyer, Joseph, 584

Eardley-Wilmot, John, 283, 524, 526
Earwaker, Louise, 62
East, Cecil Arthur Wentwood 321
Eaten, Hubert, 133
Eaves, Alfred, 194
Eaves, Samuel Hinder, 193, 477, 496
Eckbo, Garrett, 161, 355, 408, 412, 444, 445
Eckersley, Richard Hugo, 194
Eckford, Henry, 583
Ecklon, 479
Eddy (née Jamieson), Nancy Gilmour, 196, 220, 445
Edgar, James Scott, 196, 512
Edmunds, Alan, 59, 196, 197, 204, 530
Edquist, Alfred George 435
Edwards, Brian, 176
Edwards, John Sutherland 69
Edwards, Madigan Torzillo, 319
Edwards, Reginald George, 45, 61, 120, 198, 244
Edwards, Sydenham, 97
Eichler, Hansjoerg, 8, 198
Elder, Thomas, 66, 127, 198
Eldershaw, M. Barnard, 374
Ellery, Robert Lewis John, 291
Elliot (née Parry), Gwendoline Margaret, 198
Elliot, (Winston) Rodger, 47, 48, 52, 198, 244, 377, 433
Elliott, Alexander, 198, 235, 486, 540
Elliott, Brent, 81
Elliott, Joseph, 573
Elliott, Joseph William, 573
Elliott, Peter, 70
Elliott, Robert George, 199, 641
Elliott, William, 7, 43, 140, 147, 199, 202, 211, 249, 343, 359, 366, 551
Ellis, James, 481
Ellison, Thomas, 338
Elrington, William Sandys 420
Elston, Glenn, 594

Elwes, J.H. 483
Emerson, Ralph Waldo 319, 643
Engleheart, G.H. 143
Engler, Adolf, 585
Erbritch, 478
Erickson (née Sandilands), Frederica Lucy, 98, 189, 203, 250
Errey Bros, 182, 263, 477
Errey, David, 204
Errey, Edwin, 204
Errey, Gilbert Gurnett, 204
Errey, (Thomas) Henry, 204
Errey, Reginald Gilbert, 204
Errey, Sidney Arnold, 204
Errey, Thomas Peter, 204
Errey, William Gilbert, 204
Errey, William Henry, 204, 617
Eshuys family, 19
Espie, Robert, 588
Etheridge, Robert, 416
Evans, Edward, 431
Evans, Henry, 75
Evans, Obed D. 53
Evelyn, John, 273
Everett, Percy E. 339
Everist, Selwyn Lawrence, 206, 232
Ewart, Alfred James, 36, 206, 524. 645

Fagg, Murray, 650
Fairall, Arthur Robert, 209, 346
Fairbairn, Charles Osborne, 73
Fairbairn family, 73
Fairbairn, George, 309
Fairfax family, 465, 597
Fairfax, John, 584
Fairhall, Alfred Ernest, 9, 209, 534
Fairlie, Bill, 518
Fairlie, Keith, 518
Faithful family, 566
Falkner, F.A. 112
Farley, Rick, 353
Farquhar and Mackenzie, 472
Farrand, Beatrix, 166, 182, 631
Farrar, Reginald, 138, 202
Farris, A.W. 495
Fauser, Otto, 17
Fawkner, John Pascoe, 209
Feakes, Daniel, 210, 269, 346
Featherston, Gerald Henry (Tony), 61
Feint, Adrian, 32, 225, 632
Fellowes, James Edward Richards, 15
Fellowes, Walter Bennett, 15
Fenton, Cicely, 211, 639
Fenton, John, 211, 639
Ferguson, Daniel, 209
Ferguson, Francis, 19, 41, 92, 211, 385, 411, 439, 540, 548
Ferguson, William, 41, 211, 249, 286, 551

683

Index of Names

Fern, James, 212, 540
Fiedler family, 75
Field, Barron, 214
Field, Ralph, 124
Fielden, Lorna, 89
Fieldhouse family, 328
Finedon, Frank, 218
Firminger, Thomas Augustus 325
Fischer, (Detlef) Ludwig Theodor, 218, 349
Fisher, Charles Brown 304
Fisher, May, 181
Fitch, Walter, 97
Fitzalan, Eugene, 124, 219, 329, 614
Fitzgerald, John, 140
Fitzgerald, Robert David, 98, 129, 159, 219, 311, 329, 416, 453, 459, 649
Fitzgerald, William Vincent 568
Fitzhardinge (née Macmaster), Olive Rose, 219
Fitzpatrick (née Johnson), (Alice) May, 220, 445
FitzRoy, Charles Augustus, 91, 313, 414
Fiveash, Rosa, 34, 98, 221
Flannery, Tim, 145
Flaxman, Charles 21
Fleay, David, 385, 661
Flecker, Hugo, 216
Fleming, Gavin, 590, 648
Fleming, James, 221, 655
Flinders, Matthew, 53, 71, 78, 108
Flockton, Margaret Lilian, 98, 222, 395
Foley, Fiona, 32
Foott, Bethia, 19
Ford, Gordon, 47, 57, 119, 185, 228, 263, 348, 376, 434, 571, 618
Ford, Gwen, 228
Forrest, C. 155
Forrest, George, 138, 479
Forrest, John, 229, 285, 338, 346
Forrest (née Hamersley), Margaret Elvire, 230
Forrester, Sue, 57, 414, 478
Fortune, Robert, 138, 461, 479
Foster, John Harvey, 230, 250, 591
Fowler, William, 231
Fox, Paul Francis, 231, 250
Francis, George William 5, 7, 131, 232, 233, 268, 354, 377, 401, 538, 560
Francis, Jeremy Mark 296
Francis, Peter, 472
Francis, William Augustus 56, 131
Francis, William Douglas, 232, 510
Franklin, Frederick Augustus 133
Franklin (née Griffin), Jane, 63, 141, 154, 232, 266, 315, 409, 433, 526, 573, 589
Franklin, John, 141, 232, 234, 283, 409, 433, 524, 526, 589

Fraser, Charles, 40, 79, 104, 125, 139, 170, 185, 231, 234, 437, 459, 507, 517, 522, 526, 540, 573, 583
Fraser, Grace Ella, 57, 235, 260, 398, 524
Frederick, Samuel Ernest 431
Freeling, Arthur Henry 640
French, Charles, 235, 399, 541
French, Charles Hamilton 236, 470
Freschel, Gertrude, 361
Frith, Frederick, 366
Frome, Edward Charles 640
Frond, C.B. 60
Frost, Charles, 431
Frost, Phyllis, 342
Fuaux, Alexis Eric 123
Fuaux, Les, 658
Fuchs, Leonhart, 237
Furneaux, Tobias, 54

Gadd, Samuel, 516
Galbraith, Jean, 45, 47, 56, 59, 119, 241, 362, 365, 433, 617, 623, 658
Gallagher, George, 601
Gamble, Harriet Victoria 242
Gardner, Charles Austin, 53, 56, 181, 215, 254, 433, 525
Gardner, Martha, 591
Garnet, (John) Roslyn, 254, 418, 433
Garnett, Thomas Ronald, 145, 255, 300, 362
Gattenby, Ted, 591
Gatter, (James) George 256
Gatter, George Prowlin, 256
Gauba, Erwin, 62
Gaudi, Antonio, 515
Gaudichand, 231
Gawler, George, 9, 67
Gelding, John, 256, 295, 311
Gelding, William, 256
Gellatly, George L. 500
Gellert, Leon, 308
George III, 71
George IV, 15
George, Alexander Segger, 258, 518
Gibbs, May, 73
Gibbs, Vicary, 604
Giblin, Robert Wilkins 579
Gibson, Andrew, 117
Gibson (née Grassick), Emily Matilda, 3, 36, 45, 47, 116, 235, 253, 258, 260, 332, 617
Gibson, John, 82, 227, 260, 466
Gibson, Maud, 98, 277, 418, 521, 572
Gilbert, Joseph, 75, 471, 621
Gilbert, Lionel Arthur, 250, 260
Gilbert, P.A. 91
Giles, Charles (c. 1807–1887), 41, 260, 560

Giles, Charles (c. 1846-1932), 260
Giles, Charles William Wycliffe 261
Gill, Herbert Fitzmaurice 112, 262
Gill, Justin Moray, 179
Gill, (Ernest) Reginald Notton 262
Gill, Samuel Thomas, 31, 226, 261, 544
Gill and Searle, 112
Gill, Walter, 261, 262, 298, 421, 647
Gillanders, Ken, 17, 262, 589
Gillard, Joseph, 468
Gillies, William, 434
Gilmore, Mary, 538
Gilpin, William, 184, 201, 262, 473, 487, 540, 624
Gilpin, William Sawrey 262, 540, 590
Ginn, Henry, 32, 147, 173, 262, 481, 527
Gipps, George, 170
Gladstones, John, 621
Glass, Hugh, 41, 78, 212
Glass, Peter, 47, 57, 263, 348
Gleadow, John Ward 296
Gleeson, James 567
Glenn, David, 296
Glenny, George, 179, 184, 202, 264, 305
Glover, John, 31, 32, 234, 308, 332
Gloystein, Tilman Wilhelm 533
Gnuyang, see McDonald, Donald Alaster
Godfrey Spowers, 569
Goldsmith, Oliver, 108
Goldsworthy, Andy, 512
Goller, J.J. 264
Gooch Walter, 84
Good, Peter, 37, 53, 71, 78, 109, 265
Goodall family, 159
Goodman, Charles John 265
Goodman, Richard, 265
Goodman, William, 266
Goodwin, John, 268
Gordon, David Morrice, 56, 266, 291, 478, 575, 654
Gordon family, 397
Gordon, Hugh, 397
Gordon, James, 365
Gordon, William Forbes 93
Gorton, Margaret, 181
Gouan, Antoine, 351
Gould, G.R. 500
Gould, John, 614
Gowrie (née Pollok), Zara Eileen, 266, 268, 269, 313
Goyder, George, 108, 185, 269, 292, 445, 509, 518, 560, 647
Graff, Robert, 98
Graham, Joseph, 81, 270, 540
Gramp, Johann, 75
Grant and McMillan, 288
Grant, Alexander, 270, 540, 583, 655
Grant, Bob, 571

684

Index of Names

Grasby, (William) Catton, 12, 243, 639
Gray, Alexander William 142
Gray, Alfred John 47, 56, 272, 575
Gray, Alfred Kenneth, 272
Gray, Edward Waters, 173, 272
Gray, Harold Charles 272, 388
Gray, John, 52, 272
Gray, Max, 115
Gray, Roy Gordon 272
Greaves, Harold, 8, 272, 268, 573
Greenway, Francis, 28, 108, 267, 505, 567
Greenwood, Donald, 146
Gregory, Augustus, 423
Gregson, Jesse 657
Greville, Charles F. 274
Grevillea. See Kemp, Herbert John (Jack)
Griffin (née Mahony), Marion Lucy, 56, 119, 129, 130, 140, 253, 275, 367, 439, 444, 515
Griffin, Walter Burley, 18, 19, 28, 44, 45, 49, 51, 52, 56, 62, 119, 140, 231, 246, 247, 253, 260, 275, 330, 348, 352, 355, 367, 431, 432, 439, 444, 515, 566, 579, 601, 609, 617, 639
Griffiths, Alex, 661
Griffiths, Walter Scott 561
Grimes, Charles, 222, 655
Grimwade, Harold William 399
Grimwade, (Wilfrid) Russell, 45, 56, 58, 276, 277, 359, 399, 418, 473, 533
Gritten, Henry, 31, 277
Groom, Arthur 353, 430
Gropius, Walter, 412
Grounds, Roy, 569
Guérard, (Johann Joseph) Eugène von, 31, 32, 76, 142, 278, 406, 470, 638
Guertner, Beryl Greta, 60, 279, 587
Guilfoyle, John Austin, 220, 221, 279, 280
Guilfoyle, Michael, 19, 41, 279, 386, 401, 418, 439, 447, 507
Guilfoyle, William, 15, 21, 28, 36, 42, 43, 50, 56, 73, 75, 82, 98, 123, 144, 146, 149, 160, 167, 174, 185, 187, 199, 212, 221, 227, 232, 235, 250, 251, 253, 268, 279, 280, 281, 282, 286, 290, 298, 309, 332, 337, 338, 348, 349, 354, 356, 371, 376, 398, 399, 401, 402, 414, 424, 426, 434, 435, 439, 459, 461, 471, 472, 475, 501, 510, 512, 519, 522, 533, 536, 540, 577, 585, 591, 592, 605, 606, 616, 628, 635, 641, 642, 643
Gulliver, Benjamin Thomas 283
Gulliver Brothers, 496
Gulliver, Thomas Allen (c. 1809–1873), 283
Gulliver, Thomas Allen (1848–1931), 283
Gunn, J.D., 53

Gunn, Ronald, 26, 41, 54, 65, 114, 141, 231, 283, 289, 296, 315, 368, 409, 524, 526, 541
Gunson, J.M., 4
Gustav, Runge, 8, 538
Gutch, George, 567

Haase, Bernie, 51
Hackett, Brian, 161, 356, 565
Hackett, (Walter) Champion 285
Hackett (née Drake-Brockman), Deborah Vernon, 285
Hackett, E. & W. 251, 285
Hackett, Elisha W., 285
Hackett, George, 285
Hackett, George Alfred, 285
Hackett, John Winthrop, 41, 115, 209, 285, 639
Hackett, Walter, 285, 560
Haddon, Robert Joseph, 33, 285
Haenke, Fadeo, 131
Hagenbeck, Carl 661
Haigh, Richard, 464
Haines, R. Standley 499
Hall, Dianne, 437
Hall, Fiona, 32, 431
Hall, Frederick B. 19, 20
Hall, Jonathan, 437
Hall, Robert, 434
Hall, Rodney, 353
Hall, Roger, 437
Hall, Suzanne, 437
Hallstrom, Edward, 661
Halprin, Lawrence, 389
Hamer, Rupert James, 49, 286
Hamilton, Arthur Andrew 92
Hamilton, Frank, 286
Hamilton, Henry, 286
Hamilton, Richard, 286
Hammet, Ivo, 286, 376
Hammond, Eric Herbert, 47, 198, 287, 399, 403, 646, 658
Hammond, William 390
Hanbury, Thomas, 143
Handasyde, Frederick William 288
Handasyde, Gilbert, 288, 540
Handasyde, McMillan & Co, 288, 289
Handreck, Kevin Arthur, 288, 557, 558
Hannaford, Ernest Hayler 288
Hannaford, George, 288, 289
Hannaford, Samuel 109, 288, 616, 618
Hanrahan, Barbara, 374, 547
Hanson, Beverley, 571
Harding, Richard Ross 599
Hardy, James J. 289
Hardy, Thomas, 289, 342, 390, 468, 565
Hare, Harry, 193
Harper, Charles, 464, 639

Harris, Alexander, 373
Harris, George, 440
Harris, H.R. 231
Harris, Joseph, 6, 36, 41, 202, 235, 256, 289, 442, 508, 543, 575
Harris, Thistle Yolette, 45, 47, 56, 58, 98, 119, 222, 244, 287, 290, 367, 433, 440, 569, 658
Harrison, Edward James, 179, 637
Hartmann, Carl Heinrich, 290, 496
Harvey, L.J., 180
Harvey, W.H. 76, 283, 288, 289, 290, 329
Harvie, William, 263
Harwood, George, 290
Hasluck, Paul, 475
Hassall, Thomas, 181
Hassell, 509
Hatcher, William H. 583
Hateley, Garnet Alexander Stanley, 291, 376
Hathorn, Libby, 138
Haussmann, Georges Eugène 101, 231
Hawke, Bob, 353
Hawker, George Charles 114
Hawkes, Claude, 581
Hawkins, William Richard, 291, 470
Hawter, Jacob, 292, 584
Hay, William, 611
Hayes, Colin, 21
Hayes, William Brelsford, 176, 292, 307, 329, 445
Hayward, Edward, 128
Hayward (née Barr Smith), Ursula, 128
Hazelwood, Walter Gordon, 125, 250
Hazlewood Bros, 527
Hazlewood, David (Rex) 292, 431
Hazlewood, Harry H., 45, 292, 431
Hazlewood, Walter Gordon 292
Hearn, William Edward 78, 299
Hearne, Thomas, 474
Heath, Charles, 132, 210, 293
Heath, Frank, 293, 376
Hedges, (William) Henry, 294
Heinze, Kevin Carl, 295, 543, 592
Hemphill, John, 298
Hemphill, Rosemary, 298
Hemsley, G. 527
Henchman, Francis, 54, 79
Henderson, E.G. 16
Henderson, John, 524
Henderson, Robert, 40, 128, 280, 295, 390, 437, 540
Henderson, Robert Theophilus 295
Hendry, Margaret, 52, 61, 295
Henry, Augustine, 479
Henry, Frederick, 641
Henry, Kathleen Vivian (Kitty), 295, 589

685

Index of Names

Henry, Lucien, 28, 180
Henslow, John, 176, 415
Hentschke family, 75
Henty (née Tattersfield), Carol, 295
Henty, Edward, 76, 117, 296, 535
Henty, Francis, 173, 296
Henty, Stephen, 421
Henty, William, 209, 296, 315
Herbert, Daniel, 81
Herbert, Desmond Albert, 297, 497, 525, 605
Herbert, William, 90
Hester, Joy, 294
Heussler, Johann Christian 268
Hewett, Dorothy, 374
Hewitt, Mary, 441
Heyne, Carl Franz, 236, 244, 259, 301
Heyne, Ernst Bernhard, 300, 560, 585
Heyne, Franz Waldemar, 301
Heyne (née Hanckel), Maria Wilhemina Laura, 301
Heyne, Roger, 301
Heysen, Hans, 83
Hibberd, (James) Shirley, 202, 301
Hicks, David, 71
Higgins, Frances Georgina Watts (Ina), 248, 258, 299, 301
Higgins, Henry Bournes, 299, 301
Higgins, Kathleen, 138
Higgins, Walter Herbert, 301
Hill, Arthur, W., 648
Hill, (Myra) Coralie, 556
Hill, Fidelia, 373
Hill, Lancelot Leonard, 190, 364, 601
Hill, Matthew, 371
Hill, Robin Sinclair, 17, 47, 301, 343, 361, 561
Hill, Walter, 41, 67, 68, 104, 268, 302, 303, 325, 354, 402, 475, 498, 501, 540, 560, 601, 602, 605, 606
Hillary, Cyril Hamilton Corby, 303, 431
Hillary, Joan, 304
Hillier, Rob, 440
Hinder, Margel, 542
Hindmarsh, John, 16, 268
Hine, James, 386
Hirschi, Friedrich, 304, 482, 584
Hirst, C.G.S. 99
Hitchmough, James Donald, 305
Hobbs, J.J. Talbot 346
Hobbs, Jonah, 305
Hobday, John, 51, 478, 490
Hobhouse, Penelope, 202, 337
Hochgurtel, Josef, 542
Hockey, Patrick, 442
Hocking, Sidney Edwin 461
Hockings, A.J. 305, 425, 496, 605, 650
Hockings, Albert Thomas 306

Hockings, (Francis) David, 41, 146, 179, 194, 236, 244, 264306
Hoddle, Robert, 339, 493
Hodge, Leomin, 126, 274, 306, 478
Hodgins, Basil Robert 306
Hodgins, Robert Wyburn, 125, 292, 306
Hodgkinson, Clement, 14, 88, 127, 212, 220, 221, 306, 371, 405, 491, 524, 534, 536, 553, 616
Hoff, Raynor, 323
Hoffmann family, 75
Hogg, R. Bruce 91
Hogg, Robert, 485
Hogg, Thomas, 223
Hohnen, Cate, 625
Hohnen, Mark, 625
Hole, Samuel Reynolds, 142
Holford, Lord, 432
Holliday, Ivan, 306, 377, 562
Holliday, Ray, 306, 459, 467, 561, 562
Hollinsdale, Charles 307, 435
Holt, John, 291
Holttum, (Richard) Eric 405
Holtze, Maurice, 8, 176, 259, 292, 307, 445, 530, 605
Holtze, Nicholas, 15, 176, 292, 308, 314, 445
Homeyer, W.L. 626
Honey, Elizabeth, 138
Hook, Alfred, 323
Hook, Charles, 181
Hooker, Joseph Dalton, 26, 90, 164, 176, 195, 201, 219, 283, 289, 290, 390, 392, 410, 479, 507, 521, 524
Hooker, William Jackson, 53, 90, 97, 109, 170, 189, 195, 196, 201, 219, 283, 288, 290, 302, 320, 344, 359, 386, 409, 413, 415, 521, 526, 554
Hope, A.D 374
Hope, John, 555
Hope, Louis, 302
Hope, Mary, 471
Hope, Percy G.S., 272, 310
Hope, R.M. 59
Hopkins, Henry, 579
Hopkins, Isaac, 23
Hopkins, John, 231
Hordern, Alfred, 310
Hordern, Anthony (1788-1869), 310
Hordern, Anthony (1889-1970) 310
Hordern III, Anthony, 310
Hordern, Caroline, 310
Hordern, Edward Carr 310
Hordern family, 310, 562
Hordern, Lebbeus, 310
Hordern, Mary, 562
Hordern, Samuel (1849–1909), 310
Hordern, Samuel (1876–1956), 310

Hordern, Samuel (1909–1960), 310, 643
Horn and Frampton, 390
Horn, William Austin 564, 623
Hortensis, see Sangster, William
Hortle, Charles, 628
Horton, Samuel, 558
Hosking, John, 394
Hosking, Martha, 394
Hoskins, Cecil, 328, 559
Hoskins, Sidney 559, 648
Hoskins, W.G. 545
Howard, Albert, 453
Howard, Amos William, 319
Howard, Ebenezer, 151, 246
Howard, Harry Stanton, 119, 319, 388, 431, 440, 507, 515, 542
Howe, George, 16
Howie, Laurence, 180
Howitt, Alfred William 320
Howitt, Anna Mary 76
Howitt family, 78
Howitt, Godfrey, 320, 407
Howitt (née Botham), Mary, 76, 320
Howitt, Richard, 320
Howitt, William, 320
Howlett, Frederick, 320
Hucker, Wendy, 657
Hudson, Edward, 336
Hügel, Carl (Charles) Alexander Anselm von, 320, 479, 636
Hughan, Randolph, 320
Hughan, Robert, 320, 540
Hughes, (Edwin) Albert ('Elfin'), 320
Hughes, John Arthur 28, 229
Hughes, Walter Watson 320
Hughes-Jones, E., 412
Hull, George, 587
Humboldt, Alexander von, 126, 176, 479, 538
Hume, Hamilton, 15
Hume, Walter and Ernest 330
Humphrey, Adolarius William Henry, 588
Humphreys, Henry Noel 76
Humphries, Barry, 263
Hunt, John Dixon 409
Hunt, J. Horbury, 165, 310
Hunt, Leigh, 214
Hunt, Sidney Herbert, 198, 308, 321
Hunter, Edmund Harold 581
Hunter, Henry, 160, 331
Hurley, Percy Joseph (Peter), 45, 198, 321
Hussey, Christopher, 166, 474
Hutton (née Gorton), Margaret 366
Huxley, Thomas Henry 386
Hyland, Thomas Francis 468
Hyndman, William, 199, 323, 329, 540

Index of Names

Ibbotson, Charles, 294, 320
Ifould, William Herbert 431
Ingram, Collingwood, 534
Inskip, George C. 121
Iota, 373
Irvine, Hans, 87
Irvine (née Berger), Susan, 331, 517
Irving, Robert, 575
Irwin, James, 128
Isaac, Cyril Everett, 110, 135, 153, 331, 332, 433, 617
Isaac, Cyril Hampden, 332
Issacs, Isaac, 313

Jack, B. 478
Jackson, J.B. 161, 545
Jackson, Linda, 180
Jacob, William, 75
Jacobs, Maxwell Ralph 359
Jacobson, Lisa, 374
Jacques, David, 108
James, Henry Alfred, 56, 140, 224, 335, 439
James, (Thomas) Horton, 127, 335
Jamison, John, 40, 335, 378, 454
Jampijinpa, John, 3, 336, 476
Jeavons, Mary, 336
Jekyll, Gertrude, 9, 43, 68, 106, 121, 161, 162, 166, 182, 202, 226, 257, 295, 296, 336, 375, 511, 561, 589, 624, 625, 642
Jellicoe, Geoffrey, 333
Jessep, Alexander, 116, 125, 337, 471, 522, 555
Johns, Henry Isaac, 645
Johnson, Benjamin, 338
Johnson, (Thomas) George Hart, 338
Johnson, George William, 162, 322
Johnson, Lawrence Alexander Sidney, 338, 523
Johnson, Roger Kirk Hayes, 338
Johnson, Stephen, 338
Johnson, Thomas, 199, 338
Johnston, A.C. 390
Johnston, Blanche, 311
Johnston, George, 311, 437
Johnston, Julia, 31
Johnston, Lawrence, 71, 115, 149
Johnstone, Robert de Bruce, 339
Jolley, Elizabeth, 374
Jolly, Alexander, 339, 540
Jolly, Norman William, 339
Jones, Clem, 22
Jones, David Fletcher 222
Jones, David Lloyd 198
Jones, David, 52
Jones, George Sydney 515
Jones, James, 133, 134, 232, 329, 340, 618

Jones, Louisa, 508
Jones, Owen, 76, 229
Jones, Paul Osbourne, 98, 340, 632
Jones, Ron, 524
Jorgensen, Francis, 373

Kavel, August, 74
Kay, Frederick Norman, 244, 342
Kay, William Porden, 268
Keane, Edward, 637
Kearney, James, 147
Kee, Jenny, 180
Keenan, Francis (Frank), 342, 463
Kelland, William, 441
Kelly, Alexander Charles, 22, 289, 342, 390, 621
Kelly, Frances, 440
Kelly, John, 342
Kelly, Stanley, 342
Kelman, W.D. 118
Kemp, Edward 9, 41, 43, 161, 200, 202, 248, 249, 301, 342, 343, 361, 387, 451, 466, 474, 509, 536, 554, 576, 580, 604, 616
Kemp, Henry Kenneth 344
Kemp, Herbert John, 9, 15, 343, 500, 560
Kemp, Peter Frewer, 343
Kemp, Richard, 343
Kemp, Robert Frewer, 15, 343
Kempe, (Friedrich Adolf) Herman, 344
Kendall, J. 429
Kenju, Junko Morimoto 138
Kennedy, Edmund, 128
Kennedy, John, 367
Kennedy, Lewis, 366
Kenner, George, 341
Kent, William, 108, 339, 433, 454
Kermode, Robert Quayle, 409
Kermode, William, 409
Kerr, Joan, 106, 511, 520
Kershaw, George Wilkinson 431
Kerslake, George Henry Tuck, 173, 344, 477
Kerslake, Thomas Ambrose 344
Kidd, James, 91, 247, 344, 510
Kiddle, Margaret, 540, 638
Kidman family, 161
King, Helena Elizabeth (Biddy), 47, 345
King, Herbert John, 171, 345
King, Inge, 542
King, James, 321
King, Philip Gidley, 72, 124, 221, 357, 612, 620
King, Phillip Parker 20, 31, 72, 90, 170, 450
Kingdon Ward, Frank, 248, 479
Kingsley, Henry, 373

Kingston, George Strickland, 9, 28, 198, 346, 370, 640
Kirkbride, Thomas, 319
Kirkpatrick, James Barrie, 347
Klein, Edward, 304
Klem, Carl, 44, 246, 272, 310
Kneen, Thomas Hugh, 347, 463
Knight, George Robert 431
Knight, George William, 291, 348
Knight, Hattie, 553
Knight, John George 267, 348
Knight, Joseph, 54, 79, 279, 552
Knight and Perry, 614
Knight, Richard Payne 473, 487
Knox, Alistair, 47, 103, 263, 348, 434, 571, 618
Knox, Edward William, 249, 513
Knox, Margot, 348, 434, 571
Koelewyn family, 436
Koons, Jeff, 599
Kouskos, Gus, 353
Kraehenbuehl, Darrell Nairn, 348
Krempin, Frederick William, 349
Krempin, Harry Lionel 349
Krempin, John Lionel, 326, 349
Krempin, Wilhelm Frederick Johan (William John) 349
Krichauff, Friedrich, 219, 259, 300, 349, 536, 560
Kruger, Frederick, 309
Krummel, Paul, 131, 421
Kuck, Lorraine E. 605
Kuring, Peter, 349, 350
Kuwahata, Hideo, 350

La Gerche, Alfred Romeo 351, 371
La Gerche, John 351, 423
La Trobe, Charles Joseph, 33, 76, 175, 183, 185, 256, 320, 362, 423, 490, 519, 522, 524, 584, 615, 655
Labillardière, Jacques-Julien Houtou de, 37, 180, 205, 231, 351, 479, 504
Lahey, Romeo, 351, 353, 430
Lahey, Vida, 353
Laidlaw, William, 352, 522
Laird and Buchan, 339
Lamb, Charles, 214
Lambert, Aylmer Bourke, 86, 641
Lane Poole, Charles Edward, 12, 44, 146, 228, 277, 358, 582
Lane, Lauretta Caroline Maria 379
Lang, Joanna, 624
Lang, Thomas, 41, 76, 111, 199, 218, 263, 291, 338, 359, 366, 435, 441, 451, 485, 507, 540, 616
Langbecker, Albert Wilhelm, 360
Langbecker, Carl Conrad Emil Wilhelm, 360, 496

Index of Names

Langbecker, Edward Conrad, 360
Langdon, Raymond Forbes, 360
Langer, Karl, 47, 360, 412, 497
Lansell, George, 230
Larkman, Barry Howard 60
Larsen, John Will Edgard 516
Lasscock, Edward Albert, 361, 560, 561
Lasscock, Effie, 361
Lasscock, Ian Mcarthur 361
Lasscock, John Roe 361
Lasscock, Kim Genery 361
Lassetter, Frederick, 504, 530
Latham, Edward, 500
Latham, John, 307, 361
Latreille (née Dalrymple), Anne Helen, 250, 361
Latrobe, Benjamin Henry 76
Lauder, Alexander, 121
Lauder, Thomas Dick 487
Lauffer, Charles, 292
Laurence, Janet, 32
Laurie, Chris, 461
Laurie, Tina, 461
Law Somner and Co., 20, 41, 111, 147, 244, 359, 365, 439, 473, 493, 644
Law, William, 19, 365, 540
Lawn, Velvet, 364
Lawrence, D.H. 594
Lawrence, Robert William 283
Law-Smith (née Darling), Joan 58, 149, 175, 242, 365
Law-Smith, Robert 365
Lawson, Abercrombie Anstruther, 194, 366
Lawson, Daniel, 193
Lawson, Henry, 119, 373
Lawson, William, 257
Lawton, Geoff, 468
Layton, W.G. 323
Le Blanc, Lloyd 657
Le Corbusier, 515
L'Héritier, Charles 97, 204, 435, 504
Le Monnier, Louis-Guillaume 351
Le Nôtre, André 33
Le Plastrier, Constance, 194, 367, 435
Le Plastrier, Richard 28
Le Souef, Albert Alexander Cochrane 659
Le Souef, (William Henry) Dudley, 659
Le Souef, Ernest Albert, 659
Le Souef, (Albert) Sherborne, 659
Leach, John Albert, 434
Leake, John, 26, 409, 516, 534
Learmonth, Somerville, 203
Learmonth, Thomas, 203
Leason, Percy, 308
Lee and Kennedy, 54, 118, 171, 201, 366

Lee, James, 237, 366, 435, 462, 581
Lehany, Michael, 106
Lehmann, Johann Georg Christian, 367, 487
Leichhardt, Ludwig, 114, 384, 510
Leitch, Dugald, 146
Leith and Bartlett, 69
Lempriere, Thomas James 486
Lenné, Carl, 304
Lenné, Peter Joseph 78, 304
Lennon, Jane, 168
Leonard, W. 483
Leopold, Aldo, 453
Leschenault De La Tour, Jean-Baptiste, 231, 479
Leslie, George, 495
Leslie, Patrick, 440, 495
Leslie, Walter, 495
Leslie, William, 641
Lethaby, W.R. 17
Leunis, Johannes, 307
Levien, Benjamin (Goldsmidt) Goldsmith, 368
Levien, Jonas Felix Australia 368
Levien, Solomon, 366
Leviny, Ernest 112
Leviny, Hilda, 112
Lewis, Mortimer, 377, 411, 595
Lewis, Phil, 161, 356
Libeskind, Daniel, 553
Light, William, 7, 9, 28, 74, 132, 198, 347, 370, 490, 560, 567, 600
Lightfoot, Thomas, 588
Linaker, Hugh, 116, 132, 150, 269, 371, 402, 420, 617
Lincolne, Abraham, 371
Lind, Ruby, 119
Lindeman, H.J. 321
Lindley, John, 73, 90, 97, 248, 251, 342, 371, 413, 415, 509, 521, 523, 540
Lindner, Albert Edward, 56, 372, 575
Lindsay, Norman, 542, 567
Lindt, John William 299, 603
Linnaeus, Carl, 53, 71, 126, 351, 366, 372, 536, 555, 558
Linton (née Lowther), Elizabeth Helen, 146, 245, 340, 372
Linton family, 442
Linton, James, 180
Lipscombe, Edward, 372, 588
Lipscombe family, 41
Lipscombe, Frederick, 129, 166, 372, 456, 526, 589
Lipscombe, Henry, 372
Lipscombe, Leslie John 373, 533
Lipscombe, Thomas Meredith, 129
Liptus, Hugh K., 373
Lissner, Isidor Siegfried 373

Litchfield (formerly Casey, née Craig), Betty 159
Little, Alf, 211
Little, Archibald, 322
Liversidge, Archibald, 394
Llewellyn, Kate, 374
Lloyd, Christopher, 202, 296
Lloyd, Rex, 200
Lobb, William, 614
Loch, Henry, 510
Lockley, John 128, 147, 173, 199, 244, 295, 374, 375, 500
Lockyer, Dorothy Hope 17
Loddiges, Conrad, 54, 67, 385, 627
Loffler, T. 478
Logan, Patrick, 234
Longhurst, Peter, 536
Longley, George, 69, 375
Longley, William Robert 375
Lord, Clive Errol, 46, 376, 526, 645
Lord, Ernest Edward, 45, 47, 56, 112, 135, 150, 198, 244, 293, 376, 377, 399, 417, 658
Lorraine, Claude, 332, 473
Lothian, (Thomas Robert) Noel, 8, 9, 198, 244, 376, 377, 417, 421, 562
Lothian, Thomas Carlyle, 377
Loudon, Jane, 41, 76, 202, 257, 343, 377, 379, 407, 551, 619
Loudon, John Claudius, 34, 37, 41, 76, 78, 132, 171, 187, 201, 202, 209, 229, 248, 249, 250, 251, 254, 259, 268, 273, 305, 319, 325, 333, 343, 366, 368, 377, 378, 379, 387, 398, 401, 407, 411, 439, 474, 477, 490, 505, 515, 516, 530, 541, 549, 552, 576, 595, 616
Lovekin, Arthur, 346, 379
Lovett, Mildred, 180
Low, Hugh, 79, 201, 378
Lowe, Robert and Georgiana, 106
Lowenthal, David, 168
Lower, Lennie, 374
Lucas, (Beryl) Llywelyn, 379, 498, 605
Lucas-Tooth, Robert 583
Luehmann, Johann Georg, 35, 379
Luffman, Charles (Bogue), 33, 43, 116, 117, 162, 244, 379, 434, 516, 617
Lutyens, Edwin, 166, 182, 240, 252, 336
Lycett, Joseph, 31, 381, 474
Lyell, Charles, 176, 553
Lynch, Alfred, 116, 229, 381
Lysenko, Myron, 374

Mabo, Koiki (Eddie), 3, 357
Macarthur, Edward, 383, 384
Macarthur, Elizabeth, 383, 437
Macarthur family, 84, 621
Macarthur, James, 92, 383, 384, 510

Index of Names

Macarthur, John, 383, 437
Macarthur, William, 40, 41, 55, 72, 90, 92, 103, 123, 125, 147, 211, 261, 309, 320, 383, 384, 390, 415, 439, 443, 477, 504, 507, 510, 517, 548, 549, 644
Macdonald, Donald, 56, 75, 385, 418, 435
Macdonell, William, 91
Macfarlane, Walter, 198, 199, 329
MacGillivray, John, 280, 386, 459
MacGillivray, William, 386
MacIvor, (Ralph Waldo) Emerson, 12, 146, 388
Mack, Amy, 138, 388, 579
Mackay, Angus, 62, 388, 497, 529, 540
Mackay, John Bain 12, 23, 54, 79, 211, 244, 274
Mackenzie, A.J. 176
Mackenzie, Bruce, 47, 57, 119, 319, 353, 388, 389, 440, 507, 515, 571
Mackenzie, Colin, 661
Mackinnon, Clare, 585
Macleay family, 142
Macleay, George, 390
Macleay, William John 372, 392, 433
Macleay, William Sharp 128, 256, 302, 366, 390, 392, 548, 649
MacMahon, Philip, 14, 43, 103, 105, 329, 392, 393, 496, 580
Macmillan, Hugh Fraser 605, 614
Macoboy, Kenneth Stirling, 393
Maconochie, John R. 53
Macpherson, Alexander, 101, 394
Macquarie, Elizabeth, 40, 63, 78, 224, 267, 454, 603
Macquarie, Lachlan, 72, 133, 170, 185, 234, 313, 322, 357, 381, 394, 437, 463, 490, 507, 522, 562, 567, 621, 626
Magarey, Alexander Thomas 209
Maiden, Joseph, 21, 41, 43, 50, 56, 69, 87, 92, 98, 126, 131, 134, 135, 179, 216, 219, 222, 234, 250, 260, 279, 291, 340, 354, 369, 372, 379, 394, 395, 416, 425, 434, 439, 451, 456, 480, 521, 522, 523, 525, 548, 567, 574, 579, 606, 627, 632, 639, 644, 649, 657
Malaspina, Alejandro, 53, 131
Maloney, Betty Florence, 57, 119, 253, 370, 396, 397, 434, 440, 473, 618, 654
Malouf, David, 374, 409
Mangles, George, 397, 398
Mangles, James, 223, 377, 397, 398, 413
Mangles, Robert, 397, 398
Manifold family, 97, 332
Manifold, James Chester 587
Mann, Beryl, 119, 235, 398
Manning, Frederic Norton 319
Manning, George, 390

Mannix, Daniel, 500
Maple-Brown family, 566
Maplestone, Charles, 148
Marnock, Robert, 202, 211, 401, 511, 540
Maro, 439
Marriner, Crial William, 401
Marriner, George, 401
Marriner, (Noel) Leonard, 401
Marriner, Maxwell Randall, 401
Marriner, (Van) Randall, 401
Marriner, William, 401
Marriott, Neil, 402
Marsden, Samuel, 124, 222, 582
Marsh, Rose, 518
Marshall, Thomas, 92
Marshall, Valentine, 588
Martens, Conrad, 86, 322, 332, 438
Martin, Catherine, 373
Martin, James, 454
Martin, Joseph, 402, 431, 451, 541, 576
Martin, Marcus, 121, 468
Martius, Carl Friedrich Philipp von, 460
Mass, Nuri, 138
Massey & Hill, 302
Massey, Richard, 343, 561
Masson, Francis, 126
Masson, Georgina, 333
Matthews, David Reeves, 227, 402, 441
Mawson, Thomas Hayton, 202, 403, 559
Mayo, Daphne, 22
McAlister, Edward James, 383
McArthur (née Evans), Kathleen Rennie, 385
McArthur, Peter, 406
McCaw, Matthew, 7
McConnel, David Cannon 166
McConnel, Kenneth 159, 293
McCorkell, Howard, 601
McCormick, Tim, 31
McCoy, Frederick 323, 585
McCracken, Donal, 34
McCracken family, 451
McCrae, Georgiana Huntly, 385, 407
McCubbin, Frederick, 32
McDonald, Donald Alaster, 385
McDonald, Ian, 193
McDonald, John, 146
McDonald, William, 527
McEwin, George, 8, 41, 244, 366, 385, 540, 560, 562, 570
McEwin, (Robert) Hamilton, 147, 386
McEwin, John Nash 385, 540
McEwin, Joseph Nash 386
McEwin, Robert, 386
McFarland, (John) Horace 431
McFarlane, Alfred, 286
McGarvie, William, 378

McGowan, William, 130, 187, 386, 524, 540
McGrath, Raymond, 323
McGregor, John, 456
McGregor, William Peter 28, 29
McHarg, Ian, 356, 445
McHattie, John, 223
McInnis, Ronald Allison, 386
McIntosh, Charles, 19, 41, 172, 181, 229, 301, 387, 540, 596, 616, 651
McKay, Hugh Victor 255, 388, 528
McKinnon, Jon, 620
McKinnon, Karin, 191
McKinnon, Ross David, 105, 369, 389
McKirdy, Archibald James 601
McKirdy, Robert, 83
McLaren, Christine, 389, 497
McLean, John, 378
McLeay, Alexander, 40, 78, 87, 90, 125, 139, 158, 202, 224, 230, 295, 377, 390, 415, 438, 454, 474, 507, 510, 517, 549, 592
McLeay, Fanny, 390
McLennan, John P. 116
McLennan, Murdo, 512
McLeod (née Matthies), Judyth Ann, 392
McLeod, Archibald, 265
McLeod, John Norman 16
McMaugh (née Baker), Judith Lesley, 393
McMillan, Thomas, 148, 244, 288, 527, 530, 540
McMinn, Gilbert Rotherdale 267
McNab, James, 270
McNeill, Barry, 589
McNess, Charles, 570
McPhee, John, 264
Meagher, Leonard, 369
Meares, James, 546
Meason, Gilbert Lang 354
Meehan, James, 394
Meilland family, 519
Meinig, Donald, 168
Melba, Nellie, 159, 203
Meldrum, Max, 260, 263
Mellor (née Holttum), Olive, 9, 45, 60, 112, 116, 248, 258, 260, 269, 287, 405, 406, 617, 629
Melville, Andrew Wedderburn 402
Menge, Johannes, 74, 259
Menzel, Bruno, 15, 406, 556
Menzel, Ernst Wilhelm, 9, 66, 315, 406
Menzel, Oscar Ernst, 15, 406, 556
Menzies, Archibald, 71, 479
Meredith (née Twamley), Louisa Anne 41, 56, 76, 98, 138, 373, 406, 452, 474, 530, 624
Merewether, Edward, 182

Index of Names

Merfield, Bertha, 260
Mermet, Felix, 298
Merrillees, C.R. 125
Mertens Brothers, 559
Meyer, Frederick A. 378
Mezger, John, 362
Michelangelo, 565
Michell, Christine, 407
Michell, Edwin, 408
Michell, George Howard, 302, 407, 561
Michell, John Alfred 408
Michell, Patricia, 408
Michell, Patricia Mary, 408
Michurin, Ivan Vladimirovich 530
Middleton, William George Dyer, 408
Midgley, Alfred, 164, 475, 543
Miles, John Otway 409
Miles, William Wallace, 409
Millais, J.E. 76
Millard, Kathryn, 217
Miller, David, 272
Miller, Meg, 272
Millie, 3
Milligan, Joseph, 53, 283, 409, 433
Milner, Edward, 466
Milner Son and White, 260
Minchin family, 659
Mitchell, Barry, 389
Mitchell, C.W., 417
Mitchell (née Chauvel), Elyne, 410
Mitchell, James, 515
Mitchell, Jocelyn, 402
Mitchell, Josiah, 147, 199, 202, 366, 387, 410, 540
Mitchell, Thomas Livingstone, 53, 131, 170, 211, 371, 384, 411, 421, 474, 507, 562, 592, 595, 615, 649
Mitchell, W.G. 235
Mockridge, Stahle, and Mitchell, 398
Modjeska, Drusilla, 374
Moffat, John, 78, 135
Mofflin, Horace Edgar, 412, 431
Molineux, Albert, 9, 50, 209, 243, 244, 386, 412, 518, 560, 562
Mollison, Bruce Charles 468
Molloy, Georgiana, 10, 308, 371, 377, 398, 636
Molyneux, William Mitchell, 57, 414, 478
Monash, John, 402
Moon, Frank, 132
Moore, Charles, 5, 41, 43, 56, 82, 86, 87, 91, 126, 128, 133, 134, 182, 187, 219, 227, 232, 248, 249, 280, 291, 304, 328, 345, 354, 360, 369, 371, 394, 401, 414, 438, 459, 460, 494, 501, 510, 515, 523, 540, 560, 573, 585, 596, 605, 606, 618, 644, 657

Moore, David, 414, 510
Moore, Gregory, 416
Moore, Henry, 102, 133, 416, 426, 436, 440, 497, 642
Moore, James, 256
Moore, John D. 164
Moore, Percy Byron 61
Moore, Tom, 61
Mordaunt, Evelyn May 379
Morgan, John, 184
Morley, Brian, 8, 58, 417
Morres, Henry, 264
Morris, Albert, 30, 34, 151, 216, 417, 506, 648
Morris (née Sayce), Ellen Margaret, 417
Morris, William, 33, 65, 121
Morrison, (Philip) Crosbie, 56, 75, 417, 433, 435, 500
Morrison, Michael, 424
Morrow and de Putron, 310
Mort, Constance, 234
Mort, Eirene, 101, 180, 418, 579
Mort, Henry, 234
Mort, Thomas Sutcliffe, 179, 234, 280, 398, 418, 439, 577
Mortlock, James John, 146, 418
Morton, Alex, 526
Morton, Francis, 330
Mosel, Albert Edward 418
Mosel, Crawford Lampert, 418
Mosel, Ken Lampert, 9, 106, 418
Mosley, Geoff, 49
Moss, Francis, 418, 441
Moss, George William, 418
Mott(e), Hamilton Charnock, 418, 583
Moulden, Owen M. 431
Moule, William Henry 430
Moylan, John, 73
Mudd, Christopher, 422
Muecke, C.W.L. 75, 300
Mueller, Ferdinand Jakob Heinrich von, 1, 5, 6, 16, 31, 35, 41, 43, 53, 54, 56, 76, 86, 87, 88, 97, 98, 103, 108, 114, 129, 130, 135, 174, 184, 185, 187, 196, 199, 205, 206, 207, 212, 215, 218, 219, 227, 230, 235, 241, 248, 259, 260, 268, 281, 283, 288, 289, 290, 300, 307, 316, 320, 323, 338, 344, 348, 349, 362, 368, 372, 379, 388, 394, 401, 405, 420, 423, 435, 453, 456, 460, 469, 471, 474, 479, 486, 520, 521, 522, 524, 525, 526, 527, 530, 536, 541, 555, 560, 573, 575, 585, 590, 596, 616, 628, 632, 636, 638, 643, 644, 645, 648, 649
Muller, Peter, 28, 47, 302, 408, 512
Mundey, John Bernard (Jack) 272
Munro-Ferguson, Ronald 359
Murcutt, Glenn, 28

Murdoch (née Green), Elisabeth, 58, 424, 622, 625
Murdoch, James, 165
Murdoch, John Smith 22, 425
Murdoch, Keith, 381, 418, 425, 625
Murphy, Andrew, 56, 425
Murray, Hugh, 401
Murray, K.G. 60
Murray, Ron, 51
Myer (née Baillieu), Merlyn, 166, 167
Myer, Sidney, 165, 182

Nakajima, Ken, 336
Nash, John, 16, 332, 345, 505
Nash, Richard West, 244, 316, 430
Neale, Ralph, 355
Neate, Ambrose, 435
Neate, Ambrose Charles, 250, 435
Neill, Patrick, 554
Neilson, George, 116, 435, 540
Neilson, John Shaw 374
Nellie, 3
Nelson, David, 71, 435
Nelson, Tony, 160
Nesfield, William Andrews, 78, 82, 111, 141
Newman, Charles Frederick, 9, 43, 300, 436, 560, 637
Newman, Charles Lewis William 437
Newman (née Possingham), Doris, 437
Newman, Francis William, 173, 437, 526
Newman, Frederick Christoff, 437
Newman (née Bailes), Mary Ann Maria, 437
Newton, Patricia, 376
Nichol, Walter, 540, 551
Nicholas, Alfred, 116, 371, 442, 604
Nicholas, C.H. 414
Nicholas, George Richard Rich 19, 116
Nicholls, Eric Milton, 130, 276
Nicholls, George Henry 441
Nicholls, John Benjamin 441
Nicholls, Robert Uriah, 441
Nicholls, Walter Hewett, 441
Nicholls, William Henry, 18, 98, 402, 441
Nichols, Beverley, 160
Nicholson, Charles, 86
Nicholson, Harold, 149, 553
Nicolai, E., 305
Nielsen, (Mary) Fairie, 441
Nielsen, Lars, 559
Nieuwesteeg, John, 517
Ninham, Jane Laura 85
Nixon, Francis, 527
Nobelius, Carl Axel, 43, 45, 290, 442, 451, 508, 536, 582
Nobelius, Clifford Leonard 442
Noble family, 9

Index of Names

Nolan, Sidney, 294
Nolan, Stephen, 443
Norgate, Annette, 442
Norgate, Dennis Stephen, 442
Norgate, Gordon, 442
Norris, Harry, 116
North, Alexander, 130
North, Keva, 58
North, Marianne, 1, 442, 443, 520
North, Tim, 58, 61
Northey, William, 615
Norton, James, 158
Nottle, Trevor James, 250, 369, 446

O'Brien, James 420
O'Connor & Houle, 294
O'Connor, Charles Yelverton 424
O'Donnell, Deirdre, 657
O'Keeffe, Georgia 547
O'Neill, Kevin 224, 226
O'Reilly, Bernard 353
O'Shanesy, John, 329, 456, 496
O'Shanesy, Patrick Adams 329, 456, 496
Oakman, Henry Octave, 52, 102, 133, 436, 440, 449, 497, 601, 602, 605, 642
Oehme, Wolfgang, 271
Officer, Suetonius Henry 190
Oglethorpe, James, 567
Oldham, Boas, Ednie-Brown and Partners, 95
Oldham, Charles Lancelot 609
Oldham, John, 47, 242, 412, 424, 429, 450, 610, 635, 638
Oldham (née McClintock), Ruby Gertrude, 450
Oliphant, Mark, 268
Oliver, James Sylvester 430, 477
Oliver, John, 451
Olmsted, Frederick Law 187, 354, 443, 444, 451, 643
Olsen, Olive Kari 463
Onslow, Arthur Pooley 325
Orchard Stanley, 508
Ormsby Barrie, 459, 562
Osborn, Theodore George Bentley, 194, 456
Osborne, John (c.1800–1878), 12, 456
Osborne, John (c.1840–1915), 456
Osborne, John (b.1864), 456, 500
Osborne, Joseph, 456
Osborne, Wilfred Wallace 456
Oudolf, Piet, 226
Outhwaite, Ida Rentoul 138
Overall, Athol, 457
Overall, James, 457
Overell, John E. 457
Owens, John Stanley, 342, 457, 463
Oxley, John, 170, 234, 381, 507, 562

Packer family, 321
Packham, Charles Henry 485
Pagan, Jock, 344
Page, Russell, 71, 349, 476, 565
Palmer family, 174
Palmer, James, 407
Panicum, 498
Papworth, John Buonarotti 28, 619
Parcel, Henry, 74, 459, 462, 477
Park, Mungo, 108
Parker, Carol, 622
Parker, Henry Watson 548
Parkes, Henry, 94, 108, 133
Parkinson, John, 75
Parkinson, Sydney, 37, 71, 97, 462, 558
Parks, John, 517
Paronella, José, 463
Paronella (née Soler), Margarita, 463
Parry family, 56
Parry, Henry Griffith, 45, 47, 463
Parry, Percival Joseph 463
Parsons, Alfred, 226
Pascoe, John Francis 260
Paterson, Banjo, 119, 591
Paterson + Pettus, 294
Paterson, William, 72, 581
Patrick, John, 62, 464, 622
Patterson, Alfred Andrew, 159, 465
Patterson, Andrew, 536
Paul, William, 111, 359
Paull, Josiah, 461, 640
Paxton, Joseph, 41, 65, 82, 91, 133, 135, 186, 202, 248, 273, 342, 367, 371, 398, 466, 491
Paxton (née Bown), Sarah 466
Payne, Christine, 98
Payne, Ellen, 180
Payne, Frederick Cyril, 307, 466
Payne, William Herbert, 275, 556
Pearce Brothers, 84, 604
Pearce, Simeon Henry 515, 633
Pearce, William Thomas 84
Peasley, M. 15
Peate (née Wagner), Natalie Florence, 467, 478
Peck, Jill, 512
Peck, Stan, 592
Pelloe (née Sundercombe), Emily Harriet, 98, 215, 467
Pelzer, August, 10, 467, 615
Pender, William, 140
Penfold, Christopher Rawson, 468
Penfold family, 75
Penfold (née Holt), Mary, 468
Pengilly (Pengelley), William, 10, 468
Pennefather, Richard William 163
Periam, Jonathan, 146
Perkins, Arthur James 621

Péron, Francois, 620
Perrin, George Samuel, 212, 468
Perrott, Albert Victor, 469
Perrott (née Clayphan), Clara Sophie, 469
Perrott (née Gemmill), Daisy, 469
Perrott, Dorothy Daisy Elle, 469
Perrott, Douglas, 469
Perrott, Thomas, 469
Perrott, Thomas Robert 469
Perry Brothers, 256
Perry, George, 469
Perry, Richard (1825-1904), 338, 469
Perry, Richard (b.1867), 469
Perry, Thomas A., 552
Perry, William, 469
Pescott, Edward Edgar, 12, 44, 56, 75, 103, 116, 135, 147, 173, 236, 244, 250, 256, 263, 292, 418, 470, 471, 508, 510, 527, 617, 641
Pescott, Richard Thomas Martin, 280, 332, 471, 522
Petrie, Andrew Lang 90, 482
Pettigrew, William, 648
Pettit, Hugh, 121
Pfeiffer, Andrew Anthony Frederick, 321, 472
Pfeiffer, James, 422
Phillip, Arthur, 71, 72, 118, 123, 251, 318, 322, 357, 367, 522, 620
Phillips, Emma, 73
Phillips, George, 105
Phillips, Henry, 551
Phillips, E. Marie (Betty) 62
Phipson, Joan, 138
Pike, Jack, 383
Pince, R.T. 90
Pink, James, 17, 82, 105, 149, 164, 475, 496, 644
Pink, Olive Muriel, 3, 336, 446, 654
Piper, John, 40, 454
Pirie, Andrew, 621
Pitcairn, Robert, 527
Pitt, Charles, 642
Pittendrigh, Stuart, 515
Platt, Charles, 182, 333
Pluck, Patrick Joseph, 482
Plumridge, Arthur John, 483, 592
Plumridge, Charles Louis 483
Plumridge, Frederick John (1814-1855), 482
Plumridge, Frederick John (1840-1887), 483
Plumridge, Hector Harold 483
Plumridge, Henry Edward, 483
Pockett, John Bayliss 483
Pockett, Thomas William, 43, 140, 306, 430, 451, 477, 483, 617

Index of Names

Pockett, William, 483
Pockley, Diana, 369, 484
Poland, William, 117
Pollard, Edna, 376
Polya, Rosemary, 138
Pope, Alexander, 433
Porcelli, Pietro Giacomo 424
Port, Jackson Painter, 40
Porter, Hal, 374
Porter, J.H. 329
Potts, Frank, 93
Poulter, Arthur Edward, 487
Poulter, Bertie Albert, 487
Poulter, Robert Henry, 128, 182, 487
Powell, Brian Martin, 30, 487
Powell, Fay, 30, 487
Powell, Joseph, 644
Powell, Robin, 622
Power, Joseph Porter 579
Poynter, Maude, 180
Prantl, Karl, 585
Preiss, (Johann August) Ludwig, 53, 413, 479, 487, 636
Prenzel, Robert, 180
Presley, Elvis, 510
Preston, Margaret, 45, 225, 308
Price, Thomas, 81, 464
Price, Uvedale, 201, 356, 377, 411, 473, 487, 577
Prideaux, George, 431
Prior, Edward, 329, 348
Pritzel, Ernst G. 53
Proctor, Thea, 32, 225, 308
Prohaski, Eric, 592
Pryor, Lindsay Dixon, 51, 62, 146, 152, 266, 432, 490, 531, 610
Purchas, Albert, 97, 132, 405, 410, 493
Purchas and Swyer, 28, 142
Purchase, James, 493
Purchase, Samuel, 31, 439, 493
Purves, Thomas, 7, 111, 112, 493, 540
Purves, William, 493, 494
Puzzle, 180
Pye, James, 494
Pyle, Conrad, 219

Quarrell, Alfred James, 161, 315, 495, 562, 583
Quin, Tarella, 138

Raddenberry, John, 6, 42, 256, 435, 499
Rae, Frederick James, 116, 337, 471, 500, 522, 556
Rae, George, 23
Railton, David Balderston, 148, 376, 493, 500, 540, 632
Railton, James, 373, 501
Railton, Thomas, 501

Ramsay, Alexander Maurice 192
Ramsay, Ed, 60
Ramsay, Juliet, 59
Ramsay, Robert Andrew, 606
Ramsay, Thomas, 291
Ramsay, Urquhart, 414, 606
Ranicar, Betty Russell (née Barrett), 502
Rankine, Alexander, 576
Raphael, Thomas Davidson, 502
Rasp, Charles, 645
Ratcliffe, Richard, 558
Rawson, Mina, 502
Rayment, Ronald Clarence, 412, 502
Read Snr, Richard, 31
Read, Robert, 534
Reade, Charles Compton, 43, 95, 148, 246, 381, 502, 503, 509, 561, 601, 615
Reddan, William, 131
Redman family, 160
Redouté, Pierre-Joseph, 97, 205, 504
Reed, John, 294
Reed, Joseph, 78, 127
Reed (née Baillieu), Sunday, 294
Reedy, Thomas, 329, 385, 504
Reeve, Josiah Capes 146
Reeves, Herbert Trethowan 376, 418
Reeves, John, 125, 139
Regan, Danny, 576
Reid, Barrett, 294
Rennie, George Patrick 359
Rennie, Sebastian, 359
Rentoul, Annie, 138
Repton, Humphry, 40, 201, 289, 354, 356, 368, 378, 438, 474, 504, 548
Repton, John Adey 505
Resch, Edmund, 583
Retter, Michael, 180
Reuss, F. 529
Reynell, John, 289, 390, 506, 621
Reynolds, Peter, 575
Reynolds, William, 65
Rhodes, Charles, 431
Rhodes, Edith, 142
Ribbentrop, B. 325
Ricauti, T.J. 530
Richardson, C. Douglas 573
Richardson, John Matthew, 247, 507
Rickard, Bruce Arthur Lancelot, 28, 319, 388, 507, 515
Ricketts, William, 508, 542
Riddoch, John, 160
Riethmuller, Francis Lewis, 508
Rigby, John Bennett 508
Rigby, Matthew, 496, 508
Riley, Alexander, 40
Rimington, A. 110, 135
Rimington, George, 45, 290, 442, 508, 614

Rischbeith (née Earle), Bessie Mabel, 609
Rischbieth, Henry, 609
Ritchie, Antoinette, 181
Ritchie, Geoffrey, 181
Ritchie, James P. 604
Ritchie, Maria Sophie 604
Ritchie, Sylvia Noel 181
Rivers, Thomas, 359
Roberts, Ellen, 553
Roberts, Hera, 308
Roberts, James, 509
Roberts, James Fountain, 9, 135, 509
Roberts, Mary, 661
Robertson, Enid Lucy, 34, 433
Robertson, John, 444
Robertson, Naismith 90, 92, 385, 510, 540
Robertson, Neil Roderick Goldsborough, 62, 510
Robinette, Charles, 5, 277, 510, 512, 530, 656
Robinson, Robert, 421, 511
Robinson, William (1814–1889), 304
Robinson, William (1838–1935), 33, 42, 82, 121, 123, 131, 143, 149, 202, 206, 227, 232, 248, 251, 304, 340, 380, 401, 416, 434, 510, 511, 625, 642
Robinson, William Denham, 9, 421, 511
Rochlitz, Julius Albert, 511
Rodale, J.I. 453
Rodd, Tony, 422
Rodway, Leonard, 53, 171, 215, 512, 526
Roe, John Septimus, 513, 567, 636
Roessler, Henry, 175
Rofe, John, 346
Rogers, Frederick James Charles, 433, 513
Rogers, Richard Sanders, 221
Rollands, Peter, 432
Ronalds, Alfred, 514
Ronalds, Hugh, 514
Ronalds, Ivy, 514
Ronalds, Lily Agnes, 514
Ronalds, Lindsay, 514
Ronalds, Maria Emily, 514
Ronalds, Mary Ellen, 514
Ronalds, Nathaniel, 134, 135, 224, 514, 534
Ronalds, Ralph Nathaniel, 514
Rosén, Conrad Wilfred, 516
Rosén, Lars, 516, 527, 536, 622
Rose, Edwin, 155
Rose, James, 47, 161, 444, 445
Ross, Alexander, 431, 518
Ross, Andrew, 519
Ross, Deane McLaren, 431, 519
Ross, George David, 518

Index of Names

Ross, James, 16, 65
Ross, Maureen, 519
Rosser, Celia Elizabeth, 73, 98, 258, 518
Rossetti, D.G. 76
Rossi, Benvenuto Vincenzo, 43, 199, 431, 518, 519, 617
Rossi, Julius Vincent 518
Rossiter, William, 441
Rouse, Cedric, 559
Rouse, Elizabeth, 519
Rouse, John, 34
Rouse, Richard, 519
Rowan, (Marian) Ellis, 98, 443, 519
Rowcroft, Charles, 373
Royce, George, 330
Royds family, 191
Rubio. See James, (Thomas) Horton
Rudd Steele. See Davis, Arthur Hoey
Rule, John James, 41, 111, 147, 162, 288, 459, 507, 526
Rumsey, (née Nankivell), (Eva) Heather, 518, 527
Rumsey, Herbert John, 439, 527
Rumsey, Roy, 250, 518, 527
Rupp, Herman Montague Rucker, 18, 260, 433, 453, 528
Rushton, David, 431, 518
Rushton, J.J. 591
Ruskin, John, 65, 106, 642
Russell, Alexander, 558
Russell, Charles Wilfred 338
Russell family, 76, 402
Russell, James, 76
Russell, Jim, 168
Russell, (née Newton), Maude Hilary, 338
Russell, Wilfred Adams 337
Ruston, David William, 531
Rutledge, Helen, 513
Rutledge, William, 294
Ruzicka, Otaker, 412, 531
Ryan, Charles, 41, 519
Ryan, Stephen Godfrey, 58, 531

Saarinen, Esa, 620
Sackville-West, Victoria, 149, 241, 226, 553
Sadler, Arthur Lindsay 336
Sage family, 75
St John, Percival Reginald Harry, 420, 533
Salmon, A. 478
Salter, Edward, 75
Salter, William, 75
Salway, William, 182
Samson, Thomas, 359
Sanderson, Geoff, 562
Sandford, Albert, 132
Sangster, Jane Yates 591
Sangster, William, 18, 28, 36, 127, 143, 153, 230, 250, 252, 262, 398, 419, 508, 527, 540, 543, 590, 591, 616, 648
Sangwell, Alfred Henry 535
Sangwell, Jesse 535
Sangwell, Joseph Samuel 535
Sangwell, William, 15, 534
Sargeant, Harold John, 45, 535
Sargent, Charles Sprague 451
Sargood family, 593
Sargood, Frederick, 27, 78, 123, 419, 472, 508, 606
Sauer, Carl, 168
Saul, Margaret, 98
Savige, Thomas James, 250, 535
Sayce, Conrad, 18
Sayce, Joseph, 23, 185, 268, 282, 332, 536
Sayer, Victor, 129
Scarth-Johnson, Vera, 536
Schirmer, Johann Wilhelm 278
Schoenfeld, Friederich, 98
Schofield, Leo, 106
Schomburgk, Richard, 5, 7, 8, 9, 41, 43, 75, 82, 108, 149, 195, 198, 259, 300, 307, 354, 377, 517, 521, 537, 560, 573, 585
Schomburgk, Robert, 537
Schubert, Bernhardt Edlewyn, 47, 56, 539, 571, 618, 646
Schubert (née Corrie), Dulcie Lillian, 539, 646
Schultze, Frederick Hermann Heinrich 292
Scoborio, Charles, 540, 628
Scott family, 420
Scott, Helenus, 510
Scott, James, 9, 55, 235, 541, 588
Scott (née Kelly), Mary Annie, 541
Scott, T.K. 483
Scott, Thomas Sherbourne 541
Scribner, Elbridge, 223
Scrivener, Charles Robert 51
Sculthorpe, Peter, 622
Seale, Allan, 542, 591, 592
Searl, Frederick Henry 543
Searl, Frederick Rutt, 36, 224, 251, 292, 439, 447, 543, 583
Searl, John Thomas, 543
Searle (Olim Schultz), Alexander Waldemar, 262
Searle, Douglas, 534
Searle, George, 9, 496, 543
Sedding, John Dando 33, 121, 626
Seddon, George, 49, 236, 545
Seddon, John Pollard 18
Sedgley, M. 478
Sedgwick, Adam, 176
Seesle, Friedrich, 301
Seidler, Harry, 23, 47, 412
Seppelt, (Oscar) Benno Pedro 87, 546
Seppelt, Joseph Ernst, 546
Serventy, Dominic Louis 215
Sever family, 546
Sewell, Henry, 9, 15, 56, 202, 343, 477, 546, 560, 562, 647
Shackley, Ned, 73
Shannon, Mollie Glen 59, 84, 116, 160
Sharpe, Alfred, 441, 547
Shaw, Richard Norman 33, 121
Shaw, Thomas, 78
Sheath, Jeremiah, 269, 346, 547
Sheather, Silas, 385, 439, 548
Shelley, Max Robert, 343, 548
Shelton, Edward Mason, 12, 164, 497, 548, 564
Shennen, Michele, 61
Shenstone, William, 356
Shepard, Lindesay, 549
Shepard, Thomas R. 549
Shepheard, Peter, 355
Shepherd, David, 549
Shepherd, J.C., 333
Shepherd, Patrick Lindesay Crawford 549
Shepherd, Thomas, 19, 41, 55, 62, 73, 75, 108, 128, 135, 142, 158, 201, 244, 252, 280, 295, 354, 356, 359, 378, 384, 390, 402, 433, 437, 451, 474, 510, 540, 548, 550, 551, 577, 633, 646
Shepherd, Thomas (William), 549
Sheppard, Harry, 200
Sherrard, H.M. 107, 600
Shoobridge, David William 51, 62
Shoobridge, William, 550
Shum, W.A.S. (Bill) 60
Shvidkovshy, Dimitri, 530
Sibthorp, John, 78
Sicard, Francois, 323, 542
Sieber, Franz, 479
Sigsby, Don, 515
Simmons, H. George 512
Simmons, John, 650
Simmons, Richard, 512
Simons, John Joseph, 24
Simons, Phyllis Frazer, 551
Simpson, James Henry 430
Simpson, Stephen, 648
Simson, John, 76
Sinatra, James Benedict, 552
Sinclair, James, 6, 41, 81, 82, 147, 244, 410, 433, 527, 530, 540, 552, 616
Sitta, Vladimír (Tom), 553, 554
Skase, Christopher, 163
Skertchly, Sydney Barber Josiah, 340, 553

Index of Names

Slessor, Kenneth, 374
Slykerman family, 436
Smart, Richard, 621
Smart, Thomas Ware 633
Smith, Charles Hope Johnston, 387, 540, 553
Smith (née Hill), (Myra) Coralie, see Mrs Caley Smith
Smith, Edwin, 4, 9, 81, 366
Smith, Farquharson, 6
Smith, Fred Caley 15, 340, 406, 556
Smith, George, 162, 554
Smith, Grace Cossington 19, 32
Smith, Henry Arthur 366
Smith, Henry George 69
Smith, Henry Percy 192
Smith, Howard, 562
Smith, Irene, 193
Smith, M. Irvine 562
Smith, James E., 37, 112, 351, 372, 553, 555, 564, 632, 641
Smith, John, 6, 41, 325, 338, 373, 540, 555, 579
Smith, John Thomas, 221, 451, 463, 483, 555
Smith, Keith Vincent 193
Smith, Samuel, 21, 75, 556
Smith, Thomas, 555
Smith, (Sydney George) Ure, 308, 562
Smith, Walter, 373, 555
Smyth, Arthur Bowes 10, 226, 556
Snape, (née Hodgson), Diana, 556
Snelling, Douglas, 28
Snow, Frank, 83, 560
Soady, Rose, 567
Sobels family, 75
Solander, Daniel, 37, 53, 71, 73, 79, 159, 372, 395, 437, 462, 479, 536, 558
Somner, Edward, 366
Somner, William, 365, 493, 540
Sonder, Otto Wilhelm 290
Sorensen, Paul Edwin, 45, 95, 206, 266, 328, 353, 355, 361, 375, 412, 440, 512, 536, 558, 562, 626, 648
Soutter, Richard Ernest 564
Soutter, William, 17, 101, 394, 425, 475, 496, 498, 540, 563 605
Sowden, William J. 632, 648
Sowerby, James, 97, 407, 555, 564, 632
Sparnon, Norman James, 473, 564
Sparrow, George, 9, 564, 623
Spearritt, Peter, 581
Specht, Raymond L. 53
Spencer, John, 211
Spencer, Richard, 573
Spencer, Roger David, 48, 564
'Spinifex', 498

Spirn, Anne, 445
Spooner, Peter, 61, 94, 565, 648
Springbett family, 75
Spry, Constance, 225
Spunner, Suzanne, 594
Stackhouse, Jennifer, 61
Staer, John, 56, 567
Stafford, Brian, 524
Stafford, John and Valerie, 299
Stafford, Lisa, 194
Staiger, Karl, 67
Stanbridge, William Edward 648
Stanton, Gay, 622
Stead, Christina, 374, 569
Stead, David George, 56, 290, 430, 435, 568
Stead (née Harris), Thistle, 433
Stearn, William T., 462
Steedman, Harry, 661
Steele, Richard, 569
Stephen, Alexander, 82, 311, 439, 655
Stephens, William John, 433
Stephenson, Gordon, 338, 569, 610
Stephenson and Turner, 260, 569
Stevens, John, 47, 57, 139, 235, 260, 412, 569, 610
Stevenson, George, 9, 181, 315, 366, 386, 560, 569
Stevenson, John Martin, 268
Steward, Geoffrey and Robyn 264
Stewart, Thomas Adams, 15, 431, 570
Stewart, Thomas Gerrard 570
Sticht, Robert, 620
Stieglitz, Frederick Lewis von, 345
Stinton, Frederick William 570
Stinton (née Nash), Louisa 570
Stinton, William, 477, 570
Stirling, Ada Florence 534
Stirling, Edward Charles, 66, 209, 221, 507, 534, 560, 570
Stirling (née Mangles), Ellen 397
Stirling, James 234, 397, 618
Stirling, John Lancelot 570
Stoddart, Thomas, 70
Stokes, Michael, 601
Stones, Ellis, 47, 57, 116, 119, 153, 228, 287, 342, 348, 353, 412, 414, 434, 502, 512, 562, 570, 584, 607, 654, 657
Stones, (Elsie) Margaret, 98, 572, 587
Stoney, H. Butler, 579
Stopps, Arthur 219
Story, George Fordyce, 573
Stratford, Phyllis Coate, 565
Streeton, Arthur 32
Street-Porter, Tim 642
Stroud, Dorothy, 108
Stuart, Charles, 575

Stuckey, Kenneth John, 575
Sturrock, Alexander Corsar, 7, 244, 540, 575
Sturt, Charles, 392
Stutchbury & Pape, 28
Sudell, Richard, 406
Sulman (née Masefield), Annie Elizabeth, 579
Sulman, Florence, 101, 418, 579
Sulman, John, 43, 51, 141, 246, 323, 439, 579, 599, 600, 601
Summerlin, Lawrence, 194, 469, 496, 580, 641
Summerlin, Robert Lawrence, 580
Sunnyman, John, 591
Suter, Mary, 193
Suter, Richard, 193
Suttor, George, 37, 72, 139, 201, 250, 437, 581
Swaby, Arthur James, 47, 399, 556, 582, 658
Swain, (Edward) Harold Fulcher, 179, 228, 359, 582
Swainson, William, 582
Swan, Joseph, 97
Swane, Edgar Norman (Ben), 582
Swane, Edgar Norman (Ted), 582
Swane, Elwyn Lettitia, 582
Swane, Gwendoline Valerie, 582
Swane, Rudyard Kipling (Tim), 582
Swanson, Rex, 553
Sweet, Robert, 79, 288, 583
Swinbourne, Robert Frederick George, 315, 584
Swyer, Charles, 493
Sydenham, Robert, 583
Syme, David, 366, 618
Syme, Ebenezer, 618
Symonds, George 469

Talbot, Fox, 472
Talbot, Milo John Reginald, 171, 216, 329, 345, 572, 587
Talbot, Rose, 587
Tallis, Amelia, 84
Tallis, George, 84
Tallis, Jack Morton, 84
Tan, Shaun, 138
Tanner, Howard Napier, 58, 106, 250, 473, 511, 587
Tanner, John, 365
Tate, Frank, 434, 538
Tate, Ralph, 53, 91, 198, 215, 456, 525, 590
Taylor and Cullity, 520, 595
Taylor Cullity Lethlean, 596
Taylor, Charles Bowmont, 230

Index of Names

Taylor (née Parsons), Florence Mary, 112
Taylor, George Augustine, 112, 340
Taylor, Gordon, 498
Taylor, Ken, 168
Taylor, Mark C. 620
Taylor and Sangster, 18, 41, 135, 184, 199, 209, 442, 447, 507, 555, 590, 648
Taylor, Soilleux & Overend, 411
Taylor, William, 166, 230, 540, 590
'Tecoma', 499
Teese, Arnold James, 591
Temple-Poole, George Thomas, 592
Tench, Watkin, 10
Tenison, J.E. 67
Tepper, Johann Gottlieb Otto, 260, 593
Tesselaar, Anthony, 594
Tesselaar, Cornelius Ignatius (Cees), 47, 594
Tesselaar family, 436
Tesselaar, Henk, 594
Tesselaar, John, 594
Tesselaar, Kees, 594
Thoday, Peter, 278, 317
Thomas, Alfred Strickland, 45, 431, 533, 591, 594
Thomas, Henry, 101
Thomas, William, 268, 594
Thompson, John, 41, 202, 325, 377, 411, 595
Thompson, Paul, 520, 595
Thompson, Robert, 540, 596
Thompson, S.G. 388
Thomson, David, 540, 596, 639
Thomson, Estelle, 596
Thomson, Frederick, 87
Thomson, William, 387, 540, 596, 655
Thomson, William Kerr, 341
Thoreau, Henry David 643
Thorn, George, 328
Thorne, Ebenezer, 480
Thornicroft, Ira, 526
Thornton, Lindsay, 59
Thouin, André 180, 231
Thouin, Gabriel, 78
Thozet, Anthelme, 495, 596, 597, 601
Thozet, (née Berthold), Marie Isabella, 596, 597
Thunberg, Carl, 479
Tibbits, Wiliam Taylor Smith, 31, 32, 597, 623
Tiffin, Charles, 267
Tilden, Freeman, 328
Timbrell, Ann, 546
Titheradge, George, 75, 143, 429, 477, 555, 597
Togashi, Tatsuya, 336

Tongg, Richard C. 605
Tooth, Robert, 165
Topsy, 3
Totty, C.H. 483
Tovey, James Richard 206
Towns, Robert, 165, 166
Toyne, Gilbert, 45, 190, 601
Toyne, Philip, 353
Tract, 340, 601, 657
Traill, Jessie 19
Trapnell, George, 449, 602, 644
Treloar, Henry, 179, 604, 605
Treseder Brothers, 551
Treseder, John Garland, 244, 249, 343, 439, 604
Treseder, Stephen, 604
Treseder, Thomas Garland, 604
Treseder, William, 604
Trevaskis, Percival, 116, 604
Trevelyan, Walter, 509
Trigg, Ernest, 559
Triggs, Arthur Bryant 604
Triggs, (Harry) Inigo, 202, 604
Trouette and Blampied, 606
Trouette, Jean-Pierre, 87, 231 605
Tsiolkas, Christos, 374
Tuan, Yi-Fu, 168
Tucker, Cam, 592
Tuckett, Arthur Helton 606
Tuckett (née Gibson), Margaret Thomas, 43, 245, 257, 606
Tuke, Samuel, 319
Tunks, William, 266
Tunnard, Christopher, 202, 355, 412
Turner, Charles, 160
Turner, Ethel, 373
Turner, Fred, 12, 20, 44, 62, 146, 439, 606, 641, 649
Turner, George, 415
Turner, Janette, 374
Turner, John, 47, 607
Turner, Merv, 57, 478
Tuxen, Saxil, 246
'Tyro', 184

Ussher, Beverley, 121
Ussher and Kemp, 174
Utzon, Jørn, 536

Valder, George Ernest 611
Valder, Peter George, 34, 46, 344, 611
Valentien, Otto, 531
van de Velde, Henri, 206, 559
van den Broek, Barbara, 611
van der Staay family, 436
van Sweden, James 226, 271
Vancouver, George, 53, 71

Varro, Marcus Terentius 64
Vaux, Calvert, 187, 354, 443
Veale, W.C.D. 10
Veitch family, 54, 74, 201, 219, 260, 279, 285, 384, 457, 472, 474, 508, 614
Veitch, Harry James 614
Veitch, James, 74, 90, 160, 479, 499, 547, 590, 614
Veitch, John, 211, 248, 280, 338, 360, 385, 459, 462, 493, 614, 649, 650
Veitch, Peter, 614
Verdon, George Frederic 18, 19
Verey, Rosemary, 202, 226, 337
Verge, John, 28
Verschuer (née Slatyer), Jean, 47, 614
Vessey, Charles Eustace 622
Vidler, Roger, 319
Vincent, F.D'A. 325
Virgoe, William Richard 135, 291, 514
Volckers, Henry August, 622
Voller, Anne, 449
Vollmer, Martin Frederick, 292, 622
von Bibra family, 81, 409
Vorontsov, Mikhail Semenovich, 530, 552
Voysey, C.F.A. 17

W.G. Bennett and Associates, 467
Waddell, Winifred, 216, 241, 433, 623
Wade, Thomas D., 244, 488, 623
Wagner, John, 572
Waite, Edgar Ravenswood 221
Waite, Eva and Lily 106, 161, 561
Waite, Peter, 106, 624
Wakefield, Norman Arthur 433, 435
Wakefield, Priscilla, 407
Wakefield, Salvitor, 461
Wakelin, Roland, 19
Walker, Edith Campbell 655
Walker, Frank, 244, 370, 403, 507, 618, 624
Walker, (William) Frank 624
Walker, Jan, 340
Walker, (Edith) Jean, 57, 119, 245, 253, 396, 397, 434, 440, 473, 654
Walker, John, 546
Walker, Robert, 178
Walker, Stephen, 542
Walker, Thomas, 270, 655
Walker, William Alexander George, 624
Walker, William Benjamin 504
Walkley, Gavin, 80, 161, 562, 624
Wallace, Alfred Russel 36
Wallace, Ben, 422
Wallace, Roy, 477
Wallich, Nathaniel, 325, 479

Index of Names

Walling, Edna Margaret, 9, 19, 29, 33, 45, 46, 47, 49, 56, 60, 61, 69, 84, 88, 89, 97, 112, 116, 119, 137, 147, 160, 161, 162, 175, 182, 185, 191, 198, 226, 228, 229, 242, 243, 244, 248, 250, 253, 258, 266, 287, 295, 310, 333, 337, 353, 355, 371, 375, 380, 398, 399, 403, 406, 407, 412, 422, 425, 434, 442, 473, 486, 512, 555, 561, 562, 571, 574, 584, 589, 594, 607, 617, 622, 625, 626, 633, 639, 642, 646, 654
Wallis, Alexander Robert, 626
Walsh, Richard, 517, 627
Walton, William 15
Waratah, see Hurley, Percy Joseph
Ward, Edward Naughton, 65, 323, 627
Ward, Nathaniel Bagshaw, 212, 627
Ware, Charles, 560
Ware, Joseph, 540
Warmoll, Kate, 279
Warner, Sam Bass 409
Warner, William Richard, 614, 628
Warren, Joyce Noel 562
Waterer, J. 570
Waterhouse, Eben Gowrie, 45, 125, 146, 164, 208, 250, 266, 309, 340, 439, 564, 609, 630, 631, 643
Watkin, James Frazer, 85
Watkins, Dorothy, 579
Watling, Thomas, 474, 632, 641
Watters, Andrew Alexander, 632
Watters, John, 399, 632
Watters, Peter, 501, 632
Watters, Thomas, 632
Watts, Peter Roy, 58, 175, 250, 633
Way, Edward, 633
Weatherly, Lilia Margaret, 517, 633
Weaver, Charles, 16
Weaver, Lawrence, 166, 182
Weaver, Sarah, 16
Webb, Charles, 422
Webb, Danny, 591
Webb, James Hamilton 61
Webb, Philip, 126
Webley, Daniel, 634, 635
Webley, Sarah, 644
Wedgwood, John, 72
Weekes, Norman, 119, 323
Wegener, Alfred Lothar 265
Weinholt, Edward, 339
Weller, Richard, 553
Wells, W. 483
Wentworth, Charles, 128, 635
Wentworth, Emmet Charles 635
Wentworth, William Charles 612
Were, J.B. 173

Wertheimer, Ludwig, 300
West, John, 234
West, Thomas, 184
West, Winifred, 563
Weston, (Thomas) Charles George, 44, 51, 63, 110, 152, 266, 325, 359, 395, 431, 490, 541, 601, 639, 640
Weston, George, 311
Weston, Leanne, 57
Westwood, Betty Rutherford, 640
Wettenhall, (Henry) Norman Burgess, 49, 640
Wharton, Edith, 333, 375
Wheatley, Nadia 138
Whibley, David, 534, 640
Whibley, David Francis, 9, 507, 640
Whibley, David John Edward 641
Whibley, Godfrey Leslie, 641
Whibley, Henry Leonard, 641
Whibley, Herbert James, 641
White, Cyril Tenison, 53, 68, 206, 215, 232, 297, 495, 550, 641
White, James, 339, 462
White, John, 205, 318, 555, 632, 641
White, Patrick, 374, 547
White, Thomas (c. 1736–1811), 108, 201, 548
White, Thomas (c. 1764–1836), 548
Whiteby, Arthur George, 641
Whitehead, Georgina, 553
Whitely, Brett, 547
Whiting, Robert Selman 291
Whitlam, E. Gough, E 59
Whittle, Robert, 580, 641
Whitworth, Robert Percy, 21, 282, 348, 349, 642
Whyte family, 294
Wickenden, Leonard, 453
Wickham, John Clements 642
Wicks, Henry, 642
Wicks, Leonard John, 642
Wicks, (Hubert) Norman David 642
Wijaya, Made, 605, 642
Wilhelmi, (Johann Friedrich) Carl, 643
Wilkes, Annie, 464
Wilkinson, Frederick, 390
Wilkinson, Leslie, 28, 45, 310, 399, 407, 439, 468, 609, 630, 643
Willan, James, 388
William IV, 15
Williams, Alfred, 431, 496, 643
Williams, B.S. 472
Williams, George Richard, 644
Williams, James Belton, 634, 644
Williams, John, 431, 496, 644
Williams, John Theodore Austin, 644

Williams, Keith Alfred Walter, 48, 602, 644
Williams, Louis, 139
Williams, R.A. 243
Williamson, Herbert Bennett, 241, 525, 644
Williamson, Tom, 108
Willis, James Hamlyn, 53, 216, 242, 277, 376, 433, 644, 645
Willmott, Ellen, 143
Wilson, Alan 601
Wilson, Charles, 73
Wilson, Don, 646
Wilson, Edward, 5
Wilson, Ernest Henry 138, 164, 479
Wilson, George Harmston 645
Wilson, Glen Wordsworth, 47, 57, 119, 245, 630, 646, 654
Wilson, H.W. 91
Wilson, Helen, 176
Wilson and Johns, 637, 645
Wilson, Neave and Berry, 646
Wilson, R.J. 559
Wilson, Samuel, 136, 203
Wilson, William Hardy 28, 32, 45, 264, 308, 309, 311, 402, 404, 439, 630, 643, 646
Wiltshire, Helen, 592
Windeyer, Archibald, 41, 349
Windeyer, Charles, 595
Winkel, Vince, 124
Winser, Keith, 127, 287
Winston, Denis, 69
Winter Cooke family, 329
Winter Cooke, Samuel 425
Winter, Samuel Pratt, 425
Withering, William, 108
Wollaston, Morton George 648
Wollaston, Quentin Tullie 648
Wollaston, Tullie Cornthwaite, 15, 56, 377, 477, 561, 632, 647
Wood, Fred G. 103
Wood, John Frederick Francis 562
Wood, T.F. 469
Woodmason, William, 111
Woods, Clara Josephine 191
Woods, E.J. 66
Woods, William Foster 191
Woodward, Robert, 231, 630, 648
Wooff, Luke, 140, 173, 311, 386, 649
Woolley, Ken, 515
Woolls, William, 35, 41, 56, 260, 311, 372, 394, 432, 439, 649
Woolner, Charles, 541
Woolner, Thomas, 76
Woore, Thomas, 504
Wordsworth, William, 184, 214, 642

Index of Names

Wragg, Edward, 59
Wren, Chris, 562
Wright, Frank Lloyd 28, 275
Wright, G.H. 435
Wright, Judith, 374, 385
Wright, Ray, 553
Wright, Theodore, 17, 179, 244, 480, 497, 650
Wrigley, John Walter, 48, 57, 62, 350, 650
Wrixon, Henry, 500
Wulff, Rodney, 601
Wyatt, Charles, 435, 650, 651
Wynn, David, 160
Wynne, Richard, 650

Xavier, Mary Francis, 517, 653

Yanarilyi, 336
Yates, 41, 43, 45, 46, 198, 236, 244, 321, 328, 439, 451, 542, 562, 583
Yates, Arthur, 527, 656
Yates, George, 656
Yates, Guy, 656
Yates, Harold, 656
Yates, Peter, 657
Yates, Philip, 656
Yates, Samuel, 656
Yencken, David, 49, 59, 601, 657
Yencken, E.L. 555

Yeomans, Allan James, 658
Yeomans, Kenneth Bruce 658
Yeomans, Percival Alfred, 353, 630, 657
Young, Alfred, 516
Young, Blamire, 182
Young, John, 91
Young, J.R. 439, 462
Young, William H. 477, 583
Youngman, Henry John 29

Zielke, Roy, 360
Zouch, Henry, 170
Zwar, John, 51, 661